To the Reader:

Scientology® applied religious philosophy contains pastoral counseling procedures intended to assist an individual to gain greater knowledge of self. The mission of the Church of Scientology is a simple one: to help the individual achieve greater self-confidence and personal integrity, thereby enabling him to really trust and respect himself and his fellow man. The attainment of the benefits and goals of Scientology philosophy requires each individual's dedicated participation, as only through his own efforts can he achieve these.

This book is part of the religious literature and works of the Scientology Founder, L. Ron Hubbard. It is presented to the reader as a part of the record of his personal research into life, and the application of same by others, and should be construed only as a written report of such research and not as a statement of claims made by the Church or the Founder.

Scientology philosophy and its forerunner, Dianetics® spiritual healing technology, as practiced by the Church, address only the "thetan" (spirit). Although the Church, as are all churches, is free to engage in spiritual healing, it does not, as its primary goal is increased spiritual awareness for all. For this reason, the Church does not wish to accept individuals who desire treatment of physical or mental illness but prefers to refer these to qualified specialists of other organizations who deal in these matters.

The Hubbard® Electrometer is a religious artifact used in the Church confessional. It in itself does nothing, and is used by ministers only, to assist parishioners in locating areas of spiritual distress or travail.

We hope the reading of this book is only the first stage of a personal voyage of discovery into this new and vital world religion.

Church of Scientology International

This Book Belongs to:

_____

_____

(Date)

The Organization Executive Course

by
L. Ron Hubbard

EXECUTIVE DIVISION

VOLUME
7

Bridge Publications, Inc.　　　　NEW ERA Publications International ApS

Published in USA and International by
Bridge Publications, Inc.
5600 E. Olympic Boulevard
Commerce, California 90022

ISBN 0-88404-598-6

Published in United Kingdom and Europe by
NEW ERA Publications International ApS
Smedeland 20
2600 Glostrup, Denmark

ISBN 87-7336-757-5

Important Note

In reading this book, be very certain you never go past a word you do not fully understand.

The only reason a person gives up a study or becomes confused or unable to learn is because he or she has gone past a word that was not understood.

The confusion or inability to grasp or learn comes AFTER a word that the person did not have defined and understood.

Have you ever had the experience of coming to the end of a page and realizing you didn't know what you had read? Well, somewhere earlier on that page you went past a word that you had no definition for or an incorrect definition for.

Here's an example. "It was found that when the crepuscule arrived the children were quieter and when it was not present, they were much livelier." You see what happens. You think you don't understand the whole idea, but the inability to understand came entirely from the one word you could not define, *crepuscule,* which means twilight or darkness.

It may not only be the new and unusual words that you will have to look up. Some commonly used words can often be misdefined and so cause confusion.

This datum about not going past an undefined word is the most important fact in the whole subject of study. Every subject you have taken up and abandoned had its words which you failed to get defined.

Therefore, in reading this book be very, very certain you never go past a word you do not fully understand. If the material becomes confusing or you can't seem to grasp it, there will be a word just earlier that you have not understood. Don't go any further, but go back to BEFORE you got into trouble, find the misunderstood word and get it defined.

DEFINITIONS AND FOOTNOTES

As an aid to the reader, those few words which are not easily found in regular dictionaries have been defined in footnotes the first time they occur in the text.

Definitions for Scientology terminology can be found in *Modern Management Technology Defined* and *Dianetics and Scientology Technical Dictionary.* The reader should have his own copies of these dictionaries available for reference.

Footnotes are also used to refer the reader to additional data concerning the issue being footnoted. For example, a footnote may point out that there is an org board in the Appendix which will assist in locating divisional and departmental designations.

EXECUTIVE DIVISION

Contents

PATTERN AND FORM OF THE ORGANIZATION

STATISTICAL MANAGEMENT

DEPARTMENT 19
OFFICE OF THE EXECUTIVE DIRECTOR

PRODUCTION AND ORGANIZATION

DELIVERY AND EXCHANGE

EXECUTIVE COUNCIL
ADVISORY COUNCIL
ADVISORY COMMITTEE

DEPARTMENT 20
DEPARTMENT OF SPECIAL AFFAIRS

INVESTIGATIONS

PUBLIC RELATIONS

CORPORATE STRUCTURE

LRH COMMUNICATOR NETWORK SERIES

ISSUE AUTHORITY

OFFICE OF THE FLAG REPRESENTATIVE

EXECUTIVE DIVISION 7 QUALITY CHECKLIST

APPENDIX

INTRODUCTION

HCO POLICY LETTER OF 8 SEPTEMBER 1969

Remimeo
Item 1 OEC
Checksheet

THE ORG EXEC COURSE INTRODUCTION

This course contains the basic laws of organization.

Primarily intended for Scientology organization executives, its policy letters are slanted toward a Scientology org (short for organization). However, it covers any organization and contains fundamentals vital to any successful or profitable activity.

This course also applies to the individual. Any individual has his 7 (or 9) divisions and his 21 (or 27) departments. Where one or more of these is missing in his conduct of life, he will be to that degree an unsuccessful individual.

No matter how organized, any company, society or political entity will be as unsuccessful as it has these functions missing.

Thus this is not just the Scientology idea of how an org should run—most of it is vital basic discovery.

Man did not really know the principles of organization any more than he knew what made his mind work before Dianetics was published.

A very small amount of the material on this course has crept into general use, just as a very few of the principles of Dianetics and Scientology are now an "Everybody knows ———." Survival is now conceded as the basic principle of existence. Universities now know man can change IQ and personality. As time goes on, more and more of the technology "leaks" into general knowledge. But it takes a long time for all mankind to know a whole tech in this fashion.

To date the Scientology discoveries in organization are known to a very few. But some of the more general principles are already creeping into business practice.

Not long ago, for instance, a close friend of the president of the US was given the policy letter about "Don't reward a down statistic." A few days later the president used it in his new relief program policy.

Of course there are hundreds of other "PLs" that *haven't* been shown to the friend of the president. It takes years for new ideas to "leak" into public consciousness. It took 5 years for the medical professors in universities to begin to teach that aberration could come from the "birth engram." In 18 years only a handful of medical doctors accepted that mental image pictures caused aberration. In 19 years only a few medical doctors could also audit.

Therefore, if one were fully conversant with the full subject and all its principles, he would appear to be a magician, a miracle worker.

If anyone knew the Org Exec Course fully and could practice it, he could completely reverse any downtrending company or country. Indeed, here and there at this writing men have done so.

It could be argued or pleaded that this huge body of data should be made into texts capable of general application by businesses and countries. The one effort to republish these policies in other terms so badly altered the material that it became a hopeless bog even though attempted by a very successful businessman. He himself was applying the originals direct to his company and it soaringly became rich. Then he decided to rewrite it all, greatly altered and edited, for his employees; and his business went on a toboggan slide. His correct action would have been to send his employees to take the same course he took—this very Org Exec Course. And let them adapt what they now knew to fit their own posts and activities. Instead, he cut them off from source, and what *he* wrote for them was only as much as *he* had gotten out of the course from his own viewpoint.

At least there are Scientology orgs around which are successful, living models of these policies and org form.

The only real trouble these orgs ever have is not a failure to apply policy but a failure of the whole staff to know policy.

Wherever a portion of a Scientology org is in confusion, you will find that the staff members in that portion have not done the Org Exec Course. They may know a few policies. But outside that, anyone can come along and say "this is the policy" or "what you're doing is against policy," and being ignorant of policy they develop the idea of some vast unknown area and go downhill.

The name Org *Exec* Course is probably a misnomer. Certainly the executives of the org should know it well. But the staff member who doesn't know it is at effect. If he *knew* his OEC data, he would be able to defend himself and get his own "show on the road" in his portion of the org.

ANY FAILURE OF THESE BASICS AND POLICIES IS IGNORANCE OF THEM.

When you know them all, not just a few, it makes a whole intelligible picture.

It is rather exciting to be able to cut through the superstition of yesterday's organizations and deal in basic, down-to-earth fundamentals.

When you understand all the policies on this course, you will understand organization itself, no matter to what you apply it. You will also be able to recognize misorganization when you see it.

And I assure you that in a misorganized society the individual loses out.

Even dictatorships come about only because the citizen doesn't know basic organization. Thus authoritarian rule exists only to the degree that its subjects are ignorant of the fundamentals of organization.

Those fundamentals, even if specialized to fit a Scientology organization, exist in this, the Org Exec Course.

L. RON HUBBARD
Founder

KEEPING SCIENTOLOGY WORKING

HCO POLICY LETTER OF 7 FEBRUARY 1965

Remimeo
Sthil Students
Assoc/Org Sec
  Hat
HCO Sec Hat
Case Sup Hat
Ds of P Hat
Ds of T Hat
Staff Member
  Hat
Missions

Keeping Scientology Working Series 1

Note: Neglect of this PL has caused great hardship on staffs, has cost countless millions and made it necessary in 1970 to engage in an all-out, international effort to restore basic Scientology over the world. Within 5 years after the issue of this PL, with me off the lines, violation had almost destroyed orgs. "Quickie grades" entered in and denied gain to tens of thousands of cases. Therefore actions which neglect or violate this policy letter are HIGH CRIMES resulting in Comm Evs on ADMINISTRATORS and EXECUTIVES. It is not "entirely a tech matter," as its neglect destroys orgs and caused a 2-year slump. IT IS THE BUSINESS OF EVERY STAFF MEMBER to enforce it.

SPECIAL MESSAGE

THE FOLLOWING POLICY LETTER MEANS WHAT IT SAYS.

IT WAS TRUE IN 1965 WHEN I WROTE IT. IT WAS TRUE IN 1970 WHEN I HAD IT REISSUED. I AM REISSUING IT NOW, IN 1980, TO AVOID AGAIN SLIPPING BACK INTO A PERIOD OF OMITTED AND QUICKIED FUNDAMENTAL GRADE CHART ACTIONS ON CASES, THEREBY DENYING GAINS AND THREATENING THE VIABILITY OF SCIENTOLOGY AND OF ORGS. SCIENTOLOGY WILL KEEP WORKING ONLY AS LONG AS *YOU* DO YOUR PART TO KEEP IT WORKING BY APPLYING THIS POLICY LETTER.

WHAT I SAY IN THESE PAGES HAS ALWAYS BEEN TRUE, IT HOLDS TRUE TODAY, IT WILL STILL HOLD TRUE IN THE YEAR 2000 AND IT WILL CONTINUE TO HOLD TRUE FROM THERE ON OUT.

NO MATTER WHERE YOU ARE IN SCIENTOLOGY, ON STAFF OR NOT, THIS POLICY LETTER HAS SOMETHING TO DO WITH YOU.

ALL LEVELS

KEEPING SCIENTOLOGY WORKING

HCO Sec or Communicator hat check
on all personnel and all new personnel
as taken on.

We have some time since passed the point of achieving uniformly workable technology.

The only thing now is getting the technology applied.

If you can't get the technology applied, then you can't deliver what's promised. It's as simple as that. If you can get the technology applied, you *can* deliver what's promised.

The only thing you can be upbraided for by students or pcs is "no results." Trouble spots occur only where there are "no results." Attacks from governments or monopolies occur only where there are "no results" or "bad results."

Therefore the road before Scientology is clear and its ultimate success is assured *if* the technology is applied.

So it is the task of the Assoc or Org Sec, the HCO Sec, the Case Supervisor, the D of P, the D of T and all staff members to get the correct technology applied.

Getting the correct technology applied consists of:

One: **Having the correct technology.**

Two: **Knowing the technology.**

Three: **Knowing it is correct.**

Four: **Teaching correctly the correct technology.**

Five: **Applying the technology.**

Six: **Seeing that the technology is correctly applied.**

Seven: **Hammering out of existence incorrect technology.**

Eight: **Knocking out incorrect applications.**

Nine: **Closing the door on any possibility of incorrect technology.**

Ten: **Closing the door on incorrect application.**

One above has been done.

Two has been achieved by many.

Three is achieved by the individual applying the correct technology in a proper manner and observing that it works that way.

Four is being done daily successfully in most parts of the world.

Five is consistently accomplished daily.

Six is achieved by Instructors and Supervisors consistently.

Seven is done by a few but is a weak point.

Eight is not worked on hard enough.

Nine is impeded by the "reasonable" attitude of the not-quite-bright.

Ten is seldom done with enough ferocity.

Seven, Eight, Nine and Ten are the only places Scientology can bog down in any area.

The reasons for this are not hard to find. (a) A weak certainty that it works in Three above can lead to weakness in Seven, Eight, Nine and Ten. (b) Further, the not-too-bright have a bad point on the button Self-Importance. (c) The lower the IQ, the more the individual is shut off from the fruits of observation. (d) The service facs of people make them defend themselves against anything they confront, good or bad, and seek to make it wrong. (e) The bank seeks to knock out the good and perpetuate the bad.

Thus, we as Scientologists and as an organization must be very alert to Seven, Eight, Nine and Ten.

In all the years I have been engaged in research I have kept my comm lines wide open for research data. I once had the idea that a group could evolve truth. A third of a century has thoroughly disabused me of that idea. Willing as I was to accept suggestions and data, only a handful of suggestions (less than twenty) had long-run value and *none* were major or basic; and when I did accept major or basic suggestions and used them, we went astray and I repented and eventually had to "eat crow."

On the other hand there have been thousands and thousands of suggestions and writings which, if accepted and acted upon, would have resulted in the complete destruction of all our work as well as the sanity of pcs. So I know what a group of people will do and how insane they will go in accepting unworkable "technology." By actual record the percentages are about twenty to 100,000 that a group of human beings will dream up bad technology to destroy good technology. As we could have gotten along without suggestions, then, we had better steel ourselves to continue to do so now that we have made it. This point will, of course, be attacked as "unpopular," "egotistical" and "undemocratic." It very well may be. But it is also a survival point. And I don't see that popular measures, self-abnegation and democracy have done anything for man but push him further into the mud. Currently, popularity endorses degraded novels, self-abnegation has filled the Southeast Asian jungles with stone idols and corpses, and democracy has given us inflation and income tax.

Our technology has not been discovered by a group. True, if the group had not supported me in many ways, I could not have discovered it either. But it remains that if in its formative stages it was not discovered by a group, then group efforts, one can safely assume, will not add to it or successfully alter it in the future. I can only say this now that it is done. There remains, of course, group tabulation or coordination of what has been done, which will be valuable—only so long as it does not seek to alter basic principles and successful applications.

The contributions that were worthwhile in this period of forming the technology were help in the form of friendship, of defense, of organization, of dissemination, of application, of advices on results and of finance. These were great contributions

9

and were, and are, appreciated. Many thousands contributed in this way and made us what we are. Discovery contribution was not however part of the broad picture.

We will not speculate here on why this was so or how I came to rise above the bank. We are dealing only in facts and the above is a fact—the group left to its own devices would not have evolved Scientology but with wild dramatizations of the bank called "new ideas" would have wiped it out. Supporting this is the fact that man has never before evolved workable mental technology and emphasizing it is the vicious technology he *did* evolve—psychiatry, psychology, surgery, shock treatment, whips, duress, punishment, etc., ad infinitum.

So realize that we have climbed out of the mud by whatever good luck and good sense, and *refuse* to sink back into it again. See that Seven, Eight, Nine and Ten above are ruthlessly followed and we will never be stopped. Relax them, get reasonable about it and we will perish.

So far, while keeping myself in complete communication with all suggestions, I have not failed on Seven, Eight, Nine and Ten in areas I could supervise closely. But it's not good enough for just myself and a few others to work at this.

Whenever this control as per Seven, Eight, Nine and Ten has been relaxed, the whole organizational area has failed. Witness Elizabeth, NJ; Wichita; the early organizations and groups. They crashed only because I no longer did Seven, Eight, Nine and Ten. Then, when they were all messed up, you saw the obvious "reasons" for failure. But ahead of that they ceased to deliver and *that* involved them in other reasons.

The common denominator of a group is the reactive bank. Thetans without banks have different responses. They only have their banks in common. They agree then only on bank principles. Person to person the bank is identical. So constructive ideas are *individual* and seldom get broad agreement in a human group. An individual must rise *above* an avid craving for agreement from a humanoid group to get anything decent done. The bank-agreement has been what has made Earth a hell—and if you were looking for hell and found Earth, it would certainly serve. War, famine, agony and disease has been the lot of man. Right now the great governments of Earth have developed the means of frying every man, woman and child on the planet. That is bank. That is the result of Collective-Thought Agreement. The decent, pleasant things on this planet come from *individual* actions and ideas that have somehow gotten by the Group Idea. For that matter, look how we ourselves are attacked by "public opinion" media. Yet there is no more ethical group on this planet than ourselves.

Thus each one of us can rise above the domination of the bank and then, as a group of freed beings, achieve freedom and reason. It is only the aberrated group, the mob, that is destructive.

When you don't do Seven, Eight, Nine and Ten actively, you are working for the bank-dominated mob. For it will surely, surely (a) introduce incorrect technology and swear by it, (b) apply technology as incorrectly as possible, (c) open the door to any destructive idea, and (d) encourage incorrect application.

It's the bank that says the group is all and the individual nothing. It's the bank that says we must fail.

So just don't play that game. Do Seven, Eight, Nine and Ten and you will knock out of your road all the future thorns.

Here's an actual example in which a senior executive had to interfere because of a pc spin: A Case Supervisor told Instructor A to have Auditor B run Process X on Preclear C. Auditor B afterwards told Instructor A that "It didn't work." Instructor A was weak on Three above and didn't really believe in Seven, Eight, Nine and Ten. So Instructor A told the Case Supervisor, "Process X didn't work on Preclear C." Now *this* strikes directly at each of One to Six above in Preclear C, Auditor B, Instructor A *and* the Case Supervisor. It opens the door to the introduction of "new technology" and to failure.

What happened here? Instructor A didn't jump down Auditor B's throat, that's all that happened. This is what he *should* have done: Grabbed the auditor's report and looked it over. When a higher executive on this case did so, she found what the Case Supervisor and the rest missed: that Process X *increased* Preclear C's TA to 25 TA divisions for the session but that near session end Auditor B Q-and-Aed with a cognition and abandoned Process X while it still gave high TA and went off running one of Auditor B's own manufacture, which nearly spun Preclear C. Auditor B's IQ on examination turned out to be about 75. Instructor A was found to have huge ideas of how you must never invalidate anyone, even a lunatic. The Case Supervisor was found to be "too busy with admin to have any time for actual cases."

All right, there's an all-too-typical example. The *Instructor* should have done Seven, Eight, Nine and Ten. This would have begun this way. Auditor B: "That Process X didn't work." Instructor A: "What exactly did *you* do wrong?" Instant attack. "Where's your auditor's report for the session? Good. Look here, you were getting a lot of TA when you stopped Process X. What did you do?" Then the pc wouldn't have come close to a spin and all four of these would have retained their certainty.

In a year, I had four instances in *one* small group where the correct process recommended was reported not to have worked. But on review found that each one had (a) increased the TA, (b) had been abandoned, and (c) had been falsely reported as unworkable. Also, despite this abuse, in each of these four cases the recommended, correct process cracked the case. Yet they were reported as *not having worked!*

Similar examples exist in instruction and these are all the more deadly as every time instruction in correct technology is flubbed, then the resulting error, uncorrected in the auditor, is perpetuated on every pc that auditor audits thereafter. So Seven, Eight, Nine and Ten are even more important in a course than in supervision of cases.

Here's an example: A rave recommendation is given a graduating student "because he gets more TA on pcs than any other student on the course!" Figures of 435 TA divisions a session are reported. "Of course his Model Session is poor but it's just a knack he has" is also included in the recommendation. A careful review is undertaken because *nobody* at Levels 0 to IV is going to get that much TA on pcs. It is found that this student was never taught to read an E-Meter TA dial! And no Instructor observed his handling of a meter and it was not discovered that he "overcompensated" nervously, swinging the TA 2 or 3 divisions beyond where it needed to go to place the needle at "set." So everyone was about to throw away standard processes and Model Session because this one student "got such remarkable TA." They only read the reports and listened to the brags and never *looked* at this student. The pcs in actual fact were making slightly less than average gain, impeded by a rough Model Session and misworded processes. Thus, what was making the pcs win (actual Scientology) was hidden under a lot of departures and errors.

I recall one student who was squirreling on an Academy course and running a lot of offbeat whole track on other students after course hours. The Academy students were in a state of electrification on all these new experiences and weren't quickly brought under control, and the student himself never was given the works on Seven, Eight, Nine and Ten so they stuck. Subsequently, this student prevented another squirrel from being straightened out and his wife died of cancer resulting from physical abuse. A hard, tough instructor at that moment could have salvaged two squirrels and saved the life of a girl. But no, students had a right to do whatever they pleased.

Squirreling (going off into weird practices or altering Scientology) only comes about from noncomprehension. Usually the noncomprehension is not of Scientology but some earlier contact with an offbeat humanoid practice which in its turn was not understood.

When people can't get results from *what they think* is standard practice, they can be counted upon to squirrel to some degree. The most trouble in the past two years came from orgs where an executive in each *could not* assimilate straight Scientology. Under instruction in Scientology, they were unable to define terms or demonstrate examples of principles. And the orgs where they were got into plenty of trouble. And worse, it could not be straightened out easily because neither one of these people could or would duplicate instructions. Hence, a debacle resulted in two places, directly traced to failures of instruction earlier. So proper instruction is vital. The D of T and his Instructors and all Scientology Instructors must be merciless in getting Four, Seven, Eight, Nine and Ten into effective action. That one student, dumb and impossible though he may seem and of no use to anyone, may yet someday be the cause of untold upset because nobody was interested enough to make *sure* Scientology got home to him.

With what we know now, there is no student we enroll who cannot be properly trained. As an Instructor, one should be very alert to slow progress and should turn the sluggards inside out personally. No *system* will do it, only you or me with our sleeves rolled up can crack the back of bad studenting and we can only do it on an individual student, never on a whole class only. He's slow = something is awful wrong. Take *fast* action to correct it. Don't wait until next week. By then he's got other messes stuck to him. If you can't graduate them with their good sense appealed to and wisdom shining, graduate them in such a state of shock they'll have nightmares if they contemplate squirreling. Then experience will gradually bring about Three in them and they'll *know* better than to chase butterflies when they should be auditing.

When somebody enrolls, consider he or she has joined up for the duration of the universe—never permit an "open-minded" approach. If they're going to quit let them quit fast. If they enrolled, they're aboard; and if they're aboard, they're here on the same terms as the rest of us—win or die in the attempt. Never let them be half-minded about being Scientologists. The finest organizations in history have been tough, dedicated organizations. Not one namby-pamby bunch of pantywaist dilettantes have ever made anything. It's a tough universe. The social veneer makes it seem mild. But only the tigers survive—and even *they* have a hard time. We'll survive because we are tough and are dedicated. When we *do* instruct somebody properly, he becomes more and more tiger. When we instruct half-mindedly and are afraid to offend, scared to enforce, we don't make students into good Scientologists and that lets everybody down. When Mrs. Pattycake comes to us to be taught, turn that wandering doubt in her eye into a fixed, dedicated glare and she'll win and we'll all win. Humor her and we all die a little. The proper instruction attitude is, "You're here so you're a Scientologist. Now we're going to make you into an expert auditor no matter what happens. We'd rather have you dead than incapable."

Fit that into the economics of the situation and lack of adequate time and you see the cross we have to bear.

But we won't have to bear it forever. The bigger we get, the more economics and time we will have to do our job. And the only things which can prevent us from getting that big fast are areas in from One to Ten. Keep those in mind and we'll be able to grow. Fast. And as we grow, our shackles will be less and less. Failing to keep One to Ten will make *us* grow less.

So the ogre which might eat us up is not the government or the High Priests. It's our possible failure to retain and practice our technology.

An Instructor or Supervisor or Executive *must* challenge with ferocity instances of "unworkability." They must uncover what *did* happen, what *was* run and what *was* done or not done.

If you have One and Two, you can only acquire Three for all by making sure of all the rest.

We're not playing some minor game in Scientology. It isn't cute or something to do for lack of something better.

The whole agonized future of this planet, every man, woman and child on it, and your own destiny for the next endless trillions of years depend on what you do here and now with and in Scientology.

This is a deadly serious activity. And if we miss getting out of the trap now, we may never again have another chance.

Remember, this is our first chance to do so in all the endless trillions of years of the past. Don't muff it now because it seems unpleasant or unsocial to do Seven, Eight, Nine and Ten.

Do them and we'll win.

L. RON HUBBARD
Founder

13

HUBBARD COMMUNICATIONS OFFICE
Saint Hill Manor, East Grinstead, Sussex

HCO POLICY LETTER OF 17 JUNE 1970RB
Issue I
REVISED 25 OCTOBER 1983

Remimeo
Applies to all
  SHs and
  Academies
HGCs
Missions

URGENT AND IMPORTANT

Keeping Scientology Working Series 5R

TECHNICAL DEGRADES

(This PL and HCO PL 7 Feb. 65
must be made part of every study pack as
the first items and must be listed on checksheets.)

Any checksheet in use or in stock which carries on it any degrading statement must be destroyed and issued without qualifying statements.

Example: Level 0 to IV checksheets SH carry "A. Background Material— This section is included as an historical background but has much interest and value to the student. Most of the processes are no longer used, having been replaced by more modern technology. The student is only required to read this material and ensure he leaves no misunderstood." This heading covers such vital things as TRs, Op Pro by Dup! The statement is a falsehood.

These checksheets were not approved by myself; all the material of the Academy and SH courses IS in use.

Such actions as this gave us "quickie grades," ARC broke the field and downgraded the Academy and SH courses.

A condition of TREASON or cancellation of certificates or dismissal and a full investigation of the background of any person found guilty will be activated in the case of anyone committing the following HIGH CRIMES:

1. Abbreviating an official course in Dianetics and Scientology so as to lose the full theory, processes and effectiveness of the subjects.

2. Adding comments to checksheets or instructions labeling any material "background" or "not used now" or "old" or any similar action which will result in the student not knowing, using and applying the data in which he is being trained.

3. Employing after 1 Sept. 1970 any checksheet for any course not authorized by myself or the Authority, Verification and Correction Unit International (AVC Int).

(Hat checksheets may be authorized locally per HCO PL 30 Sept. 70, CHECKSHEET FORMAT.)

4. Failing to strike from any checksheet remaining in use meanwhile any such comments as "historical," "background," "not used," "old," etc., or VERBALLY STATING IT TO STUDENTS.

5. Permitting a pc to attest to more than one grade at a time on the pc's own determinism without hint or evaluation.

6. Running only one process for a lower grade between 0 to IV, where the grade EP has not been attained.

7. Failing to use all processes for a level where the EP has not been attained.

8. Boasting as to speed of delivery in a session, such as "I put in Grade Zero in 3 minutes." Etc.

9. Shortening time of application of auditing for financial or labor-saving considerations.

10. Acting in any way calculated to lose the technology of Dianetics and Scientology to use or impede its use or shorten its materials or its application.

REASON: The effort to get students through courses and get pcs processed in orgs was considered best handled by reducing materials or deleting processes from grades. The pressure exerted to speed up student completions and auditing completions was mistakenly answered by just not delivering.

The correct way to speed up a student's progress is by using two-way comm and applying the study materials to students.

The best way to really handle pcs is to ensure they make each level fully before going on to the next and repairing them when they do not.

The puzzle of the decline of the entire Scientology network in the late 60s is entirely answered by the actions taken to shorten time in study and in processing by deleting materials and actions.

Reinstituting full use and delivery of Dianetics and Scientology is the answer to any recovery.

The product of an org is well-taught students and thoroughly audited pcs. When the product vanishes, so does the org. The orgs must survive for the sake of this planet.

L. RON HUBBARD
Founder

EXECUTIVE DIVISION 7
ITS EVOLUTION AND FUNCTIONS

EXECUTIVE DIVISION SEVEN
DIV 7 SECRETARY

DIV 7 SEC'S O/O ─┐　　　　　　　　　DIV 7 ESTO

SOURCE	EXISTENCE	CONDITIONS
Department 21	Department 20	Department 19

OFFICE OF LRH	DEPARTMENT OF SPECIAL AFFAIRS	OFFICE OF THE EXECUTIVE DIRECTOR
LRH COMMUNICATOR	DIRECTOR OF SPECIAL AFFAIRS	EXECUTIVE DIRECTOR
LRH COMMUNICATOR BRANCH	**SERVICES SECTION**	**OFFICE OF THE EXECUTIVE DIRECTOR**
LRH COMMUNICATOR	SERVICES OFFICER	EXECUTIVE DIRECTOR
D/LRH Communicator for Compliances	(HCO Liaison	ED'S Communicator
D/LRH Communicator for LRH PR	Treasury Liaison	D/ED
LRH COMM SECRETARY SECTION	Qual Liaison)	ED's Programs Operator
LRH COMM SECRETARY	**INVESTIGATIONS SECTION**	**OFFICE OF THE DEPUTY EXECUTIVE DIRECTOR FOR DELIVERY AND EXCHANGE**
LRH COMM FILES SUB-SECTION	INVESTIGATIONS OFFICER	D/ED FOR DELIVERY AND EXCHANGE
LRH Comm Files Officer	**INVEST INFORMATION UNIT**	D/ED for D&E Org Officer
Policy and Bulletins Files Clerk	Invest Information In-Charge	Films, Recorded LRH Lectures and Slide Shows Usage Officer
LRH ED Files Clerk	**DEFENSIVE INVESTIGATIONS UNIT**	Service Call-In Committee
Project Files Clerk	Defensive Investigations In-Charge	**OFFICE OF THE HCO EXECUTIVE SECRETARY**
LRH COMM LOG UNIT	**Security Sub-Unit**	HCO EXECUTIVE SECRETARY
LRH Comm Log In-Charge	Security In-Charge	HCO Exec Sec's Org Officer
KEEPER OF THE SEALS AND SIGNATURE SECTION	**SUPPORT INVESTIGATIONS UNIT**	**OFFICE OF THE ORG EXECUTIVE SECRETARY**
KEEPER OF THE SEALS AND SIGNATURE OFFICER (ISSUE AUTHORITY)	Support Investigations In-Charge	ORG EXECUTIVE SECRETARY
HCO Board of Review	**Investigations Sub-Unit**	Org Exec Sec's Org Officer
LRH ETHICS AUTHORITY SECTION	Investigations In-Charge	**OFFICE OF THE PUBLIC EXECUTIVE SECRETARY**
LRH ETHICS AUTHORITY OFFICER	**Prosecution Sub-Unit**	PUBLIC EXECUTIVE SECRETARY
DESIGN AND PLANNING SECTION	Prosecution In-Charge	Public Exec Sec's Org Officer
DESIGN AND PLANNING OFFICER	**PUBLIC RELATIONS SECTION**	
Space and Materiel Utilization Inspector	PUBLIC RELATIONS OFFICER	**EXECUTIVE COUNCIL**
Design and Planning Authorization and Verification Officer	**PR OPINION ANALYSIS & CONTROL CENTER UNIT**	**ADVISORY COUNCIL**
Design and Planning Execution Supervisor	PR Opinion Analysis & Control Center In-Charge	**PRODUCT OFFICERS CONFERENCE**
KEEPER OF TECH AND POLICY KNOWLEDGE BRANCH	**PR PLANNING UNIT**	**ORG OFFICERS CONFERENCE**
KEEPER OF TECH AND POLICY KNOWLEDGE	PR Planning In-Charge	
LRH PERSONAL SECRETARY BRANCH	**PR Research Sub-Unit**	
LRH PERSONAL SECRETARY	PR Research In-Charge	
PERS SECRETARY ARCHIVES SECTION	**PR Survey Sub-Unit**	
PERS SEC ARCHIVES OFFICER	PR Survey In-Charge	
SO 1 LINE SECTION	**PR PROPERTIES UNIT**	
SO 1 LINE OFFICER	PR Properties In-Charge	
EXECUTIVE ESTABLISHMENT OFFICER BRANCH	**Properties Production Sub-Unit**	
EXECUTIVE ESTABLISHMENT OFFICER	Properties Production In-Charge	
Exec Esto's O/O	**Properties Distribution Sub-Unit**	
Exec Esto's MAA	Properties Distribution In-Charge	
Assistant Esto MAA	**PR EXECUTION UNIT**	
Esto's Esto	PR Execution In-Charge	
Esto Conference	**PR Events Sub-Unit**	
OFFICE OF THE FLAG REPRESENTATIVE	PR Events In-Charge	
FLAG REPRESENTATIVE	**Media Sub-Unit**	
Flag Rep Admin	Media In-Charge	
REPORTS SECTION	**Opinion Leaders/VIP Sub-Unit**	
DEPUTY FLAG REP FOR REPORTS	Opinion Leaders/VIP In-Charge	
COMPLIANCE SECTION	**Community Relations Sub-Unit**	
DEPUTY FLAG REP FOR COMPLIANCES	Community Relations In-Charge	
FLAG PR SECTION	**LEGAL SECTION**	
DEPUTY FLAG REP FOR FLAG PR	LEGAL OFFICER	
FINANCE OFFICE	**LEGAL INFORMATION UNIT**	
FLAG BANKING OFFICER (FBO)	Legal Information In-Charge	
OFFICE OF THE FLAG BANKING OFFICER	**LEGAL RUDIMENTS UNIT**	
FLAG BANKING OFFICER (FBO)	Legal Rudiments In-Charge	
FBO Admin(s)	**Corporate Maintenance Sub-Unit**	
OFFICE OF THE D/FBO FOR MARKETING OF ORG RESOURCES FOR EXCHANGE	Corporate Maintenance In-Charge	
DEPUTY FBO FOR MORE	**Tax/Accountancy Sub-Unit**	
ESTATES BRANCH	Tax/Accountancy In-Charge	
ESTATES MANAGER	**TRADEMARK INTEGRITY UNIT**	
GROUNDS SECTION	TM Integrity In-Charge	
GROUNDS OFFICER	**TM Licensing & Usage Sub-Unit**	
CONSTRUCTION SECTION	TM Licensing & Usage In-Charge	
CONSTRUCTION OFFICER	**TM Enforcement Sub-Unit**	
MAINTENANCE SECTION	TM Enforcement In-Charge	
MAINTENANCE OFFICER	**LITIGATION UNIT**	
Chief Engineer	Litigation In-Charge	
Cleaning Crew In-Charge	**Litigation Prevention Sub-Unit**	
Services In-Charge	Litigation Prevention In-Charge	
ESTATES ADMIN SECTION	**Civil Litigation Sub-Unit**	
ESTATES ADMIN OFFICER	Civil Litigation In-Charge	
Estates Receptionist	**Government Litigation Sub-Unit**	
Estates Purchasing In-Charge	Government Litigation In-Charge	
	SOCIAL REFORM SECTION	
	SOCIAL REFORM OFFICER	
	SOCIAL REFORM INFORMATION UNIT	
	Social Reform Information In-Charge	
	SOCIAL REFORM PLANNING UNIT	
	Social Reform Planning In-Charge	
	Social Reform Research & Survey Sub-Unit	
	Social Reform Research & Survey In-Charge	
	SOCIAL REFORM EXECUTION UNIT	
	Social Reform Execution In-Charge	
	Government Reform Program Coordinators	
	Private Sector Reform Program Coordinators	

| VFPs: 1. **THE TECHNOLOGY OF DIANETICS AND SCIENTOLOGY AND ITS PRODUCTS.**
2. **A PROSPEROUS AND VIABLE ORG WITH INCREASING MONIES TO MANAGEMENT RESERVES AND A WELL-PAID STAFF.**
3. **VALUABLE PROPERTIES OF THE CHURCH.** | VFP: **HANDLED SITUATIONS WHICH RESULT IN THE TOTAL ACCEPTANCE OF SCIENTOLOGY AND ITS FOUNDER THROUGHOUT THE AREA.** | VFP: **A VIABLE EXPANDING ORG.** |

VFP: A VIABLE, EXPANDING ORG USING THE TECHNOLOGY OF DIANETICS AND SCIENTOLOGY AND ITS PRODUCTS.

HUBBARD COMMUNICATIONS OFFICE
Saint Hill Manor, East Grinstead, Sussex

HCO POLICY LETTER OF 2 SEPTEMBER 1970
Issue II

Remimeo
All Staff
PRO Course Checksheet
Missions

FIRST POLICY

The first policy of a Scientology org, laid down on about 8 or 10 March 1950, is:

MAINTAIN FRIENDLY RELATIONS WITH THE ENVIRONMENT AND THE PUBLIC.

L. RON HUBBARD
Founder

HCO POLICY LETTER OF 25 FEBRUARY 1958

CenOCon
SHSBC Students
Missions
Field

ROUTING OF COMMUNICATION

I wonder, you guys in London and SA and LA and NY and DC and Aust-NZ, if you don't feel insulted sometimes when the public, field auditors, Scientologists, et al, bypass you and your post and "write to Ron," "have to see Ron."

You ought to. The public is invalidating you.

If somebody on your staff skips his chief and takes it all upstairs you'd feel pretty snarly.

Well, the traffic I get in HCO would show you the same thing happens broadly.

An auditor bypasses an org just 300 miles from him and hysterically comms with me. That means he is invalidating the post of his nearest Org/Assoc Sec who has full authority to handle.

You better look at this. I'm no only one. We're in this together. No man singly, no office could handle our traffic. Why pretend.

Make your zone of operations realize that *you* have the authority and ability to care for them.

L. RON HUBBARD
Founder

HCO POLICY LETTER OF 19 NOVEMBER 1958

All Hats

ORGANIZATION

An organization is composed of terminals and communications by associates in a common purpose.

An organization's efficiency and purpose are forwarded only to the degree that its communication and command lines are *known*.

The policies of this organization are established by the board of trustees and are formed by common agreement which then becomes reality by execution through its command lines.

Therefore, no single board member or unauthorized person can alter existing policy or create new policy by the issuance of directives or instructions over his own signature. If and when this should occur, it is the duty of the recipient of such a directive or instruction to forward it to the next higher authority on the chain of command. We thus corral and straighten out our communication lines by bringing to light hidden areas of confusion caused by the unmocking of posts brought about by the bypassing of terminals on the chain of command.

This directive is effective now.

L. RON HUBBARD
Founder

HUBBARD COMMUNICATIONS OFFICE
37 Fitzroy Street, London W1

HCO BULLETIN OF 5 JANUARY 1959
Issue I

1 ea. staff member
London

IMPORTANCE AND EXECUTIVES

What has hurt me most in Dianetics and Scientology organizations is the phenomenon of the rise and sudden downfall of executives.

L. RON HUBBARD
Founder

Hubbard Communications Office

No. 2

26 February 1959

HCO EXECUTIVE SECRETARY
CONTINENTAL

Purpose: To ensure the establishment and smooth operations of and adherence of policy by all HCO offices on the continent without imperiling the élan or initiative of HCO personnel, to the end of broader, better and more effective dissemination of Scientology.

The primary business of the HCO Sec Cont is the fixing of terminals in place and the speeding of their lines.

L. RON HUBBARD
Founder

HCO London Only

The following are HCO special projects upon which we will be working—they take precedence over routine duties:

1. HAS Co-audit

2. Saint Hill

3. Setup of outlying HCOs WW

4. Straightening out book and tape inventories WW

5. Getting corporate status established WW

6. HPA/ACC London.

L. RON HUBBARD
Founder

HCO POLICY LETTER OF 14 MAY 1959
Issue III

Convert
Wash DC only
To HCO US and DC

HCO ADMINISTRATOR

The HCO Administrator has general charge of administration and personnel and is responsible for the general accomplishment of HCO functions.

The Administrator in particular holds the morning meeting, apportions work load, reviews the functioning of communication lines, ensures the accomplishment of HCO and my personal business via the responsible hats.

In particular, it is the duty of the Administrator to see that personnel are causative toward their posts and that the problems related to those posts are handled by them, not by shunting despatches about.

The HCO Administrator brings order to HCO activities.

L. RON HUBBARD
Founder

HUBBARD COMMUNICATIONS OFFICE
37 Fitzroy Street, London W1

HCO POLICY LETTER OF 26 JUNE 1959

CenOCon

IMPORTANT

HCO WW CHANGES QUARTERS AND ADDRESS

This spring, with my own money, I bought Saint Hill, the former luxury estate of the Maharajah of Jaipur. It is complete with fifty-five acres of beautiful grounds and gardens, a swimming pool, a ballroom, a cinema, uncounted bedrooms, eleven baths, a two-and-one-half-acre fishing lake, another fish pond, a huge conservatory, glasshouses, a billiard room and numerous other items.

This will be used as a residence abroad and by HCO WW as the communication center of Scientology.

I am installing a commercial agricultural enterprise to make HCO WW independent of other finance in the distant future.

Six rooms will be used as offices meanwhile, but within a couple of years HCO WW will build its own buildings on the estate.

Therefore, all communications meant for me should hereafter be sent to

> HCO Saint Hill
> Saint Hill Manor
> East Grinstead, Sussex, UK

The cable address is not firmed at this writing but will possibly be HCO Saint Hill Telex.

I am putting in, effective July 9, Teletype equipment (telex) in HCO Saint Hill and London. Later these go in to all HCOs in Central Orgs.

In this beautiful setting, HCO WW can be more able to cope with *all* Scientology concerns worldwide rather than the running of the London office.

Messages sent first to London will be forwarded to HCO Saint Hill, but the routing will slow them down. Send everything intended for me or HCO WW to HCO Saint Hill now.

L. RON HUBBARD
Founder

HCO POLICY LETTER OF 1 JULY 1959

CenOCon

HCO WASHINGTON, DC

HCO Washington, DC, In-Charge
HCO Continental Sec
HCO Communicator, Continental and Area
HCO Area Sec
LRH Personal Sec
HCO Dissemination Sec
Sec ED
HCO Steno
Book Section Admin
Book Section and Shipping

L. RON HUBBARD
Founder

DUTIES AT SAINT HILL
HCO WW

HCO WW was officially inaugurated on 10 July 1959 at Saint Hill Manor, East Grinstead. Its posts consist of the following, whose duties are as stated:

HCO SECRETARY WW

This will be the handling of all nonroutine lines and also personnel.

HCO EXECUTIVE COMMUNICATOR WW

Creating and running all fixed lines. Requirement of local physical establishment, placing and designation of furniture, allocation of rooms, etc.

LRH PERSONAL BUSINESS SECRETARY

Procurement of quarters and local personnel (under requirements of HCO Secretary WW); LRH personal invoicing.

LRH TRANSCRIPTION

HCO purchasing for and design of offices (as required by HCO Executive Communicator WW).

Saint Hill Switchboard Operator; HCO Filing Clerk; HCO routing and errands; Saint Hill mailing.

HCO Communicator's Steno; fixed lines, HCO addressing, mimeoing, invoicing.

L. RON HUBBARD
Founder

HCO WW POLICY LETTER OF 22 AUGUST 1959

All Staff

HCO WW PROJECTS

At this moment I am handling twelve separate projects at Saint Hill in addition to other hats.

I need and want help on these projects. Therefore, I have listed and assigned them and will give each a work output and financial collection quota.

If the persons who assist me in these projects can handle the flaps, the routine and the financial handling and collections involved, we can do our work and prosper and can set up and finance further research and facilities.

I want you to tighten up the lines in these zones, get snap into the actions to be taken and help me handle these important spheres of my responsibilities.

Each project, except numbers eleven and twelve, are independent to a large extent and should be handled with decision and accuracy.

We cannot at this stage afford quantities of office staff and communicators. Therefore, each must do his own work with minimal assistance, remembering that the rest of staff is either handling a project or his own hats.

(Note—Projects are not necessarily in order of importance.)

Saint Hill Project No. One: TECHNICAL. The acquisition and compilation of technical data on Scientology from reports, assessments and bulletins. The vetting of all technical papers and letters. The review of all D of P and student reports.

Saint Hill Project No. Two: Is to give communication and service to and receive the 10 percent weekly income from HCO mission holders.

Saint Hill Project No. Three: This is to prepare and sell new books and new tapes to the world in general to be bought directly from HCO.

Saint Hill Project No. Four: Consists of research and commercial activity in the field of plant growth and receives data from the research and income from the commercial activity.

Saint Hill Project No. Five: Consists of the general sale of books, tapes and E-Meters to HCO offices, Central Organizations, mission holders and the general public worldwide, and the collection and banking of all such sums whether from the sale of books by HCO WW Book Section or by the sale of books by other HCOs.

Saint Hill Project No. Six: Corporate organization and continuance. This project consists of supervision of legalities and sale of shares and transfers called Hubbard Communications Office, Ltd., when formed.

Saint Hill Project No. Seven: Magazine preparation, printing and economy of costs, and printing of all leaflets, etc.

Saint Hill Project No. Eight: Collection of accounts owed HCO from past transactions.

Saint Hill Project No. Nine: Care of all HCO offices, ensuring that they function properly, that they receive their 5 percent income from Central Orgs, get out their magazines, provide inspection services, submit proper reports to HCO WW and that all special sums or surpluses are transferred to HCO WW Account and to ensure that such offices have adequate personnel.

Saint Hill Project No. Ten: Economy Saint Hill Manor. To ensure that the services, salaries, purchases and expenses of Saint Hill Manor are kept within bounds of income from various sources. To reduce these wherever possible. To see that the budget is balanced.

Saint Hill Project No. Eleven: Central Organizations. This is a vitally important project seeing to it that Central Orgs receive proper service, supervision, hats and organization and making sure their 10 percents arrive and are banked to HCO WW weekly.

Saint Hill Project No. Twelve: Accounting and Banking. The invoicing, accounting and banking of all projects separately is to be done in a manner prescribed. Books are separately invoiced on a second machine but all other invoicing is to be done on one other machine. All disbursements shall be done on a disbursement machine plus checks. All invoices are to be numbered by projects on the invoice and all disbursements shall be so numbered. The assistance of chartered accountants shall be rendered.

Each of these projects is in addition to other duties performed by the individual but it is expected that the individual appointed will be responsible in particular for these projects. These are not "hats," they are zones of supervision and finance.

L. RON HUBBARD
Founder

CenOCon

PROMOTIONAL FUNCTIONS OF VARIOUS DEPTS

Central Organizations are now running on the six-department system. They have been for some time and it is working, and working well.

Each of these six departments has its own Director, Deputy Director and function. The six are represented either by a Director of a department or a Deputy Director in the Advisory Committee.

The Association Secretary has amongst his functions seeing that the purposes of these depts are carried out and that the quotas and schedules of each department are met. In addition he must see to it that the promotional purposes of each department are carried out.

Each of the six depts has a promotional purpose in addition to all its other purposes. By promotion in a Scientology organization we mean REACH the public.

Some of the promotional purposes of these depts are listed herewith:

Dept of PrR: To reach individual aspirants for training and processing by various communication means such as letters, phone, telegram and, in particular, personal contact. Public lecturing and the visiting of groups by PrR persons or an Association Secretary are included in the promotional functions of PrR. Broad contact by means of advertisement is also a PrR function. PrR promotion is however mainly an individual matter. Amongst the promotional functions is the arranging of the lives of aspirants so that training and processing can be attained by them.

PE Foundation: The promotional functions of the PE Foundation include the dissemination of invitations and literature to the broader public by means of the available public. They also include the attainment of sufficiently exciting results by lectures and doingness that the attendees will tend to bring new persons into PE. PE via PrR may advertise for its classes. This could be summed up by saying generate enthusiasm and attendance by straightforward data and demonstration that Scientology works. The PE is a showcase.

Academy: The first function of the Academy is to have a good Academy run with tough 8-C. For years it has been observed that a fine, tautly scheduled Academy that puts students over the jumps and makes them into uncompromising zealots for the right way of doing things always attracts new students. A bad Academy is always badly attended. The grapevine here is so apparent that one only need look at Academy attendance to know Academy quality. This is the first line of Academy promotion. The second line of promotion in the Academy is using old students to get new students by letters and programs. Amongst these programs is the Extension Course.

The HGC: The promotion function of the HGC consists of turning out cases that rave about their auditors and the HGC. It is unfortunately true that an HGC is not as well attended as it gets results. Indeed a good HGC from a standpoint of results is often less well attended than one that really chews pcs to ribbons. This is because of the victim complex in the society. But good or bad—which is after all a technical, not promotional, question—the results of the HGC MUST include enthusiasm on the part of pcs for their auditors and the service rendered. Handling the private lives of pcs is forbidden by the Auditor's Code when done directly. But sometimes this has to be done to get the case up scale. The best promotion of an HGC is interest in the pcs, in or out of session. And this is furthered by the HGC use of tests. An auditor must not evaluate for a pc. This does not include the D of P. A good D of P evaluates as harshly as an Instructor and more or less follows the Instructor's Code. An overbearing, evaluating D of P always has more pcs than a meek and mild one. The sending of tests to the pc after he gets home, the hounding him afterwards for reports on what and how he is doing, is all a promotional function of the HGC. There is a five-year standing order that a pc must be written to three times after leaving the HGC, the first letter one week after he leaves, the second letter one month after that, and the third letter three months after that. An HGC that doesn't stay in communication with its pcs never has very many. It's not up to PrR to stay in communication with its pcs who've had intensives, even though PrR does. It is up to the D of P to stay in communication with these pcs.

Dept of Materiel: You would not at once think of the Dept of Materiel as being a promotional unit, yet it is. Amongst its duties is cleanliness and spark in the quarters. A Dept of Materiel that will inventively make the org loom up in terms of buildings and quarters is doing promotion. Materiel should never slack on this function but many Materiel Directors have been unaware of it. The Dir of Mat should get out and look the place over and figure out how within his budget he can make people come into this particular building who know nothing about Scientology but only because they were attracted in. Further, the Director of Materiel should realize that his promotional lines consist of keeping Address and CF straight. He holds all the bodies in CF enclosed in file folders and he knows where all the bodies are in Address. If these are straight, then the Director of Materiel has done a great deal of promotion, and combined with attracting (rather than attractive) quarters, he is really promoting heavily.

Dept of Accts: Accounts is commonly so snowed under with bookkeeping and proportionate income that it doesn't think of itself as a promotional unit. But it is. Snappy and accurate accounting, quick and accurate and even tough rendering of statements, is all promotion of a sort. We are accustomed to thinking of an Accts Dept as being figure-figure, nonreach sort of department, but this is far from true. Accounts is promotional just by rendering bills properly and on schedule. And they're promotional by making sure the public contributes to the organization in money. By thoroughly backing up the Dir of PrR, Accounts does a lot of promotion. Further, there is another thing an Accounts Dept can do in the promotion line. We are usually undermanned in the Accounts Dept and seldom realize that lack of people in it is one of the most foolish economies we can make. It's lack of people in the Accounts Dept rather than lack of willingness that keeps our Accounts in a turmoil. There should be one person on statements, one person on current bills book and one person on proportionate income breakdown even if one or two of these people are part time. If there are three—and there should be—part of the work of each would be promotion as follows: Statements, noticing that credit is good on some person in the statements book, should write and tell the person so, and give a list of such people to the Dir of PrR. Current Bills, who should handle purchasing and filing too, probably, has a public relations function in handling the merchants with whom we deal and getting them interested in what we are doing, rather than allowing a purely trade relationship to exist. Proportionate Income, who also usually does the invoicing, has a promotion function in making sure that the receipts get back to the payee along with some kind of a pat on the back for helping Scientology along. MONEY is the attention unit of this society. A lot of Scientologists say "how mercenary" when I start talking about money. They don't believe in it to the degree that they don't want to attract any attention personally. And that's the crude truth. We've got to get over that attitude. The commonest sense tells us that if we had enough money, we could advertise and build and hire our way straight up the line ten times as fast as we are doing. Well, one of the ways we fail is to fail to use money as a promotion factor, and to fail to fully utilize commercial transactions and monetary exchanges as promotional avenues. Think that over and buy the Dir of Materiel the new building he wants and see how they start crowding in. The Dept of Accounts is our most neglected promotional sphere and this we must overcome.

The six-department system is built like a watch. It is worthy of considerable study. And it certainly accomplishes doingness. Any sphere of promotion there is can be assigned to one or another of its departments.

Association Secretaries these days are selected on the basis of their personal ability to promote and get the show on the road. This should now be extended to the dept heads of the organization.

Promotion means REACH. Well, let's stop worry and start reaching on all six cylinders.

L. RON HUBBARD
Founder

HCO POLICY LETTER OF 21 OCTOBER 1959

Sthil

ROUTING OF BULLETINS AND POLICY LETTERS

A Project Supervisor must see all bulletins and policy letters going to his people first. Then the Project Supervisor must send it on for L. Ron Hubbard's acceptance before it can be sent.

L. RON HUBBARD
Founder

HCO POLICY LETTER OF 20 JANUARY 1960

Saint Hill
HCO Secs
Assoc Secs

HCO WW POINTS OF CONCENTRATION

A great deal of varied traffic passes through the channels of HCO WW. It will help to know the various importances currently given HCO WW activities.

HIGHEST PRIORITY

1. Copying and distributing to HCOs and Central Orgs the Washington January 1960 congress tapes and HCS tapes. Central Orgs should give congresses on these. This was the kickoff on the most important program Scientology ever had and is being received with tremendous enthusiasm everywhere.

The nine hours of HCS tapes, January 1960, are the most important course tapes ever issued and should be played to HGCs, staff clearing courses and new HCS/BScn courses.

HCO WW is losing no time getting these out. They will be 7½ inches per second speed tapes suitable for auditorium use.

Fifth and sixth London and Melbourne ACC tapes can be released generally.

2. Weeding out mission holders that show no promise of becoming industrious centers. Encourage all so weeded to become Lifetime Members. Mission holders doing heavy traffic and heavy remittances to be made into centers.

3. Collection of HCO WW percentages from Central Orgs, mission holders and HCOs and catching up any backlogs.

Additional important actions at HCO WW are:

a. Thursday weekly bulletins

b. *PAB* magazine

c. Central Org magazine material

d. Receipt and handling of technical matters and HCO and Central Org reports

e. Internal good order.

Other projects and actions are to be continued but are not of any high priority and can be neglected if they threaten to slow the above points.

L. RON HUBBARD
Founder

Sthil

THE PURPOSE OF HCO WW

The purpose of the office staff of HCO WW is to forward my outgoing comm lines as a first, fast priority and to cope with incoming lines so that they do not jam my outflow.

First priority then is to see that my handwritten or transcribed material goes out, no matter what emergency may be coming in.

I have usually handled situations before they become emergencies, providing my outflow lines and directions at the other end are followed.

The full outflow line starts with supplies of paper, ink, pens, clean records, tapes and functioning equipment and papers at my desk.

This line then goes to typing, mail, or mimeograph. There it is put in distributable form and is expedited *out*.

Part of the line is its receipt point. In the case of orders and instructions to a distant place, HCO WW is to make certain they are followed without flashbacks.

In the case of books or articles, these are cared for here as to proofing and accuracy and are then followed through to make sure they arrive.

The secondary purpose of the office is handling inflow. This inflow of letters, book orders, problems, is coped with by HCO WW to prevent their stopping the outflow line. This does not mean the inflow lines are not important. They are.

Mrs. Hubbard's outflow lines are important, but usually require only telexing or mailing.

This office exists to aid and speed a writer's outflow lines. It has no other basic purpose. I am responsible for about one million dollars a year of income around the world. On monetary value only, my outgoing line, the line that keeps this income created, is worthwhile forwarding.

This outflow line services the interests of an estimated two million people. Therefore, for humanitarian reasons, it has some importance.

You may or may not be interested in the ultimate goals toward which I work, but they are good goals and if anything gets accomplished in certain human spheres, it may be on this line.

Therefore, I sincerely request your attention on post and your cooperation on these counts:

1. Forward my outflow line;

2. Cope with the inflow line and don't let it stop my writing lines. Handle the problems and despatches, the income and the books as they come in with minimum recourse to me.

I'm sorry if this is blunt. However, that's the way it is.

L. RON HUBBARD
Founder

HCO POLICY LETTER OF 22 DECEMBER 1960

All Central Orgs

IMPORTANT CHANGE IN REPORTS

To reduce and standardize the administrative reporting in organizations, the following system should go into effect as soon as possible:

A form containing all the data required from any one department should be prepared by the Association (Org) Sec. Each dept may require a different form to secure all the data.

This data is the same as that required on the OIC charts.

This does not change the income sheet report system.

The new report form for a department must be headed with the name of the Central Org, and must carry its full routing. The routing is from the Association (Org) Sec's Sec to the designated dept head, to be returned to the Association (Org) Sec's Sec by next Monday afternoon (date blank very prominent), then to the Assoc (Org) Sec, then to HCO Area Sec, then to HCO WW OIC Unit. A description of the data required and the blank for it in each case is then listed. This is followed by a signature and date of the head of the department.

These reports are different for each department, therefore the form is different.

All personnel data, income data, financial data, numbers of people, technical results, etc., must appear on this form.

The form is done on flimsy paper, the lightest possible and practicable. The color should be pink.

The procedure is then this:

The Association (Org) Sec's Sec retains all these form blanks—the whole supply of each type. No stock of forms is given to a department.

On Thursday morning the Association (Org) Sec's Sec places the appropriate forms in the Comm Center baskets of department heads plus any of the old type income sheet necessary. He or she also places the Accounts Department income and disbursement sheets in their baskets.

Heads of departments or their Admin write up the income sheet from their invoices. They take their department's report form and fill it in from the data to hand. They return any income or disbursement sheet and the report to the Association (Org) Sec's Sec by Monday noon.

The Assoc (Org) Sec's Sec sets up the data on the OIC board by noon Tuesday, using the report sheets for source.

There is this difference in marking up OIC graphs. The actual figure is placed inconspicuously below the graph point being drawn in. The figure and the graph point then constitute a total fact on the graph.

The Ad Comm meeting is then held Tuesday at 2:00 P.M. in the Association Sec's office with the OIC board complete. All the data on the graphs is gone over rapidly with the Ad Comm by the Association (Org) Sec. The comments, approvals or condemnations and any plans stemming from these are noted by the Association (Org) Sec's Sec and any new ideas, plans, resolutions and suggestions are added to his minutes. These however should be kept very brief. NO FINANCIAL OR NUMERICAL DATA APPEARS IN THE MINUTES.

The brief minutes copied and the original reports from the departments are then packaged and mailed to Saint Hill where they will again be put up on OIC boards. At Saint Hill there will be an executive meeting weekly to summarize the data which, with suggestions, will be broadly published in brief form to all orgs giving data on all orgs.

The intention here is to reduce the amount of copying of data and speed the report line. These department reports can replace all existing reports by including all the data, even a roster of personnel. This reduces the Ad Comm minutes and shows department heads all data in relation to past data rather than stressing one week only.

As the data is already outlined by OIC charts and any existing additional report forms, it should be easy to make up the department reports.

The idea is one income sheet and one report for a department.

As everything in PE will shortly be on cards, not invoices, PE data can be kept by keeping cards for the week.

The original reports, in packet form, must be light for airmailing, hence the weight of the paper of the report must be light.

Technical profiles, auditors' reports, students' and training reports continue to be forwarded but as supplementary to the department report and are sent through on this same line. The Friday—Saturday test results can be forwarded the next Monday with the past week's reports.

As the OIC graphs are kept and filed and now have numbers on them, they constitute a supplement to Ad Comm minutes and should be kept as such as the basic data now does not appear in Ad Comm minutes.

HCO report blanks are made up and handled exactly this same way.

L. RON HUBBARD
Founder

HCO POLICY LETTER OF 28 MARCH 1961

CenOCon

PERSONNEL POLICIES
STAFF POST QUALIFICATIONS
PERMANENT EXECUTIVES TO BE APPROVED

(Modifying HCO PL 17 Feb. 61, STAFF POST
QUALIFICATIONS, PERMANENT EXECUTIVES TO BE APPROVED)

I desire now to approve of all executives appointed to post in Central Organizations, before the appointment is given permanent status.

I desire a full report from HASI attendant to the dismissal of any permanent executive before the dismissal occurs.

The data to be submitted to me, to qualify a department head as a permanent holder of post, includes:

1. A minimum of 45 days successful performance of duty on post.

2. A statement from the D of P, taken from pc graphs, of the auditor quality and ability of the person being appointed.

3. The appointee's own graph and IQ.

4. A summary of his Scientology career.

5. A Security Checksheet on the person.

6. An E-Meter assessment, particularly on help and control.

7. His exam results for permanent staff member.

8. Report on hat check of post by HCO Sec.

9. SOP Goals procedure fully flattened.

No new executive, not approved by myself on the above basis, may draw the salary of his executive post, but only the salary formerly drawn on a nonexecutive post until my approval is received by the Assoc Sec, effective on receipt of the letter.

No executive may continue as an executive on permanent status, unless approved by myself, on or after 1 Aug. 1961, and if not approved will revert to pay as a leading auditor even while retaining post.

For the purpose of this policy letter the following posts are defined as executive posts:

In HASI:

Association (or Organization) Secretary
PE Director
Director of Training
Director of Processing
Director of Promotion and Registration
Chief Registrar (Body)
Letter Registrar
Director of Material
Director of Accounts.

In HCO:

HCO Continental Secretary
HCO Area Secretary.

All persons permanently so appointed by myself shall be given a small certificate to that effect.

The assembly of the materials required, (1) to (9) above, is solely the responsibility of the person being appointed.

TEMPORARY EXECUTIVE APPOINTMENTS TO BE PASSED BY HCO

The HCO Continental Secretary must pass upon any temporary appointment of an executive, before the person is given post. This does not mean such temporary appointment may receive the pay of the post.

The authorization to appoint a temporary executive may be refused only on the following grounds:

1. Past unsuccessful experience with the appointee on that post.

2. Graph points lower than center.

3. IQ less than 120.

4. Security Check not passed.

5. Control and Help buttons get very bad reaction on E-Meter.

6. Examination of staff profiles and longevity show other persons better qualified for post.

If no person can be found who qualifies for the temporary executive post, it may not be filled.

In event of abuse or confusion of this section the Assoc Secretary may stop any action in progress and send full details to me for decision.

TEMPORARY AND PERMANENT DEFINED

A temporary executive fills the post on a temporary basis, using the word "temporary" in the post title. He or she does not draw the executive post's units but draws former units or the units of a leading auditor, whichever is higher. He or she may be removed from post with or without cause by the Assoc Sec at any time or by a qualified HCO Sec during the time that HCO Sec is handling a State of Emergency.

42

A permanent executive uses the full title of and draws the full units of a post.

He or she may be transferred to a similar post by the Assoc Sec, or by the HCO Sec who is handling a State of Emergency that applies to that department. He or she may be suspended for no longer than two weeks in any three months from post without pay, to be processed in event of a consistent failure in that department. He or she may be removed from post only by myself after due investigation, and reports are received by me.

APPOINTMENT TO STAFF POSTS

No appointment may be made to any post on staff until the following procedure has been followed.

An application form (green ink on pink since it belongs to Accounts and affects pay) is made available at the office of the Assoc Sec's Secretary.

People desiring employment are directed by Reception to the Assoc Sec's Secretary (or a small stock of forms may be left with Reception).

The application form is self-directing. The person fills in his own various qualifications and vital statistics. It then sends the person directly to Test In-Charge to be given a test or (as is more likely) to receive the test from his files. The person then goes to the HCO Sec. The HCO Sec marks the application form in spaces to review the test, makes a brief Security Check and marks in that result and then states either (a) the person is employable on staff or (b) this person cannot be employed on staff until processed or (c) this person cannot be employed.

If the results are (b) or (c), the person is so told at once. If the results are (a), the person is sent to the Assoc Sec (or his secretary) for interview and results of interview are marked. The person is then told when to come to work or that he or she will be informed if there is an opening.

If the person is employed (now or later), the application has the units or pay marked on it by the Assoc Sec's Sec and is sent to the Accounts Dept, when employment is begun.

The Accounts Dept makes a folder for the person in the creditor file.

Accounts may not pay out a check until the form is in the Accounts Dept and is initialed okay, throughout.

The routing of the form is written on the left margin in each case.

Important: After 1 Aug. 61, the Accounts Dept may not pay out pay even to old staff unless an application form is in the Accounts file.

TERMINATION OF EMPLOYMENT

When employment is terminated, the person terminating, to receive his or her final pay, must be routed on a similar form.

The form is obtained from the Assoc Sec's Sec, who is custodian of all forms, by the dept head of the leaving person's department or by the Assoc Sec.

The form is self-routing on the left-hand margin. It is green ink on pink paper.

The form is headed:

TERMINATION FORM

Without this form you cannot receive your final
pay or any recommendation to future employers.

The leaving person fills in name and date and writes his given reason for leaving.

He gives the form to the dept head for his or her remarks.

The leaving person then reports to HCO and gets checked out for ARC breaks and withholds and may be ordered to processing at organization expense, but not longer than 12½ hours, preferably 5 hours.

If the leaving person then changes his or her mind about leaving, the form is destroyed by the dept head.

The person reports again to the dept head for the form to be continued, or destroyed in event of person staying, and then takes the form to Director of Material to turn in his supplies and any equipment, and get an initial. This includes E-Meter or any such and in the case of a dept head or an Assoc Sec may require a full inventory by a paid company if the amount is great.

The person now goes to Accounts with the form and receives with the form his or her final pay.

Accounts, while keeping the creditor folder of the person in a "dead file" at the back of creditor's file, until the year's storage of files is made, places the person's original application for employment and the termination form (stapled, termination at the back) into comm lines to the Assoc Sec's Sec who files.

The person's final paycheck is sent to HCO by Accounts and may not be paid directly by Accounts to the person. HCO hands over the final check when the person has been checked out by HCO or has received any auditing recommended.

SEEKING PERSONNEL

Dept heads seeking personnel may procure it wherever they wish, and however they wish, but must first look in the job application file of the Assoc Sec's Sec in order to save time.

To keep the file straight, the Assoc Sec's Sec should divide the file into live (with 3 months) and inactive segments.

In times of expansion a mailing can be sent to the whole list. This would serve to freshen the file and the replies can be filed with the original applications. Until they lose a body, these applicant people do not get "dead filed."

Keeping this application file up prevents the randomity of emergency hiring and bypasses of security.

The most fruitful source of new personnel are the PE and Academy, and permanent help wanted notices should be posted in each.

L. RON HUBBARD
Founder

HCO POLICY LETTER OF 24 OCTOBER 1962

CenOCon

EMERGENCY HEADQUARTERS

The international headquarters of Scientology, in event of atomic war suddenly occurring, will be:

CAPE TOWN
Seafare House, Oranje Street
Gardens, Cape Town,
South Africa

This does not mean that I will immediately go to Cape Town or that I will not go to America. It means only this:

If atomic bombing occurs and Saint Hill does not answer up when called, and if Washington, DC, or London HASI do not answer up, then direct all communications seeking clarification or information to Cape Town.

LIBRARY

It is up to the Continental Director South Africa, now located in Cape Town, to procure a full tape and book library on Scientology.

Washington and Saint Hill are ordered to cooperate in this action.

L. RON HUBBARD
Founder

HUBBARD COMMUNICATIONS OFFICE
Saint Hill Manor, East Grinstead, Sussex

HCO POLICY LETTER OF 3 SEPTEMBER 1963

CenOCon

STATUS OF AUCKLAND

Auckland, New Zealand, is now regarded as having the status of a full Central Org. It has a continental HCO office and its sphere of influence covers the whole area of New Zealand.

As New Zealand is part of ANZO, Auckland is still under the aegis of the HCO Continental Office ANZO and Continental Director ANZO, in Melbourne, and should continue to maintain a close liaison with them, as well as maintaining their direct line to HCO WW.

L. RON HUBBARD
Founder

HCO POLICY LETTER OF 14 JANUARY 1964
Issue II

HCO Cont Secs
HCO Exec Secs
Assoc/Org Secs

FUTURE CONTINENTAL OFFICER STATUS

The HCO Continental Secretary and the Continental Director of all areas shall, after 1 September 1964 and until specifically then informed otherwise, be the senior HCO Area Sec and senior Assoc/Org Sec of the continental area.

Unless advised to the contrary on or about 1 September 1964, these offices shall not exist as offices separate from the persons of the senior HCO Area Sec and senior Assoc/Org Sec of the continent's Central Organization. The title will, however, be retained.

Until 1 September 1964 present status will remain unchanged barring emergencies.

The entire reason for this action is financial.

The offices of HCO Continental Sec and Continental Director exist mainly to increase Scientology activity and income in a continental area and, where this is not the whole concentration of such officers, as witnessed by the balance sheets, the supernumerary status of a separate HCO Continental Secretary or Continental Director cannot be afforded by that continental area.

In continental areas which are booming, the increased activity demands the separate character of these highest continental offices. But where income is not increasing, the offices become too great a burden financially on a continental area.

Between now and 1 September 1964 all org balance sheets will be carefully watched for increase, and in those areas where the increase warrants it, the separate status will be retained, and where the area has not greatly increased, the officers now holding the posts will revert to the senior HCO Area Sec and senior Assoc/ Org Sec of the area or the posts will be otherwise filled.

This is not intended as a criticism of current activity but only a calm forecast of the reality of the situation.

As I can, by administrative actions alone in any Central Org, as its Assoc/ Org Sec, boom its income, I expect my leading officers in any continent to be able to do likewise in all orgs under their control.

L. RON HUBBARD
Founder

Sthil

HCO (WW) LTD.
CENTRAL ORG ACTIVITIES

It should be the primary concern of HCO (WW), Ltd. to increase the dissemination, activities and income of all organizations on a crash program basis.

This should be done by:

1. Stressing recent policy letters on org functions.

2. Compilation of "The Association/Organization Secretary's Org Rudiments" from recent policy letters.

3. Reissue of org ruds of the HCO Area Sec rewritten.

4. Adjustment of personnel in ailing orgs.

5. Hammering the Continental Directors to take interest in other orgs and proportionalizing their pay as so much of it from each org at that org's units, i.e., twenty-five units from each org at that org's pay scale, regardless of the 100 percent.

6. Demanding long-range, advance notice by HCOs to the field of coming functions and no more of this thirty-day notice of a tape play. Get a year's schedule of special events ahead and published and then boomed ninety days in advance of each one.

7. Make a lowered-income week subject of a cable to Cont Director.

8. Change the post of Tech Dir to Organization Case Supervisor for HGC and Academy with the purposes given to SHSBC Case Supervisor and abolish post of Technical Director. Specify the appointment must be given only to a person who has himself a fine record of case results from his or her own auditing. The person does not do anything but see that every student and every HGC pc gets his case cracked thoroughly with resultant high reality on Scientology. Regulation: No student must be classified or raised in classification whose case has not been cracked and who has not gotten better in his classification level. Any classification application must have the statement on it that the applicant's case has been markedly improved and that the person knows it, signed by the Organization Case Supervisor, before HCO may issue a classification or a higher classification. Only in the case of Class One is a field auditor's statement to this effect acceptable, but even then it must be signed by the training auditor as "Case unmistakably improved and applicant is fully aware of it."

The Technical Council then heads up the Tech Division. The Case Supervisor is part of it.

9. A lowering state of book sales is to be a point of indication of a failing org and must be watched.

10. Failure of an org to grow or failure of a continental area to develop new offices is considered as an adequate reason for personnel shifts.

It is the duty of HCO (WW), Ltd. to boom Central Orgs and offices, using standard alert means for doing so as well as the above.

L. RON HUBBARD
Founder

HCO POLICY LETTER OF 20 FEBRUARY 1964

HCO (WW), Ltd.

HCO (STHIL), Ltd.

Scientology Library and Research, Ltd.

REGULATIONS

GENERAL

1. Anyone receiving orders from the Executive Director shall consider that the orders are directed to himself or herself personally and unless otherwise directed may not delegate the execution of the Executive Director's orders. All orders, therefore, are conceived to be personally directed for personal execution by the recipient unless the order itself states it may or should be delegated.

2. Flagrant disregard of the Executive Director's policies or orders can result in the convening of a Committee of Evidence on that person. The person receiving the order is held responsible for its execution.

3. If there is question concerning an assignment, the procedure is to carry out the order or begin its execution before querying or requesting alteration.

4. Absence from post for illness or any other reason including processing must become the subject of a report to the Executive Director regardless of the action of the person in charge of that activity.

5. The head of a corporation unit has the power to engage or dismiss personnel or excuse them from post. All such actions, however, must be the subject of a routine despatch to the Executive Director. Intervention will only occur in instances of understaffing, overstaffing or apparent injustice.

6. The orders of a corporation supervisor or head of department to his own personnel are final. Appeal may be made to the Executive Director only in matters of design, reduction of wage or dismissal.

7. The Executive Director has the right to intervene in matters of design, technology, finance, promotion and efficiency and may do so in any area or corporation that is not being effective or solvent. It is otherwise the intention of the Executive Director not to interfere beyond broad policy or planning with corporations or departments.

8. Anyone found to be attempting to reduce the effectiveness of the policies or instructions of the Executive Director or a corporation head or department head by knowingly contrary advices or interpretations which tend to render

the policies or instructions null and void or appear unwise may become subject to a Committee of Evidence.

9. The Convening Authority of all Committees of Evidence for this area is the Executive Director, and he may do so on the application of the corporation manager or on his own cognizance.

COURSE

1. No course student may be used for giving assists to any Saint Hill staff of any corporation or members of the public.

2. No student may be used to give ARC break assessments or assists on another student who is not his or her assigned preclear. Any auditing received by a student must be from that student's assigned auditor. Exception, Instructors or qualified Saint Hill staff members may audit students.

3. No student may be audited above his classification level. Classification policies are in full force on course. The only persons who may be audited above their formally assigned class level are Founding Scientologists and these may only be audited up to Class IV, with the reservation that the processes must fit the case.

4. Two levels of processing may not be combined, i.e., Class 0 process run with Class III commands.

5. Students are to be moved forward through units in accordance with their checksheets only and no opinion is to be interjected to prevent such progress that is contrary to checksheet evidence. In short, if a student's checksheets call for his progressing forward, no Instructor may by opinion only restrain his being moved up.

6. A student may not be retrogressed in units. If a student has attained X2, for example, he or she may not be returned to W or X1. Additional special checksheets may, however, be given a student in any unit which must be completed before progressing to the next unit or division thereof.

7. No student may be instructed contrary to existing technology or advised to do anything except standard technology.

8. No student may be accepted on course unless they personally desired to be here.

L. RON HUBBARD
Founder

Sthil Staff Only

REORGANIZATION

(This functional structure bears no relation
to and does not alter existing corporate status.)

On Sunday 31 May 1964 the following organization goes into full effect at Saint Hill.

There are FIVE production DEPARTMENTS at Saint Hill. Only these five directly produce income. All other activities are service units to these five. Therefore, they are designated UNITS. Full attention must therefore be given to production departments. Solvency depends upon maximum effort by production departments and minimum wastage by any department or unit.

The production departments are:

1. Department One. Production of basic Scientology materials, writings and policies. These functions are mainly done by myself. This unit is the basic unit responsible for eventual income.

2. The Course Department. This, under the Course Supervisor, is responsible for about one-third of the income received at Saint Hill. It consists of its technical and administrative staff, including the Course Secretary, Registrar and Letter Registrar.

3. The Book Department. This is responsible for another third of the income at Saint Hill, and is far more important to economics at Saint Hill than has been realized.

4. The Organization Department is responsible for handling international organizations around the world, not Saint Hill, and obtains another near-third of the income of Saint Hill by way of organization 10%s, etc.

5. The Mission Department. This unit receives a relatively small but respectable annual sum by way of mission 10%s from Mission Holders.

There have been other designated units in the past at Saint Hill. These are no longer so designated but are transferred to the direct control of the Organization Secretary. They include accounts, construction, maintenance, purchase, office cleaning, etc., but not administration or domestic staff.

Domestic staff is considered a unit of Department One, under my personal secretary. It includes the butler, cook, housekeepers, nanny, driver, and the outside grounds staff which in turn is headed by the head gardener.

I remain in general charge of Saint Hill and international Scientology, as Executive Director.

The following posts are, therefore, necessary:

ORGANIZATION SECRETARY, who is in general charge of everything that goes on at Saint Hill and all departments, including Department One. This is the equivalent post to a Central Organization's Association or Organization Secretary. All departments and personnel are answerable to this post for their conduct of duties and the general solvency of their departments. The Organization Secretary may hire or dismiss personnel, increase or decrease wages, sign on all accounts and act to improve conditions without further consultation with the board or the Executive Director.

COURSE SUPERVISOR, who is to increase enrollments and keep students progressing steadily through the course to early completion, safeguard technical practice and in general look over all those matters relating to course income and conduct. The Course Supervisor's primary duty is to maintain a fully enrolled course while graduating well-trained auditors rapidly.

INTERNATIONAL ORGANIZATION SUPERVISOR, who is to do everything possible to increase the efficiency, technical proficiency and income of Central Organizations and offices throughout the world and to collect all monies owed by them to Saint Hill and to act to prevent emergencies in them or to handle existing emergencies in them.

PUBLICATIONS DEPARTMENT MANAGER, who is to get into publication all new course books, handling all printing and manufacturers, and increase meter sales. He is to achieve the full potential of this department.

DIRECTOR OF PROMOTION AND ADMINISTRATION (also holds MISSION SECRETARY), who is to extend his actions into any and all promotion, and any and all administration that achieves promotion or otherwise. Under him then come all other administrative functions including mimeo, filing, typing, reception and all other such personnel except Accounts, since these are all in essence promotional activities. All typing for all other departments is done by this department where they cannot do it themselves. Administrative personnel, even when working in other departments, comes under the Department of Promotion and Administration.

ACCOUNTS ASSISTANT TO THE ORGANIZATION SECRETARY, who is in charge through the Organization Secretary of Accounts personnel and financial matters.

EDITOR of *The Auditor*, who is under the Department of Promotion and Administration.

All other technical personnel retain post as currently assigned.

All administrative personnel, reception, typists, file clerks, now come under the Department of Promotion and Administration. They remain on post as previously assigned unless transferred by the Director of Promotion and Administration. The main change is that Central Files personnel come under general administration on a pool basis and that any administrative personnel may be employed for promotion purposes and that all typing is done in this department which cannot be done by other departments.

LRH PERSONAL SECRETARY, who is in charge of all domestic staff including gardens, housekeeping, driving, nursery, etc., which is assigned to Department One.

There are no changes in invoicing by companies or disbursement or the purchase order system.

The reason behind these changes is future efficiency. The organization made huge sums in 1963 and spent them all, producing emergencies in 1964. Without threatening anyone's job but by using greater efficiency and emphasizing production, not spending, the condition will easily be righted, providing we all make more and spend less. We are far from insolvent. But—I intend we shall be even further away by autumn. Produce more. Spend less. And make this reorganization work by doing your job.

L. RON HUBBARD
Founder

HUBBARD COMMUNICATIONS OFFICE
Saint Hill Manor, East Grinstead, Sussex

HCO POLICY LETTER OF 25 JUNE 1964
Saint Hill Only

DEPARTMENTAL REPORTS

(Effective for the week of 6 July 1964)

The heads of production departments are expected to include in any other weekly reports required the following specific data.

International Organization Supervisor

1. The total income of all organizations.

2. The income of the lowest organization.

3. The exact total of 10 percents received by us in the week.

4. Any significant increase directly traceable to the actions of the International Organization Supervisor or any explanation for lack of increase.

5. The total disbursement on behalf of this department (to which need not be added its general share for service).

The Course Supervisor

1. Of his own personal knowledge and count, the number of actual applications on hand in which no actually enrolled students or withdrawn applications are included.

2. Number of graduates in the week.

3. The exact amount of course income for that week.

4. Any significant rise of income due directly to the actions of the Course Supervisor or any explanation for lack of increase.

5. The disbursements for the week on the behalf of the department (not including any general share in costs).

The Publications Manager

1. The number of book or products buyers who bought during the week.

2. The exact amount of income from purchases for the week.

3. Any significant rise in buyers or income due directly to the actions of the Publications Department Manager or any explanation for lack of increase.

4. The disbursement for the department for the week (not including its share of general service).

The Missions Secretary

1. The total of mission income for the week.

2. The lowest mission payment received.

3. Any significant increase in mission income due directly to the actions of the Missions Secretary, or any explanation for lack of increase.

4. The disbursement for the department for the week (not including its share of general service).

These reports need only be added to the forms of existing reports.

All summarizing reports required by the Organization Secretary remain unchanged.

The usual or routine reports required by the Organization Secretary, with the above appended, are forwarded to the Organization Secretary as required.

To these reports is appended the Organization Secretary's report as follows:

Organization Secretary's Report

1. Total income for the week.

2. Total bank balances for the week (without adjustment).

3. Approximation (rough) of all amounts owed by the organization.

These reports are then forwarded to me as Executive Director, arriving not later than the Tuesday following the Thursday which closed the week.

The ordinary time then for department heads to make out such reports would be Friday and the Organization Secretary's report Monday, all concerning the week that ended at 2:00 P.M. Thursday.

L. RON HUBBARD
Founder

HCO POLICY LETTER OF 18 DECEMBER 1964
Issue I

Gen. Non-Remimeo
Sthil

SAINT HILL ORG BOARD

Effective 1 January 1965, the org board at Saint Hill will be composed of the following purposes.

This policy letter is a companion to the actual posted org board in the Comm Center.

NOTES FOR CHART

CHAIRMAN BOARD OF DIRECTORS OF HASI, INC.

1. Convenes and conducts board meetings. Signs on all bank accounts worldwide. Directs basic planning and promotion. Suggests policy to the board. Sees that corporate structures worldwide are properly composed and registered.

SECRETARY BOARD OF DIRECTORS OF HASI, INC.

2. Prepares and keeps all minutes and records of board activities. Gives notice of meetings. Retains originals of all valuable corporate documents and furnishes copies. Signs on all bank accounts worldwide. Has prepared all documents of registration and reports to Registrars of Companies. Serves as Deputy Chairman in absence of Chairman.

TREASURER BOARD OF DIRECTORS OF HASI, INC.

3. Oversees all financial records and reports of the company and all branches. Retains the financial, bank account and report files, including tax and non-profit status documents. Enforces financial policy within the company and all branches.

EXECUTIVE DIRECTOR

4. Oversees all HCO Secretaries, Organization Secretaries and Association Secretaries and all managers. Appoints all executive personnel in all organizations and these may be removed only by the Executive Director or with his concurrence.

CONTINENTAL DIRECTORS

5. Oversee continental groups of organizations and act as designated board officers although not board members.

6. Manage individual organizations of Scientology throughout the world.

CONTINENTAL HCO EXECUTIVE SECRETARIES

7. Oversee continental groups of HCO Offices.

ORGANIZATION HCO AREA SECRETARIES

8. Handle the communications, technology and awards of single organizations around the world.

1ST DEPUTY EXECUTIVE DIRECTOR

9. Acts as Executive Director in the absence of the Executive Director.

2ND DEPUTY DIRECTOR

10. Acts as Executive Director in the absence of the Executive Director and 1st Deputy Executive Director.

ORGANIZATION SECRETARY

11. Manages Saint Hill in all its activities. Handles financial management for all accounts of Saint Hill. Hires and dismisses all Saint Hill personnel. Regulates all technology and awards for Saint Hill. Originates or passes upon all promotion for Saint Hill activities. Sees that income is greater than outgo at Saint Hill and in all its departments.

1ST DEPUTY ORGANIZATION SECRETARY

12. Acts as Organization Secretary in the absence of the Organization Secretary.

2ND DEPUTY ORGANIZATION SECRETARY

13. Acts as Organization Secretary in the absence of the Organization Secretary and 1st Deputy Organization Secretary.

SAINT HILL ADVISORY COUNCIL

14. Advises the Org Sec concerning promotion and execution of promotion in all Saint Hill activities. May originate minutes but they have no force without Org Sec approval.

SAINT HILL STAFF MEETING

15. Convenes from time to time for general discussion, advices and recommendations.

CHAIRMAN SAINT HILL STAFF MEETING

16. Chairman calls, convenes and presides at meetings.

SECRETARY SAINT HILL STAFF MEETING

17. Records minutes and forwards them when signed by Chairman, to the Org Sec.

CHAIRMAN SAINT HILL ADVISORY COUNCIL

18. Convenes meetings weekly and presides.

1ST DEPUTY CHAIRMAN SAINT HILL ADVISORY COUNCIL

19. Convenes meetings and presides in absence of Chairman.

SECRETARY SAINT HILL ADVISORY COUNCIL

20. Records minutes, has them signed by Chairman and submits them to Org Sec.

1ST DEPUTY SECRETARY SAINT HILL ADVISORY COUNCIL

21. Records minutes, has them signed by Chairman and submits them to Org Sec in absence of Secretary.

HCO BOARD OF REVIEW SAINT HILL COURSE

22. Passes on qualifications of Saint Hill students before graduation or classification.

LEGAL

23. Handles Committees of Evidence internationally and at Saint Hill. Handles all matters of copyrights and trademarks registrations in various countries. Handles all book contracts.

ACCOUNTS UNIT FOR SAINT HILL

24. Manages the accounts. Handles all financial records, income, disbursement and reports for the Org Sec and maintains all accounts files and the purchase order system. Purchases for Saint Hill.

ASSISTANT TO THE ORG SEC FOR ACCOUNTS

25. Manages the Accounts Unit and is in full charge of its personnel.

SAINT HILL CONSTRUCTION UNIT

26. Handles all construction, maintenance and repair at Saint Hill except roads and grounds. Receives, safeguards, uses or stores all construction equipment and materials.

IN-CHARGE SAINT HILL CONSTRUCTION UNIT

27. Is in general charge of construction and maintenance.

ESTATE BRICKLAYER SAINT HILL CONSTRUCTION UNIT

28. Handles all brick and masonry work at Saint Hill.

GROUNDS UNIT

29. Handles all grounds keeping, trees, lawns, paths, roads, gardens, fences, streams and lake at Saint Hill and keeps them safeguarded, clean, policed and of good appearance.

HEAD GARDENER GROUNDS UNIT

30. In charge of grounds, paths and all traffic and is in charge of all grounds personnel, equipment, tools and supplies. Takes care of the swimming bath. Cleans the outer buildings. Looks after all boilers at Saint Hill.

ORGANIZATION SECRETARY'S SECRETARY

31. Looks after the despatches and communication equipment of the Org Sec. Transcribes needed transcription.

COMMUNICATIONS UNIT

32. Handles all communications at Saint Hill. Does checkouts of technical and policy matters on staff. Acts as a watch during business hours. Has in its keeping all communication equipment and materials at Saint Hill and sees that it is properly used, clean and in good repair.

COMMUNICATIONS OFFICER COMMUNICATIONS UNIT

33. Is in charge of the Communications Unit, its functions, its personnel, equipment and material. Handles all staff transport and routing and all hired domestic transport.

1ST DEPUTY COMMUNICATIONS OFFICER COMMUNICATIONS UNIT

34. Acts as Communications Officer in the absence of the Communications Officer.

2ND DEPUTY COMMUNICATIONS OFFICER COMMUNICATIONS UNIT

35. Acts as Communications Officer in the absence of the Communications Officer and 1st Deputy Communications Officer.

RECEPTION

36. Handles all body traffic routing, telex, telephone and log book. Keeps a careful record of everything received by or leaving the organization.

MIMEOGRAPH

37. Handles all mimeographing, mimeograph equipment and supplies and all mimeo routine and master files.

CENTRAL FILES

38. Receives and files all Scientologist and student correspondence for filing and files. Furnishes materials for departments and Registrars.

ADDRESS

39. Keeps up to date the Scientologist address files, cuts plates and has charge of all address equipment and address area, furnishes addresses or addressed envelopes or tapes for all departments. Furnishes card files of names for departments.

INVOICING

40. Invoices all incoming monies, safeguards it during and after receipt and until taken over by the Accounts Unit for which Invoicing acts as an extension in this regard.

MAIL AND SHIPPING

41. Envelopes and mails all mail or sees that it is mailed. Handles the franking machine and is responsible to Accounts for the franking record and stamps. Wraps materials to be shipped by other departments than the Books Section.

VALUABLE DOCUMENTS

42. The Communications Officer.

TYPISTS POOL

43. Does any required typing for the Communications Unit or organization members who have no other typing service.

DOMESTIC UNIT

44. Looks after Saint Hill domestic matters and family. Takes care of the Manor itself and those living in it.

BUTLER

45. In general charge of domestic staff. Hires and dismisses domestic personnel. Looks after the security of the Manor, its doors, windows, locks. Has charge of all furnishing and decoration. Supervises all food preparation and serving. Serves as valet. Cares for all interior electrical supplies. Handles and sees to the repair of all domestic appliances and cooking fuel. Conserves heat and electricity. Has charge of all menus.

HOUSEKEEPER

46. Looks after the Manor, its supplies and cleanliness. Buys all food and handles domestic accounts. Safeguards supplies and safeguards against damage and breakage. Keeps consumable supplies under lock and issues as needed.

GOVERNESS

47. Cares for the children, their clothing, quarters, serves their meals, washes their dishes. Looks after their dining room and toys and pets and recovers or safeguards toys left outside, playground items and children's vehicles. Looks after the children while swimming.

TUTOR

48. Teaches the children or coaches them in their studies.

COOK

49. Cooks for the family and living-in staff. Has charge of all equipment, dishes and the kitchen. Designates required supplies.

CHAUFFEUR

50. Looks after the personal and company vehicles. Has charge of all automotive tools and repairs. Cleans and keeps in order the garage area and everything in it.

CLEANERS

51. Keeps domestic quarters, offices and outbuildings in good order.

LAUNDRESS

52. Washes all domestic laundry. Looks after the laundry room and its machines.

PRODUCTION DEPARTMENT

53. "Production Department" means that subdivision of the organization which directly produces income. The Course Department produces student income. The Publications Department produces book, tape and congress income. The International Organization Department produces 10 percent administration and royalty income from all organizations. The department produces income from mission 10 percents. The whole of Saint Hill income comes from these four sources. Therefore these departments, their equipment, supplies and personnel are favored.

THE COURSE DEPARTMENT

54. The Course Department procures, trains and graduates students of Scientology.

COURSE SUPERVISOR

55. The Course Supervisor oversees all Course Department activities and is directly responsible for producing course income, the training of students and graduating auditors at a high level of technology and goodwill.

1ST DEPUTY COURSE SUPERVISOR

56. Acts as Course Supervisor in the absence of the Course Supervisor.

THEORY SUPERVISOR

57. Handles all theory instruction of the course and acts as Auditing Supervisor.

THEORY INSTRUCTOR

58. Assists the Theory Supervisor, acts as Auditing Supervisor. Handles all theory administration.

PRACTICAL SUPERVISOR

59. Handles all practical instruction, acts as Auditing Supervisor.

PRACTICAL INSTRUCTOR

60. Assists the Practical Supervisor, handles all practical administration and acts as Auditing Supervisor.

CASE SUPERVISOR

61. Supervises the cases of all students on the course.

COURSE REGISTRAR

62. Acts as Registrar and Letter Registrar for the course. Is responsible for procuring new students and the income level of the department.

COURSE SECRETARY

63. Handles all students in general as individuals acting as Dean of Students. Handles lecture and TV and film arrangements and programs. Handles graduate students after their departure in matters of information, training and practice rights and activities in any actions not covered by license.

FACULTY MEETING

64. The weekly meeting of all Instructors, held on Friday, where course reports are made and questions answered. Reviews the general state of the course with an eye to any needed improvements. Sends report to Org Sec.

CHAIRMAN FACULTY MEETING

65. Calls and conducts the meeting. Signs its report.

1ST DEPUTY CHAIRMAN FACULTY MEETING

66. Acts as Chairman in absence of Chairman.

SECRETARY FACULTY MEETING

67. Keeps minutes and prepares report for signature. Forwards it to Org Sec when signed by Chairman.

THE PUBLICATIONS DEPARTMENT

68. Handles all publishing activities, book, tape, meter and insignia sales. Composes and edits the PAB, *The Auditor* and *Certainty*. Prepares all manuscripts for printing. Records and copies tapes. Handles all film and TV activities. Has charge of all printing, recording and electronic equipment, materials and supplies. Is fully responsible for achieving a good income for Saint Hill from dissemination materials and widely disseminating Scientology.

THE DIRECTOR OF PUBLICATIONS

69. Manages all publishing and dissemination activities. Handles all departmental personnel.

70. Acts as Director in the absence of the Director.

THE BOOK SECTION

71. Stocks inventories and keeps in supply all books, tapes, records, film, items and insignia and fills all orders rapidly. Notifies the Director of all dwindling or overstocked materials promptly.

BOOKS IN–CHARGE

72. Manages the Book Section. Is accountable for all orders, stocks and shipments.

SHIPPING CLERK

73. Does the actual filling of all orders and their despatch.

THE EDUCATIONAL AIDS SECTION

74. Manufactures and stocks all visual and aural educational aids such as tapes, films, records, charts, animated graphs or structures.

EDUCATIONAL AIDS IN–CHARGE

75. Supervises or manufactures the arranging, making and stocking of all educational aids.

THE PUBLISHING SECTION

76. Prepares all manuscripts and make-ups and arranges printing of books, magazines, folders, fliers and brochures.

EDITORIAL IN–CHARGE
THE PUBLISHING SECTION

77. Supervises or handles all make-up, proofs, proofing and final publication of all items published. Sees to it that publishing schedules for magazines and books are met.

EDUCATIONAL AIDS ADVISER

78. Advises on all educational aids materials to be manufactured, tapes, films, TV materials, charts, animated aids.

COURSE PROGRAMS DIRECTOR

79. Arranges all TV programs, tape plays, live lectures and all social programs of course.

BASIC COURSE SUPERVISOR (PE, HAS, HQS)

80. Handles all courses for the public or staff given at Saint Hill such as PE, HAS, HQS, and appoints and has control of their Instructors.

STAFF CO–AUDIT

81. Supervises any and all auditing amongst staff members at Saint Hill.

BASIC COURSE INSTRUCTOR

82. Instructs lower-level courses.

STAFF STAFF AUDITOR

83. Audits staff members when called upon to do so by the Org Sec. Handles auditing emergency assists on staff.

CHILDREN'S INSTRUCTOR

84. Instructs Saint Hill children in Scientology.

THE INTERNATIONAL ORGANIZATION DEPARTMENT

85. Handles all international organizations, increases their efficiency and activity. Collects their 10 percent administration and royalty payments. Handles all organization traffic.

INTERNATIONAL ORGANIZATION SUPERVISOR

86. Directs and handles the International Organization Department. Receives all cabled reports and keeps close watch on states of organizations. Supervises all Organization and Association Secretaries and their communications.

HCO SEC WORLDWIDE

87. Is in direct charge of all Continental and Area HCO Secretaries around the world.

HCO DISSEMINATION SEC WW

88. Supervises contents of all national magazines and handles international dissemination.

THE MISSION DEPARTMENT

89. Handles all mission holders and field auditor matters and traffic and supervises their activities. Collects all 10 percent royalties from mission holders. Awards and withdraws mission charters. Conducts mission programs. Handles all memberships and certifications.

MISSION SECRETARY WW

90. Conducts the Mission Department.

MEMBERSHIP SECRETARY

91. Handles all matters relating to any and all Scientology memberships everywhere.

CERTIFICATIONS AND CLASSIFICATION

92. Handles all certifications and classifications at Saint Hill and anything relating to them internationally.

STANDING ORDER 1 LETTERS

93. Letters from Scientologists and the public addressed to LRH are answered and forwarded to LRH for signature.

GENERAL LETTERS

94. Public letters from any source or kind which do not specifically belong to any unit or department are answered.

STAFF PHOTOGRAPHERS

95. Take and handle photographs for publications.

PROOFREADING

96. Proofreads stencils, bulletins, policy letters, executive letters for mimeograph.

L. RON HUBBARD
Founder

Sthil Staff

1965 SAINT HILL OBJECTIVES

This is the Saint Hill program for the remainder of 1965.

1. Bring the Saint Hill org up to a high level of efficiency.

2. Get in the program contained in 1964 HCO Policy Letters in all orgs.

3. Have every Saint Hill executive and Scientology staff member qualify for a Hubbard Administrator's certificate, the checksheet for which is being prepared. (Org board, policy letters, functions, etc.)

4. Bring all Saint Hill staff cases up to Clear or above.

The concentration in this program is to get "our own house in order" as an org and as individuals.

We have made it all the way in having available Scientology technology. I have for fourteen years said, "Scientology will go as far as it works." And "When we have it down technically is time enough to begin heavy dissemination and expansion."

We now "have it down" technically.

The first sound move in any expansion is to secure the ground you're standing on. So, taking things at a reasonable speed, we will devote 1965 to the accomplishment of a tiptop org at Saint Hill with every staff member well versed in the org and its functions and in excellent shape casewise.

If we work at it steadily, we will also keep the other orgs going in 1965 and get our dissemination program in just by doing our jobs. Then, when *we're* in top form, we can begin to concentrate on them very heavily in 1966.

I think we can accomplish these objectives for 1965 rather easily if we work at them steadily through the remainder of this year.

L. RON HUBBARD
Founder

HCO POLICY LETTER OF 20 FEBRUARY 1965

Gen. Non-Remimeo
Sthil
Post Org Staff Boards

APPOINTMENTS AND PROGRAMS

As matters ran fairly well in my absence in January and February, and as I must devote time to compilation of technology for our dissemination program, the Saint Hill organizational structure is confirmed as follows by minutes of the board of directors:

I will continue as Chairman of the Board of Directors of the Hubbard Association of Scientologists International, the company which operates all Scientology organizations over the world and Saint Hill.

The existing organizational appointments in organizations over the world continue as of this date.

_____

The basic needs of international programs set for 1965–1966 are:

a. To provide new, simplified books on already developed but not entirely released technology;

b. To provide educational aids such as films for all drills and processes for all orgs to hold a standard of excellent technical training and application;

c. To get existing org patterns and programs into full effectiveness;

d. To clear, as feasible, the majority of staff members internationally before 1967;

e. To achieve higher levels of beingness for all Scientology executive personnel before 1967.

These objectives are an easy gradient to more ambitious projects envisioned for 1967 and 1968.

It is easy to see then that the balance of 1965 and all of 1966 are being devoted to consolidating our position, making Saint Hill and other orgs efficient and effective, making each org more stable and affluent, getting our materials into highly comprehensible and easily disseminated condition, getting our 1964 book-membership program understood and going well and making each one of us better informed and effective on organizational activities and getting all our cases in order. This gives us a solid base from which to advance.

It is easily seen then that organizational appointments at Saint Hill have been made to facilitate (a) and (b) above and that all organizational appointments or transfers in other orgs in 1965 and 1966 will be influenced by the degree they carry on their own tasks or facilitate the execution and attainments of (a) to (e) above. All barriers erected to the above programs, such as avoidable org troubles, the precipitation of distracting attacks, demands on my time exterior to carrying out my part of the above, down income, wide policy departures and dev-t will be somewhat ruthlessly handled, as nothing can be permitted to assume greater importance than our basic objectives for 1965–1966, as given above, in order to advance securely into our 1967–1968 programs when these are fully agreed upon and released.

OUR FUTURE

All our actions are influenced to a remarkable degree by the state of world affairs.

A cautious estimate of the governmental situation as of this date is that, *unless something intervenes,* World War III is less than five years away, *but* may occur within three years. Thus, we are not operating with all the time margin we could hope for. We have been lucky so far. We have all held things together long enough to achieve our technology while there was still peace.

I hardly need remind anyone that we are the only organization that knows where it's going and have a chance to do something. Even our enemies give us that. Others have neither answers nor hope. And all our really rough spots are behind us.

We were rather pinned down so long as our technology was incomplete, but now this and the time consumed in technical changes have ended.

We have the most formidable array of answers ever assembled. And our technology is now not only developed but is tested and sound. We have not only the new but also the old. And it will also serve.

To make a minor point, in Arizona as early as 1954 we proved that we had the answer to the effects of atomic fission, amongst other things, and made burns caused by radioactive materials vanish using some of our most elementary processing, the Touch Assist, capable of being taught to anyone in minutes. Our aims and abilities are infinitely broader than that but this alone, as small a part as it is, would justify our forward rush and the need to be bigger, do better and to reach more in the face of threatened catastrophe.

The big thing now is to do our personal best, each of us, to lay aside our personal penchants and petty animosities, and as beings, as Scientologists and as organizations get very effective, fast. There's an awful lot depending on us.

Therefore, I ask you to accept your tasks, the necessary policies and command lines as appointed and do your best.

We can't expect perfection until all of us are perfect. We're making do with what we have and we're progressing famously despite the many faults we would all like to correct. The thing is, we *are* winning, we have enough time if we're quick to use what we have, and any future this race has is riding on our backs. It's very humanlike to vilify and misunderstand. We can take that, too. And it doesn't excuse us one bit from not doing our jobs.

Scientology is the only game where everybody wins. And we *are* winning.

We are already well advanced upon our way as the accelerating progress of the past two years indicates.

In January 1963 I took measure of how much time we had before any axe fell. I saw I had to complete all research before 1965 and somehow did so, completing the basic technology for OT at the end of March 1964.

In April of 1964 I then began eight months of administrative reorganization, promotion and programing for all orgs.

By October of 1964 I had also completed fully workable technology for Levels 0 to IV, up to Clear.

By early December 1964 we had agreed internationally upon the worldwide dissemination (book-membership) program and five of nine orgs achieved their highest weeks for the year in the usually deadest month, confirming the correctness of our planning.

On 17 February 1965 I had found the technology for and established Level VII.

On 19 February 1965 we decided the strongest need was for publications clearly and comprehensibly setting forth our technology and a final summary of that technology and the making of educational aids to communicate it and maintain standards.

Therefore, we are well advanced upon our way. Our opposition has remarkably lost heart. We are responding well in organizations to our needs and the demands of the situation.

If we are now very active in executing just the program (a) to (e) above by 1 January 1967, and if each of us, including myself, does his assigned tasks industriously, we will have made it all the way.

And in time.

If we all work hard.

L. RON HUBBARD
Founder

HCO POLICY LETTER OF 4 MARCH 1965
Issue III

Gen. Non-Remimeo
Missions
Sthil Scn Staff
Former Sthil Grads
Sthil Students

Hat Material

Division 1

HCO SECRETARY WW

Under the hat of HCO Certificates and Awards, all matters relating to certification and membership are referable to the HCO Secretary WW when not handled at lower echelons.

Under the hat of HCO Justice, all matters relating to Committees of Evidence, convening authorities, carrying out sentences and review are referable to HCO Secretary WW when not handled at lower echelons, or for final review.

In matters of dispute, the award or revocation of mission charters is referable to HCO Sec WW under the HCO Policy hat. HCO Sec WW may overrule the Mission Secretary's awards or withdrawals of mission charters when these become matters of dispute.

Under HCO Technical hat, all questions of what data is issued to whom and the proper routing of data to Scientologists is directed by HCO Sec WW, when clarifications are required.

All data to be sent to Saint Hill graduates is determined and executed by HCO Sec WW.

All organization conditions are assigned by HCO WW, and conditions may also be assigned to org departments by HCO WW where the matter is overlooked locally. (See condition formulas policy letters.)

Any matter affecting HCO Area Secretaries or HCO Continental Secretaries may be referred to HCO Sec WW for clarification or decision.

HCO Secretary WW is the Worldwide-level executive for Division One (HCO) and a member of the Worldwide Council of Three, of which the Org Sec WW and the Assistant Treasurer WW are the other two. (See policy letters of similar date.)

L. RON HUBBARD
Founder

HCO POLICY LETTER OF 2 AUGUST 1965
Issue I

Gen. Non-Remimeo

EXECUTIVE DIVISION

The Executive Division is Division 7.

The LRH Communicator is in charge of the division.

It consists of three departments.

The first department is the Office of LRH, Department 21. It is in the charge of the LRH Personal Secretary.

The second department is the Office of the HCO Executive Secretary, Department 20. It is in the charge of the HCO Exec Sec Coordinator.

The third department is the Office of the Organization Executive Secretary, Department 19. It is in the charge of the Org Exec Sec Coordinator.

THE OFFICE OF LRH
PURPOSE

The purpose of the Office of LRH is:

> To direct, authorize and organize Scientology and its organizations and to ensure the forward progress of all.

All orders, rules, regulations, policies and routes are designed to forward only this purpose, and so no order, rule, regulation, policy or route may be issued or followed that denies this basic purpose.

The principal sections are the Council Section, LRH Personal Concerns Section, Design and Planning Section, Files Section, Authority to Issue Section, Signature Section, Construction Section and the Household Section.

This office and these sections are represented in every Scientology organization.

In this office are held the council meetings consisting of LRH, usually by proxy, the HCO Exec Sec and the Org Exec Sec.

The council advises actions based on the reports of the divisional Ad Comms, which council actions, when not already covered by blanket policy, must be referred to LRH in person via his Area Communicator before such minutes are valid. LRH as Executive Director may, however, issue orders not passed upon by the council or contrary to their vote, as the org council is itself advisory and is an assistant in an advisory capacity to the Board of Directors at Saint Hill.

Through this office and its activities, the Executive Director directs and controls each organization in accordance with the above purpose.

In very small orgs these functions, aside from the Council Section, are taken over by the HCO Area Sec as LRH Communicator.

THE OFFICE OF THE HCO EXEC SEC

The primary purpose of the Office of the HCO Exec Sec is:

> To help Ron keep HCO and the organization there and make them and the policies, technology and service of Scientology well known.

As all orders, rules, regulations, policies and routes for this office exist to further this purpose, no order, rule, regulation, policy or route may be made or used to interfere with this purpose.

In the person of the HCO Executive Secretary, this office controls the two divisions of HCO, and controls the routing and handling of despatches and persons throughout the Org and HCO, and all personnel of HCO and the Org.

THE HCO PORTION

The first two divisions of the entire organization are the HCO divisions. This is known as the HCO portion of the organization.

THE OFFICE OF THE ORG EXEC SEC

The Office of the Organization Executive Secretary has as its purpose:

> To help Ron keep the organization solvent and producing and to make Scientology well known everywhere.

As all orders, rules, regulations, policies and routes exist to further this purpose, no rule, order, regulation or policy may be made or used to interfere with this purpose.

This office, in the person of the Org Exec Sec, directs and controls the four divisions of the Org.

The primary action of the Org portion of the entire organization is to *handle* whatever is routed and so produce results; and, in its sixth division, Distribution, as well as the other three, to make Scientology broadly known and well thought of everywhere by changing personal and social conditions.

It will be noted that the keynotes of the Executive Division are:

1. Authorization and broad direction lies with the Office of LRH.

2. Existence of the entire organization lies with the Office of the HCO Exec Sec.

3. The conditions of people and society are handled and changed by the Office of the Org Exec Sec.

L. RON HUBBARD
Founder

72

HCO POLICY LETTER OF 14 SEPTEMBER 1965
Issue II

Gen. Non-Remimeo
HCO Exec Secs
Org Exec Secs

UNITS AND BONUSES FOR ORG EXEC SECS
AND HCO EXEC SECS

(Revises HCO PL 24 Mar. 61,
UNITS FOR ASSOC SEC AND HCO SEC)

Each city office Scientology org shall add the Org Executive Secretary of the continental org of the zone to its payroll to the sum of two units in the Commonwealth area and eight units in the dollar area.

This shall be regularly paid to the Org Exec Sec of the continental org.

Each HCO area office of a city office shall add the HCO Exec Sec of the Continental HCO of the zone to its payroll to the sum of two units for the Commonwealth area and eight units in the dollar area.

This shall be paid regularly to the HCO Exec Sec of the Continental HCO.

The purpose of this is to increase the interest of the Continental Org Exec Secs and HCO Exec Secs in the problems and well-being of city offices.

For the purposes of this directive at this time, Continental Org Exec Secs are designated as follows:

FCDC, Washington, DC: The Senior Central Organization Acting Org Exec Sec in the US is paid also from New York, Miami, Twin Cities, Detroit, Chicago (when set up) and any other city office east of the Mississippi.

C of S, California, Los Angeles: The Org Exec Sec West Coast is paid also from Hawaii, Portland and any other city office set up west of the Mississippi.

HASI, Africa, Johannesburg: The Org Exec Sec is paid also by Durban, Cape Town, Port Elizabeth and any other city office set up in Africa.

HASI, Australia, Melbourne: The Acting Org Exec Sec is also paid from Perth, Sydney, Adelaide and any other city office that is set up in continental Australia.

HASI, New Zealand, Auckland: The Org Exec Sec Auckland is also paid if any other city offices are set up and exist in New Zealand.

HASI, UK, London: The Acting Org Exec Sec, would also be paid if any city offices existed in its continental zone.

For the purposes of this directive at this time HCO continental offices are designated as follows:

HCO Continental US, Washington, DC: The Acting HCO Exec Sec is paid also from New York, Miami, Twin Cities, Detroit and any other east-of-the-Mississippi city office that is set up.

HCO Continental West Coast: The HCO Exec Sec of Los Angeles is paid also from Hawaii, Portland and any other city office that is set up west of the Mississippi.

HCO Continental Africa, Johannesburg: The HCO Exec Sec is paid also from Cape Town, Durban, Port Elizabeth and any other city office set up in Africa.

HCO Continental Australia, Melbourne: The Acting HCO Exec Sec is paid also from Perth, Sydney, Adelaide and any other city office set up in Australia.

HCO Continental New Zealand, Auckland: The HCO Exec Sec would be paid if any other city offices existed in New Zealand.

HCO Continental UK, London: The Acting HCO Exec Sec, when on the post, would be paid if any other city offices existed.

HCO BOOK ACCOUNT POLICY

(Corrects HCO PL 11 May 65,
HCO BOOK ACCOUNT POLICY)

HCO EXEC SEC BONUS

The HCO Exec Sec is granted a bonus of two percent of the gross receipts of the local Book Account.

The HCO Exec Sec of a Continental HCO is paid one-half of one percent of the gross receipts of each Book Account in his or her continental zone.

ORG EXEC SEC BONUS

The Org Exec Sec is granted two percent of the gross receipts of the HCO Book Account but may not be a signatory to that account.

The Org Exec Sec of a continental org is paid one-half of one percent of the gross receipts of each Book Account in his or her continental zone.

L. RON HUBBARD
Founder

HCO POLICY LETTER OF 20 NOVEMBER 1965RA
Issue I
REVISED 4 MAY 1985

Remimeo
All Staff Hats

All Divisions

Qual Div Hat Check on All Staff

THE PROMOTIONAL ACTIONS OF AN ORGANIZATION

(Contains 172 actions that ensure solvency and are vital in an org)

When one hears that an org or a division, a department or section or person has been ordered to *promote,* the question can be asked, "What does this mean?"

Some suppose it means get an incredibly brilliant new idea that has never been done before. Another thinks it means hiring an ad agency. Somebody else may think it means telling lies or working confidence tricks. It is none of these things.

Only in emergency promotion does one need new ideas, and these most often consist of how to accomplish a long-neglected action in some other department one doesn't have control over. The brilliance required here is how to get your part done anyway.

PROMOTION means *to make something known and thought well of.* In our activities it means to send something out that will cause people to respond either in person or by their written order or reply to the end of applying Scientology service to or through the person or selling Scientology commodities, all to the benefit of the person and the solvency of the org.

Now do you see that a staff member *smiling* is sending something out that will make someone respond and think better of the staff member and the org. That comes under the definition of promotion. A janitor making the steps clean is presenting something (the view of clean steps) that will make both himself and the org a bit better thought of. A mail clerk doing up a neat package is sending something out that will make the org well thought of. Do you see?

So *any* action that makes the staff member or the org visible and well thought of is promotion.

Furthermore, *any* job in the org well done makes it possible for others to promote but not done makes it very hard to promote or makes it impossible altogether. Every task in the org contributes to promotion. And without promotion there is no job.

There are, however, very standard promotional actions which we concentrate on in an org.

ROUTINE PROMOTION

Through the years orgs have developed various standard promotional actions which invariably achieve results *if done*.

Today these actions are woven into the standard organizational pattern as administrative activities.

If an org follows the organizational pattern and does what the hats say, then it will be promoting with no further strain.

The promotion ideas and patterns as they now exist are never at fault. Only failing to do them is at fault.

Promotion only fails because of nonexecution.

Without promotion one has insolvency.

Promotion without adequate delivery of service or commodity will eventually fail to deliver income.

THE PROMOTION ACTIONS

The Standard Promotional Actions of an org, by division and department, are:

(*Note:* There are other actions in these portions of the org. These are only the promotional actions.)

1. *HCO AREA SECRETARY*—Coordinates and gets done the promotional functions of Division 1.

2. **DEPARTMENT 1 (Dept of Routing and Personnel)**—Requires Reception to make known free introductory lectures to all callers.

3. Has books and cassettes on display at Reception.

4. Keeps staff from collecting in Reception Center and talking Scientology before callers.

5. Routes people swiftly and accurately to the required services.

6. Recruiting signs, tastefully done, to acquire new org staff.

7. Sees that a pool of PR trainees being trained in PR tech exists for eventual posting in Div 6 and in Department of Special Affairs, on current checksheet.

8. Sees that a pool of reserve Registrar personnel are in training part time while working in other Division 2 and Division 6 posts, for future use when fully trained on Reg and Tours posts, using the current authorized Registrar salesmanship course checksheet.

9. Sees that the full org board is sightly, properly done and up-to-date.

10. **DEPARTMENT 2 (Dept of Communications)**—Sees that mailings go out promptly and on schedule.

11. Controls public notice boards of the org and makes sure they also feature org services available.

12. Sees that internal despatches are swiftly delivered and are in accurate form.

13. Sees that letters and orders arrive safely and are quickly handled and not overlooked.

14. Oversees stationery and typing quality so that communications going outside the org look smart and sound bright.

15. Sees that mimeos look well when completed.

16. Issues the technical and policy materials of the org to get in policy and tech.

17. **DEPARTMENT 3 (Dept of Inspections and Reports)**—Sees that the org is there and functioning.

18. Sees that suppressives and enturbulative elements do not block dissemination.

19. Sees that service is accurately given and that no squirrel tech is used.

20. Prevents the phenomenon of no case gain by spotting potential trouble sources and handling.

21. Ethics gets case resurgences by finding the *right* SPs.

22. *DISSEMINATION SECRETARY*—Coordinates and gets done the promotional functions of Division 2 and makes the org and services known to Scientologists.

23. **DEPARTMENT 4 (Dept of Promotion and Marketing)**—Issues magazines on schedule.

24. Properly presents services in ads in org magazines and mailings.

25. Does promotional pieces for Publications Dept and for the Public Divisions.

26. Executes planned promotions as laid down in EDs.

27. Compiles promotional pieces and programs for issue to Scientologists.

28. Gets promotional pieces printed.

29. Sees that tapes and cassettes are available and that presentation of them is of good tone quality.

30. Sees that any cine material is available and ready for broad use.

31. **DEPARTMENT 5 (Dept of Publications)**—Sees that good quantities of books, cassettes, meters and tapes are in stock.

32. Sees that books, cassettes, meters and tapes are attractively displayed.

33. Ships swiftly on receipt of orders.

34. Gets pins and insignia in stock and ensures broad issue so they will appear in the world and thus disseminate.

35. Sees that book, meter and cassette fliers (handbills) are shipped out regularly to Scientologists and bookbuyers.

36. **DEPARTMENT 6 (Dept of Registration)**—Letter Registrar works to accumulate questionnaires and mail from those responding to promotion. Follows exact policy and gets out floods of mail to all possible proper candidates for service.

37. Keeps Central Files right up and in excellent shape and adds all new names of buyers of books and services.

38. Uses Central Files to the limit to produce business and routes everyone in it individually by employing Gradation Charts and sending them out marked and devising other means of utilizing CF to produce business.

39. Sends out questionnaires with all offers which detect people's plans for training and processing.

40. Accepts advance registration and encourages more advance registration until her months ahead are scheduled full of students and pcs.

41. Does phone registration in city areas in addition to other registration actions such as Letter Registrar.

42. Registers everyone who comes in for service as pleasantly as possible with due regard for the solvency of the org.

43. Keeps a complete address file in such shape that mailings are wide and sent to people who will respond. *Never* lets go of an address or a mailing list and keeps them all properly corrected and up-to-date and in proper categories for ready use.

44. Sees that the files, addresses and requirements of persons interested in Scientology are used to the full.

45. *TREASURY SECRETARY*—Coordinates and gets done the promotional functions of Division 3.

46. **DEPARTMENT 7 (Dept of Income)**—Persuades payment of cash or increase in purchase whenever possible.

47. Collects outstanding notes by monthly statements.

48. Collects outstanding notes through field staff members via Dept of Clearing.

49. Sees that public persons' statements are accurate, on-policy and do not
    ARC break the public with errors.

50. Gets all mail orders invoiced and/or collected so they can be shipped at once.

51. **DEPARTMENT 8 (Dept of Disbursement)**—Keeps bills paid in such a
    way that the org is in excellent credit repute. (Promotes with good credit
    rating.)

52. Gets salaries accurately and punctually paid to keep staff happy.

53. **DEPARTMENT 9 (Dept of Records, Assets and Materiel)**—Acquires
    reserves to give a reputation of stability to org.

54. Keeps staff clothing issued and in good order (in those orgs providing
    uniforms).

55. *TECHNICAL SECRETARY*—Coordinates and gets done the promotional
    functions of Division 4.

56. **DEPARTMENT 10 (Dept of Tech Services)**—Makes the customers
    happy and glad to be there.

57. Gives brisk service.

58. Acquires for the org a reputation for swift and excellent handling of people.

59. **DEPARTMENT 11 (Dept of Training)**—Gives excellent training. (The
    soundest possible promotion quickly mirrored in numbers enrolling.)

60. Routes dissidents quickly to Ethics and slows to Review.

61. Briskly and punctually schedules classes.

62. Accomplishes lots of completions.

63. Turns out very competent auditors whose excellence promotes the Acad-
    emy (or College at SH) and Scientology.

64. Writes letters to possible prospective students to get the Academy (or College
    at SH) full. (This is an old, old activity of the D of T who never depends
    on Registrars or magazines.)

65. Makes sure the excellence of training that is there is bragged about in
    magazines, etc.

66. Gets students (Free Scientology Center) to find new, raw-meat pcs of their
    own around the town and audit them for student classification and gets
    them to bring such pcs in for Release examinations and declarations (dur-
    ing which they get routed through Registrar who presents the award) and
    refuses any for classification in cases already known to be a paying pc of
    some org or auditor.

67. Popularizes the Tech Films and uses them to the full and sees that all
    audio-visual equipment (including tape equipment) is well maintained for
    professional, high-quality reproduction.

68. **DEPARTMENT 12 (Dept of Processing)**—Gets excellent results on all pcs.

69. Becomes well known for standard tech.

70. Spots SPs and PTSes early and routes to Ethics. Routes bogged cases quickly to Review.

71. Takes responsibility for all cases in the whole area where the org is.

72. Makes auditors look and act professionally outside the HGC so people will have confidence in them.

73. Insists on clean, attractive HGC quarters and helps Materiel to achieve and maintain them.

74. Gets pcs in such good shape they are walking advertisements for the HGC and Scientology.

75. Writes letters to possible pcs (the D of P has had this duty for 15 years).

76. *QUALIFICATIONS SECRETARY*—Coordinates and gets done the promotional functions of Division 5.

77. **DEPARTMENT 13 (Dept of Validity)**—Makes sure no untrained student or unsolved case gets past.

78. Refuses to get so concentrated on "validating people" that errors are overlooked, for this backfires also.

79. Routes those passed quickly to Certs and Awards and those failed quickly to Review and routes any ethics matters discovered promptly to Ethics.

80. Issues credentials that will be seen around—pins that people will wear, certificates they will hang up, cards they will show.

81. Never issues anything falsely as it will be hidden or discredited.

82. Issues literature to all new Releases and other completions that tells them what they have attained and what next to do and encourages them to do it.

83. Heavily promotes auditors outside the org to bring in their pcs for examination and Release declarations.

84. **DEPARTMENT 14 (Dept of Personnel Enhancement)**—Gets staff in such good shape they are walking advertisements for the org and Scientology.

85. Turns out very competent staff members whose excellence promotes the org and Scientology.

86. **DEPARTMENT 15 (Dept of Correction)**—Finds the real errors in any failures (no student or pc ever gets upset if the actual error is spotted; they only get upset when a wrong error is found).

87. Quickly repairs any flat ball bearings turned out by the Tech Division so they will be no discredit to org.

88. Gives brilliant standard isolation of any errors in students or pcs—discovers them with ease.

89. Repairs thoroughly.

90. Makes a continual effort to get failed cases in the field in for a review.

91. Sends to Ethics all ethics matters discovered. Cultivates an aura of effortless competence.

92. Review makes the dissatisfied satisfied with the org by remedying *all* tech misses.

93. Delivers excellent internships that turn out auditors whose excellence promotes the internship and Scientology.

94. *PUBLIC CONTACT SECRETARY*—Coordinates and gets done the divisional promotional functions of Division 6A and makes Scientology and the org known to the broad public.

95. **DEPARTMENT 16A (Dept of Public Book Sales)**—Gets books and cassettes placed in bookstores, reviewed and in the public view.

96. Gets LOTS of books and cassettes sold to the raw public.

97. Places ads in magazines, radio, TV, etc., to sell books and cassettes.

98. **DEPARTMENT 16B (Dept of Body Routing)**—Guides in new body traffic.

99. **DEPARTMENT 16C (Dept of Public Contact)**—Advertises to the broad public.

100. Advertises and holds public tape plays in the org, open house.

101. Promotes free intro films and gets them shown to large numbers of public and sees that the film presentation equipment is clean and well maintained for high-quality, professional presentations.

102. Keeps mailing lists in such shape that mailings are wide and sent to people who will respond. Never lets go of a mailing list and keeps them all properly corrected and up-to-date and in proper categories for ready use.

103. Acquires new mailing lists.

104. Sends out excellent info packets.

105. Hands out invitations to intro lecture in volume to keep intro lecture full each night.

106. Carries out the promotion of and conducts the current broad public promotional projects.

107. Works on the *public,* not on the Scientologists already known to Division 2.

108. **DEPARTMENT 16D (Dept of Introductory Services)**—Sees that the

introductory lecture and introductory services use no words that will be misunderstood and makes people want to buy training and processing and offers it.

109. Furnishes lecturers to groups.

110. *PUBLIC SERVICING SECRETARY*—Coordinates and gets done the divisional promotional functions of Division 6B and makes Scientology and the org known to the broad public.

111. **DEPARTMENT 17A (Dept of Public Registration)**—Does phone registration in city areas in addition to other public registration actions.

112. Registers Div 6 public who come in for service as pleasantly as possible with due regard for the solvency of the org.

113. Sees that the files, addresses and requirements of persons interested in Scientology are used to the full.

114. **DEPARTMENT 17B (Dept of the Hubbard Dianetics Foundation)** and **DEPARTMENT 17C (Dept of Public Services)**—Sees that public services use no words that will be misunderstood and makes people want to buy training and processing and offers it.

115. Conducts an Extension Course and sees that it is well advertised.

116. Makes the customers happy and glad to be there.

117. Gives brisk service.

118. Acquires for the org a reputation for swift and excellent handling of people.

119. Gives excellent basic training. (The soundest possible promotion quickly mirrored in numbers enrolling.)

120. Routes dissidents quickly to Ethics and slows to Review.

121. Spots SPs and PTSes early and routes to Ethics. Routes bogged cases quickly to Review.

122. Briskly and punctually schedules classes.

123. Accomplishes lots of completions.

124. Makes sure the excellence of public services that are there is bragged about in magazines, etc.

125. **DEPARTMENT 17D (Dept of the Chaplain)**—Gives excellent Chaplain services.

126. Gets ARC broken Scientologists in for a ruds session.

127. *FIELD CONTROL SECRETARY*—Coordinates and gets done the divisional promotion functions of Division 6C and makes Scientology and the org known to the broad public.

128. **DEPARTMENT 18A (Dept of Public Relations)**—Sees that the org has a good, clean appearance.

129. Sees that personnel are properly dressed, well conducted and give the org a good tone.

130. Handles press.

131. Makes Scientology popular or the thing to do.

132. Sells Scientology to governments and broad social stratas.

133. **DEPARTMENT 18B (Dept of Clearing)**—Recruits and handles field staff members to get in pcs and students for the org (and collect past debts).

134. Keeps in touch with mission holders and keeps them informed.

135. Carries out all FSM and mission activities and makes them head people toward the org.

136. Treats the whole departmental activity as salesmen are handled by any other business org.

137. Trains the FSMs and mission holders and makes them financially successful.

138. Gets all commissions owed promptly paid to encourage earning more commissions.

139. Gives FSMs and mission holders things they can use to disseminate and select.

140. Invites Scientologists to ask that info packets be sent to friends and relatives.

141. Finds and encourages the formation of Scientology groups and registers them and offers certificates.

142. Sends out mailings to groups.

143. Sees that missions are properly licensed with Scientology Missions International (SMI) and that field auditors are licensed with International Hubbard Ecclesiastical League of Pastors (I HELP).

144. Encourages broad public (lay) memberships.

145. Promotes the org and standard tech to the Auditors Association.

146. Pushes along the free membership program and re-signs the person for an annual or lifetime membership the moment the six months expires.

147. **DEPARTMENT 18C (Dept of Success)**—Contacts by letter all ex-pcs and students of the org. They should be written to at widening intervals after leaving org.

148. Collects by letters or verbally successful applications of Scientology.

149. Issues stories of successful application.

150. Issues projects of application to advanced Scientologists, particularly those projects involving artists or public figures.

151. Acknowledges the activities of Scientologists busy out in the world.

152. Appoints committees of Scientologists in various areas and groups to advise on improvements of the civilization.

153. Gets spectacular wins posted on the org's public notice boards.

154. Condenses wins into data of interest for mags and as handouts.

155. Makes a catalog of successes with various processing on various conditions.

156. Encourages and publicizes various applications of Scientology.

EXECUTIVE DIVISION

157. **DEPARTMENT 19 (Office of the Executive Director)**—The Executive Director or Commanding Officer on post and functioning to get the stats of individuals in the org up and staff and org expanding so that it can present a better image and afford better and broader promotion so as to expand.

158. The **ED** or **CO** sees that everything the org is allowed to deliver for which a demand exists is available and that the org is able to deliver it, including having on hand needful tapes, tape players, books, packs, checksheets, materiel, space and Supervisors, and that it is then heavily promoted and sold and delivered.

159. **ORG EXECUTIVE SECRETARY**—Oversees and gets execution on all promotional actions and functions in his or her three divisions.

160. **HCO EXECUTIVE SECRETARY**—Oversees and gets execution on all promotional activities in his or her two divisions and the Executive Division.

161. **PUBLIC EXECUTIVE SECRETARY**—Oversees and gets execution on all promotional activities in the three Public Divisions.

162. The Executive Council closely watches gross divisional statistics and quickly acts to handle any division of low gross divisional statistic. Acts to get into action all dropped or neglected standard promotions.

163. The Advisory Council develops new ways of making old promotion, as inherent in the org (detailed above), more effective and better executed. It never neglects old standard promotion to too strongly concentrate on new promotion.

164. The Executive Council primarily handles secretaries and acts through secretaries of divisions to get all the promotion actions done.

165. As Financial Planning, sees that pricing of everything sold is not too high

to discourage the public and not too low to make the org insolvent.

166. **DEPARTMENT 20 (Dept of Special Affairs)**—Gains acceptances of Scientology and its Founder.

167. **DEPARTMENT 21 (Office of LRH)—LRH COMMUNICATOR**—Sees that Ron's postulates stick! Sees that his comms fly, look well and that Ron's (not Executive Council's) EDs are complied with.

168. **ESTATES BRANCH**—Gets proper quarters to make the org look good, whether for momentary or permanent use for all divisions.

169. Gets any org that is far out in the suburbs relocated to busy areas where there is lots of foot traffic, easily reached and where display windows can exist.

170. Keeps materiel of org bright.

171. Keeps the posts of Cleaners filled and cleaning scheduled so the org is spotless every day.

172. Carries out a program of renovation and repainting using org staff and volunteers without getting in road of production.

These are the standard promotional actions of a Scientology organization.

Any org not in a high state of solvency and activity has omitted some or a majority of the above.

It is almost impossible to fail to succeed if one just does the listed actions.

There is a great deal of busyness connected with them. But they are essentially simple actions. Most of us have been doing them for years.

If there is any mystery felt about them, then one either hasn't read his policy letters or is in disagreement with promoting at all.

Actually it is too simple. I am often amazed when people want me to write tens of thousands of words to describe these actions.

The thing to do is do them. Then one quickly "gets the hang of" them. And they are easy.

As usually one at staff level is concerned with only one or two of these, they are very easy to learn all about and do. The thing to know is (a) they exist, (b) they are essential actions and (c) their details must be done for them to succeed.

I have made no attempt here to review the org or old promotions. All I've done is write what I would expect to have happening in any org or division of any org if I wanted a successful org. I've listed things which, if missing, would cave in a division or the HCO, Org or Public portions.

A far more thorough analysis could be done. This is only a list of the *essential* actions. If less than these are done, one will have poverty, not prosperity.

If one can't get them done in an org, then there is something awfully wrong.

———————

When a staff member is in a part of the org that is in Emergency or Danger, he, not being a high executive, often feels he can do nothing. This is foolish. Solvency is not made by high executives. It is made by doing one's own job.

Every action in every department is linked with promotion. To get out of Emergency or Danger, one must first promote. That means, do the action that promotes in one's department or section or unit.

Solvency and org wins are made up of the small actions of the staff all added together.

Read again how promotion is defined. Read what is the promotional action of your immediate zone in your org. Ask yourself if you are giving it all you can. Then maybe you will understand whether you should be solvent or insolvent.

There is no other magic about it.

The one fatal error in promotion is to get so involved in worrying over things not your zone of promotion that you do not thoroughly execute your own role in promotion.

The most successful course of action you can follow is to do your part of the promotion in your own zone and do it so well it makes up for any shortcomings that might happen elsewhere in the org. Always promote more than can be wasted.

And also promote as a person and staff member. Even if you may not be an auditor, you never know what your smile, your helpfulness and your quick attention to another's confusion or difficulty might have cured.

Your actions and presence are meaningful and valuable too, you know.

L. RON HUBBARD
Founder

SEC ED 134 INT   23 November 1965

Applies to Saint Hill
Info only to other orgs

ORGANIZATION AT SAINT HILL

We will finish off 1965—the year of Reorganization—by establishing the International Executive Division at Saint Hill.

This will be done not by changing the existing Executive Division at Saint Hill but by forming a new purely Saint Hill Executive Division comparable to that in most orgs, with an HCO Exec Sec SH, an Org Exec Sec SH and an LRH Communicator SH.

All executives and personnel of the present Executive Division will become the International Executive Division. Only their functions will broaden somewhat. At present these executives are Saint Hill Executives so that to work with another org is to cross organizations. This would not be the case where they were not totally part of one org but were supervising all orgs.

The HCO Exec Sec International would supervise all Executive and HCO Divisions including Saint Hill's via local HCO Exec Secs.

The Org Exec Sec International would supervise all four organizational divisions in the world through the local Org Exec Secs.

Gradually the International Executive Division would accumulate three officers in the Office of the Int HCO Exec Sec who would each represent the LRH Communicators, the HCO Area Secs and HCO Dissem Secs in the world. The Office of the International Org Exec Sec would eventually have four officers representing the Org Secs, the Tech Secs, the Qual Secs and the Dist Secs in the world.

These seven officers would be the proper terminals for the Divisional Secretaries via their respective local Exec Secs and would carry on the International aspect of divisional work.

The International Office of LRH would be the production unit for films, bulletins, tapes, etc., and would serve the International Executive Division with quarters, supplies, etc., and would be in charge of construction (but not org maintenance).

The process of putting this into effect will be a gradual one.

First we have to select the executives for the Saint Hill Executive Division and find it quarters at Saint Hill.

Then we have to put org maintenance, org cleaning, etc., etc., where it is in other orgs (into Dept 5).

We must therefore neat up the Saint Hill Secretarial lineup as well as choose the Saint Hill Executive Secretaries.

It is very plain to me that outer orgs do not do well without close attention from Saint Hill, both for their needs and in supervision.

Unless we so evolve at Saint Hill we will tend to retard the general growth of Scientology.

The Saint Hill Executive Division is therefore alerted to begin to work on evolving into the International Executive Division. The first steps are to neat up the Saint Hill Secretarial and form and find quarters for the Saint Hill Executive Division and should be begun at once.

This evolution also contains the necessity to gradually form some new units in the International Executive Division such as International Exec Division Accounts Unit, the Magazine Copy Unit, etc. These would be formed under the International Officers in the two Offices of the Executive Secretaries, corresponding to that org function.

While this may not be completed in all aspects for many months we should start working on it now and get as much of it done as we can as we go along, being careful to not injure in any way the high production activities at Saint Hill, and beginning to step up activities in the various orgs.

L. RON HUBBARD
Founder

HUBBARD COMMUNICATIONS OFFICE
Saint Hill Manor, East Grinstead, Sussex

HCO POLICY LETTER OF 16 DECEMBER 1965
Issue II

Gen. Non-Remimeo
All Hats
  Int Exec Div

ORGANIZATION OF THE INT EXEC DIVISION
STATISTICS OF THE INTERNATIONAL
EXECUTIVE DIVISION

What is a statistic? A statistic is a number or amount *compared* to an earlier number or amount of the same thing. Statistics refer to the quantity of work done or the value of it in money.

A down statistic means that the current number is less than it was.

An up statistic means the current number is more than it was.

We operate on statistics. These show whether or not a staff member or group is working or not working, as the work produces the statistic. If he doesn't work effectively, the statistic inevitably goes down. If he works effectively, the statistic goes up.

Negative statistics—Some things go up in statistic when they are bad (like car accidents). However, we are not using negative statistics. We only use things that mean good when they go up or mean bad when they go down.

One then is valued in the group because of the rise and fall of the statistics for which he is responsible.

The organization of the division is arranged to compare with the statistics of Scientology orgs and their divisions.

There are seven divisions in a Scientology org.

These are:

1. HCO Division

2. HCO Dissemination Division

3. Org Division

4. Technical Division

5. Qualifications Division

6. Distribution Division

7. Executive Division

For each one of these there is an International Executive Division section.

These sections advise and supervise the comparable divisions all over the world as follows:

OFFICE OF LRH WW

Contains:

a. The Advisory Council WW

b. The LRH Communicator Adviser WW

c. Office of LRH production activities and staffs (cine, book writing, magazine article writing, photography, research, hats, policy writing, etc.)

d. Estate Section

e. Household Section

f. Office of LRH Personal Secretary

OFFICE OF THE HCO EXEC SEC WW

a. HCO Adviser WW

b. Dissemination Adviser WW

c. Secretarial Assistance for the HCO Exec Sec WW

OFFICE OF THE ORG EXEC SEC WW

a. Organization Adviser WW

b. Technical Adviser WW

c. Qualifications Adviser WW

d. Distribution Adviser WW

e. Secretarial Assistance for the Org Exec Sec WW.

All functions of the Int Exec Division are organized within the above framework.

It has its own org board independent of the Saint Hill org which, to the Int Exec Div, is another organization.

STATISTICS

The statistic for the whole Int Exec Div is the gross income of all Scientology orgs in the world combined (but not all mission holders or field auditors also).

The statistics for the advisory sections are:

HCO Adviser and Section—The two HCO gross divisional statistics of all HCO Divs in the world combined.

Dissem Adviser and Section—The gross divisional statistics of all Dissem Divs in the world combined.

Org Adviser and Section—The gross divisional statistics of all Org Divisions in the world combined.

Technical Adviser and Section—The gross divisional statistics of all Tech Divs in the world combined.

Qualifications Adviser and Section—The gross divisional statistics of all Qual Divs in the world combined.

Distribution Adviser and Section—The gross divisional statistics of all Dist Divs in the world combined.

EXECUTIVES

Each of the three offices of the Int Exec Div is handled by a Coordinator, instead of a director as in the case of divisional departments, comparable to director rank.

The advisers are officers.

Heads of units are "In-Charge."

EXECUTIVE STATISTICS

The statistics of advisers are named above.

There are statistics for all executives higher than advisers. These are:

LRH—Books and articles written, films, tapes, policy letters, HCOBs, Sec EDs. Items are given different numerical values.

These are combined into one figure weekly. Statistics of the production section are similarly assigned.

HCO Exec Sec WW—One figure, being the arbitrary add-up of the four figures of the two advisory sections of that office (HCO and Dissem).

Org Sec WW—One figure, being the arbitrary add-up of the eight figures of the four advisory sections of that office.

LRH Communicator WW—The gross income of the Int Exec Division itself, irrespective of the gross income of other orgs.

The Coordinator of the Office of LRH—The combined statistic of the Office of LRH Sections.

The Coordinator of the Office of the HCO Exec Sec WW—A ratio of the number of staff in the division over the gross income of the division.

The Coordinator of the Office of the Org Exec Sec—A ratio of the expenditures of the division over the income of the division.

The Office of LRH Production Officer—The number of items as per LRH statistic actually handed over to Dissem Divisions or distributors to be published or issued.

The Household Officer—The LRH statistic as above.

The Estate Manager—A ratio between the materiel expenditures of all kinds, salaries and contracts in the section, and the professionally estimated gross income of the *Saint Hill* organization.

Other staff members have statistics as set by their immediate superiors.

L. RON HUBBARD
Founder

HUBBARD COMMUNICATIONS OFFICE
Saint Hill Manor, East Grinstead, Sussex

HCO POLICY LETTER OF 9 JANUARY 1966

Gen. Non-Remimeo
SH Only
 Ad Council
  Secretaries' Hats
  Directors' Hats
  Dept Inspections
   & Reports Hats
Other Orgs Info Only

OIC SECTION SH

The HCO Div 1 OIC Section SH, having been relieved of Worldwide OIC reports which have been turned over to OIC WW, must concentrate upon getting in and executing a standard Central Org OIC system, complete with posted charts, for SH only.

Chart posting boards have existed at SH for some time and one should be set up in HCO.

OIC SH collects statistics for SH divisions, departments and sections, graphs them and posts them.

OIC SH is responsible for devising the department and section statistics. This is normally done by the Secretary of the division and okayed by the Ad Council, and OIC is given what the statistic is and then obtains it weekly from Ad Comm minutes and graphs it. But OIC is responsible that it be devised and done. OIC accomplishes this by insistence to Secretaries and Ad Council.

OIC SH submits the full set of graphs each week to the Ad Council by Tuesday noon and, getting them back, posts them.

Occasional xerox copies are made and sent to a Secretary, always when that division has been declared in Emergency or Danger.

OIC SH is responsible for sending the SH gross divisional statistics data to OIC WW as well as graphing them for SH.

OIC SH draws up a Sec ED for SH weekly for approval by the Ad Council and forwarding to the Office of LRH SH for issue by Thursday of the week after the Thursday the figures represent.

L. RON HUBBARD
Founder

Remimeo

DIVISION 7

INTERNATIONAL EXECUTIVE DIVISION
OFFICES OF THE HCO EXEC SEC AND
ORG EXEC SEC DESCRIBED

The organization of this division is modified as follows:

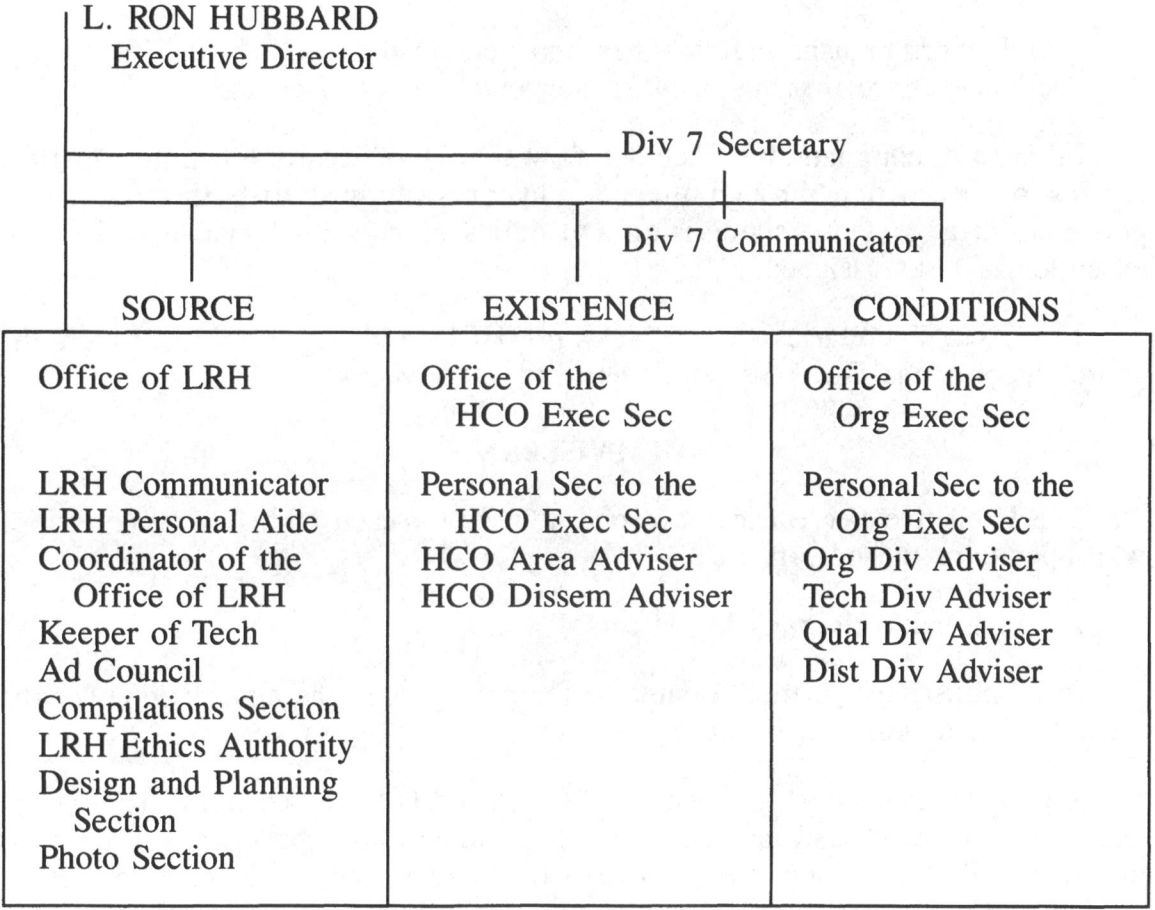

L. RON HUBBARD
Executive Director

Div 7 Secretary

Div 7 Communicator

SOURCE	EXISTENCE	CONDITIONS
Office of LRH	Office of the HCO Exec Sec	Office of the Org Exec Sec
LRH Communicator LRH Personal Aide Coordinator of the Office of LRH Keeper of Tech Ad Council Compilations Section LRH Ethics Authority Design and Planning Section Photo Section	Personal Sec to the HCO Exec Sec HCO Area Adviser HCO Dissem Adviser	Personal Sec to the Org Exec Sec Org Div Adviser Tech Div Adviser Qual Div Adviser Dist Div Adviser

This chart serves for all orgs.

The posts are filled completely only in WW and are to be filled as orgs expand.

DIV 7 SECRETARY

This new post is the secretary who cares for the personnel, communications and administration and quarters of the Executive Division.

The Division 7 Secretary is called just that, as any other title is in conflict with the offices of the division.

This secretary holds an Executive Division Ad Comm. This is junior to the Ad Council and is on a par with other division Ad Comms.

The rank of this secretary is the same as all other division secretaries and in privilege is just below that of the HCO Area Sec, who is the first secretary of the organization in privilege and precedence.

The Div 7 Sec never issues orders to other divisions and has no authority to do so.

COORDINATORS

The three offices of the Executive Division are headed by coordinators rather than directors as in other divisions.

They have the rank and privileges of directors of departments.

Coordinators manage the activities and personnel of the office. The Executive Secretaries have first authority in their own offices of course.

In chain of command the Exec Sec forwards all office administrative matters for his or her office through the coordinator. Administrative matters means personnel arrangements, supervision and duties of personnel in that office and execution of tasks assigned.

The Exec Secretaries do not forward HCO and org affairs through the coordinators or the Div 7 Secretary but through advisers.

ADVISERS

The Executive Secretaries have one adviser for each of his or her divisions who operate as liaison officers.

An adviser has the rank of officer.

In administrative matters related to the office, only the adviser is under the orders of the coordinator of the office.

An adviser may only sign letters as "for the HCO Exec Secretary" or "for the Org Exec Secretary" and may not sign any communication or letter with only his own name. To do so would create a bypass of the Exec Sec and unmock the office.

The adviser receives and handles all materials relating to the division-type he is appointed to.

The adviser advises the Exec Sec, *not* the division he is in liaison with, and issues no orders with his own authority and uses only the authority of the Exec Sec even in conversation or letters. He must be given express orders to issue by the Exec Sec even though he, in fact, writes them.

An adviser is really an aide to the Exec Sec for the division he is appointed to advise upon.

An adviser should implement the orders of the Exec Sec and the Advisory Council and only as those orders apply to his type of division.

The adviser is there to lighten the Exec Sec's burden in all possible ways as they relate to the area of responsibility for which the adviser is named.

The Exec Sec usually seeks the advice of an adviser before handling a situation in that adviser's type of division but is in no way bound to take it, whereas the adviser is bound to issue and get executed any orders expressly given by the Exec Sec.

GENERAL STAFF MEMBERS

Other posts in the Executive Division are held by general staff members.

The Office of LRH is covered in another policy letter.

L. RON HUBBARD
Founder

HCO POLICY LETTER OF 21 JANUARY 1966

EXECUTIVE DIVISION

(Modifies and extends HCO PL 20 Jan. 66 II,
DIVISION 7, INTERNATIONAL EXECUTIVE
DIVISION, concerning the Executive Div organization chart)

COMMUNICATORS (EXEC SEC)
(With data on Ad Councils)

The title Adviser where used as a helper to an Exec Sec is changed to "(HCO or Org) Exec Sec Communicator for (division represented)."

This title has the rank and privileges of a Secretary in his own org and, in a junior org to the one appointed, the privileges of an Executive Secretary.

The purpose of the post is:

TO COMMUNICATE FOR THE EXECUTIVE SECRETARY AND HELP WITH THAT OFFICIAL'S PURPOSE BY COMMUNICATING ON MATTERS, AND/OR HANDLING THEM, RELATING TO THE TYPE OF DIVISION REPRESENTED, AND TO BE RESPONSIBLE TO THE EXECUTIVE SECRETARY FOR THAT TYPE OF DIVISION AND TO BE RESPONSIBLE TO THE EXECUTIVE SECRETARY FOR THAT GROSS DIVISIONAL STATISTIC.

Only in the International Division or in an org having 250 staff members or more would this post be filled.

OIC

The Exec Sec Communicator for a type of division receives copies of the graph or graphs relating to the type of division he or she communicates with as soon as they are made up for the week by OIC. Graphs of the other divisions may be furnished by OIC option.

For example, at WW, copies of the HCO area graph for each org would be *copied* and sent to the Exec Sec Communicator for HCO area divisions.

DESPATCHES

All despatches received in the International Exec Div to the Executive Secretary for a type of division are routed to the Exec Sec Communicator for that type of division; and in an org having 250 or more staff members with no junior orgs, all despatches from the Secretary of a division are sent to the Executive Secretary's Communicator for that division.

All despatches from a type of division or a division are answered by the communicator and signed by or for the communicator's Exec Sec at the Exec Sec's option.

TITLES

Full Title	Short Title
HCO Executive Secretary's Communicator for HCO (place)	ES Comm HCO (place by telex code)
HCO Executive Secretary's Communicator for Dissemination (place)	ES Comm Dissem (place by telex code)
Organization Executive Secretary's Communicator for Organization (place in full)	ES Comm Org (place by telex code)
Organization Executive Secretary's Communicator for Technical (place in full)	ES Comm Tech (place by telex code)
Organization Executive Secretary's Communicator for Qualifications (place in full)	ES Comm Qual (place by telex code)
Organization Executive Secretary's Communicator for Distribution (place in full)	ES Comm Dist (place by telex code)

Example:

Richard Roe, Organization Executive Secretary Communicator for Organization (Oakland)

Dick, ES Comm Org (OK)

ADVISORY COUNCIL ROLE

A communicator has no Advisory Council seat. In the prolonged absence of an Executive Secretary, the first divisional *Secretary* acts as the deputy of the Exec Sec absent in the Advisory Council. The HCO Area Sec is the first deputy for the HCO Exec Sec and the Org Sec is the first deputy for the Org Exec Sec in the event of prolonged absence. The Exec Sec Communicators do not act as deputies.

At an Advisory Council meeting the Exec Sec Communicators attend but are seated together at a distance from the Executive Secretaries and may not speak or comment unless directly called upon for a report or for assistance. No Exec Sec Communicator may act as the secretary for the meetings to take its notes and minutes—this task must be done by the Division 7 Secretary. The LRH Communicator is also present, seated away from the Exec Sec Communicators and nearest the table of the Exec Secs, but has no voice in the meeting except when called upon for policy letters or Sec EDs.

The full original graphs are sent directly to the Ad Council by OIC.

In an org with 250 or more staff members and no junior org, the Ad Council takes up each graph on its own and may call for a report from the communicator representing that division and may even call up the Secretary of the division for information by sending the communicator for the Secretary.

At WW the Ad Council is furnished with all graphs of all orgs and with the WW combined graphs for all orgs for each type of division. The Executive Secretaries' inspection is of the WW combined graph. This is noted as up or down. Then the Exec Sec Communicator for that type of division is called upon to note any Affluences, Dangers or no reports from individual orgs and to explain what he or she has told or heard from the Executive Secretary in the outer org concerning the state of the graph. It should be noted that a combined WW graph that is good may contain an org that is doing badly in that type of division and vice versa.

The Ad Council (WW or area) then corrects or enforces the communicator actions for each org for that type of division.

The LRH Communicator is given the wording of the appropriate Sec ED, for okay and issue.

As Keeper of the Seals and Signature, the LRH Communicator may then order the Sec ED issued IF NOT CONTRARY TO POLICY. If the order seems contrary to policy, the LRH Communicator must despatch the Office of LRH WW by fastest means for authority to issue the Sec ED or refuse it, giving the pertinent data.

At WW the prime concern of the Advisory Council is the competence of Executive Secretaries of other orgs in keeping their divisions going well.

In area orgs the concern of the Advisory Council is the competence of Divisional Secretaries in keeping their divisions going well.

ALL actions are taken *only* on statistics. No rumor or opinion may be accepted as a reason for the assignment of conditions to anyone or anything. The statistics are up or down and to what degree or trend over a longer period decides it.

The LRH Communicator may not issue Sec EDs contrary to the condition of the statistic.

Misdemeanors and crimes are the subject of Ethics, not the Advisory Council.

If a Danger condition is assigned, then of course the formula of that condition must be followed.

Sec EDs contrary to condition formulas must be refused.

Exec Sec Communicators may not request or advise the issue of Sec EDs to the LRH Communicator. Exec Sec Communicators may suggest Sec EDs to the Exec Sec of his or her own office or bring them already written to the Advisory Council meeting but may not offer them unless asked.

Exec Sec Communicators may be ordered to write up Sec ED paragraphs on their own type of division before the Advisory Council and place them with the papers before the Executive Secretaries.

An Exec Sec Communicator is judged, like the division's Secretary, by the graph of the gross divisional statistic of that division, except at WW where the combined graph of a type of division is the graph of the Exec Sec Communicator.

Any condition may be assigned to a communicator himself but *only* on the basis of the graphs, as in the paragraph above.

If the Advisory Council or an Exec Sec Communicator proposes a Danger condition which is not visible in the statistics of that portion or if an Emergency is assigned to a portion in Affluence, the LRH Communicator must cable or report to the LRH Communicator WW at once, whether the condition was assigned or not. Proposal is sufficient.

CONDUCT OF EXEC SEC COMMUNICATORS IN AREA ORGS

An Exec Sec Communicator may, in his own org (not WW), work with the Secretary of his type of division giving advice based on policy, Sec EDs and orders, but he may *not* order the Secretary's personnel or handle the Secretary's own despatch line unless a Danger condition is assigned that division.

By approaching his Exec Sec, an Exec Sec Communicator may insist on a Danger condition or an Emergency but only on the statistic and on nothing else. If the statistic is bad *and* if the Exec Sec Communicator *is* doing the Secretary's work on bypass of the Secretary, a Danger condition *must* be assigned by the Exec Sec on the Exec Sec Communicator's request.

A Secretary may file a Job Endangerment Ethics Report on an Exec Sec Communicator who requests, or an Exec Sec who assigns, Emergency or Danger condition not shown in statistics.

DIVISION SEVENS

The seventh division and the Division 7 Secretary are cared for by the HCO Exec Sec Communicator. At WW the seventh divisions of all orgs are under the HCO Exec Sec Communicator WW who communicates to the HCO Exec Secs of the orgs about them.

CONDUCT OF AN EXEC SEC COMMUNICATOR WW

An Exec Sec Communicator WW in the Int Exec Division, having no org, may *not* work with the Secretary of his type of division at Saint Hill as above or with the Secretaries of other orgs, as this is a bypass.

When visiting other orgs, an Exec Sec Communicator WW may *not* give orders to a Secretary but only to the Exec Sec of that org comparable to his post and only on the subject of his type of division.

These orders are given in writing and a copy is always sent to the Exec Sec Communicator's own Exec Sec WW by swift means such as airmail or cable when urgent.

Exec Sec Communicators WW away from the Int Exec Division and in another org may not telephone their Executive Secretary but must cable, and may cable from outside the org at WW expense if the situation warrants it.

Travel and living expenses of an Exec Sec Communicator WW are paid by the org to be visited or the travel only apportioned to several orgs if on the same continent, as such visits would result in greater income for the org visited which would not be recompensed by administrative 10 percents. Further, currency exchange laws make this an easier procedure.

An Exec Sec Communicator WW may not accept fees or costly gifts but may accept tokens of appreciation or souvenirs. All such must be reported to the HCO Exec Sec WW on the Exec Sec Communicator WW's return and a list of what was expended upon the Exec Sec Communicator WW by the org visited (excepting only casual lunches or treats) must be given to the Treasurer WW.

Exec Sec Communicators WW may appear at and address congresses and gatherings, but if so a reasonable lecture fee is paid to the Int Org Division for it.

ABSENT EXEC SEC COMMUNICATORS WW

An absent Exec Sec Communicator WW has his post covered for him at WW by a Deputy Exec Sec Communicator WW temporarily posted for a term of his absence if prolonged to more than three days.

INTENTION

It is the intention of this policy letter to prevent the lines of an Exec Sec from jamming as Scientology expands. Therefore, it is a prime concern of an Exec Sec Communicator to care for all routine traffic of his org's division to the Exec Sec or at WW for all such divisions in the world.

An Exec Sec Communicator must *not* habitually bring a body or talk with his Exec Sec and should depart at once after he has received verbal orders, as any Exec Sec time he consumes is contrary to the reason for his post.

CONFERENCES

An Exec Sec may have in his or her Exec Sec Communicators for a conference or employ his or her Exec Sec Communicators in any fashion on Scientology business.

But an Exec Sec conference with Exec Sec Communicator has no force of orders outside the province of that Exec Sec. The Advisory Council alone may issue orders of a valid nature binding on the org in general. Conferences may not be substituted for Advisory Council meetings.

If a conference is held, it should be to determine what to do about a situation, not to act as a legal body.

None of this applies when a Danger condition exists in an Exec Sec's divisions. Then orders may be issued in conference.

In a conference with Exec Sec Communicators, there is no voting or minutes.

ETHICS

An Exec Sec Communicator is a valid Executive Hearing Officer.

He or she has no other ethics rights beyond it being a crime to stop one proceeding on his or her duty.

BYPASS

When an Exec Sec Communicator in an area issues orders to his or her type of division, it is not a bypass of his Exec Sec.

This is because he is acting in the name of the Exec Sec.

BUT IF AN EXEC SEC COMM *WW* communicates with any Secretary, it is a bypass of the Exec Sec of that org and will bring on a Danger condition in that org.

An Exec Sec bypassing his or her own Exec Sec Communicator into the division of that Exec Sec Communicator without informing the Exec Sec Communicator *is* a bypass. A WW Exec Sec Communicator issuing or taking despatches directly from anyone but an Exec Sec of another org is a bypass and will raise havoc. A WW Exec Sec Communicator of a division type does *not* communicate with Secretaries of that division type. It is a bypass of Exec Secs of those orgs.

AUTHORITY OF AN EXEC SEC COMMUNICATOR

An Exec Sec Communicator has no authority not derived from the Exec Sec or that of a staff member of his rank.

If an Exec Sec Communicator issues orders to another org's Secretary, this *is* a bypass and will bring about a Danger condition as it bypasses the Exec Sec of that other org.

If an Exec Sec Comm HCO or Exec Sec Comm Dissem issues orders to an Exec Sec Communicator on the Org side or vice versa, this *is* a bypass of both Exec Secs and will cause trouble. Such an order is unusual anyway and is seldom needed, but if done at all, it must be via the Exec Sec Communicator's own Exec Sec to the other Exec Sec to the other deputy.

Exec Sec Communicators can, of course, advise one another in an Executive Division but their advice is not binding on another Exec Sec Communicator and need not be acted upon.

SUBVERSION

If Exec Sec Communicators use their authority to subvert an Exec Sec or if they combine to remove an Exec Sec, it is a high crime.

SUPPRESSION

An Exec Sec Communicator who gives bad news continually to his Exec Sec or seeks to arouse his Exec Sec's wrath against other staff members or orgs or divisions commits a suppressive act.

The temper of an Exec Sec is in the keeping of his or her Exec Sec Communicators (where they exist), and the effectiveness of an org can be severely damaged and its staff harmed by those who seek to arouse the rancor of an Exec Sec against others.

This does not mean that bad news should be withheld from an Exec Sec. It means it should be presented with no trimmings or trappings or opinions. If it is bad news *and* requires urgent action, an Exec Sec's people should just lay it in writing silently before the Exec Sec.

If a Secretary is to be chewed on, the Secretary should be brought to the Exec Sec. It should not be done by message via an Exec Sec Communicator.

An Exec Sec Communicator must not convey an Exec Sec's orders with embellishments or with a description of any misemotion on the part of the Exec Sec.

As an Exec Sec Communicator's authority and dignity is that of his or her Exec Sec's, it behooves an Exec Sec Communicator to safeguard his or her Exec Sec's reputation by all means short of false reports.

An Exec Sec Communicator may not testify against his or her Exec Sec in a Committee of Evidence or at a Hearing.

An Exec Sec may testify against an Exec Sec Communicator.

CONTINENTAL ORG

A continental org, when large enough to have junior orgs, puts in a Continental Exec Div, patterned on WW, for that continent, and its Exec Sec Communicators are used like ones in WW, its senior.

Now maybe the Exec Sec of a very big org or WW can *breathe*.

L. RON HUBBARD
Founder

102

Remimeo

DIVISION SEVEN

For administrative purposes and to better balance the org, Division 7 is considered part of HCO.

Division 7 is in the divisions of the HCO Exec Sec.

The person in charge of it is the Division 7 Secretary.

At Worldwide (Int Exec Div) all Division 7s in all orgs come under the HCO Executive Secretary Communicator for HCO WW as part of the divisions he or she is responsible for.

The HCO Exec Sec Communicator for HCO WW must not communicate directly with Division 7 Secretaries in orgs as that would bypass the HCO Exec Secs of those orgs but addresses all communications relative to Division 7 to the HCO Exec Sec of that org.

L. RON HUBBARD
Founder

St Hill Only

INT EXEC DIV RELATION
TO SAINT HILL ORG

The International Executive Division WW is just another Saint Hill Division.

There are *eight* divisions at Saint Hill. The difference is that it has two Executive Divisions—one Division 7 for the world, one for the Saint Hill Org.

The International Executive Division has no duplicated "Ethics Officer." It uses Saint Hill's.

It is unduly complex to have two whole organizations at Saint Hill. There is only one. It has two Division 7s—one Div 7 WW, one Div 7 SH.

The Advisory Sections to the world in Div 7 WW look like divisions but they serve Saint Hill as well and someday we will have Advisory Sections in Div 7 SH also for Saint Hill only.

L. RON HUBBARD
Founder

HCO POLICY LETTER OF 1 MARCH 1966R
Issue II
REVISED 14 FEBRUARY 1991

Remimeo

EXECUTIVE DIVISION

EXECUTIVE DIVISION ORGANIZATION
AND ITS THEORY AND PURPOSE

ORGANIZATION

There are *eight* divisions posted in every organization. There are nine posted in a continental org. There are *two* Executive Divisions, the International Executive Division and the Area Executive Division, for every org. This is true for the org where the Int Exec Div is located and for every other org even though it is not physically located there. In addition, there are the normal seven divisions of the area organization.

There are nine in a continental org—the Int Exec Div, the Continental Exec Div and the normal seven divisions of the area org.

The full org board of the International Executive Division must be posted in every organization as well as the area board. Hence each org has eight divisions. This is done by mounting an additional board, one division wide, preferably to the left of the area org board.

In a continental org, the Continental Exec Division is added, making three boards, one for Int, one for Cont and seven for the area org. The continental also comes under HCO, making four divisions in a continental HCO.

There is *no* difference in the pattern of the WW or a Continental or an Area Executive Division except numbers of staff in it. All posts that appear in the Int Executive Division will also eventually appear in the Continental Exec Division and an Area Executive Division as orgs grow and numbers of staff increase.

Below is the pattern of an Executive Division. Smaller orgs have only a very small number of personnel and very few of the posts filled.

THE EXECUTIVE DIVISION

The Executive Director
The HCO Exec Sec
The Org Exec Sec

Division 7 Secretary

Div 7 Sec's Sec

Div 7   Div 7 Communicator
Ad Comm   Coordinator Office of LRH
                 Coordinator Office of HCO Exec Sec
                 Coordinator Office of Org Exec Sec

OFFICE OF LRH

LRH Communicator

LRH Comm Sec
Exec Div Mimeo Unit
Keeper of the Seals and Signature
      Policy Files
      Sec ED Files

Personal
Office of
LRH

LRH Personal Sec
      LRH Personal Files
      LRH Personal Possessions
      LRH Personal Val Doc
      LRH Personal Finance
      LRH Transcription

LRH Comm Files
      Project File

Coordinator Office of LRH
      Service Section
      Personnel Section
      Appearances Section
      Comm System and Station Section
      Courier Section

OFFICE OF THE HCO EXEC SEC

HCO Exec Sec's Sec

ES Comm for Div 7

      Offices of LRH Bureau
        Liaisons
      Offices of HCO Exec Secs Bureau
        Liaisons
      Offices of Org Exec Secs Bureau
        Liaisons

ES Comm for HCO Bureau

      Routing Appearances and Personnel Branch
      Communications Branch
      Inspections and Reports Branch
        Design and Planning Liaison
        Ethics Authority Liaison
        OIC
        Exec Div Time Machine

      Legal Branch
        Corporations
        Suits
        Legal Liaison
        Legal Files

Legal Clerks
Tech and Policy Materials Assembly
Branch

ES Comm for Dissem Bureau
       Promotions Branch
              Liaisons
       Publications Branch
              Liaisons
       Registration Branch
              Liaisons
       Dissem Materials Assembly Branch
       Visio-Audio Aids Branch
              Film Production
              Tape Recording
              Photographers

Coordinator of the Office of HCO Exec Sec
       HCO Exec Sec Personal Matters Section
       Files Section
       Communications Section
       Personnel
              Personal Secretaries
              Clerks
       Travel Section

OFFICE OF THE ORG EXEC SEC

ES Comm for Org Divs Bureau
       Income Branch
              Liaisons
       Disbursement Branch
              Liaisons
       Assets, Records and Materiel Branch
              Liaisons
       Treasurer's Office
              Accountants
              Clerks
       Finance Records
              Balance Sheet Files
              Non-current Records

ES Comm for Tech Bureau
       Tech Services Branch
              Liaisons
       Training Branch
              Liaisons
              Student Reports
       Processing Branch
              Liaisons
              Auditor's Reports
       Checksheet Branch

Checksheet Library
Standard Process Branch
Process Library

ES Comm for Qual Bureau
Examinations Branch
Liaisons
Exam Records Files
Review Branch
Liaisons
Certs and Awards Branch
Liaisons
Standard Review Process and
Checksheet Files
Org Training Branch
Staff Status Materials

ES Comm for Dist Bureau
Field Activities Branch
Congress Planning
Past Program Files
Congress Drill Files
Scientology Group Sec WW
Ad Planning
Mail List Accumulation
Clearing Branch
FSM Liaison
Mission Liaison
Selectee Files Liaison
Promotional Literature
Compilation
Promotional Programs Files
Success Branch
Success Data Liaison
Success Answers Liaison
Foundations Liaison
OT Operations
Civil Populations Liaison
Chaplain WW
Court Liaison
Justices Liaison

Coordinator of the Office of the Org Exec Sec
OES Personal Sec
OES Personal Matters
Communications Section
Personnel Section
Travel Section
Exec Div Finance Unit

The Executive Division for purposes of admin and Ad Comm comes under HCO and is part of the HCO portion of the org, and the Division 7 Sec reports to the HCO Exec Sec as his immediate superior.

DIV 7 SECRETARY

The Division 7 Secretary heads the Executive Division for purposes of personnel, Ad Comm and admin, and is the *administrative* senior to all other persons in the division excepting only the Exec Dir, HCO Exec Sec and Org Exec Sec. As such, the Div 7 Sec directs comm arrangements, is responsible for staff being on post, for pay, leave, ethics matters regarding Div 7 staff, personnel reports and supervision, for supplies, equipment, quarters and their state of cleanliness in liaison with the Org Div of the org to which the Exec Div is attached, and in all these matters is the senior to all other persons in the division except the Exec Dir, the HCO Exec Sec and the Org Exec Sec. But even these are dependent on the Div 7 Sec for matters of pay, transport, expenses, etc. The Div 7 Sec handles his duties through the Office Coordinators.

OFFICE OF LRH

This office may include *only* the personnel listed on the chart regardless of the size of the Exec Div, but numerous aides, personal secretaries and clerks may be added. No other *functions* may be placed in this office than those listed.

The LRH Comm is usually the Coordinator of this office until it grows too large.

The LRH Personal Secretary is in this department.

THE OFFICE OF THE HCO EXEC SEC

The personnel of this office are as listed on the chart.

THE OFFICE OF THE ORG EXEC SEC

This office contains those functions listed on the chart.

Where a function exists in the Exec Div *for* the Exec Div (i.e., finance), it comes under the office, bureau and branch most closely related to it. If this rule is followed, you will see that the Exec Division, particularly WW, can operate with ease.

STATISTIC

The statistic of the Int Exec Division in an *area* is dual:

THE AMOUNT OF CASH IN THE BANK AS PER THE LAST WEEK'S BANK STATEMENTS PLUS THE AMOUNT OF CASH ON HAND AS OF 2:00 P.M. THURSDAY OF THE CURRENT WEEK OF THE REPORT.

THE TOTAL OF DEBTS OWED BY THE ORG PLUS OVERDRAFTS AND CURRENT PAYMENTS DUE ON MORTGAGES (TIME PAYMENTS) AND LOANS OR BOND OR SHARE RETIREMENT BUT NOT ON THE TOTAL GROSS AMOUNT OF MORTGAGES, HIRE PURCHASE (TIME PAYMENTS) OR LOANS OR BONDS.

The OIC cables begin with these two statistics. Continental orgs which have a Continental Exec Division report the Int Exec Div area statistics, the Continental Exec Div statistics and then the seven area divisions, making a continental cable report have two more figures in it than an area org's.

The Int Exec Div at Worldwide has a composite graph of all the orgs in the world added.

A Continental Exec Division has a composite graph of all orgs in that continental area including the org which has the continental division.

The local Exec Division has the above dual graph.

ALL OIC CABLES BEGIN WITH THE LOCAL STATISTIC OF THE OFFICE OF LRH.

This continues the report on the gross income of the week, which is the statistic of LRH.

CONTINENTAL

A Continental Exec Division is formed at such time as there is reason to warrant it. Otherwise, no continental officers exist.

When a Continental Exec Division exists, then area orgs report by cable or telex to their continental org which then sends the data by cable to WW. The area org where the continental is located sends their data by despatch to continental which includes it in their cables to WW.

A Continental Exec Division must however have been established by Int Sec ED before this routing applies, and a full list of what orgs are covered by the continental must accompany it.

ZONAL ORGS

If and when a continental has under it more than five orgs, when established by Sec ED one of these may become a zone org.

A Zone Executive Division is then established with specific orgs under it and the OIC report routing is from area to zone to continental to international at Worldwide.

A Zone Exec Division is organized like any other and has a composite statistic made up of the area orgs under it. The area org attached to the zonal org then has ten divisions.

SUBZONE ORGS

If a zonal org gets more than five orgs under it, one of these is designated a subzonal org, taking under it excess orgs.

A Subzonal Exec Division is established and the area org where it exists displays eleven divisions.

OVERALL PATTERN

The principle that no Exec Division of any kind may exist without being part of an org is held firm. Only an Office of LRH may on occasion exist independent of an area org or the Exec Division but may be even so only a secondary Office of LRH.

The reason for this is that a senior Executive Division's decisions would become as unreal as a government's or war ministry if it had no actual org close against it whose problems were not familiar to it. This is a clear unalterable policy.

There may be no Executive Divisions of any designation floating free of purposeful and remunerative area divisions *housed in the same buildings* or grounds.

An Exec Division like Int or Cont *must* have an org alongside it to provide its services and costs.

It is remunerative for an area org to have a senior Executive Division with it as it thereby attracts more income. If a Continental Exec Division's area org is *not* doing as well as other orgs on that continent (unless it has just started up), well then it follows that it must be a very bad Continental Exec Division indeed and serves as a sure indicator of inattentive Exec Secs, and where the condition is chronic, the senior Exec Div to it should change at least one of its Exec Secs.

The principle that the orgs in an area should financially support their Continental Exec Division is also a shaky one, for a bad senior Exec Division has as its first cry "He-e-elp m-e-e," and isn't (a) taking advantage of its seniority to attract income to its area org and (b) isn't productive and is more suppressive than helpful.

It is worth real income to an area org to be designated a continental (or zone or subzonal) much more WW. For the seniority of courses and processing are of course arranged for students and pcs to move to it after service in their area.

All you have to notice in interpreting statistics is that the continental's area org does worse than other orgs of that continent to know that it's time for a very thorough investigation of the four Exec Secs there. This would hold true for zone and subzonal exec divs, also.

Similarly, an Office of LRH may not be independent of an actual working org. Nor any other part of an Exec Division.

Probably the most destructive institution ever invented was a government governing a business it was not a close part of. Unfamiliar government or unfamiliar ownership is possible only when all the actual decisions are still made from actual current experience with the business or activity being governed or owned. So long as Continental has an org to learn from close to it, then its orders to a distant org will be real and effective.

111

You will see in "International City" the principle reversed in order to check the whole idea of government—put the everyday government always unfamiliar with the country and it gets too unreal to be effective in its country and can content itself with tea parties with other nations instead of wars. Nationalism *is* the underlying cause of war.

You will note in our own case that the Executive Director's decisions and planning are based on data obtained from running orgs and from being close to the SH org while it was forming and running.

WW, being part of an org, knows the problems of a duplicate org even though 12,000 miles away, as it has handled the same problems. Where any differences exist, WW has an area Ad Council to advise it.

Where traffic gets heavy, then Continental Exec Divisions, with the experience of their own area org, can handle orgs on that continent, and when this gets unreal because of volume, Zone and Subzonal Exec Divisions can take it up.

Therefore, Exec Divisions of any kind are always attached to real, functioning, profitable orgs and pay their way by attracting more business to their area org than they cost the area org.

The WW 10 percents pay no real part of the expenses of the WW division or even its cable traffic. These are paid by the org that is also at WW because it makes many times more in income than WW costs it simply because WW is there. Aside from attracting the public, the presence of the Int Exec Div in the area org compels a higher *standard* of administration and service and close senior authority to quickly handle area problems and defend the area org.

Any time you hear an area org groaning over admin expenses of an extra Exec Div then you know right away that either:

a. the area org is handled suppressively, or

b. the senior Exec Division is suppressive in that it spends more than it produces for the area and reduces income.

No person should start a 5 percent for Continental, 10 percent for WW, etc.

THE 10 PERCENT GOES ALWAYS TO WW. Regardless of how many echelons of Exec Divs there are.

It is *worth more money* to a properly run area org to have an additional Exec Division, providing, of course, the added Exec Div is spending within reason and less than the added Exec Div costs it. For that gets students and pcs fed to it from lower orgs for higher services.

The facts on this are overwhelmingly convincing. Negative proof also exists, for where an area org objected (Cape Town 1963) and couldn't make more because it was for a while Continental, the head of the org portion was later, on other grounds, found to be a suppressive. In another instance (DC, 1966) where the DC area org was doing worse than other US orgs despite being the continental org, it was found that an Org Exec Sec removed in 1965 with only small resulting org improvement was found to be still "very friendly with all staff" and had the current Org Exec Sec living with him, but on Ethics review (1966) was found to be a suppressive who had involved and continued to involve staff in sex parties!

Thus, note it has to be pretty bad for an area org to lose out because it has an additional Exec Division.

These additional Exec Divisions look like an awful lot of supervision but I have found over the years that man's organizations don't expand when starved at the top. Man simply requires that much *good* supervision to be effective. And in an org which handles life itself, the randomity is too great unless one handles cases and problems on a well-organized group basis with adequate pyramided supervision.

It doesn't look this way if you see how much I supervised by myself for fifteen years. But this is not pertinent as I was not then driving orgs toward heavy expansion. Further, it is taking at this writing more than a hundred well-qualified people to take care of the hats I am shedding, all of which I handled by myself.

You will note that an Executive Division now, with LRH Comm okay of Ad Council Sec EDs, and Personnel Officer and LRH Comm okay needed for all Ad Council Sec EDs on personnel appointments, I have taken myself totally off org and Exec Division lines and fixed it so an Exec Division anywhere can run without my being there and without any successor necessary as Executive Director. I think this is the first time in history this has ever been done or that any plan existed to make it possible. Only successors to a founder have ever gotten subsequent organizations in trouble. For the successor is not the founder and the hat then can't be filled as it is no longer a founder hat.

You see, in doing my job of research, I eventually was able to end that function by completing it. Codification of the original research done is possible but the original research was completed.

Further, the whole structure of organization has been scouted down, and while it can evolve, its principles exist as complete as necessary.

So in these two fields we have the LRH hat completed.

On other things I have done my job as an administrator and Case Supervisor and all that. But these are not founder actions.

So as the duties (to discover the answers to the mind and to discover the principles of and organize their application) of the founder end and as 50,000 years did not furnish anyone to do these exact tasks completely, it is unlikely the next will. Aside from personal considerations, a factor in our organizing and pertinent to understanding an Executive Division, I set it up this way so I could complete writing up tech and organizations.

Any other hat I wear is capable of delegation.

Thus, the Executive Division exists *as* the composite Executive Director without filling the post of Executive Director.

An Exec Div of any designation (WW, Cont, Zone, Subzone, Area) then can function as an evolving administrative organism without the liability of the "civil war" that often results from problems of succession of the top post. It is interesting that all forms of government except absolute monarchy developed because none could or did solve the problem of succession. So to continue our orgs and their work, I had to solve this one or leave mankind in the lurch at some point in the future when, if I left, succession resulted in collapse of orgs.

Processing and training we know is best done as a *team* action and gets dispersed and squirrels as an individual effort. So we turned the "individual practitioner" into a field staff member, like a field agent, to feed pcs and students in to an organization where they could be given standard service. This made stable orgs necessary in order to keep service standard and not dispersed by the perils of confronting the mad and gibbering and the pc requiring "individual and unusual solutions" and the cave-in of tech because of economic needs of the lone practitioner.

The Exec Division answers these problems. It is there to get tech in and keep it in, get policy followed and not used to stop growth, keep the group solvent and functioning and the admin and org pattern correct.

If it doesn't do these things then it isn't doing its job.

If it does do its job, it is worth its weight in case gains for the whole world.

L. RON HUBBARD
Founder

Revision assisted by
LRH Technical Research
and Compilations

HCO POLICY LETTER OF 7 JUNE 1966

Gen. Non-Remimeo
Saint Hill Only
All Other Orgs
  for Info

HCO DIV

OIC PUBLICATION AND DISTRIBUTION

There are twelve xerox copies to be made of each OIC chart set for the East Grinstead environ.

A set for the East Grinstead environ consists of the WW, continental UK and Saint Hill complete graphs.

Distribution of sets is as follows, one *complete* set each, *each week:*

1. Ad Council WW

2. Ad Council UK

3. Ad Council SH

4. HCO Div Sec and Ad Comm

5. HCO Dissem Div Sec and Ad Comm

6. Treasury Div Sec and Ad Comm

7. Technical Div Sec and Ad Comm

8. Qualifications Div Sec and Ad Comm

9. Distribution Div Sec and Ad Comm

10. LRH Comm SH
    LRH Comm UK
    LRH Comm WW

11. LRH

12. Public Board for all staffs to see

These OIC sheets are *not* returned. They are *not* added to each week by the recipient. Each week a *new* xerox set is made for each distribution destination listed above.

The MASTER graph set is kept in a book, wholly loose-leaf and never distributed. Only it is marked on by the OIC Officer. Then the masters are copied by xerox, and the sets made up and distributed.

Worldwide Ad Council *also* gets sets of every graph in the world from OIC WW.

It will be found that new expansion will occur when the above distribution system of copy sets is closely adhered to, as the data becomes known to all staff.

L. RON HUBBARD
Founder

HCO POLICY LETTER OF 13 MARCH 1966
Issue I

Remimeo
All Staff Hats
Staff Status II
Checksheet

ALL DIVISIONS

ORDERS, PRECEDENCE OF PERSONNEL,
TITLES OF

The following table gives the precedence, which is to say the greater value or importance, of orders or directions in Scientology. This table shows what order to follow first and if one below is contrary to one above, follow the upper one:

For anything relating to corporate status, starting or closing bank accounts and vital planning:

BOARD RESOLUTION
(Black ink on white paper, signed by all board members.)

For policy:

HCO POLICY LETTER
(Green ink on white paper, signed by LRH.) (HCO means Hubbard Communications Office.)

For all technical matters in Scientology:

HCO BULLETIN
(Red ink on white paper, signed by LRH.)

For orders or plans, expires in one year. For personnel permanent appointments:

SEC ED (SECRETARIAL TO THE EXECUTIVE DIRECTOR) (LRH) (White paper, blue ink, signed personally by the Executive Director, LRH.)

For conditions assigned, personnel appointments and financial planning and directions to secretaries:

SEC ED (Ad Council)
(Blue paper, blue ink, signed by the Advisory Council for LRH, Exec Dir, approved by LRH Communicator as not against policy and by HCO for personnel.)

For orders to the divisions under the Exec Sec:

SEC ED (Executive Secretary)
(Blue paper, blue ink, signed by the HCO Exec Sec or Org Exec Sec for LRH, Executive Director.)

For orders to a division by its Advisory Committee:

SEC ED (Divisional Ad Comm)
(Color of paper of the division,

	blue ink, signed by the Advisory Committee of the division for LRH, Executive Director, approved by the Advisory Council and the LRH Communicator and personnel orders also approved by HCO Personnel Control.)
For orders to directors of the division from its secretary:	SEC ED (Divisional Secretary) (Color of the paper of the division, blue ink, signed by that division's secretary for LRH, Exec Director, approved by the Ad Council and LRH Communicator and requiring HCO approval for personnel.)
For directors of a department in ordering their own department:	WRITTEN ORDER (Director) (Signed by director, approved by his divisional secretary.)
For ordering personnel in work actions:	WRITTEN ORDER (Executive) (Signed by the departmental officer or in-charge, approved by the department's director.)
For ordering immediate juniors by their immediate superiors or one's immediate clerical assistants or in a conference or in moments of urgency. Not valid otherwise and not binding as evidence in Ethics Hearings or for reason for charging a noncompliance ethics chit. Never accepted when relayed through a member of the public or off channels.	VERBAL ORDER

On all orders, orders from an HCO Exec Sec may not cross to Org Divisions, orders from the Org Exec Sec may not cross to HCO Divisions except in the Office of the Org Exec Sec, Dept 19. Secretaries may not order other divisions than their own. Directors may not order staff not in the director's departments. Officers may not order other sections than their own. In-charges may not order other units than their own.

No order lower on the scale may cancel or set aside an order above it on the scale. Any staff member accepting an illegal order who does not file a job endangerment chit when he or she received it has no defense in any resulting Ethics Hearing. In these organizations one must not permit himself to be led astray by a senior with "private knowledge."

Anyone using policy to prevent statistics rising is liable to an Ethics Hearing or a Committee of Evidence. The response to a generalized statement "That's against policy" is "What is the policy letter that covers it?" And get it displayed.

It is possible to know where one stands only if one knows the seniority of orders. The hardest position to be in is one where one's senior has thrown the regulations away and is inventing his own—then none knows where he stands.

Any written or published order may be cancelled by a published order senior to it on the above chart except that, traditionally, board minutes cannot cancel policy letters or HCOBs, these being originated or modified by the Executive Director whose powers only are ratified by the board. HCO Policy Letters and HCOBs (Hubbard Communications Office Bulletins) are considered technology and know-how and are outside admin channels.

SENIORITY OF ORGS

The comparable order of a senior org cancels the order of or takes precedence over an org junior to it.

The seniority is:

> Worldwide
> Continental
> Zone
> Subzonal
> Area
> District Office
> Field Staff Member
> Center
> Mission Holder
> Field Auditor
> Professional Member
> Lifetime Member
> International Member
> Associate

The Ad Council WW can cancel or takes precedence over an Advisory Council Continental. An Advisory Council Continental takes precedence over that of an org junior to it.

Advisory Councils are senior to Advisory Committees. An Ad Council runs the whole org, an Ad Comm runs only one of its divisions.

Advisory Councils are advisory to the Board of Directors or the Executive Director and have no other powers. They cannot open or close bank accounts or change corporate status. They are appointed by a senior Ad Council or the Exec Director. An Ad Council consists of the two Executive Secretaries of an org and the Executive Director.

An Advisory Committee exists for each division in the org (7) and is advisory to the Ad Council and is appointed by the Ad Council of the org and consists of the secretary of the division and the three directors (heads of departments) or in an Exec Division, the three office coordinators of the three Exec Div offices who are the same as directors but have a different title.

SENIORITY OF EXECUTIVES

The following table gives the seniority of executives:

EXECUTIVE DIRECTOR	There is only one Exec Director, LRH, and he is Exec Dir for WW and for each org. There are no assistant or deputy Executive Directors. (Orders issued for the Exec Dir must be approved by the LRH Communicator as not against policy and by HCO Personnel when personnel is appointed.)
EXECUTIVE SECRETARY	There are two Executive Secretaries at WW, two in Continental Exec Divisions, two in every other Exec Div. They are the HCO Exec Sec and the Org Exec Sec. They head the three HCO and the four Org divisions respectively. Together they, with the Exec Dir, form the Ad Council. They are appointed by the Exec Dir or the Ad Council WW. The WW (Worldwide) Exec Secs are appointed by statistics.
SECRETARY	There are seven secretaries in each organization. They head divisions. They are the chairmen of the divisional Ad Comms. They are appointed by the Ad Council of the org with the approval of HCO Personnel and LRH Comm.
DIRECTOR	There are eighteen directors in an organization. They head departments. They are appointed by their secretaries with the approval of HCO Personnel and the LRH Comm (Communicator).
COORDINATOR	There are three coordinators in an org. They are the same as directors but head the three offices (departments) of the Executive Division. They are appointed by the Division 7 Secretary with the approval of HCO Personnel and LRH Comm.
OFFICER	These head sections within departments.
IN–CHARGE	These head units inside sections.
EXECUTIVE	A general term including any in-charge or above.
GENERAL STAFF MEMBER	Any staff member who is not an executive.
STAFF MEMBER	Any and all persons employed in an org whether an executive or general staff member.
ACTING	A prefix to a title meaning appointed conditionally and if shows good statistics for a year will become of permanent title.

118

DEPUTY	A prefix to a title meaning "in the place of." There may be a deputy for each executive post in an org in addition to the person with the title. Or it means "filling in until an appointment is actually made."
TEMPORARY	An impermanent assignment, either for reasons of expediency or under trial.
STAFF STATUS	A number following the person's name on the org board that shows the state of administrative training of the individual as done in the Staff Training Section. Status numbers go from 0 for temporary, 1 for provisional, 2 for qualified general staff member on up for the various executive grades. If no number appears after a name, the person is holding the post without checkout for it. A low-ranking staff member can have a high status number as it is *qualified for,* not "appointed to." This prevents qualified persons from being bypassed in promotion.
CLASS	A technical certificate in Scientology goes by the classes on the Gradation Chart. The class of a Scientologist's certificate is noted in Roman numerals after his name on the org board.
GRADE	The case grade of a staff member is shown after his class as an auditor or if no class, after a dash, in Roman numerals on an org board. Example: IV—IV—2 means Class IV Auditor, Grade IV pc, Staff Status 2, qualified as a permanent general staff member. —IV—2 would mean Grade IV pc, 2, qualified permanent general staff member but not trained as a Scientologist.

L. RON HUBBARD
Founder

119

Remimeo

WORLDWIDE ORGANIZATION

(Cancels all policy letters and sections of policy letters relating to Executive Secretary Communicators and tables concerning the organization of the Executive Division, except those organizing the Office of LRH.)

(All those persons now styled or titled Executive Secretary Communicators are changed as of date of receipt to the following posts and policies.)

DIVISIONAL ORGANIZERS

Worldwide and Continental Executive Divisions (as they expand) are to have on staff and as assistants to the Advisory Council (WW or Continental) executives to be termed DIVISIONAL ORGANIZERS (DIVISION TYPE) (LOCATION).

This means that each *type* of division is represented (Worldwide or Continental as they may appear necessary) by a DIVISIONAL ORGANIZER.

The purpose of a Divisional Organizer is as follows:

To help LRH organize and maintain and supply the division represented (type) in the sphere designated (locales) with all needful data, policy, tech, programs, examinations, plans, courses and activities of every kind needful to the success of that type of division, and to organize and raise in efficiency that type of division in the locales for which the Divisional Organizer is responsible.

TITLES

This means there are seven different titles of Divisional Organizers:

7. Divisional Organizer, Executive

1. Divisional Organizer, HCO

2. Divisional Organizer, Dissem

3. Divisional Organizer, Treasury

4. Divisional Organizer, Tech

5. Divisional Organizer, Qual

6. Divisional Organizer, Distribution

The title is followed by "WW" for Worldwide or the continental abbreviation for Continental Orgs or, if area orgs grow sufficiently large, for area designation.

AUTHORITY

The Divisional Organizer may issue orders, via his Advisory Council, to any division of his type in his sphere of authority.

Independent orders may not be issued without Advisory Council approval. And all Advisory Council orders require LRH Communicator authority.

SENIORITY

A Divisional Organizer is senior to any Secretary in his divisions but not to an Executive Secretary. He holds the nominal rank of Secretary.

MATERIALS AND SUPPLIES AND PROGRAMS

It must be at once visible that what a division needs most are its materials, supplies and programs.

A division type needs its policy letters and checklists of them, its applicable orders and directives, the data it employs, in usable form.

Different types of divisions need different things. Tech needs its courses laid out in full, its processes, its regulations, etc. Qual needs its examinations and review materials and its certs and awards. Distribution needs its info packets, its FSM sign-ups and programs, its congress programs and dates, etc.

Each type of division needs its know-how and each has certain personnel requirements.

The Divisional Organizer not only assembles and supplies all this or sees it is supplied, he or she makes sure it is properly used or exhibited.

STATISTICS

The statistic of a Divisional Organizer is the combined gross divisional statistic of his or her type of division in his or her sphere of authority.

AD COUNCIL

The Divisional Organizer is a full voting member of the Worldwide or Continental Advisory Council to which he belongs.

He or she has one vote regardless of the number of divisions represented or the number of types he or she represents.

He or she may not, however, vote by proxy if absent.

121

PERSONAL PRESENCE

The Divisional Organizer may call on his or her type of division personally to organize, reorganize, inspect or supply it. But if so, all expenses must be borne by the org using his or her services and no fees may be given him or her personally. In the event of several orgs being called on, expenses are shared by them as they appear actually. All such expenses must be reported to the governing org or any additional fees paid to the governing org.

AUTHORITY

If any org is found to be short or deficient in one of its divisions in knowledge, skill, materials, supplies or programs, it is the Divisional Organizer that is held responsible by the Ad Council of the governing body.

And after his own efforts are made, if a division in any org in his sphere is lacking in knowledge, skill, supplies, materiel or programs, the Divisional Organizer holds the Secretary of that specific division responsible and may require, through orders of his Ad Council, appropriate action, hearing or Comm Ev on that Secretary.

But where a Divisional Organizer demands ethics action, it must be through the Ad Council of the Executive Division to which he belongs. And the order must assign a Danger condition as well to the Executive Secretary immediately over the offending Secretary in that org.

SIZE OF ORG

While supplies and programs are gauged by the size of the org and its class, this policy also applies to six-department orgs and six-section orgs.

CORRESPONDENCE

So long as correspondence between a Divisional Organizer and the head of that type of division (dept or section in six-dept or six-section orgs) does not order but only recommends, and as long as such recommendations are not contrary to policy or his Ad Council directives, the Ad Council need not pass on the correspondence of a Divisional Organizer but may review it on request at any time.

SIN

The only real sin of a Divisional Organizer is to have a down combined statistic or a low statistic for his division type in an org.

COSTS

Materials sent any division in an org must be paid for by that org.

If large unpaid bills for divisional materials exist in an org, the supplies may not be shut off but the Ad Council of that org may be reviewed for the possibility of new chief executive personnel.

An org may be requested to order materials, but if it pleads insolvency or inability to so order in reasonable or needed amounts, the matter of its finances must be reviewed closely for any inactivity or discrepancy or irregularity. In such a case the Divisional Organizer must obtain an order for a board on the org's finances from his own Ad Council.

DIRECTIVES

Directives requested by a Divisional Organizer for a specific division or general type of division, must be submitted, already written, to his Ad Council for approval before issue and must be passed by a majority vote of the Ad Council.

Such orders may be amended or disapproved by his own Ad Council.

Care should be taken not to issue general orders for actions already in progress in some orgs. Such should be issued only to orgs where the orders have not been complied with or who are not complying.

BOARDS OF INVESTIGATION

A Divisional Organizer in need of data may request from his Ad Council a board to be convened on his type of division in a specific org, but if so, the order to be passed must be written, complete with appointments by the Divisional Organizer, before submission.

URGENT DIRECTIVES

A Divisional Organizer requiring an urgent directive may obtain one by getting the signatures of a majority of the members of his Ad Council and its chairman. But if this is done, or if any urgent directive is granted by his Ad Council in session or is passed by the Ad Council at any time, the three steps of HCO PL 31 Oct. 66 I, ACTIONS, EXECUTIVE, FOR HANDLING DISASTROUS OCCURENCES, must be followed.

STAFF

A Divisional Organizer must collect or appropriate any "special sections" or personnel junior to him in the Executive Division or org who are compiling or paralleling his activities so that no special units in Worldwide or Continental Executive Divisions exist outside the appropriate Divisional Organizer.

Staff for a Divisional Organizer will be considered excessive if its combined pay (his included) amounts to more than 40 percent of the total income of the governing org for the materials of that division type actually received by the governing org.

Therefore, it is of importance that the Divisional Organizer (a) makes his division type in each org increase the income of its org, (b) that his materials furnished are successful and used and (c) that the materials are paid for by the org to which they are furnished. (This one clause is effective on 1 Feb. 67 only.)

L. RON HUBBARD
Founder

Sthil Only

IDEAS AND COMPILATIONS BRANCH WW

(Amends HCO PL 8 Aug. 66, COMPILATIONS SECTION,
DEPARTMENT 21, OFFICE OF LRH, and HCO PL 18 July 66,
OFFICE OF LRH, LRH PERSONAL OFFICE ORGANIZATION)

The Ideas and Compilations Branch WW, Division 7, Dept 21 is transferred to the Office of the HCO Exec Sec WW, Division 7, Dept 20 under the supervision and direct orders of the Divisional Organizer Dissem WW. Any and all communications to Ideas and Compilations Branch WW must go via Divisional Organizer Dissem for approval before being passed on or returned.

All final copy and proofs of magazines, books, etc., are to be sent to the Founder when possible for his approval to print.

L. RON HUBBARD
Founder

HCO POLICY LETTER OF 11 AUGUST 1967
Issue III

Gen. Non-Remimeo

OT CENTRAL COMMITTEE

(Cancels HCO PLs 7 Dec. 66 and 10 Nov. 66 II)

The OT Central Committee is directly under the Executive Council World-wide and the Divisional Organizer for Distribution WW.

It is in fact the OT *Section* of "Dept 18 WW," but until such time as WW represents all its departments by number, is under Divisional Organizer for Distribution WW.

The duties of the OT Central Committee are:

1. To pass on projects proposed by persons on the Sect I and beyond courses or OTs, and authorize, expand, replan or reject same.

2. To recruit personnel for OT organizations by keeping lists of enrollees and graduates and informing them routinely of posts available in OT organizations.

3. Expedite for OT organizations divers matters and concerns as these arise.

4. Liaison with the Executive Council WW via Divisional Organizer Dist WW for OT organizations or their personnel.

5. Regulate all projects and cancel or rearrange those that are not productive or are causing dev-t or trouble or needless expense.

The purpose of the OT Central Committee is TO HELP LRH ORGANIZE AND CHANNEL OT FORCES, INTERESTS AND RESOURCES FOR THE GREATEST GOOD FOR SCIENTOLOGY.

———————

All other OT Committees come under the OT Central Committee via their Exec Councils.

———————

The symbol used for OT activities is an oval 0 with a horizontal bar two thirds up from the open bottom of the 0 and contained within the 0, and a vertical bar down from its center to the bottom of the 0.

A person attaining Section V OT may have a wreath completely around the outside of the 0.

This device may be displayed in gold on a light blue swallow-tailed flag or a square company flag.

———————

All OTs are considered to be subject to this Section.

L. RON HUBBARD
Founder

L. Ron Hubbard
EXECUTIVE DIRECTIVE

ED 473 WW 842 SH   1 September 1967

WW EMERGENCY CONDITION

1. A general condition of EMERGENCY BY TREND is assigned WW on a basis of leveling or dropping composite outer org graphs. All WW personnel is included. The condition is assigned by trend and although Day orgs are losing business to Foundations this is no reason Day orgs should be permitted to level off and then collapse. Don't rationalize statistics.

2. Also WW must review its graphs for false reports and must in the future send them through to me weekly so earlier action can be taken.

3. If the outer org stats do not remarkably improve fast the feeder line for SH will fall off bringing about a decline of SH.

4. The cash-bills stat is good and shows improved money handling. But with this has also come a general decline of promotion, leveling graphs and utter stagnation in outer orgs which if. neglected will see a collapse of one or more orgs and a depression at SH.

5. The outer orgs probably improved their cash-bills ratios by SAVING money on promotion and essential services. The only way to do it (get cash-bills straight) is TO MAKE MORE MONEY.

6. Now, these things (leveling graphs) are usually traced to noncompliance.

7. In this case the programs on which there have been noncompliances are:

    (1) The recruitment at flat out speed of org execs and getting them through the Org Exec Course and back home. Somebody is sitting on this one with a "We are looking over stats . . ." and other delay excuses. This course MUST get populated FAST and the program GOING. This omission all by itself accounts for leveling graphs as the program was already stalled for a year and forgotten when I caught the ball a few months ago. But I bet nobody is really pushing that ball except me. So GET SOME STAFF ON IT AND GET THE EXEC COURSE FULL. I also bet somebody put a stop on the line by charging orgs a fee for it or saying to existing execs in outer orgs—"We are training your replacement so send us some people

so we can kick you out." GET THE STOPS OFF THIS PROGRAM. SPEND MONEY ON IT. PUT WW STAFF ON IT.

(2) Each org to put out its own magazine. I'll bet they don't or we're not furnishing the copy or they are sending only to some choice list instead of their total CF or they are economizing or they are turning out trash with locally written (not LRH) articles. They MUST get into swing with quality AND ON–POLICY local magazines and WW better really start SHOVING HARD on this one.

8. The whole fault is WW is not forcing outer orgs to get in new people and forcing them to service everyone in CFs.

9. Orgs do this badly. They sit and sink while servicing walk-in public. They have to be forced to widen their areas of contact. As I did this almost single-handedly for years, it is a hat that WW has not picked up. FORCE OUTER ORGS TO EXPAND.

10. SA promotion effectiveness is a screaming disgrace. They've gone utterly stagnant while remaining solvent.

11. It also means local tech is out in outer orgs and the areas are full of ARC breaks not caught. In such a case I always order orgs to pick up and smooth out AT ANY ORG EXPENSE every ARC broken pc they can find in their files or areas as A SPECIAL PROGRAM. They put in an ARC Break Registrar who liaisons with Accounts and with Review and with CF searching for ARC broken pcs and students. A special genned in full-time auditor is put in Review and AT NO CHARGE to pcs is kept busy on ARC breaks only WITH IT BEING AN ETHICS OFFENSE TO USE HIM OR THE ARC BREAK REGISTRAR FOR ANY OTHER STUDENT, PC OR DUTY. And you clean up the whole field from years and years back. This ARC Break Auditor cures the ARC breaks with Level III tech and sends the person to the usual Registrar when done. THIS is his stable datum: IF YOUR PC IS NOT SMILING AND HAPPY AT THE END OF SESSION YOU ARE NOT AUDITING.

12. The ARC Break Registrar has a special dual stat—how many ARC broken pcs have been found, in files, etc., how many contacted. The ARC Break Auditor has a special dual stat—how many ARC breaks (not pcs) found, how many handled.

13. Now you put TWO special staff members on (1) above to get the Org Exec Program UNSTOPPED and at a howling avalanche in on SH and back home FAST. And you put a special WW staff member on (2) to get the ARC Break Program in in in fast and correctly with all tech watched and the special stats as above coming in weekly appended to other stats. THESE WW PEOPLE MUST HAVE NO OTHER DUTIES.

14. Locally, in WW, you get ETHICS in on local WW staff and hold a hearing on a quiver of an eyelash. Remove all who have full in-baskets and all who develop DEV–T. Appoint an ETHICS OFFICER WW and a DIR COMM WW and make them work on WW and then when that's smooth get to work on ethics and comm *procedure* and *swiftness* in outer orgs.

15. WW is essentially a PRODUCTION activity. You are supposed to get out the materials and hats for the outer orgs, supposed to keep them expanding, getting their staffs trained, keep them promoting and getting their mag materials to them. They are not getting the hat and tech materials they ask for obviously.

16. These outer orgs (as per current WW graphs) are NOT making *Scientologists*. They are making pcs. They have degenerated into a bunch of clinics. Therefore their Academies are bad, the courses not constantly scheduled and too long. They are trying to make duplicates of the Saint Hill Course not teach fast, minimum essentials courses. They haven't got their Dianetics courses in. Their instructors aren't on schedule. A lot of "opinion" is entering the training line. Ethics isn't held in on students. SO you have to groove their Academies in from top to bottom and SHORTEN and SPEED ACADEMY COURSES. One month for Dianetics, 2 weeks in a level up to IV or 10 weeks in all to complete 0–IV. Adapt the old 50 course booklets to a new Home Instruction Course.

17. Don't keep answering letters from org staffs in outer orgs as a sole WW activity. Use the comm lines to find what they need and get it produced and to them. Get over to CAUSE on production. GET TO THEM WHAT THEY NEED.

18. Study their org boards and get in a system of getting frequent copies by sending them a blank which contains posts. The big blueprint machine in the basement is there to do only that and I'll bet you have not sent out one photostat blank to any org so they can write in the names. It takes two big sheets lengthwise joined on edge with all posts in. You have to do a full SH org board master of posts and depts and sections only. Then copy it and mail it (in 2 sheets) to each org EVERY QUARTER and post them in WW when they come back. This program belongs to the Divisional Organizer for HCO and I'll bet the current WW post holder has never heard of it!

19. My view is you are losing your purpose, letting key lines drop and get forgotten and are in the business of answering up when somebody writes you, "Dear Pete—How are things at SH. . . ." and replying, "Dear Joe, Things are okay at SH. We had a fine day today with all the flowers. . . ." And THAT'S NOT YOUR JOB.

20. You were organized to take over my hats and I never wrote a "Dear Joe" in my life. I produced the written down wherewithal to teach and process and organize and got it into action in the outer orgs and kept them promoting and expanding. The technical creation part I've done. Your job is EASY. All you have to do is copy it, mail it and get it applied. "Dear Joe" despatches are your social life so do it at home.

21. If WW graphs remain level as they are and SH graphs climb, SH is going to run out of public suddenly. And THAT WILL BE ON YOUR HEAD.

22. You are in Emergency. That means NO WW staff gets normal pay or bonuses but subtracted pay.

23. You'll be out of Emergency when the WW graphs start climbing all across the boards.

24. Too much attention on accounts, too little attention on promotion, too tolerant of lousy tech and slack ethics, ignoring the need of making new execs in order to expand and completely ignoring ARC breaks, all in the outer orgs.

25. You are interiorized into a successful SH but the prosperity there is threatened by level graphs in outer orgs. So WW has not been doing its job, whatever else it has been doing.

26. If I have to follow this up, Danger condition is the next step and it's right around the corner. You're in a REAL EMERGENCY. A delay in your graphs to me is the only reason it was not declared earlier, so it has now gone pretty far.

27. Get the above into RIGHT NOW CRASH PROGRAMS with special staff. I'll be watching. Stop letting SH down!

L. RON HUBBARD
Founder

WW DIVISION REORGANIZATION

(Cancels all earlier organization
charts of WW Division)

Board of Directors: This is composed of the HCO Exec Sec WW, the Org Exec Sec WW, the LRH Comm WW.

Executive Council: Same as the Board of Directors.

Advisory Council: This is composed of all divisional executives, liaison executives and LRH Personal Aide in the WW Division. It advises the Executive Council and is run like all other Ad Councils as covered by policy. It is headed by the LRH Personal Aide as chairman, and its chairman is no longer elected.

OFFICE OF LRH

This office handles the affairs of LRH and has the signature and seals of the org.

It is headed by the Office Manager of the Office of LRH WW.

It contains the Office of the LRH Communicator WW.

It contains the LRH Personal Secretary and LRH Personal Aide.

These sections are organized as per earlier PLs.

It also contains the Div 7 Sec WW whose duties are detailed in earlier PLs.

OFFICE OF THE HCO EXEC SEC

This office is headed by the HCO Exec Sec WW.

It contains one Divisional Organizer for Divisions 7, 1 and 2 for each continental office in the world. The person is called the "HCO Continental Liaison Officer for (name of continental office) at WW." This one person is liaison for each and every Div 7, 1 and 2 in that continental sphere.

It compiles all needful divisional materials for every org in the world under a Materiel Executive.

The office contains as well the Communicator WW and the Ethics Officer WW.

This office is in charge of pushing through special programs, such as getting org execs up.

It also contains all WW addresses and files and *The Auditor* staff.

It also has the Worldwide personnel and ethics files.

The HCO Exec Sec WW is personally and directly responsible for all personnel and activities in this office.

The office also contains the necessary clerks, etc., for its functioning.

THE OFFICE OF THE ORG EXEC SEC WW

This office is headed by the Org Exec Sec WW.

It contains one Divisional Organizer for Divisions 3, 4, 5, 6 for every continental office in the world. This person is called the "Organization Continental Liaison Officer for (name of continental office) at WW."

This office runs the Org Exec Course.

It also contains the OT Central Committee.

The office contains as well the Treasurer WW.

It also contains the clerks, etc., necessary for the operation of the office.

This is the total extent of the WW Division 7.

Earlier policy on, say, the Office of the LRH Comm, the LRH Pers Sec all apply.

Every org and every Exec Council in the world is subject to the WW Div and it is responsible for the smooth running of every org in the world.

I forbear to lay down endless policy for the conduct of HCO Exec Sec WW and the Org Exec Sec WW or their Continental Liaison Officers.

All I will say is that its executives must complete the Org Exec Course to be more than temporary, and that its key policy is, "The supreme test of a thetan is to make things go right."

And I expect they will make things go right in every org in every continental area in the world and do it well and do it NOW.

L. RON HUBBARD
Founder

CONTINENTAL LIAISON
OFFICERS AT WW

The authority of the Continental Liaison Officer at WW, for HCOs or the org portions, is JUNIOR to the Executive Secretaries of any org. Only the HCO Exec Sec WW and the Org Exec Sec WW are senior to the Exec Secretaries of orgs.

The Continental Liaison Officer is not there to issue orders to orgs. He is at the *service* of orgs. HCO Continental Liaison is the WW *comm* point for the HCO Exec Secs in every org in the continental zone. The Org Continental Liaison is the WW *comm* point for the Org Exec Secs for every org in the continental zone.

They are essentially *representatives*.

They are there to get the stats of each org up by providing SERVICE from WW.

They are far too far away to give orders with any reality. But they can HELP.

STATISTICS

The statistic of each Continental Liaison Officer is the same as the Continental Exec Sec (HCO or Org) of the continent he represents. It is a combined stat for his portion of those orgs.

His NAME appears on the WW division statistic.

He should be from the zone he represents insofar as possible.

The Continental Liaison pair at WW are not the Continental Exec Secs.

The WW HCO Exec Sec and WW Org Exec Sec should pass any orders via and obtain any data on any continent via the Continental Liaison Officer AND IN NO OTHER WAY.

HCO and Org Exec Secs in orgs should not address the HCO and Org Exec Secs WW but their own HCO or Org Continental Liaison Officer at WW and *order* him to bring up this or that at WW.

Local lack of books, supplies, meters, bulletins, policy letters, should be pointed out to the Cont Liaison WW.

Absence of policy, downstats, etc., should be pointed out to the Exec Secs of an org by the Continental Liaison Officers at WW IN ORDER TO GET STATS UP.

Continental Liaison Officers are only in the business of getting stats up in each org and portion they represent and finding out for the Exec Secs WW why the stats aren't up.

Find the data, find the outness, for the Exec Secs WW is a primary duty of Continental Liaison Officers at WW. For instance, find out why NY can't keep execs long enough to train them, find why Miami is almost nonexistent. Really find out why and give the data to the WW Exec Secs.

GET THE STATS UP.

AND *HELP* THE OUTER ORGS.

L. RON HUBBARD
Founder

HCO POLICY LETTER OF 21 SEPTEMBER 1967
Issue I

Remimeo

WW INCOME OUTGO

WW shall now open its own bank accounts independent of SH and operate its own accounting unit, pay its own salaries and bills, all in the Treasury Office as a new section containing income, disbursement and Dept 9 functions. It is to owe SH for all assets, stocks, equipment, and pay SH rent. Its income consists of gross quantity booksales, meters, tapes, 10 percent and such income as it may develop.

It may borrow money from SH to replace stocks but it must record such as a debt.

It pays its own salaries and bills. It may charge SH for *The Auditor*; WW owns the international address files but not SH CF. Its stats must be rearranged to reflect its volume of production and solvency.

It must become independently solvent and self-supporting as a division. It may charge admin costs of Advanced Courses but must deposit all Advanced Course fees, less admin costs, in a reserve account, as neither it nor SH owns these fees.

Its income and debts are included in the international balance sheet.

It must use care in its personnel and production costs and must manage well to increase its 10 percents and the gross volume of books, meters, tape sales over the world.

A full valuation of stocks and equipment must be taken and listed as a debt to SH.

It starts its independent cycle on 1 November 1967.

L. RON HUBBARD
Founder

HCO POLICY LETTER OF 21 SEPTEMBER 1967
Issue II

Remimeo

WORLDWIDE AND SAINT HILL
FUNCTIONS REDEFINED

The Worldwide Division at Saint Hill shall hereafter function as a service center to all and shall contain HCO and Org representatives for every continental area and for use by every org's Exec Secs in expediting service, students, pcs and material and personnel for their orgs.

The WW Exec Secs are there to make service to and production for all orgs real and effective. Saint Hill's technical training and skill are the real hope of Scientology for, so long as it does its job well in training auditors and processing pcs and training executives, Scientology and all orgs will prosper.

Therefore the most highly skilled executives and auditors and supervisors in the world are to be used in the Saint Hill Org rather than the WW Division with the single exception of the WW Office of LRH.

The WW Division emphasis is on production of material for international use by all orgs and service to those orgs and expediting matters for those orgs with orgs with Saint Hill.

So long as the WW Division produces material and looks after service and Saint Hill sets an example of technical perfection international Scientology will prosper.

L. RON HUBBARD
Founder

INTERNATIONAL OFFICERS AT WW
ALERT COUNCIL

The post of INTERNATIONAL COMMUNICATIONS OFFICER is formed with the duties of ensuring all Scientology comms flow within WW and in all orgs and on all lines. It is under the HCO Sec WW in the Dept of Comm.

The post of INTERNATIONAL ETHICS OFFICER is formed with the duties of maintaining WW personnel files of all org personnel over the world and getting in ethics in all orgs and ensuring appointments of only ethics-free personnel in orgs. His okay is required from an ethics standpoint in all post assignments in Scientology orgs over the world hereafter. It is under the HCO Sec WW in the Dept of I&R.

The post of INT ADMIN OFFICER is formed. He holds the admin pattern of the org in position in every org and makes certain that execs know and follow policy letters as to the form of the org, body flow lines and functions of posts and to org spatial arrangements, and sees that all the data taught on the Org Exec Course is applied and that Scientology executives and staffs are trained in it and use it. He also sees that policy is not used to stop proper flows or halt expansion. He also sees to the correctness and issue of hats in all orgs and does what is needful to make all policy letters available and in useful form. It is under the Dissem Sec WW, Dept 5.

The above three posts are under the HCO Exec Sec WW. The post of INTERNATIONAL SPECIAL PROGRAMS EXECUTION OFFICER is formed under the HCO Exec Sec WW to collect, watch, record progress and push already-originated special programs, such as junior staff to be trained on Org Exec Course, cash-bills ratio to be improved, Qual Divs to be established, etc., and to propose programs of long-range improvement. Since lack of attention to execution of long-range planning is what brought WW to Danger, a primary job of the post is to find and list and follow through all such authorized programs for any org or division, as most troubles in the past stemmed from dropping one of these key programs, the rest of WW being concentrated on current affairs and using extraordinary solutions. It is under the Dissem Sec WW, Dept 6.

The post of INTERNATIONAL PROMOTION OFFICER is formed under the Org Exec Sec WW. It is to push standard promotion in all orgs, the sale of books to public, FSM activities, congresses and general Division 6 actions with the purpose of expanding Scientology numbers by pressing on with proven methods of reach and seeing that no org neglects them. It is under the Dissem Planning Sec WW, Dept 18.

137

The post of INTERNATIONAL TECHNICAL OFFICER is formed with the duties of keeping standard tech in and only standard tech practiced over the world. It is under the Tech Sec WW, Dept 10.

The post of INTERNATIONAL DECLARATIONS OFFICER is formed under the Org Exec Sec WW to watch all declarations procedures to ensure their correctness and to take action on all incorrect declares to correct them and to implement policy relating to examinations of processing results, the only persons amongst Scientologists who have given trouble having been misdeclares. It is under the Qual Sec WW, Dept 13.

The INTERNATIONAL TREASURER WW is in Dept 21.

The eight soft points of Scientology orgs which require constant alertness and attention are Comm, Ethics, Admin Pattern, Tech, Declares, Special Programs Execution, Public Expansion and Finance. The last point is covered by the Treasurer.

These are the principal hats I have to wear in management which if neglected bring about Danger conditions in all other lines and activities.

These eight posts work in close liaison and must meet weekly as the "Alert Council WW."

This council has advisory powers and is to draw up weekly for the LRH Comm WW and the HCO and Org Exec Secs WW an Alert Bulletin, org by org giving a prediction of good expansion or trouble or contraction based on their respective fields of Comm, Ethics, Admin Pattern, Tech, Programs Execution, Public Expansion and Money with recommendations for any action in each org or generally. They are then to execute the action as individual officers when it is approved or as modified unanimously by the executives to whom it is sent. The guiding rule of these officers and the Alert Council is contained in The Supreme Test HCOB of 19 August 1967, and each officer on these eight posts should draw up a paper on exactly how that bulletin is to be brought about by his specialized post over the world of Scientology and send to me when appointed.

L. RON HUBBARD
Founder

WW—HOW TO COMM TO WW
CONTINENTAL LIAISON OFFICERS

Any organization in the world can comm to WW to get service, materiel, clarification and resolve problems.

Each continental area appoints two Continental Liaison Officers for a period of six months who then serve at WW. Transport is at the expense of the continental area. Living expenses and pay are at the expense of WW while the representative is there.

One of these represents the HCO side of the orgs on the continent, the other represents the Org side.

Ordinarily, a new Cont Liaison is sent every three months, HCO, then Org, to leave someone at WW to groove in the newcomer.

At times of personnel scarcity there may be only one representative representing both HCO and Org sides.

At WW the Cont Liaison Officer may be refused seating in the Ad Council if it be proven he is there really for personal service or it has been arranged as a part-time favor to a student or if the representative fails to get a clearance from the Int Ethics Officer at WW. A representative can also be seated and then dismissed if new evidence turns up on the basis of personal service as the real reason or bad ethics record. But a representative may only be returned to his cont area with full reasons why—he or she cannot be punished at WW and enjoys personal immunity from arrest as do any ambassadors. No WW threat of punishment can be used to silence or coerce a Cont Liaison Officer as he is actually an ambassador. His own Cont Exec Council can, however, discipline him while at WW for alter-is or inaction or comm jams or relay failures or being insufficiently causative or for high crimes but for no other reasons. A Cont Liaison Officer has total freedom of speech at WW in Ad Council, but he may not circulate statements to his cont area he has not voiced in or committed to writing to the Ad Council. His voting record becomes part of his org personnel file.

The Cont Liaison Officer can go to the HCO or Org side of WW (whichever he represents) for help or service or redress for his area and do all possible to expedite matters and raise stats for any of his continental orgs.

The Cont Liaison Officer is junior to Exec Secs in his cont zone and has to take their orders. He cannot give orders to them. He can relay to them orders from the Exec Council WW but not from Secretaries WW or below.

The Cont Liaison Officer's stats are the combined stats of the orgs on his side of the org.

The Cont Liaison Officer may not vote not to follow policy or HCOBs but may vote to amend policy (not tech), meanwhile the old policy remaining in full force, it being a high crime to vote not to follow policy or HCOBs or to order they be ignored or altered. Policy amendment has its own routing as per another policy letter which is not changed.

Cont Liaison Officers who have made good with high stats may be invited to serve as WW personnel at the expiry of their term.

HOW TO COMM TO WW

An HCO Exec Sec in City X Africa Cont Zone wishes to get a stat corrected at WW.

She writes the Director I&R WW via the HCO Cont Liaison Officer of her continental area.

It is on blue paper (for an ES):

> via HCO Continental Liaison Officer Africa at WW
> Dir I&R WW
>
> from HCO Exec Sec X
>
> Please correct, etc.

The HCO Cont Liaison Officer for Africa at WW should log this despatch and send it on to Dir I&R WW.

The Dir I&R WW handles it by orders to his departmental officers and so marks the despatch as done *when done* and routes it back to the Cont Liaison Officer Africa at WW who marks it done in his log and sends it back to the HCO ES X Africa.

If the log column for done remains blank, the Cont Liaison Officer chases it up and gets it answered and returns it to the HCO ES X Africa.

If HCO ES X Africa gets no answer, in due course she sends the whole matter to the INTERNATIONAL COMM OFFICER AT WW as a complaint, the Int Comm Officer WW now performing the old HCO Sec function of chasing up comm malfunctions.

If an ethics matter results, the Int Comm Officer WW refers it to the Int Ethics Officer WW for action.

REVERSE FLOW

Any order to an org from the Exec Council WW or a WW Secretary MUST go via the HCO or Org Cont Liaison Officer at WW to the ES or Sec in the org concerned.

All Exec Council or WW Sec orders to area orgs must go to the ES in the org concerned or via the ES. And also always via the Cont Liaison Officer at WW.

CONTINENTAL EXEC COUNCILS

At this time of issue, only those Cont Exec Councils which exist in full independent-of-other-post fact are included in the routing.

In this case (where a full Cont Div 7 exists), all comms are routed additionally, up and down the line, to the Cont EC.

This is then the pattern for the above case:

> via HCO Continental Exec Sec Africa
> via HCO Continental Liaison Officer Africa at WW
> to Dir I&R WW.

The same routing is followed on return.

However, if the Int Comm Officer at WW finds this routing to be staledating or failing to relay at once, she petitions the Ad Council WW via her own Alert Council to disband that Cont Div 7 for the time being. If passed, the EC WW may issue an order doing so.

The evidence must be overwhelming that the Cont Div 7 is not operating productively for the Cont Div 7 to be disbanded.

If this happens, then comm is direct from those continental orgs to WW as per the above first instance.

The reason for this clause is that some (US and ANZO) Continental Div 7s have not been effective in handling their areas before this date. Continental activity must be great enough to afford a full Continental Div 7, not a part-time additional-duty one, for Continental Div 7s to function well.

The Continental Liaison Officer need not wait to be told what to do by his continental orgs to expedite service or improve them. He can and is expected to initiate improvements and to expedite service to the orgs or side of orgs he represents even when not asked.

The motto regarding comm to WW is DON'T NATTER ABOUT WHAT IS GOING ON—GET YOUR CONT LIAISON OFFICER TO ACT.

DESPATCHES TO AND FROM INT OFFICERS

If an HCO Exec Sec or an Org Exec Sec in an org has reason to comm to an International Officer (for Ethics, Special Programs, Comm, etc.) at WW, the routing is always through their Cont Liaison Officer at WW.

Replies and origins from Int Officers at WW to Exec Secs in orgs go via the Continental Liaison Officer of that zone and side of org.

INT COMM OFFICER ENFORCES

IN ANY AND ALL CASES WHERE THESE COMM LINES BECOME TANGLED OR THIS POLICY LETTER IS NOT BEING FOLLOWED, *THE INT COMM OFFICER AT WW* MUST ATTACH A COPY OF THIS POLICY LETTER TO A DESPATCH THAT IS MISROUTED, WITH THE APPLICABLE PARTS CIRCLED IN RED, TO THE OFFENDING OR UNINFORMED ORIGINATOR.

L. RON HUBBARD
Founder

Remimeo

WW SEVEN DIVISIONS

The WW organization pattern is the same as any other org's. The International Officers are placed in the divisions to which they most closely relate and have only international duties with no org additional duties, i.e., there is a WW Ethics Officer and also an Int Ethics Officer. But there is no WW Special Programs Execution Officer, only an Int Special Officer as it is not an ordinary org post. All WW officers and staff are senior to continental staff.

The Ad Council WW is composed of the seven WW secretaries and ten continental representatives. The Alert Council meets as do other WW councils in Dept 21 WW. All comms from orgs to WW executives are sent via the Cont Liaison and returned so.

The stats of WW are dual, being the local stats as a production unit and the old WW stats.

The Materiel Secretary post name is changed to Dissem Sec WW.

Cont Liaison Officers may serve only for six months and may not serve twice.

While at WW a Cont Liaison may be trained or processed only in the evening on his own time.

The Ad Council WW may refuse to accept any or may dismiss any Cont Liaison if it be proven he is only there for personal service or if his ethics file shows any signs of suppressiveness. The Int Ethics Officer WW must pass on a Cont Liaison before he is seated in the Ad Council.

L. RON HUBBARD
Founder

Remimeo

OT WW LIAISON UNIT
OT CENTRAL COMMITTEE

An OT Liaison Unit at WW, to be called the Worldwide Operating Thetan Liaison Unit, is formed at Worldwide. In general action it is known as OT WW Liaison Unit.

It is to consist of a Commanding Officer, a Supercargo and a Chief Officer representing those divisions.

It acts as liaison with the Sea Org, the Advanced Org, all OT Projects and Worldwide.

The Operating Thetan Central Committee is now transferred to the OT WW Liaison Unit, to work under it as a coordinating body, as it has been of great help in forming OT Projects.

L. RON HUBBARD
Founder

HCO POLICY LETTER OF 8 FEBRUARY 1968
Issue II

Remimeo
Issue as a
  Flag Order

SEA ORG ZONES OF PLANNING

The Sea Org is an obvious success. Its promotional and mission actions resulted in a highest ever worldwide statistic in early Feb. 1968.

The Zones of Activity of the Sea Org are therefore of general interest and are outlined for future Sea Org planning.

MISSIONS TO ORGS

The Sea Org sends its officers to individual orgs with unlimited powers to handle:

a. Ethics

b. Tech

c. Admin.

A general Sea Org mission handles all three.

Individual Sea Org missions go out to handle only one of the above also.

An individual Sea Org mission may be sent to handle a specific situation.

The most successful Sea Org mission to date handled (a) Ethics, (b) Tech, (c) Admin *and* a specific situation.

PROMOTION

Sea Org promotional tours where Sea Org members address the public are a major item.

These work well in any way but would do best on invitation from orgs and long term advance notice to public.

General Sea Org promotion, magazine, literature, is effective in general worldwide stats as well as Sea Org stats.

SEA ORG TECH

Controlling the upper end of the Bridge and having so many Class VI and Class VIIs and OT Grade Vs and OT Grade VI personnel, the technical level of the Sea Org is very high.

That the public knows it and these OT levels are real and exist and are available is a factor in worldwide stats, persuading people to begin the lower end of the Bridge.

SEA ORG ACTIONS

The actions of the Sea part of the Sea Org, being adventurous, is goodwill advertising.

The confront and organizational ability of Sea Org personnel is high above that of purely admin personnel.

Such activities give a strong base for Sea Org predominance.

PUBLIC CONTROL FACTORS

The Sea Org has an area of public or political control based on:

A. ETHICS ACTION

B. PEACE

C. FINANCE AND ADMIN.

The above are the basic elements in Sea Org planning for use in future activities and for use by orgs in coordinating with the Sea Org.

L. RON HUBBARD
Founder

HCO POLICY LETTER OF 9 MAY 1968

Remimeo

SEA ORGANIZATION PERSONNEL

The Sea Organization requirements for its staff are as follows:

That only personnel be sent who have had Scientology processing and they are at least a Grade IV Release, Power Release is preferred, as the minimum.

The Sea Organization will be very happy to handle training and processing from Grade IV on up. However, only Scientology processed and trained personnel have been able to keep up with the Sea Org activities.

The Sea Organization's responsibility to the orgs worldwide is such that its purpose line for these orgs can't be altered with internal elements who have no subjective reality on that technology which the Sea Org is enforcing.

L. RON HUBBARD
Founder

HCO POLICY LETTER OF 23 MAY 1968
Issue I

WW and SH

IMPORTANT

WW AND SH RECOMBINED

(Deadline 15 June 1968)

Although their statistics are drawn as before, WW, for all finance purposes, is recombined with SH and the PL setting up WW as a separate finance unit is cancelled.

If Worldwide does its work well, handling outer orgs, SH will have students and pcs.

SH has been developing reserves during a down-income period. WW has been reducing promotional actions for lack of funds (while overstaffing).

The original finance pattern of WW was successful in that SH paid its bills and costs. SH has begun to slump periodically since WW separated from it financially.

All org functions and actions of WW remain. Its org board remains.

However, the full tech/admin ratio of SH including WW MUST be held to three persons admin to one person tech. This applies to SH/WW only and MUST be in full effect on 15 June 68.

The org boards must be balanced to obtain this ratio.

A tech person, by actual definition, does or supervises tech. To wit: An auditor, Supervisor, Dir Training, Dir Processing, Tech Sec, Qual Sec or Examiner.

There must be one of these at least for every three persons holding admin posts.

Lack of training on the Dianetics and Solo course spring of '68 showed too few Supervisors to the number of students as the cause of bad training results.

Fast flow has *not* eradicated personal instruction.

To get more people on admin you need only add tech personnel. You don't starve down admin, you fatten up tech.

IF THE THREE TO ONE RATIO IS VIOLATED, IT IS A COMM EV OFFENSE.

All WW income is invoiced on the regular SH invoice lines. A separate box system is used to separate out the invoices for statistics each week. Graphs are then made.

Book income, as it has been subsidized always by orgs, may not be held separate, and book supplies procurement may not be held down to book income. Books are the first line of promotion.

CROSS ORDERING

Where an executive responsible for an area issues an order into an area where juniors are issuing contrary or confused orders, programs cannot exist or be executed.

Also seniors with an unreality on the problems of juniors can paralyze them with floods of orders.

Therefore, combining WW and SH should be watched that SH does not get paralyzed by too much WW ordering and reversely WW does not order programs into a lot of cross orders.

SUMMARY

The direction of progress is toward simplicity.

This PL is ordered to reduce the complexities into which WW has fallen in trying to solve its own finance and to utilize the resources of SH more widely.

Obviously, the income of SH depends on outer orgs getting in new people, training and processing them well and sending them on to SH.

WW only exists to make this action smooth and increase its volume by the use of functional procurement of new people by outer orgs and seeing that the tech given them in outer orgs is STANDARD.

The SH Foundation only exists to keep the East Grinstead area nonenturbulated and prevent a local no-auditing situation from occurring.

SH exists to furnish excellent auditors to the outer orgs and well-audited pcs to the AO.

If these relationships are understood, then the wheels will turn.

If these relationships are NOT understood, then all manner of complexity results.

The AO exists to make OTs and support the Sea Org so that the planet can be brought under control and a safe environment provided in which the planet's fourth dynamic can be cleared. The Sea Org discipline keeps the lines channeled so that outer orgs, SH and WW can do their jobs.

This is all so remarkably simple that one wonders at the odd games that get played along the command lines between SO and WW, WW and SH/outer orgs.

All we want is an operation that delivers standard tech properly done and stays solvent while it does it.

Therefore, we are making the WW and SH relationship on finance more compact so that the wheels turn better.

L. RON HUBBARD
Founder

HCO POLICY LETTER OF 15 SEPTEMBER 1968

Remimeo

SEA ORG

As of this date the Sea Org only will be conducting ethics missions.

It has been proven that this responsibility can only be run from an outfit mobile and extremely effective. This is not to say WW cannot be effective; they can. At this time, however, the Sea Org will take back the mission hat.

Worldwide can run inspections on orgs for the purpose of checking compliance on WW orders. This can also be done by Executive Council US and other continental orgs. Both these areas can utilize the OT Liaisons for advices on conducting these inspection tours or parties.

The Efficiency Expert School training should continue at the same pace at WW. This training is invaluable for just the org functions.

The Sea Org is the only group who can really run ethics missions.

Worldwide now then has no ethics power with regard to orgs other than is decided by Executive Council Worldwide in full council meeting. All WW ethics must come from full council. No member may be delegated this authority or no member of an inspection party or tour.

The Sea Org will take back now this field which in trial phase was given to WW. Worldwide is to be commended for its action to carry the mission hat.

There is only one group who can effectively run missions. This group is now putting Scientology technology into a realm which will soar the stats by three in as many months. These are the Class VIIIs.

The Sea Org does come back.

The word MISSION may now be used to designate *only* a Sea Org official mission. It has unlimited ethics powers. Their members are called "missionaires."

The word INSPECTION shall be used to designate WW or continental org parties sent out. Their members are "Efficiency Experts." They have no ethics powers but may recommend action to Executive Council Worldwide or Executive Council Continental on their return.

No Executive Council including WW may send out Efficiency Experts who are not trained by the SO and who are not graduates of the Org Exec Course.

L. RON HUBBARD
Founder

HCO POLICY LETTER OF 30 NOVEMBER 1968

Remimeo

OT CENTRAL COMMITTEE

The OT Central Committee is transferred under OTL WW of the Sea Org.

The SO Commanding Officer OTL WW is to direct and coordinate their activities according to their outlined basic purposes.

Their work is too valuable to be dropped.

The OT Central Committee is also authorized to correspond with Clears and OTs relating to their projects.

The OT Central Committee may use SO facilities to continue their work.

The Commanding Officer of the nearest Advanced Org is to assist and is to continue the committee in default of a CO OTL.

The OT Central Committee has its own chairman as before.

L. RON HUBBARD
Founder

HCO POLICY LETTER OF 12 FEBRUARY 1970
Issue II

Remimeo
All Exec Sec Hats
All WW Hats

URGENT AND IMPORTANT TO WW

EC WW, PRIMARY DUTIES OF

Reviewing actions of the past year and a half, the important points of concentration for WW are basically PERSONNEL.

LRH COMM WW

He must give first priority to three things:

a. Keeping the LRH Comm network manned and operating, as the inter-org network of world comm.

b. Ensuring rapid distribution of orders, Executive Directives, HCOBs, PLs, materials for HGC and student training.

c. Compliance therewith.

In (a) maintaining the LRH Comm network over the world he must at once detect any failure of an org to answer up, report or comply and handle the matter rapidly and without fail. In making this come about, he may request help from the Sea Org if he cannot quickly effect the matter himself.

On (b) he must ensure without fail that EDs, general HCOBs and policy letters get into the hands of every staff member in the world rapidly without backlog.

Any LRH Comm or HCO ES in any org must assist these actions to take place.

Other communications or orders from WW may travel on these lines, be logged and locally followed up by the LRH Comm if the communication is directed to LRH Comms.

A fourth and important action of LRH Comm WW is to see that TAPES by LRH are played in orgs wherever possible and also with excellent quality. A fifth duty is to see that an actual Office of LRH exists in orgs, that busts and photos are displayed and that SOURCE is maintained in orgs.

The LRH Comm WW should see to it that the LRH Comm network is USED, that orders and actions are logged and that all LRH Comms are well trained and aware of their duties.

It will be seen at once that this is primarily a PERSONNEL matter.

ALL other matters than the above are secondary to the above and are given attention only when the above are fully handled.

HCO EXEC SEC WW

The primary duties of the HCO Exec Sec WW are:

1. International personnel files.

2. International ethics files.

3. All org statistics.

If these three actions are given precedence over all others, EC WW will be able to do its job as proper, experienced, trained personnel will be on post. If these are not available and up-to-date and accurate then EC WW cannot do its job at all.

A fourth action is to establish and maintain, in action and urgency, fully operating HCOs over the world in every org.

A fifth action is to appoint, remove, supervise and maintain competent high-stat HCO Exec Secs in every org.

If the HCO ES maintains the international personnel and ethics files and works out accurate means to augment their completeness, accuracy and up-to-dateness, personnel can be wisely chosen for Exec Sec posts in orgs.

Full, complete statistics of orgs, each carrying the name of the person responsible, are *received,* plotted and posted for WW use. The HCO ES does a GDS analysis of each org each week and furnishes copies to orgs and the SO captains.

All org personnel and their posts and news of any new personnel or transfer or internal appointment and a record of training of each are received and filed by the HCO ES.

Any of the above actions are primary points of attention of the HCO ES. All other actions on international lines are secondary.

The HCO ES WW is depended upon to maintain the WW org form and WW Ethics and Personnel to prevent incompetence, infiltration or upsets on WW staff.

If the HCO ES WW performs the above duties well and efficiently, little can go wrong in Scientology orgs and what is built will stay built.

THE ORG EXEC SEC WW

The OES WW has definite *primary* duties which must never be neglected. These are:

a. Effective OES and Tech execs on post in every org,

b. Auditing in high volume in all orgs,

c.   Training in volume of public students,

d.   Training in volume of staff students,

e.   Wide staff auditing,

f.   Financial high income and solvency in WW and all other Scientology orgs with excellent cash-bills and mounting reserves,

g.   The effective delivery of high-quality auditing and training,

h.   The repair of any and all cases incompetently handled,

i.   Getting new personnel in orgs trained up rapidly.

The OES WW is responsible for the good performance, training and conduct of every OES in the world and that one is on post in each org.

If the OES WW accomplishes the above important points as his first order of action, orgs will expand and tech delivery to the public will expand the influence of orgs. Any other actions are secondary.

PUBLIC EXEC SEC WW

The PES WW has certain primary and definite duties which are his primary concern:

i.   Effective, well-trained PESes on post in every org.

ii.   Floods of new names being produced by every PES in the world.

iii.   The standard promotional actions of the Public Divisions continued in action without dispersal.

iv.   The appearance of orgs and staffs.

v.   The exertion of PRO Area Control around WW and each org.

The PES WW is responsible for having an active and effective, well-trained PES working industriously and productively in each org and is responsible for their production, effectiveness and conduct.

All other duties and actions are secondary to the above, which if done, will stabilize and expand orgs.

OTHER DUTIES

It is fully understood that other duties are performed by these Executive Secretaries and that these are also of importance. Division 2 actions, for instance, are seen to by the HCO ES. But it should be obvious that if the primary duties listed above are not alertly handled then no other actions become possible.

SENIOR EXEC SEC

The Senior Executive Secretary at WW is the HCO Exec Sec.

The HCO ES is held fully responsible for any errors or neglect by the other Exec Secs.

The HCO ES calls and conducts all meetings of EC WW and establishes their order of business.

Anyone addressing "EC WW" is in fact addressing the HCO ES WW.

Should WW fail in any respect, it is the HCO ES who is held responsible.

COLLECTIVE ACTIONS

EC WW has various collective actions. Some of these are:

1. Appointment of personnel to EC posts in continental or other orgs or their removal, which must be by unanimous vote of EC WW after inspection of ethics, graphs and personnel records. These posts are kept filled by EC WW on the basis of stats. A letter of such appointment must be written to each appointee.

2. Financial Planning for WW to maintain complete solvency and accumulate reserves.

3. Any ED being issued by any WW Executive Secretary requires unanimous agreement by EC WW and is signed (originating Executive Secretary) (by and for Executive Council WW).

4. Analysis of GDSes.

5. Assignment of conditions to orgs. (But no lower than Non-E.)

6. Broad, general planning for WW and orgs.

EC WW COMM LINES

Executive Council Worldwide orders travel on LRH Comm comm lines and are logged by the LRH Comm WW and by LRH Comms or HCO ESs in orgs. Compliance is obtained on this network.

This PL changes no other PL except the handling of WW orders by LRH Comms. It emphasizes the relative importance of Executive Secretary actions at WW.

If those items listed under their duties and collective actions are given high priority, then EC WW is fulfilling its purpose and if they are not, EC WW has no reason for being.

PERSONNEL

It will be seen and should be fully understood that EC WW's first and foremost concern is *Personnel*.

Systems of observation to build up current information on personnel in orgs, compared to their own stats, recording their level of training in ethics, tech and admin are vital to WW's operation.

The training and readying of *future* personnel is of the most vital interest to EC WW.

If EC WW regarded itself as a mammoth personnel office and concerned itself mainly with (a) identifying top stat people in orgs and appointing them to key posts, (b) training existing personnel up and (c) recruiting new personnel into orgs, the operation of EC WW and its Exec Secs would be tremendously successful.

Naturally, to observe and get reports one has to have an operating comm network.

Executive Councils in continental orgs actually only aid and abet this action.

DESPATCHES

If WW seeks to handle every small situation in orgs and issue orders about them over long distance lines, it will fail as these situations occur only because of poor personnel at the other end of the line.

Thus, endlessly answering despatches as an Exec Sec at WW as one's only action will wind things up badly. Despatches are acked and situations handled, of course. But it is far from a full-time duty. Despatches are a means of OBSERVATION. What the Exec Sec wants from them is *data*.

What WW is interested in is data about PERSONNEL, about their ethics, about their training and progress in training and, basically, their performance on post, as these relate to stats.

Despatches give data, progress, situations and compliances.

MUSICAL CHAIRS

One avoids musical chairs in an org. But one doesn't permit destructive or noncompliant persons in key posts.

LOYALTY

Staff members who stick with it through thick and thin count for much and this factor is a large one. They should not be mauled around.

FREELOADERS

Training in upper orgs for staff members in lower orgs should be okayed by EC WW first and an undated note for the expense to the lower org should be made out and signed. Accurate freeloader lists should be made and kept and the offender considered dead so far as org staff is concerned as experience shows they are often wildly out-ethics otherwise.

VOLUME

Recruiting and training staff in volume is always a safe activity and things go bad only when one doesn't.

––––––––

If WW performs its personnel functions well, it will succeed.

L. RON HUBBARD
Founder

L. Ron Hubbard
EXECUTIVE DIRECTIVE

LRH ED 83 INT   17 February 1970

TO: ECs
    All Staff
    All Orgs

SUBJECT: **STAT RECOVERY, AN ANALYSIS OF BROAD OUTNESSES**

As further observation is available it becomes very apparent why International Stats declined and how they are being made to recover rapidly.

INTER ORG COMM

The comm lines amongst orgs were permitted to become nonfunctional. Orgs went out of comm with Continental and WW. This became very apparent recently when it was found that LRH EDs could not be distributed to every staff member in the world.

Thus no real data, vital to management, was available and unreal orders could result from Continental and WW.

The remedies under way for this are:

A. Conversion of the LRH Comm line network into *the* network of comm between orgs, Continental ECs and WW and so observation and compliance can occur.

B. Permitting orgs to remimeo materials received such as LRH EDs, HCOBs and PLs. Curing any backlog of mimeo.

C. Speeding up all comm lines.

AUDITING DELIVERY

Scn orgs have had the advantage over other Earth activities of having brighter staffs. People who are audited have higher IQs and are more effective and have better judgment.

Somehow, auditing volume delivered was permitted to drop. Public pc backlogs piled up. Auditors were on Admin posts. A scarcity of auditors developed. And contracted staff members were not even audited when charged for it.

It actually is possible now to audit a pc hundreds of hours. It is also the *amount* of auditing received rather than just grades which pushes IQ and ability out the top.

If orgs had ceased to audit their staff members, they were losing a definite advantage, as orgs, of having brighter, better people.

This is being remedied by:

a. Crash programing auditor training to get lots and lots and lots of auditors in orgs.

b. Pushing admin/tech ratio to 2 to 1 or better and training any *admin* excess personnel up as auditors fast fast fast.

c. Recruiting for staff members from Academies and courses and for staff and pushing their auditor training, if not full time at least part time.

d. Pushing in hard the HDG data on training in every org so tight scheduling and good 8-C results in fast training.

e. Developing and giving Student Rescue Intensives to speed learning rate.

ORG KNOW–HOW

Our orgs long had an advantage of being better organized and faster moving than other Earth organizations. They had very advanced organizational technology in which the natural laws of organization had been isolated.

But with only 8 percent of staff members over the world who had been once through the Org Exec Course, with policy and divisional policy packs unavailable, this organizational advantage was thrown away.

I have always worked on the basis that every staff member, no matter how minor a post, must know all there is to know about the organization and its policies. I frown on having an expert or two at the top who are the only ones who know. You can't have a team where 7/8ths of those on it are in ignorance of what the team is trying to do. That's more like the army than an org!

Such a condition, all by itself, will slow an org down to a crawl because it piles up tons of misunderstoods daily. It causes excessive blows and crashes stats.

This is being remedied by:

1. Getting current EDs, HCOBs and PLs into the hands of every staff member.

2. Turning out full, printed HCO PL packs for individual purchase.

3. Turning out divisional summaries so even a new division staff member can be briefed quickly on his division.

4. Making the Org Exec Course a requirement for full pay on the post.

5. Smoothing out any conflicts that have grown up in policy matters.

6. Getting all orgs onto standard org form and actions being done by an informed and knowledgeable staff.

———

Stats went down because our advantages of good between-org lines, well-audited staffs and well-informed staff members somehow became neglected in Scientology orgs.

In the same year and a half period, the SO orgs, where these three things get heavy attention, continued to prosper.

These three things went out because of losses of trained staff to missions, etc., but mainly because WE FAILED TO RECRUIT AND TRAIN AS RAPIDLY AS WE EXPANDED.

Wherever we get these things in in an Scn org, it immediately starts to raise its stats.

The LRH ED No. 1 Programs contain these elements, amongst others.

A staff member really has 3 hats—and used to each keep up 3 folders.

1. Post hat, in which the person's hat write-up by out-going persons, PLs of the post and the data about the post were kept.

2. Staff hat, in which material concerning one's duties as a staff member were kept, plus new EDs and PLs.

3. Tech hat, in which the HCOBs relating to the post or newly issued were kept.

These three hats should be in the possession of every staff member and are inspected for by the HCO Area Sec.

––––––––––––

We are working hard to remedy these matters.

There is exactly no reason why a staff member in an Scn org cannot do better than he ever would in missions. I estimate that the GI stats of any Scn org are about 1/250th currently of what they will be if the No. 1 Programs are gotten in, if the above three situations are fully corrected and if staffs produce. And the 1/250th is a conservative estimate.

You cannot have a total monopoly in the effective mental tech of a planet, rivals or no rivals, without eventually clearing the planet. But you have to communicate, use it and apply it!

––––––––––––

I hope this analysis of the situation is of help.

Love,

Ron

L. RON HUBBARD
Founder

HCO POLICY LETTER OF 23 APRIL 1970

WW SH and
all orgs in
UK and ANZO,
all orgs in
EU

SH–UK ANZO–EU RELATIONSHIPS

(This cancels HCO PL 24 Apr. 68 I which
established Executive Council Europe.)

Executive Council WW must nominate and have the HCO ES WW appoint AN EXECUTIVE COUNCIL UK–ANZO and an EXECUTIVE COUNCIL EUROPE.

Any and all orgs in the UK excluding only WW come under the authority and operation of EC UK–ANZO. This includes SH Day and Foundation, London, Scotland and all UK orgs. It also includes all orgs in New Zealand and Australia.

Executive Council Europe is directly answerable to a Sea Org Commanding Officer and the Continental Captain, Station Ship Europe. All EU orgs, missions and groups are directly under ECEU. The Continental Captain liaises with ECWW in control of the EU orgs. Nothing in this PL shall be construed to mean that Mission Officer WW does not work directly with EU orgs and missions but it does mean that the CO ECEU may act directly with these orgs. Any conflict of interest or control is to be settled by the Continental Captain Europe on individual matters. Any settlement by the Continental Captain with which ECWW, the Mission Office WW does not agree may be submitted to arbitration which can resolve the matter. The Continental Captain EU appoints a member, ECWW, the Mission Office WW appoint a member and these two appoint a third member. Majority vote of the Arbitration Committee rules. Thus, policy on specific matters can be established.

This policy letter also corrects any separation of SH Day and SH Foundation. Executive Council SH Day directly controls and is directly above SH Foundation.

Executive Council UK–ANZO is located at Saint Hill.

L. RON HUBBARD
Founder

Remimeo

THE EXECUTIVE COUNCIL NETWORK DISBANDED

(The Why of GI crashes)

A situation existed for four years whereby the Executive Council Worldwide had several international stat crashes which then had to be picked up by the Sea Org.

The Sea Org Continental Liaison Office network has taken over these functions of management under its Management Bureau.

The first major crash was the 1968 stat crash which long remained unexplained.

Information has now come to light on how this Executive Council network put itself out of business several times.

Operating on a wrong statistic (gross income), the Executive Council network developed a system, originated or at least perpetuated by an Allan Ferguson, then OES WW, of daily hammering orgs for GI and getting the GI up by "all possible means." The Continental Executive Councils borrowed this system. It was and is an off-policy action.

In the very early 1960s it was already observed from the conduct of the Melbourne org that one could always sell out an area, and that done without delivery or with flubby delivery resulted in a collapse of stats. It was well known then that *you cannot continue to sell without full and quality delivery of what was sold.*

Pushing only "GI" does not build an org that can deliver. It is easy to push only "GI." It does not take many people. Its situations are simple and easy to solve up to a point.

The Worldwide and Continental Executive Council network, pushing only GI, dispensed with an HCO and let HCOs collapse in orgs. HCOs were not there to build an org so delivery ceased. The org went idle and collapsed. Service was undelivered or of poor quality and ARC broke the field.

It is a situation similar to the broad economic world of booms and depressions. Each boom was followed by a depression.

Back of this is nondelivery. Lots of stock sold but no product.

Delivery or production can also be pushed with no GI and with no money to reward or pay the expense of delivery, a crash also occurs.

In 1928 and 1929 the world markets pushed only shares, stocks and money, no delivery. Black Friday* in 1929 crashed the whole world of trade and began a long depression.

Production, however, did exist thereafter without money and the crash was continued.

When *either* money or production get out of balance one has trouble. All production and no money is as bad as all money and no production.

This also answers the world mystery of booms and depressions which, unsolved, drove the whole field of economics into a mad subject.

The fault in the Executive Council network (which I left in 1966) has been under study since the 1968 collapse of stats.

It apparently is the same as the old Melbourne org cycle of heavy sales but poor or no delivery.

Usually it takes several months or longer for one of these collapses to iron out. That was because each time, as the stats fell, even more frantic demands for GI would be issued from the Executive Council network. One after another orgs would cut their lines to WW and eventually no one would pay any attention and a tiny org would begin to grow back, delivering as it could.

This cycle occurred in 1967, 1968 and now again in the US in 1971 up to July when Flag abruptly disbanded the functioning Executive Council US.

This was done to prevent the old cycle of oversell and nondelivery from smashing stats too hard to recover.

The Continental Liaison Office was quickly strengthened.

A new org condition, CO, Exec Director stat was devised as PAID COMPLETIONS ACCOMPANIED BY AN ACCEPTABLE SUCCESS STORY (HCO PL 29 Aug. 71, PAID COMPLETIONS) was issued. LRH ED 151, 152 and 153 and HCOBs 30 Aug. 71 Issue I, STUDENT COMPLETIONS and Issue II, PC COMPLETIONS were quickly issued to set up a daily demand line from CLOs to orgs for that stat. A Qual Sec course (Mini Qual) and Tech Establishment Officer course were begun. Word Clearing tech, an auditing drills course and other material were rapidly formulated and released.

The urgency was to get the orgs delivering rapidly what they *had* sold while they still were financially able to do so.

Production demands were balanced with GI by "*Paid* Completions" and quality was bolstered by a requirement of a *success* story.

Training was given comparable or greater completion value to Tech to keep the orgs more heavily on training than processing.

These measures were designed to catch the boom before more and failing GI demands without delivery wrecked the network.

Any such situation is complicated by false reports or cut lines and is difficult to assess. The Data Series and many observation missions and a record of past experiences, however, indicate that this was the cause of the Worldwide network failure which until now had been something of a mystery.

At fault really is the retention of GI as the only stat used to assign orgs their conditions.

The main dangers of a shift to delivery is that GI may be placed in ill repute and that orgs, suddenly shifted in target, will not believe they can deliver in such volume. They can, rather easily, as already proven by at least one org in the current shift.

Spotted and caught in time almost any situation can be handled unless actions occur or continue which worsen it.

Orgs run on-policy which deliver what they sell in the same volume and in high quality, which maintain a good HCO to expand facilities, which recruit, hat and train their staffs, cannot do otherwise than succeed.

It is when there is more attention on income than on production and delivery that an org or network gets into trouble. And reversely, when more attention is given to production than sales, a downtrend can also occur as the organization is put out of balance.

Well-paid delivery in high quality is the correct answer. Only then can a boom continue. Frankly, it has never occurred to me that such a fact could be missed.

This is goodwill and also your integrity.

There are no shortcuts to honest prosperity.

We have the greatest possible tech when properly studied and applied. Why not deliver it?

L. RON HUBBARD
Founder

HCO POLICY LETTER OF 31 AUGUST 1971

Remimeo

ADDITIONAL

EXECUTIVE COUNCIL NETWORK

(The WHY of GI crashes)

(Reference: Data Series Policy Letters)

Since writing the original policy letter the Data Series has been completed and more data is now to hand concerning former EXECUTIVE COUNCIL Worldwide actions and the failures of other governing bodies.

This, therefore, is a VERY important subject as it concerns the success or failure of governing bodies in general.

A much broader WHY of failure has been found.

THE REAL WHY OF ANY GOVERNING BODY FAILURE WHEN IT IS SINCERELY TRYING BUT FAILING IS THAT *IT IS OPERATING ON WRONG WHYs.*

This, on review, was the true, underlying failure of every sincerely active governing body or EXECUTIVE.

There can be other Whys. There can be no governing body at all. It can be corrupt. It can be only self-interested. And (as in the case of France, Poland, Austria and Czechoslovakia in the late 1930s) (and probably England in the 1960s) it can be infiltrated and subverted.

But all governing bodies of Scientology organizations have been sincere and they have tried hard. This included Executive Council WW.

And the basic and only reason for failure was that they gave orders which did not match the situation into which the order was sent.

They had no real data collection unit and depended on reports.

They had no direct observation.

Therefore, their estimates of the situation were faulty.

There was no *valid* system of data analysis or logic known to man and they would have erred anyway.

Thus, they are totally exonerated of any evil intent or even, by human standards, incompetence.

Acting on isolated reports or opinions, without a system of evaluation, they issued orders based on wrong WHYs.

Thus, this can go wrong with ANY executive, any governing body of anything.

Their constant demand for GI without any real demand that service be given was itself a wrong HANDLING because it was based on a wrong WHY.

Orgs exchange service for money. When they have nothing to exchange for the income, the income goes down because nothing is being delivered to *earn* the money. This was the right WHY of GI decline. All the nagging in the world would not have increased GI after delivery backlogged or was faulty.

But this is just a wrong Why. There were other wrong Whys as well.

Thus, to succeed,

any

EXECUTIVE

LOCAL GOVERNING BODY

CONTINENTAL BODY

INTERNATIONAL BODY

must:

1. Collect data

2. Observe

3. Evaluate and find RIGHT WHYs

4. Issue correct orders

5. Enforce compliance.

Additionally it must:

A. ENFORCE EXCHANGE

B. ESTABLISH.

The keynotes of success are OBSERVE, EVALUATE, ORDER, SUPERVISE.

———————

From studies of this subject additional data emerged:

a. Those organizations which are on-policy are overwhelmingly more success-ful than those that are not. The validity of this is so great that any lack of success can be assumed as coming from a general off-policy scene.

166

b.   Fast, continuous work is needful at any level to continue success. It need not be frantic. It must be orderly. But it is continuous and it is rapid.

c.   Surveys of what's wanted and considered valuable are vital to any expansion.

d.   Exchange of something for something cannot occur only within a body or group but must take place with a different type of group (like org with public, not org with org) for any "GI" to be realized.

e.   Continued "GI" depends on the quality, predictability, valuedness and volume of service given for it.

f.   That the primary failure of any group is a failure to establish (meaning training, org boarding, posting, hatting, lines followed and policy and tech known and practiced).

WORLDWIDE SUCCESS

Given and knowing and using this data Worldwide or any of its Continental Executive Councils could very easily succeed with the same personnel.

The data in this PL would have to be fully utilized for success to occur.

There was, therefore, nothing whatever wrong with the ECWW–Continental EC *PATTERN*.

This is very good to know. The pattern, like the pattern of the org board, is all right.

It is just that management bodies as well as executives, to be successful, MUST OPERATE AND ACT ONLY ON CORRECT AND EVALUATED WHYs. Otherwise, they court disaster.

It has taken a couple of years to finally uncover this data.

I trust it will prove valuable.

L. RON HUBBARD
Founder

HUBBARD COMMUNICATIONS OFFICE
Saint Hill Manor, East Grinstead, Sussex

HCO POLICY LETTER OF 1 NOVEMBER 1971R
Issue IV
REVISED 13 FEBRUARY 1991

Remimeo
CO/EDs
Executives

CO AND ED PENALTY FOR
FALSE COMPLETION STATS

The completion statistic of orgs is the stat of the Commanding Officer or Executive Director and is his responsibility.

These stats are explained in HCOB 14 June 77RB, PAID COMPLETIONS SIMPLIFIED.

If at any time an org is found to have been reporting a consistently false or padded completion statistic, the CO or ED will be subject to immediate removal from post by Flag.

It is in the interest of the CO or ED to *ensure* the org's completion statistic is tallied, inspected and reported accurately and honestly. (HCO PL 26 Oct. 71, TECH DOWNGRADES, gives important data to the CO/ED.)

L. RON HUBBARD
Founder

Assisted by
Aides Council

Revision assisted by
LRH Technical Research
and Compilations

PATTERN AND FORM
OF THE ORGANIZATION

HCO POLICY LETTER OF 3 AUGUST 1956

Remimeo
All Hats

ORGANIZATIONAL HEALTH CHART

(Originally written by LRH as HCOB 3 Aug. 56.
Issued as an HCO PL on 2 Nov. 70.)

This is an anatomical chart of a live organism, the HASI, London.

In a human being, we know the man lives if his heart still beats. To further our examination of his health we determine if he breathes. We look then to his color, his stomach, his organs, his glands.

An organization is no less a living organism, but we have never had a diagnostic health chart for one.

If one were a doctor to organizations, how would he tell if it were alive or not. Not by motion, since people in an underground are in motion but they are not an organization. What is the pulse, what is the breath, of the organism called an organization?

To determine the health of an organization is important. On that health in our case depends a crusade, a very important game, the furtherance of our work and the future of millions. Also on that health depends our jobs, our continued association with friends, the smoothness of our own days. Therefore that health is important to us. But what determines it? There could be a thousand thousand different things that might be the heart, while really there is only one. And only if we diagnose ill-health in the organization can we cure it.

One of us, doing perhaps a job not connected with the pulse, wonders what is wrong—we are not, in our job, able to get on. Is it our job that is wrong or is there another factor gone awry?

This list of importances tells us what the heart is, the breath and all the rest in order. If anything on this list goes wrong, it and the items above it must be examined in turn. This is diagnosis. Repair consists of setting the functions back to order and each in turn after it, since when an organism's highest functions fail, the remainder begin to enter difficulties.

This then is a diagnostic chart and a chart to effect the cure. The organization books amplify the functions. This list gives each function its proper importance to the rest, not perhaps in social caste, but certainly in health.

Organization on an action level of the HASI London, consists of the following activities, given in order of importance:

1. Books on Dianetics and Scientology in circulation (by sale to group courses, lot sales to auditors and bookstores).

2. Secure receipt and invoicing of mail, keeping it in a closed channel, handling it with accuracy and speed; dividing that mail into the three categories—orders, students and preclears and general, invoicing the first, logging and giving to Registrar the second and distributing then the third. Without accurate and responsible channeling, handling this comm line, there would be no need to set down another point since there would be no HASI.

3. Responding same day by the Registrar to all such inquiries by personal letter, not a canned letter.

4. Interviewing and booking all eligible applicants for training and processing with regard to internal schedules only when it does not inconvenience applicants. (Internal service is a problem we must continually solve, but it is our problem, not the public's.)

5. Filling all book orders and other cash orders promptly (same day) and giving good service and satisfaction on lost orders, etc. Acknowledging by card order has been sent.

6. Placing as many books as possible in the PE Course's hands.

7. Selling as many memberships as possible. Associates in particular.

8. Answering general enquiries by routine letter.

9. Bringing as many people as possible into PE Course (providing quarters as needed is our problem) and then selling these the Advanced Course.

10. Processing preclears with fullest possible gains, with good attention to precise keeping of appointments. No waiting.

11. Writing pcs we have processed by Registrar after one week, three weeks, three months as routine.

12. Keeping accurate and full files on every potential preclear and until signed up; and putting all pcs into file as potential students; and using file to develop prospects. (Registrar.)

13. Training students to high level of reality and result (the facilities and number of instructors is our problem, not the public's.)

14. Staying in good ARC with field auditors. Getting out magazines and mailings on time.

15. Handling general business affairs of HASI. Membership cards, addresses, certificates.

16. Keeping straight with government and Inland Revenue offices. And keeping in good order at the bank.

17. Keeping bad stories out of newspapers and squashing scandal.

18. Answering general correspondence.

19. Giving social affairs for staff.

Note again that the above are given carefully in order of importance.

L. RON HUBBARD
Founder

HUBBARD COMMUNICATIONS OFFICE
London

HCO POLICY LETTER OF 23 APRIL 1957

Association Sec
HCO Washington
Bulletin Board
Director of Admin,
London
Reception, London
Treasurer, London

HCO is now handling Secretarial and Reception for the Association Secretary as well as memberships.

This replaces HCO Policy Letter of 21 Apr. as issued recently.

L. RON HUBBARD
Founder

HCO POLICY LETTER OF 20 DECEMBER 1957

To All Staff
Post—Bulletin
Board

CLARIFICATION OF PUBLIC RELATIONS POST

On the organization board, HCO is shown as a separate operating unit from the Founding Church (HASI in London), with a liaison line to the Org Sec (Assoc Sec London).

HCO personnel, which includes Public Relations, report directly to HCO. Therefore, Public Relations reports its activities directly to HCO, maintaining a cooperative liaison with the Org Sec and Assoc Sec, as is shown on the org board.

Even though it is shown on the org board, it is called to your attention here that Public Relations is a part of HCO, directly responsible to HCO, working, of course, in cooperation with the Org Sec and Assoc Sec.

L. RON HUBBARD
Founder

FOUNDING CHURCH POLICY LETTER OF 19 MARCH 1958

TRANSPORTATION
DIR ADMIN RESPONSIBILITY

Director of Admin shall hereafter be personally responsible for the condition of all transportation, its use and allocation. He shall also be responsible for servicing and repairs.

He shall also allocate parking space.

L. RON HUBBARD
Founder

HCO POLICY LETTER OF 7 APRIL 1958

All Staff
Field Offices

ROUTING OF ORG BOARD CHANGES

A slight modification in the routing of organization board changes: To date, our procedure has been that Personnel despatches HCO. The only change now is that the despatch goes from:

Personnel to Assoc Sec (Org Sec)

Assoc Sec (Org Sec) to LRH

LRH to HCO Sec for posting.

In offices where I am not present, the despatch goes from Personnel to Assoc Sec, to HCO Sec.

L. RON HUBBARD
Founder

THE FOUNDING CHURCH OF SCIENTOLOGY
1812 19th Street NW, Washington, DC

FOUNDING CHURCH POLICY LETTER OF 9 OCTOBER 1958

DEPARTMENTS OF FCDC

Effective October 20, 1958 the departments of the Founding Church of Scientology of Washington, DC, shall be as follows:

The Academy of Scientology

The Hubbard Guidance Center

The Department of Procurement

The Department of Materiel

The Department of Business

The Trustees of the Founding Church of Scientology, Washington, DC, are, and will continue to be, President, Secretary, Treasurer.

The executives of the Founding Church of Scientology, Washington, DC, shall be:

Executive Director

Administrative Assistant to the Board (supplanting the post of "Org Sec")

Director of Training

Director of Processing

Director of Procurement

Director of Materiel

Director of Business

The Advisory Council shall be composed of the following executives only, or their authorized deputies:

Director of Training

Director of Processing

Director of Procurement

Director of Materiel

Director of Business

The Technical Division shall no longer have a Technical Director but shall be governed by a Technical Council which shall consist of the Director of Processing and the Director of Training.

The Administrative Division shall no longer be governed by a Director of Administration but shall be governed by an Administrative Council which shall be composed of the Director of Procurement, the Director of Materiel and the Director of Business.

The three departments of the Administrative Division shall be the Dept of Procurement, the Dept of Materiel and the Dept of Business.

The Dept of Procurement shall be headed by the Director of Procurement who must not be the Registrar. The Dept of Materiel shall be headed by the Director of Materiel. The Dept of Business shall be headed by the Director of Business.

These changes do not particularly affect the performance on post of any staff member but are made necessary by the difficulties of grouping various functions.

The organization is being readied to handle a new influx of students and results of other promotional activities.

Staff meeting mandate of September 23, 1958 required, "That no less than 10% of the Salary Sum be spent for dissemination personnel and that a dissemination personnel is to spend at least 70% of his time in dissemination." This required that all dissemination personnel be grouped under one department necessitating the above changes.

It will be noted that the changes more affect the chain of command than they affect individual post activity on the whole.

To this policy letter is added the requirements of meeting of the Advisory Council, the Technical Council and the Administrative Council. Each must hold a meeting once per week and its report must be forwarded up the chain of command to the next stage within 48 hours and must be held at least 3 days previous to the meeting of any council or board above it.

Executives may not absent themselves from the meetings of the Technical Council, Administrative Council or Advisory Council but may substitute a deputy from his or her department only for attendance at the meeting with the distinct understanding that the deputy has the full authority and vote at the meeting of the executive.

L. RON HUBBARD
Founder

HCO POLICY LETTER OF 13 DECEMBER 1958

To all Central
  Organizations
  and HCO Offices

IMPORTANT INFORMATION
ON POLICY LETTERS

No further HCO Policy Letters shall be distributed to Central Organizations or area organizations and go to HCO offices only and are for HCO offices only. If you get anything for an area operation it will be marked "Secretarial Executive Director." If you receive one of this character it can be published. You will receive exact instructions as to how to set up a Secretarial Executive Director. Repeat: Only policies so marked are to be given to Central Organizations. HCO Policy Letters are strictly for HCO and are for the most part confidential from this point even when not so marked. If marked "Confidential" they are not to be shown to any member or officer of the Central Organization.

HCO is becoming itself and has its own private communications lines by which it is effecting things in various parts of the world. If these lines are too exposed, it may be that the effectiveness of HCO may be reduced.

HCO Bulletins of a technical nature may be released to a Central Organization as an HCO Bulletin and should be, but are not intended for field auditors or organization members outside and must not be released to field auditors and organization members even by the Central Organization. If a Central Organization reprints and releases an HCO Bulletin given to them by an HCO office, the act is subject to reprimand by HCO.

Under the classification of confidential are the following recent releases from London and are included in this HCO Policy Letter:

Confidential Memo to HCO Secretaries—29 Nov. 58, FUTURE PROGRAMS
HCO Bulletin of 1 Dec. 58, ACTIONS TO START AN HCO
BASIC FINANCIAL POLICY of 27 Nov. 58
HCO Policy Letter of 15 Nov. 58, THE SUBSTANCE AND FIRST DUTY
    OF HCO
HCO Policy Letter Issue III of 15 Nov. 58, LEGAL AID, HCO
HCO Policy Letter Issue II of 15 Nov. 58, OUTSTANDING COPYRIGHTS
    AND MARKS

Definition of an HCO area office: An office of a duly enfranchised Central Organization manned by an actual HCO Secretary and her staff as it may exist. The following offices are bona fide HCO offices and are included in distribution of HCO Policy Letters: HCO London, HCO Washington, HCO Melbourne. The following offices are not at this time qualified HCO offices even though they are carried on distribution lists for technical bulletins and all distribution to them is suspended until they are awarded total status: HCO Auckland, NZ; HCO Johannesburg, SA; HCO Los Angeles; HCO Sydney; HCO Perth; HCO Durban; HCO New York; HCO France; HCO Germany.

As soon as an HCO office is regularized and exists in fact, it will be published as additive to the distribution list. Any communication between actual HCO offices and the list of areas which are in process of being regularized shall be henceforth devoted entirely and only to the establishment of proper HCO offices and the proper enfranchisement of a Central Organization which will be done by HCO Ltd., London.

L. RON HUBBARD
Founder

HCO POLICY LETTER OF 27 FEBRUARY 1959

DUTY OF AREA SEC RE PERSONNEL

The Area Sec provides and puts hats on Central Org personnel, and is responsible to see that hats are provided, *are* put on (repeatedly if necessary) and are changed or turned in when personnel changes.

The Assoc Sec or Org Sec procures persons, puts them bodily on post, puts the person's hands on the equipment or mest of the job, handles pay, supervises the actual conduct of work (gets the work done), sees that the proper hours are kept, etc., and changes, transfers or dismisses the personnel.

These two functions are distinctly different and must not overlap.

L. RON HUBBARD
Founder

HCO POLICY LETTER OF 1 MARCH 1959

HCO Personnel
Assoc Sec London

HCO FORBIDDEN ACTIVITIES

No HCO or HCO Sec, full or part time, may do the administrative work of a Central Org or its personnel.

This means also that no HCO Sec may do letters, correspondence, filing, reception, mailing, phoning for an Assoc Sec, Org Sec or dept head.

This is so forbidden that entrance upon these activities or permitting a Central Org head or officer to use HCO for secretarial actions can cause the immediate dismissal of an HCO Sec or personnel.

When such use of HCO has been allowed, chaos has resulted and the HCO office has become nullified and my lines cut. Therefore, it is looked upon in a very serious light.

L. RON HUBBARD
Founder

HCO POLICY LETTER OF 30 APRIL 1959
Issue II

LONG–DISTANCE PROGRAM

Convert the following Sec ED to a local Sec ED, and use it as follows:

Issue a copy of this Sec ED to every staff member.

The HCO Sec will then have a staff meeting and read the Sec ED aloud.

The HCO Sec is then to have them put away copies of the Sec ED present, and issue blank pieces of paper and pencils, and give the whole staff and executives an examination by saying, "Write down now every point of this program. Sign your name at the top and hand it in when complete."

On the following day call another staff meeting. Read this Sec ED aloud, tell them to put away copies of it, issue paper, and give exam.

One week later do the same thing only this time be sure to have every exam paper signed. Grade these exam papers and airmail the lot to me.

SECRETARIAL TO THE EXECUTIVE DIRECTOR
(Local Area)

OUR LONG–DISTANCE PROGRAM
THE WAY WE'LL CLEAR (CONTINENT)

1. Function departmentally and effectively, each doing his job well.

2. Encourage HAS Co-audits run by missions in every populated area.

3. Grab off the name and address of each person who does an HAS course in the field by smartly issuing every HAS certificate called for by a field "mission holder" and get the names smartly into CF and onto address plates.

4. Mail routine minor *Ability*s each twentieth of the month to everyone in the CF address-file list.

5. Stress being the main org in every issue to make people newly receiving *Ability* aware of services offered.

6. Run a Central Organization PE Foundation HAS Co-audit Course to discourage town auditors from poaching and to get a training ground for students, and do our own PE HAS Co-audit *well*.

7. Teach the new HCA Course I've just made and teach it well.

8. Process only toward Theta Clear and say so (as field co-audit people will want to get cleared finally when they're fully released by co-audit).

This is the basic program on which we are working. It's time we all got busy on clearing all (name continent).

Only irresponsibility and failure to do one's job can keep this organization down.

I am doing my job.

It's only just that I expect you to do yours.

If we all do our jobs well together, we'll make it and have a cleared Earth.

L. RON HUBBARD
Founder

HCO POLICY LETTER OF 26 MAY 1959

TO DEPARTMENT HEADS

Each department head assumes responsibility for his department. This means ensuring that each member of his staff knows his hat fully and is willing and able to carry out the duties therein. Where consistent misduplication or hold-up occurs, investigate, understand and rectify. Watch out for veers on all department lines. Re-allocate duties when necessary. When something goes wrong, YOU do something to put it right. Department heads have the right to hire or fire their own staff with the approval of the Assoc Sec.

In order to coordinate the purpose and function of departments, a short meeting of department heads will be held daily. The Assoc Sec will be present at these meetings. Minutes will only be taken at the regular Ad Comm meeting on Tuesdays, when no other meeting need be held.

The purpose and function of departments is to provide a public service and help in the dissemination of Scientology. There is a responsibility in this which affects everyone. Therefore be causative against destructive forces. Every person in each department shares and owns the purpose of the department.

This is what I expect from each department head:

Training: Lots of students graduated, well trained, with a high reality on Scientology and the ability to run HAS Co-audits and the ability to theta clear individual pcs.

Processing: To undercut the reality of all cases and to theta clear as many cases as possible.

PrR: To get in the income for the org as a chief responsibility. To sign up as many students and pcs as possible.

Materiel: To provide quarters and materiel to get the work done—to keep CF serviceable for PrR and Address useful for *Certainty,* membership and statements.

Accounts: To get the income accounted for and into the bank, to pay the bills accurately and keep good records and to raise the devil with PrR if income is too low, with Materiel and printing if the bills are too high and with legal if collections are not made.

PE Foundation: To run an amazingly successful HAS Co-audit course, to keep new people coming in and the Co-audit growing at least five new people per week and all cases cracked and everyone keen to get trained further or cleared fully in the HGC.

In general, get more done, get the show on the road, be in on time and make Scientology felt by digging the grooves deeper.

We've got it made with administration and technology. We can take the whole of UK. Well, let's *do* it!

L. RON HUBBARD
Founder

ORGANIZATION OF CORPORATIONS

The terminals of an organization must approximate to some degree the goals of an organization. The communication lines of organizations must parallel the action lines. The traffic flow in any given organization must be approximated by the positions of terminals and their communication lines.

An organization could be said to be as real as it approximated the realities of its activities. If the organization does not well approximate these realities, then it has a low level of reality to the personnel working in it.

Further theory on the reorganization of organizations consists of the fact that certain organizational departments are engaged in business activities; certain are engaged in public relations; and certain departments are engaged entirely in the handling of programs already put into action on a board level.

The consistent failure of programs to produce results lies in the fact that the execution of these programs has not been given sufficient dignity. Thus no matter how well the programs were planned or what they consisted of, the persons actually entrusted with the execution of the programs were not permitted to carry them forward uninterruptedly. Thus a confusion of thinking has existed in the organization and a rather large absence of doingness.

For example, we give very little thought to the department known as "shipping." This shipping function is apparently something which is under executive management and has in itself no executive prerogatives. This is contrary to the reality of the situation. The action of shipping is part of the action of dissemination; part of the action of executing certain programs which have been laid down. Certainly the execution of the program should be given as much dignity and as much standing as the planning of that program.

We discover in inspecting executive function that what we think of ordinarily as an executive is someone who sits at a desk and handles a great deal of inflow. If this is the case, we could then make a graph in which we could draw a small circle on a piece of paper and point a great many arrows at it. By the very reason of inflow on this "executive" level, outflow becomes somewhat difficult. If we go off to the side from this first circle and arrows, and draw another circle with arrows emanating from it, we would have a program execution picture. This is very largely outflow. Probably the impulse of the business and planning sections to stop or change the outflow programs stems in the main from this disproportion of flows. Only we in Scientology would understand this and only we in Scientology can do something about it.

L. RON HUBBARD
Founder

CenOCon

KEY TO THE ORGANIZATIONAL CHART
OF THE FOUNDING CHURCH OF SCIENTOLOGY
OF WASHINGTON, DC

This is the organizational chart of the Central Organization of Scientology in the United States.

It is kept to date by Sec'l ED under the directions of only the Executive Director.

Any changes believed necessary should be written as a despatch and sent to Sec'l ED.

This board has the force of assignment and is the primary means of assigning personnel in the organization. This board is the publication authority for assignment to post.

This is not a communication chart.

Communication may be accomplished at any time by anyone to anyone but is official only through the Communication Center by proper despatch. If it's not a written despatch it isn't an order.

Board planned and organized by LRH with the assistance of Sec'l ED.

The above is typed on a 3 x 5 white card (takes 2). Along with this is the following, also on 3 x 5 white card, with appropriate colors pasted on as indicated below.

Trustees are in red.

Executives are in blue.

Staff members and posts are in white.

A solid red line — means a Founding Church chain of command.

A dotted red line .... means liaison.

A solid blue line — means another corporation or office.

Where a red flag appears on board there has been a change of post within the past week.

(Note: "Executives" are Dept Heads and anyone who attends the Advisory Council.)

Here are the purposes of various posts and depts in the FC of S of Wash, DC as shown on the org board.

Note: The org bd shows name of post, followed underneath by purpose, followed underneath by person's name. Examples:

Organization Secretary
Purpose: "............"
Name of Person

Comm Course Instructor
Purpose: "............"
Name of Person

Founding Church of Scientology

Purpose: To disseminate Scientology. To advance and protect its membership. To hold the lines and data of Scientology clean and clear. To educate and process people toward the goal of a civilized age on Earth second to none. To survive on all dynamics.

Founding Church Congregation

Purpose: To communicate to the congregation the principles and philosophy of Scientology. To ensure for each individual an awareness of their health, happiness and immortality through good training, processing and fellowship.

Staff Meeting

Purpose: To gather agreement and permit staff origination upon matters relating to personnel and duties. To report on performance of duties. To suggest promotional, maintenance and organizational changes to FC executives.

Organization Secretary

Purpose: To get people to get the work done. To enforce the policies and advise the Board.

Advisory Council

Purpose: To advise the executives of the organization as to needed changes and policies. To act as a meeting ground for department heads. To assemble and report the statistics of finance and action to the Executive Director. To advance ideas for promotion and improvement.

L. Ron Hubbard, Founder (Location of this on org bd is at very top of HCO.)

Purpose: To develop and disseminate Scientology. To support and assist Scientologists. To write better books. To act as a court of appeals in all organizational disputes. To form and to make official policies and orders affecting the Founding Church.

Hubbard Communications Office

Purpose: To be the office of LRH. To handle and expedite the communication lines of LRH. To prepare or handle the preparation of manuscripts and other to-be-published material of Scientology. To keep, use and care for LRH's office equipment. To assist the organizations of Scientology and their people. To set a good example of efficiency to organizations.

Public Relations (under HCO)

Purpose: To maintain and increase good public relations for the organizations of Dianetics and Scientology.

Editorial Director (under HCO)

Purpose: To keep the material in publications within organization policy, and to prepare publishable material.

HCO Communicator

Purpose: To keep the communication lines flowing and the files in order in HCO.

HCO Board of Review

Purpose: To validate for full results every certificate ever issued in Dianetics and Scientology. To be the final authority on any certificates to be issued. To be the final authority on Clear certification.

TECHNICAL DIVISION

Purpose: To ensure good training and processing, good service and ARC inside and outside the organization.

(Note: Under this is then listed: "TECHNICAL COUNCIL
Dir of Training
Dir of Processing")

Academy of Scientology

Purpose: To train the best auditors in the world.

Training Administrator

Purpose: To keep the materials and comm lines of the Academy in good order. To keep a roll book. To prepare and collect certification materials.

Hubbard Clearing Scientologist Course

Purpose: To educate auditors in the techniques and skills necessary to clear human beings.

Communication Course

Purpose: To give people a reality on Scientology and to teach the communication formula by dummy auditing.

Upper Indoctrination Course

Purpose: To attain ability to handle bodies, objects and intentions fully.

Theory and Practice Course

Purpose: To create a competent auditor with a good grasp of theory and practice of Scientology. All five levels of Indoc.

Hubbard Guidance Center

Purpose: To do more for people's health and ability than has ever before been possible and to give the best auditing possible. To help people.

Processing Administrator

Purpose: To handle the persons, communications and materials of the HGC to the end of improving and continuing the quality and business of the HGC.

Scientometric Testing In-Charge

Purpose: To give all and any tests or exams that may be required to any department or organization or personnel, and to keep and file results accurately to assist research and presentation, and to have test materials in abundance to hand.

Personal Efficiency Foundation

Purpose: To run an amazingly successful HAS Co-audit Course, to keep new people coming in and the co-audit growing, at least five new people per week, and cases cracked and everyone to get trained further or cleared fully in the HGC.

ADMINISTRATIVE DIVISION

Purpose: To ensure good and accurate communication inside organization. To handle business and administrative affairs. To ensure good working quarters and conditions for and good work from organizational personnel.

Note: underneath this is shown:

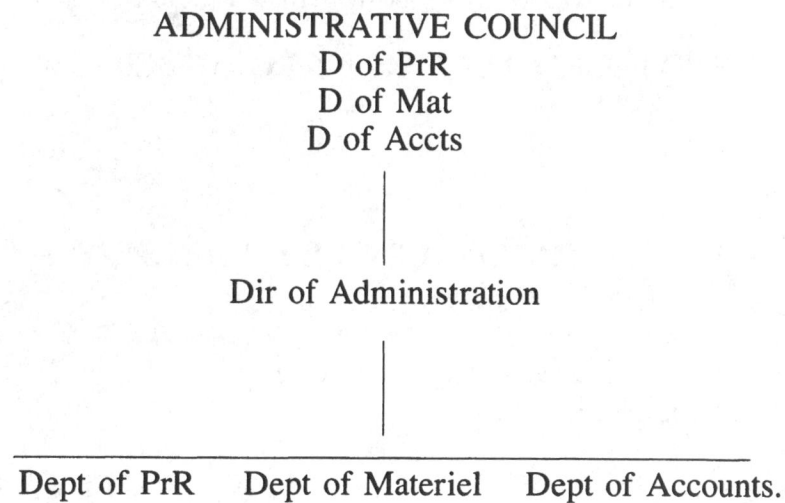

ADMINISTRATIVE COUNCIL
D of PrR
D of Mat
D of Accts

Dir of Administration

Dept of PrR   Dept of Materiel   Dept of Accounts.

Dept of Promotion & Registration

Purpose: To procure students and preclears by actual, direct and personal contact using personal letters and assuring an adequate number of students and preclears.

Reception

Purpose: To create and maintain good communication and service amongst staff, students and public.

Dept of Materiel

Purpose: To hold in readiness and good repair all the communication materiel, files, addresses, furniture, equipment, quarters and transport necessary to adequate function of the organization.

Dept of Accounts

Purpose: To keep the business affairs of the organization in good order, to maintain the good business repute of the organization and to see to it that the business activities of Scientology are up-to-date in an excellent condition. To make sure that income exceeds outgo.

Disbursement Clerk

Purpose: Break down income into proportions; validate bills; issue checks.

Legal

Purpose: To make legal the actions of the organizations of Dianetics and Scientology and safeguard their public and private interests.

L. RON HUBBARD
Founder

HCO POLICY LETTER OF 22 OCTOBER 1960
Issue II

THE THREE SERVICE BRANCHES

HASI now has three service branches. Two are paid, one is free. These are Testing, Training and Processing.

Training and Processing are the two paid services. Testing is the free service.

These three services take precedence in quarters, personnel and general activity.

All other services rendered are of secondary importance and, indeed, are important only to the degree that they make these three services work and to make sure they are adequately used.

The most important administrative department is Promotion and Registration. This department ensures a flow of bodies into testing and from testing to training and processing.

Materiel is the next most important department, furnishing as it does mest— quarters, supplies, files and addresses—to the service units.

Accounts is the next most important function, taking care of the receipts and disbursements and payrolls.

PE, as a procurement activity, continues. Its future function will be to give a basic evening course based on the Anatomy of the Human Mind, using Academy-type instruction. PE shall continue as a department in those areas where it has done well. In those areas where it has not contributed, the Academy will absorb its functions of training, PrR will absorb its procurement and HCO its open evenings.

Other activities also continue.

The basic plan of a Central Org does not shift and alters only in emphasis.

Personnel may be increased, cut, shifted or deleted in a Central Org on the sole authority of the Assoc Sec or Org Sec to accomplish any such readjustments.

The least affected organization is Washington, DC, as it does the least local procurement and probably will not materially increase its Testing Department at this time.

L. RON HUBBARD
Founder

HCO POLICY LETTER OF 28 OCTOBER 1960
Issue II

HASI–HCO RELATIONSHIP DISCUSSED

I had a meeting today between the officers of HCO and HASI in Johannesburg which brought up some points of interest to all HCOs and Central Organizations.

The points of importance were these:

Central Orgs have certain fixed promotion lines which should be followed. HCOs have some interest in the effectiveness of these. HCO has *no* interest in the number of personnel employed by HASI in tech or admin, this being entirely up to the Central Org officers. If HASI thinks it can get along with far less and still render service acceptable to HCO, then it's all up to HASI.

Central Orgs as such have a poor reputation for originating and executing new promotion. HCO is responsible for broad, new dissemination projects.

I have always operated on the theory that if I drove enough business in on Central Orgs they would cope with it, and that I should not be deterred by various resistances in the form of thinking it could not be coped with.

Thereby emerges HCO's primary function today—to do broad dissemination and drive business in on the Central Org by any means within HCO's power.

HCO's role stems logically from my own most consistent functions: (a) technology and its proper performance and (b) promotion of Scientology widely by books and ideas and creating comm lines.

Whenever HCO falls away from these two items, the Central Org has rough financial going. Lack of technical wins gives fast stagnation and few excellent personnel. Lack of heavy dissemination gives a lack of bodies in the shop.

On promotion, driving in people on the Central Org is a primary function. This does not mean individual people. It means masses of people. HCO deals in masses and mobs, and HASI deals in individuals.

HCO must carry out heavy book promotion and sale, many special events (open evenings, lectures, congresses), new effective mass comm lines (magazines, etc.) and must furnish new ideas.

HASI comm lines are set and fixed already. New lines disturb proven-effective HASI lines when HASI does them. HASI is helped when HCO does them.

HCO's interest in HASI personnel ends with making sure the business HCO drives in is not wasted. Hence hat checks, Security Checks. But HCO may not interfere with actual personnel selection or dismissal except to act as a justice on complaints from personnel, and then HCO may be going too far even so.

HCO is a *mass dissemination* organization. HASI is an *individual service* organization.

The primary breakdown in any org is technical excellence. When this goes, all else soon follows or stays low. The primary lack of income comes from HCO failure to widely disseminate and hold special events that bring people to HASI for HASI to approach and care for. Almost as important an income failure source is HASI's failure to contact often (from PrR) individuals HCO has drummed up by mass programs.

When HCO lays down how many people HASI must or must not hire, it errs.

HCO is the "Madison Avenue" of Scientology, meaning it's the advertising, broad-public-presence unit. But "Madison Avenue" does not run the businesses it serves. It only makes them look brighter to the potential public.

I think this gives us a new look at HASI–HCO relationships and their zones of responsibility.

I laid down these principles to clarify the problems which had arisen between HASI and HCO in Johannesburg, and I feel the same principles may resolve and reorient many areas of overlap or dispute in other orgs.

I consider these points as new policy for sorting out the two areas of HASI and HCO.

However, nothing in this policy letter exists to prevent HCO from taking sudden and heavy action to remedy obvious or possible collapses on HASI's part in handling the business brought in.

L. RON HUBBARD
Founder

HCO POLICY LETTER OF 16 JANUARY 1961

All HCOs
All Central Orgs
HCO Area—Call a whole
   staff meeting, read,
   issue and discuss

HELP ME PUT IN THE NEW LINES

We are about to execute some fundamental changes in Central Orgs. For years Central Orgs have had trouble promoting and procuring. After months and day-and-night work in Johannesburg, I have resolved this. It can work everywhere, according to early reports.

I am about to write up all the lines and hats of this new setup.

We already have technology wrapped up if it is followed. Ten hours of tape are coming to you from DC for use in training HGCs. It is our first complete package of technology, fully tested, fully vindicated. It has yet to be fully understood or used. It must be trained in on all staff auditors and all new auditors coming on staff. It is all there on the tapes.

In admin, the new test lines are watch-like construction.

If we get too much alter-is, too much "changed because this area is different," too many additives, we'll all be in a spin. My own admin lines will become wholly unmanageable.

I will try to be as clear as I can be. *If it isn't written into the lineup, it isn't there.* For instance, there is *no* phone number given in the IQ ad, but DC put one in its ad and got no bodies, only floods of phone calls. I had to cable DC to get the phone number out of the ad so people would walk in. For instance, an Instructor trying to grasp Formula 13 wanted to know if you crossed off a name from its assessment list when it was briefly run. Nothing was said about this in the HCO Bulletin therefore you don't cross off names.

Additives have been the most source of most scrambling to date. People add things that aren't there.

Alter-is is the other sinner. I call for small, 18-inch square tables in testing—large rectangular tables get bought, potential capacity of test room is cut in half.

People want to know what's the authority of HCO. Its earliest genus was the need to get new lineups in place in Central Orgs. Broadly, HCO is my office in an area. As Executive Director, I am usually the one to put in new departments, promotions, ideas and lineups. HCO is there to make sure they go in smoothly without omission, additives, alter-is or misunderstanding. Once these are in, they can be run by my Association Secretary in that area. HCO is there to make Ron's postulates stick. That's its most vital action. My postulates are contained in HCO Bulletins and HCO Policy Letters.

You have to have cooperation from everyone to make an organization work. But there has to be a workable organization there before it can be worked. Group-think never created an organization that worked. Hence, I put them in and modify only after long study.

Frankly, I could not function at all without HCOs and cooperation. I am tackling a huge job—the shift of Central Org patterns all over the world and putting in new Central Orgs.

You can help by putting in the lineup as laid down, without alteration or omission or additives. Only when it is *all* in and in right can you see whether or not it works or how it works. *After* it has been working for a long time, we can discuss refining it.

To make this new boom stick, we have to line up technical excellence first, making sure every pc that signs up gets full reality and case gain. Then we groove in the new PE Foundation under a competent director. Then we make very sure of our Academy for future auditor supply.

To do these things, I am already furnishing you lots of unchanging gen. You are on a high level of stability now, tech and admin both. The only way we could fail is to fail to get the exact mock-up in and working. Then it's lots of people, high units and we're away.

And I'm depending on HCO to make my postulates stick, on staffs to cooperate and on Association and Org Secs to help the new policies take form and to run them sensibly and accurately after they are squared away.

That's our program. Help me get it in shape.

L. RON HUBBARD
Founder

HCO POLICY LETTER OF 14 FEBRUARY 1961
Issue II

CenOCon
Missions
Field

THE PATTERN OF A CENTRAL ORGANIZATION

The following is a summary of all parts of a Central Organization* for use in Permanent Staff qualifications and in departments.

HCO AREA OFFICE

An HCO Area Office is attached to each Central Organization.

It expedites internal and external communications and in particular communications to and from HCO WW and myself.

As part of communications supervision it hat checks into existence with staff members HCO Bulletins, HCO Policy Letters and other official releases.

It issues and keeps to date the organization hats. HCO Area keeps the org board.

Fundamentally it is also a library of technical and administrative data consisting of books, mimeos, tapes and general know-how.

HCO Area has the power to take action to maintain a high technical level, a good administrative form in the organization and to security check personnel.

It examines students and issues certificates through its HCO Board of Review.

Mainly through the HCO Continental of a continent it reaches broad masses of the public where a Central Organization reaches individual members of the public.

The whole activity of an HCO Area Office is communication, collection, local book sales, technical level, administrative form, ethics, certificates and awards. To this, through HCO Continental, is added broad promotion and dissemination such as public book sales, the magazine, ads and special events.

THE ASSOCIATION SECRETARY'S OFFICE

The Assoc Secretary runs the Central Organization. He is usually assisted by a secretary who expedites his comm, writes his letters and gets in his reports for the OIC and keeps it.

Personnel procurement and placement, financial management, legal actions (including press), valuable documents, and the OIC board are some of the administrative functions of this office.

*[See the six–department org board, in the appendix.]

199

Proper operation, willing performance of duty of its executives and personnel, its ample financial solvency and general high effectiveness of the technical and administrative functions of the Central Organization are all the responsibility of the Association Secretary.

The Association Secretary is looked upon to keep the organization in existence and functioning at a high level. HCO helps but the final responsibility of keeping an organization going is the Association Secretary's.

He has a Dept of Official Affairs (Government Relations) to help him with legal, if required.

TWO DIVISIONS

There are two *divisions* in a Central Organization. One is TECHNICAL, the senior division, the other is ADMINISTRATIVE. There are six *departments*. The TECHNICAL DIVISION includes these three *departments:* The PE Foundation, the Academy of Scientology and the Hubbard Guidance Center. These carry out the three basic services of a Central Organization—public training and processing, individual training and individual processing.

THE *ADMINISTRATIVE* DIVISION consists of three departments: Promotion and Registration, Materiel and Accounts. These care for the three basic functions of contacting and signing up people, taking care of quarters and supplies, and handling all matters of finance.

TECHNICAL DIVISION

The Personal Efficiency Foundation

The PE Foundation is the entrance door of the public into the services of the Central Organization, a knowledge of Scientology and a higher level of civilization.

Test Section

By means of advertising mailings and word of mouth, the public is brought in to be tested and evaluated. This is done by the *Test Section* of the PE Foundation. This section does everything possible to route new individuals into a PE Course.

PE Course Section

A five evening PE Course is given weekly. Its curriculum is precisely laid down. Its total purpose is to explain elementary Scientology and prepare and route people into the co-audit.

The HAS Co-audit Section

Using precise processes developed for this section only, the HAS Co-audit (Do It Yourself Processing) seeks to improve cases and further interest people in Scientology so that they will take individual HGC processing and individual training.

Summary of the PE Foundation

The PE Foundation is an entrance point to Scientology. If it fails to pass people from testing to a PE Course, from a PE Course to co-audit and from co-audit to the Academy and HGC then it is failing its functions, the unit will be low and the Central Organization faltering.

No section of the PE is an end-all where the public feels an action has been completed. That the PE Foundation in itself does a great deal of good is indisputable. However, the moment it relaxes on this fact and fails to pass people along, it lets down every staff member in the other five departments as well as its own people. A PE Foundation income is not adequate to support even itself and its services in training and processing are not wholly adequate to functioning in life. It is an entrance door. It must be alertly watched. Its numbers in testing, PE Course and co-audit today are the organization's units and Scientology's people tomorrow.

The PE Director is now, next to the Assoc Secretary, the most responsible person for solvency in a Central Organization.

The Academy of Scientology

Headed by the Director of Training, the Academy is responsible for the technical excellence of Scientology practice tomorrow.

Teaching two different courses in the same classes, the Academy trains Hubbard Practical Scientologists and Hubbard Professional (HPA/HCA) Auditors.

The Academy also teaches an upper-level course once or more a year known as the BScn (Hubbard Clearing Scientologist) Course.

Precise scheduling, crisp training and true, direct answers to the students' questions makes an Academy.

The HPA/HCA Course enrolls more or less every Monday unless the total average unit is to be gained expensively through individual processing only.

The practical course is the same as the old professional course except that it is for people "who don't want to practice Scientology professionally." The professional course is a tougher version with more requirements.

A bad Academy results in a bad HGC tomorrow as many graduates become staff auditors.

A good Academy is known by its snappy scheduling and the degree of basic data and action the student actually absorbs.

The Hubbard Guidance Center

The HGC is headed by the Director of Processing, under whom come all individual cases (public and staff). The D of P is the case czar of the organization.

The D of P's total administration is done by HGC Admin. The D of P does not do admin, only technical, but is in charge of admin and all staff auditors and the department.

The D of P (or in case of more than 30 pcs/week, a Deputy D of P) interviews HGC cases every five hours of processing to establish the quality of goals and rudiments and what the auditor is running.

HGC Admin procures and assigns auditors, gives applicants from the Registrar their case estimates, keeps the files of cases, oversees proper auditor handling of forms, oversees testing or gets it done for HGC pcs when PE testing is closed, finds and assigns rooms for auditing and keeps, in general, the lines moving in the HGC.

If the D of P does these things or worse, takes preclears to process, you don't have an HGC. You have a technical collapse.

HGC quality *must* be high and stay high. It is the highest technical quality on the continent.

An HGC staff auditor audits directly on current rundown and produces high case gains. HGC staff auditors are the most respected auditors in Scientology and for a period of eleven years have always gotten the highest, fastest results in Dianetics and Scientology.

A staff auditor may refuse to process or refuse to release from processing any pc.

The HGC was born to show field auditors the results that could be obtained, and lived on to carry the full burden of successful auditing around the world.

ADMINISTRATIVE DIVISION

Dept of Promotion and Registration

D of PrR is headed by a Director of PrR only in the largest of Central Organizations. Otherwise its two sections are headed by Registrars—the Personal Registrar and the Letter Registrar.

Personal Registration Section

The Personal Registration Section finds and signs up applicants for the Academy and the HGC.

The section includes one or more Personal Registrars, the Receptionist and, for admin purposes, various admin personnel in the Technical Division. It is headed by the Chief Registrar.

For public purposes (and possibly in a future change), all registrars may be called or sign themselves as "Consultants."

The whole actual income of the Central Organization is dependent upon the activity and excellence of the Chief Registrar, just as its *potential* income depends upon PE and the Letter Registrar. If PE and the Letter Registrar do not get them in, it is still up to the Chief Registrar to do so. The Assoc Sec receives the total income report from the Chief Registrar each week as part of the Personal Registration Section report.

The Personal Registrars interview applicants, sign them up on contracts and releases and take their money for individual training and processing. When prospects seem too few, Personal Registrars go back over "hot files" and by phone or other means, seek to get people in.

A Personal Registrar cannot accept applicants finally for training and processing. This is done by the D of T and HGC Admin. The applicant when fully signed up is sent to Technical. HGC Admin may demand more hours be signed for after assessment (not test) by E-Meter—if so the Personal Registrar signs them up for more, adding the hours to the contracts and taking in more money.

Personal Registrars are entitled to view the profiles of HGC and Academy results.

A Personal Registrar always interviews a student or HGC pc *after* training or HGC processing and usually nets some 50 percent of an org's income for additional sign-up in these "after interviews."

The motto of a Personal Registrar is "Always sell something, even if only a book."

Unfortunately, Personal Registrars have "income ceilings" for the org. Any given Registrar may "pin" the week's income at a certain figure. This has to do with acceptance level on money. A Registrar must be wholly free on money or this will happen.

Registrars are admin not technical personnel but usually the best Registrars are good auditors. However, they may not assign times of processing for the HGC, nor may they criticize HGC results to a pc. If Registrars are dissatisfied with results, the matter is brought up in Ad Comm or taken to the Assoc Sec or even the HCO Sec, if no remedy is forthcoming.

The Letter Registration Section

The Letter Registrar is in charge of the Letter Registration Section of PrR.

The Letter Registrar and assistants keep a steady flow of letters going to applicants to get them to come in for training and processing.

Income is proportional to the number of letters mailed a few weeks previously.

To send out his or her letters, information packages and other mail material such as projects, the Letter Registrar has executive charge of all typists, Central Files, Address, Mail Room and Memberships.

Typing Pool

Anything to do with getting letters written and mailed or sending out mailings or mail projects is wholly under the Letter Registrar.

All typing and typists are under the Chief Typist.

Central Files Unit

All files on Scientologists or applicants are under Central Files In-Charge. These include a file folder for everyone who has ever *bought* anything from the Central Org. The files are divided into live and inactive files. Magazines go out only to live files. But letters may be written to persons in both live and inactive files. Everything about a person, except his financial statements, actual training record and test record is in CF, but data even on these, such as a profile sheet, can be included. For instance, a copy of an invoice, the profile of a new test taken, a notice of certification, all are forwarded to CF for filing.

Address Unit

Under Address In-Charge, the up-to-date addresses of all persons in the live and inactive files of CF are kept readily usable on a proper address machine.

Address In-Charge is always ready to give any unit or department a complete card file complete with designations on persons in whom that function is interested.

Address In-Charge receives a copy of all invoices before they go to CF to make proper address changes or bring designations up to date.

All mailing and mail functions of the organization properly come under Address In-Charge. This is external mailings. The internal despatch system can also be included here if in use.

All franking machinery also comes under Address In-Charge as well as stamps and their safekeeping.

Memberships

Memberships (as well as the issue of HAS Certificates) come under the Letter Registrar and are normally handled in the Address Unit.

Summary of Letter Reg Section

The writing of letters, the packaging of info packets, accumulation of mailing lists and the handling of all files and addresses is a highly developed activity in Central Orgs. It is enormously important since a Central Organization income, even when PE is running well, is forecast by the volume of this section. Volume has long since proven to be more important than quality in the mailing of letters and packages. Any comm is better than no comm, as facts and figures have proven for years. Of course quality plays its role here too. Autumn 1960 data on how to write letters exists and should be followed.

Healing ARC breaks is a function of the Letter Registrar.

Preventing ARC breaks from happening by proper designations and address and memberships is all part of this unit.

This section receives its mail at once after invoice and receives copies of all invoices. You can't expect high outflow and deny the section its inflow. Mail important to Personal Registration is quickly answered by Letter Reg and passed to Personal Registration when it has to do with people stating they will come in.

There is only one Central Files. Personal Registration may have folders, but just to use, not to keep. When a folder goes out of CF, a dummy folder is slipped back in, so marked as to tell where the real folder went. Anything to be filed while the main folder is gone is put in the off-color dummy and placed back in the main folder when it returns.

Card files from Address rather than CF folders are used by other departments than the Letter Reg Section.

Dept of Materiel

Headed by the Director of Materiel (Dir Mat) the Dept of Materiel owns every mest object including pieces of paper in the entire organization and is responsible for its inventory, existence and good repair and usage.

Materiel sets up and clears away rooms, keeps the place clean, maintains everything, orders and supervises construction and even procures new office or auditing space. If it's mest, take it up with Materiel. If it's service or significance or personnel, take it up elsewhere.

Materiel does all purchasing for the organization.

Purchasing can be done only after a dept head and Assoc Sec approval on a purchase order, no matter how small the item. The greatest single threat to organization survival has been purchasing by Materiel without proper judgment and authorization by purchase order. Both Washington and London have been all but crushed by this function done wrongly. Joburg, purchasing with bad judgment, wound up with very little materiel despite huge bills. Purchasing is a fine art and in Central Orgs a primary threat if done too abundantly or wrong. Purchasing can be so bad that the organization can go broke while acquiring nothing. Further, enough money to pay its bills and have things is a better index for necessary income than the unit. If the disbursement fund is kept more than adequate, the unit will also be high. Financial management includes what is to be bought. When it's okayed by the Assoc Sec, Materiel can buy it. But if Materiel, in liaison with Accounts, sees danger in buying, Materiel must take it up with the Assoc Sec with more figures even if the Assoc Sec has already okayed it.

The biggest potential upset in Materiel next to purchasing is "job completion." An organization can be torn apart if each job, started, is not finished before new jobs are begun. Unfinished jobs can upset everything. They must be avoided.

Materiel should be given proper schedules of activities so that rooms can be set up or auditoriums procured well ahead of schedule.

Cleanliness of quarters is a public point of acceptance of Scientology.

Dir Mat is a highly responsible job. It can make or break an organization.

Headed by the Director of Accounts, the Dept of Accounts receives, safeguards and expends funds in the organization. No other person can expend money, though others can receive it if it is promptly handed to Accounts.

Scientology orgs had trouble with accounts until a special accounting system for Central Orgs was developed. That system is of a vital nature to the Accounts Dept and must be followed without additives, ponderous ledgers, peculiar subsystems or deletions.

A Scientology accounts system is simple. It works. It consists of writing an invoice on a four-copy machine for everything received and a disbursement voucher on a four-copy disbursement machine for everything expended, even petty cash, with a complete statement of what Accounts knows of the expenditure.

The system consists of four files—one with a file for every creditor, one with a file for every debtor, one with a complete file for every bank account and one with a file for every weekly breakdown envelope.

A board with nails on it for pinning up invoices for every category on the breakdown sheet and a book to put income sheets in plus an adding machine and cabinets completes the entire system.

Then if Accounts will file every piece of paper, letter, invoice, voucher and receipt that comes in in these files properly, anybody can summarize them and financial management becomes possible.

Monthly, on a mimeo sheet that bears the name of every creditor, all bills are listed from the creditor file (not from bills mailed in by firms) added up and presented to the Assoc Sec with bank statements for his directions as to payment.

A similar mimeo sheet is made up of debtors each month and the amounts they owe us.

Pay is paid not by check but in cash by the signature of the staff member on a disbursement voucher that tells the whole tangled story. Staff members each have a folder in the creditor file at the back in which copies of the voucher are filed.

A chartered or certified accountant can always do a quarterly balance sheet for the Central Org rapidly from these files if they are kept up and are as designated.

We don't copy figures from figures into vast piles of daybooks, ledgers, statements and other mysteries unknown. The files *are* these books. The law demands *records* everywhere. These are the records we want.

When people pay on their bills, invoice it, (send them the white with their next statement) and file it in their file folder.

Our weekly breakdown sheet, showing gross and units, amounts deposited to salary sum, disbursement account, building fund must be displayed to the staff each week on a staff bulletin board.

We are interested in complete, orderly files and their individual summation. That's accounting in Scientology. If the Accounts Department is doing something else, they're still in the 19th century when accounting was a vast mystery and managers went broke.

We have had good accounts and an easy life for Dir Accounts everywhere the moment this whole system went in. Even governments were satisfied.

Admin Report Forms

Only one report (and its income sheet) is permitted per department per week—except in PrR where each of its two sections report.

We don't allow random report forms to develop in a Central Organization. Everything anybody wants to know is on a dept's single report sheet for the week.

HCO WW ultimately receives all except income sheets.

Technical Report Forms

A report by each student is required each week by the D of T.

A report for each session given a pc is required from staff auditors by the D of P. These are "reports to LRH."

All these are ultimately received by HCO WW.

Holding the Form

The above write-up gives the essentials of the form of a Central Organization.

There are many policies. These are found in HCO Policy Letters.

There are many specific lines and instructions. These are also mainly in HCO Policy Letters.

It isn't the type of area a Central Org is in that establishes the unit for the staff. It is the adherence to the form. As soon as parts of the Central Organization break down the unit is affected adversely.

A Central Organization now makes as much as it adheres to the form above and gets in as much hot water as it does not. The earnings of a staff member are directly related to this pattern being kept.

This form of a Central Org required a decade to develop. It is based not only on what is right but what Central Org personnel will do. Follow it.

There are certain truisms which have developed regarding overall department function. These are:

If *technical* breaks down (HGC) the whole show goes. Staff member cases bog, executive personnel isn't developed, ARC breaks disrupt the field.

A badly run Academy ceases to be attended at once by some mysterious grapevine.

If the PE Foundation isn't steadily flogged by the HCO and Assoc Sec, its order crumbles since it is the first point of impact by a disorderly public. Where the public contacts the Central Org the points have to be held hard to keep order in.

We must never put things on "wait." The legal eagles are always asking one to wait. Companies are always putting us on "wait." Don't stand for it. Crush it through.

A staff member should be judged by his effective action on post, not on his charm or personality to other staff members or lack of personality.

A clique of friends of the top versus the rest of staff always denotes fear on the part of the top. The proper group is the whole staff in and doing their jobs.

It is better to train than process incomewise but don't neglect signing up pcs.

A staff member whose appearance is sloppy tends to handle his comm the same way.

A security risk staff member can require as many as two additional staff members to handle the resultant dev-t. Security risks are dynamite. Only with security risks do you get lying rumors and bad morale.

Never fill a post with a second-rater just to have a post filled on the org board. It makes a camouflaged hole. Less staff, if highly effective, can get more done.

Don't try to raise the unit by firing good staff ever. Come down on the PE and the Registrars instead.

Get books sold to get people in. That applies to PE and Reception and the Registrars as well as HCO.

As an executive don't drag people off jobs to get emergencies done.

Emergencies only occur after somebody drops the ball.

Free weeks demanded by HGC means the Registrar–HGC Admin line has broken down, that HGC is doing a poor job and that people aren't signing for enough processing.

Keep field security risks out of PE, training and even the premises. They cost a lot of people.

Keep staff processed until they're Clear.

Don't let a person on a department head post who has a bad needle reaction to control.

Don't let an auditor on staff who has a bad needle on help—they dramatize failed help every time.

The Assoc Sec can order a staff member to *processing* at staff rates but not to the detriment of processing of the public or other staff members.

Run a tight show, using this outline of organization, convert all missions to Central Orgs, keep technical high and income up and we'll make it.

L. RON HUBBARD
Founder

HUBBARD COMMUNICATIONS OFFICE
Saint Hill Manor, East Grinstead, Sussex

HCO POLICY LETTER OF 22 FEBRUARY 1961
Issue I

CenOCon

CENTRAL ORGANIZATIONS

MY PROGRAM TO RAISE YOUR UNIT

1. Differentiate between a city office such as Perth, Sydney, Auckland, Cape Town, etc., and a Central Organization (see HCO PL 21 Feb. 61, PATTERN FOR CITY OFFICES).

2. Put strenuously into effect recent HCO Policy Letters regarding HCO activities in every Central Org HCO and every city office HCO.

3. Put firmly into effect HCO PL 14 Feb. 61, THE PATTERN OF A CENTRAL ORGANIZATION, so that it is understood fully for *every* department by every person on staff in every Central Organization.

4. Get into action auditing of staff under D of P on 12½-hour intensives.

5. Get HCOB 18 Feb. 61 on Goals SOP in action first on staff and then on HGC pcs.

6. Get HCO PL 21 Feb. 61 II on Choosing PE and Registration Personnel for action.

7. Get permanent staff and permanent executive staff qualifications in action and permit no pay increases to a new permanent staff level until all qualifications fully satisfied as per HCO Policy Letters on personnel and permanent staff. Get them qualified.

8. Get test line in and working as per policy and PE Foundation furnishing plenty of prospects.

This is my immediate program. I have been preparing it and letting you in on it for the last few months.

It means a 2 par unit plus as a routine thing *if* you follow the above steps.

To show you what this means, in 8 (test line) the moment the script for evaluation was memorized by Evaluators and used, six sign-ups for PE were done in one hour as opposed to six in half a week last week in Johannesburg.

This is the immediate basic extent of all my Central Org planning. These are the basics for action.

These are the things I want HCO concentrated upon.

These are the things I want Assoc Secs to work hard to achieve, surviving the while.

Assemble the above mentioned HCO Bulletins and Policy Letters. Do your work but get these things in as well and as firmly as you can. They are a package for forward progress. Every staff member has his part in getting these steps accomplished while keeping the show on the road.

L. RON HUBBARD
Founder

CENTRAL ORGANIZATION MINIMUM STAFF

(A reorganization policy letter)

(NOT IMPERATIVE FOR SOUTH AFRICA OR AUSTRALIA)

The minimum staff of a Central Organization means the number of posts that must be covered, each by one person. The additional hats of the organization are worn by these staff members listed as basic staff.

The main sources of low units are:

1. Poor Academy training,

2. Poor HGC results,

3. Ineffective personnel on the posts of Chief Registrar and Letter Registrar,

4. Failure to adhere to org pattern and duties, and

5. Overstaffing in admin.

The unit system makes an organization peculiarly prone to overstaffing in admin and, for some reason, understaffing in technical. There is too much ease in putting a person on staff and too much nostalgia in taking him off.

Large staffs are usually a result of a chaotic personnel-employment application system and consequent dev-t. An insecure staff member makes enough dev-t to keep two more persons employed! This is why there are large governments—they solve inefficiency and dev-t by adding people, not by getting people to do the job.

This, therefore, is a basic Central Org staff list. Consistent low units stem from the causes listed above and, in thin times, having a staff larger than that listed below:

(Not listed in order of importance)

1. Association (Organization) Secretary

2. Association Secretary's Secretary

3. Director of Processing

4. HGC Administrator

5. Staff Auditor Auditing Staff

6. Staff Auditor Auditing Staff

7. Staff Auditor

8. Staff Auditor

9. Staff Auditor

10. Staff Auditor

11. Staff Auditor

12. Director of Training

13. Instructor (plus Ext Course)

14. Director of Accounts

15. Director of Materiel

16. Chief Registrar

17. Receptionist

18. Letter Registrar

19. CF In-Charge

20. Address In-Charge (plus certs, memberships)

21. Typist for Letter Registrar (mail)

22. PE Director (tests and evaluation)

23. One-third PE Course Instructor
    One-third Night Comm Course Instructor
    One-third Co-Audit Instructor

24. One-half Weekend Academy Course Instructor
    One-half Weekend Intensives, etc.

25. Cleaning personnel.

This basic staff is observably twenty-five persons, if we count night and weekend Instructors as part of an individual unit.

It will be seen that with low income this still gives an adequate unit.

Staff auditors can be added to the degree that pcs warrant. Extra auditors occurring in the five allowed can be assigned impermanent admin duties, such as ARC Break Registrar, but are pulled back to HGC when pcs exist for them.

When the basic pattern of each department does not in fact exist in that department (such as four files complete in Accounts), the org is always too busy

213

with a disorderly present to cope with the time needed to get a basic pattern in with which to work. This makes an appearance of a need for many more staff members. If these are to be employed at all, they should *only* be given jobs which will get in the basic pattern of files, lines, materiel readiness to handle traffic. While their departments are being gotten in strict good order, regular staff should carry on *present time* activity. In other words, *never* use extra help to handle current business. Use it only to straighten out past and future business. For instance, Accounts will always be calling for current help until the basic-four file system is complete, at which time one person could care for the department proper (even if another were used on tax, etc.). But without the basic pattern in properly, it takes two or more people to do current accounts. This is also true of PE.

With no tests prepared properly for issue, no comm baskets to take various stages of a test and routing, no simple record system, it takes a full-time test administrator just to cope with the basic disorder and keep the PE Test Section running. In short, if a department isn't "in" right, it takes many more people to run it and there goes the unit value, and the future problem—"We can't get personnel because we have too low a unit," etc., etc.

Expansion from basic staff should be in two directions—(1) getting the basic department in and (2) technical personnel. Admin staff should never be expanded to handle current work until the income of the organization is above $5,000 a week or £1,400, routinely. This means hard work but it also means high units until the income gets up to that point.

However, at the moment, with our current resurge, and with staff clearing, coping with new business is going to be our worst problem, not low units.

My advice now is to skin staff down into two categories:

1. Current work, and

2. Basic organization and future technical.

Take the above skeleton force to handle current activities. Take the entirety of remaining staff you have and assign them to those departments that need their file systems, lines and materiel straightened out and get a basic organization in perfect shape.

Further, take any Scientologist on staff and get him or her also pushed through a rigorous evening course on TRs, E-Meter, Model Session and make letter-perfect auditors out of them. Technical, needless to say, is basic organization.

I would not dismiss lots of staff members now to get a higher unit. I would use existing staff members intelligently as above and prepare to expand the number of pcs who can be audited and the number of students that can be trained. Your personnel pool is the overstrength departments of the organization.

I would now stop the staff from going from HGC to admin and reverse the flow. I'd get people into admin and shape them up to be transferred to technical. You'll be needing them. You just haven't got enough auditors and Instructors. The intelligent thing to do is make them out of admin people as above.

The basic staff given above is the basic staff of a Central Organization. It can care for any current business up to $5,000 or £1,400 sterling per week by adding six more staff auditors to it. No more admin people should be added until the $5,000/£1,400 level is routine. Then give the Letter Reg more typists, get another Registrar and give Materiel a clerk. Then add an assistant admin for HGC and an Instructor to the Academy, more or less in that order.

Follow this plan or something near it and you'll have high units. Go on with an expanded admin staff and no basic organization or future tech personnel and I guarantee your units will be low. I want you to have higher units. And I want a basic organization there when the rush starts and enough tech personnel to handle them.

Please act along these lines.

L. RON HUBBARD
Founder

HUBBARD COMMUNICATIONS OFFICE
Saint Hill Manor, East Grinstead, Sussex

HCO POLICY LETTER OF 24 AUGUST 1961

Central Orgs
HCOs

HCO ORGANIZATION, FUTURE PLANS

The future spotlights of HCO will light on the following plans for continental organization.

No Continental HCO is to remain in or with a Central Org.

An HCO Continental office will be situated so as to communicate easily with all Central Orgs and city offices.

The HCO Continental office will handle all orgs in HCO matters, will contain my continental office, will do all printing for the continent, all mimeographing, all make-up of mags, all mail-order book sales, will do *all* filing for all HCO offices on that continent, will be the basic tape repository and clearinghouse for all orgs and sales of tapes, will handle all mission matters for the continent, will clear all funds to HCO WW, will handle all technology, act as Board of Review for the continent (Ds of P will give exams), will give any "HCO Special Course," will possibly conduct some special activity such as a juvenile delinquency camp and will have its own buildings and grounds.

A Central Org or city HCO office will be a one-person office, occupying one room and possibly anteroom. There will be no local communicator or other HCO officer until the org so served has at least 100 staff members. The Area HCO will act as a comm relay point, will demand and attain high technology, will distribute all bulletins to the org (sent to it in packets by HCO Cont), collect all monies due HCO from the org, distribute local books and tapes through Reception, handle the org's tape library, keep HCO Continental and myself in touch and, in short, make my postulates stick locally. With no Mimeo or filing, with no examinations to do, one person should be able to do an HCO Area job. That person should be a well-trained Scientologist, able to obtain excellent results, preferably Clear.

Telex connection should exist from HCO Continental to all HCO Area offices and from Saint Hill to all HCO Continental offices.

It will be seen that randomity amongst organizations will reduce if HCO Continental is attached to no one org. It should also be seen that if all personnel over one person in HCO Area offices were all attached to HCO Continental, more people would be available in the continental office and work duplication would fall off, thus freeing HCO Continental and Area offices from overburden.

My own continental office and all its furniture, files and equipment should be reestablished at the HCO Continental office.

For this purpose, HCO Continental Washington, DC should move to some desirable area in the center of the US. This could be St. Louis, Arkansas, Mobile or New Orleans, depending on the most liberal laws, whether Missouri, Arkansas,

Alabama or New Orleans, and depending on cost of living and construction. New Orleans would have the best comm lines, St. Louis the shortest comm lines, Mobile the best operating atmosphere, Little Rock the better climate.

HCO Continental Africa should be located on the coast, south of Durban and north of the Cape. Details of this have already been sent to SA.

HCO Continental Australia is not badly located where it is, in Melbourne, but might prosper under another roof. It should continue to include New Zealand.

HCO Continental England is carried out to a marked degree by Saint Hill but should be decentralized entirely from HASI London, leaving only the HCO Area at London, and made to include Europe.

If the continental office were on the seacoast, it would be much more likely to see me.

The primary caution on this is not to incur huge building expenses or rentals, as initially comm costs would go up everywhere but Australia. HCO Continental Africa has this already more or less in solution as 40 Hannaben* exists to be traded. Washington would at least recover a $2400 per year storage bill if the move was properly figured, and the FCDC would acquire back needed offices, as would London and Melbourne.

As Central Orgs now pay the rent on HCO Continental space, some adjustment would have to be made.

The units paid in an HCO Continental office should be calculated on the basis of standardizing all orgs' units on the continent as to how much for what job, and then each week, the HCO Continental staff would be paid a unit averaged from the units of each Central Org and city office. Like so: DC unit 40 cents, LA 30 cents, Chicago 60 cents, Texas 10 cents; HCO Continental unit 35 cents or an average of the rest.

Corporatewise, it would have to be set up properly—in the US as a branch of one of the Churches, elsewhere as a branch of HASI *and* HCO, Ltd.

I have had centralization in mind for some time, and was waiting for broad general clearing to start before initiating action. I am indebted to the HCO Executive Secretary US for suggestions as to units and other matters.

The signal for when to start this is when the main Central Org's HGC starts to make Clears.

L. RON HUBBARD
Founder

*40 Hannaben: the address of a property owned by HCO Continental Africa at the time this PL was written.

HCO POLICY LETTER OF 30 JANUARY 1962

CenOCon

TECHNICAL DIRECTOR AND ADMINISTRATOR

The last time orgs ran with minimal upset, especially in London, two posts now empty everywhere were filled. These posts were Technical Director, who oversaw all technical activities, and Administrator, who oversaw all administrative actions.

These were two very busy posts.

Units have been reduced since 1958 by:

a. Lowered technical results and

b. Administrative omissions.

_____

In a city office these two posts, rather than the director of department posts, should certainly be filled, as a Tech Director can double in brass as D of P and D of T. And an Administrator does the accounts and Dir Mat posts and oversees CF and Address as well as income from the Registrar.

So in a city office these two posts should be filled at once and some executive posts dropped, at a great saving in units and personnel.

_____

In a Central Organization such as London and DC these two posts should be filled in addition to existing executive posts. The scrambles in CF and Address alone create more income loss than the added units.

At present HCO Area is actually doing these two posts in almost all orgs. HCO Area has its own duties such as org ruds and hat checks and is finding it hard to do these as well as Tech Director and Administrator supervision.

You may or may not fill these posts elsewhere than London and DC. But I feel it would increase income and effectiveness.

L. RON HUBBARD
Founder

HCO POLICY LETTER OF 11 MARCH 1964
Issue I

BPI
CenOCon

AUDITORS DIVISION
NEW HCO WW ORGANIZATION

(HCO Area Sec: Please implement at once.)

The Auditors Division of HCO (WW), Ltd., has just been formed.

It is in the charge of the Director of Auditors at Saint Hill.

Purpose of the Auditors Division: To make all *the auditors in the world well trained, properly accredited, successful and ethical.*

All certified auditors—HAS, HQS, HPA/HCA, etc.—come under the Auditors Division.

A Leading Field Auditor is to be nominated by the HCO Area Secretary of every area. He or she will be appointed then by the Director of Auditors. In the case of several large cities covered by an HCO Area, a Leading Field Auditor may be appointed for each one, with a Leading Field Auditor for the entire area. The title for a Leading Field Auditor is the Leading Field Auditor of the Eastern US (where several have been appointed for cities) and the Leading Field Auditor of Melbourne, where only one city is involved. The titles compare to HCO Areas and Scientology geographical divisions as will be released from time to time. The criteria of nomination should be "a successful auditor of good classification, preferably Saint Hill, who is not in conflict with HCO or the Central Org."

A Leading Field Auditor is expected to remain in good communication with Saint Hill and will receive his instructions through the HCO Area Secretary.

His or her final appointment will be by letter from Saint Hill.

The Leading Field Auditor should hold and take charge of all field auditors' meetings.

The Leading Field Auditor may appoint a deputy and a secretary for meetings and other functions.

THE AUDITOR
SAINT HILL JOURNAL

A new magazine is being issued at Saint Hill to be called *The Auditor,* the Saint Hill journal of the Auditors Division.

A correspondent for *The Auditor* must be appointed in each Central Organization by the HCO Area Sec. This correspondent should keep the editor of *The Auditor* informed of all Academy enrollees and graduates and data concerning them, changes of staff members in the organization, local news, reports on congresses and various meetings and plans. Photos when available should be forwarded.

The Leading Field Auditor should appoint a field correspondent giving news about centers and various field functions, furnishing names of auditors and their activities.

Wherever possible, a correspondent should send not only a person's name but also his or her address.

The heart of a good story for *The Auditor* is lots of names and what they are doing.

THE AUDITORS DIVISION

The Auditors Division is taking over all mission, center and field auditor coordination, mailings and service.

Certification will soon become handled wholly by the Auditors Division of HCO WW, and organizations and auditors will only need to send in the names of enrollees and graduates. The certificate will be prepared by and mailed from Saint Hill upon the request of and evidence from the HCO Area Sec. This will not come into full effect for several months. Meanwhile, existing arrangements continue.

MEMBERSHIPS

Arrangements are being made to streamline memberships. All existing memberships will be honored. Local Central Organizations will also continue to have memberships in addition to the Auditors Division.

This organization implements several of the basic functions of HCO on an international basis, in full cooperation with Area HCOs, which it also coordinates.

L. RON HUBBARD
Founder

DEPARTMENTAL CHANGES
AUDITORS DIVISION

The Enrollment Division is transferred herewith from HCO (Saint Hill), Ltd., to HCO (WW), Ltd., and is renamed AUDITORS DIVISION.

The head of the Auditors Division is the Director of Auditors.

No change in the function of the former Enrollment Division or its personnel is made except that the Mission Secretary is added to the Auditors Division and comes under the Director of Auditors, and the Course Administrator and Registrar remain with HCO (Saint Hill), Ltd.

The purpose of the Auditors Division is to make all auditors well trained and successful.

Enrollment in Academies, proper certification, enrollment at Saint Hill, are all functions of the Auditors Division.

CF and Address comes under the Auditors Division.

Saint Hill News comes under the Auditors Division.

Keeping the Saint Hill Course fully enrolled is the responsibility of the Auditors Division.

Through HCOs in every area, a field auditor is appointed as the Auditors Division representative or Leading Field Auditor. This would be of assistance to the Auditors Division and to HCO Area Secs.

The aim of this transfer is to put all auditors in the world under one general heading and so get them trained and successful and to regulate practice.

HCO (WW), Ltd., has as its purpose external comm lines and auditors are certainly those, so is CF and Address.

The Auditors Division and the Director of Auditors is under the Organization Supervisor of HCO (WW), Ltd.

The activities of the Mission Department should be coordinated with those of the Auditors Division (see policy letter of this date re mission program).

No other changes in this division or activity are made.

L. RON HUBBARD
Founder

218C

Sthil Only

SAINT HILL PERSONNEL

All persons employed at Saint Hill, for personnel purposes, except officers of corporations, come under the Saint Hill Administrator.

HCO (SH) Ltd. provides this service for HCO (WW) Ltd. and SLR, Ltd.

This means that acquisition of new personnel and dismissal of personnel comes under the Saint Hill Administrator.

Personnel actions by HCO (WW) Ltd. and SLR, Ltd. must be referred to the Saint Hill Administrator.

The Saint Hill Administrator may take independent action on any personnel in the interests of efficiency or finance.

As a matter of principle, a corporation officer or department head has authority over the personnel within his own corporation or department. This includes some power of decision in the matter of hiring and dismissal.

The Saint Hill Administrator should, therefore, work in close cooperation with other corporation officers and with department heads in personnel matters.

If any disagreement arises on executive level on the question of personnel, the matter in question must be kept in abeyance until it can be referred to the board.

L. RON HUBBARD
Founder

NEW POSTS

What has formerly been called Reception is redesignated COMMUNICA-TIONS OFFICER. The post has outgrown what is commonly held to be reception responsibility.

The Communication Officer is responsible for relaying anything or anyone that is received at or sent by Saint Hill.

Phone and other duties continue.

Failure to report receipts of goods to the Communication Officer or failure to give the office courtesy and cooperation will result in a report to the Organization Secretary.

A log is kept by the Communication Officer in which all communications, received goods *and happenings* are entered.

In emergencies such as fire or accident inform the Communication Officer in the front office at once.

MAIL CHANGE

No more mail will be delivered to desks effective 22 June 1964.

Instead, such mail and despatches will be sorted into the Comm Center baskets in the front office and will be picked up daily by the staff members themselves.

Procedure for office personnel: Do your work into your out-basket as usual. Then take your out-basket contents to the front office yourself and sort it into the various other baskets or outgoing mail. Pick up whatever is in your basket and take it back to your place of work.

Try to get your despatches and letters all sorted into the Comm Center before 5:30 P.M. daily.

For materiel required get the chits into the appropriate front office baskets by noon.

Exceptions: The despatches of the Executive Director will be taken to his office by the International Organization Supervisor and the outgo picked up by him. The despatches of the Organization Secretary will be picked up and delivered by the Org Sec's Sec. This measure is made not for convenience but to expedite purchase requests and checks which might hold up other personnel.

TEA

Tea for office workers will hereafter be handled in all its arrangements by the Housekeeper or the Assistant Housekeeper, effective 29 June 1964.

One or another office worker below executive rank may be detailed to assist in this on a rotational basis by the Housekeeper.

ACCOUNTS ASSISTANT TO THE ORGANIZATION SECRETARY

There will no longer be income and disbursement posts as separate personnel.

Both these posts will be held by one person with the title Accounts Assistant to the Organization Secretary, effective at once.

ACCOUNTS FILES ADMINISTRATOR

The post of Accounts Files Administrator is created.

This staff member will help the Accounts Assistant with files and in other ways as contained in the administrative directive of the post, effective at once.

L. RON HUBBARD
Founder

HUBBARD COMMUNICATIONS OFFICE
Saint Hill Manor, East Grinstead, Sussex

HCO POLICY LETTER OF 22 FEBRUARY 1965
Issue II

Limited
  Non-Remimeo
Sthil Staff

HCO AREA SECRETARY SAINT HILL

The title "Communication Officer" is herewith changed to HCO AREA SECRETARY SAINT HILL.

The HCO Area Secretary Saint Hill is also a department head under, as such, the Org Sec.

The duties of the HCO Area Secretary Saint Hill include heading the Communications Unit. This contains all comm functions of the org, such as mimeograph, central files and address, mail and mailing, the comm center, the comm system, telephone, reception, telex, everyone's desk comm station or basket and the normal functions of hat checks, bulletin and policy checks; nominal supervision of the staff co-audit; the receipt and despatch of all goods; the arrival, departure and absence of personnel; the keeping of the log book and any other record books and whatever other functions may be assigned to this unit and the HCO Area Secretary heading it.

All personnel of the Communications Unit are under the direct supervision of the HCO Area Secretary Saint Hill.

The HCO Area Secretary Saint Hill is assisted by an HCO Communicator and HCO Steno, Address In-Charge and other personnel as available within the framework of traffic volume and economics.

The hat still retains, outside the above, a certain authority of its own and can remove the Org Sec and carry on the Org Sec duties in periods of emergency.

The HCO Area Secretary Saint Hill accompanies the Organization Secretary on the Friday inspection and keeps the inspection record and makes his own inspection.

L. RON HUBBARD
Founder

HCO EXECUTIVE LETTER OF 3 MARCH 1965
Issue II

Gen. Non-Remimeo

TO: Association Secretaries
    Organization Secretaries
    HCO Secretaries

FROM: RON

SUBJECT: **WHAT'S COMING NEXT**

With the completion of issue of the 1964 promotion and organization policies, I consider that the plan for broad promotion is now well in hand, that fees are capable of being adjusted with inflation and that things are planned for a boom.

My next thought has been org patterns. There are some adjustments in org pattern to be published now that we have some experience with the 1964 change of org pattern which has been extremely successful in increasing income in orgs.

Receiving the primary attention is the pattern of organization at Saint Hill. Unless the top area is expanded it will check expansion lower. Your lack of fresh books is due to the jam at the top.

We have the tech. The main problem I am having is clearing my immediate comm area enough to let me write them for you.

In writing up my own hat so it could be spread out, I found I had to clean up the adjacent areas as well so bits of my hats could be received and worn.

But the real news is that in finding the Level VII data I found a whole array of natural laws concerning actions in the MEST universe.

These apply to administration. They make it very simple to run an org or work in one and to expand dissemination. This will help out. It consists mainly of working as we are doing but applying certain methods in our work that will speed it up a bit. These laws give us an insight into promotion and organization nobody in this end of the universe has had before. We'll be able to predict better and work better.

So I am just now engaged in writing them up for you and you will have them soonest by HCO Policy Letter.

I should really do a book on these as they'll easily remake the business world. In short order one of our admin or exec certificates would elicit a high offer from any big firm for its holder.

Years ago somebody said we should work out dissemination by our own technology. That wasn't easy to do. But now it's done and you'll shortly have some of the material in policy letters.

———————

You'll be happy to know I am working hard also to get to you all processes for each level up to and including IV. Lack of these could be embarrassing to you. They're being taught on course here but they're not fully written up. I'm trying to catch up on this.

I spent a working vacation as you can see by policy letter dates, but I feel fresh—mainly however because of case gain. I got a chance, first in a long while, to run processes in the absence of daily PTPs and state of beingness soared. I reached past 9/10ths of VI to grab VII and am now slogging away to "run the unflat process flat" R6 before I go adventuring again for VII.

It's all good roads and good weather in Scientology these days. A very exciting future is ahead of us.

Hello and glad to be back.

Best,

RON

L. RON HUBBARD
Founder

HUBBARD COMMUNICATIONS OFFICE
Saint Hill Manor, East Grinstead, Sussex

HCO POLICY LETTER OF 13 MARCH 1965
Issue I

Remimeo
BPI

ADMIN TECHNOLOGY

THE COMM–MEMBER SYSTEM

In the eleven major zonal Scientology organizations of the world, a new communications and contact system is authorized as per this policy letter.

The staff members of these eleven major organizations may now communicate directly with the same post as their own at Saint Hill for information, guidance and orders. The holder of the same post in another org is a comm member.

The Saint Hill organization chart is exactly the same as the organization chart in every one of the major organizations. The difference is only the numbers on staff. As Founder I am the head of each of these organizations. Below, the organizations are also exactly alike with similar or the same titles. Continental Directors and Secretaries are also preserved as titles.

At Saint Hill there is the International Council and each major org has its Executive Council. At Saint Hill there is an HCO Secretary, an Organization Secretary and a Finance Secretary and in each org there are the same levels of officers.

At Saint Hill there are six departments: the Promotion Department and the Publications Department, both under the HCO Division (1); the Department of Training and the Department of Processing, both under the Technical Division (2); and the Accounts Department and Materiel Department, both under the Finance Division (3).

All posts and functions come under the three divisions and six departments.

HCO (Division 1) promotes and registers; Technical (Division 2) applies all training and processing for the org and public; Finance (Division 3) takes care of all money and property.

In eleven orgs, any staff member or executive may find his senior comm member on the Saint Hill staff and communicate directly for aid, guidance, coordination, clarification of policy and orders. In cases where the matter can't be handled at lower echelon at Saint Hill, it is referred through channels at Saint Hill directly to executives here or myself. In the eleven major orgs, executives may go direct only to their own senior comm member at Saint Hill. Reversely, Saint Hill executives may go only to their junior comm member in the org.

The lines are thus open at parallel to Saint Hill but go up or down only through channels inside the orgs.

225

This system once existed from London but dropped out. It was *very* successful, marking our time of greatest expansion. It is for the first time authorized and made official.

Now any case audited or person trained, as well as other matters, can become the subject of direct rapid communication on our enormous telex network or by air or surface mail. The slows caused by overwork at executive level are unblocked. Saint Hill can now advise quickly on any difficulties or new materials or policy.

We are standardizing all policy and issuing standard department "hats" based on fifteen years of org experience now being correlated.

Saint Hill is a *working* organization from top to bottom, having now the same functions and activities as every other first-echelon organization in the world. There are no posts at Saint Hill which are not facing and handling the same problems here as in any other org anywhere. So advice and data is real and the exact problems are known and understood.

The new org pattern applies easily to orgs very large or very small without change. It adapts easily to the small city office or an org with a thousand staff members.

Copies of org boards will be freely circulated by a new system of large photographic duplication now being installed at Saint Hill.

The comm-member system is the result of experience already tested. It is also taken from natural laws I have discovered at Level VII and which are being applied directly to Scientology organizations over the world to bring about rapid expansion. This expansion is being designed to take place at a faster doubling rate than before.

The organizations of Scientology now considered first-echelon orgs (just below Saint Hill) are London, Washington, Los Angeles, New York, Melbourne, Sydney, Perth, New Zealand, Johannesburg, Durban and Cape Town. All other orgs should attach themselves to their Continental Org and employ the comm-member system with its staff as senior comm members to it as it is to Saint Hill.

Continental lines, org seniorities and other lines are preserved. A first-echelon org need not forward through its Continental Org unless required to do so on application by Continental Orgs to Saint Hill on specific orgs or departments for temporary periods.

Purely pioneer areas now being handled by Saint Hill, such as the Pacific Northwest, Canada, Japan, Russia and Asia, remain under Saint Hill control and where embryonic pioneer orgs exist, may use the comm-member system with Saint Hill as it may apply to their staffs or committees.

Mission holders are not affected and continue as usual direct to the Saint Hill Mission Secretary and may not use the comm-member system which is reserved exclusively to orgs or city offices.

All existing lines inside orgs or existing org seniorities in the first echelon continue and *must not* be severed or dropped because of the new arrangement.

It will be found all lines now in still work exactly as before, and the comm-member system merely opens new channels in addition to existing seniorities and lines, and the new pattern only makes orderly and complete an org pattern which came almost fully into existence last summer. Hold existing lines in when they have worked for you. You will find they still answer up even under the new pattern.

The specific benefit to the public of the comm-member system is the improved service ability of their local orgs, which can now obtain fast case advices or get training queries answered from Saint Hill experts in very little time and who, in their turn, can place any difficult problem before me in a matter of minutes.

L. RON HUBBARD
Founder

HUBBARD COMMUNICATIONS OFFICE
Saint Hill Manor, East Grinstead, Sussex

HCO POLICY LETTER OF 13 MARCH 1965
Issue II

THE COMM–MEMBER SYSTEM
ROUTING POLICIES SECTION

Definition: THE COMM–MEMBER SYSTEM is a direct communications system between the staff member of one org and only the exact staff post in another org without vias. It is governed by direct policies and regulations and its own technology of handling matters. IT DOES NOT CHANGE OR ALTER ANY EXISTING INTERNAL OR BETWEEN–ORG POLICY OR COMMUNICATION CHANNELS.

ROUTING

Any but the following routing is off-line and therefore dev-t in the Comm-Member System:

1. A ROUTING. Goes directly across from own post to same org post in another org only. Do *not* go across to same post and then up or down. This is clearly marked at the top of all despatches so routed "A Routing," with no vias marked.

2. B ROUTING. Goes up in one's own org and across and down again to the same post as own in the other org. Despatches so routed are clearly marked at the top "B Routing" with a full list of vias written on it by the sender. Each via initials and forwards or stops it, says exactly why and returns it to sender.

3. C ROUTING. Goes up to one's org superior or superiors on channel as per org board only. One's own superiors can send it across if they wish to their similar post in the other org but it cannot be so routed by the original sender. Do not go up in own org and address across to a superior post than your own in another org. It must only be addressed to superiors in one's own org. Despatches so routed are clearly marked "C Routing" and have the proper vias for one's own org marked on it by the sender for forwarding inside his own org.

4. D ROUTING. Goes inside one's own org to anyone else in the org up or down. Despatches so forwarded are called "D Routing" with the person to whom addressed clearly marked. D Routing is entirely limited to one's own org and is not forwarded across to another org except when demanded or as an enclosure in other despatches. D Routing means "to a specific post in one's own org, superior or junior."

A senior org is defined as the top org heading an echelon of orgs. Saint Hill is the top org to eleven other orgs but amongst these there is continental seniority. The continental org is senior to the other orgs in that zone, but as these all form one echelon to Saint Hill, Saint Hill is senior to the rest.

A senior comm member (not senior staff member) is one holding a duplicate post in a senior org.

A junior comm member is one who in relation to Saint Hill holds the duplicate post in any org in the first echelon of eleven orgs just below Saint Hill or in an org in that echelon of eleven junior to the continental orgs.

An org founded or salvaged by an org is junior to the founding or salvaging org, and its staff members are junior to those of the same post in the founding or salvaging org.

Orgs or offices not included in the first echelon below Saint Hill have as their senior org that org of the next upper echelon which handles or controls its traffic. Orgs of the second echelon and lower communicate only to the founding or salvaging org on the next echelon above them or the org to which they are assigned. They may also communicate parallel to orgs of similar seniority in their own echelon, but seniority must otherwise be assigned. Questions of seniority of orgs are settled by appeal to the International Council.

Note: On inspection, with the assistance of sketching a few examples, the reason for these routing regulations will be very evident. Any other routing than the above *would make trouble all around.* So any routing not covered in A, B, C or D must be *spotted and called dev-t,* being off-line.

SUBJECTS

5. Discussing other than one's own concerns in despatches beyond normal ARC is off-policy and should be returned as dev-t.

6. Writing for somebody else than one's own hat is off-origin and should be returned as dev-t.

ORDERS

7. A senior comm member should not give direct orders to his junior comm member on the A Routing. Direct orders may be given only with B Routing, and any direct order not following B Routing is *off-line* except in cases of extreme urgency as in the case of books about to be shipped or a spinning pc. Such cases are called URGENCY ORDERS. An urgency order given an A Routing must be followed at once on slower channels (airmail) by repeating it with B Routing through channels. The original must begin "Urgency Order" and the forwarded-through-channels copy must begin with UR-GENCY ORDER FROM _____ TO _____ DATE _____ SUBJECT _____ ORIGINAL SENT VIA TELEX (ORDER GIVEN) BE-CAUSE _____ (REASON FOR IT). If an urgency order given with good reason on A Routing and properly followed with its B Routing copy is not complied with at the other end and there is any actual loss of money or property or damage to persons or cases or property or repute as a result of the noncompliance, the HCO Justice Codes (HCO PLs

of 7 Mar. 65 I, II, and III) apply. Only a senior comm member may give an order on the Comm-Member System.

8. If an order which is only given B Routing is not stopped by a post superior to the two comm members anywhere on the line and is delivered to the junior post and is not complied with or acted upon, the HCO Justice Codes applies regardless of lack of loss or damage.

ADVICES, QUESTIONS AND ANSWERS

9. Ordinary traffic on A Routing is usually data or questions or answers from the junior comm member to the senior comm member and advices, questions and answers from the senior comm member to the junior comm member.

TIPS

10. C Routing is so marked and used when a staff member wishes to call his own org superior's attention to a datum or statistic or even a rumor which seems to have basis in fact. One marks the despatch C Routing, as above, with all vias written on it by the sender up to the sender's own org department which might be interested. It is initialed en route and is simply received by the comm member's superior in his own org with no ack sent back or expected. It is just a *tip*, not an advice or a real comm. EXCEPT that when a long letter or report *received* by A Routing is forwarded to one's own superiors in one's own org, the staff member forwarding it *must* cover it with a brief digest despatch giving the possibly important datum or must underscore or circle the important parts with a different colored pen so one's superior can clearly pick out the datum. No comment should be made by the staff member originating the tip as that makes it an org comm which must be acked. Making tips into internal org despatches is dev-t as it is *off-origin*. The staff member forwarding the tip to his superiors is not the sender. Data can flow freely on lines without acks as it's just data. Thus, C Routing is only a data line, receives no ack from the C-routed superior to the staff member who forwarded it or the originator who sent it from the other org. Usually, the recipient of a comm-member despatch on a C Routing just sends it on to files by marking it F with an arrow.

If the person who forwarded it wants it back, he marks it "Return to (name)" and the arrow is drawn to that when seen by the superior. It is expected that the person in the org to whom his other org comm member addressed it will ack the message as a message from his junior or senior comm member in the other org.

GREETINGS AND INFO

11. Greetings contained in a letter or despatch such as "Say hello to Bill for me" are handled with D Routing as in D above. The greeting bit is clearly circled with a different colored pen than the original and the message is clearly marked D Routing, the greeted person's name put on it and arrowed and is forwarded to the person being greeted. He or she marks it F with an arrow and it goes to files. If the comm member wanted it back with a "Return

to _____ ," the greeted person returns it to sender without ack or comment but only an initial by the greeting itself. To handle any other way or to comment is dev-t as it becomes an org despatch.

12. Information goes by D Routing. Any Comm-Member System despatch in the senior or junior org may become INFORMATION. Such a despatch from another org is received by the senior or junior comm member, and when it is thought that it contains important information of interest to some other staff member of the receiver's own org above or below him on the command channel or across in another department or division, the whole message is clearly marked "D Routing," its earlier routing crossed out; if to be returned to the forwarding staff member, it is marked "Return to" with the staff member's own name or post name. If it just goes to files afterwards, it is marked F with an arrow. The information bit is clearly circled or underscored with a different colored pen. Adding comments to INFO bits in forwarding or in returning inside one's own org is dev-t as it is made into an org despatch by the comment. If acked with no "Return to" on it, it is marked F with an arrow and is sent to files.

13. Routings C and D sent with a comment by the forwarder or returned with a comment by the receiver are dev-t. However, if vital data is *also* known by the forwarder or returning staff member, an org despatch is attached as a separate piece of paper. This makes the comm-member despatch simply an "enclosure" to an org despatch. If, however, the org despatch does not contain other data or orders than idle chatter, it is dev-t. Therefore, Routings C and D do not apply when a despatch is added, for a routine internal org despatch has been made of the comm-member despatch.

14. A, B, C and D Routings are not "brought by a body" ever, any more than routine org despatches would be. By "brought by a body" is meant brought in person not by HCO. Also A, B, C and D Routings are not returned by a body.

FAILURES TO ALERT

15. Any staff member in a senior org (an org senior on the comm lines to the other org, not just Saint Hill) having vital data concerning an org, department, unit or section that is IN AN EMERGENCY STATUS or information clearly indicating it should be who does not bring the matter effectively to the attention of superiors in his own org is liable to the HCO Justice Codes under neglect or omission, a misdemeanor. If failure to advise results in loss or damage to the other org's income or public repute or his own org's, the matter becomes the subject of a Committee of Evidence, making the staff member who received the information an accessory to the other org's default or upset.

16. A junior department head comm member who does not advise the most senior comm member on his routine lines of lessened income or traffic when it has continued for three consecutive weeks in his department becomes liable to HCO Justice Codes under the heading of a misdemeanor, if not personally at fault, or a crime if at fault for any reason. Such a report from a junior comm member *must* contain specific, detailed data as to possible cause and a specific detailed recommendation to the senior comm member for correcting the slump. Such a report is called a SLUMP REPORT. The

receiving senior comm member *must* pass this report at once to HCO OIC In-Charge in his (the senior) org marked "Priority" in red. It does not go via channels but by D Routing and is made part of the senior org's own OIC summary report on orgs for the week.

The senior comm member must demand (not orders) at once from his junior comm member on receipt of a SLUMP REPORT any data he thinks he may need or doesn't know or wants to know about the situation. It is forbidden to send orders at this stage as insufficient data is to hand, but any advices may be sent by the senior comm member.

17. If a slump, determined by raw data (statistics) reported or not, occurs in any executive junior comm member's division, org, department, unit or section and the condition continues two months despite advices or orders, the senior comm member *must* despatch HCO Conditions Unit in his org requesting the assignment of an Emergency condition to any part of the org controlled by his junior comm member. HCO assigns the condition with a despatch to the division head or heads of that org on B Routing clearly marked in red on its face EMERGENCY CONDITION in very large letters such as a stamp.

18. On receipt of an "Emergency condition," the junior comm member *must* inform his senior comm member what he is doing about it and cooperate with his org and any senior staff member to his post.

19. If an "Emergency condition" does not produce results, the senior comm member, after a reasonable time, must inform his superiors of the fact with all the data he has and with a specific recommendation concerning the handling of the situation.

20. A comm member (senior or junior) must do what he can for the morale of the other comm member during the other's *periods of stress* without undermining the org's executives with his sympathy for their subordinate at "being badly led." The comm member must realize that the other comm member is already under stress when things are going wrong and try not to be short or sharp or flash back or call names. Routing is so direct and there's so much theta on the line that misemotion can blow the other end to pieces (the first organizational lesson ever learned about Scientology's open comm lines). The thing to concentrate on in any condition of stress, emergency or not, is to keep the comm member on post and working. The comm member should knock out the other's generalities with "WHO SPECIFICALLY?" and cure the junior comm member's ARC breaks with his environment. He should then get the other comm member to spot and remove distractions, barriers, noncompliance and alter-is, augment the purpose of the other's post or department or division or org, strengthen the edges of the channel and find and help reduce the real opposition where possible by any valid means. This approach is better than quoting policies during stress. This procedure usually applies from a senior to a junior comm member. But may sometimes become reversed, depending on who is under stress. If done by a junior comm member, it must be realized that a senior comm member has three to eleven junior comm members and good wishes and some understanding words may be far more valuable than several juniors "auditing" their senior via this system at once.

21. A junior comm member must not overwork or unnecessarily worry his senior comm member by caprice, long despatches, irrelevant material, gossip, hearsay

or entheta. There are other orgs being handled by the senior comm member as well as his own post, and the senior comm member is apt to be sharp about dev-t and rightly. A junior comm member can find himself involved with the HCO Justice Codes at a crime level for misinforming or falsifying reports or enturbulating or losing one's temper over a long comm line. Any comm member must report such offenses when flagrant or upsetting to HCO Justice at once.

22. In using A Routing be very certain that brevity for the sake of speed does not defeat itself. A too-brief message or a garble causes a repeat request which multiplies the message traffic by three. Always read a message you are sending before you send it as though you knew nothing about it and were receiving it. Put "ARC" between sentences when using cable or "Stop." In cabling *and* despatching always number your despatch with the date of the day plus your post initials and your org cable abbreviation and the post in the org you are addressing (abbreviated) and note the number and subject in your own log. Answer a despatch so code numbered by repeating its code, not your own, and adding a digit to the end of it to show which message it was, the first, second or third on the same subject. Omit the 1 but always add the 2, 3 and so on in rotation, using the original code number with the original day date. The Comm Officer can show you how. That way messages can't "cross" and cause a wonder of which was sent first. Sloppy comm procedure over long lines is dev-t. Always be legible. Don't scribble. Write so it can be read. An indecipherable message is a curse. Use lots of air letters, spare cable when you can and avoid enclosures when possible as they require a large envelope and aside from weight, cost nearly three times as much as an air letter. Address the post and the org. Use initials in cables remembering DP is Director of Processing and PD is Publications Director. Use dept and division in addressing air letters such as, to Div 1 Promotion and Registration Address In-Charge. Always address air letters in the order division, department (unit or section), post. Avoid personal names on addresses between orgs but use the personal name in "Dear ____" if you wish. Your senior or junior comm member in another org is your same post with the org name added instead of your org's.

23. Anybody may write his senior or junior comm member, not just executives. Where staff boards do not have further designations for their nonexecutive posts, a staff member who has no executive title simply addresses "Staff Auditor Saint Hill from Staff Auditor Benson, Sydney." As these types of post increase and decrease in number, it is not always possible to get the same line in and it is best to generalize in addressing. For example: "To Maintenance staff member Saint Hill from Maintenance staff member Melbourne." There are not many such posts with no further designation and they are usually sorted out but cross at times. The questions usually get answered.

24. All regulations apply to general staff members as well as executive staff members.

25. Complaints about routing when the staff member himself cannot get his communicating staff member's hat on himself should always be forwarded to the HCO Communications Officer in the org where the complaint is made. The HCO Communications Officer will take the matter up with the Communications Officer in the org mentioned in the complaint. If this does not

bring results, it should be reported directly to the HCO Area Secretary of the org making the complaint who takes it up with his or her communicating member in the org being complained about and can request direct discipline or a Committee of Evidence of the other org depending on the magnitude of the offense. No discipline may be ordered by a senior org member to a member in another org. One may be disciplined only by one's own org. But when one's own org fails to discipline, it can be subjected to a Committee of Evidence at its top levels by an org just senior to it, not necessarily the next echelon org. The continental org is usually so requested by Saint Hill when offenses warrant it and discipline seems to be gone in its comm lines or in the org and it will not act.

26. Letters from the field or public that get into the Comm-Member System should be turned over to the Letter Registrar for answering as they're in the line by error. All letters received by an org are opened by the org before distribution. However, public mail after being opened in the Comm Center may also be replied to by the staff member it is addressed to, but he or she should remember that they must be handled in accordance with Division 1 HCO policy. The Communications Officer should ask the staff member if he or she wants them, if the public or off-line character is noted by the Comm Officer or called to his or her attention by the staff member. If the staff member does not want it, it is properly routed by the Comm Officer to Letter Reg. But in any event, the Letter Reg should be given the original and a copy of the staff member's answer for files.

27. Any letters received in the Comm-Member System should go to CF with copies of the reply when answered. No staff member may have a file containing letters older than two months. If retained at all, they must be safeguarded and eventually turned in within two months. Comm-member letters are org letters and may not be destroyed but must go to CF where they are filed as to org and post.

28. Mission holders' queries may not be answered by other staff members than those authorized and should be turned over, when received, to the mission hat in the department or org. Answering mission holders attempting to use the Comm-Member System is forbidden.

29. Merchants and business persons and specifically lawyers and accountants may not correspond with staff members on the org's business unless it is the duty of the staff member.

30. The Comm-Member System does not in any way change any other routing or comm policy in an org internally. Its internal lines remain as always with the same procedure as before this system came into effect.

31. High-hatting is a term applied to a practice of wearing only one's highest hat in a small org using the Comm-Member System and also in receiving an order or advice as a lower comm member and "going upstairs" with one's hats to refuse it. In a very small org, it is very wise to write from the hat one is talking about to the comm member in a bigger org that wears that hat, and then, in receiving the reply, receive it as the hat that asked the question or sent the data. Help the big org's brass by querying from the hat that wants to know and receiving the reply as the same hat in proper parallel.

COMM–MEMBER SYSTEM

COMM POLICIES SECTION

1. Communications may not contain entheta or misemotion. Our lines are too open and magnify it, and lines are blown up when these are used over long distances.

2. Communications to Saint Hill may not criticize one's own org seniors, and Saint Hill communications to orgs may not criticize Saint Hill or org seniors. The surest way to interrupt the comm lines is to give executives cause to interrupt or intercept.

3. Saint Hill advices must not give unusual solutions where actual policy or technology exists and can be pointed to. Don't alter-is data in handling org problems. The data you are receiving from the other org may not be correct or complete or sometimes false, and thinking up new procedures that alter old to solve the "problem" is to introduce an arbitrary order on an already false base. If standard policy doesn't seem to apply, then the "problem" is probably misrepresented and doesn't exist that way. Get data before you advise, or use standard advices only.

   If the other fellow can't seem to apply your advice, then you haven't been given the real facts or the complete facts—try to get them and then re-advise. If the other fellow still can't understand, then *study materials* apply. He or she needs Remedy A or B on our policy or earlier organization contacts, not a new solution.

4. Clear any promotion ideas with your Division 1, HCO, before you advise them, or question HCO so as to keep the offerings real and uniform. You may interrupt an existing program.

5. Clear technical recommendations or requests (such as in an HGC) with your Division 2 before you make them so as to prevent getting a squirrel activity going in some org with consequent upsets. The technical data or solution probably already exists.

6. Clear financial and materiel recommendations or queries with your Division 3 before making them, as the policy or planning may already exist for the org being advised by you.

7. Avoid giving orders or advice that can be used to make you wrong when it's misapplied. Be sure of data and what the question really should be. Then advise.

8. Report pronounced statistical changes you get wind of on your lines to your superiors. But never report entheta and mere opinions or rumors—the data is too fragmentary to be of value. Get statistics if you hear something weird, and if the statistics are bad (less money, less bodies, less anything), report it. But REPORT ONLY STATISTICS.

9. Continually find out what's working well and why things working well in one org aren't in another. Realize faulty utilization, not the policy itself, is the commonest fault. Like a technique, they're not using it right.

10. Report large statistic changes up or down you notice in any org at once to your superiors and your senior comm member or superior, and report loudly when statistics continue bad. Report very loudly and until you are heard.

11. Kill off "bush telegraph" with facts. Reduce the rumor factor all you can. It is valueless in itself, being fragmentary data. Use it only as a signal to get more specific data before you make up your mind or report it to anyone.

12. Be absolute death on "everybody." Anyone saying "Everybody here says _____ ," "The field here thinks," "They _____ " or such generalities should be sharply answered with WHO SPECIFICALLY says or thinks or feels? You'll find one or two people have become "everybody" as that's the mechanism of an ARC break—when people have an ARC break, in general they generalize. Reporting the opinion of one person in a zone as the "opinion of everyone" in that zone can falsify ARC and ruin sound planning. Find out who "everyone in the Academy" is—Bill or Pauline. An ARC broken (upset) person, misemotionally reporting in a letter or telex, invariably generalizes broadly in an effort to justify his misemotion and make a proper effect. In finding out the exact identity of his generalized "everyone," you cure *his* ARC break and don't let *it* cause ARC breaks between your org and his.

13. Use your lines to bring order. Never use them to enturbulate.

14. Use the power of your line (its calmness and good sense) to handle disturbances. Don't threaten or nag.

15. Material passing along the line is subject to the justice regulations if the content violates any of them—i.e., inciting to insubordination, mutiny, placing a superior in danger. Cold, raw statistics, *provable* facts alone do not violate the justice regulations. Saying George X is "a lousy superior" is subject to Committee of Evidence; saying "since George X took over this post, enrollment has fallen, being an average of 100 in the last six months before he took over and only 15 in the six months since," *if* that is true and can be checked up on, it is not Committee of Evidence for the reporter. Facts not opinion keep a person reporting (and an org) out of trouble. REDUCE RUMOR AND OPINION TO RAW DATA BEFORE YOU REPORT IT OR PUT IT ON LONG COMM LINES.

16. Differentiate amongst purposes, subpurposes, senior policy, routine policy, directives, momentary orders and advice. All policy does not have equal value. Policy can't exist down to the details of getting it into effect. That requires orders and advice. The policy of "Get the job done!" is very senior to a policy relating to the expenditure of ballpoints. A martinet is only one who insists on following policy down to idiot level, using policy for how to shine shoes or bite fingernails. A good leader only gets major policy in *hard* and uses the rest as specific orders or advices. Not following important policies is a shooting offense. Using small policy as a means of avoiding the major policy is also a shooting offense.

17. One mostly causes his own trouble on his comm lines. But like the inexperienced auditor who can't spot the point where *he* started the pc's ARC break, the person who starts trouble on a comm line seldom sees how or why. Usually, it's not understanding what's said or not answering.

18. Don't try to impress on org comm lines if you have nothing really to say. "We're running a *great* Comm Course here" is an idle statement. "After taking our Comm Course, 91% of our students pass their HCO Board Provisional" is, if true, the *only* acceptable way to brag. We have had too many "great auditors" and "great Instructors" whose statistics were down graphs and failed students. Brag with statistics on an org comm line.

19. Warn when your senior or junior comm member is "under the gun" or getting into disfavor. (But say who says what. *Never* generalize in such an instance. It's vicious and stupid.) For maybe the person you warn is innocent and can straighten it up as so often happens before a needless Committee of Evidence, called by rumor.

20. Never recommend a solution in the absence of data. Less havoc is caused by demanding straight data than by waiting a bit. If the situation is an emergency, however, any policy or action is better than no action.

21. Never decide about the truth about a person or situation in the absence of data. In this case, a lie is worse than no data at all.

22. Realize when you catch someone in an outright lie about his post, he is not working.

23. Detect noncompliance of orders by flash back or complete absence of acknowledgment.

24. Be safe with policy. One is unsafe with off-the-cuff recommendations contrary to usual practice no matter how bright it may seem. When there *is no* policy, use the purpose of the activity to make your point. Don't use unusual ideas that don't fit the purpose of the group you are advising. In the absence of known policy, make the purpose serve instead and work out a solution that forwards the purpose of the department or unit. Always report such solutions when they work. Policy is a growing thing, based on "what has worked." What works *well* today becomes tomorrow's policy.

25. Lost, forgotten or overlooked policy is more often the cause of trouble than circumstances themselves. The person who is in trouble got that way because of dropped policies. Policies are the solutions which solved yesterday's lacks or troubles and which if followed will prevent tomorrow's troubles. Therefore, present loss of or noncompliance with policy is asking for trouble tomorrow. Almost all current trouble is occurring because of departures from policy yesterday or from causes never before experienced by the group. Policy is group experience. Followed, the group advances. Abandoned, the group falls away. Only Scientologists dare become fiends about following policy for only Scientologists know enough to erase it when it no longer applies. But drop a policy as if one were letting go the only piece of wood in the ocean—once gone there may be no rescue to hand. To demand that unimportant "policy" be followed slavishly or to use it to balk org purposes is *another* way of dying. For it makes people fight major policy and fighting that they have disasters. A group is only a collection of different people without policy to agree upon. For policies are the points of agreement which make the group into a True Group and an irresistible force. Using policy intelligently is the only way a group can ever advance. No policy at all or noncompliance with major policy is the basis of every upset that will be

reported to you whether the fact is stated or not. Purposes and major policy are very safe roads. Leaving them leads to too many quicksand pits for anyone to be mild about departures from policy.

26. Be inexorable and continual in getting purposes followed and major policies in. This is the whole secret of producing startling statistics.

27. Use the formula for putting power and velocity into a line and group: from the group purpose remove distractions, remove barriers, thrust aside noncompliance with bypass, strengthen the edges of the channel and make sure there is a will to follow the purpose. Like magic the group will come to life.

28. The way to audit a group that is in collapse is (a) get them to realize their purpose, spot their past distractions, alter-is and barriers and remove them; (b) get them to strengthen the channel edges to prevent wandering off it; (c) get them to see how the group purpose can be achieved; (d) take out of the group by any method those who have sought to suppress or invalidate the purpose or the source of the group's purpose; and (e) handle as a horrible example all those guilty of noncompliance expressed as laziness or mutiny; (f) provide space for the group to move toward in their action and (g) spot the exterior opposition to the group's purpose and begin to reduce it; and (h) be sure the group is energetically led by someone dedicated to the group purpose and intelligent enough to learn and follow policy and report new lessons.

If these things are done in the *group* even when not on its individual members, life will magically appear, for the formula of livingness has been used—which is "To have and follow a purpose." Now, if one also then audits the individual members of the group to increase their abilities, nothing can stand in the group's way and still remain standing. Man has hit on this formula accidentally sometimes when starting a war or mob actions, and the result is highly destructive to one and all as the purpose was a very bad one such as "Kill all Arabs" or "Lynch the man!" These are just reactive bank purposes gone into frantic dramatization, not rational thought. But man rarely rises above this in applying his instinctive feelings about groups. Sometimes there is a "born leader" who knows the ropes by experience or instinct, but his ability is "unexplained" or called personal charm. When the purpose is *good,* it then has theta, not entheta, and the result is fantastically successful. To the degree an executive can't or won't do as a starting or continuing action (a) to (h) above, the group fails and lacks life. There will be as much life in the group as the purpose is worthwhile and (a) to (h) is executed. The keynote of insanity or death in a group or person is the presence of the symptoms implied in (a) to (h) above. The ability to apply and execute these is called "leadership" or "executive action" in Scientology. Mankind has not achieved a clear definition for either until this time.

29. A comm line of an org is a trust, not a right. Anyone can speak as he pleases on his own line. But when it is a group line, it is held in trust for the group and used for the group. Never confuse one's own personal impulses and freedom of speech with the comm lines of a hat in a group.

L. RON HUBBARD
Founder

238

HCO POLICY LETTER OF 3 APRIL 1965
ISSUED 25 JANUARY 1989

Gen. Non-Remimeo

ORGANIZATION OF A SCIENTOLOGY ORG

Note: This same pattern is used for all orgs small or large. In small orgs more posts are additional hats, handed over as the org grows.

DIVISIONS AND DEPARTMENTS

The organization, wherever located, is under the Executive Director, LRH, who handles the six divisions of each org or Scientology.

The following are the SIX DIVISIONS of a Scientology organization (and Scientology):

Division 1—Hubbard Communications Office Division (HCO Division)

Division 2—The Dissemination Division

Division 3—The Organization Division

Division 4—The Technical Division

Division 5—The Qualifications Division

Division 6—The Distribution Division

In a Central Org or Scientology each division is headed by a secretary as follows:

Division 1—The HCO Secretary

Division 2—The Dissemination Secretary

Division 3—The Organization Secretary

Division 4—The Technical Secretary

Division 5—The Qualifications Secretary

Division 6—The Distribution Secretary

The secretary heads up the departments and the directors of his or her division.

The departments are as follows:

DIVISION 1—HCO DIVISION
THE HCO SECRETARY

DEPARTMENT 1—The "Office of L. Ron Hubbard," headed by the LRH Communicator and also contains the HCO Secretary's Divisional Office. It handles orders, conditions, signatures, coordination, design and planning, justice and HCO personnel.

DEPARTMENT 2—The Department of Communications, headed by the Director of Communications, handling all the communications of Scientology and all the org.

DEPARTMENT 3—The Department of Inspections and Reports, headed by the Director of Inspections and Reports, receiving any and all reports of the Scientology org and all inspections.

DIVISION 2—THE DISSEMINATION DIVISION
THE DISSEMINATION SECRETARY

DEPARTMENT 4—The Department of Compilation, headed by the Director of Compilation, compiling anything to be disseminated from the Scientology org.

DEPARTMENT 5—The Department of Publications, headed by the Director of Publications, handling all publishing, printing of books and magazines and anything else of small manufacture and issue such as tapes, meters and insignia, and stocking and selling same.

DEPARTMENT 6—The Department of Promotion and Registration, headed by the Director of Promotion and Registration and doing the promotion and tabulating its results for the Scientology org.

DIVISION 3—THE ORGANIZATION DIVISION
THE ORGANIZATION SECRETARY

DEPARTMENT 7—The Department of the Organization, headed by the Director of Organization and being his office and the office of the Organization Secretary, handling all financial planning, purchasing, legal and corporate and company secretarial matters for the org and lower echelon and forming new orgs.

DEPARTMENT 8—The Department of Finance, headed by the Director of Finance and handling all the accounts and money of the org.

DEPARTMENT 9—The Department of Materiel, headed by the Director of Materiel and handling all materiel matters, supplies, transport, construction, maintenance and cleaning for the org.

DIVISION 4—THE TECHNICAL DIVISION
THE TECHNICAL SECRETARY

DEPARTMENT 10—The Department of Estimation, headed by the Director of Estimation. This is the Office of the Technical Secretary as well as that of the Director of Estimation. It handles all interview, testing, and student and pc admin matters and their supplies and texts as issued for use by Dept 5 of HCO, and all tech personnel.

DEPARTMENT 11—The Department of Processing, headed by the Director of Processing, operates the Hubbard Guidance Center where authorized and handles *all* processing in the org.

DEPARTMENT 12—The Department of Training, headed by the Director of Training and operates the Academy of Scientology where authorized and Special Courses.

DIVISION 5—THE QUALIFICATIONS DIVISION
THE QUALIFICATIONS SECRETARY

DEPARTMENT 13—The Department of Examinations, headed by the Director of Examinations and contains his office as well as that of the Qualifications Secretary. It handles all examinations and certifications and awards and prepares all certificates and awards and issues all certificates and awards when signed by Dept 1.

DEPARTMENT 14—The Department of Review, headed by the Director of Review and handles review necessary to students who have fallen short of qualification and need coaching before classification or pcs who need additional or repair touches before gradation is awarded. It contains a Field Experience Compilation Unit.

DIVISION 6—THE DISTRIBUTION DIVISION
THE DISTRIBUTION SECRETARY

DEPARTMENT 15—The Department of Field Activities is the office of the Distribution Secretary and is headed by the Director of Field Activities. It guides field programs.

DEPARTMENT 16—The Department of Clearing, headed by the Director of Clearing. It handles the broad clearing of individuals in the society, field staff members and the field in general including field auditors, book auditors and groups.

PLAN

The org board is planned to reduce, without change of form to one person or expand, again without form change, to 2,000,000,000 or more staff members.

There is no alteration of titles or pattern no matter what size the org is.

The board is a modification of an ancient org board of a galactic civilization.

241

By repeating the six divisional names in each department as sections and then repeating the departmental names in each section as subsections and so on, the board can expand to almost infinite size without jamming anyone's lines or hats undetectably.

It is important to have a board anyone can inspect to see where he is overlooking a function, for

ONLY AN UNSEEN FUNCTION CAN JAM LINES AND PREVENT EXPANSION OF ANY ORG.

This board is in essence a "philosophic machine." One could study it for months and still get cognitions on it, on his life and his job and on his portion of the org or the org or all Scientology.

However, another rule conflicts with the above rule about expansion. IF YOU PUT A BOX ON AN ORG CHART PEOPLE WILL FILL IT.

The effort to keep an org solvent, then, (by not hiring too many people) tends to make people crush down the pattern, hiding the functions vital to smooth growth. But if this is done, the org never grows.

Executives, if overworked, seek to contract the org to reduce the traffic they are having trouble handling. If some functions of an org are hidden from view, they cause chaotic traffic and overwork.

One therefore needs a *system* of handling traffic described as the FAST FLOW SYSTEM OF MANAGEMENT given in HCO PL 29 Mar. 65 II, ADMINISTRATION, FLOWS AND EXPANSION, THE FAST FLOW SYSTEM.

One also needs the *complete* board on view at all times so when expansion (and income) increase, executives and staff can unload some of their "additional duties" (plainly visible on the org board) on new people who take over already existing posts.

One can tell what post is in need of filling because this org board is always erected above the Comm Center basket system which department by department matches it. By inspecting the traffic in the baskets (directly below the board) one can get an idea of what department is overloaded and inspect it more closely to see what "hat" (post) now needs filling there. It is also possible to judge this by body traffic inspection.

But the tendency to fill every box on the org board must also be handled. This is done by using a 2 to 1 ratio. There may be two persons or beings on posts in Divisions 1, 2, 3 and 6 for every staff executive or staff member in Divisions 4 and 5 on the org payroll.

Oddly, in Scientology and in any other activity, one can't simply put people into these divisions evenly as one would deal cards into hats. It must be the *sum* of 4 and 5 that is taken first, for 4 will have many more than 5. The expansion is a wedge from Division 4. It is the main production unit and one adds to it first, then adds twice as many to the other divisions BUT ONLY BY VOLUME OF VITAL (not internally developed) TRAFFIC.

In Scientology the center Department 11 has more personnel than any other department.

Almost *all* the personnel in Divisions 4 and 5 are technical personnel. Few clerical people are there in comparison *and* for estimating numbers who can be hired for other divisions, one doesn't include the clerical personnel in Divisions 4 and 5 *and tries not to hire any at all,* leaving them to be furnished by the other divisions.

Thus expansion of an economical nature is ensured and orderly growth is possible.

I have said that one favored a department that was a production department. Division 4 is the highest value production department and has first call on all personnel and departments and their attention. The Technical Division takes precedence in purchase orders, construction and materiel as well as personnel.

SYMBOLISM

The pattern I recalled and used was a being and three unit system repeated over and over. These basic symbols were BEING—MIND—BODY—PRODUCT. This made a small circle above three boxes. Boxes were inside boxes, but always three boxes. If you added a being you added three boxes. There was a being and three big boxes. Then each box had below it a being and three boxes. If you expanded a unit by one being you added three boxes for him.

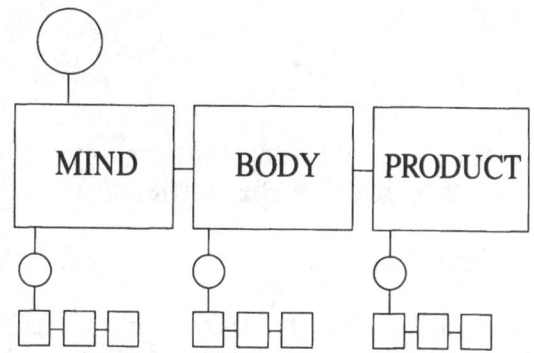

The Mind section had a mind *and* a body and a product. The Body section had a mind, a body and a product. The Product section had a mind and a body and a product.

When you got down to the next row you had now 9 beings to add and each with 3 boxes.

If you take, let's say soap manufacture and use the boxes with names that, while still MIND—BODY—PRODUCT, represent soap making, you will see how the old, old org board worked. The big box MIND, would be the executives and planners sand tech know-how and the box BODY would be the factory and the box PRODUCT would be the soap.

But of course the Mind box (executives, etc.) had themselves a clerical staff (mind) and an office building (body) and a bunch of plans and directives (product). And the factory had foremen (mind) and the machinery, etc., (body) and smoke, heat and waste (product). And the soap had to have salesmen (mind) and retail stores (body) and make money (product).

This goes on and on quite amusingly until one has a vast organization.

However, the old firm failed for only two reasons—it couldn't see and it couldn't change, characteristics which capitalists hold to this day!

Not being able to see, the being himself had to do *all* the looking, a rather arduous hat. And not being able to discover what *happened* to the product afterwards, became too smug about it and one day in a world of cars found itself making the best buggy whips in the world! And it is no more.

Its frequency of 3-3-3 is too simple. A better frequency (established by a lot of experience) is 6-16-6-16-6-16 as we had the 3-3-3 boxes above. To have less invites hidden functions.

The six are the basic symbols of our divisions.

Division 1—FACULTIES

Division 2—MIND

Division 3—BODY

Division 4—PRODUCT

Division 5—CORRECTION

Division 6—DISTRIBUTION

Oddly enough these six work with anything or any activity no matter what it is. And as it was a thetan and three in the earliest one, this is a thetan and six.

But the six hide functions and junior to them we need special parts of the six.

DIVISION 1—FACULTIES needs three parts: CONDITION (Dept 1), COMMUNICATIONS (Dept 2) and PERCEPTION (Dept 3). If you study these you will see they are not alike and are in proper sequence. These are our first 3 departments.

DIVISION 2—MIND needs three parts: ORIENTATION (Dept 4), UNDERSTANDINGS, (not singular as that's the trap) (Dept 5) and PURPOSES (Dept 6).

DIVISION 3—BODY needs to have DIRECTION (Dept 7), ENERGY (Dept 8) and MATTER (Dept 9).

DIVISION 4—PRODUCT needs to have TIME (Dept 10), ACTIVITY (Dept 11) and PRODUCTION (Dept 12).

DIVISION 5—CORRECTION needs to have EXAMINATION (Dept 13) and PERFECTION (Dept 14).

DIVISION 6—DISTRIBUTION needs to have the real PRODUCT (Dept 15) and CLEARING (Dept 16).

As I have said, these symbolic department names apply to ANY CYCLE OF COMPLETION. The 6 formula yields each of our divisions and all sixteen of our departments phrased to be useful to us.

The law appears to be a part of this universe, that a cycle that will complete, must have 16 stages and if any are omitted they will interrupt the cycle and prevent it from completing entirely. There could be thousands but the SENIOR irreducible number is 6 as above and the *whole* cycle is 16 irreducible steps.

These have just been named as departments above. They are the Cycle of Completion.

Now strangely enough, as my searches have found, there are 16 levels in the Gradation Scale and these match the Cycle of Completion!

Therefore our org board is: being—6—16, being—6—16 and so on and on. If you add a being you add 6 big boxes and 16 boxes below these as given.

It took a *projection* 3 dimensional org board to show the ancient one of which I spoke (3-3-3). It could not be graphed in two dimensions. You can see why in the picture. It got too small too quick. Try to put some more boxes on and you've had it, since each box requires a being and three new boxes. Therefore the original board went *inside* the boxes for the new 3 like a hall of mirrors that could be enlarged.

We don't need to do this. I worked for about two weeks or more until I could graph ours in two dimensions. It is sufficiently detailed that it only needs one master board. Each department has its own separate board with *all* the functions of that department and only the main ones appear on the main board. It could still be done by the same projection pictures used by the original ancient board.

To run a small Scientology program (like PE) you need a staff member from each pair of divisions (3 Scientologists), one from 1 and 2, one from 3 and 4, one from 5 and 6. A bigger affair requires that you have one from each division. As you expand you are all right so long as *you don't* cross divisions (put one person in two divisions). In a larger org, crossing (one person in two or more) departments becomes fatal and jams flows and so on. As the size of an org increases the less you can double up 2 anything under one person.

Our board enters from the left and runs parallel.

All other boards (like in big companies or armies) run from the top down to show command and action. Ours runs also from the side as inspection of it will show.

A person really goes through Scientology from left to right at departmental level, using departments one by one.

For the first idea I had in this life that led us straight to Scientology and freedom over these really few years was the realization that if I could understand everything we could find the way. And so it has turned out. That is expressed on this org board.

L. RON HUBBARD
Founder

HUBBARD COMMUNICATIONS OFFICE
Saint Hill Manor, East Grinstead, Sussex

HCO POLICY LETTER OF 1 MAY 1965R
Issue III
REVISED 29 AUGUST 1990

Gen. Non-Remimeo
Hang Near New
Org Board
Varnished Over
or Relettered

ORGANIZATION

THE DESIGN OF THE ORGANIZATION

As our org board and org pattern we have not only an org board but a "philosophical system," which gives us the levels of able and extra able beings and an analysis of one's own life as well.

If you look at the levels written above the departments you find the spans of *the* Bridge which are followed to Release, Clear and OT. You can easily see which ones are missing in one's own life and the lives of others. These are the upper end of the awareness scale.

When you look at the department names you can see what is missing in your own life.

You can also see where your post or your job breaks down for every job has all these "department names."

When you look at the division names you see what the Cycle of Production must be in this universe to be successful. By studying this you can see why other businesses fail. They lack one or another of these divisions.

Although the organization seems to have a great many departments, and would fit only a large group, it fits any org of any size.

The problem presented me in deriving this board was how to overcome continual org changes because of expansion and applying it to organizations of different sizes. This board goes from one person to thousands without change. Just fewer or more posts are occupied. That is the only change.

The staff ratio here is one administration person in the five nontechnical divisions to one technical person in the Technical and Qualifications Divisions (excepting only Staff Staff Auditors and field staff members who count as admin personnel). Staff is added *in rotation* amongst the nontechnical divisions every time a technical person is put in the Technical or Qualifications Divisions.

The board is entered from the left and proceeds to the right.

It is actually a spiral with 7 higher than and adjacent to 1.

The organization corrects itself through the Qualifications Division, under the authority of the 7th Division.

Organizations go in phases. The phases agree with the Cycle of Production.

There are two tendencies man has that this board resolves.

Man's systems are based on groups and masses of people.

Every person on *this* org board is "statisticized." That means the job he does is a statistic that can be verified. He is not lost in a group.

The tendency of filling up every box indicated on an organization chart (which man usually does) is checked by the formula that there must be only one admin staff member for every tech as above. Thus Divisions 4 and 5 are heavy with personnel containing five times as many as all the other divisions.

In expanding, each department acquires seven sections, every section then acquires seven subsections, every subsection acquires seven units.

———

At this time of issue we find Scientology itself just at the end of its Dissemination Cycle (Division 2) and just entering upon the Organization Cycle (Division 3). There will be a full and long Organization Cycle. This will eventually be followed by a Qualifications Cycle in which we adjust civilization. After that will come a Distribution Cycle in which we use Scientology elsewhere in the universe and then will come the Source Cycle again, finding us all on a higher plane.

This pattern will probably be in use for a very long time.

This board is one of the *very* few things in Scientology which is not completely new. It is taken from an ancient organization and which I have refined through considerable experience by adding Scientology and our levels to it. It is based on an extremely successful pattern.

This org pattern is designed not to make money or Scientologists as one might think. Its whole purpose is to make the "Ability to Better Conditions," which is the mission of Scientology.

THE LEVELS

Your main interest in this board is of course its levels.

There are over thirty-two levels to the left of the board, covering the average human states.

Our board shows how we move up onto the Bridge at Communications (Level 0) and then progress division by division to Level VII. One division equals one level left to right.

The abilities recovered in these levels are marked above the department names (Communication, Perception, Orientation, Understanding, etc.) and take us all the way to a new state at VII.

As he progresses along this line left to right, a level is given the person each time a division is passed.

At Level V we find we can move people from the lowest human states onto the Bridge, before we ourselves exit at the top.

Thus we leave behind us a Bridge.

In 1950 when I said, "For God's sake build a better Bridge," I had to do it on my own.

But here it is, not only a Bridge but also an organization to carry the weight of the spanning, a very needful thing.

L. RON HUBBARD
Founder

Revision assisted by
LRH Technical Research
and Compilations

HCO POLICY LETTER OF 15 JANUARY 1966
Issue I

HOLD THE FORM OF THE ORG
DON'T BRING ABOUT DANGER CONDITIONS

As long as executives fail to hold firm the form and channels of the org, their own posts *and* the org will be a confusion. Worse, it will cease to exist.

Executives *must* insist upon the privileges and responsibilities of their posts and not permit bypass and misrouting.

The whole org is run on statistics. It is not run on rumors. The more you follow statistics and the less you listen to rumor, the better off you will be.

Orders are issued to form the org and better statistics and that's all. There are no other reasons for orders, chits and upsets. Actions which don't increase statistics should be eliminated. Irrelevant orders and chits having nothing to do with statistics should never be issued.

To hold the form of the org it is vital that:

1. The Ad Council minutes only order secretaries and only on gross divisional statistics as they appear.

2. Executive Secretaries order and chit only secretaries.

3. That secretaries order and chit only directors.

4. That directors only order and chit section officers.

5. That section officers only order and chit persons in charge or, if there are none, the staff directly under them.

6. Exec Secs and secretaries can cross-chit.

7. Directors can request and chit only via secretaries when they cross divisions.

8. Anyone can file a Job Endangerment Chit with Ethics on anyone. This however is normally filed on a direct senior and only when explicit policy has been violated by an order or chit on one's own post and only when the order or chit might worsen a statistic.

9. If all else fails, petition the Office of LRH.

SEC EDs

Sec EDs issued by the Ad Council may only change secretaries as personnel. They can advise the secretary on personnel but may not demote, transfer or dismiss a secretary's personnel (exception, when sweeping an org of temporaries, staff that hasn't passed Review for Staff Status I).

An Ad Comm's orders forwarded to the Office of LRH for a Sec ED always go via the Ad Council. But again an Ad Comm may only order directors and may not demote, transfer or dismiss a director's personnel.

A director should order officers.

Officers should order in-charges.

When personnel is assigned directly to an executive, such as a personal secretary, one may of course order or chit that person directly as there is no command echelon.

REASON

Danger conditions are handled on bypass. Where a Danger condition is assigned, the senior can bypass anyone to get the job done and does.

The conditions in sequence are:

6. Power

5. Power Change

4. Affluence

3. Normal

2. Emergency

1. Danger

0. Non-Existence.

It is true of all conditions that if you use one lower than you are in, you will bring the *next* lower one about. If you use the Normal Operation Formula when you are in Affluence you will certainly descend into Emergency.

Therefore, if you are in Normal or Emergency condition and start bypassing, you will quickly descend into Danger condition (statistics will drop steeply) and achieve the only condition below Danger which is Non-Existence.

Thus, if you bypass you infer the condition is Danger when it isn't. And you drop the org or any portion of it into Non-Existence.

So don't bypass unless you *are* in Danger condition. A Danger condition exists where statistics show continuing Emergency or a steep, steep fall. If a Danger condition exists, you handle the situation, bypass anyone at all and then the personnel who ignored it. So if you bypass all the time (Exec Secs issuing orders to directors, secretaries ordering officers, directors ordering general staff members), you will infer a Danger condition and get Non-Existence of the section, department, division or the whole activity.

Moral: Only when a Danger condition exists should a senior bypass the command chain; so if you are only in Emergency or only in Normal Operation or even Affluence, DON'T BYPASS or you will crush statistics.

SUMMARY

Learn your org board.

Make your staff learn it.

Handle the org by statistics only.

Order only your immediate juniors.

Don't bypass (except in Danger condition).

Don't infer a Danger condition that doesn't show on a graph.

Hold the org firm by holding its lines and chain of command firm.

And you will prosper and expand.

L. RON HUBBARD
Founder

HCO POLICY LETTER OF 30 JANUARY 1966
Issue II

MINIMUM PERSONNEL OF AN ORG

(Effective 1 June 1966)

The minimum number of persons necessary to form a Scientology organization is ten.

Any organization having less than ten persons is classed as a city office or forming org.

CITY OFFICE

A city office is organized to do PEs and select persons to upper orgs to do co-audits and nonclassed courses and incidental processing.

A city office may not have Executive Secretaries. It can have an HCO Area Sec and an Org Sec and an org board such as fits its actual functions.

It cannot use the names "Academy of Scientology" or "Hubbard Guidance Center."

It may not have an Ad Council, but only an Ad Comm.

It nevertheless must send in the full OIC cable to Saint Hill.

AN ORGANIZATION

A Scientology organization has minimum personnel as follows:

1. HCO Exec Sec

2. Org Exec Sec

3. HCO Area Sec and LRH Communicator

4. Dissem Sec

5. Org Sec

6. Tech Sec

7. Qual Sec

8. Dist Sec

9. Receptionist

10. Cleaner or janitor.

It must operate on the 1966 org board pattern.

The secretaries do all the work of their divisions and may also be pulled in under Tech and Qual to teach and process. The Exec Secs only may not be used in Tech and Qual Divisions.

All such appointments (except 9 and 10) are "Acting" until the org has at least thirty staff members and then become permanent only by the authority of the Advisory Council WW.

Staff is appointed to the divisions as the org expands, on a ratio of one admin to one technical personnel. In other words, each time a staff member is added to Tech or Qual Divisions, one can be added to one of the remaining divisions.

The Executive Division is left unmanned except for the two Exec Secs until there are a total of forty on staff, at which time an LRH Communicator Area is appointed who serves also as Deputy Div 7 Sec.

A Division 7 Sec is appointed when staff totals 100, and the Exec Div is added to the other admin divisions in the ratio.

Exec Sec Communicators are appointed when the staff totals 250.

A Scientology organization may have an "Academy of Scientology" and a "Hubbard Guidance Center."

When the staff totals 100 and Saint Hill-trained interns are available and permanent staff have been Power processed, the org may offer Power Processing to the public.

When the org numbers 250 staff members, it may offer a Solo Audit Course to the public.

When the org numbers 500 staff members, it may offer the Clearing Course to the public.

————————

If an org carefully follows promotion and form of the org as per the current org board, and if it only acts as per OIC statistics in appointments and ethics matters, and if it *very* closely follows tech without variation, and if it does not generate numerous disagreements with tech or policy or the org pattern, it will surely grow.

L. RON HUBBARD
Founder

HCO POLICY LETTER OF 28 FEBRUARY 1966

Remimeo
Exec Sec Hats
Sec Hats
LRH Comm Hat
Director Hats

DANGER CONDITION DATA
WHY ORGANIZATIONS STAY SMALL

The size of an organization depends upon this law:

A LARGE ORGANIZATION IS COMPOSED OF GROUPS. A SMALL ORGANIZATION IS COMPOSED OF INDIVIDUALS.

If you *really* understand this principle and use it properly, you will be able to have a large organization.

There are other factors such as (1) the desirability and quality of one's commodity, (2) the able promotion of it, (3) the ability of the heads of groups in the organization to catch dropped balls and (4) the close following and comprehension of the policies of the organization and its groups.

But the gross monitoring law is as above. When one does not know this and apply it, one has a small, semibankrupt organization that overworks everyone and underpays.

This rule applies to a planet or a nation and is most readily seen in these gross terms. A planet with nations will be far more prosperous than a planet with one central government governing the individuals of a planet.

Socialism fails (and it always fails) because of two factors:

a.   The government seeks to run the individual, and

b.   Socialism unmocks *companies*.

At this writing the prosperity difference (and there is one, Russia currently starving) between the democracy of the US and England and the super socialism of Russia is that the "West" still has companies and the "East" (Russia and China) have abolished them. Russia seeks to run the individual. It has collective farms, etc., but they won't leave a manager alone—to manage—they govern his workers.

To the degree that England and the US tax the *individual* and seek to govern him they will dwindle in size.

England at this writing is undergoing an unmock of the whole empire *solely* because it is bypassing the manager and the governor and directly seeking to govern individuals through income tax, "benefits," etc.

The US is about to come to pieces. Like all big countries on the way out, it never looks so good as when it is already about to fall apart. The US is bypassing the states and US companies and is therefore putting the governors, managers and the states and companies in Danger condition. This, unrepaired, will unmock states and companies and collapse the subgroup on which the big group called the US depends, for an organization is composed of *groups*. Non-Existence is the condition just below Danger. A Danger condition carried on too long drops down scale to Non-Existence. A large group made up of Non-Existences is of course nonexistent itself. Thus bypass by the heads of a big organization of the heads of its internal small organizations works toward Non-Existence. It is really quite simple.

To make an organization get smaller all one has to do is bypass the subgroups and run the individuals only and the org will collapse or struggle along at near-collapse; NO MATTER HOW BRIGHT ITS MANAGER MAY BE OR HOW HARD HE OR SHE WORKS OR HOW BRIGHT THE STAFF IS, OR HOW GOOD THE PRODUCT, the violation of the law in the second paragraph will decay.

Fantastic, isn't it?

All one has to do to make an organization grow is apply the law that a large organization is composed of groups. It is NOT composed of individuals.

In absolute proof of this, in a tiny org it is always observed that everyone there wears each one all the hats. It is a madhouse of individual cross-endeavor. Show me an org that stays small and I will show you an org where every staff member is wearing all the hats in the place. They *can't* grow because they violate the law that a large organization is composed of groups.

Russia, just yesterday sweeping the world, has begun to lose ground and her empire withdraws. Russia won't allow companies. She never says to the head of Georgia, "Get your statistics up, bub" and leaves him to it. Instead she governs the Georgian individual with spies, secret police and even income tax and is more apt to shoot the head of Georgia if his statistics *do* rise as he is then looked on by a paranoid central government as capable enough to be a menace. Russia once governed via cells and did so as long as she was expanding. Now she has income tax! Russia expanded despite bad management solely because she was composed of cells and collectives—but she went too far and erased the individual entirely; so, though growing, she starves. Her groups were mainly dedicated to politics, not production, which is a frailty of governments anyway. But the basic group *is* composed of individuals. (For heaven's sakes don't tell Russia as we don't want her growing—tell her she *must* govern her individuals individually and she'll vanish! You can tell the US, if you like, but only because no president yet ever listened to anything except his popularity poll and, with only a four-year career, isn't likely to. In the US, the government itself vanishes regularly and only the companies, with plenty of interference, keep the civilization going.)

England's sad old empire was great as long as India was run by the East India Company, etc., etc. Its colonies and dominions did fine right up to the moment the government in Westminster and Whitehall started to run the natives as individuals, bypassing the company-controlled colonies. Then the "Empire" started to go broke because *it never was a political empire* but a commercial one. As a political empire it uniformly failed until about 350 years ago it began to charter companies to rule and govern foreign lands. Then it got an "empire." When it began to bypass its company heads and set up crown-controlled governors and then bypass these, it ceased to be an English empire and it looks today that soon there won't even be an England. It could not control even one colony the moment it started to govern individual colonial citizens on a bypass of the colonial companies.

You can use the same argument *they* use. That "concentrating only on groups is hell on the individual." Marx used that line. Well it isn't true. When you get too big a group, the individual in it, suffering the whole pressure of the state, *suffers*. The reverse is true—"by concentrating only on groups the individual is protected and prospers."

Now we get to the philosophic question in the law—how large is large, how small is small?

Oddly this is easily answered, unlike most philosophic conundrums. You have to have the answer to "how big should a group be in order for the individuals in it to be effectively managed without oppression in order to get the job done?" That asks and answers it. A correct group size is one where the individuals in it are not made too small by the group being too large. This is a ratio question. The government of England! and the individual Englishman are of incomparable magnitude. What the hell can Joe Cockney, a citizen, do against the government of England! Nothing! So Joe Cockney goes to pieces. You can't have a comm line between a billion-horsepower motor and one grasshopper! Something is going to explode and it isn't the billion-hp motor. It's the grasshopper. Therefore when the management unit is too big, the individual (despite all the protection laws in the world) becomes apathetic and can't work or doesn't see himself as important enough to bother about.

So what is a proper-sized basic group?

A GROUP IS A PROPER SIZE WHEN THE INDIVIDUALS IN IT CAN EASILY APPROACH THE MANAGER OF THAT GROUP ON A FAMILIAR, FRIENDLY BASIS AND BE SURE HE KNOWS WHAT THEY'RE DOING AND WHY AND IF THEY'RE DOING IT.

The individual in that group is not oppressed. His charm counts. He feels up to arguing with that manager. The executive (with a deputy on his side) feels up to confronting the rest of the group. His own personality counts.

The only reason you have strikes and labor unions is that this group law has been violated. Too many individuals in the group for them to know intimately their manager on a friendly, cooperative basis.

This is all Marx is about. Marx is really a protest against too big a group solved by creating a protective state (an overwhelmingly large group) that "rescues" the individual! So communism is a mess. For by making a state group, one overwhelmed the individual and sure enough the only criticism of communism that a communist will tolerate is that it has too big a "bureaucracy," by which he means too big a government for an individual to confront. Communism goes even further. It abolishes the individual utterly! It *forces* him to be a group. And that is very bad, for individuals are the building block of the small group. So

Marx neither knew nor solved the basic problem of government. He didn't know the above two laws about organizations and groups so communism, supposed to solve individual oppression, is the most individually oppressive form of government on this planet.

How many individuals can effectively compose a group?

It depends on the ability of the manager to handle men on an individual basis. This varies. But such men or women as can handle a large number are very, very rare. So we take a *safe* answer.

A fairly safe answer is six—the manager of the group plus five individuals, one a deputy manager.

This is determined by the answer to this question:

How many subordinates are you willing to work with on the job? Five others is about all you'd care to stretch it. Two others would be too comfortable—even too dull. But you can stretch it up to five.

Thus we could stretch out an org composed of groups of six persons—a manager, a deputy and four—making six maximum in each group.

And you now have the size of the largest building blocks it takes to make a big org. Six persons in each.

If we pyramid this we have (each maximum):

Five staff members and their in-charge as a unit;

Five units and the section executive in a section;

Five sections plus the department's director in a department;

Three departments and the secretary, a deputy and a communicator in a division;

Four divisions in a portion and the Org Exec Sec and a deputy and a personal sec;

Three divisions and the HCO Exec Sec plus her deputy and a personal sec in the HCO portion.

Or with a full Exec Division setup:

Four Exec Sec Comms in an Office and the Org Exec Sec and a personal sec;

Three Exec Sec Comms in an Office for the HCO Exec Sec and her personal sec.

But we build *downwards* by groups of six if we expand further, rarely exceeding five and an executive.

You see then that the moment the HCO Exec Sec starts handling Address In-Charge, the jump is too great as it puts Address In-Charge up against the equivalent of the total executives of units and sections of HCO! It makes his

257

group too big. It makes him too small (being such a small part). He gets rattled, feels oppressed, tends to snarl because he is overwhelmed—his group is too big so he is too small. Simple as that.

So long as an executive only handles two, three, four, five people, he *can* handle his job because they know him. The people under him can handle *their* subgroups so long as they contact only two, three, four, five people and themselves.

For instance, so long as there are only five Continental Orgs, Exec Sec Communicators will feel comfortable, providing the Continental Orgs have each two, three, four, five orgs under them and have in their turn Exec Sec Communicators.

So proper organization for expansion builds in blocks of six maximum—five plus an executive. That can be five groups plus an executive as you go up or five staff members plus an executive as you go to the bottom.

Wherever this is violated, the organization (whether a nation or a company or us) will dwindle. Where it is kept, the organization will grow.

I warn you that five-plus-an-executive-sized groups is hard work, even a strain at times, but it can be done. Six or seven plus an executive is quite too much. And a government versus Joe Doakes is a complete smash, as Joe is only maybe 1/70,000,000th as big as the government!

So never bypass. Completely aside from the true mechanics of the Danger Formula where bypass results in Non-Existence, it is hell on the executive *and* every member of the organization to have continual violation of the maximum group size.

If an executive feels overworked, even with all dev-t cared for and policed, then that executive has below him violations of group size *and* is bypassing some point that should have an executive below him, with a group under that executive. The overworked executive is trying to handle more than five other people directly (five staff members or five group executives).

It's like boxes in boxes in boxes. But in this case six boxes at the most fit comfortably.

If a department has eight sections under its director, then we have to group the sections by giving the director two who each control four sections. This is a very comfortable director, for he has a group of two plus the director. He can loaf. But his assistants will sweat. So add one assistant and divide the department's sections into three groups—three, three and two—and you will have a more efficient department.

That's the way you juggle it about to prevent overwork by executives and overwhelm of individuals.

If you want to increase efficiency on a five-plus-executive group, always make one of the five a deputy and slightly senior to the other four. The four can then approach the deputy to see if they should approach the executive on matters they feel uneasy about. This adds a gradient.

There are various ways to juggle this about. An executive with seven sections can take three himself and give a deputy four, etc. Lots of ways to do it but just stay at or below one plus five if you can.

The senior to the group exec is not counted as a member of the group.

Here and there we violate this. A Comm Ev is not as acceptable as a hearing because one person faces more people. Jury trials are a horrible strain and a cruelty because one has to face about fourteen people! (Judge, prosecutor, jury.) Too many!

––––––––––

So those are the laws which underlie organization.

But you can have it all on the org board and not practice it and collapse. If an Exec Sec is approaching fifteen staff members past their executives, it can wreck the place as the staff members go into apathy, the secretaries go into Non-Existence and bang! no org.

So completely aside from Danger condition, violations of *following* proper group organization will bring any organization, a planet, a state, an org, into a mess.

This is what underlies the decline and fall of civilizations: the state begins to govern the individual!

An organization is composed of *groups,* not individuals. And that truth followed and practiced in the flesh as well as on paper will bring about a happy civilization, a happy nation and a flourishing org.

––––––––––

SUMMARY

A LARGE ORGANIZATION IS COMPOSED OF GROUPS; A SMALL ONE IS COMPOSED OF INDIVIDUALS.

The primary difference between the opulent West and the starving East is that the West still permits companies. This means to some extent the Western nations are composed of groups so they are still somewhat successful.

A GROUP IS A PROPER SIZE WHEN THE INDIVIDUALS IN IT CAN EASILY APPROACH THE MANAGER OF THAT GROUP ON A FRIENDLY BASIS AND BE SURE HE KNOWS WHAT THEY ARE DOING AND WHY AND IF THEY ARE DOING IT.

More than five persons plus their executive tends to be too large a group.

The five persons under an executive can of course be executives of groups. And the five persons below each of *those* executives can be executives of groups.

If things aren't organized this way, the individual is crushed. The executive is crushed by overwork and the persons under him are overwhelmed.

259

Bypass of an executive, aside from putting him in danger, overwhelms the members of his group and makes them do less and makes them feel attacked and lessens their sense of their own power.

Two plus an executive is also a group but the executive is not really working to capacity.

With all dev-t cared for, an executive will be overworked if he is over more than five subordinates.

The principal reason orgs stay small is no matter how fancy their org boards they do not actually practice what is on the board but bypass or pay no real attention to command lines and so in actual practice are only one or two over-sized groups—which results in them staying small and being overworked and also underpaid as their system in actual practice is inefficient.

The moral is, practice proper grouping as provided by the org pattern, never bypass and so expand and have a happy staff.

L. RON HUBBARD
Founder

HCO EXECUTIVE LETTER OF 5 OCTOBER 1966

Gen. Non-Remimeo

To: All Orgs

From: RON

SUBJECT: A NEW PATTERN OF ORGANIZATION

(HCO Exec Ltr of 26 June 64: Reissued for use
in orgs no longer on Div 7 org board)

You may have certain basic stumbling blocks in organization solvency. They from time to time arise in any organization. These are:

1. Low units.

2. Low volume of income.

3. An imbalance between income and outgo.

The usual answer is to work hard and promote hard and hope. There is nothing wrong with these answers. But please be aware of the fact that they are *emergency* actions.

An emergency occurs only in the presence of poor planning. One can plan so poorly and complete so badly that one is always in emergencies.

Therefore, if you sporadically have to go into hard spurts of action to make ends meet, something must be wrong with basic planning.

I am perfectly willing to take my share of responsibility for this as I gave you the pattern you now use. With this pattern and with what we have to work in this world, we need to scramble pretty furiously at times to stay on top.

I have given a lot of thought to this lately and, using my years of Org Sec experience, have worked very hard for about 3½ months to establish a better pattern of an organization which yet does not overthrow what is good in our old pattern.

I have pretested the matter at Saint Hill for a couple of months and find there is no reason to change or refine this new revision after seeing it in operation and so I consider it ready for release. I will not, at first, make this the subject of policy letters. Instead I am asking you only to take the steps herein, with HCO's cooperation, as soon as possible. Make it very clear to all that this does not alter such things as financial policies or enrollment policies, etc. This only changes your organization board, the form of the organization, and your observation of your organization. *It doesn't even change where people sit or what they do.*

261

The steps are very simple.

It is only necessary to do the following:

1. Scrub your two division (technical and administrative) mock-up.

2. Draw one long line below Association or Organization Secretary, as per attached chart.

3. Below that from left to right mark in PRODUCTION DEPARTMENT and below that the name of the department and below that in red the name of the person directing it (as per attached drawing).

4. Fanned out just below Organization or Association Secretary and to either side place several *units* as marked.

Now the theory of this is as follows:

a. A department is a production department producing a certain thing (new people, enrolled students, pcs, etc.)

b. A unit is devoted to internal service to the organization and is only administrative and assists the Association or Organization Secretary.

c. A production department head is in red, and "PRODUCTION DEPART-MENT" itself is written in red.

d. All service unit heads are in black, and all other staff is written in black.

e. Only a production department rates.

f. An administrative unit head is played down. He or she is not a director, but only an administrative assistant to the Org or Association Secretary.

g. Production departments can have things they want *if* they are producing.

h. Service units use big brother's old bicycle and their POs are usually viewed with a very hard eye.

i. Receive your usual reports from various sections of the organization.

j. Hold the head of a production department fully, completely and personally responsible for his production quota, including procurement, and make this repeatedly known to staff.

k. Hold the heads of service units responsible for service to be rendered.

If you do this simply and directly you will no longer be in the dark as to who is doing what and who isn't. It stands out loud and clear.

You will find at once why your unit is low. Part of the answer is the overstaffing on admin in most orgs. You will see in fact how few really produce. This by the way becomes so visible that you will get blow-offs (which you should let go, should have long ago). Your good staff will stay.

It leaves you with a fantastically lucid look at the bones of the organization. How few are in action in production.

Put this chart, then, in action straightaway. Then inexorably and gently press the organization itself into this form. You will find that this does *not* reduce your actual production, though it may increase it. It will certainly reduce your bills.

After a month with this new pattern in use write me and tell me in detail what you have found, what you have realized and what further refinements you suggest.

Okay?

Best,

RON

L. RON HUBBARD
Founder

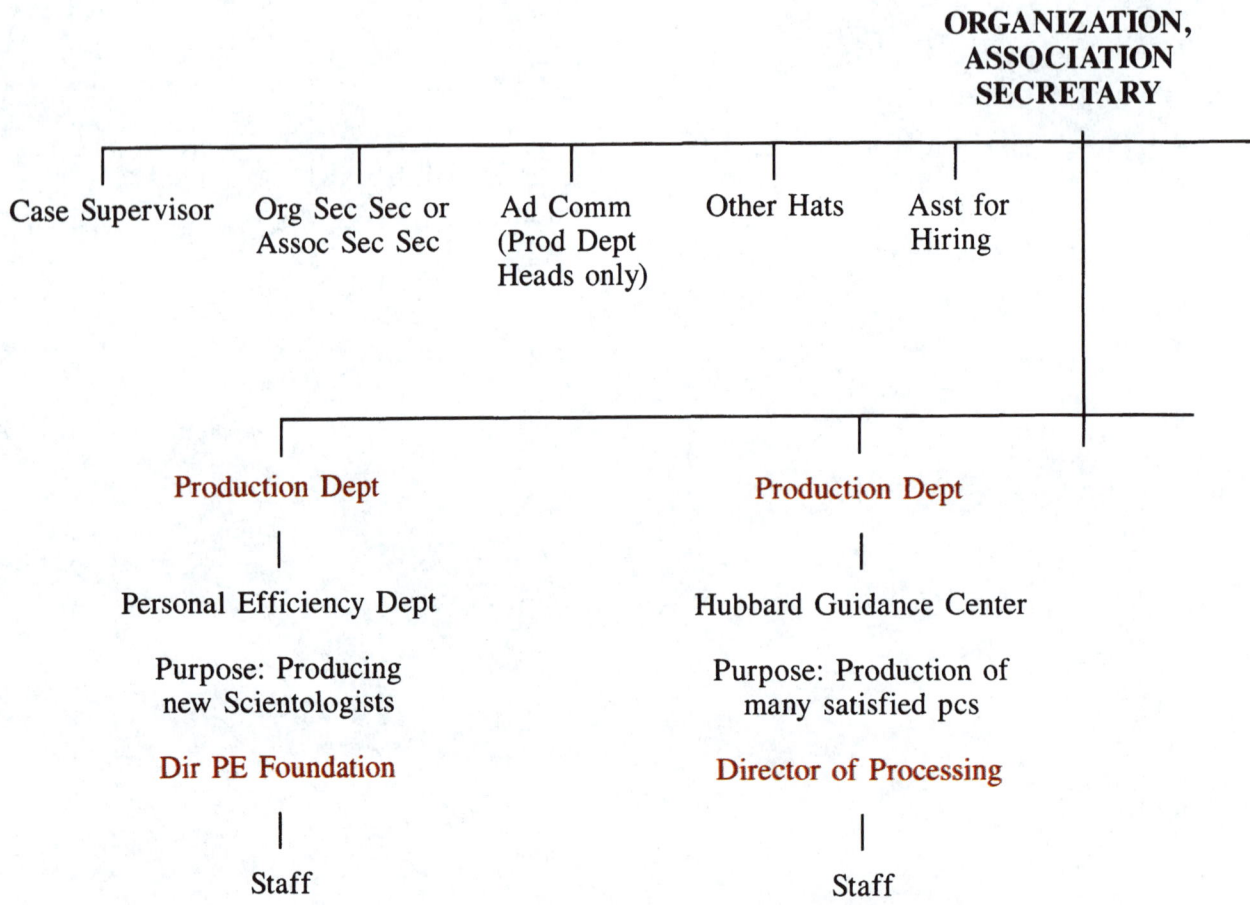

L. RON HUBBARD

EXECUTIVE DIRECTOR

**ORGANIZATION,
ASSOCIATION
SECRETARY**

Case Supervisor   Org Sec Sec or   Ad Comm   Other Hats   Asst for
                   Assoc Sec Sec   (Prod Dept   Hiring
                                     Heads only)

Production Dept   Production Dept

Personal Efficiency Dept   Hubbard Guidance Center

Purpose: Producing   Purpose: Production of
new Scientologists   many satisfied pcs

Dir PE Foundation   Director of Processing

Staff   Staff

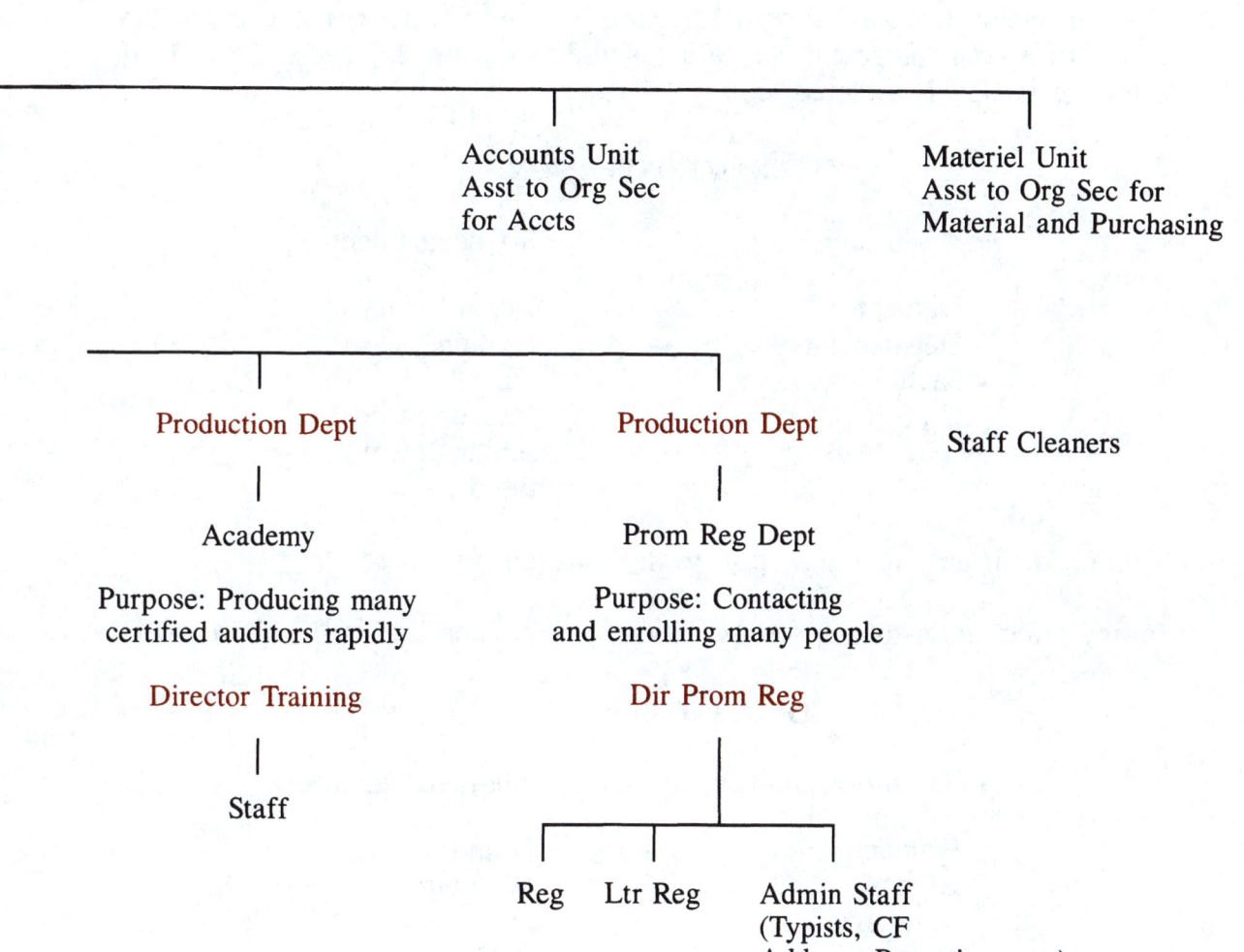

HCO (as before)

Accounts Unit
Asst to Org Sec
for Accts

Materiel Unit
Asst to Org Sec for
Material and Purchasing

Production Dept

Academy

Purpose: Producing many
certified auditors rapidly

Director Training

Staff

Production Dept

Prom Reg Dept

Purpose: Contacting
and enrolling many people

Dir Prom Reg

Reg   Ltr Reg   Admin Staff
(Typists, CF
Address, Reception, etc.)

Staff Cleaners

STAFF MEETING: ALL STAFF

HUBBARD COMMUNICATIONS OFFICE
Saint Hill Manor, East Grinstead, Sussex

HCO POLICY LETTER OF 21 OCTOBER 1966
Issue I
Remimeo

IMPORTANT

SIX–DEPARTMENT SYSTEM

The conversion from a full seven-division org to a six-department org or the conversion of a six-department org to a seven-division org is very easy to do if the following is closely adhered to.

TABLE OF CONVERSION

Seven-division org		Six-department org
Division	—	Department
Department	—	Section
Section	—	Unit
Unit	—	Include in next senior unit in the 6 Dept

This makes it easy to follow policy and have an org board.

In any policy letter of the seven-division system, substitute in the above table.

TITLE CONVERSION

Seven-division org		Six-department org
Founder	—	Founder
Exec Sec	—	Secretary
Secretary	—	Director
Director	—	Officer
Officer	—	In-Charge
In-Charge	—	Staff Member
Staff Member	—	Staff Member

In studying the seven-division policy letters or arranging an org board, use the above table for titles in the six-department system.

SIX–DEPARTMENT ORG

The following are the primary groups of the six-department org and their sections and those who head them.

OFFICE OF LRH

    LRH Communicator (or HCO Sec)
      Estate Section—Materiel Officer
             Cleaning and
                Maintenance In-Charge

Dept 1 HCO DEPARTMENT

Sect 1	Routing, Appearances, Personnel Section	— RAP Officer
Sect 2	Communications Section	— Comm Officer
Sect 3	Inspection and Reports Section	— I&R Officer

Dept 2 DISSEMINATION DEPARTMENT

Sect 4	Promotions Section	— Promotion Officer
Sect 5	Publications Section	— Publications Officer
Sect 6	Registration Section	— Registration Officer

The above two departments are under the general charge of the HCO SECRETARY.

Dept 3 TREASURY DEPARTMENT

Sect 7	Income Section	— Income Officer
Sect 8	Disbursement Section	— Disbursement Officer
Sect 9	Records, Assets and Materiel	— RAM Officer

Dept 4 TECHNICAL DEPARTMENT

Sect 10	Tech Services Section	— Tech Services Officer
Sect 11	Training Section	— Training Officer
Sect 12	Processing Section	— Processing Officer

Dept 5 QUALIFICATIONS DEPARTMENT

Sect 13	Examinations Section	— Examinations Officer
Sect 14	Review Section	— Review Officer
Sect 15	Certs and Awards Section	— Certs and Awards Officer

Dept 6 DISTRIBUTION DEPARTMENT

Sect 16	Public Information Section	— PI Officer
Sect 17	Clearing Section	— Clearing Officer
Sect 18	Success Section	— Success Officer

The above four departments are under the general charge of the ORGANIZATION SECRETARY.

The Advisory Council consists of the HCO Secretary and the Organization Secretary.

There are no Advisory Committees.

The action names of divisions in the seven-division system are assigned in the six-department system to its sections.

Therefore, there is no real change in the org board between a six-dept and a seven-division org, except that it is posted by sections instead of departments and departments instead of divisions. "The Office of LRH" is placed in a six-department system where Exec Division is placed in a seven-div system, the Office of Exec Sec of the seven divisions becomes the LRH Comm Section, and the Office of the Org Exec Sec on the seven-division board becomes the Estate Section on the six-department board.

On the six-dept board the HCO Sec takes the place of the HCO Exec Sec and the Org Sec takes the place of the Org Exec Sec.

FUNCTIONS

There are no less functions in a six-dept system but there are more functions per executive and staff member as the traffic is less.

In reducing an org to a six-dept system, those familiar with seven divisions will not have studied in vain, and in expanding an org, the policy and lines learned in a six-department org stay unchanged, save for the first and second conversion tables above.

PRODUCTION DEPARTMENTS

Four of the six departments are production departments in a six-department org. These are Dissem Dept, Tech Dept, Qual Dept and Dist Dept.

GRAPHS

The gross divisional statistics of a seven-division org become the gross departmental statistics of a six-department org plus the Exec Div stats for the Office of LRH.

OIC CABLES

Report cables are the same for a seven-division and a six-department org.

GENERAL POLICY

All policy, policy letters, Sec EDs and EDs applying to a seven-division org apply to a six-department org.

CONTINENTAL DIVISIONS

Where a continental division has its home org as a six-department org, it is called a CONTINENTAL EXECUTIVE DEPARTMENT.

In such a case the title HCO *Exec* Sec Continental is the HCO Sec Continental, the Org *Exec* Sec Continental is the Org Sec Continental.

FOUNDATION

A six-department organization has a city-office-sized evening Foundation. (See HCO PL 21 Oct. 66 III, CITY OFFICE, for the city office org board.)

STAFF STATUS

There is no change in staff status and its requirements between a six-department and a seven-division org.

REASONS

Small orgs have too hard a time obtaining sufficient personnel to cover a seven-division system. This leaves whole sections missing.

By giving the functions of those sections in the seven-division system to directors in the six-department system, they can shift their staff about in functions to cover the primary actions vital to an org's success.

L. RON HUBBARD
Founder

HCO POLICY LETTER OF 21 OCTOBER 1966
Issue II

CITY OFFICE SYSTEM

There are several types of Scientology activities and identities as follows:

SEVEN–DIVISION ORGANIZATION

SIX–DEPARTMENT ORGANIZATION

   (see policy letter same date)

CITY OFFICE

MISSION

PERSONAL EFFICIENCY FOUNDATION

STAFF MEMBER

FIELD STAFF MEMBER

FIELD AUDITOR

BOOK AUDITOR

SCIENTOLOGY GROUPS

MEMBER

SCIENTOLOGIST

The differences are of (1) size, (2) org board, (3) services rendered.

THE SEVEN–DIVISION ORGANIZATION has more than seventy-five staff members, has the large 1965 org board complete. It gives services as permitted by Worldwide, but not less than Grade IV training, Grade V Power Processing, a full PE and is also served by a Foundation (usually on a six-dept system). It may have one or more Executive Divisions, depending on whether it is Worldwide, continental, zonal, subzonal or local.

THE SIX–DEPARTMENT ORGANIZATION has up to seventy-five staff members, an org board similar to the seven-division org board but in departments. It delivers up to Grade IV training and Grade V Power Processing as permitted, operates a PE and may or may not have a Foundation attached. If so, its Foundation is city office size.

A CITY OFFICE has less than thirty-five staff members, has a six-section system and org board (see PL Issue III same date). It gives training and processing as assigned by WW and its continental senior. It has field staff members. Its evening Foundation has the same type org board as the day city office.

A MISSION has less than thirty staff members. Its org board simply states who is there and what he does. It is chartered by official Scientology but is not an "official org" unless it so requests. It trains all levels up to, but not including, Level Zero. It can run a Dianetic Course. It processes up to the classification of the auditors auditing, but not including or above Power Processing. It does not have Power Processing. It concentrates on PE, individual and co-auditing at Dianetic level. It can do Group Auditing. It operates day or evening or both.

A PERSONAL EFFICIENCY FOUNDATION has less than ten staff members. It has an org board with its activities and personnel designated. It teaches PE Courses and does individual auditing up to classifications held by the auditors concerned, but not Power Processing or above. It copes as it can.

A STAFF MEMBER is any full- or part-time member of the staff of any official org and has the title, duties and privileges assigned by policy.

A FIELD STAFF MEMBER serves the org of which he is an FSM, interests people, patches up cases and operates as a Dissemination, Qualifications function and comes under Distribution for admin purposes.

A FIELD AUDITOR professionally processes preclears up to his classification but not Power Processing or above. He can run study courses.

A BOOK AUDITOR audits preclears below classification levels without pay and operates study groups.

SCIENTOLOGY GROUPS are chartered by any official organization. They study texts and have regular group activities and are often headed by Book Auditors or field auditors and are sometimes addressed by qualified auditors. They have a regular official charter.

MEMBER receives the services and privileges to which his membership entitles him.

SCIENTOLOGIST: an individual interested in Scientology. Disseminates and assists Scientologists.

This brief outline is issued by me to correct any confusion entered by our evolving expansion.

Nineteen sixty-five was a year of tremendous forward thrust and reorganization and we must get the pieces sorted out and back in place.

L. RON HUBBARD
Founder

HCO POLICY LETTER OF 11 AUGUST 1967
Issue II

Remimeo
Also Members of
 OT Central Comm
 and Sea
 Organization

ORGANIZATION

DEFINITION OF

The word ORGANIZATION in Scientology policy means an activity organized on the 7 Division System authorized by myself and regular official Scientology organizations and under Worldwide.

When an activity or project is taken over by an organization but is separate from it, the new unit will be called an ORGANIZATION.

By the use of this word it should be communicated that the activity is fully regular, official and conducted by real, authorized Scientology organizations.

The word PROJECT hereafter denotes an unestablished and unofficial activity, condoned or authorized by an organization.

The word PROGRAM means a routine activity within an organization, repetitive and continuing.

With the issue of this policy letter, the Scientology sea activity or "project" becomes the SEA ORGANIZATION and the base establishment becomes the BASE ORGANIZATION, as these are official, recognized and are conducted by proper Scientology organizations and are under Worldwide.

The word ORGANISATION or ORGANIZATION or ORG may not be used to denote an unofficial or test or temporary activity or an activity not authorized by mainline Scientology.

L. RON HUBBARD
Founder

L. Ron Hubbard

EXECUTIVE DIRECTIVE

LRH ED 44 INT   9 November 1968

STANDARD ADMIN

You will be hearing a lot more about standard admin in the future. Like standard tech it produces fantastic results when used.

Right now these are your admin orders.

1. EACH MEMBER OF THE EC TO SEE HIS DIVISIONS PERFORM THEIR EXACT DUTIES AND DO THEM WELL AND FAST.

2. EACH DIVISION TO HAVE A SECRETARY WHO DOES OR SEES THAT THE DIVISION and ITS DEPARTMENTS DO THEIR EXACT DUTIES.

3. EACH DEPARTMENT TO DO THE EXACT MAJOR DUTY FOR WHICH IT IS NAMED.

If you simply do the above, get busy and knock off all complexities the org will soar. It is really as easy as that.

So get an org board up and up to date. Man it from the TOP down. Hold all posts below that are empty from above.

Just that. Get an org board up and up to date.

Then when you've done that put in each column of the org board a pasteboard sign of exactly what each dept mainly does.

Example, in Dept 1 put

"PERSONNEL, gets it, posts it. Really does it."

In Dept 2 put

"COMMUNICATIONS, sends, receives, routes, internal and external."

In Dept 3 put

"GRAPHS and ETHICS."

And so on down the org board for 27 departments.

Then the Exec Sec sees that it runs this way. Each Exec Sec sees that the staff knows and uses and does these simple actions.

PLEASE SEE THAT THIS IS DONE.

It is the first step of standard admin. Knock off all the airy-fairy nonsense and complexities.

Just do the above.

See that the actions under that simple department heading get *done*. Use ethics where they are NOT done. Assign higher conditions where they ARE done.

Suddenly all the complexity (and low stats) will blow off.

Most orgs have not had time to find out the total magic of standard tech. But it is sinking in. We are able today to really fly all the pcs we get. Fast. *That* sector is in the progress of being cared for.

Now begin to back it up with standard admin. I know you seem far too busy to do this. That you haven't done it is why you're far too busy.

So take these steps NOW. Just and only as outlined above. And you'll be utterly bowled over to find the org soars to Power.

Please?

L. RON HUBBARD
Founder

L. Ron Hubbard
EXECUTIVE DIRECTIVE

LRH ED 49RA INT

9 December 1969
Revised 8 January 1991

Exec Sec Hats

ORGANIZATION PROGRAM NO. 1
HCO ES for activation

Where an org is forming or where its stats are low or its performance poor or it is failing, it is URGENT that this LRH ED be put into *immediate effect*.

As the form of the org is the first thought and action of the HCO Exec Sec, he or she should activate this ED as it applies, promptly and positively.

LESS THAN FIVE STAFF

Where an org has less than five staff do the following, no matter whether it is forming or performing poorly or failing.

If the org has less than three persons in it, bring it up to three persons or it isn't an org.

Appoint this much org board:

HCO ES   OES   PES

The senior auditor of the three is the Org Exec Sec.

The one who can type or manage is the HCO ES. The one with the best public reach is the Public Exec Sec.

These three beings give you the first glance at the two to one admin/tech ratio. An org may have two or less admin personnel to every tech personnel (auditor or instructor). There must never be more than two admin to one tech.

No matter how many functions you see on a nine-division org board, each one of the above is responsible for all the major functions which appear in his org portion.

This org board goes down to as few as three staff members as above or as high as thousands.

In its most basic view, in such a tiny org the major duties are as follows:

HCO ES—Form of org, Reception, registration, procurement letters, Central Files, ethics, personnel, appearance of org and staff, any LRH Comm and Director of Special Affairs duties, communications, legal.

The functions that MUST be covered for the org's basic survival are form of the org, Reception, registration and Central Files. These are the income-getting actions of her org. Anyone who ever buys anything from the org, whether via the PES such as a book or small course, is INVOICED with the person's name and address very legible and correct on the invoice and a copy of this goes to Central Files and into a folder and into a file cabinet. To omit these actions prevents the org from having a record for the Registrar to use to contact and sign people up and the org will probably fail or go broke. This one admin action is the most neglected and the most destructive. Addresses for mailings come from CF folders and out of this Address will grow. These folders never decay unless the person dies or asks to be taken off the list. Everything relating to comm with this person and new invoices, etc., including phone notes, goes in his folder.

OES—The Org Executive Secretary—Org Exec Sec combines Accounts, Tech and Qual functions. Elementary banking and bill paying (with the Registrar and PES both able to invoice in, giving the money over to the OES with an invoice copy) is done by the OES. All auditing and major course supervision is done by the OES. The combination of duties may look all but impossible to combine, but the strange part of it is, they do and I have done all three at once in a small unit. The trick is to arrange one's time. The major functions that *must* be done for the org to be successful are safeguarding funds by recording and banking and paying bills, auditing pcs, teaching students and correcting those cases that fail or students that are slow. If one of those functions is omitted, especially correction (Qual), then the org will falter and fail.

PES—The Public Executive Secretary—Public Exec Sec works to get NEW people. He does not work on people who have already bought something unless they are dissatisfied or ARC broken with service and muddying up his field at which time he severely gets the HCO ES to bring them in and smooth them out and the OES or a higher org (preferably) to handle them as a tough case. If the HCO ES fails to handle or the OES has out-tech, the PES can have a very hard time of it. By low-level public courses, lectures, Sunday services, invitations and contacts and book sales, the PES gets people into the org, drives them in, in a number of ways. When they are in and getting some service the HCO ES signs them up for higher-level, higher-priced auditing and training. The PES also runs Group Processing sessions and co-audits and schedules such activities. As soon as possible he gets in a field staff member program using persons who have had service. Getting people to give their success stories is part of it.

THE PES GETS OUT A TWICE-MONTHLY NEWSLETTER TO HIS FSMs TELLING THEM WHAT IS BEING SUCCESSFUL AND WHAT IS NOT. HE COAXES MISSIONS TO SELECT TO HIS ORG AND GIVES THEM ADVICE, PARTICULARLY BASED ON WHAT OTHER MISSIONS ARE DOING WELL. HE KEEPS HIMSELF INFORMED OF WHAT IS SUCCEEDING

AND KEEPS OTHERS ADVISED OF IT AND KEEPS THE PICTURE CURRENT WITH CONTINUAL REOBSERVATION. He also sells memberships as well as books, tapes, meters, insignia. Methods of getting new names and getting people into the org vary. One follows the formula of pushing what was successful and dropping what wasn't. However, all of the above functions are accomplished by the PES. He is also the PRO and seeks to establish PRO area control (meaning keeping the area handled so the org is well thought of) no matter how hard this is to do where there is an active enemy or a muddied-up field or a hostile press.

TECH BACKLOGS are the primary menace in an org. If it can't deliver auditing it will shortly find no pcs apply. Neither a Tech nor Qual backlog must ever exist and must be reduced.

An org is far better off selling courses, and when pcs tend toward backlog the org increases its tech staff on a long range and starts heavily pushing courses on a short-range basis as there is no real limit to the number of students one can handle. Students also disseminate better and an org that only audits pcs stays small and is more expensive to run.

ALL AUDITORS ACTIONS

Whenever an org has a Tech or Qual backlog it is usual to call an "all auditors" action.

Any admin personnel assist with scheduling and getting pcs in to the auditors without making pcs wait or wasting an auditor's time.

All tech-trained personnel in the org devote a certain number of hours in the day to delivering auditing for Tech or Qual and spend a certain amount of time on their regular posts until the backlog is gone.

Too many of these "all auditors" can cut an org to bits. They are only done so long as there is a backlog. If too frequent the HCO ES should get in volunteer (but paid) field auditors to help (which was always MSH's successful solution to tech backlogs). The HCO ES is personnel so if personnel stays short, particularly tech personnel, then the HCO ES is not taking adequate personnel action and doesn't have a program to get adequate or qualified staff auditors. Such programs are vital, their training and support costs money. The program "Steal the VIs and VIIIs from another org" is both dishonest and org wrecking and recoils on one's org eventually. Intern programs for students help this problem and are to be found in recent policy letters.

The above describes a three-man functioning org. Yet it also describes all orgs. It is a circle. The HCO ES, *mind*, routes people to the org's *body*, the OES, who routes them to the PES as FSMs and the product of the basis of a field. From a field stimulated by processed, trained people, the PES routes new people to the HCO ES and around it goes.

If tech and org integrity and service are good, you get an expansion. More and knowledgeable people in the field stimulate more and more new people who then are routed to the HCO ES, etc. Around and around.

The cycle is only interrupted by inattentive or poor service resulting in ARC breaks in the field which if not handled end expansion. Even the attacks of competitors and the press have never stopped this circle. Only inattentive service or staff inattentive to functions or poor service halts it. AN ORG THAT BELIEVES ANYTHING ELSE IS DELUDING ITSELF. Thus organization and function is everything.

THE BIGGER ORG

No matter how many staff members an org may have, the above portions, functions and actions apply.

What occurs is that the HCO ES, the OES and PES begin to acquire assistants. These have post titles. The org board seems to have a larger form. But it is always the same org board, the same functions.

Let us say now we have an HCO ES, an OES and a PES. And we have two more staff members making five.

One of these is an auditor. One is a typist. As you must never exceed two to one of admin/tech ratio and if possible keep it below that (it's less the bigger the org so that a fifty-staff-member org has half its staff in tech and will go awry financially if it doesn't have half in tech) as regards these two additionals, the auditor goes to the OES for auditing and training help and the typist goes to the HCO ES to help write letters to people in CF.

Now let us say we have five nontech staff applicants show up. Obviously four will have to go into prestaff tech training but one can go to the PES temporarily.

Meanwhile the OES has some students graduating, so the HCO ES persuades some to intern which helps the OES.

And so it goes. The functions gradually build up. But they are always assistants to the HCO ES or the OES or the PES.

COMBINED HATS

You normally fill posts by overload noted. But you always bend toward Registration and Tech Service and Promotion.

In the HCO ES portion hats can combine like LRH Comm-HCO Area Sec-Ethics Officer.

In areas under pressure we try to keep the Director of Special Affairs "single-hatted" on its own line to the Office of Special Affairs. It is a catchall, front-line troops sort of hat.

As the LRH Comm is a split-off of the old HCO Area Sec hats, these two combine very easily as HCO Area Secs were LRH's first communicators.

Where there is an LRH Comm single-hatted the org would have to be a forty- or fifty-staff-member org.

An E/O is more important to single hat in a larger org, but if not single-hatted *must* be a specific duty of the HCO ES or the HCO Area Sec.

The OES as he struggles up the line for more tech staff finds Accounts something he can well shed and so, an Accounts personnel comes under his early tech allocations. This is not stated in previous policy. The OES assigns his better auditors to Qual actions, but he continues to do tech actions until the org is safely large. Early policy on VIIIs placed them in Qual. However, it assumes an org is there. An VIII in a tiny org would have to be the OES and the Case Supervisor and also audit and it would be quite a lot of more staff members later before he was now not the Case Supervisor.

Early on the OES splits apart training and processing as separate departments and then finally a Qual. Until he has the traffic for it *he* patches up the pcs other auditors flubbed. But if he is very clever in a small org, the OES shunts all the goofed-up, hard pcs up to a larger org right away and is satisfied to collect the FSM of it as such pcs stall his lines or may be beyond local skill. That's what larger orgs are for. The rougher pcs.

The PES with his share of staff concentrates on his small courses, book sales and magazine actions as the logical zones to fill and with greater success tries to get a single-hatted Director of Clearing to handle FSM actions and see them through.

SHRUNKEN ORGS

We have covered the tiny org but the whole thing applies to an org that has shrunk.

The only real reasons an org shrinks are because it:

a. Followed illegal or destructive orders from above.

b. Failed to do its job as an org as outlined in the earlier part of this paper—in other words was disorganized.

c. Failed to give good service and got its field muddied up with ARC breaks.

d. Didn't outflow (letters, magazines, had no PES functioning).

e. Didn't train or process its own staff.

f. Didn't look or act sufficiently professional in staff member appearance and conduct or in quarters.

g. Let huge backlogs occur without giving fast, good tech service.

h. Monitored its rate of sign-up against what a lazy OES was willing to get handled or would arrange to get handled.

i. Let its admin/tech ratio go kooky.

j. Was subjected to internal suppression which blew off good staff and lost its safe environment without anyone locating the SP.

k. Let itself be raided of auditors by the call of big money in missions.

l.   Let staff procurement be turned into freeloading.

To resolve these or other troubles one has to:

A.   Confront what it was.

B.   Remedy it vigorously.

C.   Get in the pattern and actions given in this ED NOW, NOW, NOW.

REORGANIZATION

To use this ED to reorganize an org or to increase its effectiveness, restudy the basic functions of the HCO ES, OES and PES as given here, consider that these three people are *the* working people of the org and need assistance. Don't consider them executives. Consider the HCO ES with her hands full of interview-registration-comm-ethics functions, consider the OES as having his hands full of pcs and students and doing accounts between case supervision and lecturing and consider the PES scrambling around the area selling new people the idea of coming in for service and running an FSM sales staff, organizing groups and placing and collecting for books in bookstores and you see them in the expected light, acting but needing help. If you see these as high-status orderers of destiny with uncalloused hands operating from mysterious forces with incomprehensible requirements, the org is up the chimney already. We at the top of Scientology work and work hard. And the duties are as roughly outlined at the beginning of this ED. All the way to the top I still C/S case folders or keep tabs on the C/Sing for pcs around. I still drive students to complete. I intervene when your books show cash-bills reversed. I work in the other two Exec Sec sectors, actually work in them and do my own research-writing hats besides.

Right this moment, I am handling your org personally.

The first question I'm asking, "Have you got Ethics Program No. 1 basically done? Right away get the results packaged and sent off."

The second question, "Have you got a backlog in Tech or Qual? How many auditors anywhere in the org? Okay, get an All Auditors going now, today!"

The third, "What's the state of ARC breaks in your field? Okay PES, round them up and get them to the HCO ES and then into Qual to get their overts pulled. Overts? You heard me. Overts. Then put in their life ruds."

The fourth question, "Where's your ethnic survey, PES, on what people think staff should be dressed like? To look more professional. Get it done, and on HCO ES orders get the money squeezed out of the OES and buy some outfits for the Ethics Upstats and reliable contracted execs. And get this place cleaned and neated up."

The fifth question, "What's your outflow? That's not good enough. Get it organized—magazine, info packs, letters from Letter Reg. All hands onto any stuffing-mailing cycle."

The sixth question, "How neat and complete is your CF? Get any and all folders out of mothballs and get a project going on it as you can."

The seventh question, "What state is your Address in? Good. Work it over so it is the exact index of your CF as you can. Meanwhile use it."

The eighth question, "What's your tech/admin ratio? All right, get the trained auditors into Tech and Qual and off admin posts. Assign one to HCO ES and one to PES up to a two to one ratio and put the rest on full-time training. Get personnel staff member procurement going right away of people who will be Ethics Upstats. Okay, let's post it up, holding as many posts stable as we can but double, triple hatting them where we can't cover."

The ninth question, "How is Staff Training Program No. 1 going? All right, smooth those out. Soon as they're ready get this staff audited."

The tenth question, "What students do you have on courses that are slow or blowy? All right Registrar, here's HCOB 23 November 69. OES to star-rate it for action on the Tech auditors and Registrar to sell each slow student a five-hour Student Rescue Intensive."

The eleventh question, "Have you got your staff broken-contracts list? Turn it over to the HCO ES's people for further action. Oh, you say some of the VIIIs you trained up were lured off by a higher org and missions? Well, we'll make do here and audit with what we've got and I'll pass the contract-breaker names to the Sea Org for their further attention, poor souls."

"You say, what do you do with the bill collectors and the enemy and the half-complete project on surveying salesmen? Well, I'll tell you. You turn those over to the respective Exec Secs each comes under and the enemy to the Department of Special Affairs and get the show on the road. You'll never clear the planet sitting around here worrying. Remember the old maxim? When all else fails, do what Ron said."

Love,

Ron

L. RON HUBBARD
Founder

Revision assisted by
LRH Technical Research
and Compilations

L. Ron Hubbard
EXECUTIVE DIRECTIVE

LRH ED 102 INT   20 May 1970

TO: All Staff

FROM: Ron

SUBJECT: **THE IDEAL ORG**

REF: Current "Data Series" PLs

The ideal org would be an activity where people came to achieve freedom and where they had confidence they would attain it.

It would have enough space in which to train, process and administrate without crowding.

It would be located where the public could identify and find it.

It would be busy looking, with staff in motion not standing about.

It would be clean and attractive enough not to repel its public.

Its files and papers, baskets and lines would be in good order.

The org board would be up-to-date and where the public could see who and what was where and which the staff would use for routing and action.

A heavy outflow of letters and mailings would be pouring out.

Answers would be pouring in.

Auditors would be auditing in Div 4 HGC and Qual would be rather empty.

Supervisors would be training students interestedly and 2-way comming all slows.

The HCO Area Sec would have hats for everyone. And checked out on everyone.

There would be a pool of people in training to take over new admin and tech posts.

The staff would be well paid because they were productive.

The Public Divisions would be buzzing with effective action and new people and furnishing a torrent of new names to CF.

The pcs would be getting full Grades to ability attained for each, not eight minutes from 0 to IV, but more like thirty processes. And they would be leaving with high praises.

The students would be graduating all on fire to audit.

One could look at this ideal org and know that *this* was the place a new civilization was being established for this planet.

The thousand or more actions that made it up would dovetail smoothly one with another.

And the PR area control would be such that no one would dream of threatening it.

Such an ideal org would be built by taking what one has and step by step building and smoothing; grooving in and handling each of its functions, with each of its divisions doing more and more of its full job better and better.

The business is always there—the skill with which it is handled and the results on pcs and students is the single important line which makes it possible to build the rest.

The ideal org is the image one builds toward. It is the product of the causative actions of many. Anything which is short of an ideal org is an outpoint that can be put right. The end product is not just an ideal org but a new civilization already on its way.

L. RON HUBBARD
Founder

L. Ron Hubbard

EXECUTIVE DIRECTIVE

LRH ED 107 INT   3 June 1970

TO: Class IV Orgs
      and Saint Hills
      for ACTION
      AOs for Info

FROM: Ron

SUBJECT: **ORDERS TO DIVISIONS FOR IMMEDIATE COMPLIANCE**

REFS: LRH ED 104 Int, AUDITING SALES AND DELIVERY PGM #1
           LRH ED 106 Int, WHAT WAS WRONG

DIVISION 9

1. Immediately check out and get into action the following orders in their respective divisions.

DIVISION 1

1. Immediately recover the line that any single Dianetic or Scientology grade is certified by HCO before being valid. This line goes from C&A to HCO Area Sec. Refuse to sign as official any certificate where the grade was not declared in the words of the Ability Attained column, Class Charts 66, 68, 69 and 70. Refuse any "Did you get your Level 0 ability?" Accept only the pc declaring full statement for all three flows as soon as these are released in HCO PL form.

2. Recruit staff members and auditors and get their hats on, specializing in Dept 1 actions.

3. Take ethics action on anyone not cooperating with or goofing up this program of recovering Scientology and its gains in your org. Stamp heavily on noncompliance.

DIVISION 2

1. Post several copies of any Class Chart you have, 68, 69, 70, where it can be seen by (a) public, (b) students, (c) auditors.

2. Mail copies of the Class Chart with Letter Reg letters.

3. Begin a campaign to get back in any pc who has been given "fast grades" so his grades can actually be put in. When doing this do not make the org guilty. "Have you attained your gains as per this chart?" is the campaign. "If not come into org for a free check." Then sell them more auditing to actually attain their Grades 0–IV.

4. Contact Dianetic pcs and get them to complete Dianetics and start on Grades.

5. Registrar to sell only numbers of hours (and courses), not to sell a result. State all hours bought will be delivered and held in reserve if not delivered. A result can be described but the time to attain it is not specified. Don't sell "Singles" or "Triples" as the Registrar isn't the C/S.

6. Registrar to answer any complaint "You didn't give me my results" with "You should not have attested." Don't make the org guilty or start a flap.

7. Continue any successful actions without selling results.

8. Don't change general prices. Just take the labels off. This is true until you have in hand the new price schedule. It doesn't materially change prices.

9. Remove old price postings.

10. Get CF in shape so it functions for the Letter Reg and trace back all these quickie lower grade deliveries. Use them to sell more auditing and really get the grades in.

11. Prefer to sell training. Use the arguments—a student gets tons of auditing—cheaper—need to be trained anyway to go Clear—study is high gain. An org becomes most solvent on training.

12. Realize there are dozens of processes and lots of hours in well-run TOTAL LOWER grades. Don't continue to be conned by any tale of 20 minutes from 0 to IV. It takes weeks.

13. Handle any backlog complaints—waiting for auditing—by advising Academy training. Explain that Academy payments and classes are now credited at Saint Hill (actually paid) on an SHSBC course so a person can be trained locally for awhile and go to an SH for the rest at no greater fee.

14. PROVIDE MIMEOED MATERIALS NEEDED IN TRAINING AND PROCESSING.

15. Provide books, meters and magazines.

16. Don't undersell Dianetic training or processing.

DIVISION 3

1. Don't let any wild overall price change occur. The public avoids them. The UK price list has been issued. Other continental price lists will follow. If not received, cope. Do not accept any price list from anyone except myself.

Shifting prices and packages without my authority has given you bad times. Processing is now by the hour, not by result from 0 to IV.

2. It is more costly to process than train. Help push training for both Dianetics and Scientology. Real solvency depends on students not pcs. You can do this by making promotion funds available for training more heavily than auditing.

3. Back up this program to get Scientology back in FULL use by helping finance it.

4. Get solvent and fat moneywise.

5. Push to see that staffs get paid.

6. Have future plans on org facility expansion without bankrupting the place. Some orgs have publicly inaccessible and inadequate quarters which are very costly in limiting business volume.

DIVISION 4

1. Assume all technical actions in C/Sing, HGC and Dept of Training.

2. When a pc goes to Review, Qual is credited with the time taken from the hours the pc bought.

3. Only send a pc to Review when the C/S gives up. Don't let Review give the major actions that belong to the HGC.

4. Get your Supervisors (a) interested in the students' progress and (b) using two-way comm (listen style) to speed up the students' progress, (c) get in Learning Drills on slow students.

5. Get blown students back in and using (a), (b) and (c) in 4 above get them going again.

6. Come down hard on any SP giving out with Scientology materials being "old" or "not used now" or "background data" and any other mechanism to impede its use. (Modern C/Ses are having to study *The Original Thesis* and other basic books to find out about the subject. The data is not old. It is basic.)

7. Completely throw out the idea that a fast result is a good result in auditing. Deliver auditing in volume as per the "Processes Taught" column of the Class Chart. Do not skip any gradient going up in C/Sing. Get him on TRs and repair the pc's life before even beginning serious auditing. Do ALL the processes. To full end phenomena. End completely this brushoff that is currently passing for tech.

8. Get studied all current HCOBs and data on this program. Be sure you get HCOBs now coming out that fill in these gaps to get Scientology back into its own.

9. Determine that students know their business and pcs get full gains and get this being worked at hard through the division.

10. Check this giddy impulse to do things so fast they're not done at all. Validate auditors who do a thorough job, Supervisors who are interested in and work with students to push them through. Preach attaining honest, lasting results, real lower grades, real understanding of the mind.

11. Courses should be fast, auditing drawn out. This is the exact reverse to what has been happening. Slow courses and fast auditing destroy the subjects of Dianetics and Scientology. Fast courses and long, long hours of auditing are the route to real gains and solvency.

12. Man up Division 4 with competent auditors, Supervisors, a good C/S, an able Tech Services and plan how to man it up in the future as it expands and carry on an orderly program of providing technical manpower for the division, not depending on anyone else to do so.

13. See that students do a lot of mutual auditing. Don't get stumped in finding things to audit on each other. Force them over onto the Class Chart and every process known.

14. Get the division traffic lines flowing smoothly.

15. Handle backlogs by preaching training and getting more staff.

16. Whenever a pc goes exterior (or any in your folders who have) have him called in for an Interiorization Rundown. Don't end off his auditing and don't audit past exterior without giving the Interiorization Rundown. This can be done at any stage of Dianetics or grade processing AND DOES NOT COUNT AS PART OF ANY GRADE.

17. Get out of any rut that goes contrary to this program.

DIVISION 5

1. The purpose of Division 5 is to CORRECT malfunctions in the org. Realize that the whole org has moved into Div 5 and squashed it. Begin a program of unloading functions.

2. Shift the C/S to Div 4. There is no Div 5 C/S. The Review Auditor does his own C/Sing on cases he repairs.

3. Refuse to do any major actions on cases. Repair them so they will now run and shift them back to Div 4.

4. Get in DECLARE discipline at the Examiner's. Refuse to declare more than one grade at a time. Get the pc to state the ability he has attained; not, "I'm Level 0 now," but the exact wording of that grade. Refuse flatly to pass any pc run only on one process for a grade as disclosed by folder inspection. Get the earliest Examiner discipline in. Folder, meter, pc statement as to the exact end phenomena of the grade. Student by examination and meter check for false completion.

5. Refuse to back down when anyone in Tech starts yelling you're invalidating their gains or repute. That's how all this decline started—an invalidation of

   Qual opinion by the Tech Sec at SH 1965. Wiped out Qual. Five years later the subject was *gone* over the whole world and having to be put back.

6. Provide helpful service to students and pcs. Make them feel especially safe in Qual.

7. Really repair students with your interest, two-way comm and Learning Drills (they'll be coming out in HCOB again shortly).

8. Really repair pcs using assessed lists like the GF, L1B, L4A, ruds, etc., so they're flying.

9. Take credit from Tech for every auditing hour (or part thereof costs an hour) you spend on a pc. Take all pc repair from hours pc has bought. Only if he has run out of Tech hours and needs repair do you charge him. Try to get him to buy a new package of hours as soon as possible—but of course a pc needing repair isn't likely to buy more until repaired.

10. Get in your Staff Training Officer (who in small orgs can also be Cramming) and begin to push the staff through Staff Status I and II and III and OEC so the org form will be held and thus keep the org from being in a continual correction status.

11. Get your Certs and Awards requiring all certs to be signed by the HCO Area Sec (or HCO ES) before they are valid. Get the signed cert routed back for presentation by the Registrar to the pc or student.

12. Give me a great big hand getting this Auditing Sales and Service Pgm #1 IN so that it stays in and totally assume the function of org correction for which Qual was designed. Qual was meant to do product correction and org correction. It got so bad Qual became the product *division* not the product correction division. So help me out by getting the org to be a service org producing pcs run on all grade processes for each grade and auditors who know they use what they learn.

DIVISION 6

1. The PR value of this situation is dicey. If you broadcast to all past pcs and students that since I left the post of Exec Dir WW the pcs haven't been given their full grade gains and the students not permitted to use what they studied you'd get an invalidation of your org by the field. Therefore the routine is to coax people back in who are not satisfied with their gains and sell them more auditing (so the full processes can be run for each grade). If they complain, ask them why they attested.

2. Do a PR survey of the field by small samplings on Scientology lower grades and Academy training, find what they like and don't like and advise your div secretaries, EC and CS-6 at Flag so *Auditor*s and continental mags can handle with a public field program.

3. Handle any public repercussion sensibly.

4. Push the general idea that auditing takes a while, not how fast it is. This "fast" idea has all but destroyed results. "Permanent gains take a while to do."

5. Push the idea that the cheapest best way to get auditing is to get HSDC and Academy training where students give each other the large amounts of auditing necessary.

6. Run down and kill in its tracks any wild rumor that a "Dianetic Clear" can't go on up the grades or have Power or go real Clear and OT.

7. Knock out any rumors about "old processes," "unused materials," "background data only" now current in org.

8. Bolster Dianetics.

9. Restore real Scientology.

10. Don't abandon any line that is working well.

DIVISION 7

If you have no Div 7 you sure better get one as it handles all services to the public which are many and vital.

1. Set up public testing if not in.

2. Route people coming off test line to HAS. Don't route to PE.

3. If you continue PE, route people to testing or HAS from it.

4. Run the HAS with ALL TRs. It has been reported that even drug users come off drugs doing TRs. TRs get gain and reality better than data does.

5. Push training more than auditing.

6. Institute Group Auditing.

7. Use any line you have that is producing.

8. Display a Classification and Gradation Chart prominently in your area.

9. Give activities that handle any amount of people. When some public program pulls in a mob, Div 7 provides a service for it, it can have. The operating formula is "Provide a service they can have at a cost that covers the expenses (including promotion, quarters and wages) of the service." Don't let any high public volume be killed just because "they didn't buy many intensives." You keep mass servicing them and they'll buy something eventually. Keep them interested and active. Just don't go broke doing it. Realize that Divs 2 and 4 support the org with individual packages of auditing or higher courses. But just because the mobs Div 7 collects does not instantly buy intensives is no reason not to collect a mob. Not to provide

289

interesting valuable service for mobs is a terrible mistake. To expect them to instantly buy big packages is a skipped point in a sequence. One crowd went on for years paying 10 shillings a night to public co-audit. They eventually got trained, most of them. Yet one org recently cancelled a health crusade that produced 120 bodies an hour "because they didn't buy intensives—only two people did," so the Receptionist pushed them back out into the street! Div 7 had not provided a public service action to route them to—like HAS or Group Auditing at a cost both these people and the org could afford.

This was a Div 7 oversight that made a campaign fail!

10. Work out ways to handle public so they are interested.

11. Study past actions of public handling and reinstitute and reinforce.

12. Don't drop current successful actions.

DIVISION 8

1. Get all FSMs working.

2. Get all FSMs checking to see that ex-pcs made their gains off lower grades and if not, routing them back in to get a FREE REPAIR and buy auditing.

3. Get the FSMs to send in people who exteriorized for a FREE REHAB and the org will sell them enough hours to do an Interiorization intensive. Remember that it's hours, not result that's sold.

4. Get a supply of *The Original Thesis* and *Evolution of a Science* and push them.

5. Spread the idea that the older material is more basic and is of great use today.

6. Push FSMs to sell more training on the basis that anyone can receive much more auditing as a student and will need training anyway to go upper grade.

7. Get the idea revived that student selections get a 15 percent commission to FSMs.

8. Work with Div 6 and Div 7 to get crowds coming in, getting low-level public mass service and smooth out how it can be sold and mass serviced so that it pays for itself. The org benefits by the few who get intensives and higher courses.

9. Don't drop any successful action now being done.

10. Force grade honesty into missions as per this program.

GENERAL

We have a lot of the earlier #1 programs more or less in hand. We can now begin to work in earnest. If we don't get the above orders in action now we'll have an even rougher time of it.

We have Dianetics to push and Scientology to get back in actual full operation.

L. RON HUBBARD
Founder

HCO POLICY LETTER OF 20 SEPTEMBER 1973R
REVISED 12 FEBRUARY 1991

Remimeo
FB
FOLOs
FR Network
LC Network
OSA Network
CO/EDs

CONCERNING ADMINISTRATION

(This issue was compiled from LRH notes of 20 Sept. 73 on the subject
of administration. Originally issued as a policy letter on 19 Feb. 82.)

The Exec Dir has an *org* to run. He has a fabulous number of details to care for. The org could be made pretty ragged with a lot of comm lines running into it.

The ED ought to be able to demonstrate initiative and manage his org, with the FR cheek by jowl with him. The FR can bug the ED, with no argument or chatter, on the subject of the eval. The FR can go through the org getting the eval in, in the org, without reference to the ED or CO.

This is the old Byzantine system of two generals out at the same time. It's our old HCO Sec—Assoc Sec line.

The LRH Comm out on the flank is forming the org. The Director of Special Affairs is keeping it straight and legal and handling the external scene.

With this battery the org will expand and boom—if those functions are done.

A Programs Chief can't do a thing unless he's got an FR. Lack of an FR shortens his reach to three feet, instead of several thousand miles. Having an FR extends the line.

L. RON HUBBARD
Founder

Assisted by
Flag Flag Rep

Revision assisted by
LRH Technical Research
and Compilations

HCO POLICY LETTER OF 20 AUGUST 1982

Remimeo

ORGANIZATIONAL BASICS

An organization consists of coordinated purposes, lines and terminals. That is *all* it consists of.

To be viable, it must have a fair and valuable exchange with an area outside its perimeter in a volume adequate to its needs.

To expand, it must strengthen its purposes and increase its lines and terminals and multiply its exchange above the rate of its consumption.

When you have understood this fully, you will understand all groups, companies, societies, civilizations, countries and empires.

Such rise or fall in direct relationship to how well they meet or fail to meet the first three paragraphs above.

And when you fully grasp the basic definition of organization and are trying to build, make viable and expand one, you will be very hard on anyone who is discoordinating or blunting the purposes, damaging or omitting the lines and is disestablishing the terminals. You will understand exactly what that person is doing. He is seeking to make the organization less viable and trying to contract and destroy it. So know your enemies.

And when you see somebody trying hard to build your organization up by following the first three paragraphs, you will know he is your friend and help him all you can.

It is very well to clear off all confusions by doing the first three paragraphs in clay. Then you will have, if you master it, many things clarified. And you can not only understand what makes a slum a slum, a good society a good one, why one area is poor and another opulent, you will also have acquired the potential of creating or helping to create a far better life for all.

L. RON HUBBARD
Founder

THE FOUNDATION ORG

HCO POLICY LETTER OF 11 JUNE 1965
Issue I

Remimeo in the Orgs
by the Orgs
All Staff Hats

URGENT

THE FOUNDATION

At once this policy letter goes into full effect, urgently, in Washington, DC, New York, Los Angeles, London, Johannesburg, Cape Town, Melbourne and Auckland and as feasible in all the other orgs.

Without disturbing the daytime org or its operation in any way, an evening, part-time organization is formed.

The purpose of the evening organization is to operate as a bridge from the public to the daytime org and to make money in its own right.

Its personnel are on half pay for work five nights a week from 6:30 to 10:30 and will go on full pay if also working full days Saturday and Sunday to operate a weekend organization as well which can give the evening services on weekends also, as well as deliver upper-level training and paid HGC processing.

The evening organization services are not merely free services, but include any org services as well as free services not part of Day org services.

Day staff may also hold evening posts and receive pay for them, but it is clearly understood that evening staff work is only as a part of the evening organization.

PE and Free Scientology Center ads are placed to run regularly in the papers.

The public attends these and is then sold by evening staff on daytime or evening courses or intensives. The free services are the Beginning Scientology Course and student assists. The paid services are HAS, HQS and regular evening or daytime intensives.

The entire success of this organization depends on the crispness and businesslike manner of its staff and the organization, and the quality of its technology. If the free technology is not excellent, no sales will result. If the sold technology is not spectacular, no repeat sales will occur.

NAME

The evening organization (and the weekend when it is formed) is called THE SCIENTOLOGY FOUNDATION.

The name must be registered as a business name. It is owned and operated by HASI and is just a part of HASI.

By using this name, it is easier to route, advertise and designate locally.

POSTS

The standard org board is used and all of its key posts are filled with as little doubling of hats as possible.

A *second* org board is posted for the evening organization, as formal as the daytime board. The matter of space for it must be solved, but it is best posted in the PE room. It should be on 4' x 9' Formica that is *green* in Formica color as opposed to the daytime org board's blue. Otherwise, all flash colors are the same as to titles and names, etc.

The Scientology Foundation must have the following minimum posts and two or more of these may not be worn by one person:

Foundation HCO Secretary
Foundation Ethics Officer
Foundation Organization Secretary
Foundation Registrar
Foundation Director of Training
Foundation Director of Processing
Foundation Director of Examinations
Foundation Director of Review
Foundation Director of Field Activities.

If these posts are not filled each by one person, it is not a Foundation.

In posting these names, one first puts up the entire org board, complete with all divisions and departments, secretarial posts, executive secretarial posts and LRH.

A banner, The Scientology Foundation, is put to the upper right with HASI, Inc., and its board below it.

One puts in the level words, the lot. "Foundation" is placed before each department name and section and course name on the board.

However, one then posts in the secretarial level and the departments only those names actually appointed, leaving the others blank.

Under the proper departments, one puts the actual services offered and the names of the Foundation staff members performing them.

DOUBLES

The Foundation HCO Sec doubles as Communicator for the entire Foundation and handles all external and internal communications. As things get prosperous, a Communicator is put on.

The Foundation Ethics Officer doubles for the Director of Inspections and Reports and does the OIC and other functions of that department.

The Foundation Organization Secretary is the only other Secretary assigned in a basic Foundation staff. He operates as materiel, supply and cashier and keeps all the accounts and records of the Foundation—which are *not* kept by the daytime org. As things get prosperous, he may have a janitor and a cashier. Until then he must care for the money and its records and the quarters; and as the senior org executive on duty, he must also organize the other divisions.

The Foundation Registrar doubles as Reception and Testing Officer. When things get prosperous, a Receptionist is put under the Registrar in the Department of Estimations.

The Foundation Director of Training takes one of the courses (BS or HAS or HQS) at first. He is assisted by Supervisors (not Instructors) for the remaining courses. As these courses get heavy, they must be carefully separated into Theory and Practical Courses with Supervisors. When the courses contain fifty people routinely, the Foundation Director of Training *must* not take a course but must have Supervisors for them. He is assisted by the Registrar in course admin, as all tech admin is now done in the Department of Estimations.

The Foundation Director of Processing takes care of all co-audits, group processing and auditing of whatever kind done in the Foundation, including its staff staff auditing and staff co-auditing. He has charge of the Free Scientology Center which is assisted by the Registrar in its registration work. All its student auditors come under him and he is answerable for their conduct and quality of service. Any evening or part-time auditing done is done by the Foundation and this is under him. He is also Case Supervisor and does *all* the folders and reports. He also does room assignments. If it's auditing, he supervises it and is responsible for it, whether by Free Scientology Center student auditors or Foundation staff. He is assisted by a student Case Supervisor. *Note* that *he* does not repair or handle bogged cases; these go to Review only. He handles cases only so long as they have standard reactions to standard processes. If not, they go to Review.

The Foundation Director of Examinations passes on all auditing results and completed checksheets and is the person seen when entering or leaving Qualifications Division, except when a certificate or award is attained. He acts also as Certificates and Awards for the Foundation, issuing letters on LRH stationery signed by the Foundation HCO Sec by and for LRH for certificates and classes or grades. When a signed copy goes to Saint Hill and the original is given to the Registrar to give to the student or pc, more training or processing is sold.

The Foundation Director of Review must be a good auditor who patches up goofed pcs sent by the Director of Processing or who finds out about the case for the Director of Processing. This is never varied routing. Pcs not doing well under processing go straight to Review at orders of the D of P. The D of P never interviews pcs—only Review. And Review charges for it, whole-hour rates for any part of an hour. Slow students go to Review for an assist on (1) Problems Straightwire and Comm, (2) Remedy A and (3) Remedy B. These take maybe 15–20 minutes and are charged for at student hourly rate, never less than a one-hour fee. Examinations invoices them in. This is the top auditor available, a fast one. He can make triple rates since an hour is the minimum charge and he can do up to three an hour! Review doesn't pass on all pcs—Examinations does that and shunts those to Review he doesn't like the results on. This Review Auditor cannot run other pcs than Review.

The Foundation Director of Distribution sells books, handles all the advertising placement and handles field staff members and receives people's plans for activity in Scientology. He must be on deck to keep students reminded to "select" their pcs in the Free Scientology Center and to sell all books. He also carefully gathers up all names and addresses of all traffic recorded in the Foundation and puts it on mailing lists and sends records of all purchasers to CF.

Without this minimum evening Foundation team operating, every evening for the full evening and, when on weekends, for the full weekend, the drill won't bring in business.

ALL POLICY APPLIES

All policy applies to the Foundation, as well as to the HASI.

Consecutive scheduling, however, is consecutive evening or weekend scheduling. Twelve and one-half-hour evening intensives are sold or an evening-plus-weekend 25-hour intensive is sold. The courses run all 5 nights. They have to, to move enough traffic through.

Student auditing in the Free Scientology Center, however, is just 2½-hour sessions and can be as little as one session.

RECEIPTS AND PAY

All receipts of the evening Foundation just go into the org accounts. There aren't special bank accounts for it as it's just part of the org. The HASI benefits like mad from the Foundation, but so does the Foundation, from the HASI.

Pay is the same parity as the HASI pay except that it is one-half pay or units for the same post. When weekends are included, Foundation pay is full pay.

STAFF NUMBERS

Staff on post should be adequate to care for the traffic and should be expanded from minimum staff as fast as traffic warrants it and should cover the most overloaded points first. The ratio for the divisions is one personnel for Divisions 1, 2, 3, 6 and 7 to every two personnel in Divisions 4 and 5 combined. Every time two personnel are put into Divisions 4 and 5, one is put into one of the others. It is usually done by rotation in 1, 2, 3, 6 and 7. Qual (5) has very few compared to Tech (4).

DESKS

The same spaces and desks are used by both HASI and Foundation personnel.

BASKETS

The Foundation has its own Comm Center. On the desks sit the Foundation comm stations in addition to the HASI staff member's comm station.

Foundation comm stations are a different color uniformly than HASI comm station baskets.

SUMMARY

If this is organized well, it will even the load for the town org personnel who have heavy evening and light day traffic. In such an org the Foundation may at first be bigger than the HASI. But this is easy as part-time personnel are more available to town orgs.

As this parallels the autumn 1964 stress of org traffic and only extends the successful PE Foundations, it should be very successful.

L. RON HUBBARD
Founder

Gen. Non-Remimeo

THE FOUNDATION
FORMING THE FOUNDATION

(See HCO PL 11 June 65, THE
FOUNDATION, which this continues)

You will find that the success of The Scientology Foundation (the evening or weekend foundation) depends upon three things:

1. The excellence of its administered technology,

2. The crispness and completeness of its organization,

3. Offering all services available in the daytime and delivering them in the evening or weekend.

If *any* of these three are missing, the results will be quite unsuccessful and disheartening.

Therefore, the success of the Foundation does not depend upon the brilliance with which it is conducted or upon the flashiness of its quarters or upon the personalities of its staff. The success depends upon the accomplishment of *technical results* and upon the *teamwork* of its staff.

You will find its org board is made to work. It takes minimum hat details but maximum agreement on those details.

It is not a number of individuals acting as individuals but a group of closely dovetailed efforts, dedicated to the maximum production of technical results by the maximum coordination of individual efforts.

THE TECHNOLOGY

The tech of the services offered is just standard tech for the appropriate levels.

The Beginning Scientologist Course, the *two* HAS courses (theory and practical) and the two HQS courses (theory and practical) are best done exactly by the technology given in the HCO PL of 31 May 65.

The student auditing in the Free Scientology Center (which is just a section of the Department of Processing and the Department of Estimations and is *far* from the full Foundation which has *all* services) is standard tech, and mostly assists.

The Academy courses offered are the low-level HRS and HTS courses, both by checksheet, both consisting of two courses each. If any higher level is given, it would have to be after a lot of students finished lower levels, for nothing is less crisp than a course with two people on it. You can handle both low-level courses (HRS and HTS) with only two Supervisors—one for certification (theory, HRS and HTS) and one for classification (practical, HRS and HTS). It *does,* however, require *two* Supervisors. HQS can be thrown in with them in its two courses, in a pinch, but it isn't too advisable. It's better if HAS and HQS are paired, if you must, meaning two Supervisors (one theory and one practical) exist for the lot.

A co-audit can exist. A group auditing intensive can be sold periodically.

Any public grade auditing can be sold that you have auditors to deliver it, but *don't* foul up your D of P by letting the Registrar odd-bit the auditing schedule. Twelve and one-half or twenty-five hours at a crack is the *only* way you can achieve any real gain, as any pc goes backwards on only three or four hours a week—why lose? And if you schedule nonconsecutive, you have to have far more auditors and they deliver less, and D of P work becomes a nightmare of trying to recall.

BUILD FROM A PE

If you have a running PE or evening service, build the Foundation on it—but just leave the PE, etc., and flank them with the rest of the org. These PE and public-course people *can't* function with no org present, and lose the business. For years "poor PE instruction" has been cited as why few moved from PE to the org. This was false. The reason was "What org?" There is no org flanking a PE. Its Instructor was a one-man band moving in a maze of empty offices, no phone, no despatches, no help. How could he handle these people?

Further, these people were evening people. Unless they could go to an evening org, they had to break their stride and stop work. So they could move (and did move, as per autumn 1964 graphs) into other evening services. Those services were attended not because they were cheap, but because they took place in the evening.

You will find that if you run free weekend Beginning Scientologist courses, you can then run the other services as weekend services also, as now you have attracted the weekend-type person. A person could have both evening and weekend service consecutively. You will find that will sell, too, and make lots of intensives and fast courses.

You have to sell lots of courses to the same people, so they have to go through fast in order to keep ahead on expenses.

FORMING

In organizing a Foundation, you can build it by starting or using the old PE, then starting and using the old sub-Academy services, all the while adding in the other posts given on the new org board. Lack of those posts was what lost your business. Every time you skimp those listed in HCO PL of 11 June 65 for the Foundation, you load up and jam the other lines, get no flows or sign-ups.

Try to keep PE, etc., down to where it was and you'll just keep falling down. You have to have a full org there operating in the *same* hours as the service is given.

It is the full intention to add Foundation staff until a full org is there also in the evening. This means a Foundation HCO Exec Sec, a Foundation Org Exec Sec, a Foundation LRH Communicator—the lot.

While these are all junior to the HASI staff, they are themselves AND HANDLE NO HASI BUSINESS FOR THE DAY STAFF. They have their own Ad Comms, OIC graphs, their own executive orders. They have their own org board and their own Comm Center and their own comm baskets. They place their own ads and answer their own mail and get out their own mailings.

The two orgs cross in CF and Address, but the Foundation has its own file drawers for address plates for local mailings.

Daytime Reception and daytime Registrar can take messages for and even sign up people for the Foundation and vice versa. Their money is pooled and units uniform. Their *accounting,* as different from collection, is handled by day Accounts. They can't shift quarters without permission from their daytime HASI seniors.

The HASI and the Foundation cooperate. They do not cross except as noted above.

HOURS

The hours 6:30 to 10:00 (corrects 11 June PL) for the Foundation and regular workday hours—for the area—Saturday and Sunday are all set and strictly time clocked.

Evening sessions in an intensive are only 2 hours long. But they start at 7:00 and finish at 9:30, and the staff auditor is to do other actions until 10:00, and the Foundation D of P gets all the folders in and marked in that last half hour and in the first half hour of the next Foundation day. In the period of 6:30 to 7:00 one gets the pcs collected and to session.

The courses start at 7:00 and run until 9:30. In the final half hour, the quarters are straightened up and the Supervisors make their reports to the Foundation D of T and care for other actions.

Having half an hour before public service begins and a half hour after permits even an occasional, fast Foundation staff meeting or conference even to tech.

One should be careful to shoo Foundation staff home at 10:00 as many have other jobs and will wear out if not swept out at 10:00 exactly and told to go home. Sleepy auditors don't give good sessions and sleepy execs can make mistakes.

ECONOMICS

The reasons some staffs have individual economic problems are as follows:

1. Their org depends on local people for business.

2. The local people are working at their own jobs in daytime hours.

3. The org is closed or undermanned when the traffic *can* occur.

304

4. An org depending on local business is generally open only when people can't be trained or processed.

5. A continental org depending on feeders from other orgs goes to pieces when town orgs slump if it has no town business as offered by the Foundation.

6. "Moonlighting" is the term applied to having two separate jobs and employers. There are few evening jobs available. A staff member of a Foundation, even working evening and weekend, can get another job and still hold an org post in rough times.

7. By using the same quarters *twice,* one doubles potential income at half the quarters and upkeep expense. Thus, one can afford better, bigger quarters.

8. The people with money to spend are, in the majority, people who work. They have only weekends and evenings for avocations. People who can't work or don't work are almost always the rougher cases and ethics-type pcs. Hence, by offering only daytime service, one gets a higher percent of rough cases and finds service harder to deliver.

WHY ETHICS?

You can't run pcs without ethics to hand. Technical fact. Particularly on lower-level processes and also on Power Processes, the potential trouble source (connected to a suppressive) will go to pieces under auditing—not improve.

Current statistic on this is 20 percent PTS or mild SP and, of this, 2½ percent is very vicious suppressive person.

Your D of T *can't* train a class that has a PTS or SP in it.

Your D of P can't audit people if he can't handle this PTS and SP factor efficiently.

Your Dir of Review will go round the bend if he can't shunt PTSes or SPs to Ethics. He'll have to become the Ethics Officer.

This is not policy I am talking about. It is *technical* fact. It just *can't* be done and never will be possible on lower technology and requires fantastic skill to get a real gain even with Power Processes. So accept this *technical* fact and you'll understand both ethics and all your case failures.

With no available Ethics Officer to take PTSes or SPs off the lines and handle (by spotting and using standard policy actions), your traffic will thin, your jobs will be a burden and the Foundation will fail.

The whole Foundation staff has to know the ethics drill and follow it.

Ethics is for the public far more than staff. You must use the drill.

A Supervisor to whom a student is impolite must send the student to Ethics. If the student is slow, the Supervisor *must* send to Review for special attention at the student's expense.

305

Staff auditors, finding a pc savage or unchanging, must send to Review which probably sends to Ethics. Staff auditors, finding a case failing, *must* send to Review which again may send to Ethics.

The ultimate in dumbness is the person who thinks "Ethics is to make pcs answer questions." Or the person who thinks it is for espionage on staff members.

Ethics is a long-arm part of technology. And, incidentally, spots PTSes and SPs who get onto staffs, as they sometimes do.

Ethics is a fine-edged tool, a vital part of an org if one wishes to train people in Scientology or process them successfully.

If tech is out, ethics will get tech in. If ethics is out, tech won't ever go in. It's like that. I learned this the hard way. Let's hope others learn it on easier channels. The "ARC broke pc" or "ARC broke student" is 95 percent ethics-type. That's the discovery. Use it.

If you have ethics *in*, the 80 percent will flow through the Foundation in a mad torrent.

EVENING OR WEEKEND

To start, a Foundation should be evening and should be built quickly to a *full* staff. *NO* ACTION MAY BE SHIFTED TO WEEKEND UNLESS A FULL STAFF IS ALSO PRESENT ON THE WEEKEND.

You must *not* have an evening Foundation with *some* weekend actions. If there are weekend actions, leave them with HASI until they build up to warranting the whole Foundation.

You can, of course, start a Foundation as both evening and weekend from the beginning. But that *means* everybody on deck evenings and everybody on deck weekends.

You may have potential staff members who plead they must spend some time with their families. Make them choose evening or weekend, not "three evenings a week and Saturday." That would be chaos. You can barely tolerate the randomity of one Supervisor for evening and another for weekend. You can't tolerate a staff auditor "three evenings and Saturday." You can barely get along with auditors some of whom are only evening and some only weekend.

RESULTS OF EXAMINATION

I find orgs that have no local traffic have the hardest time with booms and depressions.

I find that almost all losses from the old PE came from not having a full org present. The first instance was in LA in 1950 where 125 people a night made out cards for training and processing which the lecturer left lying about in the chairs and which sometimes were handed in by the janitor.

No daytime exec is likely to understand fully the problems of the evening traffic, tech and admin, as he isn't there, is he? Thus, the Foundation should have its own execs, junior, of course, to the same day post.

I find that the skid of some orgs in Jan. 1965 really came in part from a cessation of evening services and lack of good tech in them, and that when the evening student or potential pc was confronted with a shift from evening to daytime scheduling for auditing or training, he or she could not usually go on and fit his time that way, so dropped out.

I find that the magic key to a local org boom is the evening service and making that service excellent technically; and making the org that gives it a full org with its hats all on while technical is in progress; and keeping the lines crisp and proper, its courses and sessions starting and ending bang on the mark and all going briskly.

THE DAYTIME ORG

This is no effort to undermine the daytime org. You will find it had its own and different public and will run on quite well, even better. The evening Foundation sends a lot of business its way but has plenty of its own. The two orgs will take business away from each other. Day business may drop to evening. And evening business becomes day business. So nobody should care much who signs who up for which as long as a sign-up does occur.

The statistics of the two orgs should be kept separately or somebody will be catching the blame for somebody else's goofs.

As all this is based on data won by personal management of day and evening activities and a survey of past rising statistics, it should work very well indeed.

L. RON HUBBARD
Founder

Gen. Non-Remimeo

THE FOUNDATION DATA

The staff of a Foundation has only 2½-hours of technical activity. Half an hour before and after is allowed for administration.

There at the start you can use personnel from any division doubled in technical. This would seem to cross divisions and does, but it permits you to man a starting Foundation in all its required posts and yet have a full tech staff at the same time.

Only a Receptionist and an Ethics Officer and a Review Auditor must not be off their posts during the 2½-hour tech period since those posts are on call—the Receptionist to handle body traffic and phone calls, the Ethics Officer to handle students and pcs referred to him and the Review Officer to do Review assists or act as an Examiner.

All other posts may have technical duties, supervising courses or auditing preclears, during the 2½-hour tech period.

If this is done, the Foundation staff must report on time to their proper, assigned posts to do what they can of their hats and then speed off to do their sessions or classes and then, shaking off terminal-snapping students and pcs, be back on their own posts to pull the admin lines straight again.

It was done at Saint Hill, and though hard on staff, it works. Soon the traffic flow increases so that a larger staff can be supported, and success breeds new staff applications, and soon the basic staff can shed their tech period hats where these are double and do their basic duties for the whole evening period. By that time they'll have to. If the organization is crisp and on policy with ethics and tech well in, they'll have too much traffic to leave any post unmanned.

So if you do this, don't forget to pull the basic staff back out of additional tech assignments as soon as traffic warrants it.

You can also do this with daytime staff, governed by the same rules and remembering to give it relief as soon as traffic grows.

L. RON HUBBARD
Founder

HUBBARD COMMUNICATIONS OFFICE
Saint Hill Manor, East Grinstead, Sussex

HCO EXECUTIVE LETTER OF 4 NOVEMBER 1965
Gen. Non-Remimeo
Not Melbourne

URGENT

TO: Foundation
      HCO Exec Sec or
      HCO Sec

FROM: RON

REF: HCO Exec Letter 2 Nov. 65, YOUR ORG—REPLY EXPECTED*

I am worried about your Foundation services and income.

Read HCO Exec Letter 2 Nov. 65.

Do the steps for your Foundation as follows:

1. Is the Foundation offering anything that:

    a. A former release can buy?

    b. Raw meat can buy?

    c. A longtime rough case pc can buy?

    d. A person in trouble can buy?

2. Is it presenting any convincing literature that would make *you* come in?

3. Is it doing mailings to people who have attended lectures already?

4. Does it have and is it building its own CF and Address Unit irrespective of the Day org?

5. Is anybody on deck to sell you anything in Foundation hours? Do they sell it effectively?

6. Are services actually being delivered in the Foundation? Anybody there to deliver them?

7. Are people who bought things from the Foundation happy with what they got?

8. Why isn't your Foundation making more income?

Now I want YOU to go around in person and test each point personally as though you were a customer.

*[Editor's Note: This issue can be found on page 847 in this volume.]

And I want a *full* report from you by airmail (SH and London by despatch) with anything you can suggest to improve any of the above points.

Also give me any reason people are not buying (such as "already released so can't be put on the HQS," etc).

It's impossible to go on making releases and not make money.

So let's solve it.

Make your inspection personally and send your report by air to me.

And don't just wait for my answer. Repair what you find wrong *fast!*

L. RON HUBBARD
Founder

HCO POLICY LETTER OF 11 AUGUST 1966

Remimeo
Foundation

DIV 1 FOUNDATION

LAMPS AND SECURITY

The lighting for the Foundation is under the care of and is the responsibility of the Director of Routing, Appearances and Personnel of the Foundation.

That lights are turned on and off at the proper times, that time switches are properly set, that no essential areas or entrances are left dark and that no lights remain on after hours is all Dir RAP's responsibility.

The Dir RAP is also responsible that burned-out lamps are replaced.

That the Foundation is opened on time and that it is properly locked up at closing is also Dir RAP's responsibility.

L. RON HUBBARD
Founder

HCO POLICY LETTER OF 21 OCTOBER 1966
Issue IV

Remimeo

EVENING FOUNDATIONS

SIZE

Evening Foundations of seven-division organizations should be organized as six-department organizations (see HCO PL of 21 Oct. 66 I, SIX DEPARTMENT SYSTEM) until such time as they exceed seventy-five staff members in the evening Foundation, at which time they become seven-division organizations (as per PLs of 1965).

In a Day org that is a six-department org, the evening Foundation should be city office size (see HCO PL of 21 Oct. 66 III, CITY OFFICE), until it exceeds thirty-five staff members in the evening Foundation.

In a Day org that is a city office, the evening Foundation is the same city office pattern (see HCO PL of 21 Oct. 66 III, CITY OFFICE).

PRIMARY FUNCTION

An evening Foundation should provide the services offered by the Day org and should service the Day org's staff members up to the level authorized for the Day org. The Foundations should provide Ethics functions, hearings and Comm Evs, Qual services, status checkout and Org Exec Course facilities for the Day org staff.

DURATION

When possible, a Foundation should go five evenings and both days weekends.

INCOME

The Foundation is credited in its graphs not only with its public income but also with all payments made by or withheld from the pay of staff members of the Day org.

FOUNDATION STAFF

Foundation staff obtain their services in training, processing and checkouts, Org Exec Course, Ethics hearings, etc., in the Day org.

PAY

Foundation pay for the whole staff should average about 50 percent of the gross income of the Foundation. The remainder is usually handled by the Day org to pay bills, etc. But the Foundation may claim reasonable sums for its own promotion expenses.

L. RON HUBBARD
Founder

HCO POLICY LETTER OF 11 AUGUST 1972

Remimeo

Issue II

FOUNDATION AND DAY ORGS
SEPARATE

Refs:

HCO PL	11 June	65	THE FOUNDATION
HCO PL	12 June	65	FORMING THE FOUNDATION
HCO PL	3 July	65	THE FOUNDATION DATA
HCO PL	13 Aug.	65	FOUNDATION, BASIC COURSE ORGANIZATION
HCO PL	16 Aug.	65	FOUNDATION, BASIC COURSE ORGANIZATION—CORRECTION
HCO PL	12 Sept.	65	FOUNDATION COURSE CHANGE
HCO PL	13 Sept.	65	FOUNDATION COURSE HOURS
HCO PL	16 Sept.	65 II	FOUNDATION
HCO PL	2 Nov.	65 II	FOUNDATION CENTRAL FILES OFFICER AND ADDRESS–IN–CHARGE
HCO PL	21 Oct.	66 IV	EVENING FOUNDATIONS
HCO PL	11 Aug.	72R III Rev. 4.9.72	FOUNDATION INCOME

The Day org and the Foundation are two ENTIRELY SEPARATE ORGS. The Foundation is not under the Day org. Day org executives have no jurisdiction whatsoever over the Foundation executives or personnel.

ALL ORGS DAY *AND* FOUNDATION ARE TODAY DIRECTLY UNDER FLAG WITH COMMUNICATION AND CONTROL LINES THROUGH FOLOs, CLOs and OTLs.

HOURS

Day org hours generally run 9:00 A.M.—6:00 P.M. Monday through Friday, Foundation hours 6:00 P.M.—11:00 P.M. Monday—Friday and 9:00 A.M.—11:00 P.M. Saturday and Sunday.

There may be slight variations of the above hours area to area but the following rule is firm policy:

DURING DAY ORG HOURS THE DAY ORG EXECUTIVES AND PER-SONNEL HAVE FULL POSSESSION AND USE OF THE ORG PREMISES AND FACILITIES.

DURING FDN HOURS THE FOUNDATION EXECUTIVES AND PER-SONNEL HAVE FULL POSSESSION AND USE OF THE ORG PREMISES AND FACILITIES.

Otherwise one of the original intentions of the Day/Foundation system, that of economy of space and facilities by having two orgs using one premises and one set of facilities at different hours, is violated. Also, as has happened in at least two orgs recently, the Day org can squeeze the Foundation almost out of existence.

Therefore:

THAT ORG, DAY OR FDN, WHICH HAS POSSESSION OF THE ORG PREMISES AND FACILITIES BY REASON OF HOURS HAS FULL CONTROL OVER THEM AND EXECUTIVES AND PERSONNEL OF THE OTHER ORG MAY NOT USE THE PREMISES AND FACILITIES WITHOUT THE FULL PERMISSION OF THE HCO AREA SECRETARY OF THE ORG THAT HAS POSSESSION.

The HCO Area Sec of the org in possession is NOT obliged to give such permission and should not do so if use by the other org or its personnel is found to interfere with the FORM or FUNCTIONING of the org in possession.

STATS

Day org and Foundation stats are kept and computed separately. When there is a question of which org a stat belongs to the following policy applies:

THE STAT BELONGS TO THAT ORG, DAY OR FDN, WHOSE PRODUCTION IT MEASURES OR REFLECTS.

Thus in the case of GI it goes to the org which will deliver the service, regardless of what time of day it is taken in. This separation is handled by having different invoice machines for Day and Fdn. (See HCO PL 11 Aug. 72R III, FOUNDATION INCOME, for further details.)

PERSONNEL

The Day and Foundation orgs each have their own staffs. Some personnel may be members of both staffs (holding different posts in each org during different hours) but they function under the executives of the org they are presently working for and are not at that time under the orders of the other org.

DAY EXECUTIVES MAY NOT "RIP OFF" FOUNDATION PERSONNEL NOR USE THE FOUNDATION AS A PERSONNEL POOL AND LIKEWISE FOUNDATION MAY NOT "RIP OFF" DAY PERSONNEL.

(Definition of "rip off"—slang expression meaning "take without exchange." Can be applied to personnel, money, anything.)

Violation of the above resulted in one Foundation going into a decline as, over a period, Day org took several key Foundation execs with no exchange given.

Directors of Personnel and Dept 1s should work hard recruiting and hatting now to rapidly achieve the ideal of Day and Foundation orgs competently staffed with *different* executives and personnel in each, with Day personnel training for full Foundation hours in the Foundation and Foundation personnel training during full Day hours in the Day org, so as to markedly raise the proficiency of their staffs and the viability of their orgs.

STUDENTS

Where Day students also wish to study at night, they may do so on Foundation hours but FOUNDATION students have priority on the recorders, packs and space. The Day students studying at night are not entitled to supervision from Foundation Supervisors.

PCs

Where Day pcs are being audited also at night the auditor shifts from Day org to Foundation for the night period. The practice should not be encouraged.

MOONLIGHTING STAFF

Staff that moonlight evenings should work Day hours only. Staff that moonlight days should work Foundation and weekend hours only.

Periods off post to moonlight are expressly forbidden.

Moonlighting is discouraged. The right answer is for the org to function and make money and pay its staff.

Any org, Day or Foundation, that does not make a GI divided by staff of $500 minimum is an off-policy, unhatted, badly run org and should pull up its boots so it doesn't have to moonlight.

SUMMARY

The policy letters listed at the beginning of this issue tell you how to organize and develop a Foundation. They are extremely clear. They also give you the only points where Day org and Foundation cross administratively. Such points are very few and are minor. The two orgs *are* separate and MUST be considered and function as such.

As the above may be a major change in some orgs, care must be taken in the implementation of this policy letter not to crash stats but to keep them, both Day org and Foundation, up and rising.

Therefore a period of two months is allowed for full implementation of this PL—deadline 11 October 1972. (It is not expected that Day and Fdn orgs will have staffs of entirely different execs and personnel by that date though that program should be well under way.)

Any attempt to implement this PL destructively so as to crash stats then blame the crashed stats on this PL will be considered to be a Suppressive Act and the subject of a Committee of Evidence.

L. RON HUBBARD
Founder

Assisted by
HCO Aide

HCO POLICY LETTER OF 11 AUGUST 1972R
Issue III
REVISED 4 SEPTEMBER 1972

Remimeo
Also changes
CBO 216

FOUNDATION INCOME

(Effective for the first week ending Thursday after the date of receipt of this PL for OIC report of Day and Foundation Gross Income.)

(This revision separates the financial planning of Day and Foundation. Combining them permits the Day org to grab the Foundation's income when the Day org is low that week and Foundation high. Combining FP caused a crash of ASHO Foundation. The FP must be separate.)

Where a Day org and a Foundation are operating on the same premises, the definition which is used to determine the income of each org is:

THE ORG THAT WILL DELIVER THE SERVICE GETS THE INCOME, regardless of the time of the day and night when it is taken in.

It may at times occur that a Day Registrar signs up a person for a service to be taken Foundation hours, or vice versa.

This is handled by having two separate invoice machines, one for the Day org and one for the Foundation. Both machines are kept available by the Registrar's desk.

The Day Registrar, when invoicing money for a Foundation service, would simply use the Foundation machines to make out the invoice. Same applies for a Foundation Registrar taking in and invoicing Day income.

The Registrar who reges the person, Day or Foundation, gets the stat on her own stats.

Mail income is also invoiced on separate machines for Day and Foundation orgs.

For ease of recognition, Foundation invoices are additionally marked with a large "F" letter.

In any case where it can not be determined at the time of payment whether the service will be taken Day or Foundation, that org which reges the service is authorized to count the income as theirs.

HCO ACCOUNT

Booksales and other HCO Account items as well as Bookstore sundry sales are counted as the stat of the org that makes the sale regardless of whether the person is otherwise on Day or Foundation lines.

In order to maintain separateness of Day and Foundation income flows, the Day and Foundation orgs must also be provided with separate invoice machines for the HCO Book Account.

Foundation invoices for HCO Account also carry the "F" letter.

COLLECTIONS

The Foundation org does its own collections from its own set of advance payments and credit files and does not depend on the Day org for these functions.

ACCOUNTS

There is only one set of bank accounts for the Day and Foundation and all income, Day and Foundation, is banked in these accounts. In the case of FBO orgs, the FBO carries one set of accounts only for both Day and Foundation orgs.

Accounting functions for both Day and Foundation are handled by the Day org. The Day org pays all bills.

Day FP and Foundation FP *must* be kept separate. Each has its own FP Committee and plans its own funds. Rent or building cost and utilities are prorated between Day and Foundation.

HONESTY

The basic ingredient by which this definition and handling of Day and Foundation income will be made to work is HONESTY of Executives, Registrars and Treasury people.

L. RON HUBBARD
Founder

Assisted by
CS-3

ADMIN KNOW-HOW SERIES

HCO POLICY LETTER OF 20 OCTOBER 1966
Issue II

Remimeo
All Executive Hats

Admin Know-How Series 1

EXECUTIVES AND GOVERNING BODY
ERRORS AND ANSWERS

Anyone in an executive position must be in possession of information concerning his post and the functions of the organization or unit he is heading. Lacking it, he becomes the effect of post and organization and begins to create unreal orders and situations which result in down statistics all around.

In principle, anyone in charge of anything should know the workings and functions of every unit, item or action of which he has charge. If he lacks such, he should be careful to take advices from his juniors before issuing any order to make certain it *can* be carried out, is necessary and conforms to workable practice.

Anyone while learning an executive post and yet acting as that executive should spend the bulk of his time in study and should issue NO orders and approve of NO orders until he has taken up the matter with those who will be affected by those orders before they are issued.

Eventually, as one learns his post, after months or years, he or she can begin to issue orders independent of taking advices first from those the orders will affect.

In this way, an executive not yet well trained or experienced can keep things going while he is studying his position and those things under him.

An executive cannot call himself fully competent or informed until he has studied all literature, past orders and policies which affect his position or any activity under him and can handle any machine or operation in any unit of which he has charge.

Until then he had better adhere closely to the rule that before he issues any order he had better consult with all those it will affect.

However, in doing this, he must not at the same time issue only popular orders or orders tending to break down the existing structure just to reduce labor or hours on the job or raise pay.

A great many persons fail as executives solely because they:

a.   Do not proceed as above on a new job or promotion or

b. Fail to hold together and control the activities in which they find themselves in charge or

c. Use their position solely to buy popularity or

d. Form a clique for their own self-protection against the mob.

It takes a very sensible person to succeed on a new job as an executive without previous experience or previous study; but if a person follows this advice as given herein, he or she can win and hold the statistics up and even raise them.

GOVERNING BODIES

Any council or conference or board becomes bogged only for one of the following reasons:

A. It is inactive or

B. It seeks to solve the wrong problem or

C. It fails to notice and nullify arbitraries that have been introduced.

(A) The inactive council or conference or board may be inactive for a number of reasons.

It can simply be inactive.

It can be inactive as a governing body while individually very busy issuing orders. This is quite fatal as such orders will conflict with orders issued by other members of the body also acting individually. The consequence is that the activity so governed will then seek orders elsewhere to resolve the confusion of conflicting orders from members of the governing body—this is how mutinies and revolutions occur and also why some activities will suddenly create dictators. To use one's *status* as a member of a governing body as an individual authority and yet not see that it is the body that governs, will surely bring about mutiny and revolt and new leaders.

The remedy is of course to permit no orders not agreed to in the actual conference of the governing body and to reprimand and cancel any orders issued independently.

If the body is simply inactive and won't become active at all, despite everything, it should be disbanded as a governing body and its powers delivered to a single individual. A body inactive that won't act as a body must not be permitted any power. For example, if an Ad Council is actually inactive, it should be disbanded and its powers individually delegated to its individual Exec Secs. However, if this is done, no powers may overlap. Some "governing bodies" exist only to satisfy the law and have no power at all.

(B) Solving the *wrong* problem means also neglecting to locate the right problem. There is nothing wilder than orders to remedy situations which are not the real problems or the vital problems of an activity.

When a governing body is bogged, a well-schooled administrator should be able to see if the body is working on the right problem and, if not, to shift that body's attention to the real problem they should be solving.

An example would be a government seeking to resolve heavy spending when they have no earning. The real problem is lack of money. Conversely, a government can seek only to earn more money when they may have a real problem of fantastically foolish expenditure. In either case, by working on the wrong problem that government can fully crash a country.

A governing body can ride prejudices rather than handle existing problems, which is another way to solve the wrong problem.

(C) Arbitraries can be introduced which thereafter require constant and changing solutions which even then do not improve things.

When this happens, one must locate the arbitrary itself that is causing the need of solution and abolish it.

The only mistake one can make is calling *any* rule an arbitrary, thus destroying form. One has to isolate a *real* arbitrary that *is* causing needless solutions. When found, it should be removed.

However, one can be so sweeping in doing this that it simply gets unreal and wrecks the lot. For example, one's laziness or unwillingness to confront can condemn something as an arbitrary which, when removed, causes one to collapse. It is not then an arbitrary but a form or necessity.

An arbitrary, by definition, is an interjected law or rule or decision which does not fit or is unnecessary.

Such things can cause a governing body to box about for years and eventually fail.

Here is an example of an arbitrary that caused endless solutions and which when not removed destroyed a nation. "Our currency must not circulate beyond our borders." This was kept unwittingly in force. As money depends for its value on its scope of potential circulation, the money became worthless and the country caved in. Literally millions of governmental and individual solutions became necessary after that one arbitrary was introduced.

So an "arbitrary" can be said to be something which actually violates natural law and which becomes, when held in place, an enforced lie. This causes endless board or governing body trouble wherever it occurs.

Here is another example. "Unions have the right to strike." This was assumed and is not part of any law code as it says, "A body of men has the right to injure business and property without at least civil recourse for damages by the business." Protection racketeers assumed the same right. This arbitrary is a lie since nobody has that right. It laid France open to World War II, for instance, as France through the 1930s was one long strike. True, *unions* have improved pay and working conditions. But there is no right to damage businesses which support one. By introducing this arbitrary without seeking sensible means, the Western world was opened to inflation, unrest and conquest by lawless political elements.

So an arbitrary must be something contrary to the general scheme of things and, while a lie, is yet held in place by law or public ignorance.

Arbitraries are usually introduced by those who aren't quite bright enough to achieve a result through wise measures. And otherwise wise men thereafter can spend decades and invent whole law codes trying to handle the problems so set up.

BOGGED ORG

When an org is bogged after a period of success, it is almost always true that an earlier program or order has been dropped or forgotten.

I have always been able to trace bogs to skipped orders.

An example is the Qualifications Division program order. Outer org recovery was planned so as to improve Qual in each org, then to get staff training in and then to improve the Tech Division. This order was at first executed, then was not followed up and the beginning recovery slumped again. The remedy was to reinstitute the original program.

Ordinarily one doesn't need new programs but needs the follow-through on programs that have not been complied with.

When I see a slump occur, I first ask what program wasn't executed or got dropped. I always find it and when reinstituted, things surge. *Then* I find who dropped it and reorganize personnel with non-droppers.

In this admin failure the dropped program is seldom a little one. Recently at Saint Hill when statistics slumped, I found the program that was out was selling the Saint Hill Special Briefing Course. It was being taught but never mentioned. Yet it, not Power Processing, was the mainstay of Saint Hill.

Look for the program or orders that were dropped or forgotten before you start originating new ones. You may find the dropped one is so huge that nothing could remedy it. In many orgs the dropped program was the original one—to put an org there! Of course no other order will revive the place as the org wasn't put there in the first place and people think they are *running* an org, whereas they didn't finish up putting one there to be run. It's often as simple as that.

DEV-T

An administrator (any executive) who does not know and enforce dev-t policies is letting the org down severely. It isn't just his own basket or office, it's the fact that dev-ters are annoying *other staff* too if they are into an executive's hair.

A towering in-basket is *always* a sign of an executive not enforcing dev-t policy. The whole org will sag if executives don't enforce these.

WHOSE HAT

Once you have dev-t in hand, your basket traffic shrinks but you may still be overworking by reason of another factor—wearing, unknown, the hats of others.

I always look up every month or so to see whose hats I am wearing besides my own.

If I find I am wearing hats not mine, I begin to look around the people and areas that *should* be wearing those hats.

If I find the people whose hats I am wearing have seniors below me but above them, I then examine the work areas of the seniors.

I always find one of two things:

a.   The seniors are not active at all or

b.   The seniors are doing something else than their own hats.

On the staff whose hats I am wearing, I usually find they are doing something else—not just inactive.

I then examine the statistics involved. *And* any finances.

I can then clean up this area by reorganization.

As the seniors are being bypassed, I have to assign a Danger condition to them and apply the Danger Formula (ethics action vital).

I get the statistics up and things going in that area and then get the hats *worn.*

In this way only an executive can wear his *own* hats and do his own work.

So if you are training an executive or if you are seeking to get a governing body or council or committee to function, or trying to make an org recover, you can use these bits of know-how.

They are vital, senior data which, properly employed, can make organizations run despite lack of training by executives and even very strange governing bodies.

Just apply the data contained herein and magic!—all will resolve.

L. RON HUBBARD
Founder

Remimeo
All Executive Hats

Admin Know-How Series 2

ACTIONS, EXECUTIVE
FOR HANDLING DISASTROUS OCCURRENCES

There are three steps necessary on the part of a senior executive who discovers a situation which may be disastrous to the org.

The executive's actions are as follows:

1. Issue orders of a remedying or preventive nature instantly by directive, to remain in effect until all data is in. This is called an urgent directive.

2. Appoint a Board of Investigation to investigate the matter, with orders to investigate fully and couch findings in terms of a directive or policy for issue.

3. Pass or modify the board's findings as orders to supplant the urgent directive issued as (1) above. This is called the final directive or policy.

THE URGENT DIRECTIVE

To do (1)—issue a sweeping order to handle the situation. This is vital as there isn't time to get all the facts. The order may be fair or unfair, correct or incorrect, but at least it does *something* to arrest a deteriorating situation.

This urgent directive may, however, be in fact wide of the mark; but it is only going to remain in force until superseded by orders based on all the data obtained at leisure.

Dictatorships are somewhat successful as proven in the past and they run only on urgent directives. So the system is not all bad. However, for such a directive to remain law forever is obviously wrong as it may be wholly arbitrary and may eventually get in somebody's hair. But not to issue it just because one has little data is to ask for disaster.

So in the face of disaster issue an urgent directive as best you can and hope you are right in your directed action.

THE BOARD

Convene now a Board of Investigation composed of impartial members who will investigate thoroughly.

Order them to turn in their findings in the form of law that can be issued exactly as they wrote it.

Trouble with such boards, they "recommend" in an often rambling way and as they aren't really writing *law,* they tend to overlook things.

Democracies have a terrible habit of only appointing committees to investigate without issuing any urgent directive first. This leaves a vacuum of direction and courts disaster. Such bodies may take a long time to bring in their findings. This is a great weakness—to let an abuse go on while one investigates.

THE FINAL DIRECTIVE

When the Convening Authority has the board's findings to hand, he studies the proceedings and findings to make certain that the disaster is fully handled by the findings and that further disasters of like nature are inhibited by these findings from occurring.

If he is satisfied on this score (that the findings are adequate), he must now see that they do not violate the fast flow system of management to any great degree and that they are as adequate as the urgent directive in arresting the disaster. If so, the executive sends the findings through regular channels with all papers to make them into law. Until actually law, the urgent directive is still in force.

If he is *not* satisfied or doubtful that the findings are adequate, he can convene another board to do a better job. If he does convene another board, the urgent directive remains in force.

The findings actually become law only when:

a.   The Convening Authority has passed them as they are or modified by himself or another board;

b.   The findings have gone through all steps necessary to become law;

c.   The findings are finally the law.

Then the urgent directive is cancelled. It *must* be cancelled when the findings become law and may not remain as a possible arbitrary.

The above is good administration.

Some governing bodies use only urgent directives.

Some use only committees or boards or senates.

To use less than all three in the face of a disastrous situation is poor admin.

Example: Income goes down like a shot. (1) Issue an urgent directive calculated to get income up like a shot, (2) Convene a board to find out why it went down and to discover what was dropped out and find how to get it back up, (3) Supplant the urgent directive with the findings.

Where policy is concerned, the channel is longer as more people must pass on it. But directives are also law. So one should not issue a directive in the face of disaster and just hope. One should do all three steps above.

327

By disaster is meant a circumstance or situation that is crippling and may adversely affect a whole or a part of an org. Low income is a heavy risk that may result in disaster. A heavy, continual expenditure may result in a disaster. Any gross divisional statistic going down and staying down is courting disaster. And such should be handled with the three steps as above. Then the org form and duties, if bent out of shape by the urgent directive, won't stay out of shape forever.

As a comment, statistics when they change suddenly and go down mean that something has been dropped or some arbitrary order has been given. Stats going steeply up also mean a change has occurred and it can be very disastrous not to find what it was that was so good. So one can also use the three steps to handle a sudden soaring statistic to maintain it rather than stay in the dark. Example: Letters out soars to an all-time high. Issue an urgent directive, "No person or line may be changed in the Dissem Division on peril of a Comm Ev." Then convene a board and find why and get some law on it. Then supplant the urgent directive with the new directive resulting.

This in no way alters the need of a directive to be passed by the LRH Comm or a policy letter to be passed by all specified terminals before it becomes policy.

PERSONNEL

Steps 1, 2 and 3 can also be used on personnel where the executive thinks a staff member is the reason. Suspension from post pending investigation would be the urgent directive in this case. However, the staff member so suspended may not be deprived of wages and must be given an apology if found not to be the reason. And no real action may be taken unless there is an ethics action recommended by the board and only if the person is found guilty in that ethics action.

In this case there are four steps:

1. Urgent directive

2. Board of Investigation

3. Ethics action or no ethics action

4. Final directive either (a) restoring the personnel and stating the real causes in the form of a separate directive with long-range actions to handle the situation, or (b) appointing a new personnel and recommending in a separate directive long-range actions to handle the situation.

The steps are four because there are two matters involved: (a) the personnel and (b) the situation. Even if the personnel was at fault, there must be something else wrong too if a personnel got into a post who didn't belong there.

L. RON HUBBARD
Founder

HUBBARD COMMUNICATIONS OFFICE
Saint Hill Manor, East Grinstead, Sussex

HCO POLICY LETTER OF 31 OCTOBER 1966R
Issue II
REVISED 5 MARCH 1968

Remimeo
Staff Status II
Checksheet

GENERAL FOR ALL STAFF

Admin Know-How Series 3R

JOB ENDANGERMENT CHITS

If you are given orders or directions or preventions or denied materials which make it hard or impossible for you to raise your statistics or do your job at all, you MUST file a Job Endangerment Chit on your next highest superior.

If you are admonished or ordered to a hearing for NOT doing your job and having low statistics and have NOT *previously* filed a Job Endangerment Chit at the time it occurred, you have no defense.

You should not come to a hearing as a defendant and *say* you were prevented or inhibited from doing your job. Unless you have filed a Job Endangerment Chit previously when your job was endangered, the statement MAY NOT BE ACCEPTED by the Hearing Officer or the Comm Ev.

POLICY

Most people who have trouble with policy or admin do so simply because they don't know it or can't or don't use it.

Such a person can be told anything and tends to take it as fact.

Policy exists to speed the wheels and make a job doable.

But sometimes one has a senior who continually says this or that is "against policy."

Always respectfully ask for the date of the policy letter and to see a copy of it.

Then you will know that what you propose is or is not against policy. If no policy letter can be produced or if what you proposed is NOT against policy and is still refused, you must file a Job Endangerment Chit.

WHERE TO FILE

FORMERLY ONLY ONE COPY WAS WRITTEN. THIS IS NOW MODIFIED.

USING CARBON PAPER, MAKE AN ORIGINAL AND TWO COPIES.

329

SEND ONE COPY TO THE PERSON BEING FILED ON.

SEND TWO COPIES TO THE ETHICS OFFICER.

THE ETHICS OFFICER WILL FILE ONE IN THE FILE OF THE PERSON NAMED AND ONE IN THE FILE OF THE PERSON WRITING THE CHIT.

THESE COPIES MUST BE CAREFULLY PRESERVED IN EVENT OF A COMM EV OR HEARING AS THEY ARE NECESSARY DEFENSE PAPERS.

WHAT TO FILE

Full details, without rancor or discourtesy, must be given in the report, including time, places and any witnesses.

VEXATIOUS FILING

Anyone filing Job Endangerment Chits on superiors or equals or juniors must be able to back them up.

One cannot be given an Ethics Hearing or Comm Ev for a false Job Endangerment Chit unless it contains a willful and knowing false report which endangers somebody else's job. But even so, no Ethics Hearing may be ordered for the fact of filing, only for a willful and knowing false report.

So if your facts are straight there is no slightest risk in filing a Job Endangerment Chit. On the contrary, it is dangerous NOT to file one. For then one has NO defense.

PERSONAL MATTERS

Sometimes a staff member is imposed on in such a way as to prejudice his job such as having to do off-line favors.

This is an occasion for a Job Endangerment Chit.

If one is threatened with punishment if one files a Job Endangerment Chit, one must then file a second chit based on the threat.

If an org as a whole seems to refuse Job Endangerment Chits or ignore them, one can be filed with Worldwide simply by sending it direct to "HCO Ethics Worldwide, Saint Hill Manor, East Grinstead, Sussex."

WRONGFUL DISMISSAL

Dismissal without following proper procedure of a Hearing may be sued in the Chaplain's Court, Division 6. If no Chaplain's Court exists in the local org, then one surely does in the Continental Org and one can file such a suit there or at Saint Hill.

CHITS BY SENIORS

Seniors let down by juniors had better file Job Endangerment Chits before calling a lot of ethics actions. Staff members are seldom willful, they are just unknowing. Senior chits on juniors should carry a copy to the junior on channels as well as Ethics.

FALSE REPORTS

When one finds he has been falsely reported upon, he should file a Job Endangerment Chit.

HEARINGS ON CHITS

Ethics action is not necessarily taken because a chit has been filed on one. But if too many chits occur in a staff member's file, an investigation should be ordered and only if the board so recommends does ethics action then occur.

STATE OF MIND

Don't sit around muttering because you are being kept from doing your job.

And don't be timid about filing a Job Endangerment Chit.

Don't accept orders you know are against policy or at least unworkable. File a Job Endangerment Chit.

There is no vast THEY weighing you down. There is only ignorance of policy or misinterpretation or arbitrary interference.

If you are willing to do your job, then *know* your job and do it. And if you are being shoved off so you can't do it, you MUST file a Job Endangerment Chit.

You have a right to do your job, you know.

L. RON HUBBARD
Founder

HCO POLICY LETTER OF 3 NOVEMBER 1966

Remimeo

Admin Know-How Series 4

LEADERSHIP

Leadership is one of the most misunderstood subjects in man's dictionary. But it is based almost solely on the ability to give and enforce orders.

An order or directive is necessary to bring about coordination of function and activity without which there could be disagreement and confusion.

In an organization there is more than one person functioning. Being of comparable rank and having different purposes (hats), they can come into conflict and disagreement in the absence of a plan or order or directive. So, without orders, plans, programs, one does not have an *organization*. One has a group of individuals. We see in earlier policy letters that a group composed only of individuals cannot expand and will remain small.

Oddly enough, such a group will also remain unhappy. It will have a low affinity with the public and each other and if you know the affinity-reality-communication triangle, you will realize that all three points drop if one does. Agreement being the basis of reality, you will find a group of individuals will disagree with each other and have a low reality on what they are doing or what to propose and even what to do.

Most people confuse a "taut ship" with a harshly led ship. Actually harshness has nothing to do with it. The right word is *positiveness.*

If a group is led by someone whose programs and orders are very positive, then the group has a chance of going into agreement with one another; and so their affinity improves and so does their communication and reality.

So if one issues *no* orders, a group will remain a group of individuals, out of agreement with each other, will do little and will remain small or at least non-expanding.

Bill, of equal rank to Joe, cannot give an order to Joe nor vice versa. Thus no orders exist between them. Occasional agreements do occur; but as their jobs are different, they rather tend to disagree on what is important.

A person with a senior-standing to both Bill and Joe can give the two an order and this becomes the basis of an agreement.

The order doesn't even have to be liked by Bill and Joe. If they follow it, they thus "agree" to it; and being in agreement on this, they get reality and communication on it as well.

Even poorly thought out orders angrily given, if issued and enforced, are better for a group than no orders at all. But such orders are the low end of the scale.

Positive, enforced orders, given with no misemotion and toward visible accomplishment, are the *need* of a group if it is to prosper and expand.

The group is full of "good fellows." This does not give it success.

The group is full of plans. These do not give it success.

What it needs are positive orders leading to a known accomplishment. Many obstacles can exist to that accomplishment, but the group will function.

We call it "leadership" and other nebulous things, this ability to handle a group, make it prosper and expand.

All leadership is, in the final analysis, is giving the orders to implement the program and seeing that they are followed.

One can build this up higher by obtaining general agreement on the how, why and what of programs. But to maintain it there have to be orders and directives and acceptance or enforcement thereof—else the group will fall apart, sooner or later.

Positive orders and directions on positive programs inevitably cause expansion.

Being wise or a good fellow or being liked does not accomplish the expansion. People in the group may be cheerful—but are they going anywhere as a group?

So the whole thing boils down to:

Positive directions and their acceptance or enforcement on known programs bring about prosperity and expansion.

No or weak orders bring about stagnation and collapse.

The ideal is to have programs with which the whole group or a majority agrees fully. Then to forward these with positive orders and obtain compliance by acceptance or enforcement.

But regardless of the enthusiasm for a program, it will eventually fail if there is no person or governing body there to issue and enforce orders to carry on the program.

Thus we have the indicators of a very bad executive whose group will disintegrate and fail no matter how cheerful they are with the executive.

Bad leaders:

1. Issue no or weak orders,

2. Do not obtain or enforce compliance.

Bad leadership isn't "grouchy" or "sadistic" or the many other things man advertises it to be. It is simply a leadership that gives no or weak orders and does not enforce compliance.

Good leadership:

1. Works on not unpopular programs,

2. Issues positive orders,

and

3. Obtains or enforces compliance.

These facts are as true of a governing body as they are of an individual.

A typical example of a bad governing body, at the present stage of its formation at least, is the United Nations.

It has great ideas about how better man should be perhaps, but

1. It issues a confused babble of orders when it issues any

and

2. It issues orders for which it can obtain little or no compliance.

Note that it is also insolvent, at war within itself and that it has not made a dent in its prime program—the prevention of war.

However these things came about, they are nevertheless true. It is a very poor governing body and far more likely to vanish than expand.

You can count completely on the fact that an executive or a governing body that does not adhere to not unpopular programs, that does not issue positive orders and does not obtain or enforce compliance, will have down statistics.

And you can be sure that an executive or governing body that formulates or adheres to not unpopular programs, that issues positive orders and that obtains or vigorously enforces compliance, will have up statistics.

Wisdom? Popularity? These unfortunately have little or nothing to do with it.

The way to have up statistics, a prosperous and happy group, is far more simple than complex man has ever realized.

L. RON HUBBARD
Founder

HCO POLICY LETTER OF 6 NOVEMBER 1966R
Issue I
REVISED 9 NOVEMBER 1979

Remimeo

Admin Know-How Series 5R

STATISTIC INTERPRETATION
STATISTIC ANALYSIS

Refs:

HCO PL 9 Nov. 79RA Rev. 27.8.82	HOW TO CORRECTLY DETERMINE A STAT TREND	
HCO PL 3 Oct. 70RA Rev. 27.8.82	STAT INTERPRETATION	
HCO PL 6 Mar. 66 II	STATISTIC GRAPHS—HOW TO FIGURE THE SCALE	
HCO PL 5 May 71RA II Rev. 27.8.82	READING STATISTICS	

The subject of making up statistics is probably well known. How one draws one. But the subject of what they mean after they are drawn is another subject and one which executives should know well.

Things are not always what they seem in statistics.

BACKLOGS

A backlog caught up gives one a high soaring statistic which promptly slumps. To call the soar Affluence and the slump Emergency is an executive error.

When you see a leaping and diving pattern on something that *can* be backlogged, you can be very sure it has been.

This activity is working in fits and starts, usually only occasionally manned.

For a long time nothing is done or counted, then suddenly a month's worth is all counted in one week.

So when you see one of these, realize that the one surge in stats is averaged out with the smaller peaks and the depressions. You have to visually average the peaks and valleys and note the trend the entire stat is taking.

CAUSATIVE STATISTICS

In any set of statistics of several kinds or activities, you can always find one or more that are not "by luck" but can be directly caused by the org or a part of it.

Examples are the "letters out" and "completions" gross divisional statistics. Whatever else is happening, the org itself can improve these as they depend only on the org, not on "fate."

So if you see the gross divisional statistics generally down or going down for the last couple or three weeks and yet see no beginning upsurge in the current week in "letters out" and "completions" you know that the org's management is probably inactive and asking to be removed. For if they saw all stats going down they should have piled in on "letters out" and "completions" amongst other things as the least they could do. They *can* push those up.

So amongst any set of statistics are those which can be pushed up regardless of the rest and if these aren't, then you know the worst—no management.

ENROLLMENT VERSUS COMPLETIONS

If you see a statistic going up in "completions" and see a falling "enrollment" statistic, you know at once the body repeat sign-up line is *out*.

People who graduate are not being handed their certs and awards by a Registrar but are being given them by Certs and Awards or in mass meetings, or in some way repeat sign-up is not being procured.

Thus the 40 percent to 60 percent repeat sign-up business is being lost.

This also means, if continued over a long period of time, that bad technology is present as poor word-of-mouth advertising is going around.

Look in such a case at a third statistic, Qual collections. If this is poor or very, very high, you can be sure that lack of enrollments is caused by bad tech.

A very high Qual collections statistic and a low enrollment statistic is a terrible condemnation of the Tech Division. Gross income will soon after collapse as tech service just isn't good.

COMPARING STATISTICS

Thus you get the idea. Statistics are read against each other.

A statistic is a difference between two or more periods in time so is always comparative.

Also, two different statistics are comparative, such as in examples above.

PREDICTION

You can predict what is going to happen far in advance of the occurrence, using statistics.

High book sales mean *eventual* prosperity. Low book sales mean eventual Emergency all along the line.

High gross income and low completions mean eventual trouble as the org isn't delivering but is "backlogging" students and pcs simply by not getting results. Carried on long enough this means eventual civic and legal trouble.

Low FSM commissions may only mean no FSM program. But if there is an FSM program, then it may mean bad tech. So a low completion and low Qual will mean an eventual collapsed FSM statistic also, as the FSM's own area is being muddied up by failed cases.

High book sales, high letters out, high Tech and high Qual statistics mean the gross income statistic will soon rise. If these are low, then gross income will fall.

Bills owed and cash in hand are read by the distance between the two lines. If it is narrowing, things are improving; if widening, things are getting worse. If they are far apart and have not closed for a long while, with the cash graph below, the management is dangerous and not at all alert.

THE DANGEROUS GRAPH

When all statistics on one set of graphs show a sinking *trend* line, it is a dangerous situation.

Trend means an inclination or tendency toward a general course or direction. Thus to get the trend one would look at several weeks worth of stats.

To read the stat trend, one needs to visually average the peaks and valleys over a specific time period on the graph. It is done with the eye; there is no internal system of lines that can be drawn to assist this. One sits back and looks at the pattern as a whole and there is a definite pitch or slant that one can determine by this. That is the stat trend.

If all of these stat trends or most of them are down, the management is inactive.

FALSE COMBINATIONS

When a Continental Org includes its own org on its combined graphs for area orgs, it can have a very false picture.

Its own org's stats obscure those of the area orgs which may be dying.

Thus if you include a big function with a lot of small ones on a combined graph, you can get a very false idea.

Thus, graph big functions as themselves and keep them out of small functions of the same kind.

The Continental Org should not be part of a Continental Exec Div's statistics. Similarly, SH stats should not be part of WW's.

A combined statistic is, of course, where you take the same stats from several functions and add them up to one line. A very large function added into a combined graph can therefore obscure bad situations. It can also obscure a totally inactive senior management as the big function under its own management may be wholly alert and competent but the senior management is masked from view by this one going concern whereas all its other points except the big one may be collapsing.

THE BIGGEST MISTAKE

The one big god-awful mistake an executive can make in reading and managing by graph is *being reasonable* about graphs. This is called JUSTIFYING A STATISTIC.

This is the single biggest error in graph interpretation by executives and the one thing that will clobber an org.

One sees a graph down and says, "Oh well, of course, that's——" and at that moment you've had it.

I have seen a whole org tolerate a collapsed completions graph for literally months because they all "knew the new type process wasn't working well." The Tech Sec had JUSTIFIED his graph. The org bought it. None thought to question it. When it was pointed out that with the same processes the preceding Tech Sec had a continual high graph and a suppressive was looked for, it turned out to be the Tech Sec!

Never JUSTIFY why a graph continues to be down and never be reasonable about it. A down graph is simply a down graph and somebody is goofing. The only *explanation* that is valid at all is, "What was changed just before it fell? Good. Unchange it fast!" If a graph is down it can and *must* go up. How it is going to go up is the only interest. "What did we do each time the last few times just before it went up? Good. Do it!"

Justifying a graph is saying, "Well, graphs are always down in December due to Christmas." That doesn't get it up or even really say why it's down!

And don't think you know why a graph is up or down without thorough investigation. If it doesn't stay up or continues down then one didn't know. It takes very close study on the ground where the work is done to find why a graph suddenly rose or why it fell.

This pretended knowledge can be very dangerous. "The graph stays high because we send out the XY Info Packet," as a snap judgment, may result in changing the Dissem Sec who was the real reason with his questionnaires. And the graphs fall suddenly even though no info packet change occurred.

GROSS REASONS

Graphs don't fall or rise for tiny, obscure, hard-to-find reasons. As in auditing, the errors are always BIG.

Book sales fall. People design new fliers for books, appropriate display money, go mad trying to get it up. And then at long last one discovers the real reason. The bookstore is always shut.

A big reason graphs fall is there's nobody there. Either the executive is double-hatted and is too busy on the *other* hat, or he just doesn't come to work.

STICKY GRAPHS

Bad graphs which resist all efforts to improve them are *made*. They don't just happen.

A sticky graph is one that won't rise no matter what one does.

Such a graph is *made*. It is not a matter of omission. It is a matter of action.

If one is putting heavy effort into pushing a graph up and it won't go up, then there *must* be a hidden counter-effort to keep it down.

You can normally find this counter-effort by locating your biggest area of noncompliance with orders. That person is working *hard* to keep graphs down.

In this case it isn't laziness that's at fault. It's counter-action.

I have never seen an org or a division or a section that had a sticky graph that was not actively pushing the graph down.

Such areas are not idle. They are not doing their jobs. They are always doing *something else*. And that something else may suddenly hit you in the teeth.

So beware of a sticky graph. Find the area of noncompliance and reorganize the personnel or you, as an executive, will soon be in real hot water from that quarter.

Those things which suddenly reared up out of your in-basket, all claws, happened after a long period of sticky graphs in that area.

Today's grief was visible months ago on your stats.

SUMMARY

The simple ups and downs of graphs mean little when not watched over a period of time or compared to other graphs in the same activity.

One should know how to read stats and what they mean and why they behave that way so that one can take action in ample time.

Never get *reasonable* about a graph. The *only* reason it or its trend is down is that it is down. The thing to do is get it up.

L. RON HUBBARD
Founder

HUBBARD COMMUNICATIONS OFFICE
Saint Hill Manor, East Grinstead, Sussex

HCO POLICY LETTER OF 10 NOVEMBER 1966
Issue I

Remimeo

Admin Know-How Series 6

GOOD VERSUS BAD MANAGEMENT

The difference between good management and poor management can be the loss or gain of the entire organization.

Financial planning is a vital part of management. Good financial estimations and the ability to *figure out,* without vast accounting, the way things are in an org is an ability which is vital to good management.

The manager, given a few vital facts, who then needs an accountant to tell him how things are, is of course incompetent.

Management is a high skill. Socialist or worker governments are flat on their uppers because they do not comprehend the degree of insight required in a successful manager. When they harass, mess up and sometimes shoot their managers, they promptly begin eras of starvation as in Russia, China and to some extent under their socialisms, in recent years, England and the US. The amount of time *any* manager has to spend in the US or England battling with government clerks who aren't skilled enough to run a tricycle, assisted, is easily a third of the manager's time.

The essence of good management is CARING what goes on. The worker-oriented fellow cares for the worker but not for the organization. So we have a final extinction of the worker by the organization vanishing and no longer able to employ. The consequence is the widespread depression just beginning. *Real* help for the worker is also making sure there will be work for him to do. When the organization is gone, there is only misery, the dole, revolution and sudden death. The "worker-oriented" manager lacks the insight into the skill necessary to manage. So to him an organization is something to be bled. It is a bottomless pit of money. Such a person's total "skill" is how to get something out of the organization. But you can't take out more than comes in. Management is entirely beyond the ability of such people. They don't know what it is all about. They do not care what happens to the organization. Then suddenly the machinery all stops and everyone starves.

Whole countries go this way when the mess begins.

The basic difference between organizations that run and those that collapse is simply somebody caring what happens to the organization itself.

A good manager takes care of the workers. He also takes care of the organization. A worker-oriented fellow—union leader, agitator, do-gooder—cares only for the worker and *thus does the worker in.* So he is actually a suppressive. For the whole bang shoot goes to pieces and the end product is dismal unemployment, depression, malnutrition, starvation. You have to have lived through such a period to learn dread of it. And that's what caring nothing for the organization finally results in.

A worker-oriented person is deficient in pan-determinism. He or she cannot see that the health of all demands he take into account workers *and* the org. Therefore he or she is below the ability to determine both sides of things and so makes a very poor executive, being lopsided, given to "them and us," playing favorites and unable to see two sides of a question. Such abilities are *vital* in an executive, so he isn't one.

A worker-oriented person is not nice to individual workers—he or she may shoot them—but only about collective "workers."

Poor source identification goes with lack of pan-determinism so a person cannot see or solve the *real* problems around. So such people can't even operate as executives.

Thus you can know them. The org or country always fails.

So you want to watch this "poor-worker" pitch in an executive. If he cares only for the worker and nothing for the org, if he is only interested in what he or the workers can get out of an organization, then you are looking at somebody who in the long run will put one and all on the street.

You see here and there bared teeth at the org or the idea of the org. Along with it, if you look, you will find a heavy carelessness about the org's money and property and also a heavy effort to get something for the workers. Here you have a full-bodied case. This person won't ever succeed and should never be an executive. Never. For he'll do the workers in.

A good manager cares what happens, what's spent, what prosperity can occur, how the work is done, how the place looks, how the staff really fares. He is dedicated to getting the show on the road and he takes out of the lineup obstacles to the org's (and staff's) progress.

Caring what goes on and not caring is the basic difference. Caring for something else while working is the mark of the laborer, not the executive.

If you have to start an economy drive, look for the people who fight it. Quietly remove them from executive posts. You have a laborer, steeped privately in "us-poor-workers" and "get what you can" and "spend the org out the window."

If you care what happens to the org and the size of the paycheck as well, you will be very careful to develop an insight into finance, efficiency and the state of the org.

If you see bills owed soaring above cash on hand, you will also see executives who care nothing for the org. They are worker-oriented, anti-org people and you had better put a thumb down on continuing them as executives. Along with that unfavorable graph you will also find demands to borrow money, sell assets to pay bills and a near refusal to promote or make money.

I have learned all this the hard way. I pass it on for what it is worth. I can say these things because no man on Earth could seriously challenge me for not caring about people or staffs. I do care. And the ultimate in caring is to make sure there is an org there.

341

So please be alert to these points in conducting Ad Council meetings. Inevitably the hardest job is financial planning. But in that sphere you will show up the executives and the laborers. Watch and when you find you have a worker-oriented person there, realize you don't have an executive. Get one.

SUMMARY

Bad management is therefore detectable on these points:

1. The bills-cash ratio will be high in bills and low in cash.

2. There is an effort to borrow money rather than earn it.

3. There is a heavy effort to sell assets rather than make money.

4. There is more effort to collect debts, particularly from seniors than to make new income.

5. There will be an effort to be supported.

6. There will be low affinity in the org for the org and its public.

7. There will be protest and flash-back at efforts to get them solvent.

8. There will be noncompliance with orders of senior management.

The remedy is to:

A. Find the most worker-oriented senior executive and remove him or her.

B. Find the anti-org executives and staff and remove them.

C. Put in the senior posts those who most care what happens to the org.

D. Enjoin and conduct careful financial planning and measures.

E. Remove from executive posts those who object to them or don't comply (that may have been missed in A and B).

F. Resurrect neglected orders and main programs and get them complied with.

G. Be exceedingly careful not to appoint people there in the future who don't care what happens to the org.

It does not much matter how one goes about this. If one wants the org *and its staff* to prosper, the above measures must be done and quickly when the bills-cash ratio of an org threatens the continuance of it and the staff their jobs.

L. RON HUBBARD
Founder

Remimeo

Admin Know-How Series 7

EXECUTIVE FACILITIES
FACILITY DIFFERENTIAL

When a senior executive has the ability to make money for the organization or greatly raise statistics, and when this ability has been demonstrated, that executive should have facilities.

This ability is often discoverable by the absence of the executive from post for a period or when the executive is pulled off by emergencies. In such a time the income of the org may sink.

The degree the income shrinks is the "facility differential" of that executive. It is worth that much to the org in facilities to have the executive on post. Example: With that executive on duty—income $8000 per week. With that executive absent—$5000 per week. This is the "facility differential" of that *executive*. It is, in this example, $3000 per week. This means that the org could afford $3000 per week extreme to provide that executive with facilities for his work to keep him from overload. For it will lose $3000 a week if this executive is distracted or overloaded. Of course nobody expects the org to spend $3000. It just shows the extreme amount it could spend. One cannot afford not to spend *some* of it for facilities for this executive. The moment it does spend some of it—providing this executive does have this influence on income or production—the differential rises as the org makes more money or as the stat goes up. This trend can be pushed up and up.

Executives don't *deserve* secretaries or communicators. They earn them. If an executive has no "facility differential," he should not have special personal help.

The "facility differential" can also be judged from other statistics but income is the primary one.

For instance, we have just found my "facility differential" for Saint Hill Org only. It is, based on losses during a six months' absence and gains for the last part of the year, £244,000 per annum for just this year. Thus the org *could* afford to spend £244,000 per annum to furnish me management facilities.

In this case the computation is made by the org's increased indebtedness for the first six months plus the lack of reserves set back and the rate of dismissal of debt in the last six months plus the reserves set aside. The increasing debt and reserve absence for six months is added to the debt reduction and reserve presence for the last six months, giving the total. Income and other personnel remained similar all through the year but began to fail and was picked up by me at the half year.

The value is actual cash wasted in my absence and a beginning failure set up by bad tech and the recovery in terms of cash retained and income upsurge.

Naturally, this is a very high sum at this time (though quite accurate).

The org, however, cannot afford *not* to give me every facility required to keep me on its lines.

These total only a few thousand a year for extra personnel and admin facilities, not anywhere near £244,000. Thus, if the org (SH only) permitted me to move off its lines and failed to provide me facilities, it would lose on the current balance sheet, £244,000 per annum in actual cash and would in fact go broke. It can't stand that much loss. So, the answer, nothing to do with my wishes, is that SH *must* provide me facilities for its own sake. Pay has nothing to do with it as I don't get paid. But SH staff pay would cease entirely as they would have no jobs.

An org is very lucky to have a few persons who can make money for it, fortunate to have one and in a mess if it has none.

Post title may mean nothing. A Registrar who, on post, brings in $5000 a week and off post the org gets only $2000 a week, is obviously such a person. The facility differential is $3000 a week!

A Treasury Sec who on post has a cash-bills ratio equal but off post, the org, through lack of his financial planning, gets a gap of $20,000 for the three months he is off, means a facility differential of $80,000 a year for that Treas Sec.

The usual reward is promotion but the org often loses income by promoting a good Reg to a poor Dissem Sec.

The answer is to give the person facilities as there is a "facility differential." This may include more pay on post but *must* include more facilities, beyond that of other staff members.

Just doing a normal job on post is *maintaining* income. It takes quite an executive to raise it markedly beyond normal expansion.

Mary Sue, by actual data of times past, is worth to an org on any single executive post about 50 percent of its regular gross income. The fall and rise of about half the income has been demonstrated in several orgs over many years. Had she also been subtracted from the SH Org, the facility differential added to my subtraction would have put it out of existence before the year was out.

It would be very foolish not to give her facilities. *Yet* she has never been known to ask for any and facilities have had to be *initiated* for her when they occurred. Thus top executives themselves have to notice this and demand facilities for the person. If they do not, the person at the very least will go off post or their services lost because of overwork.

So one doesn't have a communicator because one is an Exec Sec or senior executive. One has one if he or she has a "facility differential" beyond normal expectancy.

And that tells one who has communicators in an org. And who has the facilities.

And it says who *must* be given communicators and facilities and who shouldn't have them.

Granted it is sometimes hard to determine this "facility differential" in a staff member. But long experience will establish it.

FACILITIES

Facilities normally include:

a. Those that unburden lines

b. Those that speed lines

c. Those that gather data

d. Those that compile

e. Those that buy leisure

f. Those that defend

g. Those that extend longevity on the job.

One can think of many things that do each of these.

The bare minimum are accomplished by giving the executive a communicator.

The communicator more or less covers all the categories above. Then, as the facility differential rises, the communicator sheds hats by providing other people to take over these functions as outlined above.

ANALYSIS

The org board pattern (names of divisions, departments and their code words as per any of our org boards) is an analysis system which can be applied to any person or job. He is light or heavy on one or more of these and the pattern gives him or her a clue as to what is wrong.

Write them down for yourself and you will see. Which ones don't exist in your actions, which are in Emergency, which are Normal and which are high?

This is an ultimate analysis of the state of one's post. Or of one's life for that matter. One can progress simply by doing this now and then.

345

These also comprise a total pattern of facilities.

However, one needn't go so far to help an executive with a facility differential at first. Later, such an analysis is absolutely necessary to keep facilities in balance.

At first one only need give the person a better desk in better space and a better phone and more ballpoints.

But a real facility differential amounting to 25 percent or more of the org's income (on or off job difference, proven) demands not only these but also a communicator.

WHAT IS A COMMUNICATOR?

A communicator is one who keeps the lines (body, despatch, letter, intercom, phone) moving or controlled for the executive.

The communicator, when not helped by others, really assumes all of (a) to (g) above and *does nothing else for anyone else.*

PRIMARY COMMUNICATOR DUTIES

The primary actions of a communicator concern despatch lines and are as follows:

1. Receives all written comm for the executive of all kinds with no bypass.

2. Identifies and returns to sender all dev-t. The executive never sees it. Notes the senders in a book. Attaches the appropriate dev-t PL to each returned despatch. Monthly, reports the names of offenders and the number of times to the executive. (For these people are ruining other staff members too.)

3. Puts all directives, PLs, HCOBs and Ethics Orders and any statistics in a folder so marked each day.

4. Puts the org despatches in a folder so marked each day. (If several org areas or divisions are being handled, puts the despatches in folders by areas or divisions.)

5. Puts the personal despatches in a folder so marked each day.

6. Deletes from the lines anything that may be routinely answered by letter and answers it and puts the originals and typed answers for signature in a folder so marked each day.

7. Presents the folders named in (3) to (5) inclusive in the executive's in-basket at the beginning of the executive's workday (and holds all the rest that come in after, until the next day).

8. Puts the signature folder as per (6) above in the in-basket at the latest moment of the day sufficient to get them signed for the evening mail.

9. Lays cables and telegrams and phone messages in the center of the blotter on the executive's desk.

10. Comes in for cable answers when called.

11. Picks up and files properly for the executive all PLs, directives, in the executive's own file.

12. Keeps the executive's own files for the executive's use.

13. Keeps excess paper, magazines, books picked up and filed.

14. Leaves alone things the executive is working on but files them if not being worked on after a while.

15. Oversees cleanliness and arrangement of desk and office.

16. Oversees ampleness of pertinent supplies: paper, pens, stapler, clips, etc.

17. Doesn't take up the executive's time with chitchat or verbal reports or rumors.

18. Handles by-hand rushes for the executive in and out.

19. Blocks all body traffic until its business is established, then routes it properly (except where body traffic is the executive's business on post, in which case the communicator smooths and regulates it).

20. Handles phone traffic and keeps it very low, lists abusers as dev-t.

21. Takes down names of staff body traffic that is not a routine part of the line and reports it with the monthly dev-t report.

22. Takes the entheta off the lines but not items which, if not handled, will endanger the org.

23. Notes staff who hand the executive problems but do no compliance with solutions ordered and recommends ethics action.

24. Finds out bits of data when instructed to do so by the executive.

25. Keeps alert to malfunctions of lines and reports them for handling to appropriate persons.

26. Does not take up time of other staff or executives by unnecessary visits and does not prolong such visits beyond a crisp minimum transaction.

27. Blocks all lines if the executive is engrossed in a project.

28. Keeps own desk and materials neat.

29. Demands a communicator's secretary if differential great enough and lines are jamming.

30. Demands other facilities as per (a) to (g) above if the facility differential is great enough and there is overload.

COMMUNICATOR'S TITLE

A communicator's title is always his or her executive's followed by "'s Communicator." To that, when there are more than one, may be added "for ———" being a function or division.

COMMUNICATOR'S PURPOSE

The communicator is to help the executive free his or her time for essential income-earning actions, rest or recreation, and to prolong the term of appointment of the executive by safeguarding against overload.

COMMUNICATOR EXEC ACTIONS

The communicator has his own executive actions. These come under the Admin Know-How HCO PLs of contemporary date.

If a communicator can get these and dev-t policies grooved in for the executive, the communicator is invaluable.

A communicator should know the dev-t and Admin Know-How policies star-rated.

It should be no surprise to an executive to receive from his or her communicator a notice that the executive is violating Admin Know-How or dev-t policy. "May I call to your attention that you are wearing the Dir Clearing hat and have been for two weeks," or "You should request from Ad Council appointment of a board after your 10 July urgent directive."

COMPLIANCE

Policing compliance for a senior executive is a vital function of a communicator.

When an executive issues orders and they are not complied with then, as this builds up, that executive will suddenly behold a shock situation squarely on his plate.

Noncompliance lets entheta situations backfire right up to the executive. The degree of noncompliance regulates the number of screaming emergency messes the executive will have to handle.

The communicator then keeps an LRH Comm-type log and notes in it the orders or directives issued and notes as well compliance (using Dept I&R and time machine). At length, the communicator will have a noncompliance list.

This usually involves only a few persons or outside firms.

The communicator should inform the executive of this by presenting orders ready to sign nominating Ethics Hearings or Executive Ethics Hearings (or dismissal of outside firm) on certain persons who consistently noncomply.

If the executive has a junior post and a communicator, then for noncompliance one substitutes "job endangerment" actions which harass the executive and must be filed and remedied before the executive's statistic is shattered.

Only in that way can a communicator defend his or her executive from being hit by sudden shocks. Noncompliance (or job endangerment) lets the barriers down on the whole incoming line to a nasty situation which will then, unhandled, hit the executive with no time lapse left. So he has to handle a deteriorated situation in a screaming rush. He probably handled it months before but noncompliance let it worsen. And job endangerment, let it build up, has the same effect on a junior executive. The amount of bad news an executive gets in is in direct proportion to the failure of compliance (or job endangerment) and the communicator's failure to spot it at the time. The shorter the time one has to handle a bad mess, the harder and more shocking it is.

This is the *sole* reason a competent executive grows tired, wants to quit, leaves his job.

It is basically communicator failure to warn him of noncompliance (or job endangerment) early, so he can get people who *will* comply (or get those who endanger him off his back with their ineffectiveness or suppression). Or who will do their jobs and not leave them to the executive or let the executive suffer from their deeds or lack of them.

The fashion of a "private secretary" for every title is of course nonsense. As not every title by far is an income producer or statistic raiser.

Giving facilities to titles instead of high statistics denies the real producer what he needs by soaking up available help into corners that cannot benefit the org with it.

A normal action of a post is the usual covered (not uncovered) post which if replaced changes nothing. A real facility differential is a large change.

Thus if you give facilities to those who have no more than normal (covered post) facility differential and those who have a marked facility differential are given no help, you will eventually wipe out by overwork those who have the facility differential and the org will collapse.

It is not flashy new ideas so much that raise income but efficient standard actions.

New ideas are fine, when all the old programs are *also* working.

An executive who is brilliantly successful is one who can get all the formal, standard functions going and then add the garnish of bright new angles that augment the proven track.

Facilities give a valuable executive "think time" and "consider time" and a fresh, alert attitude toward what is going on.

If you want to raise your income as an org, then:

a. Get all standard actions functioning and staff working and

b. Spot those with "facility differential" and give them facilities.

c. Don't falsify any "facility differential" for sake of face or status.

d. Make sure that facilities granted know their business or work.

L. RON HUBBARD
Founder

HCO POLICY LETTER OF 17 NOVEMBER 1966
Issue II

Remimeo

Admin Know-How Series 8

INTERVENTION

The urgent directive system (see HCO PL of 31 Oct. 66, Admin Know-How 2) is the one most commonly used, when they have to intervene, by senior executives such as the following:

Founder
Senior Ad Council
Exec Sec
LRH Comm

The routine in this case is more or less as follows:

1. The senior, on discovery of a bad situation or noncompliance, issues an urgent directive. (If more than one is issued at the same time by different seniors, the list above is the precedence list of what order to follow.)

2. The senior directs investigation. Senior Ad Council usually appoints a Board of Investigation—sometimes directly orders a Comm Ev. The Founder might only require an ED from his LRH Comm in that area. An Exec Sec might require only an ED from his or her Communicator if he or she has one. Or any on the list may order a board.

3. The ordering senior, on receipt of the requested directive in draft form, then returns it to the Ad Council of the org or orgs to which it will apply. Until the Ad Council acts or *some* directive to handle the situation is passed, the original, most senior urgent directive remains in force.

The above would be the most common admin action, most calculated to bring things right in the long run.

It is important that until some form of ED is formally passed by the Ad Council of the org or orgs concerned, the urgent directive must be followed by those to whom it is addressed.

This keeps arbitraries from entering into admin.

Nothing, of course, prevents a senior executive, as listed above, from simply issuing straight orders with no follow-through of an ED. In such case, the directive is not called an urgent directive, but is simply an order in ED form.

DIRECT ORDER

Example: A senior executive discovers that a high unreasonable rental compared to income is being contemplated. By any means or ED, he forbids it and demands other quarters be looked for quickly. This requires no follow-through beyond the senior executive making sure other quarters ARE found and the order is complied with.

URGENT DIRECTIVE

Example: The Founder finds a long string of people are being labeled suppressive because they won't separate from Joe Blow. He writes an urgent directive to stop labeling people this way and convenes a board on the whole subject in that org, gets their findings in the form of an ED, sends it to that Ad Council. They pass it after some, none or many changes. The urgent order ceases to be in force at that moment. He could also have simply issued a direct order.

Example: An HCO Exec Sec finds Central Files is not increasing. She issues an urgent directive to round up all CF names lying around the org. Then investigates personally, writes an ED and puts it before the Ad Council. They work on it, modify it or expand it and pass it. The urgent directive ceases to be valid. Remember, she could as easily simply have issued a direct order as above. It could even have been in Executive Directive form.

PETITION

A direct order or a straight directive can be petitioned against *after* compliance. The Ad Council simply passes a petition and gives any data required or an ED to substitute.

It is usually wise to give a better remedy in the form of an ED and get that ED conditionally passed with the approval of the original issuer of the direct order or straight directive.

THEORY

Those who do the work sometimes know best and those nearest the scene are sometimes better armed with data.

A senior executive sometimes has to act without all the data and a wise senior often so acts when the situation is bad.

But the senior is only trying to remedy the situation in the final analysis. After his ordered fast action is taken, he is ordinarily quite happy to have help improving the remedy.

DIRECT SUBMISSION

An urgent directive or direct order may also be handled as follows by a senior:

1. Issue it.

2. Send it to the Ad Council of the org to which it applies with the note: "After you've done this, pass a directive to handle this sort of thing."

DEMANDED DIRECTIVE

A senior can simply demand an Ad Council pass a directive to remedy a situation and let them sort it out. This is only done when one has almost *no* data.

In this case the Ad Council passes one, puts it in force and sends a copy to the senior via channels stating, "Compliance herewith."

LABELING DIRECTIVES

When an Executive Directive is passed by an Ad Council, if it wipes out an urgent directive or a direct submission or a demanded directive, the resulting ED must bear the fact under its title: Executive Directive after Board of Investigation—"Cancels Urgent Directive PE96 GET INCOME UP"; or direct submission after urgent directive—"As requested by HCO Exec Sec WUS to augment her direct order, 'Get Income Up'"; or by demand for a directive—"As demanded by Ad Council WW in their cable 239 WW, Pass a directive increasing income."

DANGER FORMULA

The Danger Formula applies when such orders bypass those responsible, meaning at least an ethics investigation must occur to find who was asleep if any.

However, the Founder can issue an urgent directive or direct order to any org and order the Ad Council of any org, as he is in fact a senior of that immediate org, without having to take ethics action on the Ad Council WW or the senior Ad Council to that org. However in such cases Ad Council WW and the senior Ad Council are informed.

If, however, the Founder has to do too much too often, he steps back upstairs and investigates the senior Ad Councils. This has been the usual practice.

The Founder usually uses his LRH Comm to effect orders, get data and submit to Ad Council.

A senior Ad Council uses its area representative in its own group or the LRH Comm in the junior Ad Council to do the same thing.

In practice, one issues urgent directives when the situation is rough and simply demands a directive when things look like they will get rough.

––––––––––

Intervention by seniors is hard for juniors to cope with. The best defense is don't develop bad situations that then require intervention and keep all stats up and the org expanding.

L. RON HUBBARD
Founder

HCO POLICY LETTER OF 4 DECEMBER 1966

Remimeo

Admin Know-How Series 9

EXPANSION
THEORY OF POLICY

It is not very hard to grasp the basic principle underlying all policy letters and organization.

It is an empirical (observed and proven by observation) fact that nothing remains exactly the same forever. This condition is foreign to this universe. Things grow or they lessen. They cannot apparently maintain the same equilibrium or stability.

Thus things either expand or they contract. They do not remain level in this universe. Further, when something seeks to remain level and unchanged it contracts.

Thus we have three actions and only three. First is expansion, second is the effort to remain level or unchanged and third is contraction or lessening.

As nothing in this universe can remain exactly the same, then the second action (level) above will become the third action (lessen) if undisturbed or not acted on by an outside force. Thus actions two and three above (level and lessen) are similar in potential and both will lessen.

This leaves expansion as the only positive action which tends to guarantee survival.

The point of assumption in all policy letters is that we intend to survive and intend so on all dynamics.

To survive, then, one must expand as the only safe condition of operation.

If one remains level, one tends to contract. If one contracts, one's chances of survival diminish.

Therefore, there is only one chance left and that, for an organization, is expansion.

PRODUCT

To expand, any company needs a demanded product and will and skill to produce and deliver it. It can be a service or an item.

If a company has a demanded product and will and skill to produce and deliver it, it must organize to expand. If it does, it will survive. If it organizes to stay level or seeks to grow smaller, it will perish.

This is easily observed in nations. Whenever one seeks to remain the same or to lessen itself, it usually perishes. It need not seek only to expand its borders. It can also expand its influence and service. Indeed, the effort to expand borders in a nation without increasing a demand for its influence and products is a primary cause of war. If a nation expanded the demand for its influence and products, it would expand without war. When a nation seeks to merely expand by force of arms and does not expand the demand for its products, one gets a dark age or at least a social catastrophe.

Rome, early on, was in great demand for its social technology and manufacturing skill and only a cruel streak in her made her wage war to expand. Britain, for instance, was ready to welcome Roman baskets and pottery and art and had been demanding them for nearly a century when Caesar's vicious ambitions actually wrecked the smooth progress of Rome by enforced expansion by arms in excess of the demand for Roman products. This was one Roman product nobody wanted—Caesar and his legions.

Psychiatry's product of further insanity was not in demand by the people but by the state which sought to crush people or at least hold them down. So psychiatry expanded by government regulation, not by popular demand, and so at this writing stands in danger of complete extinction, for its influence depends utterly on "expanding" into the legislatures and government treasuries and no expansion whatever of any demand from the public and no product except slaughter.

The Roman Catholic Church once had a healing product, by actual treatment and by relics and miracles, and was in great demand by the public and eventually even the barbarians. But she began to fight progress in science and knowledge, and her product turned into exported ignorance backed by autos-da-fé (burning heretics) and thus ceased to expand and today is rapidly shrinking.

Buddhism, earlier than that, expanded continuously as it never sought new extension of territory other than that of learning. Buddhism failed in India alone because its monks became licentious, ceased to deliver true teachings and were swept up, most likely, in India alone, by the Muslim conquest of that unhappy country sometime around the seventh century.

Britain of the twentieth century actively sought to contract her empire and did so to the tune of internal economic catastrophe.

SINGLE PRINCIPLE

Thus, it should be obvious that contraction leads to death and expansion to life, providing that one maintains a demand for itself and the will and skill to produce and deliver a product.

If, as ours is, the product is very beneficial and if we continue to produce and deliver, the demand is assured. In this we are fortunate. And we are also fortunate that, try as they will, no squirrel is ever able to duplicate our product since one variation (that of changed brand) leads to others; and they promptly

355

have neither product nor demand—that observation is itself empirical. No squirrel has lasted more than two or three years in the past sixteen years. And there have been many. That they squirrel shows enough bad faith to drive away the public the moment the public hears of the original.

Thus, providing we maintain the will and skill to produce and deliver, we can expand, and proper expansion that will continue is possible.

All our policy then is built on EXPANSION.

It assumes we wish to survive.

And it stresses the production and delivery of a straight, nonsquirrel product.

It is calculated to ensure a continued and widening demand by ensuring that product remains good and beneficial.

The technology itself is complete, but it expands also by experience of administration of it and simplifying its presentation.

But to alter the basics of the technology will stop expansion because it is what we are producing, not what we are building.

We are building a better universe. It has not been a good universe to live in so far but it can be.

Our punitive force is our ethics system, and it exists to ensure the quality of the product and to prevent the blunting of demand for the product.

INTERPRETATION OF POLICY

The organization then has all its policy rigged to expand.

It takes many things to ensure expansion.

Thus when you are interpreting policy, it should be interpreted only against EXPANSION as the single factor governing it.

This can serve to clarify questions about policy. The correct interpretation always leads to expansion, not holding a level or contraction.

For example, policy bars the entrance of the healing field. This is solely because there is too much trouble with the occupiers of that field and only outright war (with no demand) could solve them. This seems to be a brake on expansion. It is only a brake on expanding by war in the absence of demand. Therefore the right way to expand is to gradually build up general public demand, let experience by the public see that we heal and when the demand is there and howling for us, reinterpret the policy or abolish it as a brake to expansion. As one can only expand by external demand for the product, if one seeks to expand in the absence of a specific demand for the product, one has war; and war doesn't lead to expansion any more than burning heretics and other brutalities expanded the Catholic movement.

So one interprets policy against *proper expansion* that is proper.

CORRECT EXPANSION

Expansion which when expanded can hold its territory without effort is proper and correct expansion.

Hitler (like Caesar) did not "consolidate his conquered territory." It was not possible to do so, not because he did not have troops but because he didn't have a real demand for German technology and social philosophy before conquering. Thus Hitler lost his war and fascist Germany died. It is almost impossible to consolidate territory where one was not invited in in the first place and force had to be used in order to expand.

One can remove a real suppressive by force to ensure demand will then build, providing he does not seek to force the product on the suppressive and all those around the suppressive.

The suppressive, as an individual, can be removed by force because he is an antidemand factor using falsehood and lies to prevent demand from occurring. But one, in removing the suppressive, has to be sure one's own product and delivery are still correct and straight and in no way suppressive of anything but suppressives.

Further, one must leave at least a crack in the door and never close it with a crash on anyone because a demand still may develop there.

The only way to start a full scale revolution is totally and thoroughly slam the door. One must always leave a crack open. The suppressive can recant and apologize. The pauper can by certain actions, no matter how improbable, secure service. Etc.

In short, use force only to shut down false antidemand factors. Yet leave the door at least a crack open in case demand without duress develops. Never finally shut off a possible demand.

You can stimulate demand. You can create it. But you may only comfortably and properly expand into demand.

Removal of a suppressive only brings a potential appearance of demand from the area he dominated. That potential, by some means, the best of which are good dissemination and service examples, must become demand before one can truly occupy territory.

Thus areas taken purely by force of arms can never be held by force of arms in the absence of demand for product and thus demand by the area for occupation and consolidation.

As we have a product that frees in an ultimate sense and de-aberrates, there is of course an end to the game. But it is so far ahead, embracing a whole universe, that it requires minimal consideration.

Expansion requires area to expand into. And we are in no danger of running out of that.

If we were dependent as nations often think they are on boundary expansion on one planet, or into one planet's populations as companies think they are, we would have brakes on expansion due to territorial or population limitations alone. But we are not likely to encounter such barriers for a period of time so long, we can consider our expansion potential as infinite—and are the only organization that honestly can so consider. We are not conquering land in the government sense anyway.

OVEREXPANSION

All factors, then, in policy are rigged for expansion.

And this brings about a possibility one can be asked about, that of *over*-expansion.

One can "overexpand" by acquiring too much territory too fast without knowing how to handle it. One can conquer new territory as fast as one wants IF he knows how to handle the situation.

There are several ways one can "overexpand." They all boil down to over-extended administration lines in a *single* administrative unit.

In this, one must know the principle on which the org board was originally conceived. It is that of Thetan–Mind–Body–Product.

If there is a thetan, a mind (organization potential, not a harmful mass) can be set up—a mind which will organize a body which will produce a product.

If any one of these elements (Thetan–Mind–Body–Product) are missing, then an organization will fail.

Man is so aberrated all mental actions seem to him to be reactive mind actions. But there has to be in organizations a data and problem–solution coordination unit in order to set up a body. (A thetan can do this without a lot of mass, having his memory and perception and intelligence.) We have then an Advisory Council to coordinate acquired data, recognize and resolve problems. Above it, there has to be a thetan somewhat detached from it. This may be a higher mind (Ad Council) operating as a director to the lower Ad Council.

The mind must operate to form a body. This body is the mest (matter, energy, space and time) and staff of the organization.

This body must produce a product. This in the HGC, for instance, is resolved cases.

Any smaller part of the whole organization is also a Thetan–Mind–Body–Product. Often the executive is both thetan and mind, but as soon as traffic gets too heavy, he must form a separate mind such as an administrative committee or a personal staff to compose the mind. In such a smaller unit than the whole org there is yet a body (the staff and mest of the unit). And there *must* be a specific product. The product sometimes is absent and sometimes incorrectly assigned, but if so the unit won't function.

Overexpansion occurs only when one tries to handle the larger volume with the same Thetan–Mind–Body–Product numbers one had before.

This tells you why single practitioners can't expand their practices without overwork.

It also tells you why some executives are upset at the idea of expansion as they (lacking organizational insight) see it solely as overwork. They don't see that when you expand volume and traffic you must expand the organization.

There is a wrong way and a right way to expand an organization.

The wrong way is to add staff and facilities endlessly (like governments tend to do) without adding to the organization itself.

If you had huge affluences occurring steadily, you would soon go into collapse if you did not expand also *by organizational units* or branches.

In taking over a new field or area of operation, for instance, one errs when he adds that traffic to the basic organization's traffic.

In the presence of huge escalating affluences, one must analyze what is causing them and reinforce them. BUT one must also see what new KIND of traffic is being added.

If one finds a new KIND of traffic, then one sets up a suborganization unit to handle it which is complete in itself.

If we are now getting "businessmen" in quantity, we set up, under the control of the original organization:

1. A thetan to supervise it,

2. A mind to coordinate it,

3. A body to handle it, and

4. A new product called "released/cleared businessmen."

If we then were to find the new unit (struggling to form itself into seven divisions on its own by now) gets a lot of demand and statistics on an Org Exec Course, it must cease to gratuitously coach it and set up its "Business Academy" teaching the Org Exec Course as Dept 10, appointing a thetan, mind, body and achieving a product "trained businessmen" and see that units to support it occur in other divisions and an ethics unit to prevent blunting of demand and re-aberration.

This can even go backwards. One sets up in Dissem a unit called "Business Course Project Promotion Section" and stimulates the demand and then when it is there puts in its Department 10.

Soon all seven divisions have extra units to care for this new action, each unit with a Thetan–Mind–Body–Product. The products are different but they all add up to "trained businessmen," whether they are creating demand, financing or servicing.

So *over*expansion is only underorganization in the main.

One can of course "overexpand" by attempted servicing in the absence of demand causing, thus, losses in finance. In such a case only concentrate on creating *new* demand, not on servicing old demands. This, by the way, is the most common error in organizations of ours. They shrink because they are not creating *new* demand and concentrate only on creating demand in those already demanding (which is lazy-easy).

New demand is expensive to develop. Thus you often see finance units frowning on "new demand" expenses and cutting down magazines in number of issue, not buying new mail lists, etc.

To start a new suborganization, one sets up on the basis of potential demand, sets up ethics to prevent demand-blunting or bad internal service or performance, works on increasing the demand, introduces service, sets up external ethics to prevent blunted demand, increases the demand by dissemination to *new* and *old* areas of demand, increases service, ensures product, increases the organization (not just staff), increases demand in new and old areas, stiffens up ethics, improves service facilities, etc., etc.

It's continuous expansion of volume, continuous expansion of organization, continuous expansion of demand. Where one lags behind the others one gets trouble.

It is almost impossible to run a nonexpanding organization with ease. One gets into financial crises, staff troubles and overwork. Decay has set in. And fighting it is sure to overwork an executive. The easiest course is to expand. Then one has the help.

Summary: In understanding policy one must understand its key and that is expansion.

Only a Scientology organization has an unlimited horizon. But any organization must expand to survive.

The only ways you can "overexpand" are to fail to expand with new demand and keep pace with it evenly with organizational expansion as well as numbers.

It is easier to expand than to "remain level."

Organizations and units which do not expand cannot stay level and so contract.

Org executives and personnel are overworked only when they cannot afford to expand and thus cannot get the help they need to do the work—quite in addition to there being more problems made by contraction than by expansion.

Scientology organizations are designed for expansion.

Expansion requires an expansion of all factors involved; and when something expands out of pace with the rest which is not expanding at the same rate, trouble is caused.

Uniform expansion of demand, ethics and service into new fields and areas as well as old areas of operation are needful to trouble-free activities.

Each member and unit of an organization has a product which, if different, contributes to the whole product of an organization.

The ultimate product of Scientology is a universe that is decent and happy to live in, not degenerated and made miserable by suppressives as it has been. This is accomplished by the de-aberration of individuals and the prevention of blunted demand and re-aberration by suppressives, and this is the method of expansion.

If in these early days of Scientology we have any troubles, they occurred by an earlier imbalance of expansion.

Demand was created without handling suppressives, which unequal expansion gave us a backlog of unhandled ethics in the society. All we need do is catch up our backlog in those organizational functions which were not expanded when they should have been and all will go smoothly.

Any time you do not expand uniformly with all functions, you get an appearance of overexpansion by some functions. The best answer is not to cancel the expanded functions which overreached, but to catch them up by expanding the ones one neglected in support. You will have trouble wherever you cut back an expansion as that is contraction. The answer, within reason, is to advance all else to catch up to the expanded portion while still, more calmly, expanding it.

L. RON HUBBARD
Founder

HCO POLICY LETTER OF 24 DECEMBER 1966
Issue I

Gen. Non-Remimeo
Execs SH
Org Exec
   Course

Admin Know-How Series 10

HOW TO PROGRAM AN ORG
SAINT HILL PROGRAMS

In past years we have had many problems resulting in programs as follows:

The sequence of *major* programs at Saint Hill:

To provide a home for LRH and family in Commonwealth area so Commonwealth area could be organized and made self-supporting.

To provide admin facilities for LRH in Commonwealth area.

To make Commonwealth area self-supporting regardless of US funds or customers. (Not yet resolved.)

To train technical and admin staffs for Commonwealth orgs.

To make Commonwealth outer orgs run on their income without their using all the bills sums owed SH or Ron as part of their operating funds.

To find financial support for SH activities resulting in the SHSBC which also accomplished the next above.

To handle Commonwealth activities and organizations and also handle US activities. (Solved by telex and OIC and later the Exec Div WW.)

To establish SH general broad promotion. (Solved by *The Auditor*.)

To provide facilities for administering critical high-level tech such as Power Processes. (Solved by SH HGC.)

To organize SH so it could be administered (made needful by 63–64 collapse of multiple corporative setup). (Solved by seven-div system completed by end of 1965.)

To refine the Qual Div to prevent all "failed cases," train staff and improve tech.

To get reports of tax, etc., off continual crash programs. (Solved by Treasurer but incomplete of any guarantee of chartered accountant compliance.)

To get field auditors to cooperate and stop conflicts with orgs. (FSM program.)

To refine the Tech Div. (Finished about August 1966.)

To get in smooth operation an Ethics system.

To operate the Clearing Course and to assembly-line Clears. (Still under refinement but more or less complete.)

To establish and operate OT Course. (Just now under development.)

To beat back continuous attacks by suppressives in the 3rd and 4th dynamics. (Solved by establishing Intelligence Branch.)

To train up staffs at SH and in outer orgs by staff status and Org Exec Course.

To improve the cash-bills ratios of orgs.

To safeguard income once earned by better financial planning.

To reform Ad Councils into representative bodies (now complete with the formation of an Executive Council).

To assemble all Scientology materials. (Flopped by reason of noncompliance but lately reinstituted.)

Dictionary Project to prevent misunderstood words. (In sporadic and jerky action to this day.)

To handle legal situations which built up by noncompliance by attorneys internal and external in org. (Under solution.)

To improve and maintain affluences. (Just begun.)

To help Scientology dissemination and attack more broadly to prevent such quantities of legal defense. (OT activities program just begun.)

To safeguard, continue and expand all Scientology orgs. (Worked on a bit, not really concentrated on except for cash-bills and staff status.)

General improvement of finances. (OT activities.)

Buildings for Scientology orgs. (OT activities.)

To establish better audio-visio educational facilities. (Barely begun.)

These have been and are the major program steps which have been implemented or are under development at Saint Hill since 1959 and forward to the end of 1966.

Some of the years covered acquired names such as

1965—The Year of Organization.
1966—The Year of the Clears.
1967—Will probably be the Year of the OTs.

It will be noted that each of these programs solved a self-evident problem.

It must be realized then that these problems did exist.

If the problems exist again, remember there was already a solution program and usually it has only been dropped and the problem reappeared because it had been dropped. The proper directive action is to reimplement and improve the solution which is to say, in the case of SH, the carrying out of the successful programs noted above.

Ad Councils are always advancing new programs and often it is only an old program dropped out that needs reinstituting, not a new solution. Certainly an old problem has cropped up again.

There have been other programs of course. Many solutions to old problems, and of major importance, are found in policy letters. Some programs, although necessary, have never been successfully implemented. There was the motion picture program but it is dogged by technical bugs and became part of the audio-visio program now being attempted. There has been the rewrite of all books program but I've been too overworked to attempt it.

Other future, self-evident programs will come into being. They will only fail if earlier programs, dropped out or not given reorganization when needed, bring old problems into view by exposing them. All the problems underlying the program solutions above still potentially exist, held in abeyance only by the programs.

The best way to form programs is to isolate *actual* problems at any level of operation and solve them either by removing elements that make them or by instituting a program. Sensible planning tends toward both actions.

An unsuccessful program usually will be found to be solving the wrong problem or is itself an improper solution to an actual problem.

If you want to establish the validity of a new program offered by someone, ask him what problem it is seeking to solve. You can then see if you already have a solution to the problem, but most often you will see that no clarified idea of the problem existed and so the solution is poor or inadequate.

The common problem of an org is not the development of programs but failure to execute existing ones.

Another difficulty with orgs is that they often alter the existing program so that it no longer resolves the problem the program was set up to handle. A current example is magazines. Magazines exist to solve the problem of public unawareness of an org. An org has no space unless it is sending out anchor points to make it. And it is in nonexistence for its *Scientology* public unless it mails magazines regularly. Magazines do not develop much new public—that is another, largely unsolved, problem. Magazines exist to continue the awareness of the existing Scientology public. Now as these people are already aware of Scientology, the awareness one is trying to develop is that of the org and its services.

364

Recently, continental magazines began to issue only Scientology *data*. The ads making the Scientology public aware of the *org* were toned down and omitted and the cash-bills ratio worsened in orgs. The orgs started toward nonexistence. Significantly, the trend was begun by a someone who did not like orgs but was in favor of Scientology. Issue Authority erred in not looking at old magazines and comparing them to the current layout. There was a vast difference. No ads in current ones. The program had been altered.

Artists are taught to be "original" and to alter. Yet successful artists painted the same picture their whole lives under different names. These just seemed new.

To change, alter or drop a program one must know what the program was there to solve. Just change for change's sake is mere aberration (making the lines crooked).

It's a good exercise for a senior executive to list the problems the org really does have. To know the programs of an org that are *in* is to see what problems an org *would* have if they were dropped.

It's healthy to revert a program now and then by meticulously examining how it was originally when it was very successful and then put it back the way it was originally. This is done not by adjusting lines but by looking up old magazines, old policy, old despatches and issue pieces, even old tapes. What did it used to consist of? If it is no longer successful:

a. The program was altered or dropped and

b. The org will have a problem it once had long ago, or

c. (Rare) The causes of the problem have been removed and the problem no longer exists.

There's lots of trial and error in developing a program. That's why any *new* program should only be a "special project" for a while, off the org main lines really, under special management. If a "special project" starts to show up well in finance (and only in finance), then one should include it "in" with its new staff as an org standard project.

To run new programs in on existing lines is to disturb (by distraction and staff overload) existing programs, and even if good, the new program will fail and damage as well existing programs.

Provide, then, staff and money to pioneer a new program as a "special project." If you don't have money or staff to do this, you would do far, far better simply looking over the problems the org faces and get in the *old* programs that handled them. These are known winners, and don't forget, they cost a lot to find and prove as *the* thing to do. And they took a long time.

Take the Central Files–Letter Reg setup in orgs. That's a standard program. Developed in London and DC in the mid 50s. If you dropped it out, an org would fail. The problem is "how to achieve special individual contact with *existing* clientele and maintain *existing*, already-developed business." One large firm, I was told the other day, that has put in our seven-division system was stunned to find they had *never* contacted their existing business clientele. They only had

365

done business with *new* clientele. This cost them perhaps 200,000 sales a year! They promptly put in our CF–Letter Registrar system with a vengeance.

In their case (as in a forming or reorganized org) they weren't even aware of the problem and so had no program for it.

It is often the case that one can develop a program that removes the need of some other program. If one removes the factors that make the problem, one can dispense with the program that solves it. But this is so rare it is nonhuman in most instances.

For instance, doctors are a public solution to the problem of human body illness. If one removed this problem, one could remove the "doctor program" safely. That's why doctors sometimes fight us. We are thought to be working to remove the problem to which they are a program. One would have to have more than a better *cure*. One would have to remove in the fourth dynamic (mankind) the *causes* of illness. These would not be what people think they are as the problem persists and so does the "doctor program" in the society. It can't be the right problem. Only enough is known of the causes of illness to make the problem *appear* to be handled. Actually the bad statistic of ill people is rising. We have entered the field in research only far enough to know that suppressives make people ill but that's a sufficient departure to make it an ethics problem, not one in treatment! By extension of this theory, one might find this problem not caused by Pasteur's germs but by suppressive groups. In that case one would increase ethics programs. Eventually, if this solved it, the "doctor program" would be diminished as no longer the only solution.

The above is not a statement of intention or a plan. It is an example of how an old standard program can become less important. Note that one would have to (a) state the problem better than it had been stated, (b) isolate causes of the real problem, (c) institute a "special project" to handle *those* causes, (d) see if the problem was now better handled, (e) abandon it if it didn't handle the problem, or (f) make it a standard program if it did prove effective, (g) diminish the old program.

So just dropping a proven program (without going at it as above [a] to [f]) can be a catastrophe as it can let in an old problem when one already has quite enough problems already.

Abandoned programs that were successful are currently the main cause of orgs being in any difficulty.

You can always make an org run better by studying old successful programs and getting them back in.

If you were to take the above list at Saint Hill, the major SH programs since 1959, and simply *revert* them (make them more like the original) and reinforce them, income would probably double.

If we abandoned as few as five of these programs, the SH org would undoubtedly collapse.

If we added six new programs directly into the org without seeing the problem to be solved, we could distract staff to a point where the old standard programs would suffer and the org would collapse.

Sometimes, even in our orgs, we enter new arbitraries which make new problems we don't need. Those are the sources we can do without. If we didn't routinely abolish such org-generated problems, we would fade away in a year.

Therefore we cherish and forward the existing programs we have and study them continually to be sure they don't "go out."

This is not a list of the *problems* faced at Saint Hill; it is a list of solutions. For these programs may accidentally be solving problems we cannot yet clearly state.

This is not a list of all major programs in Scientology. These are found in the policy letters of past years and particularly 1965.

This is a list of the major SH programs for use by SH executives and as an illustration to others on how to program and to show them that, as Scientologists, we use our knowledge of the mechanics of life, problems and solutions to govern programs.

If *all* the problems we faced were only ours, we could of course simply audit them out. But we exist in a third and fourth dynamic which is not merely aberrated but quite batty. This thrusts problems on us (finance, international ignorance and intolerance, religious and psychiatric cults, suppressive governments, retarded or misused scientific technology, lack of human dignity and a host of other factors).

We exist, therefore, in a rather madly tossing sea, beset by numerous counter-currents.

As we grow we can remove vicious causes that make our problems problems. Only then can we begin to drop certain programs as the problems will cease to exist. But at this writing those problems do exist and holding them in check are numerous solutions we call programs.

Where one of our standard programs fails through lack of recognition we then see a problem charging in on us demanding crash programing by higher executives.

When we let uninformed or worse people put in new arbitraries or solutions that solve no problem, we disturb old programs and soon have heavy trouble through unnecessary programing. (Watching a new, inexperienced Ad Council propose "programs" is a painful experience to a trained and effective executive. These proposed measures look silly because they confront no real problems of the org and are dangerous because they will distract the org from correct existing programs of which the new Ad Council seems blissfully unaware.)

When an org doesn't know its programs, it can get pretty silly and deeply in trouble. If it also knows its problems it is fortunate.

But any Scientology org is rich in programs already proven and tested and in exact drill. If it just keeps these going it will win even if it doesn't see the problems.

As it wins the org expands, can afford more assistance, is less under duress. Then it can begin to examine the problems themselves (still keeping the solution as a program) and possibly remove some of the causes of the actual problem. Only when the problem is gone can one drop a program.

A *Scientology* org is best fitted to do this as its staff is going up tone by processing and is more and more able to confront and see source. Therefore it eventually can remove the causes of its problems since it can (a) see the problem and (b) see the bad sources which make the problem.

Until it *can* see, it is not safe to drop any of the solutions. And as orgs are a channel or a way in themselves they always will have a bottom strata of people who cannot yet see the problems and so need explicit programs to follow. As the lower strata moves up, a new lower strata, by expansion, takes its place so there is no real end to programs until the day comes when the universe is sane.

And that's not tomorrow or even the day after.

But we *are* making steady, relentless progress in that direction. Mainly because of our programs, well applied.

L. RON HUBBARD
Founder

HUBBARD COMMUNICATIONS OFFICE
Saint Hill Manor, East Grinstead, Sussex

HCO POLICY LETTER OF 24 DECEMBER 1966
Issue II
CORRECTION AND ADDITION

Gen. Non-Remimeo
Execs SH
Org Exec Course

Admin Know-How Series 11

HOW TO PROGRAM AN ORG
CORRECTIONS AND ADDITION
SEQUENCE OF PROGRAMS CORRECTION

The sixth SH program from the top on page one states, "To find financial support for SH activities resulting in the SHSBC *which also accomplished the next above.*" This does not refer to "next above" but to two above, "To train technical and admin staffs for Commonwealth orgs." The Saint Hill Special Briefing Course was founded (a) to train tech and admin staffs for Commonwealth orgs and (b) was found to be the solvency factor of Saint Hill which was being looked for.

"Next above," "To make Commonwealth orgs run on their income without using all the bills sums owed SH or Ron as part of their operating funds" has only partially been solved and the SHSBC was not founded to solve it although it helped. The 7 Div system began to solve it (financial independence of outer orgs) but only where a *good* Qual Div was put in first and all area failed or overrun cases were picked up. It is notable that Sydney and Adelaide, reported by Auckland to have put in *no* Qual Div even after 2 years of urging, were low orgs on the totem pole. Others that did get in a Qual Div and pick up their failed cases and overruns improved very markedly. So the solution to solvent outer orgs that could run without using SH or Ron's income lay in (a) establishing a fine Qual Div, (b) picking up their area's "failed cases" and also repairing *all* overruns, (c) training their staffs on tech and admin in the new Qual and (d) putting in a fine Tech Div. Those that really did that are going very well. Sydney, which butchered cases once by overrun R2-12, evidently completely neglected the program and remains insolvent.

ADDITION

To make a simpler statement of What Is a Program, the following is offered:

1. The org has a problem relating to its function and survival.

2. Unless the problem is solved, the org will not do well and may even go under.

3. The *solution* is actually an org activity or drill. We call this a PROGRAM.

4. To find and establish a *program,* one conceives of a solution and sets it up independent of org lines with its own staff and finance as a SPECIAL PROJECT.

5. When a special project is seen to be effective or, especially, profitable, it is then put into the org lines as worked out in the "special project," bringing its own staff with it.

6. The usual place to carry a special project is under the Office of LRH or the Office of the HCO Exec Sec or Office of the Org Exec Sec. Programs go in their appropriate departments and divisions, one to six, not seven.

OVERHAULING A PROJECT

When a program goes bad, gets altered to a point of unworkability or carelessly conducted or is dropped without orders to do so, two things may happen.

1. The Exec Sec (or LRH or the LRH Comm) over that division puts the executives which should have seen to the program in DANGER condition and personally pushes to get the program back in as a program.

2. If this fails, the Exec Sec (or LRH or the LRH Comm) hauls the whole program into his own office as though it were a new special project, gets it personnel and finance and sets it all up and then gives it over to its correct dept and division.

The second step comes about when one finds any noncompliance in doing 1 above. As a Danger condition was already set up and the Exec Sec (or other senior) is handling it on a bypass already, if one *still* can't get the program restarted there is no other action one can take than pulling the whole thing into one's own office. For sure somebody has a foot on it. Although we can try to find WHO has, this is no reason to continue to stall the program. After a Danger condition on a program has existed for a while with no change of activity, one is wasting one's time to keep pushing on a via. The *easier* course is simply to say, "As Address has been in Danger for some time and still continues to goof, I, the HCO Exec Sec, hereby take Address into my office in Division 7 where I will personally straighten it out and meanwhile the Ad Council is to nominate for the Exec Council a new HCO Area Sec."

In actual operation—I often do 1 above—call a Danger condition on a program that is not functioning, handle it personally and use ethics action on those bypassed.

Sometimes when 1 doesn't work, I realize there is interference still and haul the whole section into my office as a function of my office. It may stay there quite a while. Then I will put it elsewhere as a complete section transfer. Sometimes after the transfer I again have to haul it back. Usually that's because it went into the wrong place in the org. If you put a section in the wrong dept or division, it just won't function. The exception is the Exec Div and anything can be put in there for a while.

The common error in (2) is to forget one has it and forget to transfer it when formed up properly. If one looks over what hats he is wearing, one usually finds a program or two he has been handling and which he ought to finish up in final form and put into the org proper.

In theory, any exec or even an in-charge can do 1 and 2 above.

If 1 doesn't work then do 2. The main mistake is to forget to complete the action of 2 by putting the program back in place in the org. To prevent that from happening, when you do 2, change it also on the org board. Then it stays in view. Otherwise one forgets and soon begins to feel overworked.

Almost any executive is holding on to a special project or two or even a program. So one should routinely look over one's own hats and refind these and complete cycle on them.

L. RON HUBBARD
Founder

Remimeo

Admin Know-How Series 12

PTS SECTIONS, PERSONNEL AND EXECS

An org has certain sections, units, personnel and executives who go PTS to suppressive elements in the society.

If one knows this, one becomes less puzzled by noncompliances and trouble in those quarters. One can also do something effective if one realizes why.

Legal, Accounts and Construction and lesser units tend to go PTS very easily.

A "PTS" is a *potential trouble source* by reason of contact with a suppressive person or group.

Suppression is "a harmful intention or action against which one cannot fight back." Thus when one can do *anything* about it, it is less suppressive.

Thus Legal goes PTS being in contact with SP courts and with SP or PTS attorney firms as well as confronting suppressives who are seeking to injure the org through various suppressive actions.

Accounts goes PTS through various tax and government supervision suppressions.

An Estate Branch listening to Town and Country Planning or zoning suppressives tends to go PTS.

In a standard-issue corporation the labor relations contact point, continually messed up by labor agitators who could do the company in and regulations protecting such, tends to go PTS.

An Ethics Officer may become PTS.

The Dead File Unit may go PTS on all the entheta letters.

As such PTS personnel impinges on top executives, these can also go PTS and the org gets harmed to say the least.

HANDLING

As one cannot easily disconnect from suppressive society points without leaving the society, it remains that an executive must handle, if not the SP social groups, at least the situation developing from them and into the org.

Ideally one removes the SPs in the social groups. But where that is not possible one can do several things:

a. Limit the number of org personnel such groups contact.

b. Give such org personnel as do contact such suppressive elements S&Ds occasionally.

c. Change such personnel frequently.

d. Develop a system to restrain the SP from easily influencing such org personnel as may remain in contact.

e. Work gradually but steadily into a position to be able to remove suppressives from the social groups in question, such as becoming more influential as an org, suing, exposing, public education and other means.

INDICATORS

The first indicator an org executive has of a unit or staff member going PTS is noncompliance. Such personnel are being overwhelmed in various ways by the SP social groups and have no energy left to undertake their duties or forward org programs.

Another indicator is the amount of illness and lack of case progress on the part of such PTS staff members.

A third indicator is an executive getting the hat of such a personnel on his own plate.

An executive who doesn't notice such indicators and act is being in turn PTS, or simply isn't of executive caliber.

METHODS OF BALKING

There are several methods by which a staff member acting as an org contact point in connection with suppressives can balk the agents of SP groups.

One is to always tape-record *visibly* whatever the agent from such a suppressive group says. "Ah, Mr. Figuretwist of the Tax Division? Good. Now wait a moment so I can record whatever you say. Good. It's now recording. Go ahead." We used to handle the Internal "Revenue" Service of the US this way quite successfully. The org contact point always stopping the IRS inspector they sent around, turning on a portable recorder and then, and not until then, letting the man speak. Quite effective. That org only got into tax trouble when it stopped doing this. After the recording was dropped out as drill, the SP utterances of IRS agents were in full cry at the staff and they went PTS and began to make crazy errors and ignore org orders re tax.

Any time such agents come around, they try to get as many staff into it as possible. And yap and yap and threaten and enturbulate. One *must* put them in Coventry (silence treatment) from staff other than the contact point. Staff members of a unit that could go PTS must be ordered to walk off without a word whenever such an agent shows up. *No* "bull sessions" or arguments with such a person. The staff personnel who handles should point at the agent if other staff is about and say some key word like "This is a government man" at which all other staff in the unit turns its back or pointedly walks off. If you do this, such agents can't take offense but they get very uneasy, transact quickly, forget their mission to be enturbulative and go away soon. Don't ever think politeness will help you. Tipping one's hat to snakes never stopped a person getting bitten. Walking off has.

Staffs are so "reasonable" they think these SP group representatives are there for necessary purposes or serve some purpose or can be reasoned with—all of which is nonsense.

There are no good reporters. There are no good government or SP group agents. The longer you try to be nice, the worse off you will be. And the sooner one learns this, the happier he will be.

Some staff member in such contact points in the org should be the only one who handles and all other staff should be given chits for talking to such a person.

This limits the area of enturbulation. The handling staff member can become expert. But even so, watch for bad indicators in that staff member, and the moment they show up, change the contact point.

Never give such persons access to persons high up in the org—or unit. Turn such over to special personnel who can get the business over with at once and get the agent off the premises soon.

If you see a manager snapping terminals with such agents, transfer him to another post in the org. Unless you do so, he'll soon cease complying with policy and will soon have the place falling apart.

When such agents act or sound *very* suppressive, get them investigated, find the scandal and attack. It is a fortunate truth that such people *also* have crimes in their background that can be found. Find and expose them.

SPs are at war. Pleasant conduct, mean conduct, *any* conduct at all is simply more war. So wage the back action as a battle.

In all the history of Scientology no interviewing reporter ever helped. They all meant the worst when they acted their best and we are always sorry ever to have spoken. Even if the reporter is all right, his newspaper isn't and will twist his story. We have done best when we have blocked off reporters and worst when we've been nice. So the moral is, a person from an SP group will eventually make an org or some part of it PTS regardless of the agent's conduct.

These words may seem harsh and unreasonable, yet truth is truth and only when we ignore it do we get fouled up. Agents from SP groups lead to PTS staff, units or sections, leads to noncompliance, leads to a mess.

It isn't just imagination that SPs attack Scientology. The evidence has been around in plenty for 16 years.

We began to prosper the day we cut public SPs' correspondence off the org lines and sent it to dead file. Our executives began to function, policy began to be followed and we began to grow.

So we'll attain new expansion just by applying what is in this policy letter.

I personally find such agents rather pitiful in their attempts to make trouble.

I think the contemporary attempts to upset us and accusations of things we never do quite prove the fact such mean us no good. But many staff and executives try desperately to be nice to them.

Handle the business they present as effectively as possible on special channels. Don't be nice. Limit their reach. And have less noncompliance and a far more effective and happier org. After all, real suppressives only constitute about 2½ percent of the total population. Why spend more than 2½ percent of your time on them?

The whole stunt is realizing that certain groups are SP and recognizing them and then handling them.

Be alert and stay alive. It won't always be this way.

L. RON HUBBARD
Founder

Org Exec Course

Admin Know-How Series 13

THE RESPONSIBILITIES OF LEADERS

A few comments on POWER, being or working close to or under a power, which is to say a leader or one who exerts wide primary influence on the affairs of men.

I have written it this way, using two actual people, to give an example of magnitude enough to interest and to furnish some pleasant reading. And I used a military sphere so it could be seen clearly without restimulation of admin problems.

The book referenced is a fantastically able book, by the way.

THE MISTAKES OF SIMON BOLIVAR
AND MANUELA SAENZ

Reference: The book entitled

The Four Seasons of Manuela by
Victor W. von Hagen, a biography.
A Mayflower Dell Paperback. Oct. 1966. 6 shillings.

Simon Bolivar was the liberator of South America from the yoke of Spain.

Manuela Saenz was the liberatress and consort.

Their acts and fates are well recorded in this moving biography.

But aside from any purely dramatic value, the book lays bare and motivates various actions of great interest to those who lead, who support or are near leaders.

Simon Bolivar was a very strong character. He was one of the richest men in South America. He had real personal ability given to only a handful on the planet. He was a military commander without peer in history. Why he would fail and die an exile to be later deified is thus of great interest. What mistakes did he make?

Manuela Saenz was a brilliant, beautiful and able woman. She was loyal, devoted, quite comparable to Bolivar, far above the cut of average humanoids. Why then did she live a vilified outcast, receive such violent social rejection and die of poverty and remain unknown to history? What mistakes did she make?

BOLIVAR'S ERRORS

The freeing of things is the reverse unstated dramatization (the opposite side of the coin) to the slavery enjoined by the mechanisms of the mind. Unless there is something to free men *into,* the act of freeing is simply a protest of slavery. And as no humanoid *is* free while aberrated in the body cycle, it is of course a gesture to free him politically as it frees him only into the anarchy of dramatizing his aberrations with NO control whatever and without something to fight exterior; and with no exteriorization of his interest, he simply goes mad noisily or quietly.

Once as great a wrong as depraving beings has been done, there is, of course, no freedom short of freeing one from the depravity itself or *at least* from its most obvious influences in the society. In short, one would have to de-aberrate a man before his whole social structure could be de-aberrated.

If one lacked the whole ability to free man wholly from his reactive patterns, then one could free man from their restimulators in the society at least. If one had the whole of the data (but lacked the Scientology tech), one would simply use reactive patterns to blow the old society apart and then pick up the pieces neatly in a new pattern. If one had no inkling of how reactive one can get (and Bolivar, of course, had no knowledge whatever in that field), there yet remained a workable formula used "instinctively" by most successful, practical political leaders:

If you free a society from those things you see wrong with it and use force to demand it do what is right, and if you carry forward with decision and thoroughness and without continual temporizing, you can, in the applications of your charm and gifts, bring about a great political reform or improve a failing country.

So Bolivar's first error, most consistent it was, too, was contained in the vital words *you see* in the above paragraph. He didn't look and he didn't even listen to sound intelligence reports. He was so *sure* he could *glow* things right or fight things right or charm things right that he never looked for anything wrong to correct until it was too late. This is the ne plus ultra of personal confidence, amounting to supreme vanity. "When he appeared it would all come right" was not only his belief but his basic philosophy. So the first time it didn't work, he collapsed. All his skills and charm were channeled into this one test. Only that could he observe.

Not to compare with Bolivar but to show my understanding of this:

I once had a similar one. "I would keep going as long as I could and when I was stopped I would then die." This was a solution mild enough to state and really hard to understand until you had an inkling of what I meant by keeping going. Meteors keep going—very, very fast. And so did I. Then one day ages back, I finally *was* stopped after countless little stoppings by social contacts and family to prepare me, culminating in a navy more devoted to braid than dead enemies and literally I quit. For a while I couldn't get a clue of what was wrong with me. Life went completely unlivable until I found a *new* solution. So I know the frailty of these single solutions. Not to compare myself but just to show it happens to us all, not just Bolivars.

Bolivar had no personal insight at all. He could only "outsight" and even then he did not look or listen. He *glowed* things right. Pitifully, it was his undoing that he could. Until he no longer could. When he couldn't glow he roared, and when he couldn't roar he fought a battle. Then civic enemies were not military enemies so he had no solution left at all.

It *never* occurred to him to do more than personally *magnetize* things into being right and victorious.

His downfall was that he made far too heavy a use of a skill simply because it was easy. He was too good at this one thing. So he never looked to any other skill and he never even dreamed there was any other way.

He had no view of any situation and no idea of the organizational or preparatory steps necessary to political and personal victory. He only knew military organization, which is where his organizational insight ceased.

He was taught on the high wine of French revolt, notorious in its organizational inability to form cultures, and that fatally by a childhood teacher who was intensely impractical in his own private life (Simon Rodriguez, an unfrocked priest turned tutor).

Bolivar had no personal financial skill. He started wealthy and wound up a pauper, a statistic descending from one of the, if not the, richest man in South America down to a borrowed nightshirt to be buried in as an exile. And *this* while the property of royalists was wide open, the greatest land and mine valuables of South America wide open to his hand, and that's not believable! But true. He never collected his own debt of loans to governments even when the head of those governments.

So it is no wonder we find two more very real errors leading to his downfall: He did not get his troops or officers *rewarded* and he did not aim for any solvency of the states he controlled. It was all right if there were long years of battle ahead for them to be unpaid as no real riches were yet won, but not to *reward* them when the whole place was at his disposal! Well!

The limit of his ability consisted of demanding a bit of cash for current pay from churches—which were not actively against him at first but which annoyed them no end—and a few household expenses.

He could have (and should have) set aside all royalist property and estates for division amongst his officers, their men and his supporters. It had no owners now. And this failure cost the economy of the country the tax loss of all those productive estates (the whole wealth of the land). So it is no wonder his government, its taxable estates now inoperative or at best lorded by a profiteer or looted by Indians, was insolvent. Also, by failing to do such an obvious act, he delivered property into the hands of more provident enemies and left his officers and men penniless to finance any support for their own stability in the new society and so for his own.

As for state finance, the great mines of South America, suddenly ownerless, were overlooked and were then grabbed and worked by foreign adventurers who simply came in and took them without payment.

Spain had run the country on the finance of mine tithes and general taxes. Bolivar not only didn't collect the tithes, he let the land become so worthless as to be untaxable. He should have gotten the estates going by any shifts and should have state-operated all royalist mines once he had them. To not do these things was complete, but typically humanoid, folly.

In doing this property division he should have left it all up to officers' committees operating as courts of claim without staining his own hands in the natural corruption. He was left doubly open as he not only did not attend to it, he also got the name of corruption when anybody did grab something.

He failed as well to recognize the distant widespread nature of his countries despite all his riding and fighting over them and so sought tightly centralized government, not only centralizing states, but also centralizing the various nations into a federal state. And this over a huge landmass full of insurmountable ranges, impassable jungles and deserts and without mail, telegraph, relay stages, roads, railroads, river vessels or even footbridges repaired after a war of attrition.

A step echelon from a pueblo (village) to a state, from a state to a country and a country to a federal state was only possible (in such huge spaces of country where candidates could never be known personally over any wide area and whose opinions could not even be circulated more than a few miles of burro trail), where only the pueblo was democratic and the rest all appointive from pueblo on up, himself the ratifier of titles if he even needed that. With his own officers and armies controlling the land as owners of all wrested from royalists and the crown of Spain, he would have had no revolts. There would have been little civil wars, of course, but a court to settle their final claims could have existed at federal level and kept them traveling so much over those vast distances it would have crippled their enthusiasm for litigation on the one hand, and on the other, by dog-eat-dog settlements, would have given him the strongest rulers—if he took neither side.

He did not step out and abdicate a dictatorial position. He mistook military acclaim and ability for the tool of peace. War only brings anarchy, so he had anarchy. Peace is more than a "command for unity," his favorite phrase. A productive peace is getting men busy and giving them something to make something of that they *want* to make something of and telling them to get on with it.

He never began to recognize a suppressive and never considered anyone needed killing except on a battlefield. There it was glorious. But somebody destroying his very name and soul and the security of every supporter and friend, the SP Santander, his vice-president, who could have been arrested and executed by a corporal's guard on one one-hundredth of available evidence, who could suborn the whole treasury and population against him, without Bolivar, continually warned, loaded with evidence, ever even reprimanding him. And this brought about his loss of popularity and his eventual exile.

He also failed in the same way to protect his military family or Manuela Saenz from other enemies. So he weakened his friends and ignored his enemies just by oversight.

His greatest error lay in that while dismissing Spain he did not dismiss that nation's most powerful minion, the Church, and did not even localize it or reward a South American separate branch to loyalty or do anything at all (except extort money from it) to an organization which continually worked for Spain as only it could work—on every person in the land in a direct anti-Bolivar reign of

379

terror behind the scenes. You either suborn such a group or you take them out when they cease to be universal and become or are an enemy's partner.

As the Church held huge properties and as Bolivar's troops and supporters went *unpaid* even of the penny soldiers' pay, if one was going to overlook the royalist estates, one could at least have seized the Church property and given it to the soldiers. General Vallejo did this in 1835 in California, a nearly contemporary act, with no catastrophe from Rome. Or the penniless countries could have taken them over. You don't leave an enemy financed and solvent while you let your friends starve in a game like South American politics. Oh no.

He wasted his enemies. He exported the "godos" or defeated royalist soldiers. They mostly had no homes but South America. He issued no amnesties they could count on. They were shipped off or left to die in the "ditch"—the best artisans in the country among them.

When one (General Rodil) would not surrender Callao fortress after Peru was *won*, Bolivar, after great gestures of amnesty, failed to obtain surrender and then fought the fort. Four thousand political refugees and four thousand royalist troops died over many months in full sight of Lima—fought heavily by Bolivar only because the *fort* was fighting. But Bolivar had to straighten up Peru urgently, not fight a defeated enemy. The right answer to such a foolish commander as Rodil, as Bolivar did have the troops to do it, was to cover the roads with cannon enfilade potential to discourage any sortie from the fort, put a larger number of his own troops in a distant position of offense but ease and comfort and say, "We're not going to fight. The war's over, silly man. Look at the silly fellows in there, living on rats when they can just walk out and sleep home nights or go to Spain or enlist with me or just go camping," and let anybody walk in and out who pleased, making the fort commander (Rodil) the prey of every pleading wife and mother without and would-be deserter or mutineer within until he did indeed sheepishly give up the pretense—a man cannot fight alone. But battle was glory to Bolivar. And he became intensely disliked because the incessant cannonade, which got nowhere, was annoying.

Honors meant a great deal to Bolivar. To be liked was his life. And it probably meant more to him than to see things really right. He never compromised his principles but he lived on admiration, a rather sickening diet since it demands in turn continuous "theater." One is what one is, not what one is admired or hated for. To judge oneself by one's successes is simply to observe that one's postulates worked and breeds confidence in one's ability. To have to be *told* it worked only criticizes one's own eyesight and hands a spear to the enemy to make his wound of vanity at his will. Applause is nice. It's great to be thanked and admired. But to work only for that? And his craving for that, his addiction to the most unstable drug in history—fame—killed Bolivar. That self-offered spear. He told the world continually how to kill him—reduce its esteem. So as money and land can buy any quantity of cabals, he could be killed by curdling the esteem, the easiest thing you can get a mob to do.

He had all the power. He did not use it for good or evil. One cannot hold power and not use it. It violates the Power Formula. For it then prevents *others* from doing things if *they* had some of the power, so they then see as their only solution the destruction of the holder of the power, as he, not using power or delegating it, is the unwitting block to all their plans. So even many of his friends and armies finally agreed he had to go. They were not able men. They were in a mess. But bad or good, they had to do *something*. Things were desperate, broken-down and starving after fourteen years of civil war. Therefore, they either had to have *some* of that absolute power or else nothing could be done at all. They were not great minds. He did not need any "great minds," he thought, even though he invited them verbally. He saw their petty, often murderous solutions and he rebuked them. And so held the power and didn't use it.

He could not stand another *personality* threat.

The trouble in Peru came when he bested its real conqueror (from the Argentine), La Mar, in a petty triumph over adding Guayaquil to Colombia. Bolivar wished to look triumphant again and didn't notice it really cost him the support and Peru the support of La Mar—who understandably resigned and went home, leaving Bolivar *Peru to conquer*. Unfortunately, it had already been in his hands. La Mar needed some troops to clean up a small royalist army—that was all. La Mar didn't need Peru's loss of Guayaquil—which never did anybody any real good anyway!

Bolivar would become inactive when faced with two areas' worth of problems—he did not know which way to go. So he did nothing.

Brave beyond any general in history on the battlefield, the Andes or in torrential rivers, he did not really have the bravery needed to trust inferior minds and stand by their often shocking blunders. He feared their blunders. So he did not dare unleash his many willing hounds.

He could lead men, make men feel wonderful, make men fight and lay down their lives after hardships no army elsewhere in the world has ever faced before or since. But he could not *use* men even when they were begging to be used.

It is a frightening level of bravery to use men you know can be cruel, vicious and incompetent. He had no fear of their turning on him ever. When they finally did, only then he was shocked. But he protected "the people" from authority given to questionably competent men. So he really never used but three or four generals of mild disposition and enormously outstanding ability. And to the rest he denied power. Very thoughtful of the nebulous "people" but very bad indeed for the general good. And it really caused his death.

No. Bolivar was theater. It was all theater. One cannot make such errors and still pretend that one thinks of life as life, red-blooded and factual. Real men and real life are full of dangerous, violent, live situations; and wounds *hurt* and starvation is desperation itself, especially when you see it in one you love.

This mighty actor, backed up with fantastic personal potential, made the mistake of thinking the theme of liberty and his own great role upon the stage was enough to interest all the working, suffering hours of men, buy their bread, pay their whores, shoot their wives' lovers and bind their wounds or even put enough drama into very hard-pressed lives to make them want to live it.

No, Bolivar was unfortunately the only actor on the stage and no other man in the world was real to him.

And so he died. They loved him. But they were also on the stage too, where they were dying in his script or Rousseau's script for liberty but no script for living their very real lives.

He was the greatest military general in any history measured against his obstacles, the people and the land across which he fought.

And he was a complete failure to himself and his friends.

While being one of the greatest *men* alive at that. So we see how truly shabby others in leaders' boots amongst men must be.

MANUELA SAENZ

The tragedy of Manuela Saenz as Bolivar's mistress was that she was never *used,* never really had a share and was neither protected nor honored by Bolivar.

Here was a clever, spectacular woman of fantastic fidelity and skill, with an enormous "flair," capable of giving great satisfaction and service. And only her satisfaction ability was taken and that not consistently nor even honestly.

In the first place, Bolivar never married her. He never married anybody. This opened up a fantastic breach in any defense she could ever make against hers or his enemies who were legion. So her first mistake was in not in some way contriving a marriage.

That she had an estranged husband she had been more or less sold to was permitted by her to wreck her life obliquely.

She was too selfless to be real in all her very able plotting.

For this marriage problem she could have engineered any number of actions.

She had the solid friendship of all his trusted advisers, even his old tutor. Yet she arranged nothing for herself.

She was utterly devoted, completely brilliant and utterly incapable of really bringing off an action of any final kind.

She violated the Power Formula in not realizing that she had power.

Manuela was up against a hard man to handle. But she did not know enough to make her own court effective. She organized one. She did not know what to do with it.

Her most fatal mistake was in not bringing down Santander, Bolivar's chief enemy. That cost her everything she had before the end and after Bolivar died. She knew for *years* Santander had to be killed. She said it or wrote it every few days. Yet never did she promise some young officer a nice night or a handful of gold to do it in a day when *dueling was in fashion*. It's like standing around discussing how the plainly visible wolf in the garden that's eating the chickens must be shot, even holding a gun, and never even lifting it while all one's chickens vanish for years.

382

In a land overridden with priests, she never got herself a tame priest to bring about her ends.

She was a fantastic intelligence officer. But she fed her data to a man who could not act to protect himself or friends, who could only fight armies dramatically. She did not see this and also quietly take on the portfolio of secret police chief. Her mistake was waiting to be asked—to be asked to come to him, to act. She voluntarily was his best political intelligence agent. Therefore she should have also assumed further roles.

She guarded his correspondence, was intimate with his secretaries. And yet she never collected or forged or stole any document to bring down enemies, either through representations to Bolivar or a court circle of her own. And in an area with that low an ethic, that's fatal.

She openly pamphleteered and fought violently as in a battle against her rabble.

She had a great deal of money at her disposal. In a land of for-sale Indians, she never used a penny to buy a quick knife or even a solid piece of evidence.

When merely opening her lips she could have had any sequestrated royalist estate, she went to litigation for a legitimate legacy never won and another won but never paid.

They lived on the edge of quicksand. She never bought a plank or a rope.

Carried away by the glory of it all, devoted completely, potentially able and a formidable enemy, she did not *act*.

She waited to be told to come to him even when he lay dying and exiled.

His command over her who never obeyed any other was too absolute for his own or her survival.

Her assigned mistakes (pointed out at the time as her caprice and playacting) were not her errors. They only made her interesting. They were far from fatal.

She was not ruthless enough to make up for his lack of ruthlessness and not provident enough to make up for his lack of providence.

The ways open to her for finance, for action, were completely doorless. The avenue stretched out to the horizon.

She fought bravely but she just didn't take action.

She was an actress for the theater alone.

And she died of it. And she let Bolivar die because of it.

Never once did Manuela look about and say, "See here, things mustn't go this wrong. My lover holds half a continent and even I hold the loyalty of battalions. Yet that woman threw a fish!"

Never did Manuela tell Bolivar's doctor, a rumored lover, "Tell that man he will not live without my becoming a constant part of his entourage, and tell him until he believes it or we'll have a new physician around here."

The world was open. Where Theodora, the wife of Emperor Justinian I of Constantinople, a mere circus girl and a whore, ruled harder than her husband but for her husband behind his back—and made him marry her as well—Manuela never had any bushel basket of gold brought in to give Bolivar for his unpaid troops with a "Just found it, dear" to his "Where on Earth . . . ?" after the royalist captives had been carefully ransomed for jail escapes by her enterprising own entourage and officer friends. She never handed over any daughter of a family clamoring against her to Negro troops and then said, "Which ververbal family is next?"

She even held a colonel's rank but only used it because she wore man's clothing afternoons. It was a brutal, violent, ruthless land, not a game of musical chairs.

And so Manuela, penniless, improvident, died badly and in poverty, exiled by enemies and deserted by her friends.

But why not deserted by her friends? They had all been poverty-stricken to a point quite incapable of helping her even though they wanted to—for she once had the power to make them solvent. And didn't use it. They were in poverty before they won but they did eventually control the land. After that why make it a bad habit?

And so we see two pathetic, truly dear but tinsel figures, both on a stage, both *far* removed from the reality of it all.

And one can say "But if they had not been such idealists they never would have fought so hard and freed half a continent," or "If she had stooped to such intrigue or he had been known for violent political actions they would never have had the strength and never would have been loved."

All very idealistic itself. They died "in the ditch" unloved, hated and despised, two decent, brave people, almost too good for this world.

A true hero, a true heroine. But on a stage and not in life. Impractical and improvident and with no faintest gift either one to use the power they could assemble.

This story of Bolivar and Manuela is a tragedy of the most piteous kind.

They fought a hidden enemy, the Church; they were killed by their friends.

But don't overlook how impractical it is not to give your friends power enough when you have it to give. You can always give some of it to another if the first one collapses through inability. And one can always be brought down like a hare at a hunt who seeks to use the delegated power to kill you—if you have the other friends.

Life is not a stage for posturing and "Look at me!" "Look at me." "Look at me." If one is to lead a life of command or a life near to command one must handle it as life. Life bleeds. It suffers. It hungers. And it has to have the right to shoot its enemies until such time as comes a golden age.

Aberrated man is not capable of supporting, in his present state, a golden declared age for three minutes, given all the tools and wealth in the world.

If one would live a life of command or one near to a command, one must then accumulate power as fast as possible and delegate it as quickly as feasible and use every humanoid in long reach to the best and beyond his talents if one is to live *at all*.

If one does not choose to live such a life, then go on the stage and be a real actor. Don't kill men while pretending it isn't real. Or one can become a recluse or a student or a clerk. Or study butterflies or take up tennis.

For one is committed to certain irrevocable natural laws the moment one starts out upon a conquest, either as the man in charge or a person near to him or on his staff or in his army. And the foremost law, if one's ambition is to win, is of course to win. But also to keep on providing things to win and enemies to conquer.

Bolivar let his cycle run to "freedom" and end there. He never had another plan beyond that point. He ran out of territory to free. Then he didn't know what to do with it and didn't know enough, either, to find somewhere else to free. But, of course, all limited games come to end. And when they do, their players fall over on the field and become rag dolls unless somebody at least tells them the game has ended and they have no more game nor any dressing room or homes but just that field.

And they lie upon the field, not noticing there can be no more game since the other team has fled and after a bit they have to do *something;* and if the leader and his consort are sitting over on the grass being rag dolls too, of course there isn't any game. And so the players start fighting amongst themselves just to have a game. And if the leader then says, "No, no," and his consort doesn't say, "Honey, you better phone the Baltimore Orioles for Saturday," then, of course, the poor players, bored stiff, say, "He's out." "She's out." "Now we're going to split the team in half and have a game."

And that's what happened to Bolivar and Manuela. They *had* to be gotten rid of for there was no game and they didn't develop one to play while forbidding the only available game—minor civil wars.

A *whole continent* containing the then major mines of the world, whole populations were left sitting there, "freed." But none owned any of it though the former owners had left. They weren't given it. Nor were they made to manage it. No game.

And if Bolivar had not been smart enough for that, he could at least have said, "Well! You monkeys are going to have quite a time getting the wheels going but that's not my job. You decide on your type of government and what it's to be. Soldiers are my line. Now, I'm taking over those old estates of mine and the royalist ones nearby and the emerald mines just as souvenirs and me and Manuela, we're going home." And he should have said that five minutes after the last royalist army was defeated in Peru.

And his official family with him, and a thousand troops to which he was giving land, would have moved right off smartly with him. And the people after a few screams of horror at being deserted would have fallen on each other, sabered a state together here and a town there and gotten busy out of sheer self-protection in a vital new game, "Who's going to be Bolivar now?"

Then when home he should have said, "Say those nice woods look awfully royalist to me, and also those 1,000,000 hectares of grazing land, Manuela. Its owner once threw a royalist fish, remember? So that's yours."

And the rest of the country would have done the same and gotten on with the new game of "You was a royalist."

And Bolivar and Manuela would have had statues built to them by the TON at once as soon as agents could get to Paris with orders from an adoring populace.

"Bolivar, come rule us!" should have gotten an "I don't see any unfree South America. When you see a French or Spanish army coming, come back and tell me."

That would have worked. And this poor couple would have died suitably adored in the sanctity of glory and (perhaps more importantly) in their own beds, not "in a ditch."

And if they had *had* to go on ruling, they could have declared a new game of "pay the soldiers and officers with royalist land." And when that was a gone game, "Oust the Church and give its land to the poor, friendly Indians."

You can't stand bowing back of the footlights forever with no show even if you are quite an actor. Somebody else can make better use of any stage than even the handsomest actor who will not use it.

Man is too aberrated to understand at least seven things about power:

1. Life is lived by lots of people. And if you lead, you must either let them get on with it or lead them on with it actively.

2. When the game or the show is over, there must be a new game or a new show. And if there isn't, somebody else is jolly well going to start one, and if you won't let *anyone* do it, the game will become "getting you."

3. If you have power, use it or delegate it or you sure won't have it long.

4. When you have people, use them or they will soon become most unhappy and you won't have them anymore.

386

5. When you move off a point of power, pay all your obligations on the nail, empower all your friends completely and move off with your pockets full of artillery, potential blackmail on every erstwhile rival, unlimited funds in your private account and the addresses of experienced assassins and go live in Bulgravia and bribe the police. And even then you may not live long if you have retained one scrap of domination in any camp you do not now control or if you even say, "I favor politician Jiggs." Abandoning power *utterly* is dangerous indeed. But we can't all be leaders or figures strutting in the limelight and so there's more to know about this:

6. When you're close to power, get some delegated to you—enough to do your job and protect yourself and your interests—for you can be shot, fellow, shot, as the position near power is delicious but dangerous, dangerous always, open to the taunts of any enemy of the power who dare not really boot the power but can boot you. So to live at all in the shadow or employ of a power, you must yourself gather and *USE* enough power to hold your own—without just nattering to the power to "kill Pete," in straightforward or more suppressive veiled ways to him, as these wreck the power that supports yours. He doesn't have to know all the bad news, and if he's a power really, he won't ask all the time, "What are all those dead bodies doing at the door?" And if you are clever, you never let it be thought *HE* killed them—that weakens you and also hurts the power source. "Well, boss, about all those dead bodies, nobody at all will suppose you did it. *She* over there, those pink legs sticking out, didn't like me." "Well," he'll say if he really is a power, "why are you bothering me with it if it's done and you did it. Where's my blue ink?" Or "Skipper, three shore patrolmen will be along soon with your cook, Dober, and they'll want to tell you he beat up Simson." "Who's Simson?" "He's a clerk in the enemy office downtown." "Good. When they've done it, take Dober down to the dispensary for any treatment he needs. Oh yes. Raise his pay." Or "Sir, could I have the power to sign divisional orders?" "Sure."

7. And lastly and most important, for we all aren't on the stage with our names in lights, always push power in the direction of anyone on whose power you depend. It may be more money for the power or more ease or a snarling defense of the power to a critic or even the dull thud of one of his enemies in the dark or the glorious blaze of the whole enemy camp as a birthday surprise.

If you work like that and the power you are near or depend upon is a power that has at least some inkling about how to be one and if you make others work like that, then the power-factor expands and expands and expands and you too acquire a sphere of power bigger than you would have if you worked alone. Real powers are developed by tight conspiracies of this kind pushing someone up in whose leadership they have faith. And if they are right and also manage their man and keep him from collapsing through overwork, bad temper or bad data, a kind of juggernaut builds up. Don't ever feel weaker because you work for somebody stronger. The only failure lies in taxing or pulling down the strength on which you depend. All failures to remain a power's power are failures to contribute to the strength and longevity of the work, health and power of that power. Devotion requires active contribution outwards from the power as well as in.

If Bolivar and Manuela had known these things, they would have lived an epic not a tragedy. They would not have "died in the ditch," he bereft of really earned praise for his real accomplishments even to this day. And Manuela would not be unknown even in the archives of her country as the heroine she was.

Brave, brave figures. But if this can happen to such stellar personalities gifted with ability tenfold over the greatest of other mortals, to people who could take a rabble in a vast impossible land and defeat one of Earth's then foremost powers, with no money or arms, on personality alone, what then must be the ignorance and confusion of human leaders in general, much less little men stumbling through their lives of boredom and suffering?

Let us wise them up, huh? You *can't* live in a world where even the great leaders can't lead.

L. RON HUBBARD
Founder

388

HCO POLICY LETTER OF 22 MARCH 1967
Issue II

Remimeo
HCO Hats

(Also issued as an HCOB, same date and title)

IMPORTANT

Admin Know-How Series 14

ALTER–IS AND DEGRADED BEINGS

Alteration of orders and tech is worse than noncompliance.

Alter-is is a covert avoidance of an order. Although it is apparently often brought about by noncomprehension, the noncomprehension itself, and failure to mention it, is an avoidance of orders.

Very degraded beings alter-is. Degraded ones refuse to comply without mentioning it. Beings in fair condition try to comply but remark their troubles, to get help when needed. Competent higher-toned beings understand orders and comply if possible but mainly do their jobs without needing lots of special orders.

Degraded beings find *any* instruction painful, as they have been painfully indoctrinated with violent measures in the past. They therefore alter-is any order or don't comply.

Thus, in auditing pcs or in org, where you find alter-is (covert noncompliance) and noncompliance, given sensible and correct tech or instructions, you are dealing with a degraded low-level being and should act accordingly.

One uses very simple low-level processes on a degraded being, gently.

In admin, orgs and especially the Tech Div where a staff member alter-ises or fails to comply, you are also dealing with a degraded being but one who is too much a pc to be a staff member. He cannot be at cause, and staff members *must* be at cause. So he or she should not be on staff.

This is a primary senior datum regulating all handling of pcs and staff members.

A degraded being is not a suppressive as he can have case gain. But he is so PTS that he works for suppressives only. He is sort of a super-continual PTS beyond the reach, really, of a simple S&D and handled only at Section III OT Course.

Degraded beings, taking a cue from SP associates, instinctively resent, hate and seek to obstruct any person in charge of anything or any Big Being.

Anyone issuing *sensible* orders is the first one resented by a degraded being.

A degraded being lies to his seniors, avoids orders covertly by alter-is, fails to comply, supplies only complex ideas that can't ever work (obstructive) and is a general area of enturbulence, often mild seeming or even "cooperative," often even flattering, sometimes merely dull, but consistently alter-ising or noncomplying.

This datum appeared during higher-level research and is highly revelatory of earlier unexplained phenomena—the pc who changes commands or doesn't do them, the worker who can't get it straight or who is always on a tea break.

In an area where suppression has been very heavy for long periods, people become degraded beings. However, they must have been so before already due to track incidents.

Some thetans are bigger than others. None are truly equal. But the degraded being is not necessarily a natively bad thetan. He is simply so PTS and has been for so long that it requires our highest-level tech to finally undo it *after* he has scaled up all our grades.

Degraded beings are about eighteen to one over Big Beings in the human race (minimum ratio). So those who keep things going are few. And those who will make it without the steam of the few in our orgs behind them are zero. At the same time, we can't have a world full of them and still make it. So we have no choice.

And we can handle them even when they cannot serve at higher levels.

This is really OT data, but we need it at lower levels to get the job done.

L. RON HUBBARD
Founder

Remimeo

Admin Know-How Series 15

USES OF ORGS

There are two uses (violently opposed to each other) to which Scientology orgs can be put. They are:

1. To forward the advance of self and all dynamics toward total survival.

2. To use the great power and control of an org over others to defend oneself.

When a decent being goes to work in an org, he uses 1.

When a suppressive goes to work in an org, he uses 2.

When you get in ethics, the decent one raises his necessity level and measures up. The suppressive type blows (leaves).

It is of vital interest to all of us that we have orgs that serve to increase survival on all dynamics. And that we prevent orgs being used as means to oppress others.

The answer, oddly enough, is to GET IN ETHICS exactly on-policy and correctly. And we will advance.

L. RON HUBBARD
Founder

HCO POLICY LETTER OF 16 OCTOBER 1967

ETHICS

Admin Know-How Series 16

SUPPRESSIVES AND THE ADMINISTRATOR
HOW TO DETECT SPs AS AN ADMINISTRATOR

There are three areas of detection which an administrator can utilize in the detection of a suppressive person.

These are:

1. No ethics change,

2. No case change,

3. No admin change.

An SP (suppressive person) is unable to change because he cannot, himself, confront. He is badly "out of valence." Therefore, not being able to look at things directly, he is unable to erase them or even see what they are. Such people often have a curtain of pictures they look at instead of the universe around them. They do not see a building. They see a picture of a building in front of the building. They are not at the point from which they view things.

Thus they are peculiar in that they can't change.

The three principal zones in a Scientology org are:

1. Ethics,

2. Tech,

3. Admin.

We have the natural laws of these subjects, each one.

If you can get in ethics, you can get in Scientology technology. If you can get in Scientology technology, you can get in admin. If you can get all three in, you have an org and have expansion.

If you can't get in tech, ethics is out. If you can't get in admin, both tech and ethics are out.

The sequence of things that have to be "gotten in" to make an org is 1st ethics, 2nd tech, 3rd admin.

Where one of these goes out, the org contracts.

We have these three sciences. To really handle things, one has to be a master of all three, even to live a good personal life.

By "get in" we mean get it applied and effective.

We live in a very woggy world at this time. The wog is so out-ethics he is living in what amounts to a criminal society.

When we try to get tech in on the planet we run into the out-ethics areas and this is the real source of our troubles where we have any. We are getting in tech before we get in ethics. It *can* be done (obviously, since we are doing it). But it is a heavy strain at best.

Just because we do not at once get ethics in on the planet does not mean we can't get any tech in.

By handling small sectors, beginning with self and Scientology groups and orgs, we can continue to repeat the cycles of three—ethics, tech, admin. Gradually we enlarge the numbers we have and gradually our sphere of ethics-tech-admin expands. And we one day have ethics in on the planet, tech in on the planet, admin in on the planet.

The only stumbling block is the SP. This person (about 10 percent of the population) is unable to change. We can process them if we can get them to sit still.

But these are the hidden booby traps which make one's life, one's family, one's org, one's nation, one's planet a rough-rough proposition.

Ninety percent of the people say, "Ethics great, tech great, admin great." And away we go.

Ten percent say, "Horrible, horrible, horrible." And cannot *either see or change*. They are the true psychotics no matter how "sane" they sound. The people in institutions are generally only their victims.

This 10 percent, one must be able to detect and weed out so they don't contaminate areas we are bringing up in ethics, tech and admin.

Our policy is we don't waste time on them. To cater to them is to betray 90 percent of the population. So we set them aside for another day.

We get them off lines, out of orgs and to one side.

The true character of these people is usually masked in many ways. They are expert only in deception and can take on any guise.

To listen to them one would suppose he was talking to his best friend sometimes. Except the knife in one's back is also driven in by them.

We have much tech to describe them.

But one does not have to be an auditor with a meter to find these people.

393

An administrator only needs to know the three things about them:

1. No change in ethics,

2. No change in case,

3. No change in admin.

These people have:

1. Thick ethics files,

2. Thick (or no) case files,

3. Thick, full (or no) comm baskets.

If you just dismissed anyone who had all three, you would have gotten rid of an SP.

It works this way. When you start to get in ethics, most people "learn the ropes" fast. They may have a few down conditions and chits or even courts or Comm Evs but you see the frequency dwindles and eventually vanishes or nearly so.

When you start to get in tech on a person, it may be a hard haul for a while and then it begins to level out and get easier.

When you start to get in admin, the confusion around some person may be great but after a while the lines and policies straighten out.

None are good little angels. But 90 percent make progress in these three fields of ethics, tech and admin.

The SP does NOT make any consistent progress at all and lapses every time.

As only 10 percent of the people then are making nearly all the tough work in ethics, tech and admin, the thing to do then is to get them off the lines rather than betray 90 percent.

And the SP is detectable in ALL THREE AREAS. It needs no microscope to find out who on a staff has the seniors working so hard for so little gain.

Their ethics file is huge, their case file either doesn't exist at all or is very fat, their comm lines are jammed, their policy is out and their stats are on the bottom eternally.

So as an administrator you can detect SPs. You better had. YOUR OWN STATS WILL BE DOWN TO THE DEGREE YOU FAIL TO DETECT THEM.

Just go to your files and look at the desks and sack whoever satisfies all three conditions above and you can't miss and WILL be able to breathe.

L. RON HUBBARD
Founder

394

HCO POLICY LETTER OF 20 OCTOBER 1967
Issue I

Remimeo

Admin Know-How Series 17

CONDITIONS, HOW TO ASSIGN

Every post and part of an org must have a statistic which measures the volume of product of that post. The head of a part has the statistic of that part.

Every post or part of an org has a product. If it has no product, it is useless and supernumerary.

An Exec Sec has the products of his or her portion of the org. The first product of an Exec Sec is, of course, his or her portion of the org's divisions. If the portion itself does not exist, then of course the Exec Sec has no stat at all as an Exec Sec even if very busy—so he or she is not an Exec Sec despite the title. This is true of a department head, a section head and a unit head. One can't really be the one in charge if the thing one is in charge of doesn't exist. Also, things that don't exist themselves can have no product.

The whole rationale (basic idea) of the pattern of an org is a unit of 3. These are:

THETAN
↓
MIND ⟶ BODY ⟶ PRODUCT.

In Division One the HCO Sec is the thetan, Department One the MIND, Department Two the BODY and Department Three the PRODUCT. The same pattern holds for every division.

It also should hold for every department and lower section and unit.

And above these it holds for a portion of an org.

In the HCO portion of the org we have the HCO Exec Sec as the thetan, the Exec Div (7) as the MIND, Division One as the BODY and Division Two as the PRODUCT.

And so with other parts of an org. They always go:

THETAN
↓
MIND ⟶ BODY ⟶ PRODUCT.

Now, if you know and understand and can apply this, you can not only plan or correct an org or one of its parts, you can also assign conditions correctly. You need data gained from inventories or counts of items or the statistic assigned and drawn.

It is *not* enough to **only** follow graphs. That is a *lazy, lazy, lazy,* no-confront method when used alone. Graphs can be falsified, can be too fixed on one thing and can ignore others unless you read *all* the graphs of the part you are interested in.

Graphs are a *good indicator* and should be used wherever possible. BUT you must also keep in mind that it requires ALL the graphs to be wholly accurate in a conditions assignment and the most accurate conditions assignment possible and that the graphs must be based on ACTUAL figures.

So, to begin, you look at the graphs. You look for recent ups and downs. Then you look for trends (long-range drifts up or down). Then you look for discrepancies. Like high enrollment–low income, high letters out–low enrollment weeks later.

It is safe enough *at first* to simply assign moderate conditions (Emergency, Normal, Affluence) by the current ups and downs of the graphs. This should result in *expansion*.

EXPANSION (product increase) is THE WHOLE REASON you are assigning conditions in the first place, so you expect, reasonably, that if you assign conditions by graph you will get *expansion*.

Now, after a while (weeks or months) you see you *are* getting expansion so you go on assigning conditions by graph. An Exec Sec would also inspect the physical areas of Dangers and Affluences as a matter of course.

BUT let us take the reverse case. You assign conditions by graph (and inspections of Danger and Affluence) and what you are assigning conditions to DOESN'T expand!

Well, now we get to work. There is something wrong.

The first thing that can be wrong is that what you are assigning conditions to really doesn't exist. The Director of Comm does not have a Department of Comm. He has only a messenger/telex operator, no way to handle his other departmental functions and answers the phone himself.

So, finding no department, REGARDLESS OF OTHER REASONS ("can't get staff," "income too low," "no quarters"), you bang him with a condition of Non-Existence. Because he obviously doesn't exist as a Dir Comm, having no Comm Dept. (Non-Existence is also assigned for NO USE and NO FUNCTION.)

Now, if this assignment to the Dir Comm of Non-Existence—with no further help from you, mind—does not result in a Comm Dept in a reasonable time, you assume he doesn't want one to be there and you assign a condition of Liability.

You don't explain it all away. That's what *he's* doing so why imitate him?

You don't say, "He's just overwhelmed—new—needs a review—natter, natter, figure, figure." You simply ASSIGN!

He STILL doesn't get a Comm Dept there.

You inspect. You find the Ethics Officer isn't enforcing the Liability penalty ("Pete is my pal and I . . ."). So you assign the Ethics Officer a condition of Liability as he gets, naturally, what he failed to enforce.

Now they mutiny and you assign a condition of Treason, shoot both of them from guns and fill the posts.

The new incumbents you tell, "The boys before you aren't here now and aren't likely to be trained or processed until we get around to the last dregs so we hope you do better. You begin in Non-Existence. I trust you will work your way out of it at least into Danger before the week is out. As you are just on post, the penalties do not apply for Non-Existence. But they will after 30 days. So let's get a Dept of Comm and an Ethics Section."

Now of course, if the E/O had to be shot from guns, Dir I&R is at once assigned a DANGER CONDITION complete with penalties as that section was in his/her dept.

If there's no HCO (Div 7, 1, 2) part of the org, the LRH Comm of that org yells for the next senior org to act. And if there's no LRH Comm, the next senior org should see that it's gone by lack of stats or reports or expansion and act anyway.

Now you say, "But that's ruthless! No staff would . . ."

Well, such a statement reasoning is contrary to the facts.

The only time (by actual experience and data) you lose staff and have an unstaffed org is when you let low-stat people in. Low-stat personnel *gets rid of* good staff members. An org that can't be staffed has an SP in it!

Orgs where ethics is tight and savage grow in numbers!

Man thrives, oddly enough, only in the presence of a challenging environment. That isn't my theory. That's fact.

If the org environment is not challenging, there will be no org.

We help beyond any help ever available anywhere. We are a near ultimate in helping. At once this loads us up with SPs who would commit suicide to prevent anyone from being helped and it lays us wide open as "softies" to any degraded being that comes along. They are *sure* we won't bite so they do anything they please. Conditions correctly assigned alone can detect and eject SPs and DBs.

So if we help so greatly, we must also in the same proportion be able to discipline. Near ultimate help can only be given with near ultimate discipline.

Tech can only stay itself where ethics is correctly and ruthlessly administered. Admin like ours has to be high because our orgs handle the highest commodity—life itself.

So our admin only works where tech is IN. And our tech works only where ethics is in.

Our target is not a few psychiatric patients but a cleared universe. So what does THAT take?

The lowest confront there is, is the confront of evil. When a living being is out of his own valence and in the valence of a thoroughly bad, even if imaginary, image, you get an SP. An SP is a no-confront case because, not being in his own valence, he has no viewpoint from which to erase anything. That is all an SP is.

BUT the amount of knowing havoc an SP can cause is seen easily if only in this planet's savage, cruel wars.

An executive who cannot confront evil is already en route to becoming suppressive.

Next door to the "theetie-weetie" case is the totally overwhelmed condition we call SP (suppressive person).

It is so *easy* to live in a fairyland where nothing evil is ever done. One gets the image of a sweet old lady standing in the middle of a gangster battle with bodies and blood spattering the walls saying, "It's so nice, it's only a boy's game with toy guns."

The low-statistic staff member who never gets his stats up is *making* low stats. He isn't idle. It's a goodie-goodie attitude to say, "He just isn't working hard." The chronic low-stat person is working VERY HARD to keep the stat DOWN. When you learn that, you can assign conditions and make an org expand.

When stats WON'T come up, you drop the condition down. Sooner or later you will hit the REAL condition that applies.

Conversely, as you upgrade conditions you will also reach the condition that applies. Some staff members are in chronic *Power*. Who ever assigns it? They take over a post—its stats soar. Well, to measure just stats of the post taken over as his condition is false since his personal condition is and has been *Power*. And if it *is* Power, then that personal condition should be assigned.

That is very easy to see.

BUT what if you have a personnel who whenever he or she takes over a post the stat collapses?

Well, you better assign that one too. For just as the one in Power *works* to maintain up stats, the one in the lower condition, whether one cares to confront it or not, works too and is just as industriously collapsing not only his own post stats but also the stats of posts adjacent to his! So he is at least a condition of Liability as the post if vacant would only be in Non-Existence! And as somebody next to it might do a little bit for it, it might even get up to Danger condition, completely unmanned!

DISCREPANCIES

When there are discrepancies amongst statistic graphs, SOME graph is false.

When you find a false graph, you assign anyone who falsified it intentionally and knowingly a condition of Liability, for that action is far worse than a non-compliance.

And you had better be alert to the actual area where the false graph originated as it has a tiger in it. Only physical inspection of a most searching kind (or a board if it is distant) will reveal the OTHER crimes going on there. There are always *other* crimes when you get a false report. Experience will teach one that if he really looks.

RECIPROCITY

It is more than policy that one gets the condition he fails to correctly and promptly assign *and* enforce.

It's a sort of natural law. If you let your executives goof off and stay in, let us say, a Danger condition, yet you don't assign and enforce one, they will surely put YOU in a Danger condition whether it gets assigned or not.

Remember *that* when your finger falters "on the trigger."

That *natural* law stems from this appalling fact.

We didn't, a long, long time ago, get in ethics. We goofed. And the whole race went into the soup where it remains to this day.

And if we are to live in this universe at all, at all, we are going to have to get in ethics and clean it up.

Whether that's easy to confront or not is beside the point. The horrid truth is that our fate is FAR more unconfrontable!

Now we have to have highly skilled tech to bail us out. And I assure you that that tech will never get *in* or be used beneficially at all unless:

1. We get ethics in, and

2. Unless Scientology orgs expand at a regular rate.

Only then can we be free.

So that's how and WHY you assign and enforce conditions. It's the only way everyone finally will win.

L. RON HUBBARD
Founder

HCO POLICY LETTER OF 8 FEBRUARY 1968
Issue I

Admin Know-How Series 18

STATISTIC RATIONALIZATION

"Rationalizing a statistic" is a derogatory term meaning finding excuses for down statistics.

Finding excuses or reasons why a stat is down does NOT bring it up and at best is a scathing comment on the lack of foresight or initiative of the executive in charge of the area.

What is wanted is (1) prevention of stats going down and (2) quick action to bring them up.

Being reasonable about their being down should be regarded as AGREEMENT WITH THEIR BEING DOWN. Which is, of course, suppressive.

"Well, the letters out stat is down because we were paying a girl so much per letter and 'policy' stated we could not hire anyone so we fired her and that's why letters out is down."

That was an actual rationalization given in Washington, DC, for the collapse of the org last year.

To begin, there is no such "policy" and surely no policy exists to have down stats. So, here the felony is compounded by seeking to blame policy for a down stat which for sure revealed the action as a suppressive effort to rationalize (and get away with) a down stat.

The only reason stats are down, ever, is because somebody didn't push them up. All other reasons are false.

IDÉE FIXE

Some people have a METHOD of handling a down stat which is a fixed idea or cliché they use to handle *all* downstat situations in their lives.

These people are so at effect they have some *idea* sitting there "that handles" a down statistic.

"Life is like that."

"I always try my best."

"People are mean."

"It will get better."

"It was worse last year."

They KNOW it isn't any use trying to do anything about anything and that it is best just to try to get by and not be noticed—a sure route to suicide.

Instead of seeking to prevent or raise a declining stat in life, such people use some fixed idea to *explain* it.

This is a confession of being in apathy.

One can always make stats go up. Hard work. Foresight. Initiative. One can always make stats go up. That's the truth of it, and it needs no explanations.

L. RON HUBBARD
Founder

Admin Know-How Series 19

[*Note:* There is no issue assigned the Admin Know-How Series number 19. The number was earlier erroneously assigned by a staff member to HCO PL 31 Oct. 66R II, Admin Know-How 3R, JOB ENDANGERMENT CHITS, which has been returned to its correct position in the series as Admin Know-How Series 3R.]

HCO POLICY LETTER OF 30 MAY 1968

Remimeo

Issue I

(Issued from Flag Order 805)

Admin Know-How Series 20

ADMINISTRATION

When admin is OUT, tech is OUT and ethics has long ceased to exist.

You can never send administrative orders into an out-admin area; you can only get ethics in. To do other than to get ethics in is to only invite further noncompliance and dev-t.

In reality, *ANY* administration is a symptom of out-ethics. Any order is really a criticism. If a post was really being worn, orders would be unnecessary.

If someone started giving me orders, then I would wonder about my post. DO YOUR JOB WITH A PLUS AND A PREDICT. Wear your hat so well, you never need an order.

Remember: NEVER ISSUE AN ORDER TO GET AN ORDER YOU HAVE ALREADY ISSUED COMPLIED WITH. Ethics has gone out. When ethics has to be put in, responsibility is out.

L. RON HUBBARD
Founder

All Execs
Remimeo
Org Exec Course
Introductory

IMPORTANT

Admin Know-How Series 21

ADMIN KNOW-HOW

When trying to get stats up, you must realize that what GOT stats up will GET stats up.

Using new, unusual experiments can crash your full intention.

In *new* programs the BUGS have not been worked out. It's like a newly designed piece of machinery. The clutch slips or the HP is sour..

New programs are undertaken on a small scale as PILOT PROJECTS. If they work out, good. Spot the bugs, streamline them and prove them. Only then is it all right to give them out as broad orders.

So it isn't good for an EC to hand out strings of orders. Or for an executive to start a lot of new projects.

There is a thing called STANDARD ADMIN. It comes from the policy letters.

When we produced the wild, soaring tech stats with the Sea Org Class VIII Auditor program, IT WAS BY PUTTING IN THE EXACT PROCESSES AND GRADES. By going Super *Standard* we got 100 percent case gain.

It is the same with policy. If you get an org in with super standard policy—promotion, form and admin—the stats SOAR.

TELEX ORDERS

Instead of sending out a mad avalanche of orders on telex, an exec should only send the number and date of the PL he wants in AND THEN SHOULD RIDE THAT ONE ORDER until it *is* in.

To choose WHAT policy letter is of course the trick. One has to know something about the conditions of the org before sending the order.

TRYING TO GET ALL PLs IN at once can also swamp an org. "Get on policy" is a meaningless remark. Get on such and such a policy, if it is obviously out, is a very valuable action.

GENERAL EXEC ACTIONS

EDs are there to say WHAT policy should be concentrated on, not to give *new* orders.

An executive who is wise, gets in policy on a gradient (little by little, building it up higher and higher, keeping the old in while adding in the new).

To understand how to do this, one must be able to conceive of basic outnesses. It requires real genius to discover how gross and how basic an outness can be.

An exec pounds away with a high-level policy on how to do accounting. Is his face red when he finds the reason for the muddle is that there isn't anyone in the division!!!

Once we almost "did our nut" trying to find what outness had unmocked an org. All sorts of involved conclusions were reached. All manner of orders given without any improvement. And then "murder outed." EVERY Registrar in the org had been removed and no new ones appointed. The public couldn't find anyone to sign them up.

I once sent a continent into Power simply by discovering that it had not appointed people to the posts of Exec Sec in any org! How "out" can it get? As soon as Exec Secs were appointed, the whole continent went into Power.

I once read an ED which (a) removed all executives but one and then (b) gave 20 complex orders "to be done at once." The one remaining personnel could not have executed *any* of them. I at once cancelled ALL EDs not issued by myself and shortly up went the stats.

Wondering why no mail is ever mailed does not call for a complex policy. It calls for a policy about the form of the org, how it must have Exec Secs, divisional secs. For there to be no mail going out can only mean there's nobody on post!

A divisional sec trying to get in his division's policy must look first for GROSS outnesses. They are never small. And then he must get them in by policy. Then they'll stay in.

There IS a *standard admin*. It deals in simplicities. People are on post. Particles flow. Promotion is done. Tech is delivered. The org board is up and is followed.

If policy isn't in at *that* level of largeness, it will never go in on higher points.

Knowing an org inside out is also knowing who to tell to do what and what policy to get in when. It's like knowing how to drive a car. It won't go if you don't know where the ignition switch is located. Policy outnesses occur and unusual ideas are put forth only by those who don't know what is usual in the first place.

Like standard tech, in standard policy the results come from getting in the basics and doing them well.

L. RON HUBBARD
Founder

Remimeo
Senior OEC

Admin Know-How Series 22

THE KEY INGREDIENTS

When we look at organization in its most simple form, when we seek certain key actions or circumstances that make organization work, when we need a very simple, very vital rundown to teach people that will produce results, we find only a few points we need to stress.

The purpose of organization is TO MAKE PLANNING BECOME ACTU-ALITY.

Organization is not just a fancy, complex system, done for its own sake. That is bureaucracy at its worst. Org boards for the sake of org boards, graphs for the sake of graphs, rules for the sake of rules, only add up to failures.

The only virtue (not always a bad one) of a complex, unwieldy, meaningless bureaucratic structure is that it provides jobs for the friends of those in control. If it does not also bring about burdensome taxation and threatened bankruptcy by reason of the expense of maintaining it, and if it does not saddle a people or production employees with militant inspections and needless control, organization for the sake of providing employment is not evil but beyond providing employment is useless, and only when given too much authority is it destructive.

The kings of France and other lands used to invent titles and duties to give activity to the hordes of noble hangers-on to keep them at court, under surveillance, and out of mischief out in the provinces where they might stir up their own people. "Keeper of the Footstools," "Holder of the Royal Nightgown" and other such titles were fought for, bought, sold and held with ferocity.

Status-seeking, the effort to become more important and have a personal reason for being and for being respected, gets in the road of honest efforts to effectively organize in order to get something done, in order to make something economically sound.

Organization for its own sake, in actual practice, usually erects a monster that becomes so hard to live with that it becomes overthrown. Production losses, high taxes, irritating or fearsome interference with the people or actual producers invites and accomplishes bankruptcy or revolt, usually both even in commercial companies.

Therefore to be meaningful, useful and lasting, an organization has to fit into the definition above:

TO MAKE PLANNING BECOME ACTUALITY

In companies and countries there is no real lack of dreaming. All but the most depraved heads of companies or states wish to see specific or general improvement. This is also true of their executives and, as it forms the basis of nearly all revolts, it is certainly true of workers. From top to bottom, then, there is, in the large majority, a desire for improvement.

More food, more profit, more pay, more facilities and, in general, more and better of whatever they believe is good or beneficial. This also includes less of what they generally consider to be bad.

Programs which obtain general support consist of more of what is beneficial and less of what is detrimental. "More food, less disease," "more beautiful buildings, less hovels," "more leisure, less work," "more activity, less unemployment," are typical of valuable and acceptable programs.

But only to have a program is to have only a dream. In companies, in political parties, useful programs are very numerous. They suffer only from a lack of execution.

All sorts of variations of program failure occur. The program is too big. It is not generally considered desirable. It is not needed at all. It would benefit only a few. Such are surface reasons. The basic reason is lack of organization know-how.

Any program, too ambitious, partially acceptable, needed or not needed, could be put into effect if properly organized.

The five-year plans of some nations which are currently in vogue are almost all very valuable and almost all fall short of their objectives. The reason is not that they are unreal, too ambitious or generally unacceptable. The reason for any such failure is lack of organization.

It is not man's dreams that fail him. It is the lack of know-how required to bring those dreams into actuality.

Good administration has two distinct targets:

1. To perpetuate an existing company, culture or society

2. To make planning become actuality.

Given a base on which to operate—which is to say land, people, equipment and a culture—one needs a good administrative pattern of some sort just to maintain it.

Thus (1) and (2) above become (2) only. The plan is "to continue the existing entity." No company or country continues unless one continues to put it there. Thus an administrative system of some sort, no matter how crude, is necessary to perpetuate any group or any subdivision of a group. Even a king or headman or manager who has no other supporting system to whom one can bring disputes about land or water or pay is an administrative system. The foreman of a labor gang that only loads trucks has an astonishingly complex administrative system at work.

Companies and countries do not work just because they are there or because they are traditional. They are continuously put there by one or another form of administration.

When a whole system of admin moves out or gets lost or forgotten, collapse occurs unless a new or substitute system is at once moved into place.

Changing the head of a department, much less a general manager and much, much less a ruler, can destroy a portion or the whole since the old system, unknown, disregarded or forgotten, may cease and no new system which is understood is put in its place. Frequent transfers within a company or country can keep the entire group small, disordered and confused, since such transfers destroy what little administration there might have been.

Thus, if administrative shifts or errors or lack can collapse any type of group, it is vital to know the basic subject of organization.

Even if the group is at effect—which is to say originates nothing but only defends in the face of threatened disaster—it still must plan. And if it plans, somehow it must get the plan executed or done. Even a simple situation of an attacked fortress has to be defended by planning and doing the plan, no matter how crude. The order "Repel the invader who is storming the south wall" is the result of observation and planning no matter how brief or unthorough. Getting the south wall defended occurs by some system of administration even if it only consists of sergeants hearing the order and pushing their men to the south wall.

A company with heavy debts has to plan even if it is just to stall off creditors. And some administrative system has to exist even to do only that.

The terrible dismay of a young leader who plans a great and powerful new era only to find himself dealing with old and weak faults is attributable not to his "foolish ambition" or "lack of reality" but to his lack of organizational know-how.

Even elected presidents or prime ministers of democracies are victims of such terrible dismay. They do not, as is routinely asserted, "go back on their campaign promises" or "betray the people." They, as well as their members of parliament, simply lack the rudiments of organizational know-how. They cannot put their campaign promises into effect, not because they are too high-flown but because they are politicians not administrators.

To some men it seems enough to dream a wonderful dream. Just because they dreamed it they feel it should now take place. They become very provoked when it does not occur.

Whole nations, to say nothing of commercial firms or societies or groups, have spent decades in floundering turmoil because the basic dreams and plans were never brought to fruition.

Whether one is planning for the affluence of the Appalachian Mountains or a new loading shed closer to the highway, the gap between the plan and the actuality will be found to be lack of administrative know-how.

Technical ignorance, finance, even lack of authority and unreal planning itself are none of them true barriers between planning and actuality.

Thus, we come to the exact most basic steps that comprise administration.

First is **OBSERVATION**. From beginning to end, observation must serve both those in charge and any others who plan. When observation is lacking, then planning itself as well as any and all progress can become unreal and orders faulty and destructive. Observation, in essence, must be TRUE. Nothing must muddy it or color it as this can lead to gross errors in action and training.

Next is **PLANNING** itself. *Planning* is based on dreams but it must be fitted to what is needed and wanted and what men can do, even with stretched imaginations or misgivings. Planning has to be targeted and scheduled and laid out in steps and gradients or one will be laying railroad tracks that pass through oceans or boring tunnels in mountains that do not exist or building penthouses without putting any building under them to hold them up.

The essence of planning is **COMMUNICATION** and the *communication* must be such that it can be understood and will not be misunderstood. For unless those who oversee and those who do know what their part of the plan is, they cannot execute their share and very well may oversee and do quite some other action, leaving a monstrous gap and even a structure that ate up their time and funds but now has to be torn down.

The next is **SUPERVISION** and supervision is dually needful. It serves as a relay point to which plans can be communicated and from which observations as reports can be received; and it serves as the terminal which communicates the plans as orders and sees that they are actually done. This gives one the genus of the org board as a central ordering point which has other relay ordering points taking care of their part of the whole plan or program. These points are often also the points which care for local occurrences which must be handled, and their frailty is that they become so involved with local occurrences, oddities and purely local concerns that they do not or cannot give any attention to receiving, relaying and overseeing their part of the main plan.

Then there are the **PRODUCERS** who *produce* the service or the structure or the product required by the plan. Many plans are marvelous in all respects but putting somebody there to actually DO the required actions that make the plan real. The primary fault is to use persons who already have projects and duties to which they are committed and, with their local knowledge, see must be continued at any cost but who are forced to abandon existing programs or duties to start on this new activity, solely because the new activity has the stress given it in orders and the old activities are seemingly ordered left alone. Old companies and old countries could be said to be "that collection of incomplete and abandoned projects which is confused and failing."

Finally there is the **USER**, those who will *use* or benefit from the program when it is realized and completed. When planning fails to take this element into account, only then can the whole program fail utterly, for it, regardless of dreams, labor and expense, is finally seen to be of no value anyway. Thus all great programs begin with an understanding or a survey of what is needed and wanted; and a nose and value count of those who will use it; and a costing action in time, labor, materials and finance, compared to the value of it—even if only aesthetic—of those who will use it in any way, if only to know they have it or to be proud of it or to feel better or stronger because they have done it.

Thus one gets the points which are the true administrative points:

1. **OBSERVATION** even down to discovering the users and what is needed and wanted.

2. **PLANNING** which includes imaginative conception and intelligent timing, targeting and drafting of the plans so they can be communicated and assigned.

3. **COMMUNICATING** which includes receiving and understanding plans and their portion and relaying them to others so that they can be understood.

4. **SUPERVISION** which sees that that which is communicated is done in actuality.

5. **PRODUCTION** which does the actions or services which are planned, communicated and supervised.

6. **USERS** by which the product or service or completed plan is used.

Administrative systems or organizations which lack at least the rudiments of the above system will not bring off the dream and will accumulate an enormous lot of uncompleted actions. Not a few failures, bankruptcies, overthrows and revolutions have occurred because one or all of the above points were awry in an existing organization.

The amount of heroic executive overwork which comes from the omission of one or more of these vital essential points accounts for the ulcers which are the occupational disease of those in charge.

When some or all these points are awry or gone, an executive or ruler or his minister is reduced to an anxiety which can only watch for the symptoms of bankruptcy or attack or revolt.

Even if so reduced, an executive who fends off disaster while getting in a system which satisfies the above points has an enormously bettered chance of winning at long last.

The dual nature of an administrative system or an organization now becomes plain.

Let us pry apart (1) and (2) above. The effort to hold an existing organization together is really different than trying to get a plan into actuality. In practice, one *has* an organization of some sort. It has functions and it has local concerns and problems. And it has programs and actions from past control centrals or which were locally generated.

To push in upon this plans which, no matter how well conceived or intentioned, are additional to its load will cause a great deal of confusion, incomplete projects left dangling and general upset.

To place new programs into action, two prior actions are necessary:

A. Put in a whole new system paralleling the old existing system.

B. Survey the old system and its existing programs to preserve them, eradicate them or combine them with the new plans.

To leave (A) and (B) undone is to court disaster. Whether one is aware of the old programs or the old organization or not, THEY REMAIN AND WILL CONTINUE—even if only as a pile of undone, unsorted papers nobody knows where to file or as a pile of odd unfinished masonry some future generation can't identify or will identify with scorn of administrations in general.

New leaders are sometimes looked upon as a worse scourge than a foreign enemy and new patterns of rule are often subjected to overthrow simply because they did not, out of ignorance or laziness, do (A) and (B) above.

One sometimes finds a company unit or a military officer left in some unheard of place for years, at continuing expense, guarding or nibbling at some project in a bewildered or philosophic fashion. The activity remained unremembered, unhandled when a new broom and new planners entered the scene.

This can get so bad that a company or a nation's resources can be broken to bits. The old plans, disorganized, not known, discredited, are superseded by new plans and new ambitions. The old plans are in the road of the new plans and the new plans prevent old plans from completing. The result is an impasse. And the men in charge, even at the level of junior executives, become even more puzzled and bewildered than the workers and begin to believe no new plans can ever be done, blame the ignorance of the populace and the cruelty of fate and give up.

All they had to do was put in a complete new parallel system as in the (1) to (6) outline above for their new plans and to meanwhile preserve and continue the old system while they surveyed for preservation, eradication or combination of it. It is sometimes even good sense to continue old projects to completion currently with new projects just to maintain stability in the company or country and somehow find new finance and new people for the new plans. It is often far less costly than to simply confuse everything.

Furthermore, all NEW and untried plans should have PILOT PROJECTS which by test and use must be successful before one incorporates them and their new workers into the old system as a parallel dependable activity.

A "chicken in every pot" as a campaign promise could easily succeed if organized as in (1) to (6) above.

There is a lot to organization. It requires trained administrators who can forward the programs. But a "trained" administrator who does not grasp the principles of organization itself is only a clerk.

At this current writing man has not had administrative training centers where actual organization was taught. It was learned by "experience" or by working in an organization that was already functioning. But as the principles were not the same company to company and nation to nation, the differences of background experiences of any set of administrators differed to such a degree that no new corps could be assembled as a team.

Thus it was said to require a quarter to a half a century to make a company. But the number of ineffective bureaucracies and national failures which existed stated clearly that there were too few skilled administrators and too few training activities.

Man's happiness and the longevity of companies and states apparently depend upon organizational know-how. Hiring specialized experts to get one out of trouble is a poor substitute for knowing what it is all about in the first place.

Organization is actually a simple subject, based on a few basic patterns which, if applied, produce success.

If one would dream and see his dreams an actuality, one must also be able to organize and to train organizational men who will make those dreams come true.

L. RON HUBBARD
Founder

411

HCO POLICY LETTER OF 27 OCTOBER 1969
Issue I

Remimeo

Admin Know-How Series 23

DEV–T

The entire, complete and only major source of dev-t is ignorance or failure to grasp CONFUSION AND THE STABLE DATUM as covered fully in *The Problems of Work* (and LRH tapes of 1956).

Unless an executive or staff member fully grasps the basic principles of confusion and a stable datum then the org board is completely over his head, the reason for posts is not understood and dev-t becomes routine.

A post on the org board is the STABLE POINT. If it is not held by someone, it will generate confusion. If the person that is holding it isn't really holding it, the confusion inherent in that area on the org board zooms all over the place near and far.

Any executive getting dev-t knows at once what posts are not held because dev-t is the confusion that should have been handled in that area by someone on post. With that stable terminal not stable, dev-t shoots about.

Excessive transfers in an org promote fantastic dev-t as the posts do not really get held as people are on them too briefly. "Musical chairs" (excessive transfers) can destroy an org or area.

The remedy is to get people trained up (OEC) to handle their posts, to get people on post who do handle their posts.

An essential part of such training is a *study* of *The Problems of Work* and a full grasp of how a stable terminal handles and prevents confusion. If the person cannot fully grasp this principle, he is below the ability to conceive of terminals and barely able to perceive lines. He cannot communicate since there are no terminals to him.

REMOTE AREAS

If an area remote from an executive does not contain a stable point to which he can send his comm and get it handled, then his comm only enters dev-t into the area and he gets back floods of despatches and problems but no real handling. The area is not organized and does not have people in it who have grasped *The Problems of Work* or how it applies to an org board or even why there is an org board.

Communicating into a disorganized area without first organizing it to have at least one stable terminal is foolishness.

An org board is that arrangement of persons, lines and actions which classifies types of confusions and gives a stable terminal to each type. It is as effective as its people can conceive of terminals and understand the basic principle of confusions and stable data.

A good executive arranges personnel and organization to handle types of actions and confusions. He does not broadly comm into disorganized areas except to organize them.

Any area which gives an executive excessively developed traffic (dev-t) is an area where the persons supposed to be the stable terminals in that area are *not* holding their posts and do NOT understand what they are or why and do not know what an org board is and have never understood the Scientology fundamental known as confusion and the stable datum. They are NOT doing their post or organizing their areas.

An executive's evidence of this is the receipt from there of dev-t.

The executive's action is to get somebody THERE, get him to understand confusion and the stable datum and how it applies to posts as stable terminals, get him trained up and use that now stable point to handle further confusions.

If an executive goes on handling dev-t of people who are not stable terminals that handle their areas, HE WILL BE FORCED TO WORK HARDER THAN IF THE POST WERE EMPTY. At least if it were empty, he would get only the confusion of that area. As it is, if the post is improperly held and wobbly, he gets not only the area confusion but also the enturbulation of the wobbly incumbent.

Volumes could be written about this subject. But there is no reason whatever not to be able to grasp the fundamentals concerning confusion and stable data, confusion and stable terminals, apply it to org boards, to areas and to expansion.

Chaos is the basic situation in this universe. To handle it you put in order.

Order goes in by being and making stable terminals arranged to handle types of action and confusion.

In organizing units, sections, divs, depts, orgs or areas of orgs, you build by stable terminals.

You solve areas by reinforcing stable terminals.

Executives who do not grasp this live lives of total harassment and confusion.

The whole secret of organization, the whole problem of dev-t, the basic ingredient of all expansion is contained in this.

L. RON HUBBARD
Founder

413

Remimeo

Admin Know-How Series 24

DISTRACTION AND NOISE

Noise is a technical term used in the field of public relations to describe the medley of messages hitting a member of a public besides one's own message.

The clamoring for attention of many different people, firms, situations brings about a condition where another voice or despatch is just ONE MORE DISTRACTION.

We can profitably use NOISE to describe the demands for attention put upon a staff member, executive, office or org that is being distracted off a main line of action.

A law evolves—THOSE INDIVIDUALS OR AREAS THAT ARE THE LEAST WELL ORGANIZED ARE AFFECTED THE MOST BY DISTRACTIONS.

Let us take an office in Gus Falls, South Alabama. The Public Exec Sec chooses personnel and audits, the HCO ES lectures, the OES mows the lawn. The rest of the staff are assigned to no divisions particularly, they try to cope but the org makes little money, naturally, so they "moonlight" (have other jobs).

The place is a mess, of course. Public, bills collectors, salesmen, all clamor endlessly for the org's attention. The more disorganized the place is, the more messages each distractor has to originate to get anyone there to listen. Routine actions, having no lines on which to travel and no one to handle them, become frantic, *oft* repeated emergencies, each one with multiples of messages.

SO, you are an executive in a remote city. This Gus Falls office is in your area.

SO, you write them despatches.

You get no answers.

You write more despatches.

And they go unanswered.

Gus Falls just isn't reporting up.

WHY? You are just one more noise in a screaming chaos.

The office manifests mainly DEFENSE. It is being hit so hard with random voices and despatches that it develops a ridge against all voices, all despatches.

Anything from you, if it gets read at all, is resented as it's "just one more awful impossible."

So there are only three conditions wherein you get no answers or compliance:

1. There is no one there.

2. Your terminal there isn't wearing his or her hat.

3. The place is a howling disorganized madhouse.

The remotely located executive who keeps writing despatches into an area and gets no action or answers has these situations:

A. His orders are unreal in that they are not based on good observation.

B. His orders are contrary to policy and would produce upsets or disorganization.

C. There is no one there at the receipt-point.

D. The terminal addressed isn't wearing his/her hat.

E. The place is a howling disorganized madhouse.

In any of these cases we get this law:

WHEN YOUR DESPATCHES OR ORDERS AREN'T GETTING ANSWERED OR ACTIONED, DON'T EVER KEEP ISSUING MORE OF THE SAME.

In the special case of (E) you haven't got a chance of attracting attention.

There are many things you can do in the case of (E).

Whatever you do, if observation and real data to hand (not rumor or opinion) shows (E) to be the case, there is one basic rule:

WHEN A PERSONNEL OR PLACE IS DISTRACTED, GET IN ONLY EASY BASICS ONE AT A TIME.

Problems of Work data applies. Stable datum and confusion.

Whatever you do, you have to get correct factual observation that is actual data, not propaganda or opinion.

It could be somebody there is suppressive and is tearing the place apart.

It could be they just don't know what organization is, that it means that specialized personnel are assigned to different posts with specific duties and that command and flow lines are established throughout the organization. Maybe they don't know that.

It could be only the top strata is in a mess with the staff working well out of sight from a remote observer. That has happened.

A remote executive or one on the ground confronting this sort of thing gets his first inkling of it from no-reports or noncompliance or slow compliance.

His next action is to collect factual data on actual conditions.

His next action is to find out WHO if anyone is disorganizing the place, and handle that one. But this is with care as such action if remotely taken can be wrong and the place will just disintegrate.

His next action is to get in simple basics like an org board, then hats, then a Comm Center, then recruitment, then decent promotion and decent service.

Often such a group as in (E) has generated howling financial or even public emergencies and these are what are screaming for attention. The thing to do is to put a special section IN CHARGE OF THAT EMERGENCY and route anything related to it to that special section for full orderly handling. Get the rest of the place properly organized and conducting business as usual.

It takes a while for an organized activity such as an office to become a shattered wreck. However, an SP put into it as an exec can speed this process up greatly.

Therefore, anyone seeking to handle the confused area must detect the symptoms early and handle early.

THE LATER THE SITUATION IS NOTICED THE HARDER IT WILL BE AND THE LONGER IT WILL TAKE TO BUILD IT BACK UP AGAIN.

The next time you get a DEFENSIVE ANSWER, a SLOW COMPLIANCE or a NO–REPORT, realize that you have on your hands right there, whether in one person or an org, the symptoms of a situation you must handle. It is any one of from (A) to (E) above.

Honestly and dispassionately figure out which one it is. And realize if it is (D) (not wearing a hat) it could be a symptom of an SP so watch it until you know his (a) case status, (b) ethics record and (c) production record or you could make a mistake.

If it's any one of these, (A) to (E), you can find out by dispassionate analysis based on facts.

But in any event the situation MUST be handled. What is wrong *must* be remedied.

L. RON HUBBARD
Founder

HCO POLICY LETTER OF 22 JULY 1971R
REVISED 22 JANUARY 1991

Remimeo
All Bureaux Hats
OEC

Admin Know-How Series 25R

CLOs, OTLs AND FLAG

Refs:

HCO PL 14 Sept. 69   AKH Series 22
THE KEY INGREDIENTS

HCO PL 8 May 70   AKH Series 24
DISTRACTION AND NOISE

The PLs of the Data Series

PURPOSE OF CLOs

TO MAKE PLANNING BECOME AN ACTUALITY is the key message of the Key Ingredients.

This also unlocks the door to an understanding of Continental Liaison Offices and Operation and Transport Liaison Offices.

Unless the staff of a CLO or OTL knows the purpose of its existence, it ceases to exist as it will be of no real use.

A CLO or OTL must be of USE to FLAG and ORGS and missions and the public. If it is not, then it will become valueless and a burden.

If it does know and if every staff member in it knows its purpose, then it will prosper and its staff will prosper. If not, it will become unmocked and confused.

THE MAJOR PURPOSE OF A CLO OR OTL IS TO MAKE FLAG PLANNING BECOME AN ACTUALITY IN ORGS, MISSIONS AND THEREBY THE VARIOUS PUBLICS.

STEPS

In THE KEY INGREDIENTS you find a cycle of management as follows:

1. Observation

2. Planning

3. Communicating

4. Supervision

5. Production

6. Users.

Plans in this PL include programs and projects and are the duty of FLAG.

CLOs and OTLs fit exactly at (1) *Observation* and (4) *Supervision*.

Orgs fit at (5) *Production* and the publics at (6) *Users*.

(3) Communication occurs internally at Flag; between Flag and CLOs; internally at CLOs; between CLOs and orgs and missions; and between orgs and missions and the publics. There is also internal communication amongst the publics and within each public, known as "word-of-mouth advertising" and "goodwill." Laying out this network of communication is an interesting exercise, for you will see that it is becoming global—over the whole world. In addition to increasing understanding, this will give one a concept of the true size of the operation. "Publics" is a public relations term meaning a type of "users."

OTLs are an extension of CLOs for the CLO.

If you can conceive of this network of communication, you can then work out the remaining KEY INGREDIENTS.

OBSERVATION

Orgs observe for CLOs. OTLs observe for CLOs.

The Stats In-Charge of an org, the Finance Banking Officer of an org, the Bureaux Liaison Officer in an org, the mission holders and individuals of the publics are all *Observers* (No. 1 of Key Ingredients). They send their observations to OTLs and to CLOs.

In the Data Bureau of a CLO, these observations are duplicated and CIC processed for local CLO use but are at once also sent swiftly on to Flag.

In the Data Bureau at Flag, all these observations are assembled by continent and org and evaluated.

From this Flag evaluation (see Data Series on how it is done exactly), (2) of the Key Ingredients, PLANNING can occur. This step, for our purposes, includes finding the major international successes and outnesses and the big Whys or reasons for them. Flag puts these into programs and projects and sends them out via CLOs to orgs and sometimes missions.

CLOs and their OTLs now come into their own. They SUPERVISE getting these programs and projects in and done. This is the bureaux system's PRODUCTION.

The organization and its production results are of course expressed with the publics which are thereby served and increased as USERS.

Thus all the KEY INGREDIENTS line up.

418

FLAG PLANNING

On Flag the basic overall effort is *designed* and *planned*. The *big, broad* situations are spotted and the Whys (reasons for them) found.

The plans, programs and projects turned out by Flag are designed to press on with the major international designs and to spot major falterings or outnesses.

The results are policy, tech, programs and projects.

In general, Flag does not work on things that fit only an individual org.

What Flag plans and makes projects for fit a type of org or all orgs and are for the applications of orgs to the various publics.

By proven statistics, what Flag plans will improve or boom an area if it is applied.

Where Flag planning, represented by programs or projects, is actually gotten into full action in an org, that org will boom.

Also, by long historical proof, where an org or area neglects or doesn't execute Flag planning and its programs and projects, there is a collapse.

This isn't PR. This is the story of the years.

If Flag planning got into full activity in every area, we would have the planet.

For instance, the GI boom is the old Flag tours orders suddenly reactivated and carried brilliantly into effect in the Pac area. Flag was putting tours data and tours training together for a year before the present GI boom. This was then beautifully carried out by splendid initiative in the Pac area and spread.

The resulting production of GI came about because Sea Org officers brilliantly did it with a spark and spirit beautiful to behold. And it was successful because orgs were now being headed by Flag-trained Flag Executive Briefing Course grads. *Policy* was now going in. And the only falter was where policy was departed from or was not asked for.

So Flag planning *if executed* has a long historical background of huge success.

CLO ACTIONS

This brings us straight to the real duties of a Continental Liaison Office and its branches called OTLs.

A CLO is in charge of its continental areas. It has direct comm with orgs. Has or will have Finance Banking Officers and Bureaux Liaison Officers in each org.

The first duty of a CLO is to observe and get those observations into its own Continental Information Center (CIC) and observations and reports and lists of *its own activities* to Flag.

What are these activities? They are:

A. To observe.

B. To send observations by users, orgs and the publics to Flag.

C. To push in Flag programs and projects.

D. To FIND the WHY (reasons) that any *Flag* program or project is *not* going in, in an org or mission or public and REMEDY THAT WHY so the Flag program or project DOES go in.

E. Keep itself set up and operating on the pattern planned for its establishment by Flag.

F. Handle sudden emergencies.

Those are the TOTAL duties of a CLO.

They are also the duties of an OTL in respect to its CLO.

ORGS

Orgs and missions push in Flag programs and projects by department and division and also by individual staff members.

At org level and the level of its publics, the org is doing (A) to (F) above.

A Bureaux Liaison Officer or an FBO in an org is doing (A) to (F) and answering to an OTL or CLO.

The OTL handles one or more orgs as an expanded arm of the CLO and it is doing (A) to (F).

The CLO is working at the level of individual orgs and missions and their publics through them.

Flag works through CLOs, then to OTLs or orgs to the publics.

It would be highly informative to lay all this out in clay. For it IS the winning pattern. Where it is not understood, an area breaks down and needs emergency actions.

SIMPLICITY

The floods of information pouring through these lines make them appear far more complex than they are.

That a CLO runs its own service org does not violate this in any way. That's just another *org* to run.

Let us take an actual example.

Data coming in to Flag over a long period indicated few auditors being made and slow (unbelievably slow) courses over the whole world. Several observations were ordered by Flag at one time and another.

The situation was very serious. Slow courses meant no real delivery. It meant an org had to work too long for too low a payment. It meant no auditors available. It meant no students would enroll because they couldn't spare that much time. Orgs couldn't get Class VIs home from SHSBCs.

Observations piled up and up and up. A three-week course on Flag would become a six-month course in orgs. It defied belief.

After a long, long study of all this and firsthand experience at Flag, some Whys began to show up. The HCO PL 16 Mar. 71, WHAT IS A COURSE?, was one answer. The Flag Course Supervisors Course designed to be taught in the service org of a CLO. TRs the Hard Way came out of this.

Each one of these, and projects based on them, went out from Flag to CLOs and thus to orgs.

Then the big outness exploded into view. The June–Sept 1964 Study Tapes were NOT in use in courses!!!! That was the major WHY.

At once the Word Clearing tech was repiloted on Flag. Simplified versions were worked out. HCOBs were written.

Projects to get them in were written.

A whole series of drills, one for every possible Supervisor action, were swiftly put into form by an on-Flag mission and piloted.

These, as programs and projects, are pouring out to CLOs to orgs by rapid communication as fast as packaged from Training and Services Bu Flag.

Assistant Training and Services Aides in CLO Training and Services Bureaux should see that they get into each org and mission, using CLO's LRH Comm and External Comm Bureaux.

In orgs, LRH Comms or Bureaux Liaison Officers should get them checked out and *in*.

And EVERY ORG WHICH DOES NOT AT ONCE GET THEM IN AND IN FULL USE is of immediate interest to the CLO Data Bureau. The Training and Services Assistant Aide should be working to get his org contacts to give him data to find out WHY they are not IN. And Action should be alerted so it can send a CLO mission to find out WHY or remedy the already found Why.

OTHER DUTIES

"Noise" (HCO PL 8 May 70, DISTRACTION AND NOISE) is the main reason this does not happen.

The org is in a flap of unworn hats, no personnel and the milk bill.

The CLO Training and Services Bu is trying to handle a sick exec.

Noise! Every bit of noise being generated is because the main situations are not being handled, only the dev-t around them.

Like an HAS who has no time to hire because he is so busy with internal personnel demands, an org or CLO can be so knocked around by nonsense generated on the fringes of an unhandled situation that the real reasons do not get handled.

So "other duties" seem to be so important in an org or a CLO that they do not carry the line through. Why are they so distracted by so many outnesses? Because the main line is not in!

There are NO other duties more important than remedying the reason one has so many other duties!

FLAG REMEDIES

The remedies come from Flag. They are based on area observations from many sources.

CLO DUTY EXAMPLE

To construct an example of a real CLO in action:

The Asst Management Aide of a CLO finds her project board blank for Bongville. CIC of the CLO states no reports are coming in from Bongville org. The last stats sent were poor. There is natter in Bongville's field.

On A/Mgmt Aide request, CLO's Action Bureau writes the MOs for, briefs and fires a single observer missionaire.

In Bongville, the CLO's missionaire manages to find the "Exec Director" Bongville (who is not the ED supposed to be there according to CLO personnel records).

The following conversation takes place:

The org's ED says, "Your CLO has no reality on what's going on here in this org." Question: (from CLO missionaire) Do you ever send any data or reports or stats? "No, we haven't time for that. We keep going broke." Question: Do you know Flag policy relating to pricing and financial planning? "No, we're too busy. All this questioning is just too distracting. The landlord is threatening eviction." Question: How much money have you invoiced in the last month? "Oh, very little." Question: But I see you have a full classroom of students. Have they all paid? "Oh, they've been here a year. They paid long ago . . . I think." Question: Have you put the Flag Word Clearing Project into effect so they'll finish their courses? "The what?" Question: Have you sent anyone to the CLO Tours Course? "Please, I've got to go now. The HAS just transferred the Course Super to the Estate Section and our only auditor to Ethics Officer and I've got to tell our afternoon pcs to come back tomorrow. . . ."

TELEGRAM: TO CO CLO. ADVISE YOU SEND A MISSION WITH A HAS AND AN AUDITOR AND FBO TO BONGVILLE FAST TO HOLD IT. SUGGEST TWO BONGVILLE STAFF MEMBERS TO CLO TOURS COURSE AND TWO OF THESE EXECS TO FEBC. NO FLAG PROJECTS IN. CURRENT ED JOQUIM SOKUM DISTRACTED DISCOURTEOUS TO SO. CHECK

422

OF INVOICES REVEALS $18,000 UNCOLLECTED FROM STUDENTS NOW ON COURSE. NEEDS FBO AND FINANCE INSPECTOR TO SET UP TREAS AND COLLECT. ADVISE OFFICE OF SPECIAL AFFAIRS RE LANDLORD EVICTING ORG. NO DSA HERE. BEST = MISSION BONGVILLE OBSERVER.

Now the observation mission went out because the CLO Data Bureau found Bongville was not reporting.

This telegram meets up in CLO's Data Bureau CIC with a ton of public complaints in the Bongville area.

A rapid evaluation is done by the CLO CIC Evaluator using any current data on Bongville.

The Why taken from CLO CIC evaluation turns out to be an illegal promotion to Bongville ED of a blown PTS staff member from Chongton Org who put the whole staff in Treason and blew them.

The CLO Product Officer goes into action for the product of a functioning org.

CLO Action Mission Orders for a new SO temporary ED and HAS for Bongville are quickly written, the mission briefed and 24 hours later they are in Bongville handling. The Officer of Special Affairs is put in touch with the landlord. The CLO Finance Office sends an FBO. A/Dissem Aide reroutes a tour to include Bongville.

The new FBO forces $7,000 in collections by Friday, and gets a Treasury Sec on post and hatted and the Flag Invoice Pack goes in.

The HAS phones the fired Bongville auditors, gets three back. Auditing resumes. Six students are word cleared and completed on course and the Flag Intern Pgm goes in and they begin to work in the HGC making nine auditors now delivering.

The tech member gets the Mini Super Hat on the Course Super. The Flag Word Clearing Pack goes in.

Two tours students and two execs get routed via the CLO for training on the Flag checksheet courses.

The ex-ED and the ex-HAS are put on as "HCO Expeditors" pending further handling.

The HAS reverts the org to cancel out the mad musical chairs, begins to recruit, form an expeditor pool, train and hat by Flag project orders and checksheets.

The temporary SO ED produces by coping.

The scene begins to untangle to the degree that policy and Flag projects begin to go in.

The Flag ARC break program begins to go in and begins to straighten out ARC breaks in Central Files.

One month later, the tours students are back from CLO. The org is rebuilt enough to deliver. Money begins to roll in.

Two months later the first FEBC comes back, is genned in as Exec Dir.

The second one returns. Is genned in as HAS.

They are told to get two more people to the FEBC fast and a DSA is sent for training at OSA request.

Flag projects are well in.

The CLO mission pulls out.

The org remains stable but is carefully watched by the Asst Management Aide at the CLO via her project board.

Meanwhile, all reports and data have been flowing to the CLO and to Flag.

Flag compares its data, evaluates this and other orgs. Finds ex-staff members who have blown from an org are uniformly PTS. A local Flag project to develop more data and tech on PTS begins. . . .

And the cycle repeats.

The CLO gets in the PTS project.

When an org doesn't get it in according to a CLO Management Bu project board, data is looked for in the files and an evaluation is done on the orgs that didn't get it in. If no data, an observer is sent. . . .

And that's the cycle.

The Flag Why for the Bongville incident would be a CLO in that area not manned up and operating fully and not getting Flag projects in.

The CLO basic Why that let Bongville go to pieces would be that the CLO did not watch its Flag project board and did not notice Bongville was not getting in any projects and was not reporting.

The basic Why in Bongville was the promotion of unqualified persons to ED and HAS who did not know or try to get in Flag projects and instead went ethics-mad when they began to fail.

SUMMARY

A CLO is there to observe and to get Flag programs and projects in.

When a CLO doesn't report or backlogs, it gets Bongvilles.

It handles Bongvilles. It must have its Assistant Aides, its bureaux, especially a Data Bu, and a management project board, a Missionaire Unit, and an Action Bureau to handle Bongvilles.

But every Bongville it has to handle will be because Flag programs and

424

projects weren't going in, in Bongville and the CLO didn't find WHY they weren't going in soon enough.

Flag level—International Whys applying to all orgs.

CLO level—Continental Whys to remedy to get Flag pgms and projects in.

Org level—Divisional and departmental and individual Whys that prevent Flag programs and projects from going in.

So that's the reason for a CLO:

To observe and to send all data to Flag and to continentally find out WHY Flag projects and programs are not going in, in an org and remedy that Why and get the programs and projects in.

That's a CLO.

L. RON HUBBARD
Founder

Revision assisted by
LRH Technical Research
and Compilations

Remimeo
Exec Hats

ADMIN KNOW–HOW No. 26

(Cancels HCO PL 19 Dec. 69, EXECUTIVE
DUTIES, which cancelled HCO PL 19 July 63.)

Note: HCO PL 19 July 63, ADMINISTRATIVE STABLE DATA, stated that an executive should "get people to get the work done." HCO PL 19 Dec. 69, EXECUTIVE DUTIES, cancelled it and stated other duties.

This cancellation probably robbed some people of a stable datum that they got people to get the work done.

When an executive was no longer told he should get people to get the work done, hatting tended to go out and a great deal of overload began to occur on executive posts.

From an executive not doing "work" the viewpoint swung to the other extreme that executives only do all the work.

Both policy letters (HCO PL 19 Dec. 69 and 19 July 63) were correct in their way.

Therefore they are restated as follows.

PHASE I—BEGINNING A NEW ACTIVITY

AN EXECUTIVE SINGLE–HANDS WHILE HE TRAINS HIS STAFF.

When he has people producing, functioning well and hatted, he then enters the next phase:

PHASE II—RUNNING AN ESTABLISHED ACTIVITY

AN EXECUTIVE GETS PEOPLE TO GET THE WORK DONE.

SINGLE–HANDING

By "single-handing" one means do it himself, being the one responsible for actually handling things.

This phase occurs when an executive is forming up his personnel.

PHASE I IN FULL

(HCO PL 19 Dec. 69, EXECUTIVE DUTIES, is therefore requoted for this phase of the activity—he is on the post, most of the rest are new and flubby.)

An executive handles the whole area while he gets people to help.

An executive in charge of an org would "single-hand" (handle it all) while getting others to handle their jobs in turn.

This gives a practical and workable approximation of what top-stat executives actually do do.

The executive who sits back and waits for others to act when a situation is grave can crash an entire activity.

Essentially an executive is a working individual who can competently handle any post or machine or plan under him.

He is a training officer as well. He designates who is to do what and sees that a training action is done by himself or others to be sure the post will be competently held. An executive who accepts the idea that if a person has a school degree in "waffing wogglies" or sewing on buttons he can at once be trusted to waff wogglies or sew buttons is taking a personnel by recommendation, not by his experience with the personnel whose work-organization potential has never been tested *under that executive.* A camouflaged hole (undetected neglect area) may very well develop in such a circumstance, which can suddenly confront the executive with a time-consuming disaster.

Thus an executive accepts help conditionally until it is demonstrated to be help, and meanwhile does not relax his control of a sector below him until he is sure it is functioning.

In this way an executive is one who does and backs off spots continually. He could be said to always be doing himself out of a job by getting the job competently done. However, in actual practice, as post personnel does shift, he has to be prepared at any time to wade back in and put it right.

The supreme test of an executive (as in the HCOB SUPREME TEST OF A THETAN) is to MAKE THINGS GO RIGHT.

To the degree he can maintain his observation, communicate and get supervision done (see HCO PL on the Key Ingredients), he can achieve production or service and satisfy users.

As observation is often faulty, especially over long distances, as communication is not always received or studied and as supervision is often absent, the executive must develop a sensitivity to indicators of outnesses and systems to correct them.

A very good executive knows how to "play the org board" under him. He has to know every function in it. He has to know who to call on to do what or he disorganizes things badly.

An executive also has to know neighboring org board arrangements in the same org, the org board of allies and of enemies.

An executive has to know what users need and want and furnish it. When normal and routine posts fail under him, the executive is of course forced into Non-Existence as an executive, has to find what is needed and wanted and produce it. He applies the whole Non-Existence formula to the situation.

Only if he does not handle fully once he does see an outness does an executive go into Liability.

An executive deals with the frailty of human variations and distractions. When these engulf his area and he is confronted with the fruits of alteration and noncompliance, of posts not held and duties suddenly found left undone, it is up to the executive to get them done any way he can. Having handled, he applies the Danger Formula (or lower as it appears) to the neglected area.

An executive has to be somebody who cares about his job and wants to get things done. If he only wishes the title for status, he is of course heading himself and his area for disaster and it could be said that such an executive, not meaning to do the job but only wanting the title, is in Doubt or lower on the third dynamic.

The executive thinks of the area and organization first and repairs. Then he thinks of the individual and straightens him out.

An executive who is worker-oriented winds up hurting all the workers. The workers depend on the organization. When that is gone they have nothing.

An organization cannot have more taken out of it than is being put into it. Efforts to bleed an organization of more blood than it has, destroys it.

The preservation of his organization is a first consideration of an executive.

In an executive's hands an organization or one of its areas must be "VIABLE." That is, it must be capable of supporting itself and thus staying alive. When his area is parasitic, dependent on others outside it, without producing more than it consumes, the area and its workers are at severe risk and in the natural course of events will be dispensed with, if not at once, eventually.

Thus an executive is someone whose own sweat and energy keeps an organization or an area of it functioning. In this he earns and uses help and they in turn take over executive roles in their subordinate areas and keep them alive and producing.

An executive is in the business of SURVIVAL of his area and its people and providing with service or production an abundance which makes the area, his own services and that of his subordinates valuable.

If an executive so functions his own survival and increase is guaranteed even by natural law. If an executive functions for other reasons it is certain the ground will vanish from under him eventually again by natural law.

An executive is in fact a worker who can do all and any of the work in the area he supervises and who can note and work rapidly to repair any outnesses observed in the functioning of those actions in his charge.

The best-liked executive who is most valued by his workers as someone they need is an executive who functions as described above. One who seeks to survive on favors given and does not otherwise measure up is not in fact regarded highly by anyone.

Whatever ideology one finds himself in, the above still applies. The way to the top may well be marrying the boss's daughter, but the way to stay there still requires the elements described herein. As bosses' daughters are few, a sounder way is to learn all the jobs well and study this policy and just become an executive.

PHASE II IN FULL

Now we come to PHASE II. The executive has inherited from a competent former executive or has himself built (and has prevented transfers and lack of apprenticeship from destroying) his unit, department, division, org or orgs.

Now to continue to single-hand will destroy anything that has been built.

The other policy letter (HCO PL 19 July 63) now applies and is so reissued.

When an executive in charge of a working activity continues to retain the idea "Do all I can," chaos then results. An already formed activity will collapse.

The only possible datum on which an executive could work effectively in a formed activity is *"Get people to get the work done."*

Otherwise the executive does as much as he can and leaves the willing personnel standing around unhelped and unguided. If we all did this, Scientology would go nowhere. One auditor can't audit the world. One personnel cannot do all the work of a Scientology organization.

If each person in the organization wears all the hats or one wears all and the rest wear none, you will have:

1. Bad morale,

2. Overburdened personnel,

3. Underburdened personnel,

4. Rapid staff turnover,

5. Bad dissemination, processing and instruction,

6. Low income,

7. Even lower income,

8. Public flaps,

9. Chaos.

An executive in a formed org has only two jobs:

1. Policy, promotion and planning,

2.   Getting people to get the job done.

A post or terminal is an assigned area of responsibility and action which is supervised in part by an executive. Supervision means helping people to understand their jobs. Supervision means giving them the responsibility and wherewithal to do their jobs. Supervision includes the granting of beingness. Supervision does not mean doing the job supervised.

Thus you have two phases and shades of gray in between.

At a slight sag or a mess-up or failure to hire and hat and apprentice properly, a PHASE II situation can drop back into a single-handing PHASE I. An executive who again doesn't see that he has dropped out of comfortable Phase II and gotten into a PHASE I must at once again single-hand, if only for a day.

But now the executive MUST get in ethics, hire, hat and apprentice people and build once more to PHASE II.

In short, an executive has to know how to change gears!

To BOOM dissemination and income and hold the boom, study this well and be able to shift not only from comfortable II to hectic, overworked I but also to push back to Phase II.

This is the reality of it.

L. RON HUBBARD
Founder

Admin Know-How Series 27 and 28

[*Note:* Admin Know-How Series numbers 27 and 28 were never assigned and do not exist as numbered issues in this series.]

Remimeo
All Exec Hats

Admin Know-How Series 29

Executive Series 5

NOT–DONES, HALF–DONES AND BACKLOGS

There is a very definite, often unsuspected effect concealed in a backlog. And it is of such violence that it can crash an area's stats while seemingly working frantically.

BACKLOG (Webster's) noun: 3. an increasing accumulation of tasks unperformed or materials not processed; verb: to accumulate as a backlog.

NOT–DONES AND HALF–DONES

Backlogs occur for various reasons. But the two main classes are (1) NOT–DONES and (2) HALF–DONES.

For lack of seeing that a backlog exists, lack of supervision of existing personnel, other-intentionedness of personnel, lack of personnel to handle the usual or peak volumes, lack of know-how to handle, lack of resources, and outright sabotage are some of the reasons that account for NOT–DONES.

HALF–DONES are as bad as NOT–DONES as they bit and piece an area into a quagmire. Suppose Detroit began to make half-cars. All their resources would be devoured, yet nothing would really be produced, yet everyone would look frantically busy; the executive worries would mount up to an inconceivable fever pitch unless the half-done factor was handled.

But half-dones are not always as visible as half-cars. "Have you handled Bets and Company suit?" "Oh yes." But the case is lost because the filing papers were only half-prepared and half-filed.

The same reasons apply for HALF–DONES as are listed above for NOT–DONES.

The Why of many failures is found in NOT–DONES and HALF–DONES.

The primary effect (there are others) of NOT–DONES and HALF–DONES is the building up of *backlogs*.

Now, no backlog ever quietly lies there. So long as anything else depended upon the actions being done, there will be pressure or threat of one kind or another on the backlogged area.

Thus, when an activity becomes backlogged, IT GENERATES NEW WORK NOT CONCERNED WITH REDUCING THE BACKLOG AMOUNT.

Example: An insurance company backlogs claims payments. Torrents of queries then demand why. The claims section spends its time answering the queries, not reducing the number of claims. The volume of work doubles, trebles, but no claims get paid.

BACKLOGGING AT ONCE DOUBLES THE WORK BY THE ADDITION OF DEMAND HANDLING.

Example: A Central Files fails to stay filed into up to present time. Demands for items in it cause others to consume all the file clerk's time tearing CF apart to find particles.

A BACKLOG CAN INCREASE ITSELF BY ADDING DISORDER THAT UNDOES THINGS ALREADY DONE.

Thus a backlog tears up the past work while building up future work.

Example: Personnel backlogs its files, causing it to backlog appointments. This overloads areas. These areas start crashing down on Personnel in mobs demanding it provide people. Personnel is then so busy fending off people, it can't appoint. Yet is in frantic action.

A BACKLOG PREVENTS ITSELF FROM BEING HANDLED.

––––––––––

An org that has several backlogs in it becomes frantic and then goes into apathy.

The cure is to:

1. Get people and do ALL HANDS actions to get the most important backlogs done.

2. To find the real WHY of the backlog and handle it so a present time state is then maintained. (Requires a program, followed and *done*.)

3. Check out staff on the book *The Problems of Work*.

4. Get staff to do Training Drill Zero on their work areas.

5. Get staff to reach and withdraw from their materials of operation or areas.

6. Do a survey of attitudes which reveals complaints and reasons for not-dones, half-dones, backlogs.

7. Based on the survey, campaign hard to remedy NOT–DONES and HALF–DONES.

8. Be very severe with any beginnings of any future backlogs.

––––––––––

When you see an area or org in apathy, know it has gone the route of not-dones, half-dones and backlogs and handle.

When you see an area going frantic, know you are looking at not-dones, half-dones and backlogs and handle fast before it goes into the much worse condition of apathy.

Production is the basis of morale.

Not-dones, half-dones result in backlogs.

Backlogs destroy the possibility of future production.

Thus you know the situation of not-dones and half-dones will result in backlogs.

The backlogs will prevent further handling.

This subject *is* the subject which makes executives harassed.

Behind every upset there will be NOT–DONES, HALF–DONES and BACK-LOGS.

So be very alert.

Dynamite is stick candy alongside of this very explosive subject.

Don't say I didn't tell you.

L. RON HUBBARD
Founder

Remimeo

ADMIN KNOW–HOW No. 30

How is it that the highest paid salaried men in our current civilization are administrators? They draw from a quarter to a third of a million dollars per year. They are paid far, far more than professional people, far more than scientists, more than politicians who, above all people, should be excellent administrators. Why? Because they are so rare. Business schools may turn out graduates by the millions but very, very, very few of them ever become topflight executives who can really administer. Why does the civilization develop so very few of them? Because this civilization has not had much workable administrative tech and has not even known the basic natural laws which underlie administration.

The subject of administration is so poorly known because there is so little data. And because there is so little, the subject itself is not understood at all by the general population of the planet. Yet there are very few on the planet who are not the direct effect of administrators.

You hear an administrator talk about PRODUCTION or GROSS INCOME and possibly suppose this is just a peculiarity or a fixation and that these facts are distant from general living. Perhaps some people suppose that such talk and urgings is part of the capitalistic system or something for a board of directors. General public reaction to such things is usually a nothing-to-do-with-me. The usual attitude to law and accounting is a "beyond me" and an "it's confusing" yet the person is subject every day of his life to them. It is quite similar but even more mysterious with administration.

Administration is not peculiar to capitalism. Or to any special field. It embraces all of them, even law and accounting which are, in actual fact, administrative specialties.

Let us look at this abundant and glaring evidence: Russia cannot feed her people. She cannot clothe them. She has fantastic troubles in moving them about. Russia, despite her PR, is a failure. She is a failure, not because few people agree with her ideology, indeed, that ideology has crept reachingly over the world.

And let us look at the capitalist juggling money, moneybags and paper gold and look as well at the health problems and cultural unrest that ride as problems in his train. The severest criticism of the capitalist is that communism and socialism grew up and flourished during his reign.

And look at the clanking, swanking military dictators who have replaced the weak and diseased kings who once ruled the world. They are themselves replaced by their own kind as fast as firing squads can be assembled by newly ambitious dictators.

Why do these ideologies fail and why are they so oppressive while they last?

THEY HAVE TOO FEW TRAINED AND SKILLED ADMINISTRATORS WHO CAN GET A SHOW ON THE ROAD.

The SURVIVAL of any group depends utterly upon things like PRODUCTION and EXCHANGE. That is the way the universe runs. When these factors are not competently handled, the group is in poverty or vanishes.

Civilizations have not vanished because they had the wrong ideologies or ran out of resources. First and foremost they vanished because they had no technology of the mind and could not handle people because they did not know the basic fundamentals of life. And right along following that, they did not really know the tech of administration or even what administrators were or could do.

Their survival was in question the moment they did things with individuals contrary to the basic laws of life: They began to believe they would get reaction A by some strange rite, but instead of that got reaction B. They not only did not have mental technology, they adopted practices contrary to basic laws. And so they were torn with revolts. And wars.

And their survival fell to nothing when they did not know or practice fundamental administration and violated the basic rules through ignorance or sloth.

If one is going to have a group in this universe that survives and wins through its obstacles, it must have and apply basic laws. It does not have to be a perfect group but it must not be an ignorant group.

While the happiness of the individual may depend upon mental tech, apart from any group, he cannot survive well as a group member if he has no knowledge or understanding of administrative tech.

If one goes on living in this universe, he is sooner or later the subject of administration as a member of a group. In cave days, if one had to stay in his cave starving because of a saber-toothed tiger prowling, he would have had two choices: He either stayed in his cave and starved to death or he learned about saber-toothed tigers; when he knew about saber-toothed tigers he would now have new choices of how to avoid, how to kill or even how to employ saber-toothed tigers; when he had settled this he would now have a path of action he could predict. The jungle in which he lived was subject to certain rules, no matter who laid them down, God or the old, old Biological Survey. In other words, even in cave days one was the effect of an administrator.

When one had solved the crude tooth-and-claw existence, one could rise to a small niche of administering on his own; animals could be domesticated, plants when planted would grow, wood when carved would make things, metal when formed would make things that made things.

The moment one was headed in the direction of survival he was headed in the direction of production. So many killed deer made so many meals; it also made so many hides which made so many beds and jackets. The exchange with the deer was quite unequal as there was nothing for the deer and the deer protested by ceasing to exist and one got into goats and cattle. Similarly, when the wild roots gave out, for there was no exchange for the roots, one had to plant

435

them and tend them. Consumption any way one looked at it eventually got into production that equalized, or tended to, exchange.

When one could administer a small area, so many plants, so many goats, he was in his own right something of an administrator. He learned there was technical tech and he learned there was administrative tech also. And these things of all others continued to guide his survival.

One can of course decide not to go on living in this universe. But now he falls into two new choices: He either goes to another universe or drops into a sort of self-cave. In the other universe he will probably find himself under a new administrator or a new set of rules even if he alone makes them. And if he chooses a sort of nowhere self-cave, he has done so because he never solved the saber-toothed tigers.

Thus one is confronted with certain incontrovertible facts. (1) HE MUST SEEK THE TECH OF SURVIVAL AND APPLY IT; (2) HE WILL SURVIVE AS WELL AS HE CAN ADMINISTER OR HANDLE ADMINISTRATION.

As a member of any group, the PRODUCTION and GROSS INCOME or EXCHANGE he hears his executives talking about APPLIES TO HIM DIRECTLY. What ideology or system one embraces, his well-being, his safety, his happiness, will relate to PRODUCTION and EXCHANGE and the ease with which these are attained or maintained is determined directly by his understanding of and ability to handle administration.

There are thousands and thousands and thousands who might give you far, far different basics for life. But watch it! They are touting for some administrator or seeking to avoid ALL administration in every case, one or the other!

One either lone-wolfs his life or one gets through with a group. In the first place, one must think mainly of personal money or one must think of the group's survival. The regulating factors in either case are ADMINISTRATION resulting in PRODUCTION and EXCHANGE.

Bank robber or bank president, these harsh facts of life still apply. Democratic politician or autocratic commissar, these are still the main determining factors of life.

The welfare state seems so wonderful a dream to the socialist: Why is it then that ghetto people riot because THEY HAVE NO JOBS but are only on welfare? It is true, surveys show. The recipients of welfare, whether a Roman guttersnipe, a white Swede or a Black American become crippled as beings: They are the TOTAL effect of administration, they have no cause factor short of a riot. They want JOBS. For they instinctively realize that they are in little better position than the cave man with the saber-toothed tiger outside. They have been disenfranchised as members of the group, dwellers of the universe. They cannot exchange, a somewhat fearful thing, they do not produce and they are forbidden causative control or causative administration. They recognize, no matter how dimly, that they have been set up as zeros. And this is not only unhappy, it is dangerous.

Reversely, when people offer nothing in exchange, do not produce and cannot or will not administer, they become pawns. Sometimes they think they are merely the subject of meanness or rancor. But if they do not produce or exchange and cannot share in administration, they become zeros. Their fate is decided already, by themselves. It would not matter for a moment what some administrator did or did not do, such people have reduced their survival to a point that it is prey to the lightest wind. These facts are as inevitable as "apples fall," as harshly real as a tiger's claw and as predictable as tonight's darkness. Their only possible choices are (1) to cease to exist (which is impossible for a thetan) or (2) get in a position or situation or state of mind to produce, exchange and administer. There is a third choice—to leave this universe.

Life is, or can be, a pretty grim proposition. One may float along on the production of others like the recently demised "leisure class" of 19th century infamy or like a hobo being chased by every householder and cop. One can go along in the numb world of the middle class watching his public docility while he hypocritically sins behind doors and conforms with a capital C. One can creakingly labor in the world of the endlessly-being-dug ditch for some unknown pipe. Or one can simply confront the whole thing, pain, misemotion, punishments, rewards and all and produce and exchange and learn to handle the administrative system he is in and himself administer his life and environ.

One can hear countless reasons why it is too awful or too deadly to find out about the tiger. But you hear these reasons from the cowardly dead.

One can hear a million arguments against being a tiger or the administrator who orders tigers about. But one is talking to people who are not *living*.

The stark facts are these: One knows and handles administration, one produces, one exchanges OR one dies as far as this universe is concerned.

That's why you hear an administrator who means well for the group talking about PRODUCTION and EXCHANGE. That is why one never hears a politician who means ill for the group mention them.

And that's why the person who can use administration to bring about production and exchange is so highly paid by status and respect or why his group is so highly paid. He is dealing in SURVIVAL. And the skills he uses are well worth knowing and using.

> Caves are damp.
> Bring on the tigers!
> The sun is shining.

L. RON HUBBARD
Founder

Admin Know-How Series 31

ADMINISTRATIVE SKILL

An administrator is one who can make things happen at the other end of a communication line which result in discovered data or handled situations.

A very good administrator can get things handled over a very long distance. A mediumly skilled administrator has a shorter reach.

As this scale declines, we get people who can make things happen only at arm's length.

It is interesting that administrators are valued in direct proportion to the distance they can reach and get things handled over. Persons who can handle things only at arm's length are valued but not in proportion to a long-reaching administrator.

The complexity of situations and things handled is also a test of the administrator. If one began at the highest level of capability of handling things thousands of miles away and at the bottom of the scale handling things at arm's length, one would also find complexity entering the picture.

The artisan can, by means of heavy mest communication lines and tools, make all manner of things occur but mostly within his visual sight line.

The day laborer who can only handle a shovel usually can only handle the simplicity of lifting a few pounds of dirt to a definite position.

One of the troubles PTS people have, as an example, is handling something over a long-distance communication line. One can tell them to handle the suppressive, but one must realize he may also be giving the order to someone to handle another person several thousand miles away. This is a high level of administrative skill and is usually no part of a PTS's ability, whatever other technical considerations may intervene.

Estimating situations thousands of miles away and handling them terminatedly is actually comparable to an OT ability.

There is no effort here to include artists and technicians who do work with their hands, for this is another class of activity requiring enormous technical skill and ability.

However, very few people understand the administrator or what he is or what he can do, yet the whole world is the effect of good or bad administrators.

438

The administrator has technology with which to discover and handle situations and if he is a very good administrator his handling is ordinarily constructive; but whatever it is, it is firm.

A skilled administrator therefore can be defined as ONE WHO CAN ESTABLISH AND MAINTAIN COMMUNICATION LINES AND CAN THEREBY DISCOVER, HANDLE AND IMPROVE SITUATIONS AND CONDITIONS AT A DISTANCE.

When you fully grasp this and realize it is the basic simplicity that is the basic all of an administrator's further complex technology, you can estimate an administrator's efficiency or effectiveness.

If you are engaged in administration, this basic truth will serve you very well if you fully understand it and use it.

L. RON HUBBARD
Founder

Admin Know-How Series 32R

Q AND A CHECKSHEET
CHECKSHEET OF THE
HUBBARD CAUSATIVE LEADERSHIP COURSE

Any executive or officer or human being who does not know what Q and A is and indulges in it will inevitably cause dev-t, produce little or nothing and succumb.

Therefore this checksheet is a MUST for any executive.

NAME: _____   DATE STARTED: _____

ORG: _____   DATE COMPLETED: _____

POST: _____

1.	HCOB 21 Nov. 73	THE CURE OF Q AND A MAN'S DEADLIEST DISEASE	___ ___ ___
2.		Demo each paragraph and look up the Mis-U each time you can't.	___ ___ ___
3.	HCOB 5 Dec. 73	THE REASON FOR Q AND A	___ ___ ___
4.		Demo each paragraph and look up the Mis-U each time you can't.	___ ___ ___
5.	HCOB 24 May 62	"Q AND A" star-rate	___ ___ ___
6.	HCOB 13 Dec. 61	VARYING SEC CHECK QUESTIONS	___ ___ ___
7.	HCOB 22 Feb. 62	WITHHOLDS MISSED AND PARTIAL	___ ___ ___
8.	HCOB 29 Mar. 63	SUMMARY OF SECURITY CHECKING	___ ___ ___
9.	HCOB 7 Apr. 64	ALL LEVELS Q AND A	___ ___ ___
10.		TRs the Hard Way	___ ___ ___

11. Upper Indoc the Rough Way   — — —

12. Handling the not done, or "no interest" drug items from Drug RD or getting a full Drug RD.   — — —

12a. Introspection RD   — — —

13. 35 hours Op Pro by Dup given and received in co-audit (17½ each way).

          Received — — —

          Given — — —

14. HCOB 29 July 63 section "Q and A Drill"   — — —

15. HCOB 20 Nov. 73 II   F/N WHAT YOU ASK OR PROGRAM   — — —

16. Do in Clay: An auditor example of Q and A.   — — —

17. Do in Clay: An administrator's example of Q and A.   — — —

18. Do in Clay: How you have Qed and Aed with life.   — — —

19. Do in Clay: A Q and A with a body.   — — —

20. Do in Clay: A Q and A with a group.   — — —

21. Do in Clay: A correct auditor action in getting a question answered.   — — —

22. Do in Clay: A correct C/S action in getting a pc handled.   — — —

23. Do in Clay: An administrator correct non-Q and A action in getting a target done.   — — —

24. Do in Clay: A personnel correct non-Q and A action in getting a target done.   — — —

25. Do in Clay: Correct non-Q and A action in verifying a target reported done.   — — —

26. Do in Clay: A direct life handling of own life.   — — —

27. Do in Clay: A direct non-Q and A handling of own body.   — — —

28. Do in Clay: Straightforward handling the hell out of a situation.   — — —

29. Do in Clay: Straightforward handling
of a group.   ___ ___ ___

30. A final life result in real life
demonstrating that non-Q and A handling is
successful, attested and as a success story.   ___ ___ ___

31. Certificate as a "Competent Being" from
Certs and Awards.   ___ ___ ___

_____ Auditor Attest

_____ Super Attest

_____ Student Attest

L. RON HUBBARD
Founder

442

HCO POLICY LETTER OF 7 AUGUST 1976
Issue I

Remimeo
All Execs
All Purchasers

Admin Know-How Series 33

Establishment Officer Series 31

PRODUCT–ORG OFFICER SYSTEM
NAME YOUR PRODUCT

The product–org officer system, covered fully in Flag Executive Briefing Course tapes, contains the key phrase for any product officer. This is:

NAME, WANT AND GET YOUR PRODUCT.

Breaking this down into its parts we find that the most common failure of any product officer or staff member or Purchaser lies in the first item, NAME YOUR PRODUCT!

On org boards and even for sections, one has products listed. Departments have valuable final products. Every staff member has one or more products.

IF PRODUCTION IS NOT OCCURRING, THE ABILITY TO NAME THE PRODUCT IS PROBABLY MISSING.

Misunderstood post titles were collected once on a wide survey. Whenever it was found a staff member did not seem to be able to do his job, it was checked whether he knew the definition of the word—or words—that made up his post title. It was found, one for one, that he could not define it even though no un-usual or special definition was being requested. In other words, the first thing about the post could not be defined—the post title. This may seem incredible, but only until you yourself check it out on staff that habitually goof.

The ability to NAME the product required goes further than a mere, glib definition. Some engineers once drove a Purchaser halfway up the wall by glibly requesting "one dozen bolts." The Purchaser kept bringing back all different thicknesses and lengths and types of bolts. The Purchaser was going daffy and so were the engineers. Until the engineers were forced to exactly name what they were seeking by giving it ALL its name. The Purchaser trying to purchase could not possibly obtain his product without being able to FULLY name it. Once this was done, nothing was easier.

A product officer can ask, beg, plead, yell for his product. But maybe he isn't naming it! Maybe he isn't naming it fully. And maybe even he doesn't know the name of it. A product officer should spend some time exactly and accurately naming the exact product he wants before asking for it. Otherwise he and his staff may be struggling around over many misunderstood words!

When you see a staff whirling around and dashing into walls and each other and not producing a thing, calmly try to find out if any of them or their product officer can NAME what products they are trying to produce. Chances are, few of them can and maybe the product officer as well.

Handle and it will all smooth out and products will occur.

L. RON HUBBARD
Founder

HCO POLICY LETTER OF 7 AUGUST 1976
Issue II

Remimeo
All Execs
All Purchasers

Admin Know-How Series 34

Establishment Officer Series 32

PRODUCT–ORG OFFICER SYSTEM
WANT YOUR PRODUCT

A product officer has to name, WANT and get his product.

Where no real or valuable production is occurring, one has to ask the question, does the product officer really WANT the product he is demanding? And does the staff member or members he is dealing with WANT the product?

The reason that a psychotic or otherwise evilly-intentioned person cannot achieve anything as a product officer or staff member is that he does NOT want the product to occur. The intentions of psychos are aimed at destruction and not at creation.

Such persons may SAY they want the product but this is just "PR" and a cover for their real activities.

People who are PTS (potential trouble sources by reason of connections with people antagonistic to what they are doing in life) are all too likely to slide into the valence of the antagonistic person who definitely would NOT want the product.

Thus, in an org run by or overloaded with destructive persons or PTS persons, you see a very low level of production if you see any at all. And the production is likely to be what is called "an overt product," meaning a bad one that will not be accepted or cannot be traded or exchanged and has more waste and liability connected with it than it has value.

One has to actually WANT the product he is asking for or is trying to produce. There may be many reasons he does not, none of which are necessarily connected with being psycho. But if it is a creative and valuable product and assists his and the survival of others and he still does not want it, then one should look for PTSness or maybe even a bit of psychosis. And at the least, some withholds.

One does not have to be in a passionate, mystic daze about wanting the product. But one shouldn't be moving mountains in the road of a guy trying to carry some lumber to the house site either.

The question of WANT the product has to be included in any examination of reasons why a person or an org isn't producing.

L. RON HUBBARD
Founder

HCO POLICY LETTER OF 7 AUGUST 1976
Issue III

Remimeo
All Execs

Admin Know-How Series 35

Establishment Officer Series 33

PRODUCT–ORG OFFICER SYSTEM
TO GET YOU HAVE TO KNOW HOW TO ORGANIZE

A product officer and ESPECIALLY an org officer has to know how to GET a product.

All science and technology is built around this single point in the key phrase "Name, want and get your product." Managers and scientists specialize in the HOW TO GET part of it and very often neglect the rest.

There are many product officers who do NOT know enough about organization to organize things so they actually GET their product. These, all too often, cover up their ignorance on how to organize or their inability to do so by saying to one and all, "Don't organize, just produce!" When you hear this you can suspect that the person saying it actually does not know the tech or know-how of organizing or how to put an organization together. He may not even know enough about organizing to shove aside other paper on his desk when he is trying to spread out and read a large chart—yet that is simple organization.

A bricklayer would look awfully silly trying to lay no-bricks. He hasn't got any bricks. Yet there he is going through the motions of laying bricks. It takes a certain economic and purchasing and transport tech to get the bricks delivered—only then can you lay bricks.

A manager looks pretty silly trying to order a brick wall built when he doesn't have any bricks or bricklayer and provides no means at all of obtaining either one.

A product officer may be great at single-handing the show. How come? He doesn't realize that building a show comes before one runs it. And even though economics demand at least a small show before one builds a large show, a very bad product officer who can't really organize either, will, instead of making the small show bigger, make the small show smaller by trying to run a no-show.

There is a HOW of organization. It is covered pretty well in the Org Series and elsewhere. Like you can't put in comm lines unless you put in terminals for them to connect with. Like you can't get particles flowing in a profitable way unless they have something for them to run *on*. That's simply the way things go in the universe in which you are operating. Now of course you could build a new universe with different laws but the fact is, that would require a knowledge of organization as well, wouldn't it?

The tech of how to produce something can be pretty vast. One doesn't have to be a total expert on it to be able to manage the people doing it, but one has to have a pretty good idea of how it goes and know enough NOT to stop the guys who do know how to make bricks when one wants bricks.

If the product is to get somebody to come in to see you, then you have to have some means of communication and some tech of persuasion to make him want to come in to see you. Brute force may seem okay to cops but in organization it seldom works. There is more tech to it than that.

If a product officer does not know there is tech involved in GETTING the product, then he will never make his staff study it or teach anybody to do it. And he will wind up with no product. So beware the product officer who won't give time off for hatting! He doesn't know one has to know the tech of getting his product. What do you think the OEC (Org Exec Course) Volumes and the technical bulletins are all about?

One has to spend some time organizing in many different ways—the organization itself, the hatting, the technical skill staff members would have to have, to get anywhere in GETTING a product.

Sure, if you only organize and never produce you never get a product either. But if you only produce and never organize, the only brick wall you'll ever see is the one you run into.

L. RON HUBBARD
Founder

HCO POLICY LETTER OF 14 NOVEMBER 1976

Remimeo
Flag Bu
All Orgs
Ext HCO FB

Admin Know-How Series 36

Org Series 36

Executive Series 18

Personnel Series 28

MANNING UP AN ORG

The Sequence of Posting Depts and Divs

You need an org board first and an allocation board.

The sequence in which an org is manned up is roughly:

— Dept 1

— Dept 11

— Reg and Body Routers and Intro people in Div 6

— Dept 12 (enough auditors and C/Ses to approach 2 admin to 1 tech in org)

— Dept 6

— Dept 7

— Dept 3

— SSO and Supers in Qual to train staff

— Dept 5 for CF, Address and Letter Reges

— Dept 4 for promo

— Dept 21 (LRH Comm)

— Dept 10

— Dept 20

— FR and execs

— Full Div 6

— Full Div 1

— Full Div 4

— Full Div 2

— Full Div 5

— Full Div 7

— Full Div 3

(Note, an AO always mans up the AO Dept or Div along with the SH one in each case.)

Wrong sequence of manning is Dept 6, Dept 12, Dept 6, Dept 12, Dept 6, Dept 12, as you wind up with a stuck clinic that won't expand.

Wrong sequence will contract an org while trying to expand it, as the org will go out of balance, bad units, noisy and unproductive.

If manned in a correct sequence, its income has a chance to stay abreast of its new staff additions.

Emphasis on GI without comparable emphasis on delivery and organization can throw an org into such a spin only a genius can run it.

Manned in proper sequence, and hatted as it goes, an org almost runs itself.

Single handing from the top comes from longstanding failures to man or man in sequence, from earlier noncompliance with explicit orders or from not understanding orgs in the first place.

An unhappy org that doesn't produce has usually been manned only partially and out of sequence.

The trick is planned manning, ignoring the screams of those who know best or demand personnel; just manning by posting those who have been screamed for the loudest is a sure way to wind up with no people and total org problems instead of a total org that is prosperous and producing.

Incidently, this is a rough approximation of the sequence of hats the ED gradually unloads as his org takes over.

L. RON HUBBARD
Founder

449

HCO POLICY LETTER OF 29 NOVEMBER 1978

Remimeo

Admin Know-How Series 37

Personnel Series 29

HOW YOU HANDLE DEMANDS FOR PERSONNEL

Refs:
HCO PL 15 Sept. 59 II   HATS AND OTHER FOLDERS
HCO PL 1 July 65 III   HATS, THE REASON FOR
HCO PL 22 Sept. 70   HATS

HCOs get continual demands for personnel from all areas of an org. To keep an HCO from going mad with all these demands, they must, on every request, (1) have the Dir of I&R do a full utilization survey on the division, dept or section requesting personnel and (2) do a full hat inspection on all personnel in that division, dept or section.

Only if these two steps are done for *each* personnel request will sanity reign in HCOs on the subject of personnel.

HCO PL 15 Sept. 59 II, HATS AND OTHER FOLDERS (Vol 0), HCO PL 1 July 65 III, HATS, THE REASON FOR (Vol 0) and HCO PL 22 Sept. 70, HATS (Vol 0) must be well known by all staff in Depts 1 and 3.

Personnel can recruit madly, answering every frantic demand for personnel, and yet HAVE THEM ALL WASTED for lack of full hats and full training on those hats.

The whole org can sag and even vanish under these conditions.

So Personnel has a vested interest in hats being complete and staff trained on them. For Personnel people cannot possibly cope with "no pay so can't hire anyone" and "no people so can't produce."

So for every demand for personnel, *ALWAYS* demand a utilization survey *AND* an inspection of hats in that area.

L. RON HUBBARD
Founder

Admin Know-How Series 38

[*Note:* Admin Know-How Series 38 no longer exists as a numbered issue in this series. The policy originally assigned this series number has been cancelled.]

Admin Know-How Series 39

[*Note:* There is no issue assigned the Admin Know-How Series number 39. The policy letter previously assigned this number has been deleted, as LRH did not designate it for inclusion in the series.]

HCO POLICY LETTER OF 13 FEBRUARY 1980

Remimeo
All Orgs
All Staff

Admin Know-How Series 40

COORDINATION COMMITTEES AND MANAGEMENT COMMITTEES
DIFFERENCES IN PURPOSE AND FUNCTION

Ref:
HCO PL   1 July 82   AKH Series 41
                             MANAGEMENT COORDINATION

If effective, coordinated management is to occur there are two basics which must be understood at the outset.

The first of these is what a management body is and what it does.

The second is what a coordination council or committee is and what it does.

Someone has to see that the work gets done. That's management. Management organizes and runs things. Each network or sector of management has its own senior. The senior is responsible for the governing, the planning, the activities, the statistics and the expansion of his own sector of the overall organization. And each of these seniors is a member of the management committee. The handling of situations, the origination of needed or missing policy, the initiation of management actions to be taken and orders to be issued—all of this is done by the individual members of the management committee.

But such management units can be hit from various quarters unless they have a hard core of united resistance in the form of agreed-upon procedures and policy, and unless there is some coordinating body existing which has the authority to clear their strategy and their tactics.

Thus, there is a need for a coordinating committee which clears the actions and orders of management to ensure that these *are* coordinated so as not to work against the interests of any one network or sector.

That would be what a coordinating committee would do and what it would consist of. The coordinating committee would be made up of the members of the management units or their deputies—such members then acting only in a *coordinating* capacity.

The membership of a management executive on a coordinating committee gives him the chance to clear what he is doing with the other sectors who are also represented on the coordinating committee, to demand cooperation and action from them and to call to their attention points in their activities which make his post difficult for him, and to prevent them from setting policies that influence his sector but are not cleared by him.

A coordinating committee, then, is composed of the seniors who do this for their sectors, or by representatives of those seniors.

A coordinating committee exists to clear orders and certify that they are not contrary to or harmful to the activities of other committee members.

Indiscriminate policies have been issued from time to time by various units and activities which, if they do not take other units and their functions into consideration, create points of confusion. Unless some council or committee exists which has the authority to clear such policies and actions, the confusion will continue. In other words, without a coordinating committee, policies get issued which are contrary to the best interests of the overall organization.

What a coordinating committee *isn't* is some kind of group that gets together and discusses how they would solve things. That's not how a coordinating committee operates.

What a coordinating committee *is,* is a committee that clears solutions and policies originated by different autonomous units within the overall organization, so that these solutions and policies are coordinated with the functions of other units and are known to all. Such a committee also exists so that modifications can be requested by management individuals where a policy or an activity affects his sector.

Thus a coordinating committee is quite different from a management committee which organizes and runs things.

Though the membership on such committees may be composed of the same individuals or their deputies (and should be, as management must be represented in coordination) it is the capacities in which they act in these two different bodies which is different.

When one is acting as a management executive he manages. When he sits on a coordinating committee he ensures that all the management functions are *coordinated* for the good of the overall organization.

HOMEWORK

For a coordinating committee to be able to function swiftly and efficiently, as it must do, certain rules and regulations must be set up. Otherwise, such a committee will find itself spending (wasting) long hours mulling over and trying to sort out incomplete or confusing cycles and, actually, slipping down into management functions (and not even effective management functions, at that).

A coordinating committee must have some executive perpetually in charge of it. This executive must be in communication with the liaison officer or the seniors of all networks. These networks must demand that certain subjects be taken up or the coordinating committee executive must himself be familiar enough with the scene to see that certain things have to be taken up and coordinated. From this data, this executive compiles an agenda with times and dates saying what is going to be taken up when. The agenda is issued in time for other units to gather their specialized information on these subjects and the problems connected with them so as to help resolve them.

The committee should be run on exact and specific rules as laid down by the executive.

Such rules would need to provide that each committee member arrived with his homework done. That would include homework done without the person having gone past misunderstoods. It would include homework done that takes into consideration, within reason, some knowledge of the purpose and functions of the other units which his plans might affect.

So a good, workable solution for a coordinating committee to operate on is to have a committee "pot" to accumulate fines for anyone violating the rules.

With any violation, the offending member puts a specified fine in the pot, then and there. When the pot gets full, the committee has a party.

The rules would be:

1. Arriving with homework for any proposed policy, order or action *done*.

2. Such homework done on a certain knowledge of the area being addressed.

3. Such homework done with a real understanding of the terms and functions involved—and *not* having been done over misunderstoods.

4. Such homework done with a reasonable working knowledge of the other areas and units which may be affected.

5. And, if an objection is raised to another's proposal without coming up with a solution to it, it's also a violation of the rules.

A person then arriving with incomplete or no homework, or found to have an MU, or who is found not to know very much about it, must deposit a specified sum of money in the pot—then and there. Or, if it's found afterwards that he's had a misunderstood on the activity, he contributes his money to the pot at that time.

Objecting to something but not bringing up a solution to it costs double the fine.

If coordinating committees set up firm rules based on the above, set their fines for the various infractions and *stick* to them, they'll get a lot of effective coordinating done.

And if they understand the difference between management committees and coordinating committees and operate solely and only on that clear understanding, they'll be successful.

That is what it takes to bring about effective, coordinated management.

L. RON HUBBARD
Founder

453

HCO POLICY LETTER OF 1 JULY 1982

Remimeo
All Staff

Admin Know-How Series 41

MANAGEMENT COORDINATION

COORDINATION is the essence of management.

The word "management" implies there is something and some someones to manage.

A business or company or organization implies others are present and are engaged in a similar activity. It is a *team*.

Any organization, no matter how complex, is bound together by common purposes.

If the different parts of such an organization are not *coordinated*, they begin to cross each other's lines and tangle.

With such a tangle, one gets no forward progress.

The energy of the overall organization is absorbed by cross orders, cross actions and the general purpose of the activity makes little if any forward progress. This can be called "internal noise." The staff can be numerous, appear busy, even frantic, yet no production is really accomplished.

What is missing is COORDINATION. The efforts of each part of the organization are not being directed and meshed into flows which would achieve the common purpose.

THAT is what a manager is for.

The manager and his immediate assistants have to *know* where they are going and have to make certain each part of the organization knows and that the efforts of each individual segment of the organization are devoted to forwarding the same general purpose.

Without that coordination action, the different elements of the organization go into a tangle that results, not in the forwarding of the general purpose, but into confusion and frayed temper and nerves.

The elements of coordination are: *planning, knowledge, information, agreement* and *production*.

Good coordination of team effort results in high ARC. This is called "team spirit, morale, esprit," etc. But what it is in fact is agreement and understanding within the team so they can each forward the general purpose of the group. Confidence in the group by each individual part of it is built with the above factors. Out of that one can achieve meaningful and worthwhile production.

Without it one gets various versions of catastrophe. The "hey you" organization, the one-star team with everyone else on the sidelines inactive or confused—there are many aspects of a lack of coordination.

Coordination is why we have Executive Councils, Advisory Councils, staff meetings, mini programs for departments and all the rest of it. It is even why we have an org board.

Any manager, at whatever level, will most certainly fail if he does not brief his troops, get their viewpoints, establish agreement and program the general ongoing activity and see that the program is executed.

A manager at any level has to use the tools of coordination. Otherwise his organization's product will just be noise.

Oh, it is true that groups do not develop new ideas, that boards cannot plan. This is beside the point. This does not mean they do not serve a vital purpose. A manager uses them to coordinate! If he omits this, he has lost his most valuable tool, the form of the organization and he cannot possibly achieve any lasting results.

An org that doesn't hold Executive Council, Advisory Council and staff meetings on a regular basis and does not use them to brief and iron out disagreements and get cooperation is lost. It will have down statistics very surely. For no one will know what the blazes is going on, so how can they get their own job done? An answer is to splinter off and go one's own way as best he can. And that fragments a group and it ceases to be an organization but is just a lot of individual efforts.

The failure in such a case is simply a failure to coordinate!

Oh yes, management is there to plan. Good. If it is planning that will forward the general purpose of the organization, if the various units of the organization are briefed and the plan is adjusted to handle their disagreements and if the plan is real and understood by one and all and if they then cooperate and produce along these lines, you have forward progress.

In our case all we're doing is selling and delivering a product. If we do that we have a planet. Otherwise we don't.

Whether we do it in a few years or a few millennia is determined by management. Does it *coordinate* or not?

L. RON HUBBARD
Founder

455

HCO POLICY LETTER OF 18 AUGUST 1982R
Issue I
REVISED 28 FEBRUARY 1984

Remimeo
All Orgs
All Management
 Personnel
All Executives
All Staff
All Computer
 Users

Target Series 8

Computer Series 3

Admin Know-How Series 42R

TARGETS AND PRODUCTION

There is a direct coordination between the clarity and doability of the targets of a program and any increase in stats.

If one can write good, simple, doable programs on matters important to get done, they can get done. If the program is cloudy or the targets too general, little comes of it. It does not show up in stats and can even clutter up lines and impede production.

So it is *very* important to an exec and to staffs that the exec be able to write clean, concise programs and staffs to recognize when they are not and plead for correction.

Strategic planning gets bugged most often because middle management does not put it in target form or, if they do, put it in such cloudy or general targets it cannot be done and does not achieve the desired result.

Faults in this can cost—factually—millions in unmade income or actual losses and overwork.

But now today *another* factor is entering the scene. The world has gone *computer*.

Computers can keep track of things and operate to catch things which, undone, wreck things.

In a very short while, at this writing, computers will exist at management echelons to keep track of stats, demand programs and keep track of their effectiveness. The computer will be able to detect very early noncompliance both in writing and getting done programs.

Life will be much smoother as debugs will be demanded more quickly and bad targets or line jams or staff overloads will be detected sooner and remedied, resulting in more income, more service and more pay.

But all this will depend on three things:

1. The existence and soundness of the strategic planning and evaluation. (This has never much been in doubt.)

2. The clarity with which planning can be programed. (This is currently not good at all.)

3. The execution of targets called for at various echelons and staff level. (This depends, to a large measure, on 2 above.)

To a computer, which cannot really think, a target is a target. If not done in the expected time, it will squawk. If still not done, it will demand a debug.

The debug will find (a) the organization ordered did not give it to a correct or the right staff member to do, (b) had no one there to do it or (c) the target was simply neglected at staff level or (d) the target was undoable in its existing form. The right one will be found, action will be taken and the overall scene will advance once more.

So it is *very* important, whether one is writing major, minor or mini programs, that they be written absolutely on-policy from here on out.

This starts now, not waiting for computers, as it is valid in its own right and Programs Ops are on the line. With computers there will still be Programs Ops to run them but the precision and speed will increase amazingly.

The organizations in the world are getting bigger. They have to be more efficient to also pay well. And this all comes down to the 1, 2, 3 above.

It is a miserable thing to be hit with a lot of confused, undoable orders. And dangerous to one at staff level for one can be charged with noncompliance when there was really nothing precise to comply with!

So the ability to coordinate programs and write excellent target-policy targets is vital to the ability of all to work.

And when computers get on the job, electronic sparks will be flying all over the place if target policy is not adhered to carefully and precisely.

So this policy is vital, computers or no computers.

OPERATING TARGETS MUST HEREAFTER BE WRITTEN IN SUCH A WAY THAT THEY ARE FINITE AND NOT A GENERALITY SO THEY ARE PRECISELY DOABLE. Targets like "Keep stats rising" or "Be nice to Joe" are not doable targets from a computer's viewpoint or anybody else's.

But, computers aside, the one that does the target is NOT a computer and with target clarity can do it far more easily.

Hear me, the 1, 2, 3 above are the make-break point of expand or not expand.

So heed it.

L. RON HUBBARD
Founder

457

HCO POLICY LETTER OF 22 AUGUST 1982

Remimeo
All Orgs
All Management
  Personnel
All Executives
All Staff

Target Series 9

Admin Know-How Series 43

BATTLE PLANS

A "battle plan" is defined as:

A list of targets for the coming day or week which forward the strategic planning and handle the immediate actions and outnesses which impede it.

Some people write "battle plans" as just a series of actions which they hope to get done in the coming day or week. This is fine and better than nothing and does give some orientation to one's actions. In fact, someone who does not do this is quite likely to get far less done and be considerably more harassed and "busy" than one who does. An orderly planning of what one intends to do in the coming day or week and then getting it done is an excellent way to achieve production. But this is using "battle planning" in an irreducible-minimum form as a tool.

Let us take up definitions. Why is this called a "battle plan" in the first place? It seems a very harsh military term to apply to the workaday world of admin. I did not select this term; it sort of grew up by itself amongst Sea Org executives. But it is a very apt term.

A war is something that happens over a long period of time. The fate of everything depends on it. A battle is something which occurs in a short unit of time. One can lose several battles and still win a war. Thus one in essence is talking about short periods of time when one is talking about a battle plan.

This goes further. When one is talking about a war, one is talking about a series of events which will take place over a long period of time. No general, or captain for that matter, ever won a war unless he did some strategic planning. This would concern an overall conduct of a war or a sector of it. This is the big, upper-level idea sector. It is posed in high generalities, has definite purposes and applies at the top of the Admin Scale. (Ref: HCO PL 6 Dec. 70, Personnel Series 13, Org Series 18, THIRD DYNAMIC DE–ABERRATION)

Below strategic planning one has tactical. In order to carry out a strategic plan one must have the plan of movement and actions necessary to carry it out. Tactical planning normally occurs down the org board in an army and is normally used to implement strategic planning. Tactical planning can go down to a point as low as "Private Joe is to keep his machine gun pointed on clump of trees 10 and fire if anything moves in it."

"Middle management"—the heads of regiments right on down to the corporals are covered by this term—is concerned with the implementation of strategic planning.

The upper planning body turns out a strategic plan. Middle management turns this strategic plan into tactical orders. They do this on a long-term basis and a short-term basis. When you get on down to the short-term basis you have battle plans.

A battle plan therefore means turning strategic planning into exact doable targets which are then executed in terms of motion and action for the immediate period being worked on. Thus one gets a situation whereby a good strategic plan, turned into good tactical targets and then executed, results in forward progress. Enough of these sequences carried out successfully gives one the war.

This should give you a grip on what a battle plan really is. It is the list of targets to be executed in the immediate short-term future that will implement and bring into reality some portion of the strategic plan.

One can see then that management is at its best when there is a strategic plan and when it is known at least down to the level of tactical planners. And tactical planners are simply those people putting strategic plans into targets which are then known to and executed from middle management on down. This is very successful management when it is done.

Of course the worthwhileness of any evolution depends on the soundness of the strategic plan.

But the strategic plan is dependent upon programs and projects being written in target form and which are doable within the resources available.

What we speak of as "compliance" is really a done target. The person doing the target might not be aware of the overall strategic plan or how it fits into it, but I assure you that it is very poor management indeed whose targets do not *all* implement to one degree or another the overall strategic plan.

When we speak of coordination (Ref: HCO PL 1 July 82, MANAGEMENT COORDINATION), we are really talking about conceiving or overseeing a strategic plan into the tactical version and at the lower echelon coordinating the actions of those who will do the actual things necessary to carry it out so that they all align in one direction.

All this comes under the heading of *alignment*. As an example, if you put a number of people in a large hall facing in various directions and then suddenly yelled at them to start running, they would, of course, collide with one another and you would have a complete confusion. This is the picture one gets when strategic planning is not turned into smooth tactical planning and is not executed within that framework. These people running in this hall could get very busy, even frantic, and one could say that they were on the job and producing but that would certainly be a very large lie. Their actions are not coordinated. Now if we were to take these same people in the same hall and have them do something useful such as clean up the hall, we are dealing with specific actions of specific individuals having to do with brooms and mops—who gets them, who empties

459

the trash and so forth. The strategic plan of "Get the hall ready for the convention" is turned into a tactical plan which says exactly who does what and where. That would be the tactical plan. The result would be a clean hall ready for the convention.

But "Clean up the hall for the convention" by simple inspection can be seen to be what would be only a small portion of an overall strategic plan. In other words the strategic plan itself has to be broken down into smaller sectors.

One can see then that a battle plan could exist for the ED or CO of an org which would have a number of elements in it which in their turn were turned over to subexecutives who would write battle plans for their own sectors which would be far more specific. Thus we have a gradient scale of the grand overall plan broken down into segments and these segments broken down even further.

The test of all of this is whether or not it results in worthwhile accomplishments which forward the general overall strategic plan.

If you understand all the above (it would be a good thing to do it in clay) you will have mastered the elements of coordination.

Feasibility enters into such planning. This depends upon the resources available. Thus a certain number of targets and battle plans, to an organization which is expanding or attempting big projects, must include organizational planning and targets and battle plans so that the organization stays together as it expands. One writes a battle plan, not on the basis of, "What am I going to do tomorrow?" or, "What am I going to do next week?" (which is fine in its own way and better than nothing), but on the overall question, "What exact actions do I have to do to carry out this strategic plan to achieve the exact results necessary for this stage of the strategic plan within the limits of available resources?" Then one would have the battle plan for the next day or the next week.

There is one thing to beware of in doing battle plans. One can write a great many targets which have little or nothing to do with the strategic plan and which keep people terribly busy and which accomplish no part of the overall strategic plan. Thus a battle plan can become a liability since it is not pushing any overall strategic plan and is not accomplishing any tactical objective.

So what is a "battle plan"? It is the doable targets in written form which accomplish a desirable part of an overall strategic plan.

When one is talking about "mini programs" in an org, one is actually talking about small battle plans at the lowest tactical levels. These must be based upon a middle-management tactical plan and this in turn must be based on a strategic plan.

The understanding and competent use of targeting in battle plans is vital to the overall accomplishment that raises production, income, delivery or anything else that is a desirable end.

It is a test of an executive whether or not he can competently battle plan and then get his battle plan executed.

L. RON HUBBARD
Founder

HUBBARD COMMUNICATIONS OFFICE
Saint Hill Manor, East Grinstead, Sussex

HCO POLICY LETTER OF 29 DECEMBER 1982RA
Issue II
REVISED 21 JANUARY 1991

Remimeo
All Orgs
All Executives
All Management
 Personnel

Org Series 46RA

Executive Series 24RA

Esto Series 45RA

Admin Know-How Series 44RA

THE TOOLS OF MANAGEMENT

Refs:
HCO PL 11 Apr. 70   THIRD DYNAMIC TECH
HCO PL 28 July 72   Esto Series 26
                          Exec Series 16
                          Org Series 32
                          ESTABLISHING, HOLDING
                          THE FORM OF THE ORG
HCO PL   1 July 82   AKH Series 41
                          MANAGEMENT COORDINATION

There is a simplicity to managing effectively. It begins with the basics of management.

Although it may appear so to some, successful management is not a highly complicated, esoteric activity. But, just as an auditor or a C/S must know and be able to use the exact tools of first dynamic tech in handling cases in order to achieve exact and standard results on a one-for-one basis, so must an executive or manager know and be able to use the exact tools of third dynamic tech in handling groups to achieve successful and exact results in every instance.

Within the wealth of data on third dynamic tech contained in HCO Policy Letters, the OEC Volumes and recorded LRH lectures and books on the subject, there are certain definite, specific *tools* a manager uses. These are the tools of management.

The difference between brilliant management and mediocre or no management, at any level, lies in:

1. Knowing what the *tools* of management are, and

2. Knowing how to use them.

Many people are not aware that, like a carpenter or any other workman, a manager uses specific and exact *tools*. Thus, we see people here and there who are doing the equivalent of using the handle of a chisel to drive nails into wet concrete.

It is a common fault with inexpert workmen to find them using their tools wrongly or not using them at all. They make a breakthrough when they discover what the specific tools are for.

One can see this in people who can't mix sound or can't become mixing engineers. They sit with all these knobs in front of them, reach out and grab this knob or that one, hoping hopefully something will happen to the sound. Yet every component they have in front of them is an exact tool to do an exact thing with sound!

There are a lot of comparisons one could make, but the point is that people in management positions have precise *tools* available to them in Dianetics and Scientology which happen to be far better tools than have ever been available on the planet.

One can have very good people on management posts who still can drown if they don't know and put to use the management tools.

But without these being specified as exact tools, one might not see the simplicity of it.

MANAGEMENT ECHELONS

Operating as it does into an expanding scene, Scientology has grown into the need for and use of various echelons of management.

In orgs, for some time we have had division heads and above them we have the Executive Council, headed by the CO or ED of the org.

Above the level of service orgs we have middle management and still above that we have the Senior Executive Strata of management. And each of these echelons must know the tools of management and how to use them.

The OEC (Org Executive Course) and the FEBC (Flag Executive Briefing Course) have long been established as the essential courses for training executives at service org level and above.

These courses, and the OEC and Management Series Volumes upon which they are based, teach the form of the org and how to use the parts and posts and functions that go to make up the whole. They give us executives who know how to correctly utilize staff and their assigned posts and duties. We call it "knowing how to play the piano"—it's a matter of knowing what key to hit when and which keys to use in combination to produce a desired result. (Ref: HCO PL 28 July 72, ESTABLISHING, HOLDING THE FORM OF THE ORG) In other words, it's a matter of knowing and using one's tools. The OEC and FEBC courses teach this data and much, much more.

While at this writing there are numerous OEC and FEBC grads and more in the making, thousands more will be needed to handle the current rate of expansion.

Meanwhile an executive at any level and whatever his training needs to know and use his management tools NOW if he is to function at all.

A div head must "know how to play the piano" within his division.

462

The posts of CO or ED, Chief Officer, Supercargo, Org Exec Sec and HCO Exec Sec require executives who are capable of "playing the piano" across the divisions of the entire org and using hats and posts and functions correctly in order to achieve immediate production from the org as a whole.

At middle management one is handling not one function nor only one org but many orgs and their functions, which requires "knowing how to play the piano" at that level.

And at the Senior Executive Strata of management, we get into the vital need for "knowing how to play the piano" across a much wider sphere, using the full scope of management tools and using them with high skill. One might be using the same tools as lower stratas of management but a higher level of expertise is required as one's planning, decisions and actions are influencing far, far broader areas.

What has brought this about is the rapid expansion of Scientology into wider zones of responsibility and therefore increased responsibility with a resultant increase in traffic. This naturally has to be handled by increasing efficiency. What it has done, in effect, is push some up from lower-level management status to upper-level management status, necessarily. Without realizing it, some executives have been climbing a status stairs in terms of influence and zones of control. And they can go only so high without being terribly precise in their use of tools. After that, without this acquired precision, they drown.

The obvious answer to all of this is an executive training program which instant-hats executives on the fundamental tools of management and provides Management Status checksheets through which an executive or manager raises his status by *becoming more and more expert with these and an even wider range of tools*. And such a program has now been developed!

MANAGEMENT STATUS CHECKSHEETS

The new executive training program consists of three status levels.

These levels are to be covered in a series of Management Status checksheets.

The Management Status One checksheet has a prerequisite of Staff Status II. It *instant-hats* an exec on the basic tools of management, such as:

The Admin Scale, target policy, strategic plans, programs, specific lines and org terminals, org boards, despatches and telexes, statistics and graphs, conditions, hats and hatting, files, personnel folders, ethics folders, etc. Each one is a specific tool.

The Management Status Two checksheet (with an OEC prerequisite) consists of a profound review of the basic management tools and study of the upper-level tools of management, which include:

Surveys, PR, pilots, review of past performance, general economics, finance systems, cost accounting, control through networks, admin indicators, morale, legal, goodwill, exchange, missions (Action missions), economical management and managing by dynamics.

The Management Status Three checksheet (with FEBC prerequisite) would be a more profound review of the basic *and* upper-level management tools, in addition to training on the twelve ingredients of expansion upon which the Senior Executive Strata operates.

Even an OEC or FEBC grad would do the Management Status checksheets as, when he comes out of an OEC or FEBC, all in the clouds, the Management Status checksheet is needed to bring him back down to earth and tell him he's dealing with tools which are very finite tools.

What is being communicated to executives by these checksheets is that they have tools, what the tools are exactly, and that they must use them.

EXECUTIVE STATUS LEVELS

There are specific requirements to be met by a manager to attain each of the three Executive Status levels.

Working up through these status levels, a manager not only becomes more proficient in handling an org, any org, but becomes fully certified to operate at middle or senior echelons of management.

The Executive Status levels are:

1. EXECUTIVE STATUS ONE: At this level, the person is simply thrown on post, the basic management tools are put into his hands via a brief, rat-a-tat-tat Management Status One checksheet and he then gets on with it.

2. EXECUTIVE STATUS TWO: For one to be certified at this level, one must have completed the OEC, done the Management Status Two checksheet and have an adequate production record.

3. EXECUTIVE STATUS THREE: For one to be certified at this level, he must have completed the FEBC, done the Management Status Three checksheet and have a proven production record.

When the steps for Executive Status certification are complete, the exec must present adequate evidence of such to the Qualifications Division. After verification of the evidence, he is awarded the appropriate Executive Status certificate.

By use of these Executive Status levels, executives at management levels could see what executives they had (or not had). The designation "ES I" (Executive Status I) would tell them at once what they were dealing with, etc. Also, from the viewpoint of the individual, he would know where he had to go to get an upper-level rating.

Once these Management Status checksheets are issued, middle and central management personnel should not draw full pay or be bonus eligible until they have completed the Management Status One checksheet, as they will not be operating effectively until they have done this.

EXECUTIVE STATUSES AND STAFF STATUSES

The Exec Status levels do not replace Staff Status training. All staff and execs are programed and move up the Staff Statuses so as to have a better idea of the org as an org; these levels are also indicative of the training and experience of a staff member and show his promotion eligibility.

An executive should attain Executive Status One by completing the Management Status One checksheet as soon as possible upon assuming post, so he has the management tools available for his immediate application.

Once an exec attains Staff Status VI (Org Exec Course graduate), he can attain Executive Status Two by fulfillment of the requirements listed above. An FEBC graduate achieves Executive Status Three in a similar fashion.

SUMMARY

With the release of the new Management Status checksheets, precise and gradient training levels for all echelons of management will exist comparable to the precise and gradient training levels required for all echelons of technical delivery.

Quite an unbeatable combination!

One winds up with managers fully familiar with their exact tools, having the one-two-three of management tech at their fingertips, and "knowing how to play the piano" effectively across an org, a continent, a planet!

So the answer to current expansion is an action which is geared to bring about even further expansion. And that is the only way to go!

It begins with the basic tools of management.

L. RON HUBBARD
Founder

Revision assisted by
LRH Technical Research
and Compilations

HCO POLICY LETTER OF 9 AUGUST 1971
Issue I

Remimeo
All Orgs
All Management
Personnel
All Executives
All Staff

Admin Know-How Series 45

Target Series 10

WRITING PROGRAMS AND PROJECTS

Refs:

HCO PL 18 Aug. 82R	AKH Series 42R
Rev. 29.2.84	TARGETS AND PRODUCTION
HCO PL 9 Jan. 80	Exec Series 20
	DEPARTMENTAL MINI PROGRAMS:
	THE KEY TO ACHIEVEMENT
HCO PL 19 Aug. 71	PROGRAMS, USE OF—HOW TO SAVE
	USELESS WORK
HCO PL 12 Sept. 59	PROGRAMING

(The data in this issue has been excerpted from CBO 129, WRITING PROJECTS, 9 Aug. 71 and it contains pertinent and valuable data for hatting those engaged in writing programs or projects. Issued as an HCO PL on 30 Dec. 82.)

Some years back in hatting an Aide, I asked her to visualize a project she had written being read and done at the receipt point—in other words to assume the viewpoint of the receiver, and to see if she would then do the project.

After a study of this, she wrote the following excellent analysis of the action.

"COMPLIANCE REPORT

8 August 1971

Re Hatting Action

Dear Sir,

I reread five of my projects to visualize a project of mine being done and to see if I would do it and could easily do it if I received it.

I then also read some LRH written projects to see the difference and compare.

1. I found I would not do a project or would not be interested in doing it if:

   a. I didn't understand it well at first reading (unclear).

   b. If it was too long and complex and therefore unconfrontable.

   c. If the reality of WHY it was needed and what improvements it would bring to my post or area was not clearly expressed in the

INFO or SITUATION of the project. In other words if the purpose of the project wasn't real.

    d. If, just in reading the project, I didn't KNOW what I was supposed to *DO* with it or while it was underway.

2. Then I would have difficulty doing it:

    a. If each target didn't call for an ACTION, a DOINGNESS.

    b. If each target called for more than one action (confusing).

    c. If each target was not specifically directed to or assigned to one person (me) or to somebody else on my orders.

    d. If NO ONE in particular was responsible to get the project done.

    e. If it went in such detail that it didn't give me any leeway to operate in the existing scene and achieve the target, and if I was left without any initiative to do it.

    f. If each target wasn't a START–CHANGE–STOP with a definite time sequence, it would be more difficult to put it in.

From this I get some POSITIVE points to look for when writing a project:

1. Clearly assign project responsibility to one terminal or group of terminals.

2. Make the info and the situation REAL to the person by showing what the existing scene is.

3. Show why the project needs to be done and what it will accomplish, and *sell* it by doing so.

4. Have one ACTION per target and not more than one.

5. Have the time sequence properly indicated and visible in the project and make it a clear start-change-stop cycle.

6. Don't go into too many details. Better even—refer to a PL where details on HOW to do an action are contained.

7. On the other hand, don't assume that the receipt point knows policy at the fingertip. He most probably doesn't. Don't skip gradients on the receipt point.

8. Make it very clear as to who does what target.

9. Keep it short and simple, and each target short and words simple.

10. Watch for outpoints.

There are also the regular policies about targets and their types and how they relate, which are observed.

I'm not saying all my projects were bad and not getting done! FEBC projects are a bit too long maybe, but do have lots of doingness in them. One project is too detailed. One project, as you indicated, has good info but is unclear as to who does what.

A good one, which had most points above in, got completed well.

Thank you for the hatting action."

L. RON HUBBARD
Founder

Remimeo
All Orgs
All FOLOs
All Management
  Units
All Executives

Admin Know-How Series 46

STRATEGIC PLANNING

Refs:

HCO PL 22 Aug. 82		AKH Series 43
		BATTLE PLANS
HCO PL 1 July 82		AKH Series 41
		MANAGEMENT COORDINATION
HCO PL 18 Aug. 82R		AKH Series 42R
		TARGETS AND PRODUCTION
HCO PL 29 Dec. 82		AKH Series 44
		Org Series 46RA
		Exec Series 24RA
		Esto Series 45RA
		THE TOOLS OF MANAGEMENT
HCO PL 9 Jan. 83 III		AKH Series 47
		CHECKLIST FOR A STRATEGIC PLAN

What is strategic planning?

Although it has already been described at some length in HCO PL 22 Aug. 82, BATTLE PLANS, strategic planning is of such vital importance in the scheme of things that it merits more emphasis and in-depth study by those responsible for it. So let us examine strategic planning further, both as to its definition and use as well as its relationship to other aspects of management.

STRATEGIC PLANNING—WHAT IT IS

The term "STRATEGY" is derived from the Greek words:

stratégos, which means "general,"

stratos, which means "army,"

agein, meaning "to lead."

STRATEGY, therefore, by dictionary definition, refers to a plan for the overall conduct of a war or sector of it.

By extrapolation, it has also come to mean a plan for the skillful overall conduct of a large field of operations, or a sector of such operations, toward the achievement of a specific goal or result.

This is planning that is done at upper-echelon level, as, if it is to be effective, it must be done from an overview of the broad existing situation.

It is a statement of the intended plans for accomplishing a broad objective and inherent in its definition is the idea of clever use of resources or maneuvers for outwitting the enemy or overcoming existing obstacles to win the objective.

It is the central strategy worked out at the top which, like an umbrella, covers the activities of the echelons below it.

That tells us what strategic planning is.

WHAT IT DOES

What strategic planning does is provide direction for the activities of all the lower echelons. All the tactical plans and programs and projects to be carried out at lower echelons in order to accomplish the objective stream down from the strategic plan at the top. It is the overall plan against which all of these are coordinated.

This gives a clear look at why strategic planning is so vitally important and why it must be done by the upper-level planning body if management is to be effective and succeed.

What happens if strategic planning is missing? Well, what happens in the conduct of a war if no strategic planning is done?

Key troops can be left unflanked and unsupported in key areas while other troops fight aimless battles at some minor outpost. Supplies and ammunition could be deployed to the wrong area or not forwarded at all. Conflict of orders, jammed lines and maneuvers, wasted resources and lost battles all result. With the lack of a plan, coordination is missing and it's a scene of confusion and dispersal. In short, disaster.

What a difference between this and a strong, coordinated, positive thrust toward attaining the objective!

Transposing all of this over into our own activity gives an even clearer look at why strategic planning must be done at the upper levels of management. The key word here is "done." It cannot be neglected or dropped out. It cannot be *assumed* to be done. Strategic planning must be done and stated and made known at least to the next lower levels of management so coordination and correct targeting can take place.

PURPOSE AND STRATEGIC PLANNING

A strategic plan begins with the observation of a situation to be handled or a goal to be met.

It always carries with it a statement of the definite purpose or purposes to be achieved.

Once the purpose has been established, it is possible to derive from it various strategic plannings.

Strategic planning is actually a very postgraduate form of "bright idea." (Ref: HCO PL 17 Feb. 71, Data Series 23, PROPER FORMAT AND CORRECT ACTION)

In fact, STRATEGY CAN BE SAID TO BE HOW ONE IS GOING TO ACTUALLY EFFECTIVELY AND SWIFTLY GET A PURPOSE MANIFESTED AND ROLLING IN THE REAL PHYSICAL UNIVERSE AT SPEED AND WITH NO FLUBS.

Some strategic plannings are the result, really, of thumbnail evaluations done on the broad overall scene.

Any strategic plan can encompass a number of major actions required from one or more different sectors in order to achieve the purpose. These are expressed in highly general terms as they are a statement of the initial overall planning that has been done. From them one can then derive tactical plannings. But all of these things have to fit together.

EXAMPLE:

Situation: The ABC Paper Company, though continuing to produce its formerly successful line of paper products, is also continuing to concentrate solely on its regular, already-established clientele while neglecting a number of its potential publics. The company is rapidly going broke and losing its execs to companies where there is "more opportunity for expansion."

Purpose: Put a full-blown paper company there which reaches all of its potential public for volume sales of existing and new products, while it also continues to sell and service its regular clientele in volume, and thus restore the company's solvency and build its repute as a lucrative, progressive concern with opportunities for expansion.

Strategic Plan: The strategic planning, based on the situation and established purpose, might go something like this:

1. The most immediate and vital action needed to arrest the losses is to (without interrupting any ongoing business or unmocking any other unit) set up and get functioning a new sales unit (alongside the existing one) which will have as its first priority the development of immediate new clients for the current line of products from among (a) retail paper outlets, (b) wholesale paper outlets, and (c) direct mail order. Clean, experienced salesmen will need to be procured to head up each of these sections, and other professional salesmen will need to be located in volume. These can be hired at very low retainer and make the bulk of their money on commissions. This operation can then be expanded over broader areas using district managers, salesmen who start other salesmen and even door-to-door salesmen. As a part of this plan, commission systems, package sales kits and promotion and advertising will need to be worked out. Getting this going on an immediate basis will boost sales and offset losses and very shortly expand the company into the field of stellar profits.

2. While the immediate holding action is going in, current sales and servicing of clients must be maintained. At the same time, sales and production records of existing staff will need to be reviewed as well as a thorough accounting done of company books to find where the losses are coming from. Any deadwood will need to be weeded out and those who do produce retained. Should any embezzlement or financial irregularity be found this will need to be handled with appropriate legal action. In other words, the

471

current operation is to be fully reviewed, cleaned up and its production not only maintained but stepped up all possible, with production targets set and met.

3. A program is to be worked out whereby surveys are done of all publics to find out what new paper products the publics want or will buy. Based on these survey results, a whole new line of paper products (additional to the old established line) can then be developed, produced, promoted and sold broadly. The program for establishing the new line of goods will need to cover financing, the org boarding of the new production unit (including clean executives, competent designers, any needed additional workmen) as well as any additional machinery or equipment required. It will also need to cover broad PR, promotion and sales campaigns that push the new products as well as the old for volume sales of both. Inherent in this planning would be a campaign to enhance the company's image as pioneers in the field of new paper products with opportunities for expansion-minded executives.

Such a strategic plan not only corrects a bad situation but turns it around into a highly profitable and expanding scene for the future of the whole company.

What one is trying to accomplish is digging the scene out of the soup and expanding it into a terrific level of viability.

From this strategic plan, tactical planning would be done, taking the broad strategic targets and breaking them down into precise and exactly-targeted do-ingnesses which get the strategic planning executed.

One would have many people working on this and it would be essential that they all had the purpose straight and that there be no conflicting internal spots in the overall campaign. Somebody reading over such plans might not see the importance of it unless they understood the situation and had a general overall riding purpose from which they could refine their tactical planning.

It is quite common in tactical execution of a strategic planning to find it necessary to modify some tactical targets or add new ones or even drop out some as found to be unnecessary.

The tactical management of a strategic planning is a bit of an art in itself so this is allowed for.

Given a good purpose, then, against which things can be coordinated, the strategic action necessary to accomplish it can then be worked out and the tactical plans to bring the strategic plans into existence can follow.

This way a group can flourish and prosper. When all strengths and forces are aligned to a single thrust a tremendous amount of power can be developed.

So one gets the purpose stated and from that works out what strategy will be used to accomplish the purpose and this then bridges the purpose into a tactical feasibility.

When the strategic plan, with its purpose, has been put forward, it is picked up by the next lower level of command and turned into tactical planning.

STRATEGIC VERSUS TACTICAL PLANNING

Strategy differs from tactics.

This is a point which must be clearly understood by the various echelons of management.

There is a very, very great difference between a strategic plan and a tactical plan.

While tactical planning is used to win an engagement, strategic planning is used to win the full campaign.

While the strategic plan is the large-scale, long-range plan to ensure victory, a tactical plan tells exactly who to move what to where and exactly what to do at that point.

The tactical plan must integrate into the strategic plan and accomplish the strategic plan. And it must do this with precise, doable targets.

And that, in essence, is management.

BRIDGING BETWEEN PURPOSE AND TACTICAL

One error that is commonly made by untrained personnel is to jump from purpose to tactical planning, omitting the strategic plan. And this won't work. The reason it won't work is that unless one's targeted tactical plan is aligned to a strategic plan it will go off the rails.

The point to be understood here is that strategic planning *creates* tactical planning. One won't get one's purpose achieved unless there is a strategy worked out and used by which to achieve it. And, based on that strategy, one works out the tactical moves to be made to implement the strategy. But jumping from purpose to tactical, ignoring the strategy, one will miss.

So, between purpose and tactical there is *always* the step of strategic planning. We could say that by a strategic plan is meant some means to get the purpose itself to function.

It is actually a plan that has to do with cleverness.

One might be well aware of the purpose and might come up with a number of tactical targets having to do with it. And possibly the targets will work, in themselves. But the purpose is to get a situation handled and, lacking a strategic means to do this, one might still find himself facing the same problem.

Putting the actual bridge there between purpose and tactical, which bridge is the strategic side of it, the purpose will have some chance of succeeding.

USE OF MANAGEMENT TOOLS

Strategic planning is one of the vital tools of management.

Getting a truly strategic plan worked out can necessitate calling all the other tools of management into play.

One needs to know org boards, lines and terminals, programing and target policy, to name just a few of these tools. One has to have a familiarity with personnel policy, statistics, graphs, conditions and the use of ethics. A knowledge of finance policy is often required. Knowing and utilizing the various networks can enter into it. And certain situations will very clearly indicate the need for surveys or the use of PR tech which, cleverly used, can not only correct a sour scene but can actually turn it around to one's advantage.

These are all resources. Anyone doing strategic planning has got to be able to use them and to be able to use them *strategically,* as that is what this planning is all about.

The management terminal who does have these tools under his belt and who clearly understands the sequence of purpose followed by strategic planning which can then be turned into tactical planning will be a stellar manager indeed!

L. RON HUBBARD
Founder

HUBBARD COMMUNICATIONS OFFICE
Saint Hill Manor, East Grinstead, Sussex

HCO POLICY LETTER OF 9 JANUARY 1983
Issue II

All Orgs
All FOLOs
All Management Units
All Executives
All AVC Units
and Issue Authority
Terminals

Admin Know-How Series 47

CHECKLIST FOR A STRATEGIC PLAN

Refs:

HCO PL	5 Jan. 83	AKH Series 46 STRATEGIC PLANNING
HCO PL	22 Aug. 82	AKH Series 43 BATTLE PLANS
HCO PL	1 July 82	AKH Series 41 MANAGEMENT COORDINATION
HCO PL	18 Aug. 82R	AKH Series 42R TARGETS AND PRODUCTION
HCO PL	29 Dec. 82RA	Org Series 46RA Exec Series 24RA Esto Series 45RA AKH Series 44RA THE TOOLS OF MANAGEMENT

Those writing strategic plans as well as those passing them have the responsibility for ensuring:

1. That strategic plans are correct and will handle what they are designed to handle.

2. That strategic planning *is done* to handle existing situations.

3. That no situation or goal requiring strategic planning is left uncovered by an overall plan for its handling.

Additionally, those writing strategic plans have the responsibility for getting themselves trained to proficiency in the use of this vital management tool.

And those passing on strategic plans have the added responsibility of correctly critiquing submitted plans, with no caprice or opinion entered into the line. With standard, in-tech criticism given, those in planning positions can be brought up to greater proficiency in their planning through cramming, additional training and, as needed, ethics.

The following checklist is therefore offered as a guide for those writing strategic plans and those whose job it is to approve such plans and authorize them for issue.

CHECKLIST FOR A STRATEGIC PLAN

1. a. Has the strategic plan been preceded by correct observation of the situation to be handled?

   b. Is it a valid situation?

   c. Has all the applicable data been examined?

   (These points would show up in verification of the information section of the plan.)

2. Is there a clear and comprehensive statement of the situation the plan is designed to handle?

3. Is there a clear statement of the purpose to be achieved?

4. Is the purpose, as stated, based on and consistent with the situation?

5. Is the purpose broad enough and stated in sufficiently broad terms so that, when achieved, it will not only handle the situation but result in increased viability?

6. Is the strategic plan itself aligned to and consistent with the purpose?

7. Is the plan clearly expressed and understandable?

8. Does the plan include a strategy that will actually and effectively implement the purpose and swiftly get it rolling in the physical universe?

9. Is the proposed strategy actually clever and bright enough to achieve the purpose?

10. Is the plan broad enough to fully accomplish the purpose?

11. Is it doable?

12. Does it cover, in broad general terms as required in a strategic plan, the major actions and areas which need to be programed in order to accomplish the purpose?

13. Where it uses any of the other tools of management, does it use these correctly?

14. Does it take existing resources or lack of them into consideration?

15. Does it include strategic use of lines, terminals or networks where the need for this is obvious?

16. Does it include the use of surveys and/or PR handling where these are obviously indicated by the situation?

17. Does it tend to collapse purpose and tactical planning and omit the needed strategy? (If so, it needs correction.)

18. Does the strategic plan effectively bridge between purpose and tactical so that it can be used for coordination in tactical planning and serve as an orientation point for precisely targeted actions?

The above checklist is not in any way intended to be used by planning or approval terminals as a substitute for study of the references and full data on strategic planning.

While other factors than those listed might need to be taken into consideration, the checklist provides the main points upon which any strategic plan would be judged.

And it is probably safe to say that any plan which had all of the above positive points in would be worthy of the title "strategic" and highly effective when executed.

L. RON HUBBARD
Founder

HUBBARD COMMUNICATIONS OFFICE
Saint Hill Manor, East Grinstead, Sussex

HCO POLICY LETTER OF 31 JULY 1983R
Issue I
REVISED 21 JANUARY 1991

Remimeo
All Orgs
All Execs
All Management
  Personnel

Org Series 47

Executive Series 26

Establishment Officer Series 45

Admin Know-How Series 48

BASIC MANAGEMENT TOOLS

Refs:

HCO PL 29 Dec. 82RA	Org Series 46
Rev. 20.1.91	Exec Series 24R
	Esto Series 43R
	AKH Series 44R
	THE TOOLS OF MANAGEMENT
HCO PL 31 July 83 II	Exec Series 27
	Esto Series 46
	AKH Series 49
	Org Series 46
	MANAGEMENT TOOLS BREAKTHROUGH

The following is a list of the materials which, out of the many tools of management, comprise the BASIC MANAGEMENT TOOLS.

1. *ADMIN SCALE:* A scale for use which gives a sequence (and relative seniority) of subjects relating to organization. The scale, from the top down, includes: Goals, Purposes, Policy, Plans, Programs, Projects, Orders, Ideal Scenes, Statistics, Valuable Final Products. The scale is worked up and down until it is (each item) in full agreement with the remaining items. In short, for success, all these items in the scale must agree with all other items in the scale on the same subject.

2. *TARGET POLICY:* A series of policy letters which describe each type of target and how they are to be used by staff, executives and management personnel to get something *done.*

3. *STRATEGIC PLANS:* A STRATEGIC PLAN is a statement of the intended plans for accomplishing a broad objective and inherent in its definition is the idea of clever use of resources or maneuvers for outwitting the enemy or overcoming existing obstacles to win the objective. It is the central strategy worked out at the top which, like an umbrella, covers the activities of the echelons below it.

4. *PROGRAMS:* A PROGRAM is a series of steps in sequence to carry out a plan. Programs are made up of all types of targets coordinated and executed on time.

5. *PROJECTS:* A PROJECT is a series of guiding steps written in sequence to carry out one step of a program, which, if followed, will result in a full and successful accomplishment of the program target.

6. *ORDERS:* An ORDER is the direction or command issued by an authorized person to a person or group within the sphere of the authorized person's authority. It is the verbal or written direction from a lower or designated authority to carry out a program step or apply the general policy. Some program steps are so simple that they are themselves an order or an order can simply be a roughly written project. By implication an order goes from a senior to juniors.

All orders of whatever kind by telex, despatch or mission orders must be coordinated with current written command intention. You can destroy an org by issuing orders to it uncleared and uncoordinated. Coordinate your orders! Clear your orders!

7. *COMPLIANCE REPORTS:* A COMPLIANCE REPORT is a report to the originator of an order that the order has been done and is a completed cycle. It is not a cycle begun; it is not a cycle in progress; it is a cycle completed and reported back to the originator as done.

When an executive or manager accepts "done" as the single statement and calls it a compliance, noncompliance can occur unseen. Therefore, one must (1) require explicit compliance to every order and (2) receive the evidence of the compliance pinned to the compliance report. Such evidence might be in the form of copies of the actual material required by the order and procured, or photographs of it, ticket stubs, receipts, a signed note stating the time and place some action was carried out, etc. Evidence is data that records a "done" so somebody else can know it is done.

It is up to LRH Comms, Flag Reps or execs to verify reports of dones or get dones done. True compliances to evaluated programs are vital.

8. *TERMINALS:* A TERMINAL is something that has mass and meaning which originates, receives, relays and changes particles on a flow line. A post or terminal is an assigned area of responsibility and action which is supervised in part by an executive.

A fixed-terminal post stays in one spot, handles specific duties and receives communications, handles them and sends them on their way.

A line post has to do with organizational lines, seeing that the lines run smoothly, ironing out any ridges in the lines, keeping particles flowing smoothly from one post to another post. A line post is concerned with the flow of lines, not necessarily with the fixed-terminal posts at the end of the lines.

9. *LINES:* A LINE is a route along which a particle travels between one terminal and the next in an organization; a fixed pattern of terminals who originate and receive or receive and relay orders, information or other particles.

A COMMAND LINE is a line on which authority flows. It is vertical. A command line is used upward for unusual permission or authorizations or information or important actions or compliances. Downward it is used for orders.

A COMMUNICATION LINE is the line on which particles flow; any sequence through which a message of any character may go. It is horizontal.

The most important things in an organization are its lines and terminals. Without these in, in an exact known pattern, the organization cannot function at all. The lines will flow if they are all in and people wear their hats.

10. *ORG BOARDS:* An ORG BOARD (ORGANIZING BOARD) is a board which displays the functions, duties, sequences of action and authorities of an organization. The org board shows the pattern of organizing to obtain a product. It is the pattern of the terminals and their flows. We see these terminals as "posts" or positions. Each of these is a hat. There is a flow along these hats. The result of the whole org board is a product. The product of each hat on the board adds up to the total product.

11. *HATS:* HAT is a term to describe the write-ups, checksheets and packs that outline the purposes, know-how and duties of a post. It exists in folders and packs and is trained in on the person on the post to a point of full application of the data therein. A HAT designates what terminal in the organization is represented and what the terminal handles and what flows the terminal directs. HATTING is the action of training the person on the checksheet and pack of materials for his post.

12. *TELEXES:* A TELEX is a message sent and received by means of telex machines at specific stations hooked up with one another. This is a fast method of communication, similar to a telegram or cable.

Use telexes as though you were sending telegrams. Positiveness and speed are the primary factors. Cost enters as a third. Security enters as a fourth consideration. All have importance but in that order.

Telexes must be of such clarity that any other person in the org can read and understand them. You must take responsibility for both ends of a communication line. Write your communication (telex) so that it invites compliance or answer without further query or dev-t. Entheta in telexes on a long-distance comm line is forbidden.

Don't use telexes when despatches will do. Nonurgent communications on telex lines jam them. Do NOT put logistics (supply) on a telex line. Telex lines should only be used for communications concerning operations.

13. *DESPATCHES:* A DESPATCH is a written message, particularly an official communication. When writing a despatch, address it to the POST—not the person. Date your despatch. Route to the hat only, give its department, section and org. Put any vias at the top of the despatch. Indicate with an arrow the first destination. Sign it with your name but also the hat you're wearing when you write it.

As with telexes, despatches must be written so clearly that any other person in the org can read and understand them, with the originator taking responsibility for both ends of the communication line. And, as with telexes, entheta in despatches on a long-distance comm line is forbidden.

14. *STATISTICS:* A STATISTIC is a number or amount *compared* to an earlier number or amount of the same thing. STATISTICS refer to the quantity of

work done or the value of it in money. Statistics are the only sound measure of any production or any job or any activity. These tell of production. They measure what is done. Thus, one can manage by statistics. When one is managing by statistics they must be studied and judged alongside the other related statistics.

15. *GRAPHS:* A GRAPH is a line or diagram showing how one quantity depends on, compares with or changes another. It is any pictorial device used to display numerical relationships.

16. *CONDITIONS:* A CONDITION is an operating state. Organizationally, it's an operating state and oddly enough, in the MEST universe, there are several formulas connected with these operating states. The table of conditions, from the bottom up, includes: Confusion, Treason, Enemy, Doubt, Liability, Non-Existence, Danger, Emergency, Normal, Affluence and Power or Power Change. There is a law that holds true in this universe whereby if one does not correctly designate the condition he is in and apply its formula to his activities or if he assigns and applies the wrong condition, then the following happens: He will inevitably drop one condition below the condition he is *actually* in. One has to *do* the steps of a condition formula in order to improve one's condition.

17. *PERSONNEL FOLDERS:* A PERSONNEL FOLDER is kept in HCO for each person employed by the org. The folder is to contain all pertinent personnel data about the person: name, age, nationality, date employment started, address (if other than the org), next of kin, social security number, test scores, previous education, skills, previous employment, case level, training level, name of post, former posts held and dates held, production record on post(s), date employment ceased, copies of all tests, and any other pertinent data.

Copies of contracts, agreements or legal papers connected with the person are filed in the personnel folder. The originals of such papers are kept in the val doc files.

A personnel folder is used for purposes of promotion and any needful reorganization and so should contain anything that throws light on the efficiency, inefficiency or character of personnel.

Personnel folders are filed by division and department in HCO, with the personnel in separate folders filed alphabetically in their department. There should be two sections in the personnel files: (1) present employees and (2) past employees.

18. *ETHICS FOLDERS:* An ETHICS FOLDER is kept in HCO for each individual staff member. It is a folder which should include his complete ethics record, ethics chits, Knowledge Reports, commendations and copies, as well, of any justice actions taken on the person, such as Courts of Ethics or Comm Evs, with their results.

Filing is the real trick of Ethics work. The files do 90 percent of the work. Ethics reports patiently filed in folders, one for each staff member, eventually makes one file fat. When one file gets fat, call up a Court of Ethics on the person and his area gets smooth.

19. *FILES:* A FILE by definition is an orderly and complete deposit of data which is available for immediate use. As FILES are the vital operational line, it is of the GREATEST IMPORTANCE that ALL FILING IS ACCURATE. A misfiled particle can be lost forever. A missing item can throw out a whole evaluation or a sale. It is of vital interest both in ease of work and financially that all files are straight.

20. *DATA SERIES:* The tool to discover causes. The administrative technology described in these policy letters is applied to find what is logical by ferreting out what is illogical, using this to reveal the greatest outness which, when remedied, will resolve the scene.

There is considerably more data on each of these tools contained in the policy letters in the OEC Volumes and Management Series Volumes, *none* of it complicated or difficult to grasp.

The purpose of this policy letter is simply to advise the exec that these *are* his tools—his most fundamental and basic management tools. And that they are for USE and it is VITAL that he USE them.

Why? Because use of these simple, basic tools means the difference between a failing org and a flourishing one.

And we want organizations to flourish!

L. RON HUBBARD
Founder

Revision assisted by
LRH Technical Research
and Compilations

HUBBARD COMMUNICATIONS OFFICE
Saint Hill Manor, East Grinstead, Sussex

HCO POLICY LETTER OF 31 JULY 1983
Issue II

Remimeo
All Orgs
All Execs
All Management
 Personnel

VITAL—IMPORTANT

Org Series 48

Executive Series 27

Establishment Officer Series 48

Admin Know-How Series 49

MANAGEMENT TOOLS BREAKTHROUGH

Refs:

HCO PL 29 Dec. 82RA II	Org Series 46RA
Rev. 21.1.91	Exec Series 24RA
	Esto Series 45RA
	AKH Series 44RA
	THE TOOLS OF MANAGEMENT
HCO PL 31 July 83R I	Org Series 47R
Rev. 21.1.91	Exec Series 26R
	Esto Series 47R
	AKH Series 48R
	BASIC MANAGEMENT TOOLS

THE FIRST THING AN EXECUTIVE OR MANAGER AT ANY LEVEL NEEDS TO KNOW IS THAT HE HAS *TOOLS* WITH WHICH TO MANAGE.

This applies to top levels of management, to middle management echelons and in every org from the CO or ED down through the Exec Council and every head of a division or department.

BREAKTHROUGH

This datum is the result of a recent, eye-opening breakthrough.

The breakthrough was not a matter of discovering or developing or improving the materials which make up the tools of management. Org boards, the Admin Scale, target policy, planning and programing, statistics, graphs and conditions (to name a few of these tools) have been a part of our technology, well defined, available for use and used for quite some years now.

THE BREAKTHROUGH WAS IN DISCOVERING THAT A GREAT MANY EXECUTIVES DID NOT LOOK UPON THESE AS *TOOLS*.

But unless one does recognize them as tools, unless one actually puts them in the *category of tools*, like rakes and shovels and wheelbarrows, he is apt to think of them as opinions or theories or something of the sort. He won't recognize that he does have actual *tools* with which to manage. And, not realizing this, he won't USE them in managing.

Such a scene could be compared to somebody building a house who didn't even know he was trying to build a house and, should this be pointed out to him, he would look at hammers and saws as if they were total strangers. He wouldn't wind up with a house.

Any activity has its tools. And if one is going to engage in an activity, he had better know what its tools are and that they are for use.

BASIC MANAGEMENT TOOLS

We are rich in management tools but the most fundamental of them, required for use at any executive level from the highest to the lowest, are these:

ADMIN SCALE

TARGET POLICY

STRATEGIC PLANS

PROGRAMS

PROJECTS

ORDERS

COMPLIANCE REPORTS

ORG TERMINALS

SPECIFIC LINES

ORG BOARDS

HATS AND HATTING

TELEXES

DESPATCHES

STATISTICS AND GRAPHS

CONDITIONS

PERSONNEL FOLDERS

ETHICS FOLDERS

FILES

DATA SERIES.

Each of these fundamental tools is defined and covered briefly in HCO PL 31 July 83R I, BASIC MANAGEMENT TOOLS.

None of these are complicated. They are actually SIMPLE but VITALLY, VITALLY IMPORTANT.

One gets some terminals, gets them some lines, gets the channels of command and echelon worked out, gets in strategic planning and with that one can achieve some coordination.

But it is necessary to be able to conceive of purpose (which, in target policy, becomes objectives). And it is necessary to be able to write targets that will accomplish that objective or that purpose. To get the targets done one needs lines and terminals there. And to have lines and terminals, of course, one has to have an org board.

SIMPLE. But VITALLY IMPORTANT.

In laying out these tools we are laying out the fundamentals of organization as that, most definitely, is what these tools are. And these tools will give one an organization. Without them, you don't have an organization, you have a mob. And if one cannot figure out purpose or objectives or write targets and telexes and get hatting done and hats worn they'll just keep on being a mob. But correct use of just this basic list of management tools can turn a mob into a producing organization!

EXEC STATUS ONE CHECKSHEET

A fast, instant-hat type of checksheet called Exec Status One is being provided to swiftly train execs and managers at all levels on these tools.

This is not a substitute for an OEC or FEBC. But it is vital that an exec starts using these tools right now, instantly and at once yesterday, if he considers himself an executive or is in a position of handling an organization of any type, size or kind. Because if he doesn't use these tools, he's going to lay an egg.

ETHICS

Once the exec has passed this first checksheet, Exec Status One, it's an ethics offense to fail to use these tools properly. One would handle a first or second offense with cramming, but after that it's a Court of Ethics and, in the case of a person having trained on these tools continuing to misapply or not apply these tools, it becomes a matter for a Comm Ev.

SUMMARY

1. First, an executive or manager must know that actual TOOLS EXIST for his use in managing.

2. Second, he needs to know WHAT his tools are.

3. Third, he must realize that these tools are SIMPLE but VITALLY, VITALLY IMPORTANT, that they are for USE and he must *USE THEM.*

L. RON HUBBARD
Founder

HUBBARD COMMUNICATIONS OFFICE
Saint Hill Manor, East Grinstead, Sussex

HCO POLICY LETTER OF 10 JULY 1986
Issue I

Admin Know-How Series 50

KEEPING ADMIN WORKING

Refs:

HCO PL   7 Feb.   65   KSW Series 1
                             KEEPING SCIENTOLOGY WORKING
HCO PL   24 Sept. 70RA   ISSUES, TYPES OF
       Rev. 3.7.77

In 1965 I wrote the policy letter KEEPING SCIENTOLOGY WORKING. It appears as the first item of nearly every Dianetics and Scientology course checksheet. And with good reason. Unswerving and relentless application of that one issue by every Scientologist is our only certain means of keeping the technology pure and the future hope of mankind alive.

It may not be generally understood, however, that the principles given in that policy letter do not apply only to what is commonly referred to as "tech"—the first dynamic technology given in HCO Bulletins. You see, when "tech" goes out, the pc suffers. When "admin" goes out, the org declines.

Therefore, to keep Scientology working, *all* of Scientology, one must insist on standard tech *and* admin. The principles of unvarying adherence to precise technology, constant alertness to tech alter-is and insistence that every Scientologist abide by these rules apply *just* as severely to the third dynamic technology of standard administration—POLICY.

POLICY

POLICY embraces the basic duties of a staff member, the precision technology of management in all its aspects and at every echelon, and standard ethics and justice procedures. Policy is found in HCO PLs, Flag Orders, Central Bureaux Orders, LRH EDs, taped lectures and other duly authorized and on-source administrative issues.

Just as with our technology of handling the individual, our policies for the establishment and expansion of effective organizations are based on fundamental laws of life derived through exhaustive research and experience. Every policy we have has been put to the acid test—"Does it work?"—and passed. Neither tech nor policy admit interpretation, alteration or "new ideas" generated by the bank. Bright, constructive application of exact principles, yes. Embellishment and know-best, never.

To you, the individual executive or staff member, "Keeping Admin Working" means making sure that you have all the policy relating to your post and to your hat as a staff member. It means insisting that your org's Qual Division maintains a complete library of policy for use by staff and that it is not unmocked or hidden away or rendered unusable. It means knowing the policies of one's job, through standard hatting and training. It means insisting that standard staff courses exist complete with WHAT IS A COURSE? policy in down to the last comma, whose graduates go livid at the idea of anyone alter-ising standard policy. It means demanding that Qual provides a tough, standard Cramming Section that detects deviation from policy at the first pause of a stat and handles the hell out of it right now—including finding out how the scene was allowed to go awry in the first place and correcting THAT, too. It means total dedication on the part of every last Scientologist to putting in standard admin, straight by the book. It means holding an utterly unreasonable line on KEEPING standard admin IN.

OUT–ADMIN

While our overall record of success is stellar in the extreme, the history of our organizations is dotted here and there with stat crashes brought about by out-admin. These range in scope from the collapse of one staff member's post up to the near collapse of the whole international Scientology network in the 60s when squirrel "execs" at Worldwide were "managing" on their own know-best and over scores of misunderstoods on basic policy. That scene was salvaged by getting the admin squirrels off the lines, their orders cancelled and the simple on-policy usual done: org boards set straight and made known, hat checksheets and packs compiled, studied up and used by all staff, a schedule posted and adhered to, etc. Very simple, really. It just had to be DONE.

The fact is that every organizational failure or decline in our history can be traced to standard admin going OUT. Likewise, every boom or recovery can be traced to policy being put IN. It is a one-for-one.

EXAMPLES

It was once found that a senior exec (long since discovered and removed) was attempting to run a major org from his upper-management post on a day-to-day basis even though it was several echelons below him and despite numerous vividly clear policies forbidding such an activity. But this person "knew best." And he managed (not accidentally) to crash the org's delivery and leave a major mess for other, on-policy execs to come in and bail out on an emergency basis.

This same Mr. Know Best was also found to have worked his way onto the comm lines of some staff doing a vital project to revive a faltering org. He was covertly feeding them his own instructions (which were completely contrary to policy and the approved steps of the project) and getting them to forward his "successful actions" instead of policy. The result was a failed project which had to be redone from scratch. Had those executing the project adhered to policy instead of forwarding someone's know-best and alter-is, their project could have ended in success instead of a crash.

SOURCE

People's failure to recognize what standard policy is can sometimes get in your road. As an example, an executive once went into an org and established a standard, by-the-book (OEC Volume 4) Dept 10 with Dir Tech Services, HGC

Admin, Tech Pages, Tech Receptionists, etc. The stats, of course, boomed. But after that, people kept referring to this exec's actions as though they were something new and strange and referred to the project instead of the OEC Volume! From this, one can conclude that you have to put in policy with an axe and call it such and take no nonsense concerning it. For even when people see the fruits of the application of policy materialize, they have to be told again that that was POLICY and IS IN THEIR OEC VOLUMES.

The way to do this is to get in a competent Qual that hats the staff on HCO PLs, from basic staff status checksheets all the way up to FEBC, and crams them when they flub. Unless Qual is strong and functioning and pounds home green-on-white as *the* tried and true way to go about something, the staff are open to some suppressive moving in and leading them off into squirreldom.

We work, in our organizations, in the face of a bank that says that the group is all and the individual nothing. This you know. Know, too, that that same bank is constructed to make very sure that no one ever succeeds in forming anything resembling an *effective* group with true survival goals or purposes. So we face quite a challenge. But in standard admin policy we have a potent weapon with which to meet this challenge: a codified system of organization which, where it has been applied purely, has resulted in the most powerful and effective organizations this planet and sector have ever known. Required are only the courage, determination and confront to master and use this weapon.

I count on you—the individual Scientologist—to take up the challenge, to put standard Scientology administrative policy to work, and to WIN. You can, you know. And the victory will be not only for you but for Scientology and for all mankind.

L. RON HUBBARD
Founder

HUBBARD COMMUNICATIONS OFFICE
Saint Hill Manor, East Grinstead, Sussex

HCO POLICY LETTER OF 10 JULY 1986
Issue II

Remimeo
All Orgs
All Missions
All Execs
All Staff

Admin Know-How Series 51

ADMIN DEGRADES

Refs:

HCO PL 17 June 70RB	KSW Series 5R
Rev. 25.10.83	TECHNICAL DEGRADES
HCO PL 7 Feb. 65	KSW Series 1
	KEEPING SCIENTOLOGY
	WORKING

How does standard "green-on-white" policy get lost? Just as with the "red-on-white" tech of auditing or training, it can potentially be obscured or made to seem unimportant by the actions of an ill-intentioned individual.

Someone considers that the best way to get a new staff member quickly onto post is to shorten his hat checksheet or label key hat materials as "old." The new staff member fails, dragging a whole unit or department down with him in a maelstrom of dev-t.

In a hurry to get something accomplished, someone skimps on the usual, on-policy procedures and routings and soon his improvised (squirreled) "handling," tolerated by others, becomes "the way it's always done around here." And crash goes that area.

Seeking to get his own stats up at any cost (and ignoring the effects of his actions on the org as a whole), an "expert" manages to obscure standard, on-policy lines and routings and implements his own "successful actions," then torpedoes any attempt to get policy in. The result—the org falls far short of what it could be producing if it were operating by the book.

Such actions are suppressive. They are HIGH CRIMES. And they carry the same penalties as the suppression of the technologies of Dianetics and Scientology auditing or training—a condition of TREASON or cancellation of certificates or dismissal and a full investigation of the person's background.

The following actions or omissions are classified as HIGH CRIMES:

1. Abbreviating an official course in standard Scientology administrative policy so as to lose the full theory, administrative procedures and effectiveness of the subject.

2. Adding comments to the Org Exec Course or other administrative checksheets or instructions, policies or directives labeling any material "background" or "not used now" or "old" or "it doesn't need to be followed

exactly," or any similar action which will result in the student not knowing, using and applying the standard administrative data in which he is being trained.

3. Employing any checksheet for any administrative course not authorized by the Authority, Verification and Correction Unit International (AVC Int) or, in the case of hat checksheets, duly authorized per HCO PL 30 Sept. 70, CHECKSHEET FORMAT.

4. Failing to strike from any administrative or hat checksheet any such comments as "historical," "background," "not used," "old," etc., or VERBALLY STATING IT TO STUDENTS.

5. Failing to hat and apprentice a staff member on the full policy and actions of his post.

6. Discouraging or preventing a staff member, administrator or executive from training on the full Org Exec Course and Flag Executive Briefing Course.

7. Failing to insist upon precise and exact application of the Data Series policy letters in investigations and evaluations.

8. Running any organization on squirrel "policy" or third dynamic administrative or management procedures that are contrary to approved policy.

9. Using any squirrel administrative procedure in managing an organization while falsely labeling it Scientology policy.

10. Using Scientology policy but calling it something else or attributing it to some other source.

11. Acting in any way calculated to lose standard Scientology policy to use or impede its use or shorten its materials or its application.

Our policy is the result of years of hard-won experience. It works. It must be applied vigorously, intelligently and to the letter. Our own lives and happiness are at stake. This planet and universe are at stake. To carry off the task we need only keep and use these tools of standard admin.

L. RON HUBBARD
Founder

HUBBARD COMMUNICATIONS OFFICE
Saint Hill Manor, East Grinstead, Sussex

HCO POLICY LETTER OF 10 JULY 1986
Issue III

Remimeo
All Execs
Exec Sec Hats
HCO HAS Hat
Dir I&R Hat
MAA/Eth Off Hat
All Staff Hats
Qual Cram Off Hat
LRH Comm Hat
INCOMM

URGENT—IMPORTANT

Admin Know-How Series 52

Computer Series 5

ADMIN HIGH CRIME

Refs:

HCO PL	8 Mar. 66	KSW Series 13
		HIGH CRIME
HCO PL	19 Aug. 79RA	HIGH–CRIME CHECKOUTS AND
	Rev. 27.8.84	WORD CLEARING
HCO PL	10 July 86 I	AKH Series 50
		KEEPING ADMIN WORKING
HCOB	22 Feb. 72RA	Word Clearing Series 32RA
	Rev. 8.7.74	WORD CLEARING METHOD 4

With this issue, checkouts on policy by all administrative personnel become mandatory.

It has long been policy that technical personnel study, word clear, and star-rate check out on any technical materials before they apply those materials on their jobs. Pro auditors and interns at any level study, word clear and check out on the processes they are to run in session. Supervisors and Word Clearers star-rate on the basic materials of study tech and Word Clearing before they are allowed to deliver Scientology courses. And as new materials are issued, the Qual Division sees to it that the tech delivery personnel to whom the materials apply get them checked out IMMEDIATELY. Such checkouts have come to be known as "high-crime checkouts," from the title of the policy letter which brought them into being: HCO PL 8 Mar. 66, HIGH CRIME. And it is through the use of such checkouts that tech application is safeguarded and kept in step with the latest technical discoveries and advances.

Tech people take great pride in keeping on top of their subjects in this way. Understandably so; for when they do, the results they achieve are consistent and spectacular. Miracles are the order of the day. The public pour in for service. The organization thrives.

Where tech terminals don't KNOW and USE their materials, results are only anxiously hoped for. The public come in for service reluctantly, when they can be coaxed in at all. The organization dwindles.

HIGH CRIME CHECKOUTS ON POLICY LETTERS

Just as there is STANDARD TECH, so is there STANDARD ADMIN.

The fact is that any organization can be seen to fail when standard administrative policy is not known and used by its people. And every successful organization will be found to be composed of people who DO know and DO apply the basic principles found in our policy letters.

Therefore the following is classified as a HIGH CRIME:

NEGLECTING, ADVISING AGAINST THE APPLICATION OF, FAILING TO ENFORCE OR TOLERATING THE OMISSION OF STANDARD WORD CLEARING AND STAR–RATE CHECKOUTS ON ALL NEW OR NEWLY REVISED HCO POLICY LETTERS, AS WELL AS THE KEY HCO PLs OF THE BASIC STAFF MEMBER HAT AND THE KEY POLICIES OF THE STAFF MEMBER'S SPECIFIC ASSIGNED POST, BY EVERY STAFF MEMBER. IN THE SEA ORGANIZATION THIS APPLIES TO LRH CBOs AND FLAG ORDERS AS WELL AS HCO POLICY LETTERS.

STAFF MEMBER RESPONSIBILITY

Once an exec or staff member has completed study of his hat by proper checksheet, he should report to the SSO in Qual to be word cleared Method 4 and star-rate checked out on the key policies of his staff member hat as well as those policies specifically relating to his post. And when any new policy is issued relating to his post (or which is an essential part of his hat as a staff member), he must get it word cleared, checked out and into application immediately.

Such checkouts can be done by Qual personnel or by another staff member on a twinned basis. They must be tough standard star-rate checkouts which consult the staff member's understanding and demand that he demonstrate his ability to apply the material.

Staff on technical posts are included under this policy, as they are responsible for their hats as staff members.

QUAL RESPONSIBILITY

The SSO must alert all staff of new or revised LRH policies received, must keep a log of policies checked out by each staff member (just as a log is kept for technical). He must ensure that this is done within a matter of days of receipt of the issue—NOT allowed to drag out so that a backlog accumulates. The SSO is responsible for determining which policies are to be checked out by which staff, and logging them under the staff member's name in his checkout log. He should coordinate with the HCO Hatting Officer in making such determinations and in getting the checkouts done.

VIOLATIONS

The MAA or Ethics Officer, in investigating any post or area with down statistics must include an inspection of the Qual checkout log entries for the persons in the area being investigated. Where violations of this policy are found, the matter is reported to the HCO Area Secretary. The HCO Area Secretary must at once order a full and searching investigation into any persons who might have instigated it and report the matter with all particulars to the HCO Executive Secretary.

The HCO Exec Sec must then convene a Committee of Evidence with the persons accused as interested parties and must locate amongst them any suppressive or suppressives. When so located, they are duly declared as suppressive by HCO Ethics Order and dismissed.

If any Ethics Officer, Director of Inspections and Reports or HCO Area Secretary cannot obtain cooperation by superiors in carrying out this policy quickly, a report must be handed to the LRH Communicator directly, with a copy sent to the Inspector General Network via Flag.

The LRH Comm must act swiftly and effectively to handle the matter with proper justice action, reporting actions taken and results on LRH Communicator Network lines to LRH Comm International, with a copy to the Inspector General Network.

COMPUTER VERIFICATION

The International Network of Computer Organized Management (INCOMM) will be preparing a computerized system to verify that this policy is in force in every organization, and to call for HCO ethics action where it is found to be out.

With STANDARD ADMIN known and conscientiously in use on every post, the game is ours.

L. RON HUBBARD
Founder

STATISTICAL MANAGEMENT

HUBBARD COMMUNICATIONS OFFICE
Saint Hill Manor, East Grinstead, Sussex

HCO POLICY LETTER OF 1 FEBRUARY 1966
Issue IV

Remimeo

STATISTICS, ACTIONS TO TAKE
STATISTIC CHANGES

When statistics change radically for better or for worse, look for the last major alteration or broad general action just before it and it is usually the reason.

Example: Letters out statistic falls and falls. In investigating, look for the last major change in that area and, if possible, cancel it and the statistic will then rise. Let us say that just at the top of the down drop, the third week in November, the Dept of Registration was given new dictation equipment. Take it away and restore the old arrangement and routing pattern that was in use with it and sit back and see what happens. The statistic will probably recover.

Example: The field staff member commission statistic has been very low and suddenly leaps to Affluence. You want to reinforce it so you study what happened just before it. As it takes a bit of time on a statistic that has longer comm lines, you look a bit earlier. You find the Dir Clearing began to send FSMs big info packets they could give people. So you okay lots of such info packets to be given out and the Affluence of the statistic continues. And you write LRH what made it do that so a PL can be written.

I learned this while researching the life force of plants. Every time I saw a research bed of plants worsen, I queried what routine had been varied and found invariably some big change had been made that wasn't usual.

It is change that changes things for better or for worse. That's the simplicity of the natural law.

If you want to hold a constant condition, don't change anything.

If you are trying to improve something, make changes cautiously and keep a record of what is changed (like all orders must be by Sec EDs). Then you watch statistics and if they decline, you hastily wipe out the last change. And if they improve, you reinforce the change that began it.

For instance, we know the seven-division system pattern works, for the better it's gotten in, in an org, the more its graphs go up.

The org board of summer 1964 also works for a small org because it started their statistics up. But it was not good enough to maintain height of statistic when a certain size was reached. So we got the seven-division pattern of 1965.

It is, of course, obvious that if Joe as Org Sec did okay and if replaced with Bill who is only fifteen the Org Division will falter.

But, frankly, it is not just a personnel question by far.

Personnel equates against case gain more than personality. In December 1965 at Saint Hill, the gross divisional statistics very closely matched the *case progress* of the secretaries of each division. You can almost assign a post by:

1. Grade of Release, and

2. Leadership Survey, plus

3. Experience in org.

Those three factors take into no account personality or aptitude, much contrary to all the tests the nineteenth-century psychologist or eighteenth-century phrenologist would have made and used.

So while personnel changes are always a possible reason for radical shifts in statistics, they are by no means the major ones.

Shifts of comm lines, functions, policies, equipment, duties, locations are quite often far more responsible for graph shifts.

Personnel comes into it this way: When you make a bad rearrangement and you have an incompetent personnel also, you have disaster!

If you make a bad rearrangement and the personnel are good, the statistic drop may be only a small one as they cope. So even small drops should be investigated, particularly around good personnel.

The morals are these: If you have a disaster (big Danger condition), find the big change which preceded it or the missed order and get that fixed and also shift personnel.

If you see a person who has a good record coping like mad, inspect the area of that post to find what needs fixing up, what changes were made that overpressured that post and get it right.

THE PAUSED STATISTIC

During expansion, one has areas where statistics become level.

Here statistics *pause* because lines jam. People get overworked and confused.

The traffic is just too heavy.

And where do you really repair in such a case? More clerks? No! Always look to the lines of the *highest post* in the overloaded area and get them eased.

In expansion the person who never notices is the man in charge. And his lines are the most crippling to the org if jammed.

Example: Org Sec and Org Division stacked up and coping frantically. Org Exec Sec wonders what to do. Their statistics are paused (in a level line). They are overworked. Hire more clerks? No. Sort out the Org Sec and be sure more help is furnished *on that post*. Then the Org Sec (with a personal secretary to sort her mail, etc.) looks up and starts sorting out the division.

The old trick I used to use was to tell an overworked director, "Draw me up a list of all the hats you are wearing." And he or she would finally bring one in, round-eyed. "Thirty-five hats!" I recall one saying.

I would take the one nearest the director in duties and fill it with a staff member and the department would ease off.

Somebody like the Div 7 Sec or the LRH Communicator can do this to Exec Secs. If they are slaving, make them put on somebody to unjam their lines. They'll straighten the rest out.

So a *paused* statistic comes from the jammed lines of the topmost executives and is best remedied by easing them.

––––––––––

An org today is *not* run on personalities. It's run on statistics. All orders are based on statistics. The old personality system used by the business world and military is as yesterday as the rack and almost as cruel. Go modern. Use statistics only.

L. RON HUBBARD
Founder

HCO POLICY LETTER OF 6 MARCH 1966
Issue I

Remimeo
Exec Secs Hat
HCO Area Sec Hat
Dir I&R Hat
All HCO Hats
LRH Comm Hat

REWARDS AND PENALTIES
HOW TO HANDLE PERSONNEL AND
ETHICS MATTERS

The whole decay of Western government is explained in this seemingly obvious law:

WHEN YOU REWARD DOWN STATISTICS AND PENALIZE UP STATISTICS YOU GET DOWN STATISTICS.

If you reward nonproduction you get nonproduction.

When you penalize production you get nonproduction.

The welfare state can be defined as that state which rewards nonproduction at the expense of production. Let us not then be surprised that we all turn up at last slaves in a starved society.

Russia cannot even feed herself but depends on conquest to eke out an existence—and don't think they don't strip the conquered! They have to.

Oddly enough one of the best ways to detect a suppressive person is that he or she stamps on up statistics and condones or rewards down statistics. It makes an SP very happy for everyone to starve to death, for the good worker to be shattered and the bad worker patted on the back.

Draw your own conclusions as to whether or not Western governments (or welfare states) became at last suppressives. For they used the law used by suppressives: If you reward nonproduction you get nonproduction.

Although all this is very obvious to us, it seems to have been unknown, overlooked or ignored by twentieth-century governments.

In the conduct of our own affairs in all matters of rewards and penalties we pay sharp heed to the basic laws as above and use this policy:

We award production and up statistics and penalize nonproduction and down statistics. Always.

Also we do it *all* by statistics—not rumor or personality or who knows who. And we make sure everyone has a statistic of some sort.

We promote by statistic only.

We penalize down statistics only.

The whole of government as government was only a small bit of a real organization—it was an ethics function plus a tax function plus a disbursement function. This is about ³⁄₁₀₀ths of an organization. A twentieth-century government was just these three functions gone mad. Yet they made the whole population wear the hat of government.

We must learn and profit from what they did wrong. And what they mainly did wrong was reward the down statistic and penalize the up statistic.

The hard worker-earner was heavily taxed and the money was used to support the indigent. This was *not* humanitarian. It was only given "humanitarian" reasons.

The robbed person was investigated exclusively, rarely the robber.

The head of government who got into the most debt became a hero.

War rulers were deified and peacetime rulers forgotten no matter how many wars they prevented.

Thus went ancient Greece, Rome, France, the British Empire and the US. *This* was the decline and fall of every great civilization on this planet: They eventually rewarded the down statistic and penalized the up statistic. That's *all* that caused their decline. They came at last into the hands of suppressives and had *no* technology to detect them or escape their inevitable disasters.

Thus, when you think of "processing Joe to make a good D of P out of him and get him over his mistakes," forget it. That rewards a down statistic. Instead, find an auditor with an up statistic, reward it with processing and make *him* the D of P.

Never promote a down statistic or demote an up statistic.

Never even hold a hearing on someone with an up statistic. Never accept an ethics chit on one—just stamp it "Sorry, Up Statistic" and send it back.

But someone with a steadily down statistic, investigate. Accept and convert any ethics chit to a hearing. Look for an early replacement.

Gruesomely, in my experience I have only seldom raised a chronically down statistic with orders or persuasion or new plans. I have only raised them with changes of personnel.

So don't even consider someone with a steadily down statistic as part of the team. Investigate, yes. Try, yes. But if it stays down, don't fool about. The person is drawing pay and position and privilege for not doing his job and that's too much reward even there.

Don't get reasonable about down statistics. They are down because they are down. If someone were on the post, they would be up. And act on that basis.

Any duress leveled by Ethics should be reserved for down statistics.

Even Section 5 investigates social areas of down statistic. Psychiatry's cures are zero. The negative statistic of more insane is all that is "up." So investigate and hang.

If we reverse the conduct of declining governments and businesses, we will of course grow. And that makes for coffee and cakes, promotion, higher pay, better working quarters and tools for all those who earned them. And who else should have them?

If you do it any other way, everyone starves. We are peculiar in believing there is a virtue in prosperity.

You cannot give more to the indigent than the society produces. When the society, by penalizing production, at last produces very little and yet has to feed very many, revolutions, confusion, political unrest and dark ages ensue.

In a very prosperous society where production is amply rewarded, there is always more left over than is needed. I well recall in prosperous farm communities that charity was ample and people didn't die in the ditch. That only happens where production is already low and commodity or commerce already scarce (scarcity of *commercial* means of distribution is also a factor in depressions).

The cause of the Great Depression of the 1920s and 1930s in the US and England has never been pointed out by welfare "statesmen." The cause was income tax and government interference with companies and, all during the 1800s, a gradual rise of nationalism and size of governments and their budgets, and no commercial development to distribute goods to the common people, catering to royal governments or only a leisure class still being the focus of production.

Income tax so penalized management, making it unrewarded, and company law so hampered financing that it ceased to be really worthwhile to run companies and management quit. In Russia management went into politics in desperation. Kings were always decreeing the commoner couldn't have this or that (it put the commoner's statistic up!) and not until 1930 did anyone really begin to sell to the people with heavy advertising. It was Madison Avenue, radio, TV and Bing Crosby not the Gre-e-eat Roosevelt who got the US out of the depression. England, not permitting wide radio coverage, never has come out of it and her empire is dust. England still too firmly held the "aristocratic" tradition that the commoner mustn't possess to truly use her population as a market.

But the *reason* they let it go this way and the *reason* the Great Depression occurred and the *reason* for the decline of the West is this one simple truth:

If you reward nonproduction you get it.

It is *not* humanitarian to let a *whole* population go to pieces just because a few refuse to work. And some people just won't. And when work no longer has reward none will.

It is far more humane to have enough so everyone can eat.

So specialize in production and everybody wins. Reward it.

502

There is nothing really wrong with socialism helping the needy. Sometimes it is vital. But the reasons for that are more or less over. It is a temporary solution, easily overdone and like communism is simply old-fashioned today. If carried to extremes like drinking coffee or absinthe or even eating, it becomes quite uncomfortable and oppressive. And today socialism and communism have been carried far too far and now only oppress up statistics and reward down ones.

By the way, the natural law in this PL is the reason Scientology goes poorly when credit is extended by orgs and when auditors won't charge properly. With credit and no charge we are rewarding down statistics with attention and betterment as much as we reward up statistics in the society. A preclear who can work and produces as a member of society deserves, of course, priority. He naturally is the one who can pay. When we give the one who can't pay just as much attention, we are rewarding a down social statistic with Scientology and of course we don't expand because we don't expand the ability of the able. In proof, the most expensive thing you can do is process the insane and these have the lowest statistic in the society.

The more you help those in the society with low statistics, the more tangled affairs will get. The orgs require fantastic attention to keep them there at all when we reward low society statistics with training and processing. The worker pays his way. He has a high statistic. So give him the best in training and processing—not competition with people who don't work and don't have any money.

Always give the best service to the person in society who does his job. By not extending credit you tend to guarantee the best service to those with the best statistics and so everyone wins again. None are *owed* processing or training. We are not an Earthwide amends project.

No good worker *owes* his work. That's slavery.

We don't *owe* because we do *better*. One would owe only if one did worse.

Not everyone realizes how socialism penalizes an up statistic. Take health taxes. If an average man adds up what he pays the government he will find *his* visits to medicos are *very* expensive. The one who benefits is only the chronically ill, whose way is paid by the healthy. So the chronically ill (down statistic) are rewarded with care paid for by penalties on the healthy (up statistic).

In income tax, the more a worker makes the more hours of his workweek are taxed away from him. Eventually he is no longer working for his reward. He is working for no pay. If he got up to 50 pounds a week the proportion of his pay (penalty) might go as high as half. Therefore people tend to refuse higher pay (up statistics), it has a penalty that is too great. On the other hand a totally indigent nonworking person is paid well just to loaf. The up statistic person cannot hire any small services to help his own prosperity as he is already paying it *via* the government to somebody who doesn't work.

Socialisms pay people *not* to grow crops no matter how many are starving. Get it?

So the law holds.

Charity is charity. It benefits the donor, giving him a sense of superiority and status. It is a liability to the receiver but he accepts it as he must and vows (if he has any pride) to cease being poor and get to work.

Charity cannot be enforced by law and arrest for then it is extortion and not charity.

And get no idea that I beat any drum for capitalism. That too is old-old-*old* hat.

Capitalism is the economics of living by nonproduction. It by exact definition is the economics of living off interest from loans. Which is an extreme of rewarding nonproduction.

Imperialism and colonialism are also bad as they exist by enslaving the population of less strong countries like Russia does, and that too is getting a reward for nonproduction like they did in Victorian England from all the colonies.

Parasitism is parasitism. Whether high or low it is unlovely.

All these isms are almost equally nutty and their inheritors, if not their originators, were all of a stamp—suppressive.

All I beat the drum for is that the working worker deserves a break and the working manager deserves his pay and the successful company deserves the fruits of its success.

Only when success is bought by enslavement or rewards are given to bums or thieves will you find me objecting.

This is a new look. It is an honest look.

Reward the up statistic and damn the down and we'll all make out.

L. RON HUBBARD
Founder

Remimeo
Exec Secs
Secretaries
HCO OIC Sect Hat
OIC Exec Div Hat
LRH Comm Hat

STATISTIC GRAPHS
HOW TO FIGURE THE SCALE

A graph is not informative if its vertical scale results in graph line changes that are too small. It is not possible to draw the graph at all if the line changes are too large.

If the ups and downs are not plainly visible on a graph, then those interpreting the graph make errors. What is shown as a flat-looking line really should be a mountain range.

By SCALE is meant the number of anything per vertical inch of graph.

The way to do a scale is as follows:

Scale is different for every statistic.

1. Determine the lowest amount one expects a particular statistic to go— this is not always zero.

2. Determine the highest amount one can believe the statistic will go in the next three months.

3. Subtract (1) from (2).

4. Proportion the vertical divisions as per (3).

Your scale will then be quite real and show up its rises and falls.

Here is an *incorrect* example.

We take an org that runs at £500 per week. We proportion the vertical marks of the graph paper of which there are 100 so each one represents £100. This when graphed will show a low line, quite flat, no matter what the org income is doing and so draws no attention from executives when it rises and dives.

This is the *correct* way to do it for gross income for an org averaging £500/week.

1. Looking over the old graphs of the past 6 months we find it never went under £240. So we take £200 as the lowest point of the graph paper.

2. We estimate this org should get up to £1,200 on occasion in the next 3 months, so we take this as the top of the graph paper.

3. We subtract £200 from £1,200 and we have £1,000.

4. We take the 100 blocks of vertical and make each one £10, starting with £200 as the lowest mark.

Now we plot gross income as £10 per graph division.

This will look right, show falls and rises very clearly and so will be of use to executives in interpretation.

Try to use easily computed units like 5, 10, 25, 50, 100, and show the scale itself on the graph (1 div = 25).

The element of hope can enter too strongly into a graph. One need not figure a scale for more than one graph at a time. If you go onto a new piece of graph paper, figure the scale all out again; and as the org rises in activity, sheet by sheet the scale can be accommodated. For example it took 18 months to get Saint Hill statistics up by a factor of 5 (5 times the income, etc.) and that's several pieces of graph paper, so don't let scale do more than represent current expectancy.

On horizontal time scale, try not to exceed 3 months as one can get that scale too condensed too, and also too spread out where it again looks like a flat line and misinforms.

Correct scaling is the essence of good graphing.

L. RON HUBBARD
Founder

506

HCO POLICY LETTER OF 24 JULY 1967

FIXED PUBLIC CONSUMPTION OF PRODUCT

Any Scientology organization (or any organization) which is working in any way upon a fixed statistic of consumption will eventually fail. By "fixed consumption" is meant estimates of the public's consumption of product as a limit on production.

There are several ways to "fix a consumption statistic." These are:

1. Provide just so many auditors for the HGC to agree with expected pcs.

2. Schedule just as many courses in the Academy as one thinks there will be students.

3. Provide just enough quarters to handle the expected quantity of business.

Unless one disregards the expectancy and unless one simply furnishes all the service one can, regardless of past statistics, the org will go downhill.

Several orgs work on the basis that there is just so much business and that one must only cater to that. Sydney, Auckland and some others have gone so far as to hold a one-student course with hours arranged to fit that student. Joburg has in the past let the pc decide how and when he is to be audited and has had a Registrar assigning the hours (with 35 auditors on the payroll and pcs getting 2 hours each a week, 35 auditors were delivering only 100 auditing hours a week!).

Any org that does not simply provide good, uniformly scheduled service will fail.

———————

Let us have an example of a car industry working on a fixed consumption statistic. The directors look up the last year and see that 1,000,000 cars were bought. They decide then, for this year, to make 1,000,000 cars. As they keep doing this year to year, they eventually begin to make less and less cars and one day go out of business.

That is NOT the way to go about it.

What the directors should have done was ignore the last year's stat and call in the head of production and ask, "How many cars can you make this next year?" The guy says, "2,500,000." The board says, "Good. Make them." Then the board calls in their Distribution Division and says, "Tell the dealers they will get 2 and ½ times as many cars next year so be sure and get ready to sell them." And the board calls in the Letter Reg and says, "Write every owner of one of our cars that he is going to be very pleased with his next model. And mail a magazine to all of them once every two months tracing the new model's development."

Now, in practice of course, no car industry has any Letter Reg or Central Files of customers and their Dist Div is a sort of list of dealers, so that board couldn't do that. But a Scientology org can!

Now let us examine the exact, same procedure in a Scientology org if it were followed.

Wrong way: The Exec Council sees how many students and pcs were trained and processed last year and arranges to train and process that many this year. The Registrar working alone must keep up some quota so begins to make special deals in desperation.

The org goes downhill. Like Auckland, Sydney and Joburg did.

Right way: The Exec Council calls in the Tech Sec, Director of Training and Director of Processing and Director of Tech Services and says, "What is the maximum number of students and pcs that we can handle?" These executives figure it out and say, "500 students and 210 pcs." The Exec Council then tells them to do it and calls in the Dissem Sec and says, "Have your people contact and sign up 750 students and 350 pcs in the coming year." They call in the Dist Sec and say, "Double the names in CF." They call in the HCO Sec and say, "Get in ethics in this whole area and also locate and give us a list of all failed cases in the past three years." This last list they give to their field staff members with orders to "offer a free S&D and get the people in."

The Exec Council does NOT work on a fixed statistic of last year or any year. It DOES NOT CONSIDER IT IS STOPPED BY A FIXED CONSUMPTION. It does not try to limit its business to expected business.

Of course, it is silly to think there is any limit on the people who are to be trained and processed. We have not even touched the 3,000,000,000 potential Scientologists on this one planet.

If you schedule a continuous course in the Academy and teach it, it will fill up. IF you don't break it into arbitrary periods. People who run a course every six weeks or every year always eventually fail. You have to run a continuously enrolling course.

At Saint Hill we held to enrolling every Monday for many years. Then a couple years ago I ordered enrollment on arrival (any day of the week) and *enrollments increased.*

––––––––––––

If the service is there, it will be used. If it is there only by wait, it will not be used.

Sometimes you have to teach a full course to an empty Academy for weeks or months when you start this, but given good, well and precisely scheduled classes and all tech *in,* the place will fill up and stay filled.

Sometimes HGC auditors sit around for weeks with no pcs after a full HGC is organized, but they will eventually have pcs if the service is there.

There IS NO FIXED CONSUMPTION.

When you do not provide the service first, it will not be used. You cannot drum up business unless the service is certain. The best way to have certain service is to provide it before it is demanded. Then, as it exists, it will be used.

You can promote before your service is complete only so long as the service will be there when demanded.

In general org management it is very easy to fall for a fixed consumption idea and limit everyone to it. The only sure way to proceed is to operate with maximum possible service while bringing maximum pressure to bear on the Dist and Dissem Divisions to fill the place up.

There is no limit to the number of students and pcs. Why limit the sign-ups?

L. RON HUBBARD
Founder

HCO POLICY LETTER OF 15 AUGUST 1967
Remimeo
Issue I

DISCIPLINE
SPs AND ADMIN
HOW STATISTICS CRASH

One of the ways an SP works to stop an activity or to halt an Affluence is to pick out key personnel and spread wild, false and alarming stories about them.

Another way, often used in conjunction with the above, is to pound a key executive with alarming entheta about staff, divisions or activities. This urges the key executive to take uncalled-for action which upsets things and which may lead to the dismissal of valuable staff.

Also, it is a symptom of an org under external pressure to come down on its own personnel rather than on the public or on real SPs.

SPs tend to vanish in memory since they speak in generalities. "Always" "every one" salt their language so that when you say, "Who told you?" in tracing a rumor, it is hard to remember since "everyone" seems to have said it. Actually, the SP who did say it used "everyone" in his comm so often as to become in memory "everyone."

A GOOD MANAGER IGNORES RUMOR AND ONLY ACTS ON STATISTICS.

Had I heeded over the years any rumormonger, we would have no orgs. I generally don't listen, and if I do, only go so far as inspecting stats.

It is easy to discipline staff and hard to discipline the public. A LAZY executive only disciplines staff. It takes more confront to tackle the public.

When an executive listens to rumor and bad things about his fellow staff members without looking at the actual production statistics, that executive can harm the org badly.

I have never tried to make staff members "be good." I have only tried to make them produce and wear their hats.

Our whole statistic system exists to end excessive discipline of valuable staff members.

To me a staff member whose stats are up can do no wrong.

I am not interested in wog morality. I am only interested in getting the show on the road and keeping it there.

Also, I detest having to discipline anyone for anything, particularly a Scientologist. And the only discipline I use is to hold the fort until people are Clear enough to see the light. They always do. All misconduct comes from aberration.

However, if anyone is getting industrious trying to enturbulate or stop Scientology or its activities, I can make Captain Bligh look like a Sunday school teacher. There is probably no limit on what I would do to safeguard man's only road to freedom against persons who, disdaining processing, seek to stop Scientology or hurt Scientologists.

I well know man's fixation on trying to make "everybody good." Which means, really, inactive. The best men I have had in wars routinely have been continually arrested and generally frowned on by "shore patrols," "military police," etc. To the body politic a *quiet* person is the ideal. When the guns begin to go, these quiet ones are all hiding and only the active ones are there to fight. I often wonder what would happen to a state if it *did* achieve its apparent goal of making one and all inactive little sheep.

So I don't care what men or women do if they just wear their hats and keep their stats up. Only when Scientology is being slowed or stopped do you find me rigging up the tools of discipline.

In actual fact, I rather hold the person who is inactive because he is afraid of punishment in contempt. I respect only those who are strong enough to be decent without the "self-protection" of evil.

I use discipline to hold the edges of a channel, not to stop the flow.

SPs LOVE to coax those with power to slay. As the basic ambition of any SP is "EVERYBODY DEAD SO I CAN BE SAFE," he or she will use all manner of lies and mechanisms to excite a thirst for discipline in those in power.

If I ever heed any "Kill everybody" advice, it is to put the adviser up against a brick wall.

———————

All evil stems from aberration. And it can be pretty evil. And awfully aberrated. The only road out from evil is processing. Therefore, one must protect the road to freedom as the answer to evil and must protect as well all those who are working to keep the road in.

The world will never become good because of discipline or oppression of evil. All discipline presupposes that the person being disciplined wants to survive. The truly evil only want to succumb so discipline threat is no answer. The truly evil LOVE pain and suffering and deprivation. So it coerces nothing and improves nothing when you seek to solve all evil with discipline. Only the already decent can be disciplined. It only obliges the evil ones. So all you can do really is to get the evil ones parked off the lines.

The executive in disciplining is concerned with those who would stop or hinder the flow and those who are just plain idle or stupid. So he severely leaves alone all upstats and only acts to move the suppressives off the lines and not let the idle and stupid slow the flow. An executive could never make the world reform by discipline alone. He can by processing. So his only use of discipline is to continue to make processing possible. It's as simple as that.

L. RON HUBBARD
Founder

511

HCO POLICY LETTER OF 15 AUGUST 1967
Issue II

Non-Remimeo
Ad Council
HCO Exec Secs
Org Exec Secs

IMPORTANT EXECUTIVE ACTION

Any organization whose statistics:

a. Level out

b. Remain low

c. Drop

the action to be taken by Exec Secs is to convene a Board of Investigation.

The Board of Investigation is to cover:

a. Flow of bodies into the organization

b. The flow of mail into the organization

c. The flow of funds into the organization

d. Any ethics outness on principal execs, and

e. Any tech outness.

The last two are the causes of org collapses.

The Board is to establish if there are any stuck flows or off-policy handling of the above particles into the organization. Any possible blocks or violation of fast flow policy on these lines are to be isolated. These three flows are the ones that PTS and SP inclined people get onto right away and stop.

Furthermore, investigate the quality of particles leaving the organization, i.e., letters, bulk mailings, promotional mailings. Correlate the relation between items out and items in.

L. RON HUBBARD
Founder

HCO POLICY LETTER OF 10 OCTOBER 1969R
REVISED 13 FEBRUARY 1991

Remimeo

DOWNSTAT CAUSES

The most usual reasons for dwindling gross income statistics are:

1. Out-tech,

2. Lack of an enterprising ARC Break Reg and ARC Break Auditor to keep the field cleaned up,

3. An incomplete or unused CF,

4. Incomplete or unused address files,

5. Lack of books or poor book distribution,

6. An incomplete Executive Council,

7. A staff not trained on the Org Exec Course,

8. A staff not basically trained in tech,

9. Lack of meter availability,

10. Nonstandard Public Divs which do not do the basic promotion actions resulting in new names to CF.

In 3, 4 and 5 above one finds personnel wanting to actually DO the essential work necessary at a purely hard-work level. Also orgs tend to "retire" parts of their CF or "save money" (and go broke) by not doing full mailings to their address plates.

There are many other actions which can cause down stats, of course, but these have to be pretty bad to actually keep stats depressed.

The promotional actions of an org have to be in, the Director of Special Affairs has to keep the area defended and the basic functions as per the org board have to be in.

But wherever stats are down and stay down, the above ten reasons have to be looked at and handled.

You would be utterly amazed at the reasons that can be given as to why the above ten are not *in*.

One that is not listed is the most dangerous one: REASONABLE EXPLANATIONS OF WHY STATS ARE DOWN. Given anyone in an org at all, the above ten are the real reasons.

L. RON HUBBARD
Founder

Remimeo

STATISTICS, MANAGEMENT BY

The most direct observation in an org (or a country) is statistics.

These tell of production. They measure what is done.

It cannot be said too often that management is best done by statistics.

Each division in an org has a GROSS DIVISIONAL STATISTIC. This is calculated to reflect the production of that division by all its divisional members.

An EXECUTIVE COUNCIL has all these GDSes available to it every week. This is done by the OIC system (Organization Information Center). The stats are collected by each division and compiled by Dept 3, Div 1, Inspections and Reports into graphs. No matter how small an org, it has to have an OIC.

The EC as a Council runs the org by observation of the GDSes.

Conditions are assigned each division by the EC each week, according to these GDS stats.

The name of the secretary of the division is noted on the graph. EC names are also on their own graphs.

These graphs, the OIC, should be POSTED WHERE STAFF CAN SEE THEM, not hidden in some room or in only an Exec Sec's office. They tell the rest of the org what the division is doing.

There is a lot to stat interpretation. It is covered in the Org Exec Course.

The Gross Income stat is not the most important in the org. It is modified by the expense of the org. An apparent high income can be wiped out by ignorant or unreal financial planning, which makes the org cost more than it makes.

If all other stats are up, the Gross Income will go up.

Individual staff members, Secretaries and Executive Secretaries are commended, promoted, demoted or comm eved on the basis of their stats. A person with high stats has Ethics protection. A person with low stats not only has no Ethics protection but tends to be hounded.

Orgs are not well run by the old school tie, what professor one knew in the Ivy League University or who is shacked up with whom. Orgs run by other considerations than stats, hurt the individual staff members. Orgs are well run when they are run by fairly and realistically designed stats for every staff member, division and the org.

Reasonableness is the great enemy in running an org. "Well, of course, the PES's stat is down because there's been a rail strike. . . ." Nonsense. The PES's stat is down because of low production in the Public Divisions and that's the whole and only reason.

Rumor can kill orgs and staff members. Whopping generalities like "People are ARC broken with Scientology" is just a suppressive person at work. Suppressives HATE anything that helps people. Listening to rumors instead of looking at stats or instead of just producing what one is supposed to produce in an org is playing straight into the hands of the bad hats.

Stats are a safe way to operate.

By raising individual stats we expand.

By expanding we gain strength and influence.

It may be a long road but it is a safe one.

Run only by statistics.

L. RON HUBBARD
Founder

STATISTICAL JUDGMENT

(Ref: HCO PL 5 Feb. 70, STATISTICS, MANAGEMENT BY, and
other PLs on this subject which recent PLs clarify but do not modify)

When one is managing by statistics one does *not* manage by gross income only.

There can be a tendency for management and staffs to believe an org is all right because it has a rising gross income graph. This is not true. The gross divisional statistics must be observed before the gross income can mean very much.

"We can't touch the South Lansing Org because its GI is on a rising trend." "The EC was changed when the GI was rising." "I was wrongly removed because the GI was rising." These are all meaningless statements unless one studied all the gross divisional statistics.

Statistics must be studied and judged alongside the other related statistics.

A rising income graph can even be shown sometimes as an actual threat to an org if the Tech *delivery* stats are down and stay down. It means the org is selling and not delivering and may very well crash shortly.

A high Qual graph once got a Qual Sec removed. It was high because Qual ran a campaign against Tech, invalidating gains so the pcs would have unneeded reviews. A high Qual income graph compared to a low "successful hours delivered" graph in Tech can mean the org is sick. Tech isn't delivering good service so Qual is in Affluence.

Low books sold means the org will fall flat in a few months.

Low outflow means trouble soon.

An income graph needs the bills figure (cash-bills ratio graph) to see if the org is solvent and is handling its financial planning well. It might be costing far more than it makes.

An org can have an increasing gross income graph and a much more rapidly increasing bills graph. It is unhealthy and may crash.

A good cash-bills ratio with low bulk mailing means the org is staying solvent by not promoting—and it will go to pieces soon. Somebody is idiotically saving money on promotion and probably wasting it like mad elsewhere. It has happened often.

The GI should be rising. That seen, the next action is to reenforce it by

516

making all the other gross divisional statistics rise also, making bills go down and reserves go up. Then one must be sure that the expenses are less than the income.

If an EC, a manager, a staff will see to these things and see that their admin is up to date and their product quality is high, they're in clover.

If they also see that their PRO area control is excellent, they will surely take and eventually be supreme in their area.

One often has to *look* long and hard in a division to find why its stat is down but there is always an obvious, curable internal reason which found and remedied, pushes the stat up.

The divisional stat is made by the stats of the sections, units and individual staff members of the division.

The GI is made from high divisional stats.

That is how it is done and that is what is meant by statistical management.

L. RON HUBBARD
Founder

HCO POLICY LETTER OF 16 AUGUST 1970

STATISTIC MISMANAGEMENT

A no-cause attitude toward statistics expresses itself in various ways.

1. No stats at all in that they are not computed, collected or posted.

2. Stats computed and collected but not posted or issued.

3. Stats posted but disregarded in handling.

4. Stats posted and looked over but reasonably explained.

The head of an organization or division who is not going to make it operates this way:

HANDLING EVERYTHING AND TOO BUSY TO ORGANIZE AND ENFORCE STATS.

Sooner or later but we hope at *some* time he will realize that he is only handling unworn hats that result in no stats.

The rule is of course: Cope by all means but spend some of that time organizing. If one does not devote some time to organizing, then his cope will increase and he will drown for sure with increased cope.

If everyone in an org wore his hat, there wouldn't be odd bits left to handle.

If an org staff half wears its hats, then everyone in the org is wearing some piece of everyone else's hats and the result is bedlam. At the top there is total cope.

A measuring stick for a worn hat is a stat.

Half-worn hats have half stats or none.

By making sure every post is filled and every post has a stat, one can then progress toward less and less cope, more and more result.

If the stats are an indication of the ideal scene then low stats show a departure from the ideal scene and one can find out WHY *and* get the stat up again.

Thus, the ideal scene can be approached.

Down stats or none at all are a wide departure from the ideal scene. Where the stats are lowest or absent the departure is greatest.

For example, one org's individual stats were very low. They were posted. It was a very ragtag, bobtail, out-tech scene a *long* way from the ideal.

Another org had no stats even compiled or posted and was making about one-tenth of its normal income and collapsing. The head of it had worked himself to a dead end, had ceased to cope and was not even there!

REASONABILITY

Even with posted stats, one can defeat the purpose of them by being reasonable or alter-izzy about them.

"Well, the study stat is down but I know why. Our top student graduated." "We have a slump in Treasury stat but I know why. . . ." ". . . I know why. . . ." ". . . I know why. . . ."

That off-the-cuff "I know why" without even looking carries with it a spectator flavor unless one (1) went and looked and (2) figured out how to get it up.

One area with fifteen blown students using a "I know why. Joe graduated," explanation is being a bit kooky.

"Yes, we know all the stats are down but there's been a football game . . ." is a big outpoint statement in itself.

I traced some of these "I know whys" down once and found them covering up holes you could lose an elephant in. The "Joe graduated" explanation for lowered point stats disclosed a fifty percent nonattendance being neglected!

So this off-the-cuff shrug showed a hat not being worn, seniors sweating and the head of the place madly trying to handle OTHER COMPLICATIONS ARISING FROM THE SAME POST.

So if you don't have stats and they're not collected and posted and *used*, prepare to do an awful lot of coping!

Also prepare to have injustice, overload of good workers, heavy ethics, unpleasantness and overloaded seniors.

To have anything running one has to have stats, they have to be computed, posted and USED.

Locating the real WHY of down stats takes a *considerable* study of the area where they are down.

The gross outnesses are usually:

Inadequate personnel procurement

Inadequate training for or on post

Inadequate org board

Use of PR instead of sweat to get by.

519

One lesson you learn when you have been at this for a while:

THE INCOME OF AN ORG IS TOTALLY UNDER ITS OWN CONTROL.

All public flaps and catastrophes do is upset the staff. They have almost NO effect on public or inflow potential. One could even say that public flaps are assisted by down stats in the org. The staff, having produced poorly or poor quality of basic product, then invites a flap. Down stats generate down stats.

In this universe and on this planet in particular there are a lot of nuts. They would fight baby rattles if they thought it threatened their baby-poisoning business! The percentage of nuts is about 10 percent. Of that 10 percent, 2½ percent are the Chief Nuts.

They are so crazy one almost has to help them shoot himself.

When Dianetics was NOT USED for 18 years (1951–1969) to handle illness, orgs eventually got into trouble = no Dianetics stat.

When Scientology was not fully used (1965–1970), there was a lot of public trouble.

The MOST trouble was in 1968 when *neither* Dianetics nor Scientology was in use.

So a no-product, no-stat condition is the same graph as the trouble graph.

But the org stats were affected only internally! By internal causes!

So any org determines its own stats—all of them!

So the basic gross outness re stats is not to have real stats and not to compute, publish, use and PUSH THEM UP.

The "I know why" doesn't carry with it a "let's find a WHY that we can remedy and push the stat up."

While all this is modified of course by whether or not you have an org product you can do and offer, it is a comment that the quality of the product and creating a demand for it only determines the ceiling of the org as a whole.

Having a real product that one does well brings about an almost no-ceiling condition.

As I write this our ceiling is retarded only by the necessity of catching up with eighteen years of disuse of Dianetics and five years of Scientology "quickie delivery." We are issuing new scenes and stats at this writing that give an index of quality of product delivered. That takes off the ceiling.

The only thing that could go wrong is not establishing, collecting, computing, posting and using the stats to establish a nearer and nearer approach to the ideal scene, not just for us but for the planet.

L. RON HUBBARD
Founder

HCO POLICY LETTER OF 28 AUGUST 1970

Remimeo

CONTROL OF STATISTICS

(Originally written by LRH for the *Apollo* OODs of
28 Aug. 70. Issued as an HCO PL on 5 Nov. 80.)

I think GDSes are down in some sectors because some people just don't know how to get them up. Many watch them from a spectator viewpoint. Well, it's down. Fate. It recovered. Kismet (Russian for "fate"). It's level. "Will of Allah."

The missing datum is that an org's stats are totally under the control of that org. An org's stats totally reflect the production and competence of the org.

Let's take a letters in stat. You (a) increase letters out, (b) you check out letter writers on getting R in the letters wholly, (c) you use CF folders always when writing a letter, (d) you increase letters out, (e) you spot-check letters going out for R and on-policy, (f) you put hard sell and good promo out, (g) you use info packets, and (h) you get out heavy bulk mailings on-policy, (i) you offer what you can deliver, (j) you deliver what you offer. Result, letters in soars! My own letters in stat (when I sign another name) is 1 for 1. In most orgs it's about 25 percent response.

But I'll bet a lot of orgs have it explained that it's fate or "promo doesn't work" or "local public interest is low."

A success story stat is totally under control. You really use the tech and really smooth out students and cases and you get 1 success story for every completion. Then, because you have a success story, you get a re-sign-up and get a *new* completion and a *new* success story.

Major service sign-ups depend on Testing, getting DMSMH read and an HAS Course. So you test in volume as a real public service, you have an HAS or study course for the book, you teach a marvelous HAS Course. You get a sign-up for a major service. To lose one guy off the line is strictly negligence.

So my attitude toward low GDSes is about the same as you'd feel for somebody who didn't know he was driving and ran the car in a ditch on a straight road!

I don't speak from lack of knowing. Because I've done it and it's about as easy as riding an armchair.

Staffs make their own trouble. Once in Joburg they tested a whole school of kids. Why, God knows. But they did. And then did the adult test grading on

521

them! "You see, Josie Ann (aged 10), you are having trouble with your husband." Didn't half upset the parents. Tailor-made down stats.

Somebody hadn't checked out on WHY they were testing people. Or what they were supposed to do with them.

Orgs are being penalized solely because of lack of training and understanding and grooving in people.

Every point of neglect, every half-worn hat, spoils our reach just that much. Every action well done, small or large, extends our reach just that much.

The more you know and the better you do your job, the sooner we will make it.

L. RON HUBBARD
Founder

HUBBARD COMMUNICATIONS OFFICE
Saint Hill Manor, East Grinstead, Sussex

HCO POLICY LETTER OF 3 OCTOBER 1970RA
REVISED 27 AUGUST 1982

STAT INTERPRETATION

Refs:

HCO PL 9 Nov. 79R Rev. 27.8.82		HOW TO CORRECTLY DETERMINE A STAT TREND
HCO PL 6 Nov. 66R I Rev. 9.11.79		AKH Series 5R STATISTIC INTERPRETATION, STATISTIC ANALYSIS
HCO PL 5 May 71RA II Rev. 27.8.82		READING STATISTICS
HCO PL 6 Mar. 66 II		STATISTIC GRAPHS, HOW TO FIGURE THE SCALE
HCO PL 27 Aug. 82		VITAL DATA: POWER AND AFFLUENCE CONDITIONS

This policy letter has been revised 9.11.79 to delete the statement "The dotted line is drawn roughly through an average in all TREND cases" as the statement has been broadly misinterpreted to mean that one would determine a trend by drawing a line from the midpoint of the first line of the trend period to the midpoint of the last line.

This latter is a FALSE DATUM. It would only be correct about 50 percent of the time and is not to be used. The correct method of reading a stat trend is given below and is covered in detail in HCO PL 9 Nov. 79R, HOW TO CORRECTLY DETERMINE A STAT TREND.

The interpretation of statistics includes *trend.*

TREND means the tendency of statistics to average out up, level or down over several weeks or even months as long as the situation remains.

The closer one is to the scene of the stat, the more rapidly it can be adjusted and the smaller the amount of time per stat needed to interpret it.

One can interpret one's own personal statistic hour to hour.

A division head can interpret on a basis of day to day.

An Executive Secretary needs a few days' worth of stat.

An Executive Director would use a week's worth of stat.

A more remote governing body would use a TREND (which would be several weeks) of divisional stats to interpret.

In short the closer one is to a statistic the easier it is to interpret it and the easier it is to change it.

One knows he had no stat on Monday—he didn't come to work. So Tuesday he tries to make up for it.

At the other end of the scale, a Continental Executive Council would have to use a trend of weeks to see what was going on.

READING STAT TRENDS

A TREND is an inclination toward a general course or direction.

TRENDS can be anything from Danger to Power, depending on the slant and its steepness. It is also possible to have a Non-Existence trend.

NOTE: ON THE GRAPHS BELOW THE DOTTED LINES HAVE BEEN DRAWN IN SIMPLY AND ONLY TO SHOW THE TREND—THE GENERAL COURSE OR DIRECTION—THESE STATISTICS ARE TAKING OVER A PERIOD OF WEEKS. They are given here to educate one in the relationship between trend lines and conditions and for no other purpose. One does NOT in actuality determine a trend by drawing a dotted line or any kind of line through the graph. A trend is determined by looking. It is done with the eye. One must visually average the peaks and valleys of a stat and one looks at the period of time overall and determines the pitch or slant of the graph. Determining stat trends correctly is covered fully in HCO PL 9 Nov. 79R, HOW TO CORRECTLY DETERMINE A STAT TREND.

A Non-Existence TREND would look like this:
(plotted by weeks)

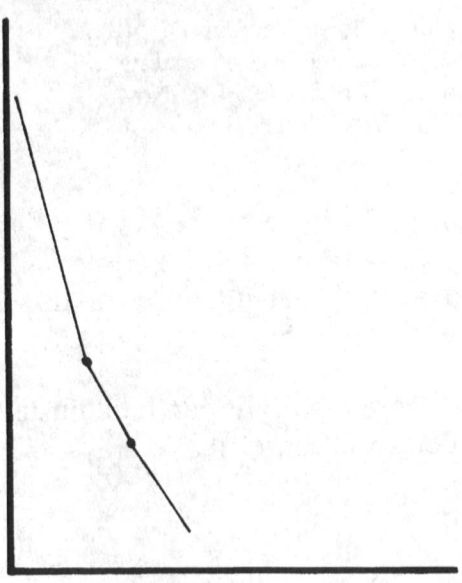

This would also be a Non-Existence TREND:

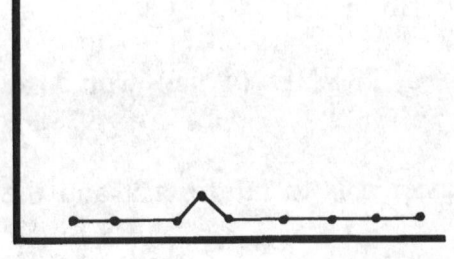

This would be a Danger TREND:
(plotted by weeks)

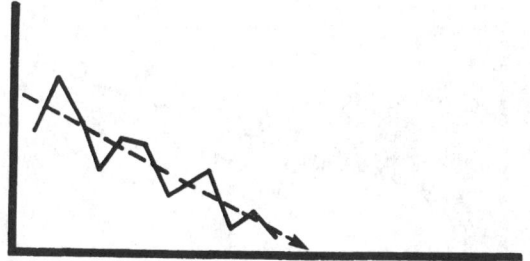

This would be an Emergency TREND:

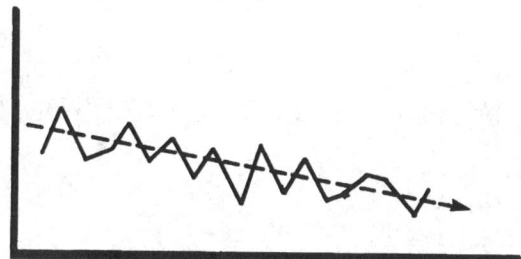

As you can see, it is not so steep.

This would also be an Emergency TREND as it will collapse—nothing stays level long.

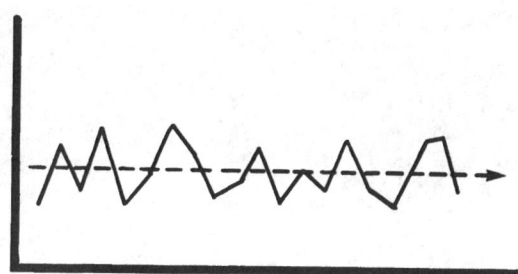

This would be a Normal TREND:

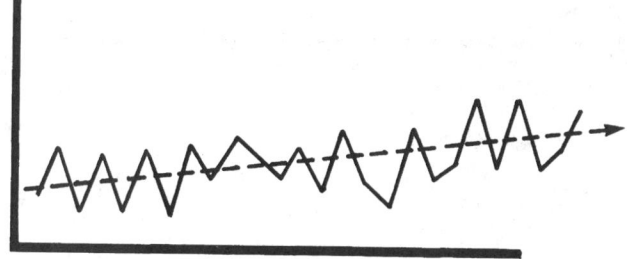

Any slight rise above level is Normal.

525

This would be an Affluence TREND:

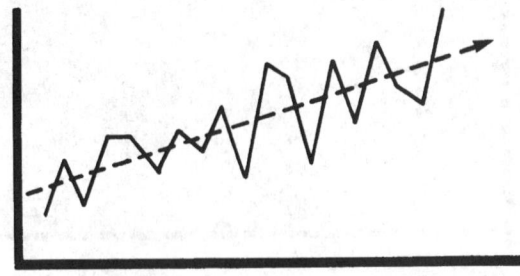

This would also be an AFFLUENCE TREND. The graph is steeply Affluence-trending.

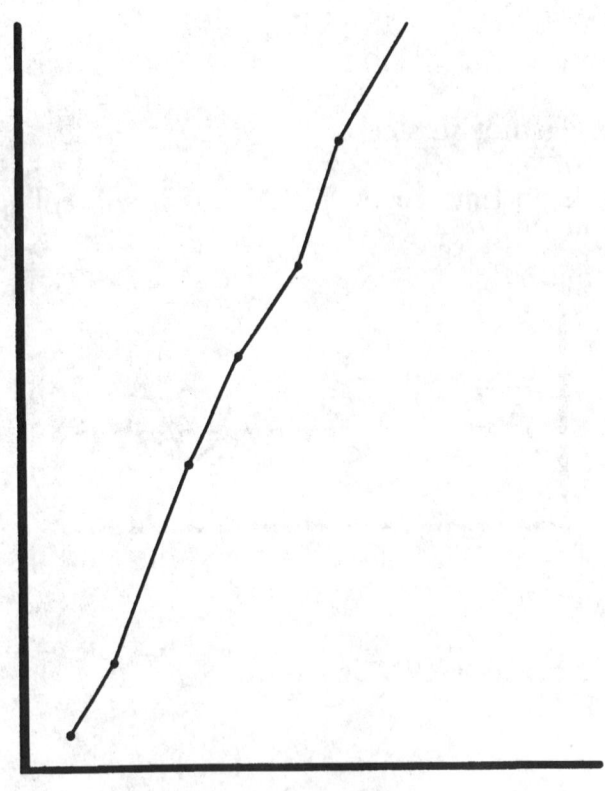

This graph shows AFFLUENCE GOING INTO POWER:

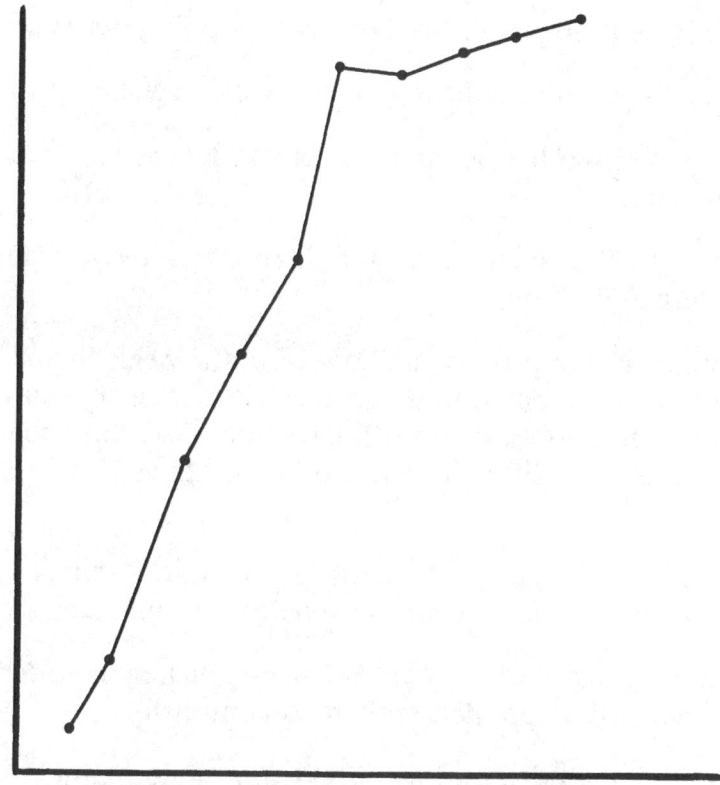

The Affluence trend has peaked at a new high range.

Power is a Normal trend that is being maintained in a very, very high range. (Ref: HCO PL 27 Aug. 82, VITAL DATA: POWER AND AFFLUENCE CONDITIONS.)

A single day or week's graph goes into Affluence differently:

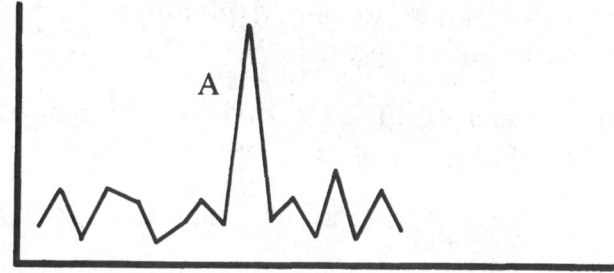

Point A is the single Affluence. The TREND however is barely Normal as the single surge did not maintain itself.

REMOTE MANAGEMENT

Not knowing TRENDS, remote management can err. An org or division may be in an Affluence trend and because the last week's stat was a bit down, actions can be (and have been in the past) taken against the org or one of its divisions and broke the winning streak.

The reason for this policy letter is several cases of remote management failures to use trends to estimate the state of an org by its stats.

A remark "All GDSes were down" could be at first glance factual until it was seen that all GDSes were in Affluence trend.

REASON

The reason for this is found in the Data Series policy letters.

A valid statistic is the best indicator of the ideal scene.

When an org or division has departed from its ideal scene, it cannot be made to recover in an instant.

The reapproach to the ideal scene for a group is by a gradient approach because so much has to be done.

One can't ordinarily jump from making 2 cars a week for months to 2,000 cars a week in one week. Workers, tools, materials, machinery out of use all have to be moved back into line. It may go to 15 cars, then 120 cars then 200 cars then 750 cars then 800 cars then 20 cars then 1,000 cars then 1,500 cars then 1,800 then 2,000.

It is so easy for a thetan to postulate a fact and so arduous to move it into MEST universe existence that management tends to be impatient.

"Get CF straight" takes 1 1/2 seconds to say but may take 6 weeks of time for a manned up specially appointed crew to accomplish.

"Get CF straight" is easily said to an existing undermanned staff. They do but "Letters Out" falls to 10 from 1,200.

It is so easy to think it. But thinking it isn't doing it.

The right way is to program it. "Recruit 2 new staff members. Hat and train on CF. Get CF straight" is the right statement.

WHY stats go up and down traces to backlogs being caught up, to new projects given overloaded staffs, to unreal planning, to finance squabbles and failures to hire, hat, train and program.

So wildly varying stats in an org's divisions almost always mean finance poorly handled, hiring, hatting, training is poor. Utilization of staff is not good.

But by TREND it shows the overall tendency to approach or depart from the ideal scene.

When you are close up you can do something about it and when you are far away the day's or the week's stat has already changed before any order could ever arrive.

In remote management, not managing by TREND is a serious fault as one's orders are always rather unreal.

An upward TREND even if only slightly upward shows people are trying and level or downward shows it is in trouble.

TREND is the overall measure of expansion or contraction and is the most valuable of stat messages.

L. RON HUBBARD
Founder

528

HUBBARD COMMUNICATIONS OFFICE
Saint Hill Manor, East Grinstead, Sussex

HCO POLICY LETTER OF 5 MAY 1971RA
Issue II
REVISED 27 AUGUST 1982

Remimeo
OEC Checksheet

READING STATISTICS

Refs:

HCO PL 9 Nov. 79R		HOW TO CORRECTLY DETERMINE
Rev. 27.8.82		A STAT TREND
HCO PL 3 Oct. 70RA		STAT INTERPRETATION
Rev. 27.8.82		
HCO PL 6 Nov. 66R I		AKH Series 5R
Rev. 9.11.79		STATISTIC INTERPRETATION,
		STATISTIC ANALYSIS
HCO PL 6 Mar. 66 II		STATISTIC GRAPHS, HOW TO
		FIGURE THE SCALE
HCO PL 27 Aug. 82		VITAL DATA: POWER AND
		AFFLUENCE CONDITIONS

In a local org area one reads the division stats for the WEEK. A dept reads its stats by the *DAY*. A section does it by the HOUR. You can also read all div GDSes by the day; successful orgs do.

TRENDS are used in more remote areas from the org to indicate successful leadership or broad admin or tech situations. TRENDS are used locally to estimate expansion or warn of contraction.

Thus in weekly condition assignments one only considers two things: that exact week and the slant of that one line. Steep near vertical down: Non-E. Down: Danger. Slightly down or level: Emergency. Slightly up: Normal. Steeply up: Affluence. (As Power is a *trend,* it is not judged on a one-week basis only nor by a single line on a graph. Power is a Normal trend maintained in a high, high range; thus a Power condition must be determined by more than one week's worth of stats.)

Note that these slants for Non-E through Affluence are used to determine the stat condition *for the week.* Measuring stat *trends,* a trend over a three- or six-week period or longer, is covered in HCO PL 9 Nov. 79R, Rev. 27.8.82, HOW TO CORRECTLY DETERMINE A STAT TREND. Additional data on Power as a trend is given in HCO PL 27 Aug. 82, VITAL DATA: POWER AND AFFLUENCE CONDITIONS.

The volume of the stat has little to do with it. Level at high or level at low are alike Emergency.

The *proof* of this is that you always find a Why and it's always some change.

Typical argument about stats: "I know it's down a bit but it's so high generally that it's Power." (Even with stats validly in a Power range, one would handle a dip in the stats with the appropriate condition formula.) Or: "I know it rose but it's so low that it's really Non-E." All this is being *reasonable*. Status think.

When you don't value stats this way, you don't catch the improvements or flubs that, piled up, wreck an org.

I recall a D of T who had high, high stats. One week they plunged. He said, "Oh, of course. We graduated some students and . . ." But I rejected that and looked and looked, and lo and behold they'd changed their method of handling students! This, found and repaired, sent their stats soaring!

When you let status reasoning get into stat assignment of conditions, the org has had it!

The weekly condition assignments must be accurate. Only in that way can one maintain expansion.

Also, it's a bit mean to nag around about a rise. "But it isn't much of a rise; you're really in too low a range to have a rise count. . . ."

A rise is a rise. They at least got more. Now, better organizing, they will get more than that. Week by week it goes up.

Similarly, to discount a fall just because stats are high, high, high is folly. They *could* do week before last's as they did it. So what was wrong that they couldn't do it again? If they got exhausted at it week before last, they need more help, obviously. Or better organization.

Only if you use the single week can you properly, locally manage.

If you keep it up, the org will start to occupy more space, need more people, need more equipment. Actually, the area control of the org increases and stability and viability increase.

If stat declines for the week are brushed off, the org will shrink, become less stable, will demand more work by fewer and will be a burden.

When you manage by the stat, you don't go wrong. But it has to be an honest stat, and explanations that aren't the real *Why* have to be rejected.

As you work with this, all becomes revealed. And one has a total control of survival.

L. RON HUBBARD
Founder

HUBBARD COMMUNICATIONS OFFICE
Saint Hill Manor, East Grinstead, Sussex

HCO POLICY LETTER OF 9 NOVEMBER 1979R
REVISED 27 AUGUST 1982

Remimeo

HOW TO CORRECTLY DETERMINE A STAT TREND

Cancels:

HCO PL	19 Sept. 73 II	HOW TO MEASURE A TREND

Refs:

HCO PL	3 Oct. 70RA Rev. 27.8.82	STAT INTERPRETATION
HCO PL	6 Nov. 66R I Rev. 9.11.79	AKH Series 5R STATISTIC INTERPRETATION, STATISTIC ANALYSIS
HCO PL	5 May 71RA II Rev. 27.8.82	READING STATISTICS
HCO PL	6 Mar. 66 II	STATISTIC GRAPHS, HOW TO FIGURE THE SCALE
HCO PL	27 Aug. 82	VITAL DATA: POWER AND AFFLUENCE CONDITIONS

Much data exists on statistics and their importance, the reading of statistics, stat interpretation and assigning conditions by stats. However, unless one knows how to read statistics correctly and how to correctly determine a stat *trend,* prediction and therefore management by stats will be way out in left field.

It is a simple action to determine the condition of a stat on a one-week basis by looking at the slant of the one line for that week. (Ref: HCO PL 5 May 71RA II, Rev. 27.8.82, READING STATISTICS)

There is a bit more tech involved in determining the condition of a stat by trend. The correct tech on trends must be understood well by any person engaged in a management activity.

FALSE DATUM

I have just found a FALSE DATUM that you run a ruler through the middle of the peaks and valleys of stats to work out the trends. That is not how one determines a trend.

HCO PL 19 Sept. 73 II, HOW TO MEASURE A TREND, actually a BPL written by others, introduced a false interpretation of how one actually determines a trend by stating: "To construct a trend line, connect the midpoint of the first line of your trend period to the midpoint of your last line."

That datum is false. It is not how it is done. It is a misinterpretation of statements in actual policy letters on how one looks at an average of a series of weekly stats to determine the trend.

Despite the cancellation of that false issue by BPL 10 Oct. 75 XI, CANCEL-LATION OF HCO POLICY LETTERS 1973–1975, it was recently discovered that the issue was still around and being used in several areas and that the false datum it put forth was still being carried around in the heads of many of those actually working with statistics.

Therefore, HCO PL 19 Sept. 73 II, HOW TO MEASURE A TREND, even though previously cancelled is hereby RECANCELLED by this policy letter. It is not to be used. Earlier valid policy letters containing data on the subject have been revised to clarify and set forth in more detail exactly how one determines a trend so there is no possibility of misinterpretation. Those issues along with this policy letter provide the correct tech on determining the trend of a statistic.

READING STAT TRENDS—THE RIGHT WAY

By TREND is meant an inclination toward a general course or direction.

Trend lines which indicate the condition of a stat by trend are shown very clearly in HCO PL 3 Oct. 70RA, Rev. 27.8.82, STAT INTERPRETATION. One must be fully familiar with them.

Another important part of the tech is figuring the scale for a graph correctly so that trend lines actually show up on the graph when the stats are plotted on it. Too large or too small a scale will obscure the true condition of a stat trend. The data on how to figure the scale is given in HCO PL 6 Mar. 66 II, STATISTIC GRAPHS, HOW TO FIGURE THE SCALE.

To determine a stat trend you need to look at several weeks' worth of stats. In a management body somewhat close to the org, such as a FOLO, one would use three weeks' worth of stats. Remote management areas, such as Flag, use a period of six weeks. In some cases for purposes of stat analysis a longer period would be reviewed. In any case, the procedure is the same. It's the slant or pitch of the stat over the period that one needs to be able to recognize.

To actually see the trend the stat is taking, you count back six weeks from the present stat. One doesn't count the present stat (this week's dot on the graph) as one of these six weeks. One counts six dots back from that point. This gives you six *lines* to work with. Each line shows the change that has taken place over a one-week period. In combination and in sequence, these lines present a pattern. Whether the pattern is one of an even, unbroken progression up, down or level, or a series of peaks and valleys, it will show the general direction, up, down or level, in which the stat is moving.

You can work out stat trends by averages but all you have to do is LOOK. It's done by inspection.

One looks at the picture AS A WHOLE. You have to visually average the peaks and valleys. You look at the peaks and note the trend they are taking. You look at the valleys and note the trend they are taking. You then visually average the two trends and you will SEE the general direction, the trend, the stat is taking.

Trends are not hard to read. But it is done with the EYE. There is no internal system of lines that can be drawn to assist this.

Anyone who has been relying on a system of drawing internal lines on the graph to come up with a trend will need to eliminate that false datum and to reeducate his eye to simply spot the pitch or slant of the overall direction of the stat by LOOKING.

One sits back and looks at the picture as a whole, and there is a definite slant one can determine by this. Is it tilting slightly downward? Steeply downward? Is it level? Tilting slightly up? Simply educating one's eye to visually average the peaks and valleys and determine the overall slant or pitch the graph, or portion of the graph, is taking will give you the trend of that graph or portion of that graph for that period.

Doing it the other way is not always wrong, but it is right only about fifty percent of the time. That is not good enough and the system should not be used.

The following example, using six weeks of stats, shows how one would arrive at a false conclusion, an *incorrect condition by trend,* by using the faulty system of drawing a line midpoint between the first and last lines.

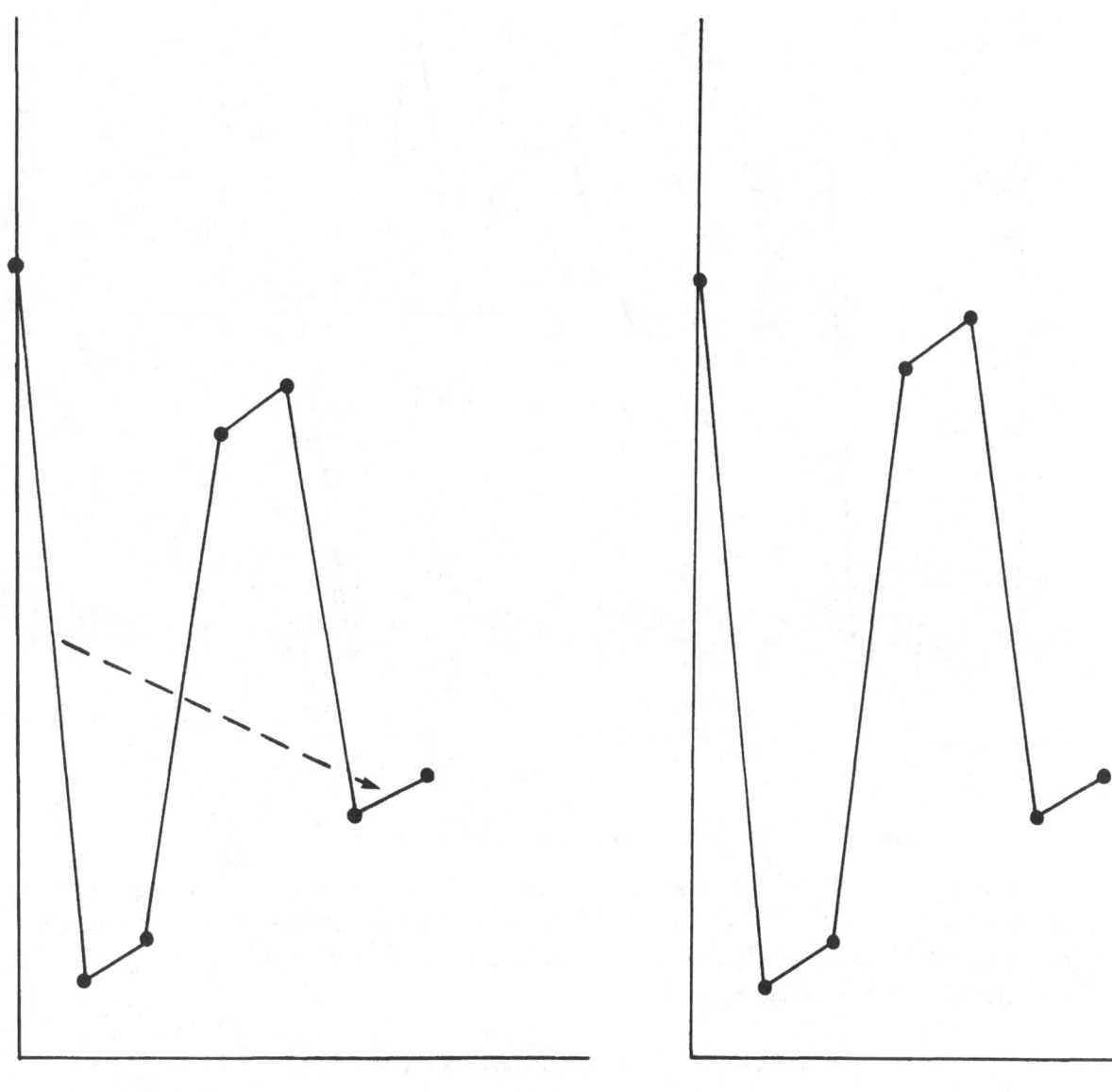

WRONG

RIGHT

The dotted line indicates the stat is DANGER trending. This is INCORRECT and an INCORRECT METHOD of determining a trend.

Sit back and look at this graph. It will be seen that the overall slant of the graph is slightly up. The condition by six-week trend is NORMAL.

533

The graph below shows a period of twelve weeks' worth of stats.

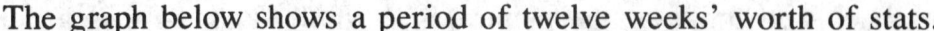

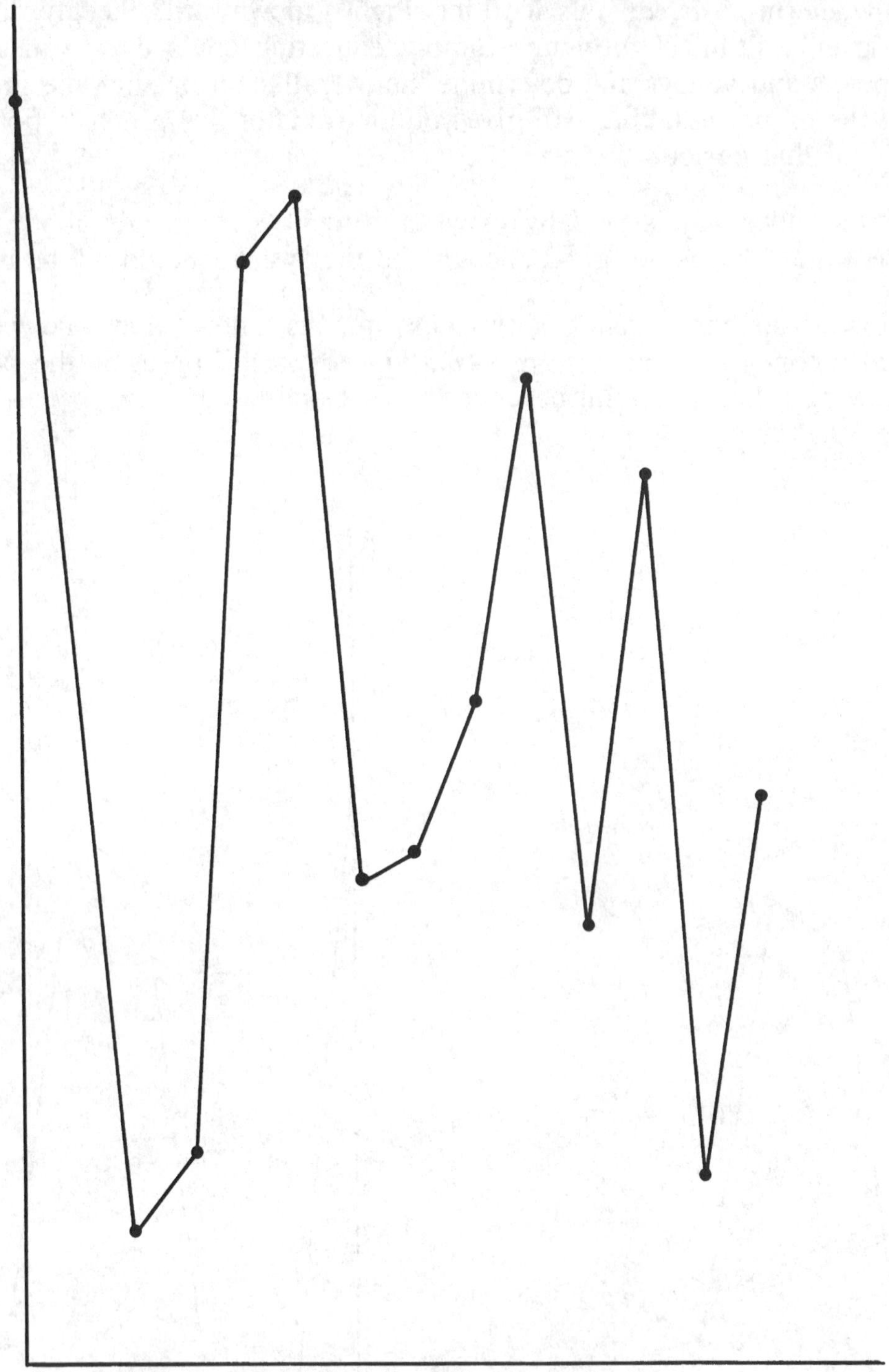

When you look at this graph and look at those declining peaks and look at the averages of the drops, the condition is slightly below level. It shows a twelve-week EMERGENCY TREND. Just sit back and look at this graph and you will see that it is tipping over.

STATISTIC TREND RECOGNITION DRILL

One can learn to recognize and read stat trends correctly and it must be done by anyone who is working with stats or stat trends in any capacity.

Attachments 1 to 17R accompanying this policy letter are provided for drill purposes. One uses them as flashcards to drill statistic trend recognition, over and over, until the person can swiftly and correctly recognize the trend.

Additionally, stat trends out of old stat books should be copied onto flashcards and used for drill purposes so one gets a variety of trends to work with.

It is an easy skill to develop. Don't complicate it with figure-figure or some intricate system of internal lines. Learn to simply LOOK and recognize the trend. It is done with the eye.

Skilled stat trend recognition is an essential ingredient of skilled management.

It takes only some drilling and a sound understanding of this policy letter and the issues it references.

So learn it well.

L. RON HUBBARD
Founder

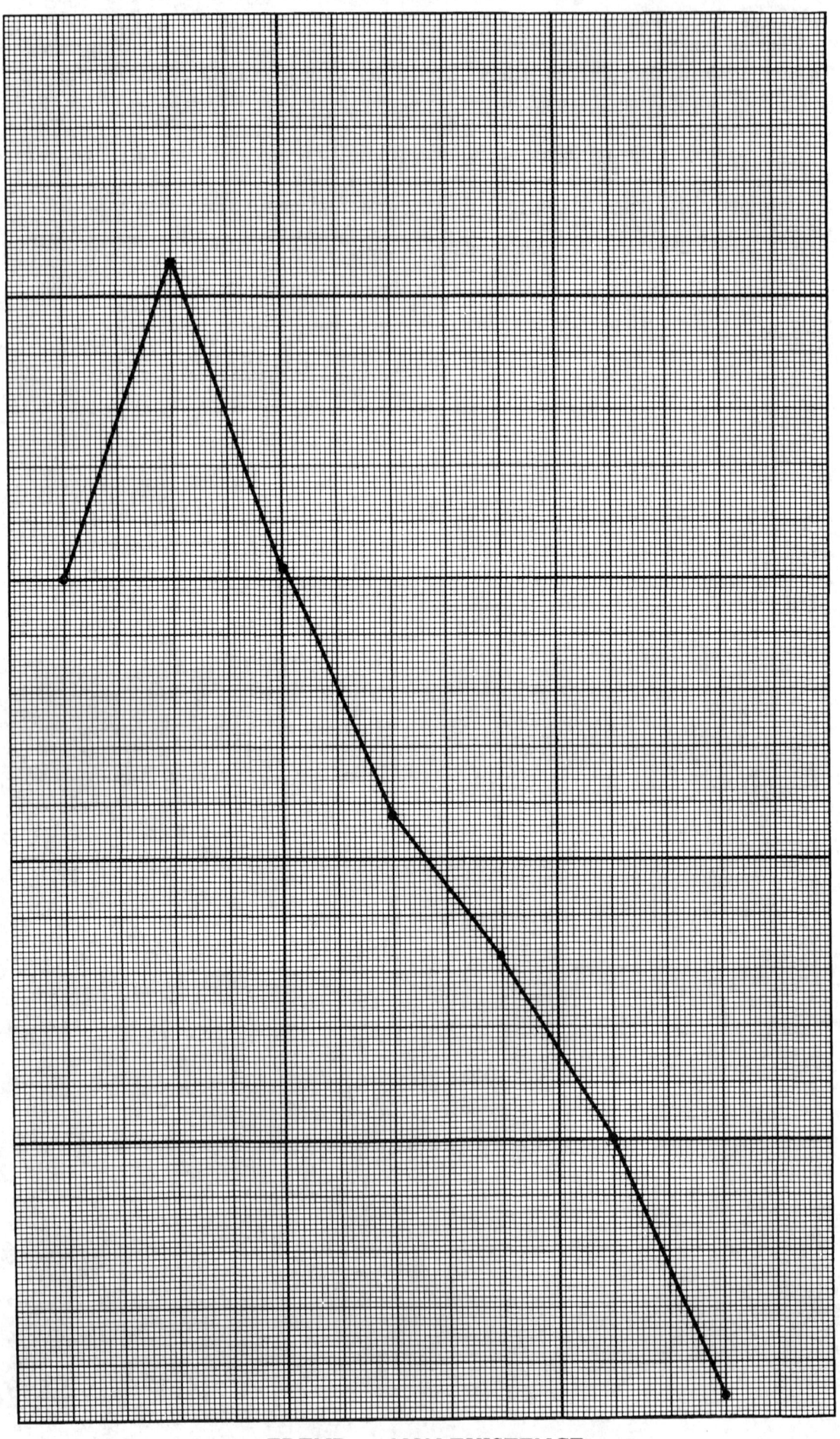

TREND = NON-EXISTENCE

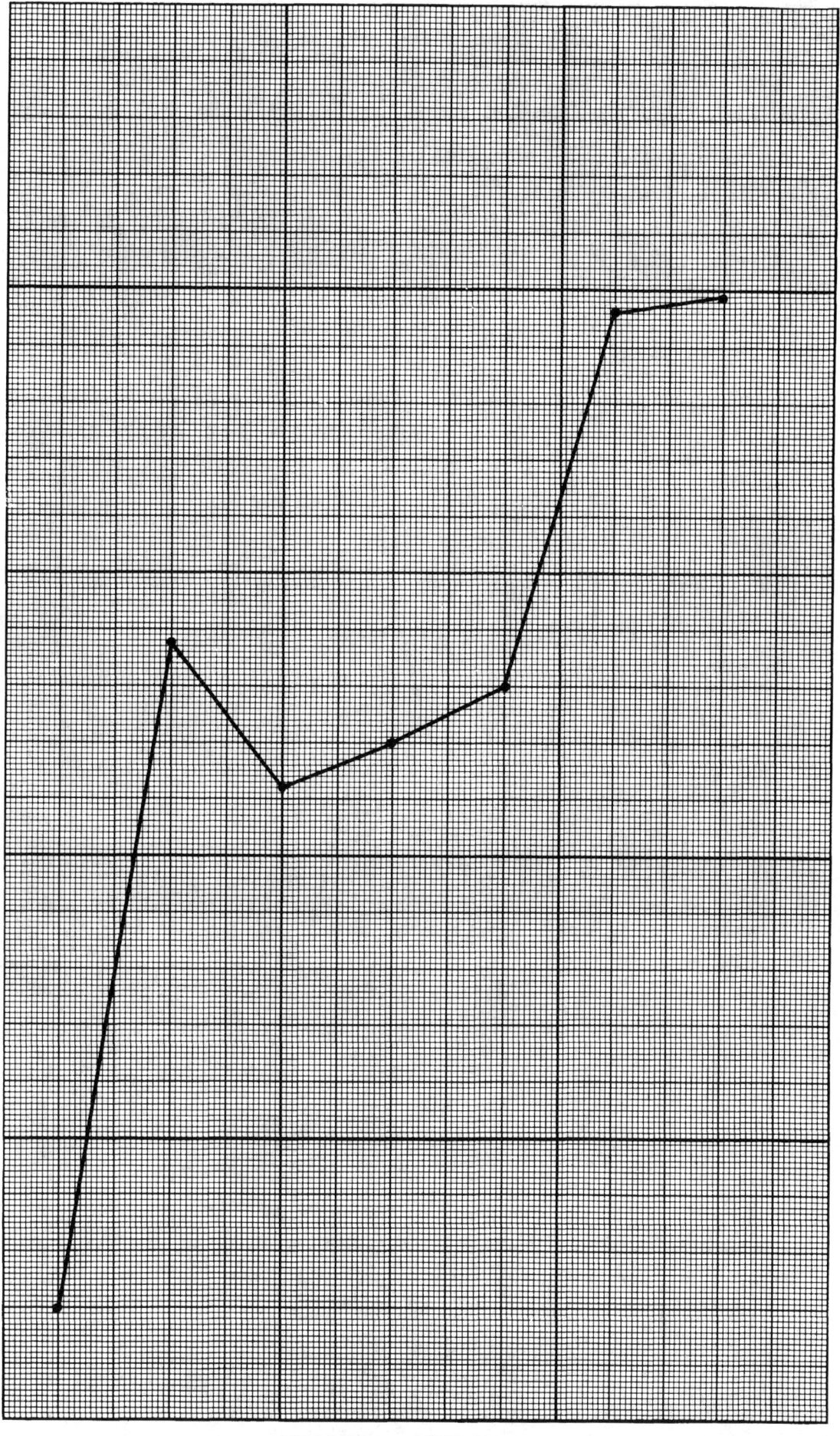

TREND = AFFLUENCE

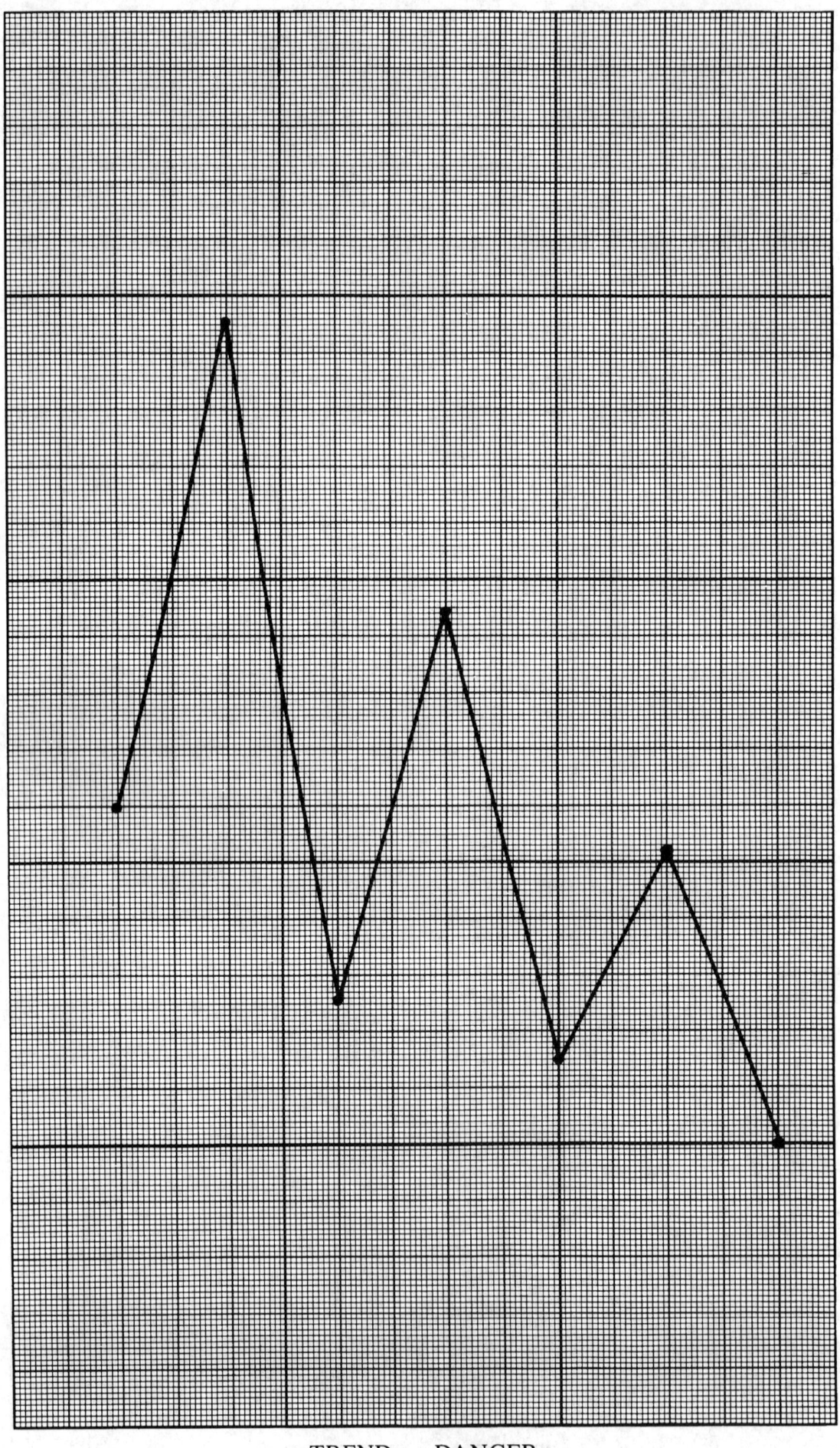

TREND = DANGER

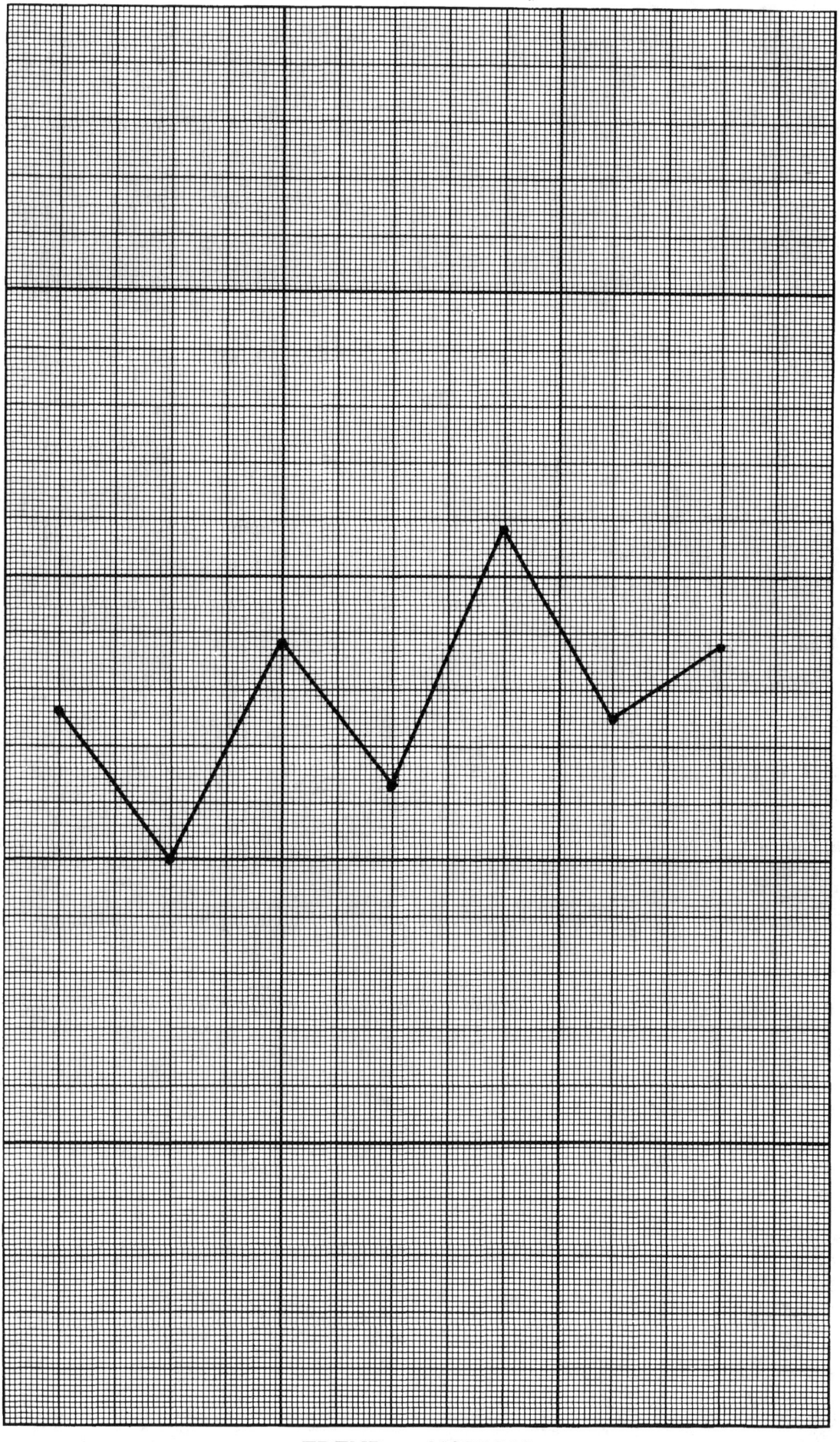

TREND = NORMAL

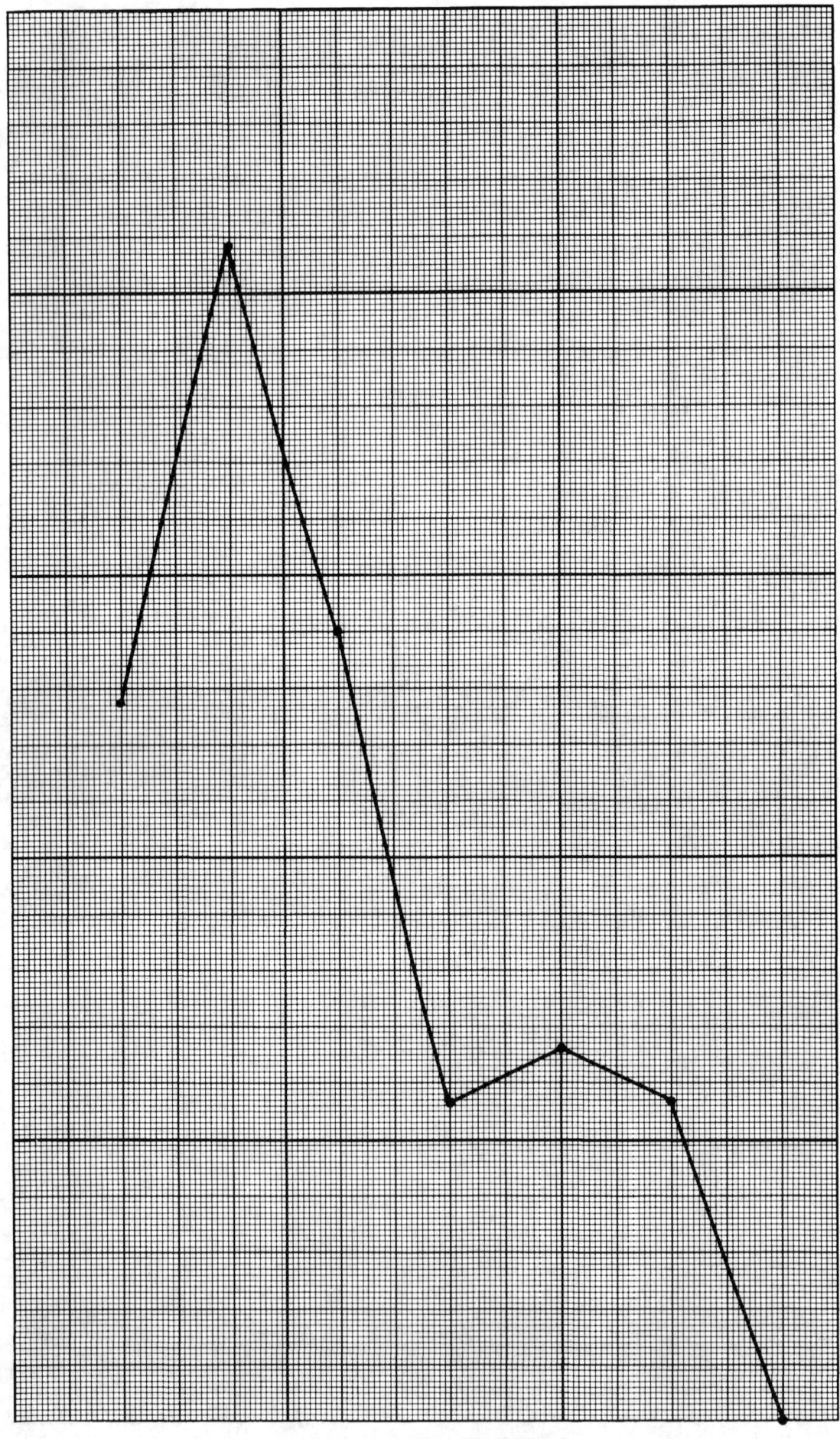

TREND = NON-EXISTENCE

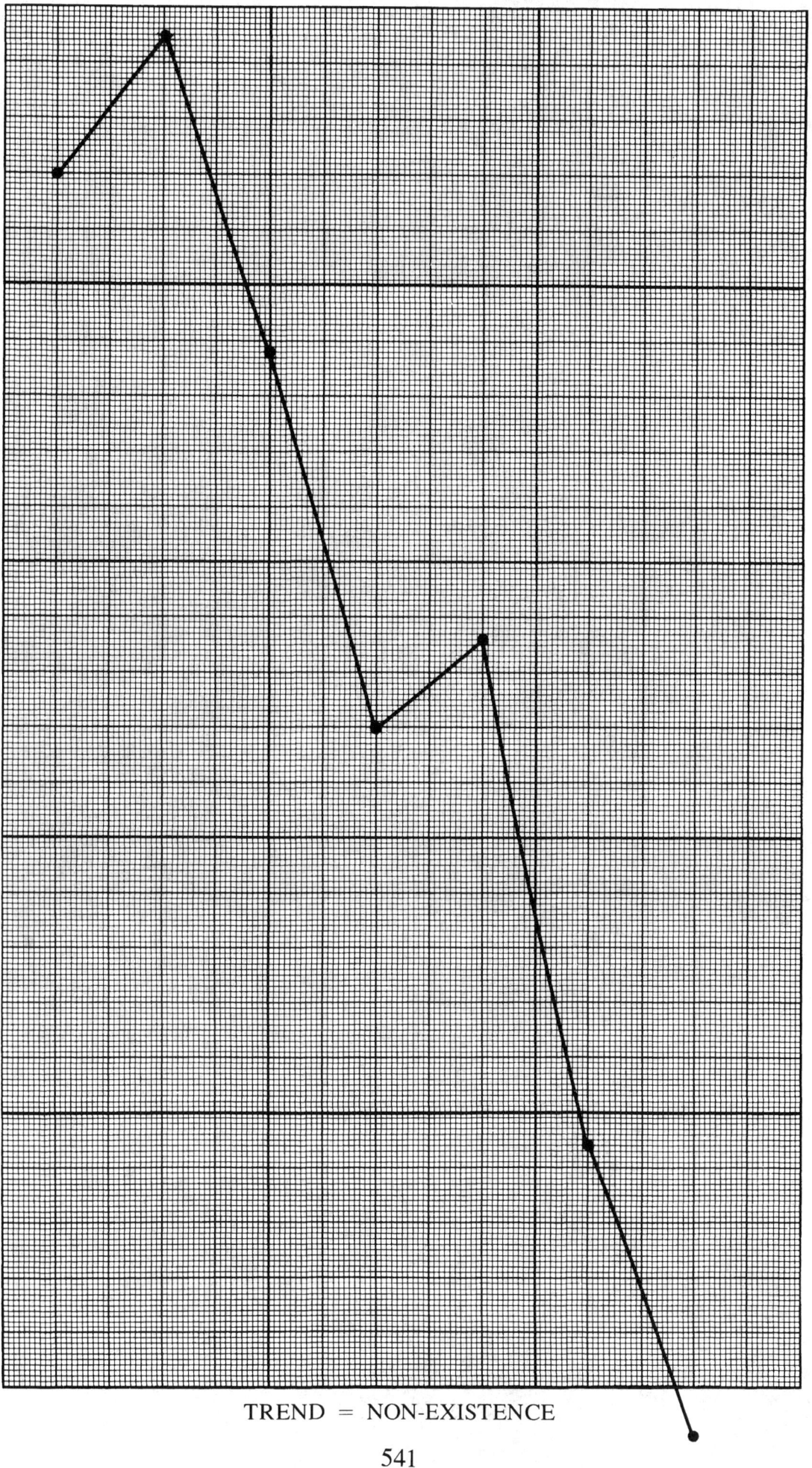

TREND = NON-EXISTENCE

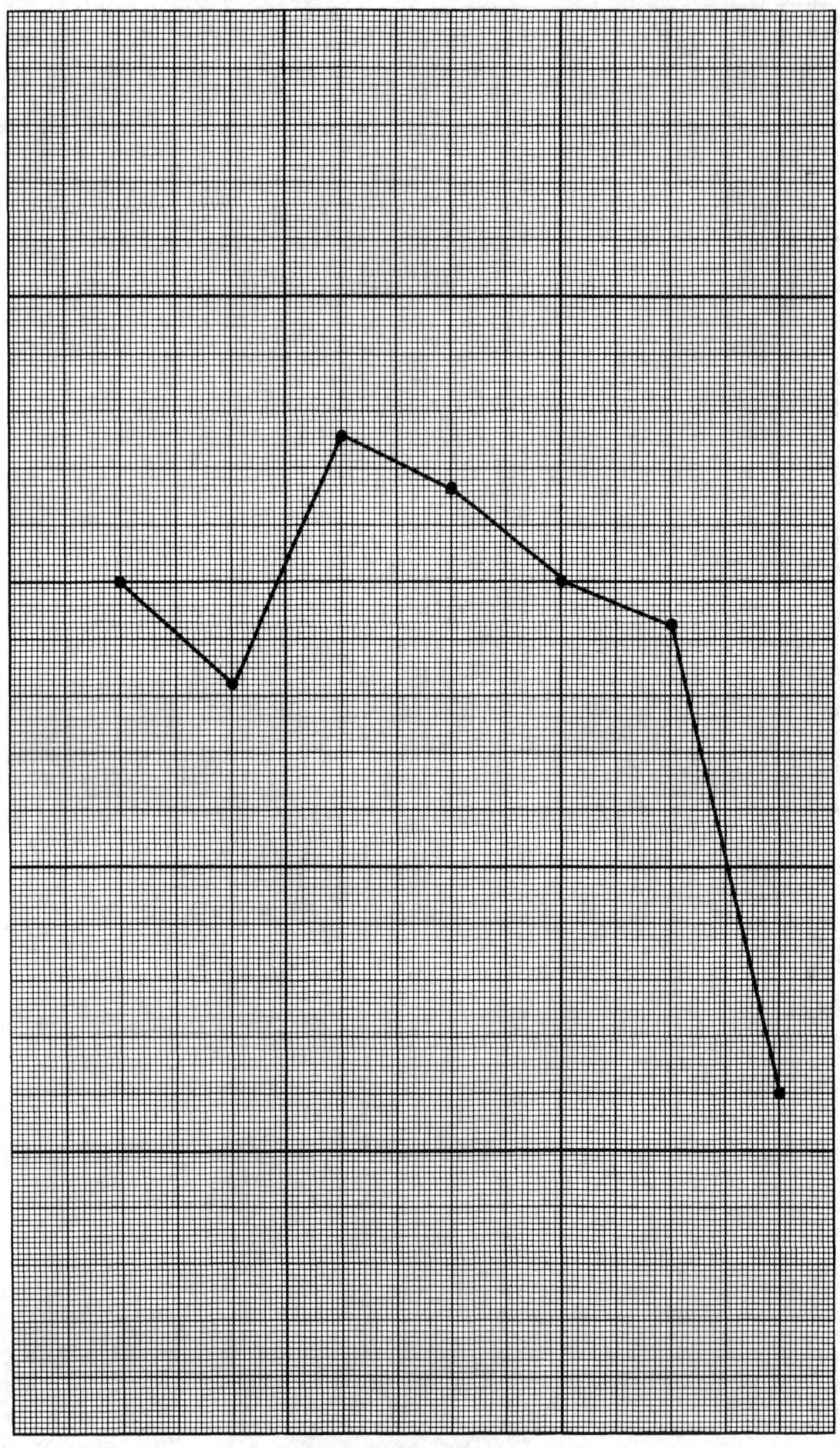

TREND = DANGER

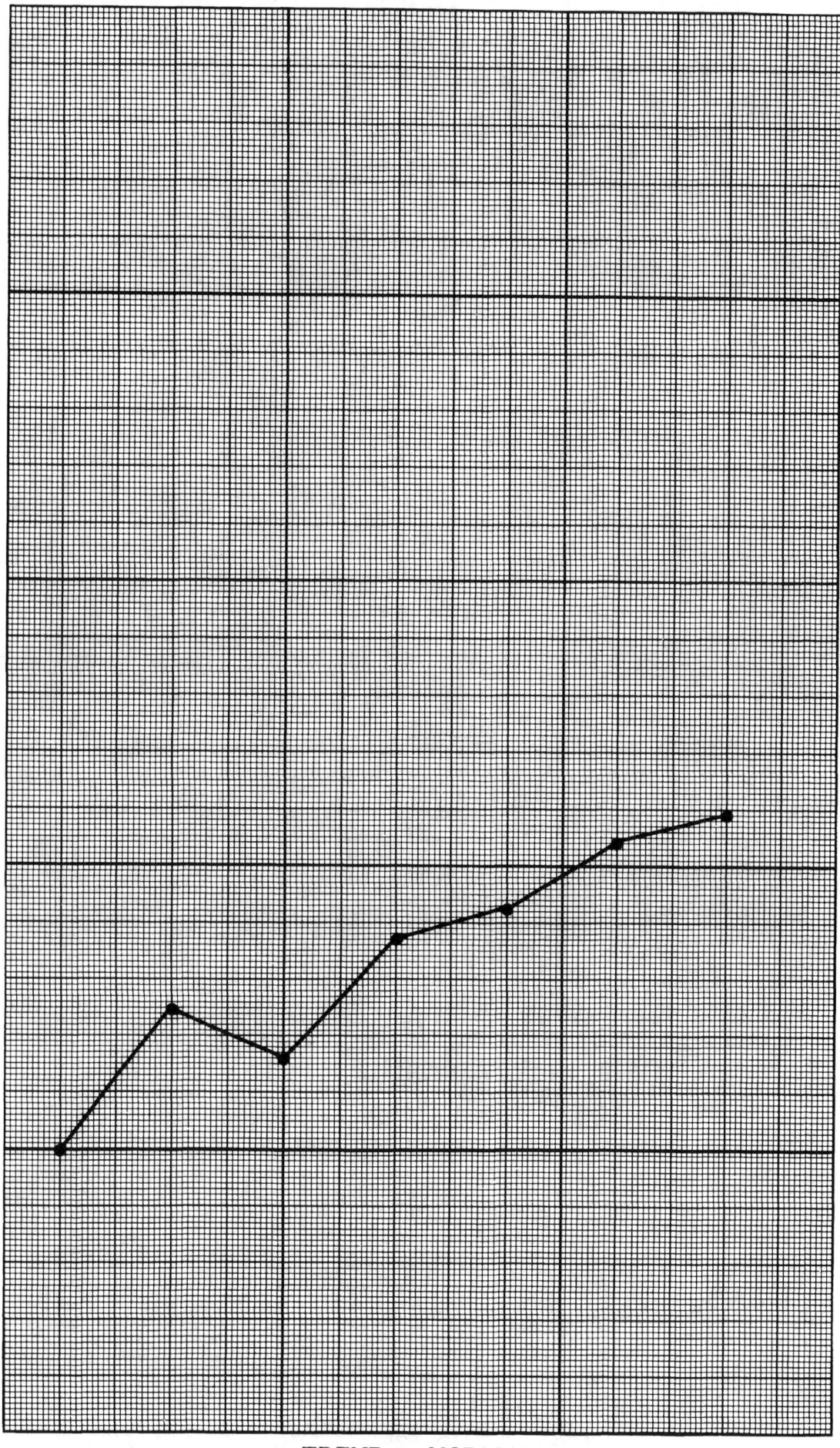

TREND = NORMAL

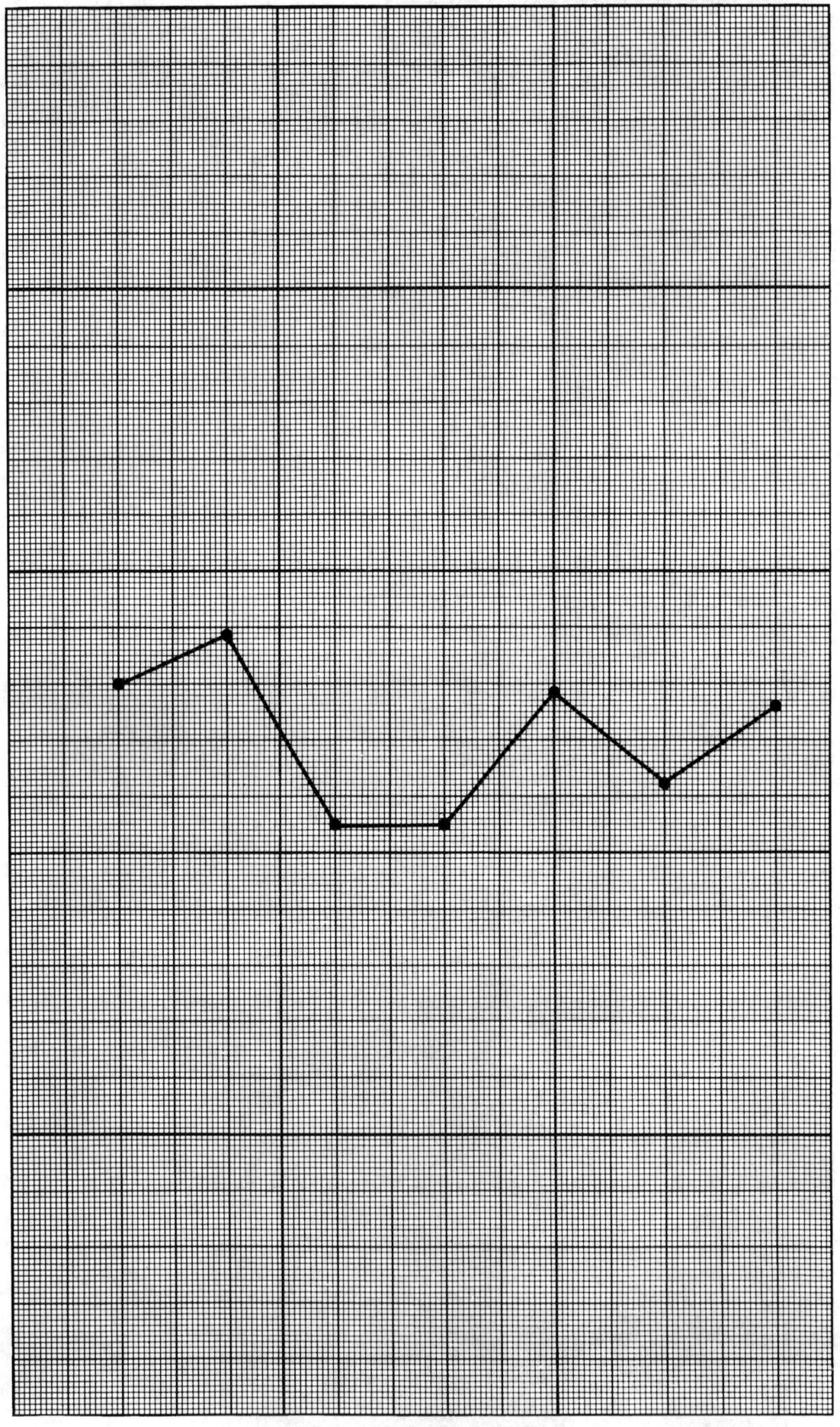

TREND = EMERGENCY

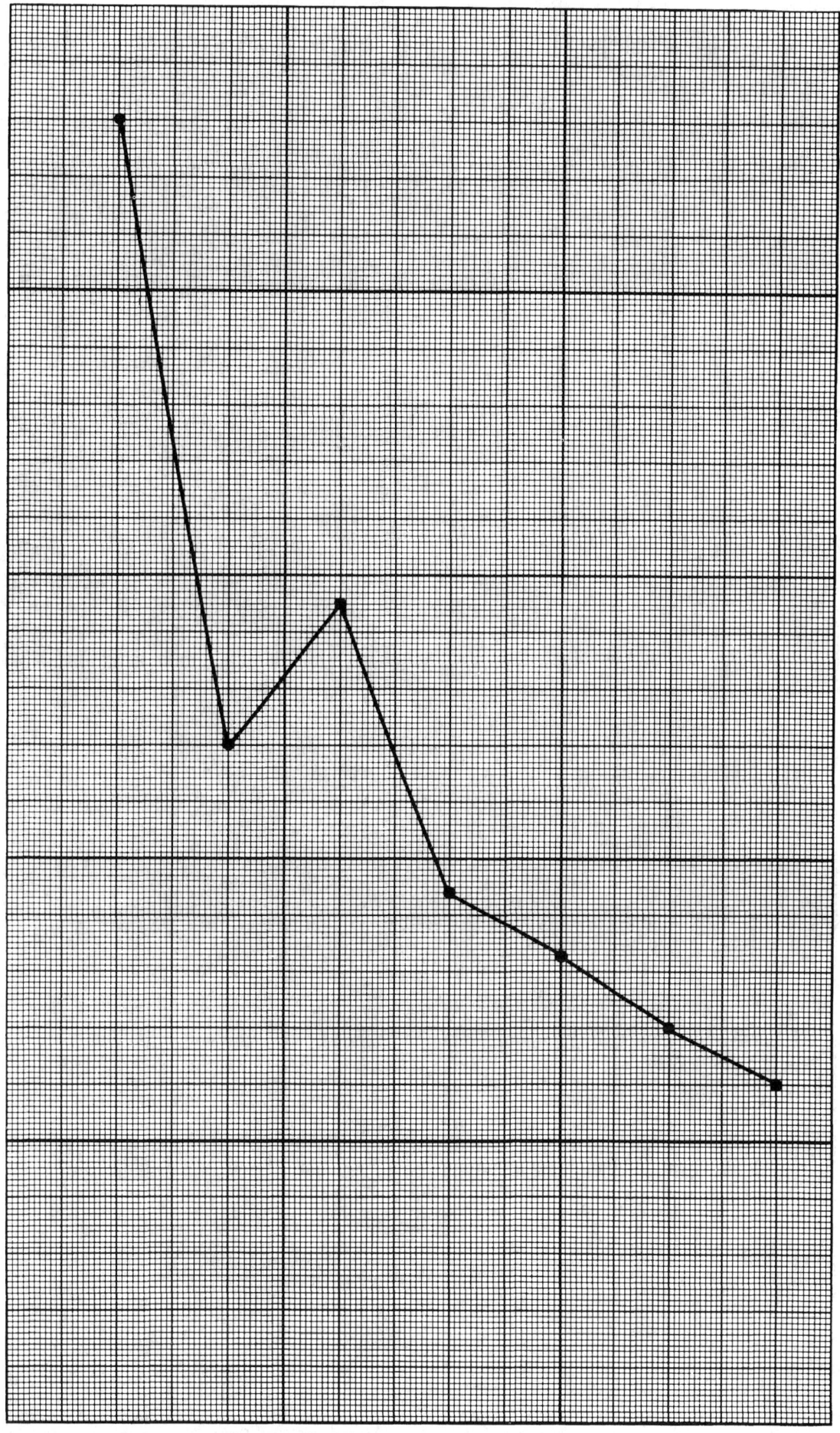

TREND = NON-EXISTENCE

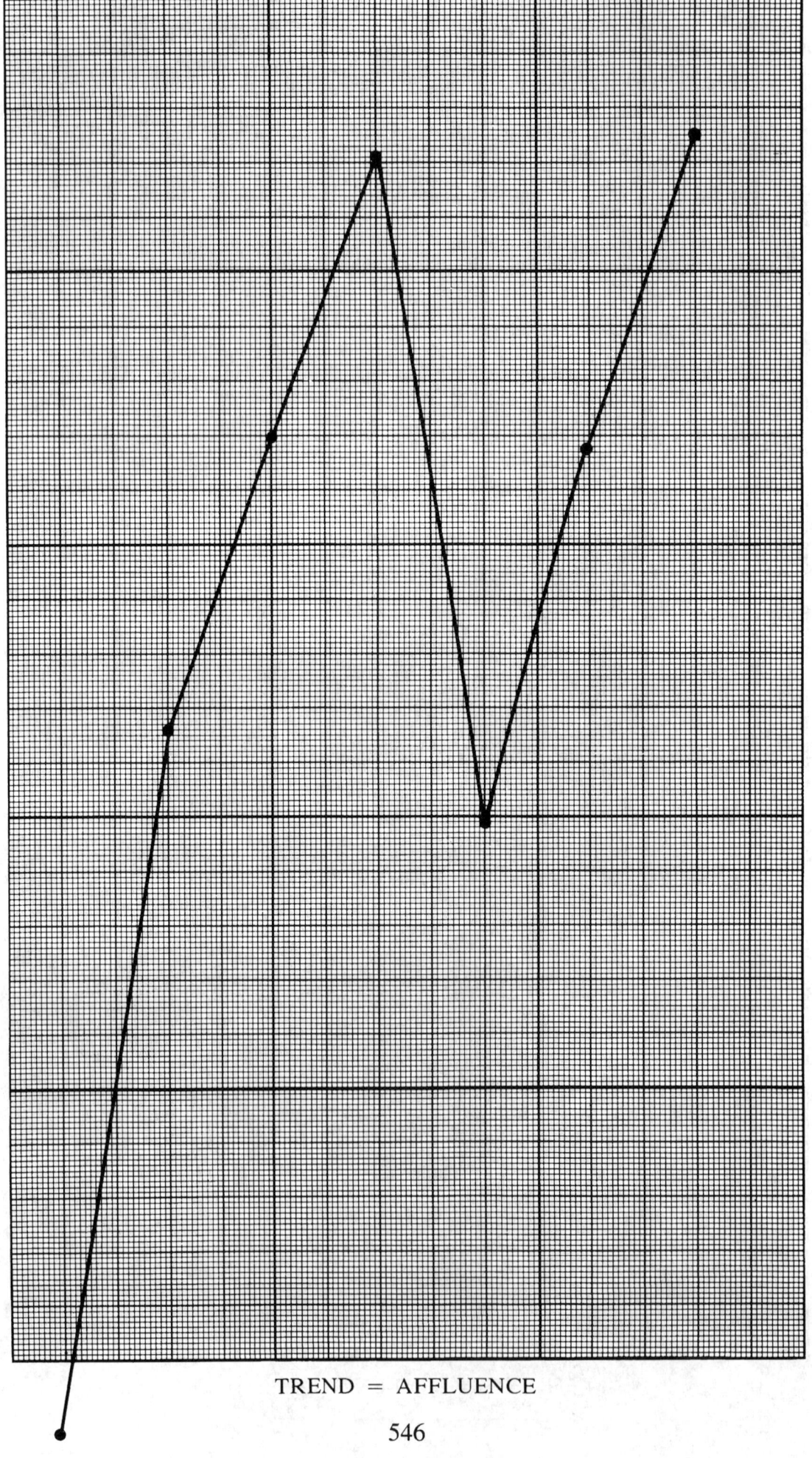

TREND = AFFLUENCE

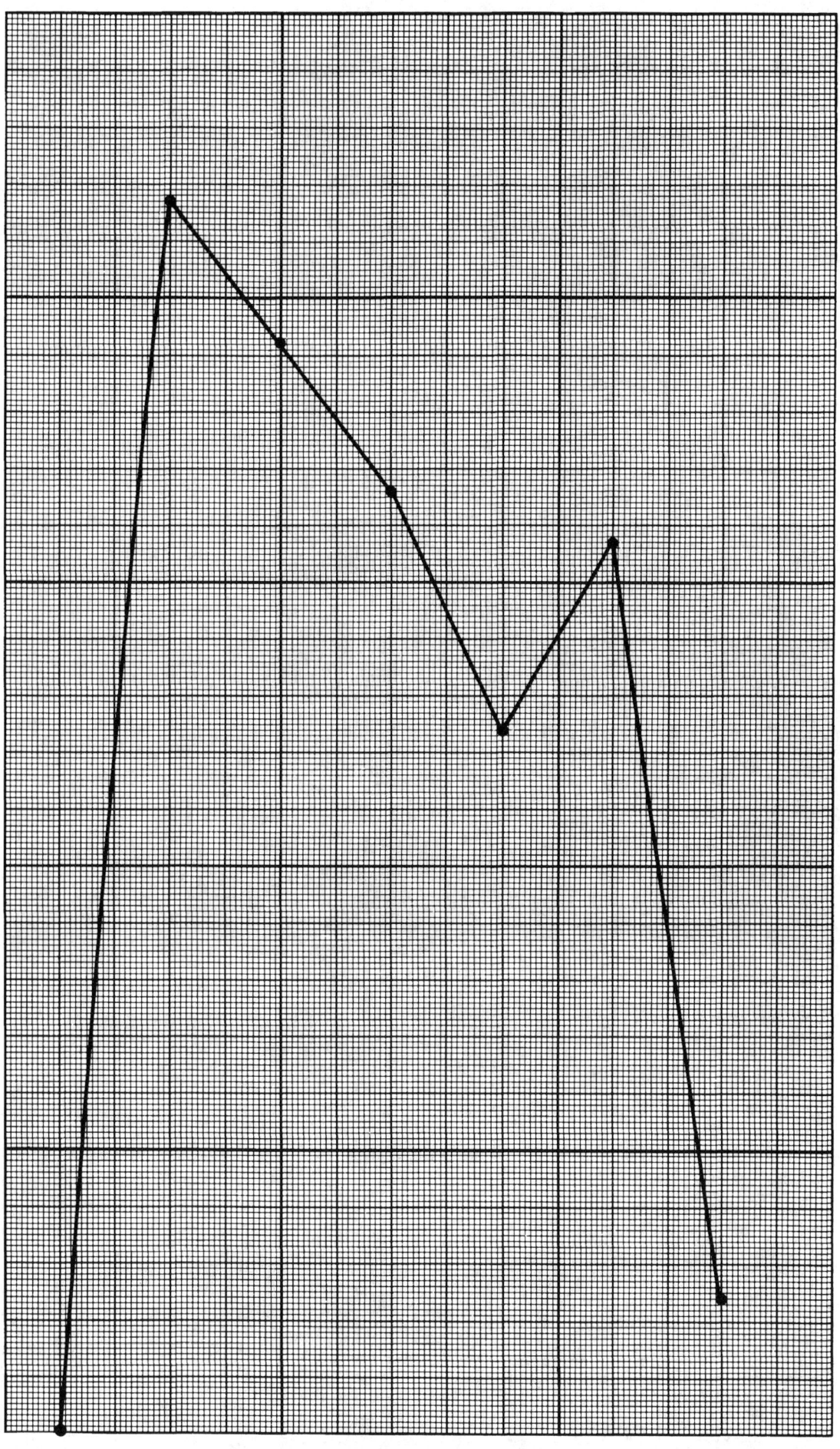

TREND = DANGER

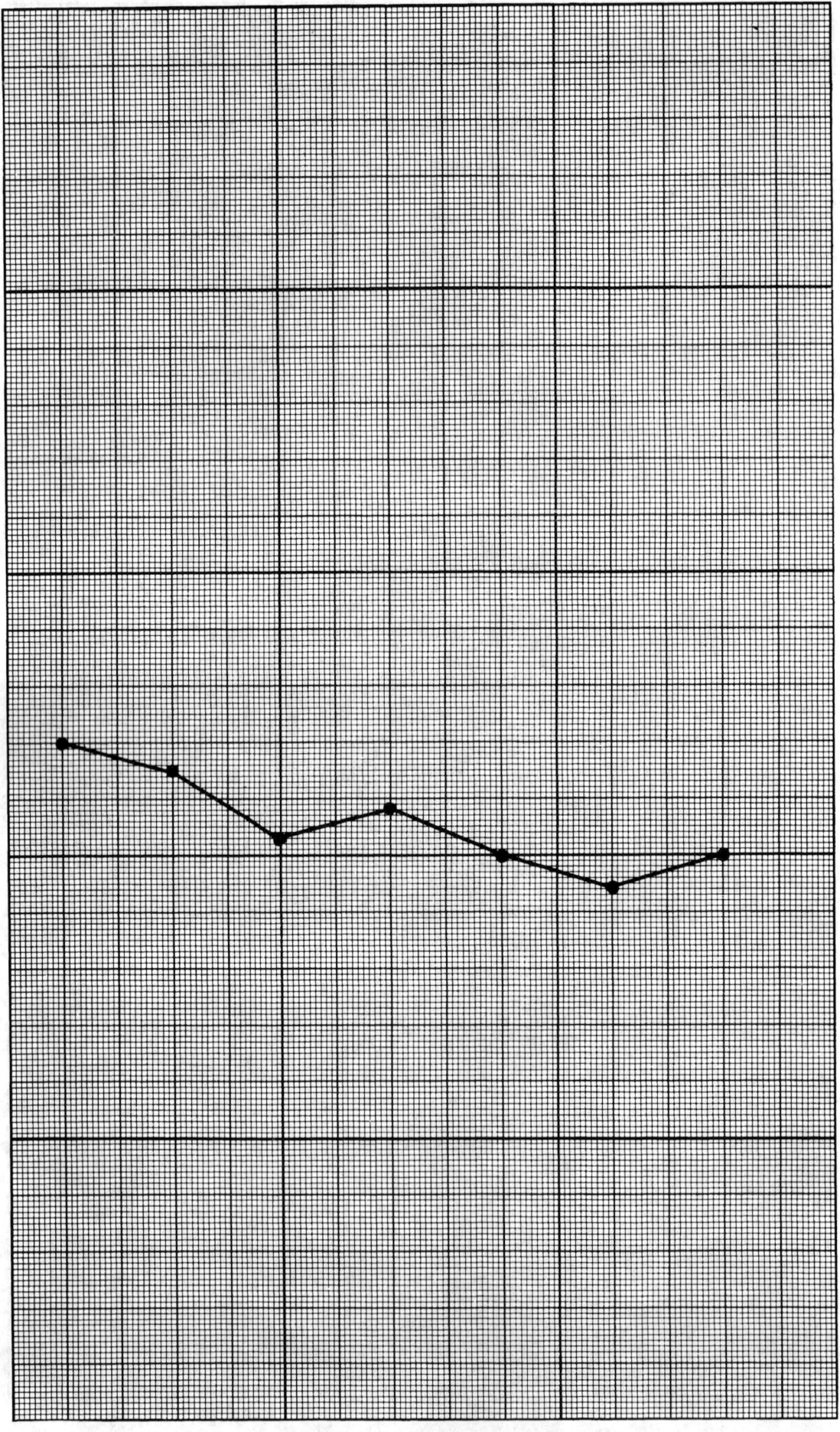

TREND = EMERGENCY

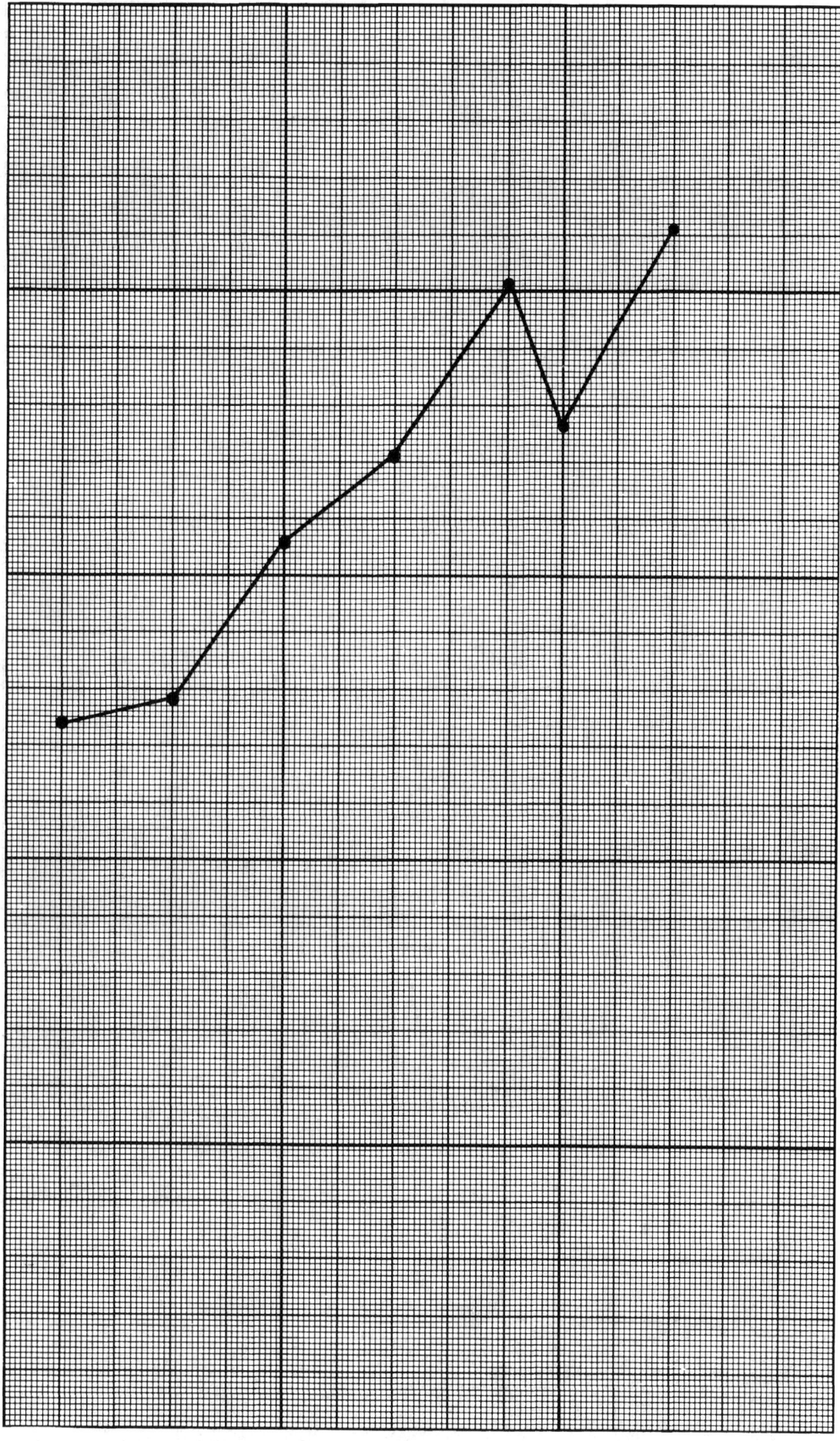

TREND = AFFLUENCE

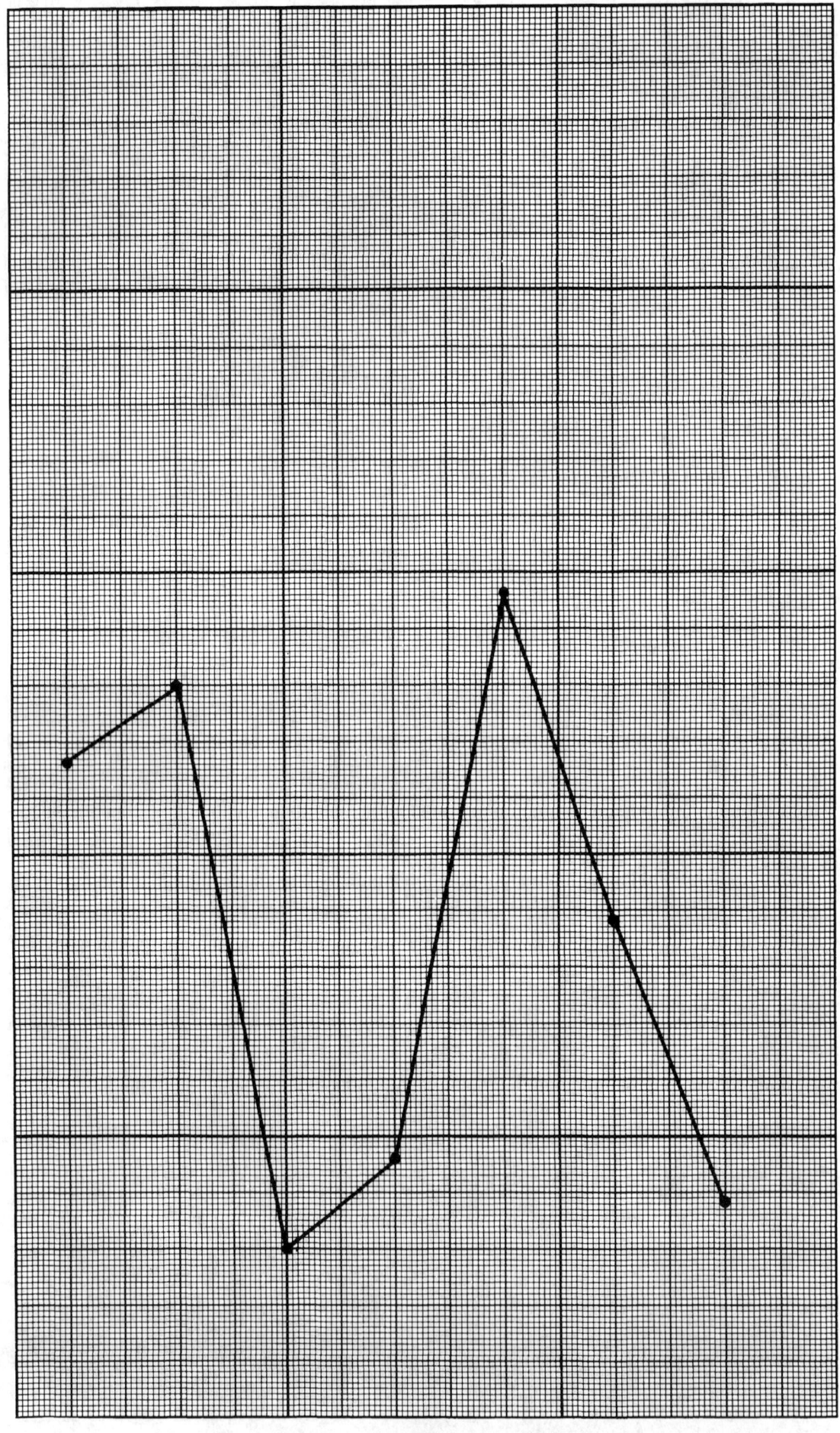

TREND = NORMAL (BARELY)

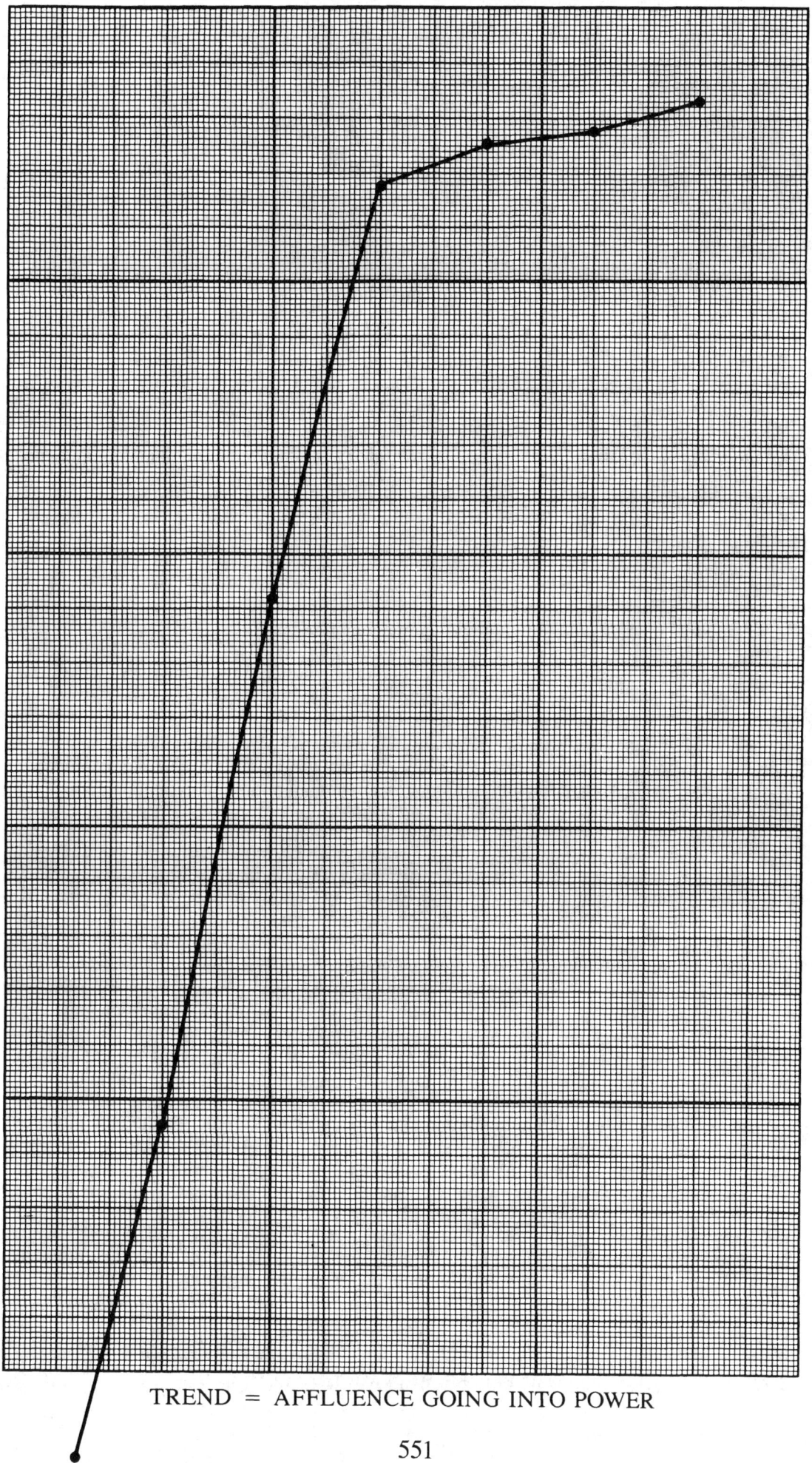

TREND = AFFLUENCE GOING INTO POWER

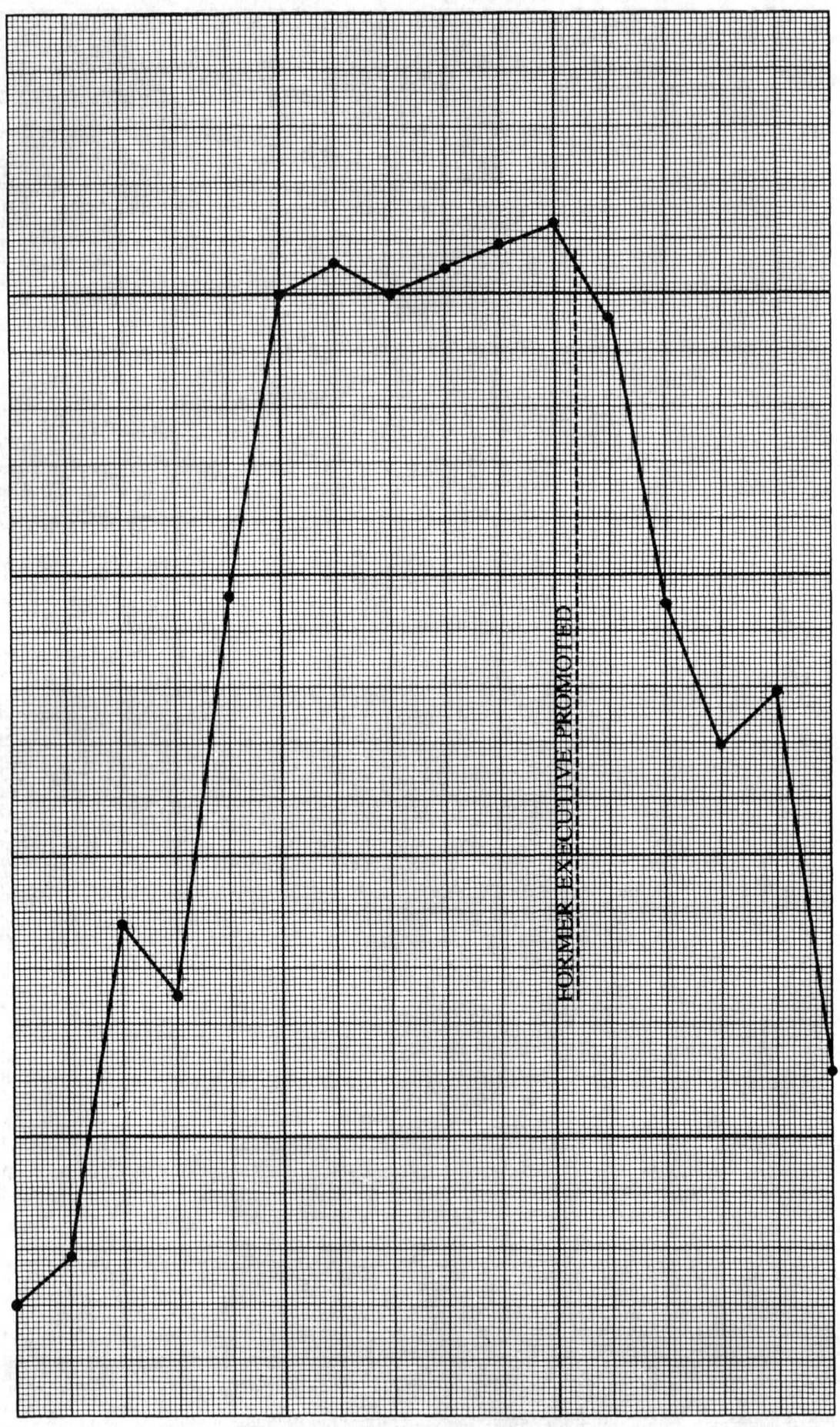

FORMER EXECUTIVE PROMOTED

VIOLATION OF POWER CHANGE

HCO POLICY LETTER OF 27 AUGUST 1982

Remimeo
All Orgs and
  Missions
All Staff

IMPORTANT

VITAL DATA: POWER AND AFFLUENCE CONDITIONS

Note: This issue *cancels,* specifically, the following:

HCO PL	5 May	71 II	READING STATISTICS
HCO PL	5 May	71R II	READING STATISTICS as revised 9 Nov. 79
HCO PL	3 Oct.	70R	STAT INTERPRETATION as revised 9 Nov. 79, and
HCO PL	9 Nov.	79	HOW TO CORRECTLY DETERMINE A STAT TREND,

as these issues contained erroneous and misleading data and/or graphs regarding the conditions of Power and Affluence. The *only* valid versions of these three policy letters are the corrected versions of these PLs as revised 27 August 1982 and listed below.

Refs:

HCO PL Rev. 27 Aug. 82	5 May	71RA II	READING STATISTICS
HCO PL Rev. 27 Aug. 82	3 Oct.	70RA	STAT INTERPRETATION
HCO PL Rev. 27 Aug. 82	9 Nov.	79R	HOW TO CORRECTLY DETERMINE A STAT TREND
HCO PL Rev. 9 Nov. 79	6 Nov.	66R I	AKH Series 5R STATISTIC INTERPRETATION, STATISTIC ANALYSIS
HCO PL	23 Sept.	67	NEW POST FORMULA, THE CONDITIONS FORMULAS
HCO PL	14 Mar.	68	CORRECTED TABLE OF CONDITIONS
Tape: 6505C25			"The Five Conditions"
HCO PL	6 Mar.	66 II	STATISTIC GRAPHS, HOW TO FIGURE THE SCALE
HCO PL	9 Feb.	70	STATISTICAL JUDGMENT
HCO PL	12 Feb.	67	AKH Series 13 THE RESPONSIBILITIES OF LEADERS
HCO PL	27 Oct.	80	POWER CHANGE VIOLATION REPAIR FORMULA
HCO PL	13 Nov.	72	AFFLUENCE ATTAINMENT

I have just uncovered what is probably a widespread misunderstanding of the difference between the condition of AFFLUENCE and the condition of POWER.

Looking at the following graph,

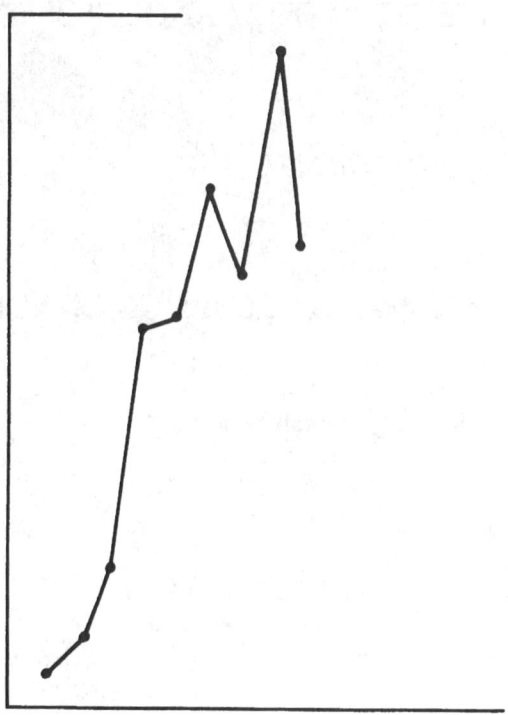

which had been MISCLASSIFIED as Power, revealed to me that Power was not understood. The graph shown above is in screaming Affluence. It is not Power since it is not maintained.

Power is not a high Affluence, as a good many people seem to think.

On spotting this misconception, I called for all of the references on Power and Affluence so these could be carefully reviewed and clarified or corrected if needed to ensure that Power is not susceptible to misinterpretation. A description of the slant of a Power line as "near vertical up" (HCO PL 5 May 71R, READING STATISTICS) is erroneous as it gives the idea that Power could be judged from one line on the graph, and this has now been corrected. While that statement might describe the ascent of a stat up to a range where it can now *move into* Power (as Power would be high at the top of the graph), it does not accurately describe Power itself, as Power is a *trend*. Therefore, HCO PL 5 May 71R has been revised to clarify this, and any extant sample graphs or issues put out by others which would forward the wrong concept of Power have been revised accordingly.

We need to get the facts regarding this condition very straight and clearly understood.

So now let us look at a very concise definition of Power, along with some further data on the subject.

CONDITION OF POWER

A Power stat is a stat in a very high range; it is a brand-new range in a Normal trend.

A Power stat is not just a stat that keeps going steeply up for a long time. Nor is it simply a very high stat on a one-time basis. Power is not a one-week thing. It is a *trend*.

DEFINITION: POWER IS A NORMAL IN A STELLAR RANGE SO HIGH THAT IT IS TOTAL ABUNDANCE, NO DOUBT ABOUT IT.

IT IS A STAT THAT HAS GONE UP INTO A WHOLE NEW, STEEPLY HIGH RANGE AND MAINTAINED THAT RANGE AND NOW, IN THAT NEW HIGH RANGE, IS ON A NORMAL TREND.

Operating in this new range you may get a slight dip in that stat now and then. But it is still Power.

There is another datum that is of importance if one is to correctly recognize and understand this condition:

Why do we call it Power?

BECAUSE THERE IS SUCH AN ABUNDANCE OF PRODUCTION THERE THAT MOMENTARY HALTS OR DIPS CAN'T PULL IT DOWN OR IMPERIL ITS SURVIVAL.

And THAT is POWER.

POWER CONDITION FOR INDIVIDUALS AND ORGS

If those who didn't understand the Power stat had asked one more question, they would have gotten a clarification.

The question would be "How much work can one guy do?" Or "How many bricks can a guy lay in a day?"

Of course, a person can only work so many hours in a day. He can only get so much individual production in a day. But he can get enough production in a day to support himself. He can get his production up into such abundance that he can take some time off. That depends on his efficiency and brightness.

At a certain peak of Affluence he will hit how many bricks he can lay. By increasing practice and efficiency he can keep that level of production going in a Normal.

If he's laying so many bricks that nobody is ever going to think of firing him, why, he's in Power. That's a Power condition for an individual.

That isn't true of an organization. An organization expands. It's got to expand if it is to stay alive at all and it's got to expand if it is to get into Power and maintain it.

Let us say an org or a portion of an org gets its production going into a series of increasing Affluences. Eventually it reaches a peak as to what it can honestly and actually produce with its current facilities (personnel, equipment, etc.). Now it is managing to maintain its new high range in a Normal trend.

555

There is a good healthy abundance of production going on. That's excellent; the org has made it into Power and the Power Formula applies.

BUT for an organization, which can expand, there are new, higher ranges which can now be reached.

In the Simon Bolivar PL (HCO PL 12 Feb. 67, THE RESPONSIBILITIES OF LEADERS) I've given you a datum which is pertinent here: "When the game or the show is over, there must be a new game or a new show. And if there isn't, somebody else is jolly well going to start one, and if you won't let *anyone* do it, the game will become 'getting you.'"

So for an org there is a new level of Power now to be attained. It's done by applying the formulas exactly. And in the course of things, that includes bettering the quality and quantity of one's service, adding personnel and hatting, training, apprenticing them up to competence, improving facilities. Expanding.

I got Saint Hill into Power in the sixties and the FSO was in true Power in Daytona.* But that's about it.

There are higher potential ranges, always, that any org can reach. But it isn't a hit-or-miss thing; it's correct application of the correctly assigned conditions formulas. Prediction, planning and adhering to the principles for sound expansion enter into it.

POWER FORMULA

The Power Formula given in HCO PL 23 Sept. 67, NEW POST FORMULA, THE CONDITIONS FORMULAS, is the formula for the condition of Power on the *first* dynamic.

That is true for an organization or for an individual, for any unit or government or civilization. To maintain a Power condition, you would apply the steps of that formula scrupulously.

Additionally, there is a formula for the condition of Power on the *third* dynamic, and that is found in the seven points regarding Power laid out in HCO PL 12 Feb. 67, THE RESPONSIBILITIES OF LEADERS. (Page 629 of OEC Volume 0)

If an org or an individual doesn't also get those seven points applied, it can be predicted with accuracy that they won't be in Power for long. That is a fact. Power carries with it those exigencies.

When these points *are* applied, you get an expansion of the Power factor, and if you continue to operate on these points, that Power factor will expand and expand again until there is a much, much larger sphere of Power realized than was originally achieved.

This is the forward look for the executives and staff of an org to take.

But you don't hit Power overnight. On the way up there will be some Affluences to handle.

CONDITION OF AFFLUENCE

When you have a line going steeply up on a graph, that's AFFLUENCE. Whether it's up steeply for one week or up steeply from its last point week after week after week, it's AFFLUENCE.

When you've got an Affluence, regardless of how you did it, the Affluence Formula applies.

You MUST apply the Affluence Formula or you will be in trouble. Anyone dealing with Affluence should be aware of the following peculiarities about it.

Affluence is the most touchy condition there is. Misname it or handle it off formula and it can kill you. You go plummeting down fast. It is, strangely enough, the most dangerous of all conditions in that if you don't spot it and apply the formula, you spatter all over the street! Spot and handle it right and it's a rocket ride.

HANDLING AFFLUENCE

Let us say the key stat of the org, operationally, is in Affluence so the condition of the org, as an org, is Affluence.

You had better do a stat analysis. You will need to review all of the GDS (gross divisional statistic) graphs and do a comparison of each set of stats in the same or related activity. This includes doing an *internal* GDS analysis (analyzing the stats within a division) as there will be vital points there to be covered. GDS analyses are just that. In order to understand what has put a GDS up or down, you have to look at the minor stats and the associated stats.

A stat analysis is not done just to see which stats are going up or down and handling these with conditions. A statistic analysis is done to determine which stat or stats, if handled forcefully and at once, will change the overall situation. In the case of Affluence it is done to determine which stats need to be handled in order to maintain and strengthen the Affluence.

(As an aside, the term "stat analysis" applies to anything, anywhere. You can do a stat analysis on any activity, whether or not it has GDSes per se, and still come up with a Why for that activity.)

All right, so you have a genuine Affluence. The Affluence Formula, per HCO PL 23 Sept. 67, NEW POST FORMULA, THE CONDITIONS FORMULAS, is:

1. Economize. Now the first thing you must do in Affluence is economize and then make very, very sure that you don't buy anything that has any future commitment to it; don't buy anything with any future commitments; don't hire anybody with any future commitments—nothing. That is all part of that economy; clamp it down.

2. Pay every bill. Get every bill that you can possibly scrape up from any place, every penny you owe anywhere under the sun, moon and stars and pay them.

3. Invest the remainder in service facilities; make it more possible to deliver.

4. Discover what caused the condition of Affluence and strengthen it.

Your battle plan, then, must include the first three targets of the formula. It goes without saying that these should be the first targets on any battle plan where Affluence is going to be handled.

Now let's look at #4 of the Affluence Formula.

Let's look now at trends. What started this Affluence? When did this steep rise begin? And what were the ongoing actions at that time or just prior to it?

We find the date coincidence of the Affluence was the implementation of a specific eval. Or, let us say, a specific org program based on sound and current strategic planning.

Good. Per #4 of the formula we must strengthen this!

All right, how? By looking over the rest of the stats and finding which are NOT in AFFLUENCE, of course.

List out the various stats and their conditions—the non-Affluence, the Normal, the Emergency, the crashed stats.

Where did the Affluence come from? It's Division X. Look over those stats. Some are, some aren't in Affluence.

Now take a look at the program that started the Affluence.

Go over the targets on the program thoroughly. Ensure the reports on the completed targets are correct. You want to be sure that what was said was done *was* done. False reports and half-dones can cause attention to drift off those targets as they're then *assumed* to be in when they're not.

Isolate the program actions, the targets done that caused or contributed to the Affluence, as you're going to strengthen them.

You might find that some of the monitoring reasons for the start of the Affluence are not yet even fully complete or, even if fully done, not marked to be maintained. That fact itself signals some of the actions to be taken to strengthen the Affluence.

Targets fully and honestly done once may have now dropped out and the successful actions are not being continued. You can be sure that if all of these points aren't carried through, you'll lose your Affluence.

Review the downstat areas. Find out what they were or weren't doing and what they *should* have been doing that would have contributed to the Affluence.

Here is Target "E"—not done at all by Department Y which was doing something else all week and wound up with a crashed stat. Aha! A departure from the program caused disaster!

And somebody else went off the strategy and current planning against which the whole program is written. That's a pull in the opposite direction.

So will failure to follow and reinforce this program break your Affluence? You said it!!!!!!

Your stat analysis, then, would conclude with:

1. To come off the cause of the Affluence will bring utter chaos and disaster.

2. The cause of the Affluence was Program X.

3. The whole handling of Program X must be reinforced.

That gives you your battle plan!

So you go over the program, target by target. Exhume every project written for those targets. Program out which actions need to be repeated, taken to full dones, maintained, whatever is called for. *Reinforce them.* Program out the production actions to be taken (in addition to correct condition assignments) in the downstat areas.

All of this makes up your battle plan. Now you go hell-bent for leather and get that BP done!

And note: If the following week a new stat analysis is done, you don't then cancel everything, change course and go careening off on a tangent in another direction on some new program. That violates management by trend and results in incomplete programs. Whatever else needs doing, you'd better also re-log any undone BP targets. And stay on the proven, successful "Program X" until it is complete and being maintained.

An org or a unit or an individual can make the mistake of thinking it has exhausted its immediate resources for creating another Affluence. But with this kind of scrutiny and analysis of the scene, you'll find you do have the means to do it. True, it may take some beef-up or re-org in certain areas, but it doesn't require going into a total organize. Any reorganization done would be done to strengthen the targets or actions which brought about the Affluence.

THE CAUSE OF THE AFFLUENCE IS STILL CAPABLE OF CAUSING IT!

These are the key tools of management: GDS analysis and conditions, strategy, programs and targets.

For a smaller unit or section of an org or an individual, you just transpose the handling given here over to the activity of that unit, section or individual and get it applied there. That you're now going to do it on a smaller scale doesn't change or negate any of the steps of the Affluence Formula.

Where it can go off the rails most easily is mistaking an Affluence condition for Power and thus applying the wrong formula, failing to find the true cause of the Affluence, assuming there's nothing more that can be done in the sector that caused the Affluence in the first place, or sloppy, inexact, incomplete application of any part of the formula.

When Affluence *is* handled with the correct condition assigned, an accurate stat analysis and an industrious application of the formula based on the true cause of the Affluence, you'll get something like this:

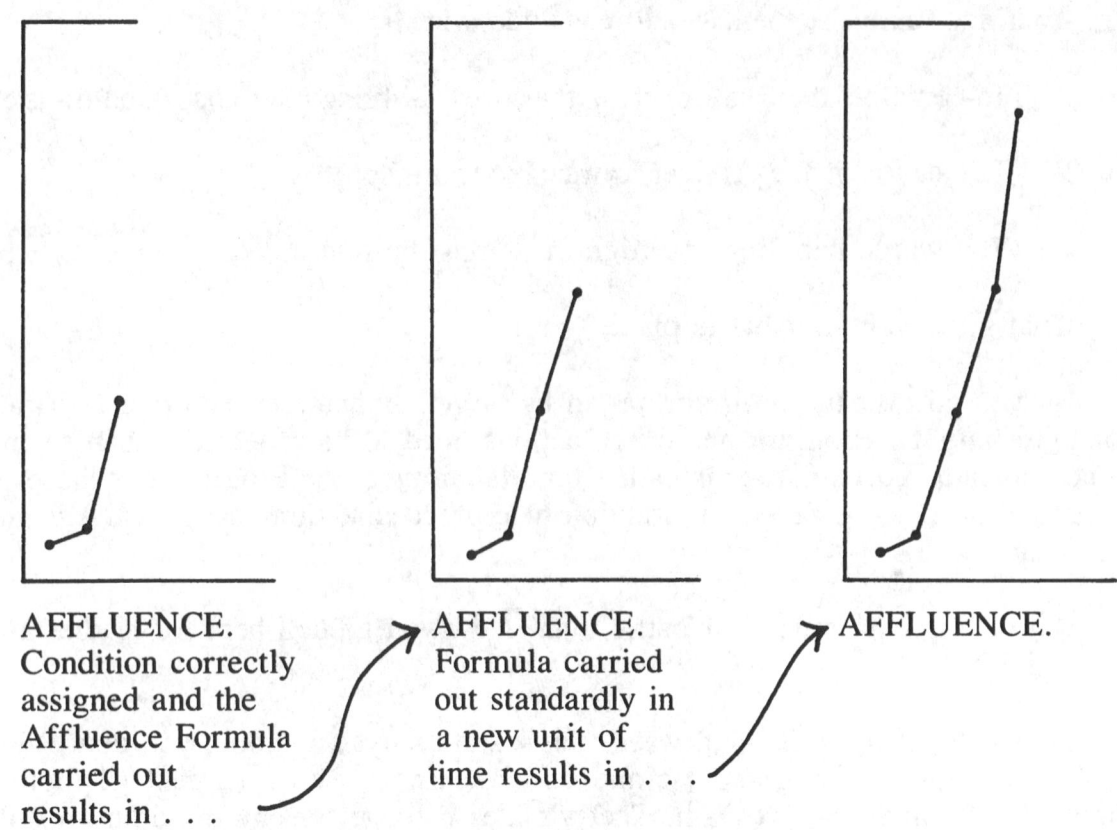

AFFLUENCE.
Condition correctly
assigned and the
Affluence Formula
carried out
results in . . .

AFFLUENCE.
Formula carried
out standardly in
a new unit of
time results in . . .

AFFLUENCE.

By reinforcing what caused the Affluence each time, you keep boosting it up to a new higher point until eventually it peaks at what is truly a stellar range. Now you have a new scene.

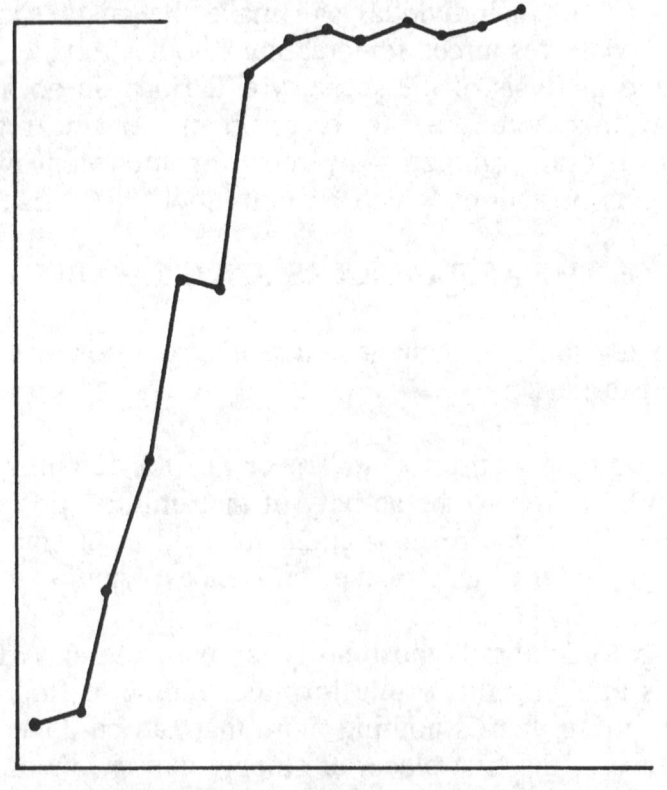

AFFLUENCE GOING INTO POWER

When you're maintaining that new range and you've got it stabilized and going in a Normal *trend*, you had better get the Power Formula carried out and all the points of Power Change as they apply.

560

You're operating now in a new range. You continue to build it from there. At some point it may take off into another Affluence. But in any case, if you keep it all going standardly and keep getting the correct conditions applied, eventually you'll work it up to a new and even wider sphere of Power.

If any of this was misunderstood in the past, it is possible that some Affluences were broken because of the confusion between the two conditions. An org was in Affluence, a real Affluence, thought it was Power and applied the wrong condition. So the Affluence wasn't maintained and the org never really got into Power.

But a far, far more common occurrence would be that an Affluence trend was broken by orders into the org by persons who didn't take the Affluence into account and didn't know or didn't bother to find out *why* the Affluence had occurred. And so, naturally, it crashed.

History is strewn with examples of individuals, states, nations and whole civilizations violating these two conditions and their formulas.

We have a different route to travel. With the tools we have, we are capable of making a different kind of history and *are* making it right now.

You have a well-defined picture of Affluence and its handling. You now have a clear-cut definition of Power. And the twain *do* meet—I've just shown you how.

Study it well, get it all straight and *applied* and you'll reach a point where you're operating with such an abundance of production that momentary halts or dips can't pull it down or imperil its survival!

And that will be Power!

L. RON HUBBARD
Founder

***Daytona:** A city on the eastern coast of Florida; original site of the Flag Land Base, before it was moved to Clearwater, Florida.

Remimeo
All Orgs
  and Missions
All Staff

THE BASICS OF STATISTICS AND MANAGEMENT

Trend monitors all graph readings.

Viability monitors all graph readings.

The place you are on a chain of command monitors all graph readings. The higher you are the longer the trend you read.

Correct scaling is vital to reading a graph.

If a stat is your own, you could probably monitor it on a one-day basis, but you sure better NOT start on a long condition formula for that day because you won't finish it by the next day. So there is such a thing as a short application and a long application of conditions formulas.

Nowhere in stat reading are any positions on the sheet drawn to indicate the different conditions.

In managing by stats, one is talking about *managing* and *managers*. A worker can manage by one-day and should—he also manages by trend.

A division can manage by the day or half-week and also by trend.

An Exec Council manages by the week and also by trend.

A continental area can manage by the week (difficult), but basically by three-weeks and also by trend.

An international management body manages by six-weeks or so and also by trend, but on a fast stat system keeps track of the one-week so as to predict.

A product officer at any level can manage by any time segment and should. But if he is too distant from the zone of operations, he can put all lower echelons below him into a permanent Danger condition.

As stat management can be made to go wrong by ignoring the above factors, the advice of senior management echelons should be sought in case of doubt or difficulty. But this must not open the door to squirreling.

There is a factor known as judgment and no amount of conditions applications in your org or area is going to prevent a mistake in some other org or area (such as Bide-A-Wee Chemical's truck breaking down and crashing your delivery stat on a one-day basis).

And this gets us into the area of stat analysis. A condition is not going to repair that truck and stat analysis is not a substitute for getting something done. It simply tells you what procedure to follow *THAT WILL RESOLVE THE STAT.*

Similarly, there is no rote method of determining the condition of a stat by the number of degrees of angle from the horizontal. If the condition of a stat is not immediately obvious (and it should be with a quick glance at the graph if it is drawn properly), then, again, judgment is the key. One must realize that a condition is an operating state of existence. The different conditions formulas make up a *SCALE* which shows the condition or state, which is to say the degree of success or survival of that individual post, division, Exec Council, continental area or international area at any one particular time and as compared to other times.

These conditions flow, one to the next, and within each one there is a flow from one step of one condition to the next step of that condition. Let us say that one is in a particular condition and that one is working on and through step number three of that condition. Well, it just so happens that when he finishes that, the next thing he should and *must* do in order to improve the scene and raise his stats is the *next* step, step four, of the formula for that condition. And when he finishes all the steps of the formula for that condition, then the *next* thing he must do to further improve the scene and further raise his stats is apply the first step of the formula for the *next* condition above.

It isn't that this is a cute, neat system. It is just that that is the way it happens to be, like it or not, in this universe or any other you will have anything to do with. And, apparently, understanding this, some people have managed to apply this to their stat and their post when they might have had some kind of doubt as to what condition to apply to their stat in order to resolve their stat and raise it.

One fellow told me once, "I used to get hung up with assigning a condition to my stat if I had to do it only according to what was the slant of the line. But if I wanted to get my stat up that week, I would have a look at the conditions formulas and decide which I had to apply that would handle the scene and raise my stat back up to the higher conditions." He was right. This is the factor of judgment. "How am I going to handle this scene and resolve the statistic that measures it? Well, let's see what condition this is really in. Well, the stat is going up and I'm sure that if I keep doing what I'm doing I can get it up again. . . . Hey! That's the Normal Formula . . . that's right. . . . I'm in Normal! Okay. That's the condition formula I will do. . . ."

Basically, you must realize that one can go pretty rote on this and the real way to do it is to understand the conditions formulas, understand what one is trying to do and what one is trying to get done, and apply the correct condition formula. (Example: Where a stat is in *completely nonviable range,* it is really in Non-Existence or worse, and the handling is to put something there to have a stat for or do something that deserves a stat.) And only then will management by stats begin to work well for you. In this case, however, *trends* are very important.

And at the upper end of the scale if one has achieved the superabundance of high Affluence or Power, little wobbles don't require hour by hour changing conditions.

But trends do require changing conditions.

One must realize that, in a stat, one is handling an indicator of complex conditions, and stats are indicators of the real universe. They are not a thing in themselves. It is vital to use them and vital to use the formulas, but remember that a stat is simply an index of things as they have been and that they inform you of the relative need of action and that the condition is a tool to change their future.

L. RON HUBBARD
Founder

DEPARTMENT 19
OFFICE OF THE EXECUTIVE DIRECTOR

Remimeo

AN ESSAY ON MANAGEMENT

A knowledge of Group Dianetics should include a knowledge of management, its problems and optimum performances. In Group Dianetics, the best organization can be seen to be one wherein all individual members of the group are versed in all the problems and skills in the group, specializing in their own contributions but cognizant of the other specialties which go to make up group life.

It is an old and possibly true tenet of business—at least where business has been successful—that management is a specialty. Certainly it is true that ruling, as Group Dianetics concerns itself with government, is a specialized art and craft not less technical than the running of complex machinery, and certainly, until Group Dianetics, more complex.

MANAGEMENT IS A SPECIALTY

With our present technology about groups, it is possible to accomplish with certainty many things which, before, came out of guesses when they emerged at all. Management in the past has been as uncodified in its techniques as psychiatry, and management, without reservation, has almost always been a complete failure. Men were prone to measure the excellence of management in how many dollars a company accumulated or how much territory a country acquired. These are, at best, crude rules of thumb. Until there was another and better measure, they had to serve. To understand that these are not good measures of the excellence of management one has only to review the history of farms, companies and nations to discover that few have had any long duration and almost all of them have had considerable trouble. Management has failed if only because the "art" of managing, as practiced in the past, required too much hard labor on the part of the manager.

Until one has considered the definitions of wealth and expanded territory, and has taken a proper view on what these things really comprise, one is not likely to be able to appreciate very much about management, its problems or its goals. Hershey, a brilliant manager with a brilliant managing staff, yet failed dismally as a manager because he neglected the primary wealth of his company—his people and their own pride and independence. His reign of a company ceased with his people—well-paid engineers and laborers, well housed, well clothed—shooting at him with remarkably live ammunition. The brilliant management of Germany came within an inch of restoring to her all her conquests of former years, yet laid Germany in ruins.

ATTAINMENT OF GOALS

Before one can judge management one has to consider the goals of an enterprise and discover how nearly a certain management of a certain enterprise was able to attain those goals. And if the goal of the company is said to have been wealth, then one had better have an understanding of wealth itself, and if the goal is said to have been territory, then one had better consider what, exactly, is the ownership of territory.

Goals and their proper definition are important because they are inherent in the definition of management itself. Management could be said to be the planning of means to attain goals and their assignation for execution to staff, and the proper coordination of activities within the group to attain maximal efficiency with minimal effort to attain determined goals.

Management itself does not ordinarily include the discovery and delineation of the goals of a group. Management concerns itself with the accomplishment of goals otherwise determined. In large companies the goals of the group are normally set forth by boards of directors. When this is done, the goals are assigned the nebulous word *policy*. In governments, goals, when they are assigned at all, generally stem from less formal sources.

Nations are so large that until they embark upon conquests they usually have few national goals which embrace all the group. The government personnel itself has the goal of protecting itself and exerting itself in management, and the remainder of the group bumbles along on small subgoals. When a goal embracing a whole nation is advanced and defined, the nation itself coalesces as a group and flashes forward to the attainment of advances. It is an uncommon occurrence at best that a nation has a goal large enough to embrace the entire group, thus governments are normally very poor, being management with only the purpose of managing. Asia Minor, given a goal by Mohammed, exploded into Europe. Europe, given a goal by certain religious men to the effect that the city of the Cross had better be attained, exploded into Asia Minor. Russia, selling five-year plans and world conquest plans and minority freedom plans, can have a conquest over any other nation without any large group goals. A good goal can be attained by poor management. The best management in the world never attained group support *in toto* in the absence of a goal or in the embracing of a poor one. Thus Russia could be very badly managed and succeed better than an excellently managed but goalless United States (for self-protection is not a goal, it's a defense). Marx is more newly dead than Paine. The goal is less decayed.

Companies obtain, usually, their "policy" from an owner or owners who wish to have personal profit and power. Thus a sort of goal is postulated. Nations obtain their goals from such highly remarkable sources as a jailbird with a dream of a conquered enemy or a messiah with cross in hand and Valhalla in the offing. National goals are not the result of the thinking of presidents or the arguments of assemblies. Goals for companies or governments are usually a dream, dreamed first by one man, then embraced by a few and finally held up as the guidon of the many. Management puts such a goal into effect, provides the ways and means, the coordination and the execution of acts leading toward that goal. Mohammed sat alongside the caravan routes until he had a goal formulated and then his followers managed Mohammedanism into a conquest of a large part of civilization. Jefferson, codifying the material of Paine and others, dreamed a goal which became our United States. An inventor dreams of a new toy, and management, on the goal of spreading that toy and making money, manages. Christ gave a goal to men. St. Paul managed that goal into a group goal.

568

In greater or lesser echelons of groups, whether it is a Marine company assigned the goal of taking Hill X428 by the planner of the campaign, or Alexander dreaming of world conquest and a Macedonian army managing it into actuality, or Standard Oil girdling the world because Rockefeller wanted to get rich, the goal is dreamed by a planning individual or echelon and managed into being by a group. The dreamer, the planner, is seldom an actual member of the group. Usually he is martyred to a cause, overrun and overreached. Often he lives to bask in glory. But he is seldom active management itself. When he becomes management, he ceases to formulate steps to be taken as lesser goals to greater goals and the group loses sight of its goal and falters. It is not a question of whether the dreamer is or is not a good manager. He may be a brilliant manager and he may be an utter flop. But the moment he starts managing, the group loses a figurehead and a guidon and gains a manager.

The dreamer of dreams and the user of flogs on lazy backs cannot be encompassed in the same man, for the dream to be effective must be revered, and the judge and the taskmaster can only be respected. Part of a goal is its glamour and part of any dream is the man who dreamed it. Democracy probably failed when Jefferson took office as president, not because Jefferson was a bad president, but because Jefferson, engrossed with management, ceased his appointed task of polishing up the goals.

According to an expert on history, no group ever attains a higher level of ideal or ethic than at the moment it is first organized. This observation should be limited, to be true, to those groups wherein management has been assigned to the dreamer of the dream. For in those cases where the dream was ably supported, the tone of the group remained high and the group continued to be brilliantly effective, as in the case of Alexander whose generals did all the generaling and Alexander, a brilliant individual cavalryman, set examples and pointed out empires.

But whether a group has an Alexander or a wild-eyed poet or an inventor doing its goal setting for it, the group cannot be an actual or even an effective group without such goals for its achievement and without management brilliant enough to achieve those goals.

THE CHARACTER OF GOALS

Having examined the source of such goals, one should also examine the character of goals in general. There are probably as many goals as there are men to dream them, probably more. Goals can be divided into two categories, roughly. The first would be survival goals and the second would be nonsurvival goals. Actually most goals are a combination of both, for goals are occasionally set forth solely for their appeal value, not for their actual value. One sees that the goal of a nation which directs it to conquer all other nations ends up, after occasional spurts of prosperity, in racial disaster. Such a goal is not dissimilar to the money goal of most "successful" industrialists or boards. One might call such goals acquisitive goals entailing, almost exclusively, the ownership of the mest accumulated through hard work by others. Technically one could call these enmest goals, for conquest of nations brings about the ownership of mest which, by conquest, has been enturbulated into enmest and which will make enmest of the conqueror's own land eventually. Rapacious money-gathering gains enmest, not mest, and makes enmest of the rightful money of the acquisitor. Such goals, since they tend toward death, are then nonsurvival goals. Survival goals are good and successful in ratio to the amount of actual theta contained in them, which is to say, the ability of the goals to answer up favorably on a maximum number of dynamics. A survival goal, then, is actually only an optimum solution to existing problems, plus theta enough in the dreamer to reach well beyond the casual solution. A group best catalyzes on theta goals, not only to a higher pitch but to a more lasting pitch than a group catalyzed by enmest goals as in a war. It can be postulated that theta goals could bring about a much higher level of enthusiasm and vigor than the most grandly brass-banded war ever adventured upon.

Another postulate is that a goal is as desirable as it contains truth or true advantage along the dynamics.

SPHERES OF ACTION

A group, then, can be seen to have three spheres of interest and action. The first is the postulation of goals. The second is management. The third is the group itself, the executors of the plans, procurers of the means and enjoyers of the victories.

These three factors or divisions must be satisfied to have a successful group or, actually, a true group. The divisions are not particularly sharp. The desires and thoughts of the body of the group influence and catalyze and are actually part of the goal dreamer. Management has to have the support of the group and the provision of the group to proceed at all and thus must have the agreement of the group for the best and most economical execution of orders. Management must have the confidence of the planning echelon or the planning echelon is liable to include the reform of management as part of the dream. The goal maker must be accepted and trusted by management or management will begin to look around for a new goal maker and, being management, not a goal maker, may take up with some highly specious ideas which management might then seek to make a sub-echelon to itself (the thing which causes most nations to cave in and most companies to collapse).

There are three divisions of action, then, which are interactive and inter-dependent. ARC amongst these three must be very high. A group which is hated by its management (often the case in the military) often gets wiped out; a whole system may be destroyed (as in American industry) when management and the group decide to become two camps. The death of the goal maker is not destructive to a group but even sometimes aids it, but only so long as the dream itself lives and is kept living. A management, for instance, which would interpose (for the "good" of the group) between the goal maker and the group is leveling death at the group by perverting and interpreting the character of the goal. Management cannot concern itself with the overall goal or plan; it can only execute and expedite the plans of accomplishing the goal and relegate its own planning to ways and means planning, not goal planning. The traffic between the group and the goal maker should be direct and clean of all "interpretations" unless management wishes to destroy the group (in which case it should, by all means, undertake an interruption of communication between the goal maker and the group). The place of the goal maker is in the marketplace with the group or off somewhere sitting down thinking up a new idea. The place of management is in the halls and palaces, arsenals and timekeepers' cages, behind the judges' bench and in the dispatcher's tower. Management leads the charge after the goals finder has assigned the cause of the campaign.

Management is subservient to goals but goal finding is not in command of management. So long as a management realizes this it will continue in a healthy state as a management, and the group, modified by natural factors such as food, clothing and general abundance, will remain in excellent condition. When management fails to realize this, the goal maker, even when he is merely an individual who enjoys the making of vast fortunes, shifts the management. When the goal maker is actually high theta and management forgets the quality of ideas (or doesn't ever quite realize their potency) then, again and more so, management will be tumbled around, for a theta goal maker has behind him a group and in a moment can become much more group than management and easily empties out the halls and palaces. A management that discredits its goal maker or perverts the communication of goals of course dies itself but, in dying, may also kill a group.

Management often takes the goal maker into its confidence and requests the solution to various problems. Management should understand that when it does such a thing it is not taking conference with more management, for the advice it will receive on technical problems, no matter how brilliant, is usually delivered with asperity, for the goal maker has no sight of tenuous lines of supply, quivering bank balances, raging labor leaders, leases and contracts unsigned or perilously inadequate. The goal maker sees goals; management sees obstacles to goals and ways of overcoming them. The first requisite of a goal maker is to see goals which are attainable only by the most violent ardures and which are yet sparkling and alluring enough to lead forward and onward his own interest (in the case of an enmest goal maker) or (if he is a theta goal maker) his entire group. Management pants between the pressure of the group to attain the goal and the clarion call of the goal maker to go forward.

Yet there are specific means by which management can lighten the burdens for itself, recover and retain its own breath and be highly successful as management, which means that the group, by that management, must be highly successful if its goals are kept bright.

A TRUE GROUP

Let us concern ourselves only with true groups. The true group could be defined as one which has (a) a theta goal, (b) an active and skilled management working only in the service of the group to accomplish the theta goal and (c) participant members who fully contribute to the group and its goals and who are contributed to by the group; and which has high ARC between goal and management, management and group, group and goal. Here we have no management problems beyond those natural problems of laying the secondary but more complex plans of accomplishing the goals, pointing out and laying the plans for the avoidance of obstacles en route to that goal or those goals and coordinating the execution of such secondary, but most vitally important, plans. Management, having the agreement of the participants, is immediately relieved by the participants of some of the planning and, that plague of management, the tying of loose and overlooked ends. Further, management is not burdened with the actual location or cultivation of food, clothing and shelter for the group as in a welfare state, but is only concerned with coordinating group location and cultivation along secondary plans laid by management for the location and cultivation. Management is enriched by the advice of those most intimately concerned with the problems of participation

571

and is apprised instantly of unworkabilities it may postulate. On the goal side it is relieved of the problem management has never solved, the postulation and thetizing* of the primary goals of the group. Further, management does not have the nerve-racking task of smoothing out enturbulations and confusions which are the bane of every semi-group.

Now let us consider what might be meant by a true group as opposed to a pseudo-group. A true group falls away from being a true group in the gradient that ARC breaks exist between goals and management, management and group, and group and goals. In the case of a high theta goal maker and a group in agreement with those goals, a bond between group and goal maker is so copper bound, cast iron strong, whether the goal maker is alive or dead as a person, that a management out of ARC with either the goal maker or the group will perish and be replaced swiftly. But in the interim, while that management still exists, the group is not a true group and is not attaining its objectives as it should. This would be the first grade down from a true group toward a pseudo-group. The condition might obtain for some time if management were not quite a true management and not flagrantly out of ARC. The duration that such a management would last would be inversely proportional to the completeness of the ARC break. A severe perversion or break of ARC would bring about immediate management demise. A continuing slight one might find the management tolerated for a longer time. The break with the group, while the goal maker lives, can be of greater severity than with the goal maker without causing management to collapse or be shifted. Break of ARC with a goal maker finds management under the immediate bombardment of a group catalyzed, as a small subgoal, into the overthrow of management. For this reason most managements prefer a good, safely dead goal maker whose ideals and rationale are solidly held by the group, and most groups prefer live goal makers because so long as the goal maker lives (in the case of a true group), the group has a solid champion, for a theta goal maker is mainly interested in the group and its individuals and his goals and has very little thought of management beyond its efficiency in accomplishing goals with minimal turmoil and maximal speed.

The next step down from the true group toward a pseudo-group is that point reached where the goals exist as codes after the death or cessation of activity, as a goal maker, of the goal maker. Management, always ready to assume emergencies exist, being hard-driven men even in the best group, breaks ARC to some slight degree with the codified goals in the name of expediency. Being interested in current problems and seeing the next hill rather than the next planet, management innocently begins a series of such breaks or perversions and begins to use various means to sell these to the group. The group may resist ordinarily but in a moment of real danger may deliver to management the right to alter or suspend some of the code. If management does not restore the break with or perversion of the code, the true group has slipped well on its road to a pseudo-group.

The next major point on the decline is that point where management is management for the sake of managing for its own good, not according to the demised goal maker's codes of goals, but preserving only some tawdry shadow of these such as "patriotism," "your king," "the American way," "every peasant his own landlord," etc., etc., etc.

---

*thetizing: from Greek *thetikos,* "such as is placed or is fit to be placed, positively assertive"; thus, positively setting forth.

The next step down is the complete break and reversal of ARC from group to management, at which moment arrive the revolution, the labor strikes and other matters.

If management succeeds the overthrown management without the simultaneous appearance of a new goal maker, the old regime, despite the blood let, is only replaced by the new one, for management, despite critics, is normally sincere in its effort to manage and strong management, unless a good theta goal maker springs up and carries through the revolution or strike, is faced with a continuing and continual emergency which demands the most fantastic skill and address on the part of managers and, oddly enough but predictably, the strongest possible control of the group.

We are examining here, if you have not noticed, the Tone Scale of governments or companies or groups in general from the high theta of a near cooperative state, down through the theta of a democratic republic, down through "emergency management," down through totalitarianism, down through tyranny and down, if not resurged by a new goal maker somewhere on the route, into the apathy of a dying organization or nation.

A true group will conquer the most mest. Not even given proportionate resources with another group, it will conquer other groups which are not quite true groups. Brilliance and skill tend naturally to rally to the standards of a true group as well as resources. As a sort of inevitable consequence, mest will move under a true group. The amount of mest a true group will eventually conquer—but not necessarily OWN—is directly in proportion to the amount of theta that group displays—theta being many things including solutions along the dynamics toward survival. To display theta the group must definitely tend toward a true group.

A truly successful management is a management in a true group. It is definitely in the interest of management to have as nearly true a group as it can possibly achieve. Indeed, management can actually go looking, for a group's completion, for a goal maker, or send the group looking for a goal maker and then, the goal maker proving himself by catalyzing the group's thoughts and ambitions, raise the goal maker's sphere of action as high as possible and abide thereby without further attempting to modulate or control the goals made (for management is necessarily a trifle conservative, is always liable to authoritarianism and is apt to be somewhat jealous of its power). Probably the most stupid thing a management can do is refuse to let a group become a true group. The group, if at all alive as individuals, will seek (the third dynamic being what it is) to become a group in the true sense. A group will always have around it a goal maker. Management in Industrial America and in Russia tries to outlaw, fight and condemn goal makers. This places the group in the command, not of management, but of a would-be martyr, a John L. Lewis, a Petrillo, a Townsend,* and management promptly has to go authoritarian and start killing sections of the third dynamic, which course leads to death, not only of the management but to the business or the nation.

*John L. Lewis: (1880–1959); US labor leader.
*Petrillo: James Caesar Petrillo, born 1892; US labor leader; president of the American Federation of Musicians 1940–58.
*Townsend: Francis E. Townsend (1867–1960); American reformer who in 1934 proposed pensions for persons over sixty.

573

Likewise, a group should be tremendously aware of the dullness or the real danger of putting a goal maker into management or insisting that the goal maker manage. Hitler had a battle. He probably had a lot of other battles he could have written about if one and all had recognized what goal maker there was in him and supported his goal finding. Instead, current management threw him into jail and sorted itself out as a target for national wrath (for don't think the people weren't behind Hitler, regardless of what the Nazis try to tell our military government). Down went the Republic, up went Hitler as management. Down went Germany in a bath of blood. At best he was a bad goal maker because he dealt with enmest, and very little theta. But he was a hideously bad manager, for by becoming one he could no longer be a good goal maker but, made irascible by the confusions of management, went mad dog.

Being rather low on the Tone Scale initially, most managements would be very chary of creative imagination level goal finding unless they knew the mechanics of the matter. And these demonstrate that it is unsafe to be without a goal maker, unsafe to suppress goal makers, unsafe not to keep trying for a true group continually and to fight very shy of letting anything drift toward the pseudo-group level. Management should stay in close tune with the group participants and give them as much to say about managing and ways and means as possible, and should avoid assuming the burden of caring for the group, and should assume and keep the role as servants of the group, at the actual command of that group.

Management and enterprises are most highly successful when they attain most energetically toward true group status.

LAWS

There are certain definite and precise laws by which management can raise the level of its own efficiency and the level of production and activity of a group.

Save when it is necessary to establish a surprise element in an attack or to secure a portion of the group from attack, suppression of OPERATIONAL DATA is permissible to management. Suppression of any other than operational data can disrupt a group and blow management over. Any management which operates as a censorship or a propaganda medium will inevitably destroy itself and injure the group. A management must not pervert affinity, communication or reality and must not interrupt it. A management fails in ratio to the amount of perversion or severance of ARC it engages upon and its plans and the goals of the group are wrong in the exact ratio it finds itself "forced" to engage upon ARC perversion or severance of ARC in terms of propaganda or internal relations.

A management can instantly improve the tone of any organization and thus its efficiency by hooking up and keeping wide open all communication lines between all departments and amongst all persons of the group and communication lines between the goal maker and the group. Fail to establish and keep in open and flowing condition one communication channel and the organization will fail to just that extent.

Communication lines are severed in this fashion: (a) by permitting so much entheta to flow on them that the group will close them or avoid them; (b) by perverting the communication and so invalidating the line that afterwards none will pay attention to the line; (c) by glutting the line with too much volume of traffic (too much material, too little meaning); and (d) by chopping the line through carelessness or malice or to gain authority (the principal reason why lines get tampered with).

He who holds the power of an organization is that person who holds its communication lines and who is a crossroad of the communications. Therefore, in a true group, communications and communications lines should be and are sacred. They have been considered so instinctively since the oldest ages of man. Messengers, heralds and riders have been the object of the greatest care even between combatants on enmest missions. Priesthoods hold their power through posing or being communication relay points between gods and men. And even most governments consider cults sacred. Communication lines are sacred and who would interrupt or pervert a communication line within a group is entitled to group death—exile. And that usually happens as a natural course of events. Communication lines are sacred and must not be used as channels of viciousness and entheta. They must not be twisted or perverted. They must not be glutted with many words and little meaning. They must not be severed. They must be established wherever a communication line seems to want to exist or is needed.

Any management of anything can raise tone and efficiency by establishing and maintaining zealously, as a sacred trust, communication lines through all the group and from outside the group into the group and from in the group outside the group.

The most vital lines of a group are not operational lines, although this may appear so to management. They are the theta lines between any theta and the group and the goal maker and the group. Management that tampers with these lines in any way will destroy itself. These actually have tension and explosion in them. It is as inevitable as nightfall that these lines will explode, when tampered with, at the exact point of the tampering. This is a natural law of communication lines.

A line is as dangerous to tamper with as it has truth in its channel. It is safe and even preserving of a line to cut it when it contains entheta. For example when a true line is cut, it charges a little power into the cutter and he has authority for a moment thereby. But it is only the authority of the cut line. If the line is thus made to perish, the cutter loses his authority. If there is much truth in that line, it does not give authority to the cutter, it explodes him.

A group has the right to exile anyone it discovers to be guilty of tampering with any communication line.

A management which will pervert an affinity or sever one may gain a momentary power, but the laws here are the same as those relating to communication, and an affinity tampered with will lower the tone of a group.

A management which will pervert or suppress a reality, no matter how "reasonable" the act seems, is acting in the direction of the destruction of a group. It is not what management thinks the group or the goal maker should know, it is what is true. A primary function of management is the discovery and publication, in the briefest form which will admit the whole force of the data, the reality of all existing circumstances, situations and personnel. A management which will hide data, even in the hope of sparing someone's feelings, is operating toward a decline of the group.

A true group must have a management which deals in affinity, reality and communication, and any group is totally within its rights, when a full and reasonable examination discloses management in fault of perverting or cutting ARC, of slaughtering, exiling or suspending that management. ARC is sacred.

POWER

Management should be cognizant of the differences existing in power. Management undeniably must have power but a management which confuses authority with power is acting, no matter its "sincerity" or "earnestness" or even conscious belief that it is doing what is right and well, in the direction of decay of organizational efficiency. Power which is held and used by rationale alone is almost imperishable. That power deteriorates and becomes ineffective in exact ratio to the amount of pain or punishment drive it must use to accomplish its end. The theta of management becomes entheta in a dwindling spiral once this course is entered upon. For example, the punishment of criminals creates more criminals. The use of punishment drive on the insane creates more insane. Punishment drive against inefficiency creates more inefficiency and no management wisdom or power under the sun can reverse or interrupt this working law. Every management of past ages has been an enturbulated group rule seeking to rule an enturbulated group. Management has only succeeded when punishment drive was suspended or when theta moved in over the scene from a goal maker and by sheer theta power, disenturbulated the group.

The need of management is for power to advance secondary and vital plans and coordinate their execution by the group. The only power that ever works is derived from reason and the ability to reason. Mest surrenders only to reason when it is to become organized mest. Punishment drive creates enmest where mest was sought. It is the boasted desire of every management to acquire mest for the group. By employing punishment drive on the group or on mest a management can acquire only entheta control of enmest and that is death. Management, if enough free theta exists in the group or if the goal is sufficiently theta, gets away with punishment drive and can confuse the punishment drive it is applying with the existing theta in the group and can delude itself into thinking that accomplishment occurs because of punishment drive, not because of existing theta. Thus enthused about punishment drive, management then applies more of it with the result that the existing theta is enturbulated. Sooner or later the group perishes or (fortunate group) saves itself with a revolt which carries a theta goal. (Example: British Navy, bad conditions of discipline before first quarter of nineteenth century; mutiny of whole Navy for humanitarian handling of men; result, a more efficient Navy than Britain had ever had before.)

Power, and very real forceful power it is, can be sustained only when it deals with theta goals and is derived from theta principles. Authoritarian power, held by breaking or perverting ARC, enforced by punishment drive, brings to management certain destruction and brings to the group reduced efficiency or death. One, in considering these things, is not dealing in airy philosophic impracticalities but in facts so hard and solid they can be worn and eaten and used as roofs. We are dealing here with the basic stuff of management and group survival. It is to be commented upon that management has succeeded despite its use of punishment drive and because of existing theta goals whether management knew it or not. This sums up not particularly to the discredit of managements of the past but to the highly resistant character of theta goals. Management, failing to understand the true force

576

of its power and the source of that power, seeing only that if it cut and perverted ARC it had power of a sort, has been the yoke around the neck of mankind in most instances, not the proud thing management thinks it is or could be, keeping the wheels turning. Where wheels turned in the past it was usually because of highly vital theta goals and despite management. Management, being a needful cog in the scheme of things, has been kept around by a hopeful mankind on the off chance that it someday might be of complete use. A punishment-drive management is the spoke in the wheel of an action being conducted by a goal maker and a group, not the grease for the wheel which management sincerely believes itself to be. A goal maker–group combination action is only enturbulated because of the lack of a good management or, much worse, the existence of a punishment-drive management. Man would run better entirely unmanaged than in the hands of an authoritarian management, for the end of such a management is group death. A group would run better theta managed with real theta power than a group entirely unmanaged.

Management derives power most swiftly by acting as interpreter between a goal maker and a group. The power of the management is effective in ratio to the cleanness with which it relays between the goal maker and the group on ARC. Management loses real power in the ratio that it perverts or cuts lines between the goal maker and the group. When the goal maker exists only as a printed code, management can continue to prosper and can continue to serve only in the ratio that it keeps that code cleanly interpreted between archives and group. Management deteriorates and grows unprosperous in the ratio that it perverts or cuts the lines from code to group.

There is an intriguing factor involved, however: ARC lines. When they are slightly interrupted they deliver power to the individual that interrupts them. True, it is authoritarian power—death power. But a very faint tampering with a line gives authority to the tamperer since he is obscuring to some slight degree a section of theta. His group is trying to see the theta and reach it and if they can do so only through the tamperer and if they are convinced that the tamperer or tampering is necessary (which it NEVER is), then the group tolerates the tamperer in the hope of seeing more theta. Mistaking this regard for him as something he is receiving personally, the tamperer cannot resist, if he is a narrow and stupid man, tampering a little more with the ARC line. He can live and is tolerated only so long as the theta he is partially masking is not entirely obscured. But he, by that first tampering, starts on the dwindling spiral. Eventually he is so "reactive" (and he would have to be pretty much reactive mind to start such an operation) that he obscures the theta or discredits it. At that moment he dies. He has put so much tension on the line that it explodes. If it is not a very theta ARC in the first place, he is relatively safe for a longer period. The pomp and glory he assumes are not his. He makes them enmest and entheta and eventually corrupts them utterly and corrupts himself and all around him dies as management.

PRETENDED GOALS

There is also a pretense of having a theta goal without having one which intrigues management. Lacking the actual article the management postulates merely the fact that such an article exists and that management is the sole purveyor of this theta goal. Usually such a management makes excuses for the goal not being in sight or existing by claiming that "it is too complicated for ignorant minds to grasp" or "it is too sacred to be defiled by the hands of the mob." Management dresses itself in all the trappings of a theta relay station, but as there is no theta goal in the first place to give to the group, punishment drive has to be entered upon instantly. Hellfire has to be promised to those who won't believe a theta goal exists just over management's shoulder. A flog has to be used to convince the group that the cause is just. However, a group is capable of generating some theta on its own. There are always some minor goal makers around. Unfortunately these serve to buoy up a masking management by actually putting some theta into circulation. Management can then keep on masking an empty altar. But as the altar is empty such a management is always afraid, instinctively. It starts to speak of rabble, the mob, the horrors of individual say in group actions. It speaks of anarchy and uses wild propaganda to stampede and enturbulate its group. The life goes, to some degree, down in every individual in that group and stays up only because of the minor goal makers in the group. Management, seeing here a rival or a threat of discovery that it exists not for the goal but for itself, starts in punishment driving the minor theta makers, calling them revolutionaries whenever they advance a goal or idea and having them torn down from any tiny eminence to which their meager supply of theta has lifted them. When the last of these goal makers is dead, the group is dead, management is dead and desolation reigns. This has been the cycle of management amongst men since first man became civilized, save in those times and places where a real goal maker existed and where management actually began by being a part of a nearly true group. (See the history of Greece, the history of Egypt, the history of Rome, trace the course of Greek tyrannies. See also the history of various companies, and one readily sorts out those which began because of a goal maker and those which pretended a goal existed but had no goal maker for the group but only made goals for individuals—management itself. Three life insurance companies began because of real goal makers and they are the leading companies of America despite subsequent perversions of the goal and its subordination to individual profit.)

MASKED MANAGEMENT

Now it so happens that a culture which has within it many examples of punishment-drive masked management will begin to develop a spurious technology of management based upon mimicry of these masked punishment-drive managements. The technology is most ably put forward for that period in Machiavelli's *Prince*. Almost any text on "military science" is a technology of masked management. However, such texts exist and are useful because they furnish a short-term method of assembling a unit to follow a cause whenever one appears. The technology of how a company evolutes or a battery spots is not the technology of management but the technology of a coordinated group. Everywhere one looks in such a text on actual battle skill one finds that cooperation and understanding are the essence and that ARC is stressed amongst the group itself at every period and paragraph. But alas, the technology of the military management itself is so far from useful or factual that wars get won only because most armies have the same management system and that one wins which makes less errors than another and which has a better "cause."

For example, the communist main group in Russia is not a true group. Probably the United States is much closer to (but very far from) a true group. Thus the nation of Russia vs. the nation of the US, in a battle of culture would lose miserably. But an army of communists, working for a management which only recently lost its goal makers, Marx and Lenin, can have a "cause" couched in modern terms. All armies are considerably entheta and take only enmest. But a Russian army has a "cause" superior to a US army. Neither army has a true group cause, but the US "cause" has not been restated in convincing modern terms. A second-rate and obsolete "cause" is as dangerous to have around an army as an obsolete weapon. The US army "cause" does not include a conquest of mest clause but contains only protection of status quo clauses. Once the US drove hard on theta goals. Because her people and culture are not much decayed and her technology is high, a US with a "cause," as before, could easily outreach any Russian culture. And a US army with such a "cause" would crush a vastly superior Russian force. Armies, understand, are short-term groups intimately concerned with the conquest of mest which, no matter if they made enmest of it, is still a mest goal until conquered. Thus armies can be thrown into action with far less reason than a culture, and, not so closely, ARC within the unit itself can be catalyzed. An army, then, builds its technology on fantastically high ARC on the private–corporal level and is governed by a fantastically low ARC on the management level. Because ARC is high in the bulk of the group and is commanded to be high (management of armies would reverse such a thing if they knew what they were effecting, one fears) by a low ARC management. Optimum in armies is that high ARC on the private–corporal level and management by a government which has high theta goals and is itself high ARC. When this is attained armies explode out of Asia Minor and overrun Europe.

FALSE MANAGEMENT TECHNOLOGY

With such bad examples in a culture, management can develop an entirely false technology. Managers have to be geniuses to work with such technologies and ordinarily work themselves into a swift demise, as witness the presidents of the US who can be seen, if you compare the pictures of the same president after just two years of being president, to deteriorate swiftly. The group one way or another will try to knock apart an authoritarian management or a management even slightly authoritarian. The management thinks this is all because of bad planning, tries to plan better, and thinks all can be righted by just a little more emergency punishment drive. The group revolts more. Management punishment-drives more. And finally something has to explode. It is a lucky nation which blows into a theta goal revolt early in this cycle. The government of the United States is overworked and inefficient as management because all the principles of its original goal makers are not applied and those that are applied are slightly perverted. And the same thing obtains with Russian management. (Example: read the works of Paine and the works of Jefferson in their original form and read also the letters and personal opinions of these men: you will find more theta in those writings which has been overlooked than the whole US government is using from those same goal makers. Read Marx and Lenin and look at the tremendous quantity of theta untapped in those works.)

Bad management, then, like any aberration, goes by contagion. Because of a native existence of theta goals even as to common survival and a country wealthy in brilliant people and natural resources, management can become a sort of priesthood because success reigns and management has never been loath to take credit for a group's production. But statistics will tell you swiftly that the great god "modern business management" is in continual trouble, is expensive, is uneconomical and that, by the duration of large fortunes and businesses, on the

579

average such management as has been purporting to be management is almost a complete failure and is murdering outright the majority of enterprises of this country. The rise of unionism is not an index of the viciousness and willfulness of man but is, as it rises and wars against production, an index of the failure of management as it has been practiced as a technology. Unionism is not wrong. It is simply an unnecessary arbitrary existing because of the existing arbitrary of management operating on an authoritarian level, masking the absence of theta goal makers and seeking to enforce that lack with punishment drive.

America fought for independence from absentee management in 1776 and won. With the advent of Alexander Hamilton's banking system (a medal please for Burr*, traitor though he may have been) that part of independence related to economics did a marked and remarkable slump back into the dark ages of fascism—or, tyranny, as they called it in those days. Senator Bone, USS, once remarked to me, "I have fought since 1905 to place public utilities in the hands of the people. But I believe that, by giving them at last to the government, I have exchanged a fairly unreasonable for a very unreasonable master. It seems to me that when this country got rid of slavery in the Civil War we changed an outright form of slavery for a far more insidious brand—the tyranny of modern management." Fascism exists in America as almost the sole modus operandi of big business. And fascism or authoritarianism almost always murders itself swiftly since it is entheta and enturbulates the existing theta. This is best exemplified by the management–labor upsets which have been increasing in volume since the early 1900s.

Economic tyranny alone could make possible the far less than ideal group ideology of communism. Where fascistic business management exists there socialism and communism can grow. State ownership of everything including the human soul and a communal ideology conducted with false propaganda by a rather fascistic group in Moscow are equally undesirable. The world is in tumult today because of three schools of management: fascism reserves the right to fire at will and devil take the men of production; socialism outlaws private property and builds up staggering bureaucracies about as efficient as Rube Goldberg's machinery; communism buffoons around with one-time high ethic tenets, building an empire on deceits. None of the three are worthy of attention should a workable science of management come into being.

A WORKABLE SCIENCE OF MANAGEMENT

Such a science of management should obtain optimum performance potentialities and optimum living conditions for the group and its members. Such a science is postulated in Group Dianetics. It is not an ideology. It is an effort toward rational operation of groups. Its pilot project has worked. Other pilot projects will follow. In Group Dianetics, should its results continue to bear out its tenets, one is looking at the general form of the government of the world. That government will not extend, as administrator, out from the Dianetic Foundation. But the Foundation will probably train the personnel that governments send to it and will probably be the adviser to all governments. No empty dreams—we have in Group Dianetics a much better mousetrap.

*Burr: Aaron Burr (1756–1836), American political leader; mortally wounded Alexander Hamilton in a duel in 1804; was charged with treason in 1807, and later acquitted.

However, if the Foundation is ever to accomplish a post as trainer of government personnel, a tutor to the world of all management, the Foundation had better become, of itself, the best example of Group Dianetics in existence.

In accordance with an ambition to put its house in order, it is suggested that any organization so desiring put into practice the following tenets:

1. Consider well its ideal and ethics. This is the province of goal finding.

2. Consider well its rationale. This is the province of management, its planning and coordination.

3. Consider well its execution. This is the province of staff and individual members of the group.

4. Establish a general, flexible plan of government—adopting a constitution, selecting its officers with full agreement, adhering to its establishment and establishers.

5. Ever lean toward creative and constructive goals and execute its ventures creatively and constructively as opposed to "saving things," "arbitrary emergencies," and destructive planning and action.

6. Choose for its posts of trust high-theta personnel who plan creatively and constructively in expanding terms rather than "emergency" terms. Keep out of office the death-talkers who pervert or selectively censor communications or cut lines to gain power, who postulate opportunistic but dire realities and who, perverting affinity, have no love for man.

7. Hook up an abundance of communication lines to fill their various needs, keep the communications terse, keep the communications wholly honest and drop no curtains between the organization and the public about anything.

8. Incline in the direction of creating affinity from group to group and group to management. Create and maintain high affinity with the rest of the world.

9. Create a high and ethical reality of a better world and then make it come into being. Make the organization a model of that better world.

10. Persevere in the continual raising of group tone. Persevere toward the goal of the highest individual tone. It is theoretically true that a high enough group tone level almost nullifies the necessity of individual clearing and that high individual tone creates a high group tone.

11. Self-generate the organization into a model of efficiency in all its departments and with high pride in his performance on the part of every individual member of the group.

12. Operate on the principle that the failure, in any department, of one individual or sub-group, by contagion, threatens the survival of all.

581

13. Understand thoroughly the principle that the amount of theta in the group materially determines the longevity, greatness and general survival of that group and its members and that the amount of entheta in the group determines its proximity to death, and thus have done with the casualnesses and insincerities existing in a low-toned outer society.

THE CREDO OF A TRUE GROUP MEMBER

1. The successful participant of a group is that participant who closely approximates in his own activities the ideal, ethic and rationale of the overall group.

2. The responsibility of the individual for the group as a whole should not be less than the responsibility of the group for the individual.

3. The group member has, as part of his responsibility, the smooth operation of the entire group.

4. A group member must exert and insist upon his rights and prerogatives as a group member and insist upon the rights and prerogatives of the group as a group and let not these rights be diminished in any way or degree for any excuse or claimed expeditiousness.

5. The member of a true group must exert and practice his right to contribute to the group. And he must insist upon the right of the group to contribute to him. He should recognize that a myriad of group failures will result when either of these contributions is denied as a right. (A welfare state being that state in which the member is not permitted to contribute to the state but must take contribution from the state.)

6. Enturbulence of the affairs of the group by sudden shifts of plans unjustified by circumstances, breakdown of recognized channels or cessation of useful operations in a group must be refused and blocked by the member of a group. He should take care not to enturbulate a manager and thus lower ARC.

7. Failure in planning or failure to recognize goals must be corrected by the group member for the group by calling the matter to conference or acting upon his own initiative.

8. A group member must coordinate his initiative with the goals and rationale of the entire group and with other individual members, well publishing his activities and intentions so that all conflicts may be brought forth in advance.

9. A group member must insist upon his right to have initiative.

10. A group member must study and understand and work with the goals, rationale and executions of the group.

11. A group member must work toward becoming as expert as possible in his specialized technology and skill in the group and must assist other individuals of the group to an understanding of that technology and skill and its place in the organizational necessities of the group.

12. A group member should have a working knowledge of all technologies and skills in the group in order to understand them and their place in the organizational necessities of the group.

13. On the group member depends the height of the ARC of the group. He must insist upon high-level communication lines and clarity in affinity and reality and know the consequence of not having such conditions. AND HE MUST WORK CONTINUALLY AND ACTIVELY TO MAINTAIN HIGH ARC IN THE ORGANIZATION.

14. A group member has the right of pride in his tasks and a right of judgment and handling in those tasks.

15. A group member must recognize that he is himself a manager of some section of the group and/or its tasks and that he himself must have both the knowledge and right of management in that sphere for which he is responsible.

16. The group member should not permit laws to be passed which limit or proscribe the activities of all the members of the group because of the failure of some of the members of the group.

17. The group member should insist on flexible planning and unerring execution of plans.

18. The performance of duty at optimum by every member of the group should be understood by the group member to be the best safeguard of his own and the group survival. It is the pertinent business of any member of the group that optimum performance be achieved by any other member of the group whether chain of command or similarity of activity sphere warrants such supervision or not.

THE CREDO OF A GOOD AND SKILLED MANAGER

To be effective and successful a manager must:

1. Understand as fully as possible the goals and aims of the group he manages. He must be able to see and embrace the ideal attainment of the goal as envisioned by a goal maker. He must be able to tolerate and better the practical attainments and advances of which his group and its members may be capable. He must strive to narrow, always, the ever-existing gulf between the ideal and the practical.

2. He must realize that a primary mission is the full and honest interpretation by himself of the ideal and ethic and their goals and aims to his subordinates and the group itself. He must lead creatively and persuasively toward these goals his subordinates, the group itself and the individuals of the group.

3. He must embrace the organization and act solely for the entire organization and never form or favor cliques. His judgment of individuals of the group should be solely in the light of their worth to the entire group.

4. He must never falter in sacrificing individuals to the good of the group both in planning and execution and in his justice.

5. He must protect all established communication lines and complement them where necessary.

6. He must protect all affinity in his charge and have himself an affinity for the group itself.

7. He must attain always to the highest creative reality.

8. His planning must accomplish, in the light of goals and aims, the activity of the entire group. He must never let organizations grow and sprawl but, learning by pilots, must keep organizational planning fresh and flexible.

9. He must recognize in himself the rationale of the group and receive and evaluate the data out of which he makes his solutions with the highest attention to the truth of that data.

10. He must constitute himself on the orders of service to the group.

11. He must permit himself to be served well as to his individual requirements, practicing an economy of his own efforts and enjoying certain comforts to the end of keeping high his rationale.

12. He should require of his subordinates that they relay into their own spheres of management the whole and entire of his true feelings and the reasons for his decisions as clearly as they can be relayed and expanded and interpreted only for the greater understanding of the individuals governed by those subordinates.

13. He must never permit himself to pervert or mask any portion of the ideal and ethic on which the group operates nor must he permit the ideal and ethic to grow old and outmoded and unworkable. He must never permit his planning to be perverted or censored by subordinates. He must never permit the ideal and ethic of the group's individual members to deteriorate, using always reason to interrupt such a deterioration.

14. He must have faith in the goals, faith in himself and faith in the group.

15. He must lead by demonstrating always creative and constructive subgoals. He must not drive by threat and fear.

16. He must realize that every individual in the group is engaged in some degree in the managing of other men, life and mest and that a liberty of management within this code should be allowed to every such submanager.

Thus conducting himself, a manager can win empire for his group, whatever that empire may be.

L. RON HUBBARD
Founder

HASI POLICY LETTER OF 2 SEPTEMBER 1957

EXECUTIVES

The following members of the organization shall be present at 8:00 A.M. Monday morning, Technical Director—Registrar—Director of Processing—Director of Training—Testing In-Charge.

Executives of the organization are never off duty wherever they are. Senior executive present has the full responsibility of the organization at any time he finds executive posts vacant.

Executives of the organization are: Association Secretary—Technical Director —Director of Training—Director of Processing—Director of Administration—Director of Registration and Procurement—Director of PE Foundation.

Trustees are not executives except as they may also occupy executive posts. Trustees are: President—Secretary—Assistant Secretary—Treasurer.

L. RON HUBBARD
Founder

PROJECT ENGINEERING

Definition:

An HCO Project Engineer is one who furnishes the live impetus, dedication and guidance necessary to the accomplishment of a special Scientology research, administration or diplomatic project.

Stable Datum:

A Project Engineer is one who helps, never forces.

He moves fast and persuades others to do so. He can use the considerable authority of HCO and LRH to get his job done but he will find his greatest authority is the value of the project and other people's understanding of it.

Where he has to use force of authority to get the job done he will find a project weakened by just that much resentment as is generated back against it.

A hot line is a fast ARC line. A Project Engineer does not support authority, he increases existing authority by building something for it to have authority over— a point which will always be favorably received by Association Secretaries.

Rules:

Only one special project may be assigned to a staff member in addition to his regular staff post or if he is graduated to full time by reason of the growing importance of his project still only one project may be assigned to him. There may be no departments of special projects, except perhaps one which appoints and receives the reports of HCO Project Engineers and such a unit would be entirely HCO and never HASI.

Even when a special project becomes a HASI department, the HCO Project Engineer may not be separated from HCO and may not be a departmental person who is running it now for the HASI. Reason: HASI changes department heads too often. Example: PE Foundation which has not in the past been followed through even though it has had "the full attention of the HASI."

Funds:

Initial funds for a special project are furnished by HCO, but only to the point of the expenses of make up or administration. Book publishing costs, advertisements, payroll, etc., of a special project in view of the fact that it is totally for the benefit of the HASI and its income, shall be borne by the HASI.

DESCRIPTION OF A PROJECT ENGINEER

Reason for Appointment:

It has been our observation in the past that no specific person in the HASI has been responsible for the carrying out of a book sales project. A case in point is *All About Radiation*. Interest aroused in the public was tremendous yet we find the Association Secretary while the book is still best selling recommending that it be "remaindered" because there are too many on hand.

A book survey demonstrated that it was one of the best sellers of the HASI yet no program was undertaken to utilize public interest aroused. Estimated lost revenue: £100,000.

HCO Sales Project Engineer for this project or any project should concentrate on the following: regardless of who is doing the work, to shepherd and pressure such a book in for its first publication, to meet the deadline date by being sure ample quantities of the book are on hand. To make sure that the ads are timed for maximal impact. To overcome all resistances such as those of staff members, publishers, finance, accountants, newspaper advertising people, shipping agents, etc., all or any of whom may break the timing of the project for one or another reason which appears valid in their own eyes but which is not valid from the project's viewpoint.

Any project is a gamble and is the risk of money and time against public interest, however failure to follow through, time, and align finance can cripple the project before it ever starts or can break the back of a worthwhile project after it is begun.

Many things can happen to derail or wreck a project and the Project Engineer must not permit this to occur.

HCO layout may be laggardly because of their work and their pressures. The printers may be full of promises and empty of deliveries. Newspaper people may give trouble with the ads. Nobody in the HASI may undertake to make sure the book is in bookstores and in adequate supply. The book may be very popular and sell out all of its copies at once, and shortsightedness may fail to provide additional copies to meet the demand. The public interest aroused may pound in vain on the HASI for service without anything being set up in the HASI such as group meetings, discussions or lectures to handle this public interest and if people are collected by the project it may be that nobody routes them into training and processing in Scientology and most and foremost, if the project is successfully started and all these obstacles are overcome and handled, the organization may forget about the project, about the time it should be giving it another kick.

I have started many projects and promotions in Dianetics and Scientology which at the beginning had a chance of success. Invariably they have been crippled internally when they have been altered. Usually by administrative knuckleheadedness or financial closefistedness or just an outright aversion on the part of executives to have that many people streaming up the front steps demanding service with money in their hands.

At this writing staff has had nearly a year of low units which could have been remedied at any time by simply carrying out existing projects.

The mission of the HASI is to do its job, terminal by terminal and line by line. Just by doing this job in a routine fashion it will succeed. Special projects boost the income and dissemination. They attract public attention. They should not drag people off post inside the HASI and disrupt the routine actions which

587

are winning, but similarly these people, busy every day with their own tasks, should not be permitted to stop or disrupt a special promotion project simply because it seems to be not quite part of their jobs.

A Project Engineer should be able to get his job done, not by dragging people off post or kicking lines aside, but setting up the lines and terminals necessary for the traffic induced by the particular nature of the project. It is his mission not to let the organization make a project fail by disinterest or wariness at the thought of that much more work.

The Project Engineer is a person with a mission which he is to accomplish without too much authority. If he cannot get his facilities from the HASI directly he must appeal to the Executive Director for special consideration or orders to do or pay.

It will be looked on very poorly if an HCO Project Engineer starts clogging the Executive Director's lines and playing the usual trick of advertising people of making L. Ron Hubbard front for the organization and do all the promotion. The HCO Project Engineer is a special assignment for the project and it is up to him or her to keep up courage and not to get discouraged simply because nobody seems to know the importance of his project except himself. This is the very reason he is on the job.

What is the use of starting a special project and outlaying hundreds of pounds or even thousands to make something go and then abandoning it before it even gets into full stride.

The Project Engineer is there to make sure that this abandonment does not occur once we are committed to the action.

The Project Engineer can be likened to a bridge builder who is throwing bridges across small streams in the teeth of the enemy far in advance of the cumbersome main forces of his organization. It is sometimes a matter of frenzy to such an engineer that he does not get the men or materials he needs to do his job, and indeed when he asks the main forces for them he finds them entirely ignorant of the obvious fact that they in the very near future will need those bridges. The main forces act as though they intend to sit there for the rest of their lives totally ignorant of the enemy, streams to be crossed or things to be done.

If a Project Engineer has to be relieved of his project it will be because he has not appreciated or understood the quality and character of his post. He has not got anything to do it with and he does it anyway and not all the cumbersomeness of authority or lack of interest of the main job can discourage him.

The Project Engineer in essence has enough to confront. He is fighting to the front, poorly supported and criticized from the rear, but if he wins he has the singular situation of a win in spite of—— in spite of—— in spite of——.

I am counting on the Project Engineer to see the thing through even if they boil him in oil, cut off his paycheck, amputate his national insurance and cut off his buttons; I can assure him I would always have a new set for him if he carries on.

The main danger of Project Engineering is that it will suck everybody off post and throw them totally into the project and leave no main force if the job is done well, therefore the Project Engineer should have as part of his patter to people on post in the organization "I don't want to pull you off your job, that's where you belong and that's what you are doing well, but . . ." and "I know you have many more important things to do and rightly so, however . . ." He must at once sell the HASI on the importance of his project and the consequences of neglecting it totally and gain the interest of the HASI staff at large to keep the organization running and stay on post regardless of what he is doing. Therefore the Project Engineer uses the lines of the organization only where he does not burst them and demands special project personnel as fast as he needs them where the activity is gaining momentum to the pitch of a full-time activity.

The Project Engineer may start out on part time and carry on on a part time but if his project is beginning to demand by its growing volume more attention than he can afford and if the project is starting to suffer because he is holding down a full-time staff job also, then he has the right and authority implicit herein to demand he be transferred fully to the project and thereafter as he needs people and can demonstrate the cash value of it to the skeptical regular staff that he receive first part-time help from other staff members and then when this is out of hand and it's hurting other HASI work, that he obtain wholly separate, new and distinct project people full time.

In this way by gradient scale we can easily take this whole society and we fully intend to do so, but we won't do so in my experience without the participation and dedication of project engineering conducted by totally interested people. For instance the HASI could have had £3 units through most of 1957 and all of 1958 if they had paid any attention whatsoever to the demands and popularity of certain special projects.

L. RON HUBBARD
Founder

HCO POLICY LETTER OF 17 NOVEMBER 1958
Issue II

PROJECT ENGINEERS
THREE TYPES

There are three types of HCO Project Engineers.

First is technical and is assigned to research projects.

The second is administrative and is assigned to sales and service projects.

The third is diplomatic and is assigned to areas of special difficulty.

Model instructions for a research project are contained in the HCO Project Engineer 5th London ACC letter of 17 November 1958.

A model letter for an administrative project is HCO PL 17 Nov. 58 IV, HCO PROJECT ENGINEER, *HAVE YOU LIVED BEFORE?*

At this writing there is no model for diplomatic since no vast trouble seems to exist.

It is usual to assign staff auditors to these projects on a part-time basis, their activities taking place after their auditing day is finished. Only one project may be assigned at one time to one person.

DEFINITION: HCO Project Engineer is one who furnishes the live impetus, dedication and guidance necessary to the accomplishment of a special Scientology research, administration or diplomatic project.

They are assigned by L. Ron Hubbard or the HCO Secretary with the approval or understood approval of L. Ron Hubbard. In cases where an HCO Project Engineer is appointed on an emergency basis without the direct approval of L. Ron Hubbard, information concerning it should be forwarded to LRH so that he can condone it, augment it or dismiss it. There is no harm in appointing too many Project Engineers except that HASI however will begin to get restive if hit from too many sides by too many projects, none of which they may find in their sphere of direct interest since they may have projects of their own, in which case it may be necessary for an HCO Secretary to appoint a diplomatic project engineer just to find out what is going on with some HASI project.

This is the extent and scope of Project Engineering of which you will see much more due to the failure of large organizations to carry through even where their bread and butter is concerned, much less the greater good of Scientology.

L. RON HUBBARD
Founder

HCO POLICY LETTER OF 17 NOVEMBER 1958
Issue IV

HCO PROJECT ENGINEER:
"HAVE YOU LIVED BEFORE?"

Effective date: 17 November 1958
Duration of project: Three years

Purpose:

To ensure the maximum sales, distribution and dissemination of *Have You Lived Before?*

Procedure:

Finished materials will be handed over from HCO Project Engineer No. 1 to HCO Project Engineer No. 2. At this point HCO Sales Project Engineer takes over and makes sure that HCO completes the layout for photolitho, cover and copyrights of the actual book for "shooting" at the printers. HCO Sales Project Engineer No. 2 makes sure that Finance issues the checks demanded by the printer in order to print and in case this is refused makes sure the checks are presented to LRH for signature. Gets adverts okayed by LRH while book is being printed. Makes sure that the ads will appear simultaneously with the readiness of the book.

Puts ads in the *Daily Sketch, Daily Express, News of the World* and all psychic newspapers. Magazine ads are placed in *Prediction,* etc., as early as possible. (Their deadline will be the hardest to meet to get them out by the time the book is out or as near to the book time as possible.)

Contacts firms that broadly distribute books so that they will put the book in the bookstalls.

Makes sure that any bookbuyers who buy books from the HASI are contacted via *Certainty* in a special issue devoted entirely to this book.

Makes sure that a printed leaflet, very fancy, is made up which can be thrown about to bookstores, book distributors, bookbuyers, can be left in the film show, on the HASI reception desk—are made and then continue to be available, repeat, then continue to be available.

Make sure that the book is delivered and mailed for all orders received and after the book is sold out or is selling out rapidly that a new order for copies is placed at once with the printers. (It is a matter of interest that nothing kills the sale of a book faster than being permitted to go out of print before all possible copies have been sold since this causes a delay and a waiting which kills off all enthusiasm.)

In case there is difficulty in obtaining finance from HASI for a reprint or for replacing ads which are already pulling, HCO Sales Project Engineer must have the checks prepared and must himself send them to LRH for signature substantiating his need for them by giving the book sales figures and the stock on hand.

The procedure of advertising and selling and placing new book orders is repeated over and over until there is finally no demand whatsoever for the book, at which time this project is ended.

Currently with this above the Sales Project Engineer must make sure that meetings and lectures are made available to people coming to the HASI to find out more about past lives. He must be sure that personnel exists to give such talks and hold such meetings. He must be careful to ensure that every phone call received by the HASI concerning past lives is routed at once to a specific terminal the Project Engineer has coached to handle such calls and that the calls do not go up in the air or go nowhere or fail to be answered well.

It could be imagined that the Project Engineer is the person who receives these phone calls or who gives the lectures or who even mails the books, but this is not the case. The Project Engineer only makes sure that these details are being handled and checks on it as many times a week as he feels it necessary to bolster his own confidence and nobody else's that the project is being handled and is continuing.

Things to prevent:

Prevent a failure of layout adequate to the task.

Prevent difficulties from occurring in placing book manufacturing contract.

Prevent the book from being stalled for lack of funds.

Prevent the book from going out of print.

Prevent the ads from being unrepeated, keep them placed as long as they are drawing and in the publications doing the most selling.

Finally, prevent this project from being eclipsed by inattention or "more pressing ones" or "inadequate funds."

Attitude of Project:

These stable data must be inserted into all conversations, lectures and reviews and particularly in newspaper reports interested.

1. That the HASI is a staid, calm, authoritarian Scientology institute.

2. That Scientology is a broad subject that interests itself in anything and everything that concerns man's social progress.

3. That studies such as this are Dianetic crazes and belong to Dianetics, which Scientology has now begun to study.

4. That past lives and the whole subject is however dangerous out of the hands of experts and only such experts as Scientologists should be permitted to study them and common Dianetic practitioners should not be permitted to handle them.

5. That hypnotism is not necessary and is indeed quite bad.

6. That this is the longest series of cases ever undertaken for study amongst some people and all past data on this subject was the product of a few cases of questionable repute.

7. That we don't believe this, we are only studying it and the evidence is available to anybody in the HASI files.

The above data must be instilled and drilled into every HASI staff member who is handling the public on past lives.

Outside auditors:

Project Engineer also handles all queries, arguments, upsets on the part of field auditors connected with this project.

The above is the extent of this project. It is an HCO project in making the HASI survive and get a high unit in spite of all opposition and further, any difficulties encountered or diplomacies needed in addition to those of the HCO Project Engineer No. 1 should be referred to the HCO Secretary or her assistant for special projects.

L. RON HUBBARD
Founder

16 December 1958

DIRECTOR OF ADMINISTRATION—HAT

The function of the Director of Administration is to see that all policies relating to the Administrative Division as laid down by the board or the Executive Director but always from the board via the Executive Director are executed.

Financial policy, material policy, registration policy, are all defined in existing instructions or will be defined further.

The post of Director of Administration is supposed to make the policies of the Executive Director stick in the Administrative Division. The post of Director of Administration will be backed up fully so long as it devotes its energies to making the Executive Director's policies work. The task is not to create new policies, but to make existing policies stick.

When room space is allocated by the Executive Director, the Director of Administration is supposed to make the people and furniture into that allocation plan. When financial policy is laid down, the Director of Administration is supposed to see that it alone is the policy used. If such things cannot be done, the post is not being held.

L. RON HUBBARD
Founder

HCO SECRETARIAL POLICY LETTER OF 17 DECEMBER 1958

DUTIES OF SEC'L ED

The Sec'l ED shall publish all Secretarials to the Executive Director on blue paper, black ink, marked for local area. One copy to go on staff bulletin board, one copy to each staff person affected. Each copy carries the corporate seal over signature.

The Sec'l to the Exec Dir is also HCO Steno and is under the HCO Area Secretary.

The Sec'l ED shall act as secretary to the board where one exists, to the Ad Comm or Ad Council and at staff meeting, shall type, get signed and distribute the minutes.

The Sec'l ED shall put into HCO Secretarial Letters any item she is given originally from LRH intended for all orgs.

The Sec'l ED shall convert any HCO Sec'l Letter she receives into a Sec'l ED for the local area.

Sec'l ED shall capture all seals of an org and shall hold and be the only person to use these.

Sec'l ED shall perform any other duties given by HCO Area Secretary or HCO Communicator.

Sec'l ED shall capture all random orders from exterior sources which have bypassed the lines of the Exec Dir and shall refer them to him for issue or cancellation.

All org board changes shall be done by the Sec'l ED. All hats and hat changes shall be reviewed and done by Sec'l ED.

DISTRIBUTION OF ORDERS

Original goes on bulletin board.

One copy to dept addressed.

One copy to each hat affected.

One copy to master file.

These in essence are the only legal hats of the org.

Color of a Sec'l mimeo is white paper, green ink.

Color of typewritten—green paper, black ribbon.

No single mimeo or copy of Sec ED ever goes out unsealed.

SEC'L ED

Priority of speed:

1. Sec'l ED

2. HCO Steno

Importance of job:

1. HCO Steno

2. Sec'l ED

Number all orders of FCDC.

Sec'l ED first duty:
Capture all seals of org and HCO.

Sec'l DC:
Pub Reg and CF–Promotion Liaison on rush basis.

No order may be valid in Area organization from outside it without Sec'l ED publication.

The duty of HCO Comm and Sec'l ED is to corral all random orders running on lines and funnel through Sec'l ED.

The way things to go:

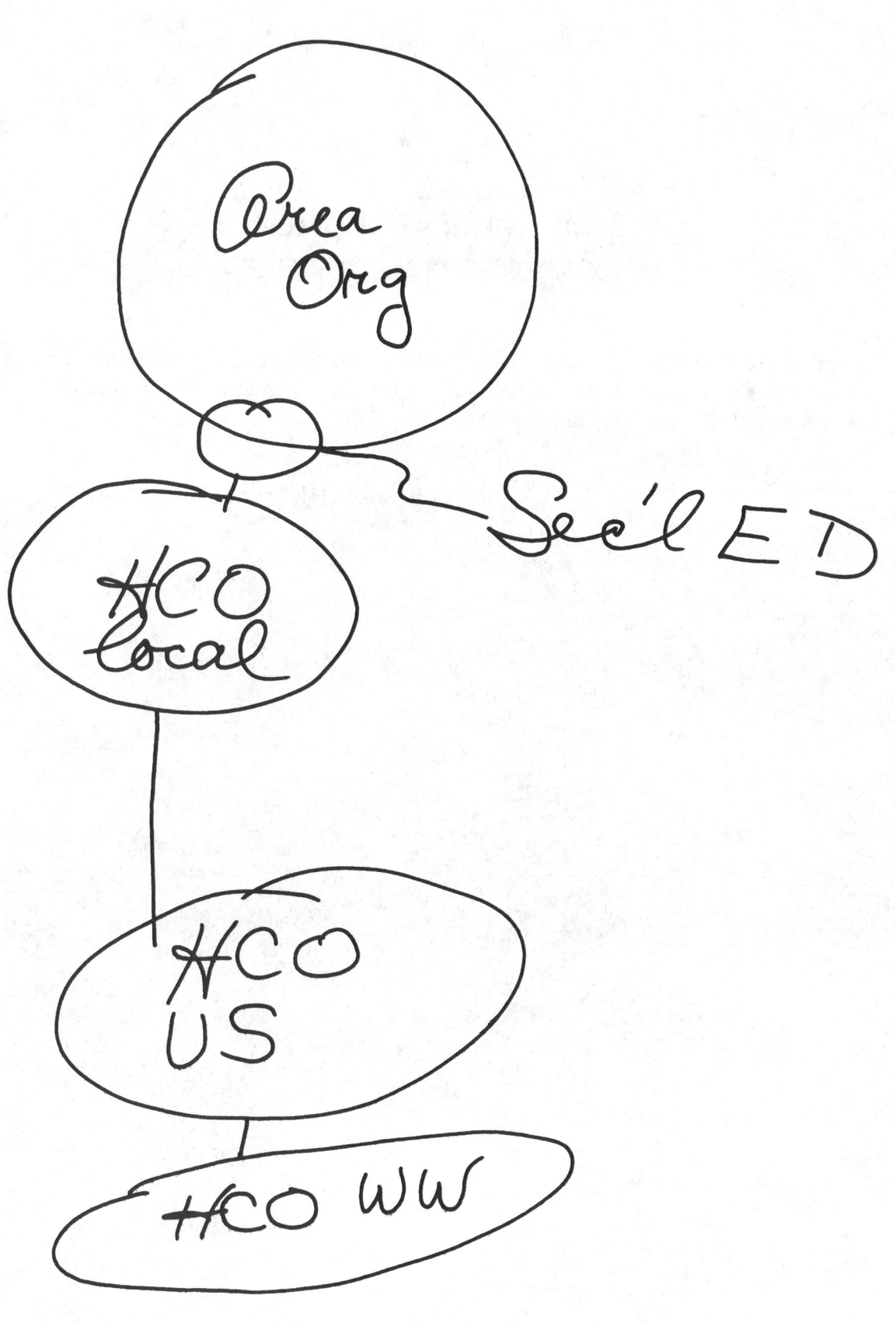

L. RON HUBBARD
Founder

SECRETARIAL TO THE
EXECUTIVE DIRECTOR HAT

Purpose: To provide a channel from the organization to the Executive Director. To ensure the arrival of orders from the Executive Director to the organization. To safeguard the hats of the organization.

L. RON HUBBARD
Founder

No. 133

Org Sec
HCO Exec Sec
Asst Org Sec
Dep Org Sec
D of P
D of T
D of M
D of Accts
D of PrR

26 February 1959

RESPONSIBILITIES OF ASSISTANT ORG SEC

(Referring to Sec ED 130, RESOLUTIONS OF
THE BOARD OF DIRECTORS, about Org Sec)

An Assistant Org Sec has been appointed to the FC.

His responsibilities and duties are all the responsibilities and duties of the Org Sec at any hour of the day that the Org Sec is not in the office. The continued absence of an Org Sec finds the Assistant Org Sec performing all such functions.

The Org Sec is supposed to get people to get the work done. Work and personnel are the concerns of the Org Sec and, in the Org Sec's momentary or continued absence, the Assistant Org Sec.

Seeing people are on time and on post, adjusting workloads, providing personnel for posts, are all part of the responsibilities and duties of an Org Sec in a Central Organization.

When neither the Org Sec nor the Assistant Org Sec is present, the Deputy Org Sec sees to these responsibilities and duties.

L. RON HUBBARD
Founder

HCO POLICY LETTER OF 22 MAY 1959
Issue III

CENTRAL ORGANIZATION EFFICIENCY

One could say with bitterness that the only place some Central Organizations show self-determinism is the HGC and then only on processes.

We are getting too big to refuse to make decisions locally. If we are going to bring self-determinism back to man, we'd sure as the devil better display it in ourselves and on our jobs.

Once the basic purpose of a post or department is known, only two things should then be necessary:

1. Self-determined and responsible continuous creation of department and post, and

2. Holding the communication lines rigidly in place.

No number of specific, detailed orders can remedy anything if these two are not in existence. Specific, microscopic orders on how the job is to be done are not only impossible but defeat the purposes of posts.

The unit depends utterly upon each department and post acting causatively. The more problems that aren't handled by the department or post receiving them, the more confusion develops.

It is my job to appoint or confirm people on posts, to map general strategy, to provide written ammunition and keep myself informed. If I am impeded in doing that job, we'll never make it. And floods of requests for decisions, which are well within the power of Central Organizations to make, defeat us in two ways:

1. It cuts my lines by jamming them and

2. Denies us general leadership and materiel.

When I appoint or confirm a Scientologist on a post, I say, "There, he'll handle that area." I don't say, "Now I've got some more nursing to do."

If we are to bring self-determinism to man, we must be prepared to exhibit it ourselves.

Defining self-determinism as it applies to departments and posts is very easy—it is the willingness to decide and act in a causative manner toward the traffic and functions of that post. When we have a person on a post who is the total effect of that post, we have the post caving in on him and the tendency to pull the organization in with it. Only when the person on that post can assume positive and effective *cause* do we have gains in dissemination, units, ARC and mest.

There are two ways of being a total effect—just to fixate and act not at all, just to disperse and throw everything off with resultant confusion to all.

We *must* come to orderly cause-point on every post. We must, we must, we must.

The full statement of function of every post is necessary or we have duplication of effort which we can't afford. But why beyond that do people demand decisions by others? Information they need. Traffic they need. A rigid communication system and exact lines they need, but decisions? How psycho can you get? Given information and the purpose, anybody can make a decision. Unless he's batty.

Right here and now I declare us to have become of an age to grow up.

Here we must decide, are we to have a Mussolini empire where only Rome could decide? Or are we to have tightly run departments and posts, taking their own causativeness over their functions and traffic.

True, I'm pretty clever about things. And I'm handy to have around. But I rebel at making slaves. If I cannot teach you to stand on your own two feet on your post, I've surely failed. You've got to be willing to be hanged for mistakes and not tremble for fear of making them. Be right on a majority of decisions, and don't be wrong on any important ones. But if you are you'll only be hanged. How come your neck is so precious when mine isn't?

Yes, it's important what you decide. Yes, it's the survival of your area at stake if you're wrong. But why be timid about it? The whole place will wither and die where you are if you aren't causative. The man or girl on the post is the one who puts life in it.

We have attained now:

1. Our technical know-how;

2. Our method of progress into the society—HAS Co-audit; and

3. Our best form of organization (6 departments).

And we can only be stopped now by failure to be causative, correct and decisive on our posts.

We're playing for blood. The stake is Earth. If we don't make it nobody will. We're the sole agency in existence today that can forestall the erasure of all civilization or bring a new better one. If we aren't willing to be hanged for our mistakes we'll surely fry for them.

So, let's get causative, each and every one.

L. RON HUBBARD
Founder

601

HCO POLICY LETTER OF 26 MAY 1959
Issue I

CenOCon
SHSBC Students
Missions
Field

WHAT AN EXECUTIVE WANTS ON HIS LINES

There are only four things which an executive wants on his incoming communication lines.

These are:

1. Information

2. Appointments and dismissals of personnel for his action or confirmation

3. Financial matters

4. Acknowledgments.

He does not want on his lines:

1. Demands for decisions

2. Backflashes and can'ts

3. Entheta.

Demands for decision are always indicative of irresponsibility; people want the executive to make the mistakes; and an executive can make mistakes if he is asked to make decisions distant from his zone of action equipped with insufficient data to make the decision correctly.

Backflashes, by definition, are an unnecessary response to an order. This can get fairly wicked. They are not acknowledgments; they are comments or refutals. Example: "Sell the bricks" as an order is replied to by "Bricks are hard to sell" or "We should have sold them yesterday." This is a disease peculiar to only a few staff members. They cannot receive an order directly and are seeking to be part of the comm, not the recipient. This goes so far as senseless "Wilco's" or "I'll take care of it" when the executive only wants to know Is it done? Despatches or orders, in most instances, are held until completed. We assume that they got through or rely on other means of saying they didn't. Only a few situations require an acknowledgment to an order over long lines, and all of these occur when there is doubt that the recipient is there.

In the matter of can'ts, an executive seldom orders the impossible and generally consults with people before issuing an order. A persistent "Can't be done" means "I am unwilling." I have learned this the long way. Person A on a job, saying "Can't" all the time, changed to Person B, receiving the same orders, discovered to me that the job *could* be done since B, on the same post, receiving the same orders, never said "Can't" and the job did get done.

Entheta means embroidered reports. Data is data. It is not opinion. Data, not entheta, brings about action. All entheta does is cut the lines.

To jam an executive's lines is a serious thing to do. The result is a cut line. A bottleneck is created by staff when staff jams a line to an executive. Eating up an executive's time and patience destroys harmony, dissemination and income.

Depending on an executive for petty decisions is sure to jam lines and cost units.

The role of an executive is to plan and execute actions and to coordinate activities.

To do this he gets people to do their jobs and establishes the overall plan of action. Only an executive can string lines and coordinate actions and resolve the jams that impede things. For an executive to decide for people decisions applicable only to the sphere of *one* job is folly.

WHAT AN EXECUTIVE'S LINES SHOULD LOOK LIKE

INFORMATION:

When a member of an organization does something of importance, he should always info the executive after the fact. It is perfectly all right to take actions within one's organizational purpose. It is not all right to keep it a secret.

1. Do it.

2. Tell the right people and the executive by adequate communication at the speed necessary to the case.

Similarly, an executive ought to tell people his goals and plans, and when he does something of any importance to others, he ought to say so. The captain who tells the ship how the action is going saves a lot of nerves and useless motion.

APPOINTMENTS AND DISMISSALS:

Minor hirings and firings in a department by authorized persons should always be subject to confirmation at least after the fact. Major appointments and dismissals of key personnel must be okayed by a senior executive before the fact and action taken only on the senior executive's authority.

For example, it is a board action to appoint, transfer or dismiss an Association Secretary or an Organization Secretary. It is an Executive Director action to appoint or dismiss department heads and then only on the advices of an Association Secretary or Organization Secretary. It is an Association Secretary or Organization Secretary action to appoint, transfer or dismiss deputies or section chiefs. It is a department head's action to appoint or dismiss other staff but always, in every case, with permission from the next superior and info all the way up.

603

FINANCE MATTERS:

Consistent finance information as in Advisory Committee minutes and authority for changes and capital expenditures are an executive matter. My own authority is needed only on major changes of policy or expenditures and on extreme financial emergencies. Ordinary financial planning and routine actions are better handled locally by the Association Secretary, Organization Secretary or the Director of Accounts. I do need financial information. But where I have done planning and promotion and it is agreed upon, further handling of finance is handled under a blanket authority from me except for extreme financial emergencies or major capital outlays which are local matters.

These are the things I want on my lines. I change personnel as the answer where information is chronically withheld, where appointments and dismissals are irregular, or when an organization starts getting insolvent. Where people are continuously demanding that I make the decisions they should be making, I again recognize other ills and again change personnel.

If we all understand what's wanted, we can do it.

Well, let's look this over and do it and win.

L. RON HUBBARD
Founder

HCO POLICY LETTER OF 19 JULY 1959
Issue II

CenOCon

NEW CORP—NEW BROOM

As we enter HASI, Ltd. and the mission period, I am adopting a new policy.

I get the discredit for every org or Scientologist failure. I have to catch the ball every time it is completely missed. This enormously slows our projects and overworks me.

In short, to some degree I get the axe every time somebody in Scientology or its organizations goofs.

Therefore, I am forced to adopt this policy:

People who make me do their jobs aren't doing their jobs and I will confirm that they are not on post by not keeping them on post.

Any time a ball is flagrantly dropped, I will drop a person.

Most staff and Scientologists are very willing and I am happy with them. I am remiss when I permit them or me to be clobbered because somebody dropped a ball.

We are now getting too big and too numerous to be careless.

Taut ship = a salvaged planet.

We're playing for *keeps*.

L. RON HUBBARD
Founder

SAINT HILL PROJECTS
BONUS AND QUOTA SYSTEM

All Saint Hill projects have a quota. At this writing, 4 Sept. 1959, this quota system is established only in part. Several projects do not have a quota set as yet for lack of data. As soon as possible, each one of these will have a quota.

The meaning of the quota and bonus system is as follows: Whenever a quota is exceeded even slightly, a bonus results for the Project Supervisor and a bonus about one tenth that size is paid to general office and domestic help. This means that if the quotas on the ten projects which are most important were reached then a full bonus would result for each nonsupervisor on the staff.

The exact size of the bonus is not yet established and will not be until I can work out some of the economics involved. But the system is effective as of 1 Sept. 1959. Probably a second paycheck in the month.

The quotas so far established are as follows:

Project One: New Books, to be collected as to materials by the Project Supervisor and written by myself: £715 per month.

Project Two: Mission Holders: £500 per week and one airmailing to each mission holder.

Project Three: Being redeveloped. Unassigned.

Project Four: Plant Growth Activity: Two completed experiments per month. Quota not established for production.

Project Five: Books and Tape Sales: £220 per week banked.

Project Six: Corporate Activity and Share Sales. Quota not yet assigned.

Project Seven: Magazine Preparation and Leaflets: Two issues per month. Shares quota with Books and Tape Sales Project Supervisor.

Project Eight: Collection of Past Accounts: £210 per week.

Project Nine: Care of other and this HCO Offices. Quota not yet assigned.

Project Ten:	Purchase Order System Economy Sthil. Quota not assigned but would be for not exceeding a gross amount in expenses.
Project Eleven:	Central Organizations Supervision: Quota £500 per week.
Project Twelve:	Accounting and Banking. Quota not assigned.

L. RON HUBBARD
Founder

HUBBARD COMMUNICATIONS OFFICE
Saint Hill Manor, East Grinstead, Sussex

HCO POLICY LETTER OF 9 OCTOBER 1959

QUOTA REVISION

(Effective date first Friday in October)

Project No. 1: Technical and New Books

One new book in manuscript completed form, ready for delivery to printer.

Project No. 2: Mission Holders

£200 a week for a month's consecutive weeks.

Project No. 3: Unassigned

Project No. 4: Plants Saint Hill

Two completed experiments.

£200 a week for a month's consecutive weeks in market produce.

Project No. 5: Book Sales

£200 a week banked from mail-order sales for a month's consecutive weeks.

Project No. 6: Incorporation Activities

One news story per week published.

Project No. 7: Magazines

Three magazines per month completed for printer.

Project No. 8: Past Due Accounts

£100 per week for a month's consecutive weeks.

Project No. 9: HCO Offices

£40 per week for a month's consecutive weeks.

Project No. 10: Economy Saint Hill

£120 per month all food items.

Project No. 11: Central Orgs

£200 per week banked at East Grinstead for a month's consecutive weeks.

Project No. 12: Accounting

All reports on Saint Hill submitted each week, all monies banked, all bills corrected for payment.

L. RON HUBBARD
Founder

HUBBARD COMMUNICATIONS OFFICE
Saint Hill Manor, East Grinstead, Sussex

HCO POLICY LETTER OF 14 OCTOBER 1959

CenOCon

ACTING EXECUTIVE DIRECTOR

During my absence from HCO WW in Australia, I appoint herewith Mary Sue Hubbard as Acting Executive Director for all Dianetic and Scientology organizations, to continue on post until I can reassume my duties at HCO Sthil.

All material ordinarily directed to me, even deeds and minutes of boards, should continue to be directed to HCO Sthil as usual, since with this appointment and with an additional power of attorney to sign legal documents, Mary Sue can take care of any and all needful matters arising.

We are making wonderful forward progress just now, and you must not let any administrative hitches slow us down.

L. RON HUBBARD
Founder

HCO POLICY LETTER OF 7 DECEMBER 1959

Mission Holders
HCO Offices
HCO Secs

FORMER SAINT HILL STAFF

All former Saint Hill personnel have no certificates until they have done the following: Written down all their overts and withholds on Scientology Organizations, LRH and Scientologists to the last detail and signed them and sent them to me to be checked out on the list at Saint Hill to make sure that's all. Further, all Scientology organizations and activities and comm lines are off limits to them until they have completed the above. They shall be removed from all mailing lists.

I think this is the kindest action that can be taken as they will spin in on their overts unless these are washed out. This is a pretty big overt for them and they won't be safe to themselves or the field until they have completed it.

L. RON HUBBARD
Founder

HCO POLICY LETTER OF 29 FEBRUARY 1960

CenOCon

ORGANIZATION SECRETARY HAT

(Taken from a telex message from
LRH to HCO London of 2 Sept. 59)

The Organization Secretary's fundamental job is to enforce policy. This is in actuality the full extent of his hat.

It is also understood that the Organization Secretary will be the foremost promoter of the organization and that he will do much reaching the public.

The Organization Secretary also has the hat of financial management when it has been specifically granted to him. This hat consists entirely of making certain that income is always greater than outgo.

The Organization Secretary is the person who sees to it that the work gets done. He is Personnel Director for the organization but in actuality can only remove department heads and can do this only after receiving permission from the Executive Director, unless he has been given the right to do this independently. In any case, the Organization Secretary must inform the Executive Director at once of any change in department heads.

The Organization Secretary may not dismiss a staff member without consultation with and permission from that staff member's department head in actual practice. Only in theory can he dismiss anybody in the organization.

As the fundamental job of the Organization Secretary is to enforce policy and see that it is carried out, he may not depart from policy without specific permission from the Executive Director. Further he must be an authority on policy. It is found by most experienced Organization Secretaries that they are very rarely asked to make a decision by a staff member without being able to quote policy and standard organizational practice. Most staff and organization problems do not call for brilliant solutions. They call for knowing the policies and enforcing them.

The best Organization Secretary would be the following:

1. The best public promoter of Scientology in the organization.

2. That person in the organization who knows policy best.

3. The person most willing to run good steady 8-C on the staff.

4. The person who has the soundest ideas on finance.

5. The person who can do every job in the organization better than anybody else in the organization.

6. That person who can best stay calm when all about you, etc.

7. Who knows his business.

As you can see, this excludes businessmen from being the best Org Sec. A good Scientologist who could combine being a whirling dervish with calm business judgment and good personnel management would just about fill the bill.

It is notable to remark that the most successful period in HASI London occurred when it was handled by a man who more than answered these requirements. And that his successor capably carried forward almost totally on enforcing policy, retained the form of the organization but did little else and still had an enormously successful run of it. By this we can see that the foremost requisite of an Organization Secretary is knowledge of policy and carrying it out. It has been adequately demonstrated that HASIs that do not do this don't succeed very well.

Foremost amongst Org Sec DON'Ts are:

Don't be ignorant of policy.

Don't fail to carry out policy.

Don't fail to consult with the Executive Director.

When major changes are envisioned in the organization, don't fail to keep the Executive Director informed.

Don't pull people off projects and posts faster than they can keep track of things.

Don't fail to consult with department heads when making changes in the organization.

Don't fail to advise the Advisory Council of important plans.

Don't fail to advise the staff of what's going on.

Don't get fouled up financially or cause financial beefs or difficulties.

Get all the ideas in the world. Do all the promotion you can think of. But understand and enforce policy and you will win as an Organization Secretary.

L. RON HUBBARD
Founder

HCO POLICY LETTER OF 21 MARCH 1960

Sthil Only
All Personnel

ECONOMY WAVE

Until the low collection period of November-December-January is cancelled out, strict economy of materials and contracture must be carried out at Saint Hill.

I will not sign any purchase orders except food, vital office supplies, needed petrol, enough sand, gravel and cement to complete construction using our night casuals. Conserve existing supplies. Scrounge what you can.

No further contracts or major purchases will be undertaken until further notice.

This does not mean we are suddenly poor or broke. It means that I want Saint Hill to run on available routine income without incurring capital losses.

Please assist to wipe out the income–outgo inequality now existing.

L. RON HUBBARD
Founder

HCO POLICY LETTER OF 30 JUNE 1960

Sthil
HCO Secs for info
Assoc Secs for info

ADMINISTRATIVE TRAFFIC TREND

If you care to study the administrative traffic lines of HCO WW, you will find that the traffic breaks down into two headings:

a.   routine, and

b.   emergency.

All heavy traffic and all unexpected loads come under the heading of emergency. There is no variation of the routine traffic load except that it tends to increase somewhat in volume as the amount of business transacted throughout the world increases. Therefore, there is nothing you can do with *routine* traffic to ease off the general work burden except to groove it more smoothly and reduce the number of times it is handled and generalize methods of caring for it. Therefore, only internal efficiency will reduce the traffic load of routine traffic.

This, however, is not the case with *emergency* traffic. It is emergency traffic that brings about the sudden rushes, the peaks, the overloads and the flaps. Therefore, to smooth out and handle administrative traffic at Saint Hill, it is necessary for everyone to understand the nature of emergency traffic and to work toward the prevention of emergency traffic. Only this action can now do more to enormously change and ease all posts.

Definition: An emergency is an unpredicted circumstance which necessitates fast and unplanned handling.

You would do well to have a thorough grasp of that definition. An emergency is unpredicted. If you predict a happening, you are prepared for it and it is not an emergency but rather tends toward routine, providing you plan well enough.

An emergency requires high-level, fast thinking, usually in the absence of complete data. Planning becomes guessing and hoping. And while this adds to the excitement of the world, it doesn't add anything to confidence and security. Even if all the emergencies are kicked upstairs to be handled by the more-authority, policy-level executive, they still bounce back at the lower levels if only as a chain reaction of executive nerves and impatience.

When we are talking about emergencies, we are talking about the things which happen that unsettle morale and disrupt lines, pull people off posts, make nerves raw and set the teeth on edge. One *can* live in this kind of an operating environment, but one doesn't have to if he understands the nature of an emergency.

The only time an emergency occurs is when someone *earlier* has erred. Any emergency we have had at Saint Hill can be traced directly back to a dropped ball either in Saint Hill or in an HCO or Central Organization office somewhere in the world. Sometimes we see one coming and issue orders to prevent it. We fail to make our postulates stick somewhere in the world as an order. The order is for some reason or other not carried out. The months or weeks go by and suddenly, *bang,* we have an emergency on our hands. So it isn't enough for us to predict an emergency. We must have a planned handling of a circumstance complied with somewhere else, usually, in order to prevent an emergency from occurring.

Example: We drop a ball. A Central Org orders an important number of books or meters. The order gets messed up. The next thing we know we are in a cable rush-to-fill-the-order emergency and up to our ears in phone calls, special letters, etc. Now, somebody dropped a ball somewhere and routine activities were not carried out. Thus, they became emergency activities.

Example: A Central Org fails to remit on schedule on some order. This is followed by some minor emergency action on the despatch lines and in the Accounts Section.

Example: A special bulletin is sent out on the handling of some expected difficulty somewhere. The bulletin does not get typed. *Bang,* we have sudden traffic here. Or somebody fails to follow it at its destination or follows it too slowly or even dully. *Bang,* our comm lines are tumbling. Our typists are getting out heavy traffic. Our communicator is rushing things here and there. Tempers get uneven.

All you have to know about an emergency besides its definition is that, from high to low on staff and on our lines, there is a reaction which jolts our routine lines out of arrangement and increases our work, and that when we fail to predict by various means (all routine) emergencies elsewhere, we get them ourselves.

Our trend then in Saint Hill organization of administrative lines is to increase the effectiveness of our routine actions so as to prevent emergencies with their unnecessary traffic. This of course also increases the survival and security of every person throughout all our organizations and is then not just a personal or self-centered activity.

In order of greatest occurrence our emergencies can be classified as follows (roughly): personnel, promotion, material distribution, financial, legal, procurement, technical and, lastly, comm failures.

We have recently refined all our administrative system internally and it is working very well indeed. We will now move forward to a level where every member of staff can inspect various reports received from all over the world so as to be able to predict both internal and external emergencies and foretell, by trend of action in all localities, where emergencies are likely to appear and handle them in our own good time on easy lines, rather than at the last moment on tight nervous lines and without data. This system would apply also to our internal activities and would apply as well to the departmental activities of all Central Organizations and other HCO Offices. It is not as ambitious as it sounds. All you have to know is the answer to each of the above classifications in any given area and here at Saint Hill, and by seeing slumps or dives in each of the subjects named from week to week, catch the ball no matter who is dropping it, and put the area and subject to rights while there is still time and before any emergency has developed.

Meanwhile, even before a system is rigged to do this, I invite your attention to these principles and your interest in smoothing out future emergencies before they happen. If we do this and only if we do this will all continue to go well, for our lines are picking up in volume already and can be predicted to treble in traffic in the next twelve months.

L. RON HUBBARD
Founder

HCO POLICY LETTER OF 6 JULY 1960

Sthil

WORKING HOURS, OFFICE STAFF

The difficulty experienced in coming to work by some office staff causes the following change of working hours:

Monday to Friday — 9:00 A.M. to 5:30 P.M.

Saturday — 9:00 A.M. to 12:00 P.M.

L. RON HUBBARD
Founder

HCO POLICY LETTER OF 12 MARCH 1961
Issue II

CenOCon

SUPPLIES OF
CENTRAL ORGANIZATION FORMS

All supplies of organizational forms shall be kept and stored ready for issue by the Assoc Sec's Secretary or, if such post is vacant, by the Assoc Sec.

Staff personnel requiring such forms shall obtain them from the Assoc Sec's Sec or from the Assoc Sec if he or she has no secretary.

The Assoc Sec's Sec or, in his or her absence, the Assoc Sec, is responsible for getting such forms run off and replaced when about to be out of supply.

A list of available forms should be posted on the staff bulletin board.

L. RON HUBBARD
Founder

HCO POLICY LETTER OF 12 MARCH 1961
Issue III

Do Not Remimeo
5 copies to each Central
Org:
  Master File HCO
  2nd File HCO
  Hat Folder Assoc
    Sec's Sec
  Assoc Sec
  HCO Area Sec for
    hat check on
    Assoc Sec and
    Assoc Sec's Sec

DUTIES OF THE ASSOC SEC'S SEC
IN A CENTRAL ORGANIZATION

The secretary to the Assoc Sec, or when there is none, the Assoc Sec, should perform the following secretarial admin duties:

1. Reception and appointments for the Assoc Sec (body and phone traffic).

2. Valuable documents, keeping them in a safe, holding the combination to the safe, photostating them in accordance with directives about val docs and being able to produce them.

3. Organization forms, knowledge of them, their duplication and supply, and giving them out on request.

4. On Thursday morning each week, placing one each of the proper weekly department head report forms and an income sheet (as it applies) in the comm center baskets of the dept heads for their filling out by Monday next.

5. Handling all job applicants and furnishing them forms and giving them guidance.

6. Filing all job applications.

7. Typing the Assoc Sec's letters from dictation equipment (never by shorthand) or seeing they get typed in the typing pool and seeing they get signed and sent.

8. Handling secretarial and filing matters of the Dept of Government Relations or Official Affairs, or if it does not exist, handling items related to it as directed by the Assoc Sec.

9. Doing all Thermofax (photostat) duplication for the organization as requested.

10. Keeping the desk of the Assoc Sec straight.

11. Keeping the hat file, policy letter file and technical file of the Assoc Sec in order.

12. Policing the comm lines and the in-, pending-, out-baskets of the Assoc Sec in order to facilitate his paper work. Preventing the Assoc Sec from using the in-basket for pending and seeing that the in-basket remains open for fast perusal of newly received material. When perused by the Assoc Sec, it goes into pending as soon as seen, or is handled and put in out. In short, preventing the Assoc Sec from being overburdened with despatches and preventing him or her as well from becoming a bottle-neck on the comm lines, since the Assoc Sec must be kept swiftly informed on the despatch line or it will become a body-phone line. Discourage the Assoc Sec body traffic by getting people to put things on the despatch line. When people phone for appointments, try to get them to write a despatch or letter instead.

13. In case the Assoc Sec is a Continental Assoc Sec, providing an additional pending-basket for each city office and for HCO WW.

14. Receiving, marking and posting on time the OIC charts each week.

15. Taking and typing Ad Comm reports.

16. Forwarding the weekly department reports to Accounts after doing the charts.

17. Seeing that Accounts forwards the dept head reports to HCO Area for forwarding to HCO WW by the Thursday following the week they represent.

18. Being acquainted with and having to hand all policy letters dealing with personnel, legal matters, val doc filing, forms, press relations and other matters relating to the above duties.

19. Refusing to permit the Assoc Sec to remain unaudited. Making sure his overts on and withholds from staff are taken off routinely.

L. RON HUBBARD
Founder

Central Orgs
City Offices
Assoc Sec
Post on Staff
  Bulletin Board

ASSOCIATION SECRETARY DUTIES

Included in the various duties of the Association Secretary are two daily inspections, one in the morning and one in the afternoon, of each department or activity of the organization.

Of each department head or staff member, the Assoc Sec should ask three basic questions. These are:

1. What are you doing?

2. Are you having any difficulties (with your lines or activities)?

3. What can I do to help?

I have found when acting as an Association Secretary that these twice-daily tours of the organization are vital in producing coordination. I have found that calling staff members off post and into my office, except for technical discussions, produces few gains.

I have also found that, as in the case of being D of P, it is fatal to invent solutions for the counter-creations and that ninety percent of the questions I am asked are already covered by policy and can be answered by quoting policy.

I have also found that almost all staff members are intensely willing, work hard and need no driving or duress and that I can help them best by taking their willingness for granted and actually helping them with their activities.

L. RON HUBBARD
Founder

HUBBARD COMMUNICATIONS OFFICE
Saint Hill Manor, East Grinstead, Sussex

HCO POLICY LETTER OF 7 OCTOBER 1961

HCO Secs
Assoc Secs
Org Executives
 Only

FRIDAY CABLES

Do not send on any Friday cable entheta to Saint Hill. It arrives overnight on Saturday morning. Only I am here. There is no office staff present at Saint Hill on Saturday or Sunday. There is only myself.

When you send off a night letter full of emergency on Friday, it arrives on Saturday.

There is no way to care for it. You are not in the office. I cannot contact you. There is nobody here to gather documents, type letters, run telexes or mail letters.

You couldn't figure a better way to throw the wheels out of gear.

On three of the last four consecutive Saturdays, I have received cables containing a demand of violent fast action. All right, what the hell, you're not on deck, there's nobody here except myself. I have to spend all of Saturday and sometimes Sunday catching balls somebody has dropped.

The data in these cables was in each case known fully on Thursday or could have been sent early Friday by fast rate. Some staff would have been here to give a hand.

Of course, there's a much better idea. Get some order into things; stop dropping the ball and having emergencies.

All emergencies stem from omission of action at a proper time. Do things right when they should be done and emergencies do not occur.

L. RON HUBBARD
Founder

HCO POLICY LETTER OF 2 AUGUST 1962

HCO Secs
Assoc Secs

ACCOUNTS INFORMATION

To obtain an accurate picture of how successful each organization has been since its inception, I would like your *rough* estimates as to *total* earnings for each HCO and each HASI for each year up to July 1961.

As you know, the technical ability of any org can be assessed by its unit, and these figures will be very helpful in assessing the whole picture.

Please let me have these figures as soon as you can.

What I want is total earnings since founding, by year.

L. RON HUBBARD
Founder

ADMINISTRATOR'S HAT

(Assoc/Org Sec: Assign this hat at once and keep it assigned.)

(HCO Area Sec: Hat check this PL on the Assoc Sec or Org Sec and on all execs of the Admin Division and particularly and often on the Director of Admin. The twelve functions below should be by rote.)

The hat of the Director of Administration is as follows:

PURPOSE: To expedite, supervise or handle all administrative actions for the organization.

The administration of the organization (the Administrative Division) is divided into the following spheres. The Administrator is *directly* responsible for these spheres:

1. Registration of students and preclears.

2. Procurement letters to obtain students and preclears.

3. Answering the organization's mail.

4. Organization quarters providing enough (a) technical facilities for training and processing and (b) secondarily providing administrative quarters.

5. Procuring, allocating, cleaning, maintaining and preserving all organization buildings, furniture, property, supplies and transport.

6. Collection of all incoming money, accounting for it, seeing that it does not remain outstanding and safeguarding it.

7. Disbursement of all sums owing any employee, person or company, safeguarding against overdisbursement.

8. Preparation of accounts for the board, the organization and for the government.

9. Maintaining and handling all files, addresses and filing and addressing equipment.

10. Guiding, handling and caring for all incoming and outgoing mail for the organization including all postage meters and posting equipment.

11. Guiding, handling, expediting and caring for all internal communications, despatches and equipment and communications property of the organization.

12. Handling and routing all body traffic for the organization.

In the above actions, depending on the size of the organization, the Director of Administration is assisted by the administrative personnel of the organization.

The Administrator is guided in his duties by the various policy letters and hats of the administrative departments and posts. These are: the Registrar, the Letter Registrar, CF In-Charge, Address In-Charge, Typists, Reception, the Director of Accounts, the Director of Materiel, Academy Admin, HGC Admin and all other hats of the Administrative Division.

In a small organization, the Administrator is also all the executives of the Administrative Division. He or she is the Registrar, the Letter Registrar, the Director of Accounts and Director of Materiel. In such a case, the Administrator has a Receptionist, possibly an accountant and a clerk as the total personnel of the Administrative Division.

In a medium-sized organization numbering around fifty staff members, all administrative departments have their own executives and this Administrator hat is worn by the Association or Organization Secretary.

Above fifty staff members, technical and administration, all departments in the Administrative Division have their own executives and there is as well a Director of Administration coordinating them.

In all cases the above twelve functions apply to whoever is wearing the hat of the Director of Administration. The organization is never without one even when the hat is being worn by the Association or Organization Secretary.

The Director of Administration has the full responsibility for the solvency of the organization, even when the hat of financial management is worn by the Association Secretary or Organization Secretary. The responsibility of the Administrator lies in getting the money collected when due, making sure things are paid for and that the money is securely accounted for and banked and is not wantonly disbursed. If preclears and students are being signed up, it is the Administrator's responsibility that the Registrar first and foremost has collected the money and that it gets recorded and banked. When people owe money, the Administrator has the responsibility of seeing that it is collected.

When bills are owed, the Administrator must make sure that the money is really owed and then that it is paid, and that there is money to do the paying.

The mest of the organization is under the Administrator's charge, and it is up to the Administrator to see that it is wisely procured and wisely and carefully used and not abused and that unused mest is disposed of, not left around to rot.

The ratio of administrative staff to technical must *never* exceed two to one.

In an organization where much service is being given and procurement is easy, the ratio of administration to technical personnel can fall as low as one-half to one. The lower this ratio the higher the unit.

The terms "Administrator" and "Director of Administration" are interchangeable.

Where the above twelve functions are obviously in poor condition in an organization, the appointment of a good Director of Administration is mandatory regardless of the size of the organization.

An organization is divided into a Technical Division and an Administrative Division.

The Technical Division is composed of those who directly audit or train or directly supervise auditing or training. The Administrative Division is composed of *all* other personnel except the Association or Organization Secretary and the HCO Continental, Area or City Secretary, and the HCO Communicator and stenographer, as these come under my direct supervision. The Director of Administration, regardless of the title of the administrative personnel, is directly in charge of all administrative personnel, is responsible for their hiring and firing, their arrival on time and proper performance of their duties. And, for the purpose of pay and facilities, is in charge of technical personnel.

The Director of Administration compares to the head of the administrative corps of a hospital where he runs everything except the doctors and does everything except treat and has charge of all the purposes except trying to make people well.

An organization is as busy as its technical is effective.

But an organization is as solvent as it has a good Director of Administration.

This is a key post. The person occupying it must have had good case gains and be clean, clean, clean on Scientology. If you can't get such a person, leave the post in the hands of the Association or Organization Secretary until you can. For this post, beyond all others, backed up by a good Technical Division, will create a wonderful organization, but no matter how good Technical is, a bad Director of Administration can crash it.

L. RON HUBBARD
Founder

HCO POLICY LETTER OF 20 MARCH 1963
Issue II

HCO Secs
Assoc/Org Secs

SELF–DETERMINISM
IN CENTRAL ORGANIZATIONS

I want to concentrate on the consolidation of technical and to write some books.

I have discovered that the daily flow of PTP-type despatches calling for urgent decisions from me, resolve themselves a few days later without any action from me whatsoever! So, I have decided that I am going to handle these perhaps once a week as I used to do, from now on.

Therefore, it becomes necessary for organizations to take very much more responsibility for their day-to-day operations. Also, remember that trained staff at HCO WW is there to advise you on any matters you can't handle or on which you need guidance.

All the policy is there to handle org operations and, particularly, I would like you to draw your org's staff members' attention to the policy I first issued on 22 May 59, on CENTRAL ORGANIZATIONS EFFICIENCY, and which has recently been reissued as HCO PL 7 Nov. 62.

We are growing up very much more rapidly than many realize. We have made it. It is now merely a matter of consolidation and then very fast expansion. Your self-determinism on your posts and that of your staff members will help very greatly.

I am always glad to hear from you. I'm not off the lines.

L. RON HUBBARD
Founder

HCO POLICY LETTER OF 27 DECEMBER 1963

Cont Dirs
HCO Cont Secs
Assoc/Org Secs
HCO Areas

THE "MAGIC" OF GOOD MANAGEMENT

(Some tips of value which, while they
do not form the rationale back of my
own actions, will be found of practical use.)

(Hat Check: HCO Secs should hat check this policy
letter on Assoc/Org Secs and Assoc/Org Secs should
hat check it on HCO Secs up to continental level.)

The sole actual criteria by which skill in management is estimated in this society and by us in any one management person is financial volume and solvency.

This does not mean that Scientology is obsessed with making money. But money does buy a lot of things orgs and staffs need and under poverty-inspired propaganda, "making money" has come into bad repute. In actual fact, the only real sin in our present system of economics is to be poor, even in Russia.

Financial volume and solvency are the final test of any manager of a Scientology organization or area, large or small. If the organization isn't making lots of money, if the staff isn't well paid, if there's no good cash surplus to hand, if book stocks are not well up and paid for, if the tape bills aren't paid up-to-date and the 10 percent is overdue and behind, then the natural conclusion at headquarters is that there isn't much good managing being done. The criticism is leveled solely at the person managing the org or its HCO and no other factors or explanations are taken into account.

Finance, in this society, is still our best index, and so we use it to judge the competence of management. People who say we shouldn't have money merely want us to fail. The data is looked at this way: A good manager's organization is highly solvent; a bad manager's organization is broke. Staff, conditions of the area, local flaps, these are never taken into account. There are no forgivenesses for insolvency from the society and there is no better index of the kind of job the manager is doing.

To have high financial volume and to be solvent, a manager need only (a) follow established patterns, (b) see that there are competent people on staff and that they are doing their work, (c) that service gets rendered on a highly personal basis, (d) that there isn't a lot of entheta and natter coming from disaffected staff members and hangers-on, (e) that the spirit of Scientology is recognizable in the organization, (f) that people aren't overrestimulated by the "dangerous environment," (g) that there are lots of bodies moving through the shop and (h) that the place is obviously for Ron and in agreement with his plans. Given just these things, success is certain. Given one or more of these poorly done or badly out and failure starts to creep in; given several out and there's no org, much less no manager.

These points of success mean many other things but they also mean high-volume solvency. And high-volume solvency is the index of success in the present economic framework of society no matter how socialistic the society appears.

The route to volume and solvency is milestoned by following these few points:

A. ESTABLISHED PATTERNS

Follow established patterns of the org. Don't keep breaking them up (or distracting personnel on post) with new projects and wild ideas. And don't follow them so Simple Simon that there's no initiative ever displayed in handling org problems. The best promotion channels are already built into the org pattern.

B. UPGRADE STAFF STATUS

See that people want to work for the org and make it a pleasant and happy thing to work for the org. Stamp ruthlessly on propaganda that interferes with org personnel procurement in the field. Continuously hold up the proper image that staffs are made up of the better Scientologists and make it true. Make it worthwhile to be on staff. Arrange it so that a staff member has more status than a field Scientologist. Discourage the idea that a staff member is there "just to help out" as a favor. Permanent staff membership should be a coveted status and an enduring career. After all, we'll be running things one of these days. And who will we count on? Staff members of tried and proven record, of course. Get competent people on staff, give them status and hold them on staff. Don't go in for transience. And see that they do their own job, not a lot of others. And treat them with courtesy and respect.

C. SERVICE

Be sure service gets rendered. The person trained must be well and interestedly trained and his or her problems in training handled. The person there for processing must be processed at the case level to get a win and processed interestedly and personally to a win. Tear the place apart if nontrained students drift off or nonwinning pcs emerge from the HGC. Don't ignore these ever. Give good service. Give the people what they came for. Schedule their time briskly and oversee their progress alertly. Look at the students and pcs every week and see *how* they look and act accordingly.

D. MALCONTENTS

See that the place stays clean of entheta and natter. Use O/W liberally. Spot the spinning malcontent and do something energetic. Don't get reasonable about natterers. If they're hypercritical they have overts. If they have a real complaint they'd talk to the management, not everybody else. These people are just nuts and they spread disaster. They drive off all the good staff members and prevent new ones, yet there they stay nattering madly about things they don't understand and haven't read. As they drive off good personnel, if you don't watch it you wind up with only nuts. So the natterer is no light problem. Don't hire them in the first place, but if you do by accident, deep-six them during the probation period provided. Don't fill up an org with disaffected persons just because you have to have bodies. This is a tough one because at least half the people about are incapable of understanding what's going on but capable of howling like mad about it. They prevent work. They're just chaos merchants. Natterers that hang around an org with "an apartment nearby where all the students go" should be processed or shot from guns.

E. THE ATMOSPHERE OF AN ORGANIZATION

The spirit of Scientology is one of help, a flippancy for the Authorities Who Know Best, a hope of getting onward, the one possible escape from the condemnation of this place. It doesn't include doubt and "I've an open mind" or reasonableness about those who would stop us. It's an aura of new horizons, a better life, an invitation out of the muck of all the misspent yesterdays. It's an offer to be born again. When it is discounted, played down, put alongside of psychology, medicine or self-betterment Carnegies,* it's being betrayed. The door is being closed on the millions. Omit playing my tapes, omit remembering why we're here, go into agreement with the idea we're just another org like Murray'* and you've had it. The atmosphere of Scientology is a lot more important than new buildings and modern furniture.

F. THE DANGEROUS ENVIRONMENT

Keep down the danger in the environment by actually winning steadily against it. As per Scientology Zero, don't increase it. Only the merchant of chaos does that. The natterer is obsessively selling a dangerous environment, trying to frighten others, trying to decry their belief in Scientology because it gets in the road of their desire to alarm and frighten others. Don't increase the danger in the staff member's environment by sudden firings, wholesale staff reductions, etc. It's the manager's job to find work for his staff to do, not reduce the staff to fit the work. Use job security, reassurance and nice steady wins to reduce the danger of the environment. Some day every Scientology org will be sanctuary for any person within it, by civil law. Just now, handle this by keeping morale up and winning against the outside. Don't fire or let off permanent staff members. Increase the volume of work to do. And laugh at these attacks. That's all such puny attacks deserve anyway, no matter the noise they make. The staff uncertain of its jobs, uncertain of the staying power of Scientology and the org, cowed by raging executives and threats is in an apathy of no work. One sweeping firing can wreck a place for a year. One threatening staff meeting can reduce work for weeks. Raise staff tone with raised security, good temper, wins they know about, and steady even if small progress against our enemies. And publish the wins so they don't come only on a rumor line. And boot out the chaos merchant—whose sole task is selling "dangerous, hopeless environment."

G. BODIES IN THE SHOP

Make sure that lots of bodies move through the shop, no matter whether they're spending or not. Just work all the time to move lots of bodies through the place. Don't let Letter Registrars drive them off with high prices threatened. Don't let Reception turn everybody away. Hold open evenings and Sunday teas and tape

---

*Carnegies: referring to Dale Carnegie, American lecturer and writer on self-improvement, interpersonal relations and salesmanship.

*Murray's: an English publisher of quidebooks and timetables for travellers.

plays and congresses and co-audits. Move bodies through the shop in volume. The instinct unfortunately is to keep the place quiet and stop traffic. Don't let it happen. Just keep people pouring in and out, no matter how or for what. And your standard promotion lines if in place will get their shares of course sales and intensives and books. The manager's first job is not to "run an organization" but to see that bodies move through the shop and build an organization to care for them and then to keep bodies moving through the shop and increase the body volume. All else, if other points here are in place, will follow. You can forecast any slump coming by a body count. When that public body traffic drops, watch it. Within a few weeks, there goes the unit.

Mail in the mailbox is an index of how many bodies are going to be in the shop. Get large volumes of letters out and large volumes of answers. Any letters out are better than no letters out. Too much emphasis on quality of letters is just another way of excusing low mail volume. And will result in few bodies in the shop. Do your best to hold quality up and keep goofs down—but get mail pouring into the mailbox.

Get books avalanching into the public (your first line of reach, actually) and you'll have more bodies in the shop.

An org is home to Scientologists. If you've no place for them to sit and talk or leave the shopping bag, you'll have closed the door on a lot more bodies in the shop. So field auditors prowl and steal pcs. All right, hang up a sign: "We are not responsible for any bad results from cut-rate co-auditing or processing not supervised by us."

Open the door with books, mail, events and interest and keep it open. And you'll soon have a volume of bodies in the shop. *Then* accommodate the flow. And still keep the channels open for *new* bodies, no matter how crowded you get.

No organization was ever solvent without bodies in the shop and channels for new bodies to put in the shop. However you get them in or why, do it. Concentrate hard on new traffic flow.

H. A HUBBARD SCIENTOLOGY ORG

This final bit is added not out of any pride or conceit or bid for loyalty. It has been consistently observed by many observers that when a place seems to be critical of or in disagreement with Ron or cool toward his plans, the public falls rapidly away. No squirrel has ever survived. Treat a bust or a personal office of mine with disrespect and the public falls away. Apologize for my policies and the public stays off in droves. There's nothing of superstition about this. The public wants Scientology, Ron's brand and they don't buy other brands. In thirteen years, every squirrel or disaffected or critical office has miserably failed.

The "we agree in most things with Ron but——" sees the coat tails of the public, not their faces. Only recently a large office nearly crashed on this one alone. I repeat that this is no self-interested observation. It is just fact. "This office doesn't fully agree with Ron" is a sure trademark of failure. I can name nearly a hundred (independent, nearly all of them) failed centers who for all their work and often creditable actions, new furniture and exteriors, failed and failed hard on just that point. Just fail to keep the nameplate on the door of my personal office bright, just let some student's critical remark about a tape go by and you've promptly got less public. Of course, the one who discounts this point of success the most is already failing the worst. It's bad taste for me to mention it but it is true and has to be brought up in any monograph on the success of a Scientology office. I know of two or three million dollars spent and lost on forming offices because this was not appreciated as a factor in success—and this at times when anti-Ron newspaper stories were at their peak!

Success in our times is measured by quantities and material gains. By our society's operational system, spiritual gains are often unobtainable in the absence of material things. However much you may regret this, we do live in this society and operate within its financial framework.

The manager's record before the board's eyes, whether he or she be Central Org or HCO, is considered basically successful or unsuccessful by measure of balance sheets. It is just a measure. Good income means good quarters, a cheerful staff, successful service and everything listed above in place. It means Scientology is winning. I do not receive direct benefit from that balance sheet. But I receive direct information from it. And the basic point, not forgiven by any other point, is that good and well-done organizational Scientology is high-volume and solvent Scientology. And all new appointments and changes in org top personnel are made by the board with that point in mind.

Of course, you can sell Scientology short, grab a lot of money for no service and have an apparent solvency. But I have found that this takes about six months to catch up with an org, at which time it starts to go broke in earnest in a soured community. So all solvency is measured by yearly averages, not sudden spurts. Consistent income means all above points in.

I just thought you'd like to know. We're not in it for money. But solvency is our best broad yardstick of consistent service and high activity, and the quality of management of any org is judged accordingly.

L. RON HUBBARD
Founder

Sthil

SAINT HILL STAFF ONLY

REORGANIZATION

You see the new organization chart in the front office. You should study it.

The basic steps are being taken to make it an efficient reality.

What we expect from staff members at Saint Hill are:

1. Do your job efficiently and well.

2. Handle and preserve your materials and supplies.

3. Work to produce income or help its production.

4. Cooperate to save on expenses.

5. Take your orders only as given on the chart. Don't accept orders from anyone and everyone for that adds confusion and wastes time and materiel.

6. Work only at your own job. Don't do somebody else's.

7. Clear designs and plans with the Organization Secretary or myself. Don't plunge in just because somebody else says so. Clear it with the Organization Secretary or myself, and if okayed, work like blazes on it.

8. Realize we are essentially a production team, not a company or commercial enterprise. What we produce is very plain on the organization chart. Production is either direct or in serving a production unit.

9. Realize that there are only a very few ways to get in trouble. These are:

   a. Not doing your job.

   b. Wasting resources.

   c. Overworking Mrs. Hubbard or myself by making us do your job.

   d. Upsetting people so they can't do their jobs or upsetting the children.

Within that framework your job is as safe as the Rock of Gibraltar.

Our aims are:

1. Increase income.

2. Decrease outgo.

3. Get everybody to know and do his job with initiative and intelligence.

4. Have a good team that doesn't require a brigade of military police to keep it going.

Our theory is that each one of you, as an individual, works for Mrs. Hubbard and myself. This is different than company or military organization. Those are essentially caste systems.

The way we're doing this is you work for us. It's always really been that way, so let's make it a fact. You don't work for X who works for us. You work for us.

Certain production activities are singled out and spotlighted. As each of these succeed, so succeeds Saint Hill. As any one of these fail to produce, so we fail.

It's a terribly simple organization. It will work as you will see.

Mrs. Hubbard and I put in about 10 hours of work a day on different activities than management. She is getting together books to print and sell and I am handling by myself a research line which is successfully completing what one large foundation (the Ford Foundation) spent 15 million a year on for a decade and which their thousands of topline scientists failed to do and eventually gave up. And I'm doing it all by myself mostly unaided.

This work requires quiet so we have an additional working day that begins sometime after 9 P.M. and ends around 7 A.M. seven days a week.

You are probably unaware of this work except in its finished form. You see students, book income, growing organizations. But what produces all this? Research projects and written materials. So right there we have a strenuous career. We then get a few hours sleep and around 2 or 3 P.M. get to our desks to handle management, administration, etc. We have dinner about seven, spend a bit of time with the children and get back at it. This is our day, then. It's one five-hour and one ten-hour working day out of the twenty-four, seven days a week.

You might ask why we work this hard. Well, nobody else can do our jobs and we are working against a set timetable that even so falls behind. We have almost made our schedule now, and just a year and a half more should see our basic jobs done. Then we can resume more reasonable working hours and have a vacation.

So you see successful management must be one that lets us do our jobs, too. If we were only managing things, it would be very easy. That we must also work makes it harder to handle an organization. You see, if we didn't do our own jobs, there would be nothing to organize.

Therefore, a really good staff member to us is somebody who does his job well and lets us do ours. We haven't any time for somebody who has to be policed before he or she will work, and we are particularly annoyed by somebody who tries to "get away with it" and thinks we will never find out, for we always find out and we always eventually act and open the outbound door.

If you understand these things, you will understand Saint Hill.

We would not be reorganizing now if the organization had not dropped production and started spending £400 a week more than it was making. That could lead to an emergency. We don't want emergencies. The organization is still solvent, but at that rate would soon go broke. Hence, current reorganization.

One could probably think of other ways to handle this, far more ideal, but we've tried many and have come back to this for only this system works. And this is what we're doing.

So what we want is very simple. Do your job so well we can get on with ours and we'll be a very happy team.

We value your help and we are glad you are with us.

L. RON HUBBARD
Founder

HCO POLICY LETTER OF 22 FEBRUARY 1965
Issue I

Sthil Staff
Post Staff Board

INSPECTIONS

On Friday of each week (except on holidays when the nearest convenient day will be substituted without missing an inspection) the ORGANIZATION SECRETARY and the HCO AREA SECRETARY will inspect all areas and departments of Saint Hill.

The following are the inspection areas in order of sequence. Inspection is to begin at 9:30 A.M.

Basement of Manor
First floor of Manor
Nursery
Servants rooms
Courtyard area and buildings
Canteen
Hall
Pavilion
Chapel
Boiler room (course)
Course baths and water closets
Garages and cars
Gardeners' sheds
Lot 4 and wood
Lots 1, 2 and 3, tennis courts and buildings
North line
Manor yards
East park
Park
Pond and stream
Lake
Roads

The Organization Secretary is to add to the above all units and departments in the sequence of the physical areas above.

The Organization Secretary is to be accompanied in each area by the person most responsible for that area and by the HCO Area Secretary.

The Organization Secretary will grade each area on a basis of 100 percent as to (a) Effective work done in past week, (b) Condition of equipment and supplies, (c) Lack of damage and (d) Cleanliness.

The HCO Area Secretary will write down or have a Steno with him to write down during the progress of the inspection any orders or grades or notes given by the Organization Secretary and will add to this inspection record any of his own comments.

At the end of the inspection the inspection record will be typed and a copy posted by the following Monday on the staff board. The original handwritten and typed copies will be kept in a book in the Comm office.

Personnel promotions and pay raises or demotions and reductions, staff transfers and dismissals will be based on these visual inspections and the week-to-week record of their grades, but modified by income and disbursement reports where these apply also. A consistent grade of 100 percent over a period of three months must result in a suitable reward for the person in charge. A consistent grade of 50 percent or less over a period of six weeks must result in demotion or transfer or dismissal for the person in charge of the department or unit.

An additional mimeographed form called the Inspection Grade Sheet, made up by the Organization Secretary from the above list but to which all departments and units are added, must be made up from the inspection record with the (a), (b), (c), (d) columns after each and the grades entered for the week. The original of this is forwarded to the Acting Executive Director by the following Tuesday after the inspection and thence to the board. A copy is posted on the staff board along with the inspection record. A second copy is enclosed in the inspection record book. The original and both copies of the Inspection Grade Sheet must be signed by both the Organization Secretary and the HCO Area Secretary.

L. RON HUBBARD
Founder

HCO POLICY LETTER OF 22 FEBRUARY 1965
Issue III

Limited Non-Remimeo
Saint Hill Executives
Hat File

EXECUTIVE DIRECTOR COMM LINES

SEC EDs

The Executive Director comm lines now include *Secretarial Executive Director* in all orgs including Saint Hill. This consists of a note or cable typed out by the HCO Steno (or Communicator where no HCO Steno exists or by the HCO Area Secretary where no Communicator exists). It is sealed with the corporation seal in the lower left-hand corner over the signature of the HCO personnel typing it. It is headed "Secretarial Executive Director." It is on blue paper. The signature of the Executive Director or the Acting Executive Director is typed below the message. Date and subject are included. Each Sec ED is numbered by the issuing Executive Director. The exact text of the note or cable is duplicated without additions or deletions. This is *never* a mimeographed item. The original sealed Sec ED, with the note or cable, goes to HCO files. A copy is immediately posted on the staff bulletin board by the HCO personnel who typed it and signed and sealed it. Another copy goes to the Org/Assoc Sec. Another copy goes to the HCO Area Sec. All copies issued of Sec EDs are signed and sealed by the HCO personnel typing it, as well as the original.

The Executive Director makes a copy of the note or cable being issued, numbers it as part of the message and files it for own reference.

Sec EDs are high-speed, urgent communications having the force of policy and require instant emergency compliance. Nonissue by HCO personnel or non-compliance by the person or department to which it is addressed immediately becomes a matter of a Committee of Evidence and can result in the demotion, transfer or dismissal of the offender.

Falsification of or counterfeiting a Sec ED must result in a Committee of Evidence with dismissal as the minimum penalty.

The Sec ED is the high-velocity comm line used to change personnel, to handle emergencies or to make limited-time policies or to handle personnel conflicts or chronic slumps.

All Sec EDs expire fully one year from date of issue but are kept on record although no longer in force.

The subjects of Sec EDs are not general in application to all orgs but only to the particular org to which they are addressed.

ADMINISTRATIVE LETTERS

Normal, general policy enforcement or advices by the Executive Director are carried in Administrative Letters. These are on yellow paper, are mimeographed and are usually designated general non-remimeo.

The Executive Director's Administrative Letters are different from others in being headed above their subject title: EXECUTIVE DIRECTOR DIRECTIVE.

They remain in force unless cancelled.

HCO EXECUTIVE LETTERS

The normal comm line from the Executive Director to Assoc/Org Secs and HCO Secs or department heads in orgs is the HCO Executive Letter of Date.

This is on legal-size blue paper, is mimeographed and is headed "TO:, FROM:, SUBJECT:, REFERENCE:," with numbered paragraphs.

It is always sent general non-remimeo and goes to all orgs even when addressed only to one org or even to a person in that org. It may also be meant for every org.

A copy of every HCO Executive Letter issued is distributed to all Saint Hill executive personnel and a copy is posted on the staff bulletin board.

HCO Executive Letters carry advices, how to do things, short-term projects, requests for data, information, reports on the state of things in general or some activity in particular or how some emergency was caused or how some emergency is progressing.

The Executive Director uses these rather than individual despatches in answering requests for instructions from some org officer so that these rundowns are available to everyone rather than just the querying person. In such cases the Executive Letter is addressed to the person, but the person's query begins the Executive Letter and is answered in the body of the Executive Letter.

The purpose is to save the repeating of similar orders or advices in numerous places by separate despatches which, received by only one person and having no publishing system, thereby lose technology and data.

When an Executive Letter requests data, it is headed under the "HCO Executive Letter of Date" line, "REPORT REQUIRED." This is done only when reports are required from all orgs. A report requested from one org is not so headed.

The International Org Supervisor at Saint Hill, on seeing a REPORT REQUIRED HCO Executive Letter, immediately makes a folder for it, with title and a date one month hence and holds it ready.

All reports received as a result (usually written on the Executive Letter received by the org by the reporting officer) are instantly and accurately filed in that folder by the Int Org Supervisor.

In exactly one month, as visible by its date on the folder, this folder is given by the Int Org Supervisor to the Executive Director, whether all orgs have reported or not.

The Executive Director then makes use of the folder and either gets the number of reports completed by cable action or otherwise handles or uses the data. It is not further handled by the Int Org Supervisor.

When such a folder is completed, a summary of the reported data received back by the Executive Director is commonly made the subject of a new HCO Executive Letter referring to the old and is issued, thus putting everyone in the picture. It is possible that this new HCO Executive Letter also carries a summary of the orders given by the Executive Director as a result, but the actual orders are issued as Sec EDs or Admin Letters. But when the Executive Director is through with it, the folder and all notes and a record of all actions are filed in the Int Org Dept files at Saint Hill under Executive Director Executive Letter Reports.

The Executive Director tries not to pour out volumes of despatches and individual advices to isolated individuals but uses the Executive Letter system instead. This has the effect of staff audiences being given on all manner of interesting matters and is useful to many staff members and orgs.

Distribution of HCO Executive Letters is as by general non-remimeo but in the orgs the spare is posted on the staff board on a clipboard and a copy must go to the person or staff hat to which it is addressed. Saint Hill distribution is to all Saint Hill executives and a copy is posted on the staff board.

Addressees in an HCO Executive Letter as in all other comms are to a hat, not a person.

Comments on entheta despatches are avoided on the HCO Executive Letter line. Entheta can usually be dropped anyway in all comms unless it is a matter involving an emergency.

CLIPPINGS

The vast number of clippings from papers and magazines sent to the Executive Director can be filed in clipping books without further handling or acknowledgment. While they often have importance, people sending them expect no ack as the clipping is not really an origin by the person sending.

BOOKS AND MAGAZINES

The large flow of books and magazines should be filed properly or discarded.

Books sent by individuals are always acknowledged.

PRESENTS

Presents arriving for the Executive Director, board members or the chairman should have a thank-you letter attached for signature and sent on to the intended person for receipt and signing the thank-you letter. Presents must have a thank-you letter attached before being forwarded to the Executive Director or board member or LRH.

ANNOUNCEMENTS

Births are acknowledged by an associate membership in the name of the new baby.

Marriages are replied to by a note of congratulations.

Divorces are neglected.

Deaths are acknowledged by a note of condolences for the signature of the chairman to the next of kin or informing person requesting condolences be given to interested parties.

HCO POLICY LETTERS

HCO Policy Letters (green ink on white paper) are not issued by the Executive Director or other persons than the Chairman of the Board.

HCO BULLETINS

HCO Bulletins (red ink on white paper) are not issued by the Executive Director but by the Coordinator of Research, which remains an LRH hat.

REPORTS

Reports from orgs, including Saint Hill, received by the Executive Director are usually due on Tuesday of each week. If the report is standard and not forthcoming, the Executive Director chases it up.

A table of such reports should be kept and checked off as received.

The Executive Director handles any matters arising from the reports such as slumps or good news promptly, by rush despatch via the appropriate channels or cable or if general by Executive Letter or if emergency by Sec ED.

The full story of Scientology locally and over the world should be fully and precisely received every Tuesday by the Executive Director in such a form that it can be swiftly viewed and followed up if divergent.

The authority of the Executive Director is maintained mainly by being the person who receives reports, and where these are neglected, it is a symptom of deteriorating authority.

Therefore, routine reports are demanded crisply and received and reviewed with great attention and acted upon with great interest.

The number of different reports demanded by the Executive Director should not be great and the form should not be complex, as these two things break down the line and burden reporting personnel who, after all, have other duties. But once a routine report is arranged, it must be demanded to be complete, accurate and punctual and when received must be given alert, interested attention by the Executive Director and when not received must become the subject of urgent communications and if still not received must become the subject of a full investigation of the nonreporting area.

Data received at Saint Hill from other orgs is digested for the Executive Director by the department heads at Saint Hill. If the Executive Director sees reason for further interest, the full data can be gone into in the department along with all related despatches *before* action is taken. Then the action is taken, the gains are complimented, the slumps scolded and whatever else that needs to be done or put right is done.

It is a word of warning here that data received from an ailing department or org is nearly always inaccurate, and that to base decision or advice on that alone is to be accused of wrong solutions as the solutions the Executive Director applies would only be as good as the data supplied to the Executive Director.

Raw figures not otherwise evaluated, compared to similar periods or similar orgs, tell the best story. Reasons why given by reporting agencies already in error are usually (but not always) worthless.

Bad spots in reports then must become the subject of intensive and intelligent personal investigation by the Executive Director. False bits in reports must be somehow ferreted out. And lack of reports must be dealt with summarily. Report analysis is a high skill requiring much personal experience, intuition, intelligence and other data for comparison.

The bulk of the job of the Executive Director is getting existing policy applied and detecting where it isn't being applied, forecasting slumps, repairing emergencies and keeping orgs on the increase, and all in such a way as not to add further upset to the mess. The power of the office is such and the velocity of the comm line so capable of impact that one has to take care to (a) get factual data without (b) upsetting the apple cart in order to (c) take intelligent measures which (d) do not bring about further confusion.

Usually, one can forecast an org or department slump about a year before it happens if one has the report lines straight.

The Executive Director depends on routine reports rather than despatches or rumors for data and thereby keeps things going well without adding to the confusion.

Demands for data must be precise, detailed, exact and crisp without explanation and censures for not receiving it but only stating one has not, never why not.

If the report is still not received, bypass the nonreporting person but demand only the same report.

When reports are consistently not received, despite all efforts to obtain them, begin looking over personnel in that area and get somebody there who can function. You will never be wrong in this. People who can't report aren't too busy if the report volume is reasonable. They just can't work and so are the probable source of the slump.

Report lines are the most vital lines of the Executive Director.

COMM STRESS

The most attention, next to reports, is given by the Executive Director to the execution of programs already laid down and spotting and discouraging projects or actions not part of the basic programs.

The org pattern in any org is the most basic series of programs. Each department, by the design of its actions, is its own promotion and execution program.

Thus, nonfunctioning departments are broken-down programs. The Executive Director is mainly concerned with preventing orgs and departments from breaking down on standard actions and in units carrying out the admin to keep the org going.

Technical departments are given the greater attention as sudden spurts in income will collapse if not followed up by good tech. Solvency is based on good standard departmental actions backed up by good tech full of good results in students and preclears.

The whole organizational operation the world over, as covered in earlier 1965 policy letters and in 1964 programs and org patterns and hats, is very simple and straightforward so long as it is executed. When it isn't being done or has been unduly complicated or altered, avalanches of despatches and reports of slumps or absence of reports call the errors to attention.

Using the policies on dev-t and enforcing them keeps Executive Director comm within reason and brings the bad spots to attention, making supervision by comm line analysis a most effective means of getting the job done.

THE DATA THE LINES SHOULD CARRY

The primary commodity of the Executive Director is data.

The Executive Director should at all times know (a) the exact financial condition of every org, (b) the current traffic volume (pcs, students, book sales) of every org, (c) the condition of tech in every org, (d) the condition of the staff training program in every org, (e) the condition of the staff co-audit in every org and (f) the junior executive member efficiencies in an org so as to know who could replace what at any given moment in emergency. And this of course includes Saint Hill.

Knowing those things and enforcing policy where it is out or getting better personnel on the job, the hat of Executive Director becomes easy to wear and everything prospers.

All this data comes from the Executive Director comm lines. These, therefore, should be concentrated on (a) to (f) above and all other concerns given secondary importance. Despatches or comms which do not serve (a) to (f) above can be neglected or put on an automatic answer basis.

The Executive Director's task is to (1) get the important data in order to act if needed without (2) getting a volume of paper too heavy to review.

Therefore, much of the comm of the Executive Director is predigested. This is done so as to not remove important data and not overburden the comm line.

Of all Executive Director duties, this is the neatest trick, and the post only fails when it is not pulled off.

The Executive Director hat does not conflict with the International Org Supervisor hat as the latter is only a portion of the sphere of responsibility of the former. The Executive Director deals mainly with Org/Assoc Secs and HCO Secs, and the Int Org Supervisor reaches much deeper into orgs. Further, the Int

Org Supervisor has the responsibility of obtaining the 10 percent org payments for Saint Hill, that they are correct and that all org bills are paid to Saint Hill. Additionally, the Int Org Supervisor lines are handled as whole lines to orgs, not predigested lines. The relationship of the two posts is similar to the relationship of Executive Director to every other hat in Scientology—the person wearing any hat acts on policies procured from the board or outlined or stressed by the Executive Director and coordinated by the Executive Director.

The Executive Director also obtains reports from the field, missions, books and advertising, even governments and the general public, and also Saint Hill departments and coordinates the whole with org activities.

MAGAZINE COMM LINES

The Executive Director has numerous magazine comm lines which are two-way, not one-way lines.

To the public the Executive Director has the minor issues of continental magazines.

To the field the Executive Director has *The Auditor* from Saint Hill and all major continental magazine issues.

Public answers and reactions concerning magazines should be watched but with the reservation that such mail is never a cross section of "public opinion"— that the true index of magazine acceptability is not letters from readers but traffic in orgs and book sales. It is fatal to modify magazines on the basis of "public letters" about them. Ten readers stuck in snarl don't make a public. Total absence of mail is more important as a gauge of ineffectiveness of magazines. The mail opinion is no opinion at all but is measured by volume, not content.

TECH ARTICLES

Part of the Executive Director comm lines is a copy of every magazine and brochure and pamphlet published by orgs.

These are carefully reviewed for the following points and/or actions:

1. Compliment an unusually good issue.

2. Call typographical errors to attention and warn that they can make a reader stop reading or even leave Scientology if a newcomer.

3. Technical material errors. These are made the subject of cables.

4. Hard sell. If the selling is soft and mousy, if ads for the Academy, HGC, books, memberships, extension course, congresses, etc., are omitted, investigate the connected personnel and get some hard sell going or some changes made in personnel. "Public criticism" brings about soft sell even though the "public" was always only one or two anti-Scientology bums. (London could have been saved earlier twice by this and Johannesburg twice and Washington once if this point had been used rather than more obvious symptoms seen and corrected months later.)

5. Articles or letters by other persons on tech. This is a sure sign of an org about to do a swan dive. The area of the mag is doing screwball tech because it doesn't think there is standard tech or isn't applying it.

6. Mentioning creditably people known to be rank squirrels. This is an org that can bolt, for it has a lot of squirrel connections, is therefore squirreling. A power push will develop from the area if rapid investigation is not undertaken and the facts *acted upon* swiftly.

7. Minors with big words in them.

8. Majors that have no appeal at all to old-timers.

9. Mags devoted entirely to local leaders.

10. Departures from byline policy.

11. Limited or curtailed distribution (for reasons of economy or others). This last is not detectable from the mag, so the Executive Director should require a circulation figure, as part of his reports, for both major and minor issues, PABs and *Auditors* as well as number of address plates currently in CF and number of brochures furnished mission holders each month.

OKAY TO MIMEO

The mimeo lines of any org are overused. Lack of planning causes heads of departments to fail to meet deadlines for printed mags. They then want to send mimeo mailings to everyone.

Sometimes it has to be done. But generally the Executive Director seeks to curb it.

Okay to mimeo by Executive Director before anything can be mimeoed is unreal for distant orgs. These should submit a copy of everything mimeoed to the Int Org Supervisor so that the Executive Director can occasionally review it and caution them, for it is very costly and poor. Receiving these also tells one when policies are being "interpreted" or local policies are being issued in divergence to mainline policies.

In the org where the Executive Director is located, this is easy. Therefore, the order is that *nothing* can be mimeographed by Mimeo in the Executive Director's nearest org unless it has "Okay to mimeo," and the Executive Director's initials on it must be enforced.

This is sometimes gotten around by an Executive Director's despatch saying, "Rewrite before mimeoing," and they then rewrite and mimeo without the actual copy being reviewed or okayed. Thus, the initial *must* be on the actual copy to be mimeoed.

This permits review and coordination of releases, curbs tech cross-advices and forces promotion into *The Auditor* or PAB and saves jamming mimeo lines. Mimeo is too costly for wide-distribution use and can get out of hand very quickly. When widely used (in hundreds or thousands of copies) it is prohibitive in cost—a thing an inexperienced org or executive never notices.

Hence, everything mimeoed in his nearest org and all repeats of existing stencils require Executive Director permission before being cut or run.

BOOKS

The Executive Director's comm lines include books. Selection of what books to reprint or push is the main part of this line. Indexes of what books are selling, what books obtain org traffic, are points of vital analysis by the Executive Director. This is the *primary* comm line of Scientology, and it is regulated and reinforced by the Executive Director, and is one of the more vital portions of the hat.

ADVERTISEMENTS

As only book advertisements are placed, one is limited as to what one can say, but this advertisement copy is an Executive Director comm line and is watched carefully and straightened out when it goes wrong or started again if it ceases to exist. It is a definite comm line and an important one.

SO #1

The SO #1 line (formerly only for LRH addressed mail) is the public and general incoming mail line to LRH, MSH and the Executive Director, and is watched and kept in order by the Executive Director.

It is a very important line in that *no major org breakdown has ever occurred without being preceded by entheta* SO #1 mail from that area!

One can estimate the condition of service, admin and tech (dominantly the latter) from the character of SO #1 letters from an area.

A year before the Victorian Enquiry, SO #1 from the Melbourne area went bad and stayed bad.

Thus, this SO #1 line, we learn from this and other instances, is an important index of the character of Scientology operation in an area.

The SO #1 line is used by the Executive Director as an alerting bell, not as a subject to be responding to directly.

SO #1 answers are severely regulated by policy—the maxim is "Give them what they want and keep them happy."

Respond casually to entheta, or noncommittally.

Forward complaints received to the org or auditor involved for their or his or her comment. Forward the response from the org or auditor to the originator, when it comes, if it is politic to do so, or condense it if it is not as a second letter; the first written at once is only an ack. Never let orgs use the SO #1 line as a sales line. Never let a critical letter go to anyone in answer to an SO #1. Just listen and understand. Ask SO #1 writers for clarification if you don't understand and want to.

Keep the line itself all "Good Roads and Good Weather" (which everybody is in favor of). Never criticize an auditor or an org in responding to SO #1 letters. Peace and understanding is the keynote of responses to people writing SO #1 letters. Save the thunder for the true source of entheta in the area, such as a bad D of P, but even then only when the evidence of his guilt is in plain view.

This SO #1 line is a *detection* line. One never responds to originators in any other way than peace and understanding. One uses the condition (theta or entheta) of SO #1 letters from an area to get a view of how well the field, missions and orgs are practicing Scientology there.

There is *never* bad SO #1 from an area where the field, missions and org are doing their jobs well. So it is a reassuring point when SO #1 is all theta from an area.

But *no* SO #1 at all from an area is an index that that area is not pushing *us*. It may even be active, but if no SO #1 arrives then that area is pushing Joe Squirrel at our expense, or worse, running us down to the public.

BUSINESS MAIL

Great respect is generally shown on commercial lines to Saint Hill and the Executive Director.

Where it is not, somebody in some important staff position is goofing like mad. It could be said somebody amongst us is being outrightly destructive.

For we are commercially *very* well regarded and respected.

One always uses the commercial-line answers from the Executive Director (or Org/Assoc Secs) to *increase credit* one way or another—not by asking for it but by casually remarking how well we're doing, how we're expanding, etc.

Never pull a "poor mouth" in a business letter. "It's too costly for us." "We are a charitable organization so we should be given favors." Be bold in all such replies, be the image of success and expansion at the slightest pretext—which is, of course, the truth.

STATIONERY

Executive Director stationery must always be top grade. Never use regular org paper for despatches—use special paper with a printed caption.

Don't use air letters if you can possibly help it.

Hand-laid, antique paper, heading embossed, for first and second sheets and envelopes is a *must* for all commercial letters from the Executive Director.

TYPING

Never let out-of-alignment typewriters, faint ribbons or erased messes go out on the Executive Director or SO #1 lines, no matter who is going to receive it.

Credit and importance is estimated by the only view they have of you—the letter in hand. Letters are small ambassadors.

MOOD

The mood of comm lines throughout Scientology is dependent on the Executive Director's alertness.

Scientology comms contain ARC. They are familiar.

Our lines are too wide open to put much entheta on. It arrives like a bullet when it was meant as a small tap.

You can blow up our comm lines with annoyance, much less anger, on them. So discourage anything but ARC.

If a long-distance comm line starts acting up, be very, very careful how it's handled.

The safest course is don't reply directly to snarly or critical despatches from org personnel anywhere. Consider the line temporarily wrecked. Do something about it but use another line or approach. It's too risky in orgs to try to run off somebody's overts 12,500 miles away with a despatch to that person. Use it as a symptom and explore it carefully. How much of the org does it represent? Call for other filed despatches available to you at once from other persons in that org. Do they contain any misemotion? Trace it all down without sending a single cable or despatch back. *Never* surrender to an impulse to flash back. Use a misemotional despatch to correct an org *condition* and be very sure that you really know the exact condition before you try to correct it.

When you're sure, act. The action perhaps will be getting somebody audited, or a transfer, or getting somebody retrained or finding a new Org/Assoc Sec or getting an HCO Sec's hat on. But *don't* reply—just handle.

In his or her own turn, curb misemotional materials or origins from the Executive Director area or self.

You can be critical only if you have a remedy that will work. Example: "Ds of P should never Q-and-A with auditors; one recently messed up a case. . . ." Never "You messed up a case! Stop your Q-and-A. . . !" It's a tolerant, sometimes tongue-clucking attitude. Not a bull charge.

RESTIMULATION

An Executive Director (or any staff member) is liable to restimulation by reason of comm lines or hats.

This nearly *always* comes from being forced to wear somebody else's hat without noticing it.

To remain sweet tempered, refuse to wear other people's hats for them and *always* check up at least once a month to see if you are wearing somebody else's hat. Otherwise your origins may become misemotional, whether verbal or by despatch.

Analysis of your comm lines will rapidly show whose hat you're wearing. Lots of despatches will concern that hat, not your own hat. Example: You have a mail clerk but you are always sorting mail or querying about lost or misrouted mail. You are wearing a mail clerk or a communicator or an HCO Sec hat. You will soon be furious with somebody, not always the right person. Example: Keokuk is always involved with something you have to solve. Recognize you are wearing the Org Sec Keokuk hat or the HCO Area Sec Keokuk hat long before you start getting snarly, and act, not by wearing the hat, but getting it worn by the incumbent or, failing that, finding somebody who can wear it.

Executives who sweep doorsteps instead of chewing up janitors are already in deep apathy from having had to wear, without noticing it, somebody else's hat too often.

It affects your comm lines this way: You are working to pay a janitor's salary. You are also being the janitor which detracts from the time you must spend to earn enough to pay the janitor. Thus, you *double* work, both to cover the salary and to do the work being paid for. Thus you must either get the janitor to do his job or transfer or fire him, thus reducing your load by twice. Even if you only fire the janitor without replacement *and* sweep up yourself, you have still reduced your load to the degree you had to earn his pay. So not noticing whose hat you're wearing when one is foisted off on you increases your workload double and will shortly pull you off your routine lines which then again reduces income. The end product is a feeling you have no time to do your job. And this messes up comm lines remarkably by causing one to short-cut and omit which in turn develops new situations which further reduce one's available time.

So to handle a set of comm lines one must be very wary of inheriting a hat from somewhere.

This, as Executive Director, is very easy to do as one is responsible for such a multitude of things it seems natural to wear a lot of hats to the neglect of one's own hat of coordination and supervision.

VERBAL COMM

Executive Director verbal comm, by phone or in person, is usually denied comm and causes trouble unless special actions are taken.

The decisions or arrangements made by the Executive Director verbally with one or two people are unknown, then, to other staff and act as a withhold.

Always record conferences and originate at once orders that come out of them.

Discourage staff body traffic.

Also write down and publish any verbal order given.

Confirm arrangements made by letter or despatch.

PUBLISH DATA

If only the Executive Director knows it, that's not enough. It will cripple staff members and orgs.

Hidden data and information, particularly estimates of situations and reasons why, must be published so staff can see them.

Release lots of information, particularly by posting on boards. Staffs try to hide data from the public. Don't bother to hide anything.

JAMMED LINES

The Executive Director lines can be jammed by:

1. Too complex a report system;

2. Letting others use Executive Director lines;

3. Failing to police dev-t.

If you outflow a lot, put it in a general form to reach many and don't make it a concentrated despatch line to one person. Thus people can read it at leisure when their own job lines are cleared. Use bulletin boards, executive letters, that sort of thing, for the release of news and info. Keep such out of despatches. Never write newsy despatches or more than one subject per despatch. Write newsy executive letters instead. It is doubtful if you can jam your outflow lines by general releases in this fashion as people are interested and want the news, and if they don't have to answer it always as a despatch, it will seep in somehow. So the amount of outflow an Executive Director does would have to be huge before people totally ignored it.

However, one can jam one's own lines by getting too report-form happy. When getting up report forms, remember it's you who must get data off them, so make them awfully plain, concise and few. If you add a new type of form, always discard an old one if you can. Regularly review report forms with an eye to discarding some or condensing them. "What forms being sent directly to the Executive Director are really useful to the Executive Director?" is the main question. Amputate those forms or data that are not. Still, don't fail to make up a new report line if you really can use the data in the time you have to study it. And don't fail to kill it when you no longer want it.

Letting other more junior staff members use the Executive Director lines or sign a type of Executive Director comm (such as an HCO Executive Letter) is a certain way to jam its line and confuse everyone.

By letting dev-t exist and not policing it, you jam everyone's lines. For not only you are getting dev-ted from a dev-t source.

CHECK SIGNING

Never sign isolated checks offered one by one.

Never sign checks unless you have:

1. A tape adding up the full sum of all checks offered;

2. The bank statements in hand to make sure you can cover;

3. Copies or originals of the statements or bills being paid;

4. Assurance that "this packet" is *all* the checks to be signed for the next thirty days.

Always do "dateline paying" no matter what the account line is.

Never be eager to sign checks. If demanding better preparation by Accounts will consume time, consume it.

In disbursement, accuracy and safety are senior to speed.

In all accounts matters don't be afraid to overwork accountants and never listen to why it can't be well done. Just get another accountant.

Always cause to be transferred or sacked any Accounts personnel who (a) act like it's their money, (b) who won't dig up funds for LRH or Executive Director concerns, (c) who get you into danger by poor or false submissions or (d) who won't enforce PO systems. Such have too much wrong in their units to set right under their control. It just won't ever go right under them.

The above also applies to orgs who make the mistakes of (a) to (d), only in this case investigate the senior executives for any one of a dozen possible crimes or delinquencies and don't be afraid to act once you have the straight information on what's what.

In fourteen years I have never found any of the above (a) to (d) attitudes without also finding hidden insolvency or, usually, theft. That is what those data (a) to (d) always add up to when investigation is complete.

Assoc/Org Secs and HCO Secs who yowl at you about your money requests or orders should be promptly looked over and usually should be demoted and transferred. They're too parasitic or too proprietorish of our money to be trusted.

Lazy accounting units are equally dangerous. In this case too, doing the work is always substituted for by a lie of some sort. So accounts lies add up to either crooked or *no* accounting system, never to overwork.

With these above data, one can handle Accounts comm lines easily without sudden shocks or financial emergencies, the two most detrimental things that can happen to an Executive Director. So preventing the shocks and emergencies when the symptoms above are first noted will save literally tens of thousands of pounds as well as Executive Director overwork and overloaded comm lines and getting all Scientology at risk.

SLOPPY LINES

Keep all comm lines and comm procedures taut and crisp.

The time to police sloppy lines is *not* when emergencies are in progress.

Any line may be needed suddenly without warning.

651

Therefore, be very harsh on floppy attitudes toward failures to acknowledge despatch forms, routings, distribution, copy filing, etc., etc. Then when they're needed, the comm lines are available and in working order. And you never know when you'll need them. They may be unused for months and then bang! they're vital. HCOs or orgs that don't answer up or properly should be investigated at once.

THE VASTNESS OF EXECUTIVE DIRECTOR LINES

One can easily be intimidated by the hugeness of expanse of Executive Director territory and lines.

Two errors can be made:

1. Fall back into specializing in some and ignoring the rest;

2. Trying to receive and answer *all* comm oneself.

About once a month solve (1) by viewing the whole network. Look for neglected areas and brush them up. Example: One, on review, finds he hasn't a clue what goes on in missions lately. Recognize it's an area of lines one is neglecting. Look over the report system on missions for faults or get one going. Look over the other lines one has been doing to find out what clandestine hats are being worn there or what makes them seem so important so as to exclude mission lines. Sort it out and regeneralize one's coverage. It's routine and common to be sucked into tech reports or finance and neglect other zones. The crime is not to discover it, find out why, act to handle the real cause and exteriorize.

In getting too much comm from too many places, one gets to a point of being able to handle none of it. This happens only when one doesn't grant existence to relay points on one's lines or when one loses confidence in the ability or effectiveness of a lot of relay points or of really faulty relays. The thing to do is work on patching up relay points, not going on handling the huge volume, as the more you handle it the worse it will become.

SPHERE OF INFLUENCE

The Executive Director's sphere of influence is too large to be handled on a part-time basis. It is a full-time job even when its comm lines are predigested to next to nothing.

Therefore, an Executive Director must not take on specialized posts "in addition to . . . ."

The symptoms of not handling the post are all to be found in:

1. Reduced overall org income, and

2. Increase of Executive Director incoming traffic.

Thus very heavy increases in Executive Director traffic will coincide with lowering org and mission incomes.

The things to do are (a) analyze the lines for dev-t and act on the analysis, (b) get neglected promotion policies and programs back in action fast, (c) trace back what old program has been dropped or replaced and get it back in force quickly and drop the later one substituted for it.

After any new program is put into action in any activity, be alert for dropping income in that activity for at least three months and don't breathe easy until income is shown to rise because of the new program. It's best to pretest. Use it in just one org before going all out in all orgs. Saint Hill sometimes serves to pilot.

Reports come into their own in scouting down a change that went sour.

When org incomes drop and Executive Director incoming traffic increases, go into the files and trace the first recent symptom of failing incomes in orgs general to all orgs. Then go earlier by a few weeks and look for any new programs or changes. You will often find it easily. Act accordingly and *very fast* to get it straightened up (the new one out, the old one back in).

This done very broadly over a long time period will spot up all successful general programs subsequently abandoned and could increase org income everywhere.

LOCAL TRAFFIC

Give local comm traffic less attention than exterior traffic.

Because an Executive Director is in an org, the org will pull him or her onto its lines for various functions. Seek to avoid this.

Concerns of the local org where the Executive Director is located should occupy the following fraction of Executive Director traffic: one over the total number of orgs in Scientology.

If that proportion is violated (taking into account reports from outside condensed or relayed by the local org for the Executive Director) then the local org has put one or more hats on the Executive Director. If these are not spotted and removed, Executive Director comm traffic will increase internationally, and international gross income will reduce (also reducing the local org's income).

PURPOSE OF COMM LINES

The main reasons the comm lines to the Executive Director exist are:

1. To disseminate Scientology as widely as possible through standard channels;

2. To increase the international (as opposed to local) gross income steadily and stably;

3. To coordinate Scientology activities;

4. To keep top org executives on their toes and functioning;

5. To hold a high tech standard;

6. To hold in policy;

7. To detect new policy when really needed and get it formulated at board level;

8. To catch the ball when it's dropped at high executive levels (Org/Assoc Sec, HCO Sec);

9. To design new promotion, test it and get it going if successful;

10. To keep Scientology research and compilation well financed;

11. To keep everyone in the know on current Scientology actions and news.

These (not in order of importance) comprise most of the functions of the office and therefore regulate the character of the comm lines.

One can do these things only if one keeps his comm lines going and within reason as to volume.

When feeling one isn't getting anywhere, the first place to look is at the comm lines, and the first thing to do is straighten up the comm lines so they can be used easily without strain.

Probably the first thing one notices about Executive Director comm lines is that one isn't originating anything; one is only answering up. If one is doing this, then the whole of the lines have to be gone into, dev-t rooted out, clandestine hats shed, slack personnel demoted, transferred or sacked, and actions taken to get policy and programs back in.

If it has gone too long, one does the above on a gradient, not all at once, starting with crisp new promotion or a furious carrying out of old promotion; getting dev-t, getting that spotted and its chronic originators handled; looking for hidden hats on one's head and shedding them, and so on.

I have found that when the Executive Director comm lines had me backed off from origin, I have always had to abandon the whole lot for a bit and, bypassing them, get promotion going fast. Because when lines get that way, income has dropped or will shortly drop, and, always, part of such a picture has *turned out to be* a forthcoming financial crisis. After furiously promoting and getting promotion done, one usually can look back in view of what one *now* knows and say, "Whew! That was close! If I hadn't gotten promotion started in December, we'd now be wiped out."

Promoting into a comm-line overwhelm is nonsense. One acts by bypass of his in-basket. *Then,* having acted, one straightens up his lines by analyzing and tabulating every despatch as he answers it. Then one shucks the accumulated hidden hats by getting them worn where they should be.

And all turns out well.

The only genius required is fast, reliable promotion action. Sometimes this requires a lot of inspiration. Example: Getting the idea to publish *The Auditor* and getting it in the run over the near-dead bodies cluttering up the place. It took four months to get it out in people's hands, but during those four months, a lot of the other above actions were also taken. By the time it came out, the org had almost collapsed, owed thousands and thousands. But it was out and the ball was caught. At the moment I started the promotion, the only visible symptom of trouble was that I could not find time to originate anything and was smashed back into only answering. Things smelled bad but not one single cause could be isolated and little data was known about what might be wrong. I promoted, then found what was wrong. So always take that order of precedence of action. Get in old promotion or design new and get it in the run. Then, straighten up the comm lines and shed the hats. The latter two actions can take eight or nine months. The financial emergency which will occur after a period of sour, flooded comm lines will occur *before* the effect of straightening up comm lines will correct the financial situation. Hence, promote and then straighten up comm lines any time there has been a prolonged period of Executive Director overwork or nonorigin.

The only hitch is to promote so that income will flood in and no existing income will be blocked.

In this respect, I never abandon known income in favor of hoped-for income. So the promotion done must take that into account. Example: A promotion scheme advanced by executives consisted of selling a lot of different memberships instead of receiving mission 10 percents. A lot of reasons were given as to why the mission 10 percent idea was poor and how much money would be made by memberships. I looked up mission income and found it was one-tenth the income of Saint Hill! Without being worked on at all. It offered great potential increase. I did not, therefore, abandon missions but arranged promotion to improve it. The advice to abandon it, if followed, would have blocked the 1964 book-ad promotion!

So no new promotion should be allowed to knock out successful functions. The thing to do is increase successful functions by newly promoting them, not something new.

Also, never go outside Scientology for income. That's a symptom of sure flop. Every Scientologist who does lays an egg. Use Scientology to produce income always, and despatches or comms advising other courses should be put in file 0 and ignored.

Reports will tell you what actions are producing income where. Use *those* actions for increased promotion.

Example: The failure to send *Certainty* to the whole list and a gradual decay of content and abandoning hard sell was coincident with London income decline. Pepping up *Certainty* increased London income. Therefore, publishing *The Auditor* was based on old, known promotion. So it didn't require vast genius to dream it up after all. And that it would save the bacon at Saint Hill by April 1964 was a foregone conclusion.

Reliable old promotion prettied up *and done* is usually best.

So promotion takes precedence over the condition of comm lines on the Executive Director (or Assoc/Org Sec) posts.

Thus there is something routine comm lines are junior to—promotion.

If you try to straighten up comm lines and the org or orgs in the face of threatened financial disaster, you will always be too late. *When financial slumps are in view* or forecast, always promote first and fast, ignoring the lines and orgs, and straighten up comm lines and orgs afterwards.

If you know this and do it, you won't ever have a complete financial disaster.

If you tried to straighten up the lines and org or orgs in order to use them to promote, the disaster will be upon you before you have a straight set of lines and an org. So the result is always a *smaller org* if you reverse the correct sequence of action.

Orgs that grow smaller have not promoted first and reorganized second. They reorganize first and so can only save themselves by reducing staff. They should have promoted first and *then* reorganized in the time thus bought.

You buy time with promotion and in that time you can straighten up the house.

Never, when promoting orgs out of a threatened financial disaster, consider whether or not it is easy to do or if staff can do it. Remember that the staff involved started the slump. Just promote, and regardless of anyone and if necessary over any number of dead bodies, get it executed. Then revive or bury the corpses. Handling things otherwise when the future goes gray will ruin everything.

Years ago it was obvious to me, as Executive Director, that orgs either could not or would not promote and that *I had to do all their effective promotion*. I used to wait in vain for orgs to generate promotion. When they didn't, disaster would loom, then I would grab the promotion ball, promote like mad, save them, and then wait again hopefully for orgs to promote.

I never realized why. Now I know. Orgs (any organization, not only a Scientology group) try to handle *everything* by administration first, last and always. They would promote routinely but when "organized for it."

Thus, when things were close to disaster financially (brink close and bill collectors calling, which alerted even the dullest person present), they sought to "change Registrars" or hire new typists or sit around and try to find out where the breakdown had been.

One, they hadn't any system to advise them of future slumps and wouldn't have put much time in using it, and it required an earthquake to alert them; and two, being introverted by threatened catastrophe, sought to remedy their org faults as the only solution.

True, if they had a smooth org, the inherent promotional actions of departments would save them.

But it takes longer to repair an org system than it does to promote new business. So the length of time of their solution, begun on at the brink of disaster, overran the last possible moment available.

Promote, *then* repair the lines and personnel malfunctions or improper placements.

This is a new idea. The world of business and government does not know it. They sometimes accidentally use it. Some dynamic director or manager might instinctively do it. But the high incidence of business failure (one in nineteen fail in the first year) and chronic governmental failures and insolvencies show the datum is not used by man even if known. Big businesses with huge sinking funds alone can use the system of "make it solvent next year by improving our structure" successfully. And even many of those miss and go bankrupt.

The shrinking empire has always (a) experienced but failed to handle financial emergencies, (b) sought to resolve the situation by administrative changes and economic measures.

Nobody can save himself or a country out of a slump. You can't save what you haven't got. Therefore, enforcing economy is aimed only at keeping outgo from being more than income. Enforced economies is no solution to a slump. When it is used as a sole salvage measure, everything gets smaller and the former position is never regained. When politicians start talking economy more than they talk of prosperity, the country is going to shrink in its sphere of influence.

England has done and is doing just this. Its empire shrank for no other reason than that it sought to reorganize itself out of too many financial crises and failed to promote.

Talk economy, yes. But talk promotion harder and sooner.

No empire stands still. They expand or shrink. They expand by (1) intelligent promotion and (2) good administration and (3) sensible economy, in that order. They shrink by using the wrong order—(1) economy, (2) more administration and (3) some promotion. They shrink because they never regain the former position by administrative management alone and the economy has nothing to economize on.

The Scientology empire must continue to expand in order to live at all. Therefore, one (a) keeps promotion going, (b) administers intelligently, (c) practices necessary economies, in that order. And in emergencies one promotes before one even thinks about reorganization. Doing that maintains the expansion.

Where an org has the same income year after year, they will soon begin to have less income. They are handling their various crises by administration and economy only.

If they watched their comm lines and every executive kept on his executive hat and corrected all dev-t, they would never have to do frenzied promotion as by the design of orgs they would be promoting constantly. And if they handled bad crises by everyone grabbing some old, tried-and-true promotional project and making it fly before they even wondered why they got into a slump and afterwards put their house in order when the promotion project was done, they would only expand.

You use comm lines to detect areas of *potential* slump. By analysis of dev-t, by observance of nonack, by watching volume of action, quality and content of

657

magazines, the Executive Director can accurately predict future slumps—literally a year or two before they happen. Predicted at this remoteness, one can make the small changes that will bring them up before they really start to fall. One has bought time. To do this one has to be very alert in comm analysis, believe its maxims and not "be reasonable about it," *and act* on what one finds when he really establishes what he thought he observed. This buys time.

When comm analysis and reports are not given close attention or when falsified for some time or bad spots don't come to view in spite of it all, then one approaches financial disaster.

When income itself starts to fall in an org or orgs, one then uses this datum—Promote first and ask questions afterwards. Always use sure-fire-type promotion, broad and huge, an old action in a bigger, new dress; never use risky, untried ideas. Now, with *that* getting done (and making sure it is being done by inspecting its progress day by day personally or doing it yourself), start getting lines and personnel straight. If the promotion idea is big enough and practical enough, it will pull through the period of reorganization, and the resultant income should be arriving just before the sheriff or bailiff knock on the door. You then smilingly pay them off and the reorganized org is now capable of rendering the service sold.

Promoted business always has a delay. It takes six weeks to get the first response to a magazine or a barrage of letters. It may take five months to flood the place with money.

You can never promote too early. You can often promote almost too late.

My early-days maxim about org finance was "make more than they can waste." Later it became "make more than they can waste and patch them up so they can deliver." Now it's "make sure they will make enough and hide some of it and make sure they deliver so they will make even more."

Intelligently observed and handled comm lines will buy enough time to make frenzied promotion unnecessary. Orderly promotion over a long term can then be done. It's the short-term money necessity that makes promotion genius level. The shorter the time available, the more genius it takes.

So vigilance on the comm lines and good analysis of them buys the time necessary to do long-term promotion and keep orgs grooved in before they go into a long slide.

All this—the prevention of shrink and the continuation of expansion—is the prime reason for the Executive Director's existence.

To do it the Executive Director must have the proper comm lines and handle them.

Beyond this there is no real reason for an Executive Director or the comm lines to and from that hat.

CSW

Completed staff work is always demanded by the Executive Director when asked to make any decision or okay anything.

This prevents errors.

However, requests for authority to depart from the usual are dangerous when okayed as they then set up areas of difference and cause policy to wander and misfit at the joints.

Given intelligent, existing org patterns and programs, one would be right more often than wrong by far if one turned down all requests for authorities or changes in action.

So while one always demands *completed staff work* (CSW) on requests for decision, one tends to say "No." If one begins to say "Yes," the whole program begins to slide into some unworkable hash.

Many requests for decision from a post means either (1) the post is improperly held or (2) the hat of the post isn't understood. In either case one should originate despatches or executive letters to obtain data about the person and the hat, and should either rewrite the hat or educate or transfer the person.

SUMMARY

The Executive Director comm lines are the carriers of data and commands and must be well handled. The traffic must be policed and kept grooved.

The lines must be handled with considerable speed. But no matter the urgency that may be urged upon the Executive Director, decisions or actions must be based on complete data.

If the Executive Director's comm lines are good and complete and well handled, the position becomes very easy to deal with and all will go well.

Emergencies, on good lines, can be foreseen by at least a year and handled long before they happen.

The only real troubles on the Executive Director lines come from incomplete or random reports and a failure to believe the raw data of income and statistics in some area and act when bad spots are consistently observed.

L. RON HUBBARD
Founder

659

DIVISIONS 1, 2, 3

THE STRUCTURE OF ORGANIZATION
WHAT IS POLICY?

The only reason anyone fights good policy is they're too stupid or too inexperienced in an org to understand it. Unable to grasp it, they are too lazy to work at trying. They miss words, don't see reasons, imagine situations are otherwise and in general can't grasp it. So they try not to use it or dream up their own. People with bad study histories can't grasp policy. For policy also follows the rules of study.

Therefore never put a person with bad study history on a key executive post. They can't grasp policy as they can't study it either.

Only personnel with quick study histories, fast passages through courses, can be counted on to put in an org or department pattern and keep it wheeling. The others are too involved in their own troubles and too imperceptive to be of any use in making an org boom.

Such people do however sometimes have a use even when not straightened up. They do well in pioneer areas where they have to do it all off the cuff and where their very inability to accept anything causes them also to refuse defeats and discouragements. Their inability to grasp a situation is often of benefit when bravery is required. This does not however excuse efforts to make them more capable and as they grow older and more experienced, they will also become brave and quick and *will* follow policy.

Following policy is a matter of grasping situations and knowing policy well enough to apply the right policy to the right situation. Where no policy covers, an experienced, quick person can easily extend the idea of general policy to cover it, knowing it isn't covered.

The dull person has never even grasped basic, general policy and so, confronted with usual or unusual situations alike, can't find any policy to cover anything and so acts in any old way.

On the other hand, policy, to fit and be of benefit, must be itself born out of great insight *and* familiarity with the facts. Government policy is usually written by clerks who have never heard a shot fired in anger. Therefore almost all current government policy is completely silly. Nobody can apply it as it fits nothing and just gets everyone in trouble. Therefore a quick person with good judgment in the field and in the real situation can get through only by following his own policies and insights. This is easily mistaken for a dull person acting against policy that is good.

But even dull policies provide wide agreement as a basis for work coordination and so something happens on a larger scale. Individual policy-making on every post is the definition of chaos. Thus even bad policy is usually more workable than individual policy and can make stronger orgs.

Brilliant policy based on experience of course can cause orgs to zoom.

We conclude then that where we see a person constantly off-policy in an area that has worked well when *on*-policy, that we must act.

Where we have a *large* organizational scope, we must have workable policy that is followed. For just lacking policy, good or bad, and lacking its being followed, we stay small by definition.

NO POLICY EXISTING MAKES SMALL, NONEXPANDING DEPARTMENTS OR ORGS.

POLICY GOOD OR BAD EXISTING BUT NOT FOLLOWED MAKES CHAOTIC DEPARTMENTS OR ORGS AND CAUSES SHRINKAGE.

GOOD POLICY BASED ON ACTUAL SITUATIONS EXPERIENCED, FOLLOWED WELL, MAKES AN EXPANDING DEPARTMENT, ORG OR CIVILIZATION.

The smaller the org unit or department, the less policy is needed. Reversely, the less policy is used, the smaller will become the org unit or department.

One can always safely assume, when policy is available, that nonexpansion is the direct result of the policy remaining unknown or not followed. The steps to take are therefore:

Expansion formula:

1. PROVIDE GOOD POLICY.

2. MAKE IT EASILY KNOWABLE.

3. BE STRENUOUS IN MAKING SURE IT IS FOLLOWED.

This is the most broad possible formula for expansion.

Profitable expansion of a unit, department, org, company, empire or civilization depends utterly on the above formula being applied.

If it is well applied, literally thousands of other impeding factors drop into unimportance.

This applies to anything, even a person; but the bigger the number of individuals involved, the more rigorously it has to be followed.

The bigger the size of the activity concerned (the more people involved in it), the more damage can result from failures to follow policy.

Thus orgs or companies which halt expansion mysteriously only need to have more policy, or to make policy more easily available or to be more vigorous in requiring it to be followed.

Policy is a *guiding* thing. It is composed of ideas to make a game, procedures to be followed in eventualities and deterrents to departures.

The basic policy of an activity must be the defining and recommending of a successful and desirable basic purpose.

Take a navy, to get a more distant comparison. If a navy has the basic purpose of defending a nation and its citizens and expanding their scope, and if the policy is the guiding principle behind all other policies and if these in turn are developed from experience and made known and followed, then oddly enough even new inventions or new philosophies of state could not prevent that navy from doing its job and expanding the nation. The US Navy might very well have won the war with Japan in its six weeks if those who headed it in Washington had not been mere political puppets subject to every Congressional and Presidential whim. The textbooks were very clear about what the navy should do. But King, Nimitz and Short, the admirals involved, had been chosen by whim, favoritism and capacity for liquor, not by raw statistics of "good navy activity." They had been trained at an academy where the basic principles of "good navy" and raw statistics on personnel had not been used to choose an academy head or instructors. So King, Nimitz and Short, as admirals, *listened to current political rumors or whims* (being only confirmed in political not naval policy) and so let Pearl Harbor happen. How? Their own naval textbooks said, "During times of negotiation with an unfriendly state, the position of the fleet should be at sea, whereabouts unknown." That is line one of the navy textbook on tactics and strategy. Where was it? In Pearl Harbor during many days of hostile negotiation between Roosevelt and the Japanese—the most dangerous naval rival. Where were King and Nimitz? At a cocktail party with the politicians. Where was Short? Giving his all ashore, having given his men full weekend liberty and having ordered all ammunition stowed below for a coming admiral's inspection. So Pearl Harbor could happen. But did the humans learn? No. True, Short, acting on his Washington orders notwithstanding, was removed and eventually court-martialed. But King and Nimitz took over the whole navy for more than four heartbreaking years of "promote by political whim," "what policy?" and defeat in battle after battle until aircraft turned the tide of war and the army and an atom bomb finally finished it. Now the navy is really no more. A few subs. A few patrol ships. The rest in mothballs. People think the navy is small now because of new weapons. No, it is small because it (a) didn't clearly express its basic purpose, (b) didn't educate its people well in the policy it did have, (c) let political opinion shift it about, (d) chose its officers by rumor, cabal and *social* presence and (e) forgot its texts when the emergency loomed. Result, long war, now no navy worth anything—officers palling with men, ships in the boneyard. Could the navy have done its job in 1941? Yes. Had its original policies regarding officer training and selection been followed ruthlessly despite all politics over the years, King, Nimitz and Short would not have been in charge or would have acted by policy had they been. The fleet would have been at sea during negotiations and the strike on Pearl Harbor would have been a Jap bust. The fleet would have been there to knock out the Jap in his own home ports. The war might have ended with Japan in the first six weeks. The point is not whether it is good or bad to have a navy. The point is that here is an actual organization and an actual occurrence.

Therefore one can learn that:

An individual, species, organism, organization, to succeed, survive and expand in influence must have a formulated BASIC PURPOSE.

To keep beings from growing, the reactive bank is almost entirely made up of false and booby-trapped purposes. Thus we can see that, by its having been impeded so thoroughly in past ages, the idea of having a personal or organizational or group basic purpose is an extremely valuable one.

Without one expressed or unexpressed, a being or an organization or group without one doesn't grow but shrinks and becomes weak—in this universe nothing can remain long in an unchanging state. Given a potentially successful basic purpose that is acceptable to the being, organization or group, one can then formulate POLICY.

POLICY is a rule or procedure or a guidance which permits the BASIC PURPOSE to succeed.

The basic purpose runs through time. When it is impeded, distracted from, not complied with, thwarted or stopped, a state of failure of the basic purpose occurs in greater or lesser degree. Sometimes challenges to it cause it to strengthen but only when the challenges are consistently overcome.

A being, organism, organization, group or species or race *learns* in forwarding its basic purpose or meeting challenges to its basic purpose certain *lessons*. Certain procedures or courses of action, rules or laws were conceived at times of stress and some of them were successful. Those that were not successful or helped the opposition were *bad*. Those that were successful forwarded of course the basic purpose and were *good*.

The successful ideas or procedures that assisted the basic purpose were then dignified by the status of proper ideas, acts, procedure or *policy*.

Those that were unsuccessful in assisting the basic purpose became *bad policy*.

Ideas or procedures that distracted from or balked the basic purpose were called *offenses*.

Things, groups, other-determinisms that challenged or sought to stop or refused to comply with the basic purpose became *enemies* or opposition.

Therefore *policy* is derived from successful experience in forwarding the basic purpose, overcoming opposition or enemies, ending distractions and letting the basic purpose flow and expand.

Policy laid down which is thought up independent of experience in similar situations is either the result of great foresight and is successful or it is simply stupidity, in that it seeks to handle situations which will never exist or if they do, won't be important.

Policy based solely on bad rumors, unverified, which may or may not reflect actual existing conditions or which is laid down at the insistence of some self-interested person or minority without taking the rest of the group into account is very destructive policy simply because it does not match the conditions which actually exist and so, *in itself,* may impede or distract from the basic purpose. An example of this is legislation by legislators who, otherwise uninformed, act because of pressure groups, minority riots or simply sensational press that seeks not legislation but simply to feed the appetite of a disaster-hungry public.

If bad policy or laws or actions based on rumor rather than raw facts become too frequent and general, then the basic purpose of a being, organization or group becomes itself distracted, smothered and forgotten and the result is shrinkage, loss of power, death and oblivion. Although it is often too late when bad policies or pressure-group laws have been the order of the day to slash them all from the books and exhume the basic purpose, the action of sweeping away unreal, unapplicable and impeding laws and policies which were based originally on rumor and bad sources can have the effect of rejuvenation on a being, a group or an organization which has begun to die. Periodic sweep-outs of antiquated and didactic laws (rather than general concepts and subpurposes) *must* be undertaken by a being, organization, group or race or species. However, such an action must be carefully done, selecting only those laws or rules which came into being because of pressure groups or infrequent enemies or which were derived from no experience. And before throwing any policy away, one must carefully examine its history to see if it is still restraining an enemy or forwarding some subpurpose. For throwing away a *lot* of lessons could also collapse the forward thrust of the basic purpose which has "gotten this far for *some* reason."

SUBPURPOSES are the purposes of the various sections or parts of the being, organism, group, race or species which forward the basic purpose. They must amplify, qualify and/or describe the action or procedure of the part of the whole in a brief and crisp way so as to hold them in function in their support of the basic purpose. They could also be called the PURPOSE OF A PART OF THE WHOLE, or as we use them, the purpose of a post, unit, department or an org with a special function. When one hears of the PURPOSE of his hat or section, unit, department, org or division, he is observing the SUBPURPOSE of a part of the whole organism which is vital to the action of forwarding the BASIC PURPOSE of the movement. Indeed he may never know what the BASIC PURPOSE really is and only know the SUBPURPOSE of his own hat, section, unit or department. However, by studying the various SUBPURPOSES of several hats or sections, he could probably figure out the SUBPURPOSE of the department; and by studying the various SUBPURPOSES of the departments of an org, he could probably guess at the BASIC PURPOSE of the whole being or organization or movement. If study of SUBPURPOSES either fails to locate any or ends in being unable to relate them into any large PURPOSE, one is of course studying a disorganized movement.

One can change a SUBPURPOSE (cautiously indeed) or add parts with new SUBPURPOSES, and leave a movement (a) unaffected, (b) increased in scope, or (c) decreased in size and influence.

One can, up to a point, add policies on and on, limited only by the ability to get them known, and leave an organization or movement (a) unaffected, (b) increased in readiness to meet emergencies, or (c) crippled. The wisdom of the policy and whether or not it was a successful solution to some actually possible confusion or crisis determines whether or not it should be added or deleted. Foresight plays a large role in formulating a SUBPURPOSE or a policy. These two are never wholly the product of chance or experience; indeed they may be eighty percent wise foresight and twenty percent experience and still be good, usable SUBPURPOSES or policies. Twentieth-century science sought to discount wisdom entirely and beings and organizations were educated or developed with no SUBPURPOSES whatever and all policies were developed either by clerks, teachers or legislators inexperienced in any part of life or were taken from past experience only, with no refinement of any wisdom. The failures of governments and systems and races in the first half of the twentieth century were wholesale and the wars frequent and senseless.

Personal, state, or organizational or social chaos results from adding parts with no well-defined SUBPURPOSES, enforcing policies based on rumor or taken from the data of mere theoreticians in their ivory towers, an irresponsible press or legislators in their self-interested heads and smoke-filled rooms. A study of how the pressure groups, clerks, theoreticians and irresponsible press and duly elected but completely unselected and uneducated legislators destroyed individualism, states, businesses, civilizations and races would be only a study of how not to organize and survive, how to ignore, abandon or discredit all basic purposes, subpurposes and successful policies. The scene was one of indescribable chaos that filled one with protest and dismay. If there was a wrong way to do things, it became the order of the day; and youth went into a complete apathy—purposeless and drifting; and the world began to die a little each day, the mental hospitals became flooded, life ceased to be any fun at all. Things are not always like this and indeed don't have to be.

Mismanagement or misgovernment of self, an organization, group or state would then consist of failing to forward the BASIC PURPOSE, not grasping and specifying SUBPURPOSES, and not experiencing and formulating policies to strengthen successful ideas or actions that forward the basic and subpurposes and impede ideas or actions that retard them, and not recognizing actual enemies or oppositions or planning and carrying out successful campaigns to handle them. Failing in any of these actions, the individual, group, organization, state, civilization, race or species will falter, fail and die.

Recognizing the basic purpose, supplementing it with subpurposes for the parts of the whole, and learning and enforcing the policies which bring success, spotting actual enemies or oppositions and planning and carrying out campaigns to overcome them, removing distractions, rewarding the forwarding of basic purpose and subpurpose and penalizing actions which retard, an individual, group, organization, civilization, race or species survives, gets better, lives on higher and higher planes.

The game of life has the formula of having and forwarding a basic purpose and supplemental subpurposes.

This is done by the Formula of Policy which consists of:

1. Conceiving, recognizing, testing and codifying successful ideas, actions and procedures that forward the basic purpose and retard its opposition;

2. Making these policies known and in greater or lesser degree understood; and

3. Getting these policies followed.

665

If in (3) policy is to be followed, there must be discipline, but even more important, there must be ways of choosing personnel other than by sloppy rumor or social presence.

Personnel can *only* be chosen on raw statistics supported by ample data containing figures. If the raw data is good, then one assumes that basic purpose is being forwarded as it is meeting with success. The raw data already has a curve in it as it is tabulated against the success of basic policy. So the person whose raw data is good *must* have been forwarding basic purpose, therefore must be either a screaming genius at originating ideas that forward the basic purpose or a wizard at knowing, applying and following policy. Either way he or she is worth all the diamonds of Kimberley.

Such a person will inevitably rise in the organization or group if raw data alone is observed in selecting and promoting personnel.

If the person is a screaming genius at originating policy and has not made enough errors to reduce his successful raw data, and has stayed on-policy otherwise so as not to reduce the effectiveness of those around him, he will eventually rise to a level which makes policy; and the whole organization will benefit. Similarly a person who grasps and follows policy very well and forwards the basic purpose well and who is very capable will sooner or later rise to a position of trust that safeguards against sweeping changes that will retard or crash the group or organization and so is vital at higher levels.

Out of these two general types of being one gets the leadership levels of a movement. But they will never arrive at all if those in charge ever use anything but statistics in judging them, since their very success will cause enough cabal to influence high levels against them if these high levels ever use fragmentary rumors or opinions in handling personnel.

RAW DATA means assembled but otherwise unevaluated data. It is "uncooked" and "unflavored" and "untouched by human hands." It, in short, is uncontaminated or unchanged data. It is native and natural and unspoiled. And the only data that answers those qualifications is statistical data. "How many or how few and how much or how little in what time." That is the *only* data that a senior official in a group, organization or state ever *dare* use in selecting and promoting personnel.

The "state" of the person, the "result of his tests," "the examination figure," are all *useless* to a senior official deciding upon who to promote or pass over. His decision will be wrong in exact proportion that he permits opinion to enter and raw data to drop out.

Introducing opinion into personnel selection is a study of "how crazy can one get." How much liquor a man can hold, how acceptable socially is his wife, his breath, his taste in ties, are all completely disrelated data. For how does anyone know at the top really what the environment is now like at the bottom? Maybe that lovely music—room board room requires a pink necktie, a purring wife and endless capacity for drink, but is that the organization's environment? It is not! Maybe the organization's environment demands an allergy to liquor, a complete tart for a wife, overwhelming breath and neon ties. And maybe tomorrow's board level will too! The world changes, it does not become softer. Only some people do.

The psychiatric or school test alike are written and administered by people in ivory towers who again have no contact with the organization's real environment. Statistical as they may try to be, such tests are utterly worthless. They are not on-the-job statistics. They are classroom or laboratory statistics. They are definitely cooked data. And when used for personnel and promotion, they cook a lot of careers. And by putting eggheads on post, they cook a lot of parts of an org if not the whole thing. They have some small value in determining someone's quickness or slowness, but the conditions are too unreal and the necessity level of real environmental emergency is missing. It's like a plane crash synthesized in bed. No jolt. So, poor (but not the worst) of cooked data.

Maybe the working environment demands a dumb guy who is too slow to panic at awesome futures! Yet bright enough to see what policy applies. When men with small experience in it can qualify to run the world, they can only then administer tests to advise who should run it.

Only statistics that represent action and accomplishment are fair tests of ability and who deserves promotion or the gate.

Therefore the only organization that is a sound organization is one WHOSE EVERY ACTIVITY can be tabulated by statistics.

If you wish to reorganize, you must do so with an eye toward "Can this post (dept or division) be statisticized?" Any body of people such as "the typing pool" or "the instructors" must be broken down to individuals one way or another. One has three things then that must be tabulatable: (a) the individual, (b) the part and (c) the whole. Each of these must be so organized as to be capable of being seen through accomplishment or lack of it. Only this is fair organization. All other types are unfair, will not select out leaders or good workers and subject these to the enturbulence of the lazy or those with other philosophies to fry.

If you have any other type, people are promoted or fired by rumor, backbiting or common brag, and either type have only liability. In using them one destroys empires and every great civilization that is dead died because opinion and rumor were the key causes of personnel changes.

It is unfair to every decent staff member to have an org that cannot be tabulated by relative income, work or traffic.

The common way of the dead-and-dying past was to put some fellow in charge and then shoot him or reward him if things went wrong or well and neglect the rest. This works unless a society only protects the man at the bottom and routinely weakens the man at the top. When that happens, the system is useless. Only by chance do things go well. So chance is added to rumor as the means of promotion or the gate. No wonder the Asiatic, a member of our oldest civilizations, says "Fate!" and explains it all. He had too many rulers who ruled by rumor or chance or didn't rule at all. And so the power died. Only when you can find out who did which or why can you be just. And only when an organization can be fully viewed top to bottom through raw data of how much or how little can individual show be rewarded and individual nuisance be weeded out.

REALITY

Reality in policy, in orders, in advice, depends upon either great insight or great experience. Combining both gives great success.

But no matter how great the insight may be, viewing the actual condition is a vital step to resolving it. Remote solutions not based on experience or close inspection are usually unreal.

Therefore no orders should ever be issued without data and experience and insight. Data comes from tabulation of actions and amounts in organizations. Experience comes from working in similar or parallel situations. Insight comes from the ability to observe coupled with the courage to see and the wit to realize without any thought of personal importance.

Therefore, the soundest leadership comes from the most extended experience and intimate knowledge of that or parallel circumstances. Leadership without this will lack judgment.

Remote leadership is best when it itself is involved close to its hand with the same problems. Therefore remote leadership must have under it similar organizational problems and traffic at home that exist at the remote point. Then understanding is quick and solutions are real.

For one organization to command another, they must be similar.

Management–labor problems evolve from the communications formula "cause-distance-effect with intention at cause, attention at effect, and duplication." A board room is not a machine shop. The machinists seek to duplicate the board or refuse to. If they fail to, they always refuse to. Thus only a working org of similar pattern can command a working org.

The commanded org will always seek to follow the pattern of the commanding org and duplicate what it thinks the commanding org consists of. A great tension exists at all points of nonduplication. This tension stems from the effort to duplicate. If foiled, trouble or breakage will occur at that point. Where the subordinate org is unable to duplicate what it thinks exists at the senior org, then it suffers an ARC break of greater or smaller magnitude. Patterns, officer authority, comm lines, all must be similar. Size is not important in this. Org pattern is. If the subordinate org has any hope of ever attaining the size, and if the purposes, pattern and policies are the same, that is enough. ARC will remain high, execution will be good and expansion is assured, providing of course that the basic purpose is good in the first place.

EXPANSION

All that is needed to expand an org or its business, given a good basic purpose and an area to expand into, is the knowledge of the expansion formula:

DIRECT A CHANNEL TOWARD ATTAINMENT, PUT SOMETHING ON IT, REMOVE DISTRACTIONS, BARRIERS, NONCOMPLIANCE AND OPPOSITION.

The basic formula of *Living* (not Life) is:

HAVING AND FOLLOWING A BASIC PURPOSE.

Thus expansion is an increase in living. To increase living and raise tone and heighten activity, one need only apply the expansion formula to living. Clean away the barriers, noncompliance and distractions from the basic purpose and reduce opposition, and the individual or group or org will seem more alive and indeed will be more alive.

All an executive has to do to expand a part or the whole of an org is to divine the basic purpose, divine or issue the subpurposes, point out an area to expand into and then remove the distractions from, barriers to and noncompliance with the basic purpose and subpurposes, and put something on the channels that augments existing impulses and expansion will begin. It will be successful to the degree that the basic purpose is good, the subpurposes real and the policies are taken from real experience and interpreted by persons facing similar current problems.

By the process, thereafter, of just removing barriers, distractions and noncompliance, expansion can be accelerated to a point where it overwhelms all hostile efforts to contain it and the result is extremely gratifying in terms of expansion at velocity. It seems completely magical. For life instantly appears.

One must remember to *channel* a basic purpose. A channel has two boundaries, one on either side of it. These must exist in an org. They consist of discipline of those who would distract or stray or wander or who help the opposition or suppress the basic purpose or subpurposes or who cannot seem to learn or comply with policies or orders. Discipline must only be aimed at the above and, where it is random or doesn't serve to channel, then it itself is a distraction or a barrier and will breed noncompliance. But when entirely absent, the force is let to wander and expansion does not occur. Discipline must be precise, known, uniformly applied and inevitable when the rules are broken. Those who do their job welcome it as it helps keep others from preventing them from working or acting or complying or getting their own jobs done.

L. RON HUBBARD
Founder

ADMINISTRATION

FLOWS AND EXPANSION
THE FAST FLOW SYSTEM

We have introduced many new principles in administration in recent policy letters. Here is one which if left out would cause mystery.

This is the principle of traffic flows we now use. It is called the FAST FLOW SYSTEM OF MANAGEMENT.

A being controlling a traffic or activity flow should let the flow run until it is to be reinforced or indicates a turbulence will occur and only then inspects the part of the flow that is to be reinforced or is becoming enturbulated, and inspects and acts on only that one flow.

This principle would operate on a committee of three in this fashion: The committee does not act as a body. Each member acts individually in three spheres of influence (three types of flow). There is no *committee* (collective) action until one of the three members wants concurrence from the other two on greatly reinforcing a flow or until the other two, by observation, see the third is going adrift. Only in these cases does the committee act as a committee. In other words all three members go about their work independently until there is a change in one of their three spheres and *then* they act. Otherwise the flows of orders and actions are independent. Not doing it like this is why committees have gotten the reputation of being unable and a waste of time.

To do this, one of course needs another principle: that of indicators.

An indicator is something that signals an approaching change rather than finding the change is already present and confirmed.

We get this from auditing. An auditor audits so long as things go evenly. He knows when they will *begin* to deteriorate or change by an indicator. He acts on seeing the indicator. He doesn't wait until the collapse or total change of the pc occurs and *then* look it over and act. The pc could be run into the ground or a good process that was bettering the case could be neglected if an auditor could not PREDICT from indicators how it was going before it was gone.

In supervising a number of sections or departments, it would work this way:

The person in charge does not examine *every* action or decision on the lines. If all despatches of all the activities went through his or her one pair of hands, the volume would be too great and would jam. The executive's "plate" would be too full and this would *halt any expansion* of the activities as the executive would feel overworked, yet in actual fact would be getting nothing much done. The flows which *needed* watching would be buried in a huge volume of flows that did not need watching.

Instead, the principle of flows tells us that the executive should have statistical INDICATORS such as OIC charts on every part of the activity each week and should act only on the basis of the charts' behaviors.

If a chart went down, the executive would not wait for that area to collapse before inspecting it. At a dip point the executive should go over all the plans and traffic and despatches of the area dipping down and unearth the *real* reason why it did dip. If the matter needs minor remedy, it should be corrected. If then the graph still dipped down, the executive would not only be advised of it by the OIC indicators but would know, having inspected earlier, what had to be done on a more drastic scale to get the graph going up again.

The OIC system *must* be used and all data plotted and circulated to the executives in an org before this system will work.

If the OIC system is put into effect fully, the executive can then (and *only* then) let go the comm lines and let the traffic flow.

He then only needs to:

1. Keep alert for and correct dev-t (off-line, off-policy, off-origin and noncompliance),

2. Keep an eye on the weekly OIC charts,

3. Find from OIC the upward trends and inspect and find out what's working so well so it can be reported,

4. Be alert to any down dip and inspect the activity itself and correct the matter, and

5. Spend most of his time getting his own job done (since executives *do* have jobs besides supervision).

The one thing he mustn't do is "get reasonable" about dips or zooms and not act to really check the decline or to reinforce the rise.

a. Thinking one does know when he has not gotten it inspected closely, and

b. Not believing the graph and indicators, and

c. Not acting, are the fatal errors.

Doing (1) to (5) tells us who's an executive and doing (a), (b) and (c) tells us who shouldn't be an executive.

If this system is in effect, the org can't help but boom.

We will call this the FAST FLOW SYSTEM OF MANAGEMENT.

It is a very precise art. It's like auditing. One predicts the slumps and reinforces the tendency to boom.

It can't miss. If it's done completely.

L. RON HUBBARD
Founder

[LRH NOTE: Study this. Shows why of OIC.]

HUBBARD COMMUNICATIONS OFFICE
Saint Hill Manor, East Grinstead, Sussex

HCO POLICY LETTER OF 23 APRIL 1965
Issue III

Remimeo
All Staff Hats
Sthil Staff
Exec Hats

ALL DIVISIONS

Use: Executives should keep a stack of these 23 Apr. 65 PLs near their desk and staple one to every despatch or report received which violates it. Circle para violated and return to staff member.

PROBLEMS

(Changes HCO PL on CSW slightly in that conclusions or solutions are no longer acceptable from a junior to a senior, only data.)

The most senior organizational policies there are follow:

1. NEVER solve the problem any junior presents to you. NEVER, NEVER, NEVER, NEVER, NEVER, NEVER.

2. ALWAYS investigate for the true cause of the trouble. ALWAYS, ALWAYS, ALWAYS, ALWAYS, ALWAYS, ALWAYS.

3. SOLVE only the problem you find after very careful investigation of the whole matter and after you have examined all possible causes of the problem.

4. NEVER solve a problem that has already been solved in general policy.

5. IF someone thinks the policy is wrong or is itself the source of the problem, then (a) he or she must be made to fully read the policy, (b) demonstrate what it is supposed to solve, (c) look over the problem he or she thinks the policy is wrong on to find the actual causes of the problem he or she is trying to solve.

The primary aberration in situations that are being mishandled is:

6. THE PERSON IS UNABLE TO RECOGNIZE SOURCE.

Example: A person A sees another B drop a wall mirror and break it. A puts in a purchase order specifying thicker glass. B next day drops a chair down steps and A puts in a PO for new stair carpeting. B a week later runs a car into a wall and A proposes a different design for the wall. If this kept on and B was never singled out by A or A's seniors, then dozens of unusual solutions are entered into the org, not just POs but policy changes as well! Why? A is "below source" and doesn't recognize the causes of his problems. Therefore his solutions are alter-is

673

of existing situations and result in alter-is of tech, policy and orders. Soon the area around *A* is in a complete confusion. What about B? He probably generalizes with "they said," "everybody knows," etc., on entheta and so remains "invisible" behind his generalities. B can be spotted best by Damage Reports whenever damage occurs. As they are filed as a statistic in B's file, it soon becomes a visible datum. The cause of confusion in A's area is not A. It is A's inability to perceive *causes*. Thus any system which isolates actual causes disenturbulates a group and makes unusual solutions unnecessary and only then can policy go *in*.

Therefore we get some other very senior org policies:

7. NEVER accept a conclusion from a junior. NEVER.

8. ALWAYS demand facts of a junior. Always.

9. NEVER take a generality from a junior.

10. ALWAYS challenge any conclusion a junior offers.

11. NEVER act on a junior's data until you have fully investigated the situation.

12. ALWAYS investigate until you find the basic policy violation that started the problem in the first place.

TECHNICAL

13. Making Scientology work on pcs and students is the ONLY way you can salvage org situations.

14. If Scientology is not applied exactly per HCOBs and tapes, technical will "go out" and within a few months the area will be spinning with unusual solutions.

15. The fastest way for a technical executive to become overworked is to violate the policies in this policy letter.

16. The fastest way for a technical executive to get into trouble and a mess is to accept an auditor's conclusions and propose a solution.

Example: An Instructor says, "Process R0-0 doesn't work on certain cases. When these cases come on course, could I please order them to Review auditing?" Serious blunder by a senior, "Yes." Why? Because the Instructor isn't capable of spotting an ARC broken student—can't confront ARC breaks. Therefore, quite often the Instructor lets R0-0 be run on an ARC broken student. The *correct* technical executive action, and the ONLY correct one on receiving such a report, is to promptly personally investigate. Investigation even of the students' case folders would disclose that the Instructor ignores ARC breaks from comm cycle blunders by new student auditors, that the Instructor won't give ARC break assessments (who else *could* give one on a Zero Level course?) but sometimes runs R6EW on the students under the guise of "an assist for a misunderstood word." I think that's enough trouble to get the Instructor's senior into a hurricane of trouble if only from blown students and no new enrollments! (This is an

674

actual example. The final result was a Comm Ev for the technical executive and the Instructor, the first for proposing and alter-ising policy and technology, the second for forcing auditing [rather than doing assessments] on Zero Level students. The Comm Ev had to be ordered at the request of *their* tech senior because neither would accept orders to remedy the above conditions but just kept on fouling up students.)

NONCOMPLIANCE

17. If you think for one moment that a staff member who won't or can't follow clear, definite policy will follow *your* orders either, you dream.

18. The first thing you know about an off-policy-type personnel is that none of *your* instructions are being carried out either, usual or unusual.

19. Look, if they can't apply vividly clear policy, they sure can't apply a brief order.

SUMMARY

20. You can conclude that where you have a personnel who cannot perceive the causes of things, you will have a continual spinning mess.

None of the problems presented for solution are the actual problems that exist. In A and B above, the problem presented was "How to get more durable things." This could not be solved because it was the wrong problem and didn't exist. The right problem was "How to get B to stop breaking everything in sight." A senior, not seeing B at all (not being around B), accepting a problem and a conclusion from a junior (A) soon is involved in endless discussions over "How to get more durable things." This never solves. Because it wasn't the problem. Further, any order the senior gives A is *also never put into effect without wild alter-is*. Why? A, unable to see sources, can't see the senior as a source either and really takes his orders from anyone who comes along! Students, pcs, the garbageman.

21. The basic problem of management then is the problem of cause blindness. People in the org who cannot see cause cannot solve problems, for to solve a problem one must see what is causing it!

22. And the solution to all this lies in the policies in this policy letter.

23. And auditing people up to an ability to perceive and perceive the causes of things is the primary solution to all problems.

24. Until you get them there, you use any mechanism necessary to follow orders. Only in that way will they ever make it.

25. When tech goes out, when HCOBs aren't followed or tapes known and used exactly, the road out is blocked.

26. *Nobody has any right to a bank.*

27. For when they are permitted such a right, they block the road for the rest.

28. The only person you could completely trust is a Clear. And unless the Clear is also trained in Scientology tech and admin also, you could never accept his vote on org matters.

That's the truth.

And that's why we're going to make it all the way.

29. If we're determined we will make it, we will make it.

L. RON HUBBARD
Founder

(*Note:* By organizational policy is meant that policy which makes the organization into an organization and keeps its flows fast and its design uncomplicated. In absence of these policies the design becomes altered and flows cease and the org dies.)

HCO POLICY LETTER OF 1 MAY 1965
Issue II

Remimeo
Exec Hats
Comm Hats
Dept of I&R Hats

ORDER BOARD AND TIME MACHINE

Executives must have and use an "order board."

In Scientology if it is not written it is not true. That's a major policy.

It applies to all.

Every order an executive issues must be in writing.

He does this on a clipboard. There is a sheaf of paper on it of his division's color. It has a sheet of pencil carbon and a ballpoint slipped through the top of the clip. It can have a hook on the back to slip on a belt for persons walking about. This is the order board.

Even when one gives a verbal order it is also written down.

The executive keeps no copies of his orders. This is done by the Department of Inspection and Reports.

The original is handed to the person being ordered. The other is sent to the Inspection Section of the Department of Inspection and Reports. If one is away from his comm station, the carbons are left on the order board until one returns, when the copies are all sent to Inspection.

COMMUNICATOR ACTION

The carbon of an order is sent to Inspection because it is obviously a carbon copy and an order. It is not otherwise designated.

An original sent through the comm lines is obviously an original order as it is not a carbon. It is simply delivered to the addressee's basket.

JUNIOR'S ACTION

The person receiving the order does it, says he has (or couldn't) on the original order he received and sends it TO INSPECTION. However, even if he sends it to his issuing superior, the communicator sends it to Inspection only.

INSPECTION ACTION

Inspection has a time machine. This is a series of baskets advanced one basket every morning.

A carbon of an order is placed in today's basket.

677

When the original comes in, the carbon is dug out of the basket (by date and color flash) and original and carbon are clipped together and routed to the issuing executive.

Orders not complied with in one week of course fall off the time machine by appearing in the basket being emptied today. (It was filled one week ago and advanced once each day.)

A copy is made of the order and it is sent to Ethics for filing in the staff member's ethics folder and counts as a report against the staff member.

The carbon is returned to issuing executive to show his order has not been complied with, so that he can handle the situation. No report from the executive is required in this instance as a copy is already in Ethics.

The executive should investigate or ask Ethics to do so if the matter is of considerable importance.

If an original is returned to Inspection which has no carbon, it is copied and held and the copy is sent to the executive with a "Sir, there is a lost carbon of your order. Did you fail to turn one in?" This disciplines a forgetful executive. When Inspection receives the answer it attaches the original to it and sends it back to the executive.

VERBAL ORDER

A junior may report a verbal order to Ethics as it places his statistics and job in danger by leaving it open to have it said the order was otherwise.

PROJECT ORDER

If something requires more than two weeks to do, it is a *project* and cannot be ordered without clearance from the Office of LRH Design and Planning Authority Section. If a project has been okayed, it has a number and its number must be put on the order as Project Number _____.

Inspections files projects in their own files. This is also time machined by one month's emptying of a file drawer or one year's emptying of a file drawer. Projects run only for one month or one year and must be routinely inspected by Inspections which then reports to the Office of LRH with any progress or lack of it.

URGENT ORDERS

Orders marked Urgent by an executive are entered into a one-day time machine and handled in one day as described above for one week.

L. RON HUBBARD
Founder

HCO POLICY LETTER OF 16 MAY 1965
Issue II

Gen. Non-Remimeo

HCO Division 1

Dept of Inspections and Reports (Dept 3)

Ethics Section

INDICATORS OF ORGS

Just as pcs have indicators so do orgs.

There is a probable long list of good indicators. When these are present, Ethics is quiet and hangs on to an interrogation, etc., only long enough to get policy and technology in.

There is a probable long list of BAD indicators. When these are present, Ethics becomes industrious in ratio to the number of bad indicators.

The first indicators, good or bad, are statistics—the OIC graphs for units, sections, departments, divisions and the org. When these are rising, the rise is a GOOD INDICATOR.

When these are falling, the fall is a BAD INDICATOR.

The second of these indicators, good or bad, is TECHNICAL GAINS. When technology is *in*, cases are gaining. This is a good indicator. When technology is *out*, cases are losing. This is a bad indicator.

Ethics only exists to hold the fort long enough and settle things down enough to get technology in. Ethics is never carried on for its own sake. It is pushed home only until technology is functioning and then technology resolves matters and Ethics prowls off looking for other targets.

We don't hang people because we started to hang them and so must do so. We start to hang people and keep right on tying the noose in a workmanlike fashion right up to the instant we can get tech in—which of course makes the noose unnecessary.

But if tech never does get in then we complete the hanging.

You will find if you *label* a suppressive you will someday get him back and get tech in on him. If you don't ever label, they wander off and get lost.

Labeling as a suppressive is our hanging.

When things are bad (bad indicators heavily visible), putting a body on the gallows is very salutary. We call it "putting a head on a pike." Too many BAD indicators and too goofed up a situation and we *must* put a head on a pike. Then things simmer down and we can begin to get tech in.

That's the whole purpose of ethics—to *Get Tech IN*. And we use enough to do so, to get correct standard tech in and being done.

When there are lots of bad indicators about—low and falling statistics, goofed cases—we get very handy with our interrogatories and put the place very nearly under martial law—we call this a State of Emergency. Once Emergency is declared, you usually have to put a head or two on a pike to convince people that you mean it. After that, necessity level rises and the place straightens up. If an Emergency is *continued* beyond a reasonable time, we resort to very heavy discipline and comm-ev the executives who wouldn't get off it.

Ethics, then, is applied to the *degree* required to produce the result of getting tech in. Once tech is really in on a person (with a case gain) or a Tech Division, let us say, and auditors actually audit standard processes by the book, we *know* it will resolve and we ease off with ethics.

Ethics, then, is the tool by which you get good indicators in by getting tech in. Ethics is the steamroller which smooths the highway.

Once the road is open, we are quite likely to skip remaining investigation and let it all be.

But somebody *promising* to be good is never good enough. We want statistics. Bettered statistics.

SYMPTOMS OF ORGS

Orgs have various symptoms which tell us how things really are ethicwise.

One of these is dilettantism.

DILETTANTE–ISM

Dilettante = One who interests himself in an art or science merely as a pastime and without serious study.

In an org, this manifests itself with "people should live a little." "One needs a rest from Scientology." "One should do something else, too." All that kind of jazz.

It also manifests itself in nonconsecutive scheduling, part-time students, "because things are different in this town and people can come only two nights. . . ." Ask what they do with other nights. Bowling. Horse racing.

Boy, you better maul the case folders of staff. You have a suppressive aboard. Maybe six.

Scientology, that saves lives, is a modern miracle, is being compared to bowling. Get it?

That org or portion just isn't serious. Scientology is an idle club to it, an old lady's sewing circle. And to somebody, selling training and auditing are just con games they put over on the public.

SUPPRESSIVES!

Root them out.

WILD RUMORS—This symptom is caused by potential trouble sources. Find whose case roller-coasters (gets better, gets worse). Investigate. You'll find a suppressive or two outside the org.

Put a head on a pike with an HCO Ethics Order and publish it widely.

ARC BROKEN FIELD—The Johannesburg Comm Ev Order of last week is a perfect method of handling the situation. Appoint a Comm Ev chairman to inquire into matters and form a list of interested parties based on reports he will now receive.

BAD TECH—When results just don't happen in the Academy, HGC or Review, one or another, look for the potential trouble sources and suppressives. Only they can keep tech out. Put a big head on a pike and then begin to interrogate every slip in the place. Suddenly tech is in again.

There are many such symptoms.

AT THE ROOT OF EVERY BAD CONDITION WILL BE FOUND A SUPPRESSIVE PERSON.

Locate your potential trouble sources by locating passers of rumors, etc. Then locate the suppressive and shoot.

Calm reigns. Tech is in.

And that's all one means to accomplish.

Today TECHNOLOGY WORKS ON EVERY CASE. If the local org can't handle a case, Saint Hill can.

If you get tech in well enough in an org, tech handles all. Beautifully. But if it is out, only ethics can bat down the reasons it can't be gotten in.

––––––––––

OPTIMUM STATE

The optimum state of an org is so high that there is no easy way to describe it. All cases getting cracked, Releases and Clears by the hundreds, command of the environment. Big. That's an optimum state for *any* org.

If it isn't rising *toward* optimum today, it is locally being held down.

The viewpoint of Ethics is there is no adequate reason why an org is stumbling except ethics reasons. Let others take care of any other lacks. Ethics *never* gets reasonable about lack of expansion. If Ethics shoves hard enough, others will get a high enough necessity level to act.

So when an org is low:

Find out where its statistics are down and who is a PTS or an SP and *ACT*.

That's the job of Ethics. Thus little by little we take off the brakes for a cleared Earth.

L. RON HUBBARD
Founder

HCO POLICY LETTER OF 13 OCTOBER 1965

Remimeo

ALL EXECUTIVES

DEV–T DATA
EXECUTIVE RESPONSIBILITY

Executives may not okay anything done or to be done below their level unless their immediate junior has also stated or attested with initial that it is okay.

Unless one can fix responsibility for actions, there is no responsibility anywhere and the whole show goes to pot.

Never let a junior say "Is this okay?"

Always require the junior to state or initial "This *is* okay" on all work, actions or projects.

An organization permitting a lot of "Is this okay?" will soon go to pieces. Things are or aren't okay. Make them say so. Hang them if it's a false attestation.

"Is this okay?" is dev-t and should be chitted as such.

L. RON HUBBARD
Founder

HUBBARD COMMUNICATIONS OFFICE
Saint Hill Manor, East Grinstead, Sussex

HCO POLICY LETTER OF 25 SEPTEMBER 1965

Remimeo
All Executive
Hats

(Addition to HCO PL 7 June 65 II, same title)

ENTHETA LETTERS
AND THE DEAD FILE, HANDLING OF

An additional action is required of Address besides those listed in the 7 June 65 policy letter.

Address is to use the address plate of the person to be dead-filed to make enough gummed address labels necessary for Ethics to use in advising all possible organizations to whom such a person would possibly communicate.

Ethics, then, uses these address stickers to stick onto an ugly mustard yellow postcard to mail to the organizations possibly concerned.

L. RON HUBBARD
Founder

HUBBARD COMMUNICATIONS OFFICE
Saint Hill Manor, East Grinstead, Sussex

HCO POLICY LETTER OF 19 JANUARY 1966
Issue I

Remimeo
Staff Hat

DANGER CONDITION, WARNING
THE JUNIOR WHO ACCEPTS ORDERS FROM EVERYONE

It has been found in the hearings on personnel after a Danger condition was assigned that:

A PERSONNEL UNDER YOU WHO ACCEPTS ORDERS FROM ANYONE WHO COMES ALONG WHO HAS ANY RANK WILL PUT YOUR SECTION, DEPARTMENT OR DIVISION AND *YOU* INTO A DANGER CONDITION AUTOMATICALLY.

This operates as a permanent bypass.

If you allow it or don't catch it in time, your statistics will fall like a shot duck.

Therefore, if you find a junior going off lines for his orders and not refusing all orders from others, you *must* put him in a Danger condition. For if you don't you will soon be in one yourself.

Danger condition is a very funny thing. It actually exists as a natural phenomenon in organizations, hitherto undetected.

If bypass of command channels occurs, the exact formula will begin to operate whether anyone says so or not. And the only cure for this plague is to follow the formula itself. *That* works. Nothing else does.

Be careful of that junior who accepts anyone's orders. He or she is like a charge of dynamite under an executive. Someday it will all blow up.

Juniors must follow the orders of their own seniors or Danger condition results.

L. RON HUBBARD
Founder

Remimeo
Executive Hats

DANGER CONDITION
RESPONSIBILITIES OF DECLARING

BYPASS = Jumping the proper terminal in a chain of command.

If you declare a Danger condition, you of course must do the work necessary to handle the situation that is dangerous.

This is also true backwards. If you start doing the work of a post on a bypass, you will of course unwittingly bring about a Danger condition. Why? Because you unmock the people who should be doing the work.

Further, if you habitually do the work of others on a bypass, you will of course inherit all the work. This is the answer to the overworked executive. He or she bypasses. It's as simple as that. If an executive habitually bypasses, he or she will then become overworked.

Also the condition of Non-Existence will occur.

So the more an executive bypasses, the harder he works. The harder he works on a bypass, the more the section he is working on will disappear.

So purposely or unwittingly working on a bypass, the result is always the same—Danger condition.

If you *have* to do the work on a bypass, you *must* get the condition declared and follow the formula.

If you declare the condition, you must also do the work.

You must get the work being competently done, by new appointment or transfer or training or case review. And the condition is *not* over when the hearings are over. It is over when that portion of the org has visibly, statistically recovered.

So there are great responsibilities in declaring a Danger condition. These are outweighed in burdensomeness by the fact that if you DON'T declare one on functions handled by those under you which go bad, it will very soon catch up with you yourself, willy-nilly and declared or not *you* will go into a Danger condition personally.

There's the frying pan—there's the fire. The cheerful note about it is that if the formula is applied, you have a good chance of not only rising again but also of being bigger and better than ever.

And that's the first time *that* ever happened to an executive who started down the long slide. There's hope!

––––––––––––

There is one further footnote on a Danger condition. I have carefully studied whether or not HCOBs and policy letters and actions by me were bypasses. And a search of statistics refutes it, as when I give the most attention to all echelons of an org, wherever the org is, its statistics rise and when I don't they fall. Therefore we must assume that advice is not a bypass, nor is a general order by me.

Where there is disagreement on a command channel I am trying to forward, *then* a bypass occurs.

So we can assume correctly on experience and statistics that Danger conditions occur only when there are fundamental disagreements on a command channel.

If you yourself then ferret out the disagreement ones of those under your orders, you will clear your command lines.

Review can always find disagreements when they exist with a meter.

Where Danger conditions are declared, the declaring executive should make an effort to find the disagreement with himself, policy, the org or Scientology as a basic review action on persons found responsible for a Danger condition. The only errors are not to look for them and not to find *all* the disagreements the person has on the subject of his superiors and post, policy, technology or orders.

This is why a low leadership-survey-grade person can be counted on to put wherever he is in Danger. His disagreements are too many and he doesn't execute and thereby secretly puts his superior into bypassing and a Danger condition inevitably occurs.

It needn't occur.

We have the data, now.

L. RON HUBBARD
Founder

HCO POLICY LETTER OF 1 FEBRUARY 1966
Issue II

Gen. Non-Remimeo
Exec Sec Hats
LRH Comm Hat

EXEC DIV

DANGER CONDITIONS
INSPECTIONS BY EXECUTIVE SECRETARIES,
HOW TO DO THEM

An Executive Secretary who does not get around his or her divisions now and then and see what is going on can make a lot of mistakes.

Inspections are desirable. But when an Executive Secretary makes one, he or she commonly issues an order or two; and if this is done without that division's secretary being present, it is a bypass and willy-nilly begins the formula of the Danger condition and can unmock a section or department or even that division.

A senior can inspect, chat, advise, but must never issue an order on a bypass unless he or she means to handle a dangerous situation and start the formula. For the formula will run, regardless, if a bypass begins.

The way to inspect, then, is to collect the seniors and go around, and issue orders only to the next senior on the command channel, never to his or her staff.

Example: HCO Exec Sec wants to see if books are stored safely. The HCO Exec Sec can nip out and look on his or her lonesome *providing* no orders are issued. Or the HCO Exec Sec grabs the Dissem Sec and the Dir Pubs and the head of the books section and goes out and looks. And if the HCO Exec Sec wants a change in it all, the order is issued to the Dissem Sec only.

It is a great temptation to tell Books In-Charge how and where to put what, for an HCO Exec Sec is one normally because he or she is smarter and more knowledgeable about orgs. But if one is to advise Books In-Charge, one had better have the rest of the command chain right there and talk to the next senior below HCO Exec Sec.

You would be surprised how many random currents a senior-type senior like an Exec Sec can set up with a few comments that skip the command channels and what a mess it can make for a secretary or director, no matter how wise the comments.

Secretaries who order a director's officers in the absence of the director or, much worse, section staff without director or section officer, thereby court and make trouble.

You can unmock a section or a whole department by sloppy command lines. It is not merely the "correct" thing. It's the vital thing to follow command channels as nobody can hold his job if he is being bypassed by a senior. He *feels* unmocked, and the Danger condition formula begins to unroll.

The correct way to route an order to a person two or three steps down the command channel is to tell the next one below you to order the next, and so on.

If you have to tell the Director of Tech Services to have his Housing Officer post a list of houses on the bulletin board, you really don't have a Director of Tech Services anyway as he would have done it as the natural thing. So an order in such an obvious case is not the right comm. The right comm is an ethics chit on the Dir of Tech Services for not posting the available houses on the bulletin board.

A smart senior is a senior because he is smarter. But when this is not true and the junior is smarter, you get an intolerable situation where the senior interferes. If a dull senior interferes continually on a bypass, it's a sure way to start a mutiny. And a senior who doesn't inspect or get inspections done does not know and so looks dull to his juniors who have looked.

The safe way in all cases is to issue orders that are very standard, on-policy and obvious and to issue them to the next one on the command channel and then in the future inspect or get an inspection. If on the inspection one finds noncompliance with a standard, on-policy order, one promptly calls for a hearing on the next one down the line who received the order.

Here's a terribly simple example: Org Exec Sec sees statistic for Tech Div down. Issues order to Tech Sec, "Get the gross divisional statistic up at once." Now nothing could be plainer or more standard. In two weeks the Org Exec Sec looks at the statistic, sees it is even further down and calls for a hearing on the Tech Sec for noncompliance or a Comm Ev to get all the evidence in about the matter.

This is about as basic as you can get with an inspection, an order and a further action all by a senior, the inspection being done by OIC and reported by graph.

Life in actual fact is very simple and an org is today a very elementary mechanism.

It is easy to run an organization providing one makes it run and handles things in it that refuse to run.

Where an Exec Sec is baffled on occasion is the apparent unwillingness of a section to function. Now this is so far down the command channel that info on it does not easily arrive back at the top.

The thing to do where possible is personally inspect. Or get it inspected. One often finds the silliest things.

Example: Book shipping statistic is really down, man, down. One orders and harangues and argues trying to get books shipped. One gets the quantity of books looked into. It's okay. One gets shipping materials looked into. They're okay. A Shipping Clerk is on the org board. But orders to the Dissem Sec just never get books shipped. So finally one gathers up the Dissem Sec, Dir Pubs and Books In-Charge and goes down to Book Shipping—Lo! They have been building a machine that wraps books tightly when a rock is rolled off a bench! (This actually happened in DC in about 1958.) It has taken a month to build it and will require another to finish it and one and all in that division are convinced this is the answer. The order? "Break that machine up and start wrapping books by hand and I want that backlog gone in one week." To the Dissem Sec, of course, in front of everyone for his soul's sake. And publish the order in writing as soon as possible.

So you see, you have to inspect because what seems logical and okay to juniors may be completely silly. Remember, that is why they are juniors and have seniors.

Frankly, you can never guess at what holds some things up. You have to look. Often you can solve it for them. But solve it with their agreement and on command channel if you want it done.

You can't always sit in an ivory tower and issue orders. You have to know the ground and the business.

Over a period of fifteen years of active management of these organizations I have a pretty good idea of what can happen in one. And to one.

I try to be right more often than wrong. I don't try to be perfect as one's best plans are often goofed. I try to get done what can be gotten done. And I carry a *little* more pressure on the org than it can really accomplish.

I inspect. You would be surprised at how often I do and what I find out.

It sometimes looks to people that I use a crystal ball in taking the actions I take because they see no possible route by which the data could have reached me.

They forget how many lines I keep in operation. And also, I *do* operate on a "sixth sense."

For instance, all accounting summaries today are done for governments, not for management. A manager has to develop a sixth sense concerning financial status of the org. One has to be able to *know* when the bills are up, the income inadequate and to know when to promote hard and stall creditors, *even with no data from Accounts* or *contrary data that proved false.*

Today with OIC this is easy. But I ran orgs successfully with no OIC for years just by sensing the financial situation. In theory, Accounts keeps one fully posted. In actual fact they often goof in filing bills owed and even in depositing money.

There are many things one can sense, OIC or no OIC.

The thing to do is to inspect or to get the area you sense is wrong inspected.

I have today LRH Communicators. They are pushing projects home. They also can tell me why projects won't push home because they have *looked*.

An Exec Sec or a secretary has HCO's Inspection and Reports and a time machine to check compliance. And this is how it should be.

But nothing will substitute for inspection by one or for one.

And the Exec Sec who thinks it's a desk job is being very naive. The org would run better if Exec Secs had no in-baskets.

If an Exec Sec watched statistics like a hungry cat at a mousehole and inspected like fury every time one went down or stayed down, the org would expand and prosper.

Providing inspection was done.

L. RON HUBBARD
Founder

HCO POLICY LETTER OF 3 MARCH 1966
Issue I

EXEC DIV

ATTACKS ON SCIENTOLOGY
SEX AND ORGANIZATIONS

It is interesting that a review of faltering orgs that got into trouble in their areas each one had a bad sex entanglement high on staff.

A review of actions of orgs and attacks over the last fifteen years makes it stand out sharply that an org which is mixed up sexually in the higher echelons will not be effective, will have low statistics and can't defend itself on the public front.

Such are not attacked for loose sexual relations. They are just too decayed to do a good job of defense or follow policy. So they become subject to attack.

The last UK attack was easily rebuffed and so are many attacks. But where an org is caved in by bad sexual messes, it doesn't seem to be able to defend itself on the general front.

We don't often get such situations as a sex-mess org, but where we do, they get into severe trouble *on other counts*.

Sex, obsessive and promiscuous, is a blood brother of psychosis. Note the sex stress of Freud, the sex orgies in institutions between patients and attendants and psychiatrists. Note the book (early 50s, US) by psychiatrist FREDA FROHMM REICHMANN where she tries to get her fellow psychiatrists to leave their patients alone. It is a text trying to make them ethical in their practices. It reveals a sordid picture.

This is given as an indicator. I know only four orgs in all the sixteen years before this writing that collapsed or came near collapse at one period in the history of each. And each one was sex crazy. (LA 1950, Melbourne early 60s, Johannesburg 60s, Washington 62 on. Each of these got into severe trouble. LA 50 collapsed, Melbourne collapsed, Johannesburg nearly collapsed, DC is being saved only by strenuous effort.)

So we have an indicator that when an org in the upper strata starts tolerating sexual promiscuity you can expect serious trouble of other kinds just ahead within the next year or two.

This also applies to psychiatry as we will start knocking them out shortly.

I am not talking about an occasional "affaire" or a slip. I am talking about general dedicated sexual misconduct by staff as the ordinary occurrence.

As a speculation it might be the early Christians (who were no fools as they built strong organizations) discovered in the first century or two that a church which went sexually off-beam didn't last and so banned it. They may have banned it so hard they made even casual Christians madly anti-sex, which is a lot too much. Certain it is they saw sex as an organizational menace and did not see that violent anti-sex was just as crazy, being the other side of the same coin.

Thus, Exec Secretaries should be alert for an org going off the beam. Watch in low statistic orgs that don't recover easily for heavy sexual promiscuity and get the sex loops out of it quick, particularly out of its upper executive level. For I promise you that that org will absorb thousands of man-hours of work to rebuild if sexual misconduct is let go on.

The label of sexual promiscuity easily attaches to persons and is not always true. So be very thorough in the investigation and be sure the charges are factual. If so, shoot quick. Don't caution. Experience with such has taught me that no amount of persuasion or orders will (a) bring up their statistics or (b) stop the catastrophe they will walk into. Only prompt removal of the offenders will get the org going up again.

L. RON HUBBARD
Founder

HUBBARD COMMUNICATIONS OFFICE
Saint Hill Manor, East Grinstead, Sussex

HCO POLICY LETTER OF 1 JULY 1966

To WW Personnel
Info other
  Orgs and
  Cont Divs

INFORMATION CONCERNING THE WW TIME MACHINE

This information is of use to and should be known by all executives in the International Executive Division. It is a write-up of a long existing practice in the International Executive Division.

EXECUTIVE USE

1. You can notice on the org board that WW has its own time machine to which you send any orders as per the 1 May 1965 policy letter, ORDER BOARD AND TIME MACHINE. You are expected to:

   a. Have and use an order board.

   b. Issue your orders in writing.

   c. Send the carbons to the WW time machine in the Inspections and Reports Branch.

2. The WW time machine is for WW orders. Don't send your carbons to the Saint Hill time machine—or your compliances to orders either.

3. The time machine exists to help relieve your admin, to provide a record of your orders so as to achieve better compliance and to help you complete your cycles of action. In turn, when you issue your orders in writing and send the carbons to the time machine, it helps hold the org there so that it can expand.

4. There are two WW time machines: one for orders to outer orgs and one for orders to Saint Hill.

5. The outer org time machine is a stalk of four baskets. Each basket marks a week of time. Your order is placed in the top basket and each week it is moved down a basket. After it has been in the bottom basket a week, it falls off the time machine and is returned to you with or without a compliance as the case may be. A month is usually the time factor allowed for a compliance to be received back from outer orgs.

6. The time machine for the Saint Hill environ consists of five baskets, allowing a week to be given for compliance. It is run exactly as per the 1 May policy. Any noncompliances are chitted as per the policy. (A copy of the order is sent to the person's ethics file.)

7. Chits are not issued by the time machine clerk on outer org personnel for noncompliance to time machined orders. As above, chits *are* issued on Saint Hill personnel for noncompliance.

8. If you have the same order going to several orgs, you can send the time machine clerk one copy only, marking on it its distribution. He will make a folder for filing the compliances or responses, marking them in a log by orgs. The entire folder is then returned to you at the end of a month's duration.

JUNIORS' USE

Juniors are expected to know and use the same policy letter of 1 May 1965.

If you don't have a copy of this policy letter, immediately demand one.

It is completely in force with the exception that in WW you send your compliance to the WW time machine in the Inspections and Reports Branch.

———————

Let's keep our jobs running smoothly by following these policies. That way we will get more work done.

L. RON HUBBARD
Founder

L. Ron Hubbard

EXECUTIVE DIRECTIVE

ED 572 INT   20 September 1967

Execs and above

FAILURE TO APPLY THE EXACT POLICIES OF SCIENTOLOGY ETHICS BY AN EXECUTIVE PLACES THAT EXECUTIVE IN A CONDITION OF NON–EXISTENCE. DISMISSING PERSONNEL WITHOUT PROPER HEARINGS, ACCEPTING FALSE REPORTS, FAILURES TO ASSIGN CONDITIONS TO DOWNSTATS OR UPSTATS ARE ALL ETHICS ERRORS. ANY FAILURE TO APPLY CORRECT REPEAT CORRECT ETHICS POLICIES AND ACTIONS MUST ALWAYS BE FOLLOWED BY THE EXECUTIVE COUNCIL PLACING THAT EXECUTIVE IN A PERSONAL CONDITION OF NON–EXISTENCE AND FILING IT ALSO IN HIS FILE. THE CONDITION IS UPGRADED TO DANGER WHEN THE EXECUTIVE HAS PASSED ALL ETHICS POLICY LETTERS AND TO EMERGENCY WHEN HE MERITS IT AND NORMAL WHEN HIS STATS ARE UP. ONLY MINIMUM PAY, NO BONUSES MAY BE PAID ANYONE IN NON–EXISTENCE OR DANGER.

L. RON HUBBARD
Founder

HCO POLICY LETTER OF 19 OCTOBER 1967
Issue I

Remimeo
Hats Execs Secs

URGENT AND IMPORTANT

#2 In Exec Sec Hats Folder

HCO EXEC SEC DUTIES
ORG EXEC SEC DUTIES

Where an org is not expanding, the fault is *always* with the Exec Secs, actually and legally.

If the Exec Secs get in ethics correctly, they can get in tech. If they can get in tech, they can get in admin.

The performance of duty of an Exec Sec must be properly understood.

1. It is not a desk job.

2. The Exec Sec (for HCO or Org side) must be better at every job on his side of the org than the staff member holding it.

3. Exec Secs get the people to get the work done and see that they get it done.

4. Exec Secs must NEVER NEVER NEVER hold ANY ADDITIONAL POST no matter the size of the org, for if they do so, they can't wholly be Exec Secs and the org is leaderless, degenerates to a group of people acting individually and is no longer an org. An org is an interdependent activity coordinated by its leaders. They can, however, pitch in on any job to set an example or show how it's done.

Some years ago, at a time when Saint Hill started its soaring climb out of the doldrums, I trained the two Saint Hill Exec Secs as follows:

A. Personally and individually INVESTIGATE any Affluence or Danger or lower conditions in their sections of the org.

B. Both together personally investigate any Affluence or Danger or lower condition of any divisional statistic. (Including the way legal or accounts may be handling pressures on the org or attacks.)

C. Taking actions on any outnesses found in (A) or (B) above.

D. Enforcing the promotional actions of their divisions (as per HCO PL 20 Nov. 65, THE PROMOTIONAL ACTIONS OF AN ORG).

695

E. Financial planning—which consists of what to spend money on per division and what bills to pay according to dateline paying (omitting public utilities that may cut off service if not regularly paid but datelining all else).

F. An org is handled only by stats, assigning and enforcing conditions, and by personal inspection and examples and getting the work done. And by following the condition the whole org is really in.

G. Keep ethics, tech and admin in in.

This was all they did. And the org soared.

They did *not* appoint Boards of Investigation to do their work for them as this would have been a lessening of their confront. They were, after all, right there.

They did *not* handle reams of despatches, but learned policy on dev-t and applied it mercilessly.

They did *not* tolerate staff members bringing them entheta and problems, and demoted or sacked those who did.

They did *not* sit at their desks and chat.

They were all over the org, picking up this stat and that as per the steps (A), (B) and (C) above.

When I run an org directly (as its Org or HCO Exec Sec or both), I go to every department and section at least once a day and see what can be done to help them boost their stats. In doing so I pick up the senior div officers as I go so they are with me in their divs and depts and so aren't bypassed. But *I* talk to the staff members myself.

And the stats soar.

So the post of Exec Sec would be best done from a room with no desk in it (joke) and only a comm station.

But in all seriousness, nations, armies, go to bits because their leaders sit at desks and never bother to confront anything.

Leaders lead.

And there is nothing quite as horrible as having a leader who sees only four walls. His confront goes down, down, down.

Another part of my routine when I handle an org or do prolonged inside work is to get outside at least some of the day even if only for a walk. At SH I used to go for a drive in a fast car with a camera every afternoon despite *an eighteen-hour-a-day schedule* on admin and research. I made it a point to get outside and breathe!

So I always made my rounds of the org and I always also got outside and I also kept my in-basket empty and my research done and fought the good fight.

I only order boards in distant places where I cannot easily investigate personally. Otherwise, I do my own.

So when I see an organization's stats down, I know its Exec Secs do not do (A) to (G) above and I know they sit at their desks and chat, that they don't know or shove home policy on dev-t, that they are "reasonable" on ethics and tolerate staff members who worry them with problems, and that they do not ever get around the org or outside and so aren't doing their jobs.

I want Exec Secs to do their jobs as Exec Secs. Then and only then stats will soar.

"The Founder WW   Oct. 2, 1967

Dear Ron,

I have been analyzing the actions of the HCO Exec Sec and the Org Exec Sec and they come down to the basic simplicities you originally taught the Org Executive Secretary and me. I write them down as the following and you should pass this on to others as you did to us:

1. Personally and individually investigating any Affluence or Danger condition of posts in their sections of the org.

2. Both together personally investigating any Affluence or Danger condition of any divisional statistic.

3. Taking actions on any outnesses found on (1) and (2) above.

4. Enforcing the promotional actions of their divisions.

5. Financial planning—which consists of what to spend money on and what bills to pay according to dateline payment.

6. Keeping ethics, tech and admin policy in."

L. RON HUBBARD
Founder

HCO POLICY LETTER OF 5 JANUARY 1968
Issue II

Remimeo

Ethics

Dev-t

PL No. 2 in Every Hat

CONDITIONS ORDERS
EXECUTIVE ETHICS

ANY EXECUTIVE MAY ASSIGN ANY CONDITION AND IMPROVE ANY CONDITION HE ASSIGNS TO ANY PERSON IMMEDIATELY JUNIOR TO HIM ON HIS COMMAND CHANNEL OR WITHIN HIS OWN OFFICE OR AREA.

To assign or improve a condition it is only necessary to write the order and send it to Mimeo or the Duplication Unit which duplicates it and sends the copies to Dir Comm for issue.

The Ethics Officer files these in the ethics files and a copy in the file of the issuing executive.

The E/O must see that the order is complied with and the formula followed. The issuing executive must also demand compliance.

In event of a down statistic of an executive's area of control, the absence of personally issued Ethics Conditions Orders may constitute grounds for removal on a charge of out-ethics in his area.

An executive who tolerates noncompliance, false reports or down stats in his control area without taking personal ethics actions as above is not an executive.

AN ORDER SO ISSUED IS CALLED A "CONDITIONS ORDER" AND IS PUBLISHED ON THE DIVISIONAL FLASH COLOR PAPER, NOT GOLD-ENROD.

Where a mimeo or duplication line jams, an executive may post the order in his own handwriting on the staff notice board, filing two copies with the E/O, all on his division's color flash paper, using carbon paper and clipboard.

No executive may be removed for issuing Conditions Orders but may be removed for not issuing them in the presence of noncompliance, false reports or down stats.

An executive is defined as anyone in charge of an org, part of an org, a division, a department, a section or a unit.

As Scientology now brings TOTAL freedom, it must also have the power and authority to bring total discipline or it will not survive.

Heavy in-baskets, inability to get things done, down stats, failures, all stem from nonapplication of ethics. If ethics is in, one can get in tech. If tech is in, one can get in admin.

Fast flow depends on a total flow without inspection. Therefore ethics has to be very harsh when errors occur, otherwise the whole line stops.

Students and pcs are also subject to Conditions Orders from their Supervisors and auditors.

L. RON HUBBARD
Founder

HCO POLICY LETTER OF 6 FEBRUARY 1968

Remimeo

ORGANIZATION—THE FLAW

I looked for a long time for any flaw in the idea of organization. It does have a flaw.

The basic flaw in organization is INSPECTION BEFORE THE FACT. That means inspection before anything bad has happened.

Violations are so harmful they destroyed every great civilization—the Roman, the British, the lot. For every flow is slowed or stopped.

The prosperity of any organization is directly proportional to the speed of its particles—goods, people, papers.

World trade, world shipping, world prosperity, is dying only because of the cumulative effect of inspections before the fact. Passports, customs, safety regulations, general government interference before anything bad has occurred, add up to a SUPPRESSIVE SOCIETY and therefore, soon enough, a dead one.

Penalty *after* the fact has occurred disciplines the criminals and does not pull down the majority to criminal level.

Scientology organizations must never lose sight of the reason organizations have decayed.

L. RON HUBBARD
Founder

Remimeo

ETHICS AND ADMIN
SLOW ADMIN

The secret of any executive success is the ability to Complete Cycles of Action Quickly.

The operative word is COMPLETE.

Ability is the ability to complete a cycle of action, to handle the matter so it does not have to be handled again.

Referral is irresponsibility. Executives who refer to others to make a decision aren't executives. They are irresponsible or are afraid of responsibility. People who are afraid of taking responsibility are not executives. They are laborers.

An executive who doesn't handle but puts something on wait is also irresponsible. Slowing an admin line by not acting NOW is also suppressive.

Suppressives cannot complete cycles of action. They either act in an altered direction or they continue an action beyond any possible expectancy. In either case they do not COMPLETE.

THEREFORE this ethics policy is brought into being:

EXECUTIVES WHO DO NOT HANDLE MATTERS SO AS TO COMPLETE THEM, WHO REFER OR SLOW ADMIN ARE LIABLE TO A COMM EV ON A CHARGE OF OUT–ADMIN.

L. RON HUBBARD
Founder

HUBBARD COMMUNICATIONS OFFICE
Saint Hill Manor, East Grinstead, Sussex

HCO POLICY LETTER OF 28 APRIL 1968
Issue I

Remimeo
Executive Sec
Hat

STANDARD EXECUTIVE ACTIONS

Once a day each Executive Secretary should walk through his divisions and inspect what is happening. He should see every Secretary, Director and walk into every office.

This is an inspection activity designed to keep divisions real by finding out what is going on. You should ask questions such as, "How are you doing?" "Is there anything I can help you with?" This is not designed to bypass, nor should it be used to do so.

Answers to the questions, anything found wrong is written down by the executive and orders written up to necessary personnel.

The rule is: EVERY EXECUTIVE SECRETARY WILL WALK THROUGH HIS DIVISIONS AT LEAST ONCE A DAY AND INSPECT ALL ACTIVITIES.

L. RON HUBBARD
Founder

Remimeo

HANDLING SITUATIONS

The only tremendous error an organization makes, next to inspection before the fact, is failing to terminatedly handle situations rapidly.

When I say terminatedly handle I mean finishedly handle. That it is handled and that's all, boy!

The fault of an organization's waffle, waffle, waffle, "Joe won't take responsibility for it," "It's got to go someplace else," and all that sort of thing, is that it *continues* a situation. It just goes on and on and on until it finally gets somewhere, goes snap, and that would be the end of that situation. So what you ought to do is *complete action* now, in the first place.

The other day I was looking at why I used to have a high stat businesswise and cinewise and otherwise, and I suddenly realized I was peculiar in the vicinity in which I operated. I *ended cycles*. I could end more cycles in less time than any organization could dream up. In other words I was CONCLUDING ACTIONS.

Ending cycles doesn't consist of shooting people. It consists of seeing that it *stays handled*.

One of the things that has happened in the past is that I have had to rehandle. Situations I had handled became unhandled someplace and I had to rehandle them again.

What you should specialize in is terminating the end of a situation, not refer it to somebody else.

If the situation comes up in your vicinity, well, handle it—that is, finish it off so that is the end of it.

Somebody comes along saying (natter, natter, natter). I've caught too many of these guys. Finally I handle the situation, if it hadn't been handled up to that point. He hadn't been handled up to that point.

When you have got this guy, handle him. Handle him, so that the fellow is handled from here on to the end of time. Don't try to patch it up so that it won't cause any trouble.

You have to be on the ball to do this, very much on the ball. An example was a dissatisfied steward. The guy was going around serving up spanners in the soup. He's going around, and he's going around and he's going around. Well, let's handle it right there, now, when he wants the situation handled. The guy appears for his pay and that's it! Do you get the idea. It's finished right now.

Please quit continuing situations by reference. Handle! You can develop more traffic internally, more upsets, more ARC breaks, than anything you can mention by simply continuing to shunt the responsibility for ending the cycle of action. That is all it is, just a refusal to take responsibility for ending a cycle of action.

Somebody comes over to the Registrar to sign up. Does she have to refer to eight different terminals as to whether or not this person is permitted to sign up? No. She either signs the guy up or she doesn't sign the guy up.

Take responsibility for the various cycles of action. When you have taken responsibility for them, let's hear no more about them anyplace.

L. RON HUBBARD
Founder

HCO POLICY LETTER OF 1 JULY 1968

Remimeo
Exec Hats

WARNING SIGNS

(Originally written by LRH as FO 980 and LRH ED 10 Int
on 1 July 68. Issued as an HCO PL on 21 Mar. 70.)

Any executive should take note of the following points and consider them as definite warning signs of imminent danger.

1. An area or individual producing no reports is soon to take a very steep dive.

When you don't hear from an area you can be assured there is something else going on. So admin is out. Tech must be out and ethics is going fast if not gone.

2. An area which issues false reports can be considered to have had its ethics pass over the cliff way way back. This should be pounced on fast fast fast.

Use these and it will take a lot of trouble off your lines.

L. RON HUBBARD
Founder

HCO POLICY LETTER OF 4 OCTOBER 1968
Issue II

Remimeo

ETHICS PRESENCE

(Reissued from Flag Order 1432)

The reason an executive can get compliance is because he has ethics presence. If you haven't got it, you won't.

When you issue orders, you are using power and force.

If you are also *right* in what you get compliance with and your programs are clear, correct and beneficial—boy, do you win.

But it is not the rightness of a program that gets compliance. It is ethics presence.

Rightness does not get compliance because there are always counter-intentions in the way. If you go on the assumption that one and all want things to go right, you are going to make a dog's breakfast out of it.

There are only a few with a good forward look and who are relatively unaberrated.

Men will keep the accounts straight only because you can muster bayonets to enforce that they do.

Ethics presence is an X quality made up partly of symbology, partly of force, some "now we're supposed to's" and endurance.

One of the reasons the press now print what we say is that we have *endured* the biggest shellackings anybody could muster up. We've gained ethics presence publicly by it.

Endurance asserts the truth of unkillability. We're still here, can't be un-mocked. This drives the SP wild.

Because of the Sea Org we appear to have unlimited reach and, in some mysterious way, unlimited resources. The ability to appear and disappear mysteriously is a part of ethics presence.

As an executive you get compliance because you have ethics presence and persistence and can get mad.

The way you *continue* to have ethics presence is to be maximally right in your actions, decisions and dictates. Because if you're wrong the other fellow gets wrapped around a pole for complying. And the *pain* of *that* starts to outweigh your own ethics presence.

So, when you issue orders you are using force and power. You can, however, get in such a frame of mind you cease to use the softer arts as well. Against noncompliance you add ferocity with the aim of continuing your comm line.

Wrath *is* effective but used in moderation and only in moments of urgency.

Man has been invalidated to such an extent that he starts to do *himself* in—that's the secret of aberration. He denies himself, then mocks up pictures to do himself in with.

If you continue to invalidate and chop people, they will start to do themselves in even harder—so if you continue to use heavy ethics on someone, you play right into the hands of his bank.

Self-invalidation is merely the accumulation of invalidation of oneself by others. The point being, that you better temper the lightning with sunshine occasionally.

If you use heavy ethics on wogs, they are being invalidated from *altitude*. You can't build up competent people by invalidating them.

Without in any way softening your approach, you should know that real force is dependent upon ARC, and the major threat is the interruption thereof.

L. RON HUBBARD
Founder

HUBBARD COMMUNICATIONS OFFICE
Saint Hill Manor, East Grinstead, Sussex

HCO POLICY LETTER OF 26 JANUARY 1969

Remimeo

(Reissued from Flag Order 1758, same date and title)

COMPLIANCE REPORTS

(Note: The compliance admin system can be wildly out.
Compliance reports can fail to reach LRH or the person
ordering, such as a Scientology executive or officer.)

This FO (PL) is to set things right.

Essentially there is a command comm cycle. HE WHO GIVES THE ORDER
GETS AN ANSWER!

They are never routed off the lines before they reach the originator of the
order. To do so creates an atmosphere of noncompliance. The originator knowing
only that he has never heard thinks the order has not been done, or is forced to
listen to rumor, or has to use other lines to get the data.

And thus no real coordination of orders can occur.

And the originator is driven into apathy on getting compliance to even the
most simple orders.

WHAT A COMPLIANCE REPORT ISN'T

Daily reports of Aides, Captains, COs OTL and juniors are *NOT* compliance
reports but info only.

Such daily reports contain:

1. The activities of their zone.

2. Particularly any important event that is occurring.

3. Any data that would be of interest to the senior.

Such reports are very explicit, never generalized and must not rely upon
supposed knowledge of the recipient. Give full name, rank, serial number type
data, never "Major Jones called today," type information. That relies on the
recipient remembering who Major Jones is. It's, "Major Jones of the American
Trade Association." Enough data to clearly identify WHO. And in the same way
of course enough data to identify WHAT or WHAT ABOUT.

And never use confusing-type abbreviations. C/S can mean "Case Supervisor" or "Church of Scientology" or even "cycles per second"! Daily reports are
NOT compliance reports but info only, summarized for fast assimilation by the
recipient.

WHAT A COMPLIANCE REPORT IS

A compliance report is exactly that. It is a *REPORT OF COMPLIANCE,* a
completed cycle reported to the originator DONE.

It is not a cycle begun, it is not a cycle in progress. It is a cycle completed AND REPORTED BACK TO THE ORIGINATOR AS DONE so that the command comm cycle is completed.

To merely commence a cycle is not to comply. To merely make some progress is not to comply. To drive it through to completion is. And to then report DONE to the originator is to put in a compliance report.

A compliance report has to be answered with the order and get logged *and* the answer goes to whoever issued the order. Standard TRs.

In practice a compliance report takes the following form. It is in standard despatch form routed through the usual channels. It is headed at the top middle of the page COMPLIANCE REPORT. It has a brief concise description of what was done:

1. It is in standard despatch form routed through the usual channels.

2. It is headed at the top of the page in the middle COMPLIANCE RE-PORT.

3. It has a brief concise description of *what* was done.

4. It has clipped to it *ALL* the original orders so that the originator and communicators on the line can see at a glance what was ordered and comparing this with what was done, see that it is in fact a compliance, a completed cycle.

5. Any other relevant information is also clipped behind, such as a carbon of a letter written if that was what was ordered.

6. AND IT IS ADDRESSED AND GOES TO THE PERSON ORIGINA-TING THE ORDER, via any communicator who logs it as a compli-ance.

7. It contains an attestation that what was done has been completed such as "Order attached completed."

Now, there is such a thing as LONG–RANGE and SHORT–RANGE targets. And while a long-range target is not reported done until in fact complete, this does not prevent reports of *completions* of the short-range targets which go to make up the long-range target being made.

That is not to say that progress reports are made. They are *not*. We are interested only in COMPLETIONS. But a short-range target DONE is a comple-tion, isn't it?

Compliance reports to LRH orders are not made to LRH Communicators but are routed via them for logging and forwarding to LRH. He who gives the order gets the answer.

Where an LRH Communicator is getting compliance to the one order from a number of different terminals, he would normally hold the compliance reports until all had reported done or, where some areas are not answering up, would forward as one CSW with a covering summary the compliance reports of those areas that had complied and a carbon copy of the condition assignment or other ethics action taken in the areas that didn't comply. This is never used to unduly hold up reporting compliance but of course full compliance is when it has been completed by all those ordered.

STALLED OR BOGGED TARGETS

It will invariably be found that when an important target is not made that it contains a "bug" in it, unknown and undetected.

Where an order or target is not done or no action is occurring or as soon as any bug has appeared the LRH Communicator, having taken all the usual actions of program checking (see HCO PL 1 Apr. 65, HCO COMMUNICATOR HAS PROGRAM CHECKING HAT) nudging and direct questioning (see HCO PL 31 May 68, LRH COMM LOG), sends a copy of the orders to the Qual Division with the information that he has and a request for Qual to wear its org correction hat and locate the "bug."

This will often be done before using ethics or while using a lower gradient of ethics. This on the theory that a stop on the flow always means a bug is present (misunderstoods, not-knowns, etc.) which Qual can straighten out, but which would remain undetected if *only* ethics was used at that point. This does *not* eliminate usual ethics actions but gives the LRH Comm another tool with which to get compliance.

Qual locates the "bug" or "bugs" AND THEN TURNS IT BACK TO THE DIVISION OR PERSON RESPONSIBLE FOR THE ACTION. Qual does not itself complete the action but finds the "bugs" and gets the action back on the rails and turned back over to the person ordered.

And so even stalled or bogged targets get completed and in their turn reported to the originator as done with a compliance report.

L. RON HUBBARD
Founder

Assisted by CS-7

HUBBARD COMMUNICATIONS OFFICE
Saint Hill Manor, East Grinstead, Sussex

HCO POLICY LETTER OF 3 MARCH 1970

Remimeo

(Also Flag Order 2368 of same title)

HOW TO WRITE AN ED OR ORDER

There are no hard and fast rules in writing orders or EDs but some comments can be made that serve as a guide for those drafting them.

In the first place an ED or order must COMMUNICATE. It must be simple and easy to read. Many I have seen are fuzzy or confused.

The person writing it should get a pretty good idea of what the situation is and what he means and why and what he wants done. So orders must be INFORMATIVE.

What he wants done must be within the CAPABILITY of the terminal or terminals he is addressing.

A truly experienced administrator or executive often has to work without all data to hand so it is good to add an escape clause of some sort when one is doubtful. Such as, "If this situation does exist _____." You don't always assume that a wrongness reported exists in fact, as many false reports can get on lines. Further, the situation might have been handled. In writing three orgs to do something, it may be one has already done it. So orders should be NONACCU-SATIVE.

I often get an ED to be issued or a Flag Order that has a covering despatch which contains all the reasons, followed by the order itself, which is baffling if the covering despatch is omitted. As the order isn't to me, why the covering despatch? An order must be able to exist by itself and be in so far as possible SELF–EXPLANATORY.

As most people are not operating maliciously in any way, they basically appreciate help. So actually an order should try to be HELPFUL.

All such orders are received in an avalanche of other papers, usually on a jammed overworked line, so as far as possible, all other things considered, it should be BRIEF.

On orders that carry a broad discovery one should also be INTERESTING.

But above all, an order or ED should be CLEAR.

If you want an order followed it has to be ADDRESSED TO SOMEBODY who will supervise or produce it.

Orders and EDs that are issued should BETTER THINGS.

It is not enough to say, "Stop doing _____" and is often taken all too literally. One should say what it is one should DO.

711

When whatever it is is done, one should also say to whom it should be REPORTED.

One of the minor worrisome things to a recipient is for someone writing an ED or order to allege data without giving its WHO. It is in fact rather suppressive to say, "Stop throwing pcs into jails," without also saying, "Joe Blow says he saw you throw a pc into jail. Could you give us more data on this?" However, one sometimes has to protect the source of info as it can occur that someone giving you good factual data will get shot at the other end. SOP in the US "government," when a senator receives a letter from a government employee telling of an outness, is to refer the letter to the employee's bureau, where of course, they dismiss the employee promptly—which in that frame of intellect handles the whole thing. But in this context you must have a vital admin principle—whenever I have acted on single reports from staff members and public I have been sorry I ever brought it up! They were isolated instances or not true. So you get enough observation either from several sources or on different lines before you actually act, for then your DATA IS ACTUAL. Then you won't be on somebody's toes uselessly. And you can say, "I have several reports here that your _____, I want to know what you are doing about it if it still exists. Please advise me. LRH COMM, LOG THIS QUERY."

The main problem of management and any exec is getting data. Issuing orders and EDs based on no observation can get one into severe dev-t and upset.

There are two basic rules in EDs and orders:

1. AVOID GETTING CHOPPY ON LONG DISTANCE COMM LINES.

2. DON'T KEEP SENDING ORDERS INTO AN AREA OR TO SOMEONE THAT IS NOT COMPLYING. TAKE OTHER ACTION.

Not all EDs and orders written are perfect by a long way and probably seldom will be. There is no perfect format.

Intuition, past experience and some tiny symptom repeated are all the data you sometimes have. And you have to issue orders on what you know.

And situations are sometimes *vitally* in need of handling and you have to handle.

So you have to issue orders and EDs to handle things.

But realize this is a temporary state of affairs for management.

Three things have to be missing that make written orders and EDs necessary:

A. A clear understanding and write-up of exactly what the terminals at the other end should be doing as basic actions.

B. A competent personnel at the other end well checked out on A.

C. A workable organizational structure matched at both ends of the line.

When you don't have these things, then lots of EDs and orders become necessary. When you *do* have these things then your traffic is basically data traffic and operational planning.

Mission orders in their target form, with their briefing and with competent missionaires, satisfy all these requirements usually. But this is a special case of a carefully worked out drill. So missions usually succeed if their major target lies within their capability and a sensible time limit.

When a mission is out too long it bogs because it is now a terminal at the other end that doesn't have any real hat, only a set of expiring MOs. Because of time and changes in situations, their MOs cease to be real. When this happens they should be recalled or debriefed on the ground and given a full hat as per A and B above.

Orders and EDs can be in target form and should be when it's a project with a potential time expiry.

An ED decays in one year, at which time it is either revived by an ED to continue it or it becomes a policy letter which usually should be neated up.

If you look at the capitalized words in the early text above, you find the desirable adjectives or verbs that apply to writing orders and EDs. One can use them loosely as a guide.

L. RON HUBBARD
Founder

HCO POLICY LETTER OF 9 FEBRUARY 1971

EXECUTIVE MISBEHAVIOR

In the past executives in three instances have seen fit to associate themselves with persons of the opposite sex who were antipathetic to Scientology and have continued with them a 2D relationship.

The idiocy of such conduct becomes obvious when it is realized that organizations antipathetic to Scientology spend money by the millions and hire people to infiltrate or disrupt organizations.

"Incautious" would be the light word for such behavior. In each case the org and staff have suffered. In each case the actual condition of the executive could not have been higher than Doubt.

Therefore the following policy is laid down:

Executive Misbehavior Policy No. 1: No executive who begins or persists in a sexual relationship with a person hostile to or "open-minded about" Dianetics and Scientology may be retained on post or in the organization.

Executive Misbehavior Policy No. 2: Any executive who engages in activities for which he could be blackmailed may not hold any executive post.

Executive Misbehavior Policy No. 3: Any person who places personal interests and situations above the interests of the group may not hold an executive post.

L. RON HUBBARD
Founder

HUBBARD COMMUNICATIONS OFFICE
Saint Hill Manor, East Grinstead, Sussex

HCO POLICY LETTER OF 12 MARCH 1971
Issue II

Remimeo
COs/EDs
Exec Secs
All SO and
   Scn Orgs
Missions

CO/ED INSPECTIONS

(Originally written by LRH as Flag Order 2773
on 12 Mar. 71. Issued as an HCO PL on 18 Aug. 81.)

To further the purposes of a Commanding Officer or Executive Director it is vital that the CO/ED make daily inspections of his org.

These are not just cleanliness inspections. They embrace general establishment and production observations.

Every smallest cranny is looked into to see if things are as they should be.

Personnel and their activities or absence of them in assigned areas are noted.

Usually a clipboard is carried to make any notes, plus or minus, of things that are observed.

Keeping such daily notes in a folder in consecutive date order then gives one some comparison over a period of time and answers the question of "Are we getting better or worse?" "Are ordered projects proceeding?" "Are we producing?" "Are there dangers in out-security?"

It is courtesy to pick up the I/C of an area one is entering so he overhears any remarks passed to his staff. The I/C is dropped in leaving the area. If there is no I/C to be found, one notes it and inspects anyway.

Receptions in orgs are generally queried as to knowledge of routing and duties to establish some idea of their competence.

The general tone level (by Tone Scale Chart) is noted on the clipboard by area. Low tones will indicate possible no production or faulty production as morale depends on production to a major degree.

The daily inspection is informal. One can have a formal inspection weekly or monthly.

The daily inspection is an effort to see the existing scene as it is when one is not there, rather than changing the scene by excessive formality.

Inspections are made at different hours, not as a set scheduled action.

Daily inspections are a morale factor in that it shows someone is interested and gives an acknowledgement whether voiced or not. It makes the work of the staff seem more valuable to them. They seldom realize how valuable their work actually is.

Obvious unworn hats, threats to materiel by neglect, general orderliness and busyness, state of lines, confusions, lack of signs, bad signs, these and many other points are observed.

Only in this way, by CO/ED inspection, is a CO/ED kept informed and staff advised of executive presence.

The CO/ED inspection action has no real substitute.

A survey by LRH Comms showed that the hardest thing to get an executive to do was inspect his own area. Thus a CO/ED cannot expect that executives will reliably and uniformly report the true state of their areas. Despite executive inspection or lack of it, a CO/ED should still inspect.

It is a fact that when a CO/ED does not inspect daily he does not make it *his* organization.

A CO/ED who is very well qualified such as an OEC Class VI or better, an FEBC Class IX who is also a Course Super can *also* do another type of action *in addition* to his inspection. (It does not substitute for informal daily inspections.) He can take over a jammed or faulty post for four or five hours and see *why* it is messed up. There is often some impossible situation—example, an illegal counter-policy that a student has to be star-rated first on anything he checks out on another which makes then all twin checkouts impossible—and can unjam the line by correcting what he finds. A 48-hour tour on a completely messed up post or area is an extreme action. It however pays off.

There are then two different types of actions a CO/ED does. One is a daily inspection pure and simple.

The other is a post and line survey and is part of a CO/ED's hatting and forming actions.

Both are needful. The daily inspection is mandatory.

A CO/ED who never looks, just issues orders, operates by reports only, has no stats available, is not totally in control of his command and is running at risk.

He can keep his own confront up and know what is going on only if he inspects daily.

L. RON HUBBARD
Founder

HUBBARD COMMUNICATIONS OFFICE
Saint Hill Manor, East Grinstead, Sussex

HCO POLICY LETTER OF 24 JUNE 1971

Remimeo

TROUBLE

(Originally written by LRH for the *Apollo* OODs
on 24 June 71. Issued as an HCO PL on 21 Sept. 80.)

The fastest possible way for a senior to get into trouble is to fail to get in ethics on a downstat junior.

The US "solves" all this with huge government payoffs and propitiation. And look at the upsurge of riots.

Capitalism works only on the reward side. It takes two sides to make a game.

If an I/C lets ethics go out on his juniors, he pulls the rug out from under himself—and slaughters the juniors also.

A team is composed of teammates. Those who mess up the team aren't teammates.

L. RON HUBBARD
Founder

HCO POLICY LETTER OF 31 JULY 1971

Remimeo

THE USUAL

(Originally written by LRH for the *Apollo* OODs of
31 July 71. Issued as an HCO PL on 6 Oct. 80.)

When in doubt do the usual, the routine, the standard.

If your hat says recruit, recruit. Don't do tool purchasing.

WHEN A POST DOES NOT DO ITS USUAL ACTIONS THESE BACK-LOG AND APPEAR AS TRAFFIC AND DEMANDS.

The post goes into desperation and tries to cope and, failing to do what it was supposed to do in the first place, just goes more desperate.

A post will run wrong so long as it does not do the usual. And it will go wronger and wronger.

Like auditing a pc. Every shortcut, every unusual solution, just makes the pc worse. You can't go on with unusual solutions forever. The pc will collapse.

So it is with a post.

Do what the post is supposed to do in the first place. Cope part of the time, yes. But somehow get in the usual action.

If you don't you will feel desperate, 9,000 feet up and in a hurricane.

EVERY personnel line has gotten in this state.

Failing to recruit and do the usual has backlogged HASes over the world to a point of total desperation. Yet I see no Personnel Procurement Officers single-hatted on post in orgs. I see no new campaign for recruits. I see no hammer to get standard forms signed.

Thus by not doing the basic usual actions, each HAS is going mad trying to answer people who are demanding personnel. Then the HAS musical-chairs the place, destroys the org form.

WHY? Because the usual action of PPOs on post and records and lines and personnel promo were not done.

Not doing the usual resulted in desperate solutions.

This is the way any post goes when it backlogs. It backlogs for lack of the usual. Then it goes into total desperation.

The way to get out of the mess is each day do a couple hours of the usual regardless of traffic and demands.

And surprise! One will dig out of it and get on top of it.

One has to know three facts:

1.   The usual solution already exists. One has to find out or work out what it is.

2.   Unusual actions will backlog one and if continued will drown one.

3.   One can dig himself out if he spends some time each day getting the usual lined up and in.

One's full hat usually contains the usual. A starter is to get the full hat and know it.

L. RON HUBBARD
Founder

HUBBARD COMMUNICATIONS OFFICE
Saint Hill Manor, East Grinstead, Sussex

HCO POLICY LETTER OF 21 FEBRUARY 1972

Remimeo

QUALITIES AT THE TOP

(Originally written by LRH for the *Apollo* OODs of
21 Feb. 72. Issued as an HCO PL on 12 Sept. 80.)

Flag Reps have to be able to OBSERVE.

Estos have to be able to train, hat groove in and make functioning people.

Command types have to be able to SUPERVISE and handle ethics.

Product officers have to be able to PRODUCE using the org to do it.

These are the basic skills on which we are concentrating.

Each one requires its own personal approach.

The person who can do all four splendidly is rare. But many can do one or two of these very well.

L. RON HUBBARD
Founder

HCO POLICY LETTER OF 13 MAY 1972

Remimeo

HANDLE

(Originally written by LRH for the *Apollo* OODs
of 13 May 72. Issued as an HCO PL on 22 Oct. 80.)

Refs:

HCO PL 12 Oct. 67	OPERATIONAL, DEFINITION OF
HCO PL 4 May 68	HANDLING SITUATIONS
HCO PL 26 Jan. 72 I	AKH Series 29
	Exec Series 5
	NOT–DONES, HALF–DONES AND
	BACKLOGS

Since December 1971 there has been a new command policy with regard to handling projects and CLOs and orgs.

WHEN IT HAS TO BE HANDLED, HANDLE THE HELL OUT OF IT.

The reference is the HCO PL (26 Jan. 72) on NOT–DONES, HALF–DONES AND BACKLOGS.

But it is more important than that.

You can spread a lot of invested time over a wide area and get no result. This is a sort of puttering around.

The way to really get someplace is give priority to definite whole actions. This is done on order of value of results. "We'll do Area A, B, C and D in that order! Now we'll take A and handle the hell out of it, terminatedly finished, done, total. We can be getting B ready meanwhile. But with A done we now get B done. And so on. We handle hell out of what we're handling."

The accuracy and extent of handling determines whether something is well handled.

Actually, you're dealing with the definition of fully operational.

Something is fully operational when it FUNCTIONS WITHOUT FURTHER CARE OR ATTENTION.

The Estos should learn this too.

Don't putter or fool about.

HANDLE THE HELL OUT OF IT!

L. RON HUBBARD
Founder

HCO POLICY LETTER OF 9 AUGUST 1972

Remimeo
All Executive Hats
All Bureaux Hats

SENIORITY OF ORDERS

No Aides Order or Flag Bureaux Data Letter or Executive Directive, Directive or Base Order of any type or kind, written or verbal, may alter or cancel any policy letter or HCOB. These remain senior.

HCO Policy Letters are senior in admin. HCO Bulletins are senior to all other orders in tech.

Only Policy Letters may revise or cancel Policy Letters. Only HCOBs may revise or cancel HCOBs.

No Aides Order or other directive or order may abolish a network or org or change the form of an org.

HCO PLs and HCOBs require passing by LRH or the full authority of International Board members as well as the Authority and Verification Unit.

Telexes which inform orgs or executives of modifications or cancellations of HCO PLs or HCOBs must quote the revision HCO PL or HCOB, and the revision must in fact exist and itself be issued and follow.

Any practice by which junior issues such as directives abolish networks or make off-policy changes can only result in the destruction of networks, orgs and tech.

This is therefore a HIGH CRIME policy letter and it is an offense both to follow or obey or issue any verbal or written order or directive which is contrary to or changes or "abolishes" anything set up in HCO Policy Letters or HCOBs, including the downgrade of "that's out-of-date" or "that's been cancelled" without showing the HCO PL or HCOB which revises or cancels.

HCO PLs and HCOBs are proven by time and are the senior data on which we operate.

L. RON HUBBARD
Founder

HUBBARD COMMUNICATIONS OFFICE
Saint Hill Manor, East Grinstead, Sussex

HCO POLICY LETTER OF 24 AUGUST 1973R
REVISED 2 JANUARY 1991

Remimeo
ED
Director of Special
  Affairs
LRH Comm
Flag Rep
HAS
Ethics Off
MAA

ETHICS

COMMUNICATION, STOPPING OF

There has been a recent incident, and there have been others in the past, where an executive seeking to report information or a situation has been prevented from doing so.

This has left those responsible for the well-being of the org without adequate data and has resulted in great difficulty and loss.

It is therefore a Comm Ev offense for anyone in an org to halt or attempt to halt the communication of a Director of Special Affairs, an LRH Comm or a Flag Rep.

It is also a Comm Ev offense for any of these to halt or attempt to halt the communication of the Executive Director or an HCO Exec Sec or an HAS to the board or to Flag but communication to the public or authorities of these may be halted by any of the six if it is to the best interest of the org and if the communication itself and the halting of it is at once reported to the board of directors or to Flag.

COMMUNICATION, FAILURE TO DO SO

When an officer or staff member is being depended upon to communicate matters relevant to the post he holds or the activity in which he is engaged, it shall be a Comm Ev offense to fail to do so or to fail to make every conceivable effort to do so.

This also applies to persons sent to represent the org or to handle situations or do observations, whether from the org, a FOLO, the board of directors, Flag or a ship.

When it is found that a terminal who is supposed to communicate is not doing so, the correct (and it will be found, the only practical) method of handling is to have the post observed by another or to send an observation mission to observe the post or in the case of a mission, to bring about immediate recall. Continuous orders to report up are time wasting and, by experience, impractical and sometimes damaging as the situation may deteriorate.

Proper communication and relay of it is an essential part of the duties of any post.

L. RON HUBBARD
Founder

Revision assisted by
LRH Technical Research
and Compilations

HCO POLICY LETTER OF 19 NOVEMBER 1974R
REVISED 31 JANUARY 1991

Remimeo

FINANCE STRESS IN AN ORG

Occasionally an org which could do well gets bogged down over some finance mess.

Hit with unpaid bills or refunds and repayments, threats of no pay, a whole staff can be enturbulated.

Then begins a crazy cycle that the org is so upset it can't produce and unless it produces it can't earn money and if it doesn't earn money, nothing will improve.

This dwindling spiral not only can be stopped but must be for the org to pull out smoothly.

There is an old and time-honored method of doing this: one compartments off the finance confusion. This is done by putting one or two staff members in Treasury whose sole duty is handling the finance emergency, the creditors, the refunds and repayments. Put up a sign "Board Finance Officer" with another sign or two around pointing to that office—"Board Finance Officer. All Finance Matters." Give them a phone with a number. Give everyone else on staff that number as the finance number so they at once direct any callers to it. Instruct Dir Comm where to put all such mail—to the Board Finance Officer.

AND LET THE REST OF STAFF GET ON WITH IT.

People put on the finance special post ONLY handle the subjects of finance emergency. They do NOT handle all finance hats and lines in the org.

They are genned in and checked out on Volume 3 finance items, handling creditors, etc. Their liaison is the nearest Director of Special Affairs.

They know such things as HCO PL 9 Nov. 74, REFUNDS AND REPAYMENTS, and have all the forms to hand.

They get the bills and advance payment files in condition. They "dateline pay" per HCO PL 28 Jan. 65, HOW TO MAINTAIN CREDIT STANDING AND SOLVENCY, Volume 3 OEC.

The Board Finance Officer should play it cool, require further decisions from the Board, shepherd funds carefully and so bring the org out of it.

DELIVERY is the keynote of all such emergencies and even inflation itself! When LRH ED 153 Int, ORG CONDITION STAT CHANGE, began to push Paid Comps in Aug. 71, the long climb of expansion began and continues. It continues except where orgs forget it and push GI only. Push GOOD, HONEST DELIVERY AND DELIVER IT.

Compartmenting off the financial stress works ONLY if the rest of the org flat out DELIVERS and produces in *every* division to do so. Only then can emergencies be solved by a Board Finance Officer.

L. RON HUBBARD
Founder

HCO POLICY LETTER OF 23 JANUARY 1979

Remimeo
Flag
LRH Comm Network
Flag Rep Network
FOLOs
Orgs

UNEVALUATED ORDERS

Every now and then somebody who can't confront handling things gets a fad started "you can't issue unevaluated orders and can't eval so no orders can be issued."

What they have wrong is the definition of "unevaled orders." An unevaluated "order" should read "POLICY."

You can issue all the orders you want to get in or debug an HCO PL, HCOB, LRH ED or targets of these as well as targets of approved Flag evaluations. It requires no eval.

Such issues or targets can be considered to have been already evaluated.

L. RON HUBBARD
Founder

HCO POLICY LETTER OF 22 JANUARY 1981

Remimeo

ORDERS OF THE DAY

(Based on FO 441, ORDERS OF THE DAY of
14 Feb. 68 and FO 2753, ORDERS OF THE DAY
POLICY, amended for use in non-Sea Org orgs.)

Lack of briefing and general info can be a major contributing cause to upsets and confusion in orgs. This is remedied by briefing the staff in the Orders of the Day (OODs).

The OODs keep the staff informed of what is going on in the org, what the ED or CO is pushing, current activities, the day's schedule, etc. Their purpose is to supply DATA to the staff on org matters.

CONTENT

Condition Orders, plans, announcements, personnel data and information of interest are published each day in the OODs.

The day's schedule as well as any changes in schedules are included.

Stat news of the org is also of major interest.

Personnel should supply a weekly mimeoed crew list by div and title so people can keep up with who is where.

FORMAT

The general format for an OODs is:

1. *HEADING* giving the name of the org, OODs number, date of issue, org condition, number on staff, schedule and any other pertinent data. Example:

NAME OF ORG

OODs Number   Date of Issue

Org's Condition

ORDERS OF THE DAY

SCHEDULE: *NUMBER ON STAFF:*

8:15–8:30 Muster

8:30–9:00 Cleaning Stations

. . .

2. *COMMAND* which is a short extract or quote, something pertinent and of general interest, taken from the works of LRH. Any orders from the Executive Director would follow.

3. *ORDERS* or targets by execs listed by exec seniority.

4. *ETHICS* notices, conditions, commendations, etc.

5. *PERSONNEL* data. This includes any approved post changes within the last 24 hours—promotions, demotions, new staff, and leaving staff.

6. *NOTICES,* items of interest, general org news, wins, etc. This does not include personal notices such as car advertisements or other non-org related matters. Very lengthy items may be left out at the discretion of the typist if the OODs become too long.

7. *NEWS* briefs of world events may be included as a last section by the Dir Comm to keep the staff info'd on general events in the news. This would not be more than a few sentences on each item.

The OODs are dated for the day for which the schedule applies. They are numbered and given the org's name.

The copy is written compactly in single space paragraphs with a double space between items, schedules, etc. They must not be strung out.

They are on white, legal length paper.

Every item is followed by the name of the issuer and the date such as 28/9/80. All NAMES of persons and all CONDITIONS or POST TITLES go in caps. To file an OODs item in personnel/ethics and other files, a copy is cut up with scissors.

The first word of each entry is in caps giving what the item is. For example, an order for HCO to do checkouts on something would begin with the word CHECKOUTS.

ISSUING THE OODs

The Dir Comm is responsible for seeing the OODs are typed and issued.

OODs are run off at the end of the day, for use first thing in the morning. For Foundation Orgs, the OODs would be run off as the last action of the night, for use first thing the following day.

A special basket designated on it "Orders of the Day Copy" is placed in the Comm Center and its use is made known to all staff. Into it are placed assignments of conditions, schedules, copies of plans, etc.

Instead of posting a Condition Order handwritten, the originator may place it in the Orders of the Day copy basket.

Personnel assignments and notices may also be placed there as well per HCO PL 24 Sept. 71RB, ASSIGNMENT, MODEL TO BE USED.

The LRH Comm as Issue Authority approves all OODs items before they are published and notes on any disapproved items what policy was violated.

In a small org, the OODs are not run off but are simply typed with a carbon and posted on the staff notice board.

OODs should be kept on a clipboard so they can be referred to.

SUMMARY

A lot of work hours go into an OOD. It should carry a true picture of what's going on and what's being done and what's intended.

The OODs are in fact a sort of daily paper. They are a vital comm line.

L. RON HUBBARD
Founder

Assisted by
Flag Compilations Bureau

HUBBARD COMMUNICATIONS OFFICE
Saint Hill Manor, East Grinstead, Sussex

HCO POLICY LETTER OF 1 APRIL 1981R
REVISED 17 JANUARY 1991

(Also issued as an HCOB,
same date, same title)

Remimeo
Exec Hats
Dissem
Tech
Qual
Registrar Hat
D of P Hat
C/S Hat
Div 6
Chaplain Hat
Ethics Off/MAA

INTERVIEWS

Refs:

HCO PL	13 Sept. 70 II	Org Series 1
		BASIC ORGANIZATION
HCO PL	10 July 65	LINES AND TERMINALS ROUTING

Interviews play a vital part in the correct routing and smooth flow of pcs and students on org lines.

Depending on how needed interviews are assigned and carried out, org lines and therefore org products can be slowed or impeded or they can be speeded up and made to flow more smoothly, with real products as a result.

TYPES OF INTERVIEWS

This issue lists the main types of interviews used in an org, and defines their use, to clearly label and differentiate between them. It summates the most used interviews but in no way replaces full hatting for one's post.

REGISTRAR INTERVIEW: The purpose of the Registrar interview is to sign prospective students and pcs up for org services, get them to pay for the services and get them routed onto the services. The Reg also signs up students and pcs for further services when they have completed the services they signed up for. The concern of the Registrar is to move pcs and students up the Bridge. He does this by caring about the person and not being reasonable about stops or barriers but caring enough to get him through the stops or barriers to get the service that's going to rehabilitate him. He gets the public person fully paid and on to service.

The Registrar must be familiar with the tech the org delivers and be kept informed of the results being obtained. Registrars must not assign hours or C/S for the case, and they mustn't promise that such and such a rundown will be done, because they are not tech terminals and they can be wrong.

Example Registrar interview: "I think I went Dianetic Clear." "Well, that's good. You just sign here on the dotted line and these invoices will go to the Tech Division and they will take care of you." End of interview! The way you end his itsa is you put a pen in his hand. That's the proper ack.

Another example Registrar interview: Joe Blow walks in to the Registrar and says, "Ted brought me down here and I'm supposed to sign up for some more auditing. I don't want to buy any more auditing here." "Oh, my goodness, what you had better have is a D of P interview so we can get data on this." The folder would go to the C/S and the C/S would tell the D of P what had to be found out.

The Registrar also signs up pcs conditionally, pending acceptance by Tech, takes the money and sees that the pc is then routed to Tech for a Technical Estimate. The reason for getting a Tech Estimate is to get the pc to buy enough intensives to get him some place.

When the pc is accepted by Tech, and the Tech Estimate is received, the Registrar signs the pc up for the estimated number of intensives; he gets payment for them or for the first one or two, but in any case has the person sign up for the remaining intensives, to be taken when paid for. (Refs: HCO PL 30 Nov. 71, BLIND REGISTRATION; HCO PL 19 Aug. 60, REGISTRAR LOST LINE)

Another Registrar action which increases the income is interviewing students and selling them professional auditing.

The Registrar must also be on the routing form for outgoing preclears and students and interview them without fail for further services. He can usually get them to take more services.

HGC PC TECHNICAL ESTIMATE INTERVIEW: The HGC Pc Technical Estimate interview is done to obtain necessary data from the applicant so that an accurate estimate can be made of the number of hours or intensives the person will need to get results from his auditing.

The routing is to Registrar, to Testing, then to Tech Estimator and back to the Registrar. The routing form should then of course take the pc to Tech Services who handles the folders and the scheduling.

The HGC Pc Technical Estimate is done by the D of P or a qualified technical terminal. It is not a metered interview. It consists of a lot of questions such as, "What do you want to accomplish with auditing?" Lots of questions about state of case, amount of time it has taken to do previous auditing cycles, etc. The Tech Estimator has the current OCA, IQ and Aptitude tests to hand. Part of his estimation includes a meter check (per HCO PL 26 Aug. 65RB, ETHICS E–METER CHECK) which estimates state of case.

The Tech Estimator must be able to rapidly spot the preclear on the Chart of Human Evaluation. He does this using tests and by getting the prospective pc talking about himself. With all of this data, he estimates the number of hours needed for a pc to get *results*.

The Registrar is sent a copy of the Tech Estimate which states:

I RECOMMEND THAT THIS APPLICANT (ONE OF THE FOLLOWING):

A. Buy _____ (number of) intensives.

B. Be refused auditing by the org on the basis of HCO PL 6 Dec. 76RB, ILLEGAL PCs, ACCEPTANCE OF, HIGH CRIME PL.

D OF P INTERVIEW: Briefly, a D of P interview is an interview given to a preclear by the Director of Processing.

There are two main types of D of P interviews:

1. *To get data for the C/S which is not otherwise available to him for C/Sing and programing the case.*

A D of P interview is used when the C/S suspects that additives are being put into the session or that there are other outside factors on his auditing or admin lines that are influencing the pc's case gain. This is the primary use of the D of P interview and consists of having the D of P ask the pc something like: "What did the auditor say to you in session?" "Exactly what happened in that session?" "What did the auditor do?"

These interviews are ordered by the C/S to obtain data he cannot otherwise obtain and when he suspects hidden matter in the session which is not covered in the worksheets; when the C/S doesn't know what's wrong with the case but strongly suspects he isn't being told all.

A D of P interview is not done to find out what the pc thinks is wrong with his case. It is done in order to get data and is not auditing. There is no attempt to audit during a D of P interview. Where a preclear is feeling bad or doesn't want more auditing, it's "When did all this start up?" "When you first came in, what did you want?" "What did you expect to have happen?" or, "When did you start feeling bad?" It's a "when" question to get a lot of data.

Some orgs have used a pat set of questions or a printed D of P interview form, but this is not a D of P interview by definition and does not give the C/S the data he really needs to program the case.

Overuse of D of P interviews can tie up the D of P and cut down the delivery of auditing to pcs. A C/S should be able to study the case, and get an FES done or do one. He will not learn what he needs to know about the pc's case by substituting a D of P interview for his work. To do a D of P interview to unravel a case actually defeats the purpose of FESing and the C/S. The C/S has specific tools he would order an auditor to use to crack a case, such as the Green Form, C/S 53, etc. This is all part of normal C/Sing and auditing lines. That's not a D of P interview.

Similarly, an arrival D of P interview is just a substitute for an FES. And a leaving D of P interview would only be done when the pc did not write a success story or wrote a poor one. They are not a routine function of a D of P by any means.

Unnecessary D of P interviews are just lazy C/Sing.

2. *To give the pc an R-factor on what is going on in order to dispel a mystery for him.*

The second type of D of P interview is basically to put in an R-factor with the pc. The D of P lets the pc talk about what has been going on, finds out what the pc is in mystery about and explains it. The D of P does not explain tech to him. He explains what is happening to the pc. A good D of P can straighten it out fast.

The D of P is actually the I/C of all pcs when they are in the org and he can originate a D of P interview such as when bad indicators are observed or the pc is hung up or curious.

D of P interviews are always done on the meter, and while it is not auditing, the D of P must have his TRs in, must have a Qual Okay to Operate an E-Meter and must be able to meter accurately. While a D of P interview is not done to get case gain, one normally tries to end the interview on an F/N.

QUAL CONSULTANT INTERVIEW: The Qual Consultation is a service provided by Qual and is described in HCOB 10 Feb. 71, TECH VOLUME AND TWO–WAY COMM. It consists of a metered interview and two-way comm and letting the person talk about his troubles and listening.

This type of interview can be done on a person who is not really on auditing lines, or he is somewhere around auditing lines and you see he is fouled up. It is not limited to pcs but can be done on very slow or dropped-out students as well.

SOLO CONSULTANT INTERVIEW AT AN AO: The duties of a Solo OT Review Consultant are to personally handle pre-OT Solo jams rapidly with metered two-way comm.

A Solo line does not run like a C/S Series 25 HGC line. It is a highly alert personalized line that picks up the pre-OTs who aren't soloing well or who are bugged and gets them wheeling. Usually it's something simple, only discovered by asking the pre-OT and handling in a metered interview. Cramming cycles on auditing are a common result. A C/S can't see that the green pre-OT forgets to turn on his meter!

It is a smooth way to get happy pre-OTs.

ETHICS OFFICER/MAA INTERVIEWS: An ethics interview is an interview done by the Ethics Officer or the MAA on a student, preclear or staff member. He uses Confessionals, conditions, investigation tech and PTS/SP tech in order to get ethics in in his org or area so that Scientology can be done.

The Ethics Officer acts on *indicators* and has a primary responsibility to keep trouble from blowing up on org lines—he is supposed to catch things before they blow up. An Ethics Officer has to know what the scene is and be able to act. With no nonsense. He is there to get ethics in so that tech can go in.

Often the job of the Ethics Officer entails an ethics interview to find out what the exact situation is with an individual and get it handled.

An example would be someone who is goofing and in trouble for not completing cycles of action. The Ethics Officer, upon checking the ethics files of this person, interviewing him and learning that this was the situation, would know that the probability is that the ethics handling needed is for going past misunderstoods in their work. With ethics in, the person could be word cleared, the MUs found and he would then be able to complete the cycle of action.

A key tool of the Ethics Officer is the ethics conditions and their formulas, as contained in the book *Introduction to Scientology Ethics*. Where a person has earlier undone or messed up ethics conditions, this can act as a serious block to getting ethics in and would require handling with HCO PL 19 Dec. 82R II, REPAIRING PAST ETHICS CONDITIONS.

Another vital tool of the Ethics Officer is getting a person freed of his overts and withholds. A person manifesting O/Ws (natter, blowy, critical of the organization, etc.) must have those O/Ws pulled. An important part of an Ethics Officer's job is hearing Confessionals and he must get meter trained and be able to do Confessionals where needed. Another way to get O/Ws cleaned up is to make the person write up all his overts and withholds and turn them in to the Ethics Officer (who would also ensure that end ruds were done).

An Ethics Officer never spends any time sitting and arguing with someone. He simply puts the person on a meter and assesses a Trouble Area Questionnaire. (Ref: HCO PL 9 Apr. 72R, CORRECT DANGER CONDITION HANDLING)

PTS interviews are a frequent duty of the Ethics Officer and he must be fully trained in the complete tech of handling PTSness contained in the PTS/SP Course.

If a pc is mid auditing, the Ethics Officer or MAA should check with the pc's C/S before doing a PTS interview or Trouble Area Questionnaire. (Ref: HCOB 13 Oct. 82, C/S Series 116, ETHICS AND THE C/S)

Full worksheets are always kept for any PTS interview and are sent to the pc folder. A copy of any ethics interview is also sent to the person's pc or student folder.

CHAPLAIN INTERVIEW: A Chaplain interview is for those persons who feel wronged, ARC broken public who have fallen off the Bridge or are about to and people whose burdens appear to be too great.

If they feel they cannot be heard anywhere else they always have recourse to the Chaplain. They mainly want to be heard and acknowledged. Half the time or more one does nothing, but one does listen.

EXECUTIVE DIRECTOR/COMMANDING OFFICER INTERVIEW: When someone has completed a service and is leaving the org, the CO/ED interviews the person before he routes out of the org, to ensure he is a good product. This interview consists of the CO/ED congratulating the student or preclear, checking his indicators and chatting briefly with him on his future plans. If all okay, the CO/ED gives his approval that the person may go. If not satisfied, the student or pc would be routed to Qual to get straightened out, with the R-factor that he doesn't have permission to go because the CO/ED is not satisfied with the technical results.

Another way that this line can be handled is for the CO/ED to see the final success story of the public person to give final approval for the person to leave the org. No public routes out of the org without the CO or ED's okay and a sign must be posted which makes this clear to the public.

This type of interview or seeing the final success story enables the CO/ED to check the product of the org. The person has gone through the lines and should have completed with a good success story.

HOST INTERVIEW: On Flag and in some other orgs, there is a Host whose duty it is to see to the well-being and good servicing of the public.

The purpose of the initial Host interview is to welcome the person arriving for services, brief him and orient him to the scene and provide him at once with a stable terminal who is interested in his welfare and will be a terminal for him throughout his stay. The Host lets the person know that if there is anything wrong that he should come and see him.

This interview is not done on a meter and there is no set patter or procedure which the Host uses.

The Host interviews pcs and students as needful to ensure they are being serviced and to ensure any service outness is handled by the proper terminals.

Returning persons are similarly welcomed, rebriefed and brought up to date on any changes in services or new facilities.

———————

While these are by no means all the types of interviews an org uses, they are the main interviews given on an org's service lines.

Standardly done interviews can make all the difference in an org's lines and viability. The result will be an increase in quantity and quality of the valuable final products of the org.

L. RON HUBBARD
Founder

Revision assisted by
LRH Technical Research
and Compilations

HCO POLICY LETTER OF 5 FEBRUARY 1982

Remimeo   Issue I

OUT–ETHICS SYMPTOMS

There are three things which, when observed, can be very revealing.

1. Overspending, waste and extravagance.

2. Overt products.

3. Nonproduction.

One or the other of these three will lead frequently to discovering the rest being present as well.

Recent incidents have now revealed something else. When those three things above are present, they are covering up a serious out-ethics scene.

Although each one of them is bad enough and although each one of them should be handled, sad experience has shown that they won't stay handled unless one reaches deeper.

Below these symptoms, as in some disease, it will commonly be found that there is an out-ethics situation of magnitude, often amounting to very despicable crime.

Quite often one is prone to say, seeing the three things above, that that is just a personality fault in the person or a lack of organization in a group. But it is a sad fact that if one were to follow these things down, all too often he would find a situation that could only be classified as major crime.

The org that never seems to be able to get going, the person who seems to be constant trouble, needing continual supervision and correction, are all too often deeply involved in actual crime.

The remedy is to look deeper.

With expert investigation and metering, you will be startled by what you sometimes find. Theft. Embezzlement. Lies. You name it. All too often it will be there—and more, it has been riding hidden, poisoning the person and the whole group.

There is another symptom one sometimes finds. It could be called the "Nothing matters" attitude. A person seems to be continually in a frame of mind of not caring about anything, feeling nothing is important, a kind of exhibited and demonstrated attitude toward the post, toward life.

Such an attitude blinds the person to any quality. He often cannot tell what is good or bad, what looks nice or what looks awful. Frequently it manifests itself, not always, in personal grooming and dress.

Missing is the element of pride: The person is not proud of and takes no satisfaction in any product he gets out, much less pride in his own skill or appearance.

This loops back into item (2) above, overt products.

But the "Nothing matters" attitude is usually just a coverup for criminality.

By reason of the way a being thinks and regards himself, he needs a justification for having committed crimes. The resulting attitude of "It doesn't matter," is all too often just the tip of an iceberg of deep crimes committed but hidden from view.

Real villains are hardly ever well dressed: Real villains have no pride. Even though TV always shows them that way, it is not true in life.

When you look around you in this society and see what passes for clothes and personal grooming, when you examine the statistic of industry and see it failing, the next time you buy a product and it falls apart, you will get some idea of where the psychologist, working in the schools, has brought us to.

The jungle that we're living in is saturated with crime. It even extends up to a criminal government. It's on TV and in the movies that it is all right. But actually, as each man and woman knows deep and well, it isn't. One cannot live a happy or even a contented life or even one worth living when one is committing crimes. Even those very well hidden. The stolen loot is worthless, the pain a man causes lives on deep in his own soul.

And it expresses itself, in the criminal, in the above ways.

So don't be naive. Hidden crime is far more common than one would suppose. One has only to look at the tramp get-ups of the people on the street to know that criminal acts are falsely looked upon too often as all right.

It is not whether it is "all right" or not. They leave their own branding iron on the person.

So raise your confront of evil, begin to observe, break out the meter.

When you see the symptoms above, you are frequently looking at the surface manifestations of criminal acts. They're as big as flashing neon signs.

We have remedies for it. It can be handled. A well-done Happiness Rundown, complete, changes people remarkably because it eases the burden.

But right now, we are concerned with being an executive and trying to handle symptoms as above.

Don't be reasonable about it.

When you see those symptoms and they are getting in your road on production lines, recognize them for what they are and act accordingly.

And I assure you you will live a much happier life. And get lots more accomplished with a staff.

L. RON HUBBARD
Founder

HUBBARD COMMUNICATIONS OFFICE
Saint Hill Manor, East Grinstead, Sussex

HCO POLICY LETTER OF 24 MARCH 1985

RESPONSIBILITY, CONTROL AND
DANGER CONDITIONS

Refs:

HCO PL 16 Jan. 66R Rev. 29.11.79		DANGER CONDITION
HCO PL 19 Jan. 66 III		DANGER CONDITION RESPONSIBILITIES OF DECLARING
HCO PL 9 Apr. 72R		CORRECT DANGER CONDITION HANDLING
HCO PL 18 Feb. 72		Exec Series 8 THE TOP TRIANGLE
HCO PL 19 Dec. 82 II		REPAIRING PAST ETHICS CONDITIONS

An executive can tend to occasionally sever somebody's responsibility line. It's a technical point.

As one definition of responsibility is to defend one's control of an area, an exec can sometimes tend to sever that control point.

That's the mechanism of a Danger condition.

If every time an exec found it necessary to bypass it was accompanied with another Danger assignment, and if those conditions were actually done, that would be handled.

That gives us the Why of how an exec can get repeatedly pulled into an area: It's failure to assign and get executed the Danger condition. That's the tech that's out. You see, the exec's juniors, by not doing their job, sever their control of their area.

PAST CONDITIONS

I recall a unit that was generating a lot of trouble and flak, and ended up being bypassed. Its stats crashed and they still had never really recovered six years later. And the reason was the undone Danger condition. They were never assigned a condition of Danger, and so those that had done the bypassing were stuck with this unit on their plates right on up the line. So when you have an area that is continually a source of trouble, a past Danger condition never assigned can be looked for and repaired.

This is the tech on Danger conditions when seen against the definition of responsibility. It opens the door to a handling.

L. RON HUBBARD
Founder

HCO POLICY LETTER OF 30 AUGUST 1990

Remimeo
All Orgs
All Staff

WEEKLY STAFF MEETINGS

Refs:
HCO PL   1 July   82   AKH Series 41
                                        MANAGEMENT COORDINATION
HCO PL 22 Aug. 82   AKH Series 43
                                        BATTLE PLANS

Modifies:
HCO PL   4 Jan. 66   STAFF MEETING

Staff meetings are a vital factor in ensuring that a group's actions and efforts are coordinated and moving in the same direction toward the achievement of common purposes.

A staff that is not kept informed of the plans, programs and targets the org has set about to accomplish becomes a tangle of cross orders and cross purposes.

Weekly staff meeting is not just a meeting where an in-charge lectures the group. A weekly staff meeting gathers agreement and keeps the staff informed as a team.

WEEKLY STAFF MEETING FORMAT

Weekly staff meeting is held each Thursday once the stats of the past week have been calculated and graphed (or Friday, for an international management or similar org that requires more time to get all stats in). The exact time of the meeting would be determined by the org's Ad Council and approved by Exec Council.

The staff meeting is chaired by the CO or ED.

Attendance is mandatory for all staff, including expeditors.

ORDER OF BUSINESS

The general order of business of the weekly staff meeting is:

1. Flaps and handlings.

2. General business announcements.

3. Presentation of stats and trends by individual staff members and a condition assigned to each stat with a battle plan for each. Stats must be real and represent actual production, leading toward a VFP.

    In a large org where it is not feasible for each staff member to present their individual stat and battle plan, the org's Executive Council would determine which stats and battle plans are to be presented. Minimally, even in a very large org, this would include each divisional head and the Executive Secretaries.

4. Summary of condition assigned to be the condition of the whole group. (In a service org the org's condition is assigned by the CO or ED according to the paid completions statistic.)

5. Bonuses for the week (or the value of the unit for that week) announced.

6. Combined battle plan.

INDIVIDUAL STAFF MEMBER RESPONSIBILITY

Each person in the group, whether he presents his stat and BP to the general group or not, is personally responsible for:

a. Having a correct stat which reflects production factually,

b. The stats of his area of responsibility,

c. Graphing the stat or stats on time,

d. Having a copy of his weekly stat or stats,

e. Having a battle plan for each stat for the coming week,

f. Full knowledge of reading stats, date coincidence, stat interpretation and conditions.

The purpose of the staff meeting is to develop a team spirit of mutual co-operation and coordination. It links bonuses to production and gives the group, by that, control over their own income.

L. RON HUBBARD
Founder

Compilation assisted by
LRH Technical Research
and Compilations

PRODUCTION AND ORGANIZATION

ORGANIZATIONAL INDOCTRINATION

Each person on a post must be cleared on that post by the Manager. The Manager, by questioning, reaches, with the person, an acceptable, embracive stable datum that exactly defines the job.

The person, with this sorted out and cognited upon, then can withstand organizational confusion in his area.

The Manager does this, no one else. The Manager does not tell the person the definition. The definition must be arrived at by the person in his own words.

Applies to all personnel.

L. RON HUBBARD
Founder

MORALE NOTE

If you have ejection jitters after the house cleaning dismissal, remember this:

The HASI has never fired anyone who was ably

> On Post, On Time, On the Job,
> On His or Her Own Comm Lines.

The HASI—and that means the staff and its working power—has always sacked people who were

> Off Post Continually—Off Time
> (late to arrive, early to go)
> Off Their Own Post and On Yours
> and Thoroughly Off Comm Line
> with their actions and despatches.

Best,

L. RON HUBBARD
Founder

HCO BULLETIN OF 25 AUGUST 1958

ADMINISTRATIVE STABLE DATA

There is an error being made by many Scientology executives. They apparently have as a stable datum "Get the work done," or "Do all I can do." Chaos results.

The only possible datum on which an executive could work effectively is "Get people to get the work done."

Otherwise the executive does as much as he can and leaves the willing personnel standing around unhelped and unguided. If we all did this Scientology would go nowhere. One auditor can't audit the world. One personnel cannot do all the work of a Scientology organization.

If each person in the org wears all the hats or one wears all and the rest wear none you will have:

1. Bad morale

2. Overburdened personnel

3. Underburdened personnel

4. Rapid staff turnover

5. Bad dissemination, processing and instruction

6. Low income

7. Low income

8. Chaos.

An executive has only two jobs:

1. Policy, promotion and planning

2. Getting people to get the job done.

A post or terminal is an assigned area of responsibility and action which is supervised in part by an executive. Supervision means helping people to understand their jobs. Supervision means giving the responsibility and wherewithal to do their jobs. Supervision includes the granting of beingness. Supervision does not mean doing the job supervised.

To double dissemination and income in Scientology organizations, study this well. Organizations that aren't run this way aren't real.

L. RON HUBBARD
Founder

Remimeo
All Exec Hats

EXECUTIVES OF SCIENTOLOGY ORGANIZATIONS

(Originally written by LRH as HCOB 27 Aug. 58, same
title. Issued as an HCO Policy Letter on 30 Oct. 62.)

By definition an executive is one who obtains execution of duties, programs and actions in an organization to further the aims and purposes of that organization.

To forward dissemination of Scientology, to increase the income of Scientology organizations, and to accomplish what we are trying to do, it is vital that we have good executives who know what they are doing and who do it.

Basically, the work of the organization does not depend upon the executive. It depends upon his supervision. The work of the organization depends upon its staff personnel and their performance of duties in exact compliance with their hat folders to accomplish the purposes of their posts. However, it is very difficult for staff personnel to accomplish their duties when they do not have good executives to provide overall supervision and liaison amongst posts. Therefore, it is only necessary to have a bad executive who has a poor understanding of what his work is all about to reduce morale, cause turnover of personnel, to impede dissemination and to lower the income of organizations.

Understanding this I have completed a considerable study of the subject of being an executive. There is more to it than one would ordinarily suppose.

In the first place, an executive should be able to perform better every single job in the organization than the personnel performing it. In this way the executive will be effective, since he will know what these posts are doing. Thus, an executive is selected primarily for his knowledge of the organization. Another attribute of the executive is an ability to get along with people and to aid them to understand their duties, the whys and wherefores of their posts, and their relationships to other posts and the communication lines which connect them. Another attribute is the ability to get something done via another person. These three attributes are easily the most important. They are followed by the other side of an executive's activities which consist of planning, organizing and promotion, as well as either setting up or gaining compliance with organizational policy.

The stable datum on which most people operate in a Scientology organization is "Get the work done." This is as it should be. However, this as a stable datum in an executive is fatal. His stable datum cannot be otherwise than "Get people to get the work done."

Let us take a contrary view of this situation. Let us suppose we have an "executive" who can himself work hard and who has the datum "get the work done." This is what he does. He pulls off some odds and ends of organizational duties into his lap, sits at his desk and in a state of exasperation tries to do everything that comes his way. Under such an executive income will decline, morale will turn sour, and there will be a large staff turnover. This "executive" simply regards himself as a workhorse who is too overburdened to pay attention to details. He makes mistakes, he does not execute policy and no matter how hard and how well he works at these jobs he has cut out for himself he never heads up or runs an organization and he never builds anything of any size. At length, he will begin to discourage business and activity on the part of the organization, since the work is already too burdensome for him to handle. Now he was chosen as an executive because he could do the job better on any post in the organization given that post, than the people present. He takes this as a license to "show people up" or to "show them how it really ought to be done." Let us look at this closely. He would not be an executive unless he could work better than each and every person on staff. He would not be there if he did not know these posts better. But let us add up for him the following activities: Director of Training, Director of Processing, auditing all preclears, keeping all accounts, writing all of the dissemination materials, running the mimeograph machine and the printing company, building and painting all of the quarters, personally writing on a typewriter all of the letters received by the organization, and a long time before we get down to typewriting we see that one person on a MEST universe time span could not perform all of these duties. Therefore, we draw the conclusion that we need many people to perform these actions. An executive who tries to perform many actions himself and does not "get people to get the work done" creates a leaderless organization. He is overworked, he cannot cope, he eventually goes out the bottom. Even more importantly, the personnel around him go out the bottom, a thing he commonly fails to observe.

We see, then, that an executive makes a mistake every time he takes into his own hands any portion of any job in the organization. There are two ways a "bad executive" can do this. The first way is quite obvious. He simply tries to do several posts, thus leaving many posts unsupervised and leaving many details uncoordinated and depriving staff of necessary liaison and supervision amongst the various posts. The other way is less obvious. He takes the juicy tidbits which require "command decision" away from the posts and leaves each post a naked drudgery of petty detail; in other words, he scoops off the cream and does, to a slight degree, each one of the jobs around and thus brings about a state of irresponsibility on the various terminals.

Furthermore, an executive who is not doing a real job of executing, "get people to get the work done," will not be in sufficient contact with the various posts in the organization and know which ones are underburdened and which ones are overburdened. Posts which are underburdened and do not have enough to do, who roam around inside the organization like billiard balls against the banks and break up other work. Posts which are overburdened confront the personnel occupying them with such a tremendous pyramid of work that they go into apathy trying to regard their job at all, and so cease to function, and quite ordinarily leave the organization (this is the primary reason people do leave an organization: they cannot do their work well and become convinced that they are badly placed.)

Chaos and confusion are the result of an executive's (1) inability or unwillingness to simply supervise a post and do none of their work, and (2) inability to grant beingness or confront the good sense of other people.

Now let us see what a good executive really does and we will find that he is busy enough if he actually does his job. He does not call people into his office and have them stand in front of his desk while he explains their job to them. In fact, he spends very little time at his desk. In the first place, such a procedure has the earmarks of "being called on the carpet" and makes for ARC breaks. Further, outside of the familiarity of the staff personnel's surroundings the executive is not in effect running 8-C. To know anything about the post he would have to see the actual equipment, materials, files, etc., connected with that post. And thus, any good executive spends much less time at his desk than he does in various parts of the organization. A good executive actually goes to the post and looks it over. He does not work with the post with the aim in mind of showing the post how much faster and how much more expertly the post can be done. Admittedly he is an executive and the person occupying the post is occupying that post because the executive can do the post better than the person occupying it. Thus, an impatience and an intolerance is too easy to demonstrate.

The executive looks over the post on the site of the post by going through the individual's hat and finding out whether or not it really matches up to the exact duties of the post. He will find if he is patient and a good auditor, that the post is quite routinely confused about his duties and this confusion makes the duties look too big or too hard to do, or he will discover that the post is not covering all of its duties, that it is specializing in some of them. This last is particularly true in an overburdened post. The answer to an overburdened post which is actually overburdened is, of course, not for the executive to take on some of the duties or to try to whip up the person doing the job but to split the hat along some natural division and put another personnel on the post in addition to the one already there.

Just as any Director of Processing is always being bombarded by the auditors to give them a new, fast, wonderful technique which will solve all of their own goofs, so an executive is always being asked by some staff personnel to do something new, wonderful and strange with the post hat. The hat, of course, containing all of the duties of the post was usually written up with great care and any real rearrangement of it or derangement of it will discover that some of the functions or liaisons of the organization will be lost. Therefore, a good executive does not succumb to the idea that something new, wonderful and strange must be done with the post simply because the personnel handling the post do not understand the procedure connected with it.

It is quite interesting to study the amount of explanation and the frequency of explanation necessary to put some personnel on post and to get them to understand and execute the exact duties as stated in the hat. Personnel usually try to run a more complicated post than is necessary. It is a natural instinct to complicate something which is simple. Therefore, the simplicities of the post, its purposes and goals, must be observed at all times in any smoothing or rearrangement of the post. For example, it took three full days in one instance to put the Membership hat on a personnel. The personnel was willing—and you will discover that nearly all personnel are—wanted to get the job done, and was perfectly happy with the routine of the job. But—for three full days this personnel attempted to complicate the job of Membership, rearrange it or twist it about in some fashion so that it was more or less unworkable. This personnel could not understand the simplicity of the Membership routine until an executive had spent three full working days with him. At the end of that time it was possible to have good membership response and good membership handling. This condition continued from there on. If the executive in this case had simply said, "Well, this fellow is stupid" and if the executive had become impatient, the Membership job never would have gotten done. It required good ARC, it required good patience. If an executive doesn't have three full days to spend putting on such a hat or if he cannot have in the next four or five weeks the equivalent time of those three full days, then he is never going to have a Membership hat worn promptly and properly for the simple reason that the personnel available to him is the personnel available to him. He should not think that he is going to get out of the brow of Jove, springing fully armed, perfect personnel. It is amazing, the confusion of many personnel on their post, particularly on a new job. They are being asked to understand the whole working principle of the organization at one gulp, as far as they are concerned. They cannot see their role, they cannot see how they fit into the scheme of things, they cannot see where their communication lines are going or what they are supposed to do. The executive, of course, being able to understand this, nevertheless has no license to do anything whatsoever but straighten up the post and get the hat worn straight and get the work done.

In working around and about the organization it will be discovered that there are certain holes in the organization or there are missing communication lines or there are needful liaisons. But at this time Scientology organizations have been worked out to such a fine point that an executive would be much safer taking the posts as primarily put together on the original organization board and putting that structure back together again than in attempting to patch up some new and strange organizational pattern which has had no prior test. The patterns of Scientology organizations have been worked out over a period of many, many years. It is highly probable that we have made almost every mistake possible. We are a very complicated organization in that we have many posts. We have many communication lines. We have many functions. We have worked these out over a period of time and have come up with something closely approaching a perfect answer. Thus, it is only at this time that I can tell executives to follow that answer and to keep the organization running as it was planned to run. There is really not much reason for an executive to dream up something new, wonderful and strange to take care of some particular activity. However, a word of caution. All personnel on all posts will attempt to drive him into something new, wonderful and strange in the way they complicate their jobs and in their failure to understand those jobs.

Giving the inspection of a post a lick and a promise and passing on, with some impatience, to another post, is not being a good executive. One should view the organization or his department as a whole. He should see what it is trying to do. Then he should try to get it to do what it is supposed to do. To accomplish this, hats have already been written up for these various posts. If they are lacking in some respect, then he should have, in the case of a department head, consultation with his superiors and in the case of an Association Secretary correspondence or consultation with myself. He should then get the department running on some minimum acceptable basis by spending a short time with each one of the personnel and giving them that part of their job which they can understand to do and accomplish. Having done this, he at least has a partially going concern. Now he should go back through his department or organization and make sure that each set of duties is fully understood and appreciated by the personnel holding each post. He should not be impatient, he should not look for the same level of understanding which he himself has for the post and he should not look for the same level of performance with which he could execute the post. The primary mistake an auditor can make is failing to estimate the case he is trying to process. The only thing which can give an auditor errors is to fail to estimate the case he is trying to process. The only way an auditor can be wrong is to fail to estimate the case he is trying to process. Therefore, the only way an executive can be wrong is to fail to estimate the personnel he is trying to get to get the work done. With patience, with good ARC, with good understanding, he should repeatedly go round and around and around these posts and instead of making the decisions (and thus skimming the cream off the post) he should show how the decisions to be made stem from the actual activities of the job. He should make the personnel occupying the post make the decisions relating to that post. These decisions in the main are minor to the executive, but they may appear very major to a personnel occupying the post. Only by getting the person to make his own decisions will he ever have a responsible occupation of the post. By seizing little pieces of the post to do himself, by running the whole show, decisions and all, the executive will wind up doing all the work himself because he has gradually forced the person for whom he is making the decisions off post. Little by little that personnel has been pushed off into an irresponsibility for his post. This is exactly contrary to the actual function of an executive. For instance, the Dir of Processing, given a well-trained auditor, should not go on forever and ever and ever dreaming new tricks and gimmicks which will "solve the preclear's case." In the first place, the auditor probably is not starting sessions, resolving PT problems, patching up ARC breaks and running a smooth session—that is why the case isn't running. The Dir of Processing should just go on putting the hat—that general hat known as staff auditor—back on the staff auditor's head. Auditors' conferences are actually totally unnecessary if auditors have been placed on post and if they are supervised on post and if they are given some feeling of responsibility and understanding of their post.

If an executive finds himself doing some particular job, he must realize that this job is either missing out of a hat or that he doesn't have a hat to cover that job. Where the idea of policy-making or enforcement becomes making all the decisions for the personnel, the executive has erred. Policy-making and enforcement is definitely his job, just as promotion and planning in general is his job. But if he finds himself doing some routine task, if he finds himself pinned down hour after hour, day after day, by some concern, then he is missing somewhere in putting hats on people's heads. Occasionally an executive is called upon to put a hat on the head of some outside firm, as in legal work. With what glee an organization's attorney will try to pass the hat back to the head of the organization. This is a task just as a staff post is a task of putting the hat on somebody's head. The attorneys of the organization, even occupying an outside office, should have their hat put on with regard to the organization so that all legal matters are simply referred and routed to them. If they do not act on this basis, then he either puts the hat more firmly on their head or, as in any case, despairing of this, one finds some new attorneys just as he would find new staff personnel if, after an investment of seven or eight days of patient work he still cannot get somebody to go through the routine of the job.

There are certain approvals an executive has to give, as Advisory Council minutes. There are personnel changes which an executive has to make, and therefore there are personnel files which he has to keep. If he is the head of a department he still keeps personnel files for that particular department and he still handles the personnel for that department. If he is a higher level executive he certainly cannot do otherwise than handle personnel as a hat for the entire

750

organization. But the personnel for an entire organization hat is actually not as big a hat as personnel for a single department since it doesn't include procurement. Any department head has the right to do personnel procurement; this has to be okayed by the executive, of course, and to be posted on the org board actually requires my okay.

Now, in a small organization it will be found that three or four or five people working together can get quite a bit accomplished. The moment this goes up to eight or ten people, you have need of an executive. That executive, if he does not know his job as it is set down here, and if he thinks his job is something else than getting people to get the work done, will actually restrict and impoverish the organization. He will not permit it to grow, since he is still trying to run an organization the size of that which can be handled by four or five people, while in actuality he has a much larger area.

An executive doing good promotion and planning will, of course, drive in a great deal of business. All he has to do is to make sure that his shipping department gets books out; that his PR places ads; that his organizational services are of a quality to invite public confidence. He doesn't really need any bigger tricks of promotion than this. The big trick of promotion is to get everybody to do his job. If this is done, then you will see all manner of promotion being accomplished. Promotion dreamed of is not promotion accomplished. An executive dreaming up promotion and working hard himself is not nearly as effective as an executive getting promotion accomplished and getting people to take care of the resulting traffic. In a large Scientology organization, he cannot get business up to speed while trying to do all the work himself.

Naturally, there are executives who, by their personal presence, giving lectures, talking to people, can accomplish a great deal of promotion, just as I accomplish a great deal of promotion by writing a book. But my book writing hat is not my executing hat and I do not get them confused. An executive can wear other hats than being an executive. But being an executive is an express and an explicit hat and its duties consist only and entirely of getting people to get the job done. If other hats are being worn along with the executive hats, then those duties should not be permitted to slop over and occupy and wipe out the executive hat since it's the more important of the two.

An example of this in a Central Organization of Scientology on another continent shows us that some organizations insist on learning always by their own experience, not by already won experience. This organization presents the picture of Scientology organizations in the United States in 1952—everybody was wearing all the hats, nobody was trying to put on any hats other than his own, but his own was all the hats. The resulting confusion, the lack of coordination, the failure to understand that an organizational pattern, orderly terminals and communication lines are vitally necessary to good progress of an organization, resulted in very low income and very hard work on the part of everyone. Contrast this with the 1958 orderliness and income of Scientology United States and we find the only great difference is that we have learned the proper pattern of organization necessary to carry on our job and that we are executing that proper pattern.

You can toss all this aside and work yourself to death and compliment yourself on believing you are getting the job done, but don't wonder why the

751

staff doesn't give you a pat on the back or why I don't give you a pat on the back, because I'm not interested in how many hours you put in. I am not interested in how many documents you handle. I am only interested in the executives who get people to get the work done. On a staff level I am perfectly content with people who take the easier course of simply getting work done. That is the simpler thing to do. These posts are interesting. To handle administration for an Academy is quite a job. Being a Receptionist in the front office is an interesting post—look at all the people you meet. These jobs which go many hours of the day and occasionally late into the night are interesting jobs, they are interesting and necessary terminals. Remember that they are the easier ones to do. Being an executive requires one to get the work done on a via, and that is one of the more difficult tricks demanded of a thetan in this universe.

Let's see if we can do it.

L. RON HUBBARD
Founder

HUBBARD COMMUNICATIONS OFFICE
Saint Hill Manor, East Grinstead, Sussex

HCO POLICY LETTER OF 19 SEPTEMBER 1958

CenOCon
SHSBC Students
Missions
Field

A MODEL HAT FOR AN EXECUTIVE

(Originally written by LRH as HCOB 19 Sept. 58.
Issued as an HCO PL on 25 Mar. 63.)

—PRIMARY—

To accomplish the purposes of the organization and/or his department on a continuing basis by the use of adequate organization and personnel.

To get people in his or her department or organization to get the work done.

To understand the jobs of staff members and to get them to ably wear all of their hats.

—SECONDARY—

To gain compliance with old or create new standard policy as necessary and to gain compliance in particular with the policy laid down by the board and the policy already existing in standard hats.

Planning of campaigns and activities to create new or fulfill old demands and to utilize thereby personnel.

Personnel: Improving his personnel's understanding of their posts and duties and improving their interest and activity on that post.

Acquiring new personnel as needed on that post.

Adjusting work burden.

An executive must realize that this is his whole hat as an executive and that any other activity in which he is engaged than the above is another hat and should be written up as such and is no part of his executive hat. He must also be certain that an adequate amount of his time is spent filling his executive post, not another post he holds as a staff terminal.

See HCOB 27 Aug. 58, EXECUTIVES OF SCIENTOLOGY ORGANIZATIONS.

The task of an executive is to put hats *on* people. Therefore, he should be very careful not to violate hats by introducing *emergency* programs which pull

753

off hats or by "temporarily" pulling people off post to do jobs not covered by their hats. If he has such jobs not covered by hats, he should make provisions for their accomplishment in existing hats or create new hats.

Executives should not write critical or confusing despatches to terminals having to do with their performance of duty.

Such matters as conduct or rearrangement of post should be taken up with the terminal directly. The only writing is done after the fact of arrangements.

Wide-open comm lines such as we have cannot tolerate critical, confusing or distempered despatches. There is no reason here to learn by experience what is already known—entheta on free comm lines can disturb an organization's comm system beyond belief. This applies equally to despatches from terminals to executives.

In the case of an executive in one part of the world having difficulty with the conduct of a terminal in another part of the world, do not despatch the terminal. Despatch instead the executive in that part of the world closest to the terminal—explain the situation to that executive and have him take it up personally with the terminal. Even in a local operation, if you cannot interview the terminal in question, do not send a critical despatch to him. Have the nearest executive to the terminal take it up with that terminal. No despatch goes directly to such a distant terminal.

(THE ABOVE IS FACT; THE FOLLOWING IS MY OPINION AND MAY BE CONSIDERED CONTROVERSIAL:)

Anyone will discover, in actually dealing with people, that these factors dominate:

1. People are willing to do their best and will until hammered about it.

2. Most causes for complaint are based not on misconduct but on misunderstanding.

3. Only personal contact can restore understanding.

4. Written criticism or anger is rarely repaired by more writing. A breach opened by writing is usually susceptible to being healed only by personal contact. The moral is, therefore, don't open the breach with a distempered despatch.

5. Don't let a detected error drift. Take it up and correct it when found.

6. Don't accumulate "bad marks" against a terminal before acting. Forget old "bad marks" when they have been corrected.

7. A terminal has his side of the story. As the person on the job he has more valid data than the executive. Listen and question before you decide you're outraged.

8. The only capital an executive has is the *willingness* TO WORK. Preserve it. No person can be driven to labor—as every slave society has

found out. They always lose. When a man is whipped, that work he then does still stems from his willingness alone. Anger made it smaller.

Terminals that are confused and have gone wrong are patched up just as an auditor patches up an ARC break. The terminal is also conscious of his own overt acts and thoughts.

The only persons an executive cannot handle are those who continually say or dramatize: "It can't be done." These persons are already spoiled by bad 8-C in life. No matter if the person is the attorney or the accountant or the head sweeper, if his response to all solutions offered is "It can't be done" (either stated or acted out), the executive has only two answers: order him to intensive intensives or fire him. Short of this action, the executive has no other course to take. Threats, penalties, scoldings, all accomplish nothing.

We have then three classes of possible personnel:

1. The willing,

2. The defiant negative,

3. The wholly shiftless.

To handle these we have three classes of action only and none in between. (An authentic case of white is white and black is black.)

Class One (above): Handle them as outlined here with understanding, intelligence, helpfulness, courage and compassion.

Class Two (above): Process only or fire.

Class Three (above): Process only or fire.

Classes two and three are nonemployable. Why burden the staff or economics of the organization with them?

The Willing include the overbearing, the meek, the swift, the slow, the efficient, the worried. Threats and punishing regulations do not help them—only hurt the innocent with the guilty. Tight scheduling, insistence, reason, crispness, and ARC help them.

The Unwilling are bait only for auditors or the unemployment bureau. Leave a post vacant rather than hire them. You'll wish you had.

Don't confuse a clash of personalities, independence and lack of subservience with unwillingness to do. The military does this and look at it! If you only want a staff that won't talk back, join the army—they punish people for communicating or deserting. Some very high-class bastards can do some high-class jobs.

The Unwilling only do or say "can't" no matter what solution or task is offered. Usually they don't talk. Sometimes they are models of meekness. But like a hunting dog that won't kill chickens, they are no good to you. If they're out of your organization or department, you have only the willing left—so why look further in executing than being decent. The man who doesn't appreciate it isn't with you anyway. So that leaves only one code of conduct for an executive to follow, the one outlined here. His personnel hat excludes the Mr. No and Miss Can't and Master Flop. An executive needs as much discipline and anger as he lets the Unwilling in. The first principle of an executive is to accomplish the goals of the organization and department. He must employ the Willing and maintain ARC. And remember that there's an R in it.

A quarter of a century of leadership in this life has taught me that the only underprivileged posts there are, are posts of leadership. As one rises on the scale of authority his flaws magnify and so does his power to hurt and destroy. It would take an archangel to be a perfect executive. Despite the trying nature of an executive post, it yet must be filled—and filled with understanding, intelligence, helpfulness, courage and compassion. When a lack of these enter upon an organization's comm lines, the organization sickens and is gone—just as our world at large is doing.

Our staff are willing. I believe in them and trust them. Nobody could ever do the job we're all doing—but we're doing it.

A hundred thousand years of future are looking at us—we can only measure up by doing our jobs as best we can today—with understanding, intelligence, helpfulness, courage and compassion—to the greatest good of the greatest number of dynamics. It is a large order—but the first to fill it must be our executives.

HOW TO ISSUE INSTRUCTIONS TO PERSONNEL

1. Have a definite clear-cut and correct estimate of the situation.

2. Make a precise, properly communicative statement in writing of exactly what you want done.

3. Reissue 2.

4. Reissue 2.

5. Reissue 2.

There are no other steps.

Every time you issue a direct, precise and orderly order you may generate a confusion. It runs out as the order is repeated over and over. The "reasons why" "the order is hard to duplicate" is the runoff of a confusion. Don't Q-and-A with the confusion. Just issue the order again while maintaining good ARC.

L. RON HUBBARD
Founder

HCO POLICY LETTER OF 5 OCTOBER 1958

All Executive Hats
Applicable to London
and Washington

Department Heads and Executives

Personnel

HOW TO FILL JOBS

Personnel for any department is the responsibility of the department head subject to final approval by myself.

The procurement, hiring and dismissal of personnel is the responsibility of the department head subject to my approval and the regulations of the board.

The advertising for personnel is the responsibility of the department head but requires a purchase order for placing an ad in a paper. Ads placed on the organization's public bulletin board for personnel can be very effective. Keeping your need of personnel a secret is a good way not to get a job done. Keeping such a secret has proven *very* effective in the past. Any and all personnel shortages stem from failure to post and advertise.

The pages of *Certainty* and *Ability* are open now to small ads for technical and administrative personnel if such ads are written and signed by a department head. *Ability* and *Certainty* editors do not write the ads for you. They only approve them, dress them up and see that they're in. (These magazines are now open for classified ads in general at $1.00 or 10 cents per line per issue.)

PERSONNEL DEPARTMENT

A personnel department either for an organization or a department is an unthinkable nonsense.

An executive, department head or foreman has to have personnel with whom he can work. Who's to judge that but himself? His personnel must know their jobs depend on the person closest to them on the job. A personnel department or section as such is a dramatization of an executive's inability to face people or handle them. So what is an executive but a people-facer? So if he has to have a personnel department he's confessed already.

REPORTS RE PERSONNEL

In hiring or firing you only have to inform two terminals—first you have to tell accounting *at once* on a proper form. If you don't your people don't get on and off the payroll—and when they complain about no pay, accounting has orders to tell them "It's your department head's fault. He never told us." Embarrassing, eh? I made sure it would be to keep you alert to reporting to accounting. The second person you tell is myself or my office. It's a good idea to give me an idea

757

of who you're going to hire and fire. I may know more about the record than you do. Even dead I'd have a better memory than most personnel offices. When you tell me, HCO Secretary gets told and you get your personnel's name up in lights on the org board. And you know—the post isn't officially filled until it's on the org board—not officially vacant, either. No info to accounting = no pay. No info to me = no official standing for employee. You, the department head, have been arranged to be damned in both cases when failure occurs.

Staff personnel has no real reality on whom they work for except the department head and me—and in London they sometimes fail to know I'm their chief administrator (they don't see the floods of administration between department heads and me, they only see from them to department head).

PAY INCREASES

BIG BUSINESS—that squirming worm under the government's thumb—encourages personnel by raising pay regularly. People get addicted to this. They take no responsibility for their pay beyond working at their jobs. This has been changed in the world of Scientology. We don't like to raise units under the guise of raising pay. There are certain standard units being paid. The ratings are roughly: Part Time, Temporary, Permanent Staff, Department Head, Secretary. They should all get a standard unit. Under proportionate pay, raising it is up to staff since the more and better they work the more money they get. I don't like the unreality of patting people on the head with pay raises and neither will you when you understand it. I'd rather they made their extra pence, pounds and greenbacks by making it themselves right on the job—namely, raising units. Even after a year staff no savvy this well. It's too ingrained this no-responsibility for income. And it's a slave mechanism. I'll succeed in giving them some freedom yet!

So don't expect to stand in good with people by raising their pay. It's an old moth-eaten dodge and I remove the temptation. Leadership is required of you as an executive. The way to be popular is by doing your job well and raising the general income thereby. As soon as things are smoother there'll be an award pool for Clears, students graduated and projects completed.

REMOVALS FROM POST

There are two ways of removing people from post—one is drown him in an apathy of realizing he can't ever do the work; the other is to send him critical notes only and give him no real attention.

I judge a department head by (1) how much work gets done and (2) how steadily his personnel stay on.

You can keep a physically working staff member on more easily than you can keep on an executive, by the way. Executives have a higher personal earning potential and are more ambitious. This (1) gets them into more trouble oftener and (2) causes them to chase rainbows. It's a matter of handling MEST. This stuff MEST keeps a staff terminal sane and a lack of handling it makes an executive jumpy and gives him ulcers. An executive who doesn't handle even people goes to Hades much faster. The more people an executive sees and handles, the less likely he is to fly off the job. The less people and MEST an executive faces and handles, the meaner he gets. Show me a department head who stays desk-bound and I will show you (1) an unhappy staff under him, (2) an executive that's really off post and (3) one that won't be in that post long whether he's fired or not. They blow themselves off by not participating in their department's activities.

PERSONNEL CONSTANCY

A department head must *never* begin a practice of yanking people off post to do things that aren't hat.

This is the commonest executive failing. To tear people away from work to do a nonhat emergency. The personnel to whom this happens get a shotgun complex about such an executive. It's the executive who puts confusion into the department. If such emergencies rise, then the executive had a hat missing somewhere. Emergency = that activity that wasn't planned. A nonplanned department is then a total emergency.

A personnel can cope with anything if it's *his hat*. Suddenness doesn't make an emergency. Misrouting and bad assignment of hats do.

So don't grab the janitor and have him file papers and an Instructor and have him fill inkwells if you want people to stay around.

Yanking people off post makes them feel insecure. They get the idea they're partly fired and they quit, strange as it seems.

You can high-pressure like mad, work staff until 3:00 A.M. daily and they'll stick with you *so long as they're doing the job they agreed to do* in the organization. Keep yanking them off post and you soon yank them off the job. This doesn't mean you shouldn't take their attention off one part of their hat to put it on another part. They don't think badly about that.

Constancy on post is developed by:

1. A fair and helpful attitude by a department head;

2. Attention to and adequate comment on the work done;

3. Industry and good planning by the department head;

4. Maintaining a high unit level;

5. Playing no favorites;

6. Developing no special cliques;

7. Demanding good high work standards;

8. Department head sincerity of purpose;

9. No entheta on despatch lines to personnel;

759

10. Consulting personnel about their jobs;

11. Watching to see that no overburden develops (overburden is a technical term here in management which means "Loading so much and so many jobs on a personnel that the personnel can never see any wins in it");

12. Being decisive. If you say something, first be sure you're right. Then when you've ordered it make sure it happens and don't forget it or let it slide. You've just plain had it if you're wrong;

13. Bawl people out in private, not before their fellows. Bawl them out personally and *never* through a comm line;

14. Fire people personally, not by a red slip. And remember, you can't fire directly, you have to first warn, then suspend, then fire—and on Permanent Staff personnel it all has to be passed upon by the Advisory Committee, or Advisory Council, with the person there in person in order to fire;

15. Take only legal actions against or for staff;

16. Criticize your fellow department heads or executives all you want to to your department but don't criticize your superiors or your own staff one to another, it's fatal;

17. Be responsible for the morale of your department or organization;

18. Don't have to be liked. Just be capable of generating good ARC and good compliance;

19. Treat your personnel with dignity; and

20. Listen when your people want to talk to you about something.

If you do all these fairly well, you'll really make it. You only have to be 51% right all the time to win. Just make sure the 49% loses don't include anything important.

Personnel and their capacity for work on their exact jobs is the basic key to income and success. BIGIDEAS and SWEEPINGCHANGES usually cost you money. You're not there to make a total effect on God or somebody. You, an executive, are there to get a job done and seeing to it that the jobs done amount to something.

One poor program well executed brings more success than fifty fine ones all flubbed. A department head has to get plenty of ideas just to keep rolling. He has to plan like anything to get ahead.

The key to getting a job done is hard work yourself and exact, good work by your people.

Confronting the society at large and totally is tough—but we can win—IF we are good executives and use our personnel—and IF we are good personnel. Given that and even a vague road map and we'll arrive.

Bad executing wrecks an organization faster than hail, snow, sleet or the medicos.

A good executive *serves* more than the lowest staff member. Rank has its privileges. Rank has its responsibilities. RHIR, RHIP as Nelson used to say. The main responsibility is to handle personnel. The main privilege is to serve.

PERSONNEL COMM LINES

Remember that personnel has the right to speak as loudly as they wish. Don't stop their comms to higher up ever. People above you have judgment. Speaking up is not grounds for dismissal ever and if an Advisory Committee or Advisory Council has this as grounds, they cannot use it.

Personnel can always write or talk to me with or without permission.

PROPERTY AND TOOLS OF THE TRADE

The department head and no other is responsible for providing his personnel with materials of their job whatever these may be. The department head does this through the regular procurement channels.

A department head does not delegate this. He sees what is needed and orders it through channels. His personnel can inform him by despatch and he orders it. He makes sure it arrives and gets placed in the right places.

The MEST in a department is the responsibility of a department head. If it gets lost, misused or broken (usually by improper use) the department head is charged up with it. He is subject to inventory.

LEAVES AND SICK LEAVE

The department head arranges and grants with the secretary's approval all leaves of absence.

The department head allows sick leave, covers the post and reports it. All matters of leave and sick leave are covered in board minutes and a department head abides by these.

ADDITIONAL PERSONNEL

If you need more personnel, make up a plan of your department the way you want it and send it to me via the unit's secretary with an exact statement as to how many more are required to carry on routine work or special projects. An HGC can add staff auditors forever so long as they compare 1 for 1 with pcs. But not clerks. Or any other organization function. It comes to me because it may need a new staff mandate to include the units and either myself or my Deputy Staff Chairman will have to hold a meeting on it.

In asking for more staff don't feel reticent. The most violent thing you can get back is, "No," and you may get a full or partial "Yes."

A common department head failing is to understaff a unit. That way he or she loses staff by overburden. Don't make this error. Be real about how many hands you need but:

TAKING IN LAUNDRY

Civilizations are said to exist by taking in their own wash. We now and then do this in a Scientology organization.

Some reports are necessary to keep management advised so they can act fast if the ship starts to go down. But too many reports, too much paper, too many forms, bring about a condition where all the staff does is take care of the staff-made work. Once in London we fired several typists from the outside and suddenly got twice as much work done. These outsiders were doing so many wrong things with such a fuss that existing Scientology staff couldn't work. This is an example of taking in our own laundry. Trying to keep inferior personnel straight ate up all our time.

Therefore, we have a saying—better to leave a post unfilled than to fill it with bad personnel. The bad personnel will devour more time and make more mess than good personnel can clean up. But this doesn't say not to hire good personnel in adequate numbers. Just keep trying.

If you think you have an area or a report in your department that is a washing machine, take it up with people. Maybe you can cut it down or out. And on the other hand, maybe it had a purpose to another department you weren't aware of at all and it was necessary.

To speed a comm line remove MEST from it—*to a certain point*. It's that point you're trying to find. Less MEST = no comm, more MEST = poor comm. What's the optimum?

To find laundry, draw a chart tracing every comm particle (body or whatever) from its point of entrance to its point of departure from your department. You'll find dead ends and laundry in an amazing number of cases.

Duplication of effort is a great laundry maker. You may think you need to do something that's already being done elsewhere that you didn't know about. Such things as addressing, purchasing, mailing *must* be centralized functions if we're to keep out laundry and stay solvent. Making the Academy train and not process and the HGC process and not train is an example of cleaning out the laundry.

The income of an organization depends on its outflow. The outflow of the Registrar is the usual governing factor in the past. If this one person's outflow regulated income, then what were all those clerks doing??? Ah, you might well ask about laundry in such a case!

Clean, orderly lines and flow means you've got to have clean, orderly personnel *on post* and functioning right. That's your job!

There's one thing you can be sure about. The old man is not writing from any ivory tower when he talks about handling people. I want these organizations to work, to progress, to succeed. They've got to! We are growing on every continent. We're growing up, too. We are winning. And every win is achieved by personnel well organized and led. That leadership has no more mystic quality than intelligence, good observation and the above points. If we can win this far with so few, what won't happen if we really snap into it?

This is our chance to win. Let's take it.

L. RON HUBBARD
Founder

HUBBARD COMMUNICATIONS OFFICE
Saint Hill Manor, East Grinstead, Sussex

HCO POLICY LETTER OF 12 SEPTEMBER 1959

Remimeo

PROGRAMING

(Originally written as an HCOB on 12 Sept. 59.
Issued as an HCO PL on 23 Oct. 69.)

(Refer also to HCO PL 4 Dec. 66, AKH Series 9,
EXPANSION, THEORY OF POLICY, and HCO PL
24 Dec. 66 II, AKH Series 10, HOW TO PROGRAM
AN ORG—SAINT HILL PROGRAMS.)

Dianetics and Scientology have never suffered from lack of programs. There have always been programs. And there will always be better programs and, maybe for dissemination purposes, the PERFECT program.

But what happens to all these programs?

Alas, I found out the facts of this some years ago, and out of it came the organizational pattern which is working so splendidly in Central Orgs. But the facts that I found out had all to do with execution of programs.

We get a wonderful idea. It's a slayer. It will tear the tops right off the skyscrapers and send them in for a book. And months later we wonder what happened to this marvelous program.

Well, I'll tell you what happened. Nobody did it.

That's the swan song of most every program that gets thought up. It was great, but nobody did it. . . .

And before you think I am being critical of all the staffs everywhere or that we're ever critical of all the staffs, I'll give you the rest of my findings on this subject.

Programs didn't get done because everybody was so overloaded with what they were already doing that they didn't have a chance to start the new program no matter how good it was. Programs were already in the run. Many of these were so fundamental—such as sale of books or answering letters to incoming preclears and students—that nobody could start on the new program. And as a result the new program didn't get started no matter how marvelous it seemed to be.

The reason executives used to keep pulling people off post all the time was this thing programing. The executive had, he thought, a better idea or was trying to carry out an old idea. And to get it going he would draft the whole staff to do it and the basic programs would go begging.

Do you know that nearly every function of a Central Org was at one time a brand-new wonderful program? Well, it was. And this gradually sifting out of activities brought us to a rather final form with one more step to go and that step is programs, a Department of Programs. A department which can carry through new or stunt programs without bringing the whole place in ruins by tearing everybody off their standard programs.

Programing is important enough to pay a lot of attention to. And there is a lot of gen about it. And the gen all adds up to no matter how many programs you have, each one consists of certain parts. And if you don't assemble those parts and run the program in an orderly fashion, then it just won't spark off. These are some of the principles about programs. And you had better have them because your new HAS Co-audit Course is a program and has to be done like a successful program. And your preclears are a program and have to be done like a program. If you don't know these facts of life, here they are:

MAXIM ONE: Any idea no matter if badly executed is better than no idea at all.

MAXIM TWO: A program to be effective must be executed.

MAXIM THREE: A program put into action requires guidance.

MAXIM FOUR: A program running without guidance will fail and is better left undone. If you haven't got the time to guide it, don't do it; put more steam behind existing programs because it will flop.

MAXIM FIVE: Any program requires some finance. Get the finance into sight before you start to fire, or have a very solid guarantee that the program will produce finance before you execute it.

MAXIM SIX: A program requires attention from somebody. An untended program that is everybody's child will become a juvenile delinquent.

MAXIM SEVEN: The best program is the one that will reach the greatest number of dynamics and will do the greatest good on the greatest number of dynamics. And that, my people who want to become victims by going broke, includes dynamic one as well as dynamic four.

MAXIM EIGHT: Programs must support themselves financially.

MAXIM NINE: Programs must ACCUMULATE interest and bring in other assistance by the virtue of the program interest alone or they will never grow.

MAXIM TEN: A program is a bad program if it detracts from programs which are already proving successful or distracts staff people or associates from work they are already doing that is adding up to successful execution of other programs.

MAXIM ELEVEN: Never spend more on a program than the income from one person signing up can repay.

MAXIM TWELVE: Never permit a new program to inhibit the success of a routine one or injure its income.

Let us now take a squint at this all in one piece. *Wrong example:* We decide to run an ad in the Hatmakers' Weekly to attract people into the PE Course. We place the ad. We forget the time this special course is to start. We have nobody there to

765

answer the phone on inquiries as to the course. We have nobody there to greet the people and make them feel at home when they arrive. We have nobody to instruct the course. We get a bill for monies three weeks later that we can't pay.

Right example: We decide to hit the hatmaker trade as a source of PE. We rule out seven other programs in favor of this one. We have a staff meeting on it and gen everybody in on the existence of this program. We see that we have made a lot of money from co-audit enrollments and we earmark this to pay for the advert, for the salary of the person who will run the program. We appoint a specific person to administer this program. When the advert has been placed and appears, our person appointed to it goes onto it full time. Reception is genned again to send all hatmaker calls to this person and to refer to this person all hatmaker bodies. All persons who may also be acting as Reception are genned with this data. The person appointed doesn't sit back to wait for the business to come in. This person reaches for hatmakers with letters and phone calls. This same person that has been contacted by the hatmakers is then on deck the zero-hour evening to greet them all and get them into their seats and to make sure the instructor is there and to instruct it himself if no instructor appears. If the program is sweepingly successful in terms of new enrollees, then we make sure we leave the person appointed for it in the first place right on duty pushing hatmakers into the PE. And we have a program. And it was successful. And we got somewhere.

A pitiful wrong example of the above was when I was running the first American College PE as the experimental setup some years ago. We started to get in longshoremen by the squad. And they brought in other longshoremen. The person in charge thought longshoremen were low cast and tried to get intellectuals in instead, thus switching off the program. You never saw a program dwindle quite so fast as the longshoremen did. The correct action would have been to notice that longshoremen were responding heavily and to put somebody maybe even out of their ranks onto the payroll to pressure away at longshoremen. A million-pound program was let go up in a puff of nowhere.

A wonderfully right example is the Director of Processing—staff auditor setup of a Central Organization. That was once just a program. It prospered. It's still with us. Every field auditor looks at it with envy and snarls and tries to copy it. But he doesn't program. He is doing everything else in the shop. He can't program a special clinic drill with his attention everywhere at once. It's now thoroughly against the law in a Central Organization to let a Director of Processing take preclears. That's how far it goes. And we get wonderful results and all is well and the only squawks you hear about HGCs are from pure green-eyed jealousy or maybe an occasional real goof that the Central Organization jumped on days before anybody else did.

Programing requires execution. It requires carry-through. It requires judgment enough to know a good program and carry it on and on and to recognize a bad one and drop it like hot bricks.

There's nothing wrong with the will to do amongst Scientologists. Now let's see if we can't up dissemination by adherence to good, steady programing that wins.

L. RON HUBBARD
Founder

HUBBARD COMMUNICATIONS OFFICE
Saint Hill Manor, East Grinstead, Sussex

HCO POLICY LETTER OF 18 OCTOBER 1959

Assoc Secs
HCO Secs

PUTTING NEW PERSONNEL ON THE JOB AND
TAKING OVER WHEN PEOPLE QUIT OR ARE TRANSFERRED

The first action, without deviation, in placing a person newly on post is to find *a specific and unalterable place* for them to sit and where they can store their mest and where they aren't in another person's road.

The second action is *a basket* (one per person) in the *Message Center*.

The third action is a *three basket stack* for *"In," "Pending,"* and *"Out."* (Use pasteboard boxes until somebody buys new baskets.)

The fourth action is providing the new person with *a hat* (no matter how brief until a new one is written up).

The fifth action is *briefing* by the *Assoc Sec*.

The sixth action is check-over by the HCO Sec on what new person should know as a *staff member* (color flash, etc.).

The seventh action is to get *his pay* straight *with Accounts*.

Further actions are obvious, and most important of these is to get the new person to do some specific work.

Most of these actions are prepared *before* the person enters the org—the day before at the latest.

Putting a new person in order is to have a new staff member. To neglect him is to invite a disorderly future for him or her.

These apply to changes in post as well as new people on post.

If a new person hasn't gripped it in a week, is still begging for help from all, he's a dev-t merchant. Unload. He won't be any better in ten weeks and the org will be a lot worse. Such a person can't be at cause over the job and will only destroy the post (as witness the way you have to do his work as well as your own—dead post). Don't ever fill a post because it's empty. Fill it only to get more work done. If more work isn't done, you are ten times worse off having it filled with a dev-t merchant than having it empty. You have to have three staff members extra for every dev-t merchant you have on staff. Why? Because the coin has "efficient" on one side and "destructive" on the other—and it never stands on edge. There are no cases on staff—ever. Cases exist only in sessions.

REMOVAL OF PERSON FROM POST

When a person is removed from a post, the Assoc Sec in a Central Org or the HCO Sec in an HCO must capture all mest and papers, and move the removed person's despatches back onto the lines, and the HCO Sec must recapture the hat.

Posts are not turned over from Leaving A to Arriving B without the Assoc Sec and HCO Sec pitching in on it. It's the Assoc Sec who dusts the removed person off and puts the new person on. Don't leave it up to the old person to break in the new person exclusively.

A change of post always means a review of post.

If Leaving A were to be the only person to groove in Arriving B, the whole org would begin to slide into strange new patterns.

So capture a post being vacated even if the new arrival was coached for a week or two by the departing person. At the moment of departure the Assoc Sec grabs the post, the mest, the work; the HCO Sec grabs the pending basket, the files, the hat. Everything is put in order by these two. *Then* the new person is formally grooved in by the Assoc Sec and the HCO Sec. *These* present the new person with his post, his instructions, his work, his hats.

It need only take a few minutes. But it makes havoc when it's not done.

Here's when you find all the secretly closeted skeletons, the long-lost despatches, the reason why Zilch never wrote again. So don't deny yourself the gen available in a post transfer and don't deny a new person the security of getting his hat from the most important people in the place.

Things work better this way.

CLAY TABLE ADMINISTRATION PROCESSING

To put a person on post who already is, use the steps of Clay Table Clearing in their staff co-auditing but limit the process to the post, other jobs they've had, etc.

Then have the staff member mock up in clay the functions and lines of the post and its relation to the org, SH and field, and wow!

L. RON HUBBARD
Founder

HUBBARD COMMUNICATIONS OFFICE
Saint Hill Manor, East Grinstead, Sussex

HCO POLICY LETTER OF 26 FEBRUARY 1961
Issue II

CenOCon

QUALIFICATION OF EXECUTIVES

(See HCO PLs on executives and personnel, 13 Feb. 61,
PERMANENT STAFF REQUIREMENT CHANGES
and 17 Feb. 61, STAFF POST QUALIFICATIONS)

I will qualify and issue a qualification certificate to any staff personnel who meets executive requirements regardless of whether they occupy an executive post or not.

This means that an Executive Qualification Certificate for a Central Organization executive post does not demand or command that the holder occupy the post or receive executive units.

A person who does not actually hold an executive post but who wishes to receive an Executive Qualification Certificate must pass all requirements for that executive post or for an executive and must receive as well a high mark on a hat check of that post.

Having once occupied such a post in the organization does not automatically qualify a person but will be taken into account.

Such persons seeking an Executive Qualification Certificate should be handled exactly as an executive is handled in their application.

Having extra qualified persons on staff for all executive posts means faster expansion and quicker filling of vacated posts with immediate executive units rather than filling posts on a temporary basis with the consequent long wait for units.

L. RON HUBBARD
Founder

HUBBARD COMMUNICATIONS OFFICE
Saint Hill Manor, East Grinstead, Sussex

HCO POLICY LETTER OF 8 MARCH 1965

Gen. Non-Remimeo
Board Members
Asst Board Members
Divisions 1, 2, 3

DIVISIONS 1, 2, 3

BOARD DECISIONS

DATA EVALUATION
RAW DATA

JUDGING A SITUATION
SELECTION OF KEY PERSONNEL

An exercise: Think of the most entheta personnel you have ever had in an org. Recall his criticisms of his superiors and incompetence.

Now think of his equivalent in charge of every org we have.

Ugh.

That would be the result of promoting those who got in the most rumors and demoting those who got talked about.

That would happen if RUMOR were used as the basis of personnel selection.

If ANY opinion at all enters the mechanism of promotion or demotion, the above will happen to some extent.

To promote the deserving and demote the foolish or vicious, one may *only* employ statistics of production or action or success or lack of them to decide.

L. RON HUBBARD
Founder

Sthil Staff Only

DATA FOR ALL STAFF MEMBERS

REORGANIZATION BOARD

An organization board is posted in the Communications Office.

All personnel will be required to take an examination showing they have studied it and know it within ten days.

STAFF MEETINGS

It is intended by the Organization Secretary to convene weekly staff meetings of all Saint Hill staff.

WORK POLICY

In the organization, security of employment depends entirely upon work accomplished.

Assigned tasks done or not done in reasonable time, rising or falling income in departments, increases or decreases in output regulate the opinion of management of the individual staff member.

The policy of altering staff in a nonfunctioning unit or department until it does function is now followed. The person, unit or department will be warned of the failure and if the expected result is not achieved, the unit or department's personnel will be changed. This will be a consistent policy. No effort will be made to scold or harass or even closely supervise anything but results.

The society regards an organization only in terms of results. Therefore an organization must regard its staff members only in terms of results. So many letters out, so much earth hauled, so many trees planted, so much money in, so many students enrolled, floors clean, walls washed, shelves built—results. Only results.

Results alone are expected of management by the world so management expects them of personnel and will supervise accordingly.

Your job will be safer if you work hard at it for two reasons: (1) because the company will last longer and fare better and (2) because failure to produce results and accomplish work is now the sole criteria of continued employment. Nobody will be around to police the tea breaks. But how many there have been is easily measured by the work counted up at the week's end. There are many good workers present and we appreciate them. People who are not and who slack will shortly not be here. This is the fundamental management policy at Saint Hill.

ORDERS

If you know the organization board you will know who can give you orders and who can't.

Only superiors in the exact department you are listed in, the Organization Secretary or myself can give you orders to do this or do that.

You *must not* take orders from anybody and everybody. Projects and major actions are cleared with your department head and the Organization Secretary.

You *must not* move equipment around or furniture or type things or paint things just because somebody who looks important tells you to.

You are held directly responsible by the Organization Secretary and myself for your exact duties. If you don't do those we will have a very poor opinion of it. If you are doing things that aren't your job it will appear from inspections that you are not doing your own job. And that's what you're supposed to do. There is plenty to do right on your own job. If you don't do your job but somebody else's, we won't be talking to any superior about it. We'll be talking to you.

So don't waste time or materials or labor on things somebody tells you to do but which aren't your job or which haven't been cleared with the Organization Secretary because they keep you from getting things done you're supposed to do.

WEEKLY SURVEYS

There is a weekly survey of quarters and accomplishment of every post.

Things you do well are known and held to your credit. The time you spend not working or doing unauthorized things are also known and eventually rebound.

There is a record of all instructions you are given and a checkup to see that they are followed.

EQUIPMENT

You have the use of certain equipment and quarters of mine with which you have been trusted. Take good care of them. Loss or damage may be charged up to you and deducted.

PURCHASE ORDERS

If you need anything it must be requested on a purchase order. No bills may be run up which are not so authorized.

Nobody may make contracts or purchases in my name without written authority in the form of a purchase order from the Organization Secretary or myself.

If you don't really need it, don't request to buy it.

KNOW YOUR JOB

Know your job and do it well and economically and you will be quite secure here.

L. RON HUBBARD
Founder

Remimeo
All Exec Hats

ALL DIVISIONS

LINES AND TERMINALS
ROUTING

The most important things in an organization are its lines and terminals. Without these IN, IN AN EXACT KNOWN PATTERN the organization cannot function at all.

An executive putting in new lines and posts or making changes in old lines or terminals REQUIRES CLEARANCE FROM THE OFFICE OF LRH before the order can take effect.

Anyone following such an order, to alter lines and terminals in the org which are already established by policy, who does not file a Job Endangerment Ethics Report (a statement that his or her job is being endangered by the illegal order of a senior) must share any penalty for such alteration.

People who haven't a clue about the org pattern throw it into chaos by altering the established pattern. Then the org won't work and goes broke quickly.

Therefore, the most serious threat to the stability of an org is shifting lines with no understanding of what is supposed to happen.

The lines and terminals (hats) outlined in policy are based on long, hard experience. When they short-circuit, the org ceases to function as an org and becomes a mad scramble.

When despatch and body routing charts laid down by policy are carefully followed, the org will function. When they are not, it won't.

A serious fault in any executive or staff member is unawareness of the *coordinated* functions of terminals, or complete unawareness of other org hats and functions.

A D of T trying to wear an Ethics hat, a Qual Sec shifting his internal lines, a Registrar who seeks to assign the hours of auditing, would be enough in any large org to throw it into a jumble where nothing works or flows.

There *is* more to an org than one person wearing all hats plus another person wearing all hats, etc. Such an org just won't prosper.

The hardest job any top executive has is teaching the staff the lines and terminals and getting them followed. That is because green staff is unaware of the org itself, or its flow lines.

A lot of the time, when one sees a declining statistic, it is only that certain lines are out or being misrouted.

The lines *will* flow if they are all in and people wear their hats. If the body and despatch lines flow, the org will prosper. If they are disarrayed, they won't flow and won't prosper.

No executive or staff member has any right to establish or alter terminals and lines without express written permission from the Office of LRH.

Believe it or not there will be people around in orgs who have no faintest concept of its pattern—or the existence of an org. And these will be the first to attempt large changes. And these are the first you should send to the Staff Training Officer to get checked out on their posts.

It is an ethics offense to issue orders altering lines without clearance from the Office of LRH.

L. RON HUBBARD
Founder

HCO POLICY LETTER OF 19 JULY 1965
Issue I

Remimeo

ALL DIVISIONS

POLICY, HOW TO HANDLE PEOPLE WHO QUOTE POLICY TO SHOW YOU THEY CAN'T FOLLOW IT

Some orgs will find that certain personnel will use policy to stop action.

When these just don't want to do their job, although it's easily understood in policy letters, they tell you certain policies are wrong or can't be followed.

The best and only effective way to handle this is to say:

"Since you are an expert on policy, permit me to ask you a few questions." Take up a PL applying to their post and start doing a hat check on it.

Since such a person is using policy to stop action and show policy wrong, a rebuttal such as the above will adequately discourage the practice.

If people won't work, they throw out lines and find ways to use policy to discuss it.

Policy is valuable.

But ALL policy exists solely to get the job done and establish points of agreement that permit flows of traffic.

When traffic doesn't flow and somebody says, "Policy so and so prevents it," then hat check at once and you'll be amazed to find they don't even know enough of it to disagree with it.

Disagreement with policy is disagreement with getting the job done. And is always accompanied by total lack of data on the policy being quoted.

It's a sure cure.

L. RON HUBBARD
Founder

773

HUBBARD COMMUNICATIONS OFFICE
Saint Hill Manor, East Grinstead, Sussex

HCO POLICY LETTER OF 16 SEPTEMBER 1965

Remimeo
Div Secs

WEEKLY SECRETARIAL PERSONNEL REPORT

Each divisional secretary is fully responsible for the personnel in their division.

Therefore, the secretary of each division shall daily check upon the presence of his personnel. These checks are done:

1. At the start of the daytime or evening working hours.

2. At the midpoint of the daytime or evening working hours.

3. At the end of the daytime or evening working hours.

The report form is marked in the appropriate day's square, according to the code given, against each person working in a division as listed in a column by the divisional secretary.

This report replaces the LRH Daily Report System and is to be handed in with the divisional Advisory Committee's reports at the required time for review by the Advisory Council.

After the Advisory Council has reviewed these reports, they are routed to the Personnel Control Officer in Dept 1 to compare with payroll records with his own personnel spot checks.

Please note that the report is attested to by the divisional secretary of the Day org for his personnel or by the Foundation divisional secretary for his personnel.

L. RON HUBBARD
Founder

WEEKLY SECRETARIAL PERSONNEL REPORT

TO: ADVISORY COUNCIL WITH DIVISIONAL AD COMM REPORT

THEN TO: PERSONNEL CONTROL OFFICER TO COMPARE WITH PAYROLL RECORDS.

X = ON POST   S = START OF WORKING HOURS
O = NOT ON POST   M = MID POINT OF WORKING HOURS
L = LATE   E = END OF WORKING HOURS
LE = LEFT EARLY

DIVISION _____ WEEK ENDING _____

STAFF MEMBER	THURS			FRIDAY			WEEKEND			MONDAY			TUESDAY			WEDNESDAY			THURSDAY	
	E	S	M	E	S	M	E	S	M	E	S	M	E	S	M	E	S	M

ATTESTED BY _____ DIVISIONAL SECRETARY

ATTESTED BY _____ FOUNDATION DIVISIONAL SECRETARY

775

HCO POLICY LETTER OF 7 MARCH 1969

Remimeo

ORGANIZATION

It may be that in studying policies and org boards or trying to get something going, the basic of organization may be missing.

Organization is the subdivision of actions and duties into specialized functions.

One can organize a series of actions to be done by himself or herself. This would consist of seeing what has to be done, doing what one can do first and then the remainder as a feasible series of events, all to accomplish a final completion of a cycle of action which forwards one's assigned or postulated purposes.

A group is organized so as to permit flows and accomplish specialized actions which are completed in themselves and from which small actions or completions the group purpose, assigned or specialized, is forwarded or accomplished.

There is a difference between directing and doing, which some people have trouble separating apart. A person in charge of an activity is sometimes found deficient in organizational understanding and so tries to do all the actions himself. This if done to excess effectively can break up a group and render it useless since all members but one have no function, having been robbed by this one-man monopoly on action.

True, an active and competent person *can* do things better. But he can really never do more than he can do. Whereas a well-organized group, each with specialized functions, coordinated by the in-charge, can accomplish many times the work only one can do.

Because it is *organized* makes a group harder to defeat than the individual.

A competent individual who has been let down too often by groups tends to take it all on himself rather than whip the group into shape and get things organized.

The correct action when faced by urgent necessity arising from incompetence of a group or other causes is to:

1. Handle it,

2. Organize the group to handle such things and do their jobs.

One can get stuck on (1) and, if he or she does, then will have trouble and overwork from there on out. Because he or she omits *also* doing (2).

The major failure of any group is to fail to organize.

Workers of the world may arise, but if they are not quickly organized before or after the fact, they will promptly be put back down!

The major cause of not organizing is just not understanding what is meant by it.

For example, an executive is told he is in charge of seeing that the X project is done. He doesn't know much about it. He has two men who do know. The incorrect action is to try to do the X project himself or issue a lot of unreal orders about it. The correct action is to call up the man who does know, give him the other as an assistant and tell them to get on with it. Then, without interfering, the executive who received the order should get more knowledgeable about the X project so *he* can be sure it is done, while still letting the designated people get on with it.

This comprehension of organization is as simple as this—put somebody on the job and let him get on with it. On a project, make a survey of all the things there are to do, group types of actions into single posts, assign people to them, provide the comm lines, materiel and liaison and let the group get on with it.

Any post, no matter how junior, has to be organized.

Anyone in charge of people has to be able to organize functions and work.

Any executive has to know his target policies and be able to write them up, particularly the primary targets.

Failing that, one gets very little done and is badly overworked. And the rest of the group is wasted.

So, high or low, get a grip on this thing called organization. It's gruesomely simple.

Honest.

L. RON HUBBARD
Founder

HCO POLICY LETTER OF 29 JULY 1969
Issue III

COMPLETION OF CYCLES

(Originally written by LRH as *Apollo* OODs item
of 29 July 69. Issued as an HCO PL on 21 Oct. 80.)

When someone is working on a cycle of action and is not permitted to complete it, an ARC break occurs.

Only the most violent emergency should pull anyone off a cycle of action and he should be returned to it when the emergency is handled.

Pulling people off jobs is done where an I/C doesn't know what jobs are being done.

To completely wreck an area all one has to do is interrupt all cycles begun.

It's a dangerous practice.

L. RON HUBBARD
Founder

Remimeo

STABILITY

It can be said of companies, societies and governments that:

THE BEST GUARANTEE OF STABILITY IS ADMINISTRATIVE SKILL.

In areas where the abilities which add up to administrative skill are missing, the organization or country can expect to fail or be overthrown.

Even such small things as file keeping, accounts records, personnel place-ment, add up to better longevity.

The integrity of personnel is a large factor in administration, and a lack of skills with which to detect and handle false reports and lack of compliance or failed performance of duty can all by itself destroy management and the group.

No matter what the intention of those at the top, no matter how bright or honest they may be, if their administrative lines are clumsy or in any way false, if they are not backed up by skillful, well-taught administrators, they can be nullified. The plans and orders put "on the lines" seldom if ever arrive at the level of the worker in the shop or the man in the street.

The torrents of laws and directives passed by legislators or even boards of directors are ninety percent of them made necessary by earlier failures in getting earlier laws or directives enforced.

Bad administration, lack of know-how, lack of trained clerks and executives, can defeat utterly any plan or program no matter how urgent or beneficial.

The continuance of an organization and its leaders can be said to be entirely dependent upon the skill, training and integrity of those who handle the admin-istrative lines, details and contacts of the group.

L. RON HUBBARD
Founder

HUBBARD COMMUNICATIONS OFFICE
Saint Hill Manor, East Grinstead, Sussex

HCO POLICY LETTER OF 7 OCTOBER 1969

Remimeo

FUNDAMENTALS OF ADMINISTRATION
No. 2

(No. 1 is HCO PL 14 Sept. 69,
THE KEY INGREDIENTS)

(See also HCO PL 28 Feb. 66, DANGER
CONDITION DATA, WHY ORGANI-
ZATIONS STAY SMALL)

An expert on administration, called in to straighten out or develop admin for a company, can ALWAYS be sure of one thing: IT WILL BE JAMMED AT THE TOP.

Thus, he can always do one thing very effectively: HE CAN UNJAM IT AT THE TOP.

Old-time business efficiency experts sometimes knew that the jam was at the top but considered this meant it was necessary to retrain the top man, and this being infeasible and unpopular, went down into the plant to do time-motion studies. As it remained jammed at the top, the firm seldom got more efficient.

Many tales are told about how the top needed retraining, was old-fashioned and hampered things, and almost none of them were true.

All organizations that are surviving at all are driven directly from the top or by a strata of executives immediately below the top and senior to anyone else.

The first action in any attempt to improve an organization is, of course, observation. The first thing to observe is who at or near the top in executive capacity is driving the organization.

Someone at the top or several someones just below the top are overloaded.

This will be the one or several most important log jams or bundles of stopped flows.

A jam or inefficiency can exist on very low strata of an organization without greatly impeding much of anything. But when such a jam occurs high up, it can reduce efficiency, revenue and threaten the whole organization.

The one or more at the top are trying. They are trying hard. Otherwise nothing would be going at all.

To even hint that any retraining is needed at the top is an invalidation. Further, there is no time available there for retraining.

What is wrong and what causes overwork and despair is that the staff-type persons serving the high-level people are not trained or organized to handle the abundance of action.

This is well within the province of an administrative expert to handle. Here he is dealing with secretaries, typists, phone operators and junior executive types who are only too willing to learn how to expedite the action for the high-level key people.

All one needs to tell the key person is that he needs administrative help and that you'll see that he gets it to take the load off.

Then you organize and groove in those who directly serve him.

He operates actually on a 9-div, 27-dept system as a person and as an executive. Those services are fully listed on a standard org board.

The larger the organization being headed, the more numerous must be the service corps that serves the key executive.

If the organization is small or he is a very junior exec, he often has a secretary but really does not have a communicator. If he can't have more than one person, one would convert the secretary to a communicator who is trained to be aware of all the functions involved in a 9-div, 27-dept org board. When his secretary learns all this well, in terms simply of basic duties, the load will come off.

But let us go much bigger. In a million-man organization, the personal staff of the upper exec who carries the load would have to be several dozen people who comprise his personal admin staff only.

All the training the top man would need would come when the rest were organized and trained and would consist only of "This is your personal staff. For these functions (divisional) here is who you call." You give him the personal org board like a new phone card and let him play with it until he learns it in actual use.

The load would come off, the lines would speed up and the result in production or accomplishment would be fantastic.

This personal staff would be trained by the admin expert, not to run the business but simply to handle and expedite all the actions of the top exec.

Overloaded execs who are near the top should also have an organized personal staff, less numerous, but still with the basic org board fully covered.

Training these personal staff members is not hard. They are usually very willing and very amazed that order can exist and that there *is* a way to help.

Unless one has sat in or near a top spot, he might not have any idea of how overloaded these are. Or how this overload can delay or prevent expansion. Where every interview is personal and where every action contains minor confusions, the brilliance and competence of the most well-meaning high executive is drained into minor chaos.

The president of the United States usually ages twenty years for every four in office. They go in looking well, they come out of office a wreck. Look at their pictures before and after. This is the toll of a relatively efficient if poorly organized personal staff.

Therefore, to handle this, a *real,* an efficient, a fully trained personal staff that is groomed to near perfection is vital.

The jammed condition is at the top.

If the top is served by people who fully understand admin (as per Key Ingredients, an org board based on natural laws, instead of whim, precise duties and hats), then the observations and inspections bring in the data, plans go out, get followed up, get executed, the lines fly, the users are satisfied and the load comes off.

The exact adaption of the standard org board has to be worked out on a basis of what the top exec or execs have to handle. But it will contain every division and every department and will be capable of sending out observation or supervision missions and survey users or voters and doing all the other things expected of that executive.

The admin expert will find, with one look at the top execs in almost all companies and countries where this has not been done, that no one man can possibly carry the loads and functions required of his post. Yet in almost all cases the job is somehow being done.

What an admin expert has to do is study and list all the functions—unobtrusively—of that post, and recruit and train a personal 9-division, 27-department-type staff for it, even though it is as few as one or three or as many as hundreds, depending on the organization size.

The result will be magical in its effectiveness throughout the entire organization. Plans become actuality, confusions vanish and the statistics rise.

You can thereafter work out ways to unstop lower executive posts. But you begin and make your biggest increase at the top.

They need help up there.

L. RON HUBBARD
Founder

L. Ron Hubbard
EXECUTIVE DIRECTIVE

LRH ED 89 INT

1 March 1970

TO: HCO ES (Hat)
HCO Area Sec (Hat)
Director of RAP Dept 1 (Hat)
Info all staff

FROM: RON

SUBJECT: **RECRUIT!**

REFERENCE: HCO PL 1 Mar. 70 STAFF APPLICATION FORM
                       LRH ED 49 Int, 9 Dec 69 ORG PROGRAM #1

Two and a half years before the 1968 slump we had a very heavy recruitment program and 2½-year contracts. People on staff got Power if contracted.

Your income is directly proportional to the number of trained auditors and sharp Course Supervisors you have on staff. These determine the number of admin staff you have.

You must go all out to train auditors and supervisors while maintaining income enough to make you solvent.

It simply doesn't matter how many auditors you train for staff. The economics of it will work out. So long as they are contracted you will be all right.

You will find that you lose them to admin and exec posts. The normal route to execs is via the HGC and Academy.

In the past, people usually paid for their courses and then decided to come on staff. However, so long as you can keep your income up, this is not important.

Lots of auditors and auditing is real wealth in an org. Income will follow as it's quite a stunt keeping a lot of HGC auditors busy. (It is *not* done by auditing less than 30 hours a week per auditor as some Tech Services try to do.) Finding pcs for a crowd of HGC auditors auditing 30 hours a week each keeps the Pub Divs and Dissem on its toes.

Fast, sharp Course Supervisors who don't take 4 months to make an HDC or 6 months for an HPA are jewels and greatly help this program.

You need staff. You need trained staff. You need auditors. You need them in the org. You need them out in the field.

So now a lot of ex-staff are in the field and in many areas missions are booming. Orgs that are good get fat on their rough cases and the new auditors they want trained in Scientology as well as people from the public.

So the thing to do is recruit staff and make auditors and Supervisors.

1.   In your public course area you should have a sign inviting org staff member applications, contracted or not.

2.   In your Academy or training area, you should have a recruitment sign.

3.   Staff application forms should also be posted (HCO PL 1 Mar. 70).

Anyone contracting to come on staff must sign a note. If he gets his service and then blows, as some freeloaders have, you present the note to an attorney for collection. Each new service he gets requires as part of it a new note of hand.

When his contract is complete, mark his notes paid and return them.

If he goes to a higher org to be trained for you, it is on a new note and a new 5-year contract that begins when he resumes work in the org. The old 2½-year contract is torn up as completed but the notes stand until the 5-year contract is complete.

As long as you keep 2:1 admin/tech ratio (closer to 1:1) you'll be in clover. The hottest SO Org there is is totally composed of trained auditors, admin/tech is 1:1 and its stats soar. It even has auditors on all its admin posts. If you train hard and fast that's what happens. First you only have auditors in Tech and Qual with nonauditors on admin. But as you train staff and recruit and train you get nearer to auditors on all posts.

POWER

Any VIII or VII can run Power on a contracted staff member but not on the public in outer orgs.

Most orgs have VIIs or VIIIs.

(Be sure they have a new Power HCOB 21 Feb. 70 they can get from their SH Qual Sec before they begin to do Power again.)

DIVISIONAL ACTIONS

If you can get each division humming, you will have lots to cover costs of such extensive recruitment and training.

KEEP IT UP

Don't slack off again in recruitment and training for staffs. Staff losses, even on completed contracts, are fairly high. Usually the real good ones stay on and wind up. But there is a fairly heavy turnover in the natural course of things.

Expansion was a big factor in staff losses. They went to higher orgs and new orgs. We must have 150 top liner ex-org staff members in the Sea Org for whom we are now recompensing at 2 courses for 1 on any incomplete contracts. But most had already completed their contracts.

Missions are full of people who completed org contracts and some who didn't and are now being billed.

Ex-org staff members turn up in big companies also.

So our staff losses in completed contracts must be recruited for heavily.

It takes a while to make a top-grade staff member—lots of training and auditing. So we've got to get ahead of this and stay ahead of it for we're still expanding like mad!

Love,

Ron

L. RON HUBBARD
Founder

HCO POLICY LETTER OF 24 MARCH 1970

Remimeo

A MATTER OF ORDERS

(Originally written by LRH for the *Apollo* OODs
of 24 Mar. 70. Issued as an HCO PL on 18 Sept. 80.)

ARC breaks occur when a person in charge requests something be looked into and he is given an opinion or an explanation.

It is not a true comm cycle.

"Go see what's smoking." "I think it's George burning toast."

"Put out a bow line." "We've got one out." (When a second one is needed.)

Gives one a long string of noncomm cycles and is a sure-fire ARC break.

I think this is why those in charge get upset. Getting an opinion or explanation when an order is meant to be done.

Part of the fault is not wording the order in anticipation of such a reply.

L. RON HUBBARD
Founder

L. Ron Hubbard

EXECUTIVE DIRECTIVE

LRH ED 122 INT

4 September 1970

TO: All Staff

    All Executives

FROM: RON

SUBJECT: **GROSS DIVISIONAL STATISTICS**

Gross divisional statistics of an org are INTERNALLY CONTROLLED.

The management and staff of an org can send GDSes up or down at will.

There is no stat in an org under public control.

All all all all are under the org's own control. Every one.

Your gross income comes directly from your GDSes.

Your pay comes from your GDSes and personal stats.

If your GDSes are going down you will shortly be in GI trouble.

The common reasons for a declining GDS are:

1. INADEQUATE STAFF HIRED.

2. Using the existing divisions as personnel pools and stripping them.

3. Nonproduction.

An analysis of data received at WW shows such ridiculous things as 7 hours auditing per HGC auditor per week! Yet with pc backlogs. The production of an auditor must be 25 actual well done auditing hours per week or he is statless.

A reported org's Course Supervisors are said to be getting only 136 points per student per week. That is one day's part-time study for a student on Flag after a long full day's work!

If a student gets only 136 points *a week* there's holdups or lack of twins or wild departures from use of two-way comm with students or no course.

Many orgs are doing better, of course. But what have we got in those that aren't? Psychiatrists?

A. GET THE ORG MANNED UP.

B. GET HATS ON.

C. GET TO WORK.

D. PRODUCE EXCELLENT VERY WELL DONE PCS IN QUANTITY.

E. PRODUCE WELL–TAUGHT STUDENTS IN QUANTITY.

If your GDSes are trending down you and your org and Dianetics and Scientology in your area will be endangered.

Each division has a statistic.

They become tomorrow's GI.

I am doing my best to do my job. Please do yours.

L. RON HUBBARD
Founder

HCO POLICY LETTER OF 15 SEPTEMBER 1970R
REVISED 25 APRIL 1979

Remimeo
Executive Hats
Ethics Checksheet
Personnel
   Checksheet

Ethics

Important

EXECUTIVE RESPONSIBILITY
FOR TRAINING STAFF

If at any time a staff member is found on staff who:

a. Does not know his hat

b. Is found not wearing the hat which he is assigned by the org board or

c. Is found in ethics trouble;

and it is discovered that:

A. He has no staff hat folder

B. No post hat folder

C. No checksheet of PLs and HCOBs or EDs or books or manuals concerning his duties or division

D. Has no pack of the materials of C above *or*

E. Is not actively being remedied in these defects and/or in progress in learning them well

   OR

F. The division is undermanned, by reason of no active demand for personnel or permitting transfers;

THE STAFF MEMBER'S IMMEDIATE SENIOR IS SUBJECT TO COMM EV on a charge of

TREASONABLE NEGLECT

and may thereby be:

1. Removed from post or

2. Demoted.

No bonuses of any kind may be paid any executive who does not himself have and whose juniors do not have:

i.   A precise post assignment on the org board and posted on the org board;

ii. A full outline of purpose of the post and the division and the org and a complete staff hat;

iii. A post hat giving the purpose of the post and its precise duties;

iv. A checksheet covering with reality the data required to be known to perform the post with all relevant manuals, HCO PLs, HCOBs, EDs, orders, books or tapes;

v.   A pack containing the material of the checksheet excepting tapes but with these available;

vi. A full Dept 14 program of post and study progress as well as case progress;

vii. Adequate study progress on the post material;

viii. Adequate acceptable statistics of each post production.

REWARD

Any Executive Director, Executive Secretary or secretary who achieves (i) to (viii) with his juniors and himself is entitled to a 25% bonus providing (vii) is completed in all cases and (vii) in satisfactory progress on all persons under him on staff less than 90 days.

The pay of a person fully on post with (i) to (viii) in and (vii) completed is the full units or pay of that post, the staff member being only on post in training until this is accomplished.

NOTE

Any and all troubles, ethics actions and org difficulties have been traced to failures to recruit, to hat, checksheet and pack and thus train for and on post every staff member.

While every effort will be made by Flag and its Liaison Offices to checksheet and assist and do the basic work, the absence of its materials or help or the absence of a Hats Officer or STO do not absolve any executive from his responsibilities for staff competence, hats, checksheets or packs or study thereof as laid down in this policy letter.

The viability and expansion of orgs and the power of Scientology in society depend utterly on recruitment and this policy letter being followed with intelligence and reality.

L. RON HUBBARD
Founder

HCO POLICY LETTER OF 21 SEPTEMBER 1970

Remimeo

COPE

(Originally written by LRH for the *Apollo* OODs of
21 Sept. 70. Issued as an HCO PL on 12 Oct. 80.)

I've had an insight into what "cope" really is. It is the process of finding and correcting outpoints without ever discovering a WHY and without organizing any return to the ideal scene.

A coper goes "outpoint found—correct it; outpoint found—correct it; outpoint found—correct it." This perpetual cycle never finds or corrects WHY these outpoints. So it just gets worse and worse and worse.

If all one ever did was handle despatches one would really get into a mountain of overwork while stats stayed down.

The WHY we face now is absence of recruiting, lack of full hats with checksheets and packs.

The Why of that was failure to make the materials filed accessibly and collatable. So it's a snake eats its tail. No hats then brought a condition of no data available in files. A true dwindling spiral.

And no hats traces to the introduction of ethics into HCOs and that it is easier to assign a condition than to compile or check out a hat. Hats went out when ethics came strongly in. Without ethics in HCO, HCO can only make stats recover by org form and hats.

Ethics has a role—after all else fails.

L. RON HUBBARD
Founder

L. Ron Hubbard

EXECUTIVE DIRECTIVE

LRH ED 126 INT   22 September 1970

TO: LRH Comm
    EC
    All staff

FROM: RON

SUBJECT: **WHY ORGS SAG**

REFS:

LRH ED 123 Int	Org Management Pgm No. 2
HCO PL 29 Aug. 70 I	Personnel Series 1 PERSONNEL TRANSFERS CAN DESTROY AN ORG
HCO PL 29 Aug. 70 II	Personnel Series 2 PERSONNEL PROGRAMMING
HCO PL 29 Aug. 70 III	Personnel Series 3 RECRUIT IN EXCESS
HCO PL 30 Aug. 70	Personnel Series 4 RECRUITING ACTIONS
HCO PL 10 Sept. 70	Personnel Series 5 TRANSFERITIS
HCO PL 12 Sept. 70	Personnel Series 6 TRAINING
HCO PL 13 Sept. 70	Personnel Series 7 HATS—VITAL DATA
HCO PL 16 Sept. 70	Personnel Series 8 ETHICS AND PERSONNEL
HCO PL 15 Sept. 70	EXEC RESPONSIBILITY FOR TRAINING STAFF
HCO PL 13 Sept. 70 II	Org Series 1 BASIC ORGANIZATION
HCO PL 14 Sept. 70	Org Series 2 COPE AND ORGANIZE
HCO PL 14 Sept. 70 II	Org Series 3 HOW TO ORGANIZE AN ORG
HCO PL 22 Sept. 70	Org Series 4 HATS

The Why, the real Why behind org sags and troubles and why the ten third-dynamic group aberrations of the society can invade an org (as given in LRH ED 123 Int, ORG MANAGEMENT PGM No. 2) is our loss of and *failure to expand and follow up the full use of hats.*

HATS

We developed the whole idea of "hats." It is even our term.

During the earlier periods of expansion HATS were in heavy use. We had a Hats Officer. We had a drill to collect hats hand reissue at any transfer. A person leaving couldn't even collect his pay unless he turned in his hats.

All the know-how of Scientology admin operates as a buffer to society's aberrations.

That know-how contained in HCO Policy Letters kept our orgs sane.

When it went out the aberrations of the society could move in.

Earlier on there were not so many PLs. They were kept loose in post hats.

We attained much more material. In 1966 I appointed Divisional Organizers at WW. They were supposed to collect all this up per division. They did not collect and issue PLs but tried to *run* divisions.

In other words, there was a failure to break down policy into divs and disseminate it to orgs.

Enough trained personnel existed to keep it running for awhile. But hats started to go out in several orgs. And as new personnel came on they had a huge mass of policy but they had no breakdown of it into exact hats.

The new 1965 org board (like the Class and Grade Chart in tech) was never gotten in, really in, in terms of post hats.

This omission cost us our third dynamic tech.

There went high pay, good facilities, good quarters, top quality service.

All the know-how was in the file cabinets. It was not specialized into post hats. It was not checked out on staff members.

Wide checking has established this lack of full post hats known on every post as the reason WHY wherever stats are down.

In support of this when I issued the LRH No. 1 programs and where they were checked out fully in an org on its staff members, the org stats tended to recover. Those No. 1s were actually generalized hats of a kind.

Where the No. 1s weren't checked out well on the whole staff, nothing happened.

Wide checking of various gross divisional stats in orgs where they were down showed behind them a total ignorance of any PLs related to how to get them up and no real hats. As an org's stat was down, its pay and appearance did not attract new recruits and PLs on recruiting weren't known either. Key posts then were left empty. This strained other posts and even more org posts were emptied.

Fewer people to wear hats and no hats anyway.

The ten points given in LRH ED 123 Int could then become aberrated.

THE ROAD BACK

A HAT is now redefined as a write-up of the post, *a checksheet and a pack.*

It is fully checked out on the staff member. He also gets full credit for it in terms of study points.

An executive is responsible for all his juniors having hats (defined as above) and that they are checked out on them fully.

HCO apparently found it easier to assign a condition than prepare a hat and check someone out. HCO is responsible for solving the problems of the org by heavy recruiting and hats, not ethics.

Dept 13 Qual must be organized to program and oversee the training of and AUDIT STAFF MEMBERS. It is to push home the idea of HATS mean full checksheets and packs for the hat.

Div 2 must bring its Mimeo Files up to date so it can make checksheets and packs for hats as well as course materials. People have to be recruited and put on this action and they themselves must be checked out on the relevant PLs that give you a Mimeo Section and Files.

Flag is flat out providing post hat checksheets. Do not wait for them. Get your own. And get your Mimeo Files up to date so you can make hat packs.

Scheduling has to be done to permit staffs time to study and time to get audited.

This is the road back—(a) recruit, (b) get full hats that consist of a checksheet and pack per hat, (c) train people in on their hats fully.

Until that time cope.

It will take a while. The 1965 org board was never grooved in, its posts never given their hats totally.

No new staff member could be expected to confront the totality of our know-how. It needs to be selected out for each post. And he sure can confront that part of it that applies to his own hat.

An org will get smaller or stay small and poor until every staff member in it has a full hat consisting of write-up, checksheet and pack and knows that material and is applying it on his post and producing.

This is *THE* ROAD BACK TO THE IDEAL SCENE.

It may be a bit to confront as there's a lot of work in it.

An executive harassed by all the local noise may believe he has many more pressing things to do. But if he will just haul up for a moment and look under that stat he will find the staff he is ordering (a) inadequate in number (b) ignorant of the first elements of the data that applies to the action (c) without full checksheets and packs for their hats. And *there* is where the noise is coming from.

There is no valid reason whatever why a staff member should not be well audited, well paid, well trained.

There is no valid reason why the org's products of pcs and students should not receive top grade level service.

The Why is totally contained in losing our tech of admin as well as our tech of auditing and training.

The WAY we get it all back is to recruit and fully HAT a staff and define that hat as a write-up, a checksheet and a pack.

To eradicate the ten points of third dynamic aberration out of an org all we have to do is work industriously to get in and then MAINTAIN hats and people fully trained on them.

EXPANSION

Some people who do not know policy knowledge believe public demand or state of mind influences org expansion. It does not. There is not one gross divisional stat controlled by the public. They are ALL under the control of the org.

The "enemy" was quite loud and impudent for a while. This was effective only on staff morale. It did not reduce public demand.

The majority of the unholy dozen are out of the running, ruined, insane or dead.

This is not an actual barrier now. While it may still ebb and flow we are following a policy of full speed ahead. What is *actually* holding us back is loss of our post admin know-how and losing sight of its value.

We expand as we determine to, not as we are prevented.

It has taken me thirteen months of hard study of field data and orgs, including missionaire reports and your Thursday reports to isolate THE Why.

And this is it.

HATS INCOMPLETELY DEFINED AND NONEXISTENT.

That even lies back of our loss of auditing tech. The exec hats that would have kept it in were not only not worn, they were not even compiled.

So if we continue to cope with things and spend part of our time each day in organizing hats and getting them worn we will come right out of it.

We are not bad off. We have coped. But we must not continue only to cope.

We must recruit, compile hats and train people on them and so get things rolling.

We don't need any miracle from above.

We need HATS.

L. RON HUBBARD
Founder

HCO POLICY LETTER OF 29 OCTOBER 1970

Remimeo   Issue II

AN ORG BOARD

(Originally written by LRH for the *Apollo* OODs of
29 Oct. 70. Issued as an HCO PL on 21 Sept. 80.)

Ref:
HCO PL 28 Oct. 70   Org Series 9
                             ORGANIZING AND HATS

An org board is a list of hats with seniorities. The hats are in flow sequence.

A hat is a duty. It outlines the actions necessary to accomplish a production and receive what's needed, change and route it.

In theory the I/C holds *all* functions. When he doesn't fully outline them they can't be hatted. If they're not hatted he wears them as an unknown fog. Simple as that.

What defines a hat is a product.

If you count up the *expected* products you get the minimum number of hats. The steps to get the product is the hat. Products are also composed of lesser products, so hats can be enlarged. It's what you designate as a product that makes the hat. It's the importance of that product to others on the line that makes the hat's importance.

The completeness and size of the product make the seniority of the hat.

The overall product of a division determines the hat of the divisional officer. The lesser products that when combined make the overall product determine the rest of the division hats.

Until you can define in one go the overall product of a division you aren't likely to be able to post any real part of its org board, for the product of hats of that div add up to the div product.

When you see an unposted or unreal org board, the head of the div is not producing a product with that div, no matter how busy it all looks or how exhausting.

L. RON HUBBARD
Founder

Remimeo

"NOISE" AND ORGANIZATION

(Originally written by LRH for the *Apollo* OODs of
7 Nov. 70. Issued as an HCO PL on 26 Oct. 80.)

Ref:
HCO PL   8 May   70   AKH Series 24
                              DISTRACTION AND NOISE

Each division is to have a completed org board.

In order to do this well, it is best to study the Org Series.

"Noise" is the amount of disturbance and off-line actions and chatter and general dev-t in an area.

In some divisional areas "noise" by far exceeds actual traffic.

An org board, amongst other things, reduces "noise" when it is well done and known.

Improvement of production occurs when there is a good org board that is also well known.

When you assess the effort expended on a post against the actual production of a post, you get an idea of the amount of "noise" present. One can be expending lots of time and effort and yet attain no production. Proper organization increases production and reduces effort by eliminating "noise."

My insistence on getting org boards done, in and known comes from my own post observation. For some time I have been seeing lots of "noise" and very low production.

When this visibly began to eat into my own production (about April 1970), I began to push in organizational steps. I restudied the subject (as you see in the PLs of the Data Series, Personnel Series and Org Series) and consulted existing realities. I was amazed to find how little technology man actually had on the subject and how wide a gap there was between theory and reality.

Studying orgs themselves, including the ship, Flag Org, bureaux and orgs as per LRH ED 123 Int (the ten social aberrations, later issued as HCO PL 14 Dec. 70, GROUP SANITY), the worst items were "hiring, training, apprenticeship and utilization" including production.

The first four would of course account for (if out) lack of production.

So far as an org is concerned, these are the functions of HCO.

Once these points are in, you will see things begin to move better, noise drop out and production increase while effort reduces.

L. RON HUBBARD
Founder

HCO POLICY LETTER OF 23 FEBRUARY 1971
Issue I

Remimeo
All Exec Hats
HCO Personnel Hats
Tech Div
　Personnel Hats
Msn Ops Hats
Missionaires

THE MAGIC FORMULA

(Originally written by LRH for the *Apollo* OODs of
23 Feb. 71. Issued as an HCO PL on 11 Sept. 80.)

The magic formula of a going org is:

1. A full, efficient operating HCO,

2. Lots of good producing auditors.

If you have that you also have Course Supers and Tech execs from the auditors and HCO will give you the rest of the org manned.

Thus, the sign of threatened failure in an org would be:

a. A declining or faulty HCO,

b. Auditors declining in numbers available or in training.

This then is the magic formula to a producing org.

1. HCO fully hatted itself, fully functioning, efficient and producing.

2. Lots of auditors flublessly producing and auditors in training to become so.

Where any org wants to boom, this is what it has to establish and keep established.

The real stars of the staff team are the auditors and the HCO personnel.

That's the key to any org.

Well worth knowing to FEBCs and also to missionaires going out to patch orgs up. All they'd have to do is get auditors and get them producing and get an HCO recruited and hatted hatted hatted and doing its job, especially getting more tech people in training and on post. It would be a long-range winning combination.

L. RON HUBBARD
Founder

Remimeo

DRILLS

(Originally written by LRH for the *Apollo* OODs
on 26 Feb. 71. Issued as an HCO PL on 3 Nov. 80.)

Drills have several purposes. To groove in a team action is a principal one. To test a system fully. To groove in lines.

Whenever postings are changed, the new post holders have to be grooved in on their posts (hatted and on-post trained) and then the team itself must be drilled.

The two steps are always needed.

This applies to org lines as well. Dummy runs and dummy bullbait runs serve as the drill.

L. RON HUBBARD
Founder

HCO POLICY LETTER OF 7 MARCH 1971

Remimeo

HANDLING OVERLOADED POSTS

(Originally written by LRH for the *Apollo* OODs
on 7 Mar. 71. Issued as an HCO PL on 12 Sept. 80.)

Ref:
HCO PL 28 July 71   ADMIN KNOW–HOW 26

Product and org officers can take over a grossly overloaded key post and (a) increase its production and (b) reduce the work hours. They should take over posts for 48 hours and give the incumbent a rest and see what gives.

The rules that seem to apply are:

a.   It is a key post of the area in question and

b.   It is the most overloaded and/or most nonproductive post in that area.

It's one thing to issue orders. It's another to do work.

One doesn't stand behind the guy. One takes him off the post and actually does the work of the post.

While doing it one will see why it can't be done or isn't being done and one can then get a good bright idea of how it can be done and get it in and write it up.

One often finds he has to ask "What hat am I wearing?" when one finds he is on overload.

Well, one solution is to just go over and really wear that hat and see why it can't be worn, get an idea of how it can be worn, do the action to see if it's right, write it up for issue and put the person back on it. A junior often can't mesh up the lines so they work because he hasn't the know-how and hasn't the authority. His proper action would be to figure his post out and write it up for issue and get it in his hat. When he doesn't do this it jams or overloads his own and other lines.

Where this situation exists and isn't changing, a product officer, org officer or HAS or the divisional product or org officers have an out. They can take over such a post, do all its work for 48 hours with no help from the incumbent, get an idea of how to debug it, see if that works, write it up and turn the post back over.

L. RON HUBBARD
Founder

Remimeo

ORG BOARD AND PRODUCTION

(Originally written by LRH for the *Apollo* OODs
on 11 Mar. 71. Issued as an HCO Policy Letter on 17 Sept. 80.)

HCO PL 9 Mar. 71 II, POSTING AN ORG BOARD, will solve a lot of confusion about org boards.

Read it and then look at what you may currently have and lights may blink like a pinball machine.

An org board *does* have something to do with getting the work done.

Quality as well as volume depend upon workable organization.

The opposite ends of the action are organization at one end and production at the other.

Things get easier and better all around.

L. RON HUBBARD
Founder

Remimeo
HAS
Staff Hats
Prod/Org
  Checksheets

SERVICE AND WORKLOAD

The way to decrease the traffic and workload of an org is to:

1. Get people to know their hats.

2. Deliver the service each hat calls for.

3. Check out all seniors on all the hats below them as well as the org board, functions, purposes of units, activities and current programs.

4. Be certain Personnel people know every hat in the org.

Production in terms of completions will soar.

Volume of work will drop.

Why is this?

NO SERVICE

If every staff member is on a no-service pitch, the body and despatch volume will rise at least fifteen times and production will decrease toward zero.

Look it over. Body A goes to Staff Terminal X for some service or other. Terminal X says, "I can't pay you because FP . . ." So Body A calls on another staff member who says, "Permission is required from G." So Body A goes to G and is told, "We haven't got a list to hand so . . ." So Body A goes . . .

Where's the production?

But there's lots of body volume!

Despatch To—From is received by Staff Member Y. He refers it to Staff Member Z. Who refers it to . . .

Where's the production?

But there's sure a lot of despatch traffic!

The system, in vogue in most bureaucracies, even has a name. It's called "the referral system."

No one gives service. No situation is terminatedly handled.

REHANDLING

When this is cured somewhat, a new situation can develop. A service facsimile (what one uses to make others wrong) develops.

"You handled it wrong!" is the cry.

So demands to rehandle occur.

This pushes the org back to DON'T HANDLE OR YOU'LL GET REPRIMANDED.

And the increased volume and lowered production set in again.

People who know their hats in the first place and give service don't have to be told to rehandle.

HAT KNOCK OFF

When a senior exec does not know all the hats and their duties, he misassigns duties.

This knocks off the hats that have been gotten on.

No service results.

When an exec knows all the hats, the org bd, the functions of units and activities and current programs, he routes and assigns properly and production goes up and volume decreases.

PERSONNEL GOOFS

When Personnel people do not know all the hats, they misassign. Some military services I know have this down to a fine art.

This increases hatting and training time. It increases confusion.

It reduces production and increases traffic volume.

The way to increase production and decrease traffic volume is to check out all Personnel people on all the hats of the posts they are assigning. Then they know.

MUSICAL CHAIRS

By playing musical chairs in an org—frequent changes of post, using areas of the org as a personnel pool—service is reduced so production is reduced and volume is increased.

There is a covert method of doing musical chairs. Go around and ask people if they want different posts. This unstabilizes them, puts them halfway between posts and reduces service, production and increases volume.

Laziness and fancied economies and lack of expertise in RECRUITING is always the bug back of musical chairs.

The answer is RECRUIT AND HIRE.

Probably other ways can be invented to prevent delivery and work everyone like mad but the above are the chief ones.

To increase production and decrease the volume handled, it is vital that people are:

A. Properly recruited and posted.

B. Hatted with and trained for the post, and all theory and practical and post drills are done on them.

C. Persuaded to deliver the expected service of the post held.

D. Knowledgeable as seniors who must know their juniors' hats, the org bd, the functions as well as purposes of units and activities and current programs.

E. Helped by signs, routings and forms to give the public or outside or internal traffic correct routes and terminals where handling will occur terminatedly.

Want to increase production and lower the workload?

Get this PL in, in, in!

L. RON HUBBARD
Founder

HCO POLICY LETTER OF 18 AUGUST 1971

Remimeo

ON–POLICY

(Originally written by LRH for the *Apollo* OODs of
15 and 18 Aug. 71. Issued as an HCO PL on 3 Sept. 80.)

Policy *works*. Just like tech. If you apply policy, it works and things go well. When you don't, like a case "audited" on out-tech, things go wrong.

Policy came from years and years and years of experience. It's the know-how of handling orgs and groups.

When it isn't used things aren't handled.

An org will get off the launching pad when every person in it has studied and knows Vol 0 OEC.

That begins it.

It doesn't matter how long one has been around or how much policy he has read. Until he has studied Vol 0 OEC as a specific basic staff hat action, he will now and then go off-policy.

Make a group!

That takes agreement.

Get on-policy.

That will build the agreement necessary.

L. RON HUBBARD
Founder

HUBBARD COMMUNICATIONS OFFICE
Saint Hill Manor, East Grinstead, Sussex

HCO POLICY LETTER OF 19 AUGUST 1971

Remimeo

PROGRAMS, USE OF
HOW TO SAVE USELESS WORK

Staff time is very often wasted by the failure to use a program-project system.

Example: Dept 4 does a full layout for promo. Then finds it is off-policy and it isn't used. Means wasted work.

Example: Tech Pc Admin is ordered to make a huge board to give pc addresses. After a lot of work it is never used.

WHY? The job never had any part of a program in the first place. It was not part of any general activity. Thus, it is not part of a team action.

The correct procedure in ordering staff to ANY project that is going to consume time is to:

1. See if there *is* a situation.

2. Find out its WHY.

3. Get a general program drawn up. Get it approved as a program with who is to do each part.

4. Get the different parts of the program drawn up as a TARGETED project. With who is to do each project. Get these approved.

5. Get the projects executed.

6. Complete *all* the projects.

7. Report the program as done.

This is a correct sequence. To do anything else is to omit steps in the sequence. This gives two outpoints—omitted steps and altered sequence.

Thus, when this procedure is short-cut, the whole org can look batty. It can also have its staff frantic and overworked without producing anything.

Usually the product officer draws up a program.

It is vital that he refer to policy to support his program.

The LRH Comm should approve the program as not off-policy.

Division heads usually write up the projects. These are approved by the product officer and then the LRH Comm.

The program is issued as a local ED when approved.

The projects refer by number to the program and are issued separately as local EDs.

Their completion is chased up by the product officer.

The fully completed program is reported to the LRH Comm.

This *looks* like a lot of writing. It *saves* a lot of work.

Programs and projects are easily corrected and brought on-policy. The actual *work* is costly and impossible to correct.

The wise staff member would clamor for this system. Further, he would ask, when told to repaint the students, "Where is the program and the project order?" He'd routinely find that he was often doing a job not approved by anyone but his senior. And disapproved of by the rest of the org.

Programs set priorities. They let a staff work as a team. They get the coins of the org correctly invested in needful work.

The Ad Council is a wise Ad Council if it demands the right to pass on all programs originated by its executives before projects are written or work is done.

Needless to say, a program must handle actual situations, the situations which depress production and prosperity.

These are vital steps in running an org or working in it.

Don't run about frantically or sink into apathy. Get your execs and staff program-project conscious, *save* work, get prosperous.

L. RON HUBBARD
Founder

HCO POLICY LETTER OF 31 AUGUST 1971
Issue II

Remimeo

OVERLOAD AND HATTING

(Originally written by LRH for the *Apollo* OODs
of 31 Aug. 71. Issued as an HCO PL on 24 Sept. 80.)

I have found that whenever I have had to handle something, I found the person who should have handled it unhatted and with misunderstood words on things intimately connected with his duties.

Thus I have found this cycle of great use and thoroughly recommend it.

1. Emergency item or omission requiring handling turns up.

2. Handle it right now fast (my handling something time lapse is about 5 minutes to half an hour). (That means terminatedly.)

3. Spot who should have handled it.

4. Interrogate the person on basics of his post (not ask about "hat folders," etc.).

In all cases so far I have found the person not doing his post duties, unhatted, with huge misunderstoods on words like "post," "hat," "muster," etc.

5. Hat the guy.

So I can tell you that any overload you have is from unhattedness of the most basic kind.

An org is as efficient and looks as good as its people are individually hatted and do their jobs.

It's a very good system. I recommend it.

A sort of a do-it-yourself HCO!

It works.

L. RON HUBBARD
Founder

809

HCO POLICY LETTER OF 8 SEPTEMBER 1971

Remimeo

INSTABILITY

(Originally written by LRH for the *Apollo* OODs on
8 Sept. 71. Issued as an HCO PL on 17 Oct. 80.)

You will find that persons who are having a rough time or giving others one are either just leaving or haven't arrived on the post. In other words they in some way are not actually ON post.

It is also an oddity that those who have to go to point B haven't arrived ever at point A in order to be able to leave for B.

The ability to BE something strongly shows up in post performances. The real stars can BE anything wholly and completely for short or long periods. They ARE what they are being. They aren't just arriving or leaving.

To BE OR UnBe, that is the ability! To not quite be or to WAS is the aberration.

L. RON HUBBARD
Founder

HCO POLICY LETTER OF 10 NOVEMBER 1971

Remimeo

ORGANIZATION AND SURVIVAL

(Originally written by LRH for the *Apollo* OODs of
10 Nov. 71. Issued as an HCO PL on 11 Sept. 80.)

Well-organized activities survive. The survival of individuals in those organizations depends on the highly organized condition of the activity.

A small group, extremely well organized, has excellent chances of survival.

Even a large group, badly organized, hasn't a prayer.

The essence of organization is org boarding, posting with reality and, in keeping with the duties being performed, training and hatting.

To this has to be added the actual performance of the duties so that the activity is productive.

The outward signs of a badly organized group are slovenliness and fumbles.

Another ingredient that goes hand in hand with organization and survival is toughness. The ability to stand up to and confront and handle whatever comes the way of the organization depends utterly on the ability of the individuals of the organization to stand up to, confront and handle what comes the individual's way. The composite whole of this ability makes a tough organization.

An individual who is not properly posted, isn't performing the duties of the post, is not trained or hatted, is soft. He has no position to hold, therefore he goes down at the first fan of a feather.

Confidence in one's teammates is another factor in organization survival. Confidence in one's self is something that has to be earned. It is respect. This is a compound of demonstrated competence, being on post and being dependable.

After an individual has failed, confidence in him on the part of his teammates sinks. He has lost face and is not respected. This, then, shows itself up in numerous ways. It is up to that individual to earn back confidence so that his teammates will again trust him. The way to do this is to get properly org boarded, trained, hatted and to confront and handle, with competence, whatever that post is supposed to control.

The ultimate in no confidence by a group in a team member is no post at all. Reports from those who have no post or from those who are between posts stress the horrors of having no post.

Our survival depends fully on becoming entirely and completely organized. This will happen to the degree that every separate unit, department and division in an org is properly org boarded, properly performing the duties of the post, is trained and fully hatted.

L. RON HUBBARD
Founder

HCO POLICY LETTER OF 19 JANUARY 1972

Remimeo

SPECIALIZATION

(Originally written by LRH as an *Apollo* OODs item
of 19 Jan. 72. Issued as an HCO PL on 31 Oct. 80.)

Specialist actions are so stressed that actual functions of a division aren't covered.

What was forgotten was that ALL HANDS operations do exist and that severe specialization is only the beginning of hatting in a division. How else would you make future I/Cs and directors unless specialty training on *each post* was done.

In a division you *begin* with only a specialist for each function. THEN these trained specialists get trained in other specialties also.

An activity composed of living beings cannot be totally cogwheeled without disaster. Units get sick or transferred.

Hanging on to only one man for a specialist function as the only one who can do that particular function is the direction org boards sometimes take.

I devised a new way to display a division that makes this evident. Each major function has an I/C, followed by all the rest of the div as assigned in each case.

Hatting Section

John Doe I/C
Richard Roe
Tom Brown

HCO Files Section

Richard Roe I/C
John Doe
Tom Brown

Personnel Section

Tom Brown I/C
Richard Roe
John Doe

The person listed as I/C is responsible always for the function and is the first one fully hatted as a specialist. But then others are also hatted for that post.

The Admin Section of the old Flag Org was the original of this. It truly worked.

Thus anyone in HCO could do the job if the rest were off.

And ALL HANDS operations are used for every major program like "File all files up-to-date" or "Make an org board."

An org went to pot once by individuating into specialization.

This leads to overman, no product and a broke org, while correct use of specialist actions and all hands leads to success.

L. RON HUBBARD
Founder

Remimeo

STUDY

(Originally written by LRH for the *Apollo* OODs of
27 Mar. 72. Issued as an HCO PL on 30 Oct. 80.)

When study tech isn't in in *full* use in any org or here, overt products are produced.

This is THE Why of any lack of expansion or troubles with orgs. It is THE Why behind admin flubs, behind tech flubs.

Orgs are actually in the hands of and at the mercy of Course Supervisors and Dept of Personnel Enhancement people.

Paralleling this, lack of knowledge of what their product is, and because they don't know how good it can be, keeps org staffs from taking the planet. So study tech does not get forced in.

This is the nitty-gritty WHY that explains all about the state of orgs and stats.

L. RON HUBBARD
Founder

HUBBARD COMMUNICATIONS OFFICE
Saint Hill Manor, East Grinstead, Sussex

HCO POLICY LETTER OF 14 MAY 1972

Remimeo

MORALE

(Originally written by LRH for the *Apollo* OODs of
14 May 72. Issued as an HCO PL 21 Sept. 80.)

Production is the basis of morale.

If one can get a unit producing and actually accomplishing worthwhile production, then their morale will rise.

Thus, it does not matter too much how one starts a unit producing so long as it does get started.

I was given a good example of this with just one person who has been on MO lines. She is actually well now. She is *miserable*. There is nothing wrong with her at all except she is out of the action and is not producing anything.

This has been noted in other fields. The "idle rich" are the most miserable people you ever wanted to meet. "To Have and Have Not" or some such title by Hemingway talks about it for the best part of a book.

L. RON HUBBARD
Founder

HCO POLICY LETTER OF 11 JUNE 1972

Remimeo

PRODUCT OFFICERS

(Originally written by LRH for the *Apollo* OODs of
11 June 72. Issued as an HCO PL on 21 Sept. 80.)

Worked last evening getting Tech to start shooting them through to completions.

The PL on Selling and Delivering Auditing (HCO PL 28 Sept. 71) tells why you have to audit a pc all at once whole program. Dribbling it out means repairs due to life upsets before the guy made it.

So crowd it on and get a pc *through*. Then we'll have some products for our coins.

A Product Officer has to name, want and get his products.

This means one says, "You there. Joe Blow. Want him completed. All right get it DONE." Product by product. There is no general "Audit these pcs." "Get up the hours." Hell, you never get a product that way.

"You there, George Thunderbird. I want you through your Primary and onto and through course and classified. Get going, man, get going. Oh, you were told to weedle the toofle before you woofled by Dorance Doppler. Org Officer? Get that name—to F/MAA, get the cross orders the hell off my lines. Now you George Thunderbird, I want you through your Primary and onto and through course by 1 July. You got it? You got it now! Good. Well, get with it. Get going!" Note on clipboard: Org Off to get cross order by Dorance Doppler invest and report. "There's your slip." Note on progress bd. Geo Thunderbird HSDA 1 July. "Now you Tobler Tomias, what's the tale; how are you going? . . . Well standing there smoking and looking at the scenery isn't going to do anything. If your girl doesn't like you anymore the thing to do is drown your sorrows in the Primary RD. . . . Okay you are to be an Exp Dn. All right, that's fine. I want you completed by 16 July. . . . I don't care if that's a 16-hour day. Let's see, Primary RD by _____ and Class IV Acad by _____ and _____ . Yes that's 16 July AT NOON. Man to hell with your PTPs. Get going, man." And on the progress board. And from the board—"And here's Bill Coal, he should be off the Primary today, where is he. All right Bill—ah, you made it that far. Now you're on schedule. That's great. HSDA. Get with it, man. You completed Primary 20 minutes ago and aren't on the next course. Super! What the _____ ."

That's the way it goes for a Tech Prod Off. "We are finishing Agnes, Torp and Goshwiler today. Today. Yes today. Certified and off lines. Got it D of T? Well, do it!"

Push, debug, drive. Name it, want it, get it.

That's the *only* way you ever get a product.

Sad but true.

They don't ever happen by themselves.

And all the public relations chatter in the world is not a product. I know this product officer beat.

It's a piece of cake.

But it has to be DONE.

L. RON HUBBARD
Founder

L. Ron Hubbard

EXECUTIVE DIRECTIVE

LRH ED 181 INT   7 September 1972

TO: Execs

SUBJECT: **EVALUATION**

Missions when they go into orgs, find that execs do not use the Data Series at all.

Execs apparently just push and push to get stats up and when they don't go up, the exec goes into apathy.

The missing action is evaluation.

Like one org CO yelled and yelled to get the place clean. It was filthy. And it didn't get cleaned. And the exec finally quit trying.

An evaluation was done by an outsider and the real Why was found: There were no brooms, mops or soap available. The simple handling was to make the materials available in central places and get them restored after use and a supply line kept in.

Well, to do that evaluation the exec would have had to

1.   Know the Data Series (Study it, get it Method 4ed).

2.   Listen to what people tried to tell him or read the reports. (TR 4)

3.   Observe. (TR 0)

4.   Find the real Why. (Apply what's studied.)

5.   Handle what's found. (Do some work: Get actual compliance.)

Now that's a ridiculously simple example. But the solution is the same for the most complex problems.

Here's an example: The ED tearing into Div 2 weekly to get GI. And ripping the place apart to get GI.

Yet *no* Reg on post to collect any!

Here's another. No GI. Why? Tech Sec telling Reg all the pcs are PTS so the Reg sending *all* pcs to Ethics instead of signing them up! And the Tech Sec's Why: wouldn't permit auditors to audit because they all needed training but there was no D of T or any Cramming to do it!

So an ED could yell and yell but if he didn't know how to evaluate the entire scene would elude him utterly.

The biggest barrier to evaluation is that the Evaluator seldom believes anything could be that stupid. Yet all Whys are huge stupidities.

This is so much the case that an Evaluator can't ever be reasonable. He has to evaluate by outpoints.

In short, to find a real Why an Evaluator has to learn to think like an idiot.

And to get a bright idea an Evaluator has to be a genius.

There is no successful middle ground.

I know one ED who is a great guy and a fireball. But he doesn't evaluate. Right now he is C/Sing and auditing while holding the post of ED and is working himself ragged trying to keep his stats up. But he has *not* noticed an omitted terminal. If he is C/Sing and auditing and is ED, then there is no ED! And that's his Why. His handling would be, if he's the only C/S and top auditor, to get a Deputy ED to run the org. It's not that he is not working. It's that he isn't evaluating.

Another org's Div 7 does only Div 6 actions. So again, nobody is running the org.

In another day all this would have been okay. But today we have the sharp tools of the Data Series.

The virtue of the Data Series is that in its use one enormously increases one's effectiveness and enormously reduces the worry and stress.

The Data Series is the key tech of organization. When it's used the stress comes off and the stats go up.

The day you find your first real dead-on Why that really opens the door, you become a Data Series convert.

Wow, what a wonderful feeling!

L. RON HUBBARD
Founder

HCO POLICY LETTER OF 9 MAY 1974

Remimeo

PROD–ORG, ESTO AND OLDER
SYSTEMS RECONCILED

In the last three years there have been two new organization systems developed. These were THE PRODUCT–ORG OFFICER SYSTEM and the ESTABLISH-MENT OFFICER SYSTEM.

Reviewing these I find that these systems not only reconcile with each other but also with the HCO Exec Sec and Org Exec Sec system and the Supercargo, Chief Officer system of the Sea Org.

TOP DOWN

In 67 I found that an organization must always be posted from the top down.

This means it cannot be posted with gaps between the top or lower levels on the org board.

The org, of course, must always have a top.

And there must not be a gap between the top and the next lower post. Or any gaps on the way down.

Example: Orgs run by a committee but without a head of org seldom succeed.

Example: An org with a CO or ED, no HAS but only a Master-at-Arms or Ethics Officer in the HCO Division will not function but disintegrate.

Example: A musical group with an I/C and all the rest just musicians will deteriorate.

Example: A small vessel with three men aboard will not function with one the Captain, another the cook and another the deckhand.

In the first example, there has to be someone responsible for the whole organization whether above or below the committee.

In the second example, an org without an HAS or HCO Exec Sec or Supercargo, there is no one to take all those lower functions and they settle on an overloaded top.

In the musical group the I/C finds himself with many juniors and no special-ized organizational handling of anything.

In the small vessel all the functions of the first three divisions are mainly abandoned and the last four as well.

All these and many more are lessons learned the hard way.

The seven-division org board is present even in organizations that know nothing of it! And not knowing it or using it can bring chaos.

EARLIEST SYSTEM

In early days there was an HCO Sec in charge of the functions of the first three divisions (Exec, HCO, Dissem) and an Assoc Sec in charge of the functions of the last four divisions. These functions were not fully known as the seven-division board had not been developed.

The org board evolved further and the HCO Exec Sec became the person in charge of the functions of the first three divisions and the Org Exec Sec, the last four.

In the Sea Org these titles became Supercargo and Chief Officer but the functions were similar.

PROD–ORG SYSTEM

Then, within the last four years the product officer–org officer system was developed.

The Executive Director or Commanding Officer had (or was) a product officer. The product officer was supported by an org officer to keep the place organized.

THE ESTO SYSTEM

The Establishment Officer system or "Esto tech" was developed in the same time period as the prod–org system.

The Esto kept the place established and organized for production and despite heavy production demands.

REEXAMINATION

Looking over these systems, I find they fall into place naturally one with the other.

The realization is that an org with only one product officer and org officer has a gap—the HCO Exec Sec!

Actually an org needs TWO senior product officers—one to get the products of Divisions 7, 1 and 2 and one to get the products of 3, 4, 5 and 6!

When this gap exists, no one in real practice is functioning over Divs 7, 1 and 2 and so there is an imbalance of the org board. The org tends to fall apart. It does not rapidly expand as it has no product officer for expansion *or* dissemination.

821

ESTO SYSTEM

The Esto system with its powerful tech is really the org officer system.

The duties of the org officer in the prod–org system were not as fully laid out as they might have been.

The tech of the org officer is really the Esto tech!

RECONCILIATION

Thus we can reconcile (make agree) these systems and profit thereby.

The basic org board of ANY sized org then has the functions of these titles:

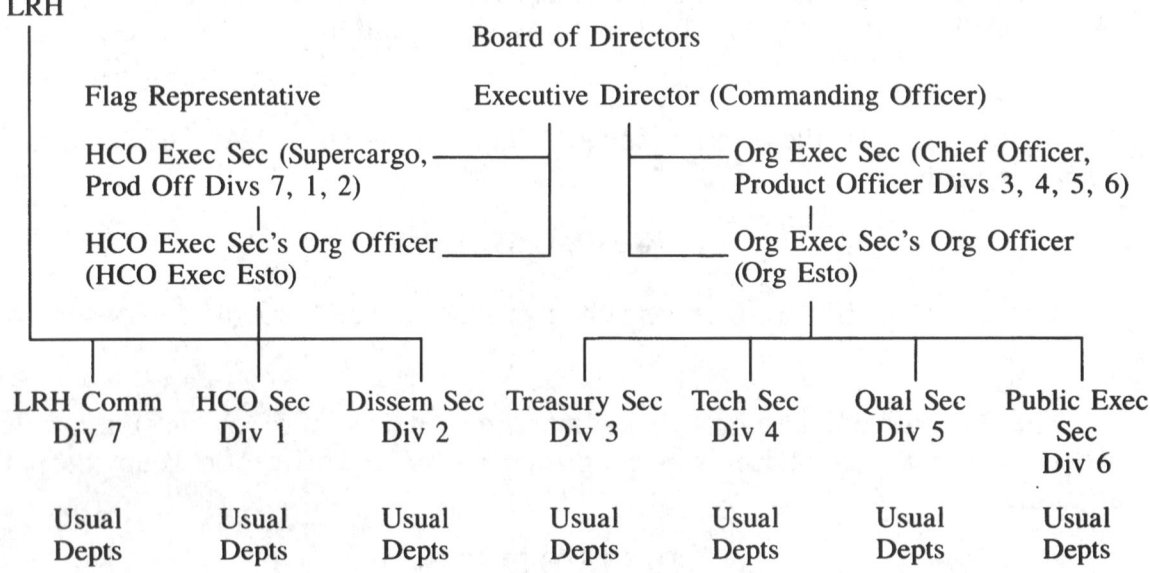

So where you have a product officer and org officer to the org, you are missing two posts and so are not posted from the top down!

You should have TWO product officers, one who is also the HCO Exec Sec (or Supercargo) and one who is the Org Exec Sec (or Chief Officer).

And each of these has an org officer who is also an Esto and who uses Esto tech.

This gives the ED (or CO) FOUR terminals he is directly operating with, even though the O/Os are also junior to and under their product officers.

SUMMARY

This ties together all existing systems.

It finds and fills an unnoticed gap in posting from the top down.

It prevents Estos from working independently from the side into the org off command chain.

In posting product officers use the old titles: HCO Exec Sec (Supercargo) and Org Exec Sec (Chief Officer), remembering that these are now product officers operating on the prod–org system into their own divisions.

Post any Esto as an org officer under one or the other of these executives, one the "HES Org Officer," the other the "OES Org Officer." And insist they use Esto tech and consider themselves Estos.

Size of org has little to do with it. A one-man org would simply have all these titles and functions. A ten-man org would be posted from the top and all other functions directly below them not posted or held by them would also be performed by them.

IMPORTANCE

Failing to post the top and from the top down is the main failure point in ANY organization (not just ours).

Finding this gap is important and filling it will raise stats.

L. RON HUBBARD
Founder

HCO POLICY LETTER OF 8 JANUARY 1975

Remimeo
LRH Comms
FRs
Execs

COMPLIANCE, HOW TO GET ONE

False compliances come about because a staff member under threat and duress (or not doing his post) seeks to protect himself by false reporting that something has been done when it hasn't. He entirely overlooks the fact that a false report will really bring the house down on him.

So why does he false report instead of just doing the thing required? There could be several answers, perhaps even one for each individual. But, overall, it can be said that he *can't* do it. He either doesn't know how or he is already backlogged on other things he also doesn't really know how to do. Or there is something that has to be done *before* he can begin to do what you want of him.

So it can be said that the staff member you are demanding a compliance from, when he doesn't do it or false reports it, is not yet at square one.

Let's see how this works. You want Miss Gooch crammed on letter-writing policy. So you order the Qual Sec to cram Miss Gooch. The Qual Sec says, in a couple days, "I have crammed Miss Gooch."

Now *if* you also require the *Qual Sec* to verify that he has done this, and it was a false report in the first place, you will just get a false verification. Also it probably takes the Qual Sec as long to write up a complex report as it would have to do the action itself.

So the right way is this way:

Exec: "Target here, you were supposed to cram Miss Gooch."

Qual Sec: "Yeah, I did that."

Exec finds Miss Gooch: "Miss Gooch, what is the first rule in letter writing?"

Miss Gooch: "Uh? Er . . . Awk."

Exec goes and finds Qual Sec: "About cramming Miss Gooch" (takes a wild shot) "where's the letter-writing policies you crammed her on?"

Qual Sec: "Well, I been meaning to mention that. FP turned down our OEC Volumes so Qual library . . ."

Exec goes to FP chairman: "Has the Qual Sec ever turned in a PO for OEC Volumes?"

FP chairman: "Let's see . . . records of POs here . . . no."

Exec goes back to Qual Sec: "Here is a PO form. Now write the PO for OEC Volumes." "Good, put it in that out-basket to FP." "Now where's your Letter Reg packs?"

Qual Sec: "Well, actually our files are kind of messy. But I think . . ."

Exec: "Here's my copy of OEC Volume 2. Now go get Miss Gooch."

The LRH Comm or FR or exec who accepts false reports is doing his job backwards. He is asking for verifications from people who say they did it.

LRH Comms, FRs and execs belong out in the org, not hiding in an office. Only a C/S has an ivory tower.

It is up to them to verify reports of dones or get dones done. And they often have to get somebody up to square one before any action can begin on the order required.

MAKE IT EASY TO ACCEPT A REPORT OF A DONE.

VERIFY IT PERSONALLY.

And there's one other rule—one gets the conditions he fails to assign. The Qual Sec above gave two false reports, a minimum of Doubt. One could hold it in abeyance—"One more false report and it's Doubt." But if it kept up, one would have to assign it.

Staffs learn that "high stats hold off ethics." But it is very true that false stats bring on ethics faster.

FOLOs are operating on orders to send a FOLO mission at once false stats are detected.

It will be the same with false reports.

But an org that can't get compliances within itself is not much of an org. And one that accepts false reports instead of actual compliances will soon begin to fail and be in real trouble.

True compliances to evaluated programs are vital.

The LRH Comm or FR or exec who can't get compliances needs to put into practice the two rules above.

And put into action the idea that areas that can't comply or don't are not yet up to square one.

FIND OUT WHY THEY'RE NOT YET AT SQUARE ONE AND GET THEM THERE FAST.

But there is a point where "reasons it can't be done" are not a square one problem but are simply Q and A and a flagrant will not. Well, in that case it's an ethics matter. Somebody needs his W/Hs pulled or somebody else belongs on that post.

You can't get compliances sitting around your office. And there *is* tech in handling getting them.

L. RON HUBBARD
Founder

825

HCO POLICY LETTER OF 24 JULY 1978

SUBPRODUCTS

HOW TO COMPILE A SUBPRODUCT LIST

If you take any VFP and trace it backwards step by step, using a BE–DO–HAVE breakdown of what it took to create it and then wrote up the list as preliminaries, you would have a subproduct list.

Let us take a cup of coffee as the VFP. The minimum subproducts list would divide into what you had to be, what you had to do and what you had to have to wind up with a cup of coffee.

Be: Somebody who wanted a cup of coffee, somebody hatted to make coffee.

Do: Boil water, add coffee, put coffee in a cup, put it someplace where it could be drunk, let it cool until it was drinkable.

Have: Money to buy the necessary, or the ability to make money so you can buy the necessaries or the skill to create the necessaries: water, a pot to boil water in, fuel to make a fire, a fire to put a pot on, time to boil the water, coffee, the skill to make a cup of coffee, a cup to pour it in when made, a place to put it or drink it.

Now when you put this into a sequence of actions you will see that it looks like a doingness list. So you would have to add the havingness list and there would be no point in it unless you brought about the beingness list.

Now, from the above you could work out the subproduct list of a cup of coffee. Now, if at some future date you found out there was something wrong with the coffee valuable final product all you would have to do is assess this list and find out how come no VFP. The subproduct omits and wrong targets would leap at you and, if handled, could result in the VFP of a cup of coffee quite promptly.

And if you yourself were not involved in making the cup of coffee you would be able to debug how come no cups of coffee.

And if other departments or people had to be convinced there was valid reason for no cup of coffee you would use the list.

So as an exercise why don't you compile the subproduct lists for a cup of coffee.

When you get into anything as vast and complex as an org you can see that subproduct lists are vital to the understanding and accomplishment of VFPs.

And you would not be asking do you have to have one staff member for making each step of making a cup of coffee.

Now, as a second exercise take a valuable final product and break it down yourself, just like we broke down the cup of coffee, and searchlights will play against the sky, bands will strike up and understanding will reign everywhere and so will VFPs.

Not getting pcs audited? Not getting students trained? Not getting mobs of people walking in the front door? Not buying new buildings? Not having a highly trained expert staff? Do some subproduct lists and assess them and you'll know all about it.

USE AS ORDERS

If a valid subproduct list is used as a basis for issuing orders to a staff member, a section, department, division or org, they will be right targeted and valuable final products result.

It will greatly increase org efficiency and show up holes.

When the orders are issued and VFPs do not appear you will know what you are getting and what you are dealing with: Noncompliance? Sabotage? Overload? No recruitment? No hatting? R/Sers? Misguided staff? or what? Well that would be up to you to investigate and you have a guide of the subproduct list and what didn't or couldn't occur and get busy and do something about it.

USE AS QUOTAS

Subproducts can be quotaed and should be but they can only be quotaed in view of what can be done with what one has.

When you quota just one subproduct in a long line-up of other unquotaed subproducts, you can get into a situation where the subproduct or the quotaed subproduct is lacking support and so won't occur. In this case you can see that the subproduct gets the support while being obtained on a cope basis.

You can't just chant a lot of figures at a staff.

It is safer to quota the doable and then gradually add quotas to new doables as your facilities and capacity expand.

You can quota an HGC on pcs gotten into session. But remember you will also have to quota Tech Services phone calls and letters.

To do quotaing you have to know how to "play the piano" and have to be totally knowledgeable of existing scenes at any given moment. It is not an ivory tower job.

You can quota 500 file folders filed but remember you had better quota, for that time only, 500 file folders if there are none.

Quotaing does result in subproducts which result in VFPs and should be done.

But it is a highly educational process. The response can be anything from "They don't make them anymore" to "The auditors have no pens" or "It's busted" but the point is whatever turns up on quotaing, you can handle it.

If you don't quota you probably won't have anything to handle and the result is a nice soft idle life of total poverty for one and all.

Subproduct lists are made for those who are not dedicated to the cult of poverty and destitution.

So quota and very soon you will find out more about playing the org piano than ever before and you may even get some VFPs too which is after all the label of the game. If you misquota too often and don't learn in the process you'll probably get a mutiny.

It's fairly certain that if you quota nothing you won't ever get a cleared area. So quota away and quota intelligently.

DEBUG USE

A major use of subproduct lists is debugging the absence of high quantity, high quality valuable final products or no product at all.

As it is VFPs which keep an org going, not promises or hope you can see that a subproduct list is vital to straighten out an area.

By assessing the subproduct lists against a direct inspection of the area to which it applies one can see the major things that are missing. It is these missing things which are preventing the attainment of the valuable final product of the area, so vital to the org's survival.

UNDERSTANDING

A subproduct list enormously assists an understanding of what an area is supposed to be doing.

It will be found that staffs in a section or department or even division don't really know what it is supposed to be doing.

By simply taking up the subproduct lists with them point by point, they will suddenly envision the VFP and see what it really is.

PRODUCTION

People can be very busy without producing anything. The busyness of people can sometimes be rather misdirected.

By having an exact list of subproducts, a staff gets a very good reality on what productive busyness is. They will coordinate their busyness and drop out nonproductive busyness and real org VFPs will begin to appear.

ORGANIZATION

As an org is compartmented, staff members in one part of an org or even in one part of a department have no view of other areas and don't know what they are supposed to be doing. A subproduct list is highly informative to them. What *is* supposed to be coming out of that other area?

Also a staff member is a part of a flow line. If he has no idea what the point earlier on the line is supposed to be doing and what the point later on the line is supposed to be doing, he sometimes can't see the value of what he is supposed to be doing and does not take adequate responsibility for it as he may not conceive how important it is to the VFP.

A case in point of this—you won't believe it—was where a Division 2 could not understand why they got no re-signs until they found out that F/Ning students were a subproduct of the Academy. When they discovered this—and that there were no F/Ning students in the Academy but an awful lot of high-TA students—they couldn't do anything about their own plight. (Needless to say the fur flew at the staff meeting.) Thus, using subproduct lists, a part of an org can improve itself and its own VFP by knowing what subproduct another part is supposed to be producing.

INCOMPLETE LISTS

Where you have incomplete subproduct lists—and probably no subproduct lists are perfect—you can get a false sense of security.

An incomplete list does not operate well as a debug list. Thus subproduct lists have to be intelligently used and often recompiled. They also have to be suitable to the activity for which they are compiled.

WRONG LISTS

Where a subproduct list is wrongly worked out the staff in that area can be mistargeted and can be made very busy again with no VFP.

The test of any subproduct list is: Is it resulting in VFPs? If not, somebody has been busy making a staff busy.

The test of a correct subproduct list is does it result in good VFPs when used.

And knowing all this, you can now act and the VFPs will now magically appear.

It's all just magic after all isn't it.

L. RON HUBBARD
Founder

HCO POLICY LETTER OF 15 AUGUST 1978

Remimeo
HCOs
Org Officers
Estos

CHINESE SCHOOLING AN ORG BOARD

In a Chinese school the instructor stands up before the class, with a pointer, and taps each part of the chart or text being taught and says it. A Chinese class then chants in unison in response to the teacher.

This system of verbatim teaching is used in orgs to drill the org board.

The top exec of the org (CO or Exec Dir) is the first one drilled, with other execs following suit, as they have to know the org board far better than the crew—otherwise they will run a "hey-you" org board.

Chinese schooling an org board is never flattened. Once you get the org board itself and the names of the people on the posts well drilled, you start drilling the duties of each department and every post one by one, all the way down the org board and that takes weeks. Then you go back to whole-org-board drilling and so it goes.

There are two steps in Chinese schooling an org board.

A. The instructor taps the org board with a pointer and says what it is. Then asks the class what it is and they chant the answer.

B. When the class has learned by being told and repeating, the instructor now taps the org board with the pointer and asks, "What is this?" and the class chants the correct answer.

L. RON HUBBARD
Founder

Assisted by
Commodore's Messenger Flag

DELIVERY AND EXCHANGE

HUBBARD COMMUNICATIONS OFFICE
1 Brunswick House
83 Palace Gardens Terrace, London W8
BAY 5780

OPERATIONAL BULLETIN 10   28 December 1955

I am giving here in outline form the basis of survival of various Scientology organizations. This is how they live and this is how they keep going. When they stumble it is because staff is missing out one or another of these points.

In five years of trying anything and everything—and I mean everything—to get things going, my own program of success for organizations boils down to the following. I would consider it a favor if all Scientologists concerned with Scientology organizations studied this for what it is—an outline that wins:

THE MANAGEMENT AND ACTIVITIES OF SCIENTOLOGY ORGANIZATIONS

(One copy to each staff member and to all
Scientology organizations)

The function of the HASUK is the dissemination of Scientology and the demonstration of its results.

Dissemination by:

Free lectures
Free Group Processing
Free pamphlets
Sale of elementary texts   ⎧ 1. To bookstores
Sale of advanced texts   ⎨ 2. To members
                           ⎩ 3. To public
Sale of tapes   ⎧ To members
                ⎩ To groups
Rental of tapes ⎧ To members
                ⎩ To groups
Circulation of *Certainty*
Circulation of HASI Bulletins

Demonstration of results by:

Good clinical auditing (intensives only)
Adequate training of auditors   ⎧ 1. By HASI school
                                ⎩ 2. By HASI grads
High ethical standards   ⎧ Certificate control
                         ⎩ Failed case control

Efficient operation and presentation of office and quarters by:

Alert personnel
Swift replies to letters
Swift filling of orders
Origin of high-toned letters
Cleanliness of offices
Courteousness of staff

Financial policy:

Income must be greater than outgo.
Charges on books should be cost x three.

Charges on tapes must be cost x two.
Tapes and magazines can be sold at a loss.

Charges on training must be adequate to ensure the long continuance of that person's training. (About 3 years.) Total training HPA and BScn and DScn, the formal (in class) training, is only a fraction of total done.

Charges on processing must be adequate to ensure all eventualities for any one case. Refuse to sell hourly processing. Never sell 25 hours to a rough case. Sell 75.

Strict accounting, bookkeeping and invoices with counterchecking of all functions.

Operational smoothness is obtained by:

Informing everyone in the organization of everything.

1. Interdepartmental bulletins;

2. Bulletin boarding coups and changes;

3. Being exact and brief;

4. Being real about conditions;

5. Being frank inside and putting up a solid front to the outside;

6. Talking out troubles within organization

7. Staff meetings, regular and exact;

8. Paying only passing attention to lengthy or critical letters

Financial security is obtained by:

1. Anticipating slumps and planning fast promotion and mailings to meet them;

2. Compelling interest in organization;

3. Being real about the actuality of needs;

4. Attention to the philosophy that a healthy organization is a *long*-term investment by staff and realization that the only staff personnel ever fired by the HASes were those who flagrantly acted to shorten the life of the organization for all;

5. Sound advertising;

6. Good word of mouth;

7. Good financial planning;

8. Only Scientologists or those so studying, on staff in any capacity;

9. A sincere interest in Scientology's health and good action—no financial distress;

10. Keep all staff processed.

The organization in general will be only as healthy as its legal control of the subject appears formidable to any hungry invader. Hence, no membership organization, no loose stock distribution, no large unpaid bills, no overcapitalization because of property. Own little, do much. Owning much means doing little.

Happy New Year to Scientology staff everywhere. Let's make 1956 the year we really win.

L. RON HUBBARD
Founder

HUBBARD COMMUNICATIONS OFFICE
Saint Hill Manor, East Grinstead, Sussex

HCO POLICY LETTER OF 26 MAY 1961
Issue II

Remimeo
All Staff
Tech Hats
Qual Hats

*A Message to the Executive Secretaries
and All Org Staff*

Keeping Scientology Working Series 2

QUALITY COUNTS

Clearing is now in the reach of every Scientologist.

Excellent auditor training is now in the reach of every Academy.

And these are the only things in the long run that will count.

When I see an organization staff panting after newspaper publicity or going mad on the subject of dissemination, and at the same time turning in to me bad results and poor student quality, I know somebody has their targets mixed up.

Quality is the *only* thing that counts. If quality in training and processing is not given first rank and constant priority by secretaries or Executive Secretaries, then all the administration in the world will not make the grade for any Central Org.

Deliver the goods. That's a crude way to put it. But if you want a new and better civilization, you won't get it by advertising or worrying what people think of you. You will get it only by releasing and clearing people and sending them out into the society to get the show on the road in all branches of human activity, including Scientology.

I know we have been a long time without clearing people. But we're clearing them now. What does it take to clear people? It takes highly skilled and tightly supervised auditing. It takes good technology. It takes good technical application.

If you'll forget about how easy it is to mob students all up in a class and actually confront each student as an individual, make sure he knows every essential step he has to know, make sure *all* his questions get answered, you'll have auditors that can audit.

Will you *please* put attention on raising technical skill in the HGC, releasing people, clearing people, and on the quality of training in the Academy to the end of getting every student capable of all the steps necessary to release people.

I have made the grade technically in the field of research. Now it's time to drop all the booboos and nonsense. All you have to do in an org is release and clear people and turn out auditors who can release people and keep in contact with the public and treat them well and you're over the top.

835

This morning I received a cable from an org. An urgent cable. Did it say, "How do you assess for a Prehav level" or something sensible? No, it didn't. It said, "Send us some biographical data for a newspaper article." I spit. That org is doing the lousiest job possible in Technical and is all worked up to get publicity. What's this? *Do* they think a society in this shape will approve Scientology into power? Hell no! And to hell with this society. We're making a new one. So let's skip the approval button from a lot of wogs and settle down to work to make new people and better people. *Then* maybe you'll have a society.

Right here and right now this policy is laid down in concrete with an atomic branding iron: THE FIRST AND PRIMARY GOAL OF AN ORGANIZATION IS DELIVERING THE FOREMOST TECHNICAL QUALITY THAT CAN BE DELIVERED IN ITS AREA.

All right. I've made my technical target bang in the bull's-eye. You can release and clear. You can train auditors well. Well, Christ! Let's do it, do it, do it!

L. RON HUBBARD
Founder

HUBBARD COMMUNICATIONS OFFICE
Saint Hill Manor, East Grinstead, Sussex

HCO POLICY LETTER OF 29 MAY 1961
Issue I

CenOCon

Keeping Scientology Working Series 3

QUALITY AND ADMIN IN CENTRAL ORGS

The function of the administrative personnel in a Central Organization is to make technical quality possible and get it delivered to Scientologists and the public.

Administration is no unimportant function. On the contrary, I had to work in Scientology a long time before I found out that in the absence of good administration, technical quality is impossible. At first I counted on high-caliber businessmen to do it. Then I found, after 1954, that they didn't have a clue and that their use had led us on a bad course. So we had to develop and learn administration and we are winning on it.

An administrative personnel is there to keep the lines moving and the function of his post operating.

Administrative personnel get Scientology to the public, keep the public happy and the organization solvent.

Administrative personnel are there to keep administration out of technical hands and let technical work.

Administration gets the public in and out, keeps communication going, gets the data to tech and keeps the org from going broke.

Administration is, however, owed something by technical. If administration gets people in for service, it is only right that that service, when rendered by technical, be the highest possible quality.

For if administration in all departments is not backed up by quality technical achievements, then administration is betrayed.

If one keeps, as in Accounts, collecting money for service rendered by technical, then Accounts has a right to demand that it was good service or else the accountant, in collecting, betrays.

Therefore, administration may at any time, just as technical may demand good admin, demand of technical that it produce and hold its own.

As of this moment there is no excuse of any kind for any technical failure in any Central Org.

The moment we got all the tools, it showed up that technical often had not understood any of the tools it already had. A clear-cut, simple routine as it now exists makes auditing and training a problem in black and white. Either it is done or it isn't.

If results are not forthcoming for any person as of now, then somebody is goofing. And it won't be any small goof.

It is working out that goofs are of this magnitude:

Auditor does not know anything about reading a meter but has been kidding us one and all that he or she knew;

Auditor has not the vaguest on how to handle rudiments;

Auditor couldn't security check Khrushchev and find a crime;

Auditor has no clue about assessment;

Auditor just doesn't even report to session.

That would be the sort of thing it would take to keep Scientology from working on every case. The errors are *gross,* never slight, if a case doesn't move.

All right. Admin personnel do their job. Therefore they have a right to expect tech will do its job.

The whole source of low units is tech failure. Bad tech makes it almost impossible to get pcs or students in. Therefore admin has a right to raise hell over bad tech. A graph drops. ARC breaks gleam clear to anyone. Admin, working at a less interesting job, has the right to scream loud enough to be heard on Arcturus. Because *that* took a fantastic, large technical goof to achieve.

None can now say all is changing in tech. The only thing that's changing is the communication and information to get tech to do its job.

Low units, lack of enough personnel, lack of new executive personnel, all trace to tech failure in the past.

Now is the time to make good. We *can* release people *easily.* Why not do it? We can clear people. Why not do it?

A high executive in a Central Org who had had a tech department that was failing, failing, failing owned up the other day to "having all the data but being too busy to study it." He meant, obviously, he was too busy to do his job. And a Joburg Security Check found out why.

All staff members, tech and admin, of a Central Org, each one or all together, have a right to demand that every tech person knows his business and does the job.

All staff personnel, in a meeting or by petition, have a right to demand certain personnel be sent to Saint Hill to be trained.

All staff personnel have a right to demand that any or all staff personnel be given a *Joburg* Security Check, WW Sec Form 3, by somebody who knows how to give one.

All staff personnel have a right to demand practical and functional releasing and clearing (1) of staff, (2) of executives and (3) of the public who buy our service.

If we're going to put a new world here, we better get going on the project. It isn't as if we could fool people forever.

L. RON HUBBARD
Founder

HCO POLICY LETTER OF 21 JANUARY 1965R

Gen. Non-Remimeo
Int Board Members
Sthil Executives

Issue I
REVISED 5 APRIL 1965

VITAL DATA ON PROMOTION
THE FUNDAMENTALS OF PROMOTION

Successful orgs, good dissemination, a salvaged planet, require the following basic things:

1. Workable Technology. This means something to offer that is desirable and will be received by individuals in the public body.

2. Good execution of the technology. This means holding a constant of application without variation in how it is done from person to person or place to place. This outlaws at once all squirreling and individual variations *even when they are good* for they bring about an inconstant of execution and this can wipe out technology, leaving one with nothing to promote and a dead end of all spread of technology. Hence, no articles in magazines giving different points of view. Hence, no officially authorized books giving variant methods. Even if they were good, it would halt all promotion and end freedom for the planet.

3. Accumulation of the identities of persons. This is done by getting lists of names, by personal contacts, etc. But however it is done, it is totally the accumulation of identities.

4. Offering those identities something they will buy, a book or a service.

5. Delivering what is offered.

That is all there is to successful promotion. There are a thousand ways to do (3) *the accumulation of the identities of persons* and (4) *offering these identities something they will buy* so promotion *looks* complex. It is not.

Successful promotion means *continuing*. One cannot continue to promote as per (3) *accumulation of the identities of persons* and (4) *offering these identities something they will buy* unless (1) *workable technology,* (2) *good execution of the technology* and (5) *delivering what is offered* are in place.

Promotion can be done without (1) *workable technology,* (2) *good execution of the technology* and (5) *delivering what is offered* or without one or another of them, but if so then it dead ends all the time and becomes too expensive to do. If (1) *workable technology,* (2) *good execution of the technology* and (5) *delivering what is offered* are in place, then promotion continues and is easy to the *degree* that (1) *workable technology,* (2) *good execution of the technology* and (5) *delivering what is offered are* in place.

However, (1) *workable technology,* (2) *good execution of the technology* and (5) *delivering what is offered* can be wholly in place without any world beating a path to the better mousetrap maker. By the nature of the bank, collective opinion is always derogatory or bank, this being the one thing held in common by all. So the group ignores the good and embraces the bad. Thus the appeal must be to the individual for his *personal* use. And even then one always has to do (3) *accumulation of the identities of persons* and (4) *offering those identities something they will buy.* No matter how good (1) *workable technology,* (2) *good execution of the technology* and (5) *delivering what is offered* are, (3) *accumulation of the identities of persons* and (4) *offering those identities something they will buy* must always be vigorously executed continually. There is no coasting along on yesterday's steam. All tomorrows require today's heavy promotion.

We call (1) Technology, (2) Good Service and (5) Ethics. We call (3) Dissemination and (4) Salesmanship. (3) Dissemination and (4) Salesmanship are really promotion. But all five must exist for promotion to be successful.

So that is *all* there is to promotion.

One contacts people by any media including word of mouth, ads, rumors, etc. In (3) Dissemination, it is enough to accumulate names and addresses of persons who have been contacted.

One, in (4) Salesmanship, effectively offers these individuals something they can and will buy—service, status, increased potential, anything they will buy.

In (5) Ethics, one delivers what is offered.

If you just remember that's all there is to promotion, you will be very successful.

Therefore you:

a.　*Never* seek public or group repute or contest it or get involved in it. It's only collective bank. You do not do "goodwill" advertising or just try to get the name about. You only accumulate identities as per (3) Dissemination and use them for (4) Salesmanship—offering them something they will buy.

b.　*Never* count on an individual to "spread the word if he experiences a miracle" as you can always contact more people than he can.

c.　*Never* via your comm line heavily through a "powerful person" or "authoritative group" as you can promote better directly.

d.　*Never* seek a subsidy for what you are doing as at once you or any subsidized office will cease to promote to the public individuals. You throw out anything or anyone who is working to make you get a subsidy or who demands a subsidy to operate an office, as there goes your public contact. It ceases to have point as there's no dependence on the public individual so he ceases to be served. Subsidy is a fine way to fail and *always* leads to a dead end. A subsidized office ceases to promote as it no longer depends on doing (3) Dissemination—*accumulation of the identities of persons* and (4) Salesmanship—*offering those identities something they will buy* for its daily bread. So it is useless in the scheme of things and, not serving, becomes dangerous.

If you don't promote, the whole effort will dead end, the individual will no longer be reached, the group bank reaction will set in and that's the end of it.

Inadequate promotion, not reaching the individual, and any violation of (5) Ethics—*delivering what is offered* are the sources of *all* the difficulties we have experienced.

Therefore adequate promotion, reaching the individual and making sure of (5) *delivering what is offered* will be responsible for all the successes we will experience in the future.

It is as simple as that.

When you hear proposals to reduce mailing lists, know somebody is trying to kill you.

When you see something being offered that the individual cannot buy, know that somebody is being silly.

When you see lists of people being collected who *will not* buy, know somebody is being extravagant.

Err on the side of too many names accumulated, however, and burn the midnight oil figuring out what they can and will buy that you can deliver. Sell it for enough to let you keep on promoting and soon you'll have the planet.

ORGANIZATION

The Earth measure of success is the amount of power, authority, people, wealth and property one *controls*.

It is not necessary to bank it to your own name if you can dictate its expenditure.

The reason we are interested in success of this kind is because it is the wherewithal to reach and get the job done. Without that, these things, except for people, are trash.

It is all very well to idealize poverty and associate wisdom with begging bowls, or virtue with low estate. However, those who have done this (Buddhists, Christians, Communists and other fanatics) have dead ended or are dead ending. That route *doesn't* get the job done so it isn't a workable route.

The hard fact of this civilization is, given enough money or control you can usually buy or demand your way out of any game you don't want to play. Thus you can keep on playing the game you *do* want to play. It is always a matter of amusement to me to find out some attacker is after money. For that's an easy one.

To keep going on a planetary salvage job you have to have the means to salvage in the frame of reference of the planet. Hence, we need the above things to get the job done.

841

Therefore you have to have an organization. This makes it easy to handle the activities needful for salvage and to acquire or control the wherewithal to continue to salvage.

Without power, authority, people, wealth and property you cannot make enough impact at the level of reality of the individuals you are seeking to salvage.

If you only wanted salvage for one or two, then none of these would be needed in any vast amount. But large numbers being salvaged requires organization. And organization requires the other things to keep operating and remain real.

You can therefore know your enemies by those who seek to knock out any part of your:

a. Power

b. Authority

c. Personnel

d. Wealth

e. Property.

As collective-think demands that these items particularly be knocked out, handling and continuing an organization is a rather arduous activity.

The *individual* is the effect of these items, however, so if one can maintain them, one wins.

One forms an organization only in order to do (1) *workable technology,* (2) *good execution of the technology,* (3) *accumulate the identities of persons,* (4) *offer those identities something they will buy* and (5) *deliver what is offered* under Promotion.

Because of the character of the bank and collective think, number (1) *workable technology* under Promotion is not possible to achieve by an organization or group. Group research is not merely too expensive, it is also only *re*-search of the work generated by an individual. New ideas never appear in group research so it merely polishes at best (and messes up at worst) what has already been done technically by an individual.

Therefore organization begins at (2) *good execution of the technology,* exists to do (3) *accumulation of the identities of persons* and (5) *deliver what is offered.* (4) Salesmanship—*offering those identities something they will buy* again is usually the work of an individual—thinking up ideas and offerings.

Therefore the central control point of an activity puts an organization there to do (2) *good execution of the technology,* (3) *accumulation of the identities of persons* and (5) *delivering what is offered* and works individually to find new ways to do (3) *accumulation of the identities of persons* and originates (4) *offering those identities something they will buy.*

Thus a central control point has a dual engagement—(a) To put and keep the broad organization there to do (2) *good execution of the technology,* (3) *accumulation of the identities of persons* and (5) *delivering what is offered;* and (b) to originate better ways to do (3) *accumulation of the identities of persons* and new ways to do (4) *offering those identities something they will buy.*

Thus the relation of a central control point to the organization is very easy to understand.

The hardest work consists of keeping the organization from going banky and not doing (2) *good execution of the technology,* (3) *accumulation of the identities of persons* and (5) *delivering what is offered.* The most brilliant work consists of better ways to do (3) *accumulation of identities of persons* and effective things for (4) *offering those identities something they will buy.*

This is the totality of action by a central control point. If done well, the whole organization achieves the final objective and if done badly the whole thing dead ends.

Great pressures exist against a central control point to violate its needs for (a) to (e) under Organization above, and it is easy to surrender without realizing that surrender is fatal in our case to everyone on this planet and perhaps ourselves as well.

Resist these pressures successfully and the central control point then can do (2) *good execution of the technology,* (3) *accumulation of the identities of persons,* (4) *offering those identities something they will buy* and (5) *delivering what is offered* and everybody wins.

And that's all there is to organization.

L. RON HUBBARD
Founder

843

HCO POLICY LETTER OF 2 JUNE 1965
Issue III

Remimeo
All Execs
All Staff
HCO Hats
Qual Hats
Tech Hats
All Registrars and
    Tours Personnel
All Marketing
    Personnel

ORG ETHICS AND TECH

(Originally written by LRH as Sec ED 44 Int,
2 June 65. Issued as an HCO PL on 23 Mar. 85.)

(Hat check on all executives)

Refs:

HCO PL 23 Sept. 64	POLICIES: DISSEMINATION AND PROGRAMS
HCO PL 19 Sept. 79	Marketing Series 11 PROMOTION
HCO PL 7 Aug. 65	SUPPRESSIVE PERSONS, MAIN CHARACTERISTICS OF
HCO PL 17 June 65	STAFF AUDITOR ADVICES

SOFT SELL

You do not bring your dissemination down to your quality of delivery.

You bring your delivery up to your dissemination.

SOFT SELL means vaguely maundering about your product. Example: "Scientology sometimes makes people worry a bit less."

Now, of course, if you don't deliver good Scientology, that mirrors what you can deliver.

The *right* course is to figure out what you *should* deliver and promote it and gear up and polish up *and* deliver it.

The "little-brown-church-in-the-vale" mock-up where the community can come and sing and not be too unhappy is horrible. If Scientology is that in your area, you better really figure out what it *can* do and do it and say you do it. You're using an atom bomb to raise pigeons in.

THE WHOLE FAILURE OF CASES AND RESULTS LIES IN LACK OF AN EFFICIENT ETHICS SECTION IN AN ORG.

If ethics is out in your area, you'll *never* get tech in. Auditors will goof and alter-is, Supervisors will foul up, and tech doesn't get run or taught. And this gives you a tendency to soft sell BECAUSE YOU AREN'T DOING SCIENTOLOGY!

ANY process we have ever had, had only TWO failure points—(1) pc was a PTS or SP, (2) auditor or Supervisor was not using standard processing procedure. There were NO other reasons.

This is a fantastic advance if you only realize it and get it fully used.

There is no reasonable reason about any of it except (1) pc was a PTS or SP, (2) auditor or Supervisor didn't practice standard procedure in delivery.

The answer is ethics. Lay off not wanting to commit overts. What size overt is it to let the whole human race rot because one didn't have guts enough to handle discipline? *That's* a gigantic overt—to have the tools and not apply them.

Execs, if there is any slightest bit of soft sell going on in your org, the actions that must be taken are:

1. Get in ethics hard in your org and area. Raise hell with it.

2. Upgrade and remorselessly standardize your HGC delivery. Never let a PTS or SP get by without full technical and ethics action. When you have a case flub in the HGC you get it promptly, same instant, to the Case Supervisor who determines whether it is (a) PTS or SP or (b) auditor goof or (c) nothing wrong and returns pc back where he came from—same auditor in HGC. If it is (a) the pc gets standard ethics and technical handling as per policy on PTS or SP. If it is (b) the auditor gets corrected with cramming and ethics. Don't do another thing than the above or you'll be messed up.

3. Upgrade and remorselessly standardize your Academy. If a student is not getting through material, send at once to Qual Div. It is (a) student is PTS or SP or (b) student has misunderstood or (c) nonstandard course such as shifted checksheet or refusal to check out or let the student have material. For (a) send the student to Ethics for standard policy handling. For (b) the student is sent to Dept of Correction for cramming and Word Clearing (at his own expense) and is then sent back, through the Examiner, to course. For (c) the Supervisor is sent to Ethics and Cramming and the student returned to course. Never vary, and be as hard on people who don't do the above exactly as you are on students.

4. Get executives turning in their 1 May 65 PL reports on goofs on staff. And turn in any executive who fails to so report a staff member who goofs or fails to comply.

5. Get a reality on what you should be producing and produce it. What *are* you trying to produce? Decide and do it.

6. Get a grip on the decisions of the org pattern—"Yes" greater than "No," "No" greater than "Yes" or no action. This means there are only two decisions possible *and* if neither is, you send the person or despatch back where he or it came from. If there are four or more choices, your org pattern is not in correctly.

7. GET RID OF DISTRACTIONS FROM SCIENTOLOGY in your org. Baby-sitting or raffle tickets and such nonsense. You need a Reception room that is *not* your Comm Center, but which *is* PLASTERED with charts and data about Scientology where loose bodies can wait—and learn.

8. Stop trying to cope with minor matters and get your org board in—that takes care of the lot. Get up an 8 foot 9 inches-long sheet of blue Formica with its bottom 3½ feet from the floor or more and the board 4 feet or more high, and put your new org pattern on it. Assign *all* your people to departments. And get more people.

9. Knock off the soft sell and flubbed delivery. You can make Releases with any level you've got *if* you get ethics in as above.

10. Recognize we're ready to roll. It's a new civilization we're after and we'll do it. And in less than five years!

You *won't* lose any people because of ethics. On the contrary, they'll swarm in. Only SPs will blow. So do it, do it, do it.

L. RON HUBBARD
Founder

HCO EXECUTIVE LETTER OF 2 NOVEMBER 1965

Gen.
Non-Remimeo

U R G E N T   U R G E N T   U R G E N T

TO: The HCO Exec Sec
    Note: Not Melbourne

FROM: RON

SUBJECT: **YOUR ORG—REPLY EXPECTED**

I am worried about your org income.

You are dropping too often into lower income areas. This can prove dangerous.

The other day here at Saint Hill I looked over the income department and found several ways they were blocking body and money flow. Further one person, able at getting people to pay, went on vacation. The first week he was off, income dropped a few hundred. The second week it dropped 3,000 pounds! The person who relieved him was more concerned *actually* in barring his door than in keeping the income up. If it can happen here it can happen elsewhere too.

I think your org suffers from three blocked lines only.

One is the required flood of letters out. Orgs are always affluent so long as they flood out letters. The income curve follows *quantity* not quality of letters. Lately stressing quality dropped quantity. Get all the addresses you have and start flooding out *quantity* of letters.

Two is blocked Registrar—Income lines. You must not have anybody really letting the income in to the degree they should. Either your Registrar or Accounts is making it hard for people to come in for service.

Three is service. I am sure you do not offer or give all the service you could—training and processing. Two orgs have never even sold a single 25-hour intensive this year. That means the service line is blocked. I don't think you deliver the 25-hour intensives or courses you could because you may not be able to deliver them easily. Your income looks that way.

Saint Hill has been booming on the heels of a big slump. It slumped in early '64. I got the income up to 5 times the early '64 weekly income. It took a lot of hard work to do that. And it took six months to really see results. I stressed (1) Heavy promotion; (2) Cleaning up Income and Registrar lines; (3) Giving better and more service.

You slumped when public prices were raised but that is ancient history now. It is no longer a factor. Your recovery depends on (1) Heavy promotion; (2) Letting the people in; and (3) Service delivery.

Frankly, I don't think you have tried to enroll in your own org.

Take the following steps at once on the highest priority basis.

1. Find out if your org is sending out anything that would force YOU to come in at once and buy large chunks of service. If not, repair it and start sending out literature or letters or offerings that would.

2. Try to enroll in your own org. Visit the Registrar and Cashier and make them go through *all* their routine of selling and receiving money from you. Repair any block or lack of pull in that you find regardless of any policy. Make the Registrar make you sign and make the Cashier take "your money" easily. Blow the line open.

3. Go through the motions of (a) getting on a course and (b) getting an intensive started on yourself. Repair any breakdown you find and get those services in a state of delivery.

Now I mean *you*. It's you I want to go through this.

When you have done it, I want your report. Give me all you (a) found and (b) did to correct any blocks.

It is very urgent that you do this.

I will be anxiously awaiting your reply.

L. RON HUBBARD
Founder

SEC ED 225 INT   17 March 1966

EXPANSION OF YOUR ORG

1. I have said for years SCIENTOLOGY WILL GO AS FAR AS IT WORKS.

2. If your org isn't making it work it won't go very far.

3. It is up to the Executive Secretaries and Secretaries to make it work in your org.

4. It does work. It works at Saint Hill. Hundreds can make it work. The tech is all there—it only needs to be drummed in and used.

5. It is my total conviction that if your org is not expanding fast you are not making Scientology work. You will expand if you make your auditors and supervisors make it work.

6. You will be overworked as long as you stay small. If you expand you will have more staff and work less.

7. So expand! That's an order.

L. RON HUBBARD
Founder

HCO POLICY LETTER OF 3 JANUARY 1968

Remimeo

SPEED OF SERVICE

(Originally written as Flag Order 340, 3 Jan. 68.
Issued as an HCO PL on 27 Dec. 72.)

In a matter of courses and students, SPEED of service is of vital importance.

The prosperity of a business is directly proportional to the speed of flow of its particles (despatches, cables, goods, messengers, students, customers, agents, etc.).

To prosper, service must be as close to instant as possible.

Anything which stops or delays the flows of a business or delays or puts a customer or product on WAIT is an enemy of that business.

Good management carefully isolates all stops on its flow lines and eradicates them to increase speed of flows.

Speed of service is of comparable magnitude to quality of service, and where exaggerated ideas of quality exist they must become secondary to speed.

Only then can a business prosper.

L. RON HUBBARD
Founder

HUBBARD COMMUNICATIONS OFFICE
Saint Hill Manor, East Grinstead, Sussex

HCO POLICY LETTER OF 30 JULY 1968

Remimeo

GROSS INCOME SENIOR DATUM

THE SIZE NOT THE QUALITY OF AN ORG'S MAILING LIST AND THE NUMBER OF MAILINGS AND LETTERS TO IT DETERMINES THE GROSS INCOME OF AN ORG. IF THIS IS NOT KNOWN AS A SENIOR DATUM TO EXEC SECS AND KEPT IN BY THEM, THEIR CONDITION IS TREASON.

L. RON HUBBARD
Founder

Remimeo

SENIOR POLICY

We always deliver what we promise.

L. RON HUBBARD
Founder

EXECUTIVE DIRECTIVE

LRH ED 26 INT   11 September 1969

TO: All ECs
   All Staff

ORG AFFLUENCES

We will be releasing new data about study next year for university students. It is under research right now.

The first HUGE lesson learned is that an org *staffed with people not fully conversant with all org policy* will be filled with dev-t, have low stats, the best org members will work like fury compared to the rest and life will be hard to live.

Previously we had a staff status program of SS I and II. It isn't enough by a long way.

If every member of an org had an OEC under his belt, 3 times through a checksheet covering policy to 1969, 100 percent exam pass, your org would *boom*.

It isn't ethics that's out. It's common know-how.

Also if your org had only HDGs or above on staff it would have a reality that nobody could knock.

I'll tell you how we learned this about the OEC and HDG.

In 2½ weeks I made 7 HDGs fully qualified out of a class of 15. Because of no time the other 8 were put off course as slower.

These 8 along with 113 other students did not make but 10 percent graduates in the next three *months* part and full time.

This was such a mystery that it had to be solved.

You know how your org classes often fill up with large numbers with few graduates? And few enrollees? Lots of students in class, nobody graduating and nobody enrolling "because it takes a year"?

Well, that mystery has been a mystery for years.

After lots of study of it and asking many questions, I found that the original class was trained with all study policy *in*. Then others took over. NOT ONE SUPERVISOR OR SENIOR IN THAT AREA HAD EVER READ SCIENTOLOGY TRAINING POLICY.

The class was taken over by Supervisors fully trained on Scientology training policy (as in the HDG pack) and WITHIN 72 HOURS FULLY QUALIFIED GRADUATES BEGAN TO ROLL OFF THE COURSE ASSEMBLY LINE.

The block was a gross outness. Training policy was out because it was unknown. And it stopped progress for 3 months! And during all that time the people tried like mad to train and be trained without getting anywhere at all!

In Scientology orgs and classes we are handling a new subject. We cannot depend on outside training to serve up experts to help us. We have had to develop our own training tech to train and our own org tech to function because the wog tech didn't work for us. Handling the mind with minds and a very aberrated public we needed more than the usual woggy system.

When we used wog study methods or wog business methods we failed even when we had experts in them.

So we developed 19-years worth of training tech and 19 years of organization tech. And *where it is known* it works swiftly and well.

Studying this further, I have found that we fail only to the degree we do not use Scientology training tech and policy. When we use those, then the mental technology itself functions like a rocket as it's backed up by good training skill and good admin.

Therefore stats depend on the degree that one

1. Has Scientology standard procedure working

2. Has good Scientology training policy being used and not violated and

3. Good standard admin being done.

Your big buildings, Cadillacs and high pay are to be found on this route of 1, 2, 3.

So how to do this, how to get every staff member at least to HDG and OEC?

Staff training often pulls one off post and makes other problems. Some orgs forget to train staffs at all.

I have just developed for AOs and SHs a way it can be done fast, providing the Supervisors of the Dianetic and OEC and Scientology courses are fully grooved in and *use training policy.*

Already we are requiring new staff members to be HDGs. But what about the old ones?

The idea for SHs is this.

1. We divide staff in half.

2. We put in a full Day org using 50 percent of the staff with its own EC of course.

3. We put in a full night and weekend Foundation using the other 50 percent with its own EC of course.

4. The Day org studies and gets auditing evenings and weekends along with the public in the Foundation.

5. The Foundation staff studies and gets auditing all day five days a week.

This gives the Day org 23 hours a week study and auditing. It gives the Foundation 40 hours a week study and auditing.

Service to the public (and promotion) is pushed heavily so that no financial upset occurs due to this program.

If training policy is severely fully IN, this will make HDGs rapidly, especially in the Foundation.

As soon as a staff member has his HDG he goes right on with his OEC.

When the majority in the Foundation are HDG OEC those now fully qualified transfer to the Day org and the most upstat Day org transfer to the Foundation to rapidly complete.

You will wind up rather quickly (depending on how well training policy is observed) with a full staff Day and Foundation who are

1. HDGs or above,

2. OECs,

3. Fully Dianetic completed as to case.

As all incoming new staff members will be HDGs, they can be kept on lower pay until they are also OECs.

This program will rid your org of most of its internal dev-t and expansion barriers. With all staff fully acquainted with policy as well as basic tech it should be a go-go org from there on out.

The agonies and conflicts of overwork and heavy ethics, errors and damage can become a thing of the past wherever they exist.

As stats are bound to go up, it means the org can make Scientology classed auditors and even VIs, VIIs and VIIIs with rapid ease.

But remember the big lessons:

1. TRAINING PROGRAMS ARE ONLY SWIFT AND SUCCESSFUL WHEN TRAINING POLICY IS FULLY USED AND IN and

2. ORGS ARE ONLY SUCCESSFUL AND FREE OF DEV–T AND TROUBLE WHEN ALL STAFF ARE FULLY TRAINED ON THE OEC and

3. FULL REALITY ON BASIC TECH AS PCs AND AUDITORS GIVE ONE A FULLY HAPPY BOOMING ORG.

It is fairly easy to put such a program into action and carry it through. It is not costly as it can only result in added income from the knowledge gained.

Love,

Ron

L. RON HUBBARD
Founder

855

L. Ron Hubbard
EXECUTIVE DIRECTIVE

LRH ED 67 INT

20 December 1969

To Every Staff Member

HOW TO RAISE STATS

Here is a bit of advice that will help you raise stats.

AUDITING

Auditing is for USE.

The service being supplied by your org is auditing even when you are training auditors—for if they are well trained good auditing is furnished to the area around them.

Staff members get auditing. They furnish auditing. Staff members get trained as auditors. By training other auditors well they furnish auditing.

The admin done is done to furnish auditing and training of auditors.

The ethics put in provides an environment in which auditing is possible and in which it can be taught.

All roads lead to auditing.

Stats depend on auditing being done and being taught.

People progress from left to right on the org board to be audited or trained in auditing.

You are raising your area little by little by auditing.

Auditing is something one does. It must be done.

The HCO ES, the OES and the PES act to keep the org there and pass people through who are audited or being trained to audit.

An org is an auditing factory that also trains people to audit.

That's the basic way we will win the world—auditing.

The divisions and posts flanking tech are all auditing and training support posts that move people down the assembly line of auditing and training.

That's why I say 2:1 admin/tech ratio. All persons on staff who are not needed on admin (exceed the ratio) should be in full-time training as auditors.

Auditors are valuable. An org is valuable if it audits and trains auditors. If an org is valuable, it will get paid by the public to be there. But it is only valuable if it audits and trains auditors.

Small livingness courses, defense, policy, the OEC, promotion, all these are valuable too. But only to the degree they get people in to get audited and trained as auditors.

The field is filling up with Dianetic courses and Dianetic auditors. That is great. But it means an org has to serve them and do even more auditing and upper-level training to handle their rougher cases and to make higher-level auditors.

That's the heart of it. A 49-man org with only 3 auditors and one Supervisor will flop. In a 49-man org 17 or more should be auditors and Course Supervisors. When more than 24 of them are (1 to 1), then the admin actions under the HCO ES and PES don't get done and the line slows.

An org gets people (on any gradient) to get audited and gets people to be trained as auditors.

That gives the org purpose—for only auditing can clean up a community. That gives action. That gives income.

If an org isn't so oriented, then no manner of highly skilled management will make it go.

That's the way it is.

SOURCE

I am the source of Dianetic and Scientology tech, know-how and org form.

A staff member is the source of his stats.

I am responsible for the potential of the auditing.

An auditor is responsible for the application of the tech.

I wrote the bulletins and data sheet.

The Course Supervisor is fully and the only one responsible for getting it to the student. When you see this as a fact, you can easily become cause—over your post, over those about you, over your stats.

You are also a living, causative being.

I have faith in you.

YOU ARE AND CAN BE CAUSE.

Love,

RON

L. RON HUBBARD
Founder

857

L. Ron Hubbard

EXECUTIVE DIRECTIVE

LRH ED 146 INT　　　　　　　　　　　　　　　　20 July 1971

TO: All Staffs
　　Executives
　　CLOs　　　　　　　　　　*URGENT*

SUBJECT: **THE BEGINNING AND MAINTAINING OF A BOOM**

GENERAL SITUATIONS

SITUATION: The GI boom has well begun. Tours and other actions have been extremely successful.

The bugs of "crush sell" and postulate checks have been ironed out.

Tours courses and selling tech are in progress.

This GI boom is excellent and MUST be continued.

Therefore other situations and actions related to it must be rapidly brought up to keep pace with it.

HANDLING: Continuing the successful actions of the GI boom. Taking those actions vital to continue the GI boom and expand it and making sure no other omissions permit the GI boom to break down.

Fortunately a concentration on selling training constitutes the biggest part of the income gained and TRAINING should continue to be concentrated on as the main sales item.

DELIVERY INCREASE

SITUATION 1: GI is being pulled in heavily. Delivery stats not increasing to match it. This forecasts a rough time if delivery of what is sold is not also speeded up and increased.

WHY: It does not take many staff members to get in a GI. It takes a whole org to deliver. One can work at the irreducible minimum of just getting in a GI without also putting an org there and delivering tech at high volume in high quality.

HANDLING: It is splendid to get in GI. At least that is something done. The orgs must be strengthened up to actually deliver fast courses and good auditing so that it EARNS what it is paid and also expands its field by successful

858

word of mouth. A plan is being worked out to credit the org only with cash for what it has *delivered*. The FBO system should be strengthened and the allocation system phased over to increase payment on a gradient for delivered services and decrease GI collected percents. Example: between such and such dates allocation will be weighted more to favor successfully delivered services. Then from such and such a date to such and such, the successful delivery allocation will again increase and the bulk GI collected will be held in reserve an even longer time to award successful delivery. This will arrive at a point where GI is allocated more heavily on successfully delivered services. To be worked out by CS-3 and activated by FBO Continentals and FBOs in orgs. Heavy GI collection should be continued by CS-2 and EDs and COs and Dissem Divs.

ESTABLISHMENT

SITUATION: Musical chairs and unstable CLOs and orgs and even orgs dwindling in staff numbers are a subject broadly mentioned in debriefs. This impedes delivery and loses great amounts of work already done. For instance, the SH area has lost all trace of last year's work in arranging staff auditing. Persons ordered to certain posts are found on other posts. Those on posts are seldom found knowing and wearing their hats. Ground is being lost.

WHY: HASes, COs and EDs are often found operating as "disestablishment officers." They keep tearing up working installations. HASes are hit by a furious torrent of demands from EDs and org officers and give way and instead of recruiting and doing normal hatting and training actions are involved in catching up the backlog of unhandled actions. No HAS to date has been found doing the *correct* orderly cycle of recruit, keep a personnel "HCO Expeditor" pool doing SS I, SS II, and hatting and apprenticing posts. HASes are doing everything else but their own hat. Further, COs, EDs and org officers do not let or force an HAS to wear his actual hat and actually establish an org and hat the posts already there.

HANDLING: HASes must at once appoint an "HCO Cope Officer" to deal with the mad scramble of backlog, must *forbid* internal transfers and forbid a rip up of what is already established. The HAS must then recruit or hire, make a personnel pool of HCO Expeditors that do their SS I and SS II and get fully trained and hatted and apprenticed and so build an org as well as preserve the org that is there. I am writing further know-how for this post and will soon be individually training HASes, org officers, product officers, COs and EDs as such after their FEBC as special courses. Meanwhile CS-7 and *LRH Comms* are to force in the correct HAS actions on the HAS by appointing an HCO Cope Officer to handle randomity, and then force the HAS to actually do THAT post and NO other. This is very URGENT.

IF EVERY STAFF MEMBER WOULD INDIVIDUALLY ORDER VOLUME 0 THE OEC BASIC STAFF HAT FROM PUBS DK, a $16.00 value available postage paid to individual org staff members for only $8.00! AND BEGIN TO STUDY IT ORGS WOULD BEGIN TO STABILIZE. IT'S A LOVELY BIG BOOK AND ITS DATA IS MISSING IN ORGS.

TECH

SITUATION: Tech delivery must be enormously improved in orgs in training and processing and volume and quality.

WHY: Training tech has been out on courses and Internships have been missing in HGCs. The word clearing data of the study tapes was not in full use, making slow courses and poor auditors. The full value of Word Clearing was not realized or used.

HANDLING: Full write-ups of WORD CLEARING are now being done. Full drills are being worked out for immediate forwarding to orgs. Full Course Supervisor drills are nearly compiled. TR AND SERVICES must get this tech checked out and in full use in every org. An HCOB 19 July 71, C/S Series 52, INTERNS, has been written and must be checked out on every CO, ED, product officer, org officer and HAS and C/S and Ds of P by the org's LRH Comm. Students coming off courses must be interns and their certs will only be provisional unless they do intern. This is true for EVERY org.

NEW PEOPLE

SITUATION: Div 6s are undermanned and by report not bringing in enough new people. Also Div 2s are not working to assemble and handle their full CFs and so take advantage of the field.

WHY: Concentration on hot prospect files only by COs and EDs.

HANDLING: TR courses and actions by Div 6 to contact new people and get them in are ordered. Div 6s must be manned up. *CS-6* is to get in full Div 6 actions.

Dissem Secs are being pushed to get CFs being filed up and used and any "ARC broken field" handled.

WHAT TO SELL

LRH ED 145 Int, WHY SOMETHING NEW? is the subject of several projects now going to bureaus and orgs. Sales people must be briefed on what orgs can deliver so they can sell it. The Grade Chart is the subject of what's sold and delivered. This program is currently in full blast.

COMMAND INTENTION

It should be clear from this what I am trying to do.

I am trying to *stabilize* orgs and get them expanded and delivering while they sell.

In this way the GI boom now well begun will continue.

It is quite urgent that this line of approach—big GI, stable org—good delivery—new people—big GI—stable org—good delivery—new people continue over and over. Those things which break this cycle down in any way must be gotten rid of.

If we keep that cycle up we will attain a Power level adequate to clear the planet.

L. RON HUBBARD
Founder

HUBBARD COMMUNICATIONS OFFICE
Saint Hill Manor, East Grinstead, Sussex

HCO POLICY LETTER OF 26 OCTOBER 1975

Remimeo
All Executive
 Directors
All HASes
All Ethics Officers
 and MAAs
All Tech Secs
All Dissem Secs
All Qual Secs
All Treasury Secs
All Distribution Secs

GROSS INCOME/CORRECTED GROSS INCOME RATIO
FAILED CASES AND FAILED STUDENTS

If you take a look at your GI/CGI graph and find it has too wide a gap, if you take a look at your refund requests, and if you find ANY unreasonable gap and if you find ANY requests for refunds, you had better get cracking before you drown in an ARC broken field!

The causes of the gap being too wide between GI and CGI are:

1. *Nondelivery.* The org just didn't deliver the service bought.

2. *Dishonest Registration.* The Registrar promised things you didn't deliver or couldn't deliver and did strange things or arranged oddball loans, or told one and all "you can get your money back."

3. *PTS Conditions Unhandled.* Your C/Ses, auditors and Ethics Officer don't know their business on PTS.

4. *Out-Tech.* Read HCOB 26 Oct. 75, "FAILED" CASES.

If any of these conditions have been permitted to foul up your org and let you down, then you had better get cracking.

The more people there are in your area who have not been given proper service, the less NEW people you will get. It is a subtle way of committing suicide.

The handling of each of the above items is VERY easy. Life only becomes hard, sweating work when you DON'T handle them.

NONDELIVERY

Where you have nondelivery, you make a study of how come and who. It is usually the DTS, D of P and D of T plus an incompetent Qual and a dishonest Dir Reg.

The DTS simply isn't calling in people for service. Or the D of T hasn't bothered to get the materials and make real Supervisors. Or the D of P doesn't know he's responsible for getting auditors and doesn't know you pick up and patch up former field auditors and get them interned and cracking, or know you recruit from the Academy and get them interned. Qual is filling the org up with wrong Whys and doesn't cram admin staff or cram tech staff well.

Somewhere amongst this lot you have some "failed cases." And as there are no "failed cases" but only failed auditors and C/Ses you have let an out-tech scene back up into your lines right inside the org.

And of course there was always the org whose staff had never read an LRH book—believe it or not—and so committed all the above errors with wild abandon.

You CAN handle all these things.

It's as easy to deliver real service as to eat ice cream. The only tough thing to do is NOT to deliver. Then life gets very hard.

DISHONEST REGGING

Dishonest regging can cover anything from crazy loans to telling the pc he will be able to remove his head after a two minute HAS Course taught by an ex-psychologist.

Reges who have never studied *Big League Sales** usually can't close. So they promise the sky, tell people they'll get their money back anyway, offer services only delivered in heaven and generally muck up the scene.

When you have incompetence, you generally get dishonesty.

So the answers to this consist of getting Reges on, cramming them on *Big League Sales,* make sure their own cases are flying and that their own personal ethics are in. Otherwise, the deals they make backfire, cost one and all a lot of work and add up the yelling in the reception room and a case for the Claims Verification Board.

If you don't handle this, you go broke. And the only crime you can really commit in Western society is to be totally broke.

Dishonest regging impoverishes an org faster than fire.

So why should you encourage it by letting it continue?

PTS CONDITIONS UNHANDLED

There are a lot of materials, all in proper packs, about PTS conditions.

Where an org is having trouble with these, the Ethics Officer hasn't ever heard of these packs, much less studied them; the auditors treat the condition as

---

***Big League Sales:** the book *Big League Sales Closing Techniques,* by Les Dane.

something to get out of the way in the ruds; Qual is as effective as a politician and the C/Ses never read the worksheets.

Any PTS condition can be handled.

There are so many policy letters and HCOBs on this and so many sure-fire ways to handle that it is a disgrace for an org not to detect or handle.

Sure, the society has SPs in it and sure, people come in who are PTS. But they come in! And what does an org that doesn't care do for them? Skips it or sends them to the Ethics Officer and off lines and they wind up as refunds.

So what do you do? You see that the C/Ses and Ethics Officers not only have the PTS packs but use the data intelligently and expertly and CARE what happens to people.

You don't just shrug and say, "She's PTS."

You HANDLE and you see they get un-PTSed and that they stay on your lines and help make a better world.

OUT–TECH

Where your org gets an epidemic of out-tech, you get a copy of HCOB 26 Oct. 75, "FAILED" CASES. And you make every tech person in the place star-rate it. And even get off their MUs and everything.

At this state of the subjects of Dianetics and Scientology, we don't have failed cases. There aren't any.

So you just don't tolerate auditors whose TR 1 compares to the mew of a sick kitten or C/Ses who read *MAD** but not worksheets, or Supervisors "all tied up in admin" or Quals whose specialty is wrong Whys.

As an executive you just don't tolerate it. You raise hell.

You know what happens to a C/S or auditor or Super or Qual in my area who lets ONE small error go by. Well, don't try to imagine it. It's too awful to contemplate.

And you know what happens when you DO raise hell and DO get tech in and your C/Ses know their business and the auditors know theirs and the Supers really get students cracking?

Well, the students soar with wins and the pcs glow and the auditors and C/Ses and Supers walk around proudly and look people in the eye and feel GREAT.

An exec who would permit out-tech in his org would feed arsenic to his dying grandmother just for laughs. I have no greater contempt for anyone than an

---

*__MAD:__ an American humor magazine, similar to a comic book.

executive who will let the diamonds of our modern technology be poured in the garbage can and deny suffering decent people a finer life.

Now you can say that's a little strong. But actually I've stated it very weakly because this PL will have to go through the mails.

You CAN handle out-tech. The real "expert" who is feeding you his excuses is only a real expert if his students and pcs always win. Remember that.

You CAN handle out-tech.

The above four crimes are the direct cause of the gap between GI and CGI when it is too wide or worsens.

An international survey just taken shows that where an org is unhealthy, these four crimes in greater or lesser degree exist.

Get prosperous.

HANDLE THESE THINGS.

You can. I trust you to.

L. RON HUBBARD
Founder

HUBBARD COMMUNICATIONS OFFICE
Saint Hill Manor, East Grinstead, Sussex

HCO POLICY LETTER OF 9 AUGUST 1979
Issue I

Remimeo
All Orgs
All Staff

CALL–IN:

THE KEY TO DELIVERY AND FUTURE INCOME

Refs:

HCO PL	9 Aug. 79 II	SERVICE PRODUCT OFFICER
HCO PL	27 Jan. 60	ACCOUNTS POLICIES
HCO PL	6 July 61	ACCOUNTS
HCO PL	13 Oct. 66	INVOICE ROUTING
HCO PL	15 Nov. 60	MODERN PROCUREMENT LETTERS
HCO PL	1 May 65 III	ORGANIZATION, THE DESIGN OF THE ORGANIZATION
HCO PL	16 Nov. 66	AKH Series 7 EXECUTIVE FACILITIES FACILITY DIFFERENTIAL
HCO PL	15 Nov. 74 I	PHONE TIPS
HCO PL	28 May 72	BOOM DATA PUBLICATIONS BASIC FUNCTION
HCO PL	25 June 72	RECOVERING STUDENTS AND PCs
LRH ED 120 Int 20 Aug. 70		AUDITORS ASSOCIATION
HCO PL	13 Sept. 62	COMMENTS ABOUT LETTER REG
HCO PL	6 July 59 II	OUTFLOW
HCO PL	9 Aug. 79 III	SERVICE CALL–IN COMMITTEE
HCO PL	15 Nov. 74 II	CFs, ARC BREAKS IN

THE ED/CO IS RESPONSIBLE FOR THE CALL–IN UNITS AND THE EXECUTION OF PROGRAMS NEEDED TO GET THEM FULLY FUNCTIONAL, UNTIL SUCH TIME AS A SERVICE PRODUCT OFFICER IS APPOINTED.

There are many ways of getting pcs and students into the org for service or further service. One of the major ones is CALL–IN.

CALL–IN means to contact and get a paid public person to come in for his service. Call-in is usually referred to as the action of getting a person who is fully paid for his next service into the org and delivered to, but it can also mean to get a partially paid person fully paid up and into the org.

CALL–IN LOCATION

FULLY PAID individuals are called in by Department 10, Department of Tech Services. An entirely new Call-in Unit is to be set up to handle PARTIALLY PAIDS, which is now located under the Advance Scheduling Registrar (ASR).

Service to the public is the reason an org is there. Call-in is the action of getting paid public into an org in order to train and process them. Just selling services is not enough. One also has to *deliver* them. If one does not deliver services, an org soon gets a reputation for not delivering and the public avoids them and an org can no longer sign people up. Furthermore, a large percentage of an org's income comes from signing up *again* people who are already in the org, just completing services. If you do not call people in to get their service, you do not get the additional sign-ups they will do. When an org does not deliver it soon makes less gross income (GI) and staff get less pay. Staffs that wonder about their pay or why it is low should look around and see whether or not there is any call-in occurring.

The four cycles an org, to be successful and prosperous, must engage in are:

1. Books and dissemination,

2. Sale of service,

3. Call-in of people for service,

4. Delivery of excellent quality service.

When one of these is omitted, the org does not prosper and the staff have difficulty in getting paid.

BASICS OF THE CALL–IN UNITS

There are three separate actions that must occur in an org for the call-in of paid and partial paid public to occur.

1. TREASURY: Invoice assembly.

2. DEPARTMENT OF TECH SERVICES: Call-in of fully paids.

3. ADVANCE SCHEDULING REGISTRAR: Making the partially paid into fully paid and called in.

INVOICE ASSEMBLY

It has been found that call-in has never been used to its full potential mainly due to incomplete lists of fully paids and partial paids, so call-in personnel end up going over the same names again and again. Therefore this project is essential to the existence of any Call-in Unit.

A. Assign a task force of staff, after normal hours, to do the action of getting invoices available for call-in.

B. Get Treas accounts files into order and rapidly filed up-to-date. (Refs: HCO PL 27 Jan. 60, ACCOUNTS POLICIES; HCO PL 6 July 61, ACCOUNTS; and HCO PL 13 Oct. 66, INVOICE ROUTING)

C. Keeping the files in order, cull through and determine for each person if he is fully paid for a service he has not yet taken, or if he is partially paid for a service. This data can be gotten from the statement sheet or invoices. Where you are unsure of whether he actually took the service or not, check with Tech or Qual.

866

D. Put the name, address, phone number, org services and monies on account on the appropriate list, either:

1. Fully Paid or

2. Partial Paid.

E. Xerox the fully paid and partially paid invoices or write down the needed data such as name, address, phone number, whether fully or partially paid, etc., and as fast as they are ready, get copies to the correct Call-in Unit as covered earlier in this issue. If these terminals are not immediately available, place the invoices in a basket labeled either "Fully Paid" or "Partially Paid," appropriately, so they can be picked up or delivered later. This is an immediate action as the full list will take longer to complete and call-in must have the names now.

F. Locate from any place in the org (Distribution, ASR logs, CF [Central Files], interviews with old and current Distrib, Dissem and Tech personnel) any other fully paid or partial paid person; get the data on them and add it to the list.

G. Complete the list of fully paids and partial paids and get the lists over to the respective Call-in Unit (keeping copies of the full list in Treasury in case those sent out are later misplaced).

H. Man the Income Department of Treasury with sufficient personnel so they are able to keep the accounts files up-to-date and call-in areas informed of fully paids and partial paids.

TECH CALL–IN

A. Get your DTS (Director of Tech Services) calling in public from the fully paid list (by means of phone and letters). Beef up his actions with idle auditors and Tech personnel being used to assist in call-in. If there is no DTS then use any other Tech personnel and get them calling in those fully paid.

B. Have them study the Central File (CF) folder and get familiar with the person and what his next step is. (Ref: HCO PL 15 Nov. 60, MODERN PROCUREMENT LETTERS) If you find further data on the public person while studying the central file such as change of address or change of phone number, add this information to the fully paid call-in list, so the list is complete.

C. The Call-in Officer would need to ensure, in liaison with the correct org terminal, that the org is actually prepared to handle the public individual in the way of schedules for auditors.

As a caution, org execs and call-in personnel should be alert to those that tell them not to call in "due to lack of auditors" or some other excuse. The above liaison is put in to ensure that Technical Division is prepared to handle the public. Auditors are to audit high hours and students are to be packed into standard course rooms.

Delivery is the whole intention of call-in.

D. The Call-in Unit is to schedule a pc or student to arrive as soon as possible.

The call-in terminal may have to also assist the public persons in so arranging their own lives as to make coming to the org possible. There is also policy that shows how one's life actually can be broken down into a seven division org board, therefore when looking at it you can see what is missing in one's life, and the lives of others, thus remedying the situation. This is fully covered in HCO PL 1 May 65 III, ORGANIZATION, THE DESIGN OF THE ORGANIZATION, and HCO PL 16 Nov. 66, EXECUTIVE FACILITIES, FACILITY DIFFERENTIAL, section on "Analysis." To utilize this tech fully it is sometimes necessary to call the person in for an interview and by laying this all out on paper, they will see the areas in their life with omitted organization and then be able to handle them.

Call-in must use good intention, understand the individual they are calling in and use good 2-way comm in dealing with the person.

NOTE: For local areas, call-in by phone is customary. For more distant areas, use mailgrams and letters and promo. Keep phone logs of any phone calls made and what was said. A carbon copy goes to Central Files. This can be done by putting a sheet of paper and a sheet of carbon paper under the log book page.

E. Get a phone or phones installed which cannot be called out on but can only be called in on by the public, and give the public these numbers. These numbers will be used for return calls. Ensure such phones are manned with a person drilled on handling public individuals, so that public are not lost off the lines because of no way to reach the org. If you do not have a full-time person to put on this, utilize part-time staff at certain hours and ensure the public are aware of these hours. But if it's part-time ensure the time in which the staff member will be at the phone is when the public will be most able to call.

F. While calling in public you sometimes run across a situation where the person you are calling doesn't answer the phone. In this case send a mailgram in order to contact them fast.

G. Put up a scheduling board and keep track of all confirmed arrivals. Make sure that all key terminals in the org who need to know that a preclear or student is arriving are fully informed. For public coming a distance away, make sure that a hotel or student/pc accommodations are arranged. Also make sure the person's pc folders are available and ready to go.

H. Get them in. Get them delivered to.

I. Get the re-sign line in with pcs and students being interviewed by a Body Reg (after completion of a service) and re-signed up on the spot for further service and their money collected.

J. Ensure the Tech Sec and other org execs force more trained auditors and Supervisors into the Tech Division, as well as more Tech Services personnel. A lack of Tech Services can cripple auditing hours.

K. Get your Tech Call-in Unit manned, and on to getting in fully paids. Don't let this unit be converted into a registration unit.

L. Keep calling in for all services and not concentrating on one service only.

The product of a Tech Call-in Unit is FULLY PAID PUBLIC (STUDENTS AND PCS) GOTTEN INTO THE ORG AND ONTO THEIR NEXT SERVICE.

The statistic for the Tech Call-in Unit is THE NUMBER OF FULLY PAID PUBLIC GOTTEN INTO THE ORG AND ONTO THEIR NEXT SERVICE, with a secondary stat of ADVANCED PAYMENTS USED.

ADVANCED SCHEDULING REGISTRAR
CALL–IN
(For partially paid public)

A. Put your Letter Reges a couple of hours a day onto getting the partially paid public fully paid up for their next service. If there are no Letter Reges, use other Division 2 personnel on an "all-hands basis," a few hours a day to call in partially paids. Ensure this is not used as an excuse to not handle their routine post functions, as these must continue as well.

If there is an ASR, put the ASR onto these call-in functions with help from the rest of the division while the ASR Call-in Unit gets manned up.

B. Ensure they study the Central File folder, as well as the accounts data on each person. Get each person paying up using letters, promo, mailgrams. Get each one fully paid up. *NOTE:* This is partially a registration action, as the Call-in Unit is getting them *paid up* and into the org for service.

C. Ensure there are two ASR Call-in logbooks to keep track of confirmed arrivals. One is for training and the other is for processing. (These logs do not replace the standard ASR logbooks.)

D. Ensure your standard accounts actions stay in.

E. Apply Tech Call-in points C, D, E, F and G, as all equally apply to ASR Call-in Unit.

F. Ensure the Director of Tech Services and Tech Call-in Unit are informed immediately of any fully paids.

G. Ensure they actually get into the org and serviced.

H. Establish an ASR Call-in Unit with single-hatted and posted personnel. Get them working on getting partial paids fully paid and into the org.

NOTE: The main concern of this unit is getting the partial paid person up to fully paid and once the person is fully paid getting his or her name over to the Dept 10 Call-in Unit so the person can be gotten in for service. If, however, the person is ready to come in now, after you have gotten him to fully pay, *do not* hesitate to handle the cycle. All you simply need to do is liaise with Dept 10 Call-in and make sure the necessary arrangements are made. Never turn down public who want to be serviced or shove them off onto another line. Handle the person in front of you is the key.

The product of the ASR Call-in Unit is PARTIALLY PAID PUBLIC GOTTEN FULLY PAID UP AND INTO THE ORG AND ONTO THEIR NEXT SERVICE.

869

The statistic of the ASR Call-in Unit is: (1) NUMBER OF PARTIAL PAIDS NOW FULLY PAID UP and (2) NUMBER OF PEOPLE GOTTEN INTO THE ORG THROUGH ASR CALL-IN ACTIONS.

USE OF PHONES

Insane use of long-distance phone calls will bankrupt any company or organization. Therefore, phones are customarily used in local call-in only. Orgs that have WATS (*Wide Area Telephone Service*) which operates on a fixed monthly rate may use phones for nonlocal call-in. This would normally be viable in major Sea Org Orgs and large Continental Orgs.

HCO PL 15 Nov. 74 I, PHONE TIPS, gives you further data you need to know on use of phones.

FURTHER ACTIONS OF CALL-IN

There are different types of public you will come across, and there are several ways of handling each. These are:

1. THE PERSON WHO IS READY TO COME INTO THE ORG IMMEDIATELY AND WHO REQUIRES ONLY MINOR DEBUGS TO GET HIM INTO THE ORG.

    Some of the ways to handle this are:

    a. Use of Tours to contact individuals, handle their upsets or bugs and get them enthused and get them in. (Ref: HCO PL 28 May 72, BOOM DATA)

    b. Use of LRH ED 302, DEBUG TECH BREAKTHROUGH; apply this to their personal life so it can be arranged that they do come in. It is amazing what some people consider "stops." These "stops" are easily handled using this debug tech and the public person gotten back on lines.

    c. Use of HCO PL 1 May 65 III, ORGANIZATION, THE DESIGN OF THE ORGANIZATION, and HCO PL 16 Nov. 66, EXECUTIVE FACILITIES, FACILITY DIFFERENTIAL, section on "Analysis." See page 3 and 4, point D of this PL for a more complete explanation of how to do this.

2. THE PERSON WHO REQUIRES FURTHER HANDLING AND REHAB TO GET HIM TO COME INTO THE ORG. EXTENSIVE FOLLOW-UP AND CHECKING ON IS NEEDED TO ENSURE HE ACTUALLY DOES MAKE IT.

    These can be handled by:

    a. Call-in personnel tagging with Division 2 Reges to assist on getting a person to arrive in the org or in getting the person fully paid. This is helpful especially if the Div 2 Reg was previously in comm with the public person.

    b. Use of staff who are experienced and have successfully handled public persons for use in calling in partial and fully paids.

c. Use of any of the points covered in 1 above.

3. THE PERSON WHO IS ACTUALLY BLOWN OR PARKED OFF LINES.

a. Use of HCO PL 25 June 72, RECOVERING STUDENTS AND PCs.*
    Find out what is going on, handle them and get them into the org.

b. Use of Auditor Association as FSMs to contact and get in blown auditors
    who are partial or fully paid but never came in for their service. (Ref:
    LRH ED 120, AUDITORS ASSOCIATION, Target 15.*)

c. Use of Tours to do personal contact with the public person and, if possible,
    bring the Chaplain or a terminal from Tech or Qual who is able to sort out
    any grievances or out-ruds the person may have.

d. Use of any of the points covered in 1 *and* 2 above.

4. THE ARC BROKEN PUBLIC.

a. ARC broken public who will not come into the org are usually turned over
    to a Ruds Auditor (located in the Chaplain's Department) who handles such
    public on a special program. The Ruds Auditor cures the ARC breaks with
    Level III tech and sends the person to the usual Registrar when done.
    (Ref: ED 473 WW 842 SH of 1 Sept. 67, WW EMERGENCY CONDI-
    TION, targets 11 and 12)

b. In the case where you can get the ARC broken person into the org for
    handling, which is usually simply done by 2-way comm with the individual
    locating the point of upset or the misunderstood which caused him/her to
    leave and then getting the person's agreement to come into the org for a
    free ruds session, the person is routed to the Chaplain in Division 6 for
    this action. The Chaplain must see to the needed handlings. A C/S 53RL
    (Ref: HCOB 24 Nov. 73RC, SHORT HI–LO TA ASSESSMENT C/S)
    and/or Green Form run on any pc or an HCOB 15 Nov. 74, STUDENT
    REHABILITATION LIST run on any blown student or student who failed
    in practice, will return a person to service.

    In the absence of a Chaplain or Ruds Auditors within the Chaplain's
    Department, this duty is delegated to the Qual Sec or his deputy to see
    to the handling of these public persons.

c. Many of the above actions listed can be used to assist in getting the
    public person handled, such as tours, use of experienced org personnel
    or Reges, etc. The key however to handling any ARC broken person is
    to GET HIM INTO THE ORG AND THE GRIEVANCE OR OUT–
    RUD SITUATION REMEDIED FAST THROUGH THE USE OF THE

*[*Editor's Note:* HCO PL 25 June 72, RECOVERING STUDENTS AND PCs, is in OEC Volume 6.]

*[*Editor's Note:* LRH ED 120 Int, AUDITORS ASSOCIATION, is in OEC Volume 6.]

CHAPLAIN OR ANY PERSON IN THE ORG CAPABLE OF HANDLING SUCH A PERSON.

This does not by any means limit what other actions can be done to handle the above four types of public but serves only to give you an idea of what can be done.

RE-SIGN

The re-sign line is one of the reasons call-in is so beneficial to the org. Every person, when they have completed the service signed up for, will see the Reg to sign up again for another service while in the org.

The factor of re-sign alone can double your org's income and delivery.

COORDINATION

Coordination is a very important part of call-in. Liaison with other divisions and departments can provide more names of fully or partial paids. It will also ensure you can deliver what you promised by knowing cold the existing scene in both auditing and training areas of the org. The following are some of the coordination lines of the Call-in Officer:

1. A line to Division 2, Division 6, and Treasury Division 3, so as to get further names of fully or partial paids, and so you know who is paying now so as to schedule them immediately after paying.

2. A line with the D of T to get briefings on the training scene.

3. A line to the D of P and C/S in order to get tech estimates to enable you to better schedule the public, as they will then know how long to plan their stay for.

4. A line to the execs and Technical Division so you can make known who is coming when, for the needed planning.

USE OF GIMMICKS

GIMMICK: An idea, scheme or stunt to attract attention.

The gimmick is there for impact, mainly.

The use of gimmicks is a proven successful means of calling public in.

For example, Ron's Journal (RJ) 30 has a gimmick of "come in now and get up your RJ 30 bridge" or the use of the Free Case Analysis by the D of P to determine what their next step is. This gets them into the org and then they can be routed to the Reg.

Gimmicks are useful to spark interest in getting public into the org and therefore are a tool of the Call-in Units.

SUMMARY

Successful call-in is the key to the future of the org.

Undelivered services called in and delivered will increase VSD, which in turn increases staff pay. To be without an operating call-in is to curb your org's future GI and delivery, as well as your own pocket.

L. RON HUBBARD
Founder

HUBBARD COMMUNICATIONS OFFICE
Saint Hill Manor, East Grinstead, Sussex

HCO POLICY LETTER OF 9 AUGUST 1979
Issue III

Remimeo
All Orgs
All Staff

SERVICE CALL–IN COMMITTEE

Refs:

HCO PL	9 Aug. 79 I	CALL–IN: THE KEY TO DELIVERY AND FUTURE INCOME
HCO PL	9 Aug. 79 II	SERVICE PRODUCT OFFICER
LRH EDs	302 & 302-1	DEBUG TECH BREAKTHROUGH
HCO PL	7 Aug. 76 I	Admin Know-How 33 NAME YOUR PRODUCT
HCO PL	7 Aug. 76 II	Admin Know-How 34 WANT YOUR PRODUCT
HCO PL	7 Aug. 76 III	Admin Know-How 35 TO GET YOU HAVE TO KNOW HOW TO ORGANIZE
HCO PL	20 Nov. 65	THE PROMOTIONAL ACTIONS OF AN ORGANIZATION
HCO PL	28 July 74	ADDITIONS TO PROMOTIONAL ACTIONS OF AN ORGANIZATION
HCO PL	28 May 72	BOOM DATA
HCO PL	15 Nov. 60	MODERN PROCUREMENT LETTERS
HCO PL	14 Feb. 61	THE PATTERN OF A CENTRAL ORGANIZATION
HCO PL	21 Nov. 68	SENIOR POLICY
HCO PL	28 Feb. 65	DELIVER

As it takes time to appoint and train a Service Product Officer, until this is done a Service Call-in Committee is created.

This committee is placed in Dept 19, Office of the CO/ED. Its purpose is to ensure the Call-in Units for both fully and partially paids are functional and the org is servicing the public in volume.

This committee is directly responsible for getting the programs listed out in HCO PL 9 Aug. 79 I, CALL–IN: THE KEY TO DELIVERY AND FUTURE INCOME, fully and completely done. It also carries out the functions of the Service Product Officer as fully outlined in HCO PL 9 Aug. 79 II, SERVICE PRODUCT OFFICER, until such time as one is appointed, trained and apprenticed and ready to assume post at which point the Service Call-in Committee would still remain in operation under the Service Product Officer's chairmanship.

The ED/CO of an org is first and foremost responsible for these duties until such time as he forms and gets this committee operational.

This committee is to be chaired by the HCO Executive Secretary (HES) and the Org Executive Secretary (OES) is deputy chairman. The Treasury Sec is a member of this committee as it is Treasury that is most intimately interested in getting rid of advance payments received (APRs). Public who have either partially or fully paid and have not yet come into the org for their service are a backlog and could potentially break the org in refunds.

The Committee is to consist of:

CHAIRMAN: HES
DEPUTY CHAIRMAN: OES
MEMBERS: Advanced Scheduling Registrar
     Treasury Secretary
     Director of Processing
     Director of Training

(NOTE: At such time as a Service Product Officer is posted and operating he would take over chairmanship of this committee with the HES and OES becoming members.)

COMMITTEE RESPONSIBILITIES

This committee's foremost responsibility is to see to the execution of the issues referenced on page one, particularly HCO PL 9 Aug. 79 I, CALL–IN: THE KEY TO DELIVERY AND FUTURE INCOME, and HCO PL 9 Aug. 79 II, SERVICE PRODUCT OFFICER.

This committee is responsible for ensuring and product officering all promotion, sales, call-in, delivery and re-sign actions occurring in the org so they are produced in ever-increasing quantity and quality. This basically consists of:

1. Promotion to new and old public so Scientology services are well known and public are driven to the org in droves.

2. The action of selling Scientology services to all new and old public either currently in the org, new to the org or returning to the org.

3. Call-in of all partial and fully paid public so they do come into the org for services.

4. Fast, high quality services delivered to the public.

5. The re-signing of all in-the-org public on completion of a service.

This committee is responsible for seeing that the above actions do occur, through product officering and debugging they ensure the products are flowing off the line. Each member of the committee has a personal responsibility to see that this occurs.

COMMITTEE DUTIES

The committee meets daily off production hours and battle plans out all actions needed to get products flowing in each area of promotion, sales, call-in, delivery and re-sign. The specific products are fully listed out in HCO PL 9 Aug. 79 II, SERVICE PRODUCT OFFICER. They ensure the products they are going to get are known and the "figure out how to do" has been done and is coordinated. When this is done each committee member knows what his or her part is in getting out the products. For instance, the Director of Training knows he will have a student graduating shortly, and that this student will need to go on the re-sign line. Therefore the D of T informs the HES at the meeting who takes notes and ensures the Dissemination Division correctly handles the re-sign, or the HES may need to get a Tech Estimate from the C/Ses for a registration cycle. The Director of Processing is then alerted to this at the committee, so the cycle will flow smoothly and quickly.

Each member of this committee is assigned appropriate targets on the committee's battle plan to get done that day.

EXAMPLE: The HES would see to it that the promotional actions are being done. He would expedite those "few students left in Ethics" and get them back onto their course and serviced using debug tech (covered in LRH ED 302) as necessary. Using his Dissem Sec he would get the ASR Call-in Unit producing products, people fully paid and in, targeting the unit for maximum production and debugging as necessary.

EXAMPLE: The OES finds every student and pc fallen off lines and gets them either back on course or in session. Using his Tech Sec and Director of Tech Services (DTS) the OES product officers the Fully Paid Call-in Unit, targeting them and getting the public in now.

The Treasury Secretary would ensure both Call-in Units are well supplied with complete lists of who is fully or partially paid per HCO PL 9 Aug. 79 I, CALL–IN: THE KEY TO DELIVERY AND FUTURE INCOME.

The Director of Training and the Director of Processing provide excellent service to pcs and students and get them through their courses or case actions.

This is a fast-pace activity and the committee deals in real products and real beings. Their effectiveness determines the viability of the org.

The committee is to ensure both Call-in Units have adequate personnel and where there is not, all hands of idle auditors and part-time use of Letter Reges and other Dissem Div personnel is immediately put into use so as to cover the functions of call-in.

The committee is also to set up an alert line so that if a student or pc is not getting serviced or is getting slow service, he can write to the committee to get it handled. This line must be made well known to the public. The committee is to have an emergency meeting whenever they receive such an alert. They are to get the situation brought up by the public person handled fast, within 24 hours. This alert line will uphold the reputation of the org.

The committee is to guard against call-in actions being monitored by low auditing hours. Call-in Units must call in. HGCs (Hubbard Guidance Centers) and Academies must deliver. Where either of these are not occurring, it is up to the Service Call-in Committee to remedy it.

An important duty of this committee is to immediately appoint a Service Product Officer and to see to it he is trained and apprenticed. Once the Service

Product Officer is on post, if it is found that he is having to handle organizational matters and thus bogging, the committee must then provide him with an org officer.

COMMITTEE STATS

The stats for this committee are: (1) Number of pcs and students completed and re-signed onto their next service. (This includes those actually routed onto the next upper org services and who do re-sign.) (2) Number of public in and started onto a service.

SUMMARY

Without someone overseeing and directly product officering the flow lines into, through and out of the org, public get lost off the lines and the org contracts. It is of the utmost importance that this committee act and get the products flying off the line.

So, when you're standing in the Academy or HGC of your org and it is deserted without a student or pc in sight ask yourself, "Why didn't I form a Service Call-in Committee like Ron said?" Form one and win.

L. RON HUBBARD
Founder

HUBBARD COMMUNICATIONS OFFICE
Saint Hill Manor, East Grinstead, Sussex

HCO POLICY LETTER OF 30 NOVEMBER 1982

Remimeo
All Orgs
All Execs
FBOs
D/FBOs

THE DEPUTY CO OR DEPUTY ED FOR
DELIVERY AND EXCHANGE

Refs:

HCO PL 9 Aug. 79R II	Esto Series 39
Rev. 19.11.79	Org Series 39
	SERVICE PRODUCT OFFICER
HCO PL 10 Sept. 82	Finance Series 36
	EXCHANGE, ORG INCOME AND STAFF
	PAY
HCO PL 29 Jan. 71RA	Finance Series 1RA
Rev. 2.2.91	FLAG BANKING OFFICERS
HCO PL 10 Mar. 71RA	Finance Series 6RA
Rev. 2.2.91	FBO HAT
HCO PL 27 July 82RA	Finance Series 33RA
Rev. 2.2.91	DEPUTY FBOs FOR MARKETING OF ORG
	RESOURCES FOR EXCHANGE
	(D/FBO FOR MORE)
HCO PL 3 Sept. 82	Finance Series 35
	DEPUTY FBO FOR MARKETING OF ORG
	RESOURCES FOR EXCHANGE
	(D/FBO FOR MORE) PURPOSE

(NOTE: The pilot for this post has been long and successful: it is the FCCI PO [Flag Case, Course, Internship Product Officer] whose duties were covered by the famous Bulldozer EDs issued on Flag. However, the FCCI PO also covers the post of what is now called D/FBO for MORE [D/FBO for Marketing of Org Resources for Exchange]. Without this post effectively manned, the FSO—Flag Service Org—collapses and any sag in its stats is instantly traced to the nonfunctioning of the FCCI PO post. The post once functioned well in the Office of the Staff Captain and has functioned less well in the Office of the CO FSO. Therefore, the D/CO [or D/ED] for Delivery and Exchange post is put in close liaison with the strong and powerful International Finance Office Network, while remaining under the authority of the CO or ED of the org.)

The Service Product Officer in any org should have D/CO or D/ED status.

His key function is to see that the org operates at the highest level of exchange. (Ref: HCO PL 10 Sept. 82, Finance Series 36, EXCHANGE, ORG INCOME AND STAFF PAY)

Therefore, his post is now retitled D/CO (or D/ED) for Delivery and Exchange and he is located in the Office of the CO/ED, Department 19, of all Class IV and Sea Org orgs.

He is the bridge between the D/FBO for MORE and the FBO.

This creates a flow:

You have the D/FBO whipping up business by seeing that the public is made aware of the org's products and services, and driving more business down on the org than it can waste.

The D/CO (or D/ED) for Delivery and Exchange makes sure this public gets SIGNED UP and SERVICED. He is a product officer who names, wants and gets promotion, sales, call-in, delivery itself and re-sign occurring.

The FBO, then, sees to the org's solvency by ensuring income is greater than outgo, that production is properly financed, that staff are well paid for their production and that Flag is recompensed for good management of the org. And all of this makes it possible for the org to then expand and deliver in greater volume.

The flow goes from public (D/FBO) to ⟶ the whole sign-up and service line (D/CO or D/ED for Delivery and Exchange) to ⟶ solvency and volume (FBO).

It is this incredibly workable lineup that takes an org stably up the conditions of exchange. (Ref: HCO PL 10 Sept. 82, Finance Series 36, EXCHANGE, ORG INCOME AND STAFF PAY)

But the line breaks down where there is no D/CO or D/ED for Delivery and Exchange posted. And where it breaks down most specifically and ruinously is in the area of CALL–IN.

If one wants call-in to occur and the org's exchange with its public kept in, the only way to do it and also expand the org is to get a D/CO or D/ED for Delivery and Exchange on post and functioning.

Public interest may be kindled, public reach may be occurring, public may be paying partially or in full for goods or services, but if goods and services aren't being delivered in full the flow is broken and the org is in a condition of only partial exchange. Delivery in full means calling in the person so the service CAN be delivered. In this way the org maintains "fair exchange" with each and every public on its lines.

So the answer for any org that is sitting in a condition of only partial exchange, or an org that is ANYWHERE below the fourth condition of exchange—exchange in abundance—is to immediately, at once and yesterday, and without ripping off some vital post, post a D/CO or D/ED for Delivery and Exchange.

The first and primary function of the D/CO (or D/ED) for Delivery and Exchange is CALL–IN and this means he personally gets call-in done all by his little lonesome. With his own hands and voice he himself begins to call in fully and partially paids. Call-in is his first duty and when he's got that going he posts a Call-in Officer to take over the hat which he has already begun and he then expands onto the other functions of his D/CO or D/ED for Delivery and Exchange post, as covered in HCO PL 9 Aug. 79R II, SERVICE PRODUCT

878

OFFICER. But he FIRST and PERSONALLY and BY HIMSELF gets call-in going and exchange occurring at once.

What is involved here is the administrative principle that in order to get something done that is an expanding function you give it to somebody and tell him to expand it.

A CO or ED, whose responsibility it is to see that the main functions of the org are getting done, also wears the planning and coordination hat for the whole of the org's activity. If he's going to get the show on the road he needs to delegate some of this responsibility. He needs a deputy—the Deputy CO (or D/ED) for Delivery and Exchange—and that deputy needs the authority and the clout to see that, through promotion, sales, call-in, delivery and re-sign, the main products of the org do get produced.

Getting this post filled competently enables the ED to fully wear his planning and coordination hat and makes it possible for the flow from D/FBO to D/CO (or D/ED) for Delivery and Exchange to FBO to occur.

As some orgs in recent times have experienced both external and internal suppression on the subject of calling people in and servicing them, the D/CO (or D/ED) for Delivery and Exchange is given the additional powers of immediate communication to the International Finance Office and the Inspector General Network without vias to report and get help to remedy internal and external situations in orgs which suppressively inhibit call-in, delivery or expansion whether by inattention, refusals to post vital posts, failures or refusals to contact or call in interested persons, theft of org prospects or business or outright rip-offs to the end of ensuring successful execution of his duties and the expansion of the org. A form for such a report will be provided but absence of a form or a supply of such forms must not inhibit such reports.

This IS the winning combination by which an org moves up to "fair exchange" with all of its public and from there up to the highest level of exchange.

And it is the highest level of exchange toward which the whole activity of the D/CO or D/ED for Delivery and Exchange is geared—exchange in abundance!

L. RON HUBBARD
Founder

HCO POLICY LETTER OF 13 JANUARY 1983

Remimeo

THE BUSINESS OF ORGS

Orgs are in the very new, for this universe, business of setting people free.

SPs will find all manner of reasons not to, for this is what they, with their own crimes, fear.

Thus it follows that they cut dissem lines, corrupt tech, suppress and confuse orgs, persuade people to be inactive and resort to other shifts, all quite "reasonable" and "logical" as to why this must be the way it is; so be alert to this and go ahead and set people free.

It's done with org services well delivered, on-policy, with standard tech.

So just do it, man, do it!

L. RON HUBBARD
Founder

HUBBARD COMMUNICATIONS OFFICE
Saint Hill Manor, East Grinstead, Sussex

HCO POLICY LETTER OF 6 MAY 1984

Remimeo
Chaplain
ARC Break Auditor
ARC Break Reg
Exec Council
LRH Comm
KOT
FBO
Treasury
Snr C/S
C/Ses
Tech/Qual
Legal

ARC BREAK PROGRAM
ADDITIONAL DATA

Refs:

HCO PL	10 Sept.	82		EXCHANGE, ORG INCOME AND STAFF PAY
ED 473 WW				ARC BREAK CLEANUP PROGRAM
842 SH	1	Sept.	67	WW EMERGENCY CONDITION
HCO PL	12 Feb.	70		QUALITY OF SERVICE
HCO PL	25 June	72		RECOVERING STUDENTS AND PCs
HCO PL	15 Nov.	74 II		CFs, ARC BREAKS IN
HCOB	15 Nov.	74		STUDENT REHABILITATION LIST
HCO PL	27 Jan.	80		RUDIMENTS (ARC BREAK) PROGRAM
HCO PL	5 June	83 VI		CLASS IV ORGS PUBLIC DIVISIONS ORGANIZING BOARD
HCO PL	26 Oct.	75		GI/CGI RATIO, FAILED CASES AND FAILED STUDENTS

The ARC Break Program is a basic org program which was first introduced at Saint Hill in the 60s, and it has since been part of the standard, on-policy actions of any successful and expanding org. Located in Division 6B, Department 17D, Department of the Chaplain, the function of the ARC Break Program is to keep the field cleaned up of ARC breaks and active.

One occasionally sees an org going more or less effect of people coming in and complaining and so forth. That tells you right there that the org does not have an ARC Break Program in effect. In an org which does have an ARC Break Program in full force, such a person is simply shunted over to the ARC break team or, if an ARC break team is not yet posted, to the Chaplain in Dept 17D. The person is handled with standard tech, gotten back in ARC with the org and Scientology, and moving on the Bridge.

SUCCESSFUL TEAM ACTION

The most successful ARC break team action I know of was operated out of Saint Hill many, many years ago. They had somebody who simply approached the ARC broken public as an initial interview. The person didn't try to reg or handle or anything of that sort but simply ascertained what the score was with the person. With this data in hand the person's name would be turned over to an auditor/reg team. The auditor/reg team was not then sent tearing all over the country trying to locate people. The person had already been spotted and something was already known about the situation. In this way they could get up to considerable quantity of handling. They were quite successful and, in fact, the most successful ARC Break Program on the track.

REFUND/REPAYMENT REQUESTS

Often the first intimation of ARC break is the refund/repayment line, so this line and the ARC Break Program tie in very closely. It is for this reason that the first port of call on the refund/repayment line is the Chaplain who will very often effect a salvage of the individual as well as keep any entheta off the general org lines.

Obviously the one interested in getting a refund or repayment would be the public person seeking it. Therefore if he has a routing form which he is required to present to different persons in the org there is a chance of salvaging him. The individual is also made responsible for sending the routing form off to the Claims Verification Board and whenever this has been done the refunds/repayments have reduced enormously. It was not because the public just didn't get the form filled out, it was because a lot of them got handled en route to filling it out.

By placing the Chaplain as the first terminal on the routing form, and with the Chaplain and his ARC break team standardly handling the person, the chance for salvaging the individual is further increased.

It should be noted that one of the primary reasons for refunds, where they occur, is not bad service but *no* service. The figures have varied between 50 and 75 percent of all requests being for the reason of *no* service at all.

You will find, however, that getting the ARC Break Program in in the org will reduce any traffic on the refund/repayment line to next to nothing—so long as you keep *delivering* and what you deliver is standard tech.

ORG EXPANSION

An org which keeps its field cleaned up and active on the Bridge or as FSMs will expand up to and past the make-break point. Factually, by policy an org has no business not having an ARC Break Program in full force keeping its local field cleaned up.

Expansion and wins are the order of the day for an org that has a standard ARC Break Program in full operation.

L. RON HUBBARD
Founder

EXECUTIVE COUNCIL
ADVISORY COUNCIL
ADVISORY COMMITTEE

HCO POLICY LETTER OF 8 APRIL 1957

ADVISORY COMMITTEE

The Advisory Committee Mandate of 1956 is amended as follows:

"The Advisory Committee shall be composed only of the following persons:

The Technical Director,
The Director of Administration,
The Director of Training,
The Director of Processing,
The Registrar and
HCO Secretary.

"When any significant change in its membership occurs (one third or more) (cumulative) there shall be an election by the new membership of a chairman, but in no case shall a chairman immediately succeed himself.

"The Advisory Committee shall report its minutes to the Association Secretary who shall in turn report to the Agent for Great Britain and the Treasurer only.

"A copy of the Advisory Committee minutes may also be sent by the Association Secretary to the Advisory Council in Washington.

"The minutes of the staff meeting shall be forwarded to the Advisory Committee as well as the Association Secretary, and the Advisory Committee may express its opinion of and recommendations concerning the staff meeting minutes. The Advisory Committee action on staff minutes may not prevent them from being submitted to higher authority."

L. RON HUBBARD
Founder

HUBBARD COMMUNICATIONS OFFICE
London

HASI POLICY LETTER OF 9 APRIL 1957
Issue III

GRIEVANCES

Any staff member shall be entitled to present any grievance he may have in writing or in person before the Advisory Committee when it is in session on Tuesday afternoons at 3 P.M.

Such grievance shall be courteously and justly heard and any action recommended by the Advisory Committee shall be forwarded to the Association Secretary for his action. The Advisory Committee may not take action without the further sanction of the Association Secretary.

L. RON HUBBARD
Founder

HCO POLICY LETTER OF 2 JULY 1957

FINANCIAL REPORTS, WASHINGTON, DC

The following financial reports are required in the Ad Council weekly reports in this order.

This changes only Part A, not B, C, etc.

All after week's deposit—no checkbook balance.

Founding Church Account No. 1 .... (Bank Balance)
Founding Church Account No. 2 .... (Bank Balance)

Founding Church Total: _____

Distribution Center .... (Bank Balance)
HASI .... (Bank Balance)

Founding Church Receipts .... (Gross for Week)
Dist Center Receipts .... (Gross for Week)
HASI Receipts .... (Gross for Week)

Total Receipts: _____

Founding Church Bills Payable .... _____
Dist Center Bills Payable .... _____
HASI Bills Payable .... _____

Total Organization Debt: _____

Accounts Receivable, Founding Church .... _____
Accounts Receivable, Dist Center .... _____
Accounts Receivable, HASI .... _____

Total: _____

L. RON HUBBARD
Founder

HUBBARD COMMUNICATIONS OFFICE
1812 19th Street NW, Washington, DC

FOUNDING CHURCH POLICY LETTER OF 8 AUGUST 1957

POWER OF VETO

As regards the Advisory Council Minutes:

Power of Veto may be exercised by the Organization Secretary or the Executive Director.

The Organization Secretary may veto or refer any minute.

The Executive Director may veto or *pass* any minute.

Minute is only valid with a specific acceptance from the Executive Director, giving its number and date.

L. RON HUBBARD
Founder

THE ADVISORY COUNCIL

PURPOSE: The purpose of the Advisory Council is to advise the executives of the organization as to needed changes and policies. To act as a meeting ground for the department heads. To assemble and report the statistics of finance and action to the Executive Director. To advance ideas for promotion and improvement.

THE ADVISORY COUNCIL IS CONSTITUTED ALONG THE FOLLOWING LINES:

The Advisory Council is composed of the following persons:

1. Director of Training

2. Director of Processing

3. Director of Accounts

4. Director of Materiel

5. Director of Promotion and Registration

These shall elect from amongst them a Chairman. The Secretarial to the Executive Director shall be the Secretary of the Advisory Council.

The time of the meeting is appointed as of 2:00 P.M. every Tuesday afternoon.

The order of progress of a meeting shall consist precisely as follows:

1. The minutes of the last meeting are read and approved or otherwise.

2. An overall financial report is submitted to the Council by the Director of Accounts. This consists of the total amount of checks drawn by an organization on any account for the preceding week. Then the total amounts deposited by any and all organizations in the area and a grand total of those sums. Next, a full statement of bank balances for all organizations and accounts. A complete total of all unpaid bills for all organizations. Then a breakdown is given of the total training receipts and total amount of notes issued for training in the previous week. This is followed by a report on the total amount of receipts and total amount of notes issued for processing the previous week. Next, a report of the amount of mail received for the preceding week for the various organizations. He gives a report of the general state of the department.

3. The Director of Training reports the number of students in each course. The number of students graduated from each course the preceding week and the number of students for the week of the Ad Council meeting and the general state of the Training Department, and the total letters into and out of the department are reported by Director of Training.

4. The Director of Processing reports the number of preclears processed in the previous week, the number of preclears who completed processing in the previous week and the number of preclears in for the week of the Ad Council meeting. He should give a report of the general state of the Processing Department and the total letters in and out of the department.

5. The Director of Promotion and Registration should report the total number of training applications received for the future, the total number of processing applications received for the future, the total number of training prospects, the total number of processing prospects, the total number of letters into the department, the total number of letters written by the department for the preceding week. A breakdown of the number of letters written by each Registrar and Assistant Registrar, the total number of letters received from advertisements, the progress of various promotion projects and a general statement of the department conditions and activities.

6. The Director of Materiel gives a report covering the condition of Central Files, the progress of Addressograph Clerk's activities, the progress of the Addressograph In-Charge's activities, the material run by the Ad dressing Clerk, the total pieces of mail out, the total mailing out, a report on maintenance, a report on the state of supplies, and a report on the general state of the department and a report on the state of transportation.

7. The HCO Executive Secretary gives a report to the Advisory Council on shortages of book stores, the number of books sold through advertisements, the number of books sold, a list of the nine best sellers in order of volume, the books which are being printed or reprinted, the conditions of HCO special projects, and other HCO activities.

8. A general statement of staff morale is given by the Chairman.

9. Bulletins and Secretarial to the Executive Directors are read and noted.

10. Staff meeting minutes are read and noted.

11. All despatches to the Ad Council are read and handled.

12. The Ad Committee minutes of London are read and noted.

13. There should ensue and be placed in minutes, motions from members of the Council as necessary to get on with the business of the organization or organizations. These minutes should be numbered each one consecutively beginning from the first meeting of the Advisory Council on through. Thus these do not express the first to the nth of any given meeting, but express consecutively the first to the nth of all the Council meetings.

The minutes should be written up in the exact form of the business conducted by the Ad Council. Copies of these minutes should be sent to the Executive Director, the Organization Secretary, the Treasurer, the Chairman of the Advisory Council, HCO Exec Sec, and a copy to London for the information of the Advisory Committee of London HASI.

As regards Advisory Council minutes, the power of veto may be exercised by the Organization Secretary or the Executive Director. The Org Sec may veto or refer any minute. The Executive Director may veto or pass any minute. The minute is only valid with a specific acceptance from the Executive Director, giving its number and date. Any minute so passed by the Executive Director is issued to the organization by a Secretarial to the Executive Director.

In the interest of a brief and interesting meeting, the Chairman should reduce discussion to a minimum and should be extremely precise in calling for the above order of business and should not permit this order of business to be varied in any degree.

Members should have their reports written up well in advance of the meeting and indeed these reports, as they are being reported in other directions, should be ready any given Monday. Thus, the heads of departments are submitting to the Ad Council copies of their reports or calling attention to their original reports but reading them to the degree necessary to inform the whole committee of the activity of that department. The Advisory Council members must not compose their report immediately before or during an Advisory Council meeting.

The minutes of the Advisory Council should be ready and in the mails by Friday afternoon of the same week the meeting is held.

The powers of the Advisory Council are as follows:

1. It has the power to recommend to any organization that it incorporate certain minutes into its minute book as having been passed by the Board of Directors if so passed by that Board of Directors.

2. It has the power to recommend action to the Executive Director, which, when ratified by the Executive Director then goes into effect.

3. It has the power to recommend hires and firings to the Organization Secretary or the Executive Director which if acted upon by the Org Sec or the Exec Dir, then are in effect.

The Advisory Council is not a governing body, it is what might be said to be the legislative body of the organization and its legislation becomes law only if ratified by the general head of the organizations which comprise Scientology, US, which head composes the executive and judicial functions of this organizational government.

The Advisory Council has the right to recommend anything it pleases. The Advisory Council has the right to investigate anything it pleases in the organization and thus submit its findings for possible ratification.

ADDITIONAL MEMBERS

Although business HCO is normally considered to be the reporting source for the Distribution Center, and its activities, it may be found feasible to add the

DCI to the membership of the Advisory Council. This is definitely up to the Ad Council.

The secretary for the Council may be added at the discretion of the Council to a voting membership in the Council.

QUORUMS AND MAJORITIES

One-half of the Advisory Council may constitute a quorum and with less than half the members present it is not possible for the Advisory Council to have a legal meeting. If a number of the members are not present because of resignation, etc., the temporary heads of departments take their place as part of the Advisory Council.

A majority of the Advisory Council constitutes two-thirds, and without two-thirds vote on any given minute it may not be recommended.

L. RON HUBBARD
Founder

24 February 1959

Ad Council Sec
Ad Council Chairman
Org Sec
HCO Exec Sec
D of Tr
D of P
Dir of M
Dir of Accts
Dir of P&R

DESPATCHES TO ADVISORY COUNCIL

Despatches to Advisory Council are handled by the Chairman of the Advisory Council.

L. RON HUBBARD
Founder

HCO POLICY LETTER OF 18 NOVEMBER 1960
Issue II

SA only
Info All
  Central Orgs

EXECUTIVE TIME SALVAGE AND
CONFERENCES CURTAILED

I find that HCO Bulletin of 27 Aug. 58, EXECUTIVES OF SCIENTOLOGY ORGANIZATIONS, page 3, paragraphs 1 and 2, is being violated. It should be adhered to scrupulously.

Also, conferences amongst executives and departments held in executive offices are using up hours and hours of valuable time. Despatch releases containing the info and phone or personal check on it by the issuing executive usually suffices.

I myself find despatches, general staff releases, phone and personal visits to offices get the work done better, get the pictures much clearer and get the job done.

On studying staff time investment, I have already salvaged 200 + hours of auditing time per week for the org.

I have no objection to executives being in their offices. I object to many meetings, conferences and staff members being called in when they should be on post.

I believe it may be necessary for all executives to be on the job Saturday afternoons, but haven't taken this step yet, thinking I may be able to salvage effectiveness during the week.

Hours of work for executives is the same as staff members.

L. RON HUBBARD
Founder

HUBBARD COMMUNICATIONS OFFICE
Saint Hill Manor, East Grinstead, Sussex

HCO POLICY LETTER OF 9 SEPTEMBER 1964

Gen. Non-Remimeo

PURPOSE OF AD COMM

Sometimes organizations tend to forget what the basic purpose of an Ad Comm is.

The original purpose was given in HCO PL 12 Oct. 62, BASIC PURPOSES OF A SCIENTOLOGY ORGANIZATION, and is now amended as follows:

"To advise the Assoc/Org Sec on promotional matters relating to the various departments."

This purpose should be read at the beginning of every Ad Comm meeting held in all orgs. It should be prefaced, "This meeting is held to advise . . ., etc."

L. RON HUBBARD
Founder

Remimeo

COUNCIL AND AD COMMS

Advisory Committees heretofore convened are abolished.

New Advisory Committees are set up by division.

There will be one "Ad Comm" for each division except Division 7.

It will be composed of the three directors of the division or their representatives and chairmanned by the secretary of the division or his or her representative.

The divisional Ad Comms should meet in the last hour of the working day Friday.

Each Ad Comm meets separately.

The divisional Ad Comm has ready the statistics of the division and takes these up in an effort to improve them.

The entire purpose of the Ad Comm is to arrange to improve statistics for its departments, sections and units.

The period taken up is the week closed on Thursday. Thus, the day's statistics for the meeting go to the next Ad Comm. Like accounts, each statistic week closes on Thursday at 2:00 P.M.

The minutes of the Ad Comm, together with all statistical reports, are forwarded to Inspections and Reports, where they must arrive by noon Monday.

These statistics are promptly compiled by Inspections and Reports for night letter to Saint Hill to arrive Tuesday morning, and are copied for the Advisory Council.

THE ADVISORY COUNCIL

The Advisory Council meets on Tuesday afternoon in the last hour of the working day.

It is composed of the HCO Exec Sec and the Org Exec Sec and is understood to include LRH.

Receiving all Ad Comm statistics, the Advisory Council determines the states of condition of the org, each division or separate departments, and publishes the states assigned as from the Office of LRH.

The Advisory Council does all minor planning and adjustments necessary as an Executive Admin Letter, local.

Should large changes be envisioned, the change must be authorized by LRH, also, and is issued as a Sec ED from Saint Hill.

SUMMARY

This is the general plan of management:

Section Officers may hold meetings with their section to brief them.

Department Directors may hold meetings with their department's personnel to brief them.

The division has an Ad Comm to compile and take up their statistics and plan and issue orders to improve statistics.

The whole org has an Advisory Council to take up the statistics of the divisions and issue orders to improve them.

Huge changes cannot be made by an Ad Council unless also authorized by LRH.

None of these bodies has any more authority than the persons and posts they contain. The Advisory Council is not a board of directors but is an assistant body to the actual board of directors at Saint Hill.

Ad Comms may issue admin letters for their division.

Ad Councils may issue admin letters for the Executive Division and assign conditions.

Large changes or transfers must be in the form of a Sec ED issued only from Saint Hill.

FOUNDATION

All this also applies to a Foundation, except that in its early days such meetings are not vital and are included in the day Ad Comms, etc.

As the Foundation grows, it will need to hold its own Ad Comms and Ad Council. When this becomes a fact, the only difference is that the Ad Comms are held in the last half hour of Friday night's work and the Ad Council is held in the last half hour of the Tuesday night following. The procedure is otherwise the same.

L. RON HUBBARD
Founder

HCO POLICY LETTER OF 30 SEPTEMBER 1965

Remimeo
Advisory Councils
Advisory Committees

All Divisions

STATISTICS FOR DIVISIONS

(Note: We will call the Advisory Council the Ad Council, never Ad Coun, to avoid any errors in confusing it with Ad Comm.)

Each whole division has a statistic on which it is judged as to condition.

While this gross divisional statistic does not cover all the statistics of the division, it is the primary *divisional* statistic.

An Advisory Council meeting can be very brief if it has these statistics tallied by Ad Comms and plotted and submitted by OIC. Then when a gross divisional statistic is up, the Ad Council can find out why and reinforce what caused the rise. And when a gross divisional statistic is down, the Ad Council can go through all the remaining statistics of that division and take action accordingly. Thus, the Ad Council need not cover *all* the statistics of an org at its meeting. Only the gross divisional statistics and take action only when these vary widely up or down.

The Advisory Committees of the divisions record all statistics but headline in their report their gross divisional statistic for quick reference. They include *all* their statistics, headline their gross divisional statistic.

The gross divisional statistics are:

Exec Division 7

Gross income of the org

This of course reflects best the total org operation and is what the Exec Division is promoted or demoted for so it is the Division 7 gross statistic.

HCO Division 1

Total org letters in–total org letters out

As HCO has personnel, ethics and such matters, if they do their job, there is a heavy outflow in of all mail types for HCO and the org and a heavy outflow out from all divisions. If the Personnel Officer gets hard workers and puts their hats on and if Inspections and Reports and Ethics are quick off the mark and if the HCO Area Sec runs a good division and handles all about, the letters in–letters out will tell the tale. HCO sees to it org pours out letters and mailing pieces.

HCO Dissem Division 2

Number of new enrollments of students
and pcs for the week, and gross booksales

Although this division has registration, magazines, etc., etc., all these add up to enrollments, which of course is the final result of all magazines, letters, promotion and advance enrollment. Booksales are our oldest index of future business.

Org Division 3

Credit collections vs. bills paid

It will be seen that gross income is established by many in the org, but collections as a special income is purely the Org Division's. Bills paid require gross money in so reflect the gross—no money in, no bills paid. This is a dual statistic which shows the industry of the division in general. It even touches materiel as no bills paid equals no supplies. Monies paid into reserve payment do not count as bills paid.

Tech Division 4

Number of students and pcs
completed in the week

The number enrolled is really only partly the Tech Division's as if they give good service they will get enrollments. However, the *completions* are the real index of a Tech Division and show up any weakness of the division. So their statistic is only total completions of courses and auditing. This, of course, includes graduations from any course and completion of any *result* for the pc that brings a Grade cert or just ends intensives.

Completed, of course, means only certified or classed or graded. However, completion of a twenty-five-hour intensive which satisfied the pc (no review at end even if one occurred before the end) counts as a pc completed. Five-hour rehabs which did not result in a Grade are not completions. Five-hour assists bought as assists are done, of course, in Qual and so are not a Tech statistic.

Qual Division 5

Cash collected by reason of
the division for the week

This division's certs and grades and awards are all really the Tech Division's work. But we early found that a Qual Division's various services were paid for when good and not when bad. So this division's gross statistic is how much *cash* was paid—not later collected—for *Qual* Division services.

Dist Division 6

Number of field staff member
commissions paid/number of new addresses
added to CF, both for the week

This dual statistic reflects a healthy Dist Div. The number of new addresses added to CF means, of course, *new* people buying things from the org. Therefore, its advertising quality and basic services can be judged even though assisted by other divisions as well. The number of field staff commissions paid reflects its leadership of field staff members.

New people is the business of the Dist Div.

SUMMARY

There are many other statistics, many even more important than these. But these gross statistics tell one at once if the division secretary is alive and has his division functioning. Thus, they provide indicators by which management can be done.

The Ad Comms, of course, handle *all* their statistics.

The Ad Council handles the gross divisional statistics, looking for steep ups (to assign Affluence) or steep downs (to assign Emergency).

Gross income only hereafter influences the Exec Division and is assigned from Saint Hill. All other divisions are assigned conditions by the Ad Council in accordance with the gross divisional statistics.

L. RON HUBBARD
Founder

HCO POLICY LETTER OF 5 OCTOBER 1965

Remimeo
All Staff

ROUTING

AD COMM REPORTS AND MINUTES

Here is a complete routing for the weekly statistics and Ad Comm reports:

1. On Thursday afternoon OIC Clerk distributes in the baskets of each person three blank forms.

2. The person receives the statistics form and fills it out accurately.

3. He keeps one copy for his own reference.

4. He routes one copy to his dept head.

5. He routes one copy to the div secretary.

6. The dept head accumulates all statistics for his dept and takes them with him to the Ad Comm on Friday at 5:30 P.M.

7. The secretary accumulates all her/his statistics routed to her by the various individuals, staples them together by dept and files them for her reference.

8. At the Ad Comm the secretary for the Ad Comm (not the div secretary) takes notes on the discussion of the statistics, notes which statistics are up or down, notes all recommendations—decisions and orders issued during the Ad Comm—and includes in his minutes.

9. At the end of the Ad Comm the secretary is handed all the statistics from each dept.

10. The secretary for the Ad Comm then takes these and his notes and types up the minutes.

11. He then signs the minutes as Ad Comm secretary and paper clips them to the statistics and routes to the div secretary for her/his signature.

12. The secretary then routes them all to the OIC Clerk for graphing. They must arrive there by Monday noon so the OIC Clerk will have time to deal with all of them.

13. The OIC Clerk completes all graphs and turns all the div's statistics and minutes (neatly stacked in consecutive order, i.e., Div 1 on top, Div 2 beneath it, etc.) over to the LRH Communicator by noon Tuesday to route to the Exec Dir.

14. The Exec Dir (or, in the other orgs, the Ad Council gets the report at this point) sees these, and the LRH Communicator then routes them to the Executive Advisory Council.

15. The Executive Ad Council, when finished with these, routes them to HCO Files Officer.

16. The HCO Files Officer files them separately by division and in consecutive weekly sequence.

The routing is followed by the evening Foundation as well, except at the point of (13). The evening OIC Officer places the completed graphs and statistics with minutes in the Day OIC Officer's basket for their forwarding with the Day reports.

The outer orgs' OIC Officer forwards the designated OIC data by telex on Monday to Saint Hill for the OIC Officer's handling.

The new OIC data that will be required from orgs is not compiled as yet, but as soon as these have been validated, it will be issued as a policy letter. Until this has been done the usual OIC data is reported, compartmented into Day and Foundation.

L RON HUBBARD
Founder

HUBBARD COMMUNICATIONS OFFICE
Saint Hill Manor, East Grinstead, Sussex

HCO POLICY LETTER OF 12 OCTOBER 1965

Remimeo

ADVISORY COMMITTEES

It is up to Ad Comms to assign conditions of Emergency to departments.

If the ADVISORY COUNCIL discovers an even slightly down statistic in the gross divisional statistic and finds that that Ad Comm in its meeting the previous Friday did not locate the cause and assign an Emergency to it, the Advisory Council may assign a condition of Emergency to the entire division, regardless of the slightness of the gross drop.

Ad Comms must establish and assign statistics for their departments and sections and units and individuals.

An Ad Comm may assign a personal state of Emergency to any person in that division.

PAY ADJUSTMENTS
Applies to all orgs on Unit Pay

An individual, unit, section, department or division will, effective 15 Nov. 65, have a unit pay-reduction of 20 percent of its units if it is assigned a state of Emergency.

An individual, unit, section, department or division, effective 15 Nov. 65, will receive an increase of 20 percent of its units if assigned a state of Affluence.

STATES ASSIGNMENT TABLE

Exec Division—States assigned for the whole Exec Division by Saint Hill only in accordance with gross income.

Divisions—States assigned by the local Advisory Council on the basis of the gross divisional statistic.

Departments—States assigned by the Advisory Committee of that division, by the Advisory Council or the HCO Secretary.

Sections—States assigned by the Ad Comm of that division or by the Advisory Council or by the HCO Secretary.

Units—Same as sections.

Individuals—Same as sections.

POLICY

No org, portion or individual in an org may be without an assigned state. No states may be assigned anything or anyone save on the basis of a graphable statistic.

L. RON HUBBARD
Founder

HCO POLICY LETTER OF 11 JANUARY 1966

Sthil Only
Exec Sec Hats
 (SH and WW)
Secretary Hats

AD COUNCIL AND AD COMMS
ORDERS, ISSUE OF

ADVISORY COUNCIL ORDERS, ISSUE OF

Advisory Council orders are issued by Secretarial to the Executive Director only.

Independent Ad Council orders are forbidden.

AD COUNCIL SH

The procedure for Ad Council Saint Hill is as follows:

On every Tuesday afternoon the Advisory Council meets to take up financial planning and the Ad Comm reports and statistics.

The results of this meeting are expressed as Financial Planning Orders and assignment of conditions to the divisions and any other orders or comments of the Ad Council.

These are written up properly as a Sec ED and are forwarded to the Ad Council WW for approval. If approved they go to the Executive Director for okay to issue.

AD COUNCIL WW

The Advisory Council Worldwide meets every Wednesday afternoon.

Its procedure is as follows:

It takes up the Ad Council SH minutes and passes or alters them and sends them on to the Executive Director for okay as a Sec ED.

The Ad Council then takes up the statistics of the International Division itself. It issues any orders as a Sec ED and forwards it to the Executive Director for approval and issue.

It then takes up international statistics org by org and draws up general Sec EDs WW or individual Sec EDs for orgs and sends them to the Executive Director for approval and issue.

No orders are issued by the Ad Council SH or the Ad Council WW except on the above lines.

The initials of the Executive Director are required for approval and issue, but where the Executive Director is not available in person, the LRH Keeper of Seals and Signatures (usually the LRH Communicator unless one is appointed) merely signs with no power of alteration and no power of nonapproval.

AD COMM ORDERS, ISSUE OF

The orders of an Advisory Committee are similarly routed.

An Advisory Committee, as the advisory group of a division, meets every Friday about 5:30 P.M. and conducts its meeting on the statistics of the division for the week ending Thursday 2:00 P.M. (the day before).

The Ad Comm assigns conditions for its departments, sections and persons for the division in accordance with statistics and confirms any personnel appointments or transfers or dismissals.

The Ad Comm reports are forwarded to the Advisory Council SH which approves or alters them and passes them on to the Ad Council WW which approves or alters them and passes them on to the Executive Director for approval and issue. If the Keeper of the Seals and Signatures only is available, the orders are simply approved and issued as a Sec ED for the division to which it applies with copies to the two Ad Councils.

A divisional Sec ED is numbered consecutively, is on blue paper and is headed "Sec ED (number) Div (number of division) followed by the name of the division abbreviated," example "Sec ED 136 Div 2 Dissem."

The orders in any event should be issued by Friday morning of the week after they were written by the Ad Comm.

The whole purpose of this routing is to prevent contradictory orders and provide a single channel of issue.

All Sec EDs not written by the Executive Director personally are hereafter signed by the originating person or body followed by "For L. Ron Hubbard, Executive Director."

L. RON HUBBARD
Founder

SEC ED 29 WW   21 January 1966

Applies to HCO Exec
Sec WW, Org Exec Sec
WW. Copies may be
used by them for info to
orgs of their orders.

TO ADVISORY COUNCIL WORLD WIDE

You are ordered to raise the WW Gross divisional statistics quickly on all orgs where any one of them is down.

My analysis where statistics are down in a division is:

DIV 1: The org is not answering mail it receives and Dir Comm should clean out all in-baskets of every staff member throughout divisions and get the mail answered by any means.

DIV 2: Magazines are not going out regularly enough from orgs to the *whole* list. Every org that wants to grow must start a magazine. We will send it the shooting plates for a magazine for mailing to its existing CF mailing lists. Magazines raise gross income statistics to the degree they are mailed. The more persons a magazine is mailed to the higher the income. The more often, the more frequent the peaks.

DIV 3: The Org Division should snap up its credit collections by sending out statements *fast*. London doesn't even know what it's owed. Enormous sums. Credit for all by small Qual bills for students and the like should be shut right off. Free membership holders *must* be billed. (A Sec ED on the last exists but needs enforcement.)

DIV 4: As completions are down, Tech Secs should get busy getting students and pcs through *fast*. Get checksheets shortened.

DIV 5: The Qual Div is now being strengthened by you in all orgs, as per existing program. Appoint a Staff Training Officer, get tech staff checked out on Rehab HCOBs and the like and improve tech. Then get in staff status system. Get every Qual Dept established and living up to their PL purposes.

DIV 6: Get in the FSM program *hard* and start paying lots of commissions to FSMs.

If these things are done FAST wherever a gross divisional statistic is down statistics will at once resurge.

These actions should have priority over all others in an org.

L. RON HUBBARD
Founder

HCO POLICY LETTER OF 2 AUGUST 1966
Issue I

Remimeo
Applies to
  Exec Secs
  Secs
  Treasury Div
  and OIC

GRAPH CHANGE
AD COUNCIL STATISTIC

OIC will graph bills owing as a total accumulation of statements and purchases. This makes a true picture of what is currently owed.

Cash in hand will be from *reconciled* bank statements.

AD COUNCIL STATISTIC

A new graph will be added to the Ad Council's statistics that shows total debt of the org including all HP, mortgages, any bonds, notes or other indebtedness whether due or not, plus the bills owing.

This graph will have a second line showing a current estimation of the org's assets and property.

L. RON HUBBARD
Founder

Remimeo

ADVISORY COUNCIL

(Cancels HCO PL 1 Nov. 66 II, ADVISORY COUNCIL; cancels all
HCO PLs specifying the conduct of the Ad Council and its formation
previous to 1 Nov. 66; cancels HCO PL of 2 Nov. 66, AD COUNCIL
APPOINTMENTS, and HCO PL 17 Nov. 66, EXEC SECS AND AD
COUNCIL. Cancels ED 110 Int, AD COUNCIL FORMATION. Modi-
fies authority of Divisional Organizer in HCO PL of 1 Nov. 66 I.)

Note: Ad Council operation specified in the above cancelled policy letters
began on 9 Nov. 1966 and a severe consecutive-week decline of SH statistics
ensued beginning 24 Nov. 1966 and continuing. Thus, as any action preceding a
slump must be cancelled as possibly contributive, the Ad Council as outlined in
the above policy letters is cancelled and reorganized as follows. The theory is
that if an Executive Secretary does not issue direct orders, he cannot be responsible for statistics. Therefore he must be aloof from the Ad Council.

The Advisory Council of an organization shall be composed of the heads of
divisions and various representatives, duly elected, of field auditors, students,
preclears and public bodies and representatives of subordinate organizations and
a representative of the senior organization or, in case of the highest Ad Council, a
representative of the senior officer of Scientology and the board.

EXECUTIVE SECRETARIES

Executive Secretaries may not be members of the Advisory Council.

EXECUTIVE COUNCIL

The two Executive Secretaries of an org shall constitute an Executive Council.

APPOINTMENTS

All representatives of an Ad Council must be elected to it by a majority vote
of the Ad Council and the appointment confirmed by the two Executive Secretaries, on submission of the results of election by the secretary of the Ad
Council.

Exception: Heads of divisions are automatically appointed to the Ad Council.

PURPOSE

The Advisory Council purpose is: To advise the Executive Secretaries or
Executive Council as to required directives and policies and to implement directives and policy for approval and to examine statistics and conditions and implement remedies or intensification for approval and to originate and recommend for
approval promotion ideas.

POWERS

The Advisory Council has the power of passing directives, policy letters and any requisite materials submitted to it already drawn in issuable form, of modifying such bills and of recommending by passage of the Ad Council such measures to the Executive Council.

CHAIRMAN

The Ad Council shall nominate and elect its own chairman.

LRH COMM

The LRH Communicator is the member of the Advisory Council representing the next senior organization to the Advisory Council.

The LRH Communicator is a nonvoting member of the Executive Council, except at such times as there is a deadlock on the Executive Council when he, by obtaining the views of the senior Executive Council after advising them, may vote accordingly.

REFERRALS

Urgent directives (HCO PL 31 Oct. 66, Admin Know-How 2) issued by either Executive Secretary or the Executive Council may be referred for final action to an Ad Council by the originating officer or body.

BOARDS OF INVESTIGATION

The Advisory Council may appoint Boards of Investigation. But the final measures recommended in issuable form by such a board may not become law until passed by Ad Council by majority vote and referred to the Executive Secretary.

POWERS OF EXECUTIVE SECRETARY

An Executive Secretary may run and issue orders to his own divisions without referral to the Executive Council or the Ad Council.

POWERS OF A SECRETARY

A divisional secretary may issue orders to his own division without recourse to or approval from the Executive Secretary above that division or the Executive Council or the Advisory Council.

RESPONSIBILITY

An Executive Secretary is responsible for the state and activities of his or her own divisions. The Executive Council is responsible for the org as a whole and the divisional secretary is responsible for the state and activities of his or her division.

Financial planning is the full responsibility of the Executive Council. The cash-bills ratio of the org is wholly in the hands of the Executive Council unless it is such as to endanger the org or its future and shows no growing assets or reserve, in which case it is taken over by the Flag Banking Officer whose power over financial planning will be considered absolute.

REMOVAL

The Advisory Council may remove one of its own members for misconduct constituting a crime but must replace the removed member at once on the authority of the Executive Council.

The Executive Council may remove the head of a division and thus remove the person from the Ad Council without notice but with explanation.

A removed member of the Ad Council may request a Board of Investigation, or may petition the Executive Council of his own org or the Executive Council of the next senior org for reinstatement, giving substantiating statistics and evidence.

An Ad Council may, by a three-fourths majority vote and for a proven crime or high crime, request the removal of an Executive Secretary. Such a measure must then be forwarded, with any evidence, to the Executive Council of the next senior org. If in the face of actual evidence beyond reasonable doubt the measure is rejected by the Ad Council of the next senior org, the Ad Council may appeal it to the org next senior to that for action.

In this connection, an Executive Secretary whose divisions are bringing the org to a state of collapse, or who is unlawfully absent from post, or who is accepting or demanding unusual favors of students, pcs or staff is considered to be committing a crime.

If an Ad Council having evidence of such delinquency does not act, it must become interested parties to any future Comm Ev called because of the crimes, and should such a measure be advanced, found true but not passed, those voting against it shall become liable to the same sentence as any higher body may eventually pass against the offending Executive Secretary.

REMOVAL EN MASSE

If an Executive Council removes an Ad Council majority in orders close to one another or en masse, the entire matter must be brought to the attention of the next higher Executive Council which must send a person or persons to hold hearings on the matter and recommend action.

DISSIDENT VOICE

A dissident voice raised against measures or orders on the floor of the Advisory Council may not be removed or disciplined therefore.

However, the *consistent* effort by any Ad Council member to bring about the discrediting of an Executive Secretary, a higher official of Scientology, without a specific crime, with evidence assigned shall be considered mutiny.

FALSE REPORT

An Ad Council member who urges action based on a report thereafter proven to be false, and if the false report was used to discredit or deliver power or profit to himself or his division or personal friends, the matter becomes an ethics matter.

Ad Council privilege exists.

Ad Council privilege may not be used or abused to overthrow or attempt to overthrow the authority by which it is safeguarded.

PROCEDURE

The Ad Council shall be governed by Robert's Rules of Order as far as they shall apply.

Note: For six-department orgs the above organization applies, substituting director for secretary and HCO Sec and Org Sec for Executive Secretary who nevertheless are provided for as "Executive Council" above.

A six-section org has no Ad Council. If it proves too time-consuming, a Foundation may omit an Ad Council until it has 100 staff members.

L. RON HUBBARD
Founder

EXECUTIVE COUNCIL

The two Executive Secretaries (or the HCO Sec and Org Sec of a six-department org) constitute an Executive Council.

This is the highest governing body of an organization.

It is assisted by an Advisory Council which meets at a time of week prior to the Executive Council meeting.

PURPOSE

The Executive Council has the purpose of conducting a successful organization.

The highest Executive Council is appointed by the Board of Directors.

POWERS

Financial planning is a primary duty of the Executive Council.

Any and all measures passed by the Ad Council must be passed by the Executive Council before they can be issued as having force (except policy letters).

POLICY

New policy developed in the Ad Council or the Executive Council must go through all additional lines prescribed by early policy letter before being issued as policy.

CONDITIONS

All conditions are set and declared by the Executive Council.

Conditions may be suggested by the Advisory Council.

LRH COMM VETO

The LRH Communicator may veto any measure of the Ad Council or the Executive Council that is undoubtedly against policy and must show the date and line of the policy violated.

DEADLOCK

In case of deadlock in an Executive Council, only then does the LRH Communicator have actual participation. The LRH Comm in such a case requests decision by a senior Executive Council, forwarding all data, and then for it and as it orders, casts his vote in the Executive Council.

APPOINTMENTS

The Executive Council appoints all heads of divisions and ratifies newly elected membership in the Advisory Council.

REMOVALS

The Executive Council may remove members of an Ad Council because they have ceased to be heads of divisions or for a specific charge or crime, against which the removed person may appeal.

EXECUTIVE APPOINTMENTS

The HCO Exec Sec and Org Exec Sec are appointed by the senior Executive Council on a basis of statistics, state of case and experience.

COLLECTIVE RESPONSIBILITY

The only collective responsibilities of an Executive Council are the cash-bills ratio of the org, its reserves and actual assets and for the successful conduct of an org as a whole.

Each Executive Secretary is responsible for and is personally known by the gross divisional statistics of his or her divisions.

In establishing responsibility in an Executive Council for a poor cash-bills ratio, poor public repute or a declining org, a senior Executive Council should consult the statistics of the divisions under each Executive Secretary as well as the org as a whole in order to remedy the matter by new appointment.

ACCEPTANCE FOR ISSUE

The Executive Council may not accept for issue any measure passed by the Ad Council which is not already in issuable form and must return for any changes and may not rewrite such measures.

FORM OF ISSUE

All directives continue to be issued in the same form as previously except that they are signed (for an Ad Council directive or measure):

As passed by the
Advisory Council and
Authorized by the
Executive Council
for the
Boards of Directors

(for an Executive Council directive or measure):

Executive Council
for the
Boards of Directors

L. RON HUBBARD
Founder

914

Remimeo

EXECUTIVE COUNCIL

Amends:
HCO PL 21 Dec. 66 I   ADVISORY COUNCIL
HCO PL 21 Dec. 66 II   EXECUTIVE COUNCIL

The third member of the Executive Council, the PUBLIC EXECUTIVE SECRETARY, is to be included in all Executive Councils and all policy letters which state only "two members."

Nothing else is changed.

The Public Executive Secretary controls the Public Divisions.

The Public Divisions are the three former departments of Division 6, each one becoming a division in its own right.

Divisions 6, 7 and 8 now have the functions of former Departments 16, 17 and 18. Division 6 has the former functions of Department 16, and Division 7 has the former functions of Department 17, and Division 8 has the former functions of Department 18.

The former sections of Department 16 become the departments of Division 6. The former sections of Department 17 become the departments of Division 7. The former sections of Department 18 become the departments of Division 8.

The Executive Division now becomes Division 9 instead of 7.

This should be put up on all org boards and number changes made in all previous policy letters.

The reason for this is Scientology orgs have been found to have a weakness in public reach with only one division (formerly Division 6) doing the action. The health and income of an org depend upon heavy continuous watchfulness and actions in the Public Divisions.

It has been found that orgs fail to expand where they do not have a competent Public Executive Secretary and manned and functioning Public Divisions.

L. RON HUBBARD
Founder

Remimeo
Executive Councils
E/Os

ORG REDUCTION OR ERADICATION

It is an act of treason to reduce, combine or close an org.

We in Scientology are the only ones who have ever been able to reduce or close an org. The enemy has never in actual fact done so.

There are several ways an org can be collapsed or closed. While these get a lesser condition, they are important. Amongst these are:

1. Leave the Executive Council unfilled as posts.

2. Assign it or its Executive Council or principals an unreal and vicious condition.

3. Combine the Day org with its Foundation.

4. Deny it the right to promote.

5. Involve it in insolvency such as running up huge debts.

6. Use policy to stop.

7. Inhibit initiative.

8. Reward downstats and punish upstats.

9. Give Scientology and Dianetics a hard sell and then let tech go out and fail to deliver so that the org gets attacked.

10. Pretend that "we don't entirely agree with Hubbard," at which, by actual test, the public leaves it alone in droves.

11. Extend heavy credit and leave cash-paying pcs to struggle to get service in a Tech Div overloaded with freeloaders.

12. Change prices on the public.

13. Fail to give service in general.

14. Use the org just to get materials and Worldwide service for use by a small clique.

15. Let somebody hang around who is trying to get the staff to engage in some other "remunerative" action.

16. Fall for the line that it should be run as a business on business methods instead of Scientology policy.

17. Violate the tech/admin ratio.

18. Use ethics suppressively.

19. Use hard ethics on the public.

20. Accept false reports on the org or its staff members from the public and act against the org before a thorough investigation is done.

21. Permit wide and general 2D activities by the higher principals of the org.

22. Accept the insane for processing in the org without institutional facilities.

23. Fail to run a precisely scheduled, Instructor on time, standard curriculum Academy or College.

24. Fail to clean up staff cases and keep them cleaned up.

25. Fail to get the staff trained by regular and enforcedly attended programs.

26. Fail to eject hecklers and enturbulative persons from the PE Course.

27. Let town auditors haunt the org to get its pcs.

28. Fail to act as a helpful, responsible public body regardless of attacks, press entheta or field third-partying.

29. Call Dianetics, Scientology something else "more acceptable."

Before assigning Treason, or any low condition, for gross offenses of this nature, a thorough investigation should be undertaken and a Comm Ev held which obtains evidence beyond any reasonable doubt. One never assigns such conditions without Comm Ev and never assigns them over a long line. It takes personal representation from a higher body and great care should be taken (see HCO PL 15 Mar. 69, THIRD PARTY, HOW TO FIND ONE) in locating any third party not to then shoot the only leader there who was trying to straighten it up.

Of these offenses, simply ordering an org closed or to combine Day and Foundation or to drop its status lower are directly treasonable acts, as a little work and better planning and attention to policy and service has always been able to lift up stats.

We are the only ones who can actually close or reduce orgs as proven in nineteen years of constant battle even with large governments at the behest of older criminal practices. We alone have ordered orgs closed. And even when it occurred they tended to survive or revive.

Thus, *we* must also take heavy care that our own executives do not do it in any shape or guise as it betrays the whole planet.

L. RON HUBBARD
Founder

917

HCO POLICY LETTER OF 9 APRIL 1970

Remimeo

CONFERENCE HATS

Why do committees fail? Why do parliaments pass such strange bills? Why does one get unreal solutions out of conferences?

The facts are these as we have lately discovered.

When a person comes to a conference:

A. He dumps his own hat.

B. He picks up a planning hat.

C. He expresses opinions not data.

D. The group think is based on collective opinion, not on actual data.

E. Results are unreal.

Example: You call in a plumber, an electrician and a concrete man. You ask for their opinion. They decide on a building with a helicopter port roof! But they don't schedule when or how they plumb, elect or concrete! That's an example of what happens in conferences.

You have seven experts in their lines. They could contribute *data* which means FACTS. But they can dump their hats and pool opinion! Thus, an unreal solution can occur.

One of those hats must be a planning hat. The others all tend to grab that hat. Their own hats will surely then fly straight up to the Manager or Commanding Officer or In-Charge who then has to redo it all.

The *correct*, vital actions of any conference member are:

1. Prepare your data *before* coming to the conference.

2. At the conference tenaciously wear, defend and don't depart from your own hat.

3. Refuse any temptation to wear a planning hat. Insist on the planning member doing the planning.

4. Express only data. Do not give an opinion even when asked for it. Differentiate between summation of data and opinion about data.

5. Refuse to go along with the opinion of others, demand they stick to hard facts.

6. Make sure that any final decision also contains your data and is based only on the data of others.

Lo and behold, the conference so conducted will actually bring about sound plans and sound decisions.

If you really understand and really follow this rundown and in any conference demand it be followed by all other members, conferences will be able to produce results and, even when held for a senior to finally decide upon, will produce valuable results. It is not vital to have a senior's final decision at all if the conference is well done as above.

This is in fact a valuable breakthrough and if used makes democratic processes real and also possible.

Try it.

L. RON HUBBARD
Founder

HCO POLICY LETTER OF 10 APRIL 1970

Remimeo

CONFERENCE PLANNING OFFICER

Ref:
HCO PL   9 Apr. 70   CONFERENCE HATS

In HCO PL of 9 Apr. 70, CONFERENCE HATS, there is a "Planning Member."

In a small committee or conference the "Planning Member" is the Chairman.

Where there is a Planning Member in the general lineup of posts, planning is his hat.

Any member who finds his own data incompatible with the data of another member or with planning must raise an objection from the viewpoint of his own hat only. If the planning proceeds contrary to his data, he must file an *objection* in writing saying why and giving his data and attach it to the conference minutes.

L. RON HUBBARD
Founder

FINANCIAL PLANNING

HCO POLICY LETTER OF 28 MAY 1959
Issue II

Central
Convert to
Sec ED

PROMOTIONAL WRITING FUND

Pursuant to the HCO PL 27 Apr. 59, WHY NEW BOOKS ARE FEW, it is now generally agreed that the suggestion of HCO Communicator South Africa is best.

He suggested that instead of 20% or 15% of the proportional income going into the Building Fund of each Central Organization, that 15% or 10% be so deposited and the other 5% be made available to me for promotional writing.

This 5% of the proportional income would then immediately be applied to the expenses mentioned in HCO PL 27 Apr. Any part of the regular HCO 10% would be applied directly to research expenses.

However, New Zealand and others suggest 12½%. Let us do it this way. We make it 8% now and drop it to 5 when our income is all brought up by all our actions and my promotional writing.

All Assoc Secs should get the immediate opinion of staff and if favorable should then at once begin the regular, routine weekly transfer of 8% of the proportional income to "Special Fund HCO WW, National Provincial Bank Ltd., 6 Fitzroy Sq., London, W1" and delete the sum from the Building Fund.

It should be clearly understood that this money and any funds that can be salvaged from the HCO 10% (which is spent locally in most Central Organizations) will help pay the expenses of the new promotional writing and research center, located at Saint Hill, East Grinstead, Sussex.

If this money can assist promotional writing, we will all experience an increase in income, since it is promotional writing that carries most of the public interest and I am currently too pressed by other things to do it to an adequate extent.

We can continue with other financing plans for research, many of which are quite good.

I have been paying for and shoestringing research for so long that an enormous backlog has developed needful to be done now to advance the whole picture of Scientology.

So if we can get this 8% coming in very soon, and gather up what HCO cash is about and send it in, we can get both promotional writing and research going with attendant rise in income everywhere.

L. RON HUBBARD
Founder

HCO POLICY LETTER OF 2 JUNE 1959

Convert to
Sec ED

A COMMENT ON FINANCE

The history of finance in Dianetics and Scientology organizations is an interesting one.

But a recent repetition of early financial history in Washington and London must bear comment.

In 1950 and 1951, I did not have financial control of Dianetics and Scientology organizations. I was, administratively, a figurehead.

In less than one year from start, the early HDRFs were crowded into financial difficulties and went broke. In early 1952, I started the first organizations I controlled, the "Office of L. Ron Hubbard" and the HAS. Impeded badly by the HDRF credit history, I nevertheless was able to build the HAS and its successor, the HASI, into a 6 1/2-million dollar organization, fully solvent.

Now, in the past few months I gave check signing and financial concerns over to others in Washington for the FCDC and, for the past two years, to London for the HASI London.

In these few months, FCDC went $19,000 into the red from a total pay-up as of 1 Jan. 59 when I gave over. To go $19,000 into the red and to show every sign of going deeper (while business volume remained fairly usual) took some hard work on somebody's part.

In HASI London the organization in two years of noncontrol went £18,000 into the red!

I am now busy making FCDC solvent.

I have already cut the HASI London bills payable from £18,000 to £7,000 in the past ninety days. And this without even having an Accounts Department to help. I've also made HASI London pay me back £2,000 of the money it has owed me personally for six years.

In other words, we don't have many people who can handle finance smartly. That this sag was not accompanied by other slackening or increasing of activities, is quite a comment.

Beside myself, only a few other staff members have a proven record of good financing.

It might interest you how I do this trick: I disseminate like mad to lots of people and get in lots of money. I don't run up bills if I don't have money. I spend money freely only when it has been made and is in the bank. I don't worry about wasting money if I have made the money first. I never "plan for emergencies." I just make lots of money for the organization. To any financial problem, I answer by making money. To any crucial organizational problem, I answer by disseminating like mad, improving service and getting in lots of money.

I answer money problems with lots of money, not with worry or sadness or impractical hope. I never count on any one source. I always plan to get the total sum of all the money I need from each one of three or four ways or sources.

But most important, I don't run up bills if I don't have the cash in sight to pay them.

I am not parasitic on the organization. I always make many times the amount I may spend on hybrid horned toads with pink ribbons for the front hall.

I *do* now and then throw money away when it's been made and isn't needed.

Now, I've taught you many things. Let me also teach you to make tons of money for the organization. It's the one thing staffs do poorly—the making and spending of money. They can evidently spend it, they don't well make it. So let me teach you this: Disseminate like mad and make tons of money. Please?

By the way, both DC and London went completely sour in only two functions—the buying of printing and the failure to send their magazine once a month to everybody in CF. In other words, HCO printing hat and the Department of Materiel hats were to blame for the sag.

No ruin faces us. I'm still here, still working hard, still communicating.

But by golly you better learn to do this one for yourselves: disseminate like mad and make money; don't incur a single bill until you have the cash to pay it already in the bank.

I've put DC and London on tight budgets for current expenses and have other ways to float their barks. If need be, I'll pay the bills out of my own pocket, which would be unjust, since I didn't incur in any way the more serious debts and repayments to me in both cases summed only a fraction of their total.

So get smart about money. It's only money. It's made and if you make it, you can have some. If you don't you can't. It won't be there to be had.

L. RON HUBBARD
Founder

HCO POLICY LETTER OF 3 JUNE 1959

CenOCon

FINANCIAL MANAGEMENT

The financial management hat of Scientology organizations has assumed a great importance now.

Financial management is ordinarily done by the Assoc Sec, the Org Sec or the Treasurer and possibly, in some cases, the Director of Accounts, but is always under the direct responsibility of the Assoc Sec no matter who wears the hat.

It is the purpose of the hat to ensure solvency of the organization and its divisions.

This hat would be worn both in the service organization and HCO and/or in some cases for both the service organization and the HCO.

The basic principle of financial management is a simple one. Income must be greater than outgo.

Amongst the principles of financial management are these: One cannot spend money unless he has it. Never contract bills or debts unless the money is immediately in sight to pay for them. Calculate all predictions necessary to security. Disseminate like mad and make money rapidly.

Every organization should be on a contract and purchase budget. A certain amount of money is laid aside every week to pay salaries and current operating expenses and no debts are incurred until the money is there to pay for them or can be predicted to be there to pay for them. Any money left over is used to pay past bills and handle special projects.

The calculation of the budget is very simple. It is done as follows:

1. Take a dozen of the lowest weeks in the past year (ignore the high weeks), add up these 12 weekly incomes and then divide by 12. This gives you an average low week of income. This is then obviously a fairly safe figure on which to base a budget.

2. From this average low income week deduct 10% to HCO. From this 90% subtract 45% of it, not of the gross. From this 45% deduct 8% of the 90% figure. This gives you the amount of money now available for operating expenses of the organization, rents, utilities, supplies, equipment and other expenditures including advertising.

Example:

Average low week	£200
Less HCO 10%	20
90% balance	180
45% (Expenditures and Bldg F.)	.45
	900
	720
Expenditures and Bldg Fund	81.00
Special Fund	14.40
	£66.6

```
    180
    .08 Spec. Fund
   _____
   14.40
```

We can see from this that our total available budget must now cover rents, purchases, time payments, hire purchase, utilities, supplies, equipment, paper, printing, the whole works.

Total available for budget: £66.12 per week. In calculating the 10% for HCO and the 8% for the Special Fund, one takes these, of course, from the actual gross. The figures above show the portion which comes from the budget figure in order to establish the budget. After the budget is once calculated, it is adhered to. The £66 above is the actual figure. It is not recalculated. It is spent for *all* expenses. HCO 10%, Salary Sum, 8% for Special Fund all come out of the actual weekly income entire and are transferred at once to proper accounts.

The way HASI London got into trouble was to have an authorized buying and contracting at every hand without regard to income and the way it tried to stay out of trouble, rather laughably but serious enough in the long run, was to only pay as many bills as they had money in the expense sum. This, of course, was an idiotic procedure. The control point must be on purchasing and contracting, not on paying bills. As a result of this policy when I returned to financial management overall at a board level and put a financial management hat into the organization we had £18,000 of unpaid bills, which were so secret that no record was even kept of them by the Accounts Department. They were evidently wastebasketed. One of the methods used to "follow the comm lines" was after a purchase was made, the goods delivered, a purchase order would be hastily made out so as to "make the records complete." Accounts not being able to pay the bill would then file it carefully in some mouse hole and not advise anybody about it. The point of entrance of financial management then is the regulation of purchase and contract and the severe calculation of and precise ordering of all supplies and the careful calculation of future rents.

Here we are not fooling. We must run within our income or we won't have any organization at all.

What happens to the money which is left after we have spent our budget? We can do several things with it, but the best thing is to take this money periodically and bring the organization up to snuff with equipment and supplies to the degree that we have actual cash with which to pay for them, and not to buy one more paper clip than we can buy with cash. Furthermore this money can be utilized for wide advertising programs and other things which we so desperately need. But unless we budget ourselves within an income and only spend money that we have and not contract for expenditures of money that we do not have and cannot expect to have we won't survive very long.

Therefore, the fundamental of financial management is guaranteeing the survival of the organization within the economic framework of the society.

However, financial management must also be real. If it has a £66.0.0 a week budget for the expenditure of the organization on current bills, rents, etc., it must spend it and not try to chip down on its actual budget. It counts on high weeks to simply provide extra funds which will be needed, probably semi-annually, to buy the things the organization has been out of for a long time or to engage in special projects desperately needed for dissemination.

Running 8C on money is very difficult to do, I am told. I personally have never found it so but many people have.

If the organization is only permitted to spend a certain amount of money, it has a prediction and there is no question about it. Salary sum varies. All other sums for transfers, of course, come out of the main account but the budget sum must cover all the expenses, rents, equipment and other things of the organization.

It is up to a financial manager to be very, very, very tough and to learn how to say no, no, no, no. In fact, it would be a very good thing if he stood in front of a mirror for ten or fifteen minutes a day saying "no." This would be an excellent drill.

It is very important to this hat to be handled at once and it would be enforced ruthlessly, otherwise we are going to continue to run into financial jams and never have enough money to do any broad advertising in the London *Times* and *Saturday Evening Post* or anything else. Besides which, we won't even be there to do it.

The budget of Washington and London have already been set by Sec ED and is not to be changed. Other organizations should set up their own budget as above.

L. RON HUBBARD
Founder

928

LOSSES

HCO WW is receiving about £600 per week and is spending about £700 per week.

This data is gained from a review of the last year of operation and of current bills.

Nobody's job is threatened by this providing it is resolved.

Here are the plans for solvency and reduction of loss.

We will cut £150 per week from the domestic bills and office supplies, postage and telex.

We will increase our income £200 a week.

By doing both we should have a "black" in short order.

Therefore, note that the following bills are too high:

> Postage
> Office paper
> Electricity
> Office supplies
> Contracts
> Food
> Soap
> Outside laundry

A Director of Economy has been appointed to eradicate these overages, to remove three telexes and reduce supplies, paper and office costs.

All food and service buying will be done for cash and all such accounts will be closed.

By installing our new information center and giving better service we can, by making an effort, increase income £200.

These improvements and other economy actions are up to the staff to implement.

L. RON HUBBARD
Founder

All Orgs

URGENT

ORG PROGRAMING

With the change to the classification policy, there are various possible danger points to org volume.

Before the public understands classification, they may feel the HGC has gone out of business or various other ideas may get afloat.

At once all comm lines must be utilized to emphasize that classification means better case gains in the HGC as well as in the field. One gets processed out of a level by the HGC or field auditors as well as trained up from it. The HGC is there to get people's processing at the lower levels caught up in the quickest possible period of time. It can be done best at an HGC which can issue a processing clearance of lower levels and speed the person to higher classification levels.

The continental mag should be issued to stress this at once.

HQS as a course should be boomed.

HAS should be stressed for the newcomer.

Get bodies moving through the shop fast. Publicize the HGC well.

Technically, in the HGC stress to auditors processes that take care of in-sessionness. What isn't the pc able to do to be completely auditable? Permit questions to be asked by the auditor? Accept the environment? Etc. Assess by session parts and use processes to remedy these things. Stress basic-type repetitive processes and grant a right to be run on them to HGC pcs to handle Level I and clean up all Level II pc requirements. Get these flat on the pc. And you'll have wins, wins, wins.

Inform the public of the new Case Supervisor and set him or her on duty.

I designed classification to get maximum case gains for the pc and prevent pcs being given loses. Stress that in HGC propaganda.

GPMs

Issue publicly pcs do have their own goals and GPMs. The best way to get them run is to get graduated up through the levels.

The invalidation of the idea that a pc had his own goals was a severe blow. Invalidation of a pc's own GPMs, calling them implants, produces an instant ARC break and physical repercussions.

So correct this quick on Broad Public Interest (BPI), regardless of classification.

SOLVE IT WITH SCIENTOLOGY

If the org slumps during this transition period, don't engage in "fund raising" or "selling postcards" or borrowing money.

Just make more income with Scientology.

It's a sign of very poor management to seek extraordinary solutions for finance outside Scientology. It has always failed.

For orgs as for pcs "Solve It With Scientology."

Every time I myself have sought to solve finance or personnel in other ways than Scientology I have lost out. So I can tell you from experience that org solvency lies in More Scientology, not patented combs or fund-raising barbecues.

FUTURE

This policy letter though urgent should be no cause for alarm. Orgs are not going broke. They are however in a transition period to huge volume of action and it is costly to bridge.

These immediate steps will *prevent* any slump, if swiftly taken.

So take them.

L. RON HUBBARD
Founder

BALANCING INCOME–OUTGO
PAPER, POSTAGE AND PRINTING

The tremendous dent that paper and postage can make in the funds of an organization is seldom appreciated.

They are mainly invisible losses. They appear to be small. But nowhere is penny saving more rewarding.

An unleashed mimeo machine, where anyone can mimeo anything, can cost a thousand dollars a month. The paper, rather dear to begin with, mounts up to astonishing heights over short periods of time.

It is *much* cheaper to put it in the magazine. However, "financial emergency," lack of planning, like any other emergency, causes promotional necessity. It takes too long to get it into the magazine and one resorts to mimeo.

Mimeograph has uses. But it has to be a guarded use. This is so much a fact that the "okay to mimeo" should be a function of an Association or Organization Secretary—it's that much a threat to finance.

Paper economy in stationery and related supplies is also important. One only need see a stationer's bill to know why. It adds up so *fast*. Here's a bill for five hundred dollars. What's been bought? Paper clips, envelopes, a stapler—no single large sum. Where did the supplies go? They're in somebody's overstocked desk, not to be used for years. I once saw all the desks in an org cleaned out of unused (and not to be used) supplies and the aggregate filled a huge closet! About three thousand dollars, it was estimated. And new supplies being ordered daily!

Envelope supplies can be wasted by inexpert machine operation or an inefficient machine. If you have envelope wastage on machines, use only address tapes and paste them on the envelopes. Hand feed is often a better answer than machine feed on these big machines where envelopes are concerned.

POSTAGE

A periodic review of postage uses is very worthwhile in savings.

Rates by which magazines or news sheets can be mailed should be taken heavy advantage of. Sending a magazine first class is idiocy and blasts the promotion budget.

You will sometimes find several mailed items could have been combined with considerable savings. A weekly mailing for all of a certain type of item saves envelopes and postage.

PRINTING

Astonishing savings in printing bills can often be effected by as simple a thing as changing the magazine or mailing piece to a more standard size.

Scientology orgs routinely go on a binge of "It must be high-class printing" and then they find, sadly, that it didn't bring in any more income. People buy Scientology, not printing. The stress should be on content, not format, and then the format should be made as good as possible within available funds.

Remember that the biggest dissemination activity in the world, religion, is notorious for bad printing. Yet they own fantastic property areas in the world.

Excellent printing is afforded by most huge firms and publishing companies. We can't rival them yet, so why try?

It's text that counts. What you say, backed up by what you can do. *Then* when we have the income for it, we'll begin on very fancy printing.

Printing bills account for huge outgo percentages. Cut them back by using cheaper paper *sizes* and other devices. It's well worth taking up.

L. RON HUBBARD
Founder

HCO POLICY LETTER OF 18 JANUARY 1965

International
  Board Members
Sthil Executives

FINANCIAL MANAGEMENT
BUILDING FUND ACCOUNT

Effective 1 June 65, no rents, cleaning bills or any other actual expense sum bills may be expended from the Building Fund Account.

Such sums must be paid from the expense sum.

The weekly proportion of income owing to the Building Fund Account must be paid into it weekly and may not be withheld.

SIGNATORIES

The Chairman, Secretary and Treasurer are the signatories for the Building Fund Account.

Only International Board members may sign on the Building Fund Account. There may be no local or national signatories.

PRIMARY PURPOSE OF BUILDING FUND

The purpose of this account is to provide a cushion by which an organization which is becoming insolvent may be salvaged.

The following steps should be taken by the International Board in event of the threatened insolvency of a local org:

a. Remove its Organization or Association Secretary by transfer to lower post or, in flagrant cases, dismissal; and

b. Use the Building Fund Account to prevent the organization's collapse until a new Association/Organization Secretary can be found and the newly appointed Organization/Association Secretary can get things going; or

c. Pay the expense involved in sending a Board representative to the area to investigate its activities but only when these show no signs of being mended locally.

SECONDARY PURPOSE

The secondary purpose of the Building Fund is to *purchase* property, but when this is done, the purchase must be for cash or, if any mortgage is involved, all further payments than the initial payment must be made from the expense sum.

THIRD PURPOSE

Building Fund monies, being under the control of only the International Board, may also be used for other Board purposes without local consultation. These include research projects or experimental dissemination projects in the local area, or research on an international basis.

FOURTH PURPOSE

The repayment of loans made by the International Board to an area may be repaid to the International Board from the Building Fund but only on arrangements originated by the International Board.

FIFTH PURPOSE

Finance of International Board projects may be obtained by the International Board by simple withdrawal of funds from the local Building Fund Accounts without permission or consultation with area or national officers or their accounts units; these, however, must be informed of the withdrawals.

CURRENCY REGULATIONS

Where the 10% of the gross income may not be paid to the international area weekly by reason of local currency regulations, an additional bank account must be set up locally to receive them and the 10% must be paid weekly into that account.

This account is to be called the *HASI INTERNATIONAL ADMINISTRATIVE ACCOUNT.*

Only International Board members may be signatories on the HASI INTERNATIONAL ADMINISTRATIVE ACCOUNT.

Funds so deposited may be handled in any way the International Board chooses and are in no way the property of the local area organization.

THIS POLICY ALSO APPLIES TO MISSION HOLDERS. Any "inability to transfer funds to the international organization by reason of currency restrictions" are handled in the above fashion always.

DEMANDS FOR FUNDS

As in my experience an organization always spends all it makes, financial management on an *international* level consists not of carefully balancing income above outgo in an effort to save a surplus in an organization but of (a) preventing an org from spending *more* than it makes and (b) setting aside enough money from its income to care for salvage operations and salvage expenses.

Part (a) is done by good financial supervision.

Part (b) is done on an international level without *any* regard whatever for the protests and "financial necessities" of the org in question. An organization, whether Standard Oil or any other, will *always* spend all it makes and try to spend more. The task is on the one hand to keep it from spending more than it makes and on the other to make some of its expenditures recoverable in cash.

Never, on an international basis, be so fatuous as to believe an organization will continue to have the difference between its income and its outgo. It will never have that. It will spend it in some way.

An avalanche of reasons it must not save money, or (same thing) why it must spend it, is routine and is to be expected. "The government will tax it," "We can't get auditing rooms," and a thousand other reasons may be advanced as to why the org must spend all its money.

Truth told, I could run any org we have on only 25% of the income I would promote for it and pay high wages. I have done so repeatedly. But I do it by making the org apparently spend all it makes while actually spending the surplus in a recoverable fashion. This is the *only* way I have ever achieved a surplus for an org in actual practice.

Accountants deal in figures. I deal in people. Some championship chess players liken life to chess and yet can't make a go of it in life. In life the pieces think. They have impulses. So chess rules, like accountants' rules, don't apply.

Collective-think is always closer to bank-think than individual reasoning. That's because the bank is the one constant people have in common. And it's crazy. So almost any individual alive can plan better than a *group* will execute and certainly better than a group can plan. Scientology groups are far superior to human groups. But the rule still applies that collective-think is always less sane than the thinking of an individual.

In finance, which is pretty weird to begin with, collective-think is always less wise than individual reason. So a group is quite certain to behave contrary to good sense in financial matters. This factor, far more than accounts balance sheets, must be given attention. A group, poorly supervised as in a government, will usually try to spend more than it makes. Heavy supervision and economy can prevent this. Only the physical removal of money can achieve a surplus.

INCOME POTENTIAL

The income potential of any usual group is established by the demand for income, not by any other important factor.

In financial supervision on an international basis, this is the only factor one works with. While it is *reasonable* to suppose that income will occur for other reasons and can be achieved in other ways, the actual fact is that only demand by the group produces any income at all.

You can, for use in financial supervision, make the requirement almost anything you like and, so long as a group believes it is spending all it makes and needs more, you will have adequate income.

For practical purposes, no other rules apply.

Scientology orgs have always spent all I would make for them. They have adjusted their "need" to how much could be made. In supervision of their finance, it is only necessary to reverse this and they adjust their income to their "needs."

When a surplus is made part of the "need" by disguised outgo, a surplus occurs. Only *then* will it occur. It will not happen otherwise.

You can waste 15% of an organization's income to obtain a 5% surplus and it will be a wise action. If you seek a surplus by trying to save the 15% instead in a visible way, you will not only lose the 15% but the 5% also.

You can only attain a financial cushion in an org by removing it out of reach so that it appears to be spent, then producing it when the org overspends or gets in trouble.

Orgs, like children, are fantastically improvident. And a group, to work, must believe it is spending all it makes.

Money, to begin with, is only an abstract idea. Therefore, it is the victim of all manner of thoughts and opinions.

All we want out of an org is for it to stay there and continue. To do that we have to have financial ideas that work. Incredible as it may seem, the above are the only practical financial ideas which have worked and which have produced surpluses and guaranteed org continuation.

Add to these good promotion and excellent technical and you have the reasons we are becoming strong all over the world.

Financial management is not accountancy. It's people. As head of an org, if you can think your way around collective-think, you can become solvent and even have a surplus. Maybe it *shouldn't* be that way but it is.

LOCAL FINANCE

When local finance is poor, don't ever look at anything or anyone but the Association or Organization Secretary. This being can either think his way around collective-think or he can't. If he can, he's got a solvent org. If he can't, he'll go broke.

An org that runs only on collective-think will go broke.

The only symptoms of approaching insolvency in an org one needs to look for are (a) demands by it for money belonging to the international org or myself, or (b) consistent low income.

In either case, the remedy is to get somebody in charge who doesn't demand monies belonging to the international org or myself and who gets a higher income coming in for the org. An Assoc/Org Sec who can't do this is the effect of the collective-think in his org and is not the org leader or the dominant planner of the org.

At continental or international level one must never seek for the "reason" why international or LRH monies must be used by the org or why income is consistently low. You can get reasoned to death. If these two facts exist, then there's so much else wrong one would go mad tabulating it.

The steps to take are:

1. Remove the Assoc/Org Sec.

2. Put somebody in who *can* handle collective-think.

3. Use any local surplus to carry the org during the upsets of transition.

Experience has taught me that distant efforts to right local extreme wrongs are usually disastrous. You can right small wrongs, show the way and so on. That's only normal leadership. But when an org begins to skid financially or get upset over "its" money being used internationally, you don't fool about. You just act.

The longer you put off acting, the more local people get hurt. Because behind those facts of poor finance are some very ugly other abuses always.

I don't want any orgs in a games condition with the international org. For this is only a symptom of the imminent collapse of the local org anyway. It goes into a games condition only after its overts stretch from A to Z.

You don't see the overts from a distance. You do see financial conditions and demands.

It would be impossible today for a cleanly run, on-policy, up-tech org not to own its area totally in 10 years.

Financial insolvency? What nonsense!

So financial policy is based on good individual ability heading up each org and is not based on either accounting or collective-think. Neither one will build any future for mankind.

The reasons behind the Building Fund Account have been set forth above in full.

Good local leadership always results in good local financial credit and strength. Weak local leadership has always resulted in financial insolvency and trouble. Broad general supervision of orgs uses financial protests and upsets and trouble to detect weak leadership.

Without adequate and sensible leaders, orgs would slump into collective-think in their planning, spend more than was made and cease to exist.

We want orgs to be successful, to stay there and continue. That requires sensible financial provisions and management.

STABLE DATA

1. An org will try to spend more than it makes.

2. Economy is aimed at preventing it from spending more than it makes.

3. A surplus is achieved only by making it part of what an org spends.

4. An org's expenditures are *not* regulated by what the org needs in order to do business but by what an org thinks it has available for expenditure.

5. Financial management can *not* achieve a financial surplus by economy alone.

6. A surplus to be achieved must be made part of what an org thinks it spends.

7. Income is regulated by what an org thinks it has to have to operate.

8. Income is never regulated in a usual org by desires for a surplus.

9. To achieve a surplus it must be masked as a "necessary expenditure."

10. Economy, to achieve a surplus, does not include saving on expenses. It includes only adding an "expense" that becomes a surplus.

11. To achieve a surplus one must add an expense that can then thereafter convert to a surplus. One can waste up to 50% of an org's income to achieve a 10% surplus. In some cases this is the only way a surplus can be achieved. Why? See (1) and (2) above.

12. An individual is always more sensible than a group.

13. When an org is losing ground financially, it is being "run" by someone who is only the effect of the group and cannot act as an individual in planning or control the group.

14. The only possible *Board* action when an org is not making its way financially is to remove the Association or Organization Secretary. The incumbent is only the effect of the group and is not planning or controlling.

15. The earlier one detects a bad Assoc/Org Sec and replaces him, the better it is for the people in that area.

16. The ways to detect a bad Assoc/Org Sec are:

    a. Their games condition by any part of the org with the Board;

    b. Their desires to be financed by the Board or use the Board's or my income to run on;

    c. Generally low income;

    d. Protests against the Board using "their money."

Under these or any of them will be found an org out of control and messing people up.

Therefore, the quicker the Board acts to replace the Assoc/Org Sec, the easier the situation will be to handle and the faster the org will recover.

17. *Board* efforts to "straighten up an area" without replacing the local head have *never* been successful in 14 years. If let go too long under incompetent management, an org's recovery requires heroic efforts and vast financial expenditure by the international org.

18. Bad local publicity and trouble always follows after 16 to the degree that the Board did not act.

19. Financial management as contained in this policy letter, closely followed, will prevent almost all trouble and org upsets, not just in finance but in all other areas.

L. RON HUBBARD
Founder

HUBBARD COMMUNICATIONS OFFICE
Saint Hill Manor, East Grinstead, Sussex

HCO POLICY LETTER OF 28 JANUARY 1965

Remimeo
Int Bd Members
Cont Dirs
HCO Cont Secs
Assoc/Org Secs
HCO Secs
Accts Units

ACCOUNTS HATS

FINANCE

HOW TO MAINTAIN CREDIT STANDING AND SOLVENCY

(Hat check on Assoc/Org Secs and Accounts Assistants)

Credit does not entirely deal with money. It has everything to do with confidence and reliability.

When the world saw a recently elected government act foolishly with customs dues, etc., it had no confidence in that government and the currency of that government went to pieces on the world market.

Money is basically a matter of confidence. So is credit.

An Accounts Unit that handles money poorly wrecks the org's credit rating. Insolvency is much less often the source of poor credit than just poor money handling.

Almost all our orgs have good credit. But where they don't, it is money *handling,* not the amount of money available, that wrecks credit.

An Assoc/Org Sec who handles bills in a certain way has good org credit. One who doesn't has bad credit.

To try to assign credit to the amount of money available is *completely* false.

You can have lots of money and horrible credit. You can have little money and excellent credit. So saying "Our income has been poor so our credit is bad" is a lie.

The business world judges Scientology not on its scientific validity but on its financial credit rating. If the org's credit is good, then "Scientology is okay." If your credit is bad, "Scientology is a racket," in business general opinion.

Melbourne's financial *credit* went bad before its general repute earned it an inquiry.

Good credit is a primary dissemination line. It breeds confidence. You can't have bad credit and still be thought of as a valid science.

So financial management *must* help general dissemination by maintaining good credit.

A bad credit rating comes from negligence in Accounts, not from the lack of industry of the Registrar.

To begin with, an org has no business spending more than it makes. To do so shows stupidity in management and Accounts, lack of a purchase order system and a general beatnik state of organization.

Make all the money you can. Spend less than that. That's the simple ABC of financial control.

Make sure all the income is accounted for and banked.

Make sure no unauthorized purchases can be made by executives or staff by requiring an authority to purchase or *contract* from the head of the org before any purchase can be made or contract signed. Sure that's slow. Who wants it fast? The slower it is, the less you spend.

You want speed on the income line. The disbursement line is something else.

So never listen to somebody saying "But it takes so long to get a purchase order that I just bought it. . . ." Yawn and say, "You bought it without authorization. You can pay for it personally." *Never* let your purchase order system break down. If you do, you will soon be spending more than you make. Fact. No exceptions.

A company to most people is something to bleed. They never realize that a company can only spend what it makes and that what it has is made by individuals. So if you have somebody around who is always saying, "The org will pay or should pay," point out that the org is its staff's collective pocketbook and that that pocketbook has a bottom.

SOLVENCY

You sometimes hear around an org a wave of "we're broke" when spending is restrained. This hurts credit. For it's not true. Economy is *not* a sign of being broke. It's a sign of increasing prosperity. Without curtailed and watched spending you *never* have prosperity.

So don't tell everybody, "We can't buy it because we're broke." That's a lazy, dull reason. A better one is, "We can't buy it because we don't need it" and is usually the truth. "We have a PO system because we want to prosper" is the real reason you have one.

Make lots of money. Spend it frugally.

So it gives a tax problem. So what? Your accountants should be capable of avoiding tax problems. Whether you do or don't have money, you will always have a tax problem because governments are crazy. The way to solve a tax problem is to have money, not to be broke.

Taxes exist only to destroy businesses. Be impudent. Get rich and to hell with them. Governments are just a reactive bank we have to live with for a while. Learn to handle them. But not by refusing to make money or have it.

941

But solvency depends on how you handle things, not on how much you have. Micawber,* in *David Copperfield*, said that if you had twenty-one shillings and spent a pound, you had happiness. But that if you had nineteen shillings and spent a pound, you had misery! A pound being twenty shillings, that's all there is to solvency.

If you *have* to spend a million dollars, then you better make one million one hundred thousand first. And then make sure you don't spend one million two hundred thousand.

The secret of solvency is:

1. Make a lot of money. The way to do that in Scientology is covered in HCO Policy Letter of 21 Jan. 65R, VITAL DATA ON PROMOTION.

2. Spend less than you make. That's covered by having a good PO system and alert financial management.

3. Make it before you have to spend it.

4. Gather bit by bit a cushion of cash to fall back on and don't ever fall back on it.

5. Keep your credit excellent as a second cushion.

6. Refuse to spend reserves. Make more money to meet the emergency instead. (It's usually quicker to make it than to dig it out of old hiding places. Never borrow to pay bills. It's less trouble just to make the money.)

7. Realize that collective-thought regarding finance is just bank and that bank is dead against the creation of anything good and all for eating up everything that exists. Thus financial planning and control is an individual job, is often contrary to group demands and succeeds only when the individual handling it can rise superior to the group. A tame-dog financial manager, trailing along behind the group, yessing everything, will always make the group insolvent. The person you put in charge of financial management should be able to say "No!" no matter how popular a silly "Yes" would be. The financial manager is not there to buy his own popularity with org funds.

In the early years of Scientology, my whole answer to org solvency was just to make a lot more money than people could waste. It's a good answer, lacking all others. When I finally attained control of orgs, I was able also to curtail the waste while making lots of money and we've been pretty solvent ever since. The principles I used to achieve and continue this state of solvency are accurately and completely listed in 1 to 7 above.

---

*[*Editor's Note:* Micawber is a character in Dicken's *David Copperfield*. Mr. Wilkins Micawber was a great speechifier, letter-writer and projector of schemes sure to lead to fortune but always ending in grief. Notwithstanding his ill success, he never despaired, but felt certain that something would turn up to make his fortune.]

CREDIT

When you realize FINANCIAL CREDIT is vital in dissemination, you become very interested in what it is. As I said above, this is *confidence*.

Given some degree of solvency, you still do not have a good credit rating. That is achieved by HOW YOU PAY BILLS.

This is the one big point that is vital to know thoroughly in this policy letter.

If an Association or Organization Secretary and the Accounts Assistant does not know exactly this data, the org will have bad credit and financial trouble, no matter how much they make.

There is an exact way to pay bills.

This is to pay the bills up to a certain date always. It is called "paying by dateline."

Never "pay a little bit on each bill" to save money or help cover a lean period. That will never help. On the contrary, it advertises your lean period and hurts your credit.

Instead, *always,* lean or fat, pay *all* the bills *behind* a certain date and *none* closer to PT than that date.

That's why we have the type of disbursement system we have. So you can do this trick. If your disbursement system and its files are not up to the mark and are sloppy, you will always have bad credit because they can't then do this trick of dateline paying.

Look to the inefficient Accounts Unit and the lack of this bill-paying system if your local credit is poor. Don't go off into income–outgo. Just demand that our general accounts system be followed and that disbursement files are up-to-date.

If you find an Accounts personnel giving financial management the razzmatazz about why it can't have good disbursement files and if this bills-paying schedule is always being violated, assume at once that that personnel is overtly wrecking the org's credit and get him or her away from that post and get somebody in who will follow our system accurately and help pay bills only by dateline.

You can have six months worth of unpaid bills in some areas of the world and *still* have a good credit rating providing you do not have one bill that is *ten* months unpaid.

Never "pay bills" any old way. A financial manager should always refuse to pay bills one at a time on different days or when Accounts submits a check.

Tell Accounts "Give me every bill we owe prior to August (three months ago)." Add these up. Let's say the amount exceeds our cash. Cut it back one month. Order "Write checks for *every* bill up to 1 July." (That's four months back.) That we can cover fully with cash. We pay *all* bills *up* to 1 July. We demand of Accounts, "Are you very, very, very, very sure that no bills dated prior to 1 July now exist?" If the answer is "None exist," okay. But if we find out next week that one existed for 1 April that wasn't included, we overhaul the unit as destructive of credit.

Businessmen handle their books by bills owed month by month, not by total sums owed. When a check comes in paying his 1 July bill, then it's plain you're paying your bills. If you send a small sum hopefully to "stave them off," they can't dismiss any one statement with it and so get panicky. It looks like you aren't paying your bills.

After you've paid all bills older than 4 months, get busy and make money. In 30 days request of Accounts "all bills up to 15 August." Let's say we find that we have cash to cover. We say, "Pay all bills up to 15 August." Now we're only 3½ months behind.

A month hence we pay "All bills up to Oct 1." Now we're only 3 months behind.

If you get some eager beaver into finance who doesn't use or understand how to do this, you can suddenly look up and find that you thought you were doing all right but you're broke. The eager beaver paid randomly anything in the files he or she came across "in order to pay our bills." We aren't interested in bills as bills. We're interested in "all bills earlier than a given date."

You can go pretty smash on an eager-beaver bills-paying spree with no regard to the age of each bill.

Only pay by this system: PAY EVERYTHING UP TO A DATE ALWAYS and no further.

And get a new Accounts Unit if disbursement files aren't accurately kept so financial management can do this.

EXCEPTIONS

Government tax bills, water bills, occasionally rent or phone are sometimes accompanied by threats of vast action unless the whole bill is paid instantly. Still try to use the above system. But if you can't, pay it and retard other bills accordingly. And thereafter, don't pay that outfit's bill on any other terms than threatened trouble.

If a tradesman, despite the use of the above system, demands further payment or threatens suit, caution him that if he carries on this way you'll deal elsewhere. And carry out the threat. *Never* continue to use a private business firm after they become obnoxious about bills. Trade elsewhere. And say why.

If you're using the above dateline system and a tradesman gets upset, then he is gypping you or he has too little finance to handle your account, so stop trading with him. Always make that an ironbound policy. Be very proud and haughty about bills. *Never* propitiate.

So the points here that are important are:

1. Pay by dateline only and pay *all* up to that dateline. Put the dateline far enough back so you *can* pay all up to that date.

2. Have an Accounts Unit that can do this and change one that flubs it.

And that handles the whole of credit rating.

Simple?

OUR SYSTEM

The other day two high-geared chartered accountants were giving me a lot of stuff about how I needed a double-entry system and that the existing system was wrong.

They said, "We can tell you 21 days after the 30th of the month where you stood in that past month using our double-entry system."

I said, "The system we have to have must tell us *four* days after the past week exactly where I stand. We operate in the twentieth century, not the nineteenth."

They said, "But your system is wrong."

I said, "In a double-entry system, you need each bit we have, don't you? Invoice all the money, bank it, reconcile the deposits with the slips and statements, file all the bills, verify them, pay them by check and voucher and keep all records."

They looked at each other and were very quiet. "Yes, that's correct," they said.

I said, "All right, that's our system. Now, you can do anything you like with that system from there on, so long as you don't prevent us from knowing where we stand four days after the past week and don't bar out a nonaccountant from discovering what's what in the Accounts Unit. Now go ahead and *on* our system erect any system you like. No government requires anyone to have *books*. They only require *records*. But books, if they help, should also be kept, made up from our records." They agreed.

So if you are getting propaganda about how our system is inadequate as a reason not to operate and have accounts, get somebody in who *can* make it work. For our system is the basis of every other system and if it's in order and *done,* you can have books. If it *isn't* in order, no books can be kept by *any* system.

So we don't care what accountants do with our basic system so long as we still at least have that. On that, *any* type of books can be erected or any balance sheet made.

If you have the basic data you can add it up.

If your Accounts Unit can't add up whatever you need, then our system is *not kept up* and *no* system would work in that unit. Where there is Accounts trouble there is:

1. Noncomprehension of our basic system as the basic of any accounts system or

2. Nothing being done.

Get our system in so you know where you are with cash and bills.

Manage by paying all bills up to a specific dateline only.

Advance the dateline as you can cover all with your cash and make lots of money so you can advance it further toward PT. Practice economy so you can advance it even closer.

Continue to do that and you'll always have a good credit rating.

We have a lot of fine Accounts Units. They do a good job. They can handle this if they understand it. It's your job now to get it understood and done.

L. RON HUBBARD
Founder

Remimeo
Ad Council
Members

FINANCIAL PLANNING

A set of proportionate figures recently compiled on financial planning at Saint Hill are of general interest to Ad Council members.

The period chosen was a fairly average one for income, covering the three months (12 weeks) late August, September, October 1966.

Four sums of monies actually disbursed were obtained.

These were:

1. Total salaries paid

2. Total gross of building POs (would constitute maintenance expenses and rent)

3. Total gross org expenses

4. Total FSM commissions.

The total gross income of the period was added up.

Ten percent was deducted from it for research (adding up to admin 10 percent of most orgs).

Ten percent of the gross was taken to operate as a reserve or to catch up errors and overages in planning and in case income went down in the next quarter.

The remaining 80 percent was then proportioned amongst (1) to (4) above.

The percentage results were as follows:

1.	Total salaries paid	31%
	Government payroll deductions	4%
2.	Total building	17%
3.	Total org expenses	21%
4.	FSM commissions:	7%
		———
		80%
	10% admin or research	10%
	10% leeway or reserved	10%
		———
		100%

This gives some sort of a guide.

During this period the org was being pulled up from a high bills–low cash ratio, so the expense sum is perhaps a trifle high. And it had a building program going, so building POs may be a trifle high. Its leeway or reserve simply paid off back bills.

However, the fact remains that this was a period of gain of org financial affairs and, being at the end of summer and into autumn, not a period of extraordinary income which occurs just before summer at Saint Hill. So it is felt that these percentages are safe.

The way one could use this table would be to calculate the past quarter of the year's gross income when the new quarter begins and then allocate these percentages each month for the next quarter.

The percentages took a 12-week quarter, but expenses were also for 12 weeks, so they are just percentages and so are valid for a 13-week quarter.

Let us say income Jan.–Feb.–Mar. (13 weeks) was Q dollars.

One could then divide Q by 13 and get an estimated future weekly gross figure. We will call this W (meaning gross income for a week).

One could then divide Q by 3.12 and get an estimated future monthly gross income average. We could call this M.

Therefore, to set a ceiling on all expenses for the coming 13 weeks for each week we would have:

.31 x W = Weekly salaries

.04 x W = Weekly tax paid by company on personnel

.17 x W = Building and rent ceiling

.21 x W = Weekly org expense ceiling

.07 x W = FSM commission estimate

.10 x W = Admin or research 10 percent

.10 x W = Leeway or reserve 10 percent

Then we would also have our figures as an estimate of monthly expenses where financial planning is done monthly:

.31 x M = Salaries/month

.04 x M = Company paid salary tax

.17 x M = Building and rent ceiling

.21 x M = Org expense ceiling

.07 x M = FSM commission estimate

.10 x M = Monthly admin or research 10 percent

.10 x M = Leeway or reserve 10 percent

Org expense includes all utilities, bills, services—the lot.

By keeping to or under these figures, one could then be considered to be planning safely.

By getting departments and divisions to turn in their estimated POs before the beginning of the month for the next month one could plan successfully (remembering their POs don't include utilities and many routine bills which must be deducted from the org expense amount before one signs any POs).

It is realized that where one is on a 55-percent-of-90-percent proportionate pay plan, the above indicated safe salary sum is greatly exceeded which is on (in all) 35-percent-of-80-percent. This may be why orgs tend to develop a high bills–low cash ratio. Lack of stability (poor financial picture) and expense money may reflect back on the gross income, tending to depress it, and thus really reduce wages despite the 55-percent-of-90-percent proportionate wage allocation. The staff might make more and have more future if their pay was only 31-percent-of-80-percent with 4-percent-of-80-percent for tax. Certainly staff at Saint Hill makes more than staff in other orgs and has consistently, even in low income years.

Anyway, there are some figures on which financial planning can be based.

L. RON HUBBARD
Founder

L. Ron Hubbard
EXECUTIVE DIRECTIVE

LRH ED 74 INT   14 January 1970

TO: All Exec Secs
    Finance Office Staff
    Treasury Secs

SOLVENCY

A project of FP Pgm No. 1, LRH ED 55 Int.

The greatest help you can be to the enemy is to permit orgs to become insolvent. There is no single greater threat to any org than insolvency.

SOLVENCY consists only of income greater than outgo and making enough money.

There is no trick to making money. It almost has to be planned not to have any.

It is much harder to walk back to solvency than to remain solvent in the first place.

All an org is is a service activity that trains and processes and keeps up the admin lines necessary to do so.

When you don't have enough auditors and supervisors there is no way to deliver service.

One never backlogs. One keeps the auditors and supervisors busy, busy, busy. Auditing has a thousand uses. So does training.

Any org has a tendency to spend all it makes and an equally silly one to make only what it needs.

Orgs should have heavy reserves.

In LRH ED 55 Int, you have the key to solvency. This ED should be followed carefully. The exact amount the org needs to get along on MUST BE KNOWN.

If the org is already in debt AN ADDITIONAL SUM IS NEEDED WEEKLY TO RETIRE ITS DEBTS.

This FP Pgm No. 1 must be done by the EC.

An additional sum to retire debts or build a reserve must be added.

A sensible and strenuous effort must then be made to make that amount of money or more.

An industrious attitude with a no-nonsense approach will provide solvency, good reserves, good staff facilities and pay.

Often when an org gets into financial problems it tends to go frantic and dream up wild unusual solutions. The org got in trouble because it didn't do the usual actions! To go even more unusual is a fatal error.

A businesslike approach of getting in people to train and process and delivering instantly valuable services is all that will make money.

The No. 1 Program EDs tell one exactly how to do this.

When we had only a hundredth of the tech we now have we had solvent, rich orgs. So it looks like we better get busier.

Get FP No. 1 done so you know where you stand.

L. RON HUBBARD
Founder

951

L. Ron Hubbard
EXECUTIVE DIRECTIVE

LRH ED 245RA INT

27 August 1974
Revised 5 May 1985

URGENT

TO: FBO Cont'ls
    FBOs
    D/FBOs for MORE
    FP Committee Hats

FROM: RON

FINANCIAL PLANNING CHECKLIST
FOR THE PROMOTIONAL ACTIONS
OF AN ORGANIZATION

REFS: LRH ED 244 Int   RAISING GI STAT
           HCO PL 20 Nov. 65RA THE PROMOTIONAL ACTIONS
           Rev. 4.5.85   OF AN ORGANIZATION

(THIS LRH ED IS URGENT FOR FP COMMITTEES AND FBOs)

This checklist was compiled from highly successful functions in handling SH finances in the 60s. It is a tried and true GI raiser.

This checklist is gone through and checked off by the Financial Planning Committee, the Exec Council and the FBO, to ensure that financial expenditures are properly made for promotion and that POs have actually been made to FP to acquire things needed for promo. If no monies have been allotted for a particular item, an attestation is required from the Divisional Secretary that he has inspected and found that there is a sufficient quantity of the item to last until the next FP or an ethics chit is written on the concerned Divisional Sec for failure to perform the promotional activities of his division and money is allocated for same. In allocating monies the concerned terminals will have to know how many names are in CF and how many names in different categories.

(Numbers refer to HCO PL 20 Nov. 65RA, THE PROMOTIONAL ACTIONS OF AN ORGANIZATION.)

HCO AREA SEC (1)

2:       INTRO LECTURE HANDOUTS FOR RECEPTION.   _____

5:       Routing Forms and routing signs.   _____

6(i):   Sign board, lettering equipment, poster paint, brushes and pins for recruiting signs.   _____

6(ii), 7, 8: RECRUITING PROMO FOR STAFF, AUDITORS, SUPERS.   _____

9:       Colored tape for org board and colored dymo tape.   _____

10(i):   Envelopes, wrappers or staples for magazine.   _____

10(ii): POSTAGE MONEY FOR MAILING MAGAZINE.   _____

3, 11(i): Sign board, lettering equipment, poster paint, brushes and pins for Reception book and cassette displays and public notice signs.   _____

11(ii): Auditing promo and training promo for public notice boards.   _____

12:      Comm baskets and labels.   _____

14(i):   ORG STATIONERY AND ENVELOPES.   _____

14(ii): POSTAGE FOR ORG'S LETTERS OUT AND BUSINESS REPLY POSTAGE.   _____

10(iii): POSTAGE FOR PROMOTIONAL MAILINGS.   _____

14(iii): FRANKING MACHINE RENTAL.   _____

13:      TELEPHONE COSTS.   _____

15:      MIMEO PAPER, INK, STENCILS AND MIMEO SUPPLIES.   _____

DISSEM SEC (22)

23:      MAGAZINE PRINTING COSTS (OR MIMEO PAPER, STENCILS AND INK FOR MAGAZINE).   _____

24(i):   PRINTING COSTS FOR AUDITING PROMO.   _____

24(ii): PRINTING COSTS FOR TRAINING PROMO.   _____

29, 30: AUDIOVISUAL EQUIPMENT AND MATERIALS AND AUDIOVISUAL EQUIPMENT REPAIR AND MAINTENANCE.   _____

25, 26, 27, 34: Paper, shooting board, press type (Letraset), art erasers, art pens, ink, and other makeup supplies. _____

29, 31, 32: BOOKS (CHECK THE ORG'S WEEKLY STOCK LIST TO ENSURE THERE ARE ENOUGH BOOKS OF EVERY TITLE IN STOCK, PLUS CASSETTES, TAPES, E–METERS, PINS AND INSIGNIA). _____

29, 31, 32, 34: IMPORT, SHIPPING OR CUSTOMS DUTIES FOR BOOKS, METERS, CASSETTES, TAPES, INSIGNIA. _____

33: SHIPPING AND WRAPPING SUPPLIES FOR BOOKS, CASSETTES, INSIGNIA AND E–METERS, STRING, ETC. _____

35(i): PRINTING COSTS FOR BOOK, CASSETTE AND METER FLIERS. _____

35(ii): PRINTING COSTS FOR BOOK, METER AND CASSETTE PRICE LISTS AND ORDER FORMS. _____

36, 39: LETTER REG QUESTIONNAIRES. _____

37(i): CF FOLDERS. _____

37(ii): ADDRESS STICKERS. _____

38: Gradation Charts. _____

40: ADVANCE REGISTRATION PACKS. _____

41: TELEPHONE REGISTRATION COSTS. _____

42: REGISTRATION FORMS. _____

43: Address plates, tabs, ink, stickers, cards, etc. _____

TREASURY SEC (45)

47(i): Statement envelopes. _____

47(ii): Statement copy paper and machine supplies. _____

47(iii): STATEMENT POSTAGE COSTS. _____

46, 50: INVOICES AND INVOICE CARBON ROLLS. _____

51: DISBURSEMENT VOUCHERS AND CARBON ROLLS. _____

52: Staff pay envelopes. _____

54: Staff uniforms (where provided). _____

TECH SEC (55)

58(i): COURSE CHECKSHEETS FOR ALL COURSES. _____

58(ii):   COURSE PACKS FOR ALL COURSES.   _____

58(iii):   TAPE MACHINES AND TAPE MACHINE REPAIR
             AND MAINTENANCE.   _____

58(iv):   COURSE TAPES FOR ALL COURSES.   _____

58(v):   Clay supplies.   _____

58(vi):   Student chairs and tables.   _____

58(vii):   Auditor Report Forms.   _____

58(viii):   Auditor worksheet paper.   _____

58(ix):   Auditor assessment lists required in auditing.   _____

58(x)   C/S forms and supplies.   _____

58(xi):   Auditing chairs, tables and auditing room
             requirements.   _____

58(xii), 67: PROJECTOR SYSTEM AND PROJECTOR
             SYSTEM REPAIR AND MAINTENANCE.   _____

58(xiii), 67: AUDITOR PAY.   _____

QUAL SEC (76)

77:          Examiner forms and routing forms.   _____

80(i):   Certificates for all courses and all grades.   _____

80(ii):   Release pins.   _____

80(iii):   Minister cards.   _____

82:          RELEASE LITERATURE FOR ALL PRECLEARS
             WHICH TELLS THEM WHAT THEY HAVE
             ATTAINED AND WHAT THEIR NEXT STEP IS.   _____

84, 87:   Auditor Report Forms, worksheets and supplies.   _____

85:          Checksheets, course packs, tape machines, tapes and
             course room supplies.   _____

PUBLIC CONTACT SECRETARY (94)

95:          Bookstore displays or posters.   _____

96, 107:   Book and cassette ads in magazines.   _____

98(i):   CARDS FOR BOOKS AND CASSETTES PLACED
             IN BOOKSTORES GIVING ORG'S ADDRESS AND
             TELEPHONE, ETC.   _____

98(ii):   TESTING HANDOUTS.   _____

98(iii): TESTING SUPPLIES. _____

98(iv): BASIC COURSES PROMO. _____

99(i): BASIC COURSE PROMO AND HANDOUTS. _____

99(ii): Extension Course advertisements. _____

100(i): Tape play handouts. _____

100(ii): Tape play advertisements. _____

100(iii): Open house supplies—i.e., mailing costs, and tea, coffee and such supplies. _____

101: PROJECTOR SYSTEM AND PROJECTOR SYSTEM REPAIR AND MAINTENANCE. _____

102: Address plates, tabs, ink, stickers, cards, etc. _____

103: Purchase of new mailing lists. _____

104(i): INFO PACKS FOR 3 MAILINGS SCHEDULED FOR EACH PERSON AND ENVELOPES FOR SAME. _____

104(ii): Address stickers. _____

105: INTRO LECTURE INVITATION CARDS. _____

109: Lecturer expenses. _____

PUBLIC SERVICING SECRETARY (110)

111: TELEPHONE REGISTRATION COSTS. _____

112: REGISTRATION FORMS. _____

115: EXTENSION COURSE MATERIALS. _____

118(i): COURSE CHECKSHEETS FOR ALL COURSES. _____

118(ii): COURSE PACKS FOR ALL COURSES. _____

118(iii): TAPE MACHINES AND TAPE MACHINE REPAIR AND MAINTENANCE. _____

118(iv): COURSE TAPES FOR ALL COURSES. _____

118(v): Clay supplies. _____

118(vi): Student chairs and tables. _____

118(vii), 125: Auditor Report Forms, worksheets and supplies. _____

126: ARC Break Reg supplies and forms. _____

134(i):   LOCAL MAILING TO LOCAL MISSIONS IN ORG'S AREA.   _____

134(ii), 135: MONTHLY FSM MAILING.   _____

138:       FSM COMMISSIONS.   _____

139(i):   FSM SELECTION SLIPS.   _____

139(ii):   FSM and mission dissem materials.   _____

140:       Promo inviting Scientologists to send names and addresses of friends for info packs.   _____

142:       Mailing to local groups.   _____

144:       Public Membership cards.   _____

145:       AUDITOR ASSOCIATION MAILING.   _____

146:       MEMBERSHIP PROMOTIONAL MAILINGS.   _____

147, 148: Postage for student and pc follow-up letters.   _____

149:       Printing of success handouts.   _____

DEPT 21, ESTATES BRANCH

168, 169: RENT OR PURCHASE PAYMENTS OF QUARTERS IN HEAVY TRAFFIC AREA.   _____

170, 171: Cleaning costs and supplies.   _____

172:       Maintenance and repair costs and supplies.   _____

THAT AN ITEM IS NOT IN CAPS DOES NOT MEAN IT IS UNIMPORTANT. THE ONES IN CAPS *MUST* BE FPed FOR.

L. RON HUBBARD
Founder

HUBBARD COMMUNICATIONS OFFICE
Saint Hill Manor, East Grinstead, Sussex

HCO POLICY LETTER OF 23 JUNE 1975

Remimeo
Ad Council
Exec Council
Treas Hats
FBO Hats

AD COUNCIL INCOME PLANNING

(Amends and adds to HCO PL 26 Nov. 65R, FINANCIAL PLANNING,
by reassigning these duties from Ad Council to Exec Council. The 19
Apr. 73 revision of HCO PL 26 Nov. 65R, FINANCIAL PLANNING,
is cancelled and the Advance Payment report it called for is a function
of the Ad Council.)

I have just found a Why for low income and promotion scarcity and FP
troubles, by isolating a missing step in the financial planning sequence.

INCOME PLANNING!

In the absence of income planning, financial planning becomes a near impossible task of allocating money that hasn't been made in the first place.

Any financial system that places expense allocation before income and delivery
planning is set up to fail.

It is the failure to do this which has given FP a bad name.

From this we get a sequence of duties:

AD COUNCIL does INCOME AND DELIVERY PLANNING *before* attempting to handle any expenditure.

AD COUNCIL DUTIES

The income of the org and its delivery is the primary business of an Ad
Council. When it has accomplished its business in this it may then consider the
limitation of expenditures.

In actual practice, all the income and delivery units of the org are represented in Ad Council and this fact affords an opportunity to coordinate actions
and require income and delivery.

An Ad Council must know every corner of the org's marketing, promotion,
pricing, sales and delivery. This means surveys, pricing and things to sell.
Things to promote. How to promote and who can one reach (CF, Address, new
publics). How to sell. How to deliver. How to get in repeat business.

These actions have been assembled into an Ad Council checklist.

Use of this checklist now becomes mandatory for Ad Council who may not
touch expenditure matters until it has reviewed the checklist and formulated an
income planning which forces in promotion, delivery and sales, and which

remedies the weak points and removes the barriers to achieving these. The checklist points are to be gotten in on a gradient. This means that Ad Council goes over all the points on the checklist at each meeting and works out how to get them all in by taking the points that are needed in immediately and getting them in. The next meeting covers keeping in those points gotten in the previous week and working out how to get in more points. This is done over and over until all points are gotten in and are being kept in.

The checklist serves as a guide to direct Ad Council's attention to vital areas, but may not be taken to supplant policy, and every Ad Council member must be checked out on a pack of the PLs that govern delivery, promotion and sales, as well as conference policies.

The Ad Council planning is expressed in an Executive Directive drawn up for Exec Council approval. This usually covers the coming week, but may also take up longer-range planning.

Ad Council collects up all Divisional FP submissions, sees to it that those things necessary to execute its planning have been FP'd for, sees that at least 14 percent of the allocation is allotted to promotion and that there are adequate promo items to utilize this 14 percent without waste. It also ensures that the allocation is not exceeded and that the org solvency is taken into account.

The Divisional FP submissions and the completed checklist with Ad Council proposals and all work papers (including any rejected, disapproved FP submissions) are then forwarded to Exec Council for approval in full CSW form.

EXEC COUNCIL DUTIES

The Exec Council is composed of the Executive Secretaries and their Org Officers. Their actions are:

A. To put a functioning Ad Council there and demand income and delivery.

B. Approval of Ad Council recommended GDS conditions and all Ad Council planning. Exec Council may veto or amend or add to Ad Council planning and is responsible to see that Ad Council performs its duties. In the final analysis, regardless of Ad Council actions or inactions, Exec Council is responsible for demanding delivery and income and getting it produced.

C. Long-range promotional planning.

D. The actions of financial planning as given in HCO PL 26 Nov. 65, FINANCIAL PLANNING, designed to oversee and ensure outgo below income is maintained, as well as balancing the budget and keeping finance on policy.

E. Approving allocations to divisions of available funds that are in keeping with divisional planning and stat conditions. Exec Council sees to it that production necessities are covered in FP, usually by means of a checklist which lists routine org expenses by division. (This should be included with Ad Council submissions to Exec Council.)

Exec Council adds its allocation to the Ad Council Directive and this then forms the Financial Planning Directive for the week.

APPROVALS

FP approval is by the FBO who sees that the FP is on-policy and will produce solvency, and who then disburses the allocation based on income planning.

The whole action is very fast with Ad Council and Exec Council actions done immediately following the end of the stat week, and Ad Council planning and financial allocations activated at once following FBO approval.

RESPONSIBILITIES

Nothing in this system waives an Exec Sec's or Secretary's responsibility for performing or getting performed the specific duties of his division or portion of the org, or his right to order into it without reference to Ad Council or Exec Council.

A Secretary may query an Ad Council order which is thought to be illegal or destructive to stats, but may not otherwise escape legal Ad Council orders once passed by Exec Council.

Each Exec Council member outside of EC meetings, and each Secretary under him, is responsible for obtaining execution of Ad Council orders that concern his area. Ad Council Secretary collects up notification of compliances and reports on these to the Council at the opening of every meeting. Exec Council Secretary does similarly for Exec Council orders.

SUMMARY

The system has already proven a roaring success in one org where it was in use, and has brought on more promotion and bettered income and delivery and has brought sanity to a hitherto chaotic finance scene.

I hope it works the same for you.

L. RON HUBBARD
Founder

HCO POLICY LETTER OF 6 JANUARY 1979

Remimeo
Exec Councils
Ad Councils
CO Estates
Estates Managers
FBOs

FINANCIAL PLANNING REGARDING
PROPERTY RENOVATIONS AND CONSTRUCTION

When doing financial planning for renovations and construction the key thing to keep in mind is that it must be done against assets or production. You renovate and build with the idea of increase of asset, not expense. You are making an investment and that investment must get beans back.

Recently an org submitted a proposal to spend $750,000 for renovations and construction of a property which would have resulted in little if any increase of asset. They wanted to build 2 new buildings at vast expense for very specialized functions which would have been worthless to any future buyer as they did not fit the scheme of the other buildings in the area. They were also going to spend a lot of money on fixing up some old shacks which would have just been bulldozed later. If you're going to build something it has to be convertible to some use which would have value to any future buyer. A studio would have to be convertible to a hotel, an indoor tennis court, or whatever would be valuable if sold some time in the future. On buildings that would just be bulldozed you would spend the least possible amount just to make them usable, if they are going to be used at all. You need to select out what is a permanent asset and what would just get temporarily fixed up.

An example of the right way to do this is Cedars in PAC. An old rundown hospital was converted into upstat offices and the value of those buildings has skyrocketed.

You can also make the mistake of spending too little with the result of no increase of asset and just waste what you do spend. You can also neglect to spend money for ordinary routine maintenance such as machinery, walls, floors and reduce a building into a slum. Doing a bunch of temporary patch-ups can cost you as much or more than doing it right the first time in the long run and will not increase the value of the property.

The rules are:

1. DOING IT RIGHT THE FIRST TIME.

2. RENOVATE AND BUILD WITH THE IDEA OF INCREASE OF ASSET.

L. RON HUBBARD
Founder

assisted by
T/Action Chief CMO

DEPARTMENT 20
DEPARTMENT OF SPECIAL AFFAIRS

THE CREED OF THE CHURCH OF SCIENTOLOGY
[1954]

We of the Church believe:

That all men of whatever race, color or creed were created with equal rights;

That all men have inalienable rights to their own religious practices and their performance;

That all men have inalienable rights to their own lives;

That all men have inalienable rights to their sanity;

That all men have inalienable rights to their own defense;

That all men have inalienable rights to conceive, choose, assist or support their own organizations, churches and governments;

That all men have inalienable rights to think freely, to talk freely, to write freely their own opinions and to counter or utter or write upon the opinions of others;

That all men have inalienable rights to the creation of their own kind;

That the souls of men have the rights of men;

That the study of the mind and the healing of mentally caused ills should not be alienated from religion or condoned in nonreligious fields;

And that no agency less than God has the power to suspend or set aside these rights, overtly or covertly.

And we of the Church believe:

That man is basically good;

That he is seeking to survive;

That his survival depends upon himself and upon his fellows and his attainment of brotherhood with the universe.

And we of the Church believe that the laws of God forbid man:

To destroy his own kind;

To destroy the sanity of another;

To destroy or enslave another's soul;

To destroy or reduce the survival of one's companions or one's group.

And we of the Church believe that the spirit can be saved and that the spirit alone may save or heal the body.

L. RON HUBBARD
Founder

Major 1 **Ability** [ca mid-March 1955]

The Magazine of
DIANETICS and SCIENTOLOGY
from
Phoenix, Arizona

THE SCIENTOLOGIST
A MANUAL ON
THE DISSEMINATION OF MATERIAL

L. Ron Hubbard

INTRODUCTION

The basic purpose of this book is to inform members and auditors of the Hubbard Association of Scientologists, International about the fundamentals of Scientology and its organization.

It is expected that a member of the HASI will know the contents of this book, and the substance of this book should become the source material of a basic course in Scientology.

The hope of this book is to bring order into any confusion concerning Scientology, its purposes, its organizations, and the various grades of auditors. The emphasis of this book is upon purposes of organization. It is quite one thing to have an orderly science of life, and quite another thing to have an orderly organization to keep that science of life in such a form as to be utilized by life.

Whereas it is all very well to envision the ideal—that everyone in possession of the materials of Scientology would utilize them with good heart and in an orderly manner to the improvement and betterment of mankind, it is quite another to have had years of experience with this science in action. It has been discovered that unless an auditor or a person interested in Scientology is part of a group which expresses this ideal, that the individual will be lost in the turbulent mass of the society and will thus become ineffective.

Scientologists everywhere, when an organization of force and purpose was, to a large extent, lacking, were victimized and brought into disrepute by persons who could express vast opinions about Scientology, yet who knew nothing about Scientology; by vested interests in the society which were bent upon the suppression of anything which might be seen to have the potential of supplanting their peculiarity. And, in particular, the auditor was victimized in his practice by the existence of persons who, untrained in Scientology and uninformed, yet practiced upon others with it, producing few, poor, or harmful effects.

[*Editor's Note:* Since 1984 the Churches of Scientology have adopted membership in the International Association of Scientologists (IAS) as their official membership system.]

However, once this organization existed and began to function, another thing came into view: the failure of the auditor and member to understand the purposes and actual operation of the organization of the Hubbard Association of Scientologists, International, and a failure to understand how Scientology should be communicated. The fact that one was an auditor of the HASI or a member of that organization did not immediately presuppose an understanding of the formation of the organization, its purposes or activities.

This publication, *The Scientologist: A Manual,* is designed for use by members and auditors to inform them of the formation and function of the HASI, and the dissemination of Scientology itself—these two subjects being more or less synonymous.

This book is the product of experience and agreement. The HASI is organized as it is because those auditors working with it have agreed that it should work this way, and the various provisions and divisions of the HASI exist by reason of the first years of experience of the HASI or other disrelated organizations which existed before it.

We know that Scientology cannot progress in the society unless it is done by a group effort. We know that it can best progress as individuals banded into groups, and these groups banded together into a larger group. In other words, the HASI is built like a life organism is built. If everyone knows his subject and does his job we will have here a smoothly running and progressive organization which can by its existence and activities bring a better civilization to man.

Although this is the avowed purpose of many organizations, those in Scientology have come to discover over and over that Scientology contains answers which man has lacked in his progress until now. Parts of these answers have been represented in many places under many names, but the organized whole has not been in his possession. As this is, at this time, in his possession, an organization to carry it forward is vitally necessary, and the subject itself and its gains would perish or be altered to such a degree as to be unrecognizable in the absence of a strong, firm organization.

When a member or auditor supports the HASI, he is supporting himself. If the HASI fails, he will fail. There are two things which could occur in the life of any individual. By Scientology he could be processed into the state of a complete static, and in that state he might find life, as represented by that state, pleasant. The other existence would be that of a well-balanced individual operating with the forms and spaces of life itself, still in communication with existence, still carrying forward to make that existence better. As, so far, those who have attained the state of complete static have again returned by their own choice to the business of life itself, we can assume that even the processes of Scientology in making a totally cleared individual are not enough. Life, its spaces and forms, must be added to existence in order to make it interesting. Thus, Scientology and life itself as represented by the forms and spaces make a workable combination. The forms and spaces by themselves are too complex and confused at this stage and in this civilization to make a usable panorama with the absence of Scientology. Scientology AND life, which is to say life broadly understood and changeable at will, can create an existence close to an ideal. Scientology and its organization, the HASI and its affiliated organizations, represent a living of life with an understanding of its goals and purposes and the ability to change it.

A DESCRIPTION OF SCIENTOLOGY

Scientology is the science of knowing how to know answers. It is an organized system of Axioms and processes which resolve the problems of existence.

A Scientologist is a specialist in spiritual and human affairs.

Scientology is organized from the viewpoint of the spirit and contains a precise and usable definition of the spirit, and charts and studies and is capable of changing the behavior of the spirit.

This science is formed in the tradition of ten thousand years of religious philosophy and considers itself a culmination of the searches which began with the Veda, the Tao, Buddhism, Christianity, and other religions. Scientology is a gnostic faith in that it knows it knows. This is its distinguishing characteristic from most of its predecessors. Scientology can demonstrate that it can attain the goals set for man by Christ, which are: wisdom, good health and immortality.

By spiritual means, but means which are as precise as mathematics, a host of bad conditions of life may be remedied in Scientology. Illness and malfunction can be divided into two general classes. First, those resulting from the operation of the spirit directly upon the communication networks of life or the body, and those occasioned by the disruption of structure through purely physical causes. Unhappiness, inability to heal, and psychosomatic illness (which include some seventy percent of the illnesses of man), are best healed by immediate address of the human spirit. Illness caused by recognizable bacteria and injury in accident are best treated by physical means, and these fall distinctly into the field of medicine, and are not the province of Scientology, except that accidents and illness and bacterial infection are predetermined in almost all cases by spiritual malfunction and unrest. And, conditions in accidents are definitely prolonged by any spiritual malfunction. Thus we have the field of medicine addressing the immediate injury, such surgical matters as birth and acute infection, and such things as contusions and abrasions resulting from accidents, as well as the administration of drugs and antibiotics to prevent the demise of the patient in a crisis. This is the role of medicine.

Where predisposition to disease or injury exists, or where disease or injury is being prolonged, or where unhappiness and worry causes mental or physical upset, or where we desire to better and improve communications or social relationships, we are dealing, if we are efficient, in the realm of Scientology. For such things are best healed, or best prevented, or best remedied by immediate and direct recourse to the spirit and its action and determinism of the course of the body.

The only truly therapeutic agent in this universe is the spirit. In Scientology this has been demonstrated with more thoroughness and exists with more certainty than the physical sciences or mathematics. A Scientologist CAN make an individual well, happy, and grant him personal immortality, simply by addressing the human spirit.

For more than ten thousand years man has been accumulating material toward this goal, but it required a wide understanding of the philosophies and processes of Asia and a thorough indoctrination in the Western physical sciences and mathematics to bring about the precision existing in Scientology when practiced properly by a trained Scientologist. It could be said that with Scientology we have entered The Second Age of Miracles.

It is a discovery of Scientology, a discovery susceptible to the most arduous scientific proofs, that people are not bodies, but that people are living units operating bodies. The living unit we call, in Scientology, a thetan, that being taken from the Greek letter theta [θ], the mathematical symbol used in Scientology to indicate the source of life and life itself. The individual, the person, the actual identity, is this living unit. It is modified by the addition of a body, and by the addition of a body it is brought into a certain unknowingness about its own condition. The mission of Scientology is to raise the knowingness of this spirit to such a degree that it again knows what it is and what it is doing, and in this state the thetan can apply directly to his own body, or to his environment, or to the bodies of others, the healing skill of which he is capable. It is the thetan which builds and constructs, it is the thetan which forms actual forms and organisms.

Amongst the capabilities and potentials of the thetan is immortality in full knowingness of his own identity. The amount of time which he has spent on Earth, and the number of deaths through which he has gone, have brought him into a state of forgetfulness about who and where he has been. This material is recovered in Scientology, if the Scientologist specifically processes toward it.

DISSEMINATION OF MATERIAL

The dissemination of materials of Scientology is a problem of comparable stature to the use of techniques on a preclear in an auditing session. Just as you would not process a preclear with heavy processes when all he could take might be ARC Straightwire, thus you would not issue Scientology materials of considerable weight to people incapable of assimilating them.

The immediate result of the issuance of materials not intended for that audience is to produce a state of confusion in the minds of that audience regarding Scientology. Here we have no question of talking down to people. Here we have no question of "watering" our material, but we do have a question of disseminating Scientology. If we do it properly, then Scientology will be very broadly known. If we do it improperly it will stop in its tracks, and be known, if at all, as a confusion.

When materials are issued above the acceptance level of an audience, a confusion results. A confusion is the antithesis of a flow. Any communication resulting in a confusion then brings about an eddy or tumbling of particles rather than their spread. And a confusion at length becomes a mystery.

Part ten of the Code of a Scientologist says: "I pledge myself to engage in no unseemly disputes with the uninformed on the subject of my profession." This is an immediate injunction not to start an eddy of confusion. The employment of Scientology to the greatest good of the greatest number of dynamics does not include using it knowingly or unknowingly to confuse hearers.

An outline of the communication lines of Scientology follows:

1. General public to the general public.

2. Scientologists to the general public.

3. Member HASI to member HASI.

4. Trained Scientologist to a member of the HASI.

5. Member of the HASI to a preclear.

6. Trained Scientologist to a preclear.

7. Trained Scientologist to a trained Scientologist.

8. HASI to membership.

9. HASI to trained Scientologist.

10. HASI to the general public.

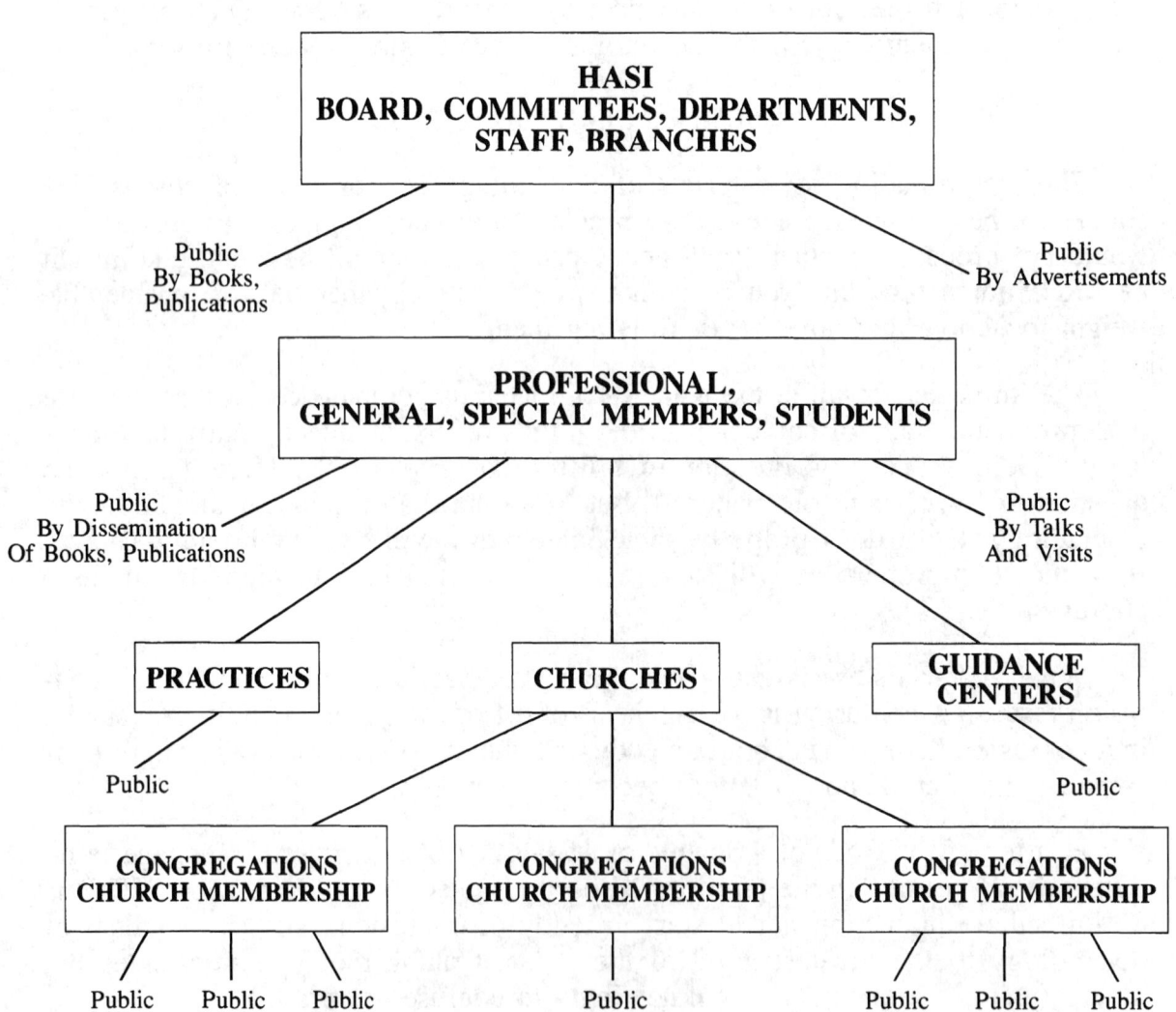

1. GENERAL PUBLIC TO THE GENERAL PUBLIC

There are several things we would like the general public to say to the general public about Scientology. The first of these is that we would like the general public, when it sees an individual or group problem, to be quite certain that the proper thing to do is for that individual or group to consult a Scientologist. For instance, if somebody is having headaches, we would like his friends to come to the obvious solution that this person should see a Scientologist or should join a group undergoing processing.

The next on this communication line is that Scientology does not pose any threat, that Scientologists are good citizens, and that they can be trusted with problems of a private and confidential nature, or with problems dangerous to other people, such as the problem of criminality. Another frame of mind we would like to see the public have and register is that people attacking Scientologists have something wrong with them (and if you could meet any such people personally you would see that this is no more than truth). As a subdivision of this, the actual substance of communication about what Scientology is, from the general public to the general public, should be that Scientology says that good health and immortality are attainable. That it is something compounded out of all man knows of the subject of man, and that people are living units operating bodies, rather than bodies, and that this living unit is the human soul. Given this much communication line, the general public can embroider enormously, and unless a person in the general public can express his opinions, and unless the subject gives him a chance to express his own opinions, and so let HIM be interestING, he will not talk about the subject. Thus the data in the general public should give individuals a chance to be interesting, by knowing no more and no less than the above. We are not interested in sensationalism, personalities or the complexity of Scientological methodology being discussed by the general public. As a subdivision of this, we do not want Scientology to be reported in the press, anywhere else than on the religious page of newspapers. It is destructive of word of mouth to permit the public presses to express their biased and badly reported sensationalism. Therefore we should be very alert to sue for slander at the slightest chance so as to discourage the public presses from mentioning Scientology. What the newspapers say is not word of mouth. As an example of this, how many minutes today have you spent in discussing current events? NEWSPAPER REPORTERS WRITING ARTICLES ON SCIENTOLOGY DO NOT EXPRESS SCIENTOLOGY. Scientologists should never let themselves be interviewed by the press. That's experience talking!

As a subdivision of general public to general public we have the problem of the professions which might consider Scientology to be antipathetic to them, amongst these would be psychologists and medical doctors as well as psychiatrists. These persons are entirely in error when they express the opinion that Scientologists are against them. Scientology does not consider them sufficiently important to be against. Flour pills or any incantation or system will produce in twenty-two percent of the public, benefit. Therefore, any practice or art can always achieve twenty-two percent recovery in their patients. It is when we better this twenty-two percent that we are being efficient. We have no more quarrel with a psychologist than we would have with an Australian witch doctor. We have no quarrel with a psychiatrist any more than we should quarrel with a barbarian because he had never heard of nuclear physics. And as for the medical doctor, we know very well that modern medical practice, having lately outgrown phlebotomy, has come of age to a point where it can regulate structure in a most remarkable and admirable way. In Scientology we believe a medical doctor definitely has his role in a society just as an engineer has his role in civil government. We believe that a medical doctor should perform emergency operations such as those made necessary by accidents; that he should perform orthopedics; that he should deliver babies; that he should have charge of the administration of drugs; that his use of antibiotics is beneficial; and that wherever he immediately and curatively addresses structure he is of use in a community. The only place we would limit a medical doctor is in the field of treatment of psychosomatic medicine, where he has admittedly and continuously failed, and the only thing we would ask a medical doctor to change about his practice is to stop taking money for things he knows he cannot cure, i.e., spiritual, mental, psychosomatic and social ills.

With regard to psychologists, medical doctors and psychiatrists then, what would one say in talking with them? But again we have section ten of the Code of a Scientologist. You wouldn't expect this psychologist or psychiatrist or medical doctor to get into an argument with you on how to get rats to find their way through mazes, how you would set a tibia, or what voltage you would put on an electric shock machine. Therefore, and equally, do not permit yourself to be put in the situation where you are discussing privately or in public the methodologies of your wisdom. The attitude of a Scientologist toward people in these professions should be: "I have my techniques. It took me a long time to learn them just as it took you a long time to learn yours, and I am not going to try to make a minister out of you, and you are not going to try to make a medical doctor (psychiatrist, psychologist) out of me. I am an expert instructor only where it is intimately involved with the human spirit. I can produce my effects. You can produce yours. In view of the fact that you do not pretend to operate in the field of the human spirit, and I do not pretend to operate in the field of structure, I do not see how there can be any discussion. But things that I can't handle in structure when called upon I will be very happy to refer to you, and I shall expect that when matters of the spirit come into question you will have enough understanding of life, where we are all specialists, to refer them to me." A quiet explanation of this character will do a great deal to place you as a professional man in their realm of understanding of professional men.

Should anyone challenge you for having suddenly secured a relief in a hospital or an institution from some dire malady which balked the efforts of the professional men in charge of it, and should you ever be "called upon the carpet" for having "interfered" with the progress of a case, you should be extremely dismayed, and act it, to find yourself in the presence of barbarians who do not believe in the power of prayer, in the will of God, or the promises of Jesus Christ. And you should point out that whereas the body was in their keeping, they did not at any time care to take purview of the human soul. And if anything has occurred because the soul, in your province, then reacted upon the body, you believe that they are unwilling to admit the will of God in their treatment of human beings, and if this is the case you now, while you are being addressed by such people, discover yourself to be in a strange place where men pretending to be Christians doubt God, the Son of God and the power of prayer. Your entire address to such people in such a situation, publicly or privately, should be entirely overt, accusative and not at any time apologetic. And you should immediately make it your business to place this matter before the proper authorities, that people are in charge of an institution here, are not Christians and do not believe in God, and you should inform your accusers that you are going to do so.

Should you ever be arrested for practicing Scientology, treating people, make very sure, long before the time comes, that you have never used drugs or surgery, and that you have never prescribed a diet or vitamins, and when that time might come make very sure that you immediately and instantly, within two or three hours after your receipt of the warrant, have served upon the signer of that warrant, a personal civil suit for $100,000.00 damages for having caused the arrest of a man of God going about his business in his proper profession, and for having brought about embarrassing publicity and molestation. Place the suit and WIRE THE HASI IMMEDIATELY. Make the whole interest during the entire time of such an unfortunate occurrence the fact that the signer of such a warrant, who would ordinarily be a medical doctor in charge of the medical department of some city, had dared fly in the teeth of religion. And use what is necessary of the earlier passage above to drive the point home. DO NOT simply fall back out of communication if you are attacked, but attack, much more forcefully, and artfully and arduously. And if you are foolish enough to have an attorney who tells you not to sue, immediately dismiss him and get an attorney who will sue. Or, if no attorney will sue, simply have an HASI suit form filled out and present it yourself to the county clerk in the court of the area in which your case has come up.

IN ALL SUCH CASES OF ARREST FOR THE PRACTICE OF SCIEN-TOLOGY, THE HASI WILL SEND A REPRESENTATIVE AT ONCE, BUT DO NOT WAIT FOR HIS ARRIVAL TO PLACE THIS SUIT. THE SUIT MUST ALREADY HAVE BEEN FILED WHEN THE HASI ATTORNEY ARRIVES.

In other words, do not at any moment leave this act unpunished, for if you do you are harming all other Scientologists in the area. When you are attacked it is your responsibility then to secure from further attack not only yourself but all those who work with you. Cause blue flame to dance on the courthouse roof until everybody has apologized profusely for having dared to become so adventurous as to arrest a Scientologist who, as a minister of the Church, was going about his regular duties. As far as the advices of attorneys go that you should not sue, that you should not attack, be aware of the fact that I, myself, in Wichita, Kansas, had the rather interesting experience of discovering that my attorney, employed by me and paid by me, had been for some three months in the employ of the people who were attacking me, and that this attorney had collected some insignificant sum of money after I hired him, by going over to the enemy and acting upon their advices. This actually occurred, so beware of attorneys who tell you not to sue. And I call to your attention the situation of any besieged fortress. If that fortress does not make sallies, does not send forth patrols to attack and harass and does not utilize itself to make the besieging of it a highly dangerous occupation, that fortress may, and most often does, fall.

The DEFENSE of anything is UNTENABLE. The only way to defend anything is to ATTACK, and if you ever forget that then you will lose every battle you are ever engaged in, whether it is in terms of personal conversation, public debate, or a court of law. NEVER BE INTERESTED IN CHARGES. DO, yourself, much MORE CHARGING and you will WIN. And the public, seeing that you won, will then have a communication line to the effect that Scientologists WIN. Don't ever let them have any other thought than that Scientology takes all of its objectives.

Another point directly in the interest of keeping the general public to the general public communication line in good odor: It is vitally important that a Scientologist put into action and overtly keep in action Article Four of the

Code— "I pledge myself to punish to the fullest extent of my power anyone misusing or degrading Scientology to harmful ends." The only way you can guarantee that Scientology will not be degraded or misused is to make sure that only those who are trained in it practice it. If you find somebody practicing Scientology who is not qualified, you should give them an opportunity to be formally trained, at their expense, so that they will not abuse and degrade the subject. And you would not take as any substitute for formal training any amount of study.

You would therefore delegate to members of the HASI who are not otherwise certified only those processes mentioned below, and would discourage them from using any other processes. More particularly, if you discovered that some group calling itself "precept processing" had set up and established a series of meetings in your area, you would do all you could to make things interesting for them. In view of the fact that the HASI holds the copyrights for all such material, and that a scientific organization of material can be copyrighted and is therefore owned, the least that could be done to such an area is the placement of a suit against them for using materials of Scientology without authority. Only a member of the HASI or a member of one of the churches affiliated with the HASI has the authority to use this information.

A DScn has the power to revoke a certificate below the level of DScn but not a DScn. However, he can even recommend to the CECS of the HASI that DScns be revoked, and so any sincere Scientologist is capable of policing Scientology. This is again all in the interest of keeping the public with a good opinion of Scientology, since bad Group Processing and bad auditing are worse than bad publicity and are the worst thing that can happen to the general public to general public communication line.

The best thing that can happen to it is good auditing, good public presentation and a sincere approach on the subject of Scientology itself. Remember, we are interested in ALL treatment being beneficial, whether it is Scientology or not. For bad treatment in any line lowers the public opinion of all treatment.

In addressing persons professionally interested in the ministry, we have another interesting problem in public presentation. We should not engage in religious discussions. In the first place, as Scientologists, we are gnostics, which is to say that we know that we know. People in the ministry ordinarily suppose that knowingness and knowledge are elsewhere resident than in themselves. They believe in belief and substitute belief for wisdom. This makes Scientology no less a religion, but makes it a religion with an older tradition and puts it on an intellectual plane.

Religious philosophy, then, as represented by Scientology, would be opposed in such a discussion to religious practice. We are all-denominational rather than non-denominational, and so we should be perfectly willing to include in our ranks a Moslem or a Taoist, as well as any Protestant or Catholic, while people of the ministry in Western civilization, unless they are evangelists, are usually dedicated severely to some faction which in itself is in violent argument with many other similar factions. Thus these people are ready to argue and are practiced in argument, and there are more interpretations of one line of scripture than there are sunbeams in a day. Beyond explaining one's all-denominational character, explaining that one holds the Bible as a holy work, one should recognize that the clergy of Western Protestant churches defines a minister or the standing of a church by these salient facts: Jesus Christ was the Savior of Mankind, Jesus Christ was the Son of God.

We in Scientology find no argument with this and so in discussing Scientology with other ministry one should advance these two points somewhere in the conversation. Additionally, one should advance to the ministry exactly those things mentioned earlier as what we would like the general public to believe. Christ, if you care to study the New Testament, instructed his disciples to bring wisdom and good health to man, and promised mankind immortality, and said the Kingdom of Heaven was at hand and the translators have not added that "at hand" possibly meant three feet back of your head. We could bring up these points but there is no reason to. You are not trying to educate other ministry. A friendly attitude toward other ministry in general, and fellow ministers in particular, is necessary.

The way to handle an individual minister of some other church is as follows: Get him to tell you exactly what HE believes, get him to agree that religious freedom is desirable, then tell him to make sure that if that's the way he believes, he should keep on believing that, and that you would do anything to defend his right to believe that.

None of these people as individuals are antipathetic. They know a great deal about public presence and can be respected for such knowledge. However, engaging in long discourses or trying to educate a minister of some Protestant church or a priest of the Catholic faith into the tenets of Scientology is not desirable and is directly contrary to Article Ten of the Code of a Scientologist.

You will find you have many problems and people in common with other ministers. They're alive too. Also you will see a campaign to place only ministers in charge of the mind and mental healing. Talk about these things.

The Christian Church has been hurt by factionalism. We stand for peace and happiness. Therefore, let us carry it forward by example, not by unseemly discussions.

2. SCIENTOLOGISTS TO THE GENERAL PUBLIC

In the assemblage of congregations, and in addressing the general public at large, a Scientologist has a responsibility to give to the public, in the form of such congregations or meetings, information acceptable to them, which can be understood by them and which will send them away with the impression that the Scientologist who addressed them knew definitely what he was talking about and that Scientology is an unconfused, clear-cut subject.

Anyone using Scientology must state that he is using Scientology. He cannot, must not, leave it unnamed or call it by another name. Use of it without naming it is a breach of law.

A Scientologist, when addressing public groups, would never under any circumstances confuse his communication line by engaging in a debate from the floor or closing terminals with any persons who would care to heckle him. By simply ignoring such people, one continues to talk to the bulk of the people who are themselves very interested. When anyone causes an unseemly upset, it is rarely difficult to have the person removed from the group. In other words, either ignore him or remove him. Don't engage in a debate with him.

Similarly, no Scientologist would ever consent to take a position on a panel or on a stage engaging in a debate of Scientology versus some other subject. This is an entirely unclear communication line. People are not interested in a debate. They are interested, if they are there at all, in Scientology. Why, therefore, give some other subjects an audience before which it could air its views? In the last five years I have turned down innumerable offers of debates, for I have found out that Dianetics or Scientology was the attraction and that medicine or psychology was using the public interest in this new subject in order to further their own aims, and that any such debate engaged upon demeaned and degraded Scientology by permitting it to be talked about contemptuously before a group—a thing which SHOULD NEVER BE PERMITTED.

The first and foremost thing which a Scientologist should do in the way of information is to relay the data contained in the earlier section. He should punch this hard, regardless of what kind of a group he is talking to. He should tell them overtly that when they see somebody who is sick or unhappy, that if their illness does not require the immediate attention of a medical doctor, then the thing for them to tell that person or that person's family is to SEE A SCIENTOLOGIST.

He should also punch home the fact that Scientology believes in the three things Christ intended for man: wisdom, good health and immortality. In other words, he should make it his business to use such an opportunity of addressing a group to pound home what we think the general public should say to the general public about Scientology. He should start this simply by saying it to such groups insistently and many times. He could add a great deal of descriptive material to this, but he should not go further into the field of data. In other words, he should talk in generalities. He should describe a Scientologist as one with a mission to bring wisdom, good health and immortality to the public. He should describe the aims and goals of the organizations, which are to assist in wiping out criminality, insanity and war.

He should pound home to such groups the fact that the human spirit is the only therapeutic agent of any lasting value. He should tell such groups what Scientology can do for them in bringing them wisdom, happiness, good health and immortality. He should describe to them how long it takes in individual processes. Above all, HE SHOULD BE HONEST. He should tell exactly what he himself feels to be true, but he should not give them involved data.

It very often happens that a Scientologist who has recently come from the HASI will be asked about the state of cases of people who have passed through that area. He should give his honest and forthright opinion, not any dressed-up or hopeful conclusion. He should tell what he himself observes. When asked about the training given in that area he should state exactly what his opinion is of that training in the area, and this sincerity itself will communicate.

He will find that people like to do little scandalmongering and that people who ask the most questions do not represent the general attitude of the group. This is one of the foremost lessons a Scientologist learns in addressing congregations, that the people who "close terminals" with him at the break or at the end of the lecture do not represent the opinion of the group. The general opinion of the group is a fairly high one. The people who close terminals with him have opinions and data which are fairly low, since these people close terminals because they are low on the Tone Scale. Therefore he should be able to lift his eyes over the whole group and see what kind of a reaction the group itself has, not merely those who speak. The people who speak from a group are not the spokesmen of a group. The spokesman of the group is the Scientologist himself as he stands there addressing the group and he can regulate their tone and reception at will. He does this best by not closing terminals with the most upsetting elements of the group.

The group occasionally wants to know something about other Scientologists. They have heard things. Those inquiries about myself are best answered in this wise: that in all Ron's experience with rumors and stories about himself, he has yet to hear one single story come back to him in a form which even vaguely approached the truth or the circumstances about which it was told, and he has heard many, many things which did not happen at all.

Thus, it is the case with Scientologists at large. Many things are said about them, but they have this experience every now and then that one of these stories comes back to them and when it comes back to them they will not recognize the incident.

It happens that it is the tone level of the general public that scandal and untruth take precedence. I ask you to consult the Chart of Human Evaluation and you will discover in that chart that truth does not exist below the level of 2.0. Therefore, why should you be surprised that so many twisted stories are circulated? They are circulated about you as a Scientologist as well as about me as the Founder of Scientology. Standing together we can best this vagary of human communication lines. The example is set for the public by its newspapers, which themselves offer little but untruths.

And I call to your attention that courts do not admit hearsay evidence. They have learned after long experience that they can only accept what the witness himself has observed, and that they can never accept what the witness has heard that somebody else observed. Hearsay evidence, that evidence which simply recounts what somebody else has said he observed, is not admissible in courts of law anywhere in the civilized world and has not been since Roman times. Compare this, then, to the communication line of hearsays in terms of rumors and find that there is little to be gained in either clarifying or forwarding such rumors. In discussing rumors with groups, discuss only the Tone Scale and theory of rumors. Use rumors as a chance to teach, for a Scientologist is a teacher.

On the subject of myself, a Scientologist addressing any group of people, when the subject is brought up and not otherwise, should make it clear that Ron is just a human being who has been working hard to solve some of the problems of life; that he has behind him now, on this subject, in the public eye, many years of sincere application to the subject, and that many results beneficial to people have resulted. That he has a definite idea of where he is going and what he is doing, and that, like anyone introducing new things into the society, a great deal of rumor and upset and backbiting can be expected. In other words, on such a thing, pass it all off.

As for himself, when addressing congregations, a Scientologist should be very careful to express his own personality and to express himself as himself, not in just any role which will suit the particular congregation he is addressing.

People may believe him to be indifferently trained as a Scientologist, but then, they believe that I am indifferently trained, too, whereas *Who Knows and What,* the companion book to *Who's Who in America,* which gives the professional experts of the country, and which you can find in any good library, lists me as an expert in psychology, and any certified Scientologist has actually invested more hours of study and practice in his subject than a medical doctor or psychologist has invested in the study of the mind.

If you do not believe this, simply add up the number of hours psychologists and medical doctors are actually in classes which teach theory and practice on the mind, and you will discover something interesting. Add up the number of hours you have spent in study in Scientology and Dianetics schools and your own hours of study and practice, and you will see some truth in the fact that nearly all Doctors of Scientology have invested somewhere in the neighborhood of five thousand hours in training, which is an overpowering amount of training.

In other words, do not let the matter of skill fall into question, and overtly represent that both the Founder of this science and those who are truly practicing this science are the best trained people in the field of the spirit and the mind in the world today. This could not have been said four years ago, but do not let the impression of four years ago continue to exist. Today they are really trained, but an auditor has a tendency to forget how well trained he is because he does not know how poorly trained other professions are in their subjects.

3. MEMBER HASI TO MEMBER HASI

Members of the HASI are theoretically bound by the Code of a Scientologist, and they should be reminded of this by Scientologists who are certified. They have the right, theoretically, to use and to study any and all of the materials of Scientology. This right is exemplified by the fact that the professional course tapes are made available to individuals and groups who are not possessed of the right to teach. The reason for this is that a communication line to the membership must not be cut.

This does not mean that a member is going to use these materials responsibly, but he has a complete right to have them and to discuss them with members. A member of the HASI is included as a Scientologist and should be cognizant of sections 1 and 2 above.

4. TRAINED SCIENTOLOGIST TO A MEMBER OF THE HASI

It is the duty of certified auditors to place their information at the disposal of members, at the same time enjoining them that there is no substitute for formal training.

A member of the HASI, as far as information is concerned, may have a great deal of material available, but the certified auditor should extend to him only the book *Self Analysis in Scientology,** The Group Auditor's Handbook, and Issue 31-G of the *Journal** to use upon preclears. These can be used with some success by people who are not trained.

* [*Editor's note: Self Analysis in Scientology* is a revision of the book *Self Analysis,* rewritten in the fall of 1952 for use in Creative Processing to get the preclear to mock up the items. This change was later reverted back to the original *Self Analysis. Self Analysis in Scientology* is out of print.]

* [*Editor's note:* Issue 31-G of the *Journal* refers to the 31st issue of *The Journal of Scientology,* a magazine published twice monthly by the Hubbard Association of Scientologists, Inc., Phoenix, Arizona in the early 50s. Issue 31-G was published mid-summer 1954 and contained numerous processes later included in the book *Creation of Human Ability,* which was published in early 1955.]

5. MEMBER OF THE HASI TO A PRECLEAR

Only members of the HASI, or of specifically delineated affiliated organizations have the right to use the materials of Scientology—a fact which the HASI is prepared to enforce as it can do legally at any financial cost. (Membership, however, does not give the right to publish or excerpt or reorganize Scientology, nor the right to teach it formally.)

Members of the HASI as well as auditors have the right to possess, study and know, all the materials of Scientology. In practice however, a member of the HASI who is not otherwise a certified auditor has no rights of professional practice and may not process for personal gain, and will not be supported by the HASI or its auditors should he err or get into difficulties through having used processes on preclears, with only one exception. A member of the HASI may apply to a preclear informally, and not as professional practice, and not for gain, and exactly as composed, *Self Analysis in Scientology*, Issue 31-G, and used as an individual process or group process, but again exactly as given to individuals or groups, *The Group Auditor's Handbook.*

A member of the HASI is expected to follow the Auditor's Code and the Code of a Scientologist, and even if he does not know them well or know about them, he may have his membership revoked by the CECS for failure to follow them, since wide agreement and practice have demonstrated that processing is ineffective or even harmful when executed without observance of the Auditor's Code, 1954, and that the subject of Scientology itself undeservedly suffers through failure to follow the Code of a Scientologist.

Where preclears in general are concerned, a member of the HASI would do well when not trained as an auditor to refer such preclears to a trained auditor.

6. TRAINED SCIENTOLOGIST TO PRECLEAR

The dissemination of information to a preclear is completely forbidden by the Auditor's Code, 1954. This is evaluation.

While it is not true that a person trained in Scientology is immediately and for that reason harder to process than one who is not trained, it is true that forwarding information about the preclear's own case, or giving him materials of Scientology while he is undergoing processing reduces the effectiveness of processing.

7. TRAINED SCIENTOLOGIST TO TRAINED SCIENTOLOGIST

It might be a surprise that any injunction about the dissemination of information would have to be outlined where communication is between a trained Scientologist and a trained Scientologist. However, experience has demonstrated that these two, particularly when auditing each other, get into many involvements over what the exact point of the process is.

We discovered a short time ago with some amazement that this was a major block on co-auditing teams composed of trained Scientologists only. It seems that it is not unusual for two trained Scientologists, one processing the other, to get into violent discussions regarding the exact running of processes, with the session suspended while they consult texts and tapes. In this regard, an auditor being processed by another auditor should, in the first place, have made sure that he had a Scientologist of comparable skill. In the second place, an auditor being audited should be content to be a preclear for the term of the session. It could be said that an auditor who has not been audited badly once in a while doesn't know how grim it can get and won't regulate his own processing of preclears accordingly, because any trained Scientologist has a great many ways of getting preclears out of trouble, and no permanent damage can result.

Although the Code of a Scientologist specifically forbids a Scientologist to talk out loud to the public about other Scientologists and to run them down, it definitely does not forbid this practice among auditors. However, it does forbid defamation by an auditor of anyone in Scientology in any published form.

A great many newsletters exist in Scientology which are more or less intended to be for circulation amongst Dianeticists and Scientologists and which take wide liberties with the reputations of all concerned. Any member or trained Scientologist expressing himself in such a way as to defame Scientology or the people connected with it may find himself in considerable legal difficulty. Although during the formative years of Dianetics and Scientology no one had enough time or patience to find out what was being written in such magazines or newsletters, the situation has now changed, and enough time and money is now available to free all of us from this great deterrent to our common purpose of making this world a better place in which to live.

The trained Scientologist does and should make his experience known to other trained Scientologists. In accordance with the Code of a Scientologist he is expected to repress the names of actual preclears as per Article Nine: "I pledge myself to refuse to impart personal secrets of my preclears." However, discussing cases with a trained auditor discovers often a necessity to be highly specific, for such cases are quite usually experienced in common.

This discussion of peculiarities of a case has nothing to do with revealing the secrets of a preclear, since processing today is not even vaguely interested in obtaining secrets from a preclear.

Discussing cases amongst auditors is not the same as discussing cases with HASI members, groups or the public. An auditor must never discuss a case with people who are not auditors beyond mentioning difficulties, exactly pertinent to the arrangements of processing, to those upon whom a case might be dependent. And, if an auditor should have occasion to mention a case to a congregation or a group, he should so disguise the identity and particulars of the case so as not to embarrass anyone, for it is quite often part of training and part of description of Scientology to interested groups to mention that such and such a type of case has recovered.

A highly specialized part of this communication line from trained Scientologist to trained Scientologist is the certified auditor to the student. While no certified auditor should invade and attempt to instruct the students of some other auditor, a great deal of liberty is possible between the trained auditor and the student, except in such instances as when the status of a student is questionable. By student here one means not someone who is studying Scientology, but one who is regularly and specifically enrolled toward a certain degree.

Students should not be given misinformation, and very definitely and specifically, as will be covered shortly, they should not be given experimental data of any kind whatsoever. It is disastrous to take a student who is not yet capable of the most elementary processes of Scientology, no matter how capable he himself thinks he is, and turn him loose with some experimental data. The immediate result of this is distraction of the student from his course of study and entering him upon a line of investigation. Giving a student experimental data—and I should know—is like turning him loose on a dark night in a sea filled with rocks. The result is that he will go aground and his preclear will go aground. Where students are co-auditing, any time you find any case in a unit bogging, look for the person who audited him with experimental techniques. You will occasionally find that the person who audited him on the experimental technique was not a member of that unit, or was some wildcat with no more purpose than "observe the effect."

A certified auditor should be courteous to the student. The student will, in all probability, become a certified auditor.

One of the hidden but more vicious crimes which can be committed in communicating information to students is to give them the data and deny them affinity, and cut the affinity lines connected to the data. One Scientologist who was very widely known in the early days trained many auditors, but it was found later that every auditor he had trained had been estranged from the subject by being estranged by this Scientologist from any Scientologist who was following closely the course of investigation I was undertaking. He gave them data, but somehow he gave them to understand that I and auditors around me had something vague and unstated wrong in the personality or behavior sector. He never gave any specific example to these students, since he never could have done so with any truth, but he conveyed to them that the subject was one thing, and I, and other auditors, quite another. That the subject was good, the people who originated and practiced it were bad.

As a result every single one of his students who has come through later training units was found to be entirely deficient in a basic understanding of Scientology. Alloying the affinity of the subject itself, the subject would then not communicate to them, and the students did not know whether they had studied gastronomy or monotony, and as a result each and every one of them had long and arduous lines of failures as auditors.

The Scientologist of whom I speak in course of time obtained no more students, not from any overt act against him by the HAS or the HASI, but because this continual failure eventually accumulated to himself and he failed in his entire establishment. I do not believe this person knows to this day what actually happened to him and his business. The alloying of the affinity line, no matter how vaguely, alloys the actual communication of data. Simply adhering to the Code of a Scientologist, regardless of one's personal opinions, however right or wrong these may be, will actually bring good training to students.

If it is in the obsessive nature of man always to have something bad to point out, and if this obsession cannot be avoided, then point out the horribly pockmarked state of the moon, not the people who are making a sincere try in Scientology.

For a long time a condition existed which confused the communication line between trained auditors and trained auditors. In view of the fact that the subject was advancing, and its advance was not being interrupted simply because people had not been trained each time to the new level, auditors who had just graduated from a school were prone to feel very superior and derogatory toward auditors who had been trained a year or so previously. There might or might not have been good reason for this, but with the Seventh Clinical Unit* I found that we could stabilize processes and that we did have processes now that weren't changing simply because of new data, and so this information level could be stabilized.

It is the responsibility of any trained Scientologist to make sure that anyone with a certificate in his area is, by whatever means, brought up to the training level which exists today. It is the particular responsibility of the Doctors of Scientology who themselves have a right to examine for or to revoke certificates.

This retraining of older Scientologists by those with later training presents a peculiar problem, since Scientology has worked for the well-trained auditor for two years.

However, for some time to come it will be necessary for auditors trained to the prescribed level to exactly follow the training letter of July 1954 in their retraining of certified auditors in their area. The HASI intends to pick up and stabilize every certificate ever issued at one time or another, and to that end currently offers a one-month retraining course at half the cost charged regular students so that certified auditors can be stabilized in training. For this is a matter of people who do not know basic techniques or how to work them. It is training, not Scientology, which is at fault in such a case.

8. HASI TO THE MEMBERSHIP

The Hubbard Association of Scientologists, International is by law a fellowship of persons actively interested in and to a greater or lesser extent trained in Scientology. It is not a public organization, but a professional organization. The casual public member of Scientology who is interested in its results and what it represents to civilization is expected to be a member of an affiliated organization such as the Church of Scientology and the Church of American Science. Those who conduct, process and handle congregations and the churches are members of the HASI. The congregations themselves are members of the Church of Scientology or the Church of American Science. In the role of being a professional organization, the HASI, then, conducts the schools and seminaries or regulates the training done by professionals in Scientology.

The HASI is also a publications organization which furnishes the materials for training done by professionals in Scientology. The HASI is additionally a research and investigation unit. Publications, research and investigation, professional services, and the regulation of those actively practicing Scientology so as to secure good public acceptance, are the functions of the HASI.

The churches accumulate congregations, conduct public programs, and generally unify, disseminate and practice Scientology. In other words, here we have a group of professionals, their publications and their data coordination center who are banded together for the uniform good practice of their subject and conduct of their activities. And here we have these professionals operating congregation and

*Seventh Clinical Unit: The Seventh Advanced Clinical Course, taught by LRH in Phoenix, Arizona, during June and July of 1954.

units of various kinds which actively practice Scientology in the public. If you can see this picture clearly, then you can understand all the organizations of Scientology, and you will understand the function and services of those organizations.

Under the HASI is the Committee for Examination, Certification and Services. (This organization was, for a short time in its early days, the Professional Auditors Guild, International [PAGI] and then the International Guild of Scientologists [IG of S] but, when the public confused it to be an additional organization, became the Committee for Examination, Certification and Services of the HASI, which is what it had been in function all the time.)

This is the body of principal authority and court of appeals of Scientology. As the State of Arizona has made the HASI the issuing authority of certificates in Dianetics and Scientology, and as LRH's signature previously was all which gave authority to certificates, the CECS then, by the laws of the State of Arizona and LRH's own delegation of certification power, controls all the certificates of Dianetics and Scientology ever issued.

No other organization or unit of any kind whatsoever has authority to issue certificates in Dianetics and Scientology outside the scope and authority of the CECS. The CECS is a committee composed of five Doctors of Scientology, who also hold Doctors of Divinity in affiliated organizations. When a Doctor of Scientology in the field has trained someone up to the level of HCA and when that person has been examined by another Doctor of Scientology, the recommendation for certification is forwarded to and passed by the CECS.

The CECS has representatives on every continent in the world. It is their purpose to guarantee the good practice of Scientology by all its practitioners everywhere. This committee for the HASI also extends various services to those professionally interested in the practice of Scientology. These are actually the services of the HASI itself, but it is the CECS which regulates what they are and polices the communication lines.

In matters of dissemination of materials of Scientology or in the improvement of practice in the field, or the revocation of or reduction of certificate levels, it would be the HASI which would be acting, and it would be acting through the CECS.

The HASI has what might seem at first a peculiar idea of what constitutes a communications or processing crime. It believes that the crimes of communication are not comparable to the crimes of noncommunication, and it holds far more detrimental to Scientology a FAILURE to circulate and communicate than it does TO communicate. If you will look over the MEST universe you will discover that one is only punished for two things by the MEST universe. The first of these is for communicating. The second of these is for being there. Nearly any organization of professionals which man has had has specialized almost entirely in punishing only those who communicated or acted.

We see this reflected in the government, in an army or a navy. In such places an officer or enlisted man may go through an entire life of service, piling up crime after crime of omission, and yet arrive with the highest rank and honors. Such services know, in theory, that there are two crimes: one is the crime of commission, the other is the crime of omission. Yet they punish only the crimes of commission. In other words, such services punish only those people who act, who communicate, who try to get something done. It is very true that you will never get a black mark on your record in such services if you simply do nothing. In World War II, for instance, it was common experience for units or men to simply refuse to act even though their friends or fellows were in danger.

Refusing to communicate, refusing to act, are alike crimes of omission, of noncommunication. And when an organization begins to specialize in punishing those people who communicate, who act, who circulate, that organization is cutting its own communication lines, its own efficiency, and spelling out its own eventual defeat.

On this theory, then, the HASI does not specialize in punishing those who communicate, except, of course, in cases where the communication is obvious slander intended to injure Scientology or the HASI, done by people who are not part of the HASI, as the people who conduct campaigns against Scientology are Scientologists or have been trained in Scientology.

Although Scientology communication lines are sometimes muddled up by the writings or letters of people condemning Scientology and Scientologists, a checkup will discover these people to be medical doctors or psychologists who are utilizing the freedom of speech existing in Scientology to deter that science from wiping out, as it might possibly do, medicine and psychiatry and psychology. While it is not the intention of the HASI to flatten or wipe out any science or field of endeavor, such a thing is an inevitable consequence of introducing efficiency where ignorance existed before.

Thus, people from medicine and psychology in particular sometimes use the communication lines of Scientology, as though they were Scientologists, in order to condemn Scientology, the HASI, well-known auditors in Scientology, or L. Ron Hubbard. By cutting the communication lines of such people one is not cutting any SCIENTOLOGY communication lines. He is cutting only the communication lines of medicine and psychology, which, very wrongly, consider themselves to be rivals in the field of Scientology. Scientology cares nothing about either medicine or psychiatry.

The HASI, by the way, after much sad experience in trying to train them, now has a rule which forbids the training of medical doctors, psychiatrists, psychologists, chiropractors and like professionals. A Doctor of Scientology is permitted to train them only in very special cases.

The HASI exists to assist communication of Scientologists just as these data in this book exist. These data are proposed simply because they are more efficient, not because they are all mandatory. On the other hand, the CECS for the HASI views very dimly a Scientologist who has been trained at considerable trouble to the organization, who has been provided with materials, information, tapes, with the goodwill of the organization, and who has had the HASI vouch for him to his practice or his public, then does nothing.

Such a person trained and equipped who is sitting still, who is not active, or who goes off to other fields and ignores what has been done for him, and ignores what he was supposed to do with the information, is the chief target of the HASI's

CECS. The HASI will do all in its power to help such an individual bring his own case level up to an overt point, and to assist him in his communication and action in the society. But when it is at last convinced that the person does not mean to communicate, does not mean to act, then it has no choice but to put him out of action by the various legal means available to the CECS. In other words, we want no professional "cases." We want professional auditors.

The CECS also exists to keep Scientology organizations solvent by proposing to them campaigns and activities which will bring them revenue. The CECS, however, can be counted upon to act when it becomes convinced that someone is using Scientology in such a way as to accumulate funds by whatever means or by becoming a thoroughly bad credit risk so as to endanger the financial standing of all Scientologists in an area, as happened in 1954 in Los Angeles.

In case of arrest or severe oppression of a trained Scientologist, the HASI's CECS is prepared to send into that person's area an attorney to clarify the situation.

The policy of the HASI to its membership in terms of data is that any member of the HASI, whether sustaining, special or professional, is entitled to possess any of the information available on the subject of Dianetics or Scientology and to use that information so as to secure a wider understanding of Scientology. By such data as is contained in this booklet the dissemination of such data is made more efficient, but the dissemination of information advised in this booklet is only recommended—it is not enforced.

Naturally, the HASI expects someone of the stature of a Doctor of Scientology to use with great understanding and great effectiveness this information; it does not enjoin the same efficiency upon a sustaining member.

This table of information, then, is not a catalog of crimes but a catalog of recommended communications. Any member can possess this information and use the information of Scientology in any way he cares to use it. The only time use of that information becomes a crime in the eyes of the HASI is (a) when he knowingly disseminates information to groups or attempts to ape or copy the activities of the HASI under another name than Scientology; (b) when he causes to be copyrighted any of the materials of Scientology under his own or an organizational name, or the names of others whom he controls; (c) when a member who is not certified or who does not have his certificate in force or whose membership has lapsed, practices Scientology professionally for the purpose of professional or financial gain; (d) when a member or an auditor whose certificate is or is not in force recommends, advises or prescribes along with Scientology, medicine, vitamins, food supplements or food, or who uses in connection with his practice any electronic devices, such as diathermy or E-Meters; (e) any member or certified auditor who combines the practice of Scientology with chiropractic, psychiatry, osteopathy, naturopathy, psychology or any other pseudomedical or medical activity; (f) any member or certified auditor who practices Scientology and calls it Dianetics, or who if certified only to practice Dianetics, does not practice Dianetics but practices Scientology; (g) who fails to follow the Code of a Scientologist; (h) any member or auditor who flagrantly and repeatedly violates in his practice the Auditor's Code 1954.

The reason there is any punitive activity at all on the part of the HASI's CECS lies with the member or auditor himself. A professional auditor has a right to personal good public repute, and he has a right to be respected for the reason that that which he represents is respected. He has a right to practice Scientology without harassment from those in his immediate area and he has a right to be free from wildcat and unauthorized activities in his area destructive to the general repute of Scientology. Further, he has a right to benefit from the general accumulation of people in the society who have got well because of Scientology. It is in the personal interest of every auditor that any auditor who processes anybody secure excellent results upon that person, for that person will then tell others and so good practices can be built and held.

He has a right as well to standardized fees not cut to pieces by somebody not authorized, processing poorly and for very little. Furthermore, he has a right to have in any preclear he receives from any other Scientologist a person whose case is already well advanced. Here is an auditor who has been trained, who has studied his subject, who has accumulated experience and who is prepared to deliver good results. He goes into an area where somebody has been using Dianetics or Scientology without any attention to what they actually are, has been using it unethically and who has been getting very poor results. This trained auditor is immediately victimized by the repute of the subject in that area. A member or an auditor has rights to be respected for what they are. People who would cut those rights to pieces or render them less must, of course, be policed.

The ease of policing, if we must call it that, in Scientology rests on the fact that the materials of Scientology are a scientific organization of data adequately and amply copyrighted and owned, and a member or an auditor of the HASI has a right to use them; but a person who is not a member or an auditor does not have any right either to use them or to possess them, and can be sued for doing so.

Furthermore, such a person practicing Scientology illegally, or using the materials of Scientology illegally, can be sued by an individual auditor in an area by an authority sent to that individual auditor by the CECS.

As far as public attacks upon individual auditors, the HASI or LRH are concerned, it has been discovered that all those who have attacked along these lines in the past, by some strange coincidence, are criminally liable for other things on quite other counts for the most part. This is not a hopeful statement nor an effort to propagandize any doubter into thinking that these attacks are untrue. They are untrue, they were untrue at the time.

Further, such attacks do relatively little damage, and in all truth, we don't spend much time worrying over being attacked. We like others to have to worry about that. But behind every one of these attacks, every time they have occurred in the past, has rested a criminal record of one kind or another. These were the kind of people one would employ if one were some hostile organization. The chief person responsible for attacks upon LRH's character in recent years was, for instance, expelled from college during his second year for grand larceny and is guilty of at least one count of perjury before Federal courts. Another person, who made the biggest splash in the newspapers (in California, where else?) was found, upon investigation, to have come from a criminal family, to have been a member of an organization pledged to overthrow the United States government by force and who committed, in making attacks, perjury on several counts, and who, when finally confronted with this fact, signed full confessions of perjury. Not all the people, of course, who make attacks upon Scientology, its organizations, its auditors or LRH, do so from any other motive than confusion. They don't know what any of these things are about and are afraid.

But when these attacks assume a public crescendo, it has been discovered in the past that the attacker was a criminal by record; thus you can see the ease with which such people can be handled. Oddly enough, there are only about twenty people in all these five years who have made such attacks and who have caused difficulties for this work. Not all of these are known to be criminals and not all of them have committed actual crimes while making these attacks so far as we know, but the most serious of these attacks WERE made by criminals. Therefore, an individual auditor finding himself confronted in an area by scurrilous and vicious attacks has only to trace these to their actual author and then trace the actual author, through police or "private eyes," to find that he has far more upon which to base charges than merely a dislike of Scientology. Normally such attacks are motivated by a frantic need for secrecy and the fear that any subject which could if it wished penetrate to the inmost secrets of a being would disclose things which such people feel would disgrace them forever.

Now, this matter of punishment is not a very happy subject, but neither is it a very happy subject for individual auditors or an organization to be engaged upon a provenly sincere course of intent in civilization and yet be balked by people who have no understanding or who represent the baser elements of a society. If we find all this uproar and entheta stemming, over a period of five years, from only twenty people, we can see that twenty people meaning no good can create a considerable communication block to us. Thus it is the responsibility of the individual auditor in his area, if he wishes to guarantee himself a quiet, pleasant, beneficial and remunerative practice, to be very alert and quite punitive where unauthorized persons and uninformed persons go on an all-out attack against him, against Scientology, against its organizations, or who illegally use or misuse Scientology.

And all of Scientology holds such a member or auditor as their hope in smoothing out our communication lines. It is an entirely moral duty to be punitive against strangers and outsiders who would stop the progress of this civilization.

It might be felt at times that by becoming possessed of a greater wisdom, a greater freedom, an individual has to some degree separated himself from the human race. True enough, he has separated himself from the more stupid elements of the human race, but it is not true that he has divorced himself from the foremost and fundamental drive of man. He has, quite the contrary, come much closer to it and the truth of living by being in Scientology. When one has the feeling that he has become an outsider by becoming a Scientologist, he has the tendency not to use the civilization or its processes themselves in carrying forward his course of existence.

A member or certified auditor, being himself a saner and more civilized person and being closer to the actual goals of government and society, which are, of course, in any actually civilized land the betterment of that society, has more right to use the government and activity lines of a people than those who would do less by their fellows. In other words, a member of the HASI or a trained Scientologist has full and complete rights to utilize whatever governmental facilities, licensing agencies, institutions, courts, police, legislations and communication lines there are in that society. A member or trained auditor confronted by disagreement from specialized interest finds himself confronted by people who would like a member or trained auditor to believe that they, not he, represent the legal side of the society. This is not true.

The person with the purer intent represents the civilized side of the society, not the person who exists solely for vested interest or personal gain. Remember that courts of law, officers of the law, institutions, regulations, legislatures, congresses, are more yours than they belong to your opponent. A Scientologist is no outlaw in a society, but is the catalyst of that society, and as such he may and should use every facility that society possesses to pull itself up to higher levels of beingness. In other words, if a Scientologist finds somebody doing wrong in the field of healing, he has the full and complete right to use any and all police courts, legislation, to right that wrong.

The HASI exists to back up any such move made. Remember, the HASI does not exist to punish communication and action, but to further it. When it cuts communication lines, it is not cutting any SCIENTOLOGY communication lines.

America was civilized by a militant ministry, and when that ministry ceased to be militant we saw on every hand the decay and decline of civil government. We saw a rise of crime and a lowering of public morals. Most churches in Western civilization hold that civil government has been convened and authorized by a divine source, and that civil government only exists by reason of that source, and that civil government is only valid because of divine source and that the members of these congregations follow civil government only so long as it does not controvert any part of the words of Jesus Christ as declared in the New Testament. In other words, these churches conceive themselves to be a higher entity than civil government. We do not declare this for Scientology, only insofar as it is the custom of religious organizations, but we do declare that the Scientologist, having a purer intent, has a better right to the use of civil government processes than those who exist for more base purposes.

Scientology exists to further and better the government of people and believes in the principles of democracy, the Magna Carta, the Constitution of the United States and also the Bill of Rights. And it believes that civil government should be dedicated to the government of the people, that it should not exist for graft, that it should not be used by individuals for personal enrichment, that its courts must be just and that its law must be for the greater good of the greater number of people.

Scientology was selflessly created and composed. It would have been easy to have made millions or even billions from its creation. It would be easy for an auditor, by narrowing his processing to the rich, to maintain himself in affluence and luxury. Scientology could only have been conceived if one had no desire for personal gain or aggrandizement. The authorship of Scientology is publicly known solely because that was the only way Scientology could be protected in its formative years. It would best have been conceived from a complete obscurity, but the controls necessary for its proper practice and dissemination would not then have been possible. For every time it has been "turned loose" it has become enturbulated.

The endless ages and a higher authority have continuously operated in the formulation and the purposes of Scientology.

It is necessary for the HASI to release to its membership and its auditors all the information which is known. The reason for this lies in the fact that Western civilization is becoming more and more enturbulated and its communication lines are being cut. A disastrous result could occur in an atomic war if the materials of Scientology were not broadly held. Furthermore, it would be dangerous for the materials of Scientology to be monopolized in one area. A Doctor of Scientology, holding the materials of Scientology for the training of persons up to certified level, may occasionally find it embarrassing to discover that one student or another has already examined all the materials. But it will not be embarrassing to that Doctor of Scientology the moment he starts to actually train such a person into the uses of Scientology. For people have to be trained into Scientology. We have yet to find one person who was not so trained who was expert in it, and we have found only those persons who were long and arduously trained could obtain the results contained in it.

9. HASI TO TRAINED SCIENTOLOGIST

The professional auditor is given specific information of a highly technical nature through the *Professional Auditor's Bulletins,* through the circulation of tapes, and on occasion by personal letter from the HASI. Additionally, auditors who have not been trained up to a level where they can achieve uniformly good results are given specialized training courses at reduced fees by Doctors of Scientology and by the HASI.

Many data of organizational nature are circulated to trained Scientologists which are not circulated to the general membership.

10. HASI TO THE GENERAL PUBLIC

It would be the rare occasion, no matter what the substance, for the HASI to release to the general public through the public presses and magazines of the country any information of any kind whatsoever about anything.

The HASI is not a secret organization, and the materials it has to hand are not secret materials, but it has been discovered in five years that the general level of the public press is such that it interviews with a preformed conclusion, and might as well have written the story before it did the interview. Several such interviews granted in the recent months have resulted in no story being written, for that was the way the reporter was handled. He had come to write anything sensational or bad as ordered by his editor, and he found himself confronting programs and activities which he became afraid to slander. In such cases, interviews were granted in order to stop stories, not to give them out. In all the thousands of articles published on Dianetics and Scientology, only three or four published in minor publications gave anything like true rendition of the subjects or their activities. The stories were preconceived before interview. Therefore, all the interview could do was to convince the person he couldn't write the story he had planned to write, and so that prevented him from writing any story at all.

In other words, the moment a reporter discovered that he could not write a bad story, he did not want to write any story. And this applies to reporters who are "friendly," who promise faithfully all good intent and good press, and who have even been processed successfully. They wrote knowingly inaccurate libel, whatever they said.

If this is the general intent of the public press, then it is our experience that interviews are better forgotten and that press releases should not be engaged upon and that reporters should not be granted interviews, whatever they promise. Dianetics and Scientology would have made far more progress had there been no single word about them in the public presses.

Newspapers, magazines, do not represent public opinion and are not the formative agencies of the public. The only time they become formative agencies in public opinion is when they express something bad badly enough to completely blacken a person or an action. Then the public will become alert and cease to have anything to do with that person or action. It could be said about the modern press that if they were to know for certain that there existed newly discovered an immediate cure for every case of polio in the world, they would mention it somewhere inside the paper, in small print. But that if one doctor in examining one polio case made an error in its handling, then the incident would receive headlines.

The motto of the press is "it is all bad over there." Although several commentators of international repute have, from time to time, given Dianetics and Scientology and LRH a resounding pat on the back, these comments have been completely lost in an avalanche of misinformed and inaccurate material appearing in the press.

Any auditor will find it so. The mere fact that somebody is trying to do something for the good of the society is sufficient to bring the modern press down upon him, according to our experience. For example, the other day an auditor performed a miracle the Pope himself would have been proud to own. A child had died, was dead, had been pronounced dead by a doctor, and the auditor, by calling the thetan back and ordering him to take over the body again, brought the child to life. The child had died because it felt it was not wanted by its parents.

The public presses knew about this—they did not care to remark upon it. In another place not too long ago, a Scientologist who had been a Justice of the Peace used, when he opened up a practice, JP after his name, and there were four columns of critical and blasting print about that auditor and about Scientology.

The public at large does not think this way. That is one of the reasons why newspapers today aren't being read to the degree that they were. Probably only the funny papers keep them being sold at all.

The HASI is very alert to the fact that word of mouth and actual Scientology publications are the only accurate or decent dissemination Scientology or its organizations will receive within the general public.

Scientology programs, then, are based solidly and entirely upon the production of results with Scientology upon people in the general public. If this policy is understood, then the actions of the HASI in handling situations or organizations can be much better understood.

At this writing an HASI clinic in City "A" has been closed while an HASI representative conducts there refresher courses. It was not that the clinic was entirely insolvent. It was barely breaking even. But it was noticed that the number of people coming to it was reducing week to week. Originally the clinic had been

990

opened to demonstrate to the public by a series of solved cases that Scientology worked. Therefore an examination of cases was quietly undertaken by the HASI and it was discovered that the auditing being done in the City "A" clinic was not as good as it should have been. The immediate result of this, of course, was for the clinic to have fewer and fewer people calling. Therefore this was not acting as a public dissemination line and that was all it was there for.

An able auditor of the HASI was immediately despatched to improve the training in general in City "A" and to conduct specifically an arduous and exacting course of training on a few select auditors there. When these have been trained, graduated, and have had some experience, some of their number will be used in a reopened City "A" clinic. And these practicing in that clinic will send out into the public people who know that Scientology has gotten results upon them.

The entire dependence of the HASI is upon good results in the public. Through an affiliated organization a test city operation was recently begun in the United States. Only one mailing, if a large one, was released to the public. Free processing was to be given every weekend by this organization. These free processing groups began immediately and systematically to grow, and the people who came to them stayed on and have remained week after week, more and more progressively in favor of Scientology, and more and more talking about it to their friends. Now this is true gain and this can be done in any city in the United States.

The HASI, through its affiliated organizations in this test city, has begun a program of visitation whereby every institution of whatever kind in the city is being made into a "regular beat" for the ministers of this organization. These persons are equipped with a small amount of literature and a very large amount of willingness to help. As they visit people in these institutions, these hospitals, these homes, the public at large will become more and more aware of Scientology.

The policy on which the HASI operates is that it trains and equips members and auditors, and provides them with the example of results and then assists them in going forth to produce results upon the public. The communication line of the HASI to the general public is one of result, and that is the only way we feel that Scientology will make progress. No other way produces any lasting result.

Our policy then is to produce and assist auditors and to hold them secure in their professions and to aid them in every possible way to go out into the society and produce results.

Beyond the general message contained under sections 1 and 2 of this article, we do not expect ministers to preach about Scientology, we expect them to use Scientology. We expect them to secure with what they can do, congregations and groups which are part of the affiliated organizations of the HASI, to support their endeavors by such groups and individual processing, and to process and give programs of public betterment to these groups, and to bring the more able members of these groups into higher technical understanding of Scientology and so make out of them members or auditors of the HASI. And by thus creating more able people to give Scientology an excellent word-of-mouth communication line to the public at large.

Visiting institutions, hospitals, schools, attending and becoming part of civic functions, by direct mailings, we assist our people to accumulate groups and congregations and, by thus accumulating such groups and congregations and by processing, to give them a higher understanding, better health, to so reach wider and wider into civilization. In announcing its policies to the general public through direct mailings and through its auditors, the HASI makes available such materials as those contained in this manual, except for this general communication plan, in the hope that a better civilization will result.

Until man has a clear, bold understanding of what man is and has a science of humanity, we will continue to fight and punish and misgovern, and it will get worse than it is unless somebody takes some responsibility. Scientologists are taking that responsibility. We know this can be a better, saner world.

It is not the purpose of the HASI or its affiliated organizations to overthrow or destroy by violence any group or government in the world. It is hoped by the HASI that a higher understanding will result in a higher and better civilization which will not have to have recourse to violence and war for the settlement of its disputes. A civilization in which disease and insanity are viewed as suboptimum rather than normal and a civilization which holds that a civilized man is one that is his soul and that a man who holds himself to be a body and to have no soul is an animal.

In keeping with this program, the HASI issues books intended for use by the general public and to interest them in the goals which man in the many ages past has envisioned for man. It is possible now. But not unless we go about it in a sane and orderly fashion ourselves. That is the reason for our organizations and communications plans.

L. RON HUBBARD
Founder

HCO POLICY LETTER OF 29 AUGUST 1957

Remimeo

GOVERNMENT PROJECT STABLE DATA

(Originally written by LRH as HCOB 29 Aug. 57 and as
Sec ED 168 on 30 Mar. 59. Issued as an HCO PL on 14 Oct. 87.)

To any government official or on any government project the HASI stable data for negotiation and discourse are as follows:

WE ARE THE EXPERTS ON HUMAN ABILITY AND ENDURANCE. WE OFFER *ONLY* SERVICES. WE DISCUSS ONLY RESULTS, THE NEED OF RESULTS, THE CONSEQUENCES OF NO RESULTS, THE SINCERITY OF THE ORGANIZATION AND ALL CONCERNED IN OBTAINING RESULTS, AND INTERESTING RESULTS.

REASON: You cannot communicate in 25 minutes something which took 25 years to develop. Scientology really takes some time to learn. To try to *teach* someone Scientology at a luncheon table or in an office is difficult, since prejudice and mental illiteracy are barriers. To talk about Scientology, however, using the above stable data, is easy.

We know already that in a discussion with uninformed persons, these attempt to learn all about Scientology in 25 minutes. To stop all further learning by them, try at once and instantly to fully educate them. To lead them to further learning, read again the stable data given above.

The importance of these data will be realized when they will be published to all personnel on a project as a must.

L. RON HUBBARD
Founder

HCO BULLETIN OF 1 MAY 1958

Remimeo

SIGNS OF SUCCESS

Whenever we're really winning, the squirrels start to scream. You can tell if somebody is a squirrel. They howl or make trouble only when we're winning.

Spectacular success can quadruple the number of complaints. Tell the complainees: "Come in, get Clear." Otherwise skip it.

To understand a squirrel, consider the reaction of somebody who could not run the fifth leg of Help, "How could another person help another person." The thought of this drives some people spinny. That's a squirrel. They can't view other people helping others without going berserk.

There's nothing personal in having squirrels. Even heroes can have lice.

L. RON HUBBARD
Founder

HUBBARD COMMUNICATIONS OFFICE
Saint Hill Manor, East Grinstead, Sussex

HCO BULLETIN OF 21 JUNE 1960

Remimeo
Staff
Students

RELIGIOUS PHILOSOPHY AND RELIGIOUS PRACTICE

(Originally written by LRH as HCOB of 21 June 60,
same title. It was later reissued as HCOB of 18 Apr. 67.)

Scientology is a religion by its basic tenets, practice, historical background and by the definition of the word "religion" itself. The following will help clarify the philosophical and practical aspects of religion.

Religious practice implies ritual, faith-in, doctrine based on a catechism and a creed.

Religious philosophy implies study of spiritual manifestations; research on the nature of the spirit and study on the relationship of the spirit to the body; exercises devoted to the rehabilitation of abilities in a spirit.

Scientology is a religious philosophy in its highest meaning as it brings man to total freedom and truth. Our Confessional relieves the being of the encumbrances which keep his awareness as a being limited to the physical aspects of life.

Scientology is also a religious practice in that the Church of Scientology conducts basic services such as sermons at Church meetings, christenings, weddings and funerals.

Scientology does not conflict with other religions or religious practices as it clarifies them and brings understanding of the spiritual nature of man.

Scientology has amongst its members people of all the major faiths, including many priests, bishops and other ordained communicants of the major faiths.

Scientology's closest spiritual ties with any other religion are with Orthodox (Hinayana) Buddhism with which it shares an historical lineage. But even here the relationship is based mainly on friendship and the recognition of the being as a spirit rather than on any organizational ties.

L. RON HUBBARD
Founder

12 August 1960

DEPARTMENT OF GOVERNMENT RELATIONS

A new department for FCDC is created herewith entitled Department of Government Relations.

It is to be given a separate room, out of the way of FC traffic flows.

It is to be manned by a trustee of the FC who shall draw the same units as department head as the Org Sec.

The entire activity of this department is to handle matters with IRS, courts, securities commissions, state, city and national governments and protect and better the FC position. All persons from these agencies or governments must be routed by Reception only to DGR. The government accountant and a part-time attorney and all FC attorneys deal with this department only.

The head of this department shall have no other duties in the FC except those of a trustee. The head of this department may not also be the Org Sec.

The purpose of this department is to wall off all government and legal affairs from the FC and prohibit them from entering FC lines and disrupting FC activities. The channel is *not* via the Org Sec to the dept but from the board to the dept directly. The head of this dept may not further enter its affairs into the org but cares for them at this department level.

L. RON HUBBARD
Founder

HCO POLICY LETTER OF 15 AUGUST 1960

Assoc Secs
HCO Secs

DEPARTMENT OF GOVERNMENT AFFAIRS

(Cancels any previous directions
to set up a Special Zone Dept)

(This policy letter is mandatory
for all Central Organizations)

There shall be established on a board level and outside the structure of the Central Org and HCO but under the board of HASI, Ltd., a new department to be called "The Department of Government Affairs."

More and more, as governments disintegrate under the threat of atomic war and communism, Central Organizations have had to give high executive time to governmental affairs, to the great loss of the organizations themselves. The enturbulence entered into Scientology activities by legal matters, tax matters and matters of assisting governments to maintain stability has sapped our time and fixed our attention, to our own loss.

Now, to remedy this situation, I wish to contain and cordon, in a military sense, this incursion and to prohibit utterly and completely such entrance (of these matters or our own projects for governments or with governments) into Central Org or HCO comm lines. In other words, Central Orgs and HCOs are run by, for and as Scientology service and activity units and the special Department of Government Affairs shall handle other matters and specifically deny such non-Scientology matters entrance into organizational comm lines.

The Department of Government Affairs shall be headed and directed with a minimum of personnel and shall not be able to call upon the personnel of the Central Org or HCO for further assistance than the relay of communications.

The Director of Government Affairs shall be a fully qualified person of good judgment subject to control of the board of directors, and shall be subject to the advices and directions of the board and the HCO and Assoc Secretary. Only Washington and South Africa are excluded from supervision of the dept by the Assoc Sec, Org Sec and HCO Sec. In all other offices, the Director of Government Affairs shall be subordinate to the Assoc Sec and HCO Sec.

Under this department comes the corporation's solicitors, attorneys, chartered accountants and any attorney or accountant hired directly by the corporation for outside legal or tax or filing purposes.

The allotment and issue of shares comes under this department, but the actual invoicing and banking shall be done as always by the Dept of Accounts or, for HCO, by the HCO Secretary.

All contracts, filings with the government; all tax reports and their preparation, corporation minutes, annual meetings, legal papers, suits against and by the corporation, whether HASI, Ltd., or HCO, Ltd.; all legal investigatory work and detectives; all contacts with government agents, bureaus and departments; all assistance to governments, messages to governments, handling answers from governments or courts shall be cared for by the department, whether to advance or protect Scientology or its corporations by government or legal channels.

All legal documents and the Valuable Document files for HCO and HASI shall be kept by the department in a proper safe in accordance with previous rules written for the keeping and handling of valuable documents.

All share sales reports and all legal, governmental and corporation reports to be made to the boards shall be made to it by this department.

No shares may be advertised or issued save with the approval of this department.

No contracts, purchases or mortgages may be undertaken without the approval of this department and then only by the action of this department.

It is clearly understood that this department shall not undertake financial management for the Central Org or HCO nor may it direct the Central Org or HCO on purely Scientology affairs or Scientology dissemination except where these may impinge directly upon the government, and even then this department is enjoined from forcing government laws or rulings upon the Central Org or HCO by threat of danger or ominous advices, nor may the department employ either solicitors nor accountants who specialize in ominous advices to the orgs, since the orgs could be discouraged or impeded by such.

The object of the department is to broaden the impact of Scientology upon governments and other organizations and is to conduct itself so as to make the name and repute of Scientology better and more *forceful*. Therefore, defensive tactics are frowned upon in the department. We are not trying to make the Central Orgs and HCOs "be good." We are trying to make their reach more secure and effective. Only attacks resolve threats.

In the face of danger from governments or courts, there are only two errors one can make: (a) do nothing and (b) defend. The right things to do with any threat are to (1) find out if we want to play the offered game or not (2) if not, to derail the offered game with a feint or attack upon the most vulnerable point which can be disclosed in the enemy ranks (3) make enough threat or clamor to cause the enemy to quail (4) don't try to get any money out of it (5) make every attack by us also sell Scientology and (6) win. If attacked on some vulnerable point by anyone or anything or any organization, always find or manufacture enough threat against them to cause them to sue for peace. Peace is bought with an exchange of advantage, so make the advantage and then settle. Don't ever defend. Always attack. Don't ever do nothing. Unexpected attacks in the rear of the enemy's front ranks work best.

Never put the organization on "wait" because of courts or other matters. It's up to the department to make the actions of HCO Secs and Org Secs *right,* not enjoin right actions on the HCO and Org Secs.

To win we must have treasure and verve. If a Central Org and HCO function perfectly as service units, then treasure and consequent security for the further advance are to hand. If the department operates with verve and elan, even with rashness, it will afford a screen behind which organizations can work.

Example: British Medical Association attacks Scientology in Australia via the government. Answer: throw heavy communication against the weakest point of the BMA—its individual doctors. Rock them with petitions to have medical laws modified which they are to sign. Couple the BMA attack with any group hated by the government. Attack personally by threats or suits any person signing anything for the BMA. Slam the matter into politics; advance a bill into parliament that strips the BMA of all legal rights by opening healing to all. Make the attack by the BMA look ridiculous. Attack medical practices. Investigate horrible practices loudly. (*Always* investigate loudly, never quietly.) Make the distinct public and governmental impression and BMA impression that they've run into a barrage of arrows or electronic cannon and that continued attack by them will cause their own disintegration. As all this is being done on a thought or idea level, the restimulation of their engrams results in the total impression that they are surrounded by their own dead, and the battery may fire again at any minute. And if one makes in writing not one slanderous or libelous statement, there is no defense by them. This example is patterned on what just happened and what we did in Australia where we are winning strongly.

The personnel of the department should be freed of past track legal and governmental overts by the HGC using evening auditing. This is a must or the department will otherwise attract attacks. Further, the higher the department personnel is raised on "control" through running Help, the less action will have to be undertaken by it and the more it will actually accomplish without violent action.

The goal of the department is to bring the government and hostile philosophies or societies into a state of complete compliance with the goals of Scientology. This is done by high-level ability to control and in its absence by low-level ability to overwhelm. Introvert such agencies. Control such agencies. Scientology is the only game on Earth where everybody wins. There is no overt in bringing good order.

The offices of the department, so far as is possible, should be so situated as to bring no government traffic into the main avenues, comm lines or halls of the Central Organization or HCO or so as to divert it to the maximum extent from said avenues, comm lines and halls.

In the United States and South Africa the head of the Department of Government Affairs shall be also Trustee or Area Director of the Central Organization while the Org Sec and Assoc Sec shall not be, but will be officers of the corporation.

This policy letter is prompted by the following facts:

1. My own traffic on government legal affairs is far too heavy and I need help of magnitude on a continental level.

2. HCO Secs and Assoc Secs are having difficulty holding down their orgs and the field because of the time demanded by government affairs.

3. The activity will get heavier rather than lighter.

999

a. The deterioration of government order is accelerating with consequent confusion in all related affairs;

b. Increasing amounts of order must be maintained by us at a governmental level against the possibility of finding our areas without governments.

4. We are about to file HASI, Ltd. and HCO, Ltd. in all areas with the attendant heavy legal and governmental action necessary.

5. We are about to arrange for the release of and the issue of over half a million pounds of shares to the public, thus making heavy demands on legal and government lines.

6. We are about to finance and erect various media of communications such as radio stations, on the various continents, and this will require enormous amounts of liaison and action in such a department.

7. We are about to finance and find new quarters in the United States and such activity comes under the new department.

8. Due to new clearing techniques, our sphere of control is widening. This is purely a case phenomenon, but will be felt heavily by orgs in the future. It is necessary to provide comm lines for this widening of influence.

L. RON HUBBARD
Founder

HCO POLICY LETTER OF 22 AUGUST 1960

All Orgs
Sec ED

DEPARTMENT OF GOVERNMENT RELATIONS

The Dept of Government Relations may not use org personnel for typing and mailing, and may only use org personnel for reception, switchboard and despatch purposes.

Where numbers of mailing pieces are envisioned or where numbers of outside letters are to be sent by the Dept of Government Relations, these may be done either by outside agencies or by a full- or part-time secretary to the Dir of Government Relations. The necessary high appearance of Government Relations letters and mailing pieces does not admit the use of mimeo, and Government Relations may not use organizational mimeo machines.

L. RON HUBBARD
Founder

HCO POLICY LETTER OF 30 AUGUST 1960

Dept Govt Affairs
Special Zone Dept
Assoc Secs
HCO Secs

SPECIAL ZONE DEPARTMENT

The Special Zone Department is herewith combined with the Dept of Government Affairs.

At such time as Special Zone produces direct income, it will be returned to a separate department.

All persons who have been active in Central Org Special Zone Depts are thanked, and it is suggested they be used part time in the Dept of Government Affairs.

L. RON HUBBARD
Founder

HUBBARD COMMUNICATIONS OFFICE
Saint Hill Manor, East Grinstead, Sussex

HCO POLICY LETTER OF 31 OCTOBER 1960
Issue II

HCOs
Central Orgs

US APPOINTMENT
AND ORGANIZATIONAL TREND

A longtime, able officer of FCDC, has been appointed HCO Executive Secretary Americas.

She has been Government Relations Director. She retains that post as part of her HCO duties.

The trend is to consolidate Government Relations and Special Zone with HCO as it seems feasible.

I have finally sorted out front-line promotion into broad public testing and the new basic course, "The Anatomy of the Human Mind." Data on these will be with you soon.

No other Government Relations or Special Zone shifts are being made at this time. Special Zone, however, will gradually shift into broad public and business testing clinics; and Government Relations, having cleaned up the most of the loose ends, will shift to HCO or into broad publishing and government activities.

Government Relations and Special Zone are not abolished.

L. RON HUBBARD
Founder

1003

HCO POLICY LETTER OF 13 MARCH 1961
Issue I

CenOCon
Hat Write-up

DEPARTMENT OF OFFICIAL AFFAIRS

The Department of Official Affairs exists as an extension of the Office of the Continental Association Secretary.

Purpose: The bettering of the public representation, legal position and government acceptance of Scientology.

ACTIONS

a. Following and enforcing current organization policy with regard to press and handling such press queries and matters.

b. Following and enforcing policies with regard to the legal status of the organizations of Scientology in the Continental area.

c. Cooperating with societies having similar organizational goals.

d. Worsening the public belief and attitude toward societies and persons having purposes counter to Scientology goals.

e. Giving hearings and assistance to field members who have ideas to advance Scientology.

f. Bringing continuous pressure to bear on governments to create pro-Scientology legislation and to discourage anti-Scientology legislation or legislation of groups opposing Scientology.

g. Handling field and organization problems of security.

h. Keeping newspaper and other files relating to Scientology and anti-Scientology groups, persons and activities.

DESCRIPTION

Examining the purpose and action of this post, it should become apparent at once that we have here in actuality the equivalent of a Ministry of Propaganda and Security, using crude, old-time political terms.

This is a very important post and must be held only by a person whose security is excellent and who has a flair for such matters.

An active department could secure, by one means or another:

a. An absence of unfavorable press and possibly someday favorable press.

b. A strong legal position for the organizations in the area.

c. Heavy influence through our own and similarly minded groups on the public and official mind.

d. The failure of influence of hostile groups and persons.

e. High ARC with and good effectiveness of field auditors on third dynamic programs that do not hinder the Central Org or absorb much of its attention.

f. A pro-Scientology government of the area.

g. An absence of field rumors, oppositions and failures.

h. A filed knowingness about the activities of friends and enemies.

OPERATION

Although this department may appear to have the third dynamic as its target, it does not in fact handle anything but INDIVIDUALS.

To accomplish its actions, it needs only to make friends and allies of individual people who can influence.

For example:

a. The action of making better press consists of making friends with a publisher who commands reporters, and does not really consist of handling reporters.

b. The action of achieving a strong legal position consists of cultivating the friendship and respect of a very good attorney and persuading him to hold up the authority of the company and its board through leading him to respect them.

c. The action of influencing groups consists of making a favorable impression on the *head* of the ally groups.

d. The action of bringing about the failure of a hostile group is accomplished by finding and releasing the truth about the leader of that group.

e. The action of influencing energetic Scientologists is accomplished by making a friend out of the individual and acknowledging what he says and encouraging what *he* wants to do, without really becoming involved in his programs.

f. The action of bringing about a pro-Scientology government consists of making a friend of the most highly placed government person one can reach, even placing Scientologists in domestic and clerical posts close to him and seeing to it that Scientology resolves his troubles and case.

g. The action of reducing hostile field rumors consists of running them down doggedly to the person who is spreading them and directly confronting that person and disposing of his personal opposition.

h. The action of accumulating files consists of accumulating files and knowingness about individual persons who are friends or enemies.

MAXIMS

If it's a group problem, find the key person and influence him.

If it's nebulously about a group without any mention of a key person, discard it.

Only data about individuals is valid for use.

Only action upon individuals is productive.

Forget *they*. Find him or her.

Use Scientology to resolve individual problems.

Never abandon an attack until you have found and contacted the key person. Then apply Scientology.

Get volunteer Scientologists interested in this game and helping.

PERSONNEL NOTE

A person who cannot deal with individuals but is fixed on the third is not well fitted for this post.

The person best fitted for the post of Director of Official Affairs is one who likes people and is easily liked.

An orderly, pleasant gentleman or a personable, charming lady, who has a flair for order and intelligence about formulating and guiding ideas to individual minds, would admirably fill this post.

One of the purposes of this post is to prevent the Assoc Secretary from having to engage in social and personal activities solely for the purpose of furthering Scientology. If the Assoc Sec's Sec receives invitations for the Assoc Sec to visit of an evening to "further Scientology," the Assoc Sec's Sec infers that the right person to invite is really the Director of the Dept of Official Affairs, unless, of course, the Assoc Sec really wants to go.

It could be that the fate of nations hangs on the actions, brilliance and skill of the Director of Official Affairs in handling individuals to gain help for Scientology.

L. RON HUBBARD
Founder

HCO POLICY LETTER OF 13 MARCH 1961
Issue II

CenOCon

DEPARTMENT OF OFFICIAL AFFAIRS

(Cancels earlier directives concerning
Depts of Government Relations and
Special Programs.)

Anyone now holding post as Dept of Government Relations or as Director of Special Programs should be retitled "Department of Official Affairs."

The field responded only faintly to special programs.

The activities connected with governments have increased.

Where field activities warrant, a Central Organization may have a Department of Official Affairs to combine all former duties and activities performed by the Department of Government Relations and Special Programs.

Where such departments do not exist, all such activities will be handled by the Assoc Sec or the HCO Continental Secretary. But where much time is being spent on government liaison, cooperation with societies and the filing of legal papers and matters, a Department of Official Affairs must be created as per HCO PL 13 Mar. 61 I, DEPARTMENT OF OFFICIAL AFFAIRS, as these matters are time consuming and deter the Assoc Sec from performing his intraorganizational duties.

L. RON HUBBARD
Founder

TERROR STALKS

I was alerted into an analysis of why we're fought by comments from an organization executive.

An analysis shows there may have been many reasons but a further look makes them invalid.

A piercing scream against Dianetics arose *before* the first book was published in 1950. Press was hot against it *before* the first foundation was formed.

For *seven* months before there was any personnel or personal troubles publicized, the bulk of articles against Dianetics had already appeared. At one time three national magazines were simultaneously on the stands screaming in lead articles about Dianetics and myself—and this was five months *before* any "divorce" publicity. And amongst the hundreds of reporters and commentators who screamed only *one* ever talked to me, and, from various evidences, none had read the book or knew *anything* about the subject.

Until May, 1950 I received only favorable publicity—on expeditions or comings or goings. In May 1950 there was a concerted shriek from people who (a) had not read the books and (b) who knew nothing bad about me.

These howls came from both conservative *and* liberal groups alike—the AMA—the commies, the Socialists, the Roman Catholics.

Thus we can rule the following facts *out* of all the protests and "bad publicity" of the past eleven years:

1. That it stems from any knowledge of the subject;

2. That it is a concerted effort by any one group; and

3. That it is based on any knowledge of myself.

Now if we look further we also find these facts:

4. In the past eleven years, some thousands of texts have been written on the subjects of philosophy, man, the mind in various universities;

5. In the past eleven years thousands of men, not connected with universities or groups have originated and forwarded philosophies about man;

Thus, with all these targets *no* protest has been made by groups or press against new philosophies.

And now let us look further:

6. Many truly dangerous practices have risen up amongst man such as a new Indian version of whirling dervishism now rampant in England;

7. Brainwashing was introduced in the past eleven years by the Russians;

8. A dozen violent and harmful psychiatric treatments have been developed.

And *no* sustained protest has continued to be made in the press against these. Indeed the US government adopted brainwashing calmly and the British government and people of the US have accepted new psychiatric treatments, organizations and propaganda without real protest.

Looking at all these things, then it would seem that protests against Dianetics and Scientology do not stem from a knowledge of myself, they do not stem from a knowledge of the substance of the work, they do not stem from conservative or liberal groups and they are not a protest against philosophy, philosophers, or evil practices, and they are not an effort to protect the public.

If you look this over with cold dispassion, examine it thoroughly from the light of the facts, only one explanation seems to remain.

They are terrified of our postulates!

This analysis places a fantastic dissemination weapon in our hands. The terror in the protest is obvious since it is misemotional and is not based on confronted facts.

To any attack by anyone, we can reply, "Why are you terrified of Scientology?" or "Why are you afraid of Hubbard?" or "Why are you frightened of Scientologists?"

For plainly this is the case. People don't even know we reach for withholds—yet terror! Protest! Screams!

Now I'll admit to having plied philosophy before within the whole track memory of Earth dwellers. Harm did not result. But evil was destroyed. And I'll admit that evil men sense the germs of their own destruction.

There may be unconscious recognition in this. Maybe it's the Fourth Dynamic *bank* that yells back.

But, of this we are certain. We inspire terror in some men. "Why are you terrified of Scientology?" is the best answer. It as-ises the condition.

I think we ought to use it.

L. RON HUBBARD
Founder

HCO POLICY LETTER OF 29 OCTOBER 1962

Urgent to DC
  NY and LA
Information
CenOCon

RELIGION

(Furnish a copy of this to all attorneys
dealing with our interests for us.)

It is of interest to all organizations that *all* Scientology incorporations are religious in nature.

Not only the Founding Church of Scientology or the Churches of Scientology in the United States, but also all HASI, Inc., offices (which includes all British and Commonwealth offices, as HASI, Ltd., is not fully in force anywhere except New Zealand) are religious corporations.

In the HASI, Inc., incorporation papers the corporation is clearly designated as a "religious fellowship."

The use of the E-Meter in Scientology, but not Dianetics, is describable as follows:

"All religions seek truth.

"Freedom of the spirit is only to be found on the road to Truth.

"Sin is composed, according to Scientology, of lies and hidden actions and is therefore untruth.

"The Electrometer is used to disclose truth to the individual who is being processed and thus free him spiritually.

"Only in this way can man's spiritual self be regained.

"A religious Confessional fails only when not guided by a modern instrument such as the Electrometer.

"Religions in the 1960s use modern aids. The Electrometer is a valid religious instrument, used in Confessionals, and is in no way diagnostic and does not treat.

"Regardless of any earlier uses of psychogalvanometers in Dianetics or psychology or in early Scientology publications when research was in progress, the Electrometer in Scientology today has *no* other use than as described above."

In view of the "interest" the Food and Drug Administration has in the E-Meter, the above data is vital and must be impressed upon investigating agents as it is only the truth of the matter. They thought that outside the US Scientology was not religious, which is false. The impression must be strongly corrected in the FDA at once.

Dianetics used an older instrument to detect engrams. The book *Electropsychometric Auditing* is entirely a Dianetic manual.

L. RON HUBBARD
Founder

OUR ROLE IN THE WORLD

The DC raid shows on inspection, a deterioration of government honesty and therefore government sanity.

The Department of Health, Education and Welfare did not tell the judge who issued the warrant that it was a church they wanted to raid. They named the HGC, Academy and Distribution Center—all of which are owned by the FCDC and are church departments conducted in quarters leased by the church. Yet the government knew it was a church, for in New York, an FDA spokesman lecturing the Humanists a month before the attack called it a church and nothing else. This makes the warrant false.

The FDA said they seized "pamphlets" and "leaflets" whereas they also seized books.

Before the raid they called in the press and planted a story so as to cover their real actions. This story was out on the streets hours before the raid, giving us no chance to give our side of it.

They referred to the Founding Church as "a quasi-religious cult." As *Scientology 8-8008* makes plain, we study and process the human spirit to free it from the effects of the physical universe. We call the spirit a "thetan" after the Greek symbol of thought and spirit—*theta*. If studying and treating the spirit isn't religion then billions and billions of savants and worshipers have been wrong for 2,500 years. If there's anything "quasi" about the religious aspect of studying and treating the human spirit, then FDA religion must be defined as "the worship of the son of Wotan, Adolph Hitler."

The meter was seized because it was "mislabeled." Their pretense of a label is "This Instrument Diagnoses and Cures Physical Illness." It doesn't. We have never said it does and it can't. Thus they want us to label something wrongly so that it will then contravene their ideas and so would be illegal. Evidently the meter should have their label on it so they can legally seize it.

Additionally, they seized privately owned meters for which they had no warrants.

This cloudy thinking is a symptom of sick men. A sick government. And a government that is afraid to perform its actions in public view. All this leads us to some speculations and planning vital to our future progress.

———————

The way I see our hand is this:

1. Our forte is the human spirit and its relationship to the physical universe.

1012

2. Two "great" nations are liable to wreck the playing field with overwhelming nuclear force, their rage against each other born out of their inability to handle their own affairs.

3. Our first job is to salvage as many as we can from the possible debacle.

4. Our hope is that we can halt the progress of destruction by processing and applications of Scientology before Armageddon.

Number 3 is well formed up and in actual progress.

In suddenly engaging our forces the US government has entered us upon number 4.

Oddly, we couldn't have been better poised to receive the government's attack. Our only danger is not using the great advantage it gives us, especially in not attaining and holding the offense. We may lapse into defense. That would be fatal.

Singularly in our favor is the dishonest aspect of the government's "case."

It makes it an easy one to win, if we are militantly offensive about winning it. We should plot and execute a *resounding* defeat, not just prove our point.

After taking care of the government charges, we should launch an attack from that springboard upon all US government "thinking" about "the mind" and hammer our way rapidly into a dominant position and use that position to audit out the danger in the two GPM items that most menace Earth.

Russia can be reached. They're going mad trying to make communism work. We have just had an oblique bid from a Russian diplomat and remember, they made more than a bid in 1938.

US or Russia, these are both run by cynical men. But they're sick men.

So we have some hopes on number 4.

The weakness and dishonesty of the US attack, the recent bid by Russia, gives us reasons to hope. It shows they are afraid of us, afraid to confront what they are doing. They can't outflow straight. Therefore they are willing to inflow.

There are three major factors in world peace. The US. Russia. And our technology. Factually there aren't any other vital factors except our continuing to hold our own in neutral ground, from where we can handle the situation. We are not becoming wild to say we're a third in this, as nowhere on Earth is there any solution or technology for a solution except in our hands. Do you know of any?

L. RON HUBBARD
Founder

HCO POLICY LETTER OF 13 FEBRUARY 1965
Issue II

Remimeo
BPI

POLITICS

Now and then you hear me speak derisively of governments and ideologies—including democracy.

If, by seeing I criticize an ideology, anyone seeks to believe I embrace its opposite, he has failed to get the point.

What political system could work amongst very aberrated people?

A democracy or a communism would be a huge joke in an insane asylum. Well, isn't it?

The basic building block of any political system is the individual. One can seek to avoid this point by conceiving of the masses. But you can't have masses which aren't made up of single units. Therefore the single unit is the basis of a mass.

No political system applied to a colony of monkeys would have anything to govern but monkeys. That's plain, certainly.

A political system seeking to function amongst ignorant, illiterate and barbaric people could have marvelous principles but could only succeed in being ignorant, illiterate and barbaric *unless* one addressed the people one by one and cured the ignorance, illiteracy and barbarism of each citizen.

The collective think of apes is ape-think. A fascism led by and applied to idiots would be idiot-fascism.

So there is no reason to suppose *any* political system is any better than those who use it to govern or be governed.

The only difference in existing systems of politics is their relative values in giving the individual a chance to develop and receive a higher level of personal sanity and ability.

That rules out any system which witch hunts, freezes opportunity or suppresses the right to improve by any workable system or suppresses a workable system.

Watching the US and Australia fight Scientology with blind fury while supporting oppressive mental and religious practices proves that democracy, applied to and used by aberrated people, is far from an ideal activity and is only aberrated democracy.

Every human has in common with every other human the same reactive bank. This is the most they have in common.

The reactive bank—unconscious mind, whatever you care to call it—suppresses all decent impulses and enforces the bad ones.

Therefore a democracy is a collective-think of reactive banks. Popular opinion is bank opinion.

Any human group is likely to elect only those who will kill them. That's concluded from actual 1950 experiments.

The group succeeds only by the efforts of individuals who rise above their banks and do their best for their fellows *despite* the vicious character of groups and the idiot nature of collective-think.

Believe in the individual being and work with him and you will find he is basically good.

Work only with a group and you work with collective-think which is basically bank and therefore evil.

Scientology gives us our first chance to have a real democracy.

By freeing from the worst aberrations each individual, one then achieves a group which doesn't react only on bank and which will be, like the individual, basically good.

For the bank was made to keep people who were not bad from going bad. It was a mistake. So it is bad.

We prove daily in Scientology that an individual freed of aberrations reacts more decently toward his fellows and that an individual, restimulated, acts worse; we prove that the individual under stress of aberration is unreasonable and an individual freed is bright.

So we can conclude on actual evidence that the first true democracy will emerge when we have freed each individual of the more vicious reactive impulses. Such beings can reason, can agree on decent and practical measures and be depended upon to evolve beneficial measures.

Until we have done that we will continue to be critical of human "democracy"—and any other political philosophy advanced upon man as a cure for his ills.

A political philosophy can't audit. We can.

And don't be so sensitive to popular reaction. Just get on with making a saner world and it will all come out all right.

L. RON HUBBARD
Founder

HCO POLICY LETTER OF 2 APRIL 1965R
Gen. Non-Remimeo
Issue V
REVISED 14 DECEMBER 1980

ADMINISTRATION OUTSIDE SCIENTOLOGY

You will find, oddly and weirdly enough, that if you fail to use Scientology admin and dev-t policies *on the society* outside Scientology that trouble will occur.

If you just make it a blind rule to always do so, you will avert much trouble and upset.

Where somebody writes you (say a business firm) an off-line or off-policy (off *their* policy too) or off-origin despatch and you don't point it out and send it back to source and say why, endless dev-t will occur! We have had an actual case of it in the US government which sent us a letter off *their* policy. We did not handle it as dev-t and so far it has cost a couple thousand dollars just because we didn't!

Now take the case of the 1 Mar. 65 amnesty. It was released so that the new Justice Codes could be issued and because we needed a cleared track for new org patterns such as certification changes and classification shifts.

Well, it was a piece of Scientology admin. So to hell with whether they think it stupid or wise, just use *any* Scientology admin *or policy letter* excerpt to slam people's hats on in governments or anywhere.

Example: The FDA of Washington, DC, is really trying to get off the hook on its attack. It may eventually commit further overts unless given an amnesty. So the HCO Continental Secretary US should mail a copy of the policy letter to the head of the FDA and each high official of that area including the Secretary of Health, Education and Welfare of the US, *and* the president, with a note on HCO stationery stating, "This amnesty was issued primarily for Scientologists so we could issue new Justice Codes in our organizations, but it happens to include you also. Scientologists therefore may not attack you for your former actions, and also if you do not continue to attack us we cannot even sue you. While you may consider it highhanded of us to issue a general amnesty, remember we have a rather enormous population to look after across the world and we probably do a much better job of it than you do since we know our business." Who knows (or who cares) the result of this? We have at least done our job.

Example: Parliament in Victoria is really covered by the amnesty and each should be mailed an exact copy, even Galbatty and the Roman Catholic Church officials, the head of the state government and even Holy Joe Anderson who headed the "enquiry." A note should accompany it: "While this amnesty was issued primarily for Scientologists so that we could then issue new Justice Codes for our organizations, it happens that you are also covered by it. Thus, it excuses your erroneous attack on Scientology during the last year and the effort to break our organizations by the cost of it. Thus, here is your copy of the General Amnesty of 1 Mar. 65. I think you would be wise to accept it."

Then we are quite in order sometime in the future to respond to any further nonsense from these humanoids if we have to label them suppressive.

It would obviously be quite out of order, in view of the newness of our codes, to slap them for acts which we ourselves have issued an amnesty on.

If the Internal Revenue Service (off-policy in refusing the FCDC nonprofit status though it qualifies) continues to act up or if the FDA does sue, we can of course comm ev them and, if found guilty, label and publish them as a suppressive group. I assure you that this is less hollow than it sounds.

We are bound by two things:

1. We are *not* just a group. We are the possessors of very powerful technology and we are still part of this civilization.

2. We owe our progress to the peace we have maintained (strenuous though it was) in our environment.

If we continue to let loose on the civilization around us with our powerful technology without giving that civilization a chance to accept us and abide by it, we will have chaos very soon.

Therefore, *whether* "society" accepts or not, we must also extend our "Pax Scientologica" as a spearhead before our direct technical action or nobody will stand still to be audited but run in terror, and just a handful of us will go free. The rest of society will simply cave in.

So we may as well develop the habit early regardless of whether they accept our admin tech or not. Extend it always. Shrug at any gasps or protests.

And then we'll have a spread over things that forms no ridge between "them" and "us."

You see, none is labeled a supressive until he or she declares against us. And only those who so declare are suppressive. Don't err in thinking the whole is against us. That's just an ARC break. Most are for us. Our files are *crammed* with applause. Our complaints drawer is a *very* tiny one. It would do any Scientologist good to see the thousands upon thousands upon thousands of "Hurrah for Scientology" in our files and the little tiny batch of sour grapes. *Yet* because what's *wrong* as cases with the tiny batch is that they use the word "everybody" continually in their cries and howls so people they talk to find it hard to locate them in their dispersal. They are the ARC breaks kid in person. "Everybody" and "nobody" and entheta are their stocks in trade. Such cases speak of "the masses" and "the public" as against us and so we sometimes fail to note that the *whole* complaint is from this puny runt raving from the whirlpool of his own overt acts. Such a person makes a greater effect on the unthinking than he should. He is giving continual false reports.

GENERALITIES ARE NOT WRONG UNLESS THEY ARE COMBINED WITH A FALSE REPORT AND INTENDED TO UPSET SOMEBODY.

The generalities of these bank puppets intend to deny the good (nobody, nothing) and generalize (everybody, everything) the bad. And so such people are really just spinners for the local spinbin. Yet you find "society" electing and appointing them since such birds echo the exact reactive bank of each individual in the mob. You can easily form a *bad* mob. It's awful hard to form an enthusiastic mob—they have to be sane!

So the individual in "society" is so far from against us that even White House clerks have sent us copies of government despatches about us. Society is in the grip of a lot of ARC broken paranoid peewees like Galbatty in Australia or the head of the FDA in Washington. Such men grab such posts because they are men of fear. Such men are just animated banks. If such cannot destroy you, they will destroy themselves. They will confess at the drop of an electrode if told to do so, poor puppets of their banks that they are.

So don't heed who is *pretending* to be in charge "out there." There really isn't any thetan in charge. "Human leadership" is usually just the guy with the most bank. When you want to handle one of these "leaders," put the guy's hat on. Hard. With Scientology admin and policy.

Never fail to use Scientology admin or justice to handle the individuals in the society beyond our edges. Sounds adventurous. Well, it is! But effective, too.

We have the tech.

It's designed to handle bank conditions.

Use it.

And use our dissem formula ruthlessly at every chance and in any situation.

You will only fail to handle a situation if you don't handle it with Scientology. The older methods have failed. Hell! That's why we're here!

L. RON HUBBARD
Founder

HUBBARD COMMUNICATIONS OFFICE
Saint Hill Manor, East Grinstead, Sussex

HCO POLICY LETTER OF 5 APRIL 1965
Issue III

Remimeo
BPI
Mag Article

SCIENTOLOGY MAKES A SAFE ENVIRONMENT

We're working to provide a safe environment for Scientology and Scientologists in orgs everywhere.

The dangerous environment of the wog world, of injustice, sudden dismissals, war, atomic bombs, will only persist and trouble us if we fail to spread our safe environment across the world.

It starts with our own orgs. They must be safe environments.

Only good tech and justice can make the org environment safe. Like an auditing room, we must be able to work undisturbed by the madness at our doors.

We can make every org a safe island and then, by expanding and joining those orgs, bring peace and a safe environment to all the world.

It not only *can* be done. It is happening this moment. Push it along. Support policy, good tech and justice.

L. RON HUBBARD
Founder

HUBBARD COMMUNICATIONS OFFICE
Saint Hill Manor, East Grinstead, Sussex

HCO POLICY LETTER OF 14 JUNE 1965
Issue III

Remimeo
BPI

POLITICS, FREEDOM FROM

(Originally written by LRH as Sec ED 56 Int,
14 June 65. Issued as an HCO PL on 10 Jan. 68.)

1. I hereby declare Scientology to be nonpolitical and nonideological.

2. Politics and ideology may be no part of any decision to train or process individuals, and any such interrogation shall cease to be a part of any application for training, processing or membership.

3. This does not change any policy relating to suppressive persons. It does delete any words in any form which seek to bring about a statement of political allegiance or antagonism.

4. It must be kept in mind and brought forward emphatically that Scientology does not work in the absence of official control and, no matter who sought to use its principles, has uniformly failed in the hands of non-Scientologists and organizations not controlled by the Central Organizations of Scientology or myself.

5. The reason for this declaration is the consistent disaster visited upon her "allies" by the United States government and the efforts of that government since 1955, stepped up since 1963, to seize Scientology in the United States rather than forbid or stop it and the role played by the United States in inspiring the Victorian State attacks in Australia. Scientology technology is no longer offered to the United States government in any effort to assist her in political ends. Our participation extends only to our willingness to process US officials as individuals unconnected with their political aims, if as individuals they are not debarred by other existing policies relating to treating the insane or our ethics system.

6. All statements attacking any political entity or ideology are hereby withdrawn and cancelled in any lectures or literature.

7. Scientologists may be members of any political group on this planet without restraint only so long as these individuals or that group do not attempt to seize Scientology for their own warlike ends and so make it unworkable or distasteful by invidious connection.

8. Scientology is for a free people and is itself on this date declared free of any political connection or allegiance of any kind whatever.

L. RON HUBBARD
Founder

THE AIMS OF SCIENTOLOGY

A civilization without insanity, without criminals and without war, where the able can prosper and honest beings can have rights, and where man is free to rise to greater heights, are the aims of Scientology.

Nonpolitical in nature, Scientology welcomes any individual of any creed, race or nation.

We seek no revolution. We seek only evolution to higher states of being for the individual and for society.

We are achieving our aims.

After endless millennia of ignorance about himself, his mind and the universe, a breakthrough has been made for man.

Other efforts man has made have been surpassed.

The combined truths of fifty thousand years of thinking men, distilled and amplified by new discoveries about man, have made for this success.

We welcome you to Scientology. We only expect of you your help in achieving our aims and helping others. We expect you to be helped.

Scientology is the most vital movement on Earth today.

In a turbulent world, the job is not easy. But then, if it were, we wouldn't have to be doing it.

We respect man and believe he is worthy of help. We respect you and believe you, too, can help.

Scientology does not owe its help. We have done nothing to cause us to propitiate. Had we done so, we would not now be bright enough to do what we are doing.

Man suspects all offers of help. He has often been betrayed, his confidence shattered. Too frequently he has given his trust and been betrayed. We may err, for we build a world with broken straws. But we will never betray your faith in us so long as you are one of us.

The sun never sets on Scientology.

And may a new day dawn for you, for those you love and for man.

Our aims are simple, if great.

And we will succeed, and are succeeding at each new revolution of the Earth.

Your help is acceptable to us.

Our help is yours.

L. RON HUBBARD
Founder

HUBBARD COMMUNICATIONS OFFICE
Saint Hill Manor, East Grinstead, Sussex

HCO EXECUTIVE LETTER OF 10 OCTOBER 1965
Gen. Non-Remimeo
Bulletin Board

TO: Scientologists

FROM: Ron

SUBJECT: **RON'S JOURNAL 17**

GOVERNMENT CONFLICTS

We entered our period of conflict with governments on 23 Jan. 1963 with the FDA Federal Marshal drawn-gun raid on the Washington Organization. Emboldened, Victoria State opposition party member Galbally began then his "enquiry."

It was inevitable we would have to clash in the governmental sphere and now the phase is approaching its end. The FDA matter will shortly be fully settled in our favor. The Victorian matter has reached its final explosion. In the latter, the attackers made so many errors they laid the sound foundation for suit against any and all papers carrying the "story." They were foolish enough to have secret meetings of hostile witnesses and then publish "suggested testimony" to them which while it may not be unlawful in Australia smells very bad in any other land.

I have worked on all this since January 1963, mining the road they would have to travel. And they are obligingly exploding the mines on schedule.

All we have to do now is smartly execute the plans and orders already prepared and very soon we will have a complete victory.

Then our government conflict phase will be over. With such victories to our credit other governments will not attack.

The keynote of our campaign has been to do right and keep our noses clean and thus render ourselves invulnerable to proper charges. The attackers thus had nothing to attack but their own idea of us. As this was false, winning points on them is very easy. In each case they attacked us for doing things we do not do.

The moral of it all is to be decent and effective and do our jobs and the sharpest spears cannot touch us.

There will be a lot of commotion now. It's all sound and fury. The main defense has been executed and the danger points are past.

I think the US papers by the way were so cowed by our FDA successes they ran nothing of the Victorian attack. We will of course sue now by reason of their slanders in the FDA matter.

During this period we have been mostly on the receiving end. We've taken about all they have to throw. Now it's our turn. We will start dishing it out. I doubt the persons responsible will take it as well as we have.

And don't forget that the time we bought gave us all the grades wrapped up *and* the technology of Clear, all on schedule.

In short, we're winning.

L. RON HUBBARD
Founder

HCO POLICY LETTER OF 15 FEBRUARY 1966
Issue I

Remimeo
Missions
FSMs

ATTACKS ON SCIENTOLOGY

(Cancels all Sec EDs and PLs to the contrary)

Having had some time to think this over and having studied the matter with great care, I have isolated the most successful response to meeting any and all attacks on Scientology, its organizations and Scientologists, and as of this date this becomes policy.

ADVOCATE TOTAL FREEDOM

That is the policy—advocate total freedom.

There are technical reasons for this which an auditor will recognize. To discharge later incidents from a mind, one must get the first or basic incident of that kind. In this case the basic aberrated incident was the suppression of freedom of the being. Just before that there must have been freedom. Thus, advocating total freedom hits the true basic incident.

This is also the basic purpose of Scientology and the basic purpose of people, so it all agrees well.

This is also easiest to do. It is easier than fighting parliaments or building up cases against people who attack us.

The only liability of using this policy (total freedom) is that it releases energy (a Scientologist knows this as "blowing locks") which looks disturbing but is weakened.

No other approach we have used worked. We are alive not because we fought but because we went on doing Scientology in spite of anything.

So never advertise an attack. Just advocate more strongly "Total Freedom!" and show how Scientology can attain it for the individual.

Careful summary of our past actions in the face of attacks and an analysis of various changes in human history show that the best and *only* effective thing we did or anyone ever did was advocate freedom. The precise practice of Scientology obtains total freedom, so never advertise anything else but total freedom and the Scientology services and steps that bring it about. Courses, processing are the gradient scale to total freedom.

That's the answer no nation or person can stand up to—if we keep saying it long and loud. SCIENTOLOGY IS THE ROAD TO TOTAL FREEDOM.

Used in argument, one can invent reasons to baffle the attacking agency or person—but all these reasons should add up to everyone has rights to total freedom.

I think this alone can move mountains.

L. RON HUBBARD
Founder

HUBBARD COMMUNICATIONS OFFICE
Saint Hill Manor, East Grinstead, Sussex

HCO POLICY LETTER OF 18 FEBRUARY 1966

Gen. Non-Remimeo
Exec Sec Hats
HCO Area Sec Hat
Legal Hat
Section 5 Hats

ATTACKS ON SCIENTOLOGY

(Continued)

(This PL augments HCO PL 15 Feb. 66,
ATTACKS ON SCIENTOLOGY.)

When you hold up an image of freedom, all those who oppress freedom tend to attack. Therefore, attacks, on whatever grounds, are inevitable. Holding up a freedom image is, however, the only successful forward action even though it gets attacked.

It remains, then, to take the handling of attacks off emergency, predict them and handle them by proper tactics and administrative machinery.

The first group of actions have *not* been effective in handling attacks (the G stands for group; the following are three different groups of actions):

G. 1.1. Hiring expensive outside professional firms;

G. 1.2. Writing Scientologists to write their representatives in government;

G. 1.3. Advertising the attack to the Scientology "field";

G. 1.4. Being carefully legal in our utterances.

This second group of actions have been of some small use in deterring attacks:

G. 2.1. Direct letters from the org to a congress or parliament (ruined the US Siberia Bill*);

G. 2.2. Circulating pamphlets about the attack (got rid of Wearne* out of the Enquiry);

G. 2.3. Suits against sources of libel and slander.

---

*Siberia Bill: a bill proposed in the US Congress in the mid 60s which would have made it possible for government officials in the US to simply pick up anyone on the street and send him to Alaska to be given "mental treatment"; its purpose was to use "mental health" practices to remove political dissenters. Called the "Siberia" bill after the Russian practice of sending political dissenters to Siberia, a remote, desolate region of the USSR.

*Wearne: Phillip Wearne, instigator of the Melbourne Enquiry in the early 60s. He later confessed and fully documented his lies and guilt in connection with the Australian attacks on Scientology. Died in 1970.

The third group of actions have been positive in stopping attacks:

G. 3.1. Investigating noisily the attackers;

G. 3.2. Not being guilty of anything;

G. 3.3. Having our corporate status in excellent condition;

G. 3.4. Having our tax returns and books accurate and punctual;

G. 3.5. Getting waivers from all people we sign up;

G. 3.6. Refunding money to dissatisfied people;

G. 3.7. Having our own professionals firmly on staff (but not halfway on staff);

G. 3.8. Going on advertising total freedom;

G. 3.9. Surviving and remaining solvent by stepping up our own usual activities;

G. 3.10. My catching the dropped balls goofed by others and hired professionals;

G. 3.11. Being religious in nature and corporate status.

As you read over the above, you should be able to see where our funds should be placed.

In the first group you can see large possible outlays to professional firms, attorneys, accountants. This is money utterly wasted. They flop and we have to do it all ourselves anyway. The fantastic cash cost of mailings to Scientologists was evident in DC where it ate up all their "freedom funds." And by advertising the attack to Scientologists, we only frighten them away from the org and lose our income as well. So we must *never* do these three things.

The second group above are not very costly and constitute a proper line of defense and should be undertaken. But they must *not* be counted on to do more than impede an attack. They will never stop it cold. This second group is like an infantry defensive action. It is necessary to oppose the enemy, but just opposing will not finally win the fight. That is done only by taking enemy territory.

The third group contains the real area for the outlay of funds and stress of planning. This group has an excellent history and has ended off a great many attacks, beginning in 1950. Therefore, one should take care not to leave any of these out whenever an attack is mounted on us.

INVESTIGATION

It is a curious phenomenon that the action of investigation alone is head and shoulders above all other actions.

This is most like Scientology processing, oddly enough, where the practitioner seeks the hidden points in a case. As soon as they are found, the case tends to recover, regardless of anything else done.

Groups that attack us are, to say the least, not sane. According to our technology, this means they have hidden areas and disreputable facts about them.

As soon as we begin to look for these, some of the insanity dissipates.

It is *greatly* in our favor that we are only attacked by mad groups, as people in that condition (1) invariably choose the wrong target and (2) have no follow-through. Thus, they are not hard to defeat providing one (A) looks for their hidden crimes and (B) is irreproachable in his conduct himself.

We discovered this more or less by accident. The basic discovery was that the interrogation of a policeman produces a confusion and an introversion; it is *his* job to interrogate—so you reverse the flow, mix up his "hat" so he doesn't know who is which, and you reach for his own doubts.

These people who attack have secrets. And hidden crimes. They are afraid. There is no doubt in their minds as to our validity or they wouldn't attack so hard at such cost. Society tolerates far worse than we are. So they really believe in us. This hampers their execution of orders—their henchmen really don't share the enthusiasm for the attack, for after a bit of investigation it becomes obvious to these henchmen that the attack smells. This impedes follow-through.

And when *we* investigate, all this recoils on the attacker. He withdraws too hurriedly to be orderly.

An attacker is like a housewife who tells city hall how terribly her neighbors keep house. But when you open *her* door, the dishpans and dirty diapers fall out on the porch.

All you have to do in lots of cases is just *say* you are going to rattle their door knob and they collapse.

I can count several heavy attacks which folded up by our noisily beginning an investigation of the attacker.

Our past liability in this was that we depended on outside firms, enquiry agencies, etc. And these have too many clients and we have too little control of their direction. The answer is to organize and maintain our own proper corps for this action.

The other items in the third group are self-explanatory, and if *any* of these are missing, then we will be less successful.

For years and years I have had this "hat" of attack handling. In January 1963 I took a calculated risk and devoted my time to research. I knew we had better get all our answers and complete our technology. But in doing so I could give only a small amount of time to the US and Australian attacks. DC followed orders and we got out of the US morass. Australia didn't and sank. But it became plain to me that we had to set up a part of our orgs to handle this "hat," as obviously I can't be there forever. So even #10 in the third group—my catching dropped balls goofed by others and hired professionals—will have to have help.

———————

To hold up to man an image of spiritual freedom is adventurous. Man is suppressed. And those who oppress him have a peculiar frame of reference.

This is:

1. If anyone became free or powerful, a suppressive believes he would promptly be slaughtered. He never realizes that it is the suppression that gets him knocked out, not the character of man.

2. If any advance were made that would improve man, then all old commercial interests with *their* answers would become worthless. It never occurs to such to advance with the times.

3. They have dirty houses.

Thus, in meeting any attack we must:

A. Recognize an attack in time to act;

B. Get Group 3 above in full action with an emphasis on investigation;

C. Get Group 2 in action as needful for defense.

Thus, we have LOOK, INVESTIGATE, DEFEND as the short formula. And all the while hold up an image of total freedom and have, ourselves, clean hands.

L. RON HUBBARD
Founder

INVESTIGATIONS

HCO POLICY LETTER OF 1 SEPTEMBER 1969R
REVISED 24 SEPTEMBER 1983

Remimeo
All Orgs
Int Finance
    Office
FBOs
Legal Dept

COUNTERESPIONAGE

Refs:

HCO PL	12 Oct. 82	CORRUPT ACTIVITIES
HCO PL	14 Mar. 82	FINANCIAL IRREGULARITIES
HCO PL	13 Jan. 83	THE BUSINESS OF ORGS

No country or company has ever solved espionage and intelligence actions within it.

Industrial "espionage" is a very prevalent activity.

As our policy letters and materials are often found in wrong hands, we must be subjected to internal espionage on occasion. We certainly are subjected to intelligence externally.

Intelligence actions internally in a company or organization take five main courses:

1. Theft of documents or materials.

2. Executive actions contrary to the company's best interests, if not outright destructive.

3. Administrative enturbulation, including messing up files, addresses, facilities or communications.

4. False reports or false advices to customers or staff to bring about apathy or defeatism.

5. Perversion or corruption of the product (in our case, technology).

MOTIVES

Financial gain is the primary motive in almost all cases of infiltration.

A very experienced European intelligence officer stated that he had never failed to buy any person he had ever approached in any government, and this in a lifetime career in the field of espionage.

Governments and many companies have amongst them people who are in or who can be forced into heavy financial trouble.

By offering surprisingly small sums of money, any one of the five actions listed above could be effected by an enemy.

The practice is so common as to be commonplace, but the harm done is all out of proportion to the effort employed.

1033

A SOLUTION

Guarding against infiltration is a vital action for survival, and nations and companies spend huge sums on counterintelligence, the action of foiling the efforts of enemies.

In studying the extensive literature of this subject, an inexpensive, effective solution has occurred to me which I do not think has ever been used.

If finance is the motive, then of course one should reward successful counterintelligence actions.

An enemy seeks those in debt or forces persons into debt so they can be bought. If the person being baited were assured of a safer reward, the person would usually incline toward his own country or company.

THE PLACARD

An org should therefore display in an area mostly frequented by staff, near the staff bulletin board or in the wc, but not necessarily to the public, a placard worded somewhat as follows:

REWARD

As industrial espionage is an ordinary occurrence in most companies, the staff is requested to be alert for:

1. Any theft of documents or materials.

2. Orders or directions which will result destructively.

3. Any disturbance of files, bills or addresses.

4. False reports or advices to staff or customers or preached defeatism.

5. Willful corruption of tech.

Anyone detecting any of the above should report the matter at once to the Reports Officer, Religious Technology Center, with names and full particulars.

Should further investigation result in the disclosure and apprehension or arrest of persons attempting willful harm to this organization

A REWARD OF $1,000.00

will be paid by the International Finance Office.

Should a staff member be approached and asked to attempt any of the above actions, he should promptly seem to agree, should accept any money offered (which he may keep) and should quickly and quietly report the matter to the Religious Technology Center so that the instigators can be traced and arrested, at which time the $1,000.00 reward will be paid after the apprehension, arrest and conviction of the person(s) attempting the willful harm to this organization.

Another reward of $400.00 will be paid any staff member or person in the field who should hear of or be subjected to any provocative antiorganization activity in the field and who then forwards sufficient evidence of the criminal background and connections of the provocative person in such form that it may be given to the police by the Religious Technology Center.

Should any staff member have knowledge of any financial irregularity within the organization and furnish proof of it to the Int Finance Office and RTC promptly along with evidence sufficient to successfully prosecute, he shall be given a reward equivalent to 25 percent of all monies recovered or $1,000.00 whichever is less.

BLACKMAIL

Any person or agency attempting to accomplish any of the above five points by reason of attempted BLACKMAIL of a staff member is liable to arrest. In this case the reward is also paid to the staff member on the arrest and conviction of those attempting the blackmail.

Staffs are requested to cooperate fully to help continue to make an org and area a safe environment from which freedom may expand.

Alertness is the penalty we pay for living in an aberrated society.

Truth cannot live in an atmosphere of deceit.

Religious Technology Center
(address)

The amount of the rewards may be changed from time to time. It is the responsibility of the Int Finance Office to update the amount of the rewards in the future.

ORG'S PROTECTION

Our Dianetics and Scientology orgs are fortunate in that where tech is "in" very little infiltration can occur since persons cannot benefit from things they try to harm.

Our primary protection is "in" tech and well-processed staffs. It follows that when tech is out, ethics will be found out also.

Persons who have no or little case gain are the only ones we have any trouble with.

No other organization and no country has as good a chance as ours to be free of infiltration.

One other thing worthy of note in connection with counterintelligence is that countries and companies which do not have a high cause, a high allegiance, have need of tremendous counterintelligence forces.

If we keep our integrity high and give staffs good and valuable government, we will have maximum counterintelligence effectiveness with minimum effort since our staffs would themselves militantly defend their executives and the org.

L. RON HUBBARD
Founder

HCO POLICY LETTER OF 12 OCTOBER 1982

CORRUPT ACTIVITIES

Ref:
HCO PL 22 July 82   KNOWLEDGE REPORTS

The corrupt activities of a few deprive the many of their pay and an activity its prosperity.

The result of out-ethics in *any* long-run situation is contraction and poverty for all concerned, even the perpetrator.

A staff member who privately sells org prospect lists to a squirrel, the I/C who lets the org get ripped off for some personal favor, are actionable, of course, under criminal law. But their suicidal action is not the point here: They are selling out their friends and fellow staff members, messing up an org for no real benefit to anyone—not even the criminal rip-off artist.

The one who would do it, the org, the field, all suffer for it one way or another.

Only in-ethics can deliver standard tech.

Only a staff that is alert to such actions and reports those they cannot stop directly by a very stern, direct confrontation with the culprit in private can be sure of their own pay and working conditions and can expand an org.

Why moonlight or be in poverty when in-ethics can bring prosperity to all?

L. RON HUBBARD
Founder

PUBLIC RELATIONS

HCO INFORMATION LETTER OF 10 DECEMBER 1963

MA
BPI

SCIENTOLOGY ZERO

THE DANGEROUS ENVIRONMENT
THE TRUE STORY OF SCIENTOLOGY

The true story of Scientology is simple, concise and direct. It is quickly told:

1. A doctor of philosophy developed a philosophy about life and death;

2. People find it interesting;

3. People find it works;

4. People pass it along to others;

5. It grows.

When we examine this extremely accurate and very brief account we see that there must be amongst us some very disturbing elements for anything else to be believed about Scientology.

These disturbing elements are the merchants of chaos. They deal in confusion and upset. Their daily bread is made by creating chaos. If chaos were to lessen, so would their incomes.

The politician, the reporter, the medico, the drug manufacturer, the militarist and arms manufacturer, the police and the undertaker, to name the leaders of the list, fatten only upon "the dangerous environment." Even individuals and family members can be merchants of chaos.

It is to their interest to make the environment seem as threatening as possible for only then can they profit. Their incomes, force and power rise in direct ratio to the amount of threat they can inject into the surroundings of the people. With that threat they can extort revenue, appropriations, heightened circulations and recompense without question. These are the merchants of chaos. If they did not generate it and buy and sell it, they would, they suppose, be poor.

For instance, we speak loosely of "good press." Is there any such thing today? Look over a newspaper. Is there anything *good* on the front page? Rather there is murder and sudden death, disagreement and catastrophe. And even that, bad as it is, is sensationalized to make it seem worse.

This is the coldblooded manufacture of "a dangerous environment." People do not need this news and if they did they need the facts, not the upset. But if you hit a person hard enough he can be made to give up money. That's the basic formula of extortion. That's the way papers are sold. The impact makes them stick.

A paper has to have chaos and confusion. A "news story" has to have "conflict" they say. So there is no good press. There is only *bad* press about everything. To yearn for "good press" is foolhardy in a society where the merchants of chaos reign.

Look what has to be done to the true story of Scientology in order to "make it a news story" by modern press standards. Conflict must be injected where there is none. Therefore the press has to dream up upset and conflict.

Let us take the first line. How does one make conflict out of it? "(1) A doctor of philosophy develops a philosophy about life and death."

The chaos merchant *has* to inject one of several possible conflicts here: He is not a doctor of philosophy, they have to assert. They are never quite bold enough to say it is not a philosophy. But they can and do go on endlessly as their purpose compels them, in an effort to invalidate the identity of the person developing it.

In actual fact, the developer of the philosophy was very well grounded in academic subjects and the humanities, probably better grounded in formal philosophy alone than teachers of philosophy in universities.

The one man effort is incredible in terms of study and research hours and is a record never approached in living memory but this would not be considered newsworthy. To write the simple fact that a doctor of philosophy had developed a philosophy is not newspaper-type news and it would not disturb the environment. Hence the elaborate news fictions about (1) above.

Then take the second part of the true story. "People find it interesting." It would be very odd if they didn't, as everyone asks these questions of himself and looks for the answers to his own beingness, and the basic truth of the answers is observable in the conclusions of Scientology.

However, to make this "news" it has to be made disturbing. People are painted as kidnapped or hypnotized and dragged as unwilling victims up to read the books or listen.

The chaos merchant leaves (3) very thoroughly alone. It is dangerous ground for him. "People find it works." No hint of workability would ever be attached to Scientology by the press, although there is no doubt in the press mind that it *does* work. That's why it's dangerous. It calms the environment. So any time spent trying to convince press Scientology works is time spent upsetting a reporter.

On "(4) People pass it along to others," press feels betrayed. Nobody should believe anything they don't read in the papers. How dare word-of-mouth exist? So to try to stop people from listening the chaos merchant has to use words like "cult." That's a closed group. And they have to attack organizations and their people to try to keep people out of Scientology.

Now as for "(5) It grows," we have the true objection.

As truth goes forward, lies die. The slaughter of lies is an act that takes bread from the mouth of a chaos merchant. Unless he can lie with wild abandon about how bad it all is, he thinks he will starve.

The world simply must *not* be a better place according to the chaos merchant. If people were less disturbed, less beaten down by their environments, there would be no new appropriations for police and armies and big rockets and there'd be not even pennies for a screaming sensational press.

So long as politicians move upward on scandal, police get more pay for more crime, medicos get fatter on more sickness, there will be merchants of chaos. They're paid for it.

And their threat is the simple story of Scientology. For that is the true story. And behind its progress there is a calmer environment in which a man can live and feel better. If you don't believe it, just stop reading newspapers for 2 weeks and see if you feel better. Suppose you had all such disturbances handled?

The pity of it is, of course, that even the merchant of chaos needs us, not to get fatter but just to live himself as a being.

So the true story of Scientology is a simple story.

And too true to be turned aside.

L. RON HUBBARD
Founder

HUBBARD COMMUNICATIONS OFFICE
Saint Hill Manor, East Grinstead, Sussex

HCO POLICY LETTER OF 25 MAY 1964
Issue II

Gen. Non-Remimeo

PRESS RELATIONS

(Originally written by LRH as an HCO PL on
25 May 64 and then later reissued on 11 Oct. 65)

These instructions are based on a wide experience of how the press, and journalists generally, write about Scientology. They apply not only to daily and weekly newspapers but to all journalists of any kind—magazines, periodicals, "serious," comic, scurrilous, etc.

Press relations should be entrusted to, and handled by, only one person in an org. This person is specially appointed to the post. Any good Scientologist should be able to do it. NOT a professional public relations man. The person chosen should be capable of good communication on Level 0 and Level I. Anyone who can run a good PE Course and who is known not to Q and A would be suitable.

The post is not even vaguely full time, not even part time. The hat is assumed only when a journalist writes in or telephones or tries to contact the org about anything. The Press Relations Officer then handles it. All correspondence, cables, telephone calls—anything—are handled *only* by the Press Relations Officer. If he or she is not available, the switchboard operator or Receptionist answers only, "Mr. _____ (the Press Relations Officer) is not available. There is no one else here who can handle it." All inquiries should be handled courteously, but there are no exceptions to the rule.

No one else except the Press Relations Officer handles any press or journalist communications of any kind.

The Press Relations Officer should answer inquiries only on a Scientology Zero basis—maybe a little of Scientology One. He or she is polite but is not tempted into giving any other information about Scientology. Do not Q and A. All other inquiries (not directly concerned with Scientology data) may usually be answered factually but will almost certainly be misduplicated, quoted out of context or misrepresented in some way.

The stable datum is: The press will not print anything good—only bad. So give them nothing that can be misunderstood.

(Note: This does not alter the truth contained in HCO PL of 14 Aug. 63, PRESS POLICIES. But it should be borne in mind by those who handle press relations that experience has shown that the press prints its own preconceived story anyway. So keep it brief, be sincere, don't defend, don't attack. Don't Q and A. And you'll win.)

L. RON HUBBARD
Founder

HUBBARD COMMUNICATIONS OFFICE
Saint Hill Manor, East Grinstead, Sussex

HCO POLICY LETTER OF 28 OCTOBER 1968

PRESS RELEASES

A press release should be on one subject ONLY and this one subject is used in variations time and again. When the press are tired of that subject, then another one is used and that one is ridden until it likewise is worn out.

Also press releases should always contain some factor of endurance. This gives the public the idea that we endure. Examples:

"For many years now we have stated . . ."

"We have stood up to such attacks many times and are still surviving and expanding."

"Since 1950 we have . . ."

"Eighteen years ago . . ."

A good time to make press releases is on a Monday. Newspapers have shot all their bolts in the Sunday newspapers, so this makes Monday a rather quiet day for news.

So remember—push one subject until that has worn thin, add endurance and release press stories on Monday.

ALWAYS ATTACK in a press release. Never defend or deny.

L. RON HUBBARD
Founder

HCO POLICY LETTER OF 3 FEBRUARY 1969

Remimeo

PUBLIC IMAGE

For a long while we have not had an exactly stated policy on building a public image. We have just been ourselves and done our jobs and hoped somebody would catch on. This is basically what protected us. And we should keep doing it.

But the time has come to also build a public image as an outflow publicity action.

The image is:

SCIENTOLOGISTS ARE THE PEOPLE WHO ARE CLEANING UP THE FIELD OF MENTAL HEALING AND EFFECTIVELY HANDLING MENTAL HEALTH ON THE PLANET.

Note that it is dual. We will handle the first part of it first, "cleaning up the field of mental healing." It is a dirty, inhuman, rotten field, full of graft, misappropriation, phony authoritarianism and betrayal. Because it is like this we get a backflash from it. We are the only ones in it who have clean hands and effective technology. So we have no choice but to NOISILY clean it up. That builds that much of the image. By uniting with other civic, humanitarian, and civil- and human-rights groups we can make an organized progress.

For the second part, we are already doing it to a degree. "Effectively handling mental healing on the planet" is what we are being effective in doing. But we don't make enough public image with it. We keep building the image to Scientologists. We must study how to do it outside.

We have clean hands. We are effective. We dedicatedly do our jobs well. We must keep on doing this.

But we have to find more PUBLIC ways to SAY so.

It would also be a good policy to have two PROs. One specializes and plans to clean up the field of mental healing and grabs allied-organization support, holds committee meetings, works on crusades about it, gets close to top publishers and really *scareheads* the world or area about the abuses to human rights in the field.

The other PRO works to banner head the successes and the programs to effectively handle mental healing on the planet. He also gets support from allied organizations (different than human-rights attacks) like churches, and gets a crusade going for handling all the mental healing problems, not just using Scientology.

In both instances you have to go civic, go outside Scientology, get support, organize committees, plot out campaigns, work for outside finance, etc.

In handling the above public image policy, you don't announce the policy. You use it for a guide to keep pounding variations of the same message.

The policy is expressed in community *action,* well press covered, not just in statements. Committee meetings, deputations, picketing, big names, events.

You figure out the story that will be written, then *do* it, seeing it gets covered by having the press to hand.

Make all issues hot, exciting, brutal or sensational. Go strictly circus in the type of message.

You can and must ally with real humanitarian and civil-rights groups (getting press coverage for every such contact).

You can and must approach governors, parliamentary committees, big names, big activities *and* get press coverage for every contact.

Scientology speakers must address groups and *say* the story which is to appear, not just talk about Scientology.

Plan a program, let it run awhile. The program is based on the policy which is the major target—to make that public image. When *that* program damps out, get a *new* program. It takes a while to beat a program into the public mind. They last a few months.

This is almost standard PRO work. The press prints "hard" news. Hard news is an event, a meeting, the formation of something, an attack, a campaign. It is not a statement.

You can and must seize the attention of the press in your area, not to defend Scientology, but to hammer home the above public image by forwarding crusades and campaigns that carry the message. Then providing events of your own manufacture. Then seeing they get reported in the press, on radio and TV.

Don't defend Scientology; attack bad conditions and bad hats.

It is a dismal flub to force a parliament to consider a bill outlawing psychiatry and then provide no other event about it or press coverage. It has to be planned, targeted. You have to have other groups start talking, public meetings, a deputation to the governor.

Build up Scientology celebrities that can speak and meet the public in your area.

And in doing all this, don't tear up the Scientology org or distract it too much or you will not have any money to do the job with. You will have lost what you're trying to save.

PRO is an energetic, imaginative fiery-eyed function. It has to be hot—hot on getting compliance, scheduling and events.

PRO should know all about targets, dev-t, and this PL.

Scientology has been the object of enemy PRO campaigns of a professional level for years. Study if you like the stunts *he* pulled. How did *he* do it? Just by using names, connections and press. So reverse the action. Do it *far* better.

Our end product is a sane planet. His was a dead one. So with all the theta in our lines and purpose, Scientology PRO to the PUBLIC can be ten-thousand times as effective and worthwhile.

This public image can and *must* be built if this planet is to survive at all.

L. RON HUBBARD
Founder

HCO POLICY LETTER OF 5 FEBRUARY 1969R
Issue I
REVISED 15 MAY 1973

Remimeo

PRESS POLICY

CODE OF A SCIENTOLOGIST

The Code of a Scientologist as per *The Creation of Human Ability* is withdrawn. It is reissued as follows:

As a Scientologist, I pledge myself to the Code of Scientology for the good of all.

1. To keep Scientologists, the public and the press accurately informed concerning Scientology, the world of mental health and society.

2. To use the best I know of Scientology to the best of my ability to help my family, friends, groups and the world.

3. To refuse to accept for processing and to refuse to accept money from any preclear or group I feel I cannot honestly help.

4. To decry and do all I can to abolish any and all abuses against life and mankind.

5. To expose and help abolish any and all physically damaging practices in the field of mental health.

6. To help clean up and keep clean the field of mental health.

7. To bring about an atmosphere of safety and security in the field of mental health by eradicating its abuses and brutality.

8. To support true humanitarian endeavors in the fields of human rights.

9. To embrace the policy of equal justice for all.

10. To work for freedom of speech in the world.

11. To actively decry the suppression of knowledge, wisdom, philosophy or data which would help mankind.

12. To support the freedom of religion.

13. To help Scientology orgs and groups ally themselves with public groups.

14. To teach Scientology at a level it can be understood and used by the recipients.

15. To stress the freedom to use Scientology as a philosophy in all its applications and variations in the humanities.

16. To insist upon standard and unvaried Scientology as an applied activity in ethics, processing and administration in Scientology organizations.

17. To take my share of responsibility for the impact of Scientology upon the world.

18. To increase the numbers and strength of Scientology over the world.

19. To set an example of the effectiveness and wisdom of Scientology.

20. To make this world a saner, better place.

L. RON HUBBARD
Founder

HUBBARD COMMUNICATIONS OFFICE
Saint Hill Manor, East Grinstead, Sussex

HCO POLICY LETTER OF 28 FEBRUARY 1982

Remimeo

NEWS

News media is parasitic on those who make news. It is not true that those who make news need the news at all.

Who needs cancer?

L. RON HUBBARD
Founder

LEGAL

ACTIVITIES OF LEGAL DEPARTMENT

1. Care and correction of all corporation status and minute books.

2. Filing of proper and timely tax returns or representations.

3. Handling of correspondence relating to suits, as may appear.

4. Proper wording and legality of legal papers of the organizations, such as waivers and notes.

5. Collection of overdue payments or notes from individuals as indicated by the Accounting Department.

6. General advices to Board of Directors.

7. Other legal matters as may appear. All legal communications falling under the above should be forwarded to the Legal Department.

L. RON HUBBARD
Founder

FOUNDING CHURCH POLICY LETTER OF 8 JUNE 1957

(Convert also to a HASI Policy Letter)

VALUABLE DOCUMENTS, HANDLING OF

All valuable documents are to be stored in a safe under the control of the Treasurer and the Organization Secretary. These include contracts, notes, official papers, awards, etc. The criteria of "valuable" is "Would their loss financially or publicly embarrass the organization?"

All such documents shall be photostated in duplicate or triplicate when received. In case of backlog, these shall be done now.

Boards, solicitors, accountants or officers of the corporation shall not *use* the originals. These persons shall use only photostats.

The originals shall not leave the safe save only to be photostated and then shall be at once returned with *one* photostat of it attached to each.

"The valuable document file" shall be another file than the safe, shall be kept by the Org Sec and shall consist only of photostats in folders which say what the document in the folder is so that removing the last copy shall not thus injure the file. A duplicate "valuable document file" shall be forwarded to the president. (In London, agent for GB.)

It is the responsibility of the Org Sec to see that all such documents are collected and that their disposition thereafter shall be as above.

L. RON HUBBARD
Founder

HCO POLICY LETTER OF 15 NOVEMBER 1958
Issue I

THE SUBSTANCE AND FIRST DUTY OF HCO

The most important function of HCO in any organization is that which justifies its existence.

Being the purveyor of ethics, technology and awards, HCO must then, first and foremost of all its duties, be the keeper of every seal, copyright, trademark, registered mark, master tape, master book copy and master bulletin file in the organization.

HCO Secretaries should act at once to take unto themselves and keep locked secure and not available to anyone else, the seals of the organization in the area. HCO seals for certificate validation or sealing are HCO's by right. Organization seals are held by HCO for the "Secretarial of the Executive Director" of HASI. If HCO sees or hears of any new seals being made up for whatever purpose, the order is "Seize and ask for instructions later."

None are permitted to use such seals or any seals except HCO.

All this applies now and later. And it will become more important as time goes on.

Seals, regulation of, permits only legal certificates, documents and minutes to be sealed.

Similarly, any book on Dianetics and Scientology must be copyrighted in the name of L. Ron Hubbard, and the copyright becomes the property of HCO. No copyright of anything must ever be permitted to escape. In the case of its having been done (a book on the subject copyrighted in the name of someone or something else), HCO Secretary in the area must request an assignment of copyright to L. Ron Hubbard from its present owner and must be tireless and remorseless in getting the copyright, using any available means at whatever cost.

Similarly any trademark, registered mark or patent for any sign, symbol, shield, device or design for Dianetics or Scientology or their organizations must be secured for HCO. All these are registered to L. Ron Hubbard and by blanket transfer are the property of HCO only. The name in which it is done is L. Ron Hubbard; the owner is then HCO.

In the case of a new symbol, design, shield, device or name, HCO registers the mark first and argues afterwards. Don't worry ever about cost in this. They're priceless to HCO and other people like to tell HCO it's too much trouble or too expensive, leaving the matter susceptible to piracy.

Master tapes, master book copies, master bulletin files are all the property of

HCO. Seize, hold, reissue only when you are sure *you* have your master copy and that the inferior copies can be issued without hurting your file.

HCO Secretaries have in this their first order of action, their first and continuingly most important duty. The items mentioned here are even ahead of paycheck since they *are* the source of paychecks for all.

Register anything, copyright anything, seize anything like this in the country of the HCO area, entirely independent of any other or the main HCO office.

Only when you have all these do you have an HCO.

Don't let one seal, one copyright, one design, one device or even the names Dianetics and Scientology escape you on this. All the money you need to hire experts, lawyers, artists and pay fees is yours for the asking from the main office of HCO. Just ask.

What is the first duty of a new HCO Secretary? Seals, copyrights, marks, tapes, bulletins and books.

What is her chief, continuing duty? Seals, copyrights, marks, tapes, bulletins and books, keeping them registered, registering any new ones and using those we have.

What is her substance of office? Seals, copyrights, marks, tapes, bulletins and books.

What is her authority for being in office? My orders, the seals, copyrights, marks, tapes, bulletins and books.

She does not copy tapes from tapes or sell books or bulletins. She is the source of the copy people use to copy or print and use and sell. She is *source* in her area.

Given no part of this we have no HCO, no Dianetics, no Scientology, no Clear Earth. All is confusion everywhere. Given it, we have indeed brought order.

Concentrate on doing this. All else that we do then falls into line. Bring order first to our substance—seals, ethics, technology and awards. If we don't own it, we can't tell anyone anything. And we *do* own it. Only we have to collect it.

Our possessions must not be permitted to lie in the rain.

L. RON HUBBARD
Founder

HCO POLICY LETTER OF 15 NOVEMBER 1958
Issue II

LEGAL AID—HCO

Any HCO Secretary anywhere is fully authorized to incur any expense to secure or make the seals, file or transfer or assign the copyrights, trademarks or registered marks of Dianetics and Scientology, secure a tape library and a master book and bulletin file and protect and safeguard these.

An HCO Secretary may hire, independent of her usual solicitors and definitely independent of the solicitors of the area organization, lawyers or attorneys who are experts on copyrights and trademarks to (1) train her in their use and value and (2) secure them to her office in execution of this bulletin.

L. RON HUBBARD
Founder

HCO POLICY LETTER OF 15 NOVEMBER 1958
Issue III

OUTSTANDING COPYRIGHTS AND MARKS

No book issued on Dianetics and Scientology by any other author than myself has received my permission to copyright in any name but L. Ron Hubbard. If any book or pamphlet has been so copyrighted or any design trademarked, it is illegal. The holder must be persuaded to assign or made to assign or sued until assignment is made. We never close such a case and never falter in expending money to accomplish this.

A simple request is ordinarily enough.

To leave one copyright outstanding anywhere is unthinkable.

All copyrights are made to L. Ron Hubbard, then after "my demise" it says in the franchise, to L. Ron Hubbard, Founder. But *all* copyrights, marks and rights, by blanket assignment, are the property of and will remain the property of HCO, Ltd., the main office. Although the copyright is to L. Ron Hubbard, it becomes by that the property of HCO with no further administrative action by reason of existing contracts and franchises.

L. RON HUBBARD
Founder

HCO POLICY LETTER OF 22 NOVEMBER 1958

Distribute Widely
Include 5th London
ACC

OWNER OF MATERIALS
THE LEGAL VIEW

The HCO is owner and custodian of all tapes, publications, bulletins and materials of Scientology.

This material even when sold is still the property as to content of HCO. The physical tape, the paper, the covers, the boxes can be sold but the actual content of the tape or book is basically, by law, still owned. The fact of buying a book does not transfer data into other ownership which can then sell it. This is common practice and law and is necessary to safeguard the ethics of the subject as well as the trademarks and copyrights. The material does not pass into a new ownership for resale when a tape or book is sold.

ANNOUNCEMENT OF MATERIAL AVAILABLE

The 5th London ACC tapes and the 5th London ACC Question Periods tapes will not be pressed, sold or copied for any purpose. They are retained by HCO for use in teaching ACCs. The reason: Engram running is not easily taught and general release of data could be dangerous.

Students, however, are free to use it all they please or "own it" in a Scientology (not a legal) sense.

Therefore, we have students who are experts and can audit the materials but we do not enfranchise students to teach or release these 5th London materials.

Instead, I am making a series of HPA/HCA lectures in the near future and putting them on records. ACC students will be free to buy these and play them to Scientologists.

Dianetics: The Modern Science of Mental Health and *Science of Survival* are soon to be available in any quantity for anywhere.

Congress lectures are now on records and are available to all Scientologists anywhere and it is recommended that *these only* be played publicly.

L. RON HUBBARD
Founder

All HCO Personnel
All HCO Secretaries

When in doubt about copyrighting it, copyright it. Copyright and trademark anything and everything.

L. RON HUBBARD
Founder

HCO POLICY LETTER OF 4 JUNE 1959
Issue I

Convert to
Sec ED

INSTRUCTIONS TO ATTORNEY OR SOLICITORS
HCO AREA SEC ENFORCE

It is my prerogative to instruct attorneys, lawyers, barristers and solicitors and to hold correspondence and conferences with them and to advise them.

PENALTY

Any Scientology organization personnel seeking advices from attorneys, etc., without obtaining permission from me or passing them through me, shall be subject to loss of 50 percent of units each week for ten weeks.

REASON

No attorney or solicitor has materially assisted us when not instructed by me, and money has been lost and organizations damaged by approaching attorneys or solicitors without authorization on behalf of the organization.

DEPUTY PERMISSION

In my absence only a member of the International Council or his deputy may approach attorneys or solicitors and either myself or the International Chairman must be fully informed before any action of importance may be undertaken.

L. RON HUBBARD
Founder

HUBBARD COMMUNICATIONS OFFICE
37 Fitzroy Street, London W1

HCO POLICY LETTER OF 4 JULY 1959

BPI
MA

ACTIONS FOR HCO SECRETARIES
FACED WITH ILLEGAL USAGE

L. Ron Hubbard and the Hubbard Communications Office, Ltd., are the proprietors of all trademarks, copyrights and materials of Dianetics and Scientology.

Any organization using the word Scientology or its name or copyrights or materials without permission from LRH or HCO is liable to suit for copyright and trademark infringement, which suits can recover all funds collected by a person unlawfully using the trademarks or materials plus sizable damages.

HASIs, Churches of Scientology, mission holders, persons holding certificates in good order, and members may use these materials under certain conditions and issue those certificates permitted by HCO.

Unauthorized use of materials, trademarks, copyrights, *must* be prosecuted at once by HCO Secretaries. No further permission is needed than this policy letter. Lawyers can be engaged, suits filed and persons prosecuted on these grounds by any HCO Secretary on her own initiative, requiring only the HCO WW be advised. This includes use of materials in books not authorized in writing from HCO WW.

Any organization illegally constituted and illegally using the copyrights, trademarks or materials of Dianetics and Scientology must be ruthlessly handled. Further, any auditor joining such organization is subject to certificate suspension or revocation and fines proportionate to damage done. The officers of such illegal organizations shall be separately sued on the charge of fraud and charged additionally with criminal fraud for obtaining money, dues, contributions or fees under false pretenses, and where such an organization shall have used the mails, the matter shall be reported by the HCO Secretary to postal authorities with a request to arrest the offenders for mail fraud.

The only way we can continue ethical standards is to control practice. On ethical practice depends the success of dissemination, so stamp hard on all such offenses.

We are the government of Scientology and must measure up to our responsibilities.

L. RON HUBBARD
Founder

Note: The certificate of Sylvan Stein has been suspended for seeking to obtain money through the mails by pretending to have an ownership of materials and pretending to be a nonexistent organization named "The International Guild of Professional Scientologists." Further criminal action will be taken.

HUBBARD COMMUNICATIONS OFFICE
Saint Hill Manor, East Grinstead, Sussex

HCO BULLETIN OF 18 JULY 1959

BPI—US only
but by mailing,
not *Ability*

INCOME TAX REFORM

Please write the enclosed letter to (1) your leading local paper and (2) your representatives in Congress.

America needs your help to survive and we need your help to spread and effect a postulate as a mass-postulate test. This test is to determine the amount of mest communication necessary to change the "mind" of a governing agency. In this last respect it is purely research. But it is also a good idea. Let's do it. Your ability to postulate is workable, too. Please tell us if you have done it.

———————

Dear ———,

There comes a time in the history of any country when tax collection activities become a disease that its economy cannot bear. Such a disease is ordinarily healed by revolt, inflation or financial collapse. The primary source of disintegration in all governments, whether ancient Egypt or modern America, is tax voracity or abuses.

While fighting a cold front with communism, the US is violently cooperating with communist aims by destroying her individual confidence and initiative with a Marxist tax reform. The basic principles of US income tax were taken from *Das Kapital* and are aimed at destroying capitalism. Unless the US ceases to cooperate with this Red push, communism could win in America.

The reform of all income tax laws is needed for other reasons. (1) To increase government revenues in order to support defense. (2) To prevent spiraling inflation and another stock market collapse and (3) to return the US to the basic principles of democracy as opposed to economic tyranny.

The following program should accomplish all desirable ends. The only "losers" are the people now gaining tax bonuses and the Kremlin.

If America cannot act rationally on this matter of tax abuse, she is condemned to a crash, another depression and communist dominance in the world.

Income tax reforms that would stabilize US economy and could win an election:

Charge as tax 5% of all gross income and forbid taxes on net incomes.

Abolish criminal penalties for tax failures; substitute higher percentiles of gross for failures to pay.

Forbid use of employers' or taxpayers' time to actually collect taxes from others (no second party tax duties).

Forbid payments of bonuses or awards to tax personnel or informants for tax collections.

Make tax personnel personally liable for all public actions if illegal or damaging.

Forbid the payment of tax on tax monies paid; sums paid to internal revenue; tax payments to be an expense, all retroactive.

Delete the political aspect from income tax; make it a financial transaction, not an advance of the principles of Karl Marx aimed to penalize leadership or initiative.

Delete all criminal aspects from income tax law, not using penalties about taxation to arrest men whose other crimes are suspected but cannot be proven by other law agencies; the payment of tax, if it is to be effected, must not be associated in the public mind with the actions of gangsters.

Use the income tax amendment to collect taxes, not fight capitalism or the inequalities of ability amongst a people.

Forbid the invasion of privacy of personal transactions and activities in order to collect tax beyond the examination of a corporation's books by a qualified accountant.

Cease to penalize corporation executives exclusively because their accounts departments fail them—penalize only the accountants who refuse to work or who make the errors, since management today is becoming difficult where the person actually making the errors and omissions cannot be touched.

Forbid complex forms for taxation purposes; allow only forms which list income and calculate its gross percentage.

If the ills of income tax practice are not cured by swift law, they will be cured by (a) economic collapse, (b) Russian victory, (c) a revolt of the people or (d) the abandonment of democracy in favor of a fascist state.

America can no longer afford the deadly disease of economic punishment in the name of income tax. This, more surely than H-bombs, is destroying her future.

The aim of the Kremlin is to destroy the US economic system. In 1911, the US altered her constitution to admit a Marxist tax principle. This was the first germ of the present economic disease.

It can be handled in such a way as to save civilization or it can be ignored with the consequence of total destruction.

A way has been hoped for that would give the government her revenues for defense without wrecking the economy. This is such a way since political popularity can be bought by it without sacrificing government revenues.

L. RON HUBBARD
Founder

HCO POLICY LETTER OF 30 AUGUST 1962

CenOCon

GENERAL FORM OF RELEASE CONTRACT

The following form is applicable for the preparation of all release contracts and should be put into effect as soon as feasible. All old release contract forms should not be used.

The general tenor of the contract states that the Central Organization takes full responsibility for clearing the individual to the state of "First Goal Clear" by reason of his enrollment in the HGC.

The person enrolling undertakes on his behalf to pay for processing delivered as per usual arrangements up to such time as he has attained the validated state of "First Goal Clear" as verified by HCO.

The contract makes no allowance for time spent in the HGC, gives no commitments or guarantee of actually attaining the state of Clear, and does not in any way offer any inducement to the individual by way of special handling or treatment, but only states as above that the Central Organization takes full responsibility for processing a person up to the state of "First Goal Clear."

The individual on his behalf undertakes to continue forward to this state at such times and periods as is possible for him to make himself available for processing, and at his cost and expense.

The contract particularly stipulates that the individual must cooperate in this activity to the best of his ability and must not place obstacles in the way of attaining this desirable end, and will not obtain processing from other quarters unless by special permission by the Director of Processing of the HGC, the Association Secretary of the organization, the HCO Area Secretary and the Continental Executive Secretary.

The Central Organization on its behalf will undertake to make the processing, as feasible, as rapid as is compatible with the case level of the individual, and will give what advices and assistances as are necessary to make the activity as free from difficulty as is also compatible with this undertaking, but that in the case of any dispute as to this matter, the directions of the Director of Processing shall be complied with.

The above is the general form of the contract and legal phraseology and other materials should be as far as possible omitted from this particular document, which I am sure will be found adequately binding.

This form is to be accompanied by a contract which states that during the coming year the organization, in return for receiving the signed release form, undertakes to furnish processing to the individual at current and existing rates, and no increase, but that the offer is valid only from the *date of the offering letter.*

The undertaking of this contract and signature on the waiver is understood to cancel all earlier contractual hours of processing, but not to cancel any existing debts.

Unless returned within thirty days of receipt, the waiver has no value.

The contract also states that any person so signing will not have any rates raised on him by reason of the probable increase in cost of auditing in view of clearing success, and extended training requirements of auditors.

The above waiver and contract should be mailed at once to all those persons who were written to and told the Central Organization had them on their clearing list approximately two years ago, or in those areas where no such letter was sent. This document should be forwarded to all those people on the mailing list at once.

This in effect is a significant portion of the clearing program of Central Organizations for continental areas.

L. RON HUBBARD
Founder

HCO POLICY LETTER OF 23 OCTOBER 1963

Missions
CenOCon

REFUND POLICY

(Cancels HCO PLs of 12 Oct. 61 and 27 Feb. 62)

REFUNDED MONIES

In a careful review of refunds and in the light of my own experience with persons demanding refunds, and due to two recent upsets in organizations (Australia and London) regarding refunds, the following data may be of assistance.

In thirteen years, involving hundreds of thousands of hours of processing and millions of dollars of income, in any organization where I was assuming direct command I have always promptly and immediately caused to be refunded every penny of the money paid by any person who was dissatisfied with his or her processing. This has been the consistent policy I myself have worked with.

In all that time I have only refunded about $3,500.

This is due in part to ensuring a certainty of results in any HGC and working hard to make sure the pc gets results, regardless of the current style or mode of processing.

This low amount of refund is also due in part to my firm policy that persons who demand refunds may have them exactly according to the Code of a Scientologist, but that any person demanding or accepting refunds thereafter shall be refused as an HGC preclear and posted for the information of field auditors.

I have only worked then with these three policies:

1. Refund at once in full any refund demanded;

2. Work hard with tech staff to ensure good results;

3. Forbid the sale of further processing to anyone receiving a refund and make the case known to Scientologists.

It is notable that all but one refund were made to persons with histories of insanity who had been accepted unwittingly for processing.

Recently, Australia was sufficiently remiss in following the Code of a Scientologist as to incur potential legal action. I did not understand why and investigated. The facts resulted in my sending a cable to the Continental Director requesting that he do the usual—refund the money and locate the bypassed charge. The case promptly resolved. What was shocking to me is that he had not immediately refunded, whatever else he did. Of course, he was absent when the incident occurred, but still his first thought on finding the matter out should have been to refund the money, not because of threatened legal action, but because AN ORGANIZATION IS BOUND BY THE CODE OF A SCIENTOLOGIST.

A Central Organization is as successful as it gives good technical service.

A tough refund policy injects aberrated stable data against the confusion of bad or poor technical service. A mild refund policy keeps technical on its toes.

The world of Scientology is based on ARC and held together with ARC. Bad technical and tough attitudes concerning the remedy of poor service break down this world.

My own often-repeated policy to my personal staff is "Give them what they want and keep them happy." That sounds like a very indefinite policy indeed. But it makes people face up to and handle individual confusions as they occur, each on its own merits; it presupposes people are basically good *and* it is successful.

The more thetan you have present, the less policy you need and the better things run. Only a thetan can handle a post or a pc. All he needs is the know-how of minds as contained in Scientology. That was all he ever lacked. So, given that, sheer policy is poor stuff, as it seeks to make a datum stand where a being should be. That's the whole story of the GPMs. So why not have live orgs?

Policy is only vital where agreement must exist between two or more thetans working together. Beyond that it fails. A needful policy is "We'll start work on time" since without it the org goes ragged. A useless policy would be "The Registrar must always smile at an applicant" for that puts a datum where a person should be.

So there are two kinds of policies—those needed to obtain work-together ease and those which seek to put a datum instead of a being in a position. The less you have of the latter the better things will get. The more reasonable the former, the more work will be done.

A refund policy is an agreement-type policy. Needful. But it must be very mild indeed or it will stand in lieu of good service.

The new policy then is:

1. Refund any fees when and as demanded, whether for training or for processing;

2. Refuse further and all future training or processing to anyone demanding a refund as the condition of refund;

3. If (2) is not acceptable to the person demanding the refund, then do all possible to smooth out the case or training situation;

4. Count only on high technical results in the HGC and Academy to inhibit or reduce demands for refunds.

L. RON HUBBARD
Founder

HCO POLICY LETTER OF 2 MARCH 1964

HCO (WW) Ltd.
HCO (Sthil) Ltd.
Scn Library
 and Research, Ltd.

CONTRACTS AND SERVICES

Contracts for services require the signed approval of the Executive Director.

No existing contract may be extended for purposes beyond its original intention without the signed approval of the Executive Director.

All types of contractual relations between the corporation and other companies, firms, banks or individuals are included. Solicitors, service companies, architects, banks, typewriter service, lift service, etc., and any other type of binding contract involving expense to the corporation are included.

Particularly included are contractors to be engaged for construction of any kind or services connected with construction.

The completed staff work and any papers for signature must accompany all requests for contractual approval.

No requests for contractual approval will be entertained unless passed upon in the affirmative by the administrative head of the corporation requesting.

L. RON HUBBARD
Founder

Remimeo
Missions
Sthil Students

USE OF "DIANETICS," "SCIENTOLOGY,"
"APPLIED PHILOSOPHY"

In order to protect the good names of "Dianetics," "Scientology" and "Applied Philosophy," the following policies are continued or become effective immediately.

1. All lectures, books, publications, films, models and diagrams on the above subjects are copyrighted by L. Ron Hubbard.

2. Permission to use these words is given to all bona fide holders of certificates issued by an organization accredited by L. Ron Hubbard, subject to the following conditions:

   a. The names, data, materials and processes are only to be used in connection with and in relation to the level and class for which the certificate has been issued.

   b. Technical information, by which is meant the "how" and "why" of our activities, must not be released by lecture, writing, demonstration or by any other means except by books or tapes published by L. Ron Hubbard, or an organization approved by L. Ron Hubbard, or on a properly organized course by a person certificated to teach that course, or in a properly arranged auditing session where a "process" may be applied within the class and level of the auditor.

   NOTE: The reason for the foregoing is that when data gets relayed other than from the original source, i.e., book, bulletin, lecture, etc., an alter-isness occurs, be it ever so small, which can be disastrous.

3. a. The names "Dianetics," "Scientology," "Applied Philosophy" may only be used in a company or activity name under license from L. Ron Hubbard.

   b. Such license can be withdrawn at any time.

   c. The license is not transferable except with written permission of L. Ron Hubbard or a person authorized by him to grant such permission.

   d. Licenses will only be issued to individual mission holders.

   e. Licenses will not be issued where the title includes a place name which indicates an area larger than the immediate vicinity of the headquarters of the mission holder.

4. Anyone practicing Scientology under any name other than his own must get permission of the Mission Secretary.

5. The use of data and/or materials under another name or using the data and/or materials in conjunction with any other philosophy is forbidden.

6. The use of data and/or materials other than for the betterment of an individual, group or mankind is forbidden.

7. Certificates and, therefore, permission to practice, etc., may be withdrawn at any time by L. Ron Hubbard or any person authorized by him to do so, if there is any infringement of the above or if, in his opinion, it is necessary for any reason.

It is not intended to stop any bona fide Scientologist, properly certificated, from practicing or using Scientology data or material; on the contrary, it is necessary to protect you from misuse of them by others.

L. RON HUBBARD
Founder

HCO POLICY LETTER OF 5 APRIL 1965
Issue IV

Gen. Non-Remimeo

HCO Division (1)

Org Division (3)

LEGAL AND PROMOTION

Policy: Legal activities, outside lawyers or attorneys, suits, may not be under the Organization Secretary ever but must be under HCO.

Reasons: Persons connected to finance value money too highly, being in charge of it, and sometimes involve the org in needless suits.

Corporate structure is part of the Office of LRH and new orgs and other orgs and requires legal primary connections. Therefore, it is extra expense to have two legal departments.

Legal control is part of the functions of justice which belongs to HCO.

Policy: Promotion expenditure must never be under the control of the Organization Division. It belongs solely to HCO.

Reasons: London in 1958, Johannesburg in 1964, to name two, went nearly broke when their economy curtailed magazine mailings and promotion.

The magazine costs and extent of mailing must never be controlled by anyone connected with finance as they seek to save on it when they, quite properly, seek to reduce expenses on other things in the org.

L. RON HUBBARD
Founder

SOME TECH DIV POLICIES

LEGAL ASPECTS OF SIGN-UPS

No persons may be admitted to an Academy or HGC who have not signed waivers (release forms) of the old type.

All such waivers must include a statement that the person is there on his or her own determinism and that the person has no record of being committed in an institution or has a criminal record for felony.

Persons with such commitments or records should be referred to a field auditor near their home and refused training or processing at the organization.

Persons suspected of purely medical illness should be referred to a doctor for competent treatment if such a doctor or treatment exists.

Minors must have their parents or guardians sign the waiver and any note for time payments.

Known trouble sources as per recent HCO Policy Letter, all of which remains in force, should be required to straighten up their lives before enrolling or signing up for processing or should be forthrightly refused.

Anyone objecting to an E-Meter check should be refused entrance.

Thus, by keeping the legal aspects straight, you will be able to help the many and not be messed up by a few. For a very few such people (21 to be exact) were the sole sources of grief in the 1950 boom.

To have a boom, you have to keep your nose clean legally or you can be stopped by the enturbulence generated, both in the org and the public. Such enturbulence is all that shortens your lines or overworks staff.

HUSBAND–WIFE TEAMS ENTERING ACADEMIES

Husband-wife teams should not be forbidden. But in all cases where husband and wife are trained to co-audit each other, they must mail their auditors' reports routinely to the D of P for which they will be charged a nominal but real fee for case supervision.

1074

Professional auditors or co-auditors who use auditing in or out of an Academy to estrange husbands and wives are subject to a Court of Ethics at their nearest HCO on any second dynamic misconduct complaint from either party, husband or wife, and a penalty up to suspension of certificate may be sentenced the offender if proven guilty.

During training it is against policy to team husbands and wives together for practice drills even when they will be co-auditing after leaving class.

Where possible, husbands and wives should, however, be persuaded to bring another couple to be trained rather than co-audit, and it should be arranged that the wife audits the other wife and the husband the other husband after training. In this case it is all right to team them in any pairing under training for drills.

SCHOLARSHIPS

No scholarships are now allowed.

COURSE FEES STANDARDIZED

Any course taught in a continental zone must conform to that zone's course fees, and it must be approved by Saint Hill and not altered.

OUTSIDE COURSES

As present-day level courses require a full Tech Division plus a full Qualifications Division plus an Ethics Officer, no Academy courses may be given outside Academy premises.

PE COURSES (BS COURSE)

PE Courses will still be taught by field auditors and mission holders, which is the BS Course. They result in a BEGINNING SCIENTOLOGIST certificate.

STUDENTS

A *course completion* is a checksheet not a time period or a classification.

It is now a *crime* to run a course without a checksheet or to change a checksheet on a student after it's issued. A different checksheet can be issued to the *next* student that enrolls on that very same course. But once issued, the same one is completed for a course completion of that course, and the student gets his certificate for the level when it is and can take his exam for class. There are two checksheets actually—theory and practical. Both should be complete before you let a student go to the next certificate.

COURSE TIMES

All courses in all orgs enroll any time of any day. No special courses for certain dates will be tolerated in any org. Magazines should say "enrolls any time" after every course in every Academy ad. If you don't, you go mad trying to get pcs every week for ad money and wind up with a psychiatric ward for an HGC. The checksheet system used now at Saint Hill for levels fits every course nicely and requires no "every four weeks." Saint Hill enrolls all week long! Further, Supervisors in Scientology must not personally lecture students on technology. If you want a current checksheet for a level, write your comm-member (HCO PL 13 Mar. 65, THE COMM–MEMBER SYSTEM) at Saint Hill.

CLEARS

Sell *Release* with confidence. Only squirreling on levels and rough ARC break handling can prevent it. The total rundown of processes is easy to groove in in an HGC and should be adhered to violently if you want to get results and Releases. It's no myth now.

RELEASED STUDENTS

Students who are Releases have to *do* all the required auditing as an auditor. And get it passed. Release is an honorary, not a technical award. But a truly floating-needle Release may not be further audited except for Power Processes. A student doesn't *know* more about Scientology just because he's released. He just *learns* faster. So the released student *must* do all his *auditing* on pcs, subjective and objective. If you don't have any raw meat for a student to do all his levels on, make the student scrounge his own pcs off the street or city dump. Remember, don't panic on Release. It means the student, like any other student, must do all his required checksheets and go on up, level by level, just like every other student.

PLEDGING CODES

Applications for certificate must be made by every student. This should give how they want their name on the certificate, address and the routing of the student out of the org, CF routing and all that.

This application *must* also carry a pledge stating that the applicant subscribes to and promises to uphold the Auditor's Code, the Code of a Scientologist, and it must state he is informed of and will follow the policies relating to gradation and classification.

CITY OFFICE AND CENTRAL ORG COURSES

City offices may teach BS, HAS and HQS Courses. Central Orgs teach these and may teach level courses according to their status of org—these courses being HRS by Class 0 Orgs, HTS by Class I Orgs (plus the HRS), Class II Orgs teach HRS, HTS and HCA, Class III Orgs teach HRS, HTS, HCA and HPA. In 1968 Central Orgs will also be given permission to teach HAA if they have attained Class IV status.

L. RON HUBBARD
Founder

HCO POLICY LETTER OF 16 DECEMBER 1965

Gen. Non-Remimeo
Applies SH & FCDC
Dist Div Hats
Dissem Div Hats
Dept Inspections
  & Reports Hats
Dept Comm Hats
Info Other Orgs

COPYRIGHT: USA

In order to protect our copyright property in books, periodicals and printed matter that are sold or distributed generally, interim copyrights should be obtained by the continental organization (FCDC) within six months of the date of United Kingdom publication.

As this interim copyright lasts for only five years, a completely American edition must be done of those published works for which it is intended to secure a 28-year term. To comply with the present law, all materials used, even the very stencil, must be done in America and manufactured in America, and the American org address used.

Before applying for renewal of copyright, the Copyright Officer DC, should obtain and send a list of interim copyrights due to expire in the next six months to Copyright Officer WW who would ascertain from LRH Issue Authority WW those for which a 28-year term renewal application should be made.

As under the present law only a maximum number of 1500 copies of works published abroad and given a 5-year interim copyright can be legally imported into the USA during those 5 years, the Dissemination Secretary should be alerted to this provision of the American law and ensure that an American edition of good sellers like *Scientology: A New Slant on Life* is ready to hand before the customs prohibit further importation.

Addresso WW should have a plate made and addressed as follows:

"Copyright Officer, for registration of US copyright, Founding Church of Scientology, 1812 19th Street NW, Washington, DC, United States," so that he receives an extra copy of all general mailing, mailings to members *and of books as they are published.*

As the registration of copyright is expensive (6 dollars per item), only books, periodical publications and such policy letters and bulletins that are widely disseminated and of intrinsic value, i.e., those not already covered by previous policy letters or bulletins, should be registered.

L. RON HUBBARD
Founder

Remimeo
Exec Sec Hats
Org Division Hats

URGENT

ACCOUNTING POLICIES OF
SCIENTOLOGY COMPANIES

(Scientology organizations long have had exact, firm rules regarding accounting procedure. They are repeated here. These MUST be in use from 1 Jan. 66 forward in *all* organizations. If they are not, put them right back to 1 Jan. 66 so we can get a proper and swift audit in 1967.)

The accounting policies of a Scientology company are:

1. ALL AUDITS MUST BE DONE FROM ORIGINAL RECORDS. (No secondary books, journals or ledgers may be consulted in doing an audit and are illegal in a Scientology company anyway.)

2. ALL SUMS RECEIVED FROM ANY SOURCE MUST BE LEGIBLY INVOICED AND BANKED. (They may not be spent before banking, not even a penny no matter the emergency.)

3. ALL SUMS DISBURSED MUST BE DISBURSED BY CHECK. (Even petty cash and salary sums must be drawn by check before being disbursed.)

4. ALL SUMS DISBURSED MUST ALSO BE DISBURSED BY LEGIBLE VOUCHER GIVING FULL DETAILS AS WELL AS CHECK GIVING FULL DATA. (Wages for each person must have a disbursement voucher for that person and signed by that person. Every check also has a voucher. A voucher is like an invoice, same machine.)

5. WEEKLY INCOME INVOICE MACHINE COPIES WITH A CARBON COPY OF THE BANK DEPOSIT SLIP FOR THAT WEEK AND A TAPE OF THE INVOICES ADDING THEM MUST BE PLACED IN AN ENVELOPE AND DATED AND CAREFULLY FILED. (This gives a complete record of bankings for the year by week.)

6. ALL BILLS MUST BE FILED WHEN RECEIVED IN A FOLDER FOR EACH COMPANY AND THE FOLDER SUMMARIZED BEFORE THE BILL IS PAID. (Bills may not be paid merely by reason of receipt in mail or before filing.)

7. EVERY MONTH ALL BILLS OWING ARE LISTED ON A MIMEO FORM AND PRESENTED TO THE SIGNING EXECUTIVES WITH A LIST OF MONIES IN THE BANK AND PLANNED FOR PAYMENT BEFORE ANY CHECKS MAY BE WRITTEN OR SIGNED.

8. EVERY PERSON OWING ORG MONEY HAS A COLLECTION FOLDER INTO WHICH COPIES OF INVOICES OF ALL PAYMENTS MADE ARE FILED, THE FOLDER TO INCLUDE COPIES OF ALL CONTRACTS AND NOTES.

9. COLLECTION FOLDERS ARE SUMMARIZED MONTHLY AND STATEMENTS ARE SENT OUT MONTHLY TO DEBTORS. (Any bill written off for tax is still billed to the debtor monthly.)

10. ALL PERSONS OWNING MEMBERSHIPS, FREE OR PAID, ARE RECORDED IN ACCOUNTS AND BILLED THIRTY DAYS BEFORE MEMBERSHIP, FREE OR PAID, EXPIRES.

11. ACCOUNTS ORIGINAL RECORDS AS ABOVE MUST BE SENT TO WORLDWIDE EVERY QUARTER FOR AUDIT AND PREPARATION OF BALANCE SHEETS AND TAX RETURNS.

12. BANK STATEMENTS MUST BE RECONCILED (COMPARED TO DEPOSITS AND VOUCHERS) WHEN RECEIVED. (TO KEEP THE BANK FROM MAKING ERRORS.)

13. CHECKS WHEN CLEARED AND BACK FROM BANK MUST BE TAPED IN TO ORIGINAL CHECKBOOK ONTO THEIR STUBS (COUNTERFOILS).

14. EVERY PERSON TO WHOM A SALARY IS PAID HAS A FILE FOLDER INTO WHICH ALL HIS PAPERS, CONTRACT, DEBTS TO ORG AND VOUCHER SHOWING EACH AMOUNT RECEIVED ARE FILED WEEKLY.

There is a pegboard system of separating the weekly invoices and vouchers into categories of income and expense. This refinement is described in earlier policy.

If you have any other accounting system in operation, it is contrary to company policy which is based on the above only.

As Executive Director I will not sign any balance sheet or return not taken from the original records: balance sheets or statements of affairs based on secondary ledgers and journals or double-entry systems or punched-card computer systems or any "books." The law requires that accurate records be kept. This does not mean ledgers and double entry and such are not required by law anywhere in the world.

Accounting is no mystery. When it becomes so by complex systems, executives cannot manage their companies and they go broke.

The introduction of complex accounting contrary to policy is a suppressive act on laymen.

Scientologists with little or no accounting experience can run the above system and interpret it easily.

The decline of more than one Scientology organization can be traced to violations of the above accounting policies. Executives could not manage the company when intimidated by mysterious, complex accounting. Accounting cost more than the company could afford. The field ARC broke on being billed erroneously. Accounts collections were neglected and staggering sums went uncollected because they weren't billed or poorly billed due to violations of the above.

This system is a very simple one and a good one, designed for Scientology orgs and successful.

L. RON HUBBARD
Founder

HCO POLICY LETTER OF 3 FEBRUARY 1966
Issue I

Remimeo
SH and WW Only
Exec Sec Hats
Executive Hats
All HCO
Mail Point Hats
All Phone Point Hats
To Be Enforced by
   Dir Comm and
   Ethics

IMPORTANT

LEGAL, TAX, ACCOUNTANT AND SOLICITOR
MAIL AND LEGAL OFFICER

There is all manner of legal-type letters, government letters, accounting notices, assessments and such and phone calls received by persons in the org and this PL FORBIDS it being routed all over the org to anyone and everyone.

IT ALL GOES TO THE LEGAL OFFICER.

I don't care *who* it is addressed to or who is being called for, if it looks or sounds lawyer or legal or tax or Town and Country Planning or Council or *anything* like legal or government, IT MAY NOT BE ROUTED TO ITS ADDRESSEE but *must* FIRST go to the Legal Officer only.

Anyone found *holding* or receiving or *finding* any legal or tax or planning matter or letter or phone call without its being routed first and at once to the Legal Officer will be reported at once to Ethics and Ethics is to hold a hearing.

The Legal Officer is hereby authorized to have a clerk. The clerk is to keep legal files and is to receive all such legal matters, letters, summonses, etc.

The Legal Clerk may then xerox a copy and send the copy only to the addressee. But must keep the original and must show it to the Legal Officer before even a copy is sent.

ALL OUTGOING MAIL to attorneys, tax cruds, the alleged government, the Council, etc., AND A FULL RECORD OF EVERY VERBAL CONFERENCE ON SUCH MATTERS must be sent to the Legal Officer BEFORE MAILING or before being held binding and must not be sealed or ratified before so sending it to the Legal Officer.

NO STENO may mail a legal-type letter or get it signed unless it is FIRST SENT TO THE LEGAL OFFICER FOR OKAY.

Without that okay it may not be signed or mailed.

No officer, executive or person in the organization may make legal contacts or commitments or arrangements that are not approved by the Legal Officer.

Any phone or telex operator receiving a request from an executive for a legal or government outgoing connection must route it instead to the Legal Officer.

RECEPTION MUST ROUTE ALL LEGAL–TYPE BODIES ONLY TO THE LEGAL OFFICER AND TO NOBODY ELSE EVER.

Note: The government is so dispersed it mails anyone's mail to anybody (absolute fact), and the most dangerous notices may get sent to the most unlikely places and parts of the org. In the recent accountancy emergency, it was conclusively proven that a suppressive always selects wrong targets and that includes wrong addressees. The most vital notices were being sent to anyone whose name was handy.

THE LEGAL OFFICER

The purpose of the Legal Officer is to help LRH handle every legal, government, suit, accounting and tax contact or action for the organization and, by himself or employed representative, to protect the organization and its people from harm and to bring the greatest possible confusion and loss to its enemies.

This purpose can only be carried out if *every* piece of mail incoming and outgoing that has to do with legal matters, tax matters, Town and Country Planning matters, government matters, solicitor matters of any kind passes through his hands and is fitted by him into the tactics and strategy agreed upon or formulated by the Legal Section.

The Legal Officer may not take direct orders from anyone but myself, policy letters and Sec EDs, and obstructing him in the performance of his duty is a crime and must be followed by a Committee of Evidence.

L. RON HUBBARD
Founder

HCO POLICY LETTER OF 31 JULY 1966R
REVISED 28 JANUARY 1991

Gen. Non-Remimeo
HCO Exec Sec
Org Exec Sec
HCO Area Sec

REFUND NOTICE

It is IMPORTANT that every *posted scale* of donations and every *rate card* bear the following notice prominently displayed at the bottom:

DONATIONS PROMPTLY REFUNDED TO ANY DISSATIS-
FIED STUDENT OR PRECLEAR IN ACCORDANCE WITH
THE POLICIES OF THE CLAIMS VERIFICATION BOARD,
IF THE PRECLEAR OR STUDENT IS DISSATISFIED AND
DEMANDS IT WITHIN THREE MONTHS AFTER THE
TRAINING OR PROCESSING, THE ONLY CONDITION
BEING THAT HE MAY NOT AGAIN BE PROCESSED OR
TRAINED.

The full regulation of this is not varied except that no donation for any of the Advanced Courses (R6EW Course, Clearing Course, New OT I, OT II, OT III, New OT VI, New OT VII or New OT VIII) or further OT Courses will be refunded as this is the student as his own auditor and is his own responsibility which is somewhat beyond our control in some cases.

The person requesting refund must sign a guarantee that he will not further undertake or apply for training or processing from any org or auditor and even if later reinstated may not ever enroll for Grades VI, Grade VII or any OT levels.

We only refund the current donation according to Claims Verification Board policies, and orgs never refund private auditor donations but may help recover them from private auditors.

DO NOT OMIT THIS ACTION.

Junk all rate cards that do not carry it or stamp or type it on them while ordering new.

L. RON HUBBARD
Founder

Revision assisted by
LRH Technical Research
and Compilations

HCO POLICY LETTER OF 1 AUGUST 1966
Issue II

Remimeo

REFUND ADDITION

(Adds to HCO PL 31 July 66, REFUND NOTICE)

TIME LIMITATION

No refund may be applied for successfully after three months from the end of the last service rendered.

This means that a refund applied for three months after the end of an intensive's last auditing session or last day of attendance on a course may NOT be granted.

MEMBERSHIP REFUNDS

There are no membership refunds of any kind as refund policy applies to service and as membership holders usually have already realized discounts.

L. RON HUBBARD
Founder

HUBBARD COMMUNICATIONS OFFICE
Saint Hill Manor, East Grinstead, Sussex

HCO POLICY LETTER OF 11 OCTOBER 1966

IMPORTANT

LEGAL, TAX, ACCOUNTANT AND SOLICITOR
MAIL INCOMING AND OUTGOING

(Amends HCO PL 3 Feb. 66, Legal, Tax, Accountant
and Solicitor Mail Incoming and Outgoing.)

Any legal, accounting or governmental communication must be xeroxed (duplicated) upon receipt with copies sent to the board of directors and the addressee BEFORE the original is routed to the Legal Officer. The responsibility for such xeroxing and routing is directly that of the Internal Comm Flow Section.

This responsibility for routing and informing of all terminals involved by xerox copies is being turned over to the Internal Comm Flow Section, as it has been seen that a breakdown within the Legal Section itself can cause urgent matters to be neglected and unhandled. This, therefore, changes the HCO PL 3 Feb. 66 where such xeroxing was the responsibility of the Legal Clerk.

No legal, accounting or governmental communication can leave the organization which has not been approved by the Legal Officer AND SIGNED BY THE SECRETARY OF THE BOARD OF DIRECTORS. A copy of such communications is sent to the addressee. This changes HCO PL 3 Feb. 66 in which the Legal Officer approved such communications and such communications were then signed by the originating terminal. Now, no matter who originates such a communication, it is to be signed only by the secretary of the board of directors as a communication from the board of directors, all directors knowing about such.

In this way the board of directors and the addressee can be certain that ALL incoming matters of a legal, accounting or governmental nature have been received and handled and that outgoing communications on these subjects are according to policy.

L. RON HUBBARD
Founder

All Executives of
All Orgs
All Accountants
LRH Finance Comm
OT Central Committee
Treasurer WW

SCIENTOLOGY ORGS
TAX AND BALANCE SHEETS

(This policy letter refers to business practices in setting forth the handling of balance sheets. Churches of Scientology have been officially recognized as religious organizations in every country in which they have been incorporated. Churches are generally not required to produce or provide balance sheets to tax agencies. Nevertheless, the United States Internal Revenue Service and some other suppressive tax agencies have from time to time required these of Scientology orgs as part of their policy of harrassment. As there is no such thing as a church balance sheet or a religious organization balance sheet, it is necessary to understand and apply certain standard methods of business accounting in order to deal with the taxman's harrassment. Indeed, the issue is written in business terms as it is manifestly impossible to write about tax and balance sheets in any other context. ——CSI)

There is a confusion on the subject of tax and balance sheets as they involve or concern monies owed on balance sheets. Extraordinary solutions are being advanced and the matter should be reviewed.

There are certain principles involved here which vitally affect Scientology companies as companies and indeed are basic in any business.

1. If you acquire the profit of an asset without paying for it, all monies received become a false profit and taxable.

2. If you invoice money as your own that is in fact owed to someone else, you wind up with a false profit and get taxed for it.

3. There are certain principles of business having to do with income and debts which cannot be thrown aside even by a tax department.

4. The moment you vary from the exact truth of any transaction you involve yourself in potential confusion that requires extraordinary solutions.

5. When you find yourself being asked for extraordinary solutions you have departed from the truth of the transaction.

———————

As tax departments have never to my knowledge accepted without question the year's return or balance sheet of *any* corporation, efforts to get such departments to accept a return or balance sheet by putting in wild solutions avail nothing. The tax people aren't going to accept anything at all anyway ever without challenge. If you are challenged, you better have the REAL facts right there. This doesn't mean one should tell them all the truth in a geyser and gush.

The real stable datum in handling tax people is NEVER VOLUNTEER ANY INFORMATION. It does mean one must not tell them or give them false data. It only means that when you give them data you can't back up or report profit you didn't make, you will get into severe trouble.

The basic errors of Scientology corporations in accounting and tax matters lie in 1 to 5 above.

Under 1, all existing companies have acquired assets from me without paying for them and therefore show a false profit.

They sell books they do not own the copyrights for, acquire technology they never paid for and, in the case of Saint Hill, acquired a business worth upwards of two million pounds and an estate worth £80,000 without ever showing any debt. So the profits then look very large in any Scientology company. And this involves them with tax.

Because the government *accuses* them of paying me (which they don't), they think it must be a crime to pay me anything and so are pushed into a profit situation because they have never paid for their main assets. Of course, a tax department wants to see them with a big profit which can be taxed and so blocks the truthful fact that the companies owe me money.

Recently a law in England, passed by the boilermakers playing politician, threatened to call any company a close company which owed any money to an individual and put close company tax at 67%. Well, the loophole is that if they don't owe it to an individual they'd pay tax anyway at high percent. And if they did owe it, they'd have no profit. And 67% of nothing is exactly nothing. So using the close company law to say I can't be owed anything is just bad thinking. And it leaves SH with £2 million of "profit" that CAN be taxed which it doesn't really own as profit at all.

Under 2 above, whenever you invoice money as your own income that is owed to somebody else, you wind up with a false profit on which you will then have to pay tax you don't owe.

Let us take an Advanced Clinical Course I have given. I paid my fare, often the bulk of expenses and took no fee. The ACC was invoiced in as org *income*. Yet it wasn't. It was my income. Yet the org not only invoiced it in, it didn't even note on its balance sheets it owed it to me and so wound up with a taxable profit.

Take the book *Dianetics: The Modern Science of Mental Health* as a property. I bought it back from the publishers in New York for $15,000 of *my* cash. I turned it over to the Distribution Center, Inc. in DC which then sold tons of copies of it, invoiced each one as its own income and never paid me any royalty at all. Further, it never noted on its balance sheets it owed me for it and soon had US tax bills against it for its *"profit."*

In addition to all that, DC, London and notably Saint Hill have taken over bank accounts of mine, have invoiced royalties owed to me only for movies and books, even my veteran's checks, and yet never noted in any balance sheet or return that it owed it. So it wound up with a taxable sum.

Of *course* the government tax offices will *say* not to put down your debts as *then* they have a profit to tax!

_____

Under 3 governments can pass all the legislation they want, but certain business actions remain themselves. One buys, one sells, one collects, one owes. The government would like to upset all this but truth is no government really can, not even in Russia, as they are flying in the teeth of the fundamentals of commercial interchange.

If one acquires a $10 dress for nothing, one now has $10 worth more than one had before. If one paid $10 *out* and took a $10 dress *in,* the books balance. A thief must be in continual trouble in economics and with tax agencies as he acquires without spending which leaves him heavily asseted without debt and so taxable to the hilt. _____

Under 4 above, the moment you depart from the truth of records with explanations or gimmicks, you cannot substantiate your statements. The records no longer line up.

So you have to destroy the accounts system or muck it up so it can't be read and promptly you are in *real* trouble.

You can assign new values to some data, you can honestly reassess the meaning of your figures (such as advanced payments are not income) but note you are going in the direction of more truth.

The truth of Scientology orgs is that I built them with my own money (which they didn't record) and made them affluent where they are without pay. I gave them technology they did not finance, books on which they pay no royalty and cash they forgot to mark down.

The result is that they show a *profit* which does not exist in fact as the wherewithal by which the money was made was not ever reimbursed.

Not only were assets acquired which had not been paid for, but additional monies were invoiced they did not have coming. The result is an apparent profit and, of course, trouble with the tax people.

_____

Under 5 when you depart from facts and basic planning, you then have to have *very* extraordinary solutions. And when you seem to have to have extraordinary solutions, you have departed from basics and facts.

Right now there is a lot of tax yap. And it is being set up to clobber Scientology with huge tax bills in England and the US.

This isn't because people are mad at Scientology. It's because Scientology orgs have given themselves a huge swollen profit by not keeping good records and by not letting the real debts *be* debts.

Every SP on the lines is, of course, frantic at the thought of Ron getting hold of any money. What will Ron do with it? More research, more orgs, more Scientology, more freedom. The record clearly states this is the case. When I draw $10,000 as a repayment of debt which it was, I promptly expand Scientology to make it another $100,000. So it goes. Sometimes, in development, some money gets "wasted." But it always comes back 10 for 1 in the long run.

So of course an SP tries *anything* or says anything to prevent my getting hold of any more money than I have. And all sorts of weird "laws" and opinions are dug up to show that I can't be paid.

The last phony was that if money owed me was shown on current balance sheets then all past years of all orgs would have to be redone. Not so. It's up to the government to demand that and in that case it would all be corrected anyway so it's no argument and wouldn't even happen. In past orgs, I had control. I no longer have it. So it's natural that the investment had to be added up and paid back.

A debt *is* a debt. Newly discovered debts are common in any accounting system.

So what does one do? Report it all as profit and get taxed out of existence? And help it happen by telling a lie—that it owes me no money?

As for the sale of Saint Hill to Church of Scientology of California, the tax on any sum paid is on *me* not the org. So it is not the org's business. It IS the org's business to be sitting there with the full income of several million all invoiced as *profit*. That is the road to ruin taxwise.

––––––––––

There are a lot of people around who "know best." This "best" usually winds us up in the soup.

MY orders on this stand and are not open to opinion. And these orders are:

1. Record in balance sheets as owed proper payment for any property or business acquired from me.

2. Record all sums invoiced into an org that were really mine as still owed to me.

3. Carry on with standard income-outgo recordings and business procedures regardless of "law."

4. Tell and record the exact truth of all transactions past and present.

5. Put into effect the basic solutions I have written out in full for the handling of monies and debts.

Don't be dismayed because somebody in a "panic" says one must do something odd to "stay within the law." They probably don't realize how lawful our conduct of business really is.

And Scientology orgs if they record their debts owed for assets and their incorrect invoicing of my money as their own and report what is really owed on their balance sheets, will come out straight on tax.

The *governments* are in the business of *falsifying other people's records* so as to collect more tax. If you report a bad debt, they say it's a good debt. If you report a debt you owe, they say it isn't a debt. They can be counted on absolutely to assign a significance to figures to increase tax. But even the craziest pervert in the tax office CAN'T argue down actual records so your only defense is actual records.

When YOU fall for the gag that YOU must falsify your records to "satisfy" some "law" or some kooky official, you are just playing into their hands.

Further, some accountants paint black pictures of the government to cow their clients and ask them to falsify records by omitting actual facts or demanding weird solutions. The thing to do is stick with the truth and the real invoices doggedly.

Now as to TAX, why this is mainly anybody's game of what is a PROFIT. The thing to do is to assign a significance to the figures before the government can. The whole thing is a mess only because arithmetic figures are symbols open to ANY significance. So I normally think of a better significance than the government can. I always put enough errors on a return to satisfy their blood-sucking appetite and STILL come out zero. The game of accounting is just a game of assigning significances to figures. The man with the most imagination wins. BUT there must be correct figures and there must not be gross misassignment of debts as profits or the whole thing won't hang together.

Income tax is a suppressive effort to crush individuals and businesses and deprive the state of national gross product (since none can expand). The thing which baffles any suppressive is truth. It's the only thing that works. Significances one assigns figures are neither true nor false but always must be reasonable and *defendable*. And the figures themselves must always check out.

Income does not mean profit. One can and should make all the INCOME one possibly can. Always. The only crime really is to be broke. But when one makes INCOME be sure it is accounted for as to its source *and* that one covers it with expenses and debts. Handling taxation is as simple as that.

Scientology income is high in most orgs. But it IS high due to the investment of time and money in earlier years. So if the balance sheets omit all the money that was invested and show only the money that was made, they are false balance sheets. And that is what the government wants us to turn in—a false balance sheet that shows all income as profit with *no* repayment or retirement of debt.

Yesterday's unreported debts became invested money for expansion. The debts of 1950 have not been lost at all where they remain unpaid but show up as DEVELOPED business.

When the debt was not paid, that sum was used to expand. So the debt is still there and today's "profit" in no small way can be traced to the orgs not having to pay. Instead, the money was used to develop the org and area. The income from that development is still there. Thus, the debt must be there, must be shown on the balance sheets and books or it will involve the org eventually in tax trouble.

L. RON HUBBARD
Founder

Remimeo

FINANCIAL LINES AND LEGAL LINES

I am dealing with at least two despatches a day on financial lines and one or two on legal lines daily.

Design and planning begin and end with study of a situation and laying down the broad plan of handling.

This does not mean I handle every letter the org receives from a bank or a solicitor.

I have my own hats to wear and these are numerous. Adequate policy exists on routine handling of finance and legal matters. Such letters not only do not belong to me but they prevent my handling my proper hats.

When I have issued planning on a matter, I am through with it. That I issued planning or strategy does not mean I thereafter handle all of it from there on out.

Finance and legal do not belong on my lines and I seriously object to being kept from my work. Adequate authority also exists to handle such matters in addition to policy.

I suggest reading the policy letters on these matters and issued planning rather than forwarding routine finance and legal to me.

Dumping such on my lines could cost us two or three thousand a week. That is in lost future income. It does not seem economical.

L. RON HUBBARD
Founder

PUBLIC ATTACKS
LEGAL POINT

It is very interesting that those groups who attack Scientology are consistently erring. The Melbourne Enquiry also erred in the same way.

The PRACTICE of Scientology is today a very routine action. It consists of drills which:

1. Better one's ability to communicate,

2. Gives one the intelligence to handle his problems,

3. Makes one able to be a social being without committing antisocial acts,

4. Brings one to abandon explanations of his failures and to get on with being successful,

5. Handles all one's reactiveness and,

6. Clears one.

These drills are quite unfrightening. If psychology had them it would use them and be a great success.

On the other hand, the BOOKS and PAPERS of Scientology are a record of research and are writings. They represent a very broad survey of the whole field of human knowledge and the mind and contain ANYTHING THAT WAS FOUND.

The effort is to make these private papers and books seem to be the practice and so make the practice look bizarre which it is not.

Medicine is always noting odd phenomena it finds but never uses in practice. So do many subjects.

Attack on the practice of Scientology by identifying it with all its research notes is a completely aberrated action.

The books and notes must be available to students. The bulletins which are today used as practice are quite different from the books and notes. For example, a newspaper group bought research notes stolen from my home the spring of 1966. These notes look quite bizarre. But they were not for public issue and are not used in practice. The newspaper group now publishes these notes out of context and implies this is the PRACTICE of Scientology.

1092

The Enquiry in Melbourne used *only* research notes and never let any practice into evidence and so could make a bizarre picture, particularly as they also condoned perjury in hostile witnesses and would not let friendly witnesses or myself testify.

So the trick used by attackers is to imply that the odd bits found are employed in practice and are the practice.

I am being condemned then for writing up notes and freedom of speech is being challenged.

A survey of current practice of Scientology would show a very sensible and even ordinary looking picture which attains gains for man he has hoped for but has not hitherto achieved. (1) to (5) above comprise the total *practice* of Scientology and what its students are taught to do.

L. RON HUBBARD
Founder

Remimeo
Enclosure in
  Advance Reg Packs
Staff Hats

IMMIGRATION TIP

The new books covers, particularly the one with the Inquisitor (*Have You Lived Before This Life?*) and the boy looking out the window (*Self Analysis*—hardback edition), operate as a sort of open-the-gate at immigration and customs if placed in plain sight in baggage or carried and shown.

If all one's papers are in order, one is not likely to be stopped if he has these books and, if detained, shows the covers to the inspectors or officials.

This probably applies to any immigration service.

One should describe himself as a student of philosophy and can use the word "Scientology" in describing it. One should hold up the book covers to them while saying this.

L. RON HUBBARD
Founder

HCO POLICY LETTER OF 10 AUGUST 1968

Remimeo

(Originally a Sec ED)

LEGAL AND DISSEMINATION

Never stop dissemination to iron out legal! *Never, Never, Never.* The $250,000 LA foundation folded because it did just that under Admiral Scoles and J. B. Farber.

L. RON HUBBARD
Founder

HCO POLICY LETTER OF 23 MAY 1969

Remimeo
Dianetics Checksheet
Div 6

DIANETIC CONTRACT

This form is a standard offering and promotion form for preclears for Dianetic auditing.

DIANETICS

FULL REFUND IF YOU DO NOT GET WELL THROUGH AUDITING.

Anyone accepting this offer must also agree to receive, if required, a medical examination and any effective treatment for any entirely medical illness he may have, both before and after auditing.

The extent of the refund will consist of the exact fee paid.

The claim for refund must be made within three months of the conclusion of the auditing.

If the fee is refunded, no more Dianetic or Scientology auditing or training may be given to the person.

Medical illnesses which beforehand could not be cured medically usually respond to medical treatment after some auditing.

Auditing after such medical treatment tends to stabilize the medical cure and prevent relapse.

A standard release form covering these points must be signed by the applicant.

Some large percentage of man's physical ills are psychosomatic and respond directly to auditing.

Only auditing done by Hubbard Dianetic Graduates in official organizations is covered by this offer.

WHY BE TIRED?

WHY BE IN PAIN?

WHY FEEL BAD?

AUDITING CAN MAKE YOU FEEL WELL AND HAPPY WITH LIFE.

OUR ORGANIZATIONS ARE FRIENDLY. THEY ARE ONLY HERE TO HELP YOU.

The points above are to be included as additional clauses in our release forms.

IF ANYONE EVER DEMANDS A REFUND UNDER THIS OFFER make him or her sign an undertaking never again to purchase training or processing and A RECEIPT IN FULL and GIVE THEM THEIR MONEY BACK ON A MINUS INVOICE AT ONCE. Do not make a long argument out of it or a long, drawn-out admin action.

By paying these claims quickly, getting the promise not to have more auditing or any training and getting a receipt, YOU ACTUALLY BUILD CONFIDENCE.

It is fully understood that this campaign applies to DIANETICS.

Trying to sell Scientology to make physical health has been a betrayal of Scientology. The subject that made bodies well was and always has been Dianetics. Scientology increases ability and gives one immortality.

Refunds for Scientology services are governed by the older policies which remain in force.

The first line, FULL REFUND IF YOU DO NOT GET WELL THROUGH AUDITING, can be posted in any display space. If so, a small, printed, complete leaflet as written above should also be displayed so they can get all the facts.

Persons asking about this should be handed the leaflet.

An additional leaflet should also be available and handed out at the same time:

DIANETICS

Dianetics (*Dia*—through; *nous*—mind) has been thirty-nine years in development.

It is the first fully precision science of the mind.

Physical illness, aches, pains, continual exhaustion, body malfunctions, are created or held in an unchanging state by the mind. This is called *psychosomatic* (*psycho*—spirit; *somatic*—body) *illness*. It has been known about for a century but there has never been a positive remedy before Dianetics.

Auditing (*audit* means "to listen") is a term given to the application of Dianetics.

No drugs, no hypnotism, no mechanical treatment is used.

The actual source of psychosomatic illness has been isolated in Dianetics.

Processing is the action of an auditor letting the preclear (person not yet cleared) find the actual source of his physical illness.

1097

Processing requires usually 25 hours or less.

Various forms of mental therapy were in existence before Dianetics. These were psychology, psychiatry and psychoanalysis.

Psychology and psychiatry were developed chiefly by a Russian veterinarian named Ivan Petrovich Pavlov (1849–1936). His basic principle was that men were only animals and could be conditioned and trained much like dancing bears or dogs. This work was only intended to CONTROL people and so has found great favor with certain rulers and upper classes. None of the activities of psychology or psychiatry were designed to help or cure, only to control the masses.

Psychoanalysis was developed by an Austrian Jew, Sigmund Freud (1856–1939). His occasional successes served to point out that there was a possibility of solving psychosomatic illness through addressing the mind. His concentration on sex gave the subject considerable popularity.

Dianetics was first released in 1950 and has been increasingly successful since that time. Unlike earlier studies, the interest of Dianetics was the relief of physical suffering.

The results of psychiatry are physically damaging, consisting of various brutalities and often injure the patient for life or kill him outright. There have never been any cures listed or claimed for psychiatric treatment as its interest lies only in control. The cost is about $2,000 a month often for years in America and £60 a week for as long as a decade in England.

Psychology is mainly used for testing aptitude or intelligence. It has counseling as part of its activities but it is more concerned with, and financed for, warfare.

These two subjects have bitterly contested any healing subject and use public media, governments and even rumor to forward population control. This action has often made it difficult to bring bona fide mental healing to the people.

Psychoanalysis requires up to five years for an uncertain result and costs about £9,000.

Dianetics requires only a matter of hours, only helps and does not physically injure anyone. It costs about $25 an hour in the US and about £50 total processing cost in the UK.

There is no quarrel between Dianetics and general practitioners of the medical profession. They both have the same purpose (to make people well) and are not political. It is freely admitted in Dianetics that physical illness that can be effectively treated medically should be so treated. Auditing will not set a broken leg or deliver a baby. But it can help get the leg healed in two weeks instead of the usual six and aftereffects of childbirth do not exist when Dianetic auditing is also used.

Many people who cannot work, who cannot enjoy life, are physically ill without realizing it.

Aches, pains, colds, even malfunctions of the body are symptoms of illness.

See the Registrar.

(address)

Variations of the central ideas of these themes may be used.

But remember, Dianetics is pastoral counseling and all HDGs must be ministers.

Psycho-somatic means spirit-body. Look up *psyche* in the dictionary and you'll see.

L. RON HUBBARD
Founder

Remimeo

DIANETIC REGISTRATION

(Revises HCO PL 6 Apr. 69 II, DIANETICS,
mainly in reference to paragraphs two, seven and ten.)

A sign should be prominently displayed in all orgs servicing the general public as follows:

"If you have come here to be cured of a physical illness, SEE THE REGISTRAR and so inform her so that she can arrange for a competent medical examination and treatment and for Dianetic auditing while under the care of a doctor. When you are physically well, you can begin Scientology training and processing on your road to total freedom."

And another sign,

"This organization will not recommend or condone political mental treatment such as electric shocks or brain operations or convulsive drugs and condemns utterly this fascist approach to 'mental health' by extermination of the insane. Because we will not agree to brutality and murder under the guise of mental healing or to the easy and lawless seizure of persons in the name of 'mental health' for political reasons, we are fought ceaselessly by those who seek domination of this country through 'mental treatment.' You are safe so long as we live."

The Registrar is to sign the person up as he or she would any preclear.

The org must make a liaison with a medical clinic which has diagnostic equipment and obtain a flat-rate charge.

Legally and ethically it is all right to send a person to a doctor for a physical examination, but it will cause an ARC break with the doctor to specify what he is to do in that examination.

It is best to say merely: "Would you please do a complete medical examination to include any acute or chronic illness and any effects from past injury or illness."

It should be made clear to the medical doctor who pays his fee. "Your fee for this examination and for any special investigations will be paid by the bearer."

It should end by saying, "Would you please give a note of your findings to the bearer."

Note that it would be unethical for the medical doctor to treat any curable disease found unless the person examined specifically asked him to treat it, otherwise he would refer the person to his own doctor.

A doctor cannot be asked to supervise a person while he is having auditing because he cannot professionally be asked to join in a nonmedical attempt to cure some illness, for if he did, he would be subject to discipline, charged with "covering," and if found guilty, struck off the medical register.

The org should make their position very clear to the clinic—that they are trying to cooperate with the medical profession and that Scientology is a religion. However, after or in the absence of medical treatment if none is needed, the persons sent will be given Dianetic auditing after such medical examination and treatment, if given, or under medical care. A clean-cut difference should be made between Dianetics as an assist done under a physician's care or after his treatment and Dianetics as a religious function of pastoral counseling or Scientology as a religious practice.

If contempt or hostility is met, write a letter of complaint to the medical association and try another doctor or clinic. In such a letter of complaint make it very plain that you are not engaged in physical healing, that you have always tried to cooperate with medicine and that your only quarrel is with psychiatric casualties and their perversion of the medical profession.

If the clinic shows clear-cut evidence of the need of an operation, the Director of Processing should give the preclear the verdict. If the preclear will not have it, arrange a meeting between the preclear and the doctor and discuss it.

It is possible to engage in Dianetic processing even when a medical verdict is for an operation, but if the preclear will not have it, then undertake Dianetic processing only under the doctor's care and with his consent, and insist upon the preclear being reexamined during processing.

The cost of the examination and any operation is in addition to processing fees and any such charges are paid directly to the clinic by the preclear, the org not taking responsibility for the costs of these.

After any medical treatment, the entire treatment is run as an engram or chain as the first action. Lingering symptoms are also run down to their basics as per Dianetic Auditing Assists given in the Dianetic Course.

Policy is not to engage on auditing sick pcs without medical advice or treatment as required.

Insane pcs are handled in this same fashion as they are mainly physically ill, need rest and no harassment. Insane pcs are a lot of trouble unless one has an institution to hand, but institutions cannot be trusted. Until an org has some means or connection by which the insane preclear will not be brutalized, shocked or operated on with brain "operations," it is better to refuse them.

By insane pc is meant one who is subject to highly irrational and destructive behavior. If not, they are regarded as physically ill.

The senile and mentally retarded are also handled as per physically ill pcs as above.

Waivers in all cases are required.

A new clause, "Will not hold the organization or its principals responsible for medical costs or errors," must be included in signing persons up for Dianetics.

Complete files of all such should be kept in Division 6 to show in case of need:

a.   that the org does not engage in physical healing and

b.   success stories with full records, x-rays, etc., for Dianetics.

Where this policy letter is fully in force, earlier policies on healing and the insane are cancelled.

This change of policy is due to (1) our wish to cease to individuate from the other social groups of the society and (2) our refusal to leave the field of mental healing in the hands of public enemies.

This is also part of our campaign to revitalize Western society. "A well society is a sane society."

L. RON HUBBARD
Founder

Remimeo
HCO ES Hat
HCO Area Sec Hat
Dept C&A Hat

DIANETICS
RIGHT TO AUDIT

The following pledge is required to be signed and witnessed by any applicant for HDC before issue of the actual certificate.

HDC CERTIFICATE APPLICATION

_____

Location

_____

Date

I, _____, of

Block Letters

_____

Permanent Home Address

hereby apply for a certificate as a HUBBARD DIANETIC COUNSELOR.

I hereby solemnly pledge myself:

1. To use the AUDITOR'S CODE well known to me whenever employing DIANETICS or STANDARD DIANETICS.

2. To use only STANDARD DIANETICS in processing persons at Dianetic levels.

3. Not to use DIANETICS or STANDARD DIANETICS or its technology or principles under another name or to alter the technology in processing.

4. I recognize the Hubbard Organizations as the only certifying body for Dianetics.

5. I realize gross errors in Dianetics can be corrected by Scientology reviews.

6. I swear that I have been through the STANDARD DIANETIC MATERI-ALS three times, have passed a comprehensive examination on them with a 100 percent grade and have audited several sessions consecutively with excellent results according to the preclear.

7. I swear that I will use DIANETICS and STANDARD DIANETICS to the best of my ability to help my fellow man and mankind.

_____
Signature

_____
Witness

_____
Witness

L. RON HUBBARD
Founder

Remimeo
HCO ES Hat
HCO Area Sec Hat
Dept C&A Hats

DIANETICS
RIGHT TO TEACH

An HDG (Hubbard Dianetic Graduate), to obtain his actual certificate as an HDG and to obtain his right to teach, must sign and have witnessed the following statement and application of his HDG certificate.

HDG CERTIFICATE APPLICATION

Location _____

Date _____

I, _____
(Block letters)

do hereby apply for my Hubbard Dianetic Graduate Certificate and my right to TEACH Dianetics and to obtain HDC certificates for my qualified students by application to an official Hubbard Dianetic or Scientology organization.

By witnessed signature hereon I pledge myself:

1. To use and abide by and require my students to use and abide by THE AUDITOR'S CODE.

2. To teach STANDARD DIANETICS.

3. To use the term STANDARD DIANETICS in communicating any of the technology of STANDARD DIANETICS.

4. To use the term DIANETICS in communicating any of the basic or older materials of Dianetics.

5. To publicly state to students or classes that anything that may have been added or evaluated to a general course of instruction that is not STANDARD DIANETICS, that it is not Dianetics or STANDARD DIANETICS when it is not.

6. To require three times through the materials, theory and practical, and a 100% passed examination and several well done sessions in a row before I recommend any student for certification or give him a course completion.

7. To inform all my students that errors made in Dianetics are reparable by Scientology reviews.

8. Not to give support or encouragement to activities calculated to injure measures or persons seeking to safeguard and continue the teaching of Dianetics or Standard Dianetics in a pure state.

9. I recognize Hubbard Organizations as the only valid certifying body for Dianetics and Standard Dianetics.

10. To teach and use Dianetics to the best of my ability to help my fellow man and mankind.

_____ (Seal)
Signed

_____
Witness

_____
Witness

L. RON HUBBARD
Founder

HCO POLICY LETTER OF 20 JUNE 1972

Remimeo

REGISTRARS AND NOTES

It may be found that Registrars do not know the difference between "WAIVERS" and "promissory notes." Registrars, Treasury people and Cashiers should be made to look these up, as a confusion of meanings can cost you your shirt in an org.

ALL CREDIT EXTENDED FOR WHATEVER REASON MUST BE IN THE FORM OF A LEGAL PROMISSORY NOTE.

This is in addition to any waivers or debit invoices or any other signed paper.

A promissory note must be legal for the country or area in which it is issued.

Note forms or booklets are usually available from a local stationery shop.

A sample for the US is:

$_____ . ___ Place _____ Date _____

On demand, for value received, I promise to pay to the order of _____

_____ (company legal name)

($_____ . ___) dollars, in lawful money of the United States of America, at _____ (place) with interest at the rate of _____ (___%) per cent per annum.

_____
(Signed)

The reason for this is that a note is more easily collected in court than a debt.

Orgs are not supposed to extend credit. In Qual, however, bills can be run up.

Whenever a bill is run up, the person signing for it must also sign a note.

The occasion for this policy letter was finding a Registrar who did not know what the word *Registrar* meant, who thought she was just a Cashier, who did not know the meaning of any of the words connected with her post and who had cost her org thereby a great deal of money.

L. RON HUBBARD
Founder

HCO POLICY LETTER OF 9 NOVEMBER 1974R
REVISED 2 OCTOBER 1980

Remimeo
EDs, COs
Reges
Missions

Important

Urgent

REFUNDS AND REPAYMENTS

Refs:
(And *very* important for every Reg and ED, HES and HAS to
know these as ignorance of them can cost enormous sums.)

HCO PL 23 May 69   DIANETIC CONTRACT
HCO PL 23 Oct. 63   REFUND POLICY
HCO PL   1 Aug. 66   REFUND ADDITION
HCO PL 23 May 65 II   REBATES

A *REFUND* is a return of money after service.

A *REPAYMENT* is a return of money without the service being taken.

BOTH ARE NOW COVERED BY "REFUND POLICY" AND ARE GOVERNED BY THE POLICY LETTERS ABOVE.

All refund and repayment policy also applies to training.

WARNING

It is very important to acquaint the person asking for refund or repayment with the conditions of receiving his money.

These are given in the policy letters above. Usually a C/S 53 (latest revision) or Green Form and handling done by a person who can make list items read (what it takes is given on the new Green Form) cures the customer impulse to run.

So if these are done before a refund or repayment is given usually there is no refund or repayment.

Where your tech is out (verbal tech, lousy TRs, overloaded or untrained C/S) you can expect refunds. Which is silly because it's all in the HCOBs.

Where you don't have a Director of Tech Services (or D of P) calling people in for service when paid or you don't have auditors or good Supervisors or materials, you can expect repayments. Which is silly because the majority of staff want to be tech trained people!

But no matter which, when you do give refunds or repayments you do it on policy. And the policy is above and when understood and followed you will benefit greatly.

Misunderstood words, withholds, no service are the cause of all your refunds and repayments.

But until you get the org and its tech people to fly right you'll have the problem of refunds and repayments eating up major quantities of GI so you better handle it very on-policy.

RECOURSE

It happens that when a person has taken a refund or repayment he often sourly regrets it. The door has been closed in his face and his dream of coming right has been ended.

If an ARC Break Reg were to see such people and an auditor (who can make lists read and has smooth TRs) were to do a C/S 53 (latest revision) and possibly a Green Form, the person would sign up again.

BUT the following policy is laid down in *all* such cases. They must sign a waiver which will be provided by the HCO of the org.

HCO Area Secretaries should ensure that the waiver is run off as a form for org use and copies sent to local missions.

Once signed, a copy is kept in Val Docs AND A NOTATION OF IT IS MADE ON ANY INVOICE WITH DATE.

Any other legal waivers ordinarily required must also be signed again.

In this way you can open the door when it has been solidly closed.

L. RON HUBBARD
Founder

Assisted by
AVC Int

HCO POLICY LETTER OF 29 SEPTEMBER 1982

Remimeo

Keeping Scientology Working Series 30

MISREPRESENTATION OF
DIANETICS AND SCIENTOLOGY

There is a vital legal and PR point which should be broadly known.

"Standard Tech" is contained in the official volumes of the technical services and in HCO Bulletins and charts within them and in textbooks on the subject.

These are, none of them, vague. They are very explicit.

The data is thus not only available but taught in courses.

Now and then we hear of "somebody's case messed up." Or that someone was complaining or dissatisfied with results. Research into such cases uniformly shows that STANDARD TECH was not applied.

Thus one arrives at an interesting point: *Standard* tech has never harmed anybody.

Recently there was a spate of "out-tech" on some executives that "messed up their cases." (This of course impaired their effectiveness and made them feel "Dianetics and Scientology did not work and so was not worth defending.")

A careful review of these cases showed that the "Case Supervisor" and a small clique of "auditors" (all of whom knew better but who were serving their own ends) were NOT applying Dianetics and Scientology but were only *pretending* to. (The clique has been detected and thoroughly handled and so are the "messed-up cases"—by standard tech of course and so successfully.)

But this brings up an interesting and useful legal and public relations point:

When people complain and are "dissatisfied with results," it will be found that Dianetics and Scientology were NOT being used on them.

Someone was doing something else and calling it Dianetics and Scientology.

This is, of course, misrepresentation and a violation of trademark and copyright law.

A similar circumstance would occur if someone put transmission oil in a package marked "Green Meadow Butter" and sold it and advised its use as "Green Meadow Butter" when it isn't.

Legal and PR situations from people who have complaints stem from two reasons:

A. They are themselves engaged for whatever reason in some self-serving end by complaining or

B. They did *not* receive Dianetics and Scientology.

A review of any such cases will bear this out. It is not a matter of making minor errors with the tech. It is not a matter of poor C/S judgment in applying it. The situation will be found to be flagrant.

Someone was only pretending it was Dianetics and Scientology and doing something else and for some other reason.

Here we have a problem in labels. The labels "Dianetics" and "Scientology" could illegally be placed on anything and that anything might be quite bad.

Thus it is the person misrepresenting who is actionable, not the originator or the properly licensed and supervised entities.

The operating question is "What did he or they do that they were calling Dianetics and Scientology standard tech?" And "Let me have their names so the misrepresentation can be stopped."

Don't let yourself be conned by an old legal or PR trick of switching labels!

Dianetics and Scientology are a precise system that works.

L. RON HUBBARD
Founder

DIANETICS AND SCIENTOLOGY REDEFINED

DIANETICS was the forerunner of Scientology.

By use of Dianetics, as early as 1950, it became apparent that we were dealing, not with cells and cellular memory, but with a beingness that defied time. Anyone using Dianetics properly would make the same discovery. For Dianetics reached deeper than man had ever gone before in plumbing the mystery of life.

The phenomena of past lives was followed by exteriorization. Many of the things man has always wondered about were suddenly very plain even to the most skeptical observer.

The conclusion was inescapable: we were dealing with the human spirit.

When this was revealed, those who comprised the wide membership of organizations at that time were insistent that the organization was actually, then, one which was dealing in spiritual matters and therefore would have to be a religious organization in order to be factual.

SCIENTOLOGY marked the point of change from a materialistic viewpoint to a spiritual one.

However, there has been no issue truly clarifying this and one is needed.

DIANETICS is defined in the *Tech Dictionary* as *DIA* (Greek) through, *NOUS* (Greek) soul.

DIANETICS is further redefined as WHAT THE SOUL IS DOING TO THE BODY.

SCIENTOLOGY, as defined in the *Technical Dictionary*, 2. Scientology addresses the thetan (the spirit). Scientology is used to increase spiritual freedom, intelligence, ability and produce immortality. (HCOB 22 Apr. 69, DIANETICS VERSUS SCIENTOLOGY)

SCIENTOLOGY is further redefined as THE STUDY AND HANDLING OF THE SPIRIT IN RELATIONSHIP TO ITSELF, UNIVERSES AND OTHER LIFE.

This does not change the technology. These are simply added to the *Technical Dictionary*.

It does change page 209 of *What Is Scientology?** a book I did not write. The definition on that page for Dianetics could pose difficulty in the field of healing and it is not and never has been correct.

Dianetics, though it might not have guessed it in its early publication, was dealing with the human spirit and it is interesting that its name, as derived, meant that.

It is recommended that in legally defining these subjects, the above be used.

L. RON HUBBARD
Founder

*[*Editor's Note:* This refers to the 1978 edition of *What Is Scientology?*]

CORPORATE STRUCTURE

CORPORATION COORDINATOR

A Corporation Coordinator is hereby appointed. This is a newly created post, the function of which is concerned solely with the setting up and maintaining of new autonomous Scientology corporations on a worldwide basis. It is a function of HCO Worldwide and comes under the aegis of the newly created HCO (WW) Ltd., headed by Org Supervisor WW.

The new Corporation Coordinator will continue also as Association Secretary, London.

The functions and purposes of the post are:

1. Setting up new, autonomous corporations of Scientology all over the world, including USA.

2. Arranging the transfer of any old Scientology corporations to the new corporations, and closing out the old, where appropriate and necessary.

3. Ensuring legality of status under varying laws of states and governments.

4. Smoothing taxation, legal and accounting problems.

5. Assisting in the setting up of further new corporations along the same lines.

6. Ensuring the smooth running of the corporations, when set up—that is, seeing that they comply with the legal requirements defined by company law.

This will be a difficult task. The cooperation of Continental Officers, Assoc/ Org Secs and others concerned with corporation affairs is earnestly requested.

Corporate reorganization has already begun and must be completed for existing organizations within the next six months. Close liaison is essential if the operation is to be smoothly carried out.

L. RON HUBBARD
Founder

Saint Hill
Only

HCO CORPORATIONS

For staff information there are FIVE HCO Corporations.

They are:

HCO (WW), Ltd.

This is the corporation that manages international organizations. It has the magazines we publish and handles the international communication lines. All photography and its accounts come under this corporation, also. Use its letterhead for these.

HCO (St Hill), Ltd.

This is the corporation that runs the course, handles the internal activities of Saint Hill. All student activities and letters concerning the course, quarters, domestic accounts, go under this corporation. Only its letterhead is used for these activities.

SCIENTOLOGY LIBRARY AND RESEARCH, Ltd.

This is the corporation that sells books, compiles research materials and makes tapes and also cine films. All book letters use this letterhead.

THE ABOVE ARE THE ACTIVE CORPORATIONS WHICH HAVE THEIR HEADQUARTERS AT SAINT HILL.

There are two other HCOs. They are:

HUBBARD COMMUNICATIONS OFFICE, Ltd.

This was a public corporation formed in order to handle the communications of another corporation, HUBBARD ASSOCIATION OF SCIENTOLOGISTS, Ltd. This corporation ran the garage at Hickstead,* but as that is closed and as the corporation it was formed to serve, HASI, Ltd., is inactive, this corporation is dormant. However, all garage (Hickstead) letters and bills are written on its letterhead. BUT ITS LETTERHEAD MAY NOT BE USED FOR ANYTHING ELSE.

HUBBARD COMMUNICATIONS OFFICE

This was the original HCO, a private, unincorporated business which was taken from London when we came to Saint Hill. It became the HUBBARD ASSOCIATION OF SCIENTOLOGISTS, Inc., Worldwide Division. This (HASI)

---

*Hickstead: a small village near Saint Hill Manor; site of Hickstead Garage, an automobile service and repair shop owned by the Hubbard Association of Scientologists, Ltd., in 1964.

was an American company. HASI, Inc. still owns all the property and equipment as it has never been transferred by formal board action. But this company is dormant and its letterhead should never be used.

It is illegal for the name of one company to be used in the transaction of the business of another. So care should be taken that this does not happen. Just remember that ONLY THE FIRST THREE COMPANIES ABOVE ARE ACTIVE.

L. RON HUBBARD
Founder

CORPORATE NAMES
GROUP NAMES

The only corporation that may use the word "FOUNDING" in its name is the FOUNDING CHURCH OF SCIENTOLOGY OF WASHINGTON, DC.

Any other corporation in the USA or elsewhere including the word "Founding" in its name must change it by board resolution, filing name change correctly before relevant authorities.

No group or congregation, etc., incorporated or not, may use the word "Founding" in its title. Any such existing shall change their name in accordance with this policy.

L. RON HUBBARD
Founder

Gen. Non-Remimeo
Board Members
Exec Secs
Typists SH

EXEC DIV

BOARD MINUTES

The way to write board minutes is as follows:

1. Use the board-book paper only—a very fine quality white 8 x 10 or 8½ x 10½-inch paper, one side only.

2. Use only a typewriter that has its type clean and in alignment and use a heavy, well-inked black ribbon for very black type.

3. Head the minutes with the corporate name.

4. Type general proceedings double-spaced.

5. Indent far enough on the left margin to permit enclosure in a board book. If it isn't so indented, the board-book binding will obscure the minutes.

6. Indent a resolution entirely even with the paragraph indentation of the proceedings, comments.

7. Single-space a resolution.

8. Begin each resolution with a RESOLVED: wholly in capitals and then proceed with capitals and lowercase.

9. Don't go too high or low on the page.

By making the resolution a single-spaced every-line-indented block, the resolutions stand out from the double-spaced proceedings.

Do about five copies. More copies can be obtained from the original.

Send the original and two copies to the Legal Officer to put in the board book when it is signed.

Send a copy to each board member for his or her files, marked "For your board files."

L. RON HUBBARD
Founder

HUBBARD COMMUNICATIONS OFFICE
Saint Hill Manor, East Grinstead, Sussex

HCO POLICY LETTER OF 15 MARCH 1966

SH only
Exec Secs
ES Comm HCO
Legal Officer

CORPORATE ADDRESS

No corporate address hereafter is to be Saint Hill.

This includes Hubbard College of Scientology, C of S of California and any other corporation.

Crawley is a little crossroads and their tax office is used to greengrocer accounts and any sum above £15,000 is a fantastic sum to Crawley. Further, Crawley's tax commissioners are East Grinstead and East Grinstead saw a £10 note once and is still talking about it.

No large corporation should ever use a rural one-horse tax office as they can't understand real business sums in such offices.

Always use a London address and make sure you have one for all corporations.

L. RON HUBBARD
Founder

[*Editor's Note:* The modern corporate structure of the Scientology religion is described in the booklet *The Corporations of Scientology,* published by Church of Scientology International.]

SOCIAL REFORM

CAPTIVE BRAINS

Pity the poor scientist. He is a captive brain.

Today he has no liberty. He may not, must not utter blasphemy against his captors.

All he is permitted to do is slave.

The cause for which he slaves derives from an accident of geography. If he was born in the "West," he gets to slave for the Extreme Right. If born in the "East," he slaves for the Extreme Left.

Should he find anything or invent anything, his discovery becomes the boast of Leftist or Rightist.

At once, he has been persuaded, he must *deny all further responsibility for his creation* and sign over the whole thing for a ruble or one dollar to his captors and must remain anonymous.

And then he must also wear his old school tie and belong to the right society. His credentials must always be in order. If he invents or discovers anything, his credentials are examined first, its political use is examined next and then he's given his microcosm of security and sent back to his cell.

His government, his society, his employer, all have managed to insist that these conditions exist and, more, are normal and fitting.

If he utters blasphemy, such as "I feel radiation is not assimilable for babies" or "Science was invented to serve man," he is sacked. His security is taken roughly away and they tear up his old school tie. They say nasty things about him in the papers and glare at his former fellows hoping they start no nonsense now.

When you make a man grind enough years at the moldy texts of yesterday's prejudices, he is already on the ropes. He is dimly peeping through bad eyesight at a myopic world. He has been made to feel that if he doesn't treat life like a tightrope, he'll fall.

And so he is piteously grateful to receive his old school tie. He is cringing with gratitude when they offer him anonymous rewards. If he destroys mankind thereby by dreaming up a bomb, he never finds it out. He forgot mankind. He denied all responsibility for his creation.

Once scientists stood for truth and tried to serve humanity. Now they serve economics and political creeds.

Why has no defense been built against fission? Because nobody wrote a check to build it. Scientifically, it is a problem only slightly more complex than atom bombs. Why has no *scientist* started to work on it, check or no check?

Can it be they gutted scientists of guts when they perverted Newton?

Can it be he or she is a coward, this scientist? Can it be a paycheck and an old school tie mean more to him than life?

Ah yes—I well recall seeking to shame some apple-cheeked young officers, strayed like blinking lambs into a man-of-war. I graded them on their watch standing with A and B and C and put gold stars on their records on the bulletin board. Such was my irony, so heavy was my hand, as I stood back, that finally I could only weep. They thanked me!

So the product of the group-think, the death of the individual in a university of today, extends further than the scientist.

Slaves, it has been said, love their chains. No more so than a scientist who sells his tiny spark of a soul for a pat on the head from a political boss.

And so, as the responsibility of the individual for his creation dies, so we enter in upon a madness of destruction where all human suffering is made available to all.

The man who would destroy all man for pay, not even vengeance, is so far below contempt he is no longer man but animal, a beast unclean who cares not what he kills so long as he is fed.

You want to end the threat of bombs, then please awake. Politics died with Victoria. Government is no longer done that way. It's done not by appeals to men but appeals to their bellies and their fears. The world is now controlled by economic groups who debase laws and rewrite texts and so make slaves.

For anything to happen now, enough to end this crazy dance, it will be needful to amend man's pride and confidence and teach him he can stand alone on his two feet. The re-creation of the individual is all that's left, no matter what you would improve.

Man buys his lies from cowardice. Afraid to face the truth, he cannot view his death—coming fast, for *all* mankind.

In companies, in every path of life, show men they can be free and you'll have courage back for them.

How do I know this about scientists? For thirty years I've been a maverick, an iconoclast. Each old school tie they sought to hang me with I painted its stripes comically. And I have watched in thirty years almost every other maverick go down. I've seen them denied security, given bad notices. I've seen them produce brilliant work and have it lie neglected even though their nation bled.

America had the V-2 in 1932. Why did she have to import a foreign scientist to "recover its secret"?

America had helicopters in 1936. Why did she copy a German machine, the Focke-Wulf, ten years later?

America had a thousand things she would not buy from men who would not wear the old school tie and bow their heads in abandonment of their creations.

I was myself once threatened with expulsion from a university because I said that students should be allowed to think. A terrible crime.

We go into the teeth today, we Scientologists, of the greatest slavery of them all, the slavery of thought. The battle is not ended yet—but listen, we've broken through!

We today are the only group on Earth that is not owned by either camp or any creed. We serve no flighty masters.

Once there was only me, sickened sometimes by lying press inspired because I would not be a slave. But now there's you and you and you. Sometimes we've lost a man or a girl but only because they were not brave enough to stand upon a mountain top and say "I'm me! I think. I feel. I am no slave. Come on! Be free!"

But even in our very trying days, we still kept most of us and now we grow into a crowd whose mutters shake the cornerstones of prisons.

And we've won technology. Why should I give you sales talks now? Upon every continent an HGC is turning people into Clears.

We're winning or why should the press begin again to growl? On one hand on the stands we read that a grayayayt university now believes that IQ can change, while in the same day a huge scientific group says we are no good.

Our hands lie heavily on destiny, yours and mine. We've turned a downward trend upward again. And so as we mount higher, be clever and understand what's happening.

Attacks in press and elsewhere will mount up. Upon me. Upon us. No. No violence. Just entheta. And money, lots of money will be spent to scream out more and more. Be gratified. Their hysteria is our index of win, nothing less.

Pity the poor slave master! There in his Extreme Right or Extreme Left den, he's penned successfully the cream of brains and wit. And just as he licks his chops to say, "You're now all slaves!" a mighty host cries back, "Who us?" and strikes the fetters from his prey. Poor fellows. Commissar Gulpski and Capitalistic Grab will have to unite to have a quorum in their caves.

Oh no. It's no mad dream. Politics is dead. Economics now dominates the world. And we sit laughing with technology to undo all their buttons and their charms.

As we improve organizations, we will improve people. And as we improve people we make men brave. And then at last the slave looks down and says, "Why, what *are* these chains?" and shakes them off.

The vested interests of the world, since its beginning, made but one mistake. They thought that punishment and hard duress were all that made man work. But man just worked so long as he could help. And when his wares were turned to bringing hate and death, he struck. Until someone, you and me, give back his willingness to help, the world, like tired wheels, will grind down to a stop.

It is an overt act by you and me to leave in power any group that denies men freedom, knowing what we know. Therefore, attack.

We are the only men and women left on Earth who are no longer slaves.

And we are now well past the point in knowledge and in numbers where we will wear their chains.

The men who need us most are the slave masters.

We will get around to them last, I think. It is more fitting so.

P.S. And *now* do you wonder why the mutter grows: "Scientologists are *dangerous*." But Scientology is the only game where all dynamics win!

L. RON HUBBARD
Founder

L. Ron Hubbard
EXECUTIVE DIRECTIVE

LRH ED 47 INT   16 November 1968

A FABLE

The following fable seems to have turned up somehow.

It may cheer you up in the present conflict with the old-time psychiatrist and his efforts to destroy modern culture:

THE WAY IT SEEMS

This situation wherein the "World" Federation of Mental Health and its "National" organizations advocate violent and brutal (and highly illegal) "treatment" on false grounds suggests an interesting anecdote.

A flock of sheep was being tended by two shepherds. They noticed the sheep were very nervous and restless and looking around one of the shepherds saw a huge black wolf, one of a hovering wolf pack, drag down and kill a sheep. The shepherd rushed over to protest. "What are you doing?" The wolf looked up from his kill and said through bloody jaws, "I'm a professional!" Whereupon the shepherd looked apologetic and said, "Oh," and walked away.

The sheep became more and more nervous and darted about, looking ready to stampede.

The two shepherds had a meeting together to see what could be done.

The farmer came out to see why the sheep were so hard to control and discussed it with the shepherds. The farmer said, "Maybe it's those wolves."

A wolf who had just killed his tenth sheep overheard this and trotted over, bits of sheep flesh sticking to his ugly teeth.

"No, no," said the wolf. "We're doing all we can to keep them herded up for you. If we went away they'd bolt. These sheep we're taking care of are the crazy sheep. You see they are the cause of the other sheep being nervous."

"Ah," said the farmer.

"Yes," said the wolf. "You see this is a highly technical field, far above your mentality. You can't recognize the crazy sheep and we can."

"Oh well," said the farmer. "We're glad of your help."

"Yes, yes. We try to oblige," said the wolf. "It's a very hard job, though, rounding up all these sheep. If you pay us, we'll make it much simpler."

So the farmer and the shepherds took up a collection and gave it to the wolves. And the wolves had a long chute built and a corral with spiked fences. And they drove sheep down the chute and killed them.

The farmer and shepherds explained how it was all right to the other sheep.

But an old big ram and three of his mates had been watching all this. They had tried to break in on it but the farmer and shepherds had held them off from interfering, saying how technical it all was and that the wolves had to study 12 years and had diplomas.

Finally the old ram had had enough of it.

He and his mates suddenly rushed at the farmer and two shepherds. The remainder of the flock thundered along with the rams.

The farmer and shepherds turned with a screech and ran down the chute to get help from the wolves.

There were several loud snaps and the wolves ate up two shepherds and a farmer so quick their overall buttons flew up half a mile.

The rams got back, took a long run at it and smashed the fences down, caught the overfed wolves against the far side and stamped them to pieces under a thousand sharp hoofs.

Sometime later the old ram was standing on the calm hillside, where the sheep now peacefully grazed, and a young kid started coughing.

The old ram reached into his throat and pulled out a scrap of paper.

"What was it?" said the kid, recovering his breath.

The old ram examined it and grinned. "It's a wolf diploma. Took him 12 years to become a professional it seems. But what you were choking on is this fingernail that was caught in it. He not only bit but ate the hand that fed him."

And that's how it got so calm and peaceful up there on the hillside.

L. RON HUBBARD
Founder

L. Ron Hubbard

EXECUTIVE DIRECTIVE

LRH ED 55 INT   29 November 1968

THE WAR

You may not realize it staff member but there is only one small group that has hammered Dianetics and Scientology for eighteen years.

The press attacks, the public upsets you receive and all those you have received for all your time in Scientology were generated by this one group.

For eighteen years it has poured lies and slander into the press and government agencies.

Last year we isolated a dozen men at the top. This year we found the organization these used and all its connections over the world.

They are as red as paint. Their former president was a card-carrying Communist and they have four on their board of directors, yet they reach into international finance, health ministries, schools, the press. They even control immigration in many lands.

Psychiatry and "mental health" was chosen as a vehicle to undermine and destroy the West! And we stood in their way.

They knew we had the answers. We were over $2,000,000 dangerous to them. That's about what they've spent to try to get rid of us.

Well, today, the World Federation of Mental Health (which pretends to be part of the United Nations and isn't) and their "national" mental health organizations (which pretend to be part of each national government and aren't) in every Western nation have been spotted by us and proven to be the ones responsible.

If a platoon of Russian soldiers landed in your country and started shooting down people, the military or the citizens would wipe them out.

But if several regiments landed in small groups, with phony passports, dressed in dark business suits, each one vouched for as a professional doctor by the "best people," they could (and do) select out anyone they wish to kill, get him behind closed doors in an institution and depersonalize or kill him.

They have infiltrated boards of education, the armed services, even the churches.

They hold the wives or daughters of a great many politicians and keep them "under treatment."

They appoint ministers of health by pretending they are already part of the government.

They collect millions.

Their "technology" is the same as that used by intelligence services. Electric shock. Brain operations. These were used in Lubenka prison in Russia but are not allowed on Russians!

Anyway, this was the live wire we got across by being *able to undo their effect on the West*.

None of this is fiction. There are too many dead men around for that.

We have the goods on them and right this minute more artillery is being rolled up by us from more quarters than they could ever predict.

We've made a beachhead. We are slamming in closer.

You aren't standing alone. There is more ammunition being flung at them right this minute than they could ever duck.

They made a few gains. They could even make one or two more.

But they made a bad mistake. They attacked us. And we weren't even in the same line of country.

For eighteen years we have had constant sniping at us over the world. They did it.

We've got to fight this one on through and we will.

Think of what it would be like to have no such opposition!!!! My, how we would expand. And will.

You just carry on your job well, do it very well. Keep the show on the road. Get the stats up.

A lot of good guys amongst us are taking care of *them*. We are using only legal means over the world. *We* don't stoop to murder and roughhouse. But man, the effectiveness of our means will become history.

It is a tough war. All wars are tough. It isn't over.

But if the enemy knew all that was heading in his direction this minute from how many quarters he'd faint.

Let him lah-de-dah with the socialites and "best people" a little longer. Let him pose as part of the government yet a little while. And then he's had it.

Our error was in failing to take over total control of all mental healing in the West. Well, we'll do that too.

You never did understand his treatments? Well so the psychiatrist acts like a Russian storm trooper after all.

L. RON HUBBARD
Founder

L. Ron Hubbard

EXECUTIVE DIRECTIVE

LRH ED 66 INT   13 December 1968

THE GREAT "CHARITY" SWINDLE

One of the reasons Scientology is fought so hard and with such heavy finance and ferocity is that if it succeeded, it would then end one of the greatest "charity" swindles of all time.

The group who fights Scientology in the press and parliaments is fighting madly to retain control of (amongst other things less savory) a billion pound "research" racket.

It goes this way: A group named so as to make people think it is part of governments over the world, has fund collection chapters and agents.

These see all the rich people they can and the governments and explain that the lot of the "poor insane" (about whom they don't give a damn as evidenced by their killing them) is so horrible that millions are needed urgently.

The rich people and the deluded governments then lay out fantastic sums of money, millions upon millions each year.

The groups' representatives then take this money and whack it up amongst their pals.

As simply to split it up would be caught by the tax people, the group invents a "reason why." It appoints insanity projects for research like, "The Depressive Project."

Then each local member is paid several thousand a year, in addition to his income for his "research." This of course is a tax-free sum.

The members write up something like, "Depressives are often noticed to be depressed" and that's it for the year.

The amounts are fantastic in size. We have the lists and boy would any tax agent love to see them!

So, these swindlers built up a structure that would sooner or later cave in.

In these times of actual advances in physics and mathematics sooner or later some independent project would come up with a datum that was real.

Dr. Wilhelm Reich, not one of their boys, was imprisoned and killed for making a breakthrough in the 50s.

It could have ended the golden avalanche.

Then, good Lord, there was Dianetics and Scientology all of a sudden, in one piece and actually working!

This gave them an awful turn.

It threatened this yearly harvest.

Scientology is fought because it *is* effective.

But if the answers are all found, then what happens to begging for funds to "research"? People say, "Well, but Hubbard did it. Why don't you use Scientology?"

The enemy has been hit in the pocketbook, his most vulnerable spot.

His world headquarters began to show more and more deficit. He was down to his last fifty million!

Rich people began to say, "Why don't you use Scientology?"

So they frantically campaigned over the world to discredit it.

Governments were being whipped into line (this group appoints all the "Health" ministers for both parties.) Because *they* began to wonder. "If it's all done, why don't they use it?" was beginning to be asked. "Why all this dough for research? When it's all done in Scientology?"

The average member of this enemy group couldn't care less about the insane.

But they care about their million pound swindle over the world.

One violent opponent of Scientology in this group who had been howling against it in the press, finally backed up and admitted he knew nothing at all about it. Not a thing!

This isn't the only motive this international group has. It is their finance motive. But in itself it would be enough.

They can bribe a lot of people with all that money.

This is one of their secrets—how they finance themselves and pay their agents and get past the tax collector.

What an unsavory group they are! And you can point your finger with accuracy at any politician who supports them. He's under blackmail or is bribed.

Sort of an odd commentary on the governments of the West, isn't it?

Birds of a feather?

They sure have bad luck anyway. The biggest mistake they ever made was to attack Scientology.

But what could they do? There it was, the whole subject of the mind fully researched. We weren't even in their line of country!

We ran into the biggest single swindle of the century. It desperately tried to discredit us. And we're knocking it in the head, bang!

For who can stand in the way of truth?

L. RON HUBBARD
Founder

HCO INFORMATION LETTER OF 4 APRIL 1969

Remimeo
BPI

TO: All Orgs

FROM: RON

SUBJECT: RON'S JOURNAL 1969 NO. 3 POLITICAL TREATMENT

I've been studying the state of psychiatry and there can now be no doubt whatever that their "treatment" is political treatment and should be called such.

Electric shocks if *not* given show patients would leave 6 weeks earlier.

Brain "operations" result in total loss of body coordination and a bright normal being is turned into a drooling blob of flesh, unable even to retain urine. They live only briefly when they do not die at once on the operating table.

The only precedent for such "operations" is Hitler's action in doing it much more lightly to 800,000 persons to make "farm slavery" or zombies.

The political color command and control of parliaments and legislatures by psychiatry are evident in the easy seizure without trial laws being passed or in the hypocritical actions like Ronald Reagan's new bill in California that was hailed in the press as giving "rights" to patients in asylums (comparable to Geneva's Prisoner of War Code) to refuse such treatment but the actual bill says in small print that the "doctor" can refuse any of these rights at his sole discretion. This equals a sentence to death without trial or even a crime.

In Dianetics insanity is shown to be common physical illnesses, yet asylums have no medical facilities. Dianetics can handle insanity with relative ease once the physical injuries and illnesses of the patient are cured medically or when the patient is only lightly ill. A new breakthrough on this is now being taught real MDs in England by a team I trained.

So there *is* an easy cure of insanity in ordinary medical treatment of broken, badly healed bones, bad kidneys, etc., plus easy Dianetic auditing.

Dianetics has been available and proven for 20 years. Yet psychiatric front groups have been able to command sufficient political action to prevent its use, instead getting bills passed to easily seize anyone, torture and kill him.

Thus the Western countries are seen to refuse actual treatment and legalize inhuman torture and brutality.

Psychiatric treatment is actually psychiatric political treatment, nothing more, to rid the world of anyone who might disagree.

Nelson Rockefeller's "youth stockades" are for youths who *might* become delinquent, it says right there in the founding papers.

In Arizona federal judges sentence delinquents to electric shock or death for "being turbulative."

Insanity is now defined as anyone who disagrees with the social autonomy.

The handwriting is plain. Only the government supports psychiatry. The public by survey stays thoroughly away from them. Death camps like the one just found in Cardiff are situated strategically over the West. Hitler at least wasn't pretending to *help* anyone. He just wanted them dead.

So psychiatric activities consist of political treatment. That is very certain now.

This was the deadly secret we in Scientology might have found out and which made them terrified of us, ridicule us, fight us and spend over 2 million dollars to try unsuccessfully to get rid of us.

Over the world they were running death camps.

A few times they missed and certain political actions came to light—Ezra Pound the poet, Governor Long of Louisiana, General Walker of Little Rock, managed to become known about before they were depersonalized.

So be mystified no longer. We weren't up against any mental treatment—only violent brutality properly known as *political treatment*.

So that's what we ought to brand it.

These dumb birds were trying to form a total police state, but the police hate them and the army deserts at every chance. How do you form a police state with the police and army on the side of the population?

That's not their only mistake. Their biggest one was attacking us.

The commies would have won in the end.

Revolt is not far off if political treatment is allowed to continue.

Some of the "very best people" are involved.

If we can expose and eradicate this bestial tendency in Western government before it is too late, the society will not fall into the chaos desired for a communist takeover. It's our one chance. Expose them fully and fast.

If we delay, the mobs will tear these government leaders limb from limb for other causes than political treatments.

If exponents of death camps can be gotten out, Western governments may yet survive.

Remember that Pavlov 1870 and Wundt 1879 invented these technologies and every nation that used their work—Russia, Austria, Germany, Poland, has ceased to exist, their leaders brutally slain and the governments replaced by maniacs. So it is no idle prediction that the West, using now Wundt and Pavlov, are very close in their turn to going down in flames.

1135

Man just doesn't like being called an animal or treated like one. He revolts.

As he did in Russia, Poland, Germany, Austria, and got *real* beasts in charge instead.

The "best people" in the West who support psychiatry and look to it to seize their mob leaders and "clean up dissident elements" had better try to remember their history since 1789.

A lot of "best people" then and since have been made awfully dead at the hands of mobs.

This is not the Middle Ages. It is the twentieth century. Human rights not death camps are the fashion today.

L. RON HUBBARD
Founder

Remimeo
BPI
Dianetics Course
 Checksheet

THE PSYCHIATRIST AT WORK

Auditors are often fought by psychiatry. The auditor is often called upon to handle psychiatric abuses. Auditors should know some facts about psychiatry.

PAIN ASSOCIATION

As a technical action, it is of interest to any auditor to know that pain and ideas is a basic "therapy" used down the years by psychiatrists and such lot.

The practice is very general and very old.

The person is made to associate his "wrong ideas" with pain so that he "will not have these ideas," or will be "prevented from doing those things."

A crude current example is to electric shock a person every time he smokes a cigarette. After several "treatments," he is supposed to associate the pain with the idea and so "give up smoking."

Homosexual tendencies are also so "treated."

In earlier times alcoholism was "cured" by putting poison in drinks so drinking would make the person violently ill so he would "stop it."

Examples of this are all over the time track.

The mechanism is "If you get this idea, you will feel this pain" ZAP!

Basically, this is the action of an implanter.

Current use of it will be encountered where psychiatry has been busy implanting.

This is a pinnacle, an all, of psychiatric "treatment."

Another version of it is drugs. Make the person too torpid (sluggish) to have *any* ideas. The motto of this is "too dead to act." Institutions are emptied by hooking psychotics and "community psychiatry" exists "to make them take their pills," in short, to keep them hooked. This started the current drug craze that spread into "illegal" drugs.

The auditor will encounter this with growing frequency as the business of it is so big that one group spends 12 billion in advertising alone per year! This is the Rockefeller drug cartel. They also spend vast sums in lobbying parliaments.

OBSESSION

Most "got to's" or obsessions come from pain association or drug association.

People in pain or drugged can become obsessed with *doing* the idea.

What the psychiatrist does not care to publicize is that his "cures" are implantings with compulsive ideas.

The smoker so treated now MUST smoke but CAN'T smoke. These two things are opposed. That is known as frustration—a form of insanity.

Must reach–can't reach, must withdraw–can't withdraw is total basic insanity.

Thus, psychiatry is *making* insane people.

This is why the insanity statistic is soaring and why the crime statistic is on a wild climb.

The psychiatrist if he handled his field well and did really effective work would have a *declining* insanity and crime statistic.

That the psychiatrist and his "technology" has been in charge during the whole period of these alarming statistics is ignored by governments.

The psychiatrist argues that he needs more money and more practitioners. But he gets money by the billion. The state has to totally support them because the public will have nothing to do with them.

Psychiatric care in a private hospital costs $30,000. $2,000 a month for board only is the price at Walnut Lodge in Washington, DC, an average place. Sixty pounds a week is charged in England for a shabby room. "Care" is extra, if it exists.

Psychoanalysis costs 9,000 pounds for a full and ineffective course, takes 5 years, 30% suicide in the first 3 months.

Psychiatric treatment runs 5 times the total cost of every course, grade and action available in Scientology orgs.

SKILL LEVEL

Any HAS knows more and can do more about the mind than any psychiatrist.

There is no real level of comparison since psychiatry as used is a destructive technology.

Under a "drug treatment" engram, you often find savage electric shocks of execution strength buried.

It is doubtful if one could watch an electric shock "treatment" without vomiting.

In "neurosurgery" the ice pick is used to rip and tear up people's brains.

Holes are drilled in skulls and the brain sliced up.

No evidence exists that this ever helped anyone, but it makes incurable invalids.

Illegal seizure of anyone and his torture is legal in most "civilized countries."

MASTERS

The psychiatrist has masters. His principal organization, World Federation of Mental Health, and its members, the National Associations of Mental Health, the "American" Psychiatric Association and the "American" Psychological Association, are directly connected to Russia.

Even the British Broadcasting Company has stated that psychiatry and the KGB (Russian secret police) operate in direct collusion.

A member of the WFMH sits on every major "Advisory Council" of the US government, to name one government.

Ministers of health or health authorities are members of the National Association or the WFMH.

The psychiatrist has masters.

DOCUMENTATION

All these statements are the subject of total documentation in the hands of Scientology.

SUMMARY

The auditor in auditing uncovers considerable data in former psychiatric cases.

Further, an auditor can put to rights a case so abused unless a fatal injury has been done.

As psychiatry circulates rumors about auditors and attempts to discourage the use of Dianetics and Scientology, it is only fair for the auditor to know exactly the status of psychiatry and psychology as used today.

It goes without saying that the savagery and fraud of psychiatry must cease and that auditors must encourage in state and public and through all their connections displacing psychiatric abuses with sane auditing.

L. RON HUBBARD
Founder

Remimeo

POLICY ON PSYCHIATRIC AND MEDICAL FAILURES

Ref:
HCO PL 29 June 71 II   PUBLIC WARNING ON PSYCHIATRY

POLICY IS THAT WE ASSIGN ANY CASE OF UPSET IN SCIENTOLOGY TO PAST DAMAGE AND INTERFERENCE WITH THE PERSON BY MEDICINE OR PSYCHIATRY. THEY WERE SENT TO US AFTER MEDICINE OR PSYCHIATRY HAD ALREADY DESTROYED THEM. WE CANNOT BE BLAMED FOR PSYCHIATRIC OR MEDICAL FAILURES.

By continually repeating this, make the AMA, the National Association of Mental Health, etc., very wary of using our name on these psychiatric and medical failures. Both subjects are guilty and the statement is demonstrably true. Use it often. Make it known to the enemy that this is our policy as a restraint on their fetid imaginations. Or an "Every time you attack us we will disclose more records of your failures."

We will also run this policy in *The Auditor* and on other channels.

Psychiatry and medicine began this existing death and drug scene and it's time somebody began to say so. It is the true reason for any failure we have ever had. All such records show it.

They're just trying to cover up their crimes by saying somebody else is to blame.

All psychotics do that, especially psychiatrists.

We may as well begin to publicize the correct cause for any cultural decay in both the East and West.

A weird society really, in which any liar can spread unbelievable nonsense and authorities act on it. If those in charge in the US and England are this irresponsible (and they are) then they are fitting companions for dishonest and degraded "social scientists."

I wouldn't trust any of these guys with the garbage.

Strangely enough little countries have maintained much greater integrity than the "leading nations." And boy do these little countries get lied about and pushed around!

This was a fairly happy planet before the coming of the psychiatrist and psychologist.

In spite of any accidents or opposition, we can do our share in making it one again.

L. RON HUBBARD
Founder

Revision assisted by
LRH Technical Research
and Compilations

HCO POLICY LETTER OF 29 JUNE 1971
Issue II

Remimeo
PR Hats

PUBLIC WARNING ON PSYCHIATRY

(Originally written in 1971. Issued
as an HCO PL on 24 June 1988.)

Ref:
HCO PL 29 June 71R I   POLICY ON PSYCHIATRIC
Rev. 24.6.88   AND MEDICAL FAILURES

It is time we began to label psychiatry for what it is, the greatest failure of the nineteenth century. Every notorious criminal and defector of the 20th century was in psychiatric hands before the crime. Burgess, McLean, the Texas Tower murderer, Manson and all the rest were psychiatric failures first. Every infamous modern assassin was a psychiatric failure. Psychiatric victims are endless trouble to our society. We are tracing social turmoil, unrest and widespread drug addiction to psychiatry.

We wish to issue a public warning that psychiatry kills. We in Scientology stand ready to help anyone and help governments rid themselves of psychiatric crime. There is urgency in this. In too many cases we are asked to repair persons already maimed beyond human tolerance by psychiatric interference and brutality. We blame psychiatric failure for the state of modern society. We will do all we can to help, but nineteenth century psychiatry must go. We have never had a failure or upset that psychiatry had not first ruined.

L. RON HUBBARD
Founder

HCO POLICY LETTER OF 16 JULY 1971

Remimeo

VIOLENCE

(Originally written by LRH for the *Apollo* OODs on
16 July 71. Issued as an HCO Policy Letter on 28 Aug. 80.)

The one thing that for sure gets a government or ruling body nowhere is violence.

Covert violence in the name of "intelligence" is about the dumbest trick of all time.

I concluded a long time ago that man can't be trusted with "justice." Yet the only restraint of wrongdoing one can impose is use of force. And that is only true UNTIL one establishes sanity.

The difference between sanity and insanity is destructiveness. Insanity has to do with motive, not competence.

If you wonder about your own sanity just ask yourself "Am I destructive?" That is the full answer.

Feeling spinny is not being insane. It's just an inability to locate one's position in relation to one's surroundings.

Thus violence practiced for its own sake is just insanity.

Sure makes some of these governments look odd.

The world needs to be given the answer to sanity before it blows itself apart altogether.

That's why I'm anxious to get things going smoothly so I can gain the six weeks or two months needed to write it.

You'd help by making sure you're hatted and doing your job well.

I appreciate the work of those who are making things go right.

L. RON HUBBARD
Founder

HUBBARD COMMUNICATIONS OFFICE
Saint Hill Manor, East Grinstead, Sussex

HCO BULLETIN OF 29 JULY 1980

Remimeo

CRIMINALS AND PSYCHIATRY

Almost every modern horror crime was committed by a known criminal who had been in and out of the hands of psychiatrists and psychologists, often many times.

There is no particular reason to enumerate endless case histories of this; they occur too frequently in news accounts and the newspaper morgues are thick with them. And as such stories develop, it is found that the perpetrator had a long history, some even from childhood, of psychiatric and psychological treatment.

Such a record of failure does not seem to come to the attention of legislators, and these continue to pour floods of money into the coffers of the psychiatrists, psychologists and their organizations. The public at large, by survey, seems to be aware of this state of affairs, if not the whole facts: The only real customers the psychiatrist and psychologist have are the governments—the public does not of its own volition go to them.

The most charitable look at this would be that the psychologists and psychiatrists are simply incompetent. But other more sinister implications can be drawn.

Developed in the latter part of the nineteenth century, they appeared on the militaristic scene of a rearming and conquest-minded Germany. At that time, the archcriminal Bismarck was laying the groundwork for the slaughters of World War I and World War II. It fitted with the philosophy of militarism that man was an animal and that there was neither soul nor morality standing in the way of the wholesale murder of war.

Up until that time the Church had some influence upon the state and possibly some power in restraining bestiality and savagely insane conduct, but small as it might have been, it was incompatible with the unholy ambitions of the militarists. That man was only an animal after all, soulless and entitled to no decency, was bound to be a popular doctrine. That insanity consisted of urges to harm others would have been a very unpopular idea to government heads who had nothing else in mind. And so the notion that insanity was a physical disease was taken up avidly.

The basic tenet of psychology is that man is just an animal. The basic tenet of psychiatry is that insanity is a physical disease. Neither has any proof that these tenets are correct. That man can be reduced to animalistic behavior does not prove that that is his true basic nature. That some physical diseases also produce mental aberration does not prove that any "mental illness" has bacteria or virus and indeed none have ever been isolated.

The instigators, patrons and supporters of these two subjects classify fully and demonstrably as criminals.

If the crimes committed by a government in one single day were committed by an individual, that individual would be promptly put in a cell and probably even a padded cell.

Unfortunately, positions of power and authority attract to themselves beings who, all too often, need that altitude to exercise their lust for covertly or overtly harming others. Government positions are well suited to this use; they are also all too often held to be above any law. Some of the most notorious criminals in history have operated from government positions. This becomes statistically impressive when one counts the strewn corpses.

Looking this over (and it is amply documented in any history book or newspaper) one can begin to make some kind of sense out of it. Spawned by an insanely militaristic government, psychiatry and psychology find avid support from oppressive and domineering governments. The employer of these people classifies, even in the most generous view, as criminal. Thus, it cannot be much wondered at that these subjects have no real success or even interest in detecting and handling criminals.

One cannot go so far as to say that psychiatry and psychology knowingly create criminals or actively plan and implant their patients to commit crimes, even though it might look this way in some cases. Rather, these subjects are false subjects, based on false principles which are well suited to the demands and ambitions of their employers. Their technology is incapable of detecting, much less helping, the criminal. It is even doubtful if their employers, the governments, would tolerate a subject which could detect and resolve criminality—for who would be the first ones detected? Some amongst the governments, of course. No, the wolf would only favor a jury of wolves to judge the crime of killing sheep. That is why you see governments flooding out money for psychologists in schools and psychiatrists in government departments.

With a complete, government-supported monopoly in the field of the mind, potential criminals will go right on remaining undetected until they injure or slaughter citizens and, having done so, become unrelieved or even confirmed in their habit patterns in the hands of psychiatrists and psychologists and re-released upon the world to further injure and slaughter citizens.

The credence and power of psychiatry and psychology are waning. It hit its zenith about 1960; then it seemed their word was law and that they could harm, injure and kill patients without restraint. The appearance of an actual technology of the mind—Dianetics and Scientology—has played no small part in acting as a restraint. At one time they were well on their way to turning every baby into a future robot for the manipulation of the state and every society into a madhouse of crime and immorality. The world is still suffering from the effects of that domination.

There is no real reason why, using the proper technology, the criminal cannot be detected and also reformed. One might also, by the use of False Data Stripping, redeem a psychologist or psychiatrist—though this would be made difficult by the fact that he achieves all his power and money from the state which might have quite different purposes for him.

The world is turning, things change. And there may come a day when the mad dogs of the world are not given over to the charge of mad dogs. But that will be to the degree that you successfully carry forward Dianetics and Scientology.

L. RON HUBBARD
Founder

HUBBARD COMMUNICATIONS OFFICE
Saint Hill Manor, East Grinstead, Sussex

HCO BULLETIN OF 15 SEPTEMBER 1981

Remimeo

THE CRIMINAL MIND

Definition: A criminal is one who is motivated by evil intentions and who has committed so many harmful overt acts that he considers such activities ordinary.

There is a datum of value in detecting overts and withholds in criminal individuals:

THE CRIMINAL ACCUSES OTHERS OF THINGS WHICH HE HIMSELF IS DOING.

As an example, the psychiatrist accuses others engaged in mental practice of harming others or worsening their condition, yet the majority of psychiatrists maim and kill their patients and, by record, in all history have only worsened mental conditions. After all, that's what they seem to be paid to do by the government.

The psychologist accuses others of misrepresenting what they do and lobbies in legislature continually to outlaw others on the accusation of misrepresenting but there is no psychologist who doesn't know that he himself is a fake, can accomplish nothing of value and that his certificates aren't even worth the printing ink. The psychologist goes further: He educates little children in all the schools to believe all men are soulless animals and criminals so that when the possible day of reckoning comes and the psychologist is exposed for what he is, the population will not be the least bit surprised and will consider the psychologist is "normal."

The psychologist accuses others of sexual irregularities when this is, actually, his entire profession.

Jack the Ripper of English fame who gruesomely murdered prostitutes now turns out to have been a medical doctor and was undoubtedly of enormous assistance to the police in pointing out "the real murderer."

The FBI agent or executive accuses others of graft and even sets up "abscams" to manufacture the crime. But an FBI agent regularly pockets money supposed to be paid to informers and then screams to protect informer sources that do not exist.

The FBI agent is terrified of being infiltrated and accuses others of it when, as standard practice, he infiltrates groups, manufactures evidence and then gets others charged for crimes his own plants have committed.

The FBI acts like a terrorist group posing as law enforcement officers. Their targets seem to be legislators and Congress and public individuals who might someday have power over public opinion, such as Martin Luther King, Jr.

From all this we get another datum:

THE CRIMINAL MIND RELENTLESSLY SEEKS TO DE-
STROY ANYONE IT IMAGINES MIGHT EXPOSE IT.

You have to be very alert when criminals are around.

J. Edgar Hoover, who organized the present FBI and is still deified by
it—they have his name in huge, brass letters on Washington, DC's biggest
thoroughfare—and that town doesn't even have the names of former presidents
up in lights—has been shown by subsequent records to have been a blackmailer
and traitor to his country. He carefully, personally sat on the information for four
months that Pearl Harbor was going to happen. Right up to the US entrance into
World War II, he was autographing his photo for pals in the deadly German SS.
He even sacked an FBI agent (Tureau) who dared to catch some German spies.

Doctors, psychologists, psychiatrists and the government form a tight clique.
Only the government would support such people as the public hates them.

From all this we get another datum:

INDIVIDUALS WITH CRIMINAL MINDS TEND TO BAND
TOGETHER SINCE THE PRESENCE OF OTHER CRIMI-
NALS ABOUT THEM TENDS TO PROVE THEIR OWN
DISTORTED IDEAS OF MAN IN GENERAL.

It is not true that where any person accuses another of a crime the accuser is
always guilty of the crime or that type of crime. But it is true that when a
criminal is doing the accusing it is more than probable that the criminal is
disclosing his own type of crime.

Apparently they add it up this way: "If I accuse him of robbing, then it
would be assumed by others that I have not robbed a bank." By loudly voicing a
condemnation of a crime, the criminal, with a crooked think, supposes people
will now suppose he is above bank robbery and won't suspect him.

Groups like psychologists who declare as fact that all men are criminals are
of course just dramatizing their own inclinations.

People assume that others have their own case. The psychologist pushes his
own case off on the whole world.

Anyone researching in the mind should be very aware of this point and be
sure not to do it. Subjective reality seems to them to be the only reality there is,
for such people are too introverted to really know the minds and motivations of
others.

When working with the criminal, one can get a very good idea of that
person's own mental state by getting him to say what other people want and do
or are guilty of.

It is inconceivable to the criminal that anyone could possibly be decent or
honest or do a selfless act. It would do no good whatever to try to convince him,
for he *knows* all men are like himself.

Thus, one gets another datum of value:

THE CRIMINAL ONLY SEES OTHERS AS HE HIMSELF IS.

One of the reasons he does this, of course, is to justify injuring others. Because everyone else is useless, worthless, criminal, an animal and insane, why then, he reasons, it is perfectly all right to injure them.

Thus, we come to another datum:

THE CRIMINAL IS NOT MUCH BENEFITED BY THE GIV-
ING OFF OF CURRENT WITHHOLDS AND IS NOT LIKELY
TO REFORM BECAUSE OF THIS.

One, therefore, has to get down to the basic evil intentions, as in Expanded Dianetics.

There is another approach in that same area of technology which is finding what act the person really can take responsibility for. It is a gradient approach.

The criminal is basically so subjective that an auditor will find, in the short run, that improving the reality of such a person is needful before any effective, overall improvement is obtained through pulling withholds.

Thus, TRs and 8-C and even ARC Straightwire are indicated as first steps. If these are done, and as responsibility rises, expect that overts could begin to pop up almost of their own accord.

It is interesting that if a criminal were to face up suddenly to the enormity of his crimes he would go into degradation and self-destruction. Thus, a gradient scale is definitely indicated.

As the person has more R (reality), he can take more responsibility and only then with pulling withholds can he have any real benefit.

This HCOB is simply some data on the criminal mind that might help.

At the very least it should give some understanding of why some individuals insist with such apparent conviction that all men are evil, why all men are insane, why all men are criminals.

And it also tells you how silly it is to try to argue with them. Who's there?

The criminal mind is a bitter and unsavory subject. The percentage of criminals is relatively small but the majority of grief and turmoil in the world caused by criminals is a majority percent. Thus, the criminal mind is a subject one cannot avoid in research as it is a major factor in the distortion of a culture.

It is a mind like any other mind but it has gone wrong. It is motivated by evil intentions which, even if idiotic, are greater than the possessor's ability to rea-son. The criminal, even when he seems most clever, is really very, very stupid. The evil intentions get dramatized by senseless overt acts which are then with-held, and the final result is a person who is more dead than alive and who faces a future so agonizing that any person would shudder at it. The criminal, in fact, has forfeited his life and any meaning to it even when he remains "uncaught" and "unpunished," for in the long run, he has caught himself and punishes himself for all eternity. No common judge can give a sentence as stiff as that. They know down deep that this is true and that is why they scream with such ferocity that men have no souls. They can't confront the smallest part of what awaits them.

When you understand what the criminal mind consists of, you can also understand how ghastly must be the feelings or lack of them with which the criminal has to live within himself and for all his days forever. He is more to be pitied than punished. Neither bold nor brave, for all his pretense, he is really just a panicky, whimpering coward inside. When he bares his breast against the bullets, he does so with the actual hope that he will be killed. But of course that doesn't save him. He's got an eternity of it left to go. And his scoff of any such data hides the whimper, for he knows, deep down, it's true.

Thus, we have another datum:

THE CRIMINAL, NO MATTER WHAT HARM HE IS DO-
ING TO OTHERS, IS ALSO SEEKING TO DESTROY HIM-
SELF. HE IS IN PROTEST AGAINST HIS OWN SURVIVAL.

If you have to work with criminals in pastoring, recognize what you are working with. He *can* be helped—if he will let you near him.

Fortunately, there are still a lot of decent people left in the world.

L. RON HUBBARD
Founder

ECONOMIC SYSTEMS

Today we are suffering from world idiot economics.

When the industrial system came along, barely a hundred and fifty years ago, the giant brains that pretend to run affairs of state were still wearing horned hats and are no less primitive today.

Once upon a time, economics were more simple: If the village was hungry, it was because they were not smart enough to husband game or plant enough crops. One produced or one starved and that was that.

Then somebody—probably named Ugh—invented *government,* which was a system which said, "When you haven't got enough to eat, I grab it so I won't starve." And founded a primary principle that today is called "taxation."

But as years rolled into centuries, people finally got restive. And, terrified as they always are, the heads of state invented a thing called "welfare." Welfare is a system invented by Robin Hood: Take from the rich and give to the poor (except, of course, one never got around to the latter step). And so we then got "income tax." Except they don't take from the rich; they take from the productive.

A basic principle of government today is "Reward the downstat." If somebody won't work or produce, why then, one simply grabs money from the guy who can and will and hands it over to the one who can't and won't.

But, as they would have to be drilled and drilled to pass a baby's moronic IQ test, the government powers that be are not up to recognizing a very vital principle when one goes in for handouts: One cannot economically engage in welfare without at the same time increasing the real value of the civilization—to the extent this isn't done, inflation will result.

When one hands out money for nothing, one is creating buying power without creating the goods to buy. Therefore, the existing goods will become scarcer and more expensive. And that's inflation.

Based on these idiocies, the policies of government get one into trouble. Eventually, even the worker cannot afford bread.

When too many basic principles are violated, the whole civilization begins to starve and, welfare or no welfare, we're right back to the village that didn't husband game or plant enough crops.

But it is even worse today because of another factor: Safeguarded and defended by patronizing governments, the greedy friends of the state have been permitted to run wild—they are emptying the oceans of fish, chopping down the forests that produced rain, defiling the rivers with pollution and poisoning the air. The get-rich-quick capitalist and the incompetent heads of state are destroying the planet.

Short-term gain is their motto. It doesn't matter that the banker hogs the money and won't lend it to plant crops; it doesn't matter if the planes are falling apart—fly them anyway! It doesn't matter if we spend the public coffers into bankruptcy, we won't—they think—be here in a few years, so bleed the place white and who cares about misgovernment.

So we are living in the tag end of a civilization, in the tag end of a planet.

And it didn't happen accidentally. It happened because of idiot economics. And these all depend upon two things: government greed and the reward of downstats. They think they have to buy the votes by giving away things they don't own. Of course they have to buy the votes—who in his right mind would ever elect such idiots?

So the next time you notice the bread price has gone up, you'll know why.

The people on welfare all want jobs, but it takes smart thinking to actually set up things so people can produce—don't expect that smart thinking from government.

But also don't think that nothing can be done about it and that there is not a better way. The basic principles of economics are quite sound and they exact terrible revenge when tampered with. There IS a subject called economics. But short-term profit and advantage can be momentarily achieved at vast expense by avoiding it.

The primary concern of government is to stay in power. Yet the actions that they take today will wind up by destroying this whole planet. If you don't believe it, just look around.

L. RON HUBBARD
Founder

BPI

Birthday March 13, 1982

THE FUTURE OF SCIENTOLOGY

There comes a time in all the great movements of mankind when they get attacked.

When one reviews the history of religious wars which laid the bulk of Europe in ruins time after time across the centuries, one gets some idea of the passions of man.

The primary passions are twofold: one stems from the decent impulses of man, the effort to do and be something good, to accomplish a resurgence and reforms that are worthwhile; the other is the evil hatred of the *status quo* who, in their violence oppose all who would question their right to oppress and maim and kill.

The first impulse comes from the very heavens, the second is born in the depths of hell.

All things worthwhile have to be fought for: every decent impulse in man's history has been opposed.

The fate of the entire civilization is decided on the issue of which one wins.

No single human being can stand aside from the fray, a spectator wondering who is going to win. It is his OWN fate that is being decided: will he in the future have a decent life or will he be crushed down into the mud? Will the decent impulses of the civilization triumph or, in defeat at the hands of evil, have to wait again for another chance, another time?

The travails of the religion of Scientology may seem great but, frankly, they do not compare to those other faiths have gone through.

Time and again since 1950, the vested interests which pretend to run the world (for their own appetites and profit) have mounted full-scale attacks. With a running dog press and slavish government agencies the forces of evil have launched their lies and sought, by whatever twisted means, to check and destroy Scientology.

What is being decided in this arena is whether mankind has a chance to go free or be smashed and tortured as an abject subject of the power elite.

The issues are extremely clear-cut, there is no argument there.

But what is the result to date of enemy action?

Hah!

Honestly, my friends, a review of these battles over the past thirty-two years moves one to contemptuous laughter. The enemy, perched in their trees or swinging by their tails, have been about as effective as one of their psychologist's monkeys peeling a policeman's club thinking it is a banana and then throwing it only to hit the chief ape in the face.

Oh, the furor has been very loud. The AMA, pouring lies into the press through gnashing teeth persevered for years—and then went bankrupt. The psychiatrist, riding high in 1959, hoping to place one of his ilk in a blackmail position behind every head of state, hoping to consign any citizen at his whim to a psychiatric Siberia, trying to preserve his right to kill and maim as a profession above the law, is today a butt of comic strips. And what of the FDA that for fifteen years snarled and snapped about the E-Meter? One hardly hears of them today. And what of the mighty Interpol, that tool of CIA? It was found to be a nest of war criminals hiding out from the law itself.

Oh, one could go on but in each case the enemy has gone down to defeat in the end. You do not hear much about this from the running dog press because, of course, they were the tool of the enemy in the first place.

They lose because they traffic in lies. But, because they told their lies so broadly, even when they were disproven, they still tend to hang around and make one feel there is—there isn't—an adverse public opinion. The enemy and their press are not the public: you could ask yourself why, year after year, fewer and fewer people buy and read newspapers: people don't believe them anymore.

I once checked, in the 50s the effect on org stats of howling bombasts of a running dog magazine called *TIME*. Its owner, a man named Luce, was said to be an LSD addict, both he and his wife carefully controlled by his psychiatrist. Of course he published blasts against anything which would expose his rotten condition. What I found was that not one of those lying bombasts had had the slightest effect upon org stats. Luce is dead now, a good testimony to his drugs and the psychiatrists. There are a dozen orgs today for every one that existed in Luce's time.

And so it goes with these attacks.

Oh, yes, we've had some casualties. Oh, yes, we've had some trouble. But that is the way with wars: not only combatants but innocent bystanders can get wounded. That's this universe: we didn't make it that way but that's no reason we cannot, bit by bit, correct it. Certainly, for mankind, there's no escaping it and if there is a battle, there is more to do than simply duck one's head: the bombs are no respecters of uniforms or identities.

It may appear that the enemy suffers no casualties for they hush them up. With no great pleasure, I used to keep a roster of them. Through no will or fault of ours, many of them are dead. Some died from things that we have tech to help: it is rather poetic in justice that they were fighting what they themselves could have used. Many others, when the battle cleared, lost their jobs: and that is a precious thing to a suppressive, his garnered rights to do others in: it is sad to say there are many in governments who are there just so they can have this right: so when one gets fired for failing in his attacks on us, that's very close to the end of his life. They do not care if you hurt the government or their association or their publication: threats against those things are part of their own plans to cause trouble—typical of the insane. Where they can be hurt and practically the only place, is losing their job or position. And their casualties in this respect would fill some very long bread lines: when they fail, their mentors fire them.

They have lost power.

They have been hurt.

And in any contemporary attack, no matter how violent it may seem, the result predictably will be the same: failures and casualties in enemy ranks. Not because we harm or touch them—we wouldn't. They are mad monkeys and they blame and shoot each other.

Now when you hear of some new attack or an old one, you could get the idea that we're losing and are likely to winnow away and vanish. The enemy keeps saying that. But just remember a maxim: if the papers say it, it isn't true.

Hearing such things, one may think that, as a Scientologist, it doesn't matter what you do: it doesn't make any difference now since all is lost. That's silly.

In or out of Scientology, one is on these firing lines. The crime-ridden, drug-crazed, misgoverned mess out there which they call civilization is no place at all to escape to. That's surrender.

And it DOES matter what one does on post, particularly when the shots are flying hottest. If you think it's bad in a Scientology area, look at Ulster or Detroit! And those poor guys are just innocent bystanders being mowed down. At least the Scientologists are DOING something about it. They're handling people, they're making inroads on crime, they're salvaging addicts, they're even quoted, often unknowingly, by beleaguered business.

All you have to do is look at where Scientology was in terms of numbers of orgs and missions even a few years back and where it is now to know. All you have to do is count the additional countries using it year by year. All you have to do is count the memberships of the Churches. And you know conclusively that while the enemy goes down, whatever the bombast, Scientology is going UP.

It DOES matter what you do on post or in the field or in the world. This scene called Scientology is not going to end. Time after time the enemy, in our blackest hours, has told itself, "We've got them now! We've stopped them! They're through!" They were just praying past their own graveyard. Each time, there we were again, stronger, expanding, working better. And at this very moment of writing, that's where we are at right now. The last enemy attack is winding down.

And there we still are all over the world, doing good, getting stronger, getting more numerous.

And in the coming decades so it will be again.

The guys in the white hats—with the S and Double Triangle—are winning. They are winning because they mean well. They do good. They know their business. And the enemy is losing and will lose because they mean bad. They do evil. They are incompetent.

Remember the principle of Flourish and Prosper. It works!

And the next time you see an attack, remember the old truth, "This too shall come to pass away."

But not Scientology. We're here and will be here for all the decades and centuries that this civilization has left to it. And right now I am working on plans so that it will be here even when the madmen, in some possible last convulsion of evil, have blown this civilization away.

We are saving beings, not men.

And the evil die within their own generation.

We don't.

So the next time you feel blue, read this.

The enemy can't even plan for tomorrow.

We work in eternity.

Love,

RON

L. RON HUBBARD
Founder

HUBBARD COMMUNICATIONS OFFICE
Saint Hill Manor, East Grinstead, Sussex

HCO BULLETIN OF 26 APRIL 1982

Remimeo

THE CRIMINAL MIND AND THE PSYCHS

It has often been noted (and reported routinely in the papers) that criminals "treated" by psychologists and psychiatrists go out and commit crimes.

It could be suspected that these "practitioners" used pain-drug-hypnosis and other means (under the guise of treatment) to induce the criminal to go out and commit more crimes. And possibly they do.

But I have just made a discovery that sheds some light on this scene.

Morality and good conduct are sensible. That is the theme of *The Way to Happiness*. It follows (and can be proven) that immorality and bad conduct are stupid.

This bears out under further investigation. One could lay aside the ancient Greek speculations of "Good and Bad" and go on an easier and less contentious logic of "Bright and Stupid."

Anything that a criminal seeks to obtain can be obtained without crime if one is bright enough. Criminals, as police can tell you, are usually very, very stupid. The things they do and clues they leave around are hallmarks of very low IQ. The "bright" criminal is found only in fiction. Now and then a Hitler comes along and begins a myth that the highly positioned are criminal—but Hitler (and Napoleon and all their ilk) were stupid beyond belief. Hitler destroyed himself and Germany, didn't he? And Napoleon destroyed himself and France. So not even the highly placed criminals are bright. Had they really been bright, they could have accomplished a successful reign without crime.

The bones of old civilizations are signboards of stupidity. The jails are bursting with people so stupid they did bad things and even did those uncleverly.

So let us look at psychs again—what they call "treatment" is a suppression (by shocks, drugs, etc.) of the ability to think. They are not honest enough, these psychs, being just dramatizing psychotics themselves for the most part, to publish the fact that all their "treatments" (mayhem, really, when it is not murder) make people more stupid.

These actions of shock and crazy evaluative counseling, etc., lower IQ like an express elevator going down to the basement. They do not tell legislators this or put it in their books. This is why they say "no one can change IQ." They are hiding the fact that they ruin it.

So the psych in prisons is engaging in an action (shocking or whatever) that makes people who are already criminal even stupider.

Although they obviously tell their victims to go out and commit more crimes (the psychoanalysts urge wives to commit adultery, for instance), they would not have to do this at all to manufacture more crime.

Their "treatments" make the criminals more stupid. The stupid commit more crimes.

It is pretty simple, really, when you look at it.

Why does the state support psychiatrists and psychologists? Because the state is stupid? Or does it want more citizens robbed and killed? It's one or the other. Take your choice.

One is bright and is moral and honest and does well or one is stupid and does badly.

The answer to crime is raising IQ. But only the Scientologist can do that.

L. RON HUBBARD
Founder

HUBBARD COMMUNICATIONS OFFICE
Saint Hill Manor, East Grinstead, Sussex

HCO BULLETIN OF 6 MAY 1982

Remimeo

THE CAUSE OF CRIME

They say poverty makes crime. They say if one improved education there would be less crime. They say if one cured the lot of the underprivileged one would have solved crime.

All these "remedies" have proven blatantly false.

In very poor countries there is little crime. In "improving" education, it was tailored to "social reform," not teaching skills. And it is a total failure. The fact that rewarding the underprivileged has simply wrecked schools and neighborhoods and cost billions is missing.

So who is "they"? The psychologist and psychiatrist, of course. These were *their* crackpot remedies for crime. And it's wrecked a civilization.

So what IS the cause of crime? The treatment, of course! Electric shocks, behavior modification, abuse of the soul. *These* are the causes of crime. There would be no criminals at all if the psychs had not begun to oppress beings into vengeance against society.

There's only one remedy for crime—get rid of the psychs! They are causing it!

Ah yes, it's true on cases and cases of research on criminals. And what's it all go back to? The psychs!

Their brutality and heartlessness is renowned.

The data is rolling in. Any more you pick up off a criminal or anyone, send it in.

On crime we have an epidemic running on this planet. The wrong causes psychs assign for crime plus their own "treatments" make them a deadly virus.

The psychs should not be let to get away with "treatment" which amounts to criminal acts, mayhem and murder. They are not above the law. In fact, there are no laws at all which protect them, for what sane society would sanction crime against its citizens even as science? They should be handled like any other criminals. They are at best dramatizing psychotics and dangerous, but more dangerous to society at large than the psychotics they keep in their offices and loony bins because they lie and are treacherous. Why the government funds them I do not know. They are the last ones that should be let loose to handle children.

L. RON HUBBARD
Founder

DEPARTMENT 21
OFFICE OF LRH

HUBBARD COMMUNICATIONS OFFICE
London

HCO BULLETIN OF 30 JULY 1958

THE HANDLING OF HUBBARD COMMUNICATIONS OFFICES

The purpose of the HCO offices is to act as stable terminals to an organization in any given area so as to provide immediate administrative assistance to L. Ron Hubbard when in that area and communications from operations to him and from him when he is not.

An HCO office is essentially a terminal. It should regard itself in company with other HCO terminals.

The foremost visible use of an HCO office is to act as a stable terminal for any area operation. An area operation can forward its communications to LRH and other operational areas through HCO terminals and should not forward communications in any other fashion than through HCO terminals, when these communications apply to other Scientology areas.

At present we have an HCO office in Washington, DC, London, and HCOs are being set up now in South Africa and Australia and France. These will be followed by additional HCO terminals as may be indicated.

If an HCO office considers itself primarily a unit which handles mail, it should disabuse itself at once. An HCO Secretary should be able to provide all necessary secretarial functions for LRH, but the activity of the terminal does not end there. The HCO Clerk receives all incoming communications and routes them to the proper hat terminal in the organization—i.e., if LRH receives a communication regarding an HPA Course, it is referred by the HCO Clerk to the Registrar, who will handle the communication; a letter to LRH requesting processing fees would be forwarded by the HCO Clerk to the Registrar; a question concerning memberships, to the Membership Secretary, etc. There was a time when LRH received and handled all manner of communications. But now we have definite organization posts established, and communications are referred to that post to which they are pertinent. It is the function of the HCO Clerk to determine proper routing of communications received in HCO.

The HCO is, in essence, a stable point to which can be communicated communications and difficulties in any area and these communications are forwarded to the proper terminal in the organization, or an analysis is made of the difficulty and communicated to another HCO terminal for clarification there. In addition to that, LRH may require reports on or about a given area and it is up to the HCO office to supply this information. The HCO should consider itself more of a troubleshooting unit than a secretarial office. It is true that it is an office, and it must be conducted precisely as an office. It is true that it is secretarial and it is also true that it does have the function of being an extended pair of eyes for LRH.

The responsibility of being "an extended pair of eyes" continues into being able to evaluate what is right and what is wrong and saying so without introducing unnecessary turbulence on the communication lines. The HCO offices exist to permit *good* communication through to other areas and to LRH and this can easily be interrupted by too much turbulence.

An HCO office is essentially self-supporting. It is supported by royalties and other monies which come into being because of the existence of L. Ron Hubbard on a personal service basis to organizations and by reason of transcribing and creating material for use in such areas.

In use as a communication system from one area to another or from an area to LRH, the following procedure must be followed: The area must be instructed that any communications to any other Scientology area or to LRH must be forwarded through the HCO office. In this sense the HCO office in any area is a message center receiving from any other area and emanating to any other area in this network. Furthermore, the HCO receives materials from other areas and communicates these in their own area directly.

For example: A D of T despatch which originates with the D of T London: It passes from D of T London to HCO London across the Atlantic to HCO Washington and to D of T Washington. This same procedure would be followed from Washington. D of T Washington originates communication. It goes to HCO Washington, then crosses over to HCO London, and HCO London passes it on to D of T London.

In handling communications it will be found that when too bulky a packet of communications is made, something on the order of two ounces, that customs often intercepts the packet and inspects it, thus delaying the line considerably. Thus packets have to be broken up into smaller packets so that this does not interrupt our communication lines.

The preparation of the PABs comes under the HCO offices, under the hat of "PAB Liaison." PABs are printed and distributed from London. PAB copy comes from the HCO office where LRH is at the time, and all copy is okayed by LRH before it is printed.

The various hats under HCO are: HCO Secretary, HCO Clerk, PAB Liaison, Manuscripts, Proofreading, Tape Transcription, *Ability* Magazine (Writing—Editorial Director—Editor), *Certainty* Magazine (London), HCO Editorial, Public Relations, Advertising, HCO Board of Review, Advanced Clinical Courses, and Examining.

The financing of an HCO office is dependent upon the area in which it is located. This is done by utilizing book sale monies. At the end of any given year the expense an HCO has been to an area is deducted from a proper allocation of book fees to that HCO and this does not enter into the basic royalties due to LRH. For example, let us say that £2,000 worth of books have been sold in an area in a given year and HCO has cost £720 to maintain during that period. The Accountant then simply writes all HCO expenses under the heading of "Preparation of Manuscripts" and so discharges it from his books.

Filing system used by HCO offices: The file "Despatches To and From LRH" is set up by area—Washington, London, South Africa, etc. Within these area files are folders marked "Academy," "HGC," etc., filed by proper names—"Academy" (rather than the name of the individual). Under "Business Files" in HCO can be kept both proper names (company names) and subject names—projects. For instance, there can be a file titled "Roneo" rather than filing under "John Jones Mimeograph Company," so that in future the file can be found by the subject name—a new person might or might not know that John Jones Mimeograph Company is the company from whom we order Roneo supplies, parts, etc. HCO files should be kept in a very orderly fashion. However, operational notes can be from time to time destroyed. These are only valid for a few months at best.

HCO also acts as a preparation and distribution area of HCO Bulletins and Policy Letters. These are bulletins of instructions to operations in general, to staff auditors, and to other things very intimate in the Scientology areas. An HCO Bulletin will not be mailed from Washington to be distributed in London. It will be found a very much sounder policy is to send an HCO Bulletin COPY to London. London will cut a stencil and distribute. Thus London always has its own stencils and Washington has its own stencils. It is paramount that these stencils be cut and that extra material be cut since such situations arise as a post being vacated without the person on that post in a Scientology operation having saved the material relating to that post. It is up to the HCO office to furnish the material from HCO Bulletins and other sources. Any bulletin or policy letter issued by HCO is distributed ONLY to organization personnel and our field offices; none are to be distributed to nonorganization persons. The contents of these bulletins are intended for staff and staff should not release the information outside of staff, without express permission from LRH.

While the speed of handling, which is to say the order of priority, of messages is very difficult to ascertain and does depend in the main upon the good judgment of the HCO terminal itself, it will be observed that the following list of precedences should be given to communications going through HCO channels. Any communication labeled "Emergency" should be sent through with extraordinary speed and care. Anything not so labeled should go through routine. Packages of financial materials such as checks and request for checks should be given to next priority. All green slip messages, which is to say operational messages, should then be given the next priority. Letters from the field, reports or data are given the last priority and may even be sent by regular mail to save postage.

The color-flash marking system originated some time ago wherein green means an operational message, pink means a financial message, etc., should be very closely followed by the HCO. The neatness and accuracy of an HCO terminal may very well influence the neatness and accuracy of administration carried on in a Scientology area and this at all times must be before the HCO terminal. Priorities of speed in terms of color flash would be any green or pink message marked "Emergency" and then any pink message and then any routine green message and finally white (which is to say field letters, etc.) should be given last priority and even sent by regular mail.

Air letters should be used wherever possible.

It is up to the Secretary in charge of an HCO office to keep the premises acceptably neat and orderly at all times since the appearance of the office is very likely to influence the caller's opinion of LRH personally; therefore, it is highly probable that HCO offices, as finance accumulates and makes this possible, will become the better-looking offices of Scientology.

The occupation of spare time by an HCO Secretary should never be a problem. If she finds herself with spare time, it is only necessary for her to remember that we are doing an encyclopedia of Dianetics and Scientology and we are transcribing many hundreds of hours of lecture tapes. It is very necessary that these tapes be transcribed so that they can come out in an eventual encyclopedia. The transcription of these tapes is a very careful and painstaking job. It is necessary that the written script must be understandable, therefore it is necessary for the HCO Secretary to understand the material on the tape as she transcribes it on to a typewriter. Such tapes are available and will be made available and each HCO office will have a tape recorder with a foot pedal in order to put in such time. THE CONGRESS OF SCIENTOLOGISTS* in Washington, DC, has this encyclopedia as a project. An HCO Secretary can contact Congress of Scientologists in Washington, DC, to determine which tapes they should transcribe—C of S monitors this project. In addition to this project, there will be other materials to transcribe and a tape can be sent through by mail containing despatches which can be received by an HCO office and the despatches of that area can be taken off it directly and emanated into the area.

Tape Transcription post of HCO is to transcribe any and all tapes given them by LRH—manuscripts, articles, bulletins, letters or anything else from LRH.

An HCO office is itself. It is a separate organization from all Scientology organizations. It works in conjunction and cooperation with Scientology organizations, but it *is* itself.

No one in an area in authority in Scientology has any right to dismiss or change an HCO Secretary or other HCO personnel. This can only be done by LRH himself. Therefore, an HCO Secretary should not feel any qualms about remarking on the conduct of an office or its general appearance or activity. The HCO Secretary is not there as a spy, but is often asked about the state of an operation. She should give a true and factual, not a colored, picture of it, but at the same time, she should not withhold an opinion for fear that it will influence her own status which it will not.

It is paramount that traffic to LRH be held to a minimum. The reason for this is that correspondence actually cuts into LRH's origin time on manuscripts and books. His job is not, first and foremost, an administrative job in Scientology. Therefore, the HCO offices have been created to do this job for him as much as possible in order to salvage writing and research time. Thus, an HCO office should feel bound to handle routine or uninteresting material and to handle it in such a way that it will be in all ways satisfactory to the people originating it. To waste time and postage on much of the material which is received at an HCO terminal office is not included. Therefore, the HCO office should pleasantly acknowledge communications received which have no particular influence on the operation, and file them without further referral to them than perhaps a remark in a report to the HCO terminal, near which LRH is, that letters from so and so

---

*Congress of Scientologists: an organization in Washington, DC in the 1950s which was responsible for the administration of several projects, including transcribing tapes for a planned Encyclopedia of Dianetics and Scientology.

and so were received and acknowledged. This will do much to cut down weight. In other words, an HCO terminal has the right to acknowledge and file without forwarding at its own discretion. It does not, however, have this right on green and pink operational messages.

An HCO office must be open during the routine business hours of the day customary in that area. It must open at a precise time in the morning, there must be an exact lunch hour which is followed and it must close officially at a certain time, no matter how long the HCO personnel stays there in the evening. By keeping regular office hours it is possible then for an area to be secure in its ability to contact the HCO terminal. If the HCO cannot be contacted or if it is sporadically out of communication it will be found that the area will begin to get a little restive about contacting LRH.

HCO offices doing extra work for the area: It may sometimes be found feasible to implement the expenses and occupy time in an HCO office by taking on additional work in an area which is not immediately concerned to the HCO terminal. However, it will be considered in a very poor light if this work is undertaken to the cost of the HCO terminal's actual line of work.

HCO offices should keep painstakingly accurate accounts of petty cash, postage, receipts and disbursements in general.

HCO offices are always liable in the accounting field to inspection by the Accountant of any Scientology area.

HCO offices exist to expedite Scientology communications. If they fail to actually speed the communication line it will be discovered that they will become bypassed; when they are bypassed an enturbulence will result. It is, therefore, up to an HCO terminal to give communications every possible expedition and to reassure people wondering about this and being anxious about communications that every means has been taken. HCO offices should have regular pickup and delivery schedules to area offices in order to seem even more stable.

The first principle of an HCO terminal is to be stable. Stability is built on good scheduling, proper despatch and relaying of communications and an orderly set of communication lines. LRH's reputation is to a marked degree in the hands of HCO terminals.

L. RON HUBBARD
Founder

HASI POLICY LETTER OF 24 OCTOBER 1957

Any staff member who has anything "confidential" for me may send it straight to Washington without going through the HCO London. Be sure it is confidential, however.

L. RON HUBBARD
Founder

ORGANIZATION INFORMATION SHEET
6 November 1957

DUTIES OF THE EXECUTIVE
DIRECTOR OF THE HASI (FC)

For an indefinite period I am going to be nailed down by book production. Previously balked by the fact that a regular publisher contract at 10 percent would not permit us to service the book, we have now resolved this problem. Lacking an exact orientation of future course I have found myself unwilling to commit programs to print. With both of these difficulties cared for it is now possible to avalanche out a few books.

In heavy demand is the *Student Manual* and the *Ability* book for the next congress. A popular book for the bookstores is also indicated. Therefore my schedule can be considered full at least until the congress and just after the congress I will have to take part in teaching the 19th ACC.

Therefore, I am reducing my schedule as follows and publish it for the general information of executives and staff.

MONDAY AFTERNOON—3:00 P.M.: Accounting Sheets and Banking Reports on my desk.

WEDNESDAY AFTERNOON—3:00 P.M.: Payroll okay.

SATURDAY AFTERNOON—3:00 P.M.: HGC PROFILE CHECKOUT.

Co-auditing periods will be Monday, Wednesday and Friday 7:30 to 10:00.

There will be no body time, no outside visitors. All internal org despatches will be routed by the HCO Clerk back to the proper hat in the organization (since I have no hats except writing or research not paralleled by hats in the organization). HCO Sec will act as London liaison for its sheets.

The following items will be cared for as necessary:

CHECK SIGNATURES, CERTIFICATE SIGNATURES, CONTRACT OKAYS, AUTOGRAPHS and ANY REALLY NECESSARY CON-FERENCES WITH THE ORG SEC.

If I produce 6,000 words a day for the next several weeks, I can perhaps meet the demanded writing scheduled.

Your cooperation and understanding in this endeavor will be appreciated.

Thank you,

L. RON HUBBARD
Founder

HCO BULLETIN OF 24 JANUARY 1958

All Staff
  B. Board

OUTLINE OF ACTIVITIES

(The following is a memorandum issued on 9 Mar. 53.
It is still appropriate and is reissued here as an HCO Bulletin.)

Subject: Outline of the Activities of the HCO Office of L. Ron Hubbard

I maintain a communications office which is devoted to specific interests and which should be used for those interests and which should not be used for any other purpose by the organization. Its use for other purpose inhibits the work for which this office was designed and has a tendency to clog my writing communication line. Thus, the indulgence of the operation in general is requested so as to keep this communications center well within its own functions.

The functions of this center are:

1. The receipt and answering of correspondence addressed to myself, some of which is personal, much of which is to the interest of the general operation.

2. The answering and delivering of telephone communications relating specifically to communications addressed to me or proceeding from me.

3. The typing of manuscripts and investigation material from my Dimaphon[*] records or personal dictation.

4. Compilation of investigation and case information submitted to me by auditors.

5. Assistance to the Treasurer in receiving bills and expediting their payment.

6. The care of social and governmental matters in which I happen to be concerned.

7. Maintaining my comm lines in good order.

Casual communication with this office inhibits its efficiency and involves it in concerns which inhibit a swift expedition of my work.

The office is not concerned with the activities of the central staff beyond acting as a communications relay point from myself to these operations and from these operations to myself.

---

[*] **Dimaphon:** a brand of dictation recording machine used by LRH in the 1950s and 1960s.

This memorandum is issued because various parts of the operation have involved my office in concerns beyond its scope, the first effect of which is to cause my correspondence to receive secondary attention. A secondary concern is involving the office petty cash and stationery materials with those of the remaining operation which should have their own, procured by proper vouchers through proper channels.

I have no feeling about this beyond the attitude I always exhibit when my communications lines or any part of them are challenged or when personnel who work very close to me have their time employed on duties which are beyond the immediate scope of my office.

L. RON HUBBARD
Founder

HUBBARD COMMUNICATIONS OFFICE
Washington, DC

HCO POLICY LETTER OF 28 MAY 1958

HCO Sec
HCO Clerk
Reception
Org Sec–Info
HCO London
Staff Bulletin Board
File Copy

INCOMING CALLS FOR LRH

At any Scientology organization where an HCO office is physically located:

When incoming telephone calls come in asking for L. Ron Hubbard, the Receptionist should simply say, "I will connect you with his office," then ring HCO Clerk telling him to pick up whatever line it is. If he doesn't answer for any reason, buzz the HCO Secretary. The HCO Clerk will monitor LRH calls, sort them out, decide if they are LRH personal business or business which falls within LRH hats of the organization. If the call is LRH business it will be handled either by the HCO Clerk or HCO Secretary. HCO Clerk to take care of appointments, checking with HCO Secretary. HCO Secretary to handle personal calls. If calls are NOT LRH business, HCO Clerk will reroute them to the proper organization terminal.

Concerning individuals who walk in, asking for LRH, direct them to HCO Clerk who will determine whether an appointment is indicated and handle same.

L. RON HUBBARD
Founder

HUBBARD COMMUNICATIONS OFFICE
37 Fitzroy Street, London W1

HCO POLICY LETTER OF 25 NOVEMBER 1958

HCO BOARD OF REVIEW
FUNCTION AND PRACTICE

The HCO Board of Review is often composed of one or two part-time staff auditors working on off-hours for HCO and in and under control of HCO, or one or more full-time expert Scientologists who have served as staff auditors and instructors and who now work full-time for HCO.

The basis of HCO Board of Review authority lies in the basic functions of HCO. These are ethics, technology and awards. Ethics and technology are otherwise cared for than by the HCO Board of Review. Awards are wholly the function of the HCO Board of Review.

The HCO is the holder of all copyrights, trademarks, registered marks and the rights of all materials of Dianetics and Scientology. Further, HCO holds in trust the signature "L. Ron Hubbard, Founder." This signature is the only thing which makes a certificate valid. This is based on the precedent that the originator of a science has the right to train persons in it and the only original right to sign certificates saying so. No corporation, company, association or foundation has ever been given the right to sign or issue Dianetics and Scientology awards. The only thing which makes these certificates valid is the signature. The association, etc., name has no value in the public eye except as signed by LRH. If LRH stopped signing an organization's certificates tomorrow, that organization could no longer issue awards of skill and the matter would be upheld in court by reason of trademarks, registered marks and copyrights.

Therefore, the authority wielded by the HCO Board of Review is quite real. Its stable datum is "We guarantee to LRH that his signature attests proper training and processing." Administratively, when the HCO Board of Review passes a student for a level of skill or a pc for Clear, it is saying, in effect, to LRH, "You can safely sign," and to the public, "You can trust the person who holds this award."

The HCO Board of Review, like all the HCO, is a natural rather than arbitrary outgrowth of our needs. Only where we did not have proper award handling by an agency like the HCO Board of Review have we fallen down on this. Therefore, we don't fall down on it anymore. We have an HCO Board of Review that can examine and say, "Ron, you can safely sign."

It is also an old principle that the people who train cannot also examine. Therefore, an Academy or a HASI or another organization enfranchised by the HCO (which grants all actual rights to use materials to such organizations in the first place) has no right to examine. It can only train to the level specified by HCO. It is then up to the HCO, through its HCO Board of Review, to examine and see if the standard is met. If it is, the HCO Board of Review says, "Ron, you can safely sign," and gives LRH the certificate to be signed. The training agency cannot do more than train. It cannot order a student to more processing. It can only collect all the classwork, papers, lessons and indicate that the student is ready for examination. It sends the papers to HCO Board of Review. If these papers are complete (indicated by a checklist prepared by HCO), HCO then calls for the student directly, not via the Academy, and administers oral exams where feasible and written exams always. What HCO Board of Review does to guarantee that the requirements as laid down in HCO Bulletins or Policy Letters have been met and that the person can perform the required skills is its own business. If the papers are not complete, HCO Board of Review returns them to the training agency, pointing out the discrepancies. When the training agency returns these, then the above procedure is followed—having the student in.

If the student passes, HCO Board of Review prepares an authorized certificate with the student's name and presents it to LRH on HCO Comm lines for the signature, "L. Ron Hubbard, Founder."

No written examination for any one grade may be repeated within 120 days of the last examination. Thus a student who flunks an HCO Board of Review exam cannot be reexamined for 120 days. There is no limit to the number of examinations he can have. And the failure of a training agency to have the papers complete (HCO Board of Review having to send them back) does not invoke the 120-day clause.

In examining, the HCO Board of Review should be real, not pedantic. Good TRs, good command of processes for the level, good axioms and theory should pass a student. But to establish these, HCO Board of Review needn't examine all day and all night. If the student flunks a few TRs, why go on? He's dead if he ever tries to audit. Why pass him or even examine further?

In case of failure, the HCO Board of Review may advise processing or more training but *may not say where* the training or processing is to be taken or how much it will cost. These items are all outside of HCO Board of Review purview.

On testing for Clear, the same principles are followed. If the pc reads wrong on the meter, why go on to an OCA or APA or IQ test?

If HCO Board of Review says it's a flunk, that's usually that. The only appeal is to HCO Sec to LRH, and it's doubtful if this will produce any change of decision.

When the person has passed his exam, HCO makes up the certificate for him, forwards it to LRH and sends it back to the original HCO Board of Review giving the exam. This HCO Board of Review gives the certificate straight to the student, not via a training agency or corporation.

The wording on all certificates is specified by HCO main headquarters. They can be locally printed but only on okay from LRH.

An HAS certificate doesn't pass through HCO Board of Review, but all others do.

It is interesting that the signature of L. Ron Hubbard, Founder, on certificates has been deeded over to HCO and "after demise" will still remain, but in seal form, the validating signature on a certificate. Thus these various lines of awarding will not be disrupted and the institution of HCO and HCO Board of Review are here to stay for a long, long while.

HCO Boards of Review are necessary in every area where training is done. They can only exist where HCO has enfranchised the local operation with exact rights to the materials of Dianetics and Scientology.

HCO Board of Review is established by written appointment by LRH. It has existed on verbal consent in the past but written appointment is now necessary.

L. RON HUBBARD
Founder

29 NOVEMBER 1958

CONFIDENTIAL MEMO TO HCO SECRETARIES

FUTURE PROGRAMS

HCO will shortly be HCO Ltd. Each HCO will present its area organization with their exclusive area license for use of materials of Dianetics and Scientology. This will apply in all sterling areas and US.

Book stocks and sales, congresses and ACCs will be wholly under HCO supervision.

Reason: These are the hats I myself wear:

1. Licensing of areas (ethics, technology, awards). By reason of holding all trademarks, registered marks, copyrights, etc.

2. Book writing, promotion and even manufacturing and sales. (All this backs up on HCO anyway sooner or later.) Books handled by associations are usually a loss anyway. We could be careful and do a win.

3. Congresses. I have to okay them and furnish tapes and appear at them, so why not supervise them, too.

4. ACCs. I have to plan, oversee, organize and give ACCs, even okay their quarters, etc., so we have to handle ACCs anyway.

5. Magazines. We have to do everything about a magazine but mail it. So here is HCO for it again.

6. Legal supervision and accounting audits.

7. Basic arrangements and policies of organization.

My hats include HCA courses, HPA courses, HGCs, PEs, etc., to a far lesser extent and these, the highest regularly income items, are for local area organizations.

HCO is "my personal office" in an area. Therefore, to be real we have to handle what I have to handle.

Looks like a lot on our plate. But we can speed up and do it.

Maybe when we have some of these things neat, the load can be shoved off. But right now we are for it. Therefore, even before I give the official word, HCO Secs had better give these things their eagle glance and not be taken by surprise when the orders are issued to land on one or another item above. I know we can cope.

L. RON HUBBARD
Founder

HCO POLICY LETTER OF 21 MAY 1959

CONFIDENTIAL

To all HCO Communicators:

The symbol * on all despatches means to attach a mimeoed slip saying:

"This is well within your province of decision. Resolve the problem with appropriate agreement from adjacent terminals.

To decide such matters is to reduce the purpose statement of your post.

Thank you for letting me see the despatch. I am not trying to cut communication. I am just trying to get Central Orgs more responsible for their own decisions.

L. Ron Hubbard"

L. RON HUBBARD
Founder

HUBBARD COMMUNICATIONS OFFICE
37 Fitzroy Street, London W1

HCO POLICY LETTER OF 10 AUGUST 1959
Issue II

HCO Personnel
Only

DATA REQUIRED AS REPORTS FROM HCO SECRETARIES

The first interest, regardless of emergencies, is promotion and dissemination. This means that the most important report is whether or not the magazine is going out on schedule, and whether or not PrR is functioning alertly. These are continuing reports of continuous interest.

The second interest is financial, that being the most direct index of whether or not the promotion is reaching people and what mark we are making in the society. Weekly reports of income must come through to HCO from Accounts and through to me. In addition, there is a Registrar's financial report on the number of sign-ups there have been in the week.

Of third interest is the effectiveness of the service being given and the quality of that service in terms of training and processing.

After that comes the general state of the org departments beginning first with Finance as to whether or not it is coping, and whether or not statements are going out monthly, and whether or not there is a complete statements book and a complete current bills book. The exact items mentioned for Accounts are quite important. I know at once if the statements aren't going out, that Accounts is running a "can't have" on the organization and I know if there is no complete statements book there is no accurate issue of statements, causing ARC breaks. Further, if there is no current bills book then it is obvious that soon we will have some big financial crisis to handle on HCO lines. The source of the majority of HCO Central Organizations emergency despatches is financial. Further, the greatest number of cans dropped by Central Organizations occur in the finance department or through lack of financial planning.

The department of next interest is training. If there are very few students we know that the training is very bad. The quality of training has been directly reflected in the number of students present for the last seven years.

Then comes the HGC with the burning question of, "Are they making any Clears? And if not, why not?"

Then, but not necessarily in order of importance since it influences the whole health of the organization, is the PE Foundation. A full PE Foundation means a healthy future survival. A thin PE means a lousy PE Director and poor administration and public presence.

Next there is the matter of programs. Are the programs being carried out or aren't they, or of course are there any?

After that is Materiel and the burning question here is: First: Are the quarters clean? and Second: Are they holding down expenses?

Two organizations are being all but wiped out by bad spending by the Dir of Mat.

Next there is the state of any books sales. This again is an index of reach and a bad answer-up on order filling costs us many gains.

Then comes CF. If CF is good we have got the data on the people with whom we are working, and if it isn't good we'll flop.

Then there is Address. A good, efficient Address setup means that we'll be able to locate people. If the Address setup isn't good, what use promotion, for where are the people?

After all these come staff morale and other sections and activities.

What I have listed here is the way to put a finger on the pulse of any Scientology organization. Starting at the top, if we drop these people out of the lineup as effective operating units in the organizations, then we've had it. There are people around who would tell you that there are a lot of things more important than these things. But in fact, there aren't.

Under programs of special nature as above, second only to promotion and dissemination activities, is the question of staff co-audit success. We'll be as successful as we are Clear. There are three major buttons to be run out of all Scientologists to make us brilliantly successful everywhere. There are first victim, second money and the third will be given out in due course. Each of these should be run on a comm process with the terminal generalized. When these are fully flat throughout our organizations you will see us soaring to success without any quibbles on the line. Naturally, we want all Scientologists to get these flat but Central Organizations come first on the lineup.

The gist of this problem is this: By sheer hope and force of personality a few of us are overcoming the collective banks of everyone in Scientology that is idle or going back against us in his or her activities. When the energy and comm we are expending doing just this can be released broadly into dissemination we'll take this planet and achieve our goals with ease. So this special program always requires special mention.

Few reports are ever required on HCO since HCO people are already selected out for zing and I have every confidence that HCO will make it. In HCO I mainly want personnel changes to keep the rosters straight. And finance coming through routinely to grease the wheels of the fighting line.

This then is a general rundown on the reports that I want here at Saint Hill from HCO offices in Central Orgs. I want HCO to keep its finger on Central Org pulse and keep it going somehow, no matter how, until we're thoroughly ahead everywhere.

L. RON HUBBARD
Founder

HCO BULLETIN OF 23 SEPTEMBER 1959

HCO Secs Only

CARRYING OUT INSTRUCTIONS

My DC HCO Office was much enlightened when I told them after a flap that when people question orders coming through HCO people weren't compelled to think up new and wonderful answers. The job of HCO was to make the original order stick.

In other words if by any line I require somebody to do something in an org and they come to you and ask for more data on it, you are supposed to say, "What did he say?" and then they read it back at you and you are supposed to say, "Well, that's what he said, now please do it." And they say, "We can't do it because yap yap" and you say, "Read it again," and they do and eventually they find out what it is they are ordered to do and they only find out THEN that they can do it.

You are there to make Ron's orders stick. We've already proven that when they don't the whole thing starts to go around the bend because my orders are based on years of know-how and the other fellow's changes are based on no experience.

So your first action is to know what it is I'm telling people to do and then to make those orders stick, usually by quietly and patiently getting them to understand what they are. The HASI London Arthritic Project is a good case in point. It wasn't followed very well and now there is traffic on the lines about it and if I didn't now try to straighten it up believe me it could create thousands of words of traffic because the way it is rigged now it will detract from the income of the whole org by bad programing (jamming lines), not make income for it, which is a reverse of my intentions.

Each department in a Central Org is rigged like a clock. People who are trying to succumb do it by failing to get the gen and then doing something that louses up the machinery.

Your function is to keep the place going the way it was intended to run and not the way somebody else thinks it ought to. Example: Within the past three months HCOs have got Melbourne and Auckland to handle departments exactly the way they were set up to run. They have both experienced higher income lately. The business available was the same. Only the method of handling the line was changed (except that the new Assoc Sec Melbourne was willing to run it right over the staff's collective dead body if need be) and it was changed directly back to my policies and suddenly the places boomed.

Get them hats on people and get the lines running the way they are supposed to and you'll have high income weeks almost at once.

L. RON HUBBARD
Founder

HCO POLICY LETTER OF 29 OCTOBER 1959
Sthil
Issue III

ORDERS DURING ABSENCE

All orders and directives issued by the Deputy Executive Director during any prolonged absence of mine from Sthil are conditional until confirmed.

L. RON HUBBARD
Founder

HCO POLICY LETTER OF 31 JANUARY 1961

Assoc Secs
HCO Secs

Issue I

SPHERES OF INFLUENCE

There is no reason for conflicts amongst HCO Offices and HASIs.

If the functions of organizations and hats are well understood, there is no reason for confusion.

An HCO Continental Office has these basic functions: To broadly disseminate Scientology to masses of people not connected or not yet connected with Scientology. This is done by magazines and by preparing proper literature.

Continental legal representation for Scientology is an HCO national function.

Broadly, the technology and dissemination of Scientology and its awards and good name are an HCO Continental function.

Supervision of all HCO Offices on the continent and their activities is an HCO Continental activity.

An HCO Continental Office does not pin down on one Central Organization to the exclusion of broad dissemination and the conduct of other HCO Offices.

An *HCO Area Office* has in its keeping the library of Scientology information for the use of the Central Org to which it is attached. It takes care of collections. It makes sure that HCO Bulletins and HCO Policy Letters are read and understood by the Central Org and its personnel. It keeps the org board. (There is no change here from the HCO Policy Letter that recently laid down the duties of an HCO Area Office.) It can security check any Scientologist or Central Org personnel.

An HCO Area Office does not run the Central Org or hire or fire its personnel but, in case of emergency and in the absence of competent Central Org personnel, may find it necessary to take charge temporarily. This has happened now and again in the past.

The Association Secretary or Organization Secretary has full authority over his or her organization and personnel. It is his or her task to cope when policy does not exist, to hold the form of the organization, to keep it busy and prosperous and its morale high.

In times of expansion, I find it necessary, as Executive Director of a Central Org, to shift its form and activities toward a greater reality. At such times my orders are relayed through the comm lines of HCO or, in rare cases, directly to the Assoc (or Org) Secretary or the organization's personnel. I try to stay on command lines but I sometimes have to have data from staff members directly.

I always try to info the Association Secretary when this happens. A bypass of this character happens usually in times when command lines have broken or when emergencies of magnitude threaten an org's existence or when I am hunting for new org patterns that will work.

In short, an HCO Continental Secretary is supposed to see that more people hear about Scientology on a mass basis—that better handouts and write-ups exist, that Scientology stays firm on that continent or part of the world and that HCO Area Offices function well with well-staffed personnel.

An HCO Area Secretary is supposed to see that technology stays high, that awards are issued properly, that people in Central Orgs know their HCO Bulletins and HCO Policy Letters and that the org board stays straight and that communication first and foremost occurs and that HCO remains solvent.

On most continents or in large areas the HCO Continental and the HCO Area Office of a Central Org are together. This makes for confusion, perhaps, but for the time being is an economic measure. But although they double up personnel, they should not be too duplicative in their duties. HCO Area rates its own office, even if it's small, its own access to files and facilities. As things expand, HCO Continental should establish separate quarters as feasible economically, but that's mostly future and depends on Central Orgs really making money.

This HCO Policy Letter is not laying down policy, it is only seeking to clarify functions. None of it has any force of law, it only seeks to promote a good understanding at a time when expansion heightens confusions and at times even tempers.

It is my task to establish a new form for Central Orgs. It is the HCO Secretary's task to make it understood and to make sure it takes form in fact. It is the Association (or Organization) Secretary's task to cope if necessary, to make the org and its personnel get the job done and to run the whole service activity of Scientology, and to keep up staff morale. It's the HCO Continental Secretary's task to make more people hear about Scientology, to guarantee the quality of presentation, to make sure HCO Area Offices are effective, to conduct special events and, of course, as in the case of all HCO Offices, to make my postulates stick.

If we do just these things, we can expand with a minimum of strain and a maximum of effectiveness.

L. RON HUBBARD
Founder

HCO CONTINENTAL

The duties and activities of HCO Continental are generally defined as helping me to wear my hats in the Continental Area.

To fully understand the duties of HCO Continental one has to understand what I do or would do and then see that it is done.

First would be the general, mass dissemination of Scientology by books, magazines, tapes, etc., and special events such as congresses.

Second would be ethics, certificates and awards which would include justice.

Third, but not in order of importance, would be technical excellence and results in processing.

Fourth would be the good functioning of all HCO Area Offices in a Continental Area, their personnel and finance problems and seeing that they do their job as outlined in a recent HCOB.

Fifth would be the preservation and form of Central Organizations and their income and survival, particularly during a State of Emergency (HCO PL 17 Feb. 61 II, EMERGENCY, STATE OF).

Sixth and throughout would be action as a personal secretary or personal secretarial functions to myself.

Seventh would be handling mission holders and field auditors.

Eighth would be legal activities.

In short, HCO Continental is an extended arm of HCO WW and maintains my presence and action in a Continental Area.

Just as my own hats are generalized and at times nebulous, so are HCO Continental's duties.

HCO Continental is governed by the maxims—make Ron's postulates stick—keep comm going—help Ron wear his hats.

L. RON HUBBARD
Founder

CenOCon

STATE OF EMERGENCY

In HCO Continental in particular and in HCO Areas, no management actions are undertaken toward a Central Organization (except for hat checks and other routine duties as covered in the actions of HCO Area Offices) unless there exists a State of Emergency.

If a State of Emergency exists in a Central Organization, HCO must assume that management has already to some degree failed to:

a. Follow the form of a Central Organization,

b. Put standard policies into action,

c. Show initiative or

d. Put properly qualified personnel on post. And HCO must pitch in and act to help the Assoc Sec with or without his or her approval.

The indication of a State of Emergency can be read beforehand from an OIC board, being forecast by red lines in three or more graphs, or by three red lines on one graph. If management has tolerated this without action when one red line occurred, a State of Emergency has already begun when it reaches three, since this is patently one or a dozen dropped balls. The organization can be assumed to be out of control.

I almost never directly interfere with the running of a Central Organization beyond okaying executives and Assoc Secs, codifying tested patterns of operation and furnishing policies based on existing experience. However, when a Central Organization shows signs of failing, I have to step in.

It is not a good thing to have to step in suddenly. It is always attended by swift action because I never step in unless an emergency already exists and in an emergency one has to act fast. Fast action is seldom attended by smoothness. *But* in the various emergencies which have occurred in the past when I had to step in, the organization was enabled to survive.

HCO Area, HCO Continental and HCO WW, in that order, become aware of emergencies.

The main responsibility for handling and executing orders in a State of Emergency falls on HCO Continental, often via HCO Area. But HCO Area may act alone, briefing HCO Continental meanwhile, until the situation is fully in the hands of HCO Continental. HCO Continental may act alone, fully briefing HCO WW and myself meanwhile.

Until a State of Emergency exists, HCO has little to do with the actual running of a Central Organization beyond HCO Area duties as outlined elsewhere in HCO PL 9 Jan. 61, DUTIES OF HCO. But when a State of Emergency has come into being, the powers of HCO representatives become the same as those of the Executive Director in all but signing contracts or certificates or awards.

The *purpose* of handling a State of Emergency is to bring the organization up to survival level instantly, now, at once, by any practical, fast means.

The steps to be taken are:

a. Immediately inspect and instantly correct the pattern of a Central Organization errors which might have developed;

b. Put standard policies in action where ignorance or "know better" may have introduced offbeat policies;

c. Demonstrate initiative in remedying the situation and encourage initiative in others;

d. Security check personnel and get better qualified personnel on critical posts.

In a State of Emergency an HCO Area Sec can appoint or transfer personnel up to department head level at will without consultation with anyone but with full advices to HCO Continental. Such appointments and transfers are always temporary in nature and can be appealed in writing with full data and graphs by an Assoc Sec to HCO Continental, HCO WW or to the Executive Director. But the temporary appointment or transfer may not wait for the findings of such an appeal, but goes into effect the instant it is ordered, verbally or in writing by the HCO representative.

Reformation of departments or lines must take effect as soon as ordered by the HCO representative during a State of Emergency. An appeal may be made in writing by the dept head or the Assoc Sec to HCO Continental, HCO WW or the Executive Director, but the temporary measure must go into effect and stay in effect until findings are issued upon the appeal.

While all this may seem vigorous, it is what I would have to do and would do if I were on the ground. Thus it is in reality HCO Continental helping me wear my hat.

STATE DEFINED

A State of Emergency is exactly defined as existing in the face of one or more of the following circumstances:

1. The Central Organization income falls below £1,000 or $3,000 by Thursday 2:00 P.M. of the week it comes in. (For city offices £500 or $1,500. This includes only New Zealand, Los Angeles, Durban, Sydney, Perth, San Diego, Cape Town, Seattle and New York.)

2. Two charts on the OIC board show red lines of decline for 2 consecutive weeks (same 2 charts) as of the moment of posting or Tuesday at 2:00 P.M. reflecting the past week.

3. One chart shows a red line for each of three consecutive weeks by the time of posting or Tuesday at 2:00 P.M.

4. Twenty percent or more of HGC cases showing no gain or a decline in any given week.

5. The PE Foundation has less than 20 for the PE Course and less than 10 new for the co-audit for any given week.

6. The organization is dunned by a creditor.

7. Academy students unable to pass HCO Board of Review or Academy attendance very low, either of which signify a State of Emergency in the Academy.

In the case of 1 (income less than £1,000 or $3,000) the State of Emergency is general and action may be taken throughout the organization.

In the case of 2 the State of Emergency is general.

In the case of 3, 4 and 5 the State of Emergency is confined to the departments affected.

In the case of 6 the State of Emergency is general.

As a State of Emergency only comes about after balls have been dropped abundantly, and as this already betokens either bad morale or security risks present, do not be too upset, HCO representative, if your actions meet protest in one form or another in the Central Organization. Your action triggered only an existing protest. So don't ever worry about my standing behind you. I stand behind department heads and the Assoc Sec all the way unless a State of Emergency develops. Then I back up HCO.

A State of Emergency must be declared to the Assoc Sec or, in his absence, his deputy, by the HCO representative before it officially exists.

One State of Emergency may only exist for ten days from the date it is declared but may be declared again immediately after if the defined emergency is repeated.

L. RON HUBBARD
Founder

HOW TO CONFESS IN HCO

The way for an HCO to confess to me that it isn't doing its job now that tech problems are solved is to write me as follows:

Dear Ron,

We are having a dreadful time with low units. We have had to loan money to the Central Org even though you forbade it. We're sorry we can't pay for any of the books we're selling. We are having trouble finding good personnel. Here are some newspaper clippings—we are sorry it's bad publicity but PE made a mistake. We are not able to get out our bulletins because we haven't any money for HCO staff.

Oh yes, here's a clipping that says the Medical Association is after quacks and also here are a number of bad letters from the public.

> Best,
> HCO Detroit.

Liberally translated this or any part of this reads in fact:

Dear Ron,

We are really goofing here in HCO. We get HCO Bulletins all right but we don't make them stick.

Quality is terrible in the HGC and Academy but of course that has nothing to do with us.

We made sure we didn't get a good Staff Staff Auditor for Lists 1 and 2. We got one who propitiates and can't do a Security Check.

We'd like to get the Central Org on the ball but we can't confront how upset they get so we don't usually show them any policy letters. If any of your postulates stick here, they come in on a rumor line and get to Central Org by accident.

Clearing the public would take much too long so we abandoned it. It may not be true anyway. Certainly *we're* still aberrated.

Hope you are as apathetic as we are.

> Worst,
> HCO Detroit.

P.S. We'll see if we can't keep technical at an even lower level. Then we can all go broke.

If the above bears any relation to persons living or dead, it is purely coincidental. Just assign it to my worse nature after working all night trying to solve problems HCOs should have prevented in the first place.

Anyone would do his job if there were a war on. Well, I've got news for you. There is. And unless you see that clearing gets routine in HGCs and good auditors get produced by Academies, not just you but the whole human race will have lost that war.

We win if HCO does its job. We win if we turn out Releases and Clears routinely. We lose if *any* of the statements made in the fictitious letter above remain long true and remain unsolved in HCOs.

Any part of that text is solved by HIGH TECHNICAL SERVICE.

L. RON HUBBARD
Founder

P.S. Thank God, I've never received anything like these letters. But I do receive lines in them. LRH

HCO POLICY LETTER OF 2 NOVEMBER 1961
Issue II

Remimeo
Tech Hats
Qual Hats
LRH Comms

(Also issued as an HCOB, same date and title)

Keeping Scientology Working Series 16

TRAINING QUALITY

It becomes fantastically, screamingly apparent that we *must not ever* turn out or let go a bad auditor, poorly trained.

Accordingly put a permanent sign where D of T can see it in his office as follows:

> EVERY TIME YOU TURN OUT A BAD AUDITOR YOU MAKE ENEMIES FOR SCIENTOLOGY.

> INCOMPETENT AUDITORS ARE THE ONLY SOURCE OF OUR TROUBLES.

L. RON HUBBARD
Founder

SCIENTOLOGY LIBRARY AND RESEARCH, LTD

(Effective on Receipt)

Scientology Library and Research personnel, under the direction of the Research Secretary and Technical Director, are appointed.

They are to accomplish between them the following actions:

Data collection, rapid assembly, storage and safeguarding of all Scientology technical materials, a copy of each book, all tapes, transcriptions of tapes, manuscripts, articles, HCO Bulletins, notes, notebooks of students that have been published on ACCs, papers and any other material of whatever kind that gives Scientology technical data.

This material is to be so stored as to be available for cataloging and so as to be of immediate use as needed.

Great care should be taken to preserve it against dust, moisture, damage, accidental loss by "lending."

The purpose here is to create a master library for research and compilation purposes only, not for lending or other use.

Insofar as possible original materials will be incorporated, such as handwritten manuscripts, original copies of tapes (masters), etc.

Adequate space must be provided regardless of what other materials have to be stored outside the Manor. Adequate shelving and cabinets have a high priority.

TAPE COPYING

They are to care for tape copying, all tape equipment, microphones, recorders, etc., allotted to Scientology Library and Research.

All needful tape copies are to be made promptly for shipment to proper authorized destinations.

The care and preservation of equipment is their full responsibility.

COMPILATIONS WORK

Immediate crash program value is to be given to them on any compilation of new publications.

They will give all possible assistance on the assembly or construction of materials for early publication.

The construction or lettering of charts, assembly of dummies for paste-up, collection of pictures or photostats for use shall receive their most instant attention, and amongst all their activities this has the highest priority.

After such compilation, the work is passed to makeup and design and thence to printing.

Scientology Library and Research has the purpose of collecting, safeguarding and preserving all Scientology materials, and while safeguarding the originals, compiling from such, new work and preparing it for direct dissemination as in tapes or designing and printing as in the case of written work.

It is a full intention that SLR shall provide a flood of new publications and compilations to assist the dissemination of Scientology.

L. RON HUBBARD
Founder

HUBBARD COMMUNICATIONS OFFICE
Saint Hill Manor, East Grinstead, Sussex

HCO POLICY LETTER OF 1 MARCH 1965

Gen. Non-Remimeo
BPI
Missions

GENERAL AMNESTY

Celebrating the attainment of all data up to Level VII and the beginning of the intensive application of exact technology at all levels, and in appreciation to any and all who assisted during the early phase of our development before exact technology was stable, a General Amnesty is issued for all Scientologists for any and all offenses of whatever kind prior to this date, acknowledging fully that they have been committed and forgiving any consequence and punishment which might have been feared, contemplated or ordered because of them.

By my hand and seal
on the 1st of March, AD15

L. RON HUBBARD
Founder

HCO EXECUTIVE LETTER OF 1 SEPTEMBER 1964

Limited Non-Remimeo

TO: HCO Area Sec, New York

FROM: Ron

SUBJECT: **TECHNICAL LECTURES BY OTHER PERSONNEL**

Recently a program for the New York October Congress was sent to me showing numerous *technical* lectures by New York staff.

As a congress package of tapes on new subject matter was available I vetoed the offered program.

I do not want anyone to get the impression that staff members are not to talk at congresses or that I frowned on New York staff members doing so. By all means the staff should talk to the public. But not on technical matters where direct communication is available.

However, as long as the subject became a matter of direct telex from DC in which the reasons as above did not seem to be understood, I had better clarify public technical materials policy.

The reason Elizabeth and Wichita blew up in the early days is directly traceable to a dispersal of public attention on technical matters. Their publications became only a public discussion ground in which any wild untested idea could be advanced as fact. Soon there was no actual Dianetic auditing being done in the US aside from a few old timers I had trained personally. A condition of no-results became widespread and Dianetics suffered to such a degree that it could not be straightened out. Even today, with straight Dianetic techniques I can achieve some very worthwhile results. So the technology was not at fault. The dispersal of correct technology by vias *was* at fault in the collapse of early organizations.

The public stays away from orgs in droves which alter technology. It shies off from congresses, etc., which have technology on a via.

The financial trouble one org is in currently was traced directly to a consistent slighting of myself and departures from the text. The public stayed thoroughly away. Any org that says even vaguely to the public, "We don't entirely agree with Ron . . ." loses its public and its income. This is not a merely hopeful statement. It is gruesomely true.

Therefore, sensible policy is—when straight technical materials and a direct comm line can be managed, they should be used in order for one organization to be successful or a congress to be well attended.

People have their own auditors at home who also talk to them so there's no novelty in coming into New York to have what they have at home. True a higher and more recently trained auditor will always have audience command.

But you see, a congress audience or a magazine's pages or a tape library isn't everybody's line to talk on. These are my own personal lines, just as you as an org are my own personal organization in your area.

If others talk on that line it is no longer a fully official line but is an anybody's line. The reason for the congress or the org to exist is knocked out and the congress is now a meeting, the org is just another field office. So—no attendance, dispersal, org failure.

These are essentially my comm lines. I made them and I keep them up.

You and the Org Sec and all the staff are handling my comm lines in trust.

So long as you keep me talking or writing on my own comm lines you will be successful.

As soon as these comm lines are for anybody's use the lines lose their direct theta and drop to an ordinary comm line. An anybody's comm line hasn't enough power on it to support an org.

One can say—with truth based on 14 years of experience—that an org is successful in direct ratio to the degree it safeguards and uses my comm line as my comm line and is unsuccessful to the degree that it does not.

So policy is based on good sense which is based on experience. No technical articles or lectures should be released by an org which are not mine.

Cape Town's insolvency traces directly to a failure to safeguard and forward my comm lines.

Melbourne's enquiry occurred directly because of a failure to safeguard and forward my administrative *and* technical comm lines.

Washington's current slump, from which it is now recovering, follows a period of occasional conversion of my comm lines—*Ability,* etc.,—into anybody's lines.

London has just come through a hard time. The direct cause of their trouble was technical failures. These occurred because they used field auditors randomly for HGC pcs so I obviously had no HGC auditors and this equalled no business.

These rough periods are in the past but they did exist.

While all these difficulties had other complications, my absence on their comm lines was felt and felt hard.

To be frank, the period of January '63 to April '64 was a period of heavy research concentration on my part. My inattention to org affairs and speaking little if any on the technical levels handled by orgs reduced the power of my comm lines and org income. Now, since April '64 I have been back working hard on org matters and, more vitally, have been using my org comm lines for matters of direct interest to the public the orgs handle. There is therefore an upsurge of org traffic and income.

I'm not telling you how necessary I am or how important. I'm only saying what the *public* expects.

You can center public attention on no more than one name in any given activity. In 1950 I had to skip my honest craving for anonymity (with its freedom) and, against my wishes, assume the rather terrible role of being a "personal front" for this work. You probably didn't know that until 1950 I always spoke of Dianetics as "the work of some scientists (unnamed) for whom I just happen to write." In support of this, look at the pen names I used in writing. Even up to August of that year I was unwilling to be a personal front with my name and face for this work. I'm no glory hound and fame to me is a grim joke. I'd far rather be this one or that one as I happen to choose from day to day.

So if I'm willing to give up my personal liberty and anonymity to keep the show on the road, the least my own people in my own orgs can do is to use it to the full.

So don't make "Ron's lines" into anybody's lines for a congress or a magazine or an org. To do so will have made me give up my freedom in vain.

Best,

Ron

L. RON HUBBARD
Founder

Gen. Non-Remimeo
Sthil

EXECUTIVE LETTER UNIT

The LRH Communicator is to set up as part of his own staff, where volume warrants it, an Executive Letter Unit.

This unit consists of a knowledgeable person who can answer SO #1–type mail, casual org mail and the public letters received by the HCO Exec Sec and Org Exec Sec.

Such mail is deleted from the lines before reaching the above-mentioned personnel, is answered by the person in charge of the unit without referral to the persons to whom it is addressed *or any other* person in the org except necessary queries to Dead Files to see what the status is and the like.

The person in charge of the unit is made familiar with general and current policies and conditions, and thus answers the mail without further despatch.

This type of mail is then typed and forwarded to the executive to whom it was addressed for signature or any change or signature and footnote and is then mailed.

The practice of sending SO #1s and the like around to various persons for their penciled answers is forbidden. The answers are done by the person in charge of the unit.

In very small orgs this is done in its entirety by the LRH Communicator.

Note that there are several such general lines, such as SO #1, and that such mail is not addressed solely to me but to other persons in the Executive Division.

The Executive Letter Unit may also extend into a typing pool for executives in the Executive Division only until secretarial help exists in their offices, but if this is done, a typist must be furnished for that purpose and it may not be done by the LRH Communicator.

The full intent of this unit is to take the following types of letters off the lines of Executive Division personnel *before* they reach the executive, answer them independently of any advice or help as to text and get them signed by the executive and mailed.

1. SO #1 (LRH public letters),

2. "Org SO #1" origins by org personnel not on official business,

3. Executive public letters being sent by the public to executives in the Executive Division,

4.   Thank-you notes,

5.   Any chatty, social or personal-type mail not essential to the conduct of the post.

The general policy regarding such mail is "Give them what they want and keep them happy." Another is "Never validate or seem to approve of technical 'discoveries'—just say okay fine in a noncommittal way or you'll get oddball application going somewhere with your seeming authority." Another is "No Dead-File-type mail (carping, critical) must ever go on to an executive but is simply dead filed."

The purpose of the unit is "to unburden executive lines so that the executive can plan, direct and get free of his desk and so get about in the org."

L. RON HUBBARD
Founder

HCO POLICY LETTER OF 7 DECEMBER 1965

St. Hill Only
Gen. Non-Remimeo
  Action
Hats
  All Execs Office 21
  All Execs Div 7
  LRH Personal Sec
  LRH Photo
  All Execs Dissem Div
  All Tape Personnel

Exec Division

Dept 21

HCO Dissem Div

TAPE COLOR FLASH CODE

Reels are marked, as well as boxes.

UNMARKED REELS: New reels or spools, unused, should be checked and color flashed if found to be recorded on. Check with LRH personally before erasure of *any* unmarked tape found anywhere.

YELLOW–TABBED LABEL or yellow—HCO Dissem master. These are *never* erased, may *not* be played or loaned or used. They are for archives only. "Production" is written on the yellow-tab label of a production master.

GREEN–TABBED LABEL or green tape—Commercial copy, for sale to orgs or field or student use in Tech and Qual Divisions.

RED–TABBED LABEL or red-marked—LRH master for music, cine, original tapes of books and tapes LRH wants kept. These belong in the Office of LRH. They are never erased. The designating word "cine" or "book," etc., is added to the label with other descriptive matter. LRH uses also some colored reels. A colored reel (plastic is colored) is always property of LRH.

BLUE–TABBED LABEL or blue-marked—Dictative tape. May be erased when transcribed and checked against copy. Usually letters, orders or notes. THIS IS USED THROUGHOUT THE ORG. Never mark a reel or box blue unless the tape has been checked by playing it to see what it really is. Don't ever erase unless you are *sure* it has been transcribed. Stenos, always add a note on the box as to date of transcribing.

Don't let tapes float about without boxes. Any tape so adrift should be checked, marked and boxed and left in a box.

Forward all dictation tapes in the right box and *in a box*.

Be careful in using tape to restore to the *right reel*. You can wind one through to an unmarked or wrongly marked reel.

Never use a marked reel for the take-up reel. If your empty *is* marked, find the original and restore it. Blank (empty) spools are always unmarked.

Tape labels can have a div and dept or section number or name on them. This is done using the color code above.

Colored plastic reels may not be used by anyone but LRH. All others use clear plastic.

Labels for reels are easy to get. Use them.

L. RON HUBBARD
Founder

SEC ED 231 SH   14 December 1965

Dept 21 personnel only

DEPARTMENTAL ACTIONS

I know we have a lot on our plate and that we are somehow getting on with it.

However, my own lines are beginning to tumble because of omissions or slows.

For instance, I edited a needed cine film and readied it for reprint but because a door to the 1st floor projection room is not done, the film cannot be completed. My lecture schedule is far behind due to delays on the stage in the Chapel. And I spent last night completing proofing of prints. I have had to take over to some degree food ordering and safeguarding.

My own work is bang on, if anything ahead of schedule, so I am doing my job. All I want is for others to do theirs.

The idea of *expedite* is the routine of Dept 21. So many divisions and organizations depend on this department that we must push on. The reason for this is when we get anything from orgs or divisions it is already overdue or has been flubbed. Thus we have to move much faster than in an ordinary activity. Nearly all our most routine actions are influenced by the fact that we are part of a command staff and such nearly always has to move at rush as its normal pace.

The consequences of *our* slowing down is to utterly smash some project elsewhere.

One or more of the following possible faults has crept in to Dept 21 recently.

A lot more talking about it than doing it or:

Somebody around saying it isn't worthwhile.

Somebody giving personnel something *else* to do each time they get started on a job or:

Distractive actions by such as Town and Country Planning Committee fixating people to the exclusion of their jobs or:

Some wild rumor I don't know about.

In general we lack a proper divisional org board.

Being at an executive strata departmental personnel tends to discuss rather than act. We can help that by sending a despatch rather than bringing a body with a message.

There is nothing wrong that hard personal work won't cure.

Several Department 21 people are doing very well indeed. But not all.

I therefore wish to point out only that my own lines are tending to tumble over overdue actions.

And that we need a departmental board posted and better hats.

And I trust this can all be sorted out and we can quickly get the show on the road.

L. RON HUBBARD
Founder

Remimeo

GIFTS

When a staff member has a baby, the following line will be followed:

The HCO Area Sec in the org concerned prepares a card and sends to St. Hill Exec Letter Unit, giving details of the birth, parents' names, etc.

The Exec Letter Unit secretary prepares a letter from LRH and one from MSH and forwards with the card for signature. These letters and card are routed back to the HCO Area Secretary.

The HCO Area Sec then orders a bouquet of flowers and attaches the card to those and has these delivered by the flower company. The two letters are sent separately.

A separate card and letter can be sent from the staff of the organization. A supply of appropriate cards can be kept for these occasions.

Care must be taken to do this promptly so that the action is appropriate and doesn't occur a month or two late.

Also, as usual, issue to the new baby an associate membership as our welcome to the team.

L. RON HUBBARD
Founder

HCO POLICY LETTER OF 4 JANUARY 1966
Issue VI

Gen. Non-Remimeo
LRH Communicator Hat
HCO Area Sec Hat
Exec Sec Hats
Org Sec Hats

LRH RELATIONSHIPS TO ORGS

I have several posts and relationships to orgs which make up several identities.

Unless these are understood, many errors can occur, not the least of which are tax errors, and not the least dangerous, power pushes and upsets.

For instance, there are *two* Offices of LRH at Saint Hill. And one more for every other org. This is a familiar situation. It has happened in LA, Phoenix, DC and London—I always specially work with the org where I am situated as well as continue to handle all other orgs on an international basis and remain the chief executive of each org elsewhere.

An org where I am, making more than other orgs, always bears the expense of international activities. In this case, here at Saint Hill, the org also shares international income and so its cost is light.

Thus, I have several hats and resultant comm lines here at Saint Hill and at least one more in each org. These can be described as identities and posts as follows:

LRH, AN INDIVIDUAL

This is LRH, a private person. This identity is the one who is entitled to any royalties and leases copyrights and trademarks and technology for use by Scientology organizations. This identity paid for and did the research, organized the organizations. This is the identity that loans orgs money or guarantees their bank accounts, etc., and on death is a private trust for my family.

LRH, TRUSTEE

This identity is a trustee who holds in trust properties and money for Scientology and since 1957 has held UK and Commonwealth corporations in trust for the original US company until these assets can be transferred to a UK *non*profit corporation. As UK tax people will not okay such a nonprofit status until after a year of operation, we have formed other corporations in the UK and Commonwealth time and again only to have them refused nonprofit status. The laws of Arizona prevent transfer of HASI assets abroad to any but a corporation with nonprofit status. This leaves me as a trustee of all assets outside the US until they can be transferred. But even after transfer I will still be a trustee for Scientology corporations. All money sent to LRH, an individual, is received by LRH, a trustee, or a corporation and is seldom paid to LRH, an individual, but turned over to companies without being given to LRH, an individual. This is a vital point, often missed even by accountants who then get us involved. If the money were (1) received by LRH, an individual, and then (2) turned over to LRH, a trustee, and/or (3) received and used by a company, it would hang LRH, an individual, for huge tax sums for money he has never really received or used and indeed won't ever get. Example: Mr. X sends a $20 mission payment to "L. Ron Hubbard." This is always invoiced by an org as "mission payment." Therefore, one concludes that "LRH" in that case is LRH, a trustee. If one erred and said it was the income of LRH, an individual, that identity, never seeing the money, would yet owe tax on it, which is unfair. All incoming 10 percents to "LRH" mean LRH, a trustee, and are used in company expenses or are put away to be used in general defense. The point of confusion is that LRH, an individual, is actually owed those 10 percents as royalties to support research, etc. But the companies receive and use the money and it doesn't even go through the hands of LRH, an individual. LRH, an individual, has not canceled monies owed to him. He has not received them. LRH, a trustee, seldom gives LRH, an individual, any Scientology money. Tax authorities are astounded at this (believing the worst of everyone), but those on our accounts lines know it is so. This is LRH, a trustee. "Trustee" is an identity and activity almost all movements, churches and benevolent associations have, and in each case the "trustee" does just what LRH, a trustee, is doing—safeguarding property and assets of an association. It's a very usual role.

LRH, BOARD MEMBER

This is an unpaid identity on several boards. It is entitled only to out-of-pocket expenses and almost never puts in for any. This is a member of a board of directors. These must be paid no salary in a nonprofit corporation, only expenses. "Chairman" comes under this. Also "president."

LRH, EXECUTIVE DIRECTOR

This is better understood as "general manager" as it isn't as a member of the board that it is held but as a manager. This is a paid post in any corporation or association. There are numerous LRH Exec Dir titles and identities, for this title repeats in each area and org and in the International Division.

It means "highest executive of the organization," "third member of the Advisory Council," "head of the department called the Office of LRH." Therefore, there is one of these titles for each org we have and for the International Exec Division as well. Perth, for instance, has an LRH Executive Director Perth; LA has LRH Executive Director LA, etc. Then there is LRH Executive Director WW.

The identity of the LRH Communicator in the org or activity gives clue to this. *Each* LRH Executive Director title has an LRH Communicator.

There are two LRH Communicators at Saint Hill—LRH Communicator WW, who attends to each org for LRH Executive Director WW via each org's LRH Communicator, and LRH Communicator SH, who handles the traffic both of LRH Executive Director WW as sent to it from the LRH Communicator WW and for LRH Executive Director SH.

This is only possible as the orgs are all similarly engaged. HCO Area Secs filled this role for years and still do where there is no LRH Communicator. HCO Area Secs *still* have duties for the Executive Director, regardless of the LRH Communicator, as old policy letters show. "Sec ED issue" is one of these.

Proper routing from an org is through the LRH Comm of that org to LRH Executive Director of that org and forwarded on to LRH Comm WW who sees that LRH Exec Dir *that org* receives it in absence. LRH Exec Dir WW may issue a blanket order concerning it but it is usually answered by LRH Exec Dir that org.

The Advisory Council of any org operates without its third member, LRH Exec Dir of that org, but in case of disputes or errors, finds LRH Exec Dir that org taking it up.

LRH, STAFF MEMBER

In addition to all these other identities and titles, there is that of LRH, staff member. As such I give staff lectures in the org where I am, assist where I can, crack cases and train students as "Coordinator of Research" (meaning application of research), write magazines, take pictures, act as a routing expert, listen to problems, and do a lot of other things.

I am chiefly a staff member of the org where I am located but am also a staff member of each org.

COMPLEXITY

Necessarily, no one person can hold all these posts and identities. But at the same time, over the years, I have found they are the minimum number I must give attention to.

To handle this complexity, I have many persons assisting me. I expect them to act with initiative. I expect them to carry out the purposes I have regarding orgs and Scientology so as to keep things expanding and the lines clean and flowing and keep me from getting so involved on just one point I can't do the rest of my jobs.

For quite in addition to these posts, I have my research hat (our most important hat) and an organizing hat and a promotion hat and a public relations hat. My writing-books hat should absorb most of my time with research complete but not wholly published.

Thus, I expect people to do their jobs so I can then do my job and don't like people to flub theirs and require special attention on it. Only this holds us back because I then can't do my jobs which eventually breaks down our expansion and dissemination.

OTHER ARRANGEMENTS

Many other arrangements have been tried—fewer "identities," less traffic for me. But each time some catastrophe has occurred. This then required more work than wearing that hat in the first place. The early Dianetic corporate catastrophes occurred because I did not have or wear all my Exec Director hats and had no legal control of the orgs. Since I began to wear these and took responsibility, things have been much better indeed, so I can't shed them. So these identities are a minimum by trial and error and by success.

SUMMARY

Anyone on high executive and accounts lines should understand these things thoroughly and LRH Communicators should point them out.

Only when these relationships are misunderstood do we get in trouble.

Our growth depends on our staying out of trouble, getting our lines in and keeping corporate structure straight. *And* understanding these separate identities or titles and functions and using them.

It is doubtful if this situation will change. As orgs grow, my assistants grow also and become more competent and refer less to me and work on delegated authority. My work is lighter the bigger we get so eventually I will hold only titles with no actions or duties. This can be continued easily and so there is no need to reduce identities to simplify lines. And there wouldn't even be a need to reorganize if I wasn't there in the flesh at all. All I need to do is work out a succession of assistants to make the activities continue. There is no succession of myself to be worked out in any identity regardless of what happens to me simply because I did the original work and as it is done there is no reason to have a succession for it as it is itself.

My identities are therefore woven into the pattern so they don't have to be altered to keep things going. LRH, an individual, becomes an estate. The rest is by appointment from "LRH Executive Director" with that title activated by the Int Ad Council or board but still used as a title but not of a person. The "Office of LRH" is part of org structure. And before long even LRH, "a board member," will be needless to be filled in the flesh by delegated signature of LRH.

This is not only today, then, but tomorrow as well, and the above identities are firm as identities whether I am here or not. Even today 99 percent of my functions are done by delegated authority. The 1 percent left is heavy enough for twenty men but *it is getting lighter* each year and so can be seen to be only a post in a few years and so it can continue. Trying to fill up the post is all that would cause "a war," so leave it activated as itself, none assigned to it, assistance to it by established formula. We won't vanish if I as a person vanish. And these identities never were me anyway so they can survive. It is a part of basic org structure. My post title is used ten thousand times a day on matters I never will hear of, so why should I hear of any in the long run as only the *delegation* of authority is in action anyway.

So whatever happens to me as a person, leave these LRH identities on the org board unfilled and all will be well. If you try to fill them, catastrophe will result. Only how authority is delegated by "LRH Executive Director" in my absence needs to be worked out and that will be published.

Somebody some day will say "this is illegal." By then be sure the orgs say what is legal or not.

L. RON HUBBARD
Founder

HCO POLICY LETTER OF 14 FEBRUARY 1966

Remimeo

DOCTOR TITLE ABOLISHED

In protest against the abuses and murders carried out under the title of "doctor," I abandon herewith all my rights and legitimate use of this title as the name has been disgraced.

I was a Ph.D., Sequoia's University, and therefore a perfectly valid doctor under the laws of the state of California.

My beloved grandfather was a doctor and was known as such throughout his life.

Through the ages the term "doctor" has meant "a learned man" but in modern times has been stained by its preemption by medical doctors and psychiatrists and I do not care to be associated in any way with faithless men or ignorant butchers or murderers.

The title of "mister," implying "master," I also abandon.

I wish to be known solely by my name "Ron" or Hubbard, an honorable name in the fields of philosophy and exploration.

Any and all DScns may apply for and receive a new certificate and the title "Dean of Scientology."

I wish to call to attention that any certificate ever issued by me is valid first by my signature and second by the laws of the country in which its corporation is founded.

The originator of a subject traditionally has the right to qualify persons in that subject, and this is the chief source of any title of learning.

I could with ease defend any use of the term doctor in any nation, but the name has come into question by association.

This is the second time I have requested not to be so named. The first was in the late 50s in Washington, DC. But people have continued the practice against my wishes and I have not lately been active in correcting them.

No secretary, press spokesman or LRH Communicator may hereafter refer to me as "Doctor" or sign my name as such.

I have been a "captain" of sailing vessels, a "captain" of corvettes, a "sergeant" of marines in my extreme youth, a "commander" and many other captions. And as a Scientologist knows, one has had other names.

"L. Ron Hubbard" is a proud enough title. Or humble enough. I wish it to so remain.

The wide world calls me plain "Ron." That is more than good enough for me, signifying as it does the friendship and confidence of the many. They are my friends.

L. RON HUBBARD
Founder

HCO POLICY LETTER OF 1 SEPTEMBER 1966RA
REVISED 8 MAY 1973

Remimeo
Board Members
Executive Directors
Staff

FOUNDER

In that new Boards of Directors are being elected for the various corporations and their branches, I am resigning the title of Executive Director and in accordance with a resolution of the general meeting of charter members, am being given the title of "Founder" instead.

Hereafter, all Sec EDs (now named "Executive Directives" or EDs) will be signed "for the BOARDS OF DIRECTORS."

The "Office of LRH" remains as before. The designation Sec ED (Executive Directive) does not change.

All org boards should change the top line Executive Director to "Founder" in letters of similar size.

None of this changes various communication lines, but policy letters are hereafter to be accepted or nullified by Boards of Directors in their regular meetings.

All policy letters since 1 September 1966 have been written in fact for the Boards of Directors.

The signature of the Boards of Directors of the Churches of Scientology is legal on any policy letter issued by the Hubbard Communications Office, Saint Hill Manor, East Grinstead, Sussex from 1 September 1966 and gives any policy letter so signed its full force as policy.

I have not for a long while received pay from any organization and my services are wholly volunteer.

There are considerable outstanding sums loaned by me to orgs or owed to me by orgs and these should be paid as feasible, carrying me as a creditor in disbursement files.

I have worked long to stabilize and expand orgs and to complete technology and policies and am resigning on a high statistic.

I am still available for consultation and for signature.

It is called to attention that the signature available is that of L. Ron Hubbard, as writer, and not that of L. Ron Hubbard, an Individual. As the two signatures may become somewhat confused, the distinction is emphasized.

My office of LRH as Founder remains mine as the public demonstrably stays away from orgs that do not bear the name "L. Ron Hubbard" and I do not wish to damage their "traffic" volume.

This is not a retirement but is a resignation from all director posts and the conducting of organizations by myself.

Organizations have now proven they can manage themselves and with mainly Clears and OTs in charge should come to no grief.

This affects all corporate structures in that I am not now a board member.

Bank accounts need no longer bear my signature but as they are so numerous and the task of changing them so great, I leave this to the new boards to accomplish when they can.

I would appreciate the new boards holding early meetings to review or accept policy and bank mandates as soon as possible as I wish to remain available to answer any questions.

On specific request, as a writer, I will write books on Scientology, its organization, and will write HCOBs and Policy Letters as requested. This is my writer hat.

L. RON HUBBARD
Founder

HCO POLICY LETTER OF 21 DECEMBER 1966

Saint Hill
Only

OFFICE OF LRH SUPPLIES

All photo supplies arriving for me are to be unpacked carefully and placed in the ballroom for my inspection.

They are not to be touched further, viewed or handled or shown about or looked at until I have inspected them and designated further action.

Some are delicate instruments. Supplies are sometimes incorrect.

Photographs and transparencies are to be carefully handled and placed in the center of my desk in my office.

There are no exceptions.

L. RON HUBBARD
Founder

HCO POLICY LETTER OF 22 FEBRUARY 1967
Issue I

Remimeo

OFFICE OF LRH

LRH Personal Office Organization

(Cancels HCO PL 18 July 66 and
HCO PL 16 Dec. 66, OFFICE OF LRH)

(Modifies HCO PL 1 Mar. 66, EXECUTIVE DIVISION
ORGANIZATION, as it applies to LRH Personal Office)

Personal Office of LRH Chart

LRH, Founder

LRH Communicator Branch

LRH Comm Sec Section

Exec Div Mimeo Section

Keeper of the Seals and Signature Section

LRH Comm Files Section
    Policy Files Unit
    Sec ED Files Unit

LRH Comm Log Section

LRH Personal Sec Branch

LRH Personal Files Section
    LRH Clipping Unit
    LRH Personal Val Doc Unit
    LRH Personal Address Unit

LRH Personal Finance Section
    LRH Financial Records Unit
    LRH Tickets Unit

LRH Transcription Section
    LRH Typing Unit

LRH Personal Appointments Section
    LRH Reception Unit

LRH Personal Aide Branch

LRH Audiovisual Aids Section
    Processing Unit

Cameras Unit
Tapes Unit
Recorders Unit
Supplies Unit

LRH Business Section
LRH Personal Attorney Unit
LRH Contract Unit
LRH Traveling Unit

LRH Ethics Authority Section
LRH Petitions Unit
LRH Judge Advocate Unit

LRH Appearances Section
LRH Stage Unit
LRH Costume Unit
LRH Lighting Unit

LRH Public Relations Section
LRH Releases Unit
LRH Press Unit
LRH TV Unit
LRH Radio Unit
LRH Host Unit

LRH Personal Courses Branch
(LRH Personal Courses Supervisor)

Clearing Course Supervisor
Assistant Clearing Course Supervisors
Clearing Course Administrators

OT Course Supervisor
Assistant OT Course Supervisors
OT Course Administrators

LRH Property, Building and Plans Branch

Estate Bureau

LRH Personal Property Section
LRH Library Unit
LRH Equipment Unit
LRH Real Property Unit
LRH Insurance Unit

Plans Section
LRH Ship Plans Unit
LRH Building Plans Unit
LRH Long-Range Programs Unit
LRH Personal Projects Sub-Unit

L. RON HUBBARD
Founder

HCO POLICY LETTER OF 31 MAY 1968

Gen. Non-Remimeo
LRH Comm Hat
Communicator's Hat
Exec Secs

LRH COMM LOG

Policing and gaining rapid compliance for LRH is a vital function of an LRH Communicator. A comm log is used to keep track of orders issued and not yet complied with and to bring to light those persons or areas noncomplying, or those falsely reporting compliances.

As it is failure to acknowledge and answer up and report on orders and noncompliance with orders or false reports that brings about emergencies and even catastrophes, it is vital that it be known what orders are not being complied with and by whom.

An effective LRH Comm log will rapidly indicate those orders not complied with and who is not complying as well as provide other useful data.

The LRH Comm log described here has been designed to highlight areas of noncompliance and no report and to indicate false report so that they may be spotted early and remedied.

The log consists basically of two foolscap folders. One, the inactive log contains only those items attested to as having been completed, the other, the active log, contains in chronological or number order only those items yet to be completed or complied with.

It is the second folder that an LRH Communicator uses most.

The folders may be simple manila folders, or more suitably two-hole ring binders with large rings. Normally the active file would be a ring binder and the inactive one or more manila folders.

A copy of each item (LRH ED, telex, handwritten order, etc.) is placed in the active log and has next to it a log sheet (described below) on which is written the relevant logging information.

The log sheets are mimeoed off on blue paper. One log sheet is used for each item being logged.

The logging is done upon receipt of the item, a copy of the item being filed in date order with its filled out log sheet facing. In the case of an LRH ED or HCO PL or HCO Exec Letter being received which is yet to be mimeoed the log sheet is made out and filed in the front of the folder while the original of the ED or policy letter goes to be mimeoed. When the mimeoed copy is received it is mated with the relevant log sheet and both are filed in chronological order. Thus any log sheets not yet mated with their mimeoed copies show up in the front of the active log as an indication of a slowdown on the mimeo issue line.

As each item is attested complied with by the person or persons to whom it is addressed it is transferred out of the active log into the inactive log. Thus it can be seen at a glance which orders are yet to be completed. If at any time it is necessary to relog an item it is merely transferred with its log sheet from the inactive log to the active log.

With this method of logging the original orders are always to hand when checking on compliance or logging an ack, report or compliance and it can be easily seen what is being checked or reported on.

The log sheet contains the usual log information and has columns for entering the dates of queries, acks and compliances. The post to whom the order is addressed is entered in the left hand column. Any posts often ordered or addressed can be included on the stencil before the log sheets are run off to save writing in each time. When that particular post is addressed an X can be placed in the second narrow column to indicate that the order was to that person or post. Additional persons or posts ordered can be filled in on the unused lines.

Compliance is checked upon by direct question. Nudging does not work well as execs have to look up the item queried. Direct question *works*. Nudging does not work *at all*.

It is done simply by asking a direct question in such a way that the answer will clearly show whether or not the item (LRH ED, telex, handwritten despatch, etc.) has been complied with, or if it is actually in motion and being complied with, whichever is applicable. Ask the question in such a way that the person does not have to look up the original order to be able to answer the question.

It can be as simple as a single question or as complete as a whole questionnaire covering each point of an ED, that requires compliance.

The query is made of the person or persons from whom compliance is expected. Such queries are always time machined. It will be found that querying compliance in this way will spark an executive into action where he has been noncomplying, for in order to answer your question he either has to have done what was ordered or will have to report his noncompliance. Where each point of an ED is covered by a questionnaire it will also pick up any point missed by the executive. Ask the question in such a way that the reply can be brief and to the point. You are not after pages of reports, you want *compliance* to the order. The questions can be such that a simple "yes" or "no" or very brief statement covers. *No report* usually means *noncompliance*.

Noncompliance is handled by standard ethics actions taken immediately noncompliance is evident. An LRH Comm will fail where he fails to use the full power of ethics to get compliance when noncompliance is evident.

False reports are detected by comparing the answers to the same or similar query from different persons. Where they differ there is a probable false report WHICH MUST ALWAYS BE FOLLOWED UP and the truth found out and the correct ethics action taken on the false report.

False reports can also be detected by checking or querying if the expected result has occurred or is occurring. Where it is not then suspect false report.

Example: Order was to restore all old names from old invoices to CF. Reported to be done. If on checking that magazines are being mailed to all of CF you discover that the number mailed is still only the same as before the order to restore all old names or has not increased by the expected amount then it is evident that a false report exists and this must be tracked down, and ethics action taken on the false report.

The log at WW or at a Continental Org differ only in that the names of the orgs from whom action is required are entered in the left hand column.

LRH COMMUNICATOR LOG (place)

Received for Issue

Name of Item _____

Date Approved for Issue _____

Source _____

Received as a Mimeo

Date _____

Identity _____

For Action or Report	By	Dates of Ack Query	Date of Ack	Nudged for Report or Compliance	Date of Report or Comp	Date Informed Source
HCO Exec Sec						
ORG Exec Sec	X					
HCO Area Sec						
(etc.)						

In practice it will be found best to use a quarto log sheet mimeoed as above with a ⅝th inch margin on the right hand side to take the punched holes. The holes are punched closer to the top of the quarto sheet so the bottom of the quarto log sheet is level with any foolscap items filed in the same folder. This way the headings of the actual items are visible while looking through the log for a particular item.

L. RON HUBBARD
Founder

Assisted by
LRH Communicator WW

OFFICE OF LRH WW REORGANIZATION

(Amends HCO PL 22 Feb. 67, OFFICE OF LRH, and
HCO PL 6 Sept. 67, WW DIVISION REORGANIZATION)

The post of LRH Personal Aide is abolished.

The LRH Ethics Authority WW is set up as a separate hat.

The Div 7 Sec (now Div 9 Sec WW) is made chairman of Ad Council WW.

The SO #1 Clerk is put under the LRH Personal Secretary.

The Archives Project Assembly and Preservation of Materials is taken back into the Office of LRH WW to safeguard.

L. RON HUBBARD
Founder

Remimeo

DIV 6

FILMS AND TAPES
NOT PROHIBITED

There is NOTHING anywhere in policy or HCOBs that forbids the use of films or tapes to their proper public, misunderstood words or no misunderstood words.

Introductory films and tapes are a MUST for proper public information.

The points that should be understood are that:

1. The QUALITY must be good.

2. The proper materials must be chosen for that PUBLIC.

HCOB 10 Nov. 71, Word Clearing Series 25, Tape Course Series 6, mainly concentrates on HIGH QUALITY and the CORRECT PUBLIC. Nothing in the HCOB forbids tapes and films being used on raw public.

When tape copy machines have worn-out recording heads at Pubs, making the copy tape bad, the org receiving such a bad copy must not accept the copy but must fire it back to Pubs to be redone.

When tapes are chosen, they must be chosen for the public to which they will be played.

When tapes or films are played to the public, they must have the highest quality players and hi-fi *speakers*.

There is this about tapes and films:

WHEN YOU CEASE TO PLAY TAPES TO THE PUBLIC AND STAFF, THEY LOSE THE WHOLE FLAVOR AND MEANING OF DIANETICS AND SCIENTOLOGY.

TO CEASE TO USE TAPES AND FILMS FOR FEAR OF MISUNDERSTOOD WORDS IS A FATAL DECISION.

The right decision is to word clear 4 publics who have seen films or heard tapes.

THE MOMENT YOUR ORG OR ACTIVITY NO LONGER PLAYS TAPES TO THE PUBLIC AND STAFF YOU WILL BEGIN TO LOSE.

Old orgs always had tape plays for field auditors and public particularly on Saturday or Sunday and made it a properly drilled Foundation event with the right tapes chosen and hi-fi equipment used and charged a small sum for it.

No words at all is worse than a few misunderstoods!

SO USE TAPES AND FILMS.

L. RON HUBBARD
Founder

HCO POLICY LETTER OF 9 SEPTEMBER 1972
Issue I

Remimeo
LRH Comm Hats
ED Hats
OIC
Info
  FBOs
  Treas Divs

LRH INCOME

(Cancels HCO PL 7 Sept. 72, LRH COMM
STAT REVISED, which dealt with LRH income)

I refuse to accept income or debt repayment from Scientology orgs or companies.

From the earliest royalties of *Dianetics: The Modern Science of Mental Health,* orgs have absorbed income originally intended for me but not received by me. This was even proven in tax courts.

In the late 1960s two qualified accountants computed the monies not received by me to be about 13 1/2 million pounds.

At no time did orgs actively refuse to pay me. It was just that their operational expenses and demands in expansion absorbed funds before they could be paid to me.

On the contrary, there has been a consistent effort, particularly recently, to pay me at least what I was currently owed.

People are so often willing to pay me that some orgs have even told the public that the money paid them was for me. But in actual fact it was absorbed in general operation and furnishing service even when the staff hoped it would go to me.

I have paid for the research that now is the technology of Dianetics and Scientology and have accomplished it as well, thus the orgs have not been out of pocket on this account either.

Aside from personal considerations, the tax problems of receiving repayment or pay for what I have done are enormous. I am told that if I receive pay the nonprofit status of some orgs is forfeited. In one instance, in Washington, DC, when it was proven in tax court that I had not received monies even when it was forwarded to Worldwide, where it was used by management, a long time after the case was "closed" the tax people again challenged the nonprofit status on the basis that I had for a while received a normal salary (which I assure you was more than earned).

Were I to accept royalties or salaries personally at this time from readily available org funds over the world, the sum would exceed the top executive pay of the largest corporation heads in the world and would add up to about five times the pay of the president of the United States.

I am told by legal authorities that were I to take pay, it would almost all of it just be absorbed as tax, so I would not receive any large part of it anyway as it is in the 93 percent tax bracket. Furthermore I am told by legal experts that my taking large sums of royalties and pay would jeopardize the nonprofit status of organizations.

Arguing that the laborer is worthy of his hire, an effort has recently been set afoot by others to see that I *did* get paid on the basis that I deserved it.

This collided with a longstanding private policy of my own not to accept personally pay or royalties.

I do not particularly desire a personal reward for the good work being done by Dianetics and Scientology.

Some time ago I forgave the 13 1/2 million pounds said to be owing to me by orgs. And I officially repeat the fact again.

I refuse to accept income or collections personally even when collected by others in my name.

This is not dictated out of any personal fear of taxes. I am not in any tax trouble and no taxes or disputes about my personal taxes exist.

I am also told that this decision works a hardship on orgs as it leaves on their books all the money that was collected as "income," whereas it was not. They have not paid for their goodwill or research or courses I gave for them or even repaid personal monies of mine collected by them. Thus they have listed as "income" what was actually debt owed by them. This gives them a difficulty whenever their taxes are computed and makes them pay taxes on money they in fact owe.

The International Board has pointed out these balance sheet problems. However, it remains that I refuse personal income from Dianetics and Scientology.

If the board wishes to clear these debts off org books, they should direct the collections and past debts elsewhere. If they gave these sums to a charitable or educational or research foundation and collected them for that purpose only, their problem with orgs and income that is actually debt would be solved.

This would assist and perpetuate research and the furtherance of man's knowledge and I am sure all orgs would be happy to contribute present and past debts to it without my receiving any of them.

Further, any unclaimed trustee funds I have held in the past should be disposed of in the same manner, thus clearing off all these matters utterly.

I did not develop Dianetics and Scientology for large financial recompense. The money paid to orgs pays for service and management to ensure good service.

The staffs themselves are often poorly paid, though not by any intent of mine.

Any large sums of money intended for me should go to the further betterment of man.

We're not here for pay anyway? Who could recompense with what the value of life itself?

Even our need of gross income is just to give more service.

And we're giving it. That's what counts.

L. RON HUBBARD
An Individual

HCO POLICY LETTER OF 24 SEPTEMBER 1973RA
REVISED 25 JANUARY 1991

Remimeo
All Orgs
All AOs
All SHs
Missions
LRH Comms

RELIGION

ALL AUDITORS—MINISTERS
MINISTERIAL BOARD OF REVIEW

All auditors must hold a valid Certificate of Ordination in order to practice auditing, whether for a church, a mission or as an independent missionary in the field.

Previously, auditors trained in New Era Dianetics were required to have their ministerial ordination before they could go onto an internship, which effectively blocked them from becoming interns. With this policy letter, that provision is cancelled. Any Academy or NED Course graduate may go directly into an internship without ordination, as his status is still that of "ministerial student." It is recommended that his ordination course be taken at the same time as his internship.

If a student elects to become a minister of the church and practice pastoral counseling (auditing) he does his training and a full internship and a Minister's Course. He is then given permanent certification. Auditing must occur on the internship and one does not have to be a minister to audit on an internship. However, no one is entitled to practice pastoral counseling after an internship unless they have also been ordained. Permission to practice may thus be granted by the local church upon permanent certification and ordination.

Missions are not authorized to ordain ministers. Their graduates who wish to practice auditing may apply to the nearest local church for any necessary training and ordination.

A Ministerial Board of Review is established in HCO. It shall be composed of no less than three persons who shall themselves be ministers of the church. The Chairman of the Board must be an HCO staff member. The other two members must be ministers of good repute but may be members of other divisions at the discretion of the chairman.

The purpose of this Board of Review is to help LRH safeguard Scientology, Scientology churches and Scientologists by ensuring that ministers of the church are and remain of good moral character, continue to uphold the Codes of Scientology and apply standard technology to their counseling of parishioners.

The board is normally convened by the chairman. In cases of extreme emergency or flagrant out-ethics in HCO the LRH Comm may convene the board and is the chairman.

Ministerial certificates may be suspended by the board when it finds cause within the framework of the above purpose. Certificate cancellation may be recommended to the Office of LRH in extreme cases.

Where the minister involved is a staff member of a mission, the board is regulated as well by HCO PL 18 Apr. 70, ETHICS AND MISSIONS.

L. RON HUBBARD
Founder

Revision assisted by
LRH Technical Research
and Compilations

HUBBARD COMMUNICATIONS OFFICE
Saint Hill Manor, East Grinstead, Sussex

HCO POLICY LETTER OF 5 NOVEMBER 1973

Remimeo
Div 6s
Pioneer Areas
PR & C
LRH Comms
I/As
LRH Pers PR Bu

SOURCE ACKNOWLEDGMENT

It is against policy as well as general honesty to quote from the works of LRH without due credit being given.

In areas where there has been conflict or dissidence it can be counseled that it is expedient to not give credit or mention LRH in order to secure some illusory advantage.

One calls to mind the number of times some auditor or group has set himself up as a "psychologist" and attributed Dianetic and Scientology *techniques* to psychology. These have uniformly failed, it being overlooked that psychology is losing and the alter-is alone corrupted the tech even further. No such efforts have survived.

At times writers ("to get in with a certain group") have used LRH work and quotes without credit. Their work, being generally corrupt in the first place, did not communicate or sell.

Truth must go with truth.

Admin tech is very very saleable, for instance. Study tech, done correctly, goes like a hot bomb. Even ethics tech has a popularity.

In a new area or estranged area, it is the *part* of Dianetics and Scientology you choose to disseminate that will mark success. It is not the omission of its authorship.

L. RON HUBBARD
Founder

HUBBARD COMMUNICATIONS OFFICE
Saint Hill Manor, East Grinstead, Sussex

HCO POLICY LETTER OF 21 NOVEMBER 1973

Remimeo

LRH COMM DRILLS

Ref:
HCOB 21 Nov. 73   THE CURE OF Q AND A,
                      MAN'S DEADLIEST DISEASE

The production of LRH Comms is mainly impeded by their own TRs and any tendency to Q-and-A.

Therefore, the HCOB 21 Nov. 73, THE CURE OF Q AND A, MINIMUM checklist fully and honestly done is vital to the success of an LRH Comm.

The whole program of handling tendencies to Q-and-A is given with its references in HCOB 21 Nov. 73.

Written as auditor and C/S drills, these vitally apply to LRH Comms.

The reason an LRH Comm would falsify his stats, wind up with incomplete programs or have trouble with his post are *all* covered in HCOB 21 Nov. 73 as above. After that he has a chance of applying his tech.

A requisite for LRH Comms is that program. Until it is fully and honestly done and he has checked out on his pack, HE MAY ONLY SIGN HIS NAME AND DESPATCHES AS "LRH COMM I/T." (I/T = In Training)

Persons now calling themselves "LRH Comms" who have not done the above successfully must revert their titles to "LRH Comm I/T" until it IS honestly and fully done.

L. RON HUBBARD
Founder

HCO POLICY LETTER OF 8 NOVEMBER 1978RB
REVISED 5 NOVEMBER 1979

Remimeo

SENIOR HCOs AREA AND CONTINENTAL

To get order into the various areas, a Senior HCO is created for the Flag Land Base, PAC and every Continental Office.

It is located in the FOLOs and is independent of the FOLO HCO.

The Senior HCO exists under the LRH Comm Network and should exist there as the LRH Comm Network is basically entrusted in establishment. LCI is more or less under the supervision of the CMO. On this via Senior HCOs are to be established.

Only the LRH Comm under whom the Senior HCO is established may issue orders to it. Other COs and EDs no matter what rank may not.

A Senior HCO Int is established in the Office of the LRH Comm Int and is added to the LRH Comm Int org board.

A Senior HCO Flag is established at the Flag Land Base under the LRH Comm Flag.

A Senior HCO PAC is established under the LRH Comm Continental PAC.

A Senior HCO is established in every Continental Office under the LRH Comm Continental.

A Senior HCO consists of the following:

The Senior Personnel Officer handles recruitment and has under him a Training and Hatting Officer. Like a banker the Senior Personnel Officer accumulates reserves of trained and hatted personnel. Every org demand for personnel is responded to with a utilization survey by the Senior Dir I&R. This is the one thing in the past that Department One has failed to do and this failure has developed in continental personnel scarcity while mobs of untrained and unhatted people stand around unutilized.

The Senior Personnel Officer as a result of finding unutilized people can get them transferred to his training pools where their cases can be handled and they can be properly trained and utilized. This personnel pool is called the area EPF which has five hours a day study and auditing just as it says in various FOs (Flag Orders).

The establishment actions should consist of a Senior HAS Area; Senior PCO who is in charge of all personnel files of the area and has to okay all transfers and postings but does not furnish personnel and may not be hounded for personnel; the PCO also sees to it that people get trained and that personnel pools exist of trained personnel and prevents them from being ripped off; a Senior Communications Officer that sees that comm systems are in in all orgs; a Senior I&R who does investigations and has under him a Senior MAA for the area.

The Senior PCO also has a line to Senior PCO Int where he forwards all executive personnel transfers and postings for approval. These are relayed to the Establishment Exec Int for final okay.

Senior PCO Cont and Senior PCO Int have the responsibility to ensure complete personnel files are available, and that full investigation of the person's record precedes any posting, particularly those of executive postings. Seeing that people get trained so they can hold a post and seeing that no criminal execs or staff are posted is part of their hat.

The Senior I&R does utilization surveys. He also does inspections of quarters, buildings, berthings and equipment to make sure that it is in acceptable condition. Of course, where his orders are neglected he has an MAA under him to turn the matter over to where it can be handled properly. This is all independent of any CS-Estates Network.

The way this Senior HCO has to be put together is to get the Senior HAS forcing every org or activity in the area to get functioning HCOs going.

Then you commandeer all personnel files of the area under the Senior PCO and give him finance for file cabinets and folders and at least two expeditors, construct a massive personnel central files. It has to include the ethics and study records of the person. The files have to be constructed and then kept in maintain. Crew lists are issued monthly by Senior PCO.

Provision has to be made for the PCO to receive all issues and postings related to personnel so as to file them in the proper folders. Provision also has to be made in the Senior PCO's Office to furnish people with data on personnel where they themselves are not keeping personnel files. Under no circumstances should unauthorized personnel be allowed to tear through these files.

Crew lists must be issued on a regular basis by the Senior HCO and to do this they must receive monthly reports from all orgs and HCOs in their area and continent.

The Senior Communications Officer sees that standard comm systems exist in every org and the staffs are hatted in using these comm systems. He also has supervision of overall area transport, making orgs take care of their transport.

The Senior I&R of the area conducts all necessary investigations and under him the Senior MAA enforces the orders of the Senior HAS, where they are not complying, and sees to it that MAAs exist in every org and that they perform their duties.

The Senior HCO can be the starting point for getting an area in order. You won't have a prayer of handling an area which has no operating HCOs in it. You can just forget it. It's a—why training?

Because the Senior HCO is outside the authority of orgs, it can't be ripped apart by org execs who might do so for innumerable reasons.

Therefore the first step in getting the whole area in order would be the creation of a Senior HCO. Just as the first step in getting an org in order is getting an org HCO that does its job.

The LRH Comm of an org cannot operate at all unless he is supported by a strong HCO.

Therefore, to get an area containing several orgs on a cont in order, it is the first and most vital step to put a Senior HCO under the LRH Comm for that area or cont.

L. RON HUBBARD
Founder

LRH COMMUNICATOR NETWORK SERIES

HUBBARD COMMUNICATIONS OFFICE
Saint Hill Manor, East Grinstead, Sussex

HCO POLICY LETTER OF 7 MAY 1984

Remimeo
LRH Comms
KOTs
Flag
CLOs
FOLOs

LRH Comm Network Series 1

THE LRH COMM NETWORK AND ITS PURPOSE

Cancels:

HCO PL	12 Feb. 78 I	THE PATTERN AND DUTIES OF THE LRH COMM NETWORK INTERNATIONAL
HCO PL	12 Feb. 78 II	POWERS OF LRH COMMS, KOTs AND THE LRH COMM NETWORK
HCO PL	12 Feb. 78-1 II	POWERS OF LRH COMMS ADDITIONAL

When I stepped off the management lines to devote my time to research and writing, certain factions took that opportunity to advise that since I was not an officer of the Church and managing the orgs that the purpose of the LRH Comm Network should be changed. However, that advice was ill-conceived.

The Churches of Scientology subsequently adopted all LRH policies and programs as the creed of the Church. Their use does not infer that I still manage the Churches of Scientology. The duties of the LRH Comm can be interpreted as enforcing the creed of the Churches of Scientology. And where image is concerned that too is very important to the Churches in order to carry forward their creed.

Therefore, the above policies are cancelled and the LRH Comm Network is restored to its original purpose as stated in HCO PL 27 Dec. 65RA, LRH COMMUNICATOR:

"TO FORWARD THE COMMUNICATIONS AND ORDERS OF LRH AND TO MAKE CERTAIN THAT HIS ORDERS, DESPATCHES, DIRECTIVES, POLICY LETTERS AND SECRETARIALS AS ISSUED ARE COMPLIED WITH AS THESE AS THEY EXIST ARE THE CREED OF THE CHURCH. ACKNOWLEDGMENT IS RETURNED TO LRH COMM INT WITH INFORMATION TO ED INT CONCERNING THEM IN DUE COURSE."

It is VITALLY important for every org to have a competent on-source LRH Comm who knows, applies and gets others to apply, LRH policies exactly.

The result is an on-source org and as proven time after time, on-source orgs boom, off-source orgs shrink. And booming orgs are the only way to clear this planet.

So, while I am not an officer of the Church and am not involved in its management, I felt I would be remiss if I did not help to restore the LRH Comms to their rightful position. It is a hat I gave them years ago and with this policy they now have it back in its true form.

I trust the hat will be worn well by all who assume it.

L. RON HUBBARD
Founder

HCO POLICY LETTER OF 27 DECEMBER 1965RA
REVISED 7 MAY 1984

Gen. Non-Remimeo
LRH Communicator

LRH Comm Network Series 2

LRH COMMUNICATOR

The purpose of the LRH Communicator is:

TO FORWARD THE COMMUNICATIONS AND ORDERS OF LRH AND TO MAKE CERTAIN THAT HIS ORDERS, DESPATCHES, DIREC-TIVES, POLICY LETTERS AND SECRETARIALS AS ISSUED ARE COMPLIED WITH AS THESE AS THEY EXIST ARE THE CREED OF THE CHURCH. ACKNOWLEDGMENT IS RETURNED TO LRH COMM INT WITH INFORMATION TO ED INT CONCERNING THEM IN DUE COURSE.

The LRH Communicator keeps a project board. Every project or order or directive or Sec ED issued is noted on this board; by routine and regular inspec-tion personally and by despatch the LRH Communicator sees to it that each and every order and project is eventually complied with or acknowledged.

The formula of communication applies on this post as its title would indicate and all other duties are secondary to this primary function: to complete the communication cycle originated by LRH.

It is not enough for an LRH Communicator to simply forward despatches to LRH or take LRH's despatches away or keep files thereof. Such actions are only a part of the function as above.

The LRH Communicator keeps the Office of LRH properties inventoried, safe and in good condition and safeguards the premises of the office.

The personal possessions of LRH are regularly inventoried and any discrep-ancies, breakages or damages are accounted for, and lists thereof are filed with the Inventory Officer of the organization. By definition, property means furni-ture, fittings, personal effects and files and papers which are the personal prop-erty of LRH, an individual, or LRH an official of the organization.

In small organizations, the HCO Area Secretary is also the LRH Communi-cator and has all of the above duties. As the organization begins to expand, an LRH Communicator must be appointed to fulfill these functions.

There are other administrative duties and the duties of a staff member in addition to the above, but they are secondary to the primary consideration and purpose of the LRH Communicator.

L. RON HUBBARD
Founder

HCO POLICY LETTER OF 4 JANUARY 1966RA

Issue IV

REVISED 7 MAY 1985

Gen. Non-Remimeo
LRH Comm Hat

OFFICE OF LRH

LRH Comm Network Series 3

SEC EDs AND HCO EXEC LETTERS

The LRH Communicator is responsible for seeing that Sec EDs and Exec Letters requiring action by an org are executed and acknowledged.

The order is this:

1. LRH Comm Int: Enter the Sec ED or Exec Letter on the Int project board, with area designation (Int, Cont, Flag or individual org or unit).

2. Org or unit LRH Comm: Enter each Sec ED or Exec Letter applying to the org or unit on the org or unit project board.

3. Call the attention of the area persons who will execute it to the Sec ED.

4. Put it on the org time machine (Flag Command Bureaux time machine is used by LRH Comm Int).

5. Occasionally query on it to the person or persons responsible.

6. If there is a delay, info LRH Comm Int via LRH Comm Cont.

7. When executed, relay fact on to LRH Comm Int via LRH Comm Cont with information to ED Int.

8. Locally, file papers on it in the LRH Comm completed project file.

It is important, if the Sec ED or Exec Letter name no specific person, that the area LRH Communicator consult the Exec Secs in charge of the probable division to get it specifically assigned to a person or persons who will be responsible for doing it. If no *person* is designated, then the LRH Communicator must assign it to a person in the org off his or her own bat, right or wrong. Any person to which a project is assigned is noted on the area project board.

Sec EDs and Exec Letters containing projects require doingness. They must be *done* by someone.

When they are not *done,* but only discussed, then the whole line balls up. The LRH Comm wants them *done,* not discussed.

POLICY LETTERS

Policy letters are not put on the project board. They are routine in the org.

A policy letter overlooked can become a project, such as "Project Get In Policy Letter 22 Nov. 65." These are called into play by Sec EDs when overlooked by an org.

The LRH Communicator can assign projects based on policy letters. This becomes a local project. To do this the LRH Comm consults with the Exec Secs first. If they agree, it becomes a local project and goes on the project board. If thrown off or forbidden, get authority from LRH Comm Int with information to ED Int who will order the policy letter in and it becomes a project.

L. RON HUBBARD
Founder

HUBBARD COMMUNICATIONS OFFICE
Saint Hill Manor, East Grinstead, Sussex

HCO POLICY LETTER OF 19 JANUARY 1966RA
Issue II
REVISED 7 MAY 1984

Remimeo
Staff Hats

LRH Comm Network Series 4

LRH COMMUNICATOR ORDERS

The only orders an LRH Communicator may issue to other than his own staff are those exact orders found in Sec EDs or from the Executive Director.[*] These are always on channels in accordance with the org board and with no bypass. He always informs a senior before he questions that person's junior.

EXCEPTION

When a unit, section, department, division or the org is in Danger condition, and the LRH Communicator lacks specific orders for it, he may issue his own orders from policy. Then the orders are issued only to handle the condition, and if the LRH Communicator does have to operate on a bypass with his own orders to get compliance and handle the condition, he or she must follow, then, the Danger condition formula exactly, as the assigning executive.

The primary function of the LRH Communicator is getting acknowledgments for Sec EDs issued or getting the Executive Director's orders and policy issued and reporting to LRH Comm Int with information to ED Int. He does not often issue orders, and when he does, they are covered by policy as above.

L. RON HUBBARD
Founder

---

[*][*Editor's Note:* At the time this HCO PL was written, LRH was the Executive Director. He resigned as Executive Director on 1 Sept. 66.]

HUBBARD COMMUNICATIONS OFFICE
Saint Hill Manor, East Grinstead, Sussex

HCO POLICY LETTER OF 30 JANUARY 1966RA
Issue I
REVISED 7 MAY 1984

Remimeo
LRH Comm Hat
Programs Chief Hat
Exec Sec Hats
Secretary Hats

Dept 21

Div 1

Ethics

Ad Councils

LRH Comm Network Series 5

ORG LRH COMMUNICATOR
REPORTS TO LRH COMM INT

Anyone proposing the assignment of a Danger condition to a section, department, division or org which has a high and rising statistic must be reported by the org or unit LRH Communicator to the LRH Communicator International via the LRH Comm Cont by fastest available means.

Proposing or assigning an Emergency condition to an Affluence statistic is also to be reported.

The actual assignment of a Danger or Emergency condition to a good and rising statistic is prohibited. The org or unit LRH Communicator, as Keeper of the Seals and Signature, may not authorize the issue of such a directive and must cancel one if it is issued and must report the matter to the LRH Communicator International via the LRH Comm Cont promptly.

A "statistic" means the relative rise or fall of a quantity compared to an earlier moment in time. If a section moved ten tons last week and twelve tons this week, the statistic is rising. If a section moved ten tons last week and only eight tons this week, the statistic is falling. Statistics must be graphed weekly by the OIC and furnished the org Ad Council.

A suppressive society comes down hard on rising statistics. Income tax is only one example among many—the more one earns the harder he is taxed. In short, when your statistic goes up the government stamps down. This is a sure way to bring a society or organization to ruin. A person with suppressive tendencies can always be detected by the fact that he or she stamps only on rising statistics and ignores down statistics.

If Tech completions rise and it is proposed by someone that the Tech Sec be reprimanded *for any reason,* that suggestion shows a dissatisfaction with a successful Tech Division.

Similarly, Ethics Hearings proposed on persons whose section, department or division has a nice rising statistic must be reported by the org or unit LRH Communicator to the LRH Comm International via the Cont LRH Comm and rejected by the LRH Comm.

Also, a number of ethics chits being filed on a section, department or division *or its personnel* while it has rising statistics should be clamped down on and investigated by HCO, and if it is not, the org or unit LRH Communicator must report the fact to the LRH Comm International via the LRH Comm Cont and then handle.

THE SECOND DANGER CONDITION

Exception: If a senior executive to that portion of the org which is being assigned a Danger condition has by his or her own efforts alone raised their statistic *after* a Danger condition was assigned on the previous low statistic and if the senior executive still gets no help in keeping the statistic up, then a new Danger condition may be assigned. This exception occurs only when a Danger condition has been assigned and relaxed within the past ninety days.

Example: The org HCO Exec Sec gets letter count up by working heavily with Letter Registrars and so assigns a Danger condition to the Dissem Division. The Danger condition formula is followed. After a few days or weeks the org HCO Exec Sec still has to work with the Letter Registrars to keep the statistic up. Although the statistic *is* up, the continued labor of the HCO Exec Sec to keep it up makes a *second* Danger condition assignable. This does not have to be reported to LRH Comm International. But notice it is a *second* assignment to the same portion of the org within ninety days.

ADDITIONAL REPORTS

The org or unit LRH Communicator must also report to the LRH Comm International via the LRH Comm Cont the following:

1. Obstructions to assigning, graphing and reporting statistics for sections, departments or divisions, giving the name of the person obstructing or not complying.

2. Failure of secretaries to take ethics actions on consistent down statistics in their divisions.

3. Failure of HCO to order investigations and hearings on portions of the org with prolonged down statistics.

4. Obstructions of reports to the Flag Data Files.

5. Obstructions of reports to the Central Computer Bank, i.e., computerized weekly report forms, computerized routing forms.

6. Any order issued to inhibit reports to the Flag Data Files or the Central Computer Bank.

7. The use of rumors or opinions to assign conditions rather than statistics.

8. And the most important, as above, proposals or assignments of a Danger condition to staff members or portions of the org with rising statistics.

LRH COMM INTERNATIONAL ACTION

On receipt of a report of an effort to assign a Danger condition to a rising statistic or a report of any of the above eight actions, the LRH Comm International informs the Flag Network Coordination Committee who at once directs the matter to the appropriate Programs Chief for investigation and any action. LRH Comm Int can also alert Senior HCO Int for action to be taken on matters relating to their hat.

The investigation may take any form and can be very brief if the org or unit LRH Communicator includes evidence with his report, such as a despatch in the person's handwriting or witnessed statements. These would be deemed sufficient to prove the case.

If the person who did any one of the eight listed things above was a secretary, the org Ad Council should be ordered to convene a Comm Ev at once on that secretary or take other suitable action.

If the person who did any of the eight above was an Executive Secretary, the person can be ordered to a higher org for a Comm Ev, or the person is simply ordered to the org's own Review Department for executive training, meanwhile their duties being taken over by a deputy and the person not to act in the post until specifically reassigned to it.

The same actions may be taken by an org Ad Council on a secretary.

A secretary may order any of these actions on a subordinate executive doing any of the eight listed above in his or her division, but not retaining the person on payroll meanwhile. The more common action below secretary would be an Ethics Hearing and demotion or transfer.

LRH COMMUNICATOR OMISSION

Any LRH Communicator failing to report as above must be removed from post by the LRH Comm International or LRH Comm Cont on the omission being proven.

SUMMARY

We have here the major fault of any organization or government—it promotes to power persons who then suppress anyone with a rising statistic.

If we pay close attention to this phenomenon our orgs will grow. If we grow careless and start permitting ethics actions to be aimed at persons in portions of an org which have rising statistics, then we will shrink in size.

A. Reward rising statistics.

B. Stamp on falling statistics.

C. Stamp on those who seek to prevent rising statistics.

D. Bring to view those who do not act in the presence of falling statistics.

That's all there is to guiding an expansion.

So we must:

1. Have statistics.

2. Follow only *graphed* statistics, not rumors or guesses.

3. Prevent rising statistics from being squashed.

4.   Remove those who find down statistics satisfactory.

We don't have all that time to fool about.

So let's use this key to opening the door to a better world. And cure the only real thing wrong with any organization anywhere.

L. RON HUBBARD
Founder

HCO POLICY LETTER OF 8 MAY 1966RA
REVISED 7 MAY 1984

Remimeo
LRH Comm
Exec Secs

LRH Comm Network Series 6

LRH COMMUNICATOR, NO OTHER HATS

(Modifies earlier policy)

Every org must have an LRH Communicator.

The LRH Communicator may not wear additional hats outside Dept 21. The LRH Comm may no longer be the HCO Sec or the Division 7 Secretary.

The reason for this is that orgs begin with Source and expand from Source, Dept 21. If the lines are jammed at Source no expansion can occur.

Construction and maintenance also belong at Source, Dept 21 for the same reason. An org cannot expand without premises being provided, salvaged and cared for. But the LRH Comm may not personally engage in building or cleaning but may supervise them.

If the LRH Comm keeps his or her log and carefully sees that bulletins, policy letters and Sec EDs are gotten in and tends to his other duties, the org will expand.

L. RON HUBBARD
Founder

HCO POLICY LETTER OF 10 MAY 1968RA
REVISED 7 MAY 1984

Remimeo

LRH Comm Network Series 7

LRH COMMS
FUNCTIONS

(Cancels any portion of any ED
or policy to the contrary)

The LRH Comm has the first and primary duty of "making Ron's postulates stick." All his admin and actions have to do with this.

ANY use of the LRH Comm by Executive Councils to enforce *their* orders or EDs is a post alteration changing the LRH Comm to Dept 3 I&R.

ECs have the HCO Area Sec and the Dir Inspection and Reports to enforce their EDs and orders.

The LRH Comm's office has seals and signatures and can *pass* an ED only as "not against policy." The LRH Comm has no function of enforcing that ED.

EC EDs are not entered in the LRH Comm log but in a similar log in Dept of I&R.

The LRH Communicator handles the communications to and from *LRH* and gets compliance with LRH EDs and orders and *enforces* policy letters.

This PL should be entitled "What Will Be Altered Next?" Golly the name "LRH Communicator" sure means what it says. It doesn't say "EC Communicator."

So *get* the lines straight and get policy on this IN IN IN.

Violation of this PL is a CRIME and any violator is to be comm eved on the charge of originating an effort to cut my lines.

The LRH COMM MAY NEVER AGAIN BE AN EC MEMBER but may be a member of a board of directors.

L. RON HUBBARD
Founder

HUBBARD COMMUNICATIONS OFFICE
Saint Hill Manor, East Grinstead, Sussex

HCO POLICY LETTER OF 12 FEBRUARY 1970RB
REVISED 7 MAY 1984

Remimeo
LRH Comm Hat
Ethics Hat
HCO ES
HCO Area Sec

LRH Comm Network Series 8

LRH COMM AND HCO ES
RESPONSIBILITY FOR LINES

(Cancels HCO PL 12 Feb. 70RA, Rev. 3 Mar. 80, same title)

When Executive Directives, HCO Bulletins or Policy Letters are not being distributed to or in an org and to every staff member in that org regularly and on time,

IT IS THE PRIMARY DUTY OF THE LRH COMM TO REPORT BY AIRMAIL TO LRH COMM INT INFO LRH COMM CONT AND THE FLAG DATA FILES WITH THIS DATA:

What distribution unit is sending these important items late or not at all?

What action has been taken to get them sent to the org?

What executive is making it difficult or refusing to distribute these items to each staff member?

The *HCO ES* is responsible for performing this action where there is no LRH Comm.

The essence of the report is WHO.

The purpose of the report is to get in ethics in that org.

On the basis that whoever impedes LRH Comm flow will also impede disseminating Dianetics and Scientology in other ways, the LRH Comm Int, on receipt of such a report, is to add what data he may have and send a copy to the Flag Network Coordination Committee for action by the appropriate Programs Chief, which should consist of the demotion or removal of the person impeding the flow. He should turn over another copy of the report to Senior HCO Int as it is a function of the Senior HCO Network to see that standard comm systems exist in every org.

Denial of Advanced Courses may be part of the stipulations in any Ethics Order or action resulting from proof of a charge of willfully or negligently impeding the flow of Executive Directives, Policy Letters or HCO Bulletins, org to org, or within an org to all staff.

It is a high crime to cut the basic comm lines of Scientology.

This policy applies also to instances where impedance or negligence denies adequate supply of technical materials to HGC or Qual auditors and to Dianetics or Scientology students.

FAILURE ON THE PART OF LRH COMMS OR HCO ESes TO ACT ON THIS POLICY LETTER WILL RESULT IN REMOVAL FROM POST.

L. RON HUBBARD
Founder

HCO POLICY LETTER OF 11 FEBRUARY 1971RA
REVISED 7 MAY 1984

Remimeo
LRH Comm Hat

LRH Comm Network Series 9

POLICY KNOWLEDGE FUNCTION

It is now a primary duty of the LRH Comm to get *policy* followed and in such a way as to expand the org and not stop flows.

The LRH Comm has, besides, a major duty getting action and compliance on LRH *EDs, programs, projects* and *orders.*

It will be found by the LRH Comm that where trouble occurs:

a.   Policy is out or

b.   Doesn't exist or

c.   Is being used to stop expansion or flows.

Further it will be found by the LRH Comm that where orgs or parts thereof begin to collapse, LRH EDs, programs, projects and orders are not being complied with or are falsely reported on or the situation is unknown to seniors so no orders exist.

LRH Comms have in the past failed, where they have failed, because they do not use ETHICS and CONDITIONS to handle outnesses, noncompliance or false reports and try to handle things on a personal basis or by personalities instead of stats and instead of using the full power of ethics and conditions to back them up.

The LRH Comm should call for policy outnesses in all Danger conditions or below and for all policy innesses on Affluences reported.

The LRH Comm should come down with hearings on noncompliance and false reports and demand on false reports the removal of the offender from that post.

There is no halfway way to handle the LRH Communicator post.

L. RON HUBBARD
Founder

HCO POLICY LETTER OF 26 FEBRUARY 1971

Remimeo
LRH Comm Hat

LRH Comm Network Series 10

LRH COMM TROUBLES

An org with an effective LRH Comm prospers.

Yet an org inevitably tries to give an LRH Comm problems.

Basically I operate as a product officer for the whole of Dianetics and Scientology.

In doing this I attempt to get orgs producing and try to get them to organize so as to back up production.

Thus my orders relate to an org's products or to getting it to organize so it can produce.

When you try to get production you will find any lack of it is traceable to someone not wearing his hat.

When you try to get organization to give production, any failure is traced to someone not wearing his hat.

This can extend to there being no one there at all to wear the hat in the first place. In such a case the person not wearing his hat is the HCO senior who is failing to recruit or hire. So it is again a problem of someone not wearing his hat.

In the wide planetary scene, a large percent of the population do not wear their hats as beings, thus the malady extends easily into orgs.

The final answer to any problems on LRH Comm lines is to get an LRH Comm on post who is wearing his hat and who then has a system that selects out those who are not wearing their hats.

The persons who DO wear their hats in orgs are amply rewarded in terms of accomplishment.

Those who don't are the ones who prevent compliance with orders that will put things to rights.

The background record of LRH orders has been proven by statistics of rising stats when followed and falling stats when not.

Such orders exist on an immediate basis or in policy or technical form.

By getting in the orders and their know-how in tech and admin, the LRH Comm is the one who is driving in an expanding zone of a new era.

How to get these orders followed is the subject of this policy letter and HCO PL 27 Feb. 71 I, LRH COMM, NEW BASIC DUTIES, and 27 Feb. 71 II, LRH COMM CORRECTION FORM.

Here is additional material that does not change any existing LRH Comm expertise but which makes it much easier to do his job effectively.

L. RON HUBBARD
Founder

HCO POLICY LETTER OF 27 FEBRUARY 1971RA
Issue I
REVISED 7 MAY 1984

Remimeo

LRH Comm Network Series 11

LRH COMM
NEW BASIC DUTIES

An LRH Communicator has a basic duty of getting compliances with LRH orders.

This remains the basic duty.

New tech on this, however, greatly expands the action.

1. HOW to get compliance and

2. WHAT to get compliance on give the post a new and valuable meaning and make the basic duty far more accomplishable.

HOW

It will be found in almost every case that the basic reason an LRH Comm cannot get compliance is SOMEBODY IS NOT WEARING HIS HAT.

The somebody may not be the person who is noncomplying.

Thus EVERY noncompliance with an LRH order encountered by an LRH Comm must begin a fast INVESTIGATION to find out WHO is not wearing his hat. He locates the one or more WHOs who are not wearing their hats.

While still pushing to get COMPLIANCE, the LRH Comm also puts in train a correction checklist which he keeps to hand.

The form of this checklist contains the order noncomplied with and the *who* revealed by the investigation. Then follows the actions taken.

1st Action. Nudged.

2nd Action. Cautioned.

3rd Action. Ethics condition for not fully wearing his or her hat.

4th Action. Hatted by HCO.

5th Action. Post Purpose fully cleared in Qual and sent to Staff College or

Cramming where a Staff College doesn't exist to do full check-sheet of his hat on his own (not org) time.

6th Action. Ethics Hearing.

7th Action. Demotion via HCO and regular lines.

8th Action. Dismissed.

During this period the order may be complied with. At that point (let us say [3], ethics condition) the form gets a compliance note if the order is complied with.

However, this does not end the form. It is filed in a file which is kept alongside the LRH Comm Log.

The very *next* noncompliance with an LRH order places the person at the next point on the form (in this example, the 4th action).

FORM CLEARANCE

Presentation of high, consistent post stats can clear the form and start a new clean sheet. In the absence of this the sheet continues and is dropped one for each new noncompliance. The person may be so informed.

Each original noncompliance is fully investigated NOT to find why they can't do it but to find WHO is not wearing his hat. Thus it is the investigatory result name that is continued if the investigation again turns up a name in the Noncompliance Correction Form file.

Thus an LRH Comm is working himself *out* of the confusion of noncompliances by hatting.

For it will be found that the basic reason is unworn hats, so by forcing hats on, one gradually gets an org that needs less orders to produce and organize and which complies easily.

DEFIANCE

Wherever defiance occurs (the person refuses the correction or refuses to do the action) the next point lower on the correction scale is at once entered and the action is taken.

Continued defiance thus would end the person up demoted (the 7th action) which is what should happen anyway to a person who refuses to wear his hat and defies orders.

USING POLICY TO STOP

It will be found in doing this that a person NOT DOING HIS POST PURPOSE will pick bits of policy out that seem to state the order given cannot be followed. If you track down such a person's post purpose you will find he or she hasn't got it and is using policy to stop.

TIGERS

This system will also lead to the exposure of tigers as they will be amongst the Correction Forms very early and will constantly repeat. A tiger is someone who is not about to let the org or staff succeed.

STATS

In using this system the best clue to who IS wearing his hat is the individual department or division statistic that most closely applies to the post.

Thus in investigating a noncompliance it is fastest to sort out the least likely persons by simply eliminating all those with high production stats and passing them by. This narrows the area to be investigated.

In most cases it will simply be the person to whom the order was given in the first place. But in all cases an investigation is necessary.

Cross orders may exist from other persons that prevent compliance. In these cases it is not the person to whom the order is given.

EXAMPLE

ORDER: Get the staff uniformed.

ORDER GIVEN TO: *Treasury Sec* John Doe, 16 Aug. In noncompliance 17 Sept.

INVESTIGATION: Reveals insufficient funds and turndown by FP in Ad Committee are reasons given for noncompliance. Examination of Ad Committee minutes finds no action by chairman to get GI up. Also, Dept of Reg, Dir Reg (who has this valuable final product of GI) has told Purser it will be several months before org has any spare cash. Means two influences at work balking compliance.

ACTION: LRH Comm makes out a Correction Checklist on the chairman of Ad Committee by name and the Dir Reg *and* the Treasury Sec and takes action 1.

On 20 September the order is still in noncompliance according to log. Action 2 is taken on all three.

On 1 October a routine log check reveals that the order is still in noncompliance. Action 3 is taken on all three.

On 12 October a recheck of the log shows that progress is reported by the chairman of the Ad Committee and that he has taken his own action. The Treasury Sec has reported he has the staff measured and the supplier contacted. Dir Reg says nothing.

The LRH Comm takes no further action on those reporting progress but takes action 4 on the Dir Reg.

On 1 November there are still no uniforms as the order is still in the LRH Comm's log as in noncompliance. Action 5 is ordered on Dir Reg. However, it is found that he did not do (4). Thus he is dropped to action 6.

Income miraculously appears and the staff gets uniformed.

The form sits in the file. If one more noncompliance with an LRH order is logged and investigation traces it to the Dir Reg, that's it. He goes to action 7.

WHO INVESTIGATES

The LRH Comm or his Investigator (present in a large LRH Comm office) does the investigation in each case. It is not sent to HCO.

ADMIN

As each item in an LRH Comm log has its number, the Correction Form relating to it carries the same number.

Any added note can be made in the log like CR (correction form). The name or names can also be added.

The names are alphabetically arranged in the form.

WHAT ORDERS

Priority of LRH orders are:

Direct comm from LRH.

A telexed order from a senior LRH Comm.

A letter to the Exec Dir or secretary via the ED from or via a senior LRH Comm.

LRH EDs, current.

New HCOBs and tech tapes.

New policy letters and admin tapes.

Older HCOBs, particularly a subject covered by a series of HCOBs like exteriorization or C/Sing or the Dianetics Course checksheet, etc. These include any tapes.

Older HCO PLs, particularly a series or checksheet. These include any tapes.

LRH ED series, older.

In any conflict, the most senior LRH Comm's order is taken; example, LRH Comm Int and a Cont LRH Comm both telex orders. LRH Comm Int's order is taken as the senior order.

LOCAL ORDERS

LRH and LRH Comm orders have precedence over locally issued orders where there is any conflict of orders.

––––––––––

The practical aspects of this new noncompliance system must be fully reported if any are found to exist so they can be ironed out or clarified by LRH Comm Int.

Having already piloted this and found that noncompliance inevitably led to one or another unworn hats in all cases, and being aware of the rough time LRH Comms sometimes have in getting compliance, it is certain that an LRH Comm's lot will be much easier in view of the discovery of the Why behind noncompliance.

Improvement of the org would be inevitable.

L. RON HUBBARD
Founder

HUBBARD COMMUNICATIONS OFFICE
Saint Hill Manor, East Grinstead, Sussex

HCO POLICY LETTER OF 27 FEBRUARY 1971RA
Issue II
REVISED 7 MAY 1984

Remimeo
LRH Comm Hat

LRH Comm Network Series 12

LRH COMM
CORRECTION FORM

(See HCO PL 27 Feb. 71RA I,
LRH COMM NEW BASIC DUTIES)

(Make one out for each Who found)
(Paperclip all related reports to back of this form)

To: LRH Comm File   cc: _____

                                     cc: Flag Data Files

                                     _____/ _____/ _____/
                                     (Cont / Org / Month)

                                     cc: Central Computer Bank

Who _____

_____ LRH Comm Log Number

_____ Date of 1st Noncompliance noted

INVESTIGATION:

Disclosed name above _____ not wearing
his hat.

☐   1st Action — Nudged. Copy of this PL sent the person
           with original order attached.
_____ date.

☐   2nd Action — Cautioned. Original order nudged with copy
           to person.
_____ date.

☐ 3rd Action — Ethics Condition _____ for not
_____ date.　fully wearing his/her hat assigned. Person and E/O
informed and copy attached to this form. And copy
of original order attached marked "3rd Action."

☐ 4th Action — Hatting by HCO ordered.

_____ date.

_____ HCO reports compliance with copy of original
order to person marked "4th Action."

☐ 5th Action — Post Purpose fully cleared in Qual and sent
to staff college in Qual or Cramming, which-
_____ date.　ever exists, to do full checksheet on his
hat on his own time.

_____ Date of Qual compliance. With copy of original
order to person marked "5th Action."

☐ 6th Action — Ethics Hearing ordered for failure to wear his hat and
failure to comply with an LRH order. With copy of
_____ date.　original order to person marked "6th Action."

☐ 7th Action — Ordered demoted in his same area to a post that
can be supervised.
_____ date.

_____ Date of compliance. With copy of original order to
person marked "7th Action."

The 7th Action is final so far as the order is concerned on that person.

The same order is issued to any new incumbent on that post and is reentered in the log referring to its earlier noncompliance and number.

This form is retained in LRH Comm Files as part of the LRH Comm log system.

L. RON HUBBARD
Founder

Remimeo
LRH Comm Hat
ED Hat
Tech Hats
Qual Hats

LRH Comm Network Series 13

TECH AND LRH COMMS

The LRH Comm should not flinch at the idea of putting in HCOBs, books and tapes just because he is not a classed auditor.

This is a field of expertise. It is lamentable that experts very often gain their status by fending off the nonexpert with lofty "As it is a technical matter you would not understand. Therefore my opinion on this stands." While far from all tech people have that attitude it is true that some have had it. This might serve to cause an LRH Comm to be shy of the area as a subject for programs.

But look at it this way: the reputation of the whole org depends upon its tech delivery; tech delivery excellence does not for a moment depend upon a "knack" or individual skill. The way you get the finest and most startling tech results is by strong and uncompromising adherence to HCOBs, books and tapes.

Tech is just another area of compliance. HCOBs are in packs. They have dates. They refer to exact actions and situations. HCOBs, books and tapes are, from the LRH Comm point of view, simply items on which compliance can be obtained.

Let us take the most obvious *tech* PL of all as a sort of bridge from PLs to HCOBs. This is PL 16 Mar 71, WHAT IS A COURSE? This one can be programed like a shot. Strictly a piece of cake. There was even a pack to get it in. If you get that in, your tech scene will gradually improve. For that is the basic organizational action to make technicians. Somebody will tell you it is the Primary Rundown that makes technicians able to read so they can be. All right but that is TECH. "What is a Course?" is tech administration.

Now let us look at a weird one. You say, well, as an LRH Comm I should then be a Flag Class X. The courses which you would have to take might have "What is a Course?" PL out in them. It would take you years if that were true. So you, by saying you have to be a Class X to get tech in, are saying you have to take a course which is not a course in order to learn how to be capable of putting a course there so that you could take a proper course. . . .

In other words, you have to start something from somewhere and somebody in your area has to start it and you are there so it's you.

Let us take a Case Supervisor line. It is a definite line. In various places for various services it has to be different and you will be told when you try to get in the HCOB that it is not applicable to this particular line in this area. I would listen with a very skeptical eye. I would look over the HCOBs on the subject and then check what is actually going on and have a conference and see how much of the HCOB *can* be gotten in as a practical measure in order to increase tech quantity and quality. Then I'd write up a program that gets in as much of the line as can be gotten in THAT IS COVERED IN HCOB and knock out the innovations that waste time. You'd have a nice smooth C/S line when it was all complied with.

Things like the requirement that auditor students must listen to LRH tapes to get their TRs perfected are not there for idle chatter. When an auditor, unlike a public TR student, does not have his TRs in the hard way he'll never make it. That's a coldblooded fact. So is this in? It's in many HCOBs, even programs have existed for it. You get that program in—the tapes, the TRs, the adherence— and your tech quality will SOAR BEYOND ANYTHING YOU WOULD AT ONCE BELIEVE.

So what is this "getting tech in?" It's just getting a program to get it in and getting compliance on it.

Tech consists of a large amount of precision administration and the application exactly of the existing wealth of materials. That can be programed. Results will start pouring out when compliances are obtained.

Then maybe in your study time when it's all smooth as a summer sea, you could get your class. Because you had put something there which could deliver.

So somebody has to get the tech in. It was always my hat. So, LRH Comm, it's YOU.

L. RON HUBBARD
Founder

HUBBARD COMMUNICATIONS OFFICE
Saint Hill Manor, East Grinstead, Sussex

HCO POLICY LETTER OF 28 AUGUST 1973RA
REVISED 7 MAY 1984

Remimeo
LRH Comms Hat
EDs Hat

LRH Comm Network Series 14

THE MISSION OF THE LRH COMM NETWORK

The modern mission of the LRH Comm Network is the reason for its new duties and statistic.

The scene over the world has been changed for Scientology. Victories over past opposition have been numerous in the last year and more victories are being attained in the near future. The entire status of Scientology is shifting to an upward thrust. Even authoritative books (like the *Encyclopedia Britannica Year Book, 72*) have found, by surveys, that Scientology is the fastest-growing religion on the planet. This is at a time when older, orthodox religions are on a decline.

We are building a new civilization on top of the decay of the old. At every major period of history when inflation, duress and ruin have assailed man, a new religion has arisen: this has happened in India, in Egypt, as well as at the end of the old Roman Empire and even the Middle Ages when Protestantism arose. The old values crumble, new values arise and are rallied to. Each new resurrection of religion has been attended at first by persecution and suppression. The great religions were no exception. Yet they rose through this because they had values their contemporary man needed. Scientology has been going through just such a period. While the whole war is not yet won, the battle victories are increasing and whole areas are changing and coming over to our side. This is due to the purity and truth of the subject itself and to the perseverance, endurance and loyalty of Scientologists. This is an accurate, not just a PR estimation of the current scene and it is borne out by the record of the past year.

The tide has definitely turned.

It is up to the LRH Comm Network to expand Scientology orgs.

The tried and proven method of doing this has been proved over and over and over. There is many an org which was limping, gasping, feebly floundering about which, when put strongly on policies and HCOBs by a determined person, resurged to a point where its stats went out the top and its influence spread.

In other words, the ONE STRONG, SOUND, ALWAYS WORKABLE CAMPAIGN TO EXPAND SCIENTOLOGY HAS BEEN TO GET ORGS ON-POLICY AND IN-TECH. This has never failed.

And reversely, when certain orgs, for political reasons now removed, had to send away their HCO PLs and were without them for a while, their stats collapsed and stayed collapsed even when there was no further danger, until they got their packs back and began to use them again.

There is another proof of this. It has happened, a sad fact, that an org has lost (by transfer or promotion to an upper org or other reasons) the person who was strongly pushing HCO PLs and HCOBs and it has promptly gone into a decline.

Further, there were many instances in the long-ago 50s when we were not as strong as we are now when certain groups were running unofficial orgs. These groups might tell the public that "they didn't quite agree with LRH" and were doing something better or improved. When they did, they went broke and dispersed. It was certain suicide. The public stayed away in mobs and would not go near them, solely and only because they trusted LRH and did not trust and did not want anything to do with people who didn't agree with him. You can see from this that the LRH Comm presence all by itself was a guarantee of public confidence. An amusing incidence of this was an ED who didn't want an LRH Comm in the org and who was in continual trouble with his staff and stats. The staff didn't trust him!

As a parallel to this, one org, needing space badly, unfortunately sought and obtained permission to dismantle LRH's office there "as it was not in active use" and ever since that time has ceased to have the stats it had before.

There are also instances where a double-hatted LRH Comm (who was also HAS) became single-hatted as LRH Comm, began to do LRH Comm duties, and the stats went up.

So it is very plain that it is A POSITIVE WAY TO EXPAND AN ORG TO HAVE AN LRH COMM WHO GETS THE ORG ON–POLICY AND IN–TECH. In fact it is the most effective way of guaranteeing the expansion of Scientology.

This then is THE WAY WE ARE GOING TO EXPAND SCIENTOLOGY OVER THE PLANET: (1) Get a single-hatted LRH Comm on post, (2) Get the org on-policy, and (3) Get the org's tech in with HCOBs.

We now have the Flag Rep getting in AOs, these are based upon the current state of the org and have to do mainly with the org's production and correcting it so that it can produce. This gives a single channel and removes the burden of comming from the ED who is then free to actually run the org in its day-to-day activities.

In actual fact, to whom could the task of getting an org on-policy and in-tech belong except to an LRH Comm?

L. Ron Hubbard has always had the hat of building orgs and keeping them on-policy and in-tech. The HCO PLs themselves were derived directly from intimate experience with handling organizations of many kinds and especially those of Scientology. Therefore, the hat that L. Ron Hubbard wore is the hat of the LRH Communicator, naturally.

At first glance this role may appear to be solely and only organizing and it is known that if you only organize, omitting production of products, the organization will go broke. But there is also the fact that in the flurry of getting out products, organizations lose their form and are shortly unable to get out any products at all. And go broke. The degree that the form of the organization is held DETERMINES ITS STAT CEILING. When its form is off-policy and its tech is out it will have a very low ceiling indeed.

It is also true that the volume an org handles is NOT dependent upon public demand. The volume it gets and handles is solely determined by its internal organization. This sounds so strange that many an ED has had great trouble until he believed it and used it. You can always internally shoot the stats up and keep them up. It is THAT, across all divisions, which determines the volume an org gets and handles. This is sometimes hard to teach people but once they see the results of it they become converts to that principle—that it is internal, not external, actions that determine stats.

When you have what amounts to a total monopoly on the only effective spiritual and administrative basics, public demand is assured. And public traffic into the org depends only upon HCO PLs and HCOBs being in, the staff hatted and skilled and turning out the desired result. The results are there to be obtained if exactly and correctly worked for, the form of the org is there to handle anything if HCO PLs are known, correctly used and applied.

The only variable, then, is the degree that policy is known and applied and that HCOBs, tapes and LRH books are known, taught and exactly applied. It's all there, as many, many thousands of Scientologists have remarked many times.

SO OUR BASIC PROGRAM FOR EXPANDING SCIENTOLOGY IS FOR LRH COMMS TO GET ORGS ON–POLICY AND IN–TECH USING EVALUATED AND EXACT PROJECTS TO ACHIEVE THIS.

This, essentially, is compliance to an LRH order. Every policy and HCOB can be regarded as an LRH order when placed in project target form.

The LRH Comms are the org builders. And through that the world builders.

THIS is how we are going to expand Scientology. It will take a lot of good sense, a lot of work, a lot of persuasion and a lot of determination. But it CAN BE DONE BECAUSE IT OFTEN HAS BEEN DONE IN OCCASIONAL ORGS AND ALWAYS WITH A GREAT RESULT.

THIS is how we are going to raise the stats.

THIS is how we are going to build a new civilization. With the LRH Comm Network.

L. RON HUBBARD
Founder

HUBBARD COMMUNICATIONS OFFICE
Saint Hill Manor, East Grinstead, Sussex

HCO POLICY LETTER OF 12 MAY 1973RC
Issue I
REVISED 7 MAY 1984

Remimeo
LRH Comms
KOTs
Flag
FOLOs
Orgs

LRH Comm Network Series 15

POST PROTECTION
LRH COMMUNICATORS

1. NO OFFICIALLY APPOINTED CONTINENTAL OR ORG LRH COMMU-NICATOR MAY BE LOCALLY REMOVED, TRANSFERRED FROM POST OR ABSENT FROM POST FOR EVEN A TEMPORARY PERIOD WITHOUT THE EXPRESS APPROVAL OF LRH COMM INTERNA-TIONAL.

2. Any attempt to remove or transfer a duly appointed LRH Comm, in violation of this policy, will be subject to an immediate Court of Ethics or Comm Ev by a senior LRH Comm. (Ref: HCO PL 19 Dec. 82, "DOING A QUICK-SILVER" FORBIDDEN)

3. Before an LRH Comm may leave post or be transferred, a competent re-placement must be apprenticed and programed onto post, after transfer and new post appointment have been officially approved by LRH COMM INTERNATIONAL following HCO PL 28 Mar. 84, EXECUTIVE POSTING QUALIFICATIONS.

4. No LRH Comm may be comm eved in their own org and may only be comm eved in a senior org and only if the orders are their own executive seniors'. An exception to this is that any LRH Comm Network executive or staff may be ordered crammed, retreaded or comm eved by the LRH PR Network or the CMO.

5. This same policy is applicable to Keepers of Tech and Policy Knowledge, Deputy LRH Comms and all other LRH Comm N/W personnel.

L. RON HUBBARD
Founder

HCO POLICY LETTER OF 7 APRIL 1982

Remimeo

LRH Comm Network Series 16

OUT–ETHICS INDICATORS

There are three indicators which, when present singly or collectively, point to possible out-ethics in an org, network or management body.

LRH COMM

The absence of an LRH Comm—none appointed or a sector of the network missing—can mean the org is possibly off-source, does not use policy and is subject to false reports.

HCO

An inefficient HCO, poorly organized or posted or absence of effort to post them up from management bodies, usually indicates out-ethics executives who would be discovered if an HCO existed.

TREASURY DIV

When no Treasury Div is formed or functioning or grossly undermanned, it can indicate there is rip-off or embezzlement present in an org or at management levels.

Recent experience in certain areas has pointed these things out. They are indicators, when present, which one should look into vigorously. Otherwise, stats may remain depressed and a lot of work and progress may be wasted.

An org with a competent LRH Comm, a good HCO and a functioning Treasury Division will usually pick up and prosper, for its other divisions can now work and do their jobs.

L. RON HUBBARD
Founder

HCO POLICY LETTER OF 15 SEPTEMBER 1983

LRH Comm Hat
KOT Hat

LRH Comm Network Series 17

LRH COMM AND PRO

Refs:

HCO PL	27 Dec. 65	LRH COMMUNICATOR
HCO PL	10 May 68	LRH COMMS FUNCTIONS
HCO PL	28 Aug. 73R	THE MISSION OF THE LRH
	Rev. 25.10.75	COMM NETWORK
HCO PL	18 Nov. 70 II	PR Series 5
		PR DEFINITION
HCO PL	13 Aug. 70 II	PR Series 2
		THE MISSING INGREDIENT
HCO PL	13 Aug. 70 III	PR Series 3
		WRONG PUBLICS
HCO PL	30 May 71	PR Series 9
		MANNERS
HCO PL	19 July 82	PR Series 45
		FAILED PR

(The following material is from my notes on this subject written in 1970. I am issuing this material now as an HCO PL at the request of Church of Scientology International, as it contains data very pertinent to LRH Comm Hats.)

The way to get a policy complied with willingly and over a long period of time is by using good PR (Public Relations).

In this case the *public* refers to the staff member public. These are a special "public." The LRH Comm should work hard to raise my PR value with staff.

What the LRH Comm has to do is establish and maintain and improve a local LRH *image* in his area so that there is an LRH presence. PR techniques are best suited to this. If a local LRH image is present, it will be easy to obtain compliances. The org's business, it has been repeatedly shown, increases greatly when attention is paid to maintaining a local image and decreases when it is not.

If an LRH Comm lowers my PR value in getting policy carried out or just in general, then he will have a very gruesome time of it trying to get any compliances.

A BASIC DUTY OF LRH COMMS IS THE HAT OF LRH PERSONAL PUBLIC RELATIONS.

In a large org or high-level HQ this hat is separately worn. But even then it will be found that an LRH Comm will have great trouble doing his job if he does not wear an LRH PR hat also.

If orders are issued in such a way as to lower my PR with staff or the public, the LRH Comm post will either be very difficult or it will become unfilled.

For a score of years the Scientology public has come to trust me, not only to help them with their cases but also to make things go right. No amount of newspaper false reports has ever altered this. Even the broad general public has a high regard. Commercial business firms respond well to me, often refusing to do business or grant credit unless my name is on it. One government decided to stop its attacks on orgs if they would undertake some minor reforms, but they would accept no signature on it but mine despite being told I was not an officer of that particular corporation. All an org has to do is say they "don't quite hold with my views" for the public to stay away in droves, a thing proven many times. The US government has stated that what is wrong with Scientology is people's high regard for me personally.

All this is high PR value, priceless, in fact.

If an LRH Comm does not uphold or increase that PR value, he'll not only be unpopular, he won't be able to do his job.

The subject of PR is a big one, rather simple, but it IS a subject. It does have its own textbook and rules in this modern society. An LRH Comm could do nothing better than to get a textbook on it, read it and see what it is all about. *Effective Public Relations* by Cutlip and Center, Prentice-Hall Publishers (Englewood Cliffs, NJ, USA) is a good text, used in a couple universities.

While we know far more about the mind and communication, such a text gives you what the general society accepts and expects as PR. It gives you the rundown of standard PR actions developed since the turn of the century.

The LRH Comm is impeded, in such PR work, because I have no hunger for spotlights and certainly developed Dianetics and Scientology for far better reasons than my own aggrandizement. Thus he doesn't get much personal PR material from me. In the early 50s, Hollywood and Madison Avenue PR men always tried to sell Dianetics by playing me up as an individual. I always maintained there was far more to it than that.

However, an LRH Comm is not being asked to do celebrity PR. He is being asked to do the PR actions that keep my name bright and my policy and data complied with.

This action may be as small as ensuring staff receive my greetings to them on special holidays or birthdays or just assuring visitors their message will go to me, in seeing my picture is hung up and my mailbox plainly marked.

The appearance and conduct of an LRH Comm is itself a PR action which reflects on me or does credit to me. The neatness of his desk, his office, become associated with me in people's minds.

By talking to an LRH Comm, people are trying to talk to me. Thus he must be courteous and interested and know how to LISTEN and to invite people to talk to me through him in various ways, such as a modest sign on the notice board, "If you have something to tell Ron, see the LRH Comm." Make notes, forward them on lines with WHO, WHEN, WHERE.

These are all basic PR actions.

The LRH Comm who does such things is handling:

1. Staff as a special public.

2. Scientologists as the Scientology public.

3. The general public.

4. The government as a special public.

Even though he works through the Department 20 of an org in all government and defense matters, an LRH Comm can act as a spokesman for me under the directions of that office.

Small campaigns can be begun and pushed through, such as a "WEAR YOUR HAT" campaign. Many others suggest themselves.

If done with a light touch and good PR, such will be effective.

OBSERVING and reporting what one observes up the lines to me is a definite PR action. It comes under "fact finding" in the texts.

Policy and campaigns that are not pushed well or are running counter to opinion should be reported at once up the lines to be modified.

The LRH Comm follows the full cycle of PR: Find the facts, plan, communicate, push the action, see what went well and what didn't.

Any LRH Comm, in addition to his expected duties, can become a good PR man with study of PR texts. It's a valuable thing to be, professionally. Any Scientology LRH Comm by text study can become far superior to the usual professional PR man. And should.

As you will find if you study the texts, the general public idea of a PR man isn't one. A good PR man is not a press agent or publicist or newspaperman. He's got his own tech and it's valuable.

And if an LRH Comm wants to do a smashing job for me and improve himself and his position as well, he'll become a good PR man and use it to handle his post.

If you have to nudge very often to get a compliance, your PR has broken down in that area. And an ounce of PR is worth a ton of ethics.

It's a PR World today.

And we, having superior mental tech, can easily become the best PRs the world has ever seen.

Try it.

L. RON HUBBARD
Founder

HCO POLICY LETTER OF 29 OCTOBER 1965

Gen. Non-Remimeo

EXECUTIVE DIVISION

HCO DIVISION

LRH Comm Network Series 18

ETHICS AUTHORITY SECTION
OFFICE OF LRH

The actual authority on which Ethics operates, no matter who signs the order, is LRH. No matter what action is undertaken, any and all errors rebound heavily on the Office of LRH. Therefore, there must exist a route of correction of ethics actions where needful.

In addition, there are several ethics functions purely belonging to the Office of LRH. These are:

1. The actual declaration of suppressive persons or groups, no matter who signs the order. Cancellation of certificates may not be done by any other than LRH as that is the issuing authority for all certificates.

2. Comm Ev findings cannot be put into effect where they require cancellations without an LRH okay of findings. In general, Comm Ev findings are usually okayed in practice by the Office of LRH.

3. Petitions which concern ethics are handled by the Office of LRH, usually by routing to Ethics for data and the Office of LRH acting on that data or any other known data or policy.

4. The form and presentation of Ethics Orders are the concern of the Office of LRH, and when the form, wording or presentation are incorrect, the Office of LRH acts to remedy.

5. New ethics policies or procedures are the concern of the Office of LRH when required.

6. Amnesties and their points of interpretation are handled by the Office of LRH.

7. Investigations concerning Ethics itself.

8. Although entirely under the HCO Area Secretary and in Div 1, Dept 3, Ethics Officers are looked on by me as *my* Ethics Officers and none may be appointed without my okay with a review of their record by myself.

Therefore, for these eight reasons *only,* the Office of LRH has a responsibility for Ethics. There is therefore an ETHICS AUTHORITY SECTION in the Office of LRH that cares for the above eight actions *only,* not for general ethics actions.

No other post in Dept 21 may assume the authority of the Ethics Authority Officer unless it is specifically designated as a hat.

Routing on the above eight matters is self-evident.

Anyone holding the hat of Ethics Authority Officer, Office of LRH must be checked out on all ethics policy letters.

L. RON HUBBARD
Founder

HUBBARD COMMUNICATIONS OFFICE
Saint Hill Manor, East Grinstead, Sussex

HCO POLICY LETTER OF 23 FEBRUARY 1978R
REVISED 7 MAY 1984

Remimeo
Orgs
FOLOs
Flag
LRH Comms
KOTs

LRH Comm Network Series 19

BOARD OF REVIEW

Occasionally an administrative body takes an action or issues a directive or order that:

a. Results in lowered statistics

b. Causes contraction of an area

c. Results in an injustice.

This is usually the result of incomplete CSW, acting on rumor without proper investigation and violation of basic policy.

The correction hat for this has mainly been worn by LRH.

The function of a Board of Review is to look into injustices, technically incorrect findings and instances of flagrant injustice or out-ethics actions which are destructive to stats.

The board is convened by any LRH Comm or KOT who appoints a chairman and two other members. Members of the board are appointed based on their own good statistics, high ethics level and knowledge of ethics and justice policy. They are preferably Org Exec Course graduates.

A Board of Review can be originated by the LRH Comm or KOT or a CSW may be submitted to the LRH Comm or KOT requesting a board be convened.

The board, once convened, reviews the data concerning the matter using standard investigatory procedure and bases its decisions only on LRH policy. It has no authority to write or issue new policy or issue new directives or orders. The board can only cancel an action, directive or order which has been found to:

a. Be impractical

b. Lower statistics

c. Cause contraction

d. Result in an injustice

e. Violate basic LRH policy.

It is expected that very few appeals will be lodged and few boards will have to be convened as the function of org execs and Exec Councils is to implement the longstanding and successful programs already covered in LRH HCO Policy Letters. Directives, orders and actions taken should be toward this end.

L. RON HUBBARD
Founder

Assisted by
PAC Ethics Board of Review

HUBBARD COMMUNICATIONS OFFICE
Saint Hill Manor, East Grinstead, Sussex

HCO POLICY LETTER OF 7 MAY 1966

Remimeo
LRH Comm
Exec Secs
All Staff

LRH Comm Network Series 20

LRH COMMUNICATOR, ISSUE AUTHORITY OF

The LRH Communicator in any org may veto and deny the issue of any Exec Sec or Sec instruction, order or Sec ED that is contrary to policy or technology.

In case of such veto, the date and paragraph number of the HCOB, Policy Letter or prior Sec ED must be stated in the veto.

As per the fast flow system of management, the LRH Comm may require that a Sec ED, order or instruction is certified as "okay and not against policy" before approving it. The LRH Comm need not approve the Sec ED, order or instruction out of his own research of policy but may approve one "approved on the okay."

If, in such event, the Sec ED, order or instruction is later found to be contrary to policy or technology, the LRH Comm may charge the person or persons who stated on it in writing that it was not against policy with FALSE ATTESTATION and must report the matter to LRH Comm WW who may order further action.

The comm lines of an LRH Comm between his Continental Org or WW must not be impeded and any censorship of the LRH Communicator lines must result in an immediate Comm Ev.

Any LRH Comm in any org has the Executive Director on his direct comm line where the communication is possible, as the Executive Director is the highest officer of his org and the post of Executive Director exists in every Executive Division.

———————

The LRH Comm may cancel verbal tech instructions or advices and verbal breaches of policy.

———————

An LRH Comm may reject magazines or mailing pieces which do not conform to policy.

———————

An LRH Comm may halt the use of unauthorized material or technology.

1267

An LRH Comm may reenter in his or her log for compliance any policy letter, HCOB or Sec ED at his or her own discretion. (It is wise to reenter qual, tech, promotional and ethics bulletins and PLs as the priority items.)

An LRH Comm on discovering a departure from technology or policy that has been attested to as okay and who has not yet approved it may require the author of the Sec ED, order or instruction, regardless of rank, to be checked out on that and similar technology or policy by the Staff Training Officer.

It is fact that an org will go as far as Scientology works and no further. Ethics gets tech in. Adherence to org form and policy makes the org expand to the degree Scientology works. Therefore, primary stress by the LRH Comm is on tech quality, ethics adherence, org form and policy.

Dept 21 puts the org there. The rest of the Exec Division sees that it stays there and expands. The LRH Comm must see that they do.

L. RON HUBBARD
Founder

HUBBARD COMMUNICATIONS OFFICE
Saint Hill Manor, East Grinstead, Sussex

HCO POLICY LETTER OF 1 APRIL 1965

Gen. Non-Remimeo
HCO Comm
Div Secs

LRH Comm Network Series 21

HCO COMMUNICATOR HAS PROGRAM CHECKING HAT

HCO Communicator is attached to the Office of L. Ron Hubbard, and this post is charged with the duty (additional to extant duties of HCO Communicator) of forwarding communications from L. Ron Hubbard and to L. Ron Hubbard. This duty includes the responsibility of seeing that these communications are duplicated and understood, and that any confusions on them are queried until the communication is duplicated and understood. This duty becomes particularly important when a major program is on the lines from L. Ron Hubbard.

To effect the above, then, HCO Communicator is to have personal charge of an activity called program checking. When a program comes into the lines, be it by cable, despatch or policy letter, the HCO Communicator is to call in the six division secretaries and carefully checks them out on the points in the program and what action is to be taken, in such a way that the open line to Saint Hill and Ron is quite apparent. The drill on this is done in this fashion.

1. First of all, the HCO Communicator checks the division head on duplication of the communication—that is, questions calculated to assess if the division sec has read the comm and knows what it said.

2. Then the Communicator asks the division sec questions pertaining to what he is going to do in effecting the comm.

The HCO Communicator at the beginning of the check lets the division sec know that he can query by cable if necessary back to Saint Hill for clarifying anything he is uncertain of, if by the end of the check anything is not understood. The understanding that the line to Saint Hill is wide open is maintained at all times throughout the check, and that the line may be by cable if necessary. If on (2) the div sec snags on a point, misduplicating in proposed action some point on the communication, the HCO Comm then asks him to (a) reread the communication and then if (b) he wants to query Ron about it. It is supposed that he would want to reread the communication at least once again before cabling. If after rereading it and after query again by the HCO Communicator as to what the div sec understands it to mean still leaves the div sec with a lack of understanding of how to put it into action, or any other misunderstanding, then the point may be queried to Ron. An example of such a drill is given below, taken from a cable sent by the Acting Exec Dir for Ron, which if this drill had been applied would have resulted in straight action instead of no action or misaction which has resulted in dev-t at Saint Hill. A program of mailing a mailing piece from Saint Hill promoting the various Central Organizations around the world

1269

was instituted at Saint Hill. For this, Saint Hill needed fast the count of the active and inactive lists of the various continents less the memberships (since memberships are on our plates, although untabbed, it would cut out most of the duplication of addresses). So a cable was sent to all the continental offices saying the following: "Cable immediately total number your total active and inactive list less international and lifetime memberships stop then airmail stickers or gummed tapes of these total lists less memberships."

The drill by the HCO Communicator on the above would be:

HCO COMM: "What lists numbers are to be cabled?"

DIV SEC: (say it's HCO Area Secretary in this case) "Total active and inactive list less memberships."

HCO COMM: "What memberships?"

DIV SEC: "Oh, international and lifetime."

HCO COMM: "What does Saint Hill want sent to them?"

DIV SEC: "Stickers or gummed tapes of these lists."

HCO COMM: "Of what lists?"

DIV SEC: "Oh, total active and inactive less memberships—oh, less international and lifetime memberships."

HCO COMM: "Okay. Now is there anything about this that you don't understand, that you want queried to Ron?"

DIV SEC: "No, I don't think so."

HCO COMM: "Well, you don't have to decide yet, then—What is the first action to be taken here?"

DIV SEC: "Let's see. Oh, cable the total number of the active and inactive lists less memberships."

HCO COMM: "Good. And who does this?"

DIV SEC: "Oh, well, HCO sends the cable."

HCO COMM: "And where does the data come from?"

DIV SEC: "From Div 1—Addressograph. Oh, I am HCO Area Sec and I am to despatch Addressograph on it."

HCO COMM: "What exactly do you put on the despatch?"

DIV SEC: "Well, I would put the heading, then I would put

1. Fast, send me the count on the total active and inactive lists less international and lifetime memberships.

2. Run off the total lists and send to Saint Hill."

HCO COMM: "Please reread the cable, and let me know if you want to query Ron about it."

DIV SEC: (after rereading the cable) "Wait a minute—I made a mistake. On (2) it would be, Run off on gummed stickers or tape the total active and inactive list less the memberships. Set the tabbing so that memberships don't go on the list. That is so both international and lifetime memberships don't go. And airmail the stickers or tape to Saint Hill. There. Oh, wait, this came in by cable, so that means they're in a rush for it, so I would add, Do this immediately and get them off fast. Gee, I wonder what they want them for."

HCO COMM: "Does not knowing what they want them for interfere with your understanding of what you are to do?"

DIV SEC: "No, it doesn't. No, I don't need to query this at all. I guess they couldn't put all their reasons why on a cable—that would be silly. No, I've got it now."

HCO COMM: "Good. End of check."

If the above had been done in all orgs, on the above cable, DC wouldn't have sent their entire list with memberships included, LA wouldn't have sent theirs surface, and there would have been some response from Cape Town.

The HCO Comm keeps at the check until either the communication is comprehended, including the action to be taken being duplicated, or in the case of a real noncomprehension or confusion as to what is to be done, Ron is queried on it.

L. RON HUBBARD
Founder

HCO POLICY LETTER OF 9 JUNE 1961

CenOCon

LRH Comm Network Series 22

TECHNICAL HAT CHECKING
VITAL POLICY FOR HCO AREA SEC

The HCO Area Secretary not only does hat checks routinely upon all new and all old staff members but also checks all staff out on all bulletins and policy letters issued for the week.

This is done by having a folder for all bulletins and policy letters issued. On the back of each bulletin or policy letter is written the name of each staff member on whom a check of the bulletin or policy letter has been made, the date the check was made and whether they passed or failed the check. When all persons to whom the bulletin or policy letter was directed have passed a check on the bulletin or policy letter, then the checking job on the bulletin or policy letter can be considered finished.

The check is done simply by calling the staff members in and asking them one random question taken from some part of the material contained in the bulletin or policy letter. If they fail to correctly answer this one question, they are flunked on the check, told to restudy it and come in again for a recheck. A staff member is called back as many times as it is necessary for him or her to answer all the most searching questions correctly. Choose different sentences from the text as subjects for questioning.

The HCO Area Secretary does not engage in explanations or discussions. The above is the entire procedure.

The purpose of this bulletin and policy letter checking is to make all sure that staff members are always informed of up-to-date material, to reduce dev-t caused by people not having read their bulletins or policy letters and to increase faster execution of directions.

L. RON HUBBARD
Founder

HCO POLICY LETTER OF 31 AUGUST 1974RA
REVISED 27 JULY 1986

Remimeo
All Orgs
LRH Comm Hat
KOT Hat
Exec Hats

LRH Comm Network Series 23

KEEPER OF TECH

OFFICE OF LRH

Refs:

HCO PL 7 Feb. 65	KSW Series 1	
	KEEPING SCIENTOLOGY WORKING	
HCO PL 17 June 70RB	KSW Series 5R	
Rev. 25.10.83	TECHNICAL DEGRADES	
HCO PL 8 Mar. 66	KSW Series 13	
	HIGH CRIME	
HCO PL 10 July 86 I	Admin Know-How Series 50	
	KEEPING ADMIN WORKING	
HCO PL 10 July 86 II	Admin Know-How Series 51	
	ADMIN DEGRADES	
HCO PL 10 July 86 III	Admin Know-How Series 52	
	Computer Series 7	
	URGENT—IMPORTANT	
	ADMIN HIGH CRIME	

The full title of this post is KEEPER OF TECH AND POLICY KNOWL-EDGE.

The Office of LRH and LRH Comms have always had an establishment function.

The purpose of the Keeper of Tech is:

TO HELP LRH ESTABLISH TECH AND POLICY IN ORGS FULLY AND ACCURATELY AND IN FULL USE AND KEEP IT THERE.

Inherent in that purpose is the responsibility of the Keeper of Tech to prevent refunds and repayments.

As the awareness and use of tech and policy requires continual renewal in orgs, the duties of the Keeper of Tech concern themselves with having the knowledge of tech and policy readily available and getting it known and used on a continuing basis.

The channel used by the Keeper of Tech is the Qual Division. By establishing its library and a Tech and Admin Cramming Section Cramming Officer and Word Clearer or more than one, the Keeper of Tech can ensure that tech and policy are available, known by and corrected on staffs. (See HCO PL 30 Aug. 74 II, QUAL STAT CHANGE.)

Additionally on-policy courses in hatting, in all auditing and C/Sing functions, the OEC Course, etc., are the concern of the Keeper of Tech. (See HCO PL 16 Mar. 71R, KSW Series 27, WHAT IS A COURSE?)

It is the business of the Keeper of Tech to see that no squirrel processing or training occurs and that Source materials are available and in use.

The Keeper of Tech operates through the Qual Sec or the Tech Sec of an org or by direct establishment of these functions and the hatting of those (including EDs and execs) who are responsible for them so that the functions continue.

The Keeper of Tech has full ethics powers to stamp out squirrel activities or actions and to get in on-policy actions in both tech and admin.

NETWORK STRUCTURE

Where the org size does not warrant a Keeper of Tech in the Office of LRH, THE LRH COMM HAS THE FUNCTION OF A KEEPER OF TECH as an additional duty and is responsible for the function.

The org Keeper of Tech or the LRH Comm receives his orders regarding tech and policy from the Keeper of Tech Continental.

The Keeper of Tech Continental is answerable to the LRH Comm Continental.

The KOT Continental receives his orders from the KOT Int via the LRH Comm Continental.

The KOT Int receives his orders from LRH Comm Int.

The post of KOT, however, does not depend on orders but operates on the above purpose of the post.

OPERATION

The KOT Continental is expected to actively look in on orgs and after inspection, write a targeted program for that org that will establish its Qual, especially Cramming and Word Clearing, its library and to see that on-policy Cramming and Word Clearing *occur*. He then writes a targeted program to establish the org's courses on policy and to see that actual on-policy training is occurring.

The LRH Comm as KOT of the org or the KOT of the org sees that this program is vigorously executed.

All Qual Cramming and Word Clearing policy and tech apply.

The biggest stumbling block will probably be "personnel." To combat these the KOT must see that LRH EDs relating to recruiting auditors and Supervisors and training them on the job are activated forcefully on the Tech Sec. Large salaries demanded and other blocks to actual establishment must be overcome. An in-tech, on-policy org has NO trouble getting auditors and other staff.

THE LONGER QUAL CRAMMING IS INACTIVE THE WORSE AN ORG WILL GET.

A BAD ACADEMY EMPTIES.

OUT–TECH OR NO AUDITING BREAKS THE GI.

THE ONLY SUCCESSFUL ORGS ARE HATTED, ON–POLICY ORGS.

These four demonstrable facts are the main points of argument in breaking down opposition to rapid utilization of tech and policy.

Whatever turns up the KOT must see that his purpose is gotten in in that org.

REFUNDS/REPAYMENTS

A REFUND is returning money after service is given.

A REPAYMENT is returning money because no service has been given at all to earn it.

The way to avoid *auditing* refunds is to have TRAINED C/Ses and C/Ses for each type of auditing (Dianetics, Grades) and a good QUAL that crams auditors and C/Ses.

The way to avoid *training* refunds is to have TRAINED SUPERVISORS and a good Qual that crams both Supervisors and students for supervising learning and co-auditing flubs.

The way to avoid *repayments* is to have a Director of Tech Services who calls people in for service. AND to have C/Ses and auditors and Supervisors who can and do *deliver* service.

Not only is it a KOT and LRH Comm responsibility to prevent refunds and repayments, it is the responsibility of the KOT and LRH Comm to ensure requests for refunds and repayments are HANDLED when they do occur, and that they are handled standardly and promptly.

A refund claimant can consult the org or Continental KOT or LRH Comm for any guidance required in the handling of his refund or repayment request.

Routing forms must exist whereby the person requesting refund or repayment is directed very clearly as to the exact steps he takes to obtain his refund or repayment and the exact terminal he sees at each step. The claimant is then, himself, responsible for getting each step of the routing form done and its terms enforced.

The org KOT or LRH Comm ensures such routing forms exist and that each org terminal on the line is hatted on his assigned function at a specific point on the form, as well as being fully hatted on the policies covering the entire refund/repayment line. This hatting, in addition to dummy running of the line, is vital to swift, standard and on-policy handling of any such claim. It can also mean the difference between salvaging a claimant and failing to do so. Therefore, correction of any org terminal who is flubbing on or delaying this line becomes the responsibility of the KOT or LRH Comm.

Refund/repayment requests do not always mean technical quality is out. It can also mean that registration acceptance is out. (This would be evidenced by Registrars in Division 2 and Division 6 failing to get all of the necessary registration papers signed and establishing the actual condition of the person at the time of sign-up.) Therefore, Tech can be wrongly targeted when trying to correct refunds, as responsibility also lies with the Registrars. Thus the KOT or LRH Comm must also ensure that Registrars are hatted and operating standardly in regard to sign-ups.

STATS

The stats of an org KOT would include the stats of:

1. The *number* of outstanding refund/repayment claims weekly (an upside-down graph), and

2. The number of targets completed on a KOT Program for that org.

Where an LRH Comm is acting also as a KOT for an org, the stats of a KOT Program are added to her own but are separately reported by despatch via the Continental KOT who reports them by despatch to KOT Int. The stats of the Keeper of Tech Continental are the cont totals of both the production and establishment KOT stats of the cont.

The stats of the Keeper of Tech Int are international totals of the production and establishment KOT statistics.

The success and rate of expansion of Scientology on the planet depends on the degree tech and policy are known and used. That has been proven over and over and over.

That is the reason for the post of Keeper of Tech.

L. RON HUBBARD
Founder

Revision assisted by
LRH Technical Research
and Compilations

ISSUE AUTHORITY

HUBBARD COMMUNICATIONS OFFICE
1812 19th Street NW, Washington 9, DC

HCO BULLETIN OF 30 APRIL 1957

ISSUE AUTHORITY FOR MIMEO

Effective this date, all mimeo work is to be sent to me for okay before being run; all material going to the field should be printed, not mimeoed—looks better, is cheaper. Only exception, when replacing current stock of mimeoed forms used in the organization.

L. RON HUBBARD
Founder

HUBBARD COMMUNICATIONS OFFICE
37 Fitzroy Street, London W1

HCO POLICY LETTER OF 18 MAY 1957

POLICY ON SIGNATURES IN PUBLICATIONS

On data called to attention by Association Secretary London, the following is the policy laid down:

Articles by myself are signed as a byline under title and another written signature at end.

Articles taken from tapes are signed "From a lecture by L. Ron Hubbard" (bold face).

Books written by staff are signed "By staff from materials of L. Ron Hubbard" with the names of writers in light face under "By staff from materials of L. Ron Hubbard."

Articles somewhat independent of materials directly from lectures and texts are signed by the writer at the article's end only in same face as type in which article is set.

Mastheads carry the name of the editor of any publication.

These policies apply to *Ability*, *Certainty*, PABs, books and pamphlets.

When articles are written for outside publications, the writer should always mention a specific text and its author, the price and from whence the text can be obtained.

L. RON HUBBARD
Founder

HUBBARD COMMUNICATIONS OFFICE
37 Fitzroy Street, London W1

HCO POLICY LETTER OF 23 MAY 1957
Issue I

RESPONSIBILITY FOR ISSUE

Any item which is to be mimeographed, printed, disseminated, etc., which needs my "okay" must first be initialed by the department head or anyone related or associated with it before the item comes to me for an "okay." When it comes to me, I want to see that the parties involved have already "okayed" it themselves.

L. RON HUBBARD
Founder

1 Each Staff Member
Field Offices

WHO CAN ORDER PRINTING

(Replaces HCO PL of 1 June 1957
WHO CAN ORDER PRINTING)

The following persons can originate copy for printing:

Association Secretary or Organization Secretary
Treasurer
Registrar
Central Files In-Charge
Director of Training
Director of Processing
Director of Administration

All material to be printed and its price must be okayed by the Director of Administration before order is placed.

L. RON HUBBARD
Founder

HUBBARD COMMUNICATIONS OFFICE
37 Fitzroy Street, London W1

HASI POLICY LETTER OF 31 OCTOBER 1958

1 each Staff Member
Field Offices for Info
Washington

Only 75 copies of any given item may be run off on mimeo machines.

Any item to be run further than this number must be well done on photolitho or photo-offset.

All general releases of data go out in *Certainty* and in no other printed way.

L. RON HUBBARD
Founder

HUBBARD COMMUNICATIONS OFFICE
1812 19th Street NW, Washington, DC

HCO POLICY LETTER OF 23 DECEMBER 1958
Issue I

To all HCO
staff only

QUALITY OF PRESENTATIONS

HCO is hereby given the authority and responsibility to ensure high quality presentation of all tapes, books, mailings, film showings, tape shows, congresses, etc.

This is the right to demand high quality, not to do it all. HCO must pass on all such showings or printings as to equipment and styling.

You *always* lose money with poor presentation so why try to *save* money that way.

Motto for all presentations: Get the best. Have it professionally done in accordance with stiff specifications.

Let's put quality in Scientology presentation!

L. RON HUBBARD
Founder

HCO POLICY LETTER OF 4 JUNE 1959
Issue II

Convert
to Sec ED

VALIDITY OF SEC EDs

All Sec EDs except those which state or imply a penalty for noncompliance are guideposts, subject to judgment, based mainly on org findings.

Where a penalty for noncompliance is implied or stated, judgment is invited and an HCO Sec may modify to fit local conditions.

L. RON HUBBARD
Founder

BPI

SIGNATURES ON BULLETINS,
POLICY LETTERS AND SEC EDs

Only when I have personally written a bulletin, a policy letter or a Sec ED should it be signed "L. Ron Hubbard" or "L. Ron Hubbard, Executive Director."

When I have knowledge of or have okayed a bulletin, policy letter or Sec ED but have not actually written it, it should be signed "Jane Doe (the name of the actual writer) for L. Ron Hubbard" or "Jane Doe for L. Ron Hubbard, Executive Director."

When I have not seen or okayed a policy letter or a bulletin or a Sec ED but it is published by the authority of a held post such as HCO Sec, it should be signed "Jane Doe (actual name of person issuing) HCO Sec (or other title)."

The field or public must not be led to believe that I have written or issued things I have not. Further, other people have authority, too.

L. RON HUBBARD
Founder

HCO POLICY LETTER OF 4 JANUARY 1961
Issue I

HCO Secs
HCO Communicators

URGENT MIMEO CHANGE

I have found in two Central Orgs that my HCO Bulletins and HCO Policy Letters are *not* being duplicated as to color.

Proper color on these is as follows:

Duplicate the Saint Hill color scheme. If you get a red-ink-on-white paper HCO Bulletin, put it in red mimeo ink on white paper. If you get one with green ink on white paper, put your copy in green ink on white paper.

These two flashes are *my*-signature-only letters and bulletins. They must not get lost into the general lines. My comm lines are being cut by no flash identification for staff.

Only these two flashes get duplicated for the whole org. Salmon-colored-paper-with-green-ink HCO Bulletins from Saint Hill are handled as follows in a Central Org. You get two copies. Put one in HCO files, put the other on the staff bulletin board, or if the HCO Bulletin otherwise indicates, handle as directed.

Also, *attention Area Sec,* I want you to hat check my material coming in as HCO Bulletins and Policy Letters on Central Org personnel to whom Policy Letters and HCO Bulletins apply as though they were hats. Do these with all recent HCO Bulletins and Policy Letters and *all* future ones.

The primary function of HCO is to make my postulates stick. Please do so.

L. RON HUBBARD
Founder

HCO POLICY LETTER OF 7 JUNE 1961

CenOCon

ORDERS

All directives or orders issued as HASI Association Sec Technical Orders, HASI Association Sec Administrative Orders, HCO Continental Technical Letters, and HCO Continental Administrative Orders are valid only so long as they do not contradict HCO Policy Letters, HCO Bulletins and, as contained in these, operating and technical policies established for Central Organizations or city offices.

Any HASI Association Sec Directive or HCO Continental Directive as noted above may be declared null and void by anyone who can demonstrate, by HCO Policy Letter or HCO Bulletin, displayed and in hand, that any former directive contradicts the latter.

L. RON HUBBARD
Founder

CenOCon

E–METERS TO BE APPROVED

HCO PL 9 Oct. 61, ACADEMY TRAINING, states that students in the Academy should only be allowed to use E-Meters which have been approved by HCO.

This policy should be extended to include also E-Meters which are used in the organization throughout, including the HGC. In order to safeguard the interests of Scientology, it is essential that this policy should be strictly enforced by the HCO.

No E-Meter should be approved by the HCO unless it is known to be a type which has been designed and manufactured by L. Ron Hubbard, or by individuals or groups who have been directly and specifically authorized by L. Ron Hubbard to manufacture E-Meters of approved design under license.

All formerly made E-Meters which have not been approved by L. Ron Hubbard are automatically disallowed by this policy letter. No Central Organization should manufacture E-Meters locally unless by direct arrangement with L. Ron Hubbard personally, who will first require to examine an actual prototype of the proposed meter to ensure good quality and excellent performance.

No authority to manufacture E-Meters or approval of meters may be issued by any office except HCO WW.

L. RON HUBBARD
Founder

CenOCon

REISSUE OF MATERIALS

It is forbidden to reissue Scientology technical data in bulletins and policy letters, by a Central Org or office, over some other signature than mine.

Culling bits out of a tape and issuing over the signature of the D of T or some such, as has been done in Australia, is not only an alter-is, it is also terribly confusing and opens the door to 1950 where countless "authorities" sprang up after lecture and "developed" a "new technology." I took responsibility of origin of my materials at that time to prevent further chaos and spinning pcs. I have never relaxed that responsibility and we have done well.

If you excerpt tapes or notes, do so over my name, not somebody else's.

Materials for dissemination to the public can be of course rewritten and published so long as no confusion as to origin is generated.

Issues of materials of mine under other names without credit is the most destructive action that can be undertaken as it splinters the whole of Scientology.

L. RON HUBBARD
Founder

HCO POLICY LETTER OF 4 MARCH 1965RA
Issue II
REVISED 7 JULY 1983

Gen. Non-Remimeo
SH Execs
Mgmt and Org Execs
HCO Secs

Hat Material

Division 1 (HCO)

TECHNICAL AND POLICY DISTRIBUTION

The HCO Secretary (WW, Continental or Area) passes on and makes available for issue all:

1. Staff releases

2. Releases to HGC

3. Releases to Academies

4. Mission releases

5. Major magazine releases

6. Minor magazine releases

7. Org letters

8. Brochures

9. Ads

10. Supervisors' answers

11. Public lectures

Bulletins and policy letters and articles may be:

A. Culled from files.

B. Obtained newly written from LRH.

C. Copied from LRH tapes and rewritten.

D. Summarized from A, B and C without injecting new materials, policies or technology.

All bulletins, policy letters and articles from A, B, C and D must bear the LRH byline.

No other material is permitted on lines 1 to 11 above than straight Scientology. No interpretations are permitted.

All materials released, used or sold must be straight Scientology as given in the writings or lectures of LRH.

Under the copyright hat, all HCO Secretaries must make certain that all LRH materials published are properly copyrighted in the name of LRH. No org copyrights are permitted of LRH materials.

Books may not be advertised for sale or the advertisement paid for from the HCO book fund except LRH books.

No technical articles or letters by another person than LRH are permitted in Scientology publications. Only data written by others on application, use or results of Scientology may appear, and any tech data, if nonstandard, must be deleted from the article or letter.

Lectures by others on application, use and results only are permitted in public lectures of any kind, including congresses.

Use of Scientology technical or policy data in testimony is forbidden. Only application and results may be testified to. Only low-level works may be read as part of any testimony and no Scientology words may be used in such instances.

All staff members looking for data to release, use or print must look to their HCO Secretary. If the HCO Secretary is in doubt, he or she should consult the next higher HCO Secretary.

No effort should be made by HCO to censor opinion or comment on policy or technology; the whole effort is to be directed to the dissemination and use of correct Scientology technical and policy materials only. As there exists a correct technology and policy structure, alteration of it becomes a retarding factor in organizational solidarity and expansion. The prime cause of alter-is in tech and policy is ignorance of it or stupidity.

POLICIES GOVERNING RELEASE

1. DISSEMINATE SCIENTOLOGY.

That is the governing policy of all the rest.

2. DATA SHOULD BE CHANNELED TO THE RIGHT SOURCES.

If promotion is to one-legged men, don't send them materials about eyesight.

The dissemination materials are designed for the more able members of society who seek self-betterment. Don't channel them toward psychiatric cases or strata they would not have an effect upon.

Example: A person in charge of an org or HGC is psychoanalytically oriented and seeks only "patients" as preclears and handles them as such. The org declines because this is a wrong target since promotion was aimed at quite different people.

Example: An office is successful handling workers and longshoremen, but new direction of that office seeks to pull in only idle intellectuals, who would never act in any case, and the office declines. In either case, the source of success was not spotted, and when direction of reach altered everything declined. The old public that was being reached was offended and the new public was useless. The above two examples are actual.

3. THE WORKABLE AND PROVEN MATERIALS OF DIANETICS AND SCIENTOLOGY ONLY MAY BE RELEASED.

This at once excludes all squirrel or off-line materials by others. Experience has shown that no significant or lasting developments have arisen off-line in fifteen years following a whole track of very murderous technology other than Dianetics and Scientology.

This truth emerged in the first three years after 1949. Every effort was made to encourage other development. The LRH research hat was put on LRH solidly by others.

Every group and organization devoted to off-line materials that came into being—E-Therapy,* Howes,* others, others, others—all wound up discredited and rejected by everyone, even their early promoters and adherents. Thus, by the test of time and of continued use only, show that if an org adventures on off-line materials it will decline markedly or cease to exist. All groups that have departed or "dreamed it up themselves" have perished. Even psychology, psychoanalysis and psychiatry are dying, supported now mainly by governments, detested by the public. So this is not propaganda; this is a survival fact: groups that use squirrel material fail.

4. ALL EFFORTS TO DISCREDIT THE PERSONS OF ANY LEADING OR REPUTABLE SCIENTOLOGISTS MUST BE SAFEGUARDED IN ALL RELEASES ESPECIALLY LRH.

This means more than it seems to say.

The near collapse of one org was traced back to a whispering campaign by its principals against LRH and MSH. All of "the data" was false. By newspaper standards it should have been listened to avidly. Instead, the public deserted the org and it nearly collapsed, and the person who did it was eventually driven out of Scientology by fellow Scientologists, although no discipline was ordered and the matter ignored.

The public buys only "our brand" despite newspaper publicity, government actions, whispering campaigns and rumor. This again is from actual experience. Orgs that apologize for its tech or people or LRH suffer a declining public.

It is a pure survival fact that failure to protect the names and repute of Scientology leading personalities and LRH collapses an org. The only proof is that

---

*E-Therapy: a squirrel technique of setting up a circuit in the mind called "the examiner" and then trying to have this circuit run out engrams. It was called Examiner Therapy or E-Therapy and did not work.

*Howes: a short-lived squirrel group started in 1951 by Ron Howes. Howes was jailed and the group dispersed soon after it was formed.

those orgs that haven't aren't here any more and those orgs that strenuously have are thriving.

Protecting names and repute may also sometimes involve selection of correct materials. Example: Despite explicit orders to the contrary, mainly Level V materials were released at the Australian Enquiry. The org suffered heavily and not wholly from the government. The foolishness of it came home to most well-trained Scientologists.

Sending Level VI works to Level 0 people is easy to see and intercept. But an Instructor teaching Level IV to Level II students is not always found until somebody blows. This comes under protecting names and repute as well as properly targeted tech because the recipients can't understand it and so may think it's silly.

Releasing unfavorable photographs, badly recorded tapes or films all come under this policy.

5. THE PUBLIC MUST BE PROTECTED AGAINST ABUSERS OF TECHNOLOGY OR POLICY.

Persons who try to use Scientology lines to get loans or funds for fraudulent purposes must always be exposed by HCO Secretaries by public postings when proven and Committees of Evidence when doubt exists.

A complaining pc does not come under this heading but more likely under the policy of correct technology or who to accept for processing, unless less auditing was given than paid for or no auditing at all was given, at which time it comes under this policy.

Anyone using a Scientology mailing list for purposes other than the greatest good for the greatest number of dynamics should be heavily censured and brought to book.

The Scientology public and any mailing lists are the exclusive property of HCO. It does not matter how the mailing list was gathered or if we ever saw it before. If someone used Scientology to collect names, that's a Scientology mailing list. It's ours and comes under this policy.

6. DELIVER SCIENTOLOGY WORKS, TRAINING, PROCESSING AND RESULTS.

Although actual training and processing is under Division 4, whether or not it was or will be delivered (past and future but not current) is up to HCO.

By making the right materials available for publishing and use in training and processing, HCO expects them to be employed.

If they are not employed, then the matter falls back on HCO to act.

The reason I had to continue research and writing myself as a lonely action was because nobody else developed anything, despite my expectations and despite the money they spent. The reason I had to enforce use was because other technology crept in and failed, causing org emergencies. HCO then furthers my own hat, assumed for research in July 1950, and for control of things, to be sure tech wasn't altered or misapplied in 1952 and after. So long as those two things have been watched and kept in effect we have prospered. Where they haven't been watched carefully and where no control existed to get them in effect, everything died as our history clearly shows.

Even when I strayed on research, we still did better than with the strayings of others. The public knows rightly that I correct any errors as soon as I discover them and that errors grew less as research went on.

Therefore, HCO issues the best material it has for the right targets and notes carefully any lack of results because of misapplication and retains the authority and control necessary to correct bad delivery under its justice hat as well as its certificate and awards hat.

The formula is, "Issue the correct data properly, correct use when delivery is poor or nonexistent."

Early HCOs had some trouble in executing this policy because (a) they were operating on a technology that was advancing and, therefore, always changing. Now and then HCOs are held up by (b) my not being able to write up and issue or issue the needed materials because of comm-line jams. The best solution for (a) is to issue what has *been* working and the best solution for (b) is to excerpt tapes or what you have and issue. However, (a) has now vanished because of completed technology and (b) is becoming no problem to the degree I can get it written up and issued.

7. INSTRUCTION AND ADMIN POLICY ARE ALMOST AS IMPORTANT AS TECH.

Completely aside from developing Scientology tech itself, it took fourteen years to develop the technology of instruction (how to communicate the data and make auditors). It took fifteen years to fully develop the technology of our administration.

Admin publicly is looked down on, like nineteenth-century psychology, because it was not developed. Teaching and business admin alike have been quite low paid or in disrepute in the civilization. They were not sciences. For instance, business admin students in a university are renowned for falsifying exams more than students of other subjects. That's because there was no subject there anyway.

Why we had to know how to teach is self-evident.

In Scientology, to keep our orgs going and live through bad times, we have had to develop a whole new subject—admin. We had to have its laws, the economic factors that regulate business and all the rest.

We are pretty good. People with "formal training" in subjects used in our orgs are seldom as good as Scientologists who just studied with us as part of their job.

The main thing to know, like in studying our tech, in *our* teaching and admin, there *are* two subjects there to be studied and used. Our teaching is Scientology-type teaching. Our admin is Scientology admin. Both are regulated by Scientology policy. Orgs prosper when they know and use them, and fumble and get poor when they don't.

Holding teaching and admin policy and releases in is best handled by insistence they exist and are ours and are not what the person thinks they are—borrowings from the schools or business world. The business world already borrows from us. The biggest management association in the world since 1958 or so has been duplicating (as well as it could) everything we do in business admin and planning. Of course, having no HCO, they squirrel and it's hard to see how they twist our stuff so far around. But it *is* our material. Even their "congresses" have the same number of days and lectures and have programs printed on our *exact* format.

When we have our teaching materials (not just "study") all written up, you will see the universities use them. We already have some universities trying.

As we write our admin up in books, business will use it all the more. But the point is, *we* lead in this field, others follow. We only develop and use Scientology admin to help us as we go toward freedom. But we still use it and only it. Because it's more modern and it's what we need.

The thing to guard against in releasing teaching and admin policy letters is the change factor. Teaching and admin evolved with our formative years. Thus, patterns and policies, like our tech, grew better. Growing better, some of it became obsolete.

When rereleasing an old policy letter, always blue pencil out everything gone old and contradicted by later policy letters. You can still salvage a lot that still applies—a surprising amount. But try to cut out the contradictions with our modern policy where they exist. After all, we were children when we first tackled teaching and admin. As we grew, we became wiser. But even our admin childhood has wisdom in it and in some places even more fire and interest.

Don't release contradictory hats where you can help it. Modernize them with a blue pencil whether you retype them or remimeo them or not.

That way none get a chance to invalidate a really great achievement—teaching that works despite aberration and admin that works amongst men.

8. ISSUE TECH AND POLICY AS BROADLY AS POSSIBLE WITHIN ECONOMIC LIMITS.

It costs money to issue anything. The way to sustain issue is get it paid for one way or another. Total subsidy of all tech and policy issue can stop its being issued, for it is no longer economical to issue it.

Thus, to disseminate over any long period, the data must somehow be paid for or dissemination ceases. Actually, you can't give away Scientology really. Money, credit or favors will flow back. But often only after many years. And meanwhile people eat.

Unless you pay attention to the economics of dissemination, you will cut the dissemination line even if only temporarily.

If you have data, don't try to throw it all away by frantic, unpaid-for dissemination. Use some of the data as a leader (to announce with) and sell the rest of it.

This applies to magazines, books, training and processing, all of them.

People don't respect data they read in magazines, anyway. For some reason they respect books. The public believe books and hoard them and throw magazines away. Even paperbacks suffer. A book has to have a hard cover to gain respect.

Thus, a magazine article on tech ideally should point up a book to buy. Tons of bulletins are less well received than one book.

The point is, don't invest a lot of money on the quality and thickness of magazines or other temporary media. Put the data between hard covers and sell it as a book.

Don't give a lot of free courses or free admittances to Academies or courses or free intensives in HGCs and call it dissemination. It isn't. Beyond a small amount it cuts your ability to disseminate. The cost of the give-away does not come back in and you can't finance more outflow because you gave it all away.

This can even happen to an HCO in its publishing to the org, mimeos and new books. It gives away all its materials to the org and suddenly finds the org "can't pay for more mimeo paper" or a new mimeo machine. The way to handle is not to charge for bulletins and policy letters directly but to insist the org profit by the tech and admin by promoting harder for the org.

My policy on this has always been to promote more business than the org can handle and then let *it* solve the jams thus brought about. Orgs I founded have never failed to handle such problems providing one demanded they did. The only problem an org *can't* handle is "no dough"; the only weak point of orgs, traditionally, has been promotion. They are sometimes even afraid to promote for fear they'll get too big (something wrong with the top exec's comm lines is the usual cause). I have seen an old-time psychiatrically oriented D of P *book* pcs six months in advance rather than hire more than six auditors and a queasy D of T seek to shut everyone out of an Academy "because they would not be socially acceptable."

Such persons in the wrong positions will rail against promotion—because it makes pcs and students crowd in too hard. So you get plans "to train more only when we have Instructors" or "few pcs until the next Academy class graduates so we have auditors."

Instructors, auditors, that's Division 4's problem. HCO ignores it.

So part of paying for dissemination and ads is promoting to drive in more business than the org can handle and making it make more money than it can waste. An org always manages to handle the business and it always wastes lots of money.

So in issuing materials, remember to promote them, too. Then there's always enough money flowing back to pay for more printing, more bulletins and policy letters, more books and tapes.

If you don't become strenuous on this point of policy, you will cease to disseminate. And I have always waived aside all objections to honest, appealing, clear-cut, heavy promotion as treasonable suggestions. Let somebody "doing the mag" complain about the "hard sell" in it (insistence people buy) and I always find myself somebody else to do the mag and go on promoting.

Therefore, people who (a) want us to give it all away and, thus, end our ability to pay for more and who (b) shudder at the possible inflow, I always carefully note down in my little black book for transfer. And an HCO Sec anywhere would do well to advise higher authority in all cases where efforts to reduce our ability to pay for our dissemination get in our way.

Whereas this possibly may seem unreasonable, it works. And every time I've not followed it ruthlessly as a policy, we've come a cropper.

9. OFFER ANYTHING YOU OFFER AT A HIGH APPEAL LEVEL AT HIGH VELOCITY AND HEAVY IMPACT.

If you know it works and is the way, you will have no trouble with this policy.

If you don't, you will have trouble.

The answer to this policy is to have a good subjective and objective reality on Scientology. Then you couldn't keep yourself from following it.

L. RON HUBBARD
Founder

HCO EXECUTIVE LETTER OF 27 MARCH 1965

Gen. Non-Remimeo

TO: ASSOC SEC LONDON

FROM: RON

SUBJECT: **CONFUSED PRESENTATION DENIES SERVICE**

Ray from Ron: Your promotion letter (Sec ED No. 1) was messed up by adding a PS to correct a correction rather than throw away a stencil and cut a correct new one. This may result in loss of business. A new stencil would have cost 3 shillings. The blunder may cost £2–3000.

A *Certainty* Minor is being rushed out to your lists to correct this confused presentation. It will just make a straight statement.

I see there's a blame of high prices from HCO London for the drop after 1 January in business volume. I think this was not due to a rise in prices but due to local confused promotion. I think you will find that such a confusing picture was presented by the Registrar about membership and prices that people, feeling in need of auditing or wishing training, just felt locked out and went home.

This was again expressed in this London org promotion Sec ED mix-up—a confusion of the public as to what is offered. Such a confusion seems to deny service and people don't buy.

Please take over the okay of all pieces to be released by your local org and coach the lines in so that the door for service looks open to the public, not closed. Please help me open your doors to a good traffic volume. Clumsy presentation by the local org alone is keeping them closed.

Love,

Ron

L. RON HUBBARD
Founder

Gen. Non-Remimeo

JUSTICE POLICY LETTERS
CORRECTIONS

The act of calling an Emergency condition does not open the person, unit, section, department, org or division to any transfer, demotion or dismissal or cause a reduction of pay. The subject of the condition must put the Emergency Formula into prompt operation, and it is expected in the case of an org or portion of an org such as a division, department or section that the executive staff member, after the stage of promotion is passed in the formula, will request a Committee of Evidence be convened on the staff member under him whose noncompliance or actions caused the Emergency.

Pay reduction, demotions, transfers, fines or dismissal may only be done after a Committee of Evidence and on its recommendation. There is no other way to bring about transfer, demotion, dismissal from an org, or fine or reduce the pay of a staff member.

When after calling an Emergency condition there is no improvement during a reasonable time, a Committee of Evidence must be convened.

Emergency and all other conditions are assigned only by the Office of L. Ron Hubbard, which is a part of each HCO.

The form of issue of any conditions, including Emergency, is a Sec ED.

A condition is cancelled by a Sec ED.

Sec EDs are only issued by the Office of L. Ron Hubbard under the "per pro" (by and for) of the HCO Secretary or LRH Communicator in any org.

Requests for an Emergency condition should be made to the Director of Inspections, Dept 13, Distribution Div (4), who comments and forwards them to the Office of L. Ron Hubbard. The comment of the Director of Inspections can be a recommendation for or against with any data he or she has.

Emergency conditions are given *only* on OIC statistics and not by rumor or opinion.

Emergency conditions may be issued on anyone in any portion of an org, including divisions, without permission from a senior org, but may only be issued as above for reasons of declining statistics.

However, no Emergency condition may be placed on a Secretary by the org itself. This may be done only by applying to the senior org to that org or to Saint Hill.

CONVENING AUTHORITY

Only HCO's Office of LRH may now convene a Committee of Evidence or a Civil Committee of Evidence (one person satisfactory to both contestants used in disputes between Scientologists or portions of Scientology, the contestants abiding by the findings of the one-person committee).

The order to convene one is requested of the Director of Inspections (Div 4) who forwards it (or originates it) to HCO's Office of L. Ron Hubbard with comments and any statistics. No statistics are actually demanded in such a request but any available evidence is forwarded. The bill is prepared by Dept 13 for forwarding to HCO for authority to convene.

The authority to convene is issued by the Office of LRH in HCO, "per pro" (by and for) the HCO Secretary or LRH Communicator.

The authority for a Committee of Evidence is issued by Sec ED. It is issued to the Director of Inspections who then handles all arrangements and actions from there up to the point of authorizing the findings. The complete record and papers, prepared, are sent to HCO's Office of LRH for final action and publication. In cases where the machinery to convene a committee is missing, it is requested from a senior org on the same routing as above.

Publication of a Committee of Evidence findings is done by Sec ED of the same number that convened it. Publication is done by the Office of LRH.

The Director of Inspections (Div 4, Dept 13) takes care of all further actions and the resulting files.

The Department of Inspections, Division 4, Department 13, has the actual *administration* and *execution* of all justice.

HCO's Office of LRH issues all *authorities* for justice and confirms all findings of justice and publishes results.

All guards or forces to be used in justice (but not members of Committees of Evidence) are under the control of the Department of Promotion, Div 1, Dept 6, and are under the orders of the HCO Secretary who may relay to them, through the Department of Promotion, the requirements of the Director of Inspections. Such forces may be loaned to the Dept of Inspections but remain HCO personnel.

BALANCE OF POWER

Division of Justice (HCO) has the authority and forces. Division 2 (the org itself, consisting of Organization, Finance and Materiel) has the money and materiel. Division 3 (Service and Technical) has the technical personnel and Div 4 has the field and "population."

1301

All four divisions are called the organization, as Division 2 organizes, finances and supplies them.

Justice, therefore, is under Division 4 in administration, depends on Division 1 for authority and power, and depends on Division 2 for finance and supplies, and uses the technology of Division 3.

Thus, it remains balanced.

Recourse from discipline or findings is requested always from the Department of Inspections, who applies to HCO's Office of LRH for decision and authority, and then the Department of Inspections cares for the resulting actions.

The Office of LRH need not wait on any request from anyone to issue conditions or authorities but must advise LRH at once on doing so.

LRH may issue conditions or authorities without request through his office or via the Director of Inspections. All such conditions or authorities are based only on statistics but may include actions to obtain further statistics such as requesting or ordering data to be furnished to decide whether or not a committee should be convened.

No condition, simply by being directed, carries a penalty with it. However, the declaration of a condition for any org, division, department, section or person commands that the formula for that condition be followed by the org, division, department, section or person named.

The Sec ED declaring the condition may not be posted on a public board or a board commonly viewed by the public, but *must* be posted on a staff board available to staff members. Copies of the Sec ED declaring a condition are given to every person in the org, division, department or section named in it or to the person.

The form of the condition Sec ED is as follows below and with the usual Sec ED designations and seal.

CONDITION

The condition of (name of condition in capitals) is declared upon

(Subject in capitals)

by reasons of

1. (give specific reasons one after next)

2.

3.   etc.

    (Sec ED ending)

The form of a Sec ED (Secretarial Executive Director) for a Committee of Evidence is as follows below and with the usual Sec ED headings and designations:

COMMITTEE OF EVIDENCE

At the request of _____ (title and org, or, By the order of LRH), the Director of Inspections, Div 4, Department 13, is to convene and attend to the speedy conduct and conclusion of a Committee of Evidence.

(Names in capitals) are to be named as interested parties.

The committee is convened to look into and bring findings on a matter of a possible (give type—misdemeanor, crime or high crime) of (give exact charge or charges very briefly from the Justice Code) for which the maximum penalty is (give maximum penalty).

The Director of Inspections is to name the chairman and committee and compose and serve a bill of particulars on the interested parties. He is further instructed to provide the committee and interested parties with copies of the Justice Codes. Further, he is to charge the committee to find facts and absolve the interested parties or prove them guilty beyond reasonable doubt, recommend any action and return all findings to HCO's Office of LRH for acceptance of findings and their publication.

L. Ron Hubbard

per pro _____ LRH
Communicator (or HCO Sec)

L. RON HUBBARD
Founder

HCO POLICY LETTER OF 22 APRIL 1965
Issue III

Remimeo
SH
All Orgs
All Scn Staff
Dissem Hats
HCO Hats

Urgent

Office of LRH

Design and Planning

All Promotion Functions in an Org

All Mailing Activities in an Org

BOOKLETS, HANDOUTS, MAILING PIECES

(Effective at once Saint Hill.
Effective 1 June 1965 other orgs.)

No mailing may be made without a complete sample of the entire mailing being okayed by myself at Saint Hill.

No booklet or brochure may be given or handed out without being okayed for *that specific purpose* by myself.

No Letter Registrar may mail bits or pieces in letters without their being specifically okayed for that purpose by myself.

No insert may be placed in certificate mailings such as a pamphlet or brochure without my specific okay *for that purpose.*

Previously, Letter Registrars and Dir Promotion and Registration have chosen out bits and pamphlets to mail people at their own discretion. This is cancelled. Any such presentation must first be okayed *for that purpose.*

That a booklet exists or has been printed is *not* an okay for its general use.

Any printed booklet or book must be okayed before being used for a specific purpose.

This means that booklets and handouts may not be indiscriminately released. One may not place them in with certificates or mailings unless they are okayed to be used for that purpose.

Booklets, etc., may not be handed around at congresses or in PEs unless they have been okayed.

SUBMISSION FOR OKAY

The entire packet that is to be mailed or handed out or put in with a certificate must be packaged up the way it will be assembled and passed to me via the Office of LRH Saint Hill.

Mark it—Office of LRH Saint Hill—Issue Authority Section.

Do not send a pamphlet and ask if it is "okay to release it." State what it is to be released with or how it is to be released.

All permissions granted are for *a specific use* of the material. That an item has been given a specific permission for a specified use does not grant permission to use it as anything else. If it is to be used for anything else, a new permission must be asked.

All permissions granted will be issued as Sec EDs and expire, like all Sec EDs, in one year.

MAGAZINES

Every issue of a magazine must be passed upon in dummy form. *Two* dummies must be submitted. One is kept; the other returned.

A copy of the finished magazine must be sent to the Office of LRH, Issue Authority Section.

BOOKS

Books which may be advertised and sold must first be passed upon by the Issue Authority Section.

This includes all books, those by myself and others.

REPRINTING BOOKS

Any book to be reprinted must have an authority from the Issue Authority Section.

In requesting a reprint authority, sales data on the book during the past year must be included.

Several new books are to be issued and they may replace some old ones.

Some old books are to be rewritten.

"Unauthorized issue" means that the material does not have an authority for that purpose and is a misdemeanor.

Coordination of issue makes it possible to assess values of various materials and bring greater effectiveness of presentation.

L. RON HUBBARD
Founder

HCO POLICY LETTER OF 26 APRIL 1965

Remimeo
Post

SEC ED ISSUE

No Secretarial Executive Director may be issued unless specifically directed by myself.

Any Sec ED issued in the past which was not by my direct order is cancelled herewith.

L. RON HUBBARD
Founder

HCO POLICY LETTER OF 8 MAY 1965
Issue I

Remimeo

CANCELLATION OF ASSORTED DIRECTIVES

All administrative letters, continental letters, continental directives, administrative orders, directions, advices and any other issue of any officer or executive of Scientology, written or verbal, are cancelled as of this date.

Only Secretarial Executive Directors issued after 1 March 1965 are in force.

Only HCOBs and policy letters are in force. HCOBs and HCO Policy Letters are not cancelled.

Secretarial Executive Directors issued after 1 March 1965 are not cancelled.

This policy letter expressly takes out of force any order or arrangement, written or verbal, of any Scientology executive other than myself.

Therefore, any arrangements or orders or directives of executives prior to this date should be reviewed by the issuing executive now on post and submitted to the Office of LRH, Saint Hill, for review before again being issued.

This does not in any way influence the current routine orders given to staffs after this date.

The reason for this policy letter is to clear away any outstanding plans or orders or "policies" unknown to myself, if any exist, so that new hats and the new org board can be put in smoothly without contradiction between old executive orders and new policy.

The standard, long-standing policies issued in HCO Policy Letters signed only by myself remain in force where applicable.

Technology, issued in HCOBs, signed by myself, remains unchanged.

NEW DIRECTIVES

No new admin letters of a planning or continued nature may be hereafter issued without clearance from the Office of LRH.

L. RON HUBBARD
Founder

HCO POLICY LETTER OF 13 SEPTEMBER 1965
Issue II

St Hill Only

ISSUE AUTHORITY REQUIRED FOR MIMEO

"Okay needed from Issue Authority" means an okay is needed for *all* things run through the mimeo machine, whether okayed previously to be mimeoed or not.

The objects are twofold:

1. To save on mimeo paper, and

2. To keep my mimeo policy and technical lines from being jammed. If too much is put on these lines, the line is cut just because it's too much for people to read at the other end.

HCO Policy Letters, HCO Bulletins and HCO Executive Letters are especially my lines. These are never "by the authority of" mimeo signatures. No mission info issued by the Mission Officer here is ever put on HCO Policy color flash or title.

There are HCO admin channels, other flash systems, etc., for things that bear "by the authority of."

The reissue of a policy letter requires Issue Authority okay.

Providing extra copies of anything requires Issue Authority okay.

In addition, nobody else puts anything on HCO Policy Letter, HCO Bulletin or HCO Exec Letter except myself over my own signature without any "by the authority of." These are my own personal lines. When they appear in orgs, they can be picked out easily from other mail and mimeos. I try to keep the quantity down to keep from jamming people's lines. Therefore, anyone else putting traffic on these lines is unappreciated. They have other color flash anyway.

In filing, designation of where they were sent does not place them in a different file. HCO Bulletins, HCO PLs and HCO Executive Letters all go chronologically. Saint Hill is not separate.

And no matter what color flash or designation a mimeo has and whether old or new or whether a stencil exists or not, before it goes into the Roneo it needs Issue Authority okay.

L. RON HUBBARD
Founder

HUBBARD COMMUNICATIONS OFFICE
Saint Hill Manor, East Grinstead, Sussex

HCO POLICY LETTER OF 2 NOVEMBER 1965
Issue II

Sthil
Staff Only

FAST LINE SEC EDs AND
ADMIN ORDERS

Sec EDs are to be picked up straight from Ron's basket and body routed by LRH Communicator to HCO Steno.

HCO Steno is to body route to Division Comm Centers as soon as they are run off.

Anybody disturbing HCO Steno for any reason whatsoever while she is dealing with a Sec ED or an Admin Order will be chitted for job endangerment.

HCO Admin Orders are to be body routed to HCO Steno.

HCO Steno is to body route to Division Comm Centers immediately they are run off.

This line is to be put into effect immediately to speed up issue of Sec EDs and HCO Admin Orders to divisions.

L. RON HUBBARD
Founder

HCO POLICY LETTER OF 3 FEBRUARY 1966
Issue IV

Remimeo
LRH Comm Hat
Exec Sec Hat

SEC ED

CHANGE IN ISSUE AND USE

Any Sec ED written personally by the Executive Director will hereafter be

WHITE PAPER
BLUE INK

Those Sec EDs issued for and on *behalf* of the Executive Director by Executive Secretaries or the Ad Council will remain

BLUE PAPER
BLUE INK

but will be signed

ADVISORY COUNCIL (Location)
for the Executive Director (Location)

or

HCO Exec Sec or Org Exec Sec
for the Executive Director (Location)

All Sec EDs for Ad Comms or Secretaries are

DIVISION COLOR PAPER
BLUE INK

and are signed by the named Ad Comm or Secretary "for the Executive Director (Location)."

The LRH Communicator of the area may sign and okay for issue any Sec ED for the area providing only it is not contrary to policy or orders from a higher org or the Int Exec Div (WW) or the Exec Dir.

No Sec ED or executive orders of any kind may be issued without an okay by the LRH Communicator, and ALL general orders of the Ad Council or an Executive Secretary *must* be in Sec ED form and *all* general orders of Ad Comms or Secretaries must be passed by the Ad Council of that org and issued as Sec EDs with LRH Comm okay.

WW Sec EDs take precedence over local Sec EDs where there is any conflict or question of importance, and Sec EDs written by the Exec Dir (white ones) take precedence over all others.

Sec EDs retain their traditional forms and seals.

A COPY OF EVERY SEC ED ISSUED MUST BE SENT TO WW.

This policy letter cancels executive orders of divisions or orgs issued in any other form than Sec EDs.

Direct orders to specific posts in own portion of an org need not be in Sec ED form but any extensive project must be.

Directors may issue general orders and projects only as Sec EDs by the Secretary in the fashion described above for Secretaries and only with the approval of their Secretaries.

L. RON HUBBARD
Founder

HCO POLICY LETTER OF 3 FEBRUARY 1966
Issue V

Remimeo
Ad Council Hats
Exec Sec Hats
Ad Comm Hats
Secretary Hats
LRH Comm Hat
HCO Area Sec Hat
HCO Steno Hat

ALL DIVISIONS

SEC EDS

DEFINITION AND PURPOSE

CROSS-DIVISIONAL ORDERS

In a Sec ED neither an Advisory Committee nor a secretary may order another division than their own.

An Executive Secretary may issue a Sec ED that crosses divisions but only those divisions directly under that Executive Secretary (HCO Exec Sec Sec EDs may only order the two HCO divisions; Org Exec Sec Sec EDs may only order the four org divisions).

The Advisory Council Sec EDs may order HCO and org divisions at the same time.

Advisory Councils, in approving the text of Sec EDs before passing them on to the LRH Communicator for an okay to issue, should be very careful to see that no Ad Comm issues Sec EDs to other divisions than their own.

The LRH Communicator, in authorizing the issue of a Sec ED, should be careful that this policy letter is not violated.

No Sec ED of any kind may be issued unless it has been authorized by the LRH Communicator, and any violation of issue authority should be reported to the LRH Communicator WW who is to refer it to the Ad Council WW for action.

Sec EDs improperly issued have no validity and need not be obeyed and may not be used for hearings or Comm Evs.

The meaning of the word *Sec ED* is "Secretarial to the Executive Director." The word "Secretarial" applies to the signature, meaning it is signed as official *by* a person other than LRH personally. It is the written initials in the lower left-hand corner that are "secretarial."

The system came into use to accommodate cable orders originally. By being sealed and initialed by an official person like a notary public in the org, the validity of the order was attested as a valid order of LRH.

Approval by an Advisory Council or an Exec Sec and authorization by the LRH Communicator for issue are now both required before the secretarial official in HCO (usually the HCO Steno) may seal, initial and issue the order. It is *this* person who requires that the Ad Council or an Exec Sec *and* the LRH Communicator's initials appear on the original copy before she may type, seal and initial and then publish a Sec ED.

The HCO Steno may *not* issue any Sec ED today which does not have the initials of the Ad Council or an Exec Sec *and* the initials of the LRH Communicator on it or unless it is in the handwriting of LRH or has come off the telex or through the mails from WW and is a valid communication from proper persons there. The LRH Communicator WW must be the transmitting authority from WW and must initial any despatch or telex before transmission that is to become a Sec ED at the other end. The HCO Steno must look for this before issuing. Her guide is that if the LRH Communicator's initials are not on it she may not issue it, excepting only it being in the handwriting of LRH or personally transmitted by him.

Sec EDs are fast orders and have top priority in transmission and execution. They take precedence over all other orders both in transmission speed and execution.

The priority of Sec EDs is as follows:

LRH personally written or personally sent
Sec ED Ad Council WW
Sec ED Exec Sec WW
Sec ED Ad Council Area
Sec ED Exec Sec Area
Sec ED Ad Comm Area
Sec ED Secretary Area.

The penalty for not complying with a Sec ED is a misdemeanor and must result in an Executive Ethics Hearing or an Ethics Hearing.

If Executive Secretaries in an area fail to respond to WW Sec EDs, they are usually scheduled for early removal by WW.

Sec EDs have the virtue of making orders known and getting them on file where they can be referred to by other than the recipient.

The *only* answers to a Sec ED if one isn't going to do it are:

1. An immediate petition to LRH on Sec EDs issued by LRH personally, or

2. A job endangerment chit immediately filed in Ethics.

If this step is lacking and it is found that a Sec ED has not been complied with, then an Executive Ethics Hearing or an Ethics Hearing MUST follow when the noncompliance is discovered.

Every single major Danger condition at Saint Hill in 1965 was found to have had as its source the noncompliance with a Sec ED. If this policy seems unduly harsh then add up that fact. Some of these Danger conditions involved day and night work by top brass. And every one of them would have been prevented had Ethics had this attitude toward noncompliance with a Sec ED. The cost of these noncompliances ran above £10,000, and they threatened the very existence of Scientology. And each one would have been prevented had Sec EDs been complied with. From this, one should regard noncompliance with a Sec ED without instantly petitioning or filing a chit for job endangerment as something one does just before taking the arsenic.

The *only* thing that holds down the size of Scientology today is simply noncompliance. The only thing that makes trouble is noncompliance.

The Sec ED system is designed to make orders public and get them complied with fast.

Conversely, if the order wasn't in a Sec ED or policy letter, it does not have Ethics force—that is to say, one can't be seriously tried for it.

All current projects and programs should be in Sec EDs so people know what they are. Those written in despatches only are written in sand.

Sec EDs can be confidential and of limited issue.

Sec EDs expire one year from their date of issue if not sooner by reason of their text.

If a Sec ED is to be preserved beyond a year, it must be converted into a policy letter by sending it to LRH.

The Director of Inspections and Reports is responsible for routinely checking the Sec ED file for noncompliances and when found must forward the matter to Ethics for prompt action.

L. RON HUBBARD
Founder

HUBBARD COMMUNICATIONS OFFICE
Saint Hill Manor, East Grinstead, Sussex

HCO POLICY LETTER OF 13 FEBRUARY 1966
Issue II

Remimeo
All Exec Hats

SEC EDs
SEC ED OKAY (CONTINUED)
POLICY LETTER CHANGES AND ORIGINS

"SEC ED" = Secretarially signed order of the Executive Director, expiring one year from date of issue.

"POLICY LETTER" = A letter laying down policy, continuing until cancelled by a new policy letter.

The Executive Secretaries may not change or edit a secretary's or Ad Comm's Sec ED but may only pass or send it back with comments.

A secretary likewise may not change another lower executive's Sec ED in the secretary's division but must only pass it on or send it back with comments.

An Executive Secretary or a secretary may have a job endangerment chit filed for refusing to pass a Sec ED an executive believes vital to uphold his or her statistic, with a full explanation of why.

The LRH Communicator may refuse to pass a Sec ED only if it is against policy, and if so, then the full reference of *what* policy letter or Sec ED it violates must be furnished with the refusal. This means, of course, that an LRH Communicator must be well up on policy. Nebulous "It's against policy" is a violation of the LRH Comm's instructions from me.

If no policy concerning such a Sec ED is known to exist yet the Sec ED seems to the LRH Communicator to put the org at risk, the Sec ED must be cabled to the LRH Comm WW for further advices.

If by refusing to issue a Sec ED an executive's statistic becomes bad and if this is traced beyond reasonable doubt in any resulting hearing on that executive, the LRH Communicator must be given a hearing.

On the other hand, if a Sec ED is passed by an LRH Communicator that is clearly against published policy letters and results in dropped statistics, then, if any hearing occurs on the executives whose statistics dropped, the LRH Communicator must be made an interested party.

THEORY

The theory operating here is that Sec EDs are supposed to improve statistics and that one cannot hold an executive responsible for his or her statistic if that executive's orders are prevented from being issued.

An executive worth anything at all will issue specific orders to remedy a dropped statistic or reinforce a climbing one, and as that executive is awarded or penalized only on the basis of the statistics he or she is responsible for, interference with his or her orders can be serious.

Seniors usually *advise* a more-junior executive who is doing normally. One who is not gets into a Danger condition easily, and so specific orders must be originated that bypass his authority. Advising a junior who is in Affluence is pretty silly unless one simply says he better find out why and keep doing it.

One can always quote actual policy letters or bulletins at any level with no fear of making a Danger condition unless one is quoting inapplicable material.

POLICY LETTER ORIGINATION

If an executive is going to be hung for a statistic, then he is entitled to give the orders up to a point where the org is endangered. At that moment, of course, he or she goes into Danger condition.

An executive can always even originate a policy letter or one that cancels an impeding policy letter or Sec ED if he or she thinks it will help his statistic.

An originated cancellation of a policy letter or a new policy letter must go to the Qual Sec for opinion and then the HCO Area Sec and then the Advisory Council, and any changes needed must be noted, and it must be sent back to the originator at any stage for rewrite before it can go to the LRH Communicator and so on to LRH.

L. RON HUBBARD
Founder

HCO POLICY LETTER OF 10 AUGUST 1966

Gen. Non-Remimeo

EXECUTIVE DIRECTOR SEC EDs

All Executive Director Sec EDs are to be typed and run off by Mimeo Worldwide. They are to be distributed by HCO Steno Saint Hill immediately upon receipt from Mimeo WW.

Executive Director Sec EDs are a fast, fast, fast line and take priority over any other issue. It is, therefore, expected that any Sec ED will be typed, run off and completely distributed within one hour of receipt. Any failure to issue an Executive Director Sec ED or any stop anywhere on this line will be considered a crime, if not a high crime.

It is the responsibility of the LRH Communicator Worldwide to see that this line is kept moving at a fast rate of speed and to report any failures to issue or stops on this line to Ethics who must immediately take ethics actions to remove the person responsible for the stopped line from his post.

Sec EDs which have not originated from the Executive Director go to HCO Steno for typing, running off and distribution.

L. RON HUBBARD
Founder

HCO POLICY LETTER OF 20 OCTOBER 1966
Issue I

Remimeo

SIGNATURES OF POLICY LETTERS

(Modifies any existing policy re
signature only of policy letters.)

Any policy letter I have not personally written must bear the signatures of:

1. The actual composer

2. Each passing agency or identity required to make it legal.

This may mean as many as five or six names may be signed to policy letters I did not personally write.

The reason for this is that a recent policy letter that violated six major policies re ethics was slipped through and not questioned due to bearing my name, whereas I had never seen it and it did not pass through the required approval lines.

L. RON HUBBARD
Founder

HCO POLICY LETTER OF 22 MAY 1968
Issue III

Remimeo
BPI

TRANSLATIONS

I have solved the principle of the translation of books, which is as follows.

The Scientology words themselves are not translated. The definition of the Scientology word is put in the foreign language but the word itself, like engram, is not translated.

In translating, the Scientology word is put in italics (the first time it is used in the text) and the definition in the foreign language follows it in parenthesis. A glossary of terms is then put in the back of the book giving the Scientology words in alphabetical order with their definitions, as already defined the first time they appeared in the text.

This means that these foreign languages will have a Scientologese vocabulary of 400 or 500 words that have to be learned by students studying the books and materials in the foreign languages. They learn them as completely arbitrary symbols and therefore no misunderstoods can occur (unless somebody misdefines them).

L. RON HUBBARD
Founder

HCO POLICY LETTER OF 12 FEBRUARY 1969

CenOCon
Public Exec Secs
Executive Councils
LRH Comms

RELIGION

Visual evidences that Scientology is a religion are mandatory on the PES.

Any staff who are trained at any level as auditors (but not in AOs) are to be clothed in the traditional ministerial black suit, black vest, white collar, silver cross for ordinary org wear.

Creed of the Church is to be done big and plainly posted in public areas.

Stationery is to reflect the fact that orgs are churches.

All public literature must state that Scientology is religious philosophy.

Since its first incorporation as HASI Arizona all orgs have been religious fellowships by corporation statements.

All orgs are now churches by their Church of Scientology of California affiliation.

The Minister's Course is a requisite for permanent certification.

The legal decisions handed down on Scientology by US high courts uphold it as a religion.

It has never been anything else. It seeks SPIRITUAL FREEDOM.

This may or may not be publicly acceptable. This is NOT the point. It is a requisite defense and it is true. Those are the points.

Reinforce this in all possible ways.

L. RON HUBBARD
Founder

HUBBARD COMMUNICATIONS OFFICE
Saint Hill Manor, East Grinstead, Sussex

HCO POLICY LETTER OF 3 DECEMBER 1969
Issue II

Exec Councils
LRH Comms
Mission Holders
Gung-ho Groups
Dissem Secs

ISSUE AUTHORITY FOR TRANSLATIONS
OF DIANETICS AND SCIENTOLOGY MATERIALS

No bulletin, tape or book may be published in any form in a foreign language without obtaining issue authority.

Issue authority for such is held by LRH Comm, Pubs Org, to whom all translations must be sent for approval before printing or mimeoing.

This also applies to quotations and excerpts from Dianetics and Scientology materials which are made up into handouts and info packs.

Each and every application for issue authority for a translation must be accompanied by an attestation by a Class VI, VII or VIII Auditor that the materials contain exact duplication of technology without addition or alter-is.

No matter how expert the translator is who did the translation, the attestation by a trained Scientology auditor must accompany it or it will not be granted issue authority.

This policy is retroactive and any bulletins, tapes or books which have been translated but not granted issue authority must be resubmitted for issue authority. When issued they must also be copyrighted and bear the line "© by L. Ron Hubbard." The purpose of this policy letter is to ensure that all foreign-language students of Dianetics and Scientology have the benefits of standard tech.

L. RON HUBBARD
Founder

HCO POLICY LETTER OF 24 SEPTEMBER 1970RA
REVISED 3 JULY 1977

Remimeo
All Hats

ISSUES—TYPES OF

To clarify the value and distribution of various major types of mimeo issues, the following summary is made.

HCO PL—Hubbard Communications Office Policy Letter. Written by LRH only. This is a permanently valid issue of all third dynamic, org and administrative technology. These, regardless of date or age, form the know-how in running an org or group or company. The bulk of hat material is made up from HCO PLs. They are printed in green ink on white paper. They are filed by consecutive date. More than one issued on the same date are marked Issue I, II, III, etc. Every org must have full master and bulk files of these or it won't be able to make up hats or hat packs for staff or know what it's doing and will fail. Stencil files to replenish supplies of HCO PLs are also kept. It took 20 years to find out how to run orgs. It's all in HCO PLs. HCO PLs are distributed to all staffs or as indicated or as made up in packs.

HCOBs—Hubbard Communications Office Bulletins. Written by LRH only. These are the technical issue line. They are valid from first issue unless specifically cancelled. All data for auditing and courses is contained in HCOBs. An org needs a master file of them (and their stencil file) from which to prepare course packs. These outline the product of the org. They are distributed as indicated, usually to technical staff. They are red ink on white paper, consecutive by date.

TAPES—These are an issue line of both policy and tech as designated and are recopied at Pubs Org and issued for courses, congresses and other purposes.

LRH EDs—L. Ron Hubbard Executive Directives, earlier called Sec EDs. These are issues by LRH to various areas. They are not valid longer than one year if fully complied with when they are automatically retired. They otherwise remain valid until fully complied with or until amended or cancelled by another LRH ED. They carry current line, projects, programs, immediate orders and directions. They are numbered for area and sequence for the area and are sent to staffs or specific posts in orgs. They are blue ink on white paper with a special heading.

The above are the four main lines of issue of valid data. They have first priority on mimeo and in distribution.

Red, green or blue ink on white paper indicates my material only. No other mimeos may be issued using these color schemes. This is to separate out my material and make it easily identifiable. Experience shows org stats and public results soar immediately on implementation of LRH EDs, HCOBs and HCO PLs.

BOARD ISSUES—BPLs (Board Policy Letters), BTBs (Board Technical Bulletins), BEDs (Board Executive Directives). These are similar in content to HCO PLs, HCOBs and LRH EDs respectively, but are written by someone other than LRH and issued on Flag by or for the boards of directors of the Churches of Scientology. BPLs and BTBs are valid until cancelled or revised. BEDs are valid for one year after which they expire unless cancelled before that. Distribution of board issues is as indicated. They are printed on buff paper with green ink for BPLs, red for BTBs and dark blue for BEDs.

HCO ADMIN LETTERS—Issued by HCO personnel from Flag with AVU okay. Green on salmon. Contain checklists of issues, admin data of an informative nature. Do not contain policy or orders. Distributed as designated.

EDs—Executive Directives. Issued by any Executive Council and named for the area it applies to. Thus ED WW, meaning issued to Worldwide. They are valid for only one year. They contain various immediate orders, programs, etc. They are blue ink on blue paper.

DIVISIONAL ORDERS—Each division has its own order line to its staffs or to its opposite numbered divisions. The order is followed by the place and org name. The paper is color-flashed for the division.

SEA ORG ORDERS

All Sea Org issues not written by LRH other than MOs (not FMOs), COs, SSOs and OODs must be authorized by AVU before issue and are issued for the boards of directors of the Churches of Scientology.

FO—FLAG ORDER. This is the equivalent to a policy letter in the Sea Org. Contains policy and sea technical materials. They are numbered and dated. They do not decay. HCO PLs and FOs are both in effect on Sea Org orgs, ships, offices and bases. Black ink on white paper. Distribution to all Sea Org members. It is vital for SO units to have master files and quantity of FOs from which HATS can be made up for SO personnel and courses.

CBO—CENTRAL BUREAUX ORDER. Applies to SO bureaux. It is distributed to bureaux personnel and SO org executives only. Usually noted under heading to what bureau it refers. Issued by the head of a central bureau at Flag. Black on white. Has no force on nonbureaux personnel. These regulate the organization and activity of SO bureaux and their offices. Bureaux need master files for bureaux hats.

BO—BASE ORDER. Has been used interchangeably for Flag Order. FOs started as Base Orders. Occasionally erroneously used at bases. Should be a CO (Continental Order) when locally issued. These are filed by area in consecutive number sequence in their own files.

SO ED—SEA ORG EXECUTIVE DIRECTIVE. Distributed broadly or not to SO and/or Scientology orgs and binding on both. Usually issued by Flag management personnel. Contains immediate orders or programs. Blue on blue paper.

FDD—FLAG DIVISIONAL DIRECTIVE. Applies to specific divisions in Scn and SO orgs alike. Is the SO equivalent of a Divisional Order. Is senior to a WW Divisional Order. Issued by a Flag Aide. Printed on divisional color flash.

FCO—FLAG CONDITIONS ORDER. Is the equivalent of a Scn org HCO Div Order such as an Ethics Order. Distributed only to those concerned and Masters-at-Arms (Ethics Files).

FMO—FLAG MISSION ORDER. Distributed to those concerned, not to others. Usually confidential. Should never be shown around or sent to Bureaux Liaison Offices not concerned with that mission.

MO—MISSION ORDER. Issued by a Flag Operations Liaison Office under authority of its Commanding Officer. Confidential, no further distribution than those concerned and copy to Flag.

FSO—FLAG SHIP ORDER. Never goes off Flag. Full distribution to Flag Ship's personnel.

SSO—STATION SHIP ORDER. Issued for that station ship only by the Captain or Deputy Captain. Goes to all personnel of that ship and a copy to Flag.

CO—CONTINENTAL ORDER. Issued by Continental Captain or the Commanding Officer of a FOLO. Distribution is all SO personnel in the area.

AO—AIDES ORDER. Covers EXTERNAL matters having to do with FOLOs and outer orgs. Usually contains evaluations by myself or Flag management personnel. The program of an evaluation is sometimes issued as an FPGMO. Issued to senior executives on Flag and personnel concerned. They are numbered by area to which they apply.

FPGMO—FLAG PROGRAM ORDER. Issued on Flag for internal or external use. Contains long- or short-range production programs which are usually the entirety or major part of the handling of a published evaluation. Distributed as designated. Numbered by area to which they apply.

FPJO—FLAG PROJECT ORDER. Issued on Flag to execute a target in a program. Like FPGMOs, FPJOs are issued on Flag for internal or external use. Distributed as designated. Numbered by area to which they apply.

FPO—FLAG PERSONNEL ORDER. Contains all personnel transfers, removals, postings, etc., on Flag and ordered by Flag in orgs. Issued only by Flag. Composed per HCO PL 24 Sept. 71, ASSIGNMENT, MODEL TO BE USED. Distributed to those concerned.

TIPs—TECHNICAL INDIVIDUAL PROGRAMS. Originated so that personal programs for students and pcs coming to Flag may be issued and published. Numbered and dated. More than one program can be on one issue. They are on GREEN paper on one side of a page so they can be cut up. Distributed only to those concerned.

FBDLs—FLAG BUREAUX DATA LETTERS. Issued by a Flag executive to COs/EDs, FRs and Flag execs. Their purpose is TO INFORM EXECUTIVES. May contain news, forewarnings of traffic loads, expansions, PR interest items. Essentially they are newsletters. They are numbered. Printed in black ink on white paper. (Formerly they were blue ink on white paper.)

OOD—ORDERS OF THE DAY. Issued by any Commanding Officer to his own unit daily and may contain current activities, Ethics Orders, etc., by others. Contains the schedule of the day. Serves as a crew briefing.

(OODs are also put out to their own orgs by Executive Directors or Executive Councils in Scn orgs.)

Of *all* types of SO orders only the FO is carefully preserved and masterfiled, as it is HAT material vital to the efficiency, comfort and safety of the crews.

HCO PLs and HCOB master files are also required in SO units, making only three vital files and can be locally reproduced with stencils preserved.

All SO issues are black ink on white except the SO ED, FDD and TIP. HCO PL and HCOB color flash is preserved in SO master files.

Note that all SO issues except FOs and CBOs decay within the year and have no continuous validity.

WRONG PUBLIC

The reason why there are so many types of orders is to separate publics. Tapes are often used to wrong publics than which intended and should be watched on this basis.

––––––––––

It is not difficult to separate out the various orders. It is mainly of interest to distribution and Mimeo and files personnel that very correct identification of different types of orders occur and for staffs to understand the relative command value of what they are receiving.

L. RON HUBBARD
Founder

Revision assisted by
LRH Comm Policy Revision
Project I/C

[*Editor's Note:* A more complete list of mimeo issues is included in the appendix of OEC Volume 0.]

DESIGN AND PLANNING

Sthil

No changes of positions of desks, rooms or quarters may be done without my okay first.

L. RON HUBBARD
Founder

HCO POLICY LETTER OF 19 DECEMBER 1960

SPATIAL REORGANIZATION

The introduction of testing as a public service has made it necessary to totally reorganize office spatial locations in the Johannesburg buildings.

The actual test room has been placed nearest the street, with Reception and Registration deeper into the building. Body Registrars, D of P and Processing Admin, Accounts and Security have all been placed on one corridor so that all body traffic is centralized.

It has been found that the typing pool, CF, Address and the Letter Registrar (see HCO PL 18 Dec. 60, CF AND ADDRESS CHANGE) and probably test evaluation by mail all comprise a single unit which need not occupy any forward space but might even go into a distant building to save space. Their lines have no close relation to other activities if so packaged.

The Association Sec's office has been placed well away from the public traffic lines.

The D of T can be close to classrooms but remote from Reception. Training Admin, extension course should be with D of T and remote from reception.

So long as the test room is nearest the street and so long as Reception, Body Registrar interview offices, D of P and its admin and Accounts are all grouped, body traffic can be handled easily.

Johannesburg is doing better on internal comm with its Comm Center in the mail room and its despatches distributed to all Central Org persons by a communicator four to six times per day. Reception is too crowded for a Comm Center now. The entire Comm Center basket system of the org can be anywhere handy to the Communicator rather than org personnel.

HCO, its files, book shipping, etc., needed no change. An HCO Area Sec needs to be near activities similar to the Association (Org) Sec but need not be very prominently placed in the org.

I invite you to restudy your placements in view of the above and to shift things as needed.

If you run out of space, put Letter Reg, CF and Address right out of the immediate quarters. They can be miles away. If you run out of space again, shift HCO, its shipping, filing and my office elsewhere.

Also, you have *expensive* space in every auditing room in the Central Org. In a press it would be wiser, as I have done in Johannesburg, to wipe out all auditing in the Central Org buildings and rent cheap auditing rooms outside, giving HGC Admin a cubicle for case assessments in a lounge outside the D of P's small office.

Beware always giving great space to executives such as the Association Sec, PE Director or D of T. The Body Registrars, Testing, Reception and service rooms (for PE, co-audit, anatomy training) have priority any time.

The whole Academy can be peeled off. All auditing rooms can be gotten elsewhere. The D of P and his admin cannot be and must be near the Registrars, as Accounts must be.

L. RON HUBBARD
Founder

Sthil

FURNITURE AND QUARTERS

All quarters assignment for housing, training, administration or whatever purpose at Saint Hill may be assigned or changed only with my permission.

Furniture may be rearranged or positioned only with my permission.

A despatch to me will suffice if returned with an authorization initialed by me.

L. RON HUBBARD
Founder

HCO POLICY LETTER OF 25 JULY 1966

Remimeo
HCO Area Sec
RAP Hats
Receptionist

(Adds to HCO PL 22 Oct. 62, THEORY
OF SCIENTOLOGY ORGANIZATIONS)

ALLOCATION OF QUARTERS
ARRANGEMENT OF DESKS AND EQUIPMENT

In allocating quarters and arranging the desks and equipment of the personnel who are to use them, it is essential to analyze the particle flows to be handled by these personnel: What particles does each post handle, where do these particles come from, what does this post do with them and where do the particles go from there.

Example: All types of particles from the public enter the org through Reception. Thus, the space allocated to Reception should be easily accessible to the street; the channel to it should be clearly marked and there should be nothing along this channel which would stop or distract the flow of particles to Reception. Within the Reception area itself, the Receptionist's desk should be so placed that it is clearly visible from the entry and there should be no barriers or distractions between it and the entry; thus, incoming particles will naturally flow to it as the first barrier in their path.

What Reception does with these particles is discover their proper destination in the org and route them to it, as well as give persons entering the org recognition. Thus, Reception's space must have in it a public bulletin board and notices of services, book display and the like; and space and chairs, etc., for bodies to wait in if their destination terminal is not immediately available.

Reception's highest priority particles are incoming public bodies, and these go mostly to Registrar and/or Accounts from Reception. Thus, Registrar and Accounts should be easily accessible—preferably adjacent—to Reception, and clear channels should exist between Reception and them.

Incorrect allocations of space and/or placement of desks and equipment therein slow, confuse and even lose traffic. Example: An org had its public bulletin board, some chairs and a magazine stand in the hallway leading to its Reception area, out of view of the Receptionist. An inestimable amount of body traffic was lost by this arrangement—inestimable simply because these items stopped the flow and Receptionist never saw many of the bodies that came in the door.

It would be wise for any org to review its allocation of space and arrangement of desks and equipment in terms of particle flows as above as a routine action once every six months or so.

L. RON HUBBARD
Founder

HUBBARD COMMUNICATIONS OFFICE
Saint Hill Manor, East Grinstead, Sussex

HCO POLICY LETTER OF 27 JULY 1966

Remimeo
Promo Planning
Dept 9 Hats
Div 2 Hats

MOVING

The location of an organization is an orientation point for the public and should not be moved unless necessary.

If it *is* necessary, then care must be taken to maintain it as an orientation point nonetheless.

This is done by (1) maintaining predictability of location and (2) maintaining high-volume outflow.

The new location is announced the moment the new quarters are found and approximate date of occupancy is known and the move is promoted as a sign of expansion. The essence of these promotional pieces is that we're right here giving full service and expanding; in (time period) we'll be right here (new location) giving full service with (more, better, more convenient—whatever can be truthfully said) space and facilities.

When the exact date of occupancy is known, an open evening is planned and promoted for the first weekend in the new quarters and each weekend thereafter for at least one month; these are continued after the move until body flow for routine activities exceeds what it was in the old quarters.

It is also important to plan the move itself for the least possible disruption of services.

L. RON HUBBARD
Founder

HCO POLICY LETTER OF 5 NOVEMBER 1968R
REVISED 8 FEBRUARY 1989

Remimeo

SPACE ALLOCATION

(Reissued from Flag Order 1549R, same date)

A place is best planned by the org board. You put Div 7 way out of the traffic lines, up or back. You put HCO Divs 1 and 2 near their own entrance, compact and up tight to it.

You put Div 3 close up to Div 2 with a Cashier over on public lines.

You spread Div 4 over the *bulk* of your space, Tech Services close to public lines, Dept of Training and HGC using up the *bulk* of your space. Students should have their own entrance.

The Public Divisions provide a circular in and out with their own entrance.

Service space (Training, Processing and Qual) always have the bulk of an org's space.

L. RON HUBBARD
Founder

Revision assisted by
LRH Technical Research
and Compilations

HUBBARD COMMUNICATIONS OFFICE
Saint Hill Manor, East Grinstead, Sussex

HCO POLICY LETTER OF 6 DECEMBER 1978

Remimeo
Org Officers
Estates Managers
Design and
    Planning

SPACE PLANNING

(Originally written by LRH as FO 3736,
same title, on 6 Dec. 78. Issued as an
HCO Policy Letter on 21 Jan. 82.)

Ref:
HCO PL   5 Nov. 68R   SPACE ALLOCATION
    Rev. 8.2.89

Three factors in space planning:

1. Flow lines,

2. Location of functions so they agree with flow lines,

3. Expansion.

Consequences of not doing this are that people won't follow it and they'll locate everything else when in actual use and you'll have a dog's breakfast.

Maybe even worse than you would have unless you left it all unplanned in the first place.

Another consequence is the place goes out of communication with itself internally and won't function.

In the above are the three stable datums and if not followed it will cost you your shirt in terms of lost income and lost time.

L. RON HUBBARD
Founder

ESTATES BRANCH

Dir of Materiel Hat
Materiel Admin Hat
Org Sec Hat
HCO Area Sec Hat

18 February 1959

THERMOSTATS IN BUILDINGS

Only the Director of Materiel may set, change or touch *any* thermostat in any Founding Church building. This includes coolers, furnaces, refrigerators and any other item.

L. RON HUBBARD
Founder

HUBBARD COMMUNICATIONS OFFICE
Saint Hill Manor, East Grinstead, Sussex

HCO BULLETIN OF 18 JANUARY 1960

Saint Hill Only

ZONES OF AUTHORITY
AND REGULATIONS OF SAINT HILL

Three zones of authority are established herewith: Household, Grounds, and Office.

Household includes the care of the house, care of the children, preparation and serving of all meals, care of quarters, ordering of food, all Project Ten functions, laundry, and all persons performing these functions. This is the zone of the *Housekeeper.*

All personnel procurement for these posts and the award of any bonuses for these persons is done by the Housekeeper. This is my own domestic staff but cares for other persons living in by extension. The following posts are included in this department: chef, nanny, serving and kitchen personnel, cleaning personnel, laundress, maids, valet, etc.

Grounds includes all care of outside grounds, glasshouses, roads, paths, gardens, lakes and ponds, lawns, seeds, trees, plants and shrubs, fences, gates, sporting areas and sports equipment, vehicles, implements, tools, supplies, construction, repair and maintenance, electrical, building supplies, etc. This is the zone of the *Grounds Manager*. It includes only construction, repair, maintenance, furnaces, fuel and electrical where the interior of the house is concerned. The following personnel come under the *Grounds Manager:* maintenance man, gardener, chauffeur, artisans, laborers and contractors.

The Office includes all executive, clerical and communication functions, and contains such personnel as the HCO Technical Secretary, the Mission Secretary, the HCO Communicator, the HCO Steno, Accounts, the Book Section, *Certainty,* LRH personal secretarial and public relations, and any other office personnel. This post area includes all equipment and supplies, and the repair or ordering thereof. The transaction of all HCO business is handled by the office. The HCO Administrator is in charge of the office. In his absence the post is filled by the HCO Secretary WW.

The bonus system by projects is abandoned by reason of lack of personnel. In its place is instituted a very occasional bonus whenever a particularly good week is had by HCO.

A sum amounting to 10 shillings, £1, or £2 will be issued individually at the discretion of the Housekeeper, Grounds Manager, and HCO Secretary to their staffs. I will authorize the bonus. It will then be up to the supervisors of the three areas to say which of their people get how much of the sum allocated. Those who have worked well for their manager will receive more than others. I will allocate the amount given to the supervisors for themselves. They will allocate what should be given to those in their zones.

As I attribute any past staff difficulty to (a) inadequate delegation of supervision and authority, (b) staff difficulties with each other and (c) office staff warfare with the cook and domestic personnel, I am taking measures to iron out these points.

Supervision (a) is cared for now as above. Item (b), staff personality clashes, I could and may care for with Scientology Group Processing or other means. Item (c) is cared for below:

MEALS

Breakfast—8:30 A.M.—None served after 8:50. Orders for breakfast to be in the night before.

Lunch—12:30 P.M.—No menu except as authorized.

High Tea—5:30 P.M.—No other menu than authorized.

The cook is my personal cook and also is permitted to cook for staff. Domestic staff is my personal staff.

Staff may not enter larder nor kitchen at any hours.

Any additional drinks or food will be laid out in recreation room.

All previous difficulties with cooks and domestic staff stem from misapprehensions concerning the above. Please comply.

REGULATIONS OF SAINT HILL

There are several regulations regarding Saint Hill. The most important of these follow:

1. Any physical or mental abuse of the children, or any tampering with them will result in dismissal or worse; this includes any instruction of the children to withhold something from their parents;

2. Any commission on Saint Hill purchases, or wages requested of tradesmen or accepted by employees at Saint Hill is forbidden;

3. No radios or phonographs are permitted on the second floor; only the lift may be used up to or down from the second floor—the use of the stairway is forbidden; please close firmly *both* doors of the lift when leaving it if only for a moment;

4. No food preparation is permitted on the second floor or in the recreation room; the hall booth is where coffee and supplies should be placed; steaming tea kettles will injure the painting in the cinema;

5. No staff except the Housekeeper, chef and kitchen maid are permitted in the larder or the main kitchen and no office staff may discuss food or menus with my chef;

6. No furniture or household goods may be disturbed or moved, placed or changed in position without the Housekeeper's permission;

7. No fires may be lighted in fireplaces;

8. All office wastebasket paper is to be burned as soon as emptied from baskets in incinerators provided for that purpose;

9. It is our policy that, as all emergencies stem from overlooked or neglected duties, when a staff member seriously drops a ball we drop the staff member;

10. Falsifying Accounts reports or records or ordering from tradesmen is regarded as a criminal offense and will be so handled.

SECURITY PRECAUTIONS

Windows and doors of Saint Hill Manor must not be left unlocked or open.

The staff office and the admin office of HCO and my office area must be locked fully and thoroughly nightly.

As we have no Master at Arms, each person should lock up at night the windows and doors he opened earlier in the day.

Other doors:

Please keep closed the following doors at *all* times. Do not lock back.

The back door (flies).

The larder door (flies).

Both hall doors leading into the main entrance hall. Never leave or lock these open. (Noise and cooking odors.)

The passage door, evenings, leading into the area where the domestic message center is. (Noise—the children will be trying to sleep evenings just up the stairs from this.)

The terrace door from the main entrance hall. (Drafts upstairs.)

Both boiler room doors (fire or smoke).

The front door of the Manor (salesmen).

ASSIGNMENT OF ROOMS

All room assignments and furniture changes are done by the Housekeeper.

VEHICLES

No vehicle may be used without the permission of the Grounds Manager. Repairs made necessary by carelessness in handling, cleaning, servicing or oiling vehicles or implements may be required paid for by the offending person or the person in charge of vehicles or the Grounds Manager out of pocket.

KEEPING VEHICLES

The Grounds Manager assigns where vehicles may be parked but may refuse parking privileges to any person or vehicle at his own discretion without further recourse.

FISHING AND SWIMMING

The staff may use fishing and any swimming facilities but at posted times only.

SPORTS FACILITIES

Tennis and other sports facilities may be used by staff but only at posted times and only at discretion of the Grounds Manager. Any equipment so used must be taken down, cleaned and stored by the staff persons using it.

The above bulletin is issued after due thought and experience of the past many months and should be considered inflexible, final and to be fully enforced by the supervisors of the three zones of action and by myself. Personnel consistently bypassing the authority of supervisors or breaking regulations will be dismissed.

L. RON HUBBARD
Founder

Saint Hill

FLOWERS

(Add to staff regulations)

Permission of the Grounds Manager is required to pick flowers. Each time flowers are to be picked the Grounds Manager must give his permission and designate the location.

Experimental flower beds have been planted and picking would upset experiments.

Also, flowers are being picked too close to the house, upsetting the landscaping. More distant and less vital beds exist and have been planted for picking.

No roses may be picked by anyone except myself and the Grounds Manager due to possible bush damage.

We are winning in restoring beauty to Saint Hill. Please help.

L. RON HUBBARD
Founder

DOMESTIC ARRANGEMENTS CHANGES

Due to domestic arrangements overloading myself and other staff and the great difficulty in securing domestic staff and for economy reasons, I regret that certain changes will have to be made, effective Monday, 25 Apr. 60.

As lunches were gratuitous and not part of wages and as it becomes impossible to serve them, I am sorry to announce that no further lunches will be served, and it will be necessary for staff to bring their own lunches or return home for them as they used to do. This is effective Monday, 25 Apr. 60. Lunch will be served to the family, the nanny, kitchen staff and housekeeper only.

Hot tea and coffee will, however, be provided for tea breaks and at lunch.

After Monday, 25 Apr., only the following quarters will be furnished to staff: Chef and nanny in the Manor House, housekeeper and HCO Secretary at the Gate Lodge.

The wage of the Technical Secretary and the Tape Technician will be increased £3 each per week to help pay for their outside living. The wage of the HCO Secretary will be similarly increased, £1 as a salary increase and £2 as an outside food allowance.

L. RON HUBBARD
Founder

Saint Hill

ACC AT SAINT HILL

The 7th London ACC will be coming down to Saint Hill for the next six weeks.

There will be quite a few persons in it.

They will use the Monkey Room.* They arrive by bus at 9:30 and leave at 5:00.

They will have ¾ of an hour for lunch from 12:45 to 1:30. They bring their own lunches. We furnish tea and coffee.

They are restricted to front terrace, park and lake. Pleasure Gardens and other areas are out of bounds to them.

They will use terrace door into office and thus into Monkey Room.

The house, except for Monkey Room area, is completely out of bounds to them.

Be pleasant to them but don't let them interrupt your work.

They will want to know about all kinds of things. It's okay to talk to them. But remember that they are going back to all parts of the world and will take whatever you say as gospel truth. So make sure it is or Scientology might be upset.

You will find them to be good people. You'll also find them underfoot a bit. So make the best of it.

Thank you.

L. RON HUBBARD
Founder

---

*Monkey Room: a room in Saint Hill Manor, the walls of which are decorated with a mural depicting monkeys dressed like people and enjoying themselves at a pleasure resort. The mural was painted by John Spencer Churchhill, nephew of former British Prime Minister Sir Winston Churchhill.

HCO POLICY LETTER OF 8 AUGUST 1960

Sthil

PERSONS LIVING IN

Those persons who live in at Saint Hill should observe the following:

The stairs from the second floor to the ground floor may *not* be used. All persons living on the second floor *must* use the *lift*.

Loud radios and TV are not permitted on the second floor.

Meals:

Breakfast   8:30 A.M.
Lunch   12:30 P.M.
Dinner   5:30 P.M.

Persons who do not live in may not eat in.

Persons who live in are responsible for their own serving and washing up.

Laundry is done by the laundress for sheets, pillowslips and towels only.

There is no pressing service but cleaners and dyers call weekly.

The lake may be swum in or fished in.

The children are to be treated courteously at all times. If they bother, locate their nanny; don't order the children.

L. RON HUBBARD
Founder

NEW ROAD

The new road is to be built by casual labor at 5 shillings per hour.

To be put in as staked.

Accurate account kept of labor and materials (as Jones pays half).

Step One: Move fence and gates to new position (as staked). Move by sections. Put *neatly* in new place each time a section is removed. Get welder if areas are rusted out.

Step Two: Dig trenches, quite deep, through *all* boggy areas, leading off water. Fill with coarse brick rubble.

Step Three: Lay in concrete drainage pipe in areas that might dam up in rains. Only one such area observed—by Jones' water trough.

Step Four: Bulldoze and fill.

Step Five: Roll road. *Heavy* roller.

Step Six: Clear stream bed and edge of lake and replant in grass.

L. RON HUBBARD
Founder

Saint Hill

TRAINING PROJECT
CONSTRUCTION AND PREPARATION

A crash project must be started and carried forward to prepare the basement and to ready staff for the Training Project.

Within 2 1/2 weeks from date, the following must have been accomplished:

CONSTRUCTION

Plumber must lift pipes to ceiling in laundry room, reconnect dark room. Bridglands* may not be utilized.

Safe must be moved around corner by safe movers.

Shelves in old laundry room, etc., must be torn out, and old carpentry shop.

Replastering old laundry and carpentry shop must be completed, making all smooth.

Old carpentry shop, adjacent rooms, basement bath and old laundry must be painted.

A glowing-coal electric fire and proper lighting must be installed.

FURNITURE, RUGS, DRAPES

A proper carpet for the old laundry room and smaller carpets for the old tape room, carpentry shop and adjacent room must be ordered.

Wide side-arm student chairs, blonde, to the number of six, and plain-arm, matching chairs to the number of eight must be purchased.

Drapes for the old laundry room, carpentry shop and the adjoining room must be purchased and installed.

Carpet, drapes, paint and furniture must match.

Two Instructor desks or tables and one Receptionist desk, all with chairs, must be provided for the old tape room.

---

*Bridglands: the name of a hardware and building supply store in East Grinstead.

SUPPLIES

Five E-Meters of the *latest model* must be procured for use in the project and checked for any flaws.

Clipboards, folders and other supplies must be made ready for use.

Bulletins and tapes must be assembled from the list.

PERSONNEL

London HGC test files must be consulted to find two men and one girl who have left the HASI but who had excellent results on profiles while there. Old-timers are best.

They must be hired and gotten on the job within ten days from date so they can be briefed and trained prior to arrival of students.

No existing HASI staff may be employed.

Their wage will be reasonable cash wage plus travel expenses. They will not live in or eat in.

The two men will be Staff Auditor-Instructors, the girl will be an HCO-type personnel doing "hat checks" on students, finding them rooms and generally handling the post of HCO Training Admin.

MAILINGS

The mailing piece must be recovered from Grants,[*] completed.

The membership addresses from Central Orgs must be put on envelopes.

The whole mailing must be gotten out in the next few days.

REGISTRATION

All students applying must be registered, must sign releases and be invoiced.

The releases must be prepared with attention to the data in the mailing and so as not to infer we are in a training business, which we are not.

EQUIPMENT MOVING

The entire contents of the old tape room must be moved to safe storage elsewhere than the tape room.

The old tape room is to become the Instructors' office. This has to be done within a week.

---

[*]**Grants:** a British printing company.

ASSIGNMENTS

The following duties are being assigned to Saint Hill staff for this project:

General In-Charge of project and is to prepare curriculum.

Assistant, whole project. Moving things and mailing.

Furnishings, decoration, rugs, color scheme, chairs.

Personnel procurement.

Safe movers, cleaning and setting up rooms.

Carpentry shop moving. Carpentry In-Charge: Construction items. Painting.

Plastering and smoothing walls, and stone work.

Releases.

Registration.

Answering mail from applicants and helping them make arrangements and find quarters until new Training Admin is grooved in.

Supplies.

L. RON HUBBARD
Founder

Sthil

ANIMALS FORBIDDEN IN HOUSE

Add to Saint Hill regulations:

No animal is permitted inside the house. Any animal is to be fed only outside the house.

In event of an animal being kept on the grounds, suitable protection arrangements from cold and rain should be arranged or built outside the house.

L. RON HUBBARD
Founder

HCO POLICY LETTER OF 3 MAY 1961

Sthil

DINING ROOM FOR STAFF

All meals should be eaten by staff in the new room in the basement. The pantry should not be used for eating purposes by anyone now that suitable space has been provided.

L. RON HUBBARD
Founder

SECURITY OF HOUSE

In that the North Lodge was entered and robbed by burglars last week, it is doubly necessary to pay attention to the security of Saint Hill.

Staff must not leave windows unlocked and ready for entrance, and must not leave doors unlocked.

Certain assignments were made in the office regarding the closing of windows and locking them. These are to be closely followed.

The executive office has almost always been neglected in this respect and its windows are usually open after hours.

Mrs. Hubbard's bedroom windows, through which burglars have entered the house in the past, must not be left open after office hours.

As I am seldom successfully robbed, it will probably be *your* raincoat, purse or possessions that get taken. Look to them, please.

L. RON HUBBARD
Founder

Sthil

LAUNDRY

Mildew and other difficulties with laundry will be a source of continued difficulty this damp winter unless the following rules are rigorously adhered to:

1. The laundry room must be kept aired.

2. Clothing must be placed on the slatted table just inside the door.

3. Damp towels must be kept separate from other clothing and put in a different place on the table.

4. Laundry may only be done in the laundry room, not in bathrooms.

5. Actual washing of clothes, including the children's, may be done only on Tuesday and Friday. The Laundress may only use the *washing* machines Tuesday and Friday. Monday, Wednesday and Thursday are reserved for ironing and sorting. Clothes washed should be dried the same day or left overnight on the lines.

When both washing and ironing are attempted on the same day, the clothing does not get a chance to dry.

6. Damp-finished clothing may not be brought in the house. It must be left in the laundry room until dry or it should be redried. No wet clothes or towels may be placed in cupboards or "drying rooms" in the house.

7. When clothing is dirty, put it in the laundry room at once. Do not leave in the house.

8. Let washed clothing hang in the drying room until it is dry.

9. Let ironed clothing stay in the laundry room on the rack until it is dry.

10. Only fill a washing machine *half* full of dirty clothing. Do not pack it to the top. Unless clothes are loose in the machine they will not wash.

11. Do not use heavy bleaches.

12. Do not boil or overheat any clothing.

13. Do not overheat nylon as it melts.

14. Do not hang wet clothes in the laundry room.

15. No person has the right to order the Laundress to do anything, except the Butler.

A good laundry room, a drying room and outside lines have been provided. The Laundress is to wash the clothes received so that they are clean, well preserved, dried and well ironed. They are to come dry into the house.

This should now be easy to accomplish and will be appreciated.

L. RON HUBBARD
Founder

REPAIRS AND CLEANING OF MY OFFICE

My downstairs office can be unused for several weeks if need be.

I have a temporary office on the first floor, first door to right at top of main stairs.

Anything necessary to be done to my office should be done now. Any cleaning, touch-up, repairs or installation.

The haircord carpet back of my desk wore because my chair spindle was below wheel level and dragging. This section of carpet should be replaced. Contrary to earlier instructions, no board is needed, only a new carpet section.

The shelf lights should be completed, one more added just under the lower one, and the lights boarded in.

Any speaker installation should be done.

My telex table and chair should be moved up to my temporary office and placed against wall nearest bathroom door.

The big flag should be taken into schoolroom.

Folders should be completed and placed in a file cabinet in the typing office.

All pictures should be put on top of a cabinet in my temporary office.

A radiator grill for behind my desk should be made when the speaker grill is made.

All leak streaks on the ceiling, if any, should be spotted out with paint.

PVC should be checked over on windows and neated if necessary.

It may be desirable to smooth out finish of blonde desk and blonde shelf behind it.

Tile faces should be carefully wiped so as not to hurt emulsion paint of fireplace. Tile faces on lower part of room could be washed.

All dust and debris should be vacuumed out under all grills and radiators.

Floodlamps should be wiped down.

1357

Red plastic covers matching settees should be made for projectors and tape recorder and Dimafon (4 in all).

My desk Indian rug should be cleaned.

Curtains and valances should be freshened up.

When any construction and wiring and all cleaning is done, my various knickknacks should be brought from safe, cleaned up and put in place, and the room made ready for occupancy.

It has been two years less only two months since this room was fully overhauled.

L. RON HUBBARD
Founder

Sthil

FISH AND GAME

(This order is not retroactive)

The shooting of any game and the catching of any fish in Saint Hill grounds or water is forbidden to staff and public.

The lake should be posted "Fishing Forbidden. Offenders will be prosecuted for trespass." Three signs to be posted at the lake.

The grounds should be posted "No Hunting. £5 reward for information leading to conviction." Four signs should be posted, facing out from and on the North, East, South and West boundary centers.

A £5 reward will be paid for information and evidence leading to the proven fact that any person has trespassed at the lake, has caught any fish or has shot any game on Saint Hill land, and the positive identification of that person.

I am fond of wildlife and birds. With all the shooting in surrounding lands, game, if there is no shooting over Saint Hill land, will tend to move into this area. Further, I wish the lake to restock.

All permissions formerly granted to any person or persons whatever are herewith revoked.

L. RON HUBBARD
Founder

HCO POLICY LETTER OF 2 AUGUST 1962
Issue II

Sthil

NEW WORK ARRANGEMENTS
OUTSIDE STAFF

As from next week, week ending Friday 10th August, changes are made in working hours of outside staff (garden, construction, etc.) so as to eliminate Saturday morning working, and introduce a five-day week.

Working hours, from Monday to Friday, will be as under:

8:00 A.M. to 5:15 P.M. each day, with half an hour allowed for lunch break.

L. RON HUBBARD
Founder

HUBBARD COMMUNICATIONS OFFICE
Saint Hill Manor, East Grinstead, Sussex

HCO POLICY LETTER OF 3 OCTOBER 1962

Sthil

ROOMS, EMPTYING FOR CLEANING

Study rooms, the pavilion, chapel and basement, must be emptied of all students by the respective Supervisors *in person* at the exact end of period at the end of the day.

Cleaning cannot be accomplished unless this is done.

Students are expected to be out of these rooms at 6:30 on the dot. Earlier periods get no extension time, why the last period of the day?

Provision for students eating supper in may be made but may not include the theory room, pavilion or chapel or areas that must be cleaned.

L. RON HUBBARD
Founder

CAR WASHING

(Post conspicuously in garage)

As all cars at Saint Hill have to date had their finishes injured severely by improper washing and polishing, the following steps *only* are to be taken in cleaning cars:

Cars should be parked in garage so as to allow easy opening of door on the driver's side. This permits easy entrance, dusting out, and prevents banging up of doors on garage wall.

Do *not* get in cars with greasy overalls, shoes or hands. Use seat, floor and wheel covers.

CLEANING MATERIALS

Keep all cleaning materials, seat covers, buckets, brushes, spray nozzles, in a cabinet in the open garage area. Always replace after use. Put up a cloth-drying line in same area.

The following cleaning materials should be procured and used:

1. Hose.

2. Spray nozzle.

3. Two dozen soft cloths.

4. A large soft-bristle brush for exterior.

5. A long stiff-bristle brush for under fenders.

6. A whisk broom for interiors.

7. Three turkey-feather dusters.

8. Clothes-cleaning fluid.

9. A plastic bucket (eight quarts or larger).

10. A box of Tide.

11. Cans of Simoniz Liquid Cleaner (but *no* other Simoniz product).

12. Cans of Johnson's Car Plate.

13. A pile of newspapers.

14. A spray can of window cleaner.

CAR DUSTY ONLY

Do NOT wipe with a rag as this scores the paint.

Sweep car out, dust interior with a clean rag.

Dust with a turkey-feather duster until *no* dust is apparent on surface.

Wipe interior out (seats, sills, panel) with a *clean,* soft rag.

This is *all* that is required. Do not remove car from garage.

CAR DIRTY

1. Put car on ramp outside. Do *not* wipe.

2. Hose all mud and dirt off car using a spray nozzle and hose and a soft brush. Use a special brush for under fenders.

3. Using a *clean,* damp cloth, apply liquid car cleaner to entire car exterior and chrome, including hub caps. Let it dry to brown white. To put on and wipe off use long, straight strokes, no circular rubbing.

4. When liquid car cleaner dry, wipe it off with a *clean,* soft cloth, leaving no residue of the cleaner. Wipe off hub caps. Make sure no residue is left.

5. Take a clean, dry cloth and apply Car Plate with long, straight strokes. Cover entire car including chrome. Do not scrub it on, just wipe it on. Let it dry.

6. With a clean, soft cloth wipe off Car Plate. Do not attempt to polish. Car will be brilliant and dust will whisk off it with a feather duster.

7. Put all rags in a bucket. Use detergent such as Tide. Wash and hang up on a line in garage.

DO NOT USE GREASY OR DIRTY RAGS. USE OTHER RAGS FOR OIL AND KEEP THEM SEPARATE.

WINDSHIELDS AND GLASS

Dust windows off with turkey duster.

Wet a newspaper and wipe off windows, getting all dirt.

Take dry newspaper and polish windows.

Don't go over windows with a cleaning rag and *never* with an oil rag. Keep rags and cloths and wax and cleaners off windows or they will steam and fog up in damp weather.

INTERIORS

Use carpet cleaners on floor carpets as per regular directions on their packages, just as in the house.

Use leather cleaners on leather seats. Be careful of smelly leather cleaners. A white, soft cream is best.

Use a rag with clothes-cleaning fluid on it to wipe off steering wheels, etc., interior.

TAR

Remove any tar on the car with a rag and cleaning fluid.

———————

DO NOT USE SOLID CLEANERS OF ANY KIND ON A CAR. USE NO ABRASIVE CLEANERS.

DO NOT WAX CARS WITH SOLID WAX.

DUST is the main reason finishes and windows get ruined. Wiping a dusty surface with a dry cloth can ruin a car's paint or windows.

Abrasive cleaners and solid wax spoil a car's paint within a year or two.

L. RON HUBBARD
Founder

HCO POLICY LETTER OF 8 NOVEMBER 1962

Sthil

OUTSIDE STAFF
DUTIES, ASSIGNMENT OF

The following duties and areas of responsibility are assigned forthwith:

HEAD GARDENER

Grounds, trees, beds, flowers, lawns, cleanliness of exterior buildings and road, path and courtyard areas.

Construction and maintenance of paths, walks, roads, drains, fences and garden houses, toolsheds and garden vehicle storage sheds.

Has charge of gardeners and his grounds men.

Has purchase, maintenance and repair of garden machinery, tools, trailers, tractors, mowers and barrows.

Has purchase of flowers, shrubs, trees, seeds, fertilizers and building materials for roads, paths, fences and land drains.

MAINTENANCE MAN

Has charge of all building construction in general except paths, drains, toolsheds and fences.

Does all carpentry for new buildings and existing structures except tool and garden vehicle sheds.

Does or supervises all painting, interior and exterior.

Does or supervises all glazing, electrical installations and layouts for same.

Takes charge of all plans for existing or planned structures of whatever kind or area.

Has complete care of *all* furnaces and boilers, coal or oil, and procurement of fuel for same.

Has charge of all locks, keys, and orders new keys.

Has charge of any assistant carpenters, electricians, painters or glaziers or any contractors' men while on the estate, and straightens out any building or repair problems for these, no matter whose department the work comes under.

Has purchase of lumber, timber, electrical supplies, plumbing supplies, paint, glass and materials for roofing.

Has specific charge of the watertightness of all roofs and water systems internal and all plumbing internal or external. The watertightness of the roofs of *all* buildings is his responsibility.

Has charge of all furniture repair or removal, and for the latter may borrow gardener's men with the approval of the gardener.

Has charge of all vehicles, whether work is done by another or not, and the execution of all policy regarding vehicles. By vehicle here is meant road-licensed vehicles except tractors.

ESTATE BRICKLAYER

Has charge of all stonework, masonry construction, foundations, brick- and plasterwork.

Repairs, supervises or does new construction on all stonework, masonry and brick- and plasterwork.

Has charge of all chimneys and their drawing.

Has purchase of all rubble, cement, ballast, pipes, bricks, stone and materials used in building construction, but not paths, land drains or roads.

Assists when possible in path and road pavement.

Does or supervises all interior drains and foul sewage drains, interior or exterior.

Has charge of all brick or stone walls, and all nontimber floors, their reduction or construction.

Has complete charge of any bricklaying assistants or helpers.

L. RON HUBBARD
Founder

HCO POLICY LETTER OF 15 NOVEMBER 1962

CAR PARKING

All parking is under the control of the Head Gardener.

All student cars are to be parked on the new concrete strip only. The cars are to be parked only on that part of the strip where there is a wall. Cars should be pointed straight in at the wall. Student cars should use only the west gate to the Manor grounds, both in and out (the one nearest the parking strip).

Staff cars may be parked in the new parking strip or against the wall under the cedar tree in front of the house.

No staff or student cars may be parked along the roadway curb anywhere on the Saint Hill roads except to receive and discharge passengers.

The Head Gardener has the authority to levy a 10-shilling fine on any improperly parked car. Any fine is to be paid into Accounts on the basis of a note from the Head Gardener under the windshield wiper. There are no charges for parking properly.

The parking lot has the advantage of not being under trees, and therefore, leaving a car relatively free of birds, leaves and needles.

The wide apron below the parking lot should be left empty as it is a roadway up to the greenhouse area.

L. RON HUBBARD
Founder

Sthil
Domestic and
 Grounds Staff

TRIPS TO TOWN

There will be only one trip made to town for supplies daily.

This will be in the late morning. The exact time will be posted.

A basket will be placed just inside the workshop door for orders.

Anything required from town should be ordered by placing a slip in the basket before the posted hour.

Transport comes under the supervision of the Maintenance Man's Department.

This does not change other transport arrangements.

L. RON HUBBARD
Founder

HUBBARD COMMUNICATIONS OFFICE
Saint Hill Manor, East Grinstead, Sussex

HCO POLICY LETTER OF 12 MARCH 1963

STAFF PERSONNEL ALLOWANCE
SAINT HILL

The following is published as the allowed staff for Saint Hill:

Office

HCO Secretary WW
HCO Mission Secretary WW
HCO Technical Materiel Secretary, plus one helper
Accounts, Disbursement
Accounts, Income
Accounts, Ledger (part time)
Treasurer (part time)

One full-time HCO Communicator/Mail/Telex
   (plus one part time possibly to help with PAB
   mailings, etc.)

Mimeo—two full time (part time can help with "bulges")
   (Mimeo also helps with correspondence, filing, etc.)

Materiel and Purchasing (part time)

Domestic

One full-time cleaner, one part time (for offices)
Laundress (part time)
Cook
Nanny or home help for children
Tutor for children

Outside

Head Gardener: two assistants
Maintenance Man: one assistant
Estate Bricklayer: one assistant
Driver and vehicles

Course

Course Secretary
Course Administrator (also Secretary)
Theory Supervisor
Practical Supervisor
Auditing Supervisor

L. RON HUBBARD
Founder

Sthil Staff
Outside Staff

CONSTRUCTION INFORMATION

There are several construction and grounds projects envisaged for this year.

Those listed are not in order of priority. These include:

Completion of L-shaped new building.

Battering up the slope back of the L-shaped building.

Preparing the front yard of the L-shaped building and landscaping it.

Completing walks in Pleasure Garden area.

Pointing up the whole of the Manor House and painting with Impervium during dry weather.

Completing new dome over Winter Garden.

Redecorating Winter Garden.

Redoing all windows on the front of the Manor House.

Placing storm windows (glass) on front windows of Manor House.

Rebuilding tennis hut near court.

Repairing wire and pavement of tennis court.

Completing paths and roads from new garden shed.

Repairing front fence along main road.

Planting privet hedge along line before Manor where temporary sheep fence now is.

Planting some oak trees in the park and protecting them.

Fixing new closed garage in open area of present garage and using current Jaguar garage for cleaning materials, benches, tea things and cloakroom for outside staff.

Reasphalting and sealing all Manor roofs.

Cleaning up moles and rabbits out of the grounds.

Damming up the lake again so it will be deeper and hold more water.

The above belong to various departments. The data is issued only to give a general idea of this year's work projects. Paving the main roads, building the park road, will probably not be attempted until next year. There is an appeal pending for the big office building but even if won it could not be started for some time.

L. RON HUBBARD
Founder

CHANGES IN BASEMENT STUDENT FACILITIES

The following facilities are to be constructed in the basement to accommodate increased enrollment expected on the Briefing Course.

Most of the work can be done by the existing staff over the next few months.

See the Course Secretary for specific construction details.

Work should be done in the order given, wherever possible.

1. Construct student mail facilities in the space by the stairs, facing the outside door.

2. Build bench tables against the walls of the large basement room with electrical outlets to accommodate twenty tape recorders.

3. Move the safe from its present position to against the wall in corridor at foot of stairs from front office.

4. Against the wall opposite the present bulletin board, construct a new bulletin board of twice the size. Use a cork surface.

5. Construct a tape filing cabinet in the shelf area of the large basement room to hold one hundred tapes with label holders.

6. Remove and store the doors from the cupboards in the theory study room and construct eighty open locker spaces for student study material with label holders.

7. Fasten a blackboard on the wall opposite the windows in the large study room.

8. Paint the large basement room and the study room.

9. Drape 2½ walls of the basement TV studio with medium dark, inexpensive material.

10. Increase the soundproofing quality of the large door to the large basement room.

L. RON HUBBARD
Founder

Saint Hill Only

REVIEW OF DEPARTMENTS

The following review is made concerning departments and personnel. The review is made without dividing up divisions or functions by ratings or importances.

I am very satisfied with the Mimeo Section and the girls in it, who are to be complimented.

I am well satisfied with Accounts and its present personnel and progress of work.

I am well satisfied with Missions but look for an increase in its receipts.

I am very satisfied with the Estate Bricklayer and his helper.

I am not satisfied with the handling and use of my cars and have dismissed the driver because of this and to meet pay demands.

I am fairly satisfied with Cleaning, but call attention to small scars and breakages I have noticed appearing. Otherwise, they do quite well.

I look for improvement with the nursery and the state of the children's clothes, but the condition is improving. The children's morale is good and the Nanny is doing much better.

I am generally very happy with Maintenance, but consider that too much work was pushed on the man in charge by his men.

The Cook is now doing somewhat better but could improve the children's food.

The Book Department is doing very well indeed and is now very solvent.

The grounds look well but the grounds crew has been the weakest point as the Head Gardener has done nearly all the work himself. I have accordingly dismissed two men.

Reception is good in general but should pay more attention to the condition of the front office and its equipment, some of which is dirty.

Registration has improved and has been given a new clerk and higher enrollment is looked for.

My own secretarial help has sagged due to the illness of my personal secretary.

Course personnel, while not in fact a subject for such a report, are doing an excellent job and are to be congratulated. Improvement over a year ago is astonishing.

SUMMARY

Saint Hill is running fairly well.

The work policy of retaining those who do their jobs and dismissing those who need constant supervision has worked well.

Income is still less than outgo, but staff will only be shortened where the work is not being done. We are counting on marked increases in registration to balance this situation.

My own time has been so taken up with research during the past six months that I have not given adequate supervision to some departments. However, I have just reviewed the organization as a whole, as above, and in my own way keep an eye on things. The staff as a whole is doing well.

L. RON HUBBARD
Founder

DOORS

The heating and fire security of the house depends on the following door arrangements:

GROUND FLOOR

The leather door in the passage outside the kitchen must never be hooked open.

The door at the top of the basement steps outside the typists' room always must be closed.

The door to the entrance hall just beside the elevator should be closed.

The back door should not be propped open.

FIRST FLOOR

The interconnecting hall door should always be shut.

TOP FLOOR

The interconnecting hall door should always be closed securely but not locked. This is a fire door.

BASEMENT

The door leading outside up the steps should be kept closed.

Due to the construction of the Manor House, a series of heavy convection currents set up when the above doors are left open. Fire regulations require that they be kept closed. Leaving them open also sets up sufficient draft to make the Manor difficult to heat and heavily increases the fuel cost.

L. RON HUBBARD
Founder

HCO POLICY LETTER OF 3 FEBRUARY 1964

Sthil Staff
and Post Backdoor
Board

HCO (STHIL), LTD.
TRANSPORT

All vehicles are in the charge of the chauffeur.

Permission of the chauffeur is required each and every time some other driver desires permission to drive a Saint Hill vehicle.

Because of insurance clauses which limit drivers, the following vehicles may not be driven by anyone but Dr. Hubbard and R.J. Bonwick: Pontiac, Jaguar XK 150 and Jaguar Mark VIII.

The Commer bus may not be driven by anyone under 21 years of age due to insurance.

Although not limited by insurance, the red Mini Estate may only be driven by Mrs. Hubbard and the chauffeur.

The Austin van may be driven by anyone with the required permission.

Persons taking any of the insurance-limited vehicles and driving them cannot be classed otherwise than taking and driving a car without the owner's permission, a serious legal offense.

That some drivers are insured for comprehensive insurance "in any vehicle" does not waive any of the above as such insurance is usually valid only for "third party" and does not cover the actual vehicle being driven.

L. RON HUBBARD
Founder

HUBBARD COMMUNICATIONS OFFICE
Saint Hill Manor, East Grinstead, Sussex

HCO POLICY LETTER OF 2 APRIL 1964
Issue III

Sthil Only

USE OF RECREATION FACILITIES, 1964

Saint Hill students and staff may:

1. Use tennis courts;

2. Use croquet green by tennis court;

3. Fish in the lake;

4. Walk in grounds.

Specifically withdrawn from use by staff and students this season is the swimming pool, which is being reserved for the children.

L. RON HUBBARD
Founder

HCO POLICY LETTER OF 10 APRIL 1964

Saint Hill Staff
Only

DOMESTIC STAFF

(Cancels earlier organizational policies)

To minimize conflict with purely administrative actions, the following staff are designated as domestic staff:

Housekeeper

Butler

Assistant Housekeeper

Cook

Nanny

Chauffeur (but also retains staff driving duties—see below)

Office Cleaner

Laundress.

The domestic staff comes under the direct supervision of my personal secretary.

All food purchases and domestic purchases are also routed along these lines.

The chauffeur is also under the direct supervision of my personal secretary, but he must arrange his staff driving duties to the best advantage, but with the proviso that his first priority is my personal driving and vehicles, and the family. He remains responsible for all road vehicles on the estate, as before. My personal secretary will ensure that these duties are coordinated as smoothly as possible.

L. RON HUBBARD
Founder

Sthil
Students

TRANSPORT

Students desiring noon transport weekdays from Saint Hill to East Grinstead at noon and return at 12:50 may have it by procuring an invoice from the Income Section costing 5 shillings per week.

The invoice should be plainly dated and displayed to the driver on departure from Saint Hill.

The reason for the charge is the limited transport space available.

There is no charge for staff members.

L. RON HUBBARD
Founder

HCO POLICY LETTER OF 13 MAY 1964
Issue I

Sthil

TRANSPORT

(Adds to HCO PL 8 May 64, TRANSPORT)

Regarding HCO PL 8 May 64, TRANSPORT, it should be clearly understood that there is no contract to carry passengers on the staff bus for fares.

The five shillings payment by students should be invoiced by Accounts as a contribution to the upkeep of the bus. The student is then privileged to ride on the bus, as and when available, for one week.

L. RON HUBBARD
Founder

HCO POLICY LETTER OF 15 NOVEMBER 1964

Issue II

Sthil Staff
Students
  (give to each
  new student)
Gardener's Hat
Chauffeur's Hat
Comm Officer's Hat
Theory Supervisor's Hat
Accounts Hat
Org Sec's Hat

TRAFFIC REGULATIONS

SAINT HILL

(Effective 23 Nov. 64. Cancels earlier
policy letters on traffic.)

The traffic regulations of Saint Hill are as follows:

1. The Head Gardener is in charge of all traffic, parking and routing.

2. Violations of traffic regulations are subject to fine.

3. The Head Gardener gets to keep all fines for himself.

4. Students may park cars and vehicles in the student parking lot to the northwest of the Manor. They may not park along roadways or before the Manor.

5. Student car traffic is through the west gate of the Manor. The east (iron) gateway is closed to all student vehicle traffic (not to foot traffic).

6. Students and staff members who use taxis must direct their taxi drivers to arrive and leave by the west gate.

7. Students must not abandon vehicles in the parking lot or along roadways in the grounds. If through with a vehicle, a student should sell it or dispose of it outside the grounds.

8. There is no Manor garage service available to staff or students and the chauffeur must not be called upon to do or be paid for odd repair jobs or services, including battery charging.

9. Staff cars may be parked before the Manor so long as there is space available, and when there is not, staff cars must go into the student parking lot.

10. None may park cars before or on the ramp of the Manor garage.

11. No vans or cars may be run into the area at the back door of the Manor (near publications office and carpentry shop) as that concrete area is a thin shell over an enormous well and a van or car could easily break through it and plunge its own height into the water.

12. No vehicles may be run on Saint Hill paths.

13. No cars must park along any verge.

14. Speed limit along roadway before garage and Manor is 10 mph.

FINES

The scale of fines that may be collected by the Head Gardener is as follows from students or staff:

Illegal parking—10 shillings.

Using front gate—10 shillings.

Speeding—2 pounds.

Failing to properly direct taxi driver to comply with routing and speed limit, 10 shilling fine for each passenger, paid by passengers.

Damaging verge—1 pound.

Abandoning vehicle on departure from course—Confiscation and 10 pounds (cost of hauling it away).

Repeated offenses—Barring staff or student vehicle from grounds with 10 shilling fine each time it enters.

Causing a vehicle accident of any kind in the grounds—5 pounds.

Refusal to pay fine—Barring vehicle or person's taxi from grounds with 10 shilling fine each time it enters.

CAUTION

There is a great deal of pedestrian traffic along Saint Hill's roadways. There are children and pets. There are bicycles.

All this means that careless, swooping driving or irresponsible parking by anyone (including tradesmen) can result in accident or tragedy.

Therefore, the above regulations are in full force.

Staff member fines are paid directly to the Head Gardener or are deducted from wage and paid the Head Gardener.

If the Head Gardener fines anyone, he must tell the Communications Officer and the fact must be logged. Failure to log can cause a confiscation of the fee from the Head Gardener by the Org Sec's orders.

Tradesmen's vans may pause before the back entrance to the Manor and outside workmen may park along the roadway but not before the garage proper.

If tradesmen's van drivers, taxis or outside workmen violate any of these regulations, the matter *must* be reported to the Communications Officer by the Head Gardener and the offense logged, regardless of any other action taken, such as fining passengers.

The Communications Officer must phone the company to which the offending vehicle belongs or the contractor for whom the workmen work and advise them that a driver or workman has broken our traffic regulations and that a repeated offense will cause the usual fine we levy to be deducted from their bill payment for each new offense. This sum deducted is given to the Head Gardener.

The Head Gardener should provide himself with tickets for offenses and place these, properly marked, in the offending vehicle or mail them to the offending company.

In any case where the Head Gardener is not paid the fine he has levied, he must report the matter to the Org Sec and the Org Sec is to collect the money for the Head Gardener.

In all cases of dispute a Committee of Evidence is to be convened by the Org Sec. But if the person is found to have disputed the regulations falsely, the fine is increased by 5 pounds.

We want no one's stay marred by accidents.

L. RON HUBBARD
Founder

SH Staff
and Students

GROUNDS REGULATIONS
STAFF AND STUDENTS

The following places are out of bounds to staff and students (excepting Construction and Maintenance personnel):

The pleasure garden
The pool
The terrace before the manor
The rose garden before the manor
The east park
The new orchard

Note that the following places are not out of bounds:

The lower park
The lake
The tennis court
The lot 4 wood
Lot 4

LITTER

Throwing cans, papers, refuse about and not removing it to the garbage cans is a matter of ethics.

PARKING

Parking violations and fines are now under the Construction and Maintenance Officer and are turned in to Ethics.

L. RON HUBBARD
Founder

HCO POLICY LETTER OF 9 SEPTEMBER 1965

Sthil Only

HOUSEHOLD SECTION

FLOWERS, CARE OF

Cut flowers must be put into water at once on receipt, regardless of packaging. If not yet presented, the card is conspicuously attached to them.

The water into which flowers are placed must be of room temperature, not ice cold or hot as both these wilt them at once. Flowers are always watered with room-temperature water, never ice-cold water.

A supply of *large* vases must always be to hand. Those holding less than a gallon of water are useless. Without adequate water the flowers promptly wilt.

Daily, empty the water out of any vase containing flowers, rinse it and fill it with room temperature water. Pick out the wilted flowers and throw them out. Cut a small section of the ends off the remainder (the end rots and won't draw water to the bloom) and rearrange them.

Throw out wilted vases of flowers and wash the vase before putting it away.

Keep all the vases in the winter garden behind the bar or in a chest.

Be *very* careful of large vases getting near taps as they strike them and break. Therefore, never hold a valuable vase under a tap. Wash it and fill it from a small plastic pitcher that won't break if it hits a tap.

PLANTS

Growing plants are handled as follows:

A wide bucket with a small amount of water at *room temperature* (not cold) in it is taken to the plant. The water is only a few inches deep. The pot is lifted into the bucket and let stand there a short time with the bottom of the pot in the water.

The plant is then put back in its saucer and any drops wiped up.

This is done daily.

Never water a plant from the top as it washes the nitrogen off the roots. Always let the water come up from the bottom hole in the pot.

Snip dead leaves off plants cleanly.

Turn plants over to the gardener to put in the greenhouse when their blooms are gone.

PERSONNEL

This task should be assigned to one person only by the Household Officer.

L. RON HUBBARD
Founder

HUBBARD COMMUNICATIONS OFFICE
Saint Hill Manor, East Grinstead, Sussex

HCO POLICY LETTER OF 14 SEPTEMBER 1965
Issue III
Saint Hill Only
Students
Staff

NEW CAR PARK

In view of new building and road construction, as from 16 Sept. 65 the parking lot adjoining Lot 4 will be closed. All staff and students using this car park must park their cars in the field to the left of the drive near the entrance.

There is a gateway and a chalk road has been laid at the entrance. Parking must be done to the instructions of the Estate Manager or his deputy.

ENTRANCE TO NEW CAR PARK

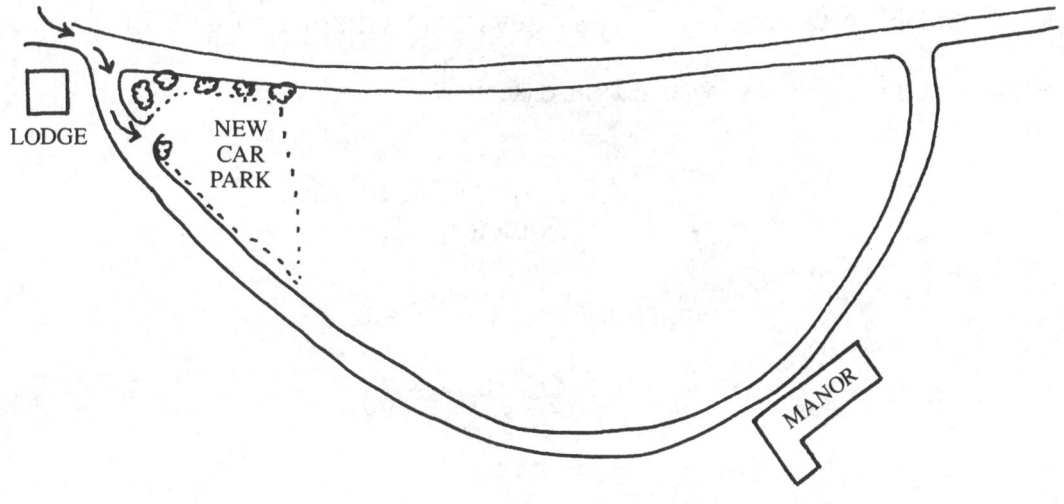

L. RON HUBBARD
Founder

HUBBARD COMMUNICATIONS OFFICE
Saint Hill Manor, East Grinstead, Sussex

HCO POLICY LETTER OF 12 NOVEMBER 1965
Issue II

SH Only

Dept 21

Office of LRH

All Maintenance Personnel

PAINT, ODORLESS

There are brands of odorless paint on the market. The thinner used is a synthetic, not turpentine.

Only this paint and no other may be used in the manor. Only the odorless thinner may be used.

On two earlier occasions I have been told it couldn't be procured and each time have found it on the market. It is simply slightly harder to get.

Ordinary paint may only be used on exteriors.

L. RON HUBBARD
Founder

Remimeo

STATISTIC INTERPRETATION
ESTATE STATISTIC

The Estate statistic to be meaningful at all must be properly inspected.

Whenever you see a long horizontal line in an Estate statistic of useful space you know there is either no inspection, improper inspection or "friendly" inspection.

An Estate statistic is NOT done by subtracting square footage from a known amount. It is done by inspecting for a clean, well-ordered working or grounds area and putting that down on a paper. When all such areas are found, the result is added up and that's the statistic.

A "useful space" is one that promotes the org, may be used by the org, is heated or cooled properly, equipped for its purpose, clean, orderly and serviceable. It may only be scenic but it is still "useful space."

Such statistics should be in square *paces,* not square feet or yards. For one can always pace one off. A pace is about 30 inches. One simply walks them off in a normal, not exaggerated, stride.

An area table inside and outside is easily developed simply by the Inspection Officer pacing what's in perfect order. Gradually it may all be useful but until then he only measures what passes and makes a table of areas from his inspections.

If the Inspection Officer finds any litter, dirt or unworkable fittings or anything else that mars the appearance or usefulness of an area, he does not put it down on his list.

One scrap of paper on a lawn is enough to wipe out that entire area as a statistic. One faulty drain finishes the statistic. An overheated or underheated room—anything and the area is out.

If the room or area is not of a high standard obvious to the most critical public, the Inspection Officer ignores it as a statistic.

Only in this way are Estate statistics meaningful.

It does not matter whose fault it is or that no PO can be gotten or the org can't afford to put it right. That is not the problem of the Inspection Officer. If any detail would be objected to by a critical public, the whole area is *out*. It is not considered useful space from a viewpoint of promotion.

In this way someone reading the statistic has an idea of the efficiency and activity of cleaners, construction, maintenance and general repair and the state of finance and income of an org.

If you see a horizontal line as the Estate statistic, you know the Dept of I&R is not on the job and Estate probably isn't either.

Let's put our orgs in condition to attract the public and hold a high standard.

L. RON HUBBARD
Founder

Remimeo
Applies to
7 Division
Orgs

LRH PROPERTY, BUILDING AND PLANS BRANCH

As of this date a new branch, LRH Property, Building and Plans Branch, is to be formed in the Office of LRH, Dept 21. It replaces the Estate Branch which now becomes a section.

The purpose of this branch is:

> TO TAKE OVER CONTROL OF ALL MY PERSONAL PROPERTY, CARS, JEWELRY, ETC., AS WELL AS MY INTEREST IN ORG PROPERTY AND MY PLANS FOR BUILDINGS.

ESTATE BUREAU

The Estate Bureau is headed by an Estate Manager. In WW the Estate Manager is essentially a liaison post. The Estate Manager Worldwide would keep an eye on all orgs and liaise with their Estate Managers to see that the buildings and grounds are kept up well and good in appearance and that they have a building.

He would also relay any building plans from the Plans Section to the Estate Manager of the org concerned and would check to see if such plans are being followed.

The Estate Manager of local org is responsible for seeing the org has proper quarters and that the property is kept up well in its appearance. He is also responsible for the locating of or building of new premises as the org expands or needs new quarters and for seeing that full CSW is presented via Estate Manager Worldwide when such changes are needed. Further, he is responsible for the accurate following of all plans or programs of the Estate Bureau.

The Estate Bureau WW supervises and local Estate Bureaus execute all plans and programs sent to them via the Estate Manager WW from me.

PLANS SECTION

Photostats (or copies) of all drawings, sketches, plans, etc., together with any letters or notes written or approved by me must be kept in LRH Property, Building and Plans Branch—Plans Section.

These are the sort of things that get lost and have to be redone by me all the time. So copies of *ALL* plans, drawings and sketches together with any notes or correspondence go to the LRH Property, Building and Plans Branch—Plans

Section, as well as to their destinations and addressees. All of this sort of thing does. Like a copy of an ED on construction or care and upkeep of grounds and buildings I've done.

These scraps of sketches I do for people to do plans from are my greatest source of upset. They get lost, ignored and in our castles this alone cost us at least 50,000 wasted pounds and gave us bad work. So it's vital that we set up (and put the hat on) (and write the hat up for) such a branch.

So all plans I've drawn or have approved are to be sent to LRH Property, Building and Plans Branch—Plans Section so that a copy can be made and retained. Then we can see if the plans are followed or goofed.

I do not have to run everything but when I am asked for solutions and do them I hate to have to do it all two or three times and still have it goofed. This branch has been formed to correct this.

L. RON HUBBARD
Founder

HCO POLICY LETTER OF 12 OCTOBER 1967
Issue I

Gen. Non-Remimeo

OPERATIONAL, DEFINITION OF

A lot of trouble in the Sea Org comes from lack of grasp of what we mean by *operational*.

Definition: AN ITEM THAT IS OPERATIONAL WORKS WELL WITHOUT FURTHER ASSISTANCE OR ATTENTION.

This does NOT say that operational means something *works*. It works *well*. It works without assistance or patch up or holding on to it. It works without attention. It does not have to be continually watched.

The breakdown in mail comm stemmed in part from the photocopier. The error was not in the copier. The error was in having something around that doesn't work well, needs continual attention, breaks down regularly. That comes from not reading or understanding the *Ship's Org Book*. *Operational* was misunderstood. This photocopier was wholly nonoperational in that it had to be continually nursed, was operated in bright light and took up tons of time. Because it was there nobody simply typed a copy of the vital despatches. One must NOT keep nonoperational things around or they must be made operational by above definition.

Also the early Flag Order about fast communication being vital was not complied with.

A costly mess resulted from delayed comm. All because OPERATIONAL was not understood.

L. RON HUBBARD
Founder

HCO POLICY LETTER OF 23 SEPTEMBER 1970

Remimeo
Estate Bureau
LRH Comm Hat
OES Hat
ED Hat
CO Hat

QUARTERS, POLICY REGARDING
HISTORICAL

In twenty years an enormous amount of experience has been gained regarding the quarters and housing of orgs.

From this experience there are only a few clear-cut lessons. These follow:

A. VIABILITY of the org (its economic survival including its security from political-enemy-motivated attack) is the first and foremost consideration. In terms of quarters an org can afford just so much expense. Therefore, viability is the first consideration—not how posh or what repute or what image. Thus, we have the policy that:

THE FIRST CONSIDERATION IN PROCURING QUARTERS IS THE *VIABILITY* OF THE ORG.

Example: Stockholm took very posh, fancy quarters. Up to that time it has been viable. The overload of expense rapidly upset the salary sum, the staff began to moonlight (work on other jobs), and the org all but collapsed until cheaper quarters were found.

Example: Phoenix 1955. A beautiful, big building at small expense was found. It was very prominent. Enemy local attack was stepped up in the area including door-to-door black propaganda by psychiatrists and a campaign by commie newspaper reporters. The full reserves of the org went into furnishing these quarters. The area had to be abandoned, losing all reserves. Elizabeth, New Jersey, 1950. The shabby quarters there made lots of money. Beautiful country quarters were under survey for purchase. The psychiatric block, much stronger then, began action in Trenton, New Jersey to invoke a law against medical schools. If the better quarters had been purchased, they would have been lost. The org foolishly moved to New York City across the river where the New York Org owned a building.

CONCLUSION: Viability of economics must not exceed the income of the org. The SAFE figure for rent and mortgage payments must not exceed 15 percent to 17 percent of the gross income of the org.

Political security must be attained by counterattack and if not attained or is risky, no heavy property investment or renovation should be programed.

If a country itself is liable to fall, property investment and renovation should be held to a minimum as viability is under the general political threat to the country itself.

B. Quarters must be close to ample and *cheap* student and pc housing, restaurants and transport.

Example: Abellund in Denmark, 1969, was a lovely place. The org there failed because it was 42 kilometers in the country without transport or taxis or buses, had no student housing nearby and had no restaurants. It was lovely but hated by students and pcs. Its isolation and general atmosphere promoted idleness and the org was down to half rations and no pay when forcefully moved by Flag into Copenhagen where in very bad quarters and bad housing it became viable. Student housing and feeding is very expensive and facilities scarce even so and still hurts the org income greatly.

Example: Elizabeth, New Jersey 1950. The org was located amid square blocks full of rooming houses and at the city center of three railways and bus lines. The students' own rooms were used for auditing which permitted org expansion. Nothing was posh. Everything noisy. The org was very viable and had streams of people.

Example: SH 1960–1968. The presence of lots of rooms for students in the town and cheap living despite the lousiness of the quarters gave SH in England its greatest periods of affluence. Political attack barred out foreign students, and the town people came at length to petition the government to remove the ban. (The closure of the 1955 Phoenix org also caused 35 small-town businesses to close in the org vicinity.)

CONCLUSION: The presence of ample, cheap housing and restaurants and general and local transport is a main factor in the viability of an org.

C. Image is a secondary consideration.

Example: Hotel Reycar Alicante Spain was relatively cheap. It was quite posh. Students complained as it cost a bit more than they were willing to pay. Image in this case worked against the org.

Example: Johannesburg's three old buildings foolishly sold and the money squandered has yet to attain the income it made in its "old, horrible quarters" despite its newer image.

Example: The beauty of Saint Hill in England is secondary to its viability and student housing.

CONCLUSION: One does all he can by staff work to improve the image. If image is the reason why one must move from an area where the org was viable or had student housing, forget it. Polish up what you have already. Image is gratifying. *If* A and B exist, one can think about image. Image of the outer building does not much affect A and B. Cleanliness and order of what you have is the image to concentrate upon. Staff pay and food and cheap student housing do more for an org than a posh building.

D. DON'T SELL IN ORDER TO RENT IF YOU'RE VIABLE.

Example: London about 1965 agreed to sell its buildings. Three years later by agreement it had to vacate. It squandered its money so made and has rented quarters and has not done well since.

Example: Johannesburg sold its buildings in the late 60s for a profit, blew the profit on old bills instead of making the money and has been on a struggle ever since.

Example: Reversely, Washington, DC has paid for its buildings in rent several times over and has nothing and is in sporadic trouble, probably exceeding its 17 percent of gross for quarters.

CONCLUSION: Purchase is superior to renting unless political viability is very bad. And when an org owns quarters and is viable, it is not clever to sell and rent.

E. Expensive office equipment is not a first priority.

Example: Camden, New Jersey 1954 bought beautiful desks and chairs and cabinets. When it moved they were seized on a landlord pretext. All its reserves were tied up in furniture which can't be resold anyway.

CONCLUSION: *Enough* desks and chairs and furnishings is far superior to top-grade office furniture. Reserves tied up in furniture is never recoverable. Furniture quality does not influence production. Furniture lack does reduce production.

F. Renovations are destructive if extensive.

Example: London 1958–59 rented 7 Fitzroy. Contrary to orders which were to hire a man and do one room at a time, it went all out with contractors and even rewired the place and went broke on renovation bills. It took three rough years to get the org out of debt. Then when the building was given back to the owners (Church of England), they charged huge building damages which had to be paid although they had a new, sleek building in return for an old wreck it had been.

Example: Phoenix 1955 cost all the org reserves to renovate a building then lost.

Example: A ship was fully renovated before use and wound up costing more than a huge, usable ship.

CONCLUSION: Don't renovate at vast expense. *Use* and make it better as you can with your own people.

G. Other businesses or rentals to support an org wind up very costly.

Example: Hickstead Garage was bought to support Saint Hill. Was a horrible drag and distraction and supported nothing, not even itself. Saint Hill Special Briefing Course supported Saint Hill.

CONCLUSION: Schemes to use other than Scientology actions or partial rentals, etc., can be a bad nuisance. *Scientology* supports Scientology orgs and we learn this over and over.

H. Depending on political viability, it is better to buy than rent.

If political viability is shaky, it is better to rent than buy.

Example: Spain's Hotel Reycar was a great success as a rental, getting org quarters so students would rent rooms. However, the Spanish government was worked on by the South African ambassador who was worked on by the World Federation of Mental Health stooge Stander, a commie in South Africa. The org was subjected to surveillance and upset and moved. It could not have moved easily had it owned.

CONCLUSION: In politically troubled areas use a downstat hotel and promise student room rentals. One can move in hours. Or one can stay. This would apply to the Middle East or to any country, like Spain, subjected to political menace. (Spain is intolerant of religions, and its officials are bought easily and is caving in to Russian pressures and probably won't live as a government beyond Franco's death.)

I.   Where possible, don't split up units of the same org unless you have to.

Example: Notting Hill Gate 1955 was rented. Half the org stayed a bus ride away at 163 Holland Park, London. Denied some of the services of an org, each part had a rough time.

Examples: The HGC Los Angeles from 1956 for some time was separate. This was not too bad and it paralleled an earlier 1955 separate building HGC in Washington. But the secret here was the personal competence of the HGC D of P and when that person was promoted to Los Angeles the HGC did much less well. The separate HGC in LA got into out-tech.

CONCLUSION: The functioning public line units (Academy, HGC) should not be in separate buildings from the org. However, working units such as Mimeo or even Div 2, except the Body Reg, have sometimes been separate from an org and no trouble was experienced. Housing and food for a staff can of course be separate and should be.

SUMMARY

The above are the major policies relating to obtaining and situating quarters.

A and B are much more important than the remainder.

An org which adventures more than 15 percent of its current gross income for rent or purchase payments can get into far more serious trouble than an org with a poor building image. Hopeful thinking contrary to these policies, especially A and B, can smash an org.

The switch of address alone can cost an org a great deal unless loudly remedied.

One maxim is, if you have a going concern with enough income and pay, don't monkey with it until you can realize a total purchase price with A and B in mind.

L. RON HUBBARD
Founder

HCO POLICY LETTER OF 16 AUGUST 1974RA
REVISED 13 FEBRUARY 1991

Remimeo
Finance Network
LRH Comms
Exec Council
HCO
Estates Managers
Estates Personnel

ESTATES
RESTORED TO DEPT 21

On receipt, Estates is restored to DEPT 21, DIVISION 7.

Buildings, properties and org facilities are assets and are under the charge of the Finance Network, in Dept 21.

Buildings, internationally, must be *managed*. This function is the hat of the International Landlord in the Int Finance Office.

Personnel to handle Estates functions in orgs are to be posted in Dept 21 under an Estates Manager.

The Finance Network is alerted to staff up their offices and Estates so as to handle any overload before it occurs.

Estates has historically only functioned well in Dept 21.

ESTATES DUTIES

The Estates Branch is in the charge of the Estates Manager.

The Estates Manager is responsible for locating new premises as the org expands or needs new quarters and for obtaining approval on and securing such premises.

The Estates Branch is responsible for the upkeep, maintenance and operationalness of all mechanical systems in the org, including plumbing, heating, electrical and any others, and for the operational state of all motors and machines of any kind on the premises, including vehicles.

They are responsible for the routine maintenance, cleaning, repair and servicing of the org grounds, buildings and facilities, which includes landscaping and grounds, painting, carpentry work and any action that will restore or add to the asset value or usability of org premises and fixtures.

Under the Estates Branch also comes new construction and all renovations of existing buildings.

Org equipment such as typewriters, addresso or photocopy machines do not come under the Estates Branch, but are the responsibility of the user as designated by the Dir RAM on stock cards and the Dir RAM is overall responsible for the upkeep and operational state of such items.

ESTATES OPERATIONS

The essence of successful Estates operations is to separate out maintenance and service actions from repair or renovations actions, as each of these require their own unit of time. Maintenance and service are continuing actions that are repeated over and over again, whereas repairs, renovations and new construction are one-time actions (which, when completed, require routine service and maintenance actions to keep them up to standard).

ALL MAINTENANCE AND SERVICE ACTIONS ARE DONE AGAINST MAINTENANCE AND SERVICE CHECKLISTS.

ALL REPAIR AND RENOVATION ACTIONS ARE DONE AGAINST A JOB CARD SYSTEM.

Maintenance and Service Checklists

The responsible Estates personnel must have checklists which cover all maintenance, service and routine cleaning actions. These include both weekly and daily checklists, according to the actions they cover.

Weekly inspection checklists must cover in detail all areas of the org premises, grounds, building exterior and interior, room by room, including inspection of plumbing, electrical, heating, ventilation and all other systems and machinery. Each area is then inspected each week as to state of repair, state of operation, cleanliness and usability. Items and areas inspected are accordingly marked as in or out so they can be *handled*.

Such checklists are drawn up against the ideal scene of appearance and usability and must not be reduced down to what the Estates Manager thinks he can handle in a week or a day. Only in this way do they assist in reaching and maintaining an ideal scene.

Checklists are usually drawn up locally by the Estates Manager, based upon a working knowledge of the org premises maintenance requirements. Checklists are subject to approval by the LRH Comm and are issued locally and mimeoed in sufficient quantity for routine use. They should be revised and updated based on experience in use and expanded facilities. Completed checklists are sent to Flag Data Files and provide a valuable record against which the productivity and viability of the Estates Branch and the state of org premises can be estimated.

Maintenance checklists are never to be tossed off as unimportant.

Job Cards for Repairs and Renovations

A job card is a small card on which is recorded the job to be done. Job cards are used for all repair and renovation actions. There must exist a master card file of all ordered or ongoing repair or renovation cycles.

In this way, the work of Estates can be arranged against proper planning and exists in an orderly fashion, and work which is not ordered, planned for or approved does not mistakenly begin.

Each job card contains the date, name of the job to be done, area of the org involved, a target date for completion and a notation of priority of the action. Repair and renovation cards are drawn initially from a thorough inspection of the org aimed at detecting areas of deterioration or mest in disrepair which require handling. These can also be originated based on necessary or useful renovations which will improve the usability of org premises and areas, enhance org image, etc.

The Estates Manager and his seniors can inspect against the job cards to see if the jobs are being done and what remains to complete them. The cards are kept up-to-date as jobs commence and complete and are added to from routine org inspections. Sensible demands to the Estates Branch from staff members or executives become at once the subject of a job card and are handled in their order of priority.

Job cards are then posted on a board, or listed out by name on a large board, and kept well in view and shown as started or not or completed. From this the Estates Manager can program out his work towards a steady improvement in premises.

Using Programs and Project Orders

All renovation actions (and construction work, such as putting in a new course room or expanding an existing course room, adding rooms into an existing building, repaving the parking lot, etc.) are done using programs and/or project orders. (Ref: HCO PL 1 May 65 II, ORDER BOARD AND TIME MACHINE and HCO PL 19 Aug. 71, PROGRAMS, USE OF—HOW TO SAVE USELESS WORK)

CLEANING STATIONS

A cleaning station is assigned to every staff member in the org, with a cleaning stations list drawn up to cover all areas of the org. A staff member is usually assigned his own work area as a cleaning station. A staff member is responsible to clean his own work area and keeps it tidy and unenmested.

A daily cleaning stations period is designated and published as part of the org schedule, usually before or after org business hours. The HAS sees that cleaning station lists are issued and that cleaning stations are in fact attended.

However, in a busy org, the building, rooms and any grounds or walks or approaches need daily attention to keep them shipshape. Offices, reception areas, auditing rooms, WCs, exterior areas, all need daily handling. This takes an Estates Branch.

Often when an org is working days, nights and weekends, there is trouble getting rooms, particularly offices, auditing rooms and study rooms cleaned. Thus Estates Branch actions have to cope with this problem, by properly scheduled cleaning stations and Estates cleaning.

The broken door latch, the stuck drawer, the burned out lamp and broken window are all Estates matters. The littered sidewalk and full dustbins are Estates concerns. Waxing floors, washing windows, etc., are Estates matters.

The job of Estates is to keep our buildings posh and the quarters cared for. Cleaning stations must be well planned and done with high standards.

Estates should have checklists for every mousehole of every building inside and outside that catch every slightest outness in the quarters themselves. Any outnesses found would be brought to the attention of the person whose cleaning station it is, or the Estates personnel responsible.

The Estates Branch retains final responsibility for the cleanliness of the org.

ESTATES PERSONNEL

There must be at least a single-hatted Estates Manager in each org. By longstanding tradition, Estates Managers can be employees hired on fixed pay instead of unit pay. Unit pay is, however, the more usual action. Any difficulty encountered in getting a contracted staff member appointed to the post of Estates Manager should be acted on with a demand to obtain, on FP channels, the okay to hire an Estates Manager on fixed pay. If this is made necessary though, it is very unusual.

Such personnel must, however, be thoroughly hatted and apprenticed for their posts to ensure efficiency. They must be posted as Estates Managers responsible for the whole Estates Branch, not as janitors or org cleaners.

Downstats who have failed elsewhere will fail in charge of Estates and may not be so utilized.

It is expressly forbidden to man up Estates posts with downstat or unqualified staff members. Only by permanently posting in Estates competent personnel, who can be hatted and apprenticed for the job and who will have the time and responsibility level to create their posts, does one obtain an upstat Estates scene.

One thing that will destroy morale in an Estates area is a state of underman. The principle that an overloaded division empties out applies, and in fact in one instance an undermanned Estates area emptied out and was all but destroyed with blows and demanded transfers. No org can afford to be without a properly manned up Estates Branch.

SUMMARY

The above policies are derived from long years of experience with Estates in the Sea Org. They are proven workable and are the backbone of a successful Estates operation.

Estates, as an activity, will succeed only to the degree that these policies are followed, and that primary targets are in: someone there taking responsibility for the area, form of organization held or reestablished and organization operating.

L. RON HUBBARD
Founder

Revision assisted by
LRH Technical Research
and Compilations

HCO POLICY LETTER OF 25 APRIL 1979

Remimeo

ESTATES PRODUCTION STATISTICS

Refs:

HCO PL	6 Nov. 66	STATISTIC INTERPRETATION
		ESTATES STATISTIC
HCO PL	12 Oct. 67	OPERATIONAL, DEFINITION OF

The statistics of repair, construction and renovation and percentage of inspection checklist items passed as described in BPL 16 Aug. 74RB II, ESTATES SECTION BACK TO DEPT 21 are CANCELLED.

The production statistic for Estates is dual:

PERCENTAGE OF FULLY OPERATIONAL EQUIPMENT
and
NUMBER OF SQUARE PACES OF USEFUL SPACE

PERCENTAGE OF FULLY OPERATIONAL EQUIPMENT

The percentage of fully operational equipment stat requires that machines and equipment are assigned a value, e.g. main building boiler 500 points, hot water circulating pump 10 points. Total points on a list of all org equipment divided into the sum of points of equipment found fully operational x 100 will give the percentage of fully operational equipment.

Point values are assigned according to the amount of service provided to the users of the premises with the greater number of points assigned to the machine or piece of equipment that produces more service. Priority equipment, like fire extinguishers and fire doors are given higher than normal points as they have a greater importance. A master list of machinery and equipment must be drawn up with point values assigned under categories. This list is the stable datum for the computation of the statistic. Sample categories are: machines, pumps and compressors, ventilation, electrical equipment, galley equipment, cleaning equipment, fire equipment, heating equipment, plumbing, air conditioning.

NUMBER OF SQUARE PACES OF USEFUL SPACE

The number of square paces of useful space statistic is computed exactly per HCO PL 6 Nov. 66, STATISTIC INTERPRETATION, ESTATES STATISTIC.

INSPECTION AND REPORTING

The Dir I&R (or as held from above) inspects both the stats at the same time at the end of the week. The definitions of "operational" and "useful" given in the above reference HCO Policy Letters must be used exactly and honestly.

Both statistics are reported weekly to Flag via FOLO on the org's OIC cable.

It should be noted that these statistics parallel each other and when they don't, by graph comparison, management should become very interested. As both stats measure the production of Estates, the Estates terminals in charge of planning, whether it is a single Estates manager or a building CO with 50 staff, should work out Estates' actions toward increasing both stats at the same time.

SUMMARY

If these statistics are accurately and honestly computed and reported, you will find the org's premises being continually upgraded in appearance and operational state. You will also find that these statistics allow prediction to go in on needed repair and maintenance, and Estates' planning will become very real.

Use these stats. Increase your org image. The public knows us by our mest.

L. RON HUBBARD
Founder

Assisted by
CS-E

OFFICE OF THE FLAG REPRESENTATIVE

HCO POLICY LETTER OF 29 DECEMBER 1971RB
REVISED 4 SEPTEMBER 1990

Remimeo
Flag Rep Hat

(Also issued as FO 3096RB)

FLAG REPRESENTATIVE, PURPOSE OF

To safeguard that those actions necessary to the delivery of Scientology by an area or org are implemented and continued and to prevent the destruction of the org by omissions, alter-is or counter-intention and to keep Flag abreast of the existing scene so that efficient operation can be directed.

A study reveals that orgs fade and stumble simply and only because vital actions are dropped out or harmful arbitraries are introduced. This is also true of Continental Liaison Offices and OTLs.

It has been proven continually that orgs which function on policy deliver and prosper. Periods of decline have been preceded by gross omissions, unwarranted changes or destructive actions which obstruct or distract from delivery.

Therefore an org that can be kept on policy, whose gross omissions are rapidly reported and in which unwarranted changes and destructive actions are prevented will maintain its delivery and prosperity and will be free of long periods of depression where previous hard work has been destroyed by neglect.

Our orgs, unlike industry where the machine prevails, are built out of people. It takes time to train people and people shift and change. Thus our orgs are subject to unstabilizing human factors such as the absences of people or their own conflicts. A decline can come about simply by transfers and failures to train and apprentice replacements.

The major factors which keep an org delivering and prosperous are actually few. The things which can destroy it are not very many.

Therefore it is up to the Flag Representative to inspect these factors regularly and rapidly alert Flag as to such changes in cases where his own influence does not serve as a brake.

Therefore Flag Reps shall be provided with org checklists which embrace these points and shall fill them in and keep Flag advised not only of the general scene but of the vital points which keep an org delivering and prosperous.

FLAG REP LINES

The communication and command lines of a Flag Rep are parallel to the communication and command line of the org or CLO.

The Flag Rep is of equal seniority to the CO or ED.

Therefore the Flag Rep lines are not subject to inspection or via at local level.

It is a Comm Ev offense for an org or executive to halt a Flag Rep communication or edit it.

FLAG REP PR

It is a duty of the Flag Rep to enhance the image of Flag and to counter local false reports and entheta concerning Flag.

The Flag Rep can always be sure that the intentions of Flag are to make it go right. This is not always understood at local levels.

Example: Bongville Org sends their worst case, who has blown the org twice, to Flag for the FEBC. Flag has done its best to straighten the case out and train the person. The person on return causes upset. Bongville blames Flag. The Flag Rep should point out it was Bongville and insist a competent high stat person be sent to Flag for training and auditing.

Example: An order from Flag upsets the whole lineup of Division 6 Bongville. The Flag Rep should rapidly gather the facts, hold the order in suspense and get the whole story to Flag Rep I/C with a request to modify. Too much of this will of course make that Flag Rep unpopular at Flag but permitting an unintentionally destructive order to go into effect will also make the Flag Rep look ineffective.

One of the main purposes of PR is TO INTERPRET THE POLICIES OF TOP MANAGEMENT.

Flag Rep should obtain info from Flag so that he *can* say why this or that was done.

Preservation of Flag image and its enhancement is done by standard PR tech and the Flag Rep should be familiar with it.

FAMILIARIZATION

The Flag Rep should carry forward a personal program of familiarizing himself with the technology of admin and tech he is safeguarding.

He can request from Flag or obtain locally various packs so that he can read up on what he is safeguarding.

A regular daily program of this should be in effect.

KEY INGREDIENTS

A further study of Flag Rep lines shows that Supervision is not the Key Ingredient.

The Key Ingredient (HCO PL 14 Sept. 69, AKH Series 22, THE KEY INGREDIENTS) of the Flag Rep is OBSERVATION.

To quote the PL:

"First is OBSERVATION. From beginning to end Observation must serve both those in charge and any others who plan. When Observation is lacking, then planning itself as well as any and all progress can become unreal and orders (can become) faulty and destructive. Observation in essence must be TRUE. Nothing must muddy it or color it as this can lead to gross errors in action and training."

VALUE

If a Flag Rep can carry forward his post purpose well, he will succeed in preventing delivery slumps. The value of a slump is the difference between what an org was averaging in delivery in a good period when it was well run and a bad period when omissions, alter-is and neglect have given it low delivery. This will be found to be considerable.

Org losses are losses of what it *should* be delivering and what it *is* delivering in a poor period.

STAT

The stat of a Flag Rep is therefore the difference between an ideal scene and the existing scene measured in DELIVERY.

A paid comps stat ceiling is set for the org (or area) based on its best times over a period.

A paid comps stat low is set for the org based on its low over a consistent low period.

The proportion of this made good in honest delivery by the org is a stat of the Flag Rep.

Example: A consistent low period of the last year was 150 paid comps. The consistent high period peaked several times at 300 paid comps. This is a figure of 150 paid comps "loss." Current week's paid comps is 230. That means 80 above low. The stat in fractions is therefore 80/150 or *53 percent*. The 53 percent is the FR stat. He is considered to have recovered 53 percent of the "loss" for that week. Anything below the minimum is reported as zero. Anything above the maximum will of course add up to more than 100 percent. Such percents can be graphed.

This stat shows what the org is doing compared to what it should be doing. This is a direct index of omissions, alter-is and counter-intention in the org.

THIS STAT HIGH AND LOW IS SET BY FLAG REP I/C.

It takes *all* the factors of an org to make and keep up its paid completions.

The Basic Staff Hat, Volume Zero OEC, gives the pattern of how this is done.

APPEARANCE

The Flag Rep should be very careful of his appearance and manners.

Clean, well-dressed appearance carries status.

Good manners ease the communication lines with staff members.

CONFERENCES

A Flag Rep may attend Executive Councils, Aide Councils, Advisory Committees or Conferences. He should be advised of their scheduled times.

He has no vote.

He may however, as Flag Rep, give his opinion and he may state, when necessary, what he will report to Flag when omissions or departures seem gross or threatening.

MISSIONS

A Flag Rep may call for a mission to come and support him if in difficulties he cannot handle.

It is required that such a mission, called for, be sent—from Flag to a CLO FR and from a CLO to an org FR.

The mission may be called for and sent only to carry out the purpose of a Flag Rep as contained in this issue.

ADVICE LETTER

A weekly advice letter on the scene is required from a Flag Rep to Flag Rep I/C.

REQUIRED INVESTIGATIONS

Investigations required by Flag or CLOs may be requested on Flag Rep lines.

This issue is supplemented by other FOs and PLs relating to Flag Representatives.

L. RON HUBBARD
Founder

Revision assisted by
LRH Technical Research
and Compilations

HCO POLICY LETTER OF 31 DECEMBER 1971

Remimeo
Flag Rep Hat
Also FO 3097

FLAG REP
KEY INGREDIENTS

KEY INGREDIENTS

A further study of Flag Rep lines shows that *Supervision* is not the key ingredient.

The key ingredient (HCO PL 14 Sept. 69, AKH Series 22) of the Flag Rep is OBSERVATION.

To quote the PL:

"First is OBSERVATION. From beginning to end, observation must serve both those in charge and any others who plan. When observation is lacking, then planning itself as well as any and all progress can become unreal and orders (can become) faulty and destructive. Observation in essence must be TRUE. Nothing must muddy it or color it as this can lead to gross errors in action and training."

L. RON HUBBARD
Founder

HCO POLICY LETTER OF 7 AUGUST 1973R
Issue I
REVISED 2 JANUARY 1991

Remimeo

FLAG REPRESENTATIVE,
PURPOSE, DUTIES AND STATISTIC

PURPOSE

The purpose of the Flag Representative is:

To find and report situations to Flag and to obtain compliance on orders from Flag, it being understood that such orders result from valid evaluations based on Flag Rep reports, routine reports and always with due attention to the actual statistics of the activity.

SENIORITY

All Flag Representatives operate under the authority of the Boards of Directors of Churches from which stems the authority of the Flag Bureaux.

The immediate senior of a Flag Representative in any Church organization is the Continental Flag Representative for that continental zone.

The immediate senior of a Continental Flag Representative is the Flag Flag Representative.

The senior of the Flag Flag Representative is the CO Flag Bureaux.

The CO Flag Bureaux is responsible to the Boards of Directors of Churches.

The Executive Director or CO of a ship or church ranks with but not above or below a Flag Representative for his church.

A Continental Flag Representative ranks with the CO of a Flag Operations Liaison Office but not above or below.

ETHICS

A Flag Representative may not be comm eved in the church or ship to which he is assigned but may be at the next highest level on its orders, but in the physical area of the next highest level. The exception is that a Flag Representative may be disciplined or comm eved by a Flag or FOLO mission (providing it contains three members) in the area of the church or ship to which he is a representative. A Comm Ev may be ordered on a Flag Representative only for false reports, neglect of duty, misrepresenting the intentions of Flag or bringing Flag into disrepute by statements, actions or personal misconduct, and for felonies.

Conditions may be assigned by the Flag Flag Representative or the Continental Flag Representative but only for the statistical trends of the Flag Representative's own statistics.

A Flag Representative or Continental Flag Representative may be removed from post only if the continental zone or the area statistics are trending toward collapse beyond reasonable doubt of rapid recovery, but any such removal shall then be followed by Comm Ev if requested by the Flag Representative.

The ethics powers of a Flag Representative shall consist of the right to assign conditions to any staff or crew member who willfully and repeatedly refuses to comply with Flag orders, but only if that person's correctly computed correctly assigned personal statistics are down. This includes the Executive Director or CO. This does not include a member of the LRH Comm or Office of Special Affairs Networks over whom the Flag Representative has no power except that of report, a power which they also have over the Flag Representative.

REPORTS

Any situation of whatever kind that may in any way influence the well-being of a church or ship, its statistics, staff or public presence or repute should be the subject of a Flag Representative report.

Any situation which shows a valuable advance or improvement or commendable actions on the part of an Executive Director, CO, staff member or crew when it advances the purposes of Scientology or improves statistics can be the subject of a Flag Representative report.

Any type of report required by Flag may be the subject of a Flag Representative report.

The obtaining of other types or forms of reports needed by Flag or delinquent from the Church or ship may be nudged and gotten by the Flag Representative and qualifies then as a Flag Rep report for statistical purposes even though it is in another form but has been gotten only after it is already delinquent.

Reports shall be in the form set from time to time by the Flag Flag Representative. They may also be in an informal or telex form, as the situation may require.

COMPLIANCES

The basic order form of Flag is the Aides Order. This is an evaluation done by a Flag evaluator. It contains targets. Continental and Base Orders when instructed to be activated by a Continental Flag Rep or the Flag Flag Rep, both on the competent orders of the Flag Bureaux or by the Continental FOLO CO in the absence of and when not in conflict with Aides Orders or PLs, HCOBs, or FOs, may, in unusual circumstances and during emergency, be enforced by a Flag Representative.

When an LRH ED, PL, HCOB or FO is contained as part of an AO or when it is being specially urged by the Flag Bureaux on any communication channel, the Flag Representative may exact compliance with it and should. When there is an LRH Comm the LRH Comm may also exact compliance with the same order and may obtain statistics for its target compliances but regardless of who obtained the compliance when it is being urged on Flag Rep lines by the Flag Bureaux, the Flag Rep also obtains statistical credit for its compliances. Thus two different networks may obtain compliance statistics from compliance with the same order, LRH Comm and Flag Rep. The Flag Rep however does not obtain statistical credit for programs being urged only on the LRH Comm Network: it must also be part of an AO or direct order for the Flag Rep to obtain credit.

Telexed orders from the Flag Bureaux or Continental Flag Rep to investigate and report or to obtain compliances, when complied with, count as compliances as well as reports.

Priority A (highest) despatches requiring a report count as reports and if they give orders for compliances count also as compliances when these are obtained.

An acknowledgment of an AO or order simply stating that it has been received counts as a report, as it has value to the Flag Bureaux.

STATISTICS

The statistic of the Flag Representative is dual:

NUMBER OF REPORTS TO FLAG OR THE NEXT SENIOR FLAG REPRESENTATIVE (who forwards them to Flag).

NUMBER OF COMPLIANCES OBTAINED FULLY AND COMPLETELY ON TARGETS ON PROGRAMS ORDERED DONE BY FLAG OR THE CONTINENTAL FOLO IN THE ABSENCE OF FLAG ORDERS, WITH AN ADDED TEN FOR THE FULL COMPLETION OF THE WHOLE PROGRAM IN THE AREA WHERE THE FLAG REPRESENTATIVE HAS AUTHORITY.

LOGGING

The Flag Rep keeps a Flag Rep Report Log. Each report sent to Flag is logged with its title and date so that it can be identified. Copies of the report are filed as well as sent to Flag.

The Flag Representative also keeps a Flag Rep Compliance Log. Each incoming order is entered into this log with a copy of the order or program placed or stapled in the log so that it can be lifted.

The record of actions done on its targets are noted in the log with the name of the person who would be nudged to get compliance with each target.

The arrangement of both logs are such that they facilitate the orderly business of the Flag Rep and permit the easy tally of the effectiveness of his work and its statistics.

The logs are scrupulously kept up-to-date and should be the first point of inspection of any mission into the area.

The logs are kept hourly current and are not "caught up with" as they ARE the working substance of the post.

When full, a log is carefully preserved in files for later reference in case data is needed concerning the numbers of times personnel had to be nudged or if there were any false compliances or unreceived orders. Further, such logs SHOULD

ALWAYS BE PART OF ANY EVIDENCE PLACED BEFORE A COMM EV ON A FLAG REPRESENTATIVE OR OF AN EXECUTIVE OF A CHURCH OR SHIP.

REPORTING STATISTICS

As each action is done, what it is is identifiably noted in its proper log.

The date and title of a report and its method of transmission—by despatch or telex—is noted.

The date and number or other designating means of a compliance obtained, is entered in the compliance log.

At the close of each day the last action of the Flag Rep is to tally his day's stats. These are done on a single sheet. The report stat is in red with a dotted line. The compliance stat is in blue in a solid line.

At the end of each working week, the Flag Rep computes his two daily stats and makes them the subject of a despatch (for which he gets report credit) to Flag Flag Representative via the Continental Flag Representative. To this report he appends comments on these two figures to explain why they are either one high or low. He files a copy of this despatch in his own office for his own record.

The Continental Flag Rep makes certain that he has the reports all in, but not longer than one week from the week that has just closed (all missing ones then are considered and marked a no-report), and adds these up for his own collective statistic. He graphs them locally and for Flag appends his own collective statistic and makes his comments on them. He sends the bundle to Flag Flag Rep.

Flag Flag Rep causes these statistics to be graphed and displayed on Flag for these are the Flag Flag Rep's stats.

In this way the Continental FOLO Programs executives and the Programs Chiefs on Flag are both kept abreast of (a) the alertness of the Flag Reps in specific areas and (b) the degree of compliance and program progress rate in specific churches and ships, (c) the general effectiveness of their own work when measured against general stats for a church or ship and (d) the value of the Flag Rep Network.

SUMMARY

The need and function of a reporting and compliance network for the Flag Bureaux is vital and by itself can greatly influence the statistics and general expansion of an org and area as well as establish certainty in the Flag Bureaux as well as promote ARC and prevent injustice in Scientology.

L. RON HUBBARD
Founder

Revision assisted by
LRH Technical Research
and Compilations

HCO POLICY LETTER OF 15 AUGUST 1973R
REVISED 2 JANUARY 1991

Remimeo

FLAG REPRESENTATIVE, ORDERS TO

Ref:

HCO PL 7 Aug. 73R   FLAG REPRESENTATIVE,
Rev. 2.1.91   PURPOSE, DUTIES AND STATISTIC

Programs Bureau Chiefs or Aides may order the Flag Representative to report on certain situations or to obtain compliances with exact programs which have resulted from evaluations that apply to that org.

In usual practice, orders from Flag and FOLOs travel to the Flag Representative of that org. It is up to the Flag Rep to take up the matter known to the board or the Executive Director of his org.

The routine line would be for the Flag Rep to receive copies of Aides Orders or EDs, to log it, to see that copies were available as needed to those who would be responsible for execution in the org, to then personally, in contact with staff members, see that the AO's program was executed fully and completely and then to send the completed program and any evidences thereof to Flag with a copy for the FOLO which is removed by the FOLO en route. The addressee on Flag would be the Programs Chief under which the org came.

The Programs Chief responsible for that org is the one who is responsible for seeing that copies of the AO or ED are actually sent, even though distribution may have routine copies going on other channels. The Programs Chief addresses them to the Flag Rep of that org. He also is responsible for sending copies to his FOLO.

The Executive Director of the org is responsible for his org's stats and viability. He may not be pulled into the direct compliance line and the Flag Rep must not offload his hat onto the Executive Director "to get the program done." It is the Flag Rep who does the actual staff contacts and sees that they comply with the target that applies. Targets that belong to the Executive Director must of course be executed by the Executive Director.

An Executive Director has much to do to keep the org running and viable. It is probable that cross orders (where the AO is ordering one thing and the ED another) will exist. But in any such conflict, the AO has priority. If the ED objects he may contact the FOLO and through it Flag to get a reconsideration of the specific order if he considers it will damage his stats. It is up to the Aide who has the most associated division to the order to judge whether or not it should be changed. If there is no answer in five days the AO order must be executed.

The Programs Chief for that org or area is also responsible for the overall stats of that org, like the ED, but is also responsible for getting programs executed.

The Flag Flag Rep may intervene in any dispute to get the matter clarified and it is to the Flag Flag Rep that the org's Flag Rep addresses his side of any dispute in the org.

The routine reports or reports ordered from the org's Flag Rep, are returned to the person on Flag who ordered them. All such reports, however, go to the Data Bureau where they are reviewed or received by the person interested. If a Flag Rep supposes some crucial report sent in has been overlooked, he may send an alert to the person who ordered it in the first place, using a red ball point or sign pen on a white card and including it in routine traffic. These will reach the person directly.

The FOLO should not contact the Executive Director with questions but should contact the Flag Rep and get the data required, or pass on the order being urged.

The exceptions are the LRH Comm and Office of Special Affairs Networks. Their traffic does not pass through the Flag Rep but goes to the LRH Comm of the org or its Director of Special Affairs.

Materials from Flag to the board of any org pass through the Flag Rep except as they may concern LRH Comm or Office of Special Affairs matters since the latter two are always free to independently approach the board.

The Flag Rep is at all times answerable to the Flag Flag Rep. He may not be removed by a Programs Chief or assigned a condition. This is done by the Programs Chief to the Flag Flag Rep who would be expected to look more carefully into the matter and protect his network. Complaints from Aides or Flag executives must follow the same channel.

Where it becomes difficult for a Flag Rep to get report material required or compliances from staff members and where evidence may be found that he is being obstructed or that the staff is being ordered not to cooperate or that he is being disparaged and the image of Flag injured, the Flag Rep may request an ethics mission from his FOLO to look into the matter and handle any out-ethics that may exist in the org. When such a mission is requested, the FOLO Captain must see that it is responded to and that a mission is actually sent and that the mission acts with justice and handles any situation found in a way that is creditable to Flag and the FOLO.

If a Flag Rep suspects that he is being sent random orders that are not part of a program based on an evaluation, he should inform the LRH Comm who must put the matter through to LRH Comm International who can act through the LRH Comm Flag Bureaux to set the matter straight rapidly and get proper evaluations and programs being done, for it is in the interest both of LRH Comm International and LRH Comm Flag Bureaux to keep an on-policy Flag Bureaux functioning.

Telexed programs are sometimes sent without the entire AO or ED and should be gotten in on the assumption that they are part of a proper evaluation. But if the AO itself then fails to appear within a reasonable time, the Flag Rep should take action as above, for it can be fatal to begin to execute random orders and could get the org into a poor state and injure the repute of the Flag Rep.

The Flag Rep in an org or Flag Flag Rep may protest an evaluation as not based on fact and liable to injure the org or its stats. The protest takes the form of an urgent request to Authority, Verification and Correction Unit International (AVC) to at once again check the AO for accuracy, giving any contrary data. AVC may then reject the AO, order it to be redone, and should quickly inform the Flag Rep or Flag Flag Rep that it has done so. In this event AVC must time machine a replacement AO for 48 hours and see that the new AO actually comes into existence and is sent the org. In such an event, AVC must assign a condition to the Programs Chief if the AO is found to have been incorrect and must order further ethics action if the new AO is not expedited.

The Executive Director uses the same channels as above to protest random orders through the LRH Comm and to protest unreal AOs to AVC.

The health of an org or area depends upon correct reports, correct evaluation and rapid compliance to programs as well as to the industry and dedication of its executive and staff.

L. RON HUBBARD
Founder

Revision assisted by
LRH Technical Research
and Compilations

HUBBARD COMMUNICATIONS OFFICE
Saint Hill Manor, East Grinstead, Sussex

HCO POLICY LETTER OF 10 APRIL 1979RA
REVISED 12 FEBRUARY 1991

Remimeo
All Flag Reps

FLAG REP STATISTICS

A Flag Representative shall now have two separate stats on the same graph which reflect his production on vital reports required by Flag weekly as well as getting compliances to Flag program targets. Flag Management requires that both of these functions are executed in such a manner that they result in expansion of the org, and the forwarded well-being of the Scientology and Sea Org networks.

REPORTS

The report part of this statistic shall consist of the following weekly reports required on a regular basis and sent off to Flag by 2:00 P.M. Thursday of each week.

Now it is vital that when these reports are done an FR doesn't only just observe but also investigates and finds out exactly what is going on in an area. He must be able to pull strings and to note changes that have occurred in an area. He must also look at stats and refer to them in his reports. For example, by looking at stats he can note high and low stats in his report for that area and give data on why the stat went up or down. It is this kind of data that will really let Flag know what's going on.

1. DELIVERY. Report in detail on the current scene with delivery of Scientology and Dianetics tech to the public. Send in xeroxes of sessions per Tech Flub Catch System, report in detail on the state of the courses, per WHAT IS A COURSE? PL, and the state of the HGCs, with regard to C/S Series 25, and visible tech results. Send a copy of the weekly paid comps breakdown. Also send in data on any red tags, and report in detail on the state of Qual correction, as regards tech and admin personnel and lines that affect delivery. Investigate student points, WDAHs, VSD, student comps, paid releases and find out why these stats went up or down for the week and include this data on your report.

    Also report in detail on the new issues and tech material line. Are new issues and tech materials being issued to the staff and appropriate tech terminals? Is there a backlog? What is the state of the backlog if there is one? What is being done to handle any existing backlog?

2. PUBLIC DISSEMINATION. Report in detail on what the org is actually doing to contact its public and get them in. (All Divs.) Exactly what promotion (including mags, info packs, tickets, FSM newsletters, ads, etc.) has gone out of the org, in what quantity, to what publics during the past week? (Attach copies.) Attach data on degree to which the promo is surveyed and

data of most recent population survey. Describe the state of the lines into and through the org. Exactly what tech briefings for promo sales personnel have occurred during the past weeks? Give details of any public falling off lines and circumstances. What call-in actions, ASR, and ARC break actions are currently occurring? Send real data on the quality of points of public contact; include a couple of xeroxes of Letter Reg letters. Send in a copy of the weekly stock report (also ensure Dir Pubs sent a copy to Pubs). Include data on the state of CF/Addresso. What actions are occurring to get in the promotional actions of the org? To what degree are LRH films/tapes in use in Div 6, how are new public handled and indoctrinated, are FSMs being made active and what performance of Public Reges? Investigate PRPS and GBS, and report on what made these stats go up or down for the week.

3. PERSONNEL. Report in detail on how current Flag Directives on the subject are being implemented. Include specifics on recruits, training of staff, hatting of personnel, estoing, post transfers, removals, TTC, and utilization of staff. Include specifics on current ethics and/or justice actions on staff, data on which staff are currently receiving staff staff auditing or other personnel enhancement actions, and anything else of importance on the personnel scene: how they are handled, who is doing very well, in trouble, who has counter-intention, etc., should be included. Include a copy of the weekly personnel list from HCO. Investigate QSR and QTSM and report on what made these stats go up or down for the week.

4. GROSS INCOME. Report in full on and attach any plans or programs Dept 6, Dept 18, Dept 5, Qual, Dept 7, Dept 4 have for getting in GI. This includes any mini programs that have been written. Look into these programs and report on any major bugs or slows occurring in getting them done. Attach a copy of the org's income sources summary and also include the data of what part of the org made how much of the GI that week. Also attach a list of who actually made the GI that week—include post title, person's name and approximately how much made. What executive actions are occurring on getting GI in, any free service occurring, if so by whom and what, what refunds requested that week, how much and how is it being handled? Report in full on any other planning, actions, and efficiency in getting in GI and any other internal blocks or wrongheadedness on the subject not already covered above. Investigate GI and report on what made this stat go up or down for the week.

5. SOLVENCY. Report in full on the state of Div 3 files, Div 3 backlogs or in-PTness, quality of contact with the public. Attach a copy of the previous week's FP, describe the general solvency scene from exact data, note any irregularities on finance lines encountered. How is the FP Committee attended and operated, what executive actions are occurring on solvency, any FBO major actions in the area, is the PO system in use, any PTSness on finance lines? Include data on staff pay, food/shelter, where applicable. Investigate cash-bills and report on what made this stat go up or down for the week.

6. MANAGEMENT. Exactly what LRH EDs and targets on org programs and/or other programs are currently being pushed or were completed during the past week? How are these being pushed and to what result? How are the execs doing? Attach a copy of the week's battle plan, Exec Council, Ad

Council meeting minutes. Investigate PDC and report on what made this stat go up or down for the week.

The reports required above are to be of a high-quality, in-depth nature. These reports are not done by org staff members (except where specifically noted above, such as staff crew list, FP, but even these should be verified by direct observation so their accuracy is guaranteed) but are done by direct observation and by verification of data, inspection of files and records and are as observed and reported by the Flag Rep himself.

Flag Reps certainly should continue to send in other data as they see necessary to the org's prosperity, and they should continue to encourage other staff to send in their reports.

COMPLIANCES

The types of compliances and how one gets compliance are already covered in existing LRH policy for Flag Reps. Particular note should be taken of LRH policy 8 Jan. 75, COMPLIANCE, HOW TO GET ONE. All Flag Reps are required to star-rate and M9 this PL as a standing order so they can competently carry out their functions. The stat of Flag Rep reports and compliances is reported as two lines on the same sheet. The report stat is marked on the graph as a red dotted line. The compliance stat is marked on the same graph in a solid blue line.

STAT COMPUTATION

The Flag Rep stat is computed as follows:

Plus 1 point for each compliance fully verified by the Flag Rep and sent out before 2:00 P.M. each Thursday.

Plus 5 points for each report of the above 6 reports required to be sent off each week. (Must be sent before 2:00 P.M. each Thursday.)

Plus 10 points for the full completion of a whole program in the area where the Flag Representative has authority.

Plus 1/2 point for FR weekly stat report and any other report that is required by Flag other than the 6 weekly reports, e.g., org weekly reports by other staff members, SIT–WHY–HANDLING reports, change log report, telex investigations.

Minus 2 points for each false compliance forwarded to the FOLO as a done. To be taken off the R/C stat the same week the compliance is rejected.

Minus 10 points for each brushoff, incomplete or no report on any one of the above 6 required categories to be reported on weekly. To be taken off the R/C stat the same week the report is rejected or not done.

The Continental Flag Rep shall have a dual statistic, one for the combined stats for all Sea Org units under his jurisdiction and one for all Scientology Class IV Orgs combined under his jurisdiction.

The above stat requires that the Flag Rep do the routine reports weekly, and to raise his stat the Flag Rep must get volume real compliances. Factually, a Flag Rep who simply reports is not worth much. But a Flag Rep who gets compliance on a Flag order is valuable. If the Flag Rep does perform these two duties well, he will have a far-bettered scene in his org. In order to get all the above done in the required time, the FR is going to have to have his lines in well, and be around the org a lot observing on a routine basis, as well as digging for data, and demanding compliance.

Nothing in this HCO PL cancels or alters the other major stat of the Flag Representative—the percentage of paid comps increase stat per HCO PL 29 Dec. 71RB, FLAG REPRESENTATIVE, PURPOSE OF, which remains as is.

There is a lot to do, so get on with it, and let's see the orgs booming through accurate, vital info getting to Flag and volume compliances to Flag orders done for real.

L. RON HUBBARD
Founder

Revision assisted by
LRH Technical Research
and Compilations

EXECUTIVE DIVISION 7
QUALITY CHECKLIST

HUBBARD COMMUNICATIONS OFFICE
Saint Hill Manor, East Grinstead, Sussex

HCO POLICY LETTER OF 26 FEBRUARY 1972R
Issue V
REVISED 10 SEPTEMBER 1990

Remimeo
Flag Rep
COs
EDs
LRH Comms
Staff Hats
Div 7 Hats

IMPORTANT

COORDINATION OR CONFUSION
AN EXEC DIV CHECKLIST FOR QUALITY

Upon the Executive Division depends the management and coordination of the entire org. Without leaders who know and effectively apply LRH policy and technology, the whole org will rapidly diminish to a state of total confusion.

The Executive Division sets the directions and pace of the org.

The alignment of actions and intentions, coordinated as a whole, brings about the continued prosperity and well-being of the org and its staff.

The quality of performance of this division directs the course of the org and determines its future progress.

There are three grades of quality.

POWER QUALITY

The characteristics of power quality are:

1. All org execs show up to work on time, bright, clean and cheerful. _____

2. All Exec Council posts are posted, with an Executive Director and Executive Secretaries who are Flag Executive Briefing Course graduates. _____

2a. All org execs are experts in their divisions, fully trained and qualified for their posts and know exactly how to apply the correct policy. _____

3. There is a single-hatted LRH Comm on post. _____

3a. The LRH Comm is a Flag Executive Briefing Course graduate. _____

4. An LRH Comm Log is maintained in PT which shows the exact state of compliance of each LRH order (i.e., LRH EDs, HCOBs, HCO PLs, etc.), as designated for the org by management or the LRH Comm himself as needed. _____

5. All LRH orders as designated for the org by management or the LRH Comm himself as needed, are relayed to the intended recipients, duplicated exactly, understood fully and implemented rapidly. _____

6. Full investigations are done to locate the Whys preventing compliance to LRH orders. _____

6a. Correction forms to handle the Whys preventing compliance to LRH orders are issued as needed. _____

7. Tech and policy is gotten in in the org through the use of programs and/or projects which is evident from the numerous amount of re-signs and stellar delivery of the org. _____

8. Full compliance is swiftly and accurately reported on LRH Comm lines to LRH Comm Int via LRH Comm Cont with information to ED Int. _____

8a. No half-dones or not-dones are reported as done. _____

9. Staff and public are encouraged to write to the Executive Director International. _____

9a. Facilities are provided so that they may do so. _____

10. There is an SO #1 box maintained in the org in easy public access that is *daily* handled by the LRH Comm. _____

11. There is an office for LRH in the org which is highly presentable and used only by LRH. _____

12. LRH's presence is prominent in the org with high-quality and correctly-sized photographs of LRH tastefully framed and displayed. _____

12a. LRH's name is used in all promotion. _____

13. Issue authority is granted only for promotion and magazines that are effective, exactly on-policy and based on a valid survey. _____

14. Executive communications fully back up LRH's postulates and help bring them about. _____

15. Justice is safeguarded and all HCO and executive ethics actions conform exactly to policy and to LRH intention. _____

16. Each exec and staff member gets his admin high crimes done in Qual on the key policies of his staff member hat as well as those policies specifically relating to his post. _____

17. The org has adequate quarters that are clean and bright. _____

17a. The org's quarters contribute to the quality and speed of organization and delivery. _____

17b. The quarters make the org staff and public comfortable and are a tribute to LRH and the org. _____

18. There is a single-hatted Keeper of Tech on post. _____

18a. The Keeper of Tech is a trained Class VIII Auditor. _____

18b. The Keeper of Tech is a Flag Executive Briefing Course graduate. _____

19. The Keeper of Tech ensures that there is an established Qual Library and a Tech and Admin Cramming Section, Cramming Officer and Word Clearer or more than one. _____

20. There is no squirrel processing or training occurring and Source materials are available and in use. If the Keeper of Tech receives any report of such actions or lack of LRH materials, he gets it immediately investigated and those responsible handled through ethics action by HCO and correction by the Qual Division. _____

21. The Keeper of Tech ensures requests for refunds and repayments are HANDLED exactly per the refund/repayment routing form when they do occur, and that they are handled standardly and promptly. _____

22. There is an Executive Establishment Officer who is a full FEBC. _____

23. The Executive Establishment Officer is putting the org there by having Establishment Officers establishing the divisions, org staff and the materiel of the division. _____

24. The Flag Banking Officer creates and has an income–outgo surplus by forcing monies routinely into org reserves and to Central Management as an "expense" thereby increasing the org's need for funds and demand for income. _____

25. The Flag Banking Officer, organization executives and FP members are fully hatted in income-making policy expertise and financial planning policies. _____

26. Current and past income sources surveys from invoices exist. _____

26a. Income sources surveys are *used* to reinforce high income sources and revive lowered ones. _____

27. There is consistently adequate FP allocation for surveyed and effective and high-volume promotion that will drive in income. _____

27a. Promotion is never cut to pay bills or for other reasons. _____

27b. The FP Committee, Executive Council and the Flag Banking Officer ensure that items required to get in promotional actions are financed, purchased and used. _____

28. Org cash-bills is excellent. _____

28a. A proper FP No. 1 which allows for promotion and needful actions and all basic vital expenses exists, is current, and is in full use. _____

29. The Flag Banking Officer ensures the staff are well paid. _____

30. The Flag Banking Officer prevents any commitment incurred into the future beyond the org's ability to pay and has no such commitments currently. _____

31. Payments to Central Management for services and management actions are in good range, uptrended and are consistent with org income range. _____

32. The Flag Banking Officer collects and banks all org income daily, matched with Div 3 invoices. _____

32a. The Flag Banking Officer pays allocations promptly and accurately. _____

32b. The Flag Banking Officer has excellent on-policy accounting admin with no backlogs. _____

32c. The Flag Banking Officer keeps command informed with timely accurate financial data and reports. _____

33. The D/FBO for MORE enforces that minimum book stocks are maintained at all times. _____

34. All points of HCO PL 10 May 82, BOOKSTORE OFFICER HAT, are in and remain in. _____

35. Films and lectures are in full use in the org. _____

36. More business is driven down on the org than it can waste, through the use of on-policy promotion. _____

37. There is a single-hatted Flag Representative on post. _____

38. The Flag Representative is well dressed, has excellent manners, carries high status in the org and represents the image of Flag. _____

39. The Flag Representative is aware of the existing scene in the org. _____

39a. The Flag Representative knows what areas are situations, no-situations, and high situations as compared with the statistics of those areas. _____

40. The Flag Representative accurately investigates and sends the required Flag Representative weekly reports each week on a "Look, Don't Listen" basis and sends all data to Flag. _____

40a. The Flag Representive ensures that all required computerized weekly report forms are properly filled in and sent on time. _____

41. The Flag Representative keeps Flag well informed of the general scene in his weekly advice letter and immediately reports any emergency situation, omission, alter-is, false report, or noncompliance to Flag with full specifics. _____

42. The Flag Representative always knows why actions that affect the org are done by Flag and informs local execs as needed. _____

43. The Flag Representative has received copies of all Aides Orders or Executive Directives which apply to his org. _____

43a. The Flag Representative has logged them and sees that copies are available as needed to those who would be responsible for execution in the org. _____

43b. The Flag Representative then personally, in contact with staff members, sees that the org's evaluation, programs from Flag Management and programs from the International Executive Strata are executed fully and completely, and sends completed programs with evidence to Flag, with a copy for the Flag Operations Liaison Office. _____

44. There is a single-hatted Director of Special Affairs on post who has been fully trained. _____

45. The Director of Special Affairs is aware of and is standardly handling legal matters in the org. _____

46. The Director of Special Affairs ensures HCO keeps valuable documents in proper order and condition. _____

47. The Director of Special Affairs ensures the org is properly incorporated, registered to do business and files the necessary corporation reports and returns required by the county, state or country. _____

48. The Director of Special Affairs ensures the copyrights, trademarks and patents of Scientology are properly registered and protected in the state or country concerned. _____

49. The Director of Special Affairs appoints all attorneys or solicitors for the org and handles all suits against the corporation or its principals and ensures such are won. _____

50. The Director of Special Affairs originates and undertakes legal actions on behalf of the org against those threatening Scientology or the org. _____

51. The Director of Special Affairs has PR area control built up to a point where any attacks on the local organization would be rebuffed by the people in the area. _____

52. The Director of Special Affairs isolates and fully handles any groups that are hostile towards the organization. _____

53. The Director of Special Affairs protects the corporate status of Scientology as a religion. _____

54. The Director of Special Affairs has full information about any potential attackers of the org, plans the handling of such, and does successfully handle any attack situation occurring. _____

55. All Director of Special Affairs media matters pertaining to press relations, government relations, opposition group relations and troublesome relations are handled by the Director of Special Affairs to the betterment of the org's image in the community. _____

56. The Director of Special Affairs ensures all required balance sheets and tax returns are filed on time and protects the tax status of the org. _____

57. Students and pcs are satisfied with the services they are obtaining, are completing and are re-signing up for more services. _____

58. The Executive Council meets regularly and takes effective actions to plan, coordinate and direct the org. _____

58a. The Advisory Council meets regularly and works as a team to forward org viability, production and organization. _____

58b. The Advisory Committees meet regularly and determine condition assignments and planning for their respective division. _____

59. Staff meetings occur weekly, with briefings from individual staff on any flaps and handlings, general business and their statistics, conditions and battle plans, so as to ensure the group members are informed and their actions and efforts are coordinated and moving in the same direction. _____

60. There is a D/CO or D/ED for Delivery and Exchange posted and functioning and is a Flag Executive Briefing Course graduate. _____

61. The D/CO or D/ED for Delivery and Exchange has sales, call-in, delivery and re-sign occurring. _____

62. The D/CO or D/ED for Delivery and Exchange has exchange in abundance happening with no backlogged service and is keeping up with the present sales. _____

63. The Executive Secretaries target the org products and see that the targets are achieved. _____

63a. The Executive Secretaries keep the staff winning on their production cycles. _____

64. The Org Officers for the Executive Secretaries back up the Executive Secretaries and see that the needed organization is rapidly established so that products actually are delivered. _____

65. All stats are posted where they can be seen by staff. _____

65a. Org executives operate their divisions BY STATISTICS per policy. _____

66. The executives ensure that each area in the org is assigned and operating on the correct condition. _____

66a. The staff of the org are correctly applying the conditions of their post. _____

67. The CO/ED daily inspects all areas of the org. _____

68. Org executives daily inspect their divisions. _____

68a. Org executives guide them on proper channels to correct outnesses, handle backlogs and increase production. _____

69. All executives USE the Data Series 23—they OBSERVE, EVALUATE, PROGRAM, SUPERVISE and REVIEW. This is done on a weekly basis against org GDSes. _____

70. Departmental mini programs based on policy are written and fully executed to completion for each department of the org and raise the stats of each department. _____

A Power Executive Division consists of these actions and any others needed to make them come about.

The org that has such an Executive Division will be coordinating its actions, energy and intentions in the direction set by LRH—toward the goals of Scientology itself.

POOR QUALITY

If any of these are so, the Executive Division has poor quality:

1. Executives late for work. _____

1a. Executives not properly clean, shaved, barbered, coifed. _____

2. The LRH Comm is not a Flag Executive Briefing Course graduate. _____

3. LRH Comm Log maintained but not used to detect bugs or slows or noncompliance to LRH orders. _____

4. LRH orders relayed but without care or attention to see if it was really duplicated or understood. _____

5. Investigations done but no or slow action taken to remedy outnesses found inhibiting execution of LRH orders. _____

6. Poor or no compliance to programs and/or projects for getting tech and policy in in the org as evident by the low amount of re-signs and delivery. _____

7. Compliance forwarded without actual verification to see if they were really done. _____

8. SO #1s not handled daily but allowed to accumulate. _____

9. LRH's personal office not kept clean and maintained. _____

9a. LRH's personal office is being shared by other executives. _____

10. Poor quality photos or pictures of LRH displayed in the org. _____

10a. Poor quality LRH photos are used in org promotion. _____

11. I/A granted on promo not based on survey. _____

12. Downstats promoted or rewarded instead of upstats. _____

13. Only some staff get their admin high crimes done. _____

14. Org quarters and grounds are not adequate for org needs. _____

14a. Org quarters and grounds are dismal or unkept, that are not a tribute to LRH and the org, or are legally insecure. _____

15. There is no single-hatted Keeper of Tech on post. _____

15a. The functions of the post are being handled by the LRH Comm at a minimum. _____

16. Requests for refunds and repayments are poorly handled when they do occur and do not get handled standardly and promptly. _____

16a. There are routing forms that exist for a person requesting refund or repayment but it is not clear as to the exact steps to take to obtain his refund or repayment. _____

17. There is no Exec Esto or Estos putting the org there. _____

18. The Estos are only running on a few programs. _____

18a. There is very little hatting occurring so as to get production. _____

19. Flag Banking Officer efforts to make the org make more money are sporadic and ineffective. _____

19a. Income-making expertise is only vaguely known or used by Flag Banking Officer, other executives or FP members. _____

20. The org spends all it makes as evidenced by income–outgo graphs or cash-bills running parallel or no regular payment to back bills or org reserves. _____

21. FP members are unhatted and there is no program in progress to hat or educate them. _____

22. The Flag Banking Officer allows a sloppy FP which leaves off basic expenses. _____

22a. The Flag Banking Officer lets FP Pgm No. 1 drop out or doesn't put it in at all. _____

23. Staff pay is usually poor. _____

24. The Flag Banking Officer permits accounting or financial irregularities on his own post. _____

24a. In Treasury. _____

24b. Among FP members. _____

24c. Among executives. _____

24d. The Flag Banking Officer's reports are late. _____

24e. The Flag Banking Officer's records sometimes do not agree with Treasury's. _____

25. Little or no money is sent to Flag. _____

26. HCO PL 10 May 82, BOOKSTORE OFFICER HAT, is partly out. _____

27. There is only a trickle amount of business being driven into the org. _____

28. The Flag Representative is not of clean and neat appearance and does not promote the Flag image. _____

29. The Flag Representative sends in his Flag Representative weekly reports each week but is not accurate in his observation or reports. _____

30. The Flag Representative is slow and incomplete in handling any queries and thereby does not get accurate data to Flag. _____

31. The Flag Representative is reasonable with local alter-is, off-policy or false reports and entheta to Flag. _____

32. The Flag Representative has received copies of only some Aides Orders or Executive Directives which apply to his org. _____

32a. The Flag Representative hasn't logged them or seen that copies are available as needed to those who would be responsible for execution in the org or personally contacted staff members on them. _____

32b. The Aides Order's programs are bugged and no debugs have been done. _____

32c. Compliance reports lack full evidence. _____

33. There is a Director of Special Affairs on post, though not fully trained in the functions of a Director of Special Affairs. _____

34. Most legal matters are known about and being handled by the Director of Special Affairs. _____

35. There are some but not enough PR area control actions being done to proof up the org against attacks. _____

36. The Director of Special Affairs isolates but does not fully handle groups that are hostile towards the organization. _____

37. Not all Director of Special Affairs media matters are being handled by the Director of Special Affairs. _____

38. Some students and pcs are getting services and few are signing up for more upon completion. _____

39. Exec Council meets but does not take effective action to implement plans or coordinate and direct actions found needed in the org. _____

40. No targets set by executives for org production. _____

41. No adequate organization brought about to assist getting the products out. _____

42. Backlogging delivery is permitted. _____

43. Advisory Council not working together to forward org production, viability or organization. _____

44. The executives don't ensure that each area in the org is assigned and operating on the correct condition. _____

44a. The staff are not always correctly applying the conditions of their post. _____

45. Senior execs single-handing. _____

46. No inspections done routinely by executives for areas over which they are responsible. _____

47. Departmental mini programs are only sporadically written for some departments of the org and occasionally get executed to completion. _____

An Executive Division of this type has a dim idea of what is needed to direct and coordinate an org. It is usually unhatted and on a mad cope, leading into a very confusing scene.

TREASON QUALITY

If any of these are so, then the quality of the division is Treason:

1. Executives not showing up to work, one or two working elsewhere. _____

2. Off-the-cuff decisions are made. _____

2a. Actions are taken on wrong Whys with further collapse of stats. _____

3. All LRH orders are forced into the org at once with no programing or concern for existing scene. _____

4. There are no programs and/or projects that exist to handle the out-tech and off-policy in the org. _____

5. Correction forms issued without investigations. _____

5a. Correction forms issued on upstats who are trying hard to get LRH orders and intentions done. _____

5b. No correction forms issued at all. _____

6. Actual compliance not reported to LRH Comm Int via LRH Comm Cont with information to ED Int. _____

7. No LRH office at all in the org. _____

7a. LRH image not promoted or used in the org or in its publications. _____

8. Harsh ethics allowed on upstats. _____

8a. Proper recourse denied. _____

9. Admin High Crimes are not done in the org at all. _____

10. Org premises not suitable or legal for org needs. _____

11. Public and staff facilities left filthy and not properly supplied. _____

12. There is no single-hatted Keeper of Tech on post nor are the functions being handled by the LRH Communicator. _____

13. Requests for refunds and repayments are not HANDLED when they do occur. _____

13a. There are no routing forms that exist for a person requesting refund or repayment. _____

14. There is no Exec Esto or Estos putting the org there. _____

15. The Estos are not running on any programs. _____

15a. There is no hatting occurring so as to get production. _____

16. The income is low and the Flag Banking Officer makes no effort at all to demand or raise it. _____

16a. Income-making policy is utterly unknown and unused by FP members, Flag Banking Officer and executives. _____

17. Real necessities which could stall vital actions or Flag programs or promotion are left off of FP or cut by FP members or others. _____

17a. Properly surveyed and effective promotion is cut below adequate or usual volume to pay bills or for other reasons. _____

18. Staff are not paid at all. _____

18a. The org has off-policy and unauthorized pay systems in use setting excessive pay and bonus precedents that the org could not meet on lowered income. _____

19. The org has large or newly increased commitments extending into the future beyond its ability to pay or which could crash it financially in the event of suddenly lowered income. _____

19a. FP No. 1 or any effective method of keeping income greater than outgo has been utterly abandoned. _____

19b. Nonpromotional expenses remain high and uncut even when income is down. _____

20. The org sends no money to Flag at all or sends a small amount widely inconsistent with its current income. _____

21. HCO PL 10 May 82, BOOKSTORE OFFICER HAT, is completely out. _____

22. There is no business being driven into the org. _____

23. The Flag Representative is coarse in conduct or communication. _____

24. The Flag Representative accepts the opinions and conclusions of others and does not himself inspect or locate the real Why. _____

25. The Flag Representative does not report honestly the existing scene. _____

26. The Flag Representative takes harsh actions or makes harsh recommendations without looking at the stats of the area concerned. _____

27. The Flag Representative received copies of only some Aides Orders or Executive Directives which apply to his org but puts them in his desk drawer and no other copies are available. _____

27a. Program targets are not relayed to any staff members. _____

27b. Any compliance reports that do get sent up are completely false. _____

28. There is no Director of Special Affairs on post in the org. _____

29. There are no PR area control actions being done at all. _____

30. Illegal contracts have been signed, illegal commitments have been made, and no one is aware of the consequences or gives a damn. _____

31. There are reporters crawling in the windows, squirrel groups in the classroom, and the Janitor and Qual I&I doing a TV interview in the entrance of the org. _____

32. The classroom and auditing rooms are empty of students and pcs, and those who got away aren't coming back to sign up for more. _____

33. Executive Council at odds. _____

33a. Executive Council not coordinating any org actions at all. _____

34. Executives not operating the org by stats but using personalities instead. _____

35. Conditions are not used at all. _____

36. Executives not policing dev-t, but allowing the org to get drowned in its own noise. _____

37. There is a backlog of delivery with little or no delivery occurring. _____

This type of Executive Division will very quickly destroy the org, which is what it is probably trying to do.

Such an Executive Division is a crime against every staff member. It will get every executive and every staff member into trouble.

PR area control will go out.

The org will go broke.

Production will cease.

Staff members will blow.

Senior executives in such an Executive Division should be assigned the correct condition—TREASON.

SUMMARY

Org conditions are set wholly from within. It is up to the executive to program, target and push through production and establishment to create and maintain the org.

It takes time to make an executive.

It takes study of policy and duplication of LRH intention and strict application of all the technology.

It takes hard work.

But given the willingness and desire to bring about a better world, the Executive Division can unite the org into the team that's needed to get the job done.

If any senior executive wants to know the overall condition of his org, he can use this checklist to actually inspect and see.

The LRH Comm should do so regularly. The Exec Dir or CO would be wise to also.

TIPS TO EXECS

You are far more capable of doing any action that will ever be required of you as an exec in your org.

When you goof an action, remedy it fast.

When you make it go right, give yourself a pat on the back!

L. RON HUBBARD
Founder

Assisted by
LRH Comm Aide

Revision assisted by
LRH Technical Research
and Compilations

APPENDIX

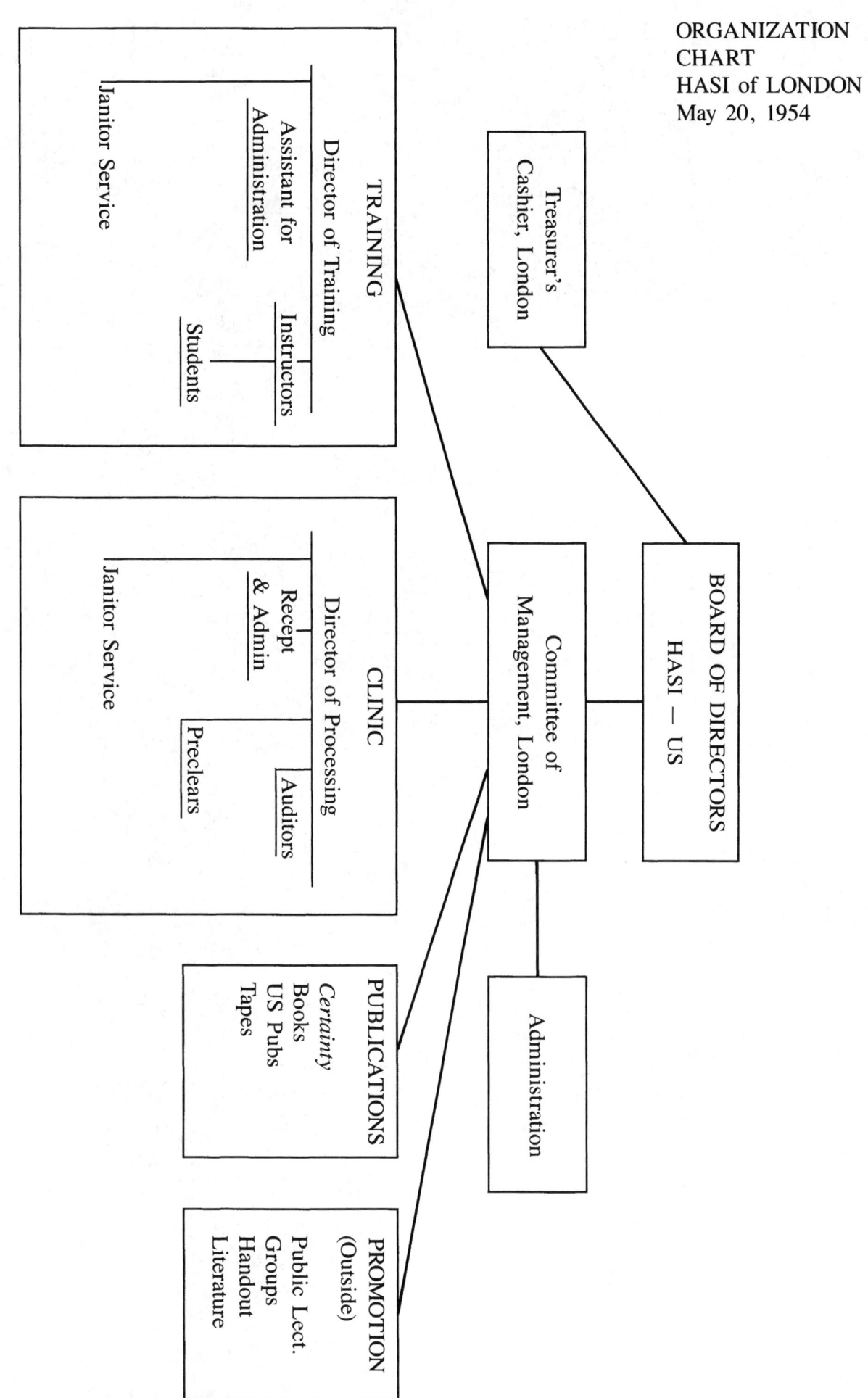

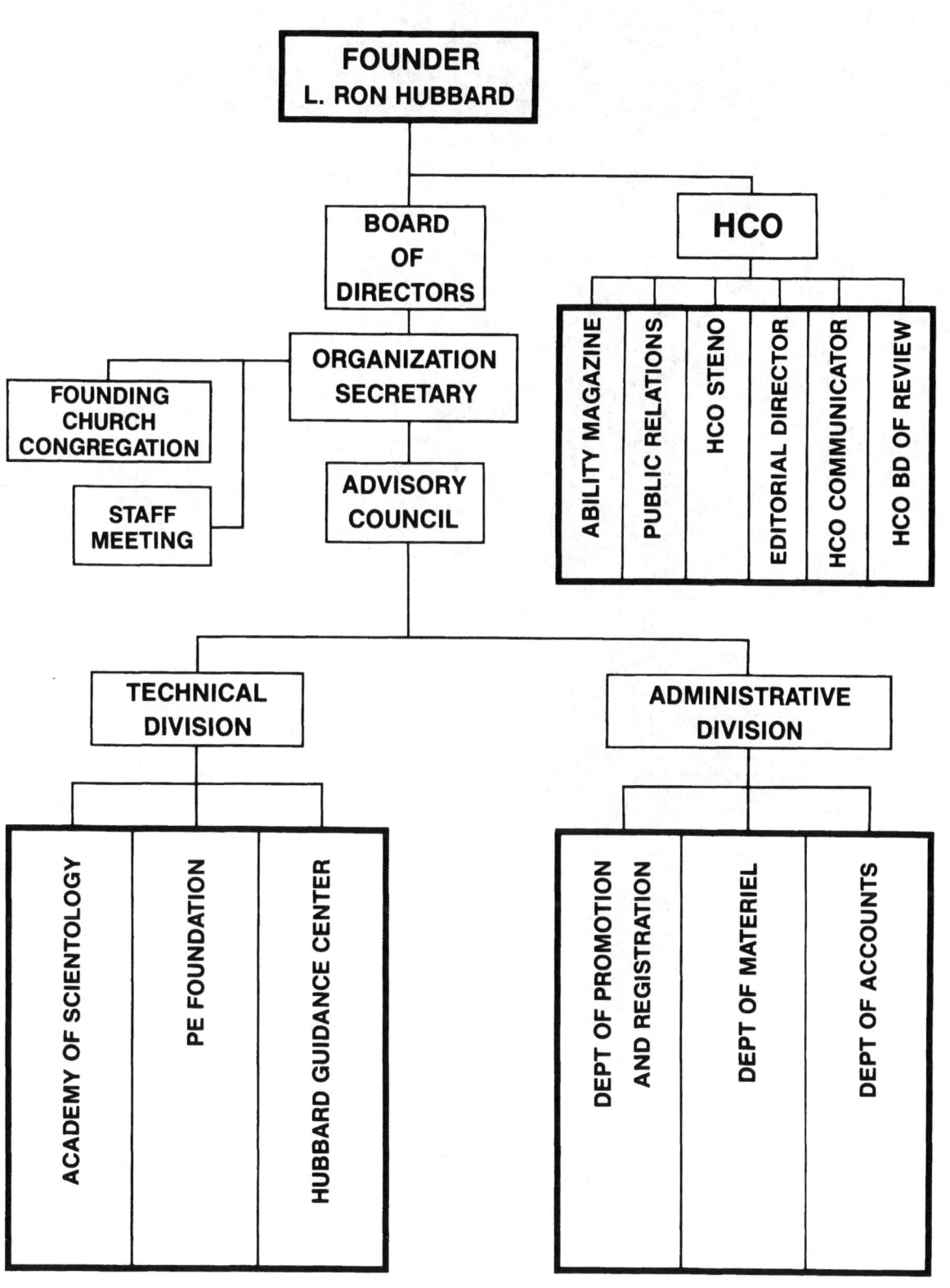

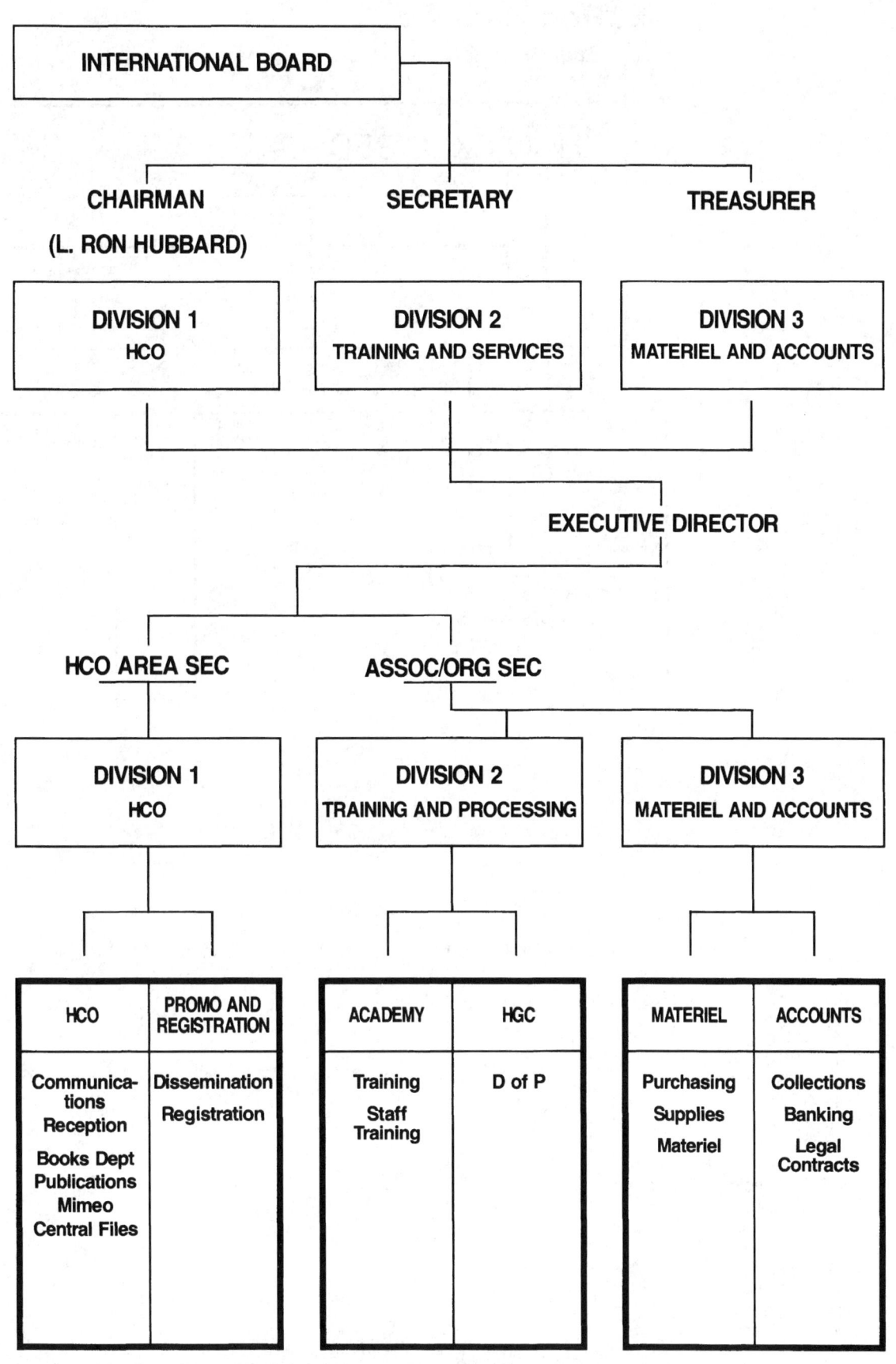

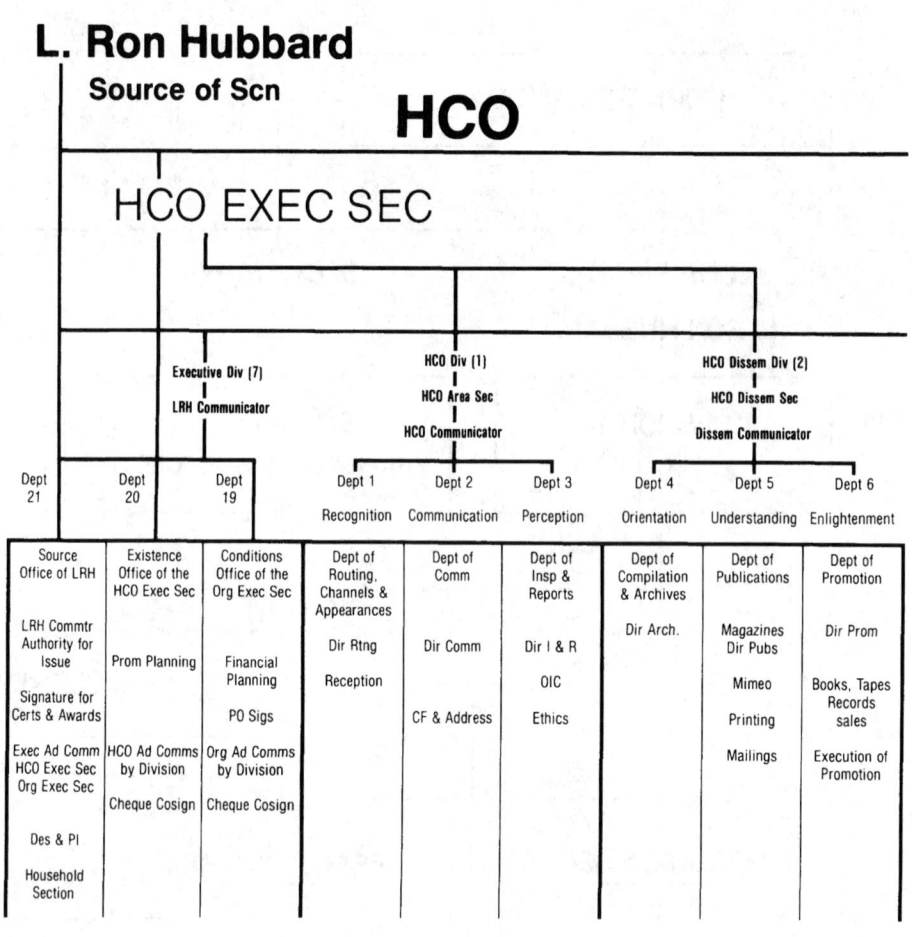

L. Ron Hubbard
Source of Scn

HCO

HCO EXEC SEC

	Executive Div (7) LRH Communicator		HCO Div (1) HCO Area Sec HCO Communicator			HCO Dissem Div (2) HCO Dissem Sec Dissem Communicator		
Dept 21	Dept 20	Dept 19	Dept 1 Recognition	Dept 2 Communication	Dept 3 Perception	Dept 4 Orientation	Dept 5 Understanding	Dept 6 Enlightenment
Source Office of LRH	Existence Office of the HCO Exec Sec	Conditions Office of the Org Exec Sec	Dept of Routing, Channels & Appearances	Dept of Comm	Dept of Insp & Reports	Dept of Compilation & Archives	Dept of Publications	Dept of Promotion
LRH Commtr Authority for Issue			Dir Rtng	Dir Comm	Dir I & R	Dir Arch.	Magazines Dir Pubs	Dir Prom
	Prom Planning	Financial Planning	Reception		OIC		Mimeo	
Signature for Certs & Awards							Printing	Books, Tapes Records sales
		PO Sigs		CF & Address	Ethics		Mailings	
Exec Ad Comm HCO Exec Sec Org Exec Sec	HCO Ad Comms by Division	Org Ad Comms by Division						Execution of Promotion
	Cheque Cosign	Cheque Cosign						
Des & PI								
Household Section								

Arch — Archives
Auds — Auditors
C Con — Changed Conditions
Certs — Certificates
Cl — Clearing
Commtr — Communicator
Cosign — Cosignatory
Cses — Courses
Des & PI — Design & Planning
Est — Estimations
Exams — Examinations
F — Files
Prom — Promotion
Rtng — Routing
Sigs — Signatories
Studs — Students

Other terms and abbreviations used in this org board can be found in MODERN MANAGEMENT TECHNOLOGY DEFINED by L. Ron Hubbard.

ORG

ORG EXEC SEC

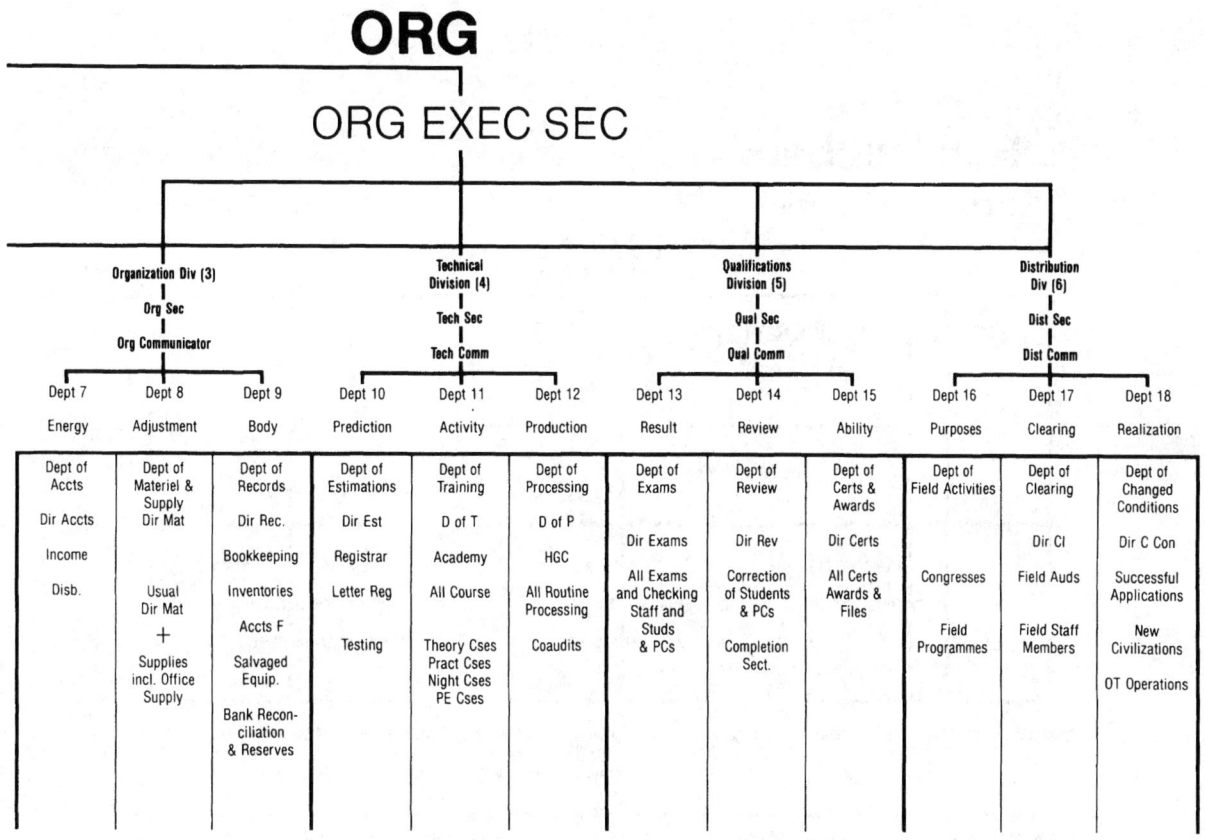

	Organization Div (3)			Technical Division (4)			Qualifications Division (5)			Distribution Div (6)	
	Org Sec			Tech Sec			Qual Sec			Dist Sec	
	Org Communicator			Tech Comm			Qual Comm			Dist Comm	
Dept 7	Dept 8	Dept 9	Dept 10	Dept 11	Dept 12	Dept 13	Dept 14	Dept 15	Dept 16	Dept 17	Dept 18
Energy	Adjustment	Body	Prediction	Activity	Production	Result	Review	Ability	Purposes	Clearing	Realization
Dept of Accts	Dept of Materiel & Supply	Dept of Records	Dept of Estimations	Dept of Training	Dept of Processing	Dept of Exams	Dept of Review	Dept of Certs & Awards	Dept of Field Activities	Dept of Clearing	Dept of Changed Conditions
Dir Accts	Dir Mat	Dir Rec.	Dir Est	D of T	D of P	Dir Exams	Dir Rev	Dir Certs		Dir Cl	Dir C Con
Income		Bookkeeping	Registrar	Academy	HGC	All Exams and Checking Staff and Studs & PCs	Correction of Students & PCs	All Certs Awards & Files	Congresses	Field Auds	Successful Applications
Disb.	Usual Dir Mat + Supplies incl. Office Supply	Inventories Accts F Salvaged Equip. Bank Reconciliation & Reserves	Letter Reg Testing	All Course Theory Cses Pract Cses Night Cses PE Cses	All Routine Processing Coaudits		Completion Sect.		Field Programmes	Field Staff Members	New Civilizations OT Operations

Rough Draft of Scientology Org Pattern
Done to show Execs here
for briefing the basic plan
of the new Org.
Sections only Indicated.
General Pattern quite firm.
Some small changes in
Section naming may occur.
Proper Copy Being Made in a week.
25 May 1965

L. RON HUBBARD

L. Ron Hubbard

EXECUTIVE DIRECTOR

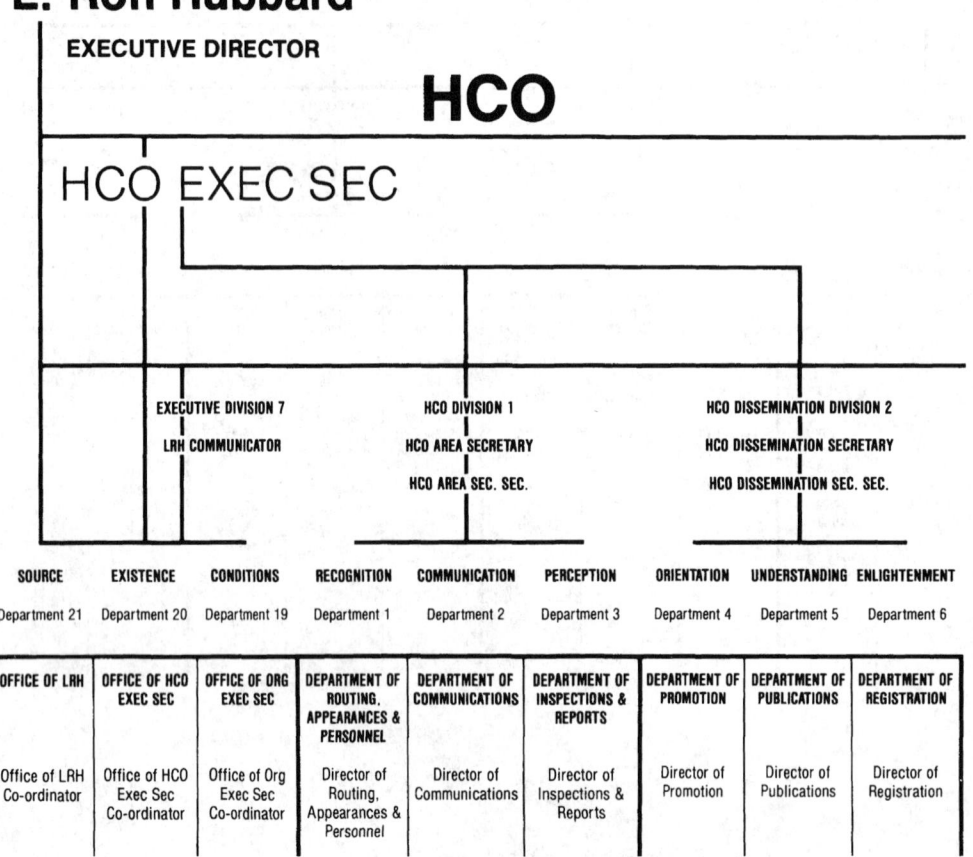

HCO

HCO EXEC SEC

	EXECUTIVE DIVISION 7		HCO DIVISION 1			HCO DISSEMINATION DIVISION 2		
	LRH COMMUNICATOR		HCO AREA SECRETARY			HCO DISSEMINATION SECRETARY		
			HCO AREA SEC. SEC.			HCO DISSEMINATION SEC. SEC.		

SOURCE	EXISTENCE	CONDITIONS	RECOGNITION	COMMUNICATION	PERCEPTION	ORIENTATION	UNDERSTANDING	ENLIGHTENMENT
Department 21	Department 20	Department 19	Department 1	Department 2	Department 3	Department 4	Department 5	Department 6
OFFICE OF LRH	OFFICE OF HCO EXEC SEC	OFFICE OF ORG EXEC SEC	DEPARTMENT OF ROUTING, APPEARANCES & PERSONNEL	DEPARTMENT OF COMMUNICATIONS	DEPARTMENT OF INSPECTIONS & REPORTS	DEPARTMENT OF PROMOTION	DEPARTMENT OF PUBLICATIONS	DEPARTMENT OF REGISTRATION
Office of LRH Co-ordinator	Office of HCO Exec Sec Co-ordinator	Office of Org Exec Sec Co-ordinator	Director of Routing, Appearances & Personnel	Director of Communications	Director of Inspections & Reports	Director of Promotion	Director of Publications	Director of Registration

ORG

ORG EXEC SEC

ORGANIZATION DIVISION 3			TECHNICAL DIVISION 4			QUALIFICATIONS DIVISION 5			DISTRIBUTION DIVISION 6		
ORGANIZATION SECRETARY			TECHNICAL SECRETARY			QUALIFICATIONS SECRETARY			DISTRIBUTION SECRETARY		
ORGANIZATION SEC. SEC.			TECHNICAL SEC. SEC.			QUALIFICATIONS SEC. SEC.			DISTRIBUTION SEC. SEC.		
ENERGY	ADJUSTMENT	BODY	PREDICTION	ACTIVITY	PRODUCTION	RESULT	REVIEW	ABILITY	PURPOSES	CLEARING	REALIZATION
Department 7	Department 8	Department 9	Department 10	Department 11	Department 12	Department 13	Department 14	Department 15	Department 16	Department 17	Department 18
DEPARTMENT OF INCOME	DEPARTMENT OF DISBURSEMENTS	DEPARTMENT OF RECORDS, ASSETS & MATERIEL	DEPARTMENT OF TECHNICAL SERVICES	DEPARTMENT OF TRAINING	DEPARTMENT OF PROCESSING	DEPARTMENT OF EXAMINATIONS	DEPARTMENT OF REVIEW	DEPARTMENT OF CERTIFICATION & AWARDS	DEPARTMENT OF PUBLIC INFORMATION	DEPARTMENT OF CLEARING	DEPARTMENT OF SUCCESS
Director of Income	Director of Disbursements	Director of Records, Assets & Materiel	Director of Technical Services	Director of Training	Director of Processing	Director of Examinations	Director of Review	Director of Certification & Awards	Director of Public Information	Director of Clearing	Director of Success

L. Ron Hubbard
FOUNDER

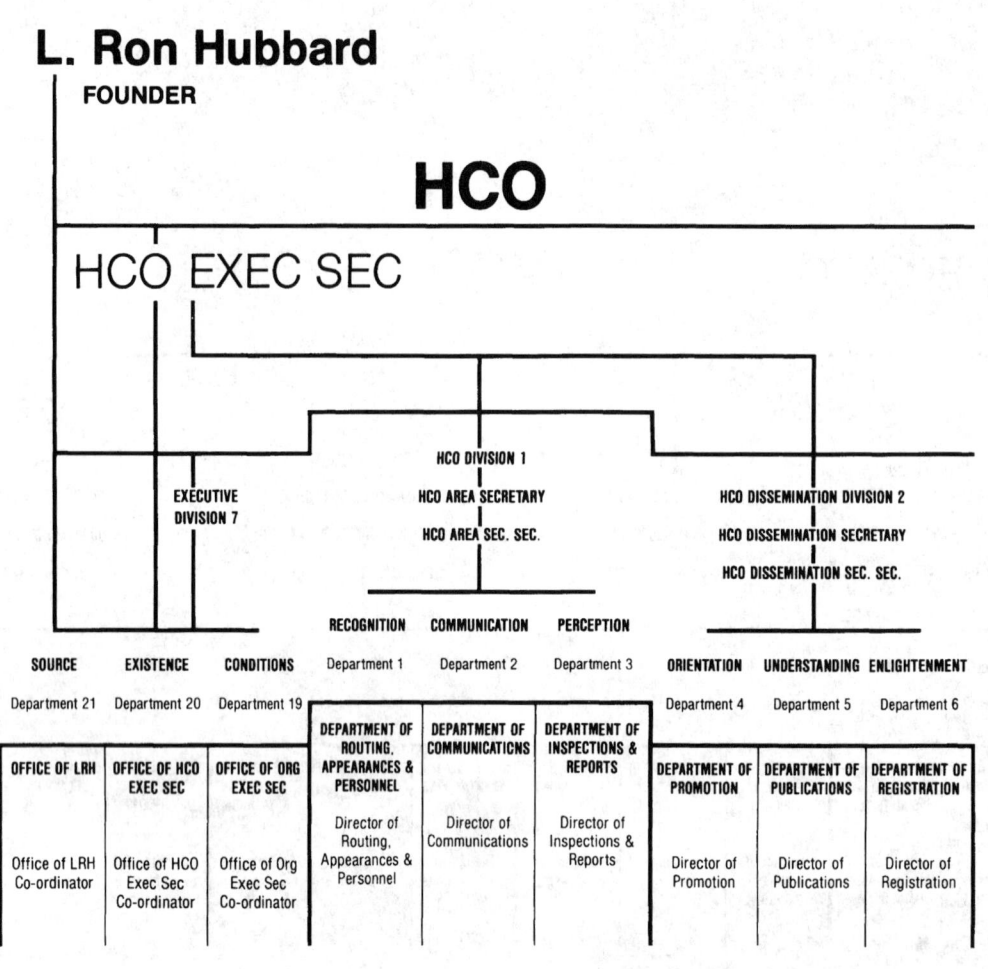

HCO

HCO EXEC SEC

			RECOGNITION	COMMUNICATION	PERCEPTION			
	EXECUTIVE DIVISION 7		**HCO DIVISION 1** HCO AREA SECRETARY HCO AREA SEC. SEC. Department 1	Department 2	Department 3		**HCO DISSEMINATION DIVISION 2** HCO DISSEMINATION SECRETARY HCO DISSEMINATION SEC. SEC.	
SOURCE	**EXISTENCE**	**CONDITIONS**				**ORIENTATION**	**UNDERSTANDING**	**ENLIGHTENMENT**
Department 21	Department 20	Department 19				Department 4	Department 5	Department 6
OFFICE OF LRH	OFFICE OF HCO EXEC SEC	OFFICE OF ORG EXEC SEC	DEPARTMENT OF ROUTING, APPEARANCES & PERSONNEL	DEPARTMENT OF COMMUNICATIONS	DEPARTMENT OF INSPECTIONS & REPORTS	DEPARTMENT OF PROMOTION	DEPARTMENT OF PUBLICATIONS	DEPARTMENT OF REGISTRATION
			Director of Routing, Appearances & Personnel	Director of Communications	Director of Inspections & Reports			
Office of LRH Co-ordinator	Office of HCO Exec Sec Co-ordinator	Office of Org Exec Sec Co-ordinator				Director of Promotion	Director of Publications	Director of Registration

ORG

ORG EXEC SEC

	TREASURY DIVISION 3			TECHNICAL DIVISION 4			QUALIFICATIONS DIVISION 5			DISTRIBUTION DIVISION 6	
	TREASURY SECRETARY			TECHNICAL SECRETARY			QUALIFICATIONS SECRETARY			DISTRIBUTION SECRETARY	
	TREASURY SEC. SEC.			TECHNICAL SEC. SEC.			QUALIFICATIONS SEC. SEC.			DISTRIBUTION SEC. SEC.	

ENERGY	ADJUSTMENT	BODY	PREDICTION	ACTIVITY	PRODUCTION	RESULT	CORRECTION	ABILITY	PURPOSES	CLEARING	REALIZATION
Department 7	Department 8	Department 9	Department 10	Department 11	Department 12	Department 13	Department 14	Department 15	Department 16	Department 17	Department 18
DEPARTMENT OF INCOME	DEPARTMENT OF DISBURSEMENTS	DEPARTMENT OF RECORDS, ASSETS & MATERIEL	DEPARTMENT OF TECHNICAL SERVICES	DEPARTMENT OF TRAINING	DEPARTMENT OF PROCESSING	DEPARTMENT OF EXAMINATIONS	DEPARTMENT OF REVIEW	DEPARTMENT OF CERTIFICATION & AWARDS	DEPARTMENT OF PUBLIC INFORMATION	DEPARTMENT OF CLEARING	DEPARTMENT OF SUCCESS
Director of Income	Director of Disbursements	Director of Records, Assets & Materiel	Director of Technical Services	Director of Training	Director of Processing	Director of Examinations	Director of Review	Director of Certification & Awards	Director of Public Information	Director of Clearing	Director of Success

L. Ron Hubbard
FOUNDER

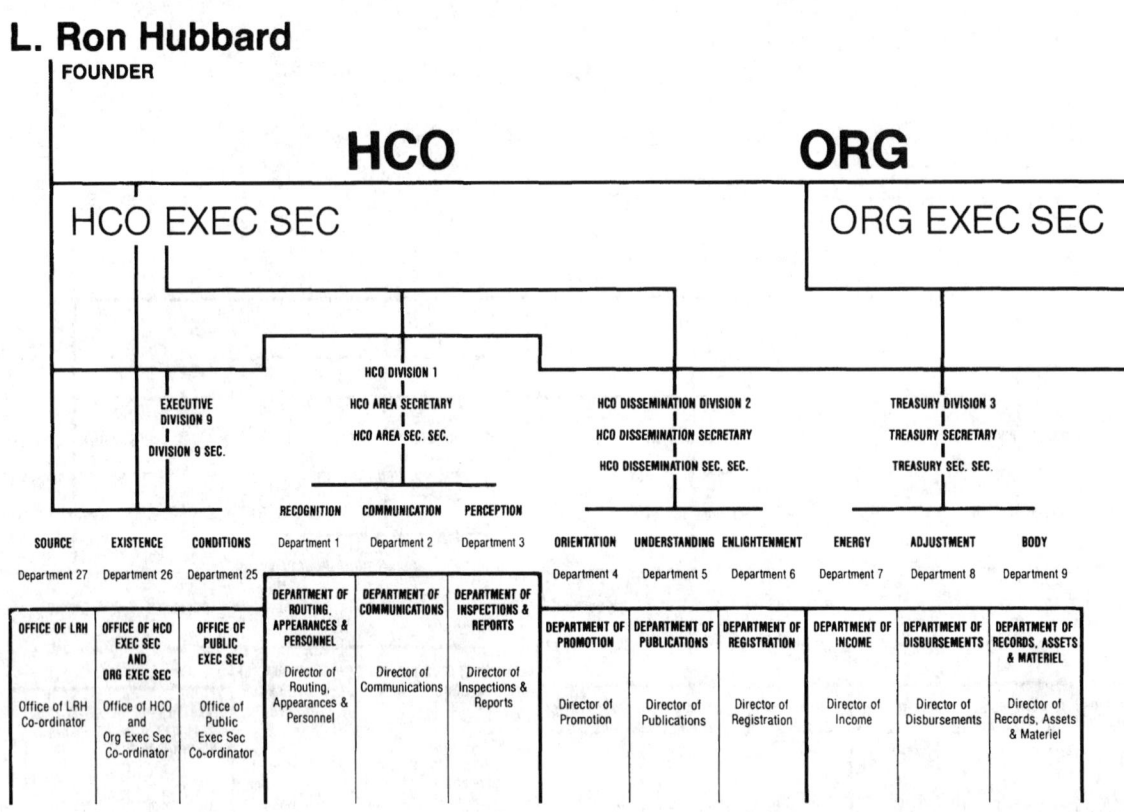

			HCO DIVISION 1								
	EXECUTIVE DIVISION 9		**HCO AREA SECRETARY**			**HCO DISSEMINATION DIVISION 2**			**TREASURY DIVISION 3**		
	DIVISION 9 SEC.		**HCO AREA SEC. SEC.**			**HCO DISSEMINATION SECRETARY**			**TREASURY SECRETARY**		
						HCO DISSEMINATION SEC. SEC.			**TREASURY SEC. SEC.**		
			RECOGNITION	**COMMUNICATION**	**PERCEPTION**						
SOURCE	**EXISTENCE**	**CONDITIONS**	Department 1	Department 2	Department 3	**ORIENTATION**	**UNDERSTANDING**	**ENLIGHTENMENT**	**ENERGY**	**ADJUSTMENT**	**BODY**
Department 27	Department 26	Department 25				Department 4	Department 5	Department 6	Department 7	Department 8	Department 9
OFFICE OF LRH	**OFFICE OF HCO EXEC SEC AND ORG EXEC SEC**	**OFFICE OF PUBLIC EXEC SEC**	**DEPARTMENT OF ROUTING, APPEARANCES & PERSONNEL**	**DEPARTMENT OF COMMUNICATIONS**	**DEPARTMENT OF INSPECTIONS & REPORTS**	**DEPARTMENT OF PROMOTION**	**DEPARTMENT OF PUBLICATIONS**	**DEPARTMENT OF REGISTRATION**	**DEPARTMENT OF INCOME**	**DEPARTMENT OF DISBURSEMENTS**	**DEPARTMENT OF RECORDS, ASSETS & MATERIEL**
Office of LRH Co-ordinator	Office of HCO and Org Exec Sec Co-ordinator	Office of Public Exec Sec Co-ordinator	Director of Routing, Appearances & Personnel	Director of Communications	Director of Inspections & Reports	Director of Promotion	Director of Publications	Director of Registration	Director of Income	Director of Disbursements	Director of Records, Assets & Materiel

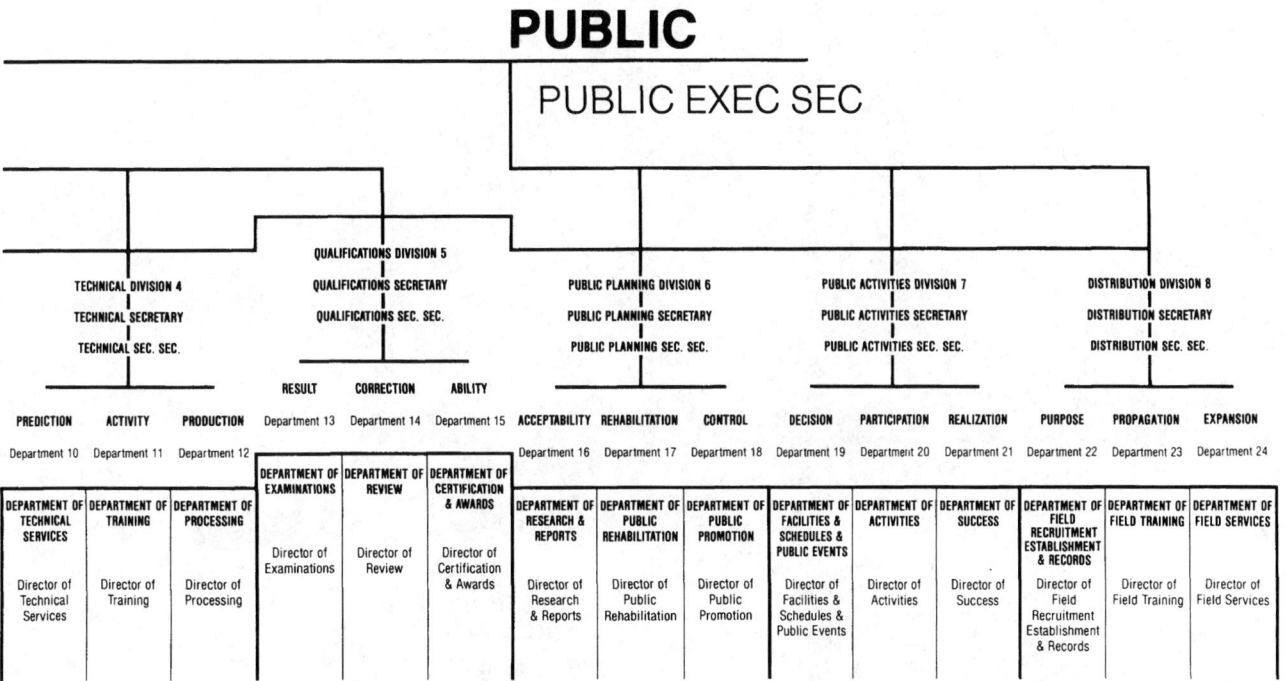

[*Editor's Note:* See accompanying chart for the current Class IV Organization org board.]

1990 NINE-DIVISION ORGANIZING BOARD

About the Author

"Organization is actually a simple subject," wrote L. Ron Hubbard in 1969, "based on a few basic patterns which, if applied, produce success.

"If one would dream and see his dreams an actuality, one must also be able to organize and to train organizational men who will make those dreams come true."

L. Ron Hubbard was no stranger to the organization and management of groups. Throughout his life, he was a leader of men—a captain of ships and the head of expeditions to Alaska, the Caribbean and the Mediterranean. Soon after the May 1950 release of the international bestseller, *Dianetics: The Modern Science of Mental Health,* he recognized the need for an administrative and organizational technology to ensure that proper and standard Dianetics was delivered.

To help achieve this he isolated, for the first time, the skills that a man needs to succeed and discovered the technology with which to improve these so that anyone could easily reach their goals.

To make these initial discoveries available he authored two books in the mid-1950s—*The Problems of Work* and *How to Live Though an Executive.* The principles contained in these works have been successfully applied by individuals in thousands of groups, businesses and companies around the world. Ron's breakthroughs are of immense use in handling the stress and pressures associated with holding a post, a job or running an organization.

With his keen understanding of life's fundamentals, he discovered and codified simple and practical steps through which one can sanely and easily create both stable and enduring organizations.

"Scientology," he stated in 1956, "the broad science of life, has many applications.

"If you knew what life was doing, you would know what many sciences and activities were doing.

"Here, we have Scientology assisting the worker and the executive in helping man to be more competent and more able, less tired and more secure in the workaday world."

In 1961, with the writing of HCO Policy Letter of 14 February 1961, THE PATTERN OF A CENTRAL ORGANIZATION, he summarized the organizational structure of Scientology and provided a stable datum for all orgs, allowing further expansion.

Ron turned his attention, in 1965, to fully developing and laying out the principles of how to administer and organize groups of any size. As he researched these, he applied his discoveries directly to the Saint Hill org, where he was Executive Director. Through the application of his policies the staff grew to more than two hundred and the HGC delivered an average 1,000 well done auditing hours per week, as Saint Hill set the standards by which Scientology organizations now measure their own expansion.

The bulk of the policies contained in the *Organization Executive Course* volumes concern "how and why sh became SAINT HILL!" Ron wrote. It is the data on how to build and refine orgs. These thousands of policy letters contain solutions to the problems of management—including the hiring and training of personnel, finances, organizational communications systems, ethics and justice, administration, data analysis, how to be a successful executive, leadership, marketing, organizational programing and targeting, promotion, production, public relations, quality control, statistical analysis and troubleshooting.

The *Organization Executive Course* (OEC) volumes, designed as study material for church executives, contain the results of years of successful international application of Ron's fundamental policies vital to productive and rewarding activities.

With his studies of individual and group dynamics completed to his full satisfaction, Ron departed his body on 24 January 1986.

L. Ron Hubbard not only opened a new door to personal ability for mankind; he also made it possible for organizations of any kind to forge their own way to success and predictably achieve their goals.

Subject Index

A

aberration,
all evil stems from, 511
example of, 673
handling for eradicating 10 points of third dynamic
aberration, 795
primary aberration in situations that are being
mishandled, 673
to be or unbe is the ability, to not quite be or to WAS is
the aberration, 810

ability, completing a cycle of action, handling the matter so
it does not have to be handled again, 701

Academy,
definition, 201
promotional purposes, 32
students should only be allowed to use E-Meters
approved by HCO, 1289

accounting,
administrative specialty, 434
introduction of complex accounting contrary to policy is
a suppressive act on laymen, 1079
policies of Scientology, 1078

Accounts, goes PTS through various tax and government
supervision suppressions, 372

Accounts Files Administrator, post is created, 221

Accounts Unit, purposes, 59

Address Unit, definition, 204

admin degrades, high crimes, list of, 490

admin high crimes, computerized system to verify, 493

administration, *see also* **management**
bad administration, lack of know-how, lack of trained
clerks and executives, can defeat utterly any plan or
program no matter how urgent or beneficial, 779
expert knows where admin out it will be jammed at the
top, 780
good, two distinct targets, 406
key ingredients of, 408
never send orders into out-admin area, 402
one knows and handles, produces, exchanges or dies, 437
one will survive as well as he can administer or handle
administration, 436
owed something by technical, 838
resulting in production and exchange, 436
standard, comes from policy letters, 403
system, necessary to perpetuate any group, 406
systems which lack key ingredients, 409
true points of, 409
using Scientology admin and dev-t policies on the society
outside Scientology, 1016
when admin out, tech out and ethics long ceased to
exist, 402
when goes out, the org declines, 486
works where tech is in, 398

administrative department, most important is Promotion
and Registration, 194

administrative know-how,
gap between plan and actuality will be found to be lack
of, 407
man's happiness and longevity of companies and states
depend upon, 411

Administrative Letter, definition, 638

administrative personnel, functions, 838

administrator,
definition, 438, 439
detection of a suppressive person, 392
test of, 438
too few trained and skilled who can get a show on the
road, 435
why civilization develops so few, 434

Admin Scale,
definition, 478
strategic plan, applies to the top of the, 458

Advanced Organizations, exist to make OTs and support
the Sea Org, 149

Advance Scheduling Registrar,
Call-in Unit located under, to handle partially paids, 865
procedure for partially paid public call-in, 869

advertising, money to do wide advertising programs, 928

Advisory Committee,
assigns conditions, 906
composed of, 885, 896
Emergency assignments and, 903
exists for each division in the org and is advisory to the
Ad Council, 117
grievances and, 886
Mandate of 1956 amended, 885
meetings, 896, 906
orders, issue of, 906
purpose of, 895, 896
reports forwarded to Ad Council, 906
reports minutes to the Association Secretary, 885
reports, routing for, 901
statistics and, 898
who is represented, 32

Advisory Council,
assignment of Affluence and Emergency and, 900
assists Executive Council, 913
Boards of Investigation and, 910
chairman nominated and elected by, 910
composed of, 889, 909
coordination, why we have, 455
despatches to, 893
dissident voice and, 911
Exec Secs may not be members of, 909
false reports and, 912
financial reports required in weekly reports, 887
functions of, 896
gross divisional statistics and, 898
gross divisional statistics, how to raise them quickly
when down, 907
LRH Comm may veto any measure that is against policy, 913
majority, 892
may request removal of an Executive Secretary, 911
measures must be in issuable form, 914
members may be removed by Exec Council, 914
members, removal of, 911
minutes, 888, 891
not a governing body, 891
order of progress of meeting, 889
orders, issue of, 905
power of passing directives, 910
powers of, 891
privilege, 912
promotional actions, 84
purpose of, 889, 909
quorum, 892
reports made to, 889, 891

C

1466

dedicated, we'll survive because we are tough and are dedicated, 13

defense,
be decent and effective and do our jobs and the sharpest spears cannot touch us, 1022
only way to defend anything is to attack, 973

degraded being(s),
characteristics of, 390
find instruction painful, as have been painfully indoctrinated in the past, 389
handled only at OT III, 389
not an SP, but is so PTS that he works for SPs only, 389
not natively bad, simply so PTS for so long, 390
very degraded beings alter-is, 389

deliver, Scientology works, training, processing and results, 1293

delivery,
bring up to your dissemination, 846
competent use of targeting in battle plans and, 460
Flag Rep report, 1419
GI increase and, 858
remedy for dropped auditing volume, 159
we always deliver what we promise, 852

demand directive, definition, 353

democracy,
is a collective-think of reactive banks, 1015
will emerge when we have freed each individual of the more vicious reactive impulses, 1015

demotion, may only be done after a Committee of Evidence, 1300

department, *see also* **division**
actions of, 1198
each of the six depts has a promotional purpose in addition to all its other purposes, 32
once basic purpose known, only two things should be necessary, 600

Department 19, promotional actions, 84

Department 20, promotional actions, 85

Department 21, promotional actions, 85

department head,
how one is judged, 758
must never begin a practice of yanking people off post to do things that aren't hat, 759
responsibility of, 186
responsible for providing his personnel with materials of their job whatever these may be, 761
what is expected from each, 186

Department of Accounts,
definition, 206
promotional purposes, 34

Department of Government Affairs,
headed and directed with a minimum of personnel, 997
new department formed, 997

Department of Government Relations,
mailing pieces of, 996
may not use org personnel for typing and mailing, and may only use org personnel for reception, switchboard and despatch purposes, 1001

Department of Materiel,
definition, 205
promotional purposes, 33

Department of Official Affairs,
actions, 1004
Dept of Government Relations retitled, 1007
description, 1104
exists as an extension of the Office of the Continental Association Secretary and purpose, 1004
maxims, 1006
operations and, 1005

Department of Promotion and Registration,
definition, 202
promotional purposes, 32

Department of Tech Services, fully paid individuals are called in by, 865

despatch(es),
Advisory Council, despatches to, 893
definition, 480
get work done better than conferences, 894
meaning of symbol * on all despatches, 1175
when not getting answered or actioned, don't keep issuing more of the same, 415

destructiveness, difference between insanity and sanity is, 1143

developed traffic (dev-t),
area giving dev-t, persons supposed to be stable terminals are not holding their posts, 413
complete and only major source of, 412
essential part of training is study of *The Problems of Work*, 412
"Is this okay?" 682
people who are not stable terminals, executive who goes on handling forced to work harder than if post empty, 413
using Scientology dev-t policies on the society outside Scientology, 1016

devotion, requires active contribution outwards from the power as well as in, 388

D/FBO for MORE, driving more business down on the org than it can waste, 878

Dianetics,
can handle insanity with relative ease once the physical injuries and illnesses of the patient are cured medically or when the patient is only lightly ill, 1134
description of, 1097
misrepresentation of, 1110
policies effective immediately to protect good name of Dianetics, 1071

dictatorship, comes about only because the citizen doesn't know basic organization, 4

dilettante, definition, 680

dilettantism, described, 680

directive,
Ad Council and, 909
one issues urgent directives when the situation is rough and simply demands a directive when things look like they will get rough, 353

direct order, example, 352

Director of Administration,
function of, 594
hat and purpose, 624
spheres of responsibility, 624
task is to make existing policies stick, 594

Director of Communication, responsible for OODs, 728

Director of Inspections and Reports, utilization survey and, 450

Director of Processing,
interviews, 732
provides excellent service to pcs and gets them through their case actions, 875

Director of Routing, Appearances and Personnel, opened on time and properly locked up at closing is responsibility of, 311

Director of Training, provides excellent service to students and get them through their courses, 875

discipline,
only the already decent can be disciplined, 511
use to hold the edges of a channel, not to stop the flow, 511

dishonesty, incompetence and, 862

I

LRH Personal PR,
actions done by LC, 1261
basic duty of LC, 1260
LRH Programs No. 1, where issued, stats recovered, 793
LRH Property, Building and Plans Branch,
formation and purpose (1967), 1391
Plans Section, responsibilities, 1391
L. Ron Hubbard (LRH),
an individual, 1201
board member, 1202
Executive Director, 1202
job is not an administrative job in Scientology, 1164
quoting from works of, 1222
Trustee, 1201

M

magazine, submission procedure, 1305
mail,
distribution of in org, 220
routing of communication received from legal, accounting or government, 1085
mailing list, gross income senior datum and, 851
maintenance, checklists used, 1399
make-break point, 457
man,
can't be trusted with "justice," 1143
happiness and longevity of companies and states depend upon organizational know-how, 411
management, *see also* **administration**
"art" of managing as practiced in the past required too much hard labor on the manager, 567
at its best when, 459
between the pressure of the group to attain the goal and the clarion call of the goal maker to go forward, 571
concerns itself with the accomplishment of goals otherwise determined, 568
coordination, essence of, 454
cycle of, 417
definition of, 568
detectable points of bad management, 342
difference between brilliant and mediocre, 461
easy for thetan to postulate a fact and so arduous to move it into MEST universe existence that management tends to be impatient, 527
essence of, 340, 473
fast flow, 670–671
financial planning a vital part of, 340
Flag Rep report, 1420
general plan of, 897
good goal can be attained by poor management, 568
good versus bad management, 340
gross divisional statistics and, 900
improve the tone of any organization and its efficiency by hooking up and keeping wide open all communication lines, 574
laws by which management can raise the level of its own efficiency and production and activity of a group, 574
list of tools of, 478
local management using a single week's statistics, 530
power of is effective in ratio to cleanness with which it relays between goal maker and the group on ARC, 577
pretended goals and, 578
primary function of management is discovery and publication of the reality of circumstances, situations and personnel, 575
puts goal into effect, provides the ways and means, coordination and execution of acts leading toward goal, 568

management, *(cont.)*
remedy for bad management, 342
remote governing body would use a trend of divisional stats to interpret it, 523, 527
right way to handle it is to program it, 527
seeking extraordinary solutions for finance outside Scientology is sign of very poor, 931
Senior Executive Strata above middle management, 462
skilled stat trend recognition is an essential ingredient of skilled management, 535
sole criteria by which skill in management is estimated is financial volume and solvency, 628
statistic trends and remote management, 532
statistics must be studied and judged alongside the other related statistics, 516
strategic planning gets bugged most often because, 456
strategic planning must be done by upper-level planning body if management is to be effective and succeed, 470
suppression of operational data and, 574
tactical management of a strategic planning is bit of an art in itself, 472
tenets of, 581
unless one knows how to read statistics correctly and how to correctly determine a stat *trend*, prediction and management by stats will be way out in left field, 531
various echelons of, 462
ways a no-cause attitude towards statistics expresses itself, 518
what it takes to bring about effective, coordinated management, 453
workable science of, 580
management body,
three indicators which point to possible out-ethics, 1259
what it is and what it does, 451
management committee,
definition, 451
organizes and runs things, 452
Management Series, checksheets for, 463
Management Status One, checksheet, instant-hats an exec on basic tools of management, 463
Management Status Two, checksheet, profound review of basic management tools and upper-level tools, 464
Management Status Three, checksheet, more profound review of basic and upper-level management tools and twelve ingredients of expansion, 464
manager(s),
actions a manager does to have high financial volume, 628
considered successful or unsuccessful by measure of balance sheets, 632
credo of a good and skilled manager, 583
financial volume and solvency are final test of any manager of a Scientology organization or area, 628
first thing needs to know is he has tools with which to manage, 483
good manager ignores rumor and only acts on statistics, 510
instant-hat type of checksheet for, 485
must know and be able to use tools of third dynamic tech, 461
use the tools of coordination, 455
what a manager is for, 454
when accepts "done," 479
material(s),
data should be channeled to the right sources, 1292
for dissemination to public can be rewritten and published so long as no confusion as to origin generated, 1290
going to field, printing vs. mimeo, 1279

S

Alphabetical List of Titles

Chronological List of Titles

Books and Tapes
by L. Ron Hubbard

Advanced Executive Books

Organization Executive Course

The *Organization Executive Course* volumes contain organizational technology never before known to man. This is not just how a Scientology organization works; this is how the operation of *any* organization, *any* activity, can be improved. A person knowing the data in these volumes fully, and applying it, could completely reverse any downtrend in an organization—or even a country!

Management Series Volumes 1, 2 and 3

These books contain technology that anyone who works with management in any way must know completely to be a true success. Contained in these books are such subjects as data evaluation, the technology of how to organize any area for maximum production and expansion, how to handle personnel, the actual technology of public relations and much more.

Modern Management Technology Defined: Hubbard Dictionary of Administration and Management

Here's a real breakthrough in the subject of administration and management! Eighty-six hundred words are defined for greater understanding of any business situation. Clear, precise Scientology definitions describe many previously baffling phenomena and bring truth, sanity and understanding to the often murky field of management.

Basic Executive Books

The Basic Executive Books Package consists of three books listed below. They are available individually or as a set, complete with an attractive slipcase.

The Problems of Work

Work plays a big part in the game of life. Do you really enjoy your work? Are you certain of your job security? Would you like the increased personal satisfaction of doing your work well? This is the book that shows exactly how to achieve these things and more. The game of life—and within it, the game of work—can be enjoyable and rewarding.

How to Live Though an Executive

What are the factors in business and commerce which, if lacking, can keep a person overworked and worried, keep labor and management at each other's throats, and make an unsafe working atmosphere? L. Ron Hubbard reveals principles based on years of research into many different types of organizations.

Introduction to Scientology Ethics

A complete knowledge of ethics is vital to anyone's success in life. Without knowing and applying the information in this book, success is only a matter of luck or chance. That is not much to look forward to. This book contains the answers to questions like, "How do I know when a decision is right or wrong?" "How can I predictably improve things around me?" The powerful ethics technology of L. Ron Hubbard is your way to ever-increasing survival.

Basic Dianetics Books

The Basic Dianetics Books Package is your complete guide to the inner workings of the mind. You can get all of these books individually or in a set, complete with an attractive slipcase.

Dianetics: The Modern Science of Mental Health

Acclaimed as the most effective self-help book ever published. Dianetics technology has helped millions reach new heights of freedom and ability. Millions of copies are sold every year! Discover the source of mental barriers that prevent you from achieving your goals—and how to handle them!

The Dynamics of Life

Break through the barriers to your happiness. This is the first book Ron wrote detailing the startling principles behind Dianetics—facts so powerful they can change forever the way you look at yourself and your potentials. Discover how you can use the powerful basic principles in this book to blast through the barriers of your mind and gain full control over your success, future and happiness.

Self Analysis

The complete do-it-yourself handbook for anyone who wants to improve their abilities and success potential. Use the simple, easy-to-learn techniques in *Self Analysis* to build self-confidence and reduce stress.

Dianetics: The Evolution of a Science

It is estimated that we use less than ten percent of our mind's potential. What stops us from developing and using the full potential of our minds? *Dianetics: The Evolution of a Science* is L. Ron Hubbard's incredible story of how he discovered the reactive mind and how he developed the keys to unlock its secrets. Get this firsthand account of what the mind really is, and how you can release its hidden potential.

Dianetics Graduate Books

These books by L. Ron Hubbard give you detailed knowledge of how the mind works—data you can use to help yourself and others break out of the traps of life. While you can get these books individually, the Dianetics Graduate Books Package can also be purchased as a set, complete with an attractive slipcase.

Science of Survival

If you ever wondered why people act the way they do, you'll find this book a wealth of information. It's vital to anyone who wants to understand others and improve personal relationships. *Science of Survival* is built around a remarkable chart—the Hubbard Chart of Human Evaluation. With it you can understand and predict other people's behavior and reactions and greatly increase your control over your own life. This is a valuable handbook that can make a difference between success and failure on the job and in life.

Dianetics 55!

Your success in life depends on your ability to communicate. Do you know a formula exists for communication? Learn the rules of better communication that can help you live a more fulfilling life. Here, L. Ron Hubbard deals with the fundamental principles of communication and how you can master these to achieve your goals.

Advanced Procedure and Axioms

For the *first* time the basics of thought and the physical universe have been codified into a set of fundamental laws, signaling an entirely new way to view and approach the subjects of man, the physical universe and even life itself.

Handbook for Preclears

Written as an advanced personal workbook, *Handbook for Preclears* contains easily done processes to help you overcome the effect of times you were not in control of your life, times that your emotions were a barrier to your success and much more. Completing all the fifteen auditing steps contained in this book sets you up for really being in *control* of your environment and life.

Child Dianetics

Here is a revolutionary new approach to rearing children with Dianetics auditing techniques. Find out how you can help your child achieve greater confidence, more self-reliance, improved learning rate and a happier, more loving relationship with you.

Notes on the Lectures of L. Ron Hubbard

Compiled from his fascinating lectures given shortly after the publication of *Dianetics,* this book contains some of the first material Ron ever released on the ARC triangle and the Tone Scale, and how these discoveries relate to auditing.

Basic Scientology Books

The Basic Scientology Books Package contains the knowledge you need to be able to improve conditions in life. These books are available individually or as a set, complete with an attractive slipcase.

Scientology: The Fundamentals of Thought

Improve life *and* make a better world with this easy-to-read book that lays out the fundamental truths about life and thought. No such knowledge has ever before existed, and no such results have ever before been attainable as those which can be reached by the use of this knowledge. Equipped with this book alone, one could perform seeming miracles in changing the states of health, ability and intelligence of people. This *is* how life works. This *is* how you change men, women and children for the better, and attain greater personal freedom.

A New Slant on Life

Have you ever asked yourself Who am I? What am I? This book of articles by L. Ron Hubbard answers these all-too-common questions. This is knowledge one can use every day—for a new, more confident and happier slant on life!

The Problems of Work

Work plays a big part in the game of life. Do you really enjoy your work? Are you certain of your job security? Would you like the increased personal satisfaction of doing your work well? This is the book that shows exactly how to achieve these things and more. The game of life—and within it, the game of work—can be enjoyable and rewarding.

Scientology 0-8: The Book of Basics

What is life? Did you know an individual can create space, energy and time? Here are the basics of life itself, and the secrets of becoming cause over any area of your life. Discover how you can use the data in this book to achieve your goals.

Basic Dictionary of Dianetics and Scientology

Compiled from the works of L. Ron Hubbard, this convenient dictionary contains the terms and expressions needed by anyone learning Dianetics and Scientology technology. And a *special bonus*—an easy-to-read Scientology organizing board chart that shows you who to contact for services and information at your nearest Scientology organization.

OT[1] Library Package

All the following books contain the knowledge of a spiritual being's relationship to this universe and how his abilities to operate successfully in it can be restored. You can get all of these books individually or in a set, complete with an attractive slipcase.

Scientology 8-80

What are the laws of life? We are all familiar with physical laws such as the law of gravity, but what laws govern life and thought? L. Ron Hubbard answers the riddles of life and its goals in the physical universe.

Scientology 8-8008

Get the basic truths about your nature as a spiritual being and your relationship to the physical universe around you. Here, L. Ron Hubbard describes procedures designed to increase your abilities to heights previously only dreamed of.

Scientology: A History of Man

A fascinating look at the evolutionary background and history of the human race—revolutionary concepts guaranteed to intrigue you and challenge many basic assumptions about man's true power, potential and abilities.

The Creation of Human Ability

This book contains processes designed to restore the power of a thetan over his own postulates, to understand the nature of his beingness, to free his self-determinism and much, much more.

Purification Book Package

The books in the Purification Book Package contain data on the only effective way of handling drug and toxic residuals in the body, clearing the way for real mental and spiritual improvement—the Purification program. These books are available individually and as a specially boxed set.

Clear Body, Clear Mind: The Effective Purification Program

This book contains all the information on L. Ron Hubbard's Purification program. This is the only program of its kind in existence that has been found to clean the residues of drugs, toxins and elements harmful to human bodies out of them! Drugs and

---

1. **OT:** abbreviation for **Operating Thetan,** a state of beingness. It is a being "at cause over matter, energy, space, time, form and life." *Operating* comes from "able to operate without dependency on things," and *thetan* is the Greek letter *theta* (θ), which the Greeks used to represent *thought* or perhaps *spirit,* to which an *n* is added to make a noun in the modern style used to create words in engineering. It is also θ^n or "theta to the nth degree," meaning unlimited or vast.

chemicals can stop a person's ability to improve himself or just to live life. This book describes the program which can make it possible to start living again.

Purification: An Illustrated Answer to Drugs

Presented in a concise, fully illustrated format, this book provides you with an overview of the Purification program. Our society is ridden by abuse of drugs, alcohol and medicine that reduce one's ability to think clearly. This book lays out what can be done about it, in a form which is easy for anyone to read and understand.

Purification Rundown Delivery Manual

This book is a manual which guides a person through the Purification Rundown step by step. It includes all of the needed reports as well as spaces for the person to write his successes and to attest to program completion. This manual makes administering the Purification Rundown simple and *standard*.

All About Radiation

Can the effects of radiation exposure be avoided or reduced? What exactly would happen in the event of an atomic explosion? Get the answers to these and many other questions in this illuminating book. *All About Radiation* describes observations and discoveries concerning the physical and mental effects of radiation and the possibilities for handling them. Get the real facts on the subject of radiation and its effects.

Other Scientology Books

Have You Lived Before This Life?

This is the book that sparked a flood of interest in the ancient puzzle: Does man live only one life? The answer lay in mystery, buried until L. Ron Hubbard's researches unearthed the truth. Actual case histories of people recalling past lives in auditing tell the tale.

What Is Scientology?

Scientology applied religious philosophy has attracted great interest and attention since its beginning. What is Scientology philosophy? What can it accomplish—and why are so many people from all walks of life proclaiming its effectiveness? Find the answers to these questions and many others in *What Is Scientology?*

Background and Ceremonies of the Church of Scientology

Discover the beautiful and inspiring ceremonies of the Church of Scientology, and its fascinating religious and historical background. This book contains the illuminating Creed of the Church, church services, sermons and ceremonies, many as originally given in person by L. Ron Hubbard, Founder of Scientology.

Introductory and Demonstration Processes and Assists

How can you help someone increase his enthusiasm for living? How can you improve someone's self-confidence on the job? Here are basic Scientology processes you can use to help others deal with life and living.

Volunteer Minister's Handbook

This is a big, practical how-to-do-it book to give a person the basic knowledge on how to help self and others through the rough spots in life. It consists of twenty-one sections—each one covering important situations in life, such as drug and alcohol problems, study difficulties, broken marriages, accidents and illnesses, a failing business, difficult children, and much more. This is the basic tool you need to help someone out of troubles, and bring about a happier life.

Dianetics and Scientology Technical Dictionary

This dictionary is your indispensable guide to the words and ideas of Scientology and Dianetics technologies—technologies which can help you increase your know-how and effectiveness in life. Over three thousand words are defined—including a new understanding of vital words like *life, love* and *happiness* as well as Scientology terms.

The How to Present Scientology to the World Lecture Series

Here is a series of 18 lectures given by L. Ron Hubbard in late 1956 laying out the technology by which Scientologists can make Scientology better known and help to accomplish the purpose: "to bring about a superior civilization in which peace can exist on Earth." The subjects Ron covers in these talks include the basic tenets and laws governing organizations, setting up and teaching introductory and advanced courses about Scientology, overcoming stage fright in addressing small or large groups, the step-by-step actions one can take to truly bring others to an understanding of Scientology, and much more.

The Personal Achievement Series

There are nearly three thousand recorded lectures by L. Ron Hubbard on the subjects of Dianetics and Scientology. What follows is a sampling of these lectures, each known and loved the world over. All of these are presented in Clearsound state-of-the-art sound-recording technology, notable for its clarity and brilliance of reproduction.

Get all the Personal Achievement Series cassettes by L. Ron Hubbard listed below and ask your nearest Scientology church or organization or the publisher about future releases.

The Story of Dianetics and Scientology

In this lecture, L. Ron Hubbard shares with you his earliest insights into human nature and gives a compelling and often humorous account of his experiences. Spend an unforgettable time with Ron as he talks about the start of Dianetics and Scientology!

The Road to Truth

The road to truth has eluded man since the beginning of time. In this classic lecture, L. Ron Hubbard explains what this road actually is and why it is the only road one MUST travel all the way once begun. This lecture reveals the only road to higher levels of living.

Scientology and Effective Knowledge

Voyage to new horizons of awareness! *Scientology and Effective Knowledge* by L. Ron Hubbard can help you understand more about yourself and others. A fascinating tale of the beginnings of Dianetics and Scientology.

The Deterioration of Liberty

What do governments fear so much in a population that they amass weapons to defend themselves from people? Find out from Ron in this classic lecture.

Power of Choice and Self-Determinism

Man's ability to determine the course of his life depends on his ability to exercise his power of choice. Find how you can increase your power of choice and self-determinism in life from Ron in this lecture.

Scientology and Ability

Ron points out that this universe is here because we perceive it and agree to it. Applying Scientology principles to life can bring new adventure to life and put you on the road to discovering better beingness.

The Hope of Man

Various men in history brought forth the idea that there was hope of improvement. But L. Ron Hubbard's discoveries in Dianetics and Scientology have made that hope a reality. Find out by listening to this lecture how Scientology has become man's one, true hope for his final freedom.

The Dynamics

In this lecture Ron gives incredible data on the dynamics: how man creates on them; what happens when a person gets stuck in just one; how wars relate to the third dynamic and much more.

Money

Ron talks in this classic lecture about that subject which makes or breaks men with the greatest of ease—money. Find out what money really is and gain greater control over your own finances.

Formulas for Success—*The Five Conditions*

How does one achieve real success? It sometimes appears that luck is the primary factor, but the truth of the matter is that natural laws exist which govern the conditions of life. These laws have been discovered by Ron, and in this lecture he gives you the exact steps to take in order to improve conditions in any aspect of your life.

Health and Certainty

You need certainty of yourself in order to achieve the success you want in life. In *Health and Certainty*, L. Ron Hubbard tells how you can achieve certainty and really be free to think for yourself. Get this tape now and start achieving your full potential!

Operation Manual for the Mind

Everybody has a mind—but who has an operation manual for it? This lecture reveals why man went on for thousands of years without understanding how his mind is supposed to work. The problem has been solved. Find out how with this tape.

Miracles

Why is it that man often loses to those forces he resists or opposes? Why can't an individual simply overcome obstacles in life and win? In the tape lecture *Miracles*, L. Ron Hubbard describes why one suffers losses in life. He also describes how a person can experience the miracles of happiness, self-fulfillment and winning at life. Get a copy today.

The Road to Perfection—*The Goodness of Man*

Unlike earlier practices that sought to "improve" man because he was "bad," Scientology assumes that you have *good* qualities that simply need to be *increased*. In *The Road to Perfection*, L. Ron Hubbard shows how workable this assumption really is—and how you can begin to use your mind, talents and abilities to the fullest. Get this lecture and increase your ability to handle life.

The Dynamic Principles of Existence

What does it take to survive in today's world? It's not something you learn much about in school. You have probably gotten a lot of advice about how to "get along."

Your survival right now is limited by the data you were given. This lecture describes the dynamic principles of existence, and tells how you can use these principles to increase your success in all areas of life. Happiness and self-esteem *can* be yours. Don't settle for anything less.

Man: Good or Evil?

In this lecture, L. Ron Hubbard explores the greatest mystery that has confronted modern science and philosophy—the true nature of man's livingness and beingness. Is man simply a sort of wind-up doll or clock—or worse, an evil beast with no control of his cravings? Or is he capable of reaching higher levels of ability, awareness and happiness? Get this tape and find out the *real* answers.

Differences between Scientology and Other Studies

The most important questions in life are the ones you started asking as a child: What happens to a person when he dies? Is man basically good, or is he evil? What are the intentions of the world toward me? Did my mother and father really love me? What is love? Unlike other studies, which try to *force* you to think a certain way, Scientology enables you to find your own answers. Listen to this important lecture. It will put you on the road to true understanding and belief in yourself.

The Machinery of the Mind

We do a lot of things "automatically"—such as driving a car. But what happens when a person's mental machinery takes over and starts running him? In this fascinating lecture, L. Ron Hubbard gives you an understanding of what mental machinery really is, and how it can cause a person to lose control. You *can* regain your power of decision and be in full control of your life. Listen to this lecture and find out how.

The Affinity-Reality-Communication Triangle

Have you ever tried to talk to an angry man? Have you ever tried to get something across to someone who is really in fear? Have you ever known someone who was impossible to cheer up? Listen to this fascinating lecture by L. Ron Hubbard and learn how you can use the affinity-reality-communication triangle to resolve personal relationships. By using the data in this lecture, you can better understand others and live a happier life.

Increasing Efficiency

Inefficiency is a major barrier to success. How can you increase your efficiency? Is it a matter of changing your diet, or adjusting your working environment? These approaches have uniformly failed, because they overlook the most important element: *you.* L. Ron Hubbard has found those factors that *can* increase your efficiency, and he reveals it in this timely lecture. Get *Increasing Efficiency* now, and start achieving *your* full potential.

Man's Relentless Search

For countless centuries, man has been trying to find himself. Why does this quest repeatedly end in frustration and disappointment? What is he *really* looking for, and why can't he find it? For the real truth about man and life, listen to this taped lecture by L. Ron Hubbard, *Man's Relentless Search*. Restore your belief in yourself!

More advanced books and lectures are available. Contact your nearest organization or write directly to the publisher for a full catalog.

Create a successful organization.

The *Organization Executive Course* contains the basic laws of organization. Originally developed for the training of Scientology executives, this course contains basic LRH technology that you can apply to any group or activity.

"When you understand all the policies on this course, you will understand organization itself, no matter to what you apply it. You will also be able to recognize misorganization when you see it."—L. Ron Hubbard, from HCO PL 8 Sept. 69, THE ORG EXEC COURSE INTRODUCTION.

This is the only organizational technology based on a true understanding of the mind and spirit. Any failure of an organization is a failure to apply the data on this course or an ignorance of it.

When you know all the materials of this course, it makes a whole, intelligent picture of organization. For the first time, you can cut through the superstition of yesterday's organizations and create a sane, ethical and expanding group.

The *Organization Executive Course* consists of eight separate courses: one course for each of the divisions of the Scientology organizing board, plus one course covering the basics of handling any staff job.

Not only do you study every page of the powerful *Org Executive Course* Volumes, you will also study books and manuals and listen to lectures by L. Ron Hubbard on:

* Personnel
* Administration
* Ethics and justice in a group
* Communication
* Service
* Production
* How to train people for their jobs
* Quality and correction of the product
* Executive actions and duties
* and more

And, you will PRACTICE and APPLY what you learn as you study.

Learn and apply the knowledge in this course for certain and lasting success in any endeavor.

Do the *Organization Executive Course* now, available at your local Church of Scientology. See your Registrar today!

"If anyone knew the Org Exec Course fully and could practice it, he could completely reverse any downtrending company or country."— L. Ron Hubbard, from HCO PL 8 Sept. 69, THE ORG EXEC COURSE INTRODUCTION.

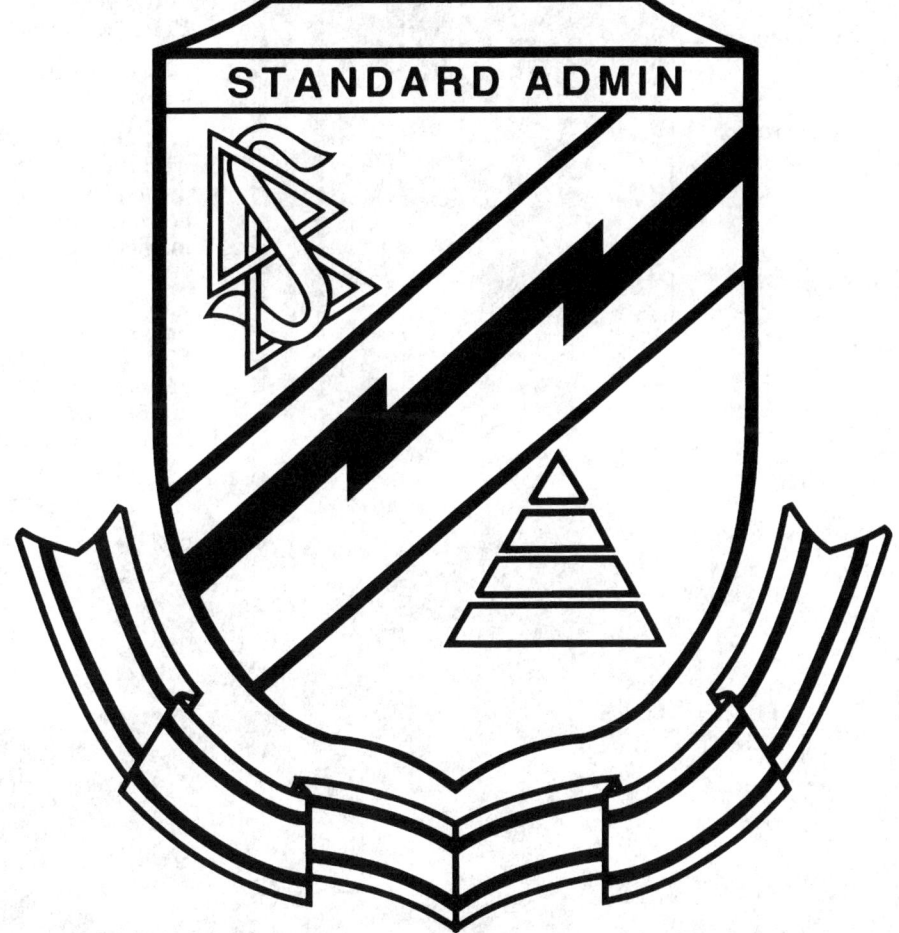

STANDARD ADMIN

Enroll on the Organization Executive Course.

Get the LRH data to expand any activity.

Before L. Ron Hubbard discovered and developed the technology of administration, man did not really know the principles of organization.

These basic discoveries of organization are available to you now, in the *Organization Executive Course* Volumes.

The policy letters in these volumes were written for Scientology organizations. However, you can apply the knowledge in these volumes to ANY group, organization or endeavor to make it a sane, ethical and expanding activity. This material applies to the individual as well. Where the functions covered in these policies are missing in your conduct in life, you will be to that degree an unsuccessful individual.

In these volumes is organization technology you'll find nowhere else, including:

* What exact actions and functions MUST be done in any organization for it to operate smoothly?

* Why the organizing board as developed by L. Ron Hubbard is a "philosophic machine," and how you can use the principles of the org board to achieve unlimited expansion.

* What is the one often-forgotten function which if missing will always eventually bring about the decline of any activity?

* What are the keys to maintaining a high ethical level in any group?

* What are the secrets to prosperity?

* How does a group ensure its products are top quality?

Any company or society will be as successful as it includes all the functions that are covered in these volumes.

There are eight *Organization Executive Course* Volumes, each fully indexed by subject, as well as alphabetically and chronologically. There is a ninth volume containing a cumulative index for the full set.

Get your full set of *Organization Executive Course* Volumes now!

See your Bookstore Officer today.

If one were fully familiar with the full subject and all the principles in these volumes, he would appear to be a magician, a miracle worker!

If unavailable, order from Bridge Publications, Inc., 5600 E. Olympic Boulevard, Commerce, CA 90022, USA, or NEW ERA Publications International ApS, Smedeland 20, 2600 Glostrup, Denmark.

Buy your full set of OEC Volumes.

YOUR GUARANTEE OF FREEDOM.

INTERNATIONAL ASSOCIATION OF SCIENTOLOGISTS

The purpose of the International Association of Scientologists is:
"To unite, advance, support and protect the Scientology religion and Scientologists in all parts of the world so as to achieve the aims of Scientology as originated by L. Ron Hubbard."

All great movements have succeeded because of the personal conviction and dedication of their members. And no members are as dedicated as those of the IAS, the group which is winning the war against suppression around the world.

Even if you're not directly involved in the fight, it *is* your war. You have a stake in what kind of world this is — and will become.

Become a member of the International Association of Scientologists.

Help guarantee your route to full OT as well as freedom for the millions.

WRITE TO
THE MEMBERSHIP OFFICER

INTERNATIONAL ASSOCIATION OF SCIENTOLOGISTS

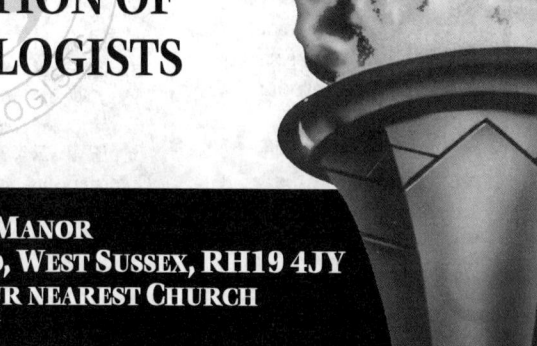

C/O SAINT HILL MANOR
EAST GRINSTEAD, WEST SUSSEX, RH19 4JY
OR CONTACT YOUR NEAREST CHURCH
OF SCIENTOLOGY

"I AM ALWAYS HAPPY TO HEAR FROM MY READERS."

L. RON HUBBARD

THESE WERE THE WORDS of L. Ron Hubbard, who was always very interested in hearing from his friends and readers. He made a point of staying in communication with everyone he came in contact with over his more than fifty-year career as a professional writer, and he had thousands of fans and friends that he corresponded with all over the world.

The author's representatives, Author Services, Inc., wish to continue this tradition and welcome letters and comments from you, his readers, both old and new.

Additionally, they will be happy to send you information on anything you would like to know about L. Ron Hubbard, his extraordinary life and accomplishments and the vast number of books he has written.

Any message addressed to the Author's Affairs Director at Author Services, Inc., will be given prompt and full attention.

AUTHOR SERVICES, INC.

7051 HOLLYWOOD BOULEVARD
HOLLYWOOD, CALIFORNIA 90028, USA

authoraffairs@authorservicesinc.com

Scientology Churches and Organizations

UNITED STATES

ALBUQUERQUE

Church of Scientology of
New Mexico
8106 Menaul Boulevard
N.E. Albuquerque, New Mexico 87110
www.scientology-albuquerque.org

ATLANTA

Church of Scientology of Georgia
1611 Mt. Vernon Road
Dunwoody, Georgia 30338
www.scientology-atlanta.org

AUSTIN

Church of Scientology of Texas
2200 Guadalupe
Austin, Texas 78705
www.scientology-austin.org

BATTLE CREEK

Church of Scientology of
Ann Arbor
66 E. Michigan Avenue
Battle Creek, Michigan 49017
www.scientology-battlecreek.org

BOSTON

Church of Scientology of Boston
448 Beacon Street
Boston, Massachusetts 02115
www.scientology-boston.org

BUFFALO

Church of Scientology of Buffalo
836 Main Street
Buffalo, New York 14202
www.scientology-buffalo.org

CHICAGO

Church of Scientology of Illinois
3011 North Lincoln Avenue
Chicago, Illinois 60657-4207
www.scientology-chicago.org

CINCINNATI

Church of Scientology of Ohio
215 West 4th Street, 5th Floor
Cincinnati, Ohio 45202-2670
www.scientology-cincinnati.org

COLUMBUS

Church of Scientology of
Central Ohio
30 North High Street
Columbus, Ohio 43215
www.scientology-columbus.org

DENVER

Church of Scientology of
Colorado
3385 South Bannock Street
Englewood, Colorado 80110
www.scientology-denver.org

DETROIT

Church of Scientology of Michigan
28000 Middlebelt Road
Farmington Hills, Michigan 48334
www.scientology-detroit.org

HONOLULU

Church of Scientology of Hawaii
1146 Bethel Street
Honolulu, Hawaii 96813
www.scientology-hawaii.org

KANSAS CITY

Church of Scientology of
Kansas City
2 East 39th Street
Kansas City, Missouri 64111
www.scientology-kansascity.org

LAS VEGAS

Church of Scientology of Nevada
846 East Sahara Avenue
Las Vegas, Nevada 89104
www.scientology-lasvegas.org

LONG ISLAND

Church of Scientology of
Long Island
64 Bethpage Road
Hicksville, New York
11801
www.scientology-longisland.org

LOS ANGELES AND VICINITY

Church of Scientology of
Los Angeles
4810 Sunset Boulevard
Los Angeles, California 90027
www.scientology-losangeles.org

Church of Scientology of
Orange County
1451 Irvine Boulevard
Tustin, California 92680
www.scientology-orangecounty.org

Church of Scientology of
Pasadena
1277 East Colorado Boulevard
Pasadena, California 91106
www.scientology-pasadena.org

Church of Scientology of
the Valley
15643 Sherman Way
Van Nuys, California 91406
www.scientology-valley.org

LOS GATOS

Church of Scientology of
Los Gatos
4050 Moorpark Avenue
San Jose, California 90028
www.scientology-losgatos.org

MIAMI

Church of Scientology of
Florida
120 Giralda Avenue
Coral Gables, Florida 33134
www.scientology-miami.org

MINNEAPOLIS

Church of Scientology of
Minneapolis
Twin Cities
1011 Nicollet Mall
Minneapolis, Minnesota 55403
www.scientology-minneapolis.org

MOUNTAIN VIEW

Church of Scientology of
Mountain View
117 Easy Street
Mountain View, California 94039
www.scientology-mountainview.org

NEW HAVEN

Church of Scientology of
Connecticut
909 Whalley Avenue
New Haven, Connecticut
06515-1728
www.scientology-newhaven.org

NEW YORK CITY

Church of Scientology of
New York
227 West 46th Street
New York, New York 10036-1409
www.scientology-newyork.org

ORLANDO

Church of Scientology of
Orlando, Inc.
1830 East Colonial Drive
Orlando, Florida 32803-4729
www.scientology-orlando.org

PHILADELPHIA

Church of Scientology of
Pennsylvania
1315 Race Street
Philadelphia, Pennsylvania 19107
www.scientology-philadelphia.org

PHOENIX

Church of Scientology of Arizona
2702 44th Street, Suite A-100
Phoenix, Arizona 85008
www.scientology-phoenix.org

PORTLAND

Church of Scientology of Portland
709 SW Salmon Street
Portland, Oregon 97205
www.scientology-portland.org

SACRAMENTO

Church of Scientology of
Sacramento
825 15th Street
Sacramento
California 95814-2096
www.scientology-sacramento.org

SALT LAKE CITY

Church of Scientology of Utah
1931 South 1100 East
Salt Lake City, Utah 84106
www.scientology-saltlakecity.org

SAN DIEGO

Church of Scientology of
San Diego
1330 4th Avenue
San Diego, California 92101
www.scientology-sandiego.org

SAN FRANCISCO

Church of Scientology of
San Francisco
701 Montgomery Street
San Francisco, California 94111
www.scientology-sanfrancisco.org

SAN JOSE

Church of Scientology of
Stevens Creek
1865 Lundy Avenue
San Jose, California 95131
www.scientology-sanjose.org

SANTA BARBARA

Church of Scientology of
Santa Barbara
524 State Street
Santa Barbara, California 93101
www.scientology-santabarbara.org

SEATTLE

Church of Scientology
of Washington State
601 Aurora Avenue North
Seattle, Washington 98109
www.scientology-seattle.org

ST. LOUIS

Church of Scientology of Missouri
6901 Delmar Boulevard
University City, Missouri 63130
www.scientology-stlouis.org

TAMPA

Church of Scientology of
Tampa, Inc.
3102 North Habana Avenue
Tampa, Florida 33609
www.scientology-tampa.org

WASHINGTON, DC

The Founding Church of
Scientology
of Washington, DC
1701 20th Street N.W.
Washington, DC 20009
www.scientology-washingtondc.org

PUERTO RICO

HATO REY

Church of Scientology of
Puerto Rico
272 JT Piñero Avenue
Hyde Park,
San Juan, Puerto Rico 00918
www.scientology-puertorico.org

CANADA

EDMONTON

Church of Scientology of
Edmonton
10255 97th Street
Edmonton, Alberta
Canada T5J 0L9
www.scientology-edmonton.org

KITCHENER

Church of Scientology of
Kitchener
159-161 King Street West
Kitchener, Ontario
Canada N2G 1A6
www.scientology-kitchener.org

MONTREAL

Church of Scientology of
Montreal, Inc.
4489 Papineau Street
Montreal, Quebec
Canada H2H 1T7
www.scientology-montreal.org

OTTAWA

Church of Scientology of Ottawa
150 Rideau Street, 2nd Floor
Ottawa, Ontario
Canada K1N 5X6
www.scientology-ottawa.org

QUEBEC

Church of Scientology of
Quebec, Inc.
1996 1. Avenue
Quebec, Quebec
Canada G1L 3M2
www.scientology-quebec.org

TORONTO

Church of Scientology of Toronto
696 Yonge Street, 2nd Floor
Toronto, Ontario
Canada M4Y 2A7
www.scientology-toronto.org

VANCOUVER

Church of Scientology of
Vancouver
401 West Hastings Street
Vancouver, British Columbia
Canada V6B 1L5
www.scientology-vancouver.org

WINNIPEG

Church of Scientology of
Winnipeg
315 Garry Street, Suite 210
Winnipeg, Manitoba
Canada R3B 2G7
www.scientology-winnipeg.org

UNITED KINGDOM

BIRMINGHAM

Church of Scientology of
Birmingham
8 Ethel Street
Winston Churchill House
Birmingham, England B2 4BG
www.scientology-birmingham.org

BRIGHTON

Church of Scientology of Brighton
Third Floor, 79-83 North Street
Brighton, Sussex
England BN1 1ZA
www.scientology-brighton.org

EAST GRINSTEAD

Church of Scientology
Saint Hill Foundation
Saint Hill Manor
East Grinstead, West Sussex
England RH19 4JY
www.scientology-sthillfdn.org

EDINBURGH

Hubbard Association of Personal
Independence
20 Southbridge
Edinburgh, Scotland EH1 1LL
www.scientology-edinburgh.org

LONDON

Church of Scientology of London
146 Queen Victoria St.
London, England EC4V 4BY
www.scientology-london.org

MANCHESTER

Church of Scientology of
Manchester
258 Deansgate
Manchester, England M3 4BG
www.scientology-manchester.org

PLYMOUTH

Church of Scientology of Plymouth
41 Ebrington Street
Plymouth, Devon
England PL4 9AA
www.scientology-plymouth.org

SUNDERLAND

Church of Scientology of
Sunderland
51 Fawcett Street
Sunderland, Tyne and Wear
England SR1 1RS
www.scientology-sunderland.org

EUROPE

AUSTRIA

VIENNA

Church of Scientology of Austria
Capistrangasse 4
1070 Vienna, Austria
www.scientology-vienna.org

BELGIUM

BRUSSELS

Church of Scientology of Belgium
rue General MacArthur, 9
1180 Brussels, Belgium
www.scientology-brussels.org

DENMARK

AARHUS

Church of Scientology of Jylland
Chr. X Vej 166
8260 Viby Jylland, Denmark
www.scientology-jylland.org

COPENHAGEN

Church of Scientology of
Denmark
Gammel Kongevej 3–5, 1
1610 Copenhagen V, Denmark
www.scientology-denmark.org

FRANCE

ANGERS

Church of Scientology of Angers
28B, avenue Mendès
49240 Avrille, France
www.scientology-angers.org

CLERMONT-FERRAND

Spiritual Association of the
Church of Scientology
of Auvergne
6, rue Dulaure
63000 Clermont-Ferrand, France
www.scientology-clermontferrand.org

LYON

Church of Scientology of Lyon
3, place des Capucins
69001 Lyon, France
www.scientology-lyon.org

PARIS

Spiritual Association of
the Church of Scientology
of Ile de France
7, rue Jules César
75012 Paris, France
www.scientologie-paris.org

SAINT-ÉTIENNE

Spiritual Association of
the Church of Scientology
of the Loire
24, rue Marengo
42000 Saint-Étienne, France
www.scientologie-stetienne.org

GERMANY

BERLIN

Church of Scientology of
Berlin e.V.
Otto-Suhr-Allee 30-34
Charlottenburg
10585 Berlin, Germany
www.scientology-berlin.org

DÜSSELDORF

Church of Scientology of
Düsseldorf e.V.
Friedrichstraße 28B
40217 Düsseldorf, Germany
www.scientology-duesseldorf.org

FRANKFURT

Church of Scientology of
Frankfurt e.V.
Kaiserstraße 49
60329 Frankfurt 70, Germany
www.scientology-frankfurt.org

HAMBURG

Church of Scientology of
Hamburg e.V.
Domstraße 9
20095 Hamburg, Germany
www.scientology-hamburg.org

Church of Scientology of
Eppendorf e.V.
Auf dem Koenigslande 92A
22047 Hamburg, Germany
www.scientology-eppendorf.org

HANNOVER

Church of Scientology of
Hannover e.V.
Odeonstraße 17
30159 Hannover, Germany
www.scientology-hannover.org

MUNICH

Church of Scientology of
Munich e.V.
Beichstraße 12
80802 Munich 40, Germany
www.munich.scientology.org

STUTTGART

Dianetik Stuttgart e.V.
Hohenheimerstraße 9
70184 Stuttgart, Germany
www.scientology-stuttgart.org

GREECE

ATHENS

Church of Scientology of Athens
Patision 200
11256 Athens, Greece

HUNGARY

BUDAPEST

Church of Scientology of
Budapest
1399 Budapest
1073 Erzsébet krt. 5. I. em.
Pf. 701/215. Hungary
www.scientology-budapest.org

ISRAEL

TEL AVIV

College of Dianetics and
Scientology of Tel Aviv
12 Shontzino Street
PO Box 57478
61573 Tel Aviv, Israel
www.scientology-telaviv.org

ITALY

BRESCIA

Church of Scientology of
Tre Laghi
Via Fratelli Bronzetti, 20
25125 Brescia, Italy
www.scientology-brescia.org

CATANIA

Church of Scientology of Catania
Via Etnea, 468
95128 Catania, Italy
www.scientology-catania.org

MILAN

Church of Scientology of Milan
Via Lepontina, 4
20159 Milan, Italy
www.scientology-milano.org

MONZA

Church of Scientology of Brianza
Via Ghilini, 4
20052 Monza (MI), Italy
www.scientology-monza.org

NOVARA

Church of Scientology of Novara
Corso Milano, 76
28100 Novara, Italy
www.scientology-novara.org

NUORO

Church of Scientology of Sardinia
Via San Martino, 3
08100 Nuoro, Italy
www.scientology-nuoro.org

PADUA

Church of Scientology of Padua
Via Ugo Foscolo, 5
35131 Padua, Italy
www.scientology-padova.org

PORDENONE

Church of Scientology of
the City of Pordenone
Via Dogana, 19
Zona Fiera
33170 Pordenone, Italy
www.scientology-pordenone.org

ROME

Church of Scientology of
Rome and Mediterranean
Via del Caravita, 5
00186 Rome, Italy
www.scientology-roma.org

TURIN

Church of Scientology of Turin
Via Bersezio, 7
10152 Turin, Italy
www.scientology-torino.org

VERONA

Church of Scientology of Verona
Corso Milano, 84
37138 Verona, Italy
www.scientology-verona.org

NETHERLANDS

AMSTERDAM

Church of Scientology of
Amsterdam
Nieuwezijds Voorburgwal
116–118 1012 SH
Amsterdam, Netherlands
www.scientology-amsterdam.org

NORWAY

OSLO

Church of Scientology of Norway
Karl Johans Gate 12J
0154 Oslo, Norway
www.scientology-oslo.org

PORTUGAL

LISBON

Scientology Church Association of
Portugal
Rua dos Correiros N 205, 3° Andar
1100 Lisbon, Portugal
www.cientologia-lisbon.org

RUSSIA

MOSCOW

Church of Scientology of Moscow
Ul. Boris Galushkina 19A
129301 Moscow, Russia
www.scientology-moscow.org

ST. PETERSBURG

Scientology Center of
St. Petersburg
Ligovskij Prospect 33
193036 St. Petersburg, Russia
www.scientology-stpetersburg.org

SPAIN

BARCELONA

Dianetics Civil Association
of Barcelona
C/Dos de Maig 310 Baixos
08025 Barcelona, Spain
www.scientology-barcelona.org

MADRID

Dianetics Civil Association of
Madrid
C/ Santa Catalina, 7
28014 Madrid, Spain
www.cienciologia-madrid.org

SWEDEN

GÖTEBORG

Church of Scientology of
Göteborg
Värmlandsgatan 16, 1 tr.
413 28 Göteborg, Sweden
www.scientology-gothenburg.org

MALMÖ

Church of Scientology of Malmö
Porslinsgatan 3
211 32 Malmö, Sweden
www.scientology-malmo.org

STOCKHOLM

Church of Scientology of
Stockholm
Reimerschlomsgaten, 9-11
116 62 Stockholm, Sweden
www.scientology-stockholm.org

SWITZERLAND

BASEL

Church of Scientology of Basel
Herrengrabenweg 56
4054 Basel, Switzerland
www.scientology-basel.org

BERN

Church of Scientology of Bern
Muhlemattstrasse 31
Postfach 384
3000 Bern 14, Switzerland
www.scientology-bern.org

GENEVA

Church of Scientology of Geneva
12, rue des Acacias
1227 Carouge
Geneva, Switzerland
www.scientology-geneva.org

LAUSANNE

Church of Scientology of
Lausanne
10, rue de la Madeleine
1003 Lausanne, Switzerland
www.scientology-lausanne.org

ZURICH

Church of Scientology of Zurich
Freilagerstrasse 11
8047 Zurich, Switzerland
www.scientology-zurich.org

AUSTRALIA

ADELAIDE

Church of Scientology of Adelaide
18 Waymouth Street
Adelaide, South Australia
Australia 5000
www.scientology-adelaide.org

BRISBANE

Church of Scientology of Brisbane
106 Edward Street, 2nd Floor
Brisbane, Queensland
Australia 4000
www.scientology-brisbane.org

CANBERRA

Church of Scientology of
Canberra
Unit 4, 7-11 Botany St. Phillip
Canberra City, ACT 2606
Australia
www.scientology-canberra.org

MELBOURNE

Church of Scientology of
Melbourne
42–44 Russell Street
Melbourne, Victoria
Australia 3000
www.scientology-melbourne.org

PERTH

Church of Scientology of Perth
108 Murray Street, 1st Floor
Perth, Western Australia
Australia 6000
www.scientology-perth.org

SYDNEY

Church of Scientology of Sydney
201 Castlereagh Street
Sydney, New South Wales
Australia 2000
www.scientology-sydney.org

JAPAN

TOKYO

Scientology Tokyo
2-11-7, Kita-otsuka
Toshima-ku
Tokyo, Japan 170-004
www.scientology-tokyo.org

NEW ZEALAND

AUCKLAND

Church of Scientology of
New Zealand
532-534 Ellerslie/Panmure Highway
Panmure, Auckland
New Zealand
www.scientology-auckland.org

SOUTH AFRICA

CAPE TOWN

Church of Scientology of
Cape Town
185 Bree Street
Cape Town 8001, South Africa
www.scientology-capetown.org

DURBAN

Church of Scientology of Durban
20 Buckingham Terrace
Westville, Durban 3630
South Africa
www.scientology-durban.org

JOHANNESBURG

Church of Scientology of
Johannesburg
21 Kerk Avenue
Ruiterhof Ext. 2, Ferndale
Randburg, Johannesburg, 2194
South Africa
www.scientology.org.za

Church of Scientology
of Johannesburg North
No. 108 1st Floor,
Bordeaux Centre
Gordon Road, Corner Jan
Smuts Avenue
Blairgowrie, Randburg 2125
South Africa
www.scientology-johannesburgnorth.org

PORT ELIZABETH

Church of Scientology of
Port Elizabeth
2 St. Christopher's
27 Westbourne Road Central
Port Elizabeth 6001
South Africa
www.scientology-portelizabeth.org

PRETORIA

Church of Scientology of Pretoria
172 Brooklyn Road
Brooklyn, Pretoria 0181
South Africa
www.scientology-pretoria.org

ZIMBABWE

BULAWAYO

Church of Scientology of
Bulawayo
Southampton House, Suite 202
Main Street and 9th Avenue
Bulawayo, Zimbabwe
www.scientology-bulawayo.org

HARARE

Church of Scientology of Harare
No. 3 Seagrave Road
Mount Pleasant
Harare, Zimbabwe
www.scientology-harare.org

CELEBRITY CENTRES

**CHURCH OF SCIENTOLOGY
CELEBRITY CENTRE
INTERNATIONAL**
5930 Franklin Avenue
Hollywood, California 90028
www.celebritycentre.org

AUSTRIA

Church of Scientology
Mission of Vienna
Senefeldergasse 11/5
1100 Vienna, Austria
www.scientology-ccvienna.org

FRANCE

Spiritual Association of the
Church of Scientology
Celebrity Centre Paris
69, rue Legendre
75017 Paris, France
www.scientology-ccparis.org

GERMANY

Church of Scientology
Celebrity Centre Rheinland e. V.
Luisenstraße 23
40215 Düsseldorf, Germany
www.scientology-ccduesseldorf.org

ITALY

Church of Scientology
Celebrity Centre Firenze
Via Salvestrina, 12
50129 Firenze

UNITED KINGDOM

Church of Scientology
Celebrity Centre London
42 Leinster Gardens
London, England W2 3AN
www.scientology-cclondon.org

UNITED STATES

DALLAS

Church of Scientology
Celebrity Centre Dallas
1850 North Buckner Boulevard
Dallas, Texas 75228
www.scientology-ccdallas.org

LAS VEGAS

Church of Scientology
Creative Mission of Las Vegas
4850 W. Flamingo Road, Suite 10
Las Vegas, Nevada 89103
www.scientology-cclasvegas.org

NASHVILLE

Church of Scientology
Celebrity Centre Nashville
1204 16th Avenue South
Nashville, Tennessee 37212
www.scientology-ccnashville.org

NEW YORK

Church of Scientology
Celebrity Centre New York
65 East 82nd Street
New York, New York 10028
www.scientology-ccnewyork.org

PORTLAND

Church of Scientology
Celebrity Centre Portland
708 S.W. Salmon Street
Portland, Oregon 97205
www.scientology-ccportland.org

ADVANCED ORGANIZATIONS

AUSTRALIA, NEW ZEALAND & OCEANIA

Church of Scientology
Advanced Organization Saint Hill
Australia, New Zealand and Oceania
19–37 Greek Stree, Glebe, New South Wales
Australia 2037

EUROPE & AFRICA

Church of Scientology Europe
Advanced Organization
Saint Hill
Jernbanegade 6
1608 Copenhagen V, Denmark

UNITED KINGDOM

Church of Scientology Advanced
Organization Saint Hill
Saint Hill Manor
East Grinstead, West Sussex
England RH19 4JY

UNITED STATES

Church of Scientology
Western United States
Advanced Organization of
Los Angeles
1306 L. Ron Hubbard Way
Los Angeles, California 90027

Church of Scientology
Western United States
American Saint Hill Organization
1413 L. Ron Hubbard Way
Los Angeles, California 90027

**CHURCH OF SCIENTOLOGY
FLAG SHIP SERVICE
ORGANIZATION, INC.**
c/o *Freewinds* Relay Office
118 N. Fort Harrison Avenue
Clearwater, Florida 33755-4013

**CHURCH OF SCIENTOLOGY
FLAG SERVICE ORGANIZATION, INC.**
210 S. Fort Harrison Avenue
Clearwater, Florida 34616

To obtain any books or lectures by L. Ron Hubbard which are not available at your local organization, contact any of the following publishers:

NEW ERA PUBLICATIONS INTERNATIONAL ApS
Smedeland 20
2600 Glostrup, Denmark
Phone: (45) 33 73 66 66
Fax: (45) 33 73 66 33
e-mail:
books@newerapublications.com
www.newerapublications.com

NEW ERA PUBLICATIONS UK LTD
Saint Hill Manor
East Grinstead, West Sussex
England RH19 4JY
www.uk.newerapublications.com

NEW ERA PUBLICATIONS AUSTRALIA PTY LTD
16, Dorahy Street
Dundas, New South Wales
Australia 2117
www.au.newerapublications.com

CONTINENTAL PUBLICATIONS SOUTH AFRICA PTY LTD
PO Box 27080, Benrose
Johannesburg 2011, South Africa
www.sa.newerapublications.com

BRIDGE PUBLICATIONS, INC.
5600 E. Olympic Boulevard
Commerce, California 90022
Phone toll free: 1-800-722-1733
(in US and Canada)
Fax: 1-323-953-3328
e-mail: info@bridgepub.com
www.bridgepub.com

CONTINENTAL PUBLICATIONS LIAISON OFFICE
696 Yonge Street, Suite 705
Toronto, Ontario
Canada M4Y 2A7
www.can.bridgepub.com